The Charities Acts Handbook

A Practical Guide

The Charities Acts Handbook

A Practical Guide

General Editor

Alice Faure Walker

Editor

Julian Blake

Contributors

Tamsin Anderson
Stephanie Biden
Erica Crump
Augustus Della-Porta
Pippa Garland
Jamie Huard
Viral Kataria
Mairead O'Reilly
Sarah Payne
Christine Rigby
Victoria Schneider
Lawrence Simanowitz
Laura Soley
Simon Steeden
Jaqui Symcox

The general editor, editor and contributors are all solicitors in the Charity and Social Enterprise department at Bates Wells Braithwaite

LexisNexis®

Published by LexisNexis

LexisNexis
Regus
Terrace Floor
Castlemead
Lower Castle Street
Bristol BS1 3AG

British Library Cataloguing-in-Publication Data

A catalogue record for this book is available from the British Library.

ISBN 978 1 84661 577 1

Typeset by Letterpart Limited, Caterham on the Hill, Surrey CR3 5XL

Printed in Great Britain by Hobbs the Printers Limited, Totton, Hampshire SO40 3WX

This book is dedicated to the memory of

STEPHEN LLOYD

Former partner at Bates Wells Braithwaite

A much missed colleague and one of the leading figures in the development of charity law in the UK over the past 30 years

PREFACE

The previous edition of this book was published almost a decade ago, in the wake of the Charities Act 2006, which was billed as the biggest shake-up in charity law for 400 years.

Much has happened since then. Most of the changes introduced by the 2006 Act, including the new rules on public benefit, the Charity Tribunal and the charitable incorporated organisation, have now had a chance to bed in. The Charities Act 2011 consolidated most charity legislation into a single statute, making the law much easier to navigate. We also have a new Charities Act: the Charities (Protection and Social Investment) Act 2016 received Royal Assent in March 2016. We comment on all these developments, as well as Lord Hodgson's wide-ranging review of charity law in 2012. This book states the position as at 31 July 2016, but we highlight where more change may be on the horizon, including areas covered by the Law Commission's 2015 consultation on technical issues in charity law which is due to report in 2017.

We are all too aware that although this book is about charity law, charities also need to stay on top of a myriad of rules and regulations relating to their day to day operation: employment, data protection, health and safety, consumer protection, to name but a few. We recognise that this is a huge challenge, particularly for the smaller charities which make up the vast majority of the sector. We are supportive of any attempts to cut down the bureaucracy and regulation which threaten to engulf us all.

This book has been a team effort. Based on the original work by Stephen Lloyd and Fiona Middleton, and the significant contributions of Christine Rigby to the last edition, many of our colleagues have contributed to the new edition. We are grateful to Christine, in particular, and to co-authors Tamsin Anderson, Stephanie Biden, Erica Crump, Augustus Della-Porta, Pippa Garland, Jamie Huard, Viral Kataria, Mairead O'Reilly, Sarah Payne, Victoria Schneider, Lawrence Simanowitz, Laura Soley, Simon Steeden and Jaqui Symcox. Thanks are also due to our colleagues Rebecca Bruce, Jim Clifford OBE, Chinonso Denwigwe, Rupert Earle, Lucinda Ellen, Luke Fletcher, Louise Harman, Oliver Hunt, Caraline Johnson, Emma Knuckey, Jess Long, Thea Longley, Rosamund McCarthy, Rob Oakley, Brennie Richards and Chris Theobald for their help, as well as other colleagues who have commented on the text and our former colleagues Lindsay Driscoll, Sarah Cannings and Talhit Aziz.

We would like to thank Ben Harrison of the Office for Civil Society and Innovation for his updates on the progress of charity law reform, and the Charity Commission, in particular Kenneth Dibble and Stephen Roberts, for helping us with a number of queries. We are also grateful to the Judicial Appointments Commission for help with queries on the Charity Tribunal and to Gareth Morgan, Emeritus Professor of Charity Studies at Sheffield Hallam University.

We dedicated the last edition of this book to Fiona Middleton, who died tragically in 2004. Stephen Lloyd, who edited the last edition, was involved in reviewing some of the very early drafts of this edition, but died suddenly and unexpectedly in August 2014. This edition is dedicated to Stephen. Both we and our co-authors at Bates Wells Braithwaite were privileged to work alongside and be inspired by Stephen. He was well known and loved throughout the sector. He was committed to making the law accessible to charities – not only through legal publications but by the knowledgeable and practical advice he gave to clients. One of his many achievements was to serve as independent adviser to Lord Hodgson during his statutory review of charity law in 2012. Without Stephen this book would simply not exist, and we hope that this edition does his legacy justice.

Alice Faure Walker and Julian Blake, October 2016

TABLE OF ABBREVIATIONS

'the 1992 Act'	Charities Act 1992
'the 1993 Act'	Charities Act 1993
'the 2006 Act'	Charities Act 2006
'the 2011 Act'	Charities Act 2011
'the 2016 Act'	Charities (Protection and Social Investment) Act 2016
'the Commission'	The Charity Commission
CIO	Charitable Incorporated Organisation
Attorney General	Her Majesty's Attorney General
HMRC	Her Majesty's Revenue and Customs

CONTENTS

TABLE OF CASES

References are to paragraph numbers.

TABLE OF STATUTES

References are to paragraph numbers.

TABLE OF STATUTORY INSTRUMENTS

References are to paragraph numbers.

CHAPTER 1

INTRODUCTION – BACKGROUND TO THE CHARITIES ACTS

THE CHARITIES ACT 2011

1.1 The Charities Act 2011 is now the main charity legislation in England and Wales. The 2011 Act, which came into force in March 2012, was consolidating legislation, bringing together most of the provisions of the Charities Acts 1993 and 2006 into a single Act of Parliament.

1.2 Prior to the 2011 Act, the most significant charity legislation had been the Charities Act 1993. The 1993 Act had been amended significantly by the Charities Act 2006 which deleted some parts of the 1993 Act, amended others, and introduced new stand-alone provisions. Navigation of charity legislation had become something of a minefield, particularly given the staggered implementation of much of the 2006 Act. The 2011 Act represented a vast improvement.

1.3 The 1993 Act was completely repealed by the 2011 Act, as was the Recreational Charities Act 1958, which dealt with certain charitable purposes.

1.4 However, the Charities Act 1992 was not affected by the 2011 Act. The 1992 Act deals with fundraising, not only for charitable purposes, but also for philanthropic and benevolent purposes. Government therefore considered that it was beyond the scope of legislation designed to consolidate the law in relation to charities. There was considerable opposition to this in the sector: the Charity Law Association described it as a glaring omission.

1.5 The Charities (Protection and Social Investment) Act 2016 (see **1.17-1.21**) amends the 1992 and 2011 Acts.

1.6 Charity legislation is, therefore, now set out primarily in the 2011 Act and in the 1992 Act. Some provisions of the 2006 Act remain on the statute book, but apart from those relating to public charitable collections (which are not currently in force, and may never be brought into force: see **18.25–18.26**), they are very minor.

1.7 Readers should be aware of a complication which affects some of the provisions of the 2011 Act. Where provisions of the 1993 Act had been amended by the 2006 Act, but those amendments were not in force on the commencement date of the 2011 Act,[1] the effect of the amendments is suspended by the detailed provisions of Sch 9 to the 2011 Act. Relevant provisions include those relating to certain exempt charities (see Chapter 5) and voluntary registration with the Charity Commission (see **4.42–4.53**): at

---

1 14 March 2012.

the time of writing these are still subject to the 'transitory modifications' in Sch 9. Equally, most of the provisions relating to charitable incorporated organisations (see Chapter 14) were not effective when the 2011 Act came into force, by virtue of Sch 9, but were subsequently commenced in early 2013. This complication is one of the less straightforward aspects of the consolidation exercise.

THE CHARITIES ACT 2006

1.8 Many of the provisions of the 2011 Act have their origin in the Charities Act 2006. The 2006 Act was described by some as the biggest shake-up in charity law for 400 years. It had its origins in a report of the Prime Minister's Strategy Unit, *Public Action, Private Benefit*, published in 2002.[2] Many of the recommendations in the report were endorsed by Government and a draft Charities Bill was published in 2004. Following detailed scrutiny by a Joint Committee of the House of Lords and House of Commons[3] and subsequently in Parliament, particularly in the House of Lords, the 2006 Act finally received Royal Assent in November 2006.

1.9 The 2006 Act made some sweeping changes. These included:

- a new statutory list of the purposes which the law regards as charitable;
- a statutory requirement to the effect that charitable purposes must be for the public benefit, and an obligation on the Charity Commission to produce guidance promoting awareness and understanding of this requirement;
- changes to the charity registration requirements: meaning that smaller charities were no longer obliged to register, but larger so-called 'excepted' charities were brought within the scope of registration;
- changes to the framework for the regulation of 'exempt' charities;
- the introduction of a new Charity Tribunal designed to hear appeals from decisions of the Charity Commission;
- a new corporate legal form for charities, the charitable incorporated organisation or CIO.

1.10 Very few of the provisions of the 2006 Act came into force immediately. Implementation was staggered, with many of the changes taking effect in 2007 and 2008. The regime for CIOs was finally introduced, alongside detailed regulations, in 2013. Some changes, such as those dealing with exempt charities, and some of the provisions on conversion to CIO status, are still not completely in force.

1.11 One of the notable features of the 2006 Act was a commitment to a review of the impact of the legislation after five years. Under s 73 of the 2006 Act, Parliament was obliged to appoint a person to review the operation of the Act, with particular focus on some specified areas, including the Act's effect on public confidence in charities. There was a requirement for the report to be laid before Parliament.

---

2 *Private Action, Public Benefit, A Review of Charities and the Wider Not-For-Profit Sector* (Strategy Unit, Cabinet Office, September 2002).

3 The Joint Committee on Draft Charities Bill JL 167/HC660.

LORD HODGSON'S REVIEW AND OTHER DEVELOPMENTS

1.12 In November 2011, Lord Hodgson of Astley Abbots was duly appointed to carry out the review of the 2006 Act. His terms of reference were more wide ranging than those set down in the legislation: his aim was not only to report on the operation and effectiveness of the 2006 Act, but also to consider whether further changes could be made to improve the legal and regulatory framework for charities. Lord Hodgson's detailed report, *Trusted and Independent: Giving Charity Back to Charities*, was published in July 2012. He made 14 pages of recommendations.

1.13 In September 2013 Government issued a detailed response to Lord Hodgson's recommendations, in a report which also addressed a number of issues which had been raised by the Public Administration Select Committee (see **1.14**). Government committed to implementing many of the recommendations, and has since been in the process of following up this commitment through a combination of consultation, discussion and legislative change.

1.14 In July 2012 the House of Commons Public Administration Select Committee (PASC) announced a review of certain aspects of charity law, and the role of the Charity Commission. Its report, *The role of the Charity Commission and 'public benefit': Post-legislative scrutiny of the Charities Act 2006*, was published in May 2013. Government responded to the PASC's recommendations when it responded to Lord Hodgson's review.

1.15 The House of Commons Public Accounts Committee in turn published two reports on the Charity Commission in June 2013 and February 2014, which commented on the Charity Commission's regulatory approach.[4] The National Audit Office issued its own report on the Charity Commission in December 2013,[5] and a further report in January 2015 following up on its findings, and those of the Public Accounts Committee.[6]

1.16 In the summer of 2015, intense media focus on fundraising practices by charities triggered a response from both the sector and Government. This included reviews by various sector bodies and an inquiry by the Public Administration and Constitutional Affairs Committee.

CHARITIES (PROTECTION AND SOCIAL INVESTMENT) ACT 2016

1.17 The scrutiny of the Charity Commission's regulatory approach mentioned above led the Commission to call for an increase in its powers. In December 2013 the Cabinet Office published a Consultation on the Charity Commission's Powers to Tackle Abuse in Charities. This led to publication of a draft Protection of Charities Bill in October 2014: the draft Bill was scrutinised by a Joint Committee of both Houses of Parliament which reported in February 2015.[7]

---

4 *Charity Commission: the Cup Trust and tax avoidance*, June 2013. *The Charity Commission*, February 2014. A follow-up evidence session was held in January 2015. See **2.43**.

5 The regulatory effectiveness of the Charity Commission. See **2.43**.

6 Follow up on the Charity Commission.

7 Joint Committee on the Draft Protection of Charities Bill – Report HL Paper 108/HC 813 Published 25 February 2015.

1.18 In May 2015 the Charites (Protection and Social Investment) Bill was introduced into Parliament and had its first reading in the House of Lords. The legislation was based on the draft Protection of Charities Bill but also included provisions facilitating social investment by charities, in line with recommendations made by the Law Commission (see **1.23**).

1.19 As the Bill made its way through Parliament, the Government introduced further amendments designed to improve charity fundraising practices.

1.20 The Charities (Protection and Social Investment) Act 2016 received Royal Assent on 16 March 2016. Most of the substantive provisions of the 2016 Act came into force on 31 July 2016; further provisions will come into force on 1 October and 1 November 2016.[8] The remaining provisions are not likely to come into force until at least April 2017.[9]

1.21 The Minister for the Cabinet Office is required to review and report on the operation of the 2016 Act at five yearly intervals, including on how the 2016 Act affects public confidence in charities, the level of charitable donations and people's willingness to volunteer. The first review must begin within 3 years of the Act being passed and the report must be published within 4 years of the Act being passed.[10]

THE LAW COMMISSION

1.22 A further development in recent years has been the Law Commission's interest in charity law. The Law Commission is an independent body, created by statute to keep the law under review and to recommend reform where needed. In 2011 the Law Commission announced that its Eleventh Programme of Law Reform would include a review of various aspects of charity law concerning the constitution and regulation of charities and their activities. This was timely: Lord Hodgson's review highlighted a number of areas where he felt the law could be clarified or reformed, and identified a list of issues which he suggested be addressed by the Law Commission.

1.23 In April 2014, the Law Commission consulted on social investment by charities, and it produced a report in September 2014. Its recommendations led to the inclusion of social investment provisions in the Charities (Protection and Social Investment) Bill: see **1.18**.

1.24 In March 2015, the Law Commission published a further detailed consultation paper on Technical Issues in Charity Law. The stated aim of the project was to remove unnecessary regulation while safeguarding the public interest in ensuring that charities are properly run. The paper made a number of provisional recommendations designed to remove complexities in the law which impose unnecessary administrative and

---

8 The Charities (Protection and Social Investment) Act 2016 (Commencement No 1 and Transitional Provision) Regulations 2016, SI 2016/815.

9 See the implementation plan for the 2016 Act first published by the Office for Civil Society and Innovation in May 2016 and currently available at www.gov.uk/government/uploads/system/uploads/attachment_data/file/541788/charities_act_implementation_plan_29_july_2016.pdf and the Bates Wells Braithwaite 'is it in force' page for the 2016 Act at www.bwbllp.com/knowledge/2016/08/03/charities-protection-and-social-investment-act-2016-is-it-in-force/.

10 Section 16 of the 2016 Act.

financial burdens on charities. The Law Commission expects to produce a report in the first half of 2017. Legislative change may be possible in 2017/18, subject to the Parliamentary timetable.

WHAT NEXT?

1.25 This book sets out the law as at the end of July 2016 (although we have included references to the explanatory notes to the 2016 Act which were published in September 2016). Lord Hodgson's review has already led to some changes to the law and practice. The Law Commission's work may well lead to further change. Throughout the book we have highlighted areas where the indications are, at the time of writing, that there may be further amendments to the existing legislation.

1.26 As mentioned at **1.21**, the 2016 Act includes obligations for regular review of the legislation. The Joint Committee reviewing the draft Protection of Charities Bill suggested that a wider review of charity legislation after five years would be more valuable. However Government responded that in the light of recent developments, including the work of the Law Commission, there was not a pressing need for a wide review of charity legislation.[11] So as things stand it seems that although charities can expect some changes to the 2011 Act in the forthcoming years, a wholesale review of the legislation is not on the horizon.

---

[11] Government Response to the Joint Committee on the Draft Protection of Charities Bill, March 2015.

CHAPTER 2

THE CHARITY COMMISSION

INTRODUCTION

2.1 The Charity Commission is responsible for regulating charities in England and Wales. Charities in Scotland are regulated by the Office of the Scottish Charity Regulator: see 23.5. Charities in Northern Ireland are regulated by the Charity Commission for Northern Ireland: see 23.20.[1]

2.2 The Commission has a raft of statutory powers to assist charities and investigate their activities. It has been reformed and modernised over the years, with major changes introduced in 1992, and the 2006 Act and the 2016 Act making further changes to its constitution and role. These reforms have transformed the Commission from being principally a registrar into a modern regulator undertaking a wide range of activities. The work of the Commission includes:

- maintaining the register of charities (see Chapter 4);
- scrutinising charity information for the purposes of monitoring charities and providing information to the public;
- investigating the activities of existing charities and publishing the details where appropriate (see Chapter 9);
- engaging with charities in areas where the Commission's consent is required by law;
- producing guidance for charities and charity trustees;
- involvement in appeals and references to the Charity Tribunal (see Chapter 10);
- working with partner organisations and with other regulators; and
- consulting on policy and guidance.

A vast amount of information, including the online register of charities, reports, guidance, blogs and Commission-related news is available on the Commission's website.[2]

2.3 The work of the Commission is underpinned by the statutory framework in the 2011 Act, which sets out how the Commission is constituted and its statutory objectives, functions and duties. These provisions are explored in this chapter. Chapter 9 covers the more specific powers of the Commission.

---

1 Charities working throughout the United Kingdom may therefore be subject to the oversight of more than one charity regulator.

2 www.gov.uk/government/organisations/charity-commission.

2.4 In recent years the role of the Commission and where its focus should lie has been the subject of considerable public scrutiny. A desire to allow the Commission to regulate abuse in charities more effectively prompted the introduction of more significant powers in the Charities (Protection and Social Investment) Act 2016. At the same time, in common with other government departments, the Commission has been subject to major cuts in its funding since 2007. These cuts have necessarily affected how the Commission prioritises its resources.

HOW IS THE COMMISSION CONSTITUTED?

2.5 The Commission is a non-ministerial government department and part of the Civil Service (see **2.32**).

2.6 Prior to the 2006 Act, the Commission was made up of a body of individual Commissioners: the 2006 Act modernised the status of the Commission by recreating it as a body corporate.[3]

2.7 The 2011 Act[4] provides for a Commission comprised of a chair and at least four, but not more than eight, other members. They are commonly referred to as board members. All board members are appointed by the Minister for the Cabinet Office. The Commission's governance framework, published in December 2015, states that board members are appointed following fair and open competition, and that each appointment is regulated and overseen by the Office of the Commissioner for Public Appointments.[5] At least two board members must be legally qualified. At least one board member (not including the chair), with knowledge of conditions in Wales, must be appointed following consultation with the Welsh Assembly. The Minister for the Cabinet Office must ensure that the knowledge and experience of the Commission board members includes charity law, charity accounting and the financing of charities, and the operation and regulation of charities of different sizes and descriptions: this requirement was introduced in the 2006 Act in a bid to ensure that the charitable sector itself is properly represented.

2.8 The Commission may establish committees including persons who are not board members.[6]

2.9 Board members can serve for up to 3 years. Although they can be reappointed, there is a statutory bar on any board member serving for more than 10 years in total.

2.10 The Minister for the Cabinet Office decides the levels of pay and other benefits of board members.[7]

---

3 Section 13(1) of the 2011 Act.

4 Schedule 1, para 1 of the 2011 Act.

5 The 2015 governance framework also states that the chair's appointment is subject to a pre-appointment hearing before the Public Administration and Constitutional Affairs Select Committee. In April 2015 the National Council for Voluntary Organisations put forward proposals to reform the process of appointment of the chair of the Commission: see **2.36**.

6 Schedule 1, para 6 of the 2011 Act. The Charity Commission's Annual Report 2015/16 refers to an Audit and Risk Committee, a Governance and Remuneration Committee, a Public Interest Litigation and High Risk Cases Committee, a Policy and Guidance Committee and a Transform Programme Oversight Committee.

7 Schedule 1, para 4 of the 2011 Act.

2.11 The Commission may regulate its own procedure.[8] The Commission's December 2015 governance framework includes details about the board's governance arrangements, including how formal board meetings are conducted and how conflicts of interest are managed. A register of board members' interests and details of board expenses are published on the Commission's website.

2.12 The Commission is required to appoint a chief executive who is not a board member, and may appoint such other staff as it deems appropriate.[9]

2.13 The Commission has freedom to decide the salary levels and terms and conditions of service of the chief executive and other Commission staff, but this is subject to the approval of the Minister for the Civil Service.[10]

2.14 The Commission has offices in Liverpool, London, Newport and Taunton.

WHAT IS THE ROLE OF THE COMMISSION?

2.15 The 2006 Act introduced a clear statement of the objectives, functions and duties of the Commission, which is now contained in the 2011 Act.

Objectives

2.16 The Commission's five objectives are set out in s 14 of the 2011 Act. They are:

- *the public confidence objective:* to increase public trust and confidence in charities;
- *the public benefit objective:* to promote awareness and understanding of the operation of the public benefit requirement (described in detail in Chapter 3);
- *the compliance objective:* to promote compliance by charity trustees with their legal obligations in exercising control and management of the administration of their charities;
- *the charitable resources objective:* to promote the effective use of charitable resources; and
- *the accountability objective:* to enhance the accountability of charities to donors, charities and the general public.

2.17 The objectives provide a framework against which the Government, and the public, can assess the Commission's performance as regulator. The Commission must address the extent to which it believes its objectives have been met each year in its annual report.[11]

2.18 In May 2013, the Public Administration Select Committee (PASC) reported on the role of the Commission.[12] Its assessment of the Commission's statutory objectives was that they are 'far too vague and aspirational in character' representing 'an ambition

---

8 Schedule 1, para 7 of the 2011 Act.
9 Schedule 1, para 5 of the 2011 Act.
10 Schedule 1, para 5(2) of the 2011 Act.
11 Schedule 1, para 11 of the 2011 Act.
12 See **1.14**.

which the Commission could never fulfil, even before the budget cuts were initiated'.[13] Lord Hodgson, in his 2012 review of charity law, had been more sympathetic, noting that:[14]

> '(E)ven in a world where the focus is on regulation alone, the Commission's objectives continue to make sense ... While it is the compliance and accountability objectives that should be prioritised in future, the other three objectives are, in many ways, necessary and ancillary to those two goals.'

2.19 In responding to the PASC and Lord Hodgson, the Government did not agree that legislative change to the Commission's objectives was needed, saying that this 'would be a distraction from the Charity Commission's focus on its priorities'.[15]

2.20 As Lord Hodgson's report indicates, in recent years cuts in the Commission's resources have forced it to prioritise some of its objectives over others. In its Strategic Plan 2012–15 the Commission stated that in the light of its reduced resources it would focus on its accountability and compliance objectives.[16] This approach continues: in 2014 the Commission published a statement of regulatory approach, mission and values which states that:

> 'We consider that we can best fulfil all our statutory objectives, with the resources at our disposal, by concentrating on promoting compliance by charity trustees with their legal obligations, by enhancing the rigour with which we hold charities accountable, and by ensuring that we uphold the definition of charity under charity law.
>
> We also believe that this is the best way for the Commission to promote public trust and confidence in charities, and thereby encourage charitable giving and endeavour in all its forms.'

This was endorsed in the Commission's Strategic Plan 2015-18.

2.21 The scope of the Commission's objectives means that, in practice, its reach extends beyond pure charity law into areas of public, media and political interest (see 2.35).

General functions

2.22 The Commission's objectives are complemented by six general functions describing the activities the Commission is to carry out in seeking to achieve its objectives. The functions, which illustrate the scope of the Commission's role, are set out in s 15 of the 2011 Act. The five functions in force at the time of writing are:

- determining whether institutions are or are not charities;
- encouraging and facilitating the better administration of charities;
- identifying and investigating apparent misconduct or mismanagement in the administration of charities and taking remedial or protective action in connection with misconduct or mismanagement in the administration of charities;

---

13 Public Administration Select Committee (PASC) Report 2013, para 22.
14 *Trusted and Independent, Giving Charity Back to Charities*, para 5.16.
15 Government response, p 7.
16 Introduction to Charity Commission Strategic Plan 2012–15, p 1.

- obtaining, evaluating and disseminating information in connection with the performance of any of the Commission's functions or meeting any of its objectives. This specifically includes maintaining an accurate and up-to-date register of charities; and
- giving information or advice or making proposals to any Minister on matters relating to the Commission's functions or meeting its objectives.

A further function, set out at para 4 of s 15(1), is that of determining whether public collections certificates should be issued, and remain in force, in respect of public charitable collections. However, this provision is not in force,[17] as it is linked to the provisions in the 2006 Act dealing with public charitable collections which are now unlikely ever to be brought into force (see Chapter 18).

2.23 The Commission must report on the discharge of its functions in its annual report.[18]

2.24 The Commission's dual role as regulator and supporter to charities, which has long been the subject of debate, is illustrated in its range of functions. The second function highlights the assistance the Commission provides to charities with their administration, while the third deals with its powers to investigate and intervene in charities' activities.

2.25 In his 2012 review of charity law, Lord Hodgson asked whether the Commission's role as both a supporter and regulator can, or should, continue. Whilst he noted there was evidence from across the sector that the advisory work of the Commission is greatly valued, he concluded:[19]

> 'for all the benefits this advisory work delivers, it cannot be seen as essential to the core work of the Charity Commission, which is to ensure that charities comply with charity law. In a time of significantly reduced resources, the "friend" side of the Commission's work can only be seen as an extra and its regulatory role must come to the fore.'

He recommended that the Commission:[20]

> 'should prioritise its core functions:
>
> a. Registering charities (and maintaining an accurate register);
> b. Identifying, deterring and tackling misconduct and abuse of charitable status; and
> c. Providing the public with information (in a relevant form which is easily understood by the public) about charities, and charities with information about charity law.'

2.26 In 2013 the Public Administration Select Committee, in turn, concluded that: '[T]he core role of the Charity Commission must be the regulation of the charitable sector'[21] and that its 'reduced budget means extra tasks, outside of its statutory objectives, are an unaffordable luxury ... Furthermore, by seeking to be an advice service to charities, the Commission also risks a conflict of interest: it cannot

---

17 Schedule 9, para 1 of the 2011 Act.
18 Schedule 1, para 11 of the 2011 Act.
19 *Trusted and Independent*, para 5.9.
20 *Trusted and Independent*, ch 5, recommendation 2.
21 Public Administration Select Committee (PASC) Report, May 2013, para 20.

simultaneously maintain public trust in the charitable sector while also acting as champion of charities and the charitable sector.'[22]

2.27 In practice, the Commission's focus on accountability and compliance, mentioned above, and on its core regulatory functions does mean that there is now far less opportunity for direct engagement between the Commission and charities, particularly smaller charities, than has been the case in the past. At the time of writing the Commission's telephone helpline is only open on weekdays in the mornings. Charities are encouraged to communicate with the Commission via its website, and where seeking advice are often likely to be referred to generic guidance rather than given bespoke advice. The Commission's Annual Report for 2015-16 states that it 'can rarely offer one-to-one advice'.

General duties

2.28 The 2011 Act sets out the general duties which the Commission must comply with in performing its functions or managing its affairs. The Commission's duties, which were introduced by the 2006 Act, and are now contained in s 16 of the 2011 Act, are as follows:

- in performing its functions, to act in a way which is compatible with its objectives and which it considers most appropriate for the purpose of meeting them;
- in performing its functions, to act in a way which is compatible with encouraging all forms of charitable giving and volunteering;
- in performing its functions, to have regard to the need to use its resources in the most efficient, effective and economic way;
- in performing its functions, to have regard to the principles of best regulatory practice, including those under which regulatory activities should be proportionate, accountable, consistent, transparent and targeted only at cases in which action is needed;
- in performing its functions, in appropriate cases, to have regard to the desirability of facilitating innovation by or on behalf of charities; and
- in managing its affairs, to have regard to generally accepted principles of good corporate governance.

The Commission must report on the performance of its general duties in its annual report.[23]

2.29 In his 2012 review of charity law, Lord Hodgson's view of the duties was that they 'provide a framework against which to judge the Commission's performance in terms of not just what it has done, but the way in which it has done it. They serve as a restatement and reminder of good practice'.[24]

2.30 During the debates on the legislation which became the 2006 Act, the Government consistently resisted pressure to include a specific statutory duty on the Commission to act fairly and reasonably, arguing that as a public body the Commission is obliged to act fairly and reasonably in any event. The duty to have regard to the

---

22 Ibid, para 23.
23 Schedule 1, para 11 of the 2011 Act.
24 *Trusted and Independent*, para 5.20.

principles of best regulatory practice and therefore to act in a way which is proportionate and accountable was introduced as an amendment to the Bill in the House of Lords. This duty is reinforced in the Legislative and Regulatory Reform Act 2006 which imposes a duty on regulators, including the Commission, to have regard to the principles that regulatory activities should be carried out in a way which is transparent, accountable, proportionate and consistent, and should be targeted only at cases in which action is needed. In addition, the Commission, in common with other regulators, is subject to the Regulators' Code. The code sets out a number of key principles, including basing regulatory activities on risk, and ensuring that clear information, guidance and advice is available to help those being regulated to meet their responsibilities.[25] The Deregulation Act 2015 also contains provisions obliging regulators to have regard to the desirability of promoting economic growth: at the time of writing these are not in force, but it is conceivable that some of the Commission's functions may be brought within their scope.[26]

2.31 The Commission's 2014 statement of mission, regulatory approach and values states that it 'will be an efficient, objective and proportionate authority that seeks to deliver just and reasonable outcomes'. However, the new powers for the Commission in the 2016 Act have given rise to concerns that a political focus on making the Commission a stronger regulator, with enhanced powers, is not being balanced with accountability safeguards.

THE COMMISSION'S INDEPENDENCE AND ACCOUNTABILITY

The Commission's status

2.32 As mentioned at 2.5, the Commission is a non-ministerial government department (or NMD). This means that government ministers have no legal power to give directions to the Commission, whose decisions can only be overturned by the courts. Section 13(3) of the 2011 Act provides that 'the functions of the Commission are performed on behalf of the Crown', but it is clear from s 13(4) that 'in the exercise of its functions the Commission is not subject to the direction or control of any Minister of the Crown or of another government department'.

2.33 In the debates on the legislation which became the 2006 Act, the question of the Commission's status was hotly debated in both Houses of Parliament, with different contributors flatly disagreeing on what was best for the sector. Lord Phillips of Sudbury argued that:[27]

> 'The Charity Commission is a quasi-judicial body and, just as the judges in the courts have to be seen to be independent as well as being independent, so the greater constitutional distance one can create between the Commission and the Government, the better for the Commission and the Government ... The public will not believe that, if the Charity Commission has non-ministerial departmental status, it is completely free of influence from, or behind the arras of, government or, indeed, senior opposition politicians.'

---

25 Sections 21 to 24 of the Legislative and Regulatory Reform Act 2006 and the Legislative and Regulatory Reform (Regulatory Functions) Order 2007, SI 2007/3544.

26 Sections 108 to 111 of the Deregulation Act 2015.

27 Lords Hansard text for 10 February 2005 (50210–24).

2.34 In the event, the 2006 Act made no changes to the Commission's status and it remained as a non-ministerial government department. However, the issue was considered again in 2012, as the review conducted by Lord Hodgson was specifically charged with considering the status of the Commission as a government department.[28] Lord Hodgson duly considered a range of alternative options for the status of the Commission, concluding that:[29]

> 'its current status as an NMD is "the least worst option." To turn the Commission into an arm's length body or non-departmental public body would most likely require it to become accountable to a Minister, which would reduce its level of independence. To make it accountable to Parliament, in a similar way to the National Audit Office, would increase its independence from Government but would be otherwise inappropriate as the Commission exercises some executive and judicial functions.'

2.35 Yet Lord Phillips' concerns remain relevant. Charities are often subject to intense media and political scrutiny and, as mentioned above, the Commission does operate in areas which are of public and political interest and which can be highly emotive and controversial. The Commission is also challenged and pressurised publicly in politically motivated ways, while endeavouring to fulfil its politically neutral responsibilities. It is vulnerable to accusations of political bias, however unfounded.

2.36 In April 2015 the National Council for Voluntary Organisations published a paper on the independence of the Commission.[30] Like Lord Hodgson, it concluded that there was no case for a change of status, but argued that the perception of independence could be addressed by improving the current process of appointment of the Commission's chair in a way which distances the role of the chair from executive control. It suggested that Parliament should have a greater involvement in the process.

2.37 In his Review, Lord Hodgson also recommended that consideration should be given to whether the name 'Charity Commission' was sufficiently well-matched to the Commission's role going forward to support public and sector understanding of that role. He suggested the name 'Charity Authority' as an alternative.[31] The Government did not accept this recommendation, commenting that it might undermine current improvements in public awareness of the Commission, and it was not a priority in a time of limited resources.[32]

Accountability

2.38 A number of practical and legal mechanisms are designed to ensure that the Commission is accountable to Parliament and to the public at large.

2.39 Schedule 1, para 11 of the 2011 Act imposes an obligation on the Commission to publish an annual report on the discharge of its functions, the extent to which it believes its objectives have been met, the performance of its general duties and the management of its affairs. The report must be laid before Parliament.

---

28 Section 73 of the 2006 Act.
29 *Trusted and Independent*, para 5.4.
30 Charity Commission Independence NCVO Discussion Paper April 2015.
31 *Trusted and Independent*, ch 5, recommendation 6.
32 Government response, p 26.

2.40 Under Sch 1, para 12 of the 2011 Act, the Commission must hold a public meeting each year within three months of the date of publishing the report in order to allow charities and the wider public to discuss the report and ask the Commission questions about its content. The Commission must try to ensure that all registered charities have notice of the meeting, and that it receives as much general publicity as possible.

2.41 As a government department, the Commission has its accounts audited by the National Audit Office, and is subject to periodic Value for Money examinations by the National Audit Office and Public Accounts Committee, which lead to published reports.[33]

2.42 The Commission's work falls within the remit of parliamentary committees: see for example the work of the Public Administration and Constitutional Affairs Committee (which succeeded the Public Administration Select Committee in 2015).[34] In May 2016 the House of Lords set up a Select Committee on Charities.

2.43 In recent years the Commission's effectiveness as a regulator has come under intense scrutiny. The Public Accounts Committee published two reports on the Commission in June 2013 and February 2014, concluding that 'the Commission's approach to regulation and enforcement lacks rigour' and 'the Commission has not regulated the charity sector effectively'.[35] In a report in December 2013 the National Audit Office described the Commission as reactive rather than proactive and said that the Commission was neither regulating charities effectively nor delivering value for money.[36] The National Audit Office and the Public Accounts Committee have since carried out follow up work with the Commission, both acknowledging the work which the Commission has done in addressing their recommendations.[37]

THE COMMISSION'S RESOURCES

2.44 The changes introduced by the 2006 Act imposed a number of additional responsibilities on the Commission. These included its obligation to issue guidance on public benefit, the registration of excepted and exempt charities for the first time and dealing with appeals to the new Charity Tribunal.

2.45 The Joint Committee scrutinising the draft legislation which became the 2006 Act echoed the concerns of many in querying 'whether the Charity Commission is properly organised and properly resourced to make it effective in its new tasks'.[38]

---

33 See, for example, the 2013 and 2014 Public Accounts Committee reports, and the 2013 National Audit Office report, which are referred to at **1.15**.

34 See, for example, the PACAC Report 'The 2015 Charity Fundraising Controversy: Lessons for Trustees, the Charity Commission, and the Regulators' published in January 2016, and the PASC Report 'The Role of the Charity Commission and "public benefit": Post-legislative scrutiny of the Charities Act 2006' published in May 2013.

35 PAC Report 'Charity Commission: The Cup Trust and Tax Avoidance 2013', p 5 and PAC Report 'The Charity Commission 2014', p 5.

36 The regulatory effectiveness of the Charity Commission, National Audit Office, December 2013.

37 See, for example, Follow-up on the Charity Commission, National Audit Office, January 2015 and the PAC follow-up evidence session with the Charity Commission in January 2015, and subsequent correspondence, available at www.parliament.uk/business/committees/committees-a-z/commons-select/public-accounts-committee.

38 Paragraph 215 of the Joint Committee on Draft Charities Bill HL 167/HC660.

2.46 These concerns have been exacerbated by substantial cuts to the Commission's budget since 2007. In his report, Lord Hodgson's recommendation regarding the funding of the Commission was:[39]

> 'The Commission needs to be adequately funded to properly regulate the sector. Some analysis of financial efficiency and requirements needs to be undertaken as reductions in the Charity Commission's budget take place.'

2.47 He suggested that the Commission should develop a charging system for filing annual returns and for the registration of new charities, which would increase the Commission's resources.[40] The Government responded that it 'continues to believe that the Charity Commission has sufficient resources to effectively regulate charities, provided it focuses on its core regulatory functions'.[41] It was not supportive of charging by the Commission.[42]

2.48 The Commission has been clear that its ability to regulate charities has been adversely affected by cuts to its funding. In responding to the February 2014 report of the Public Accounts Committee, the chair of the Commission, William Shawcross, argued that:

> '... Parliament has granted us a broad regulatory remit. If we are to fulfil all the expectations placed on us while at the same time increasing our serious case work, we must be adequately funded. Our current funding position is simply unsustainable.'[43]

2.49 The Commission has since been in receipt of some additional funding. But a freeze on the Commission's funding was announced in the November 2015 spending review. And the debate over the Commission's role, effectiveness and resources continues. In the Commission's Strategic Plan 2015-18, the Commission identified reduced dependence on taxpayer funding as a strategic priority and noted that it would be consulting on alternative funding options, including an annual charge for registered charities. The Commission's Annual Report 2015-16, published in July 2016, indicated that a consultation on its funding would be launched later in the year. Discussions about resources and charging by the Commission are therefore set to continue.

---

39 *Trusted and Independent*, ch 5, recommendation 5.
40 *Trusted and Independent*, ch 6, recommendation 18.
41 Government Response to the Lord Hodgson Review and PASC Report, part 3, para 22.
42 Government response, p 33 and see also **4.67–4.69** and **21.92**.
43 Commission press release dated 10 April 2014.

CHAPTER 3

CHARITABLE PURPOSES AND PUBLIC BENEFIT

INTRODUCTION

3.1 The 2006 Act introduced, for the first time, a statutory list of charitable purposes. Together with the new provisions about public benefit, these were high profile and hotly debated elements of the new legislation. These provisions are now set out in the 2011 Act. This remains an evolving area of the law. The legislation specifically contemplates the development of new charitable purposes which are analogous to or within the spirit of existing charitable purposes. Recent cases in the Charity Tribunal have provided a degree of clarity as to the interpretation of the provisions about public benefit.

CHARITY DEFINITION BEFORE THE 2006 ACT

3.2 Prior to the 2006 Act the definition of what was charitable was a matter of case law. A charitable organisation had to have exclusively charitable purposes and be established for public benefit.

3.3 Accepted charitable purposes were originally based on the preamble to the 1601 Statute of Elizabeth which contained an illustrative list:

> 'The relief of aged, impotent and poor people; the maintenance of sick and maimed soldiers and mariners, schools of learning, free schools and scholars in universities; the repair of bridges, ports, havens, causeways, churches, sea-banks and highways; the education and preferment of orphans; the relief, stock or maintenance of houses of correction; the marriages of poor maids, the supportation, aid and help of young tradesmen, handicraftsmen and persons decayed; the relief or redemption of prisoners or captives; and the aid or ease of any poor inhabitants concerning payment of fifteens, setting out of soldiers and other taxes.'

3.4 Over the years, the courts refined that list into four 'heads' or categories of charitable purpose:

- relief of poverty;
- advancement of education;
- advancement of religion; and
- other purposes beneficial to the community.

3.5 The advantage of this common law definition was that there was flexibility for new purposes to be added as social and economic circumstances changed. Any new purpose had to be analogous to an existing charitable purpose or to the 1601 preamble.

3.6 It was commonly thought that for the first three heads, public benefit was presumed unless there was evidence to the contrary. For the fourth head, public benefit had to be demonstrated.

OVERVIEW OF THE CHARITY DEFINITION IN THE 2011 ACT

3.7 The 2006 Act did not introduce an entirely new definition of what is charitable, but restated and developed existing case-law. However, the 2006 Act did remove the link to the preamble in the 1601 Statute of Elizabeth and new purposes may now be accepted by analogy with existing charitable purposes.

3.8 Significantly, the 2006 Act was heralded as removing the presumption of public benefit for the first three heads or categories of charitable purpose so that for the first time all charities would have to demonstrate that their purposes are for the public benefit. However, the question of whether there was, in fact, such a presumption prior to the 2006 Act is now less clear (see 3.86).

3.9 In essence the 2011 Act:

- retains the definition of a charity as an organisation that is established for exclusively charitable purposes and is for public benefit (s 1(1));
- lists 13 descriptions of charitable purposes, which replace the four previous heads of charitable purpose. The list is designed to reflect the range of purposes that were already charitable under the fourth head. In some areas, the definition is expanded or clarified, but all existing charitable purposes are included. The flexibility to add new categories, as social and economic circumstances change, is retained (s 3(1));
- requires all charities to demonstrate that their purposes are for public benefit. Pre-existing case law relating to public benefit is preserved;
- requires the Charity Commission to publish guidance about public benefit, which charity trustees must have regard to, and consult where necessary before publishing or revising its guidance.

Scotland and Northern Ireland

3.10 The charity definition in the 2011 Act applies only to England and Wales. In Scotland the Charities and Trustee Investment (Scotland) Act 2005 introduced a slightly different definition of charity and an alternative public benefit test. It requires charities to 'provide' public benefit, placing greater emphasis on activities rather than purposes, and sets some statutory criteria which the Office of the Scottish Regulator ('OSCR') must have regard to when considering whether public benefit is provided by a body's activities. These include considering private benefit, 'disbenefit' which is likely to be incurred by the public and whether the conditions on obtaining benefit (including fee-charging) are unduly restrictive.

3.11 In Northern Ireland, the Charities Act 2008 (Northern Ireland) (as amended by the Charities Act (Northern Ireland) 2013) sets out a definition of public benefit which is based on English law and is linked to an organisation's purposes, rather than its activities.

Definition of charity for tax purposes

3.12 Section 1(2) of the 2011 Act states that where there is a different definition of 'charity' in other legislation, this will be retained. Schedule 6 of the Finance Act 2010 provides a definition of charity for UK tax purposes. To receive tax relief a charity must be established for charitable purposes only (as defined in the 2011 Act) and it must also meet three further conditions relating to jurisdiction, registration and management). These provisions ensure that tax relief for charities in Scotland and Northern Ireland links back to charitable purposes as they are defined in English law, although charities established in Scotland and Northern Ireland must also comply with the requirements to register in those jurisdictions to meet the registration condition (see **4.81**).

CHARITABLE PURPOSES

3.13 The list of descriptions of charitable purposes is set out at s 3(1)–(4) of the 2011 Act:

(a) the prevention or relief of poverty;
(b) the advancement of education;
(c) the advancement of religion;
(d) the advancement of health or the saving of lives;
(e) the advancement of citizenship or community development;
(f) the advancement of the arts, culture, heritage or science;
(g) the advancement of amateur sport;
(h) the advancement of human rights, conflict resolution or reconciliation, or the promotion of religious or racial harmony or equality and diversity;
(i) the advancement of environmental protection or improvement;
(j) the relief of those in need by reason of youth, age, ill-health, disability, financial hardship or other disadvantage;
(k) the advancement of animal welfare;
(l) the promotion of the efficiency of the armed forces of the Crown, or of the efficiency of the police, fire and rescue services or ambulance services; or
(m) any other purposes recognised as charitable under the law before the 2006 Act, or analogous to or within the spirit of existing charitable purposes.

3.14 Section 3(2) of the 2011 Act gives further clarification about some of the categories listed. In general, terms used in the list are to be interpreted in the same way as they were under charity law before the 2006 Act (s 3(3)). This means that the extensive body of case law is retained.

3.15 Section 3(1)(m)(i) of the 2011 Act states that any existing charitable purpose not explicitly listed will continue to be charitable. This includes recreational charities: see **3.64**.

3.16 The expanded list of charitable purposes extended what was considered charitable before the 2006 Act. The practical effect of this is that:

- some organisations that previously could not register may now be able to do so;
- charities such as grant-giving trusts that have general charitable objects can now fund or undertake work in these new areas; and
- some existing charities can apply to the Commission to expand their objects to include newly accepted purposes, if they wish.

3.17 The Commission has published guidance linked to each category as well as guidance on drafting charitable objects and a number of example objects for different types of charity. The guidance includes key Commission decisions relating to each category.

The prevention or relief of poverty: s 3(1)(a)

3.18 The relief of poverty was expanded to include the prevention of poverty and charities may now give help to those who are not poor but who without the charity's help would become so. Charities can also tackle the root causes of poverty by, for example, equipping people with skills, knowledge and resources to lift themselves out of poverty.

3.19 Poverty continues to be interpreted broadly to include the disadvantages and difficulties arising from, or which cause, the lack of financial or material resources. The Commission recognises that it is generally charitable 'to relieve either the poverty or the financial hardship of anyone who does not have the resources to provide themselves, either on a short or long-term basis, with the normal things of life which most people take for granted.'[1] The category includes:

- famine relief and overseas development charities;
- charities which undertake research, education and healthcare projects directed towards alleviating social conditions that can lead to, or can be caused by, poverty;
- organisations which make grants or small loans to those in poverty in an area of particular deprivation; and
- charities concerned with relieving the poverty of people who are particularly vulnerable and who have a particular need (for example, refugees and asylum seekers or the elderly).[2]

The advancement of education: s 3(1)(b)

3.20 Education continues to be interpreted widely to include:

- formal education by institutions such as schools and universities;
- less formal education such as playgroups, vocational training and in community groups;
- developing individual capabilities, competences, skills and understanding;

---

1 Charity Commission guidance *Charitable purposes*.

2 See the Charity Commission's publication 'The Prevention or Relief of Poverty for the Public Benefit' for further guidance.

- undertaking academic research and publishing the results;
- providing mentoring and coaching;
- physical education and development of young people;
- educating the general public by publishing educational information or running libraries, museums and art galleries; and
- making grants available to students for books or other equipment, or support to enable them to be taught in mainstream classes.[3]

3.21 Educational charities are similarly broad, including schools, universities, pre-schools, youth sporting organisations, those developing life skills training, such as the Duke of Edinburgh Award schemes, research charities, think tanks, museums, galleries, libraries, learned societies, and those which educate the public in a particular subject. Note that there is an overlap with the advancement of the arts, culture, heritage or science (see 3.37–3.38).

3.22 To be charitable, education must go beyond merely providing experience or information. It does not have to be value free and completely neutral – it may be based on broad values that are uncontroversial and which would generally be supported by objective and informed people – for example, a view that the countryside, in general, is beneficial (upheld in the Commission's decision to register The Countryside Alliance Foundation as a charity).

The advancement of religion: s 3(1)(c)

3.23 This category includes:

- providing a place of worship including provision of property for retreat;
- providing religious instruction and raising awareness of religious beliefs and practices;
- religious devotional acts including visiting the sick;
- outreach and missionary work; and
- inter-faith charities.[4]

However, the promotion of a particular religious doctrine is not necessarily charitable (as determined in the Commission's decision on Good News for Israel, which found that promoting the doctrine of Aliyah, being 'the promotion of the return of Jewish people to the land promised to them by God' was not charitable).

3.24 The vexed question of how to define a religion was considered by the Charity Commissioners when they published their reasons for not registering the Church of Scientology in 1999. The Commissioners concluded that to be a religion there must be:

- a belief in a Supreme Being;
- expression of that belief through worship of the Supreme Being.

---

3 See the Charity Commission's publication 'The Advancement of Education for the Public Benefit' for further guidance.

4 See the Charity Commission's publication 'The Advancement of Religion for the Public Benefit' for further guidance.

3.25 With non-deity faiths such as Buddhism and multi-deity faiths such as Hinduism, prior to the 2006 Act the question of how to deal with charity registration was not always straightforward. Some Buddhist organisations, for example, had to register with the Commission as educational charities advancing the teachings of the Buddha. However, this was not consistently applied and some charities were registered with promotion of Buddhism as their object.

3.26 To comply with the Human Rights Act 1998, it was important that all the world's major religions were included in the charity law definition. However, there was disagreement as to what, if anything, was necessary to address this. The result was s 3(2)(a) which states that 'religion' includes multi-deity and non-deity faiths.

3.27 There was some confusion in Parliament when the 2006 Act was being debated about how a non-deity religion could meet the criteria of worshipping a Supreme Being, even though the Commission in practice had long accepted religions which did not involve belief in a deity. The position was clarified in 2013 when the Supreme Court recognised a Scientology chapel as a place of meeting for religious worship.[5] The case concerned whether a valid marriage ceremony could be held at the chapel and did not consider the charitable status of Scientology or any other religion. However, it is influential in how religion is defined for the purposes of charity law because it overturns a previous case[6] which had decided that Scientology did not involve religious worship since it did not involve reverence for or veneration of a Supreme Being or entity. Lord Toulson's 2013 judgment defined religion as 'a spiritual or non-secular belief system, held by a group of adherents, which claims to explain mankind's place in the universe and relationship with the infinite, and to teach its adherents how they are to live their lives in conformity with the spiritual understanding associated with the belief system. By spiritual or non-secular I mean a belief system which goes beyond that which can be perceived by the senses or ascertained by the application of science.' As a result, it is likely to be easier for organisations to establish that they are advancing a religion, but they will still need to meet the public benefit test to be charitable.

3.28 The Commission also states that a religion must also have a degree of cogency, cohesion, seriousness and importance and an identifiable positive, beneficial, moral or ethical framework.[7] Clearly this is a complicated area and, while it tends to be taken for granted in the case of more mainstream and long-established religious groups and traditions, there is still argument on the fringes as to whether certain organisations are religions, and therefore charitable (provided they also meet the public benefit test), or not.

3.29 The Government was keen not to expand the definition too far and rejected a proposed amendment to the Bill which became the 2006 Act to define religion in terms of a belief in 'a supernatural principle, being or thing' in case it would broaden the definition to allow palmistry, horoscopy and tree worship to qualify. Spiritualism, including the promotion of mediumship and clairvoyancy has nevertheless been recognised by the Commission as charitable (before the 2006 Act) where is it sufficiently incorporated into religious practices.[8]

---

5 *R (on the application of Hodkin and anor) v Registrar General of Births, Deaths and Marriages* [2013] UKSC 77.

6 *R v Registrar General, ex parte Segerdal* [1970] 2 QB 697, [1970] 3 All ER 886, [1970] 3 WLR 479.

7 *Charity Commission guidance Charitable purposes.*

8 Decision of the Charity Commissioners to register Sacred Heart Hands Spiritual Centre as a Charity.

3.30 Since the 2006 Act the Commission has refused to register The Gnostic Centre as a charity with objects to advance the Gnostic religion on the basis that its founders had not identified a positive, beneficial, moral or ethical framework which was being promoted, although the Commission accepted that Gnosticism met the other characteristics of a religion.[9] However, it registered The Druid Network, a charity with objects 'to provide information on the principles and practice of Druidry for the benefit of all and to inspire and facilitate that practice for those who have committed themselves to this spiritual path' as a charity for the advancement of religion.[10]

3.31 The Government had also resisted proposed amendments to the Bill which preceded the 2006 Act to expand the definition to include belief systems such as humanism, which fell within the catch-all category 'advancement of moral improvement'. In 2008 the Charity Commission consulted on draft guidance on public benefit and the advancement of moral or ethical belief systems, but did not proceed with publishing formal guidance. However, in November 2011, the Commission approved the new objects of the British Humanist Association, which was previously registered as an educational charity, which expressly include the advancement of humanism as 'a non-religious ethical life stance'. The decision marked a significant change in approach to non-religious beliefs.

The advancement of health or the saving of lives: s 3(1)(d)

3.32 The advancement of health explicitly includes the prevention or relief of sickness, disease or human suffering (s 3(2)(b)). Using the term 'advancement of health' rather than the traditional 'relief of sickness' demonstrates the growing emphasis on preventing disease before it occurs. This category covers a broad range of charities, including hospitals, medical research organisations and charities set up to help individuals with a particular disease, as well as charities that promote activities which have a proven beneficial effect on health, and organisations offering complementary or alternative therapies (provided their efficacy can be demonstrated). The category also covers charities that advance health indirectly, for example by ensuring proper standards in medical practice or providing facilities and services for nurses or other medical practitioners. It also covers assistance to victims of war or natural disasters. There is therefore overlap between this head and s 3(1)(j) 'relief of those in need by reason of … ill-health [and] disability' and the relief of poverty.

3.33 The saving of life covers purposes such as the provision of life saving or self defence classes and the provision of lifeboats, mountain rescue services and first aid, although there is also an explicit reference to rescue services in s 3(1)(l).

The advancement of citizenship or community development: s 3(1)(e)

3.34 The advancement of citizenship or community development covers a broad range of charitable purposes mainly directed towards support for community and social structures, rather than individuals.

---

9 Charity Commission Decision made on 16 December 2009 on the application for registration of The Gnostic Centre.

10 Charity Commission Decision made on 21 September 2010 on the application for registration of The Druid Network.

3.35 Section 3(2)(c) states that this category includes rural or urban regeneration and the promotion of civic responsibility, volunteering, the voluntary sector or the effectiveness or efficiency of charities. The following Charity Commission guidance gives more details about what activities charities with these objects can undertake:

- RR2 – 'Promotion of Urban and Rural Regeneration';
- RR3 – 'Charities for the Relief of Unemployment';
- RR5 – 'The Promotion of Community Capacity Building';
- RR13 – 'Promotion of the Voluntary Sector for the Benefit of the Public';
- RR14 – 'Promoting the Efficiency and Effectiveness of Charities and the Effective Use of Charitable Resources for the Benefit of the Public'.

3.36 This is a mixed bag of purposes that would cover organisations such as:

- Scout and Guide groups, which promote civic responsibility and good citizenship;
- organisations regenerating particular geographical areas or funding such work;
- umbrella organisations supporting other charities;
- the promotion of community capacity building; and
- charities concerned with social investment.

Note that the Commission does not generally accept that advancement of community development itself is a charitable purpose, so when drafting objects it is necessary to spell out which purpose(s) within this heading a charity will be furthering. It is not clear to the authors why the Commission sees advancement of community development as different from other descriptions of purposes, which can be directly incorporated into charitable objects.

The advancement of the arts, culture, heritage or science: s 3(1)(f)

3.37 Many of the activities covered by this category were, prior to the 2006 Act, included within the advancement of education. The separate head reflects and highlights the wide range of charitable organisations that operate in this area. 'Art' includes numerous forms of art from a national and/or professional level to a local and/or amateur level, provided a criterion of merit is satisfied. 'Heritage' includes local or national history.

3.38 The category includes:

- charities that promote or encourage high standards of the arts;
- charities for the preservation of historic land or buildings or concerned with maintaining a particular tradition such as carnivals or folk dancing;
- museums, art galleries, art festivals (see Charity Commission publication RR10);
- theatres and cinemas;
- the promotion of crafts and craftsmanship;
- local arts and drama groups; and
- charities connected with learned societies and institutions.

Note that there remains an overlap with the advancement of education and charities which are working in this area often have both purposes in their charitable objects.

The advancement of amateur sport: s 3(1)(g)

3.39 Prior to the 2006 Act, the advancement of sport was only recognised as being charitable so far as it was a means to further other charitable purposes. The 2006 Act expanded the law in this area as it reversed *Re Nottage, Jones v Palmer*,[11] where it was held by the Court of Appeal that the promotion of sport was not charitable. As a result of this case, for many years single sports clubs could not register as charities, although multi-sports clubs and leisure centres were able to do so under the Recreational Charities Act 1958. The Commission relaxed the position in 2002 by accepting 'the promotion of community participation in healthy recreation' as a charitable object. This allowed single sport clubs to register, provided they were open to the whole community regardless of their ability, and provided fees were kept at a reasonable level.

3.40 The proposals made by the 2002 Strategy Unit report which were enacted in the 2006 Act were intended to allow sports clubs that select members on the basis of their aptitude or fitness to register for the first time. Having social (non-playing) members should also no longer be a barrier. However, clubs that select on an arbitrary basis, such as personal connections, would continue to be excluded. However, this has not been followed in practice by the Commission, which continues to apply the same tests used prior to the 2006 Act, which are set out in its guidance note RR11 'Charitable status and sport'.

'Sport'

3.41 The 2011 Act defines the advancement of amateur sport as the advancement of amateur sports or games which promote health by involving physical or mental skill or exertion (s 3(2)(d)). The Act does not further define 'sport', 'game' or 'amateur' which continue to bear their ordinary and natural meaning, having no particular meaning in charity law. It reflects changes introduced in the 2006 Act, which broadened the law by including reference to games, but also made promoting physical or mental health a necessary element of the definition.

3.42 The health benefits of most sports have already been accepted by the Commission. For sports not previously accepted such as angling, ballooning, billiards, crossbow or rifle shooting, flying, gliding, motor sports and parachuting, it will be for each sport to make its case.

3.43 In 2011 Hitchin Bridge Club, which provides facilities for the playing of duplicate bridge, was entered onto the register of charities as the Commission was satisfied as to the potential health benefits which might arise from the mental skill and exertion involved in the regular playing of bridge. In comparison, the Ferryhill District Angling Club, which exists to promote participation in recreational activity for the public benefit through the provision of angling facilities, was found not to have been established for charitable purposes. In 2015 the First-tier Tribunal decided that the Cambridgeshire Target Shooting Association was not a charity. The Tribunal held that activities which represented a material proportion of the Association's shooting activities were not shown to have any physical skill or exertion, such as to promote general health. It also

---

11 [1895] 2 Ch 649.

decided that the evidence before it had not shown that there was sufficient mental skill or exertion involved in the range of shooting activities promoted in pursuance of the Association's objects.[12]

'Amateur'

3.44 'Amateur' is not defined in the 2011 Act, but the Strategy Unit report which preceded the 2006 Act suggested that the Treasury's definition of amateur in what was then Sch 18 of the Finance Act 2002[13] should apply, which prohibited payments to players but allowed:

- payment for costs of obtaining coaching qualifications; and
- reimbursement of reasonable travel expenses incurred by players and officials travelling to away matches.

General

3.45 This category should therefore include:

- a range of single sports clubs, and clubs such as chess clubs;
- organisations promoting amateur sport, such as governing bodies; and
- organisations funding improvements to sporting facilities.

3.46 The Commission consulted some time ago about republishing its guidance RR11 'Charitable Status and Sport', to take account of the changes brought in by the 2006 Act. However at the time of writing the revised guidance has not yet been published and it remains to be seen how far the Commission will be prepared to expand the current approach in light of s 3(1)(g) and s 5 of the 2011 Act (see **3.64**).

Community amateur sports clubs

3.47 The Finance Act 2002 introduced favourable tax treatment for community amateur sports clubs that meet certain criteria and register with HMRC (commonly referred to as CASCs).[14] It was feared that introducing the promotion of amateur sport as a charitable object might mean that some CASCs had constitutions that looked charitable and they would be forced to register with the Commission. Section 6 of the 2011 Act deals with this issue and states that a CASC registered with HMRC cannot be a charity.

3.48 Unfortunately, there is no provision for CASCs to become charities if they wish. This means that if a CASC wishes to become a charity, it must set up a new charitable club and transfer its assets. Surprisingly, the Commission accepts that it may be possible for a charitable sports club to register as a CASC and cease to be a charity, but details of when this would be acceptable remain unclear.

---

12 *Cambridgeshire Target Shooting Association v Charity Commission* (CA/2015/0002).

13 Similar provisions now appear in s 660 of the Corporation Tax Act 2010.

14 The legislation relating to CASCs now appears in the Corporation Tax Act 2010, Part 13, Chapter 9 and the Community Amateur Sports Clubs Regulations 2015, SI 2015/725.

The advancement of human rights, conflict resolution or reconciliation or the promotion of religious or racial harmony or equality and diversity: s 3(1)(h)

3.49 The Commission previously accepted that advancing human rights and promoting religious or racial harmony or equality and diversity were charitable because these activities were analogous to the pre-existing charitable purpose of promoting moral improvement. The inclusion of this head in the 2006 Act provides a statutory basis for this.

3.50 The advancement of conflict resolution or reconciliation had been also recognised as a charitable purpose before the 2006 Act.[15] It includes the resolution of international conflicts and relieving the suffering, poverty and distress arising through conflict on a national or international scale by identifying the causes of the conflict and seeking to resolve such conflict. The Commission also includes within this head the promotion of restorative justice, defined as being where all the parties with a stake in a particular conflict or offence come together to resolve collectively how to deal with its aftermath and its implications for the future. Charities established to promote mediation, conciliation or reconciliation as between persons, organisations, authorities or groups involved or likely to become involved in dispute or inter-personal conflict are also included. It should be noted that this is not the same as promoting peace, which continues to be outside the scope of charity in England and Wales.[16]

3.51 The Commission published guidance on promoting human rights before the 2006 Act in its leaflet RR12. The scope of this purpose has subsequently been considered by the First-tier Tribunal in relation to the Human Dignity Trust, as the Commission asserted that its meaning was unclear. The Tribunal held that 'the term "human rights" is to be given its ordinary natural meaning … which may evolve and change from time to time.' It concluded that the rights set out in the Universal Declaration of Human Rights, the International Covenant on Civil and Political Rights and the European Convention on Human Rights were all included.[17]

3.52 Charities can carry out a political activity in pursuance of their charitable objects, but charities cannot have political objects: this is often a particular issue for organisations wishing to register in this category. More detail on this can be found in the Commission's guidance CC9 Speaking out: guidance on campaigning and political activity by charities.

The advancement of environmental protection or improvement: s 3(1)(i)

3.53 There are many charities set up to preserve the natural environment in general or specific flora or fauna and these will be covered by this category. The Charity Commission leaflet RR9 deals with 'Preservation and Conservation' in more detail. This category includes organisations:

- concerned with conservation of a particular geographical area;

---

15 Charity Commission Decision made on 23 July 2004 on the application for registration of Concordis International Trust.

16 *Jonathan Bishop on behalf of Crocels Community Media Group v Charity Commission* (CA/2015/009).

17 *Human Dignity Trust v Charity Commission* (CA/2013/0013).

- promoting sustainable development and biodiversity;
- promoting recycling and sustainable waste management;
- researching the use of renewable energy; and
- running zoos, botanical collections etc.

The relief of those in need by reason of youth, age, ill-health, disability, financial hardship or other disadvantage: s 3(1)(j)

3.54 Section 3(2)(e) states, rather unnecessarily, that this includes relief given by the provision of accommodation or care to persons mentioned in this category.

3.55 Again, this is an eclectic mix of objects that in places overlaps with the relief of poverty and advancement of health (see above). This category includes charities:

- running children's care homes or homes for elderly people;
- that are registered social landlords or housing associations; and
- providing services or care for people with disabilities.

The purposes within this category evolved, prior to the 2006 Act, as purposes analogous to, or within the spirit of, purposes within the relief of poverty head and as applications of the 'other purposes beneficial to the community' head.

The advancement of animal welfare: s 3(1)(k)

3.56 The advancement of animal welfare includes any purpose directed towards the prevention or suppression of cruelty to animals or the prevention or relief of suffering by animals. This category was not included in the list put forward by the Strategy Unit when making the recommendations that led up to the 2006 Act. The Government, no doubt responding to pressure from the animal welfare lobby, decided that it should be included when they published their response to the Strategy Unit's report. The rationale for its inclusion is that the list should reflect major areas of charitable endeavour which have 'strong public recognition'. This category includes:

- animal sanctuaries; and
- the provision of veterinary care and treatment.

3.57 In the Parliamentary debates on the legislation which became the 2006 Act, the Government Minister, Lord Bassam of Brighton, confirmed that this category would not give charitable status to anti-vivisection organisations, nor would it place any restrictions on medical charities that experiment on animals.[18]

---

[18] Official Report of the Grand Committee on the Charities Bill, HL Deb, vol 669, col 56GC (3 February 2005).

The promotion of the efficiency of the armed forces of the Crown, or of the efficiency of the police, fire and rescue services or ambulance services: s 3(1)(l)

3.58 Promoting the efficiency of the armed forces has long been an accepted charitable purpose; the 1601 preamble includes 'the setting out of soldiers'. Although it did not originally appear in the list proposed for inclusion in the 2006 Act, the Government eventually relented to requests to insert it.

3.59 The Commission considers it is charitable to promote the efficiency of the armed forces of the Crown as a means of defending the country. A wide range of charities fall within this description including those which promote the physical fitness or technical knowledge of the armed forces, and those providing military band instruments and equipment and war memorials, chapels and museums. In the debates on the legislation which became the 2006 Act, the Government Minister, Lord Bassam of Brighton, stated that the inclusion of the reference to the armed forces was not inconsistent with the promotion of conflict resolution at s 3(1)(h).

3.60 It is charitable to promote the efficiency of the police, fire, rescue or ambulance services as they exist for the prevention and detection of crime, the preservation of public order and to protect the public. 'Fire and rescue services' is further defined at s 3(2)(f) as fire and rescue authorities provided under Part 2 of the Fire and Rescue Services Act 2004.

Any other purposes within s 3(1)(m)

3.61 This section covers:

- all existing charitable purposes accepted in the law of England and Wales as in force immediately before 1 April 2008 (which is when the relevant provisions of the 2006 Act came into force);
- any purpose that is analogous to or within the spirit of any of the purposes listed in the 2011 Act; and
- any purpose that is analogous to or within the spirit of a purpose accepted as charitable after 1 April 2008.

3.62 This was an extremely important provision of the 2006 Act, now consolidated into the 2011 Act, because it ensured that all existing charitable purposes not explicitly mentioned in the statutory list remain charitable. This category covers a wide range of purposes including recreational charities, public amenities, the promotion of moral or spiritual welfare, promotion of the sound administration of the law, relief of unemployment, rehabilitation of ex-offenders, prevention of crime and promotion of agriculture, industry or commerce.

3.63 Crucially, this section also provides the flexibility to allow further purposes to be added in the future by analogy to or within the spirit of existing purposes. This will mean that the law can expand and change to reflect changes in society, in much the same way as it has over the last 400 years.

Recreational Charities Act 1958

3.64 Section 5 of the 2011 Act originates from the Recreational Charities Act 1958 and confirms that charities previously registered with purposes covered by that Act, namely charities that provide, or assist in the provision of, facilities for recreation or other leisure-time occupation (if the facilities are provided in the interests of social welfare[19]), such as village halls and Women's Institutes, will continue to be charitable. However, the provisions of the 1958 Act have been amended in the following ways to ensure compliance with the Human Rights Act 1998:

- recreational facilities available to men only are now charitable, whereas previously just women only facilities were covered.
- miners' welfare trusts are no longer specifically mentioned as being charitable and as a result the Commission requires them to widen their objects to make their facilities available to other inhabitants of the local community.

Existing charitable trusts

3.65 Sections 2(2) and 2(3) of the 2011 Act ensure that charitable constitutions which refer to charitable purposes or institutions having purposes that are charitable under English law are construed as referring to purposes charitable under the 2011 Act. This is to ensure that, for example, grant-giving trusts with general charitable objects can give grants to all charities accepted as charitable under the 2011 Act.

The relationship between the list of charitable purposes and a charity's objects

3.66 It is the Commission's view that s 3(1) of the 2011 Act sets out a list of descriptions of charitable purposes and not purposes themselves.

3.67 This means that there are instances where the Commission will not accept the wording of the description of the purpose as set out in the 2011 Act as part of a charity's objects. For example it will sometimes but not always reject charitable objects including 'the promotion of amateur [football/other charitable sport]' requiring instead the pre 2006 Act wording 'to promote community participation in [football]'. Lord Hodgson noted in his 2012 review of charity legislation that it is difficult to see how this approach helps organisations with legitimately charitable aims to frame their objects in a way that will be acceptable to the Commission.[20]

Future amendments to the list of charitable purposes

3.68 It has been widely identified that, in many respects, the statutory list of charitable purposes has been helpful to clarify the broad range of purposes which can be charitable. However, as with any list, and particularly considering the diversity of the charity sector, there have been purposes which do not fit neatly into one of the available categories. In the Commission's response to the call for evidence to review the 2006 Act in 2012, recreation charities (which include community village halls and recreation

---

19 Section 5 of the 2011 Act contains more detail about what is meant by facilities provided in the interests of social welfare.

20 *Trusted and Independent: Giving Charity Back to Charities: Review of the Charities Act 2006*, July 2012, para 4.15.

grounds) were highlighted as purposes which represent a large part of the sector but do not appear at all in descriptions 3(1)(a)–(l), although they are provided for in 3(1)(m): see **3.61–3.63**.[21]

3.69 There have been a number of calls to expand the statutory list of purposes. A report from the House of Lords Select Committee on Communications recommended that investigative journalism be recognised as a charitable purpose.[22] However, the Culture Secretary, in his evidence to the Select Committee stated that 'the government is not currently inclined to legislate'[23] and in March 2012, the Bureau of Investigative Journalism, a not-for-profit organisation which exists to promote independent public interest investigative journalism, had its application for charitable status turned down for a second time by the Commission.

3.70 The recent growth of social investment, which is broadly investing for social as well as financial returns (see Chapter 11), has prompted some to argue that new categories could be added to the list to facilitate social finance projects.

3.71 Nevertheless, Lord Hodgson noted in his 2012 review of charity legislation that submitted views 'were almost unanimously against expanding the list of charitable purposes … and there appears to be no need to revisit the list of charitable purposes again at this juncture'.[24] As mentioned above, s 3(1)(m) of the 2011 Act specifically allows for continued development of further charitable purposes (see **3.61–3.63**).

Exclusively charitable purposes

3.72 To be a charity all of an organisation's objects must be exclusively charitable as defined in the 2011 Act and be for the public benefit. A charity cannot have some purposes which are charitable and others which are not.

3.73 In late 2011, the Commission refused to register Uturn UK as a charity on the basis that one of its objects, which concerned the promotion of street associations, was not exclusively charitable. The First-tier Tribunal upheld the Commission's decision, sharing the Commission's concerns that there can be no guarantee that the activities of street associations would be restricted to activities that are exclusively charitable.[25] The Tribunal found that the question is not whether an organisation's purposes are capable of being for the public benefit, but whether there is sufficient evidence from which it can be concluded that they will result in such benefit.

3.74 Full Fact, a not-for-profit organisation which independently verifies the accuracy of the facts used by the media and politicians, applied to the Commission to be registered as a charity with the words 'civic responsibility and engagement' in its objects. Its application was rejected. The Tribunal considered that the charity's activities were capable of being charitable but dismissed the appeal, finding that the word 'engagement'

---

21 Charity Commission submission, Charities Act 2006 Review 'Call for evidence: response from Charity Commission for England Wales: The definition of charity and the public benefit'.

22 House of Lords Select Committee on Communications 'The future of investigative journalism: 3rd Report of Session 2010–2012', 16 February 2012, p 52.

23 Ibid.

24 *Trusted and Independent*, para 4.15.

25 *Uturn UK CIC (formerly Uturn UK Ltd) v Charity Commission* (CA/2011/0006).

permits a range of charitable and non-charitable activities.[26] Full Fact was subsequently registered as a charity with objects relating to the advancement of education.[27]

3.75 The Commission can use The Charitable Trusts (Validation) Act 1954 to amend trust provisions created before 16 December 1952 where trust property has been used exclusively for charitable purposes, but where the objects declared in the charity's governing document allow use for non-charitable purposes. The legislation is often used by the Commission to amend the trust deeds of village halls which have been operating for some time, with an old trust deed, but are seeking to register for the first time. Numerous trusts were established with model objects that contained references to the provision of a village hall for the non-charitable purposes of promoting 'social, moral or intellectual development' or 'entertainment'. Where trust objects contain non-charitable wording the Commission can apply the 1954 Act, with the consent of the trustees, to strike out non-charitable provisions.

3.76 In determining whether an organisation is charitable, it should be noted that where an organisation is established with clearly stated charitable purposes, the motives and intentions of the founders are technically irrelevant, although the Commission will analyse intended activities and reject applications where proposed activities would not necessarily be exclusively charitable means of promoting the technically charitable objects.[28]

PUBLIC BENEFIT

3.77 As Lord Hodgson encapsulated, 'The intention of the 2006 Act was always to re-emphasise the importance of public benefit and to encourage charities to consider how they deliver that benefit.'[29]

3.78 The 2006 Act therefore specified, in a provision which now appears at s 2(1)(b) of the 2011 Act, that in order to be charitable a purpose must be for the public benefit. This requirement is known as 'the public benefit requirement' (s 4(1)). It means that all charities, when applying to the Commission for registration, must demonstrate that their objects are for public benefit. Although the test is of the charity's purposes, in most cases the Commission will examine both its charitable objects and its proposed activities.

3.79 The 2006 Act also provided that it is not to be presumed that a purpose of any particular description is for the public benefit (s 4(2) of the 2011 Act), meaning that all charities must demonstrate that their purposes are for public benefit. It was thought that this provision changed the law for religious, education and poverty charities, where public benefit was previously presumed unless there was evidence to the contrary. However, there is now doubt about whether there was, in fact, a presumption of public benefit prior to the 2006 Act (see **3.86**).

3.80 The Scottish legislation is much bolder and provided a definition of public benefit. The Government rejected this approach and the 2006 Act provided, in what is

---

26 *Full Fact v Charity Commission* (CA/2011/0001).

27 Charity Commission Decision made on 17 September 2014 on the application for registration of Full Fact.

28 *James Miller and Partners Ltd v Whitworth Street Estates (Manchester) Ltd* [1970] AC 583 and *Helena Partnerships Ltd v HMRC*, Upper Tribunal (Tax and Chancery) [2011] STC 1307 [16–22], cited in the Charity Commission's 'Analysis of the law relating to public benefit' at p 8.

29 *Trusted and Independent*, para 4.8.

now s 4(3) of the 2011 Act, that the existing case-law on public benefit remained in place, subject to the removal of the presumption.

3.81 The 2006 Act also charged the Commission with the objective of promoting awareness and understanding of the public benefit requirement (s 14 of the 2011 Act), and obliged the Commission to issue guidance in pursuit of its public benefit objective (s 17 of the 2011 Act). Charity trustees must have regard to the guidance (s 17(5) of the 2011 Act: see **3.101**) and report on public benefit in their annual trustees' report (see **3.101–3.104**).

3.82 The idea of providing a level playing field where all charities must demonstrate public benefit was first put forward in an NCVO consultation document in 2001. This was a popular proposal and its inclusion in the Charities Bill which became the 2006 Act was broadly welcomed by the sector. However, as this part of the Bill was scrutinised and debated, it emerged that there was no consensus on what its effect would be, particularly in relation to fee-charging charities such as public schools. Questions were also raised about the assumption that the existing case-law on public benefit was clear and whether it would be possible to rely on it once the presumption was reversed.

3.83 When giving evidence to the Joint Committee scrutinising the legislation which eventually became the 2006 Act in 2004, the Commission's view was that the removal of the presumption of public benefit would probably not change the law and in particular would not affect the charitable status of independent schools. The Home Office in contrast believed that the Act would affect charities charging high fees and would force them to provide some access to the less well-off through bursaries or sharing facilities. As a result, a Concordat was reached between the Home Office and Commission, expressed in a letter to the Joint Committee stating that the Commission would look at public benefit on a case-by-case basis and follow the approach set out in *Re Resch*[30] with regard to fee-charging charities. The Concordat states:

> 'These principles are that:
>
> (a) both direct and indirect benefits to the public or a sufficient section of the public may be taken into account in deciding whether an organisation does, or can, operate for the public benefit;
>
> (b) the fact that charitable facilities or services will be charged for and will be provided mainly to people who can afford to pay the charges does not necessarily mean that the organisation does not operate for the public benefit; and
>
> (c) an organisation which wholly excluded poor people from any benefits, direct or indirect would not be established and operate for the public benefit and therefore would not be a charity.'

3.84 However, the debate continued over whether the 2006 Act would leave the public benefit test unchanged or raise the bar. In particular, it was pointed out that *Re Resch* accepted that if a charity relieved the public purse, as a fee-charging school does by taking a child out of the state system, this counted as a charitable public benefit.

[30] *Re Resch's Wills Trusts (Le Cras and the Perpetual Trustee Co Ltd & ors)* [1969] 1 AC 514.

Lord Phillips of Sudbury described the common law as 'confused and sparse'[31] and said of *Re Resch* 'read, and read, and read ye may, but a certain conclusion you will not find ...'.[32]

3.85 Since the implementation of the public benefit provisions in the 2006 Act, two significant cases in the Upper Tribunal have considered the impact of the changes. The first ('the ISC case') was a challenge by the Independent Schools Council to the first version of the Commission's public benefit guidance, published in 2008.[33]

3.86 One of the key aspects of the judgment in the ISC case was a commentary on whether the 2006 Act had, indeed, reversed a presumption of public benefit. The Upper Tribunal concluded that in the case of educational purposes there had, in fact, never been a presumption that they were for the public benefit. Instead, any analysis of an educational purpose would start with a 'pre-disposition' that such a purpose was for the public benefit, which is different from a legal presumption. As explained at **3.113**, in order to be for the public benefit a charitable purpose must benefit the public in general or a sufficient section of the public. The Upper Tribunal also decided that there had not been a presumption that purposes of any kind were for 'a section of the public': this would all depend on the circumstances of the particular case. This meant that the public benefit rules as applied to educational charities were not, after all, altered by the 2006 Act. The Tribunal said that the 2006 Act had brought 'into focus' what is required from a public benefit perspective.

3.87 The judgment in the ISC case, which is over 100 pages long, contains a detailed analysis of the law on public benefit. While, strictly, the case only relates to educational charities, the principles set out in the case are of wider relevance and have informed the latest version of the Commission's public benefit guidance: see **3.106–3.124**.

3.88 Shortly after issuing its judgment in the ISC case, the Upper Tribunal considered the status of relief of poverty charities with a restricted class of beneficiaries and, in particular, whether they remained charitable following the implementation of the 2006 Act ('the Benevolent Funds case').[34] The Upper Tribunal held that the so-called abolition of the presumption of public benefit in the 2006 Act had no impact on whether a trust for the relief of poverty is charitable or not. The Tribunal made it clear that even before the 2006 Act, there was no presumption of public benefit for relief of poverty charities in practice and whether or not a relief of poverty charity is for the public benefit will turn on the evidence.

3.89 The practical point, as it always has been, is that charity trustees must act to ensure that their charities operate for the public benefit in pursing the constitutionally defined charitable objects, that what is for 'the public benefit' is to a significant degree open to reasonable interpretation and that in the past some charity trustees have not had this principle in mind to the degree the charity law principle, now given expression in statute, demands.

---

31 HL Deb, vol 674, col 310 (12 October 2005).
32 HL Deb, vol 672, col 794 (7 June 2005).
33 *Independent Schools Council v Charity Commission & ors* [2011] UKUT 421 (TCC).
34 *Attorney General v Charity Commission & ors* [2012] UKUT 420 (TCC).

Guidance as to the operation of the public benefit requirement

General

3.90 Sections 14 and 17 of the 2011 Act oblige the Commission to issue guidance about public benefit in pursuance of its public benefit objective. The Commission's public benefit objective is to promote awareness and understanding of the operation of the public benefit requirement (see **3.78**). Charity trustees are obliged to have regard to the guidance, and report on compliance with the public benefit requirement (see **3.101–3.104**).

3.91 The Commission's guidance may still properly raise interpretive questions and the ISC case (see **3.85–3.87**) did agree that the Commission's published guidance was too prescriptive, even though it did not agree with all the arguments advanced in that case about the presumption of benefit.

3.92 The Commission must carry out such public and other consultation as it considers appropriate (s 17(3)):

- before issuing any guidance; or
- before revising any such guidance (unless it considers that it is unnecessary to do so).

3.93 The Commission published its first guidance on public benefit in January 2008. It was followed by supplementary 'sub-sector' guidance, including guidance for religious, fee-charging, poverty and educational charities, in December 2008.

3.94 The ISC case (see **3.85–3.87**) was a challenge to certain aspects of the guidance. The Upper Tribunal decided that the Commission's guidance was wrong in some respects, and parts of the guidance were effectively quashed by the Tribunal's decision. In the summer of 2012, the Commission issued new draft public benefit guidance for consultation, reflecting the judgments of the Upper Tribunal in both the ISC case and the Benevolent Funds case. New, revised guidance was published in September 2013. Some changes have since been made to some parts of the guidance.[35]

3.95 The statutory guidance (which trustees must have regard to) is now contained in three quite short documents, as follows:

- Public benefit: the public benefit requirement (PB1): see **3.107–3.115**.
- Public benefit: running a charity (PB2): see **3.116–3.122**.
- Public benefit: reporting (PB3): see **3.123–3.124**.

3.96 The Commission has published a number of other documents dealing with public benefit, which may also be helpful for trustees. However, they do not form part of the statutory guidance which trustees have a legal obligation to have regard to. The previous sub-sector guidance (see **3.93**), which has been amended in some respects following the ISC Case, remains available (listed as 'supplementary public benefit guidance' on the Commission's website). However, it no longer has the status of statutory guidance.

---

35 For example, in 2015 the guidance was updated in relation to how trustees of charitable schools should report on their approach to public benefit.

3.97 A major criticism of the Commission's original public benefit guidance was that it was unduly prescriptive about how trustees should be satisfying the requirement of charity law that a charity's purposes must be for the public benefit. This was one of the concerns raised in the ISC case (see **3.85–3.87**). In that case, the Tribunal was clear that, while charities may not exclude poor people from benefit, beyond that it is up to the trustees to decide how they provide for their beneficiaries.

3.98 In line with the judgment in the ISC case, it is now clear from the Commission's revised public benefit guidance that trustees have freedom to decide how they carry out their charity's purposes:

> 'When making decisions about how to carry out their charity's purposes for the public benefit, many trustees are concerned about what is "the right" decision. In many situations there is no one "right" decision to be made.
>
> ... however, trustees must make decisions that are within the range of decisions that trustees could properly make in those particular circumstances.
>
> Provided that the trustees make a decision within that range, then they will have made a "right" decision.
>
> It is not for the courts or the commission to tell trustees which decision to make where there is a range of decisions open to them.'

3.99 In its overview of the guidance (which does not itself form part of the statutory guidance) the Commission acknowledges that its guidance is not the basis on which it makes decisions about public benefit, because high level guidance cannot cover all the complexities of the law relating to public benefit.

3.100 Whilst it is appropriate that the guidance's status is not elevated to equate it with legal requirements, this creates some difficulty for trustees in being able to understand and apply the public benefit requirement in the context of their charity. This was noted by the Upper Tribunal in the Benevolent Funds case (see **3.88**):

> 'the authorities do not provide a comprehensive statement of the public benefit requirement but provide rather a series of examples of when the public benefit requirement is or is not satisfied. There is no application of some overarching, coherent, principle by which the Courts have been guided.'[36]

Duties of charity trustees

3.101 Under s 17(5) of the 2011 Act all charity trustees must have regard to the Commission's public benefit guidance when exercising any powers or duties to which it is relevant. This means that trustees should be able to show that:

- they are aware of the guidance;
- they have taken it into account when making a decision to which the guidance is relevant (see **3.117**); and
- if they have decided to depart from the guidance, they have good reasons for doing so.

---

36 *Attorney General v Charity Commission & ors* [2012] UKUT 420 (TCC) para 32.

3.102 Charity trustees are also obliged to mention public benefit in their annual report (see Chapter 21).[37]

3.103 The report must contain a statement by the trustees as to whether they have complied with the duty in s. 17(2) to have due regard to guidance by the Commission.

3.104 The trustees must also report on activity which furthers the charity's purposes for the public benefit, although the level of detail required depends on whether the charity's accounts are audited. A charity which is not required to have its accounts audited must include a brief summary setting out 'the main activities undertaken by the charity to further its charitable purposes for the public benefit'. Where an audit is required, the report must include 'a review of the significant activities undertaken by the charity ... to further its charitable purposes for the public benefit or to generate resources to be used to further its purposes', including a range of specified information.

3.105 In practice, these requirements emphasise the general charity law responsibility of the charity trustees to interpret the legal principles reasonably, in the relevant context, now taking due account of the statutory guidance and demonstrating that they have undertaken their responsibility through complying with the statutory disclosure obligations.

Substance of the guidance

3.106 The Commission's guidance breaks public benefit down into two parts, the 'benefit aspect' and the 'public aspect'.

The benefit aspect is about whether the purpose is beneficial. To satisfy this aspect:

- a purpose must be beneficial;
- any detriment or harm that results from the purpose must not outweigh the benefit.

To satisfy the public aspect the purpose must:

- benefit the public in general, or a sufficient section of the public;
- not give rise to more than incidental personal benefit.

Public benefit: the public benefit requirement (PB1)

3.107 This guidance is stated to be relevant to those 'thinking of setting up or registering a charity', or for trustees of existing charities wishing to change their purposes.

3.108 Where a charity has more than one purpose, the Commission will look at each purpose on its own to decide if it is for the public benefit.

3.109 For a purpose to be charitable it must be beneficial in a way that is identifiable and:

---

37 Regulation 40 of the Charities (Accounts and Reports) Regulations 2008, SI 2008/629.

- capable of being proved by evidence if necessary,
- not based on personal views.

3.110 In some cases the purpose is so clearly beneficial that there is little need for trustees to provide evidence to prove this. The example given is emergency aid in the context of a natural disaster. Examples given of when evidence may be required include the merit of a training programme.

3.111 It should always be possible to identify and describe how a charity's purpose is beneficial, whether or not that can be measured. If it cannot be shown that an organisation's purpose is beneficial 'based on evidence that a court could accept where necessary' it will not be a charitable purpose.

3.112 A purpose cannot be charitable where any detriment or harm resulting from it outweighs the benefit (this is also part of the benefit aspect). Detriment or harm will be taken into account where it is 'reasonable to expect that it will result from the individual organisation's purpose. ... Where the benefit of a purpose is obvious and commonly recognised, there is an even greater need for evidence of detriment or harm to be clear and substantial, if it is to outweigh that benefit.'

3.113 For a purpose to be charitable it must benefit either:

- the public in general, or
- a sufficient section of the public.

3.114 What is a sufficient section of the public is decided on a case-by-case basis, but the guidance sets out some relevant factors. For example:

- Except in relation to poverty charities, the number of people who can benefit should not be 'numerically negligible', although there is no set minimum number.
- In most cases people living in a geographical area will be a sufficient section of the public (except if the area is very narrowly defined).
- Defining who can benefit by reference to a 'protected characteristic' must satisfy the requirements of the Equality Act 2010.[38]
- Defining beneficiaries by reference to a person's occupation or profession can be a sufficient section of the public, depending on the circumstances.
- The definition of who can benefit must not be 'capricious' when related to the purpose.
- Unless the purpose is for the relief (or possibly prevention) of poverty (see **3.125–3.126**), a purpose which exists for the benefit of the organisation's members will not be charitable unless a sufficient section of the public can access those benefits by becoming members and membership is a suitable way of carrying out the charity's purposes for the public benefit.

3.115 A charitable purpose may only confer personal benefits if these are incidental to carrying out that purpose. This means personal benefit must be a necessary result or by-product of carrying out the purpose.

---

[38] Protected characteristics are age, disability, gender reassignment, marriage and civil partnership, pregnancy and maternity, race, religion and belief, sex and sexual orientation.

Public benefit: running a charity (PB2)

3.116 This guidance is expressed to be relevant for charity trustees when running their charity. It reiterates the 'benefit aspect' and 'public aspect' of public benefit as stated above.

3.117 It explains that trustees must have regard to the guidance when making 'relevant decisions', which are defined as those which impact on the way in which people benefit from the charity's purpose or who can benefit from it.

3.118 According to the guidance, decisions must:

- ensure that the charity's purpose provides public benefit;
- manage risks of detriment or harm to the charity's beneficiaries or to the public in general; and
- ensure any personal benefits are no more than incidental.

3.119 Helpfully, the guidance confirms that in many situations there is no one 'right' decision to be made.

3.120 Annex A deals with benefits accessed through membership of a charity. In this case, it must be possible for a sufficient section of the public to access benefits by becoming members, and the membership structure must be a suitable way of carrying out the charity's purposes for the public benefit. Trustees must ensure that any changes to membership criteria do not have the effect of turning the charity into a private members' club.

3.121 Annex C deals with charities which charge for their services. In line with the judgment in the ISC case, it is clear that trustees may not run their charity in a way that excludes the poor from benefit. They must, therefore, consider whether the charges are more than the poor can afford. As articulated in the Tribunal judgment, 'poor' is a relative term and does not just mean the very poorest in society, although this depends on the circumstances of individual cases: 'in general it will usually mean charges that someone of modest means will not find readily affordable'.

3.122 If charges are not of a level that the poor can afford, the trustees 'must ensure that the poor can benefit'. The level of benefit must be more than minimal or token. However, the guidance reaffirms that it is for a charity's trustees to decide what provision to make to enable the poor to benefit – this cannot be prescribed by the Commission or the courts.

Public benefit: reporting (PB3)

3.123 This guidance is relevant for trustees when preparing their annual report. It gives examples of how charity trustees can report on public benefit and refers to example annual reports prepared by the Commission. The Commission states that a general failure to report may be considered as a possible indication of other problems that the Commission might wish to explore. Where persistent non-reporting is brought to the Commission's attention, this would be considered as a potential regulatory issue.

3.124 In his 2012 review of charity law, Lord Hodgson recommended that charities should recognise the importance of public benefit reporting both to public confidence and their own ability to attract supporters. This was endorsed by Government in its response to the review.

Public benefit and relief of poverty charities

3.125 Relief of poverty charities have always been a special case. Prior to the 2006 Act it had been accepted that relief of poverty charities could be charitable even where they were established for a restricted pool of beneficiaries defined by a relationship to an individual or an employer, or membership of an unincorporated association.

3.126 In the Benevolent Funds case (see **3.88**), the Upper Tribunal confirmed that the 2006 Act had not affected the law in this respect. The Tribunal found that what satisfies the public benefit requirement may differ markedly between different types of allegedly charitable purpose. Relief of poverty charities must have a purpose which must be by nature beneficial to the community, but the Tribunal made it clear that this test does not look at the section of the public to be benefited. In the ISC case, the Tribunal had determined that to be charitable, public benefit must also be provided to a 'sufficient section of the public'. However, in its decision in the Benevolent Funds case, the Tribunal concluded that relief of poverty for a narrow beneficiary class is an exception to this requirement. This is reflected in Annex A to the Commission's guidance on the public benefit requirement (PB1) which acknowledges that poverty charities (but no other charities) may define who can benefit by reference to:

- their family relationships (ie descent from one individual)
- their employment by a particular employer, or
- their membership of an unincorporated association.

Public benefit and religious organisations

3.127 When the 2006 Act purported to remove the presumption of public benefit for organisations which exist to advance religion, there was disquiet amongst religious organisations which feared that congregations would be asked to demonstrate measurable public benefit and would only pass the test if they were undertaking community work, as opposed to recognition of the public benefit that is inherent in religious worship and teaching. The Government was keen to refute this, and its spokesman and Government Minister, Lord Bassam of Brighton, reiterated, at least twice, in the Parliamentary debates which preceded the 2006 Act, that removing the presumption was not intended to narrow down the range of religious activities seen as charitable.

3.128 The question of public benefit and religious charities was scrutinised when in 2012, Preston Down Trust, a Plymouth Brethren meeting hall, was denied charitable status because the Commission was not satisfied that it met the public benefit requirement. Members of the Plymouth Brethren adhere to a doctrine of 'separation from evil', which the Commission found resulted in both a moral and physical separation from the wider community and limited interaction with the wider public. The Commission had also received allegations of detriment or harm arising from the church's disciplinary practices.

3.129 The Trust appealed to the Charity Tribunal, but the appeal was stayed while the Trust and the Commission discussed the issue further. Ultimately the Preston Down Trust was registered as a charity in January 2014 on the condition that the Trust adopt a revised governing document which stated more clearly and transparently its doctrine and practices. The Commission's decision[39] includes an analysis of the law on public benefit and the advancement of religion. This affirms that 'public benefit must enure to the wider community not simply to the particular adherents of any religion' but acknowledges that there may be public benefit where a religious group is not wholly shut off from the wider community, and appears to set quite a low threshold for religious groups to meet the public benefit test. The decision concluded that, 'public benefit for a religious charity would be determined by the extent to which its moral and ethical teaching impacted on the community leading to a betterment of society generally.'

3.130 However, the unusual doctrines and practices of the Plymouth Brethren and the fact that no Tribunal hearing took place means that the decision is of limited use in clarifying the law on public benefit and religious charities.

A statutory definition of public benefit?

3.131 As the Bill which led to the 2006 Act progressed through Parliament, various options to clarify the public benefit requirement were considered and rejected, including a non-exclusive list of criteria, non-binding statutory guidance issued by the Secretary of State, and including a clause stating that the Commission must take into account the effect of charging when assessing public benefit.

3.132 The call for evidence for Lord Hodgson's 2012 review asked respondents to consider whether the current definition of public benefit based on case law should be retained or if there should be a move to a statutory definition.

3.133 The Commission's submission acknowledged that a statutory definition has the potential to provide for greater clarity and certainty particularly because case law in relation to some aspects of public benefit is patchy. However, it concluded that a definition enshrined in statute would be less able to respond quickly to changing social and economic circumstances and its preference was to have a system that allows the law to develop organically.

3.134 Lord Hodgson agreed but identified the tensions between the purposive approach taken by the Commission and the role of backward looking precedents in the Tribunal's decision-making. One of Lord Hodgson's recommendations to the Government was to consider ways in which the Tribunal could be empowered to take account of changing social and economic circumstances as well as case-law precedents.[40]

3.135 The Public Administration Select Committee scrutinised the provisions of the 2006 Act on public benefit in 2013, concluding that the Act is 'critically flawed on the question of public benefit and should be revisited by Parliament'.[41]

---

39 Charity Commission Decision made on 3 January 2014 on the application for registration of the Preston Down Trust.

40 *Trusted and Independent*, para 4.14 and Chapter 7 recommendation 11.

41 The role of the Charity Commission and 'public benefit', May 2013, para 92.

3.136 Government, in responding to Lord Hodgson and the PASC, agreed with Lord Hodgson's recommendation not to pursue a statutory definition of public benefit 'at this time', noting that 'the case law definition of public benefit has served us well for over 400 years'.[42]

[42] Page 13 Government response, September 2013.

CHAPTER 4

REGISTRATION

INTRODUCTION

4.1 One of the Charity Commission's key functions is the maintenance of a register of charities. Its fifth general function under the 2011 Act, that of 'obtaining, evaluating and disseminating information in connection with the performance of any of the Commission's functions or meeting any of its objectives',[1] specifically includes the maintenance of an accurate and up-to-date register of charities.[2]

4.2 The 2006 Act made a number of changes to the rules about charity registration. These included raising the financial threshold for registration and widening the Commission's net to include many previously exempt and excepted charities. Not all of the changes which affect exempt charities have yet been fully implemented.[3]

4.3 Lord Hodgson also made a number of recommendations in his 2012 review of charity law in relation to registration, but most of these were not adopted by government.

THE REGISTER OF CHARITIES

4.4 Sections 29 to 34 of the 2011 Act deal with the register and its contents. These provisions are adapted in so far as they apply to charitable incorporated organisations, or CIOs, by virtue of the Charitable Incorporated Organisations (General) Regulations 2012:[4] a version of s 29 to 34, showing the amendments, is included in Appendix 7 of this book.

4.5 The Commission is required to keep a register of charities, in such manner as it thinks fit. The register must contain:

- the name of every registered charity; and
- such other particulars of, and such other information relating to, every registered charity, as the Commission thinks fit.[5]

4.6 In practice, the register, which is accessible online via the Commission's website, contains a range of facts and figures about a charity's work and finances. This includes the name and any working names of the charity, the name and address of its

---

1 Section 15(1) of the 2011 Act.
2 Section 15(4) of the 2011 Act.
3 See Chapter 5.
4 SI 2012/3012. See Chapter 14.
5 Section 29 of the 2011 Act.

correspondent, its registration number and date of registration, details about its governing instrument and its objects, the names of its trustees, summary financial information, often including access to its accounts, and details of its filings with the Commission. Where registered charities are late in filing accounts, reports and returns with the Commission, it is the Commission's practice to highlight this fact very clearly on the online register entry. If a charity is subject to a statutory inquiry (see Chapter 9) this will also be noted on the register. The online register can be searched by charity number, name, objects, activities and area of operation. The Commission also keeps a register of charity mergers: see Chapter 16.

Access to information on registered charities

4.7 Section 38 of the 2011 Act provides that the register, including details of charities removed from the register, must be open to public inspection in legible form at all reasonable times, unless the Commission determines that certain information should not be accessible to the public. The Commission might decide, for instance, that it is inappropriate for the names of charity trustees to be publicly accessible if this might put them at risk.

4.8 The Commission is obliged under s 38(4) of the 2011 Act to keep copies, or particulars, of the constitutions of every registered charity as supplied to them by the charity under s 35 (see **4.56** and **4.70**). These must be publicly accessible, together with copies of certain constitutional documents already in the Commission's possession, such as schemes made by the Commission.[6] Under s 18 of the 2011 Act, the Commission must, on request, provide copies or extracts from documents in the Commission's possession which are open to public inspection under the Act. Thus, copies of governing documents may be requested from the Commission.[7]

4.9 Section 18 also applies to charity accounts held by the Commission, as these are open to public inspection for as long as they are retained by the Commission.[8] In practice, at the time of writing, where a registered charity has filed accounts with the Commission they are available to download from the Commission's website for no charge.

4.10 Under s 19 of the 2011 Act, the Minister for the Cabinet Office can make regulations regarding the fees charged for providing copy documents: these are currently contained in The Charity Commissioners' Fees (Copies and Extracts) Regulations 1992[9] and relate to the provision of hard copy documents, and extracts from the register.

4.11 At the time of writing the Commission fulfils its obligations to provide public access via its website. It does not have the resources to allow physical inspection of the register at its offices. Neither does it supply hard copy documents, but will provide copies of governing documents electronically free of charge on request.

---

6 Sections 35(4), 38(4) and 38(5) of the 2011 Act.

7 For charitable companies, it is often quicker to obtain a copy of the Articles of Association from Companies House: there is no charge.

8 See **21.94** and s 170 of the 2011 Act.

9 SI 1992/2986.

Registration number

4.12 In general, each registered charity is given a unique registration number. However, under s 12(1) of the 2011 Act the Commission can direct that an institution established for any special purposes of or in connection with a charity can be treated as forming part of that charity (or as forming a distinct charity) for any of the purposes of the 2011 Act. In addition, under s 12(2) of the 2011 Act the Commission can make a direction to the effect that two or more charities with the same trustees should be treated as a single charity for all or any of the purposes of the 2011 Act. Where the Commission has made a direction linking two or more charities for registration purposes under either of these sections, those charities may be grouped under the same registration number (currently the reporting charity has one registration number, while charities linked to it also use that number, with a linked suffix).[10]

THE REQUIREMENT TO REGISTER

4.13 Under s 30(1) of the 2011 Act 'every charity' must be registered unless it falls within s 30(2).[11]

4.14 Under s 30(2) of the 2011 Act the following charities are not required to register:

- Exempt charities (s 30(2)(a)). Exempt charities are dealt with in detail in Chapter 5.
- Excepted charities whose gross annual income does not exceed £100,000 (ss 30(2)(b) and (c)). Excepted charities are dealt with in more detail at **4.25–4.40**.
- Small charities, whose gross annual income does not exceed £5,000 (s 30(2)(d)). These are dealt with in more detail at **4.16–4.24**.

The categories of charity which do not need to register were changed in some important respects by the 2006 Act: although not all of these changes affecting exempt charities have been implemented (see Chapter 5).

4.15 Section 30 does not apply in relation to charitable incorporated organisations (see Chapter 14 and **Appendix** 7).

SMALL CHARITIES

4.16 Charities, other than charitable incorporated organisations, are not required to register unless they have a gross annual income of more than £5,000.

4.17 Section 30(4) of the 2011 Act makes it clear that the gross income threshold refers to the gross income for the charity in the last financial year or, if the Commission decides, the amount which the Commission estimates as the likely gross income of the charity in any financial year specified by the Commission, which is likely to be the

---

10 There is detailed guidance on linking charities in Charity Commission operational guidance OG 555 'Linking Charities'.

11 See 4.54 for the meaning of 'charity'.

current or next financial year. Gross income is defined in s 353(1) of the 2011 Act as the charity's gross recorded income from all sources, including special trusts.[12]

4.18 Prior to the 2006 Act, charities were required to register if they had an annual income from all sources of more than £1,000, or if they held permanent endowment or had the use or occupation of land (regardless of the level of their income). The 2006 Act raised the income threshold to £5,000 and removed the requirements relating to permanent endowment and the use or occupation of land irrespective of income. The alteration in the income threshold sprang from a desire to avoid bureaucracy where possible: the Strategy Unit, when reviewing charity law before the 2006 Act, felt that smaller charities present the least regulatory risk, yet often have limited capacity to cope with the burden of regulation by the Commission. It was originally proposed that the threshold should be raised to an income of £10,000, but Government reduced this to £5,000.

4.19 Under s 32(1)(b), the Minister for the Cabinet Office has power to change the £5,000 threshold by order if he considers it expedient to do so as a result of inflation or in order to exclude more charities from compulsory registration.

4.20 In his 2012 review of charity law, Lord Hodgson considered whether the registration threshold should be changed. He noted that the evidence to his review had highlighted the value of having a registered charity number 'or, more accurately, the challenges associated with not having one', due to 'an apparent lack of understanding in the wider world that an organisation can be a charity without being on the charity register'.[13] However, he took into consideration the fact that while charities with income over £5,000 are required to register, they are not required to file annual returns with the Commission until their income is over £10,000, and they are not required to file annual reports and accounts with the Commission until their income exceeds £25,000.[14]

4.21 Lord Hodgson recommended that the registration threshold should be increased to £25,000, although charities below that threshold would be obliged to register if they wished to obtain tax relief, and would also be able to register voluntarily if they wished (see **4.42–4.53**). However, Government disagreed. Noting that 'the clear message from the charity sector is that registration should be required of small charities to help protect the reputation of the ... sector as a whole', Government decided that the £5,000 registration threshold should remain.[15]

4.22 The reduction in the registration threshold in the 2006 Act meant that many smaller charities were no longer obliged to remain registered. Registered charities with an annual income of £5,000 or less may ask to be removed from the register (see **4.87**), although given the value of a charity registration number many clearly choose to remain registered: at the time of writing there were over 47,000 registered charities whose annual income did not exceed £5,000.[16]

12 For more information on special trusts see Chapter 12.

13 *Trusted and Independent: Giving Charity Back to Charities*, para 5.41.

14 See Chapter 21.

15 Government response to Lord Hodgson's review, September 2013, p 9.

16 A search of the Charity Commission register just prior to publication of this book in 2016 indicated there were around 10,000 registered charities with income of £1 or less, around 14,000 with income of between £2 and £1,000, and around 23,000 with income of between £1,001 and £5,000.

4.23 Charities which are not registered because they fall below the registration threshold nonetheless need to ensure that they are registered with HMRC in order to qualify for tax relief (see **4.81–4.82**).

4.24 Charities which do not register initially because their annual income is below the £5,000 threshold should note that they will need to apply for registration once their income looks likely to reach this level.

EXCEPTED CHARITIES

Introduction

4.25 Excepted charities are in a special position. Prior to the 2006 Act, excepted charities were not required to register at all: the rationale for this was, generally, that they were already registered with their own umbrella or support groups.

4.26 However the Strategy Unit, in its review of charity law before the 2006 Act, concluded that 'in the context of today's more extensive reporting and monitoring regime for registered charities, designed to improve accountability for charitable funds, these exceptions no longer make sense'.[17] The 2006 Act therefore introduced a requirement for excepted charities to register, but at the time of writing this only applies where an excepted charity's annual income exceeds £100,000.

4.27 Note that there is a significant difference between *excepted* and *exempt* charities. Excepted charities are subject to the Commission's jurisdiction in most respects, but smaller excepted charities need not register, and do not have to file annual reports and returns with the Commission. Exempt charities may not register and the Commission's jurisdiction over them is limited in some ways: see Chapter 5 for more detail.

Which charities are excepted?

4.28 Charities are excepted, either temporarily or permanently, by Charity Commission order or regulations made by the Minister for the Cabinet Office.[18]

4.29 At the time of writing excepted charities fall into four categories:

- churches and chapels belonging to many Christian denominations, including registered places of worship under the Places of Worship Registration Act 1855;[19]
- some charities which provide premises for certain schools;
- Scout and Guide groups (with some exceptions where they hold certain property); and
- certain armed forces charities.

17 *Private Action, Public Benefit*, para 7.90.

18 Section 30(2)(b) and (c) of the 2011 Act.

19 Many of these charities are due to lose their excepted status in 2021: The Charities (Exception from Registration) Regulations 1996, SI 1996/180 (as amended).

4.30 The legislation dealing with excepted charities at the time of writing is:

- The Charities (Exception of Voluntary Schools from Registration) Regulations 1960 (SI 1960/2366) (school charities);
- The Charities (Exception of Certain Charities for Boy Scouts and Girl Guides from Registration) Regulations 1961 (SI 1961/1044) (scout and guide groups);
- The Charities (Exception from Registration and Accounts) Regulations 1965 (SI 1965/1056) (armed forces charities);
- The Charities (Exception from Registration) Regulations 1996 (as amended) (SI 1996/180) (church charities);
- The Charities Act 1993 (Exception from Registration) Regulations 2008 (SI 2008/3268) (educational institutions and places of worship);
- Section 23, School Standards and Framework Act 1998 (school charities); and
- The Charities (Exception from Registration) Regulations 2010 (SI 2010/502) (formerly exempt charities).

4.31 As mentioned at **5.27**, s 31(3) of the 2011 Act ensures that previously exempted charities also become excepted charities, since the Minister for the Cabinet Office must make regulations ensuring that they fall within the scope of s 30(2)(c). This currently affects some religious and educational institutions, and students' unions.[20]

4.32 Since 1 January 2009, when the parts of the 2006 Act dealing with registration of excepted charities came into force, no other new categories of excepted charity can be created.[21]

Registration of excepted charities

4.33 Excepted charities only need to register once their annual income is over £100,000. Under s 30(2)(b) and (c) of the 2011 Act, charities are not required to register if they are permanently or temporarily excepted by Charity Commission order or by regulations made by the Minister for the Cabinet Office and their gross income does not exceed £100,000, provided they comply with the conditions of the exception.

4.34 Under s 30(4) 'gross income' means gross income in the last financial year or, if the Commission decides, the Commission's estimate of likely gross income in any financial year which it specifies: see **4.17**.

4.35 In 2012 the Commission was reported as stating that around 4,000 excepted charities had registered following the introduction of this requirement in the 2006 Act.

4.36 The idea when the 2006 Act was enacted was that the £100,000 income threshold should be reduced over time to bring excepted charities completely into line with other (non-exempt) charities. Under s 32 of the 2011 Act the Minister for the Cabinet Office may amend the £100,000 figure by order if he considers it expedient to do so with a view to reducing the scope of the exception. However, this power could not be exercised until after the 5-year review of the 2006 Act, undertaken by Lord Hodgson in 2012 (see **1.11–1.12**), was laid before Parliament.

---

20 See 5.12–5.14.

21 Sections 31(1) and (2) of the 2011 Act, although orders and regulations concerning excepted charities in force before that date may be varied or revoked, by virtue of s 31(4) and (5).

4.37 Under s 73(2) of the 2006 Act, Lord Hodgson's review was specifically charged with addressing the effect of the legislation on excepted charities. Lord Hodgson duly reported on the experience of those excepted charities which had been required by the 2006 Act to register with the Commission for the first time. He said:[22]

> 'Excepted charities are generally content with their situation and many are, by and large, similarly relaxed about the likely eventual lowering of the registration threshold to match the general level. Some positively welcomed registration and its benefits, in particular an increase in public trust and confidence and the helpful discipline of having to submit annual reports and accounts. A few had also experienced the problems of not having charity numbers, and felt registration would help in this respect. Others were unconcerned as they felt no need to look beyond their members or beneficiaries for support.'

4.38 Lord Hodgson echoed the Strategy Unit[23] in saying that 'the existence of the current exception adds confusion and complexity to the charity sector landscape and has long outlasted its original justification'. His view was that a further reduction in the registration threshold for excepted charities would have a positive impact on 'the wider interests of transparency, accountability and equal treatment across the sector as a whole'. Lord Hodgson recommended that the registration threshold for excepted charities should continue to be reduced until it matches the general compulsory registration threshold (which, as noted at **4.21**, Lord Hodgson had recommended should be increased to £25,000). He recommended that the reduction should be staggered, with reductions to £50,000 and then £25,000 over a three year period (commencing when all existing organisations wishing to convert to charitable incorporated organisation status had had two years to do so).[24]

4.39 However, this recommendation was not taken up by Government, which responded that:[25]

> 'We are inclined to take view (sic) that now is not the right time to require smaller excepted charities to register with the Charity Commission. Our main concern is that to do so would impose an unnecessary regulatory burden on several thousand small charities at a time when many may be under pressure.'

4.40 Section 33 of the 2011 Act allows the Minister for the Cabinet Office to order that the provisions of ss 30 to 33 which relate to excepted charities should no longer have effect: this will allow references to excepted charities to be removed from the legislation if and when the £100,000 threshold is reduced to the level which applies to other charities.

CHARITABLE INCORPORATED ORGANISATIONS

4.41 Charitable incorporated organisations, or CIOs, are a special case: see Chapter 14. A CIO only comes into existence on its registration with the Charity Commission and must, therefore, always be registered. There is no minimum income threshold for CIOs to register.

---

22 *Trusted and Independent*, para 5.54.
23 See **4.26**.
24 *Trusted and Independent*, para 5.56 and ch 5, recommendation 9.
25 Government response, p 27, para 26.

VOLUNTARY REGISTRATION

4.42 As the evidence to Lord Hodgson's review illustrates, while some may view registration with the Charity Commission as a burden, many regard it as a distinct advantage: see **4.20**.

4.43 The 2006 Act contained a new provision allowing non-exempt charities falling below the registration thresholds to register voluntarily: this provision is now contained in s 30(3) of the 2011 Act. However, at the time of writing, s 30(3) is not yet in force.[26]

4.44 In the meantime, reg 6 of the Charities Act 2006 (Commencement No 5, Transitional and Transitory Provisions and Savings) Order 2008[27] provides that:

> 'The Commission may enter a qualifying excepted charity in the register if that charity requests to be so registered …'

4.45 A 'qualifying excepted charity', under reg 1, is a charity within s 30(2)(b), (c) or (d) of the 2011 Act (see **4.14**).

4.46 This means that charities below the registration thresholds may apply to register (unless they are exempt charities), but there is currently no obligation on the Commission to admit them to registration. In practice the Commission will only register charities below the relevant registration threshold in exceptional circumstances.[28]

4.47 The practical solution for new small charities which would prefer to operate under a registered charity number, but which fall below the £5,000 income threshold, would be to seek to register as a charitable incorporated organisation, as there is no minimum income threshold for registration of a CIO.

4.48 The original intention had been for a right for charities to register voluntarily to be implemented once the Commission had dealt with the large numbers of formerly excepted and exempted charities which were required to register following implementation of the relevant provisions of the 2006 Act. Voluntary registration was considered by Lord Hodgson in his 2012 review. As part of his package of recommendations, which included an increase in the general registration threshold to £25,000 and a reduction in the threshold for excepted charities to the same level within a relatively short timeframe (see **4.21 and 4.38**), Lord Hodgson recommended that there should be a staged introduction of the right to voluntary registration, by bringing s 30(3) into force. He suggested that voluntary registration should commence once the process of registering excepted charities with an income over £25,000 had been completed, and when all existing organisations wishing to convert to a charitable incorporated organisation had had 2 years to do so.[29]

---

26 See Sch 9, para 8 of the 2011 Act.

27 SI 2008/3267.

28 Charity Commission publication CC21b, 'How to register your charity' sets out the Commission's positon in relation to non-excepted charities below the £5,000 threshold. The Commission has confirmed in correspondence with the authors that it takes the same approach to excepted charities below the £100,000 threshold.

29 *Trusted and Independent*, ch 5, recommendation 11.

4.49 While Government did not accept an increase in the general registration threshold to £25,000, nor an imminent reduction in the registration threshold for excepted charities, it did, in principle, accept Lord Hodgson's recommendation regarding voluntary registration.[30]

4.50 Exempt charities cannot register voluntarily, and there is no suggestion that this should change.

4.51 The register of charities does, in practice, include a number of charities operating under the minimum income registration threshold (see **4.22**). These may have registered before the reduction of the income threshold from £5,000 to £1,000 under the 2006 Act, may have registered while their income was above the registration threshold but since seen a drop in income, or may have persuaded the Commission to register them voluntarily.

4.52 An excepted or small charity which is registered even though it falls below the relevant income threshold may be removed from the register on request,[31] or by the Commission without a request from the charity.[32] In practice, the Commission has confirmed in correspondence with the authors that it will not, as a matter of course, seek to remove a charity from the register without a request from the charity simply because its income has dropped below the relevant income threshold.

4.53 Once s 30(3) of the 2011 Act is in force, it will be open to a charity which is registered voluntarily to ask to be removed from the register if it so requests: s 34(3) of the 2011 Act provides that a charity which is for the time being registered under s 30(3) must be removed if it so requests.[33]

HOW TO REGISTER WITH THE COMMISSION

Eligibility

4.54 To be eligible for registration, an organisation must be a charity within the meaning of s 1 of the 2011 Act. It must be an institution, corporate or not,[34] which is established for charitable purposes only and which falls to be subject to the control of the High Court in the exercise of its jurisdiction with respect to charities. Charitable purposes are defined in ss 2 to 4 of the 2011 Act (for more detail see Chapter 3).

4.55 An institution established under the laws of another legal system will not usually be subject to the High Court's jurisdiction.[35] A corporate charity established in England and Wales will meet the jurisdiction requirement, as will an unincorporated charity whose constitution provides that it is governed by the law of England and Wales. If there is no such provision in the constitution of an unincorporated charity, other factors, including the residence of the trustees, will be relevant in determining jurisdiction.[36] The

30 Government response, p 28.
31 Section 34(3) of the 2011 Act as modified by reg 7 of the Charities Act 2006 (Commencement No 5, Transitional and Transitory Provisions and Savings) Order 2008, SI 2008/3267.
32 Regulation 8 of the Charities Act 2006 (Commencement No 5, Transitional and Transitory Provisions and Savings) Order 2008, SI 2008/3267.
33 At the time of writing s 34(3) is subject to transitory modifications: see note 31.
34 See the definition of 'institution' in s 9(3) of the 2011 Act.
35 *Gaudiya Mission v Brahmachary* [1997] 4 All ER 957.
36 See, eg, *Armenian Patriarch of Jerusalem v Sonsino* [2002] EWHC 1304 (Ch).

authors' view is that it is not a technical rule of charity law that one of the trustees must be resident in England and Wales, but the Commission takes a generally reasonable position (subject to possible case-by-case exceptions) in considering that, for its regulatory function to be meaningful, it must be able to engage with at least one of a charity's trustees within the jurisdiction.

Application for registration

4.56 Section 35 of the 2011 Act specifies the duties of charity trustees in connection with registration. The trustees of a charity which is required to be registered must apply for registration and supply the Commission with copies of the charity's trusts (or, if they are not in documentary form, particulars of them) and such other documents or information as the Commission may require or as the Minister for the Cabinet Office may prescribe by regulation. Under s 353(1) of the 2011 Act a charity's trusts are the provisions establishing it as a charity and regulating its purposes and administration. In most cases, the trustees will be able to provide a copy of the governing instrument of the charity. Very rarely, evidence of the trusts may be in some other form, for example a statutory declaration where the original deeds are lost.

4.57 The Commission requires applicants to complete an online application form providing information about the activities of the charity, how its purposes are for the public benefit, the charity trustees and other relevant information. The Commission may call for more information or ask further questions when assessing the application. The Commission may, in some cases, make registration conditional on compliance with certain conditions. It may also carry out post-registration monitoring.

4.58 If an application for registration is successful, the charity will be given a registration number (see **4.12**) and entered in the register. Registered charities can obtain a registration certificate by logging into their account on the Commission's online services.

Challenging a registration decision

4.59 If an application for registration is unsuccessful, the Commission can be asked to review the decision. The decision is also subject to appeal to the Charity Tribunal.

4.60 An application to the Commission for decision review must be made within three months of the date of notification of the original decision: see Chapter 10 for more detail about the decision review process. The process is likely to be more cost-effective than an appeal to the Tribunal, and may allow more scope for dialogue with the Commission about possible amendments to the organisation's governing document and activities in order to achieve registration.

4.61 An appeal to the Tribunal must be made no later than 42 days after the decision was sent to the appellant, or was published: see Chapter 10 for more detail. This is a shorter time frame than that which applies to the Commission's decision review process. The Commission has confirmed that where the Commission's decision not to register an organisation as a charity is subject to a decision review, time for a Tribunal appeal will run from the date of the decision review decision, and not from the date of the original decision. However, potential applicants may nonetheless wish to file a protective application with the Tribunal, which can then be stayed while the decision review process is ongoing, or at the very least seek confirmation from the Commission within the 42-day period that an application for decision review in their particular case will effectively defer the start of the 42 days until the outcome of the decision review.

4.62 The appeal to the Tribunal may be made by the charity trustees (or those who claim to be the charity trustees), the organisation (if it is a body corporate) and any other person who is or may be affected by the decision. The Tribunal may quash the decision and (if appropriate) remit the matter to the Commission and/or direct the Commission to rectify the register.[37]

4.63 At the time of writing the Tribunal has issued substantive judgments in relation to six appeals from decisions of the Commission not to register charities under s 30 of the 2011 Act.[38]

4.64 It is also possible for a successful registration to be challenged: see **4.93**.

4.65 The Commission may reconsider any question affecting the registration of a charity notwithstanding the Tribunal's decision, and may make a different decision to the Tribunal if there has been a change of circumstances, under s 36(5) of the 2011 Act.

Registration with HMRC

4.66 A charity which is seeking registration with the Commission is also likely to wish to be registered with HMRC for tax purposes (see **4.81–4.82**). At the time of writing, this entails a separate application to HMRC. In his 2012 review Lord Hodgson recommended that the processes for registration with the Commission and HMRC should be joined up into a single process[39] and Government agreed that this should be explored.[40] This has been discussed by HMRC and the Commission: it is the authors' understanding that the proposals may be implemented in the course of 2016.

Charging for registration

4.67 There is no charge for registering a charity. None was recommended in the discussions preceding the passing of the 2006 Act, although s 19 of the 2011 Act does allow the Minister for the Cabinet Office to make regulations about the payment of fees (which must be approved by Parliament, under s 348).

4.68 In his 2012 report Lord Hodgson, while recognising that 'charging by the Commission remains a very divisive subject',[41] recommended that Government should work with the Commission to develop a fair and proportionate system for the registration of new charities (and for filing annual returns[42]). Government decided,

37 Sections 319 and 323 and Sch 6 of the 2011 Act.

38 In *Full Fact v Charity Commission* (CA/2011/0001), *Uturn UK CIC (formerly Uturn UK Ltd) v Charity Commission* (CA/2011/0006), *Harrogate Fairtrade Shop v Charity Commission* (CA/2013/0009) and *Cambridgeshire Target Shooting Association v Charity Commission* (CA/2015/0002), the appeals were dismissed. In *The Human Dignity Trust v Charity Commission* (CA/2013/0013) and *Wilfrid Vernor-Miles & ors v Charity Commission* (CA/2014/0022) the appeals were allowed and the Commission was directed to register the charity. See also *Jonathan Bishop on behalf of Crocel's Community Media Group v Charity Commission* (CA/2015/0009) which was an appeal against the Commission's refusal to register a charitable incorporated organisation under s 207 of the 2011 Act.

39 *Trusted and Independent*, ch 5, recommendation 12.

40 Government response, p 28, para 28.

41 *Trusted and Independent*, para 6.59.

42 See **21.92**.

however, that in view of the complexities and sensitivities around charging, and the risk that charging could deter charities from being registered, this recommendation would not be taken forward for the time being. Government said that any introduction of charging would be subject to full consultation with the charity sector.[43]

4.69 However, more recent reports from the Commission, including the statement in the Commission's Strategic Plan for 2015 to 2018 to the effect that the Commission would be consulting on proposals for alternative funding options for the Commission, including an annual charge for registered charities, mean that charging for registration is by no means off the agenda (see **2.49**).

THE IMPLICATIONS OF REGISTRATION

Obligations following registration

4.70 Once a charity is registered, the trustees must keep the Commission informed about any changes in the constitution (except those effected by Charity Commission scheme), or other registered particulars of their charity. Under s 35(3) and (4) of the 2011 Act the trustees are obliged to inform the Commission of any change in a charity's trusts (which will include documents dealing with its purposes and administration: see **4.56**) or the particulars of the charity entered in the register, for example an amendment to its governing document.[44] So far as appropriate, the Commission must be sent particulars of the change and copies of any new trusts or alterations of the trusts.[45]

4.71 Registered charities are required to file annual reports and returns with the Commission (see Chapter 21).

Disclosure

4.72 Under s 39 of the 2011 Act, a registered charity with a gross income in the previous financial year in excess of £10,000 must state that it is a registered charity on certain documents. The rationale behind this provision is to alert people dealing with a registered charity to the fact that it is subject to the supervisory regime of the Commission and to the legal constraints which bind charities.

4.73 The documents to which the provision relates are set out in s 39(2). They are:

(a) notices, advertisements and other documents issued by or on behalf of the charity and soliciting money or other property for the benefit of the charity;
(b) bills of exchange, promissory notes, endorsements, cheques and orders for money or goods purporting to be signed on behalf of the charity; and
(c) bills, invoices, receipts and letters of credit.

4.74 Under s 39(4), the requirement in relation to documents soliciting money or other property applies whether the solicitation is express or implied, and whether or not the money or other property is given for consideration. Therefore, it applies not only to

43 Government response, p 9 and para 47, p 33.
44 Certain changes to a charity's governing document may require prior Charity Commission consent: eg see Chapter 13 in relation to charitable companies.
45 These obligations are modified slightly in relation to CIOs: see Chapter 14.

direct fundraising material, but also to newsletters providing information about projects which have the indirect purpose of raising funds. It applies to documents seeking outright donations, and to those inviting contributions in exchange for some benefit, eg admission to some fundraising event, or soliciting membership subscriptions. The rules apply to paper documents and to appeals appearing on websites, or sent by email. Since the provision relates to solicitations issued on behalf of a charity, it is also relevant to solicitations issued on behalf of a charity by professional fundraisers and commercial participators (see Chapters 19 and 20).

4.75 With the exception of documents in Welsh, the statement of registered charity status must be in English in legible characters, even if the literature of the charity is normally published in another language. In that case, the charity may wish to make the statement in both English and in the language which it would normally use. Charities are permitted to use the words 'elusen cofrestredig' on documents in Welsh.

4.76 The Minister for the Cabinet Office has power to change the £10,000 threshold mentioned at **4.72**, under s 40.

4.77 Section 41 of the 2011 Act imposes criminal sanctions for failing to comply with s 39. Under s 41(1) any person who issues or authorises the issue of any document mentioned in (a) or (c) at **4.73** which does not carry the necessary statement is guilty of an offence and liable on summary conviction to a fine. Section 41(2) imposes a similar penalty on any person who signs a document mentioned in (b) at **4.73** – a cheque being the most obvious example – without the necessary statement of registered charity status. Liability rests on the individual who issues, authorises or signs the document, whether a trustee or an employee of the charity, or even, in the case of an advertisement soliciting funds, a professional fundraiser or a commercial participator. The individual is guilty, whether or not the default was committed knowingly.

4.78 No proceedings may be instituted except by or with the consent of the Director of Public Prosecutions, under s 345 of the 2011 Act. At the time of writing the authors are not aware of any prosecutions having been made under s 41.

4.79 There are further disclosure obligations for charitable companies under s 194 of the 2011 Act (see Chapter 13) and for charitable incorporated organisations under s 211 of the 2011 Act (see Chapter 14).

Other implications of registration

4.80 Section 37(1) of the 2011 Act provides that an institution which is registered is conclusively presumed to be a charity for all purposes at any time when it is or was on the register, other than for the purpose of rectification of the register. When an appeal to the Tribunal against the Commission's decision to register a charity is pending, the entry in the register may be suspended: see **4.95**.

4.81 Registration has tax implications. In order to be recognised as a charity for most UK tax purposes, an organisation must satisfy four conditions, set out in Sch 6 to the Finance Act 2010. These are:

- it must be established for charitable purposes only (as set out in s 2 of the 2011 Act): since this is also a condition of registration with the Commission (see **4.54**), a registered charity will meet this condition;

- it must be subject to the control of a relevant UK court (which includes the High Court in England and Wales) in the exercise of its jurisdiction with respect to charities (or a similar court in various European countries): again, since control by the High Court in the exercise of its jurisdiction with respect to charities is a precondition of registration with the Charity Commission (see **4.54**), a registered charity will meet this condition;[46]
- if the organisation is a charity within the meaning of s 10 of the 2011 Act (which means a charity within s 1 (see **4.54**) or certain ecclesiastical organisations), it must have complied with any requirement to register with the Commission. The effect of this condition is that if an organisation which is required to register with the Charity Commission fails to do so, HMRC may deny it the tax reliefs and exemptions available to UK charities. The implications of failure to register could, therefore, be significant; and
- the persons with general management and control of the charity's administration (which, for HMRC's purposes, can include employees as well as trustees) must be fit and proper persons to be managers of the organisation. More information about this requirement is available from HMRC.[47]

4.82 HMRC is the final arbiter of whether a charity qualifies for UK tax reliefs, so any registered charity would be well advised to ensure that it is registered with HMRC in order to confirm its eligibility.

4.83 Local authorities are also likely to accept that a registered charity is eligible for the reliefs from business rates available to charities under s 43(6) of the Local Government Finance Act 1988, although a slightly different definition of charity applies for the purposes of that legislation.

REMOVAL FROM THE REGISTER

General

4.84 Once registered, there is scope for a charity to be removed from the register in several ways.

4.85 Under s 34(1) of the 2011 Act the Commission must remove from the register any institution which it no longer considers is a charity and any charity which has ceased to exist or does not operate: see **4.97-4.103**.[48] This process may be initiated by the Commission itself, or an interested party may prompt the Commission to exercise its power to remove by objecting to registration under s 36: see **4.90-4.91**. A decision to remove a charity from the register may be appealed to the Tribunal.[49]

4.86 If the Commission's decision to register a charity is appealed to the Tribunal and is successful, this may result in the institution's removal from the register.

---

46 This means that there is scope for charities established outside the United Kingdom to benefit from UK charity tax reliefs. At the time of writing, the relevant territories whose charities may benefit include all countries in the European Union plus Norway, Iceland and Liechtenstein. Further territories may be added by statutory instrument. In practice very few non-UK charities have been accepted by HMRC as satisfying the definition.

47 www.gov.uk/government/organisations/hm-revenue-customs.

48 In 2015–16, 4,800 charities were removed from the register: Charity Commission Annual Report 2015/16.

49 Sections 319 and Sch 6 of the 2011 Act.

4.87 As discussed at **4.52–4.53**, charities which are not required to register, but are nonetheless registered, may ask to be removed from the register and the Commission currently has the right to remove them even if no such request is made.

4.88 The register of charities continues to contain information on institutions which have been removed from the register, under s 38(1) of the 2011 Act.

4.89 It is possible for a charity which has been removed to be reinstated: for example in 2013 the Commission decided to reinstate the Ellenborough and Netherton Reading and Recreation Room Charity[50] (formerly known as the Miners' Welfare Reading and Recreation Room) to the register following its removal in 1997.

Application for removal

Application to the Commission

4.90 Under s 36(1) of the 2011 Act 'a person who is or may be affected by the registration of an institution' may, on the grounds that it is not a charity, object to its registration or, if it has been registered, apply to the Commission for its removal from the register. This can cause the Commission to consider whether it should exercise its power of removal under s 34(1).

4.91 There is a question as to who has standing to make an application under s 36. Section 36 uses similar wording to the test used to determine who has standing to appeal a decision to the Tribunal (see below), although in the case of s 36 the question is whether a person is affected by registration, rather than by the decision of the Commission which is sought to be appealed. However, even if the Commission considers that an applicant lacks standing under s 36, the fact that an application has been made may well prompt the Commission to consider the status of the charity in any event under s 34.[51]

Application to the Tribunal

4.92 A positive decision by the Commission to register a charity may be challenged by making an appeal to the Tribunal: the challenge can be made by the charity or its trustees (which is clearly unlikely) or by 'any other person who is or may be affected by the decision'.[52] The challenge must be made within the 42-day time limit for making an appeal to the Tribunal: see Chapter 10.

4.93 In addition, a decision by the Commission not to remove a charity from the register, taken under s 34 of the 2011 Act, may be appealed to the Tribunal.[53] The appeal can be brought by the charity trustees, the charity itself (if a body corporate)[54] or by 'any other person who is or may be affected by the decision'.

---

[50] Charity decisions can be accessed on the Government website: www.gov.uk/government/collections/charity-commission-regulatory-decisions-by-year.

[51] See the Charity Commission's December 2013 decision in the case of the JNF Charitable Trust, JNF Educational Trust and KKL Charity Accounts (which was appealed to the Charity Tribunal in *Nicholson v Charity Commission*: see **4.94**).

[52] Section 319 and Sch 6 of the 2011 Act.

[53] Section 319 and Sch 6 of the 2011 Act.

[54] See, eg, *Regentford v Charity Commission* (CA/2013/0014).

4.94 The meaning of 'any other person who is or may be affected by the decision' in this context has been considered by the Upper Tribunal in the case of *Nicholson v Charity Commission*.[55] The Upper Tribunal decided that Mr Nicholson, who wished to challenge the Commission's decision not to remove three charities from the register, did not have standing to appeal the decision as a person 'affected by' it. The Tribunal said that neither the fact that Mr Nicholson had originally asked the Commission to consider the issue and was therefore an 'addressee' of its decision not to remove the charities, nor the fact that he was a taxpayer, necessarily meant that he was 'affected by' the decision in the way required by the legislation.[56]

4.95 If an appeal to the Tribunal challenging the status of a charity on the register is pending, and the Commission is not satisfied as to whether it will remain on the register, its entry is suspended and it is not regarded as a charity under s 37 of the 2011 Act.[57]

4.96 The Commission may reconsider any question affecting the removal of a charity notwithstanding a decision by the Tribunal, and may reach a different decision if circumstances have changed in the interim, under s 36(5) of the 2011 Act.

Grounds for removal by the Commission

Charity has ceased to exist or does not operate

4.97 A charity may be removed under s 34(1)(b) because it has ceased to exist, or does not operate.

4.98 Under s 35(3)(a) of the 2011 Act the charity trustees must notify the Commission if their charity ceases to exist. The charity trustees can expect that once they have made this notification, their charity will be removed from the register. A charity which has closed, or merged with another charity or (as an unincorporated charity) transferred its assets and liabilities to a successor incorporated charity may wish to be removed, although there will sometimes be a question as to whether such a charity should remain in existence, and on the register, for the purposes of receiving possible legacies.[58]

4.99 There are a number of examples of situations where removal under s 34(1)(b) has been considered. For instance:

- in the case of *Regentford v Charity Commission*,[59] the charity challenged the Commission's decision not to remove it from the register. In upholding the Commission's decision, the First-tier Tribunal said that as a properly constituted company with separate legal personality, the charity had existed at the time of the decision. Even though it had very low levels of activity, few resources and little capability to act or carry out the activities which would be expected of a normally functioning charity, it was still operating for the purposes of s 34(1)(b);

---

55 [2016] UKUT 0198 (TCC). See **10.61–10.67**.

56 The Upper Tribunal decided that the earlier First-tier Tribunal case of *Lasper v Charity Commission* (CA/2010/006) had been wrongly decided. In that case Mr Lasper had been allowed to appeal the Commission's decision not to remove a charity from the register, as a person affected by the decision, on the basis that it was Mr Lasper's approach to the Commission which had precipitated the Commission's decision. See Chapter 10 for more information about the Charity Tribunal.

57 Sections 36(3) and (4) and 37(2) of the 2011 Act.

58 See Chapter 16.

59 CA/2013/0014.

- in 2015 the Commission removed Yoruba Language and Cultural Heritage from the register following a statutory inquiry, having found no evidence of charitable activity or funds being applied for charitable purposes;[60]
- in July 2014 the Commission removed 10 charities from the register on the basis that they did not operate, having discovered that there were fraudulent features in the documents submitted when the charities applied for registration;
- the Tribunal case of *Lasper v Charity Commission*[61] concerned whether the charitable trusts affecting the Town Field charity had been extinguished by the operation of the Commons Registration Act 1965, meaning that the charity had ceased to exist. The First-tier Tribunal decided that the principal asset of the charity was no longer held on charitable trusts, so quashed the Commission's decision not to remove the charity from the register.[62]

Institution no longer considered to be a charity

4.100 Under s 34(1)(a) the Commission must remove any institution which it no longer considers is a charity from the register. These cases may well be controversial. The Commission has said that 'the decision to remove an institution from the Register on the grounds that it no longer appears to be a charity is not one the Commission would reach lightly'.[63]

4.101 A charity may be removed on this ground because it was placed on the register in error, or because its objects are no longer charitable, either as a result of a change in social circumstances, or as a result of a constitutional change.

4.102 There is a common misconception that if a charity loses its charitable status its assets need no longer be used for charitable purposes. This is not the case: broadly speaking, where the removal results from a loss of charitable status rather than a mistaken registration, the assets continue to be held for charitable purposes, and it may be appropriate for them be applied cy-près (see Chapter 17).[64]

4.103 The Joint Committee considering the legislation which became the 2006 Act recommended that the Act should include provisions to clarify the effect of the loss of charitable status on the assets of a charity – possibly influenced by concerns that the new provisions on public benefit in the 2006 Act might mean the loss of charitable status for some charities.[65] The Government did not accept this recommendation, arguing that the existing law, as set out in RR6, Maintenance of an Accurate Register of Charities (then dated November 2000), was an adequate basis for determining what should happen to a charity's assets in these circumstances.

---

60 Charity Commission inquiry report published March 2016.

61 CA/2010/0006.

62 See also Charity Commission operational guidance OG 531-1 'Removal of Charities from our Register: Dissolutions and Voluntary Removal' and OG 531-2 'Removing Charities from our Register: Inactive Charities'.

63 Charity Commission publication RR6, 'Maintenance of an Accurate Register of Charities', December 2012.

64 RR6, 'Maintenance of an Accurate Register of Charities', December 2012.

65 See Chapter 3.

CHAPTER 5

EXEMPT CHARITIES

INTRODUCTION

5.1 Some charities, known as exempt charities, are subject to a lesser degree of regulation by the Charity Commission than other types of charity. They are not required, nor indeed able, to register with the Commission, and the Commission's powers to oversee and intervene in their activities are more limited than for other charities. Exempt charities are subject to this special regime because, historically, another regulator has been charged with their supervision.

5.2 In its review of charity law prior to the 2006 Act, the Strategy Unit found that some exempt charities were not being monitored in relation to charity law requirements.[1] As a result, the 2006 Act introduced significant changes to the regulation of exempt charities. A number of charities lost their exempt status. For those charities that remained exempt, a 'principal regulator' was given responsibility for promoting their compliance with charity law and the Commission was given more significant powers in relation to them.

5.3 However, at the time of writing not all of the changes introduced by the 2006 Act (and now in the 2011 Act) are in force: some charities which were due to lose their exempt status have not yet done so. This means that different regimes apply to the following:

- charities that remain exempt, following the changes in the 2006 Act which have been implemented. In this chapter, we refer to these charities as 'exempt charities with a principal regulator';
- charities which lost their exempt status, following the changes in the 2006 Act which have been implemented; and
- exempt charities whose status is undecided because the 2006 Act was due to make changes to their status, but the relevant provisions have not yet been implemented. In this chapter, we refer to these charities as 'exempt charities whose status remains undecided'.

There is more detail on the differing rules below.

5.4 In his 2012 review of charity law, Lord Hodgson estimated that there were around 10,000 exempt charities,[2] as compared with 162,000 registered charities.[3] However, the size of the exempt charity sector, in terms of income, is very significant.

---

1 *Private Action: Public Benefit*, p 87.
2 *Trusted and Independent: Giving charity back to charities*, para 6.2.
3 *Trusted and Independent*, para 5.25.

National Audit Office figures from 2012 gave a figure of £55.4 billion for the income of registered charities in 2009/10, alongside income of an estimated £57.3 billion for exempt charities.[4] It is worth noting that the size of the exempt charity sector has been significantly affected by increases in the number of academies and free schools, which are exempt charities.

5.5 Exempt charities should not be confused with excepted charities. The two are different: exempt charities do not register with the Commission, and are subject to a lesser degree of regulation by the Commission; excepted charities do not need to register nor submit reports and accounts to the Commission if their annual income does not exceed £100,000, but they are subject to the Commission's jurisdiction in all other respects (see **4.25–4.40**).

WHICH CHARITIES ARE EXEMPT?

The legislation

5.6 Under s 22(1) of the 2011 Act, 'exempt' charities are those institutions which fall within Sch 3 to the 2011 Act, so far as they are charities. However, s 22(1) is 'subject to any other enactment by virtue of which a charity is an exempt charity'.[5] It was explained, in evidence to the Joint Committee on Consolidation Bills reviewing the legislation that became the 2011 Act,[6] that this reflects the fact that there is legislation outside the 2011 Act which confers exempt status, such as s 143 of the Learning and Skills Act 2000.[7]

5.7 In addition, at the time of writing, common investment and common deposit funds which only admit exempt charities are exempt under ss 99 and 103 of the 2011 Act, as amended by para 2 of Sch 9 to that Act (although their future status is undecided).

5.8 For the most part, however, the categories of exempt charity are set out in Sch 3.

Exempt charities with a principal regulator – charities that remain exempt following the changes made in the 2006 Act

5.9 The charities that remain exempt following the changes in the 2006 Act which, at the time of writing, have been implemented include a number of national galleries and museums, most English universities[8] and higher education institutions, further education and sixth form college corporations, academies (including free schools) and the governing bodies of foundation and voluntary schools.[9]

---

4 *Regulating charities: landscape review*, National Audit Office, July 2012, www.nao.org.uk/wp-Content/uploads/2012/07/Regulating_charities_facts_sheet.pdf.

5 Section 22(2) of the 2011 Act.

6 Joint Committee report on Consolidation Bills, First report of session 2010-12, pp 18–20, www.publications.parliament.uk/pa/jt201012/jtselect/jtconsol/168/168.pdf.

7 For example, St David's Catholic College, a designated further education provider in Wales: exempt status was conferred by statutory instrument.

8 Universities in England can be added to the list of exempt charities if the Queen makes a declaration to that effect by Order in Council: see for example Exempt Charities Order 2015, SI 2015/210 and Exempt Charities (No 2) Order 2015, SI 2015/1894.

9 Schedule 3 to the 2011 Act.

5.10 'Principal regulators' have been appointed to each of these charities in order to ensure their compliance with charity law (see 5.30-5.36).

5.11 Institutions administered by or on behalf of exempt charities and established for the general purposes, or special purposes of or in connection with the exempt charity, are also exempt (with some exceptions such as students' unions).[10] At the time of writing, the Commission's internal operational guidance on how to identify these so-called 'connected institutions' is available on the Commission's website.[11]

Charities that lost their exempt status in the 2006 Act

5.12 Schedule 3 to the 2011 Act reflects the significant changes to the list of exempt charities which were precipitated by the 2006 Act. The key changes were the removal of the representative body of the Welsh Church, Winchester College, Eton College, the Church Commissioners, the Museum of London, the colleges and halls of the universities of Oxford, Cambridge and Durham, students' unions and universities and other higher education institutions in Wales from the list of exempt charities.

5.13 In identifying these charities, Government was influenced by the fact that it was not possible to identify an acceptable principal regulator for them: the Government Minister, Lord Bassam of Brighton, stated in early debates on the Bill which became the 2006 Act that the Government had 'tried where possible to identify suitable main regulators to take on the role of monitoring basic charity law compliance, but for some exempt charities it has not proved possible'.[12]

5.14 These charities are now subject to the full range of the Commission's powers, although at present they are subject to a more relaxed registration threshold than other charities (see 5.27).

Exempt charities whose status remains undecided

5.15 Not all of the changes anticipated in the 2006 Act have been brought into force. At the time of writing, the following remain 'in limbo' as exempt charities which were, for the most part, due to lose their exempt status but have not yet done so:

- common investment and deposit funds which only admit exempt charities;
- Church of England and Methodist Church Investment funds; and
- charitable community benefit and cooperative societies (formerly called industrial and provident societies)[13] and friendly societies.

5.16 The 2006 Act had provided that most of these charities should lose their exempt status, but these provisions had not been implemented by the time the 2011 Act came into force. The relevant provisions of the 2006 Act were replicated in the 2011 Act, but subject to Sch 9, which suspends the effect of some of the provisions of the 2011 Act for the time being. At the time of writing, the relevant provisions are still not in force.

---

10 Schedule 3, para 28 of the 2011 Act.

11 OG 717-2 'Exempt charities: connected institutions and how to identify them'.

12 HL Deb Official Report of the Grand Committee, vol 670, col GC 400 (14 March 2005).

13 As a result of the Co-operative and Community Benefit Societies Act 2014 industrial and provident societies are now referred to as either cooperative societies or community benefit societies.

5.17 This means that at the time of writing these charities are exempt from registration with the Commission for the time being, but they currently have no principal regulator, and the expansion of the Commission's jurisdiction over exempt charities which was brought in by the 2006 Act (see 5.37-5.64) does not yet apply to them (see 5.65).

5.18 In his 2012 review of charity law, Lord Hodgson noted that there was a need to accelerate the implementation of the legislation for these charities.[14]

5.19 The intention was that common investment and deposit schemes and funds which only admit exempt charities, and church investment funds, should cease to be exempt charities. However, at the time of writing no firm decision has been made on the future of these charities.

5.20 It was also intended that charitable community benefit societies and cooperative societies (formerly called industrial and provident societies) and friendly societies should lose their exempt status, except those which are registered providers of social housing or registered social landlords under Part 1 of the Housing Act 1996. Lord Hodgson recommended that the Office for Civil Society and the Commission should begin discussions with the Homes and Communities Agency about the possibility of it becoming the principal regulator for charitable social housing providers in England.[15] The Government supported this recommendation and reported in its response to Lord Hodgson's review that discussions were underway and that similar discussions had also begun with the Welsh Government in respect of equivalent charities in Wales.[16] Lord Hodgson also recommended that charitable community benefit societies should be required either to register with the Commission or resign their charitable status.[17] Government responded that it would consider the possibility of appointing a principal regulator for these societies, and the alternative of requiring larger societies to register with the Commission. It said that 'relinquishing charitable status is not an option without relinquishing all assets so that they can be applied for similar charitable purposes'.[18] Again, at the time of writing, these charities remain exempt.

5.21 Some community benefit societies which are currently treated as charities for tax purposes by HMRC have power to pay interest to members on their share capital. In many cases, payment of interest is out of profits. There were concerns that this could be a barrier to registration with the Commission, as and when these charities lose their exempt status, since the Commission regards a power to distribute profits as fundamentally incompatible with charitable status. However, after some discussion the Commission indicated that there could be circumstances where a power to pay interest on shares would not be incompatible with charitable status, provided certain restrictions were imposed under the rules of the society, including a condition that the payment be made as a revenue expense, before any surplus is determined.[19]

---

14 *Trusted and Independent*, para 6.8.
15 *Trusted and Independent*, para 6.8.
16 Government response, September 2013, p 29.
17 *Trusted and Independent*, ch 10, p 122, recommendation 1.
18 Government response, p 45.
19 See Charity Commission guidance on industrial and provident societies issued in May 2013 and para 6.36 of the Financial Conduct Authority's publication FG15/12: Guidance on the FCA's registration function under the Co-operative and Community Benefit Societies Act 2014, November 2015.

Power to change the list of exempt charities

5.22 There is some scope to alter which charities are exempt and which are not.

5.23 Under s 23(1) of the 2011 Act, the Minister for the Cabinet Office may order that a particular charity, or charities of a particular description, should become exempt charities, or that a particular charity, or charities of a particular description, should cease to be exempt.[20] However, that power may only be exercised if the Minister is satisfied that the order is desirable in the interests of ensuring appropriate or effective regulation of the charities concerned in connection with the trustees' compliance with their legal obligations in exercising control and management of the charities' administration.[21]

5.24 The Minister may make appropriate changes to other legislation following an order under s 23(1).[22]

5.25 The Minister for the Cabinet Office may also remove organisations that have ceased to exist from Sch 3, by order.[23]

REGISTRATION WITH THE COMMISSION – EXEMPT AND FORMERLY EXEMPT CHARITIES

5.26 Exempt charities are not required to register with the Commission.[24] This applies to both exempt charities with a principal regulator and exempt charities whose status remains undecided. Indeed, an exempt charity may not register with the Commission even if it wishes to. An exempt charity may not set itself up as a charitable incorporated organisation,[25] nor, once the relevant legislation is in force, apply to be converted to a charitable incorporated organisation.[26]

5.27 Charities which were exempt prior to the changes effected by the 2006 Act, but which have since ceased to be exempt,[27] must register with the Commission, but only if their annual income exceeds £100,000. This is because where charities cease to be exempt, regulations must be made which ensure that they become excepted charities.[28] Regulations have been made to this effect in relation to charities which have lost their exempt status as a result of the 2006 Act.[29] As explained in Chapter 4, excepted charities are not currently required to register so long as their gross income is less than £100,000. The £100,000 registration threshold for excepted charities may reduce over time:[30] any reduction would apply equally to formerly exempt charities which are now excepted.

---

20 Orders under s 23 are subject to the prior approval of both Houses of Parliament under s 349 of the 2011 Act.
21 Section 23(2) of the 2011 Act.
22 Section 23(3) and Sch 8, para 15 of the 2011 Act.
23 Section 24 of the 2011 Act.
24 Section 30(2)(a) of the 2011 Act.
25 See reg 5 of the Charitable Incorporated Organisations (General) Regulations 2012.
26 Sections 228 and 229 of the 2011 Act. See Chapter 14 for more information on charitable incorporated organisations.
27 See **5.12–5.14**.
28 Section 31(3) (which replaced s 3A(4)(b) of the 1993 Act) and Sch 9, para 9 of the 2011 Act.
29 The Charities Act (Exception from Registration) Regulations 2008, SI 2008/3268 and 2010, SI 2010/502.
30 See **4.36–4.39**.

5.28 As and when any exempt charities whose status is currently undecided cease to be exempt, the Minister for the Cabinet Office will be required to make similar regulations to ensure that those charities become excepted charities.

REGULATION OF EXEMPT CHARITIES

General

5.29 The 2006 Act introduced a system under which all exempt charities would have a 'principal regulator'. The Commission's powers to intervene in the activities of these charities were also significantly expanded. However, at the time of writing these rules do not yet apply to those exempt charities whose status remains undecided.

Principal regulators

5.30 All exempt charities (except those whose status remains undecided) now have a 'principal regulator', designated in regulations made under s 25 of the 2011 Act.[31] Generally, the regulators that were chosen already had a regulatory relationship of some kind with the relevant charities before taking on the additional role of principal regulator, but not in respect of charity law issues. The following principal regulators have been prescribed for the following exempt charities:[32]

Qualifying academy proprietors (which includes free schools), sixth form college corporations, governing bodies of foundation, voluntary and foundation special schools, foundation bodies established under s 21 of the School Standards and Framework Act 1998	Secretary of State for Education
Further education corporations in England	Secretary of State for Business, Innovation and Skills
Further education corporations in Wales, governing bodies of foundation, voluntary and foundation special schools in Wales, foundation bodies established under s 21 of the School Standards and Framework Act 1998 in Wales	Welsh Ministers
Universities and higher education corporations in England	Higher Education Funding Council for England (HEFCE)

---

31 Under s 348 of the 2011 Act, regulations under s 25 are subject to the prior approval of both Houses of Parliament.

32 The Charities Act 2011 (Principal Regulators of Exempt Charities) Regulations 2013, SI 2013/1764, the Charities Act 2006 (Principal Regulators of Exempt Charities) (No 2) Regulations 2011, SI 2011/1727, the Charities Act 2006 (Principal Regulators of Exempt Charities) Regulations 2011, SI 2011/1726 and the Charities Act 2006 (Principal Regulators of Exempt Charities) Regulations 2010, SI 2010/501.

The boards/trustees of the Victoria and Albert Museum, Science Museum, Royal Armouries, National Museums and Galleries on Merseyside, British Museum, Natural History Museum, National Gallery, Tate Gallery, National Portrait Gallery, Wallace Collection, Imperial War Museum, National Maritime Museum and British Library	Secretary of State for Culture, Media and Sport
The trustees of the Royal Botanic Gardens, Kew	Secretary of State for Environment, Food and Rural Affairs

5.31 The principal regulator of an exempt charity has responsibility for ensuring its compliance with charity law: under s 26 of the 2011 Act the relevant principal regulator must do all that he, she or it reasonably can to meet the compliance objective in relation to the charity. The compliance objective is to promote the charity trustees' compliance with their legal obligations in exercising control and management of the administration of the charity.

5.32 The principal regulators may clearly use their existing powers and influence to encourage the exempt charities for which they take responsibility to comply with charity law. Under s 27 of the 2011 Act, regulations under s 25 may make any changes to existing legislation which the Minister for the Cabinet Office considers appropriate to facilitate, or otherwise in connection with, the principal regulators' discharge of their duties.[33]

5.33 However, the 2011 Act does not give principal regulators any powers to take enforcement action under charity legislation. They must work with the Commission to resolve any charity law concerns about an exempt charity.

5.34 The Commission has entered into Memoranda of Understanding with all the principal regulators of exempt charities, which are available via the Commission's website. These set out how the Commission and the relevant principal regulator will work together, with a view to clarifying the roles of the respective regulators and promoting effective working and communication between them. At the time of writing an informal Principal Regulators' Forum meets annually to support and inform the regulation of exempt charities.

5.35 Some principal regulators hold public lists of the exempt charities which they regulate.[34]

5.36 Lord Hodgson recommended that the term 'principal regulator' should be changed to 'co-regulator', to reflect the cooperative nature of the relationship between

33 For example, this power was used to allow the Young People's Learning Agency, when it existed, to assist the Secretary of State for Education as principal regulator of sixth form colleges and academies: Charities Act 2006 (Principal Regulators of Exempt Charities) Regulations 2011, SI 2011/1726.

34 See, for example, the list maintained by HEFCE, www.hefce.ac.uk.

the Commission and the respective principal regulators.[35] However, Government responded that there are no plans to make this change, which would require primary legislation.[36]

Charity Commission jurisdiction over exempt charities – charities with a principal regulator

5.37 A further significant change introduced by the 2006 Act was an increase in the scope of the Commission's powers to intervene in exempt charities' activities. Most, but not all, of the Commission's powers now apply to exempt charities with a principal regulator. (The Commission's powers in relation to exempt charities whose status remains undecided are still more limited.)

5.38 However, under s 28 of the 2011 Act, the Commission must consult the charity's principal regulator before exercising any specific power in relation to an exempt charity. This is an obligation of consultation only, which means that the principal regulator cannot veto action by the Commission. In the lead up to the 2006 Act, the Government stated that 'we see the consultation requirement as a requirement on the Commission to explain to the principal regulator what action it intended to take, and why; and to take account of the principal regulator's views'.[37]

5.39 Significantly, the Commission may only open a statutory inquiry into an exempt charity under s 46 of the 2011 Act[38] where this has been requested by the charity's principal regulator.

5.40 The Commission's powers in relation to exempt charities with a principal regulator include those set out below.[39]

Change of name

5.41 The Commission's power to require charities to change their names under s 42 of the 2011 Act (see Chapter 6) applies to exempt charities.

Inquiry and information powers

5.42 The Commission may conduct formal inquiries into the activities of exempt charities under s 46 of the 2011 Act (see Chapter 9), but only where the charity's principal regulator has asked the Commission to do so. This means that the Commission cannot act on its own initiative in opening an inquiry: the request must come from the principal regulator.

5.43 The Commission's powers to intervene in a charity's affairs following the institution of an inquiry, including the powers to appoint an interim manager (see Chapter 9) generally apply to exempt charities.

---

35 *Trusted and Independent*, ch 6, recommendation 6.

36 Government response, September 2013, p 30.

37 The Government reply to the Report from the Joint Committee on the Draft Charities Bill Session 2003-04, HL Paper, 167/HC 660, para 44.

38 See Chapter 9.

39 At the time of writing, Charity Commission operational guidance OG 717-1 'Exempt charities and principal regulators' contains detailed information on the Commission's powers in relation to exempt charities.

5.44 The Commission's powers to demand documents and search records under ss 52 and 53 of the 2011 Act (see Chapter 9) apply to exempt charities.

Failed charity appeals

5.45 The Commission may exercise its powers in relation to failed charity appeals under ss 63–66 of the 2011 Act (see Chapter 17) in relation to exempt charities.

Schemes, change of trustees and vesting of property

5.46 The Commission may exercise its scheme making powers under s 69 of the 2011 Act in respect of exempt charities.

5.47 The charity trustees of an exempt charity, and the Attorney General, may ask the Commission to exercise its powers under s 69 of the 2011 Act to make schemes, change trustees and vest property. The court can order the Commission to make a scheme in relation to an exempt charity. The Commission's powers under s 69 in relation to charities with income of £500 or less[40] (see Chapter 17) also apply to exempt charities. However, the Commission's powers to establish a scheme on its own initiative under s 70(4) and (5) of the 2011 Act (see **17.73**) do not apply to exempt charities.

5.48 The Commission's powers to make schemes which are given effect by Ministerial order under s 73 of the 2011 Act (see **17.93**) apply to exempt charities.

5.49 The Commission's powers to remove or appoint charity trustees under s 80 of the 2011 Act apply (see Chapter 9), but only after a s 46 inquiry has been commenced.[41]

5.50 The Commission may vest the property of an exempt charity in the Official Custodian under s 90 of the 2011 Act (see **22.2**).

Direct application of charity property

5.51 The Commission's powers to direct the application of charity property under s 85 of the 2011 Act (see Chapter 9) apply to exempt charities.

Authorise action and give advice

5.52 The Commission's powers to sanction action which is expedient in the interests of the charity (s 105 of the 2011 Act), authorise ex gratia payments (s 106 of the 2011 Act) and give advice (s 110 of the 2011 Act) (see Chapter 9) apply to exempt charities.

Charity trustees

5.53 The Commission's powers to grant a waiver from disqualification from charity trusteeship under s 181 of the 2011 Act (see **9.214–9.218**) apply to exempt charities.

---

40 Section 70(3) of the 2011 Act.

41 Section 80(4) of the 2011 Act.

5.54 The Commission's power under s 184(3) of the 2011 Act to demand repayment of benefits by a trustee who has acted while disqualified apply to exempt charities (see **9.232**).

5.55 The Commission's powers to make an order in relation to remuneration of a trustee under s 186 of the 2011 Act apply to exempt charities (see Chapter 7).

5.56 The Commission may relieve the trustees and auditors of exempt charities from liability for breach of duty under s 191 of the 2011 Act (see Chapter 9).

Regulated alterations

5.57 The provisions in s 198 of the 2011 Act apply to exempt charities, meaning that certain alterations to the Articles of Association of exempt charities which are charitable companies are ineffective without the prior written consent of the Commission (see Chapter 13).

Determining membership

5.58 The Commission has power under s 111 of the 2011 Act to determine the membership of exempt charities (see Chapter 9).

Miscellaneous

5.59 The requirement in s 115 of the 2011 Act to obtain the Commission's consent before bringing charity proceedings (see Chapter 9) applies to exempt charities. The Commission's power under s 115(7) of the 2011 Act to ask for the Attorney General to become involved also applies.

5.60 Dormant bank accounts of exempt charities fall within the Commission's remit (see **9.203**).

5.61 The Commission's powers to consent to the costs of promoting a Bill in Parliament being paid out of charitable funds under s 74 of the 2011 Act apply to exempt charities.

5.62 The Commission's powers to present winding-up petitions, bring legal proceedings or compromise claims under ss 113 and 114 of the 2011 Act (see **13.29** and **9.164**) apply to exempt charities.

5.63 The Commission may establish common investment and deposit schemes and funds for exempt charities, under ss 96–104 of the 2011 Act (see **11.62–11.64**).

5.64 As mentioned at **5.38**, the Commission must consult with the principal regulator before exercising any power in relation to an exempt charity.

Charity Commission jurisdiction over exempt charities whose status remains undecided

5.65 The changes to the Commission's powers over exempt charities brought about by the 2006 Act do not apply to those exempt charities whose status remains undecided.[42] Most significantly, the Commission has no power under s 46 of the 2011 Act to institute inquiries into these charities.

Other charity law provisions affecting exempt charities[43]

5.66 Most of the other provisions of the 2011 Act apply to exempt charities. For example, the following provisions apply to both exempt charities with a principal regulator and those whose status remains undecided, although in the case of the former, the Commission must consult the principal regulator before exercising any specific powers:

- The charity trustees of all exempt charities have a duty to take steps to apply charitable property cy-près where appropriate under s 61 of the 2011 Act (see Chapter 17).
- The provisions of the 2011 Act relating to the disqualification of charity trustees (see Chapter 9) apply.
- Exempt charities are required to include statutory statements in documents dealing with the disposal or mortgage of land under ss 122 and 125 of the 2011 Act, although not all of the provisions of the 2011 Act relating to the disposition of land apply to exempt charities (see Chapter 8).
- Charitable companies that are exempt charities remain subject to the disclosure requirements set out in s 194 of the 2011 Act, and as mentioned at 5.57, require the Commission's consent to any regulated alterations to their Articles of Association (see Chapter 13).
- Section 197 of the 2011 Act, which restricts the effect of amendments made to a body corporate's constitution, applies.
- The provisions of the 2011 Act relating to the incorporation of charity trustees apply (see **15.69–15.73**).
- The powers of unincorporated charities to transfer property, change their purposes and spend permanent endowment contained in ss 267–292 of the 2011 Act (see Chapters 15 and 12 respectively) apply.

5.67 Notably, the provisions of the 2011 Act restricting the disposal and mortgage of charity land (see Chapter 8) do not apply to exempt charities, including those whose status remains undecided (although as mentioned at 5.66 the documentation must include certain statements).

---

42 Transitional provisions apply by virtue of Sch 9 to the 2011 Act. At the time of writing, the Commission's operational guidance OG 717-1 'Exempt charities and principal regulators' contains detailed information on the Commission's powers in relation to exempt charities whose status remains undecided.

43 At the time of writing, Charity Commission operational guidance OG 717-1 'Exempt charities and principal regulators' contains detailed information on charity law provisions applying to exempt charities.

5.68 An exempt charity should not describe itself as registered nor use a registered charity number.[44]

5.69 The accounting regime for exempt charities is different to the regime which applies to other charities. They do not need to file accounts nor annual reports with the Commission, nor produce a trustees' annual report under the 2011 Act. However they will be required to comply with the accounting rules under their own legal frameworks or regulatory regimes, which may include audit requirements (see Chapter 21).

5.70 The rules on fundraising in the 1992 Act apply equally to exempt charities (see Chapters 19 and 20).

Disclosure of information to and by principal regulators

5.71 Sections 54–59 of the 2011 Act deal with the disclosure of information to and by the Commission (see Chapter 9). Section 58 applies specifically to disclosure to and by the principal regulators of exempt charities.

5.72 Information may be disclosed to the principal regulator of an exempt charity by relevant public authorities (as defined in s 54), including HMRC, for the purpose of enabling or assisting the principal regulator to discharge its functions as principal regulator in relation to a particular exempt charity. A principal regulator may, in turn, disclose information to relevant public authorities if it is relevant to the discharge of the public authority's functions. Information disclosed by HMRC may not be further disclosed without HMRC consent: it is an offence for a 'responsible person' to make an unauthorised disclosure in these circumstances and the regulations prescribing principal regulators for the various categories of exempt charity define 'responsible person' for these purposes (see note 32). Under s 58 of the 2011 Act the regulations prescribing principal regulators may also make changes to other legislation in order to make sure that disclosure obligations which would otherwise apply to principal regulators do not apply in relation to them when they act in the capacity of principal regulator.[45]

THE FUTURE

5.73 In his 2012 review, Lord Hodgson specifically reviewed the current regime for exempt charities. He commented that:[46]

> 'in many ways, principal regulators, and the notion of "exempt charities" are an anomaly, and it is true that the structure can cause confusion as regards their status and role in the sector. However, against this must be balanced that many of the groups of charity falling within this system have a primary role that requires its own special form of regulation (eg as a school or university) and so single regulation by the Charity Commission would be highly inappropriate. The alternative, dual regulation, would place a heavy burden on the organisations involved and should only be undertaken if no alternatives remain.'

---

44 Under s 63 of the 1992 Act, when fundraising it is an offence to represent that an institution is a registered charity if it is not.

45 For example, the Charities Act 2006 (Principal Regulators of Exempt Charities) Regulations 2011, SI 2011/1726 amended the provisions of the Education Act 1996 in relation to disclosure of information under that Act.

46 *Trusted and Independent*, para 6.6.

5.74 He commented that the arrangements in place for principal regulators appeared to have so far been in many ways successful, although the extent to which principal regulators emphasised the charity element of their role clearly varied. He suggested that there might perhaps be a need for the Commission to increase its focus on and communication with those principal regulators who may not be discharging their duty as fully as others, but commented that 'on the evidence received, the challenges are not sufficiently serious to merit the removal of the system'.[47]

5.75 As mentioned at 5.18, he called for the legislation to be accelerated for those exempt charities whose status still remains undecided.[48]

FURTHER GUIDANCE

5.76 The Commission, at the time of writing, has published a detailed guidance document for exempt charities, CC23. Operational guidance on exempt charities is also accessible via the Commission's website.[49]

---

47 *Trusted and Independent*, para 6.7.
48 *Trusted and Independent*, para 6.8.
49 OG 717-1 'Exempt charities and principal regulators'; OG 717-2 'Exempt charities: connected institutions and how to identify them'.

CHAPTER 6

CHARITY NAMES

INTRODUCTION

6.1 A charity has an interest in ensuring its name is appropriate and not misleading, and that it reflects the charity's purpose, nature and preferred style of presentation. However, there are some limitations on the names which charities may use. This chapter explores the Commission's powers under the 2011 Act to require a charity to change its name and outlines certain restrictions on the names that can be used by charitable incorporated organisations (or CIOs) and charitable companies. It also explains the procedure which charities should follow on a change of name.

6.2 In selecting names, charities must, in addition to the provisions of the 2011 Act and (where relevant) company law, take account of business name regulation and existing intellectual property rights. Names cannot be used which infringe trade marks.

6.3 Name licensing also raises issues for charities to consider – both where a charity's name is licensed to a commercial organisation for fundraising purposes, and between connected organisations such as corporations and their charitable foundations, charities and their trading companies, and national charities and their local associates.

6.4 Registered charities are affected by rules which require disclosure of their status to the public: see **4.72–4.78** and, in relation to CIOs, **14.133–14.137**. Charitable companies are also subject to particular disclosure requirements under the 2011 Act and under company law: see **13.2-13.8**.

RESTRICTIONS ON CHARITY NAMES

The 2011 Act

6.5 When choosing a name, both new and existing charities would be well advised to consider the circumstances in which a charity's name might be changed by the Commission, in order to avoid the risk of the Commission issuing a direction to change the name under s 42 of the 2011 Act (see **6.13-6.28**). Where the charity is a charitable incorporated organisation, or CIO, it should be aware of the Commission's powers to refuse to register a CIO or an amendment to a CIO's name (see **6.29**).

Charitable companies[1]

6.6 Part 5 of the Companies Act 2006 and regulations made under it impose restrictions on company names, which affect charitable companies.[2] These include:

- a company must not have a name which is the same as the name of an existing company (some words and expressions are disregarded for this purpose);
- there is a general prohibition on offensive names;
- a name suggesting a connection with government, a local authority or certain public authorities may not be used without prior authorisation; and
- certain 'sensitive' words or expressions may not be used in a company name without appropriate authorisation. These include association, charitable, charity, foundation, society and trust.

6.7 There is scope for a person to apply to the Company Names Tribunal to object to a company's registered name on the grounds that it is the same as a name in which the applicant has goodwill, or it is sufficiently similar to such a name that its use in the United Kingdom would be likely to mislead.[3] There have been several cases before the Tribunal involving charities.

6.8 Since the Tribunal was established, the majority of cases have been undefended, and there are two such examples involving charities. The RSPCA objected to a company registering with the name RSPCA Ltd and The Royal British Legion objected to a company registering with the name Poppy Travel Ltd. In both cases, the respondents did not file a defence and were therefore treated as not opposing the applications: the Tribunal ordered that their names be changed.

6.9 To date, there have been two defended cases involving charities. The first case involved the charity International Ministerial Council of Great Britain, which had been trading under its full name, 'IMCGB', or 'IMC' since 1968. The charity filed an application in 2010 objecting to the name of a company named IMCGB. The Tribunal upheld the application in 2012, finding that the name was not actually available to the respondent company at the time of registration, that the respondent had assumed the name in bad faith (specifically that the founder of the company was a former trustee of the charity, who must have known that the name IMCGB would have been misleading) and that the charity had considerable goodwill attached to the name, having traded under the name since 1968 and having been registered as a charity since 1975.

6.10 The second case involved the charity Friends of Devonport Park, which filed an application in 2014 objecting to the name of a company named Friends Of Devonport Park Limited. The Tribunal upheld the application in 2015, finding that the charity had goodwill under the name (the name had originally been used by a voluntary association established in 2005 which subsequently registered as the charity in 2014), that its interests were adversely affected by the company registering the same name and that the name was adopted in bad faith. Specifically both directors of the company had been

---

1 More detailed information is available from Companies House, in particular in publication GP1 Incorporation and Names.

2 The Companies Act 2006, the Company, Limited Liability Partnership and Business (Names and Trading Disclosures) Regulations 2015, SI 2015/17 and the Company, Limited Liability Partnership and Business Names (Sensitive Words and Expressions) Regulations 2014, SI 2014/3140.

3 Sections 69–74 of the Companies Act 2006 and the Company Names Adjudicators Rules 2008, SI 2008/1738.

members of the voluntary association and there had been a breakdown in the relationship at committee level, which appeared to lead to one of the respondents registering the company with the same name.

6.11 The Companies Act 2006 requires that the name of a private limited company must end in 'limited' or 'ltd' (or the Welsh equivalent). However, charities (and companies limited by guarantee with restrictions in their Articles of Association relating to the objects, distribution of profits and distribution of assets on winding up) are exempt from this requirement, and may choose to take advantage of the exemption by making an application to Companies House.[4] However, they still need to disclose their limited liability status on various documents: see **13.8**.

Other restrictions

6.12 Part 41 of the Companies Act 2006 and regulations made under it[5] impose restrictions on the use of business names, which are relevant to charities. To some extent these overlap with the restrictions on company names. In addition, when choosing a name, any charity should consider whether there might be other restrictions on a proposed name such as under laws preventing passing off and/or trade mark infringement. Charities registered with the Office of the Scottish Charity Regulator or the Charity Commission for Northern Ireland will need to check the relevant legislation for any additional restrictions. For example, Scottish charities may not have the same name as any other charity.

THE COMMISSION'S POWERS OVER CHARITY NAMES

6.13 Under ss 42-45 of the 2011 Act the Commission has power to require charity trustees to change the name of their charity. This power was introduced in the 1992 Act: prior to that there had been a lacuna in the Commission's powers in that it could not refuse to register a charity with a name similar to that of another charity or with a name which was misleading in some way. For example, the name of a local charity might suggest that it was associated with some national charity, when in fact there was no connection.

6.14 When these provisions were first introduced, it was anticipated that the Commission would issue orders requiring a change of name to charities that were already in existence at that time. Therefore, the legislation gave the Commission the power to require a charity to *change* its name. There was no specific power to refuse to *register* a charity on the grounds that its name was unacceptable (although the Commission does now have this power in relation to CIOs: see **6.29**). However, in practice the Commission does request a charity with an inappropriate name to change its name prior to registration, on the basis that it would require the charity to change its name if the charity were to be registered.

6.15 In his 2012 review of charity law, Lord Hodgson recommended[6] that this power should be extended to allow the Commission to require any charity to change its name as a condition of registration. The Law Commission duly proposed that the Commission

---

[4] Chapter 2, Part 5 of the Companies Act 2006 and the Company, Limited Liability Partnership and Business (Names and Trading Disclosures) Regulations 2015, SI 2015/17.

[5] See note 2.

[6] *Trusted and Independent, Giving charity back to charities*, Appendix A(i)(10).

should be given power to refuse an application for registration as a charity if any of the criteria in s 42(2) apply, and should be able to stay an application for registration pending an inquiry into compliance with the criteria in s 42(2).[7]

6.16 When a registered charity changes its name, the Commission does not have power to refuse to enter the new name on the register for any reason (unless it is a CIO: see **6.29**). The Law Commission has also proposed that the Commission should be able to refuse the registration of a change of name of any registered charity if any of the criteria in s 42(2) apply, and to stay the registration of a change of name pending an inquiry into compliance with the s 42(2) criteria.[8]

Which charities does the power apply to?

6.17 For the most part, the powers of the Commission to require a change of name apply to all charities, whether registered or not. However, the power in s 42(2)(a) of the 2011 Act (see **6.19**) is concerned specifically with changing the registered name of a registered charity. The Law Commission, in response to a recommendation by Lord Hodgson, has proposed that this power should be amended so that it applies to unregistered charities too.[9]

6.18 In the case of an exempt charity with a principal regulator, the Commission must consult with the charity's principal regulator before exercising its power to direct the charity to change its name. The Commission's powers under s 42 do not apply to exempt charities without a principal regulator.[10]

Reasons for requiring a change

6.19 There are five sets of circumstances when the Commission may require a change of name. The first currently[11] only applies where the charity is registered.

(a) If the registered name of a charity is the same as or too like the name of another charity at the time the registered name is entered in the register: s 42(2)(a). The key points of this power are as follows:
   (i) the registered name is the name entered in the register of charities, not an acronym or working name used as an alternative;
   (ii) the other charity, whose name is protected by the Commission's action, need not be a registered charity;
   (iii) the similarity must exist when the name is entered in the register of charities. This power cannot be used to protect the former name of an existing charity which has been changed and no longer used, or the name of a charity which has ceased to exist.

   Under the 1993 Act, the Commission had a specific power to disregard minor differences in the names of two charities in reaching a conclusion that the names are the same or too alike. This provision was removed in 2009 and has not been

7 Chapter 14, Technical Issues in Charity Law: A Consultation Paper, Law Commission, March 2015.
8 See note 7.
9 See note 7.
10 Schedule 9, para 10 of the 2011 Act. See Chapter 5 for more on exempt charities. The Law Commission has asked for views on whether the Commission's power should be extended to all exempt charities: Chapter 14, Technical Issues in Charity Law: A Consultation Paper, March 2015.
11 See **6.17**.

replicated in the 2011 Act, although its removal does not appear to prevent the Commission from disregarding minor differences.

In a case concerning the Thomson Reuters Foundation in 2009,[12] the Commission was asked to give a direction requiring the registered name of the Thomson Reuters Foundation to be changed on the ground that it was 'too like' the name of The Thomson Foundation. Whilst not having a constitutional or operational connection, the organisations both bore the family name of Roy Thomson who founded The Thomson Foundation and the media group Thomson Corporation. The latter acquired the Reuters Foundation which subsequently changed its name to the Thomson Reuters Foundation. Both provide journalism and media training in developing countries. The Commission was concerned that supporters and beneficiaries might be confused. However, it concluded that whilst the name 'Thomson Reuters Foundation' was similar to, it was not 'too like' the name of 'The Thomson Foundation'. It did not order the Thomson Reuters Foundation to change its name but instead to distance itself from The Thomson Foundation in the field of journalism training. It also requested both organisations to engage in mediation to find ways of avoiding the risk of public confusion.

(b) If a charity's name is likely to mislead the public as to the true nature of the purposes or activities of the charity: s 42(2)(b).

In the case of the Island and Royal Manor of Portland Historical Association (incorporating the Friends of Portland Museum) ('the Association'),[13] the Commission was asked to review its decision not to make a direction requiring the Association to change its name. At issue was whether the name would mislead the public or give an incorrect impression that the charity was connected with the Portland Museum Trust ('the Trust'), when it was not so connected. Following submissions from both the Association and the Trust, the Commission was satisfied that there was some ongoing contact between the organisations and that the charity did offer some support to the Trust and the Portland Museum. It therefore decided there were insufficient grounds for directing the charity to change its name.

(c) If a charity's name includes a word or expression specified in the Charities (Misleading Names) Regulations 1992[14] and the Commission is of the opinion that this is likely to mislead the public as to the status of the charity: s 42(2)(c). Examples are words which denote national or international status or royal patronage. (The Minister for the Cabinet Office has power to make regulations under s 42(2)(c).)

(d) If a charity's name is likely to give a misleading impression that it is connected in some way with HM Government, a local authority or some other body or individual: s 42(2)(d).

(e) If a charity's name is offensive: s 42(2)(e). There is no statutory indication of what may be regarded as offensive.

Time limits

6.20 The Commission must give the direction to require a charity to change its registered name under s 42(2)(a) within 12 months of the date when the name was entered in the register. However, the powers to require change under s 42(2)(b)-(e) are

12 Charity Commission Decision: Thomson Reuters Foundation 2009.

13 Charity Commission Decision: Island and Royal Manor of Portland Historical Association (Incorporating the Friends of Portland Museum) 2010.

14 SI 1992/1901 (see **Appendix 8**).

not subject to any time limit. These powers could be used by the Commission to require a charity to change a name which has been in use for some time.

The direction

6.21 The Commission exercises its power to require a charity to change its name by giving a formal direction to the charity trustees under s 42(1). Under this direction the charity trustees are required to change the name of the charity. The new name is to be determined by the trustees, with the approval of the Commission. The direction will also specify the period within which the change must be effected.

6.22 Section 338 of the 2011 Act deals with directions of the Commission generally. The principal features of a direction are:

(a) a direction must be in writing, but does not require any other formality – a letter will suffice;
(b) the Commission can vary or revoke a direction by a further direction;
(c) a direction can be enforced by contempt proceedings in the High Court under s 336 of the 2011 Act.

6.23 There is a right to appeal to the Charity Tribunal against a direction to a charity to change its name, under s 319 and Sch 6 of the 2011 Act.[15]

The resolution

6.24 If the Commission makes a direction, the charity trustees must pass a resolution to change the name of the charity, regardless of any provisions in the trusts or constitution of the charity: s 43.[16] They cannot refuse to comply on the grounds that they have no power to amend the trusts or constitution or that the power to amend rests with others or is subject to the consent of some other individual. In particular, s 45 of the 2011 Act makes it clear that, in the case of a charitable company, the name is to be changed by resolution of the directors rather than by special resolution of the members, which would be the normal procedure under company law (unless its Articles of Association specifically grant that power to the directors).

6.25 Note that if the Commission does not have the power to issue a formal direction, but has informally refused to accept a charitable company's name, the charitable company will have to pass a members' resolution to change its name (or use any other means provided for in the company's Articles of Association: see **6.30**).

6.26 Any resolution to change the name of a charitable company must be filed with the Registrar of Companies and the change of name will not take effect until a certificate of incorporation on change of name has been issued.[17] Charitable companies will also need to observe the restrictions on company names: see **6.6-6.11**.

---

15 However, it is not possible to appeal against the Commission's refusal to make a direction under s 42, as illustrated by the case of *Hospice Aid UK v Charity Commission* (CA/2016/002). For more on the Charity Tribunal see Chapter 10.

16 See s 353 of the 2011 Act for the meaning of 'trusts'.

17 This is the official name of the document recording a change of company name, which is a replacement, updating certificate of incorporation.

6.27 Under s 43(2), the charity trustees must notify the Commission of the charity's new name and of the date on which the change occurred. If the charity is a registered charity, the Commission will then enter that new name in the register.

Checklist for charities directed to change their name

6.28 Charity trustees should take the following steps if they receive a direction from the Commission to change the name of their charity:

(a) Consider whether there is evidence to justify the name and, if so, submit this to the Commission with a request that they revoke the direction.

(b) If this request is refused, the trustees may request a review of the direction using the Commission's internal procedures, and may appeal the direction to the Charity Tribunal under s 319 and Sch 6 to the 2011 Act: (see Chapter 10).

(c) If the direction is to be complied with, select a new name and if the charity is a company, check that the new name is not the same as or too like that of a registered company and that it complies with the other requirements of the Companies Act 2006 (see **6.6-6.11**).

(d) Consider whether there might be other restrictions on using the name such as under laws preventing passing off and/or trade mark infringement.

(e) Submit the new proposed name to the Commission for approval.

(f) Once approved, pass a trustees' resolution to change the name, following the trustees' normal rules of procedure.

(g) If the charity is a company, file the appropriate information and fee with the Registrar of Companies (see **6.31**) and await the receipt of the certificate of incorporation on change of name.

(h) Notify the Commission of the name change by completing the online form on the Commission's website. If the charity is a registered charity, check the online register to confirm that it has been amended.

(i) If it is not possible to complete the change of name within the time limit specified by the Commission in the direction, ask the Commission to vary the direction so as to permit more time.

Charitable incorporated organisations

6.29 The Commission has slightly different powers in relation to charitable incorporated organisations, or CIOs. It has power to refuse an application to register a CIO if the proposed name is the same as, or (in the Commission's opinion) too like the name of any other charity, or if the proposed name falls within any of the categories listed in s 42(2)(b)-(e): see **6.19(b)–(e)**.[18] It must refuse to register a change of name for a CIO in the same circumstances.[19] The Commission also has the power to refuse an application for amalgamation of two CIOs (see **14.153-14.163**) and, once the relevant provisions of the 2011 Act are in force, an application for conversion into a CIO by a charitable company or registered society (see **14.210-14.224**) on the same grounds.[20] There are also particular disclosure requirements for CIOs: see **14.133–14.137**.

---

18 Section 208(2) of the 2011 Act.

19 Section 227(3)(b) of the 2011 Act.

20 Sections 237(3) and 231(2)(a) and (b) of the 2011 Act, respectively.

PROCEDURE – VOLUNTARY NAME CHANGES

6.30 In the absence of a direction from the Commission under s 42 of the 2011 Act or under legislation in Scotland or Northern Ireland a charity's procedure for changing its name will depend on its legal form:

- Charitable companies can change their name by special resolution, although the Articles of Association may provide for the name to be changed by other means.[21]
- Unincorporated charities may have power to change their name in their governing document, and may also use the statutory power of amendment conferred by s 280 of the 2011 Act (see Chapter 15).
- A CIO wishing to change its name should follow the procedure for making any constitutional amendment (see Chapter 14).

Charities registered with the Commission in England and Wales do not require the Commission's consent to change their name. Similarly, charities registered with the Charity Commission for Northern Ireland do not need to seek its consent to any name change. However, charities registered with the Office of the Scottish Charity Regulator in Scotland are required to obtain prior consent from OSCR, and must give OSCR at least 42 days' notice of the proposed change.[22]

6.31 Charitable companies registered in England and Wales must notify the Registrar of Companies of any change of name: the change of name takes effect from the date on which the Registrar issues a new certificate of incorporation of change of name which bears the new name. If the new name includes the word 'charity' or 'charitable', the Commission's consent is required.[23]

6.32 A charity registered with the Commission in England and Wales must notify the Commission after the change of name has taken place,[24] using the Commission's online form.

21 Section 77 of the Companies Act 2006.
22 Section 11 of the Charities and Trustee Investment (Scotland) Act 2005.
23 See 6.6.
24 Section 35(3) of the 2011 Act.

CHAPTER 7

REMUNERATION OF CHARITY TRUSTEES

INTRODUCTION

7.1 It is a well-established principle of charity law that a charity may only confer benefits on its trustees if the benefit is authorised by the charity's constitution, by statute, by the Charity Commission or by the court. A trustee may be required to reimburse the charity for any benefits which are received in breach of this rule.

7.2 This means that it is very common for charities to have specific provisions in their constitutions allowing some level of benefit to be conferred on their trustees on the basis that such benefits are consistent with the best public benefit interest of the charity. Several such provisions are standard, for example, allowing for reasonable interest on loans or rent. Others may cover particular circumstances, for example limited payment for an especially demanding chair's role, or a chief executive also being a member of the board. See **7.31-7.32.**

7.3 As a result of changes introduced in the 2006 Act, the 2011 Act extends the principle of legitimate expectations to the general rule against trustee benefits by providing a statutory power for trustees to be paid for services provided to the charity, subject to a number of safeguards ensuring their provision is in the charity's best interests. The statutory power does not extend to remuneration for actually acting as a trustee, and it does not allow payment under a contract of employment (such matters would still require bespoke constitutional provision). The statutory power is described in detail in this chapter: see **7.7-7.30.**

7.4 The 2006 Act also introduced a statutory power for charities to purchase trustee indemnity insurance for the benefit of their trustees: see **7.40-7.44.**

7.5 The Commission's main guidance on payments to trustees is 'Trustee expenses and payments' (CC11). This deals with the statutory power and other areas such as trustee expenses, small payments to trustees, and the factors the Commission will consider when considering whether to approve a proposed payment to a trustee: these issues are explained further at **7.33-7.37.**

7.6 Both Lord Hodgson in his 2012 review and the Law Commission in its 2015 consultation made a number of proposals regarding the remuneration of trustees: see **7.45-7.48.**

THE STATUTORY POWER TO REMUNERATE TRUSTEES

7.7 The statutory power to remunerate trustees for services which they perform for the charity is set out in ss 185–188 of the 2011 Act.

When does the statutory power apply?

7.8 The statutory power applies to any person who will be remunerated (including remuneration in kind) for providing services to a charity or for providing services on behalf of a charity who is either:

(a) a trustee of that charity; or

(b) connected with a trustee of that charity and the remuneration might result in that trustee obtaining any benefit (whether direct or indirect).

Provided the conditions set out in s 185 are met, the trustee or connected person may be remunerated.

7.9 Section 188 sets out the following list of those who are treated as 'connected' to a trustee:

Box A	Box B	Box C
Trustee	Person in business partnership with a person in Box A (s 188(1)(c))	Institution controlled either individually, or collectively, by any person or persons in Boxes A or B (s 188(1)(d))
Trustee's spouse or civil partner (s 188(1)(b))		Body corporate in which any persons in Boxes A or B individually or collectively have a substantial interest (s 188(1)(e))
Trustee's parent or grandparent, child or grandchild, brother or sister or a spouse or civil partner of any such relative (s 188(1)(a) and (b))		

7.10 Note that the general legal definition of 'person' means human individuals or corporate entities with their own legal identity. Sections 350–352 clarify that:

- 'child' includes a stepchild or illegitimate child;
- a person living with another as that person's husband or wife is treated as that person's spouse;
- where two persons of the same sex are not civil partners but live together as if they were, they are treated as if they were civil partners;
- a person controls an institution if he/she/it is able to secure that the affairs of the institution are conducted in accordance with his/her/its wishes; and

- as a general rule of thumb, a person with more than one-fifth in value of the share capital of a company, or who has control of more than one-fifth of the voting power at any general meeting is treated as having a substantial interest – see s 352 for the full test.

7.11 The statutory power extends to payment for goods supplied by a trustee or connected person, but only where they are supplied in connection with services. In his 2012 review of the 2006 Act, Lord Hodgson recommended that the statutory power should be extended to apply to the provision of goods alone. This recommendation was endorsed by the Law Commission which has proposed a new statutory mechanism mirroring s 185 which would allow trustees to be remunerated for the supply of goods even where it is not linked to a supply of services.[1]

How does a charity comply with s 185?

7.12 Section 185(2) sets out four main conditions which must all be met before a trustee or connected person may be remunerated under the statutory power.

Condition A – written agreement

7.13 The amount or maximum amount of remuneration must be set out in a written agreement between the person providing the services and the charity. The amount must not exceed 'what is reasonable in the circumstances'. This is for the trustees to assess, subject to their general duties.

7.14 The agreement must be entered into before the services are provided – it is not sufficient for the agreement to be entered into retrospectively, either after the services have been provided or after payment has been made.

7.15 Before entering into any agreement, the trustees must 'have regard to any guidance given by the Commission concerning the making of such agreements' (s 185(4)): in practice this means taking the guidance reasonably into consideration. At the time of writing, the Commission's guidance is set out in section 4 of 'Trustee expenses and payments'. It deals with the form of the agreement, how to deal with conflicts of interest and how to decide whether the arrangement is in the best interests of the charity (see Condition B at **7.16-7.18**). It sets out factors to take into account when assessing the level of payment: these include affordability, how much other organisations pay in similar circumstances and reputational implications.

Condition B – best interests of the charity

7.16 Before entering into the agreement, the charity trustees must have decided that they were satisfied that 'it would be in the best interests of the charity for the services to be provided by' the person in question 'for ... the remuneration set out in the agreement'.

7.17 A further condition is imposed by s 185(5) which provides that when making this decision, the charity trustees are under the special duty of care set out in s 1(1) of the Trustee Act 2000. This states:

---

1 *Trusted and Independent*, Appendix A, para 14. Chapter 10, Technical Issues in Charity Law: A Consultation Paper, Law Commission, March 2015.

> 'Whenever the duty under this subsection applies to a trustee, he must exercise such care and skill as is reasonable in the circumstances, having regard in particular–
> (a) to any special knowledge or experience that he has or holds himself out as having, and
> (b) if he acts as a trustee in the course of a business or profession, to any special knowledge or experience that it is reasonable to expect of a person acting in the course of that kind of business or profession.'

This duty is consistent with the general duties of charity trustees.[2]

7.18 Guidance from the Commission[3] sets out various factors to be taken into account when deciding whether the payment is in the best interests of the charity. The trustees should be satisfied that the service is required by the charity. They should be able to show that there is a clear advantage to using a trustee to perform the service rather than someone else. Other factors include value for money and the possible impact on the charity's reputation, level of support and funding. In practice, trustees should ensure that their decision, and the reasons for it, are specifically recorded in the minutes of the relevant trustees meeting.

Condition C – minority of trustees to benefit

7.19 At any time, the number of trustees who have an agreement with the charity under which they may be remunerated (either under the statutory power or otherwise, and including any trustee connected to a person who is entitled to remuneration) must constitute a minority of the total number of trustees of the charity.

Condition D – no prohibition

7.20 The charity's constitution must not expressly prohibit the relevant person from receiving the remuneration. In practice, this can be a significant barrier to use of the statutory power. Many charitable constitutions include a prohibition on payments to trustees, often accompanied by a list of exceptions. The Commission's guidance, at the time of writing, suggests that where authority to pay trustees is expressed in a charity's constitution to be subject to the Commission's prior consent, this is not an express prohibition and does not, in the Commission's view, prevent use of the statutory power.[4] However, the position is not certain. In the authors' view the clear practical approach would be to secure the Commission's consent to constitutional amendments facilitating use of the statutory provision: in most situations this would be a technical formality.

7.21 Charities wishing to take advantage of the statutory power may therefore need to seek amendments to any existing provisions which explicitly prohibit trustee benefit. Charitable companies amend their Articles of Association by resolution of the members: if there are enough members (who are not also trustees) to form a quorum to consider the alteration, it can be made without involving the Commission. Otherwise the

---

2 Trustees of unincorporated charities are subject to this statutory duty in relation to a number of their powers, particularly as regards investment (see Chapter 11). A similar statutory duty is imposed on the trustees of charitable incorporated organisations, or CIOs, when performing their functions (see Chapter 14).

3 'Trustee Expenses and Payments', March 2012, para 4.7.

4 CC11 'Trustee Expenses and Payments' and Charity Commission operational guidance OG 515-2 'The Statutory Power to Pay for Services Provided by a Trustee'.

Commission's consent will be needed. An unincorporated charity will generally need to involve the Commission when seeking to remove a relevant prohibition.[5]

7.22 At the time of writing, charities can use an online form on the Commission's website to help determine whether a proposed payment falls within the scope of the statutory power: if it does they can print written confirmation to this effect.[6]

Managing conflicts of interest

7.23 Section 186 requires that conflicts of interest are managed appropriately when a charity uses the statutory power, by providing that any trustee who is or would be entitled to remuneration, or is connected with a person so entitled, is 'disqualified from acting ... in relation to any decision or other matter connected with the agreement' (s 186(2)). This would include, for example, taking part in trustees' discussions about the settling of the terms of the agreement, the decision to appoint, the review of performance, the 'signing off' of any work, or any strategic decisions which are connected with the services. The trustee concerned should withdraw from discussion of these issues and not vote, and will not count towards the relevant quorum necessary to validate any meeting at which such discussions take place. The Commission's view is that it would not be a breach of this requirement if the trustees simply ask the person concerned to provide any information necessary to help make a decision.

7.24 There is a safeguard in s 186(3) in that the mistaken involvement of a trustee or connected person in a decision while disqualified will not affect the decision's validity. However, the trustee or connected person will still themselves have acted wrongfully and there is a risk that they will be required to reimburse the charity if the Commission makes an order under s 186(4). This gives the Commission power to order trustees to reimburse the charity where:

(a) a trustee has done an act which he or she was disqualified from doing under s 186(2) (see **7.23**); and
(b) the disqualified trustee or a person connected with him or her has received or is to receive from the charity any remuneration under the agreement in question.

The Commission can make one of two orders:

(a) that the disqualified trustee or connected person should reimburse to the charity all or part of the remuneration received – and if the remuneration was a benefit in kind, the Commission can determine an equivalent monetary value (s 186(5));
(b) that the disqualified trustee or connected person should not be paid the whole or part of the remuneration (s 186(6)).

If the Commission makes one of the above orders, the order effectively extinguishes the person's right to be paid.

7.25 The provisions restricting the involvement of trustees in decisions to exercise the statutory power are in addition to any other rules on how to deal with conflicts of

---

5 'Trustee Expenses and Payments', March 2012 and Charity Commission operational guidance OG 515-2 'The Statutory Power to Pay for Services Provided by a Trustee'.

6 Charity Commission operational guidance OG 515-2 'The Statutory Power to Pay for Services Provided by a Trustee'.

interest which may apply in the circumstances of the particular charity. These may appear in the charity's constitution, or may apply as a matter of law.[7]

7.26 Early drafts of the Bill which became the 2006 Act contemplated the creation of criminal offences for trustees or connected persons who approved arrangements for remuneration in breach of s 185. However, the proposed offence was ultimately not included in the legislation on the basis that such penalties could be counter-productive (most importantly they could be a significant deterrent to those thinking of volunteering as a trustee).

Exceptions

7.27 It is important to note that the statutory power cannot be used to pay a trustee just for being a trustee or to pay a trustee under a contract of employment (s 185(3)). This means that charities that wish to pay their trustees for serving on the board, or that wish to allow trustees to be employees of the charity, must have specific authority either in their governing document, or from the Commission or the court.

7.28 The provisions of s 185 do not apply to any existing provisions, ie payments or benefits properly made under existing constitutional provisions, by court or Commission order, or under a different statute (s 185(3)).

Situations where the statutory power can apply	*Situations where s 185 cannot be used*
Trustee or connected person to be paid for providing services to the charity	Trustee or connected person to be paid for acting as a trustee of the charity, eg a director's salary, an honorarium or allowance
Trustee or connected person to be paid for providing services on behalf of the charity	Trustee or connected person to be a paid employee of the charity
	Reimbursement to a trustee of loss of earnings whilst carrying out trustee business
	Gifts to retiring trustees
	Trustee who is an accountant providing services to act as auditor for the charity

7.29 The authors' view is that s 185 should, in an appropriate case, allow payment to a trustee for services rendered in the management of a charity's subsidiary trading company.

Charitable companies

7.30 Section 185 applies to the trustees of charitable companies. An amendment to the Articles of Association of a charitable company which simply authorises benefits which would be permitted by the statutory power will not require the prior written consent of the Commission under s 198 of the 2011 Act (see **13.12**). However, if the Articles

[7] See, for example, the conflicts of interest rules for charitable incorporated organisations, or CIOs: Chapter 14.

contain a prohibition on payment of trustees, which may well be the case, removal of the prohibition may require the Commission's authority (see **7.21**).

OTHER TRUSTEE BENEFITS

Powers in the constitution

7.31 Many charities include provisions in their constitution which authorise the conferring of benefits on trustees. The Commission's model constitutions for charities, for example, allow trustees to be paid for goods or services, and to be paid rent on premises let to the charity, or interest on money lent to the charity, all subject to various conditions and safeguards.[8]

7.32 Constitutional powers to remunerate trustees are interpreted restrictively. For example, in the case of *Fowler v Fenland Area Community Enterprise Trust*, Cambridge County Court determined that the terms of the professional charging clause under which one of the trustees was seeking to be paid for services he had performed for the charity had not been complied with, because his appointment and remuneration had not been approved at a meeting from which he was absent, or had withdrawn.[9]

Consent from the Commission[10]

7.33 If an existing charity wishes to amend its constitution to increase the level of benefit conferred on its trustees to something over and above what is permitted under the statutory power, it is likely to need to involve the Commission.[11]

7.34 In the Tribunal case of *Roger Thomas v Charity Commission*,[12] a scheme made by the Commission which increased the level of benefit which could be conferred on trustees was quashed on an appeal to the Tribunal. The First-tier Tribunal decided that, in the circumstances, a sufficient case had not been made to the effect that the change was expedient in the interests of the charity.

7.35 The Commission may be prepared to approve one-off payments to trustees, without a constitutional amendment. An application should be made to the Commission, setting out why it would be to the charity's advantage to make the payment.

7.36 The Commission does not usually require charities to seek its authority where the total value of all trustee payments (excluding expenses) is less than £1,000 in any financial year. The Commission's rationale for this is that it is not a good use of the resources of the Commission or a charity to seek and grant authority for small payments to trustees where the charity is being properly administered and the total of all payments to all trustees during the financial year will be below this figure.[13]

---

8 Note that some dispositions of land to trustees require consent from the Commission: see Chapter 8.

9 The Court of Appeal refused leave to appeal the decision: [2010] EWCA Civ 1571.

10 See 'Trustee Expenses and Payments' and the Commission's series of operational guidance OG 515 for an indication of the factors which the Commission will take into account.

11 For example, in the case of charitable companies the Commission's prior written consent will be needed under s 198 of the 2011 Act: see Chapter 13.

12 CA/2012/0001.

13 'Trustee Expenses and Payments', March 2012, and OG 515-7 'Small Payments to Charity Trustees'.

Expenses

7.37 All trustees are entitled to legitimate expenses while engaged on trustee business. It is not necessary for the constitution to contain a provision to this effect. Reasonable travel and childcare costs are legitimate expenses, but compensation for loss of earnings while carrying out trustee business is not covered.[14]

SCOTLAND

7.38 The Scottish rules on the payment of trustees are set out in ss 67 and 68 of the Charities and Trustee Investment (Scotland) Act 2005. These apply to charities registered with the Office of the Scottish Charity Regulator (OSCR). The position in Scotland is slightly different to that under the 2011 Act and OSCR-registered charities should ensure that any benefits conferred on their trustees are compliant with the Scottish legislation. Importantly, unlike the Charity Commission, OSCR has no power to authorise a payment to a trustee which is not permitted under the charity's constitution.

TRANSPARENCY AND ACCOUNTING

7.39 The Statement of Recommended Practice for Charities requires the disclosure of benefits received by trustees in the accounts.[15] At the time of writing, the Commission's guidance recommends that all charities (irrespective of whether they have to comply with SORP) disclose benefits received by trustees in their accounts.

TRUSTEE INDEMNITY INSURANCE

7.40 Section 189 of the 2011 Act allows any charity (except those whose constitutions contain an express prohibition against the purchase of such insurance) to pay for trustee indemnity insurance, subject to a few specific safeguards. Prior to the 2006 Act this was possible under specific constitutional authority or by obtaining the Commission's approval following a self-certification by the trustees of a charity to the effect that trustee indemnity insurance was in the best interests of the charity.

What type of insurance does the statutory power apply to?

7.41 The statutory power applies to insurance designed to indemnify the charity trustees against any personal liability in respect of:[16]

> '(a) any breach of trust or breach of duty committed by them in their capacity as charity trustees or trustees for the charity, or
>
> (b) any negligence, default, breach of duty or breach of trust committed by them in their capacity as directors or officers of–
>
> (i) the charity (if it is a body corporate), or
>
> (ii) any body corporate carrying on any activities on behalf of the charity.'

---

14 'Trustee Expenses and Payments', March 2012 and OG 515-1 'Trustee Expenses'. The trustees of a CIO have a statutory right to expenses: see 14.63.

15 See Chapter 21 for more on the SORP.

16 Section 189(1) of the 2011 Act.

7.42 But the insurance must exclude any indemnity in respect of:

(a) a fine imposed in criminal proceedings;
(b) any sum due to a regulatory authority as a penalty;
(c) any criminal proceedings in which the trustee is convicted of an offence arising out of his or her fraud, dishonesty or wilful or reckless misconduct; or
(d) any liability that arises out of any conduct which the trustee knew (or must reasonably be assumed to have known) was not in the interests of the charity, or where the trustee did not care whether the conduct was in the best interests of the charity.

What must the charity do to comply with s 189?

7.43 Before purchasing insurance, the trustees must decide that they are satisfied that it is in the best interests of the charity for them to do so (which in practice should be noted specifically in the minutes of the relevant trustees meeting). The duty of care in s 1(1) of the Trustee Act 2000 applies to each trustee when making the decision – this is identical to the duty of care arising in relation to trustee remuneration (see **7.17**).

7.44 Note that if the charity's constitution expressly prohibits the purchase of trustee indemnity insurance, then the charity cannot seek to rely on s 189. In the authors' experience such an express prohibition would be extremely rare.

FUTURE REFORM?

Relief of liability

7.45 A charity trustee who has obtained a profit from the charity in breach of fiduciary duty is liable to account to the charity for that profit. The court may effectively relieve a trustee of liability by awarding the trustee an equitable allowance. The Commission has no such power, and does not consider that its power under s 191 of the 2011 Act to relieve a trustee from liability for breach of trust (see **9.197–9.200**) allows it to relieve a trustee from liability to account for a profit made in breach of fiduciary duty.[17]

7.46 The Law Commission, in its 2015 consultation, considered that the Commission should have more extensive powers in this respect and has proposed that it should have a statutory power to relieve a trustee, in whole or in part, from liability to account for a profit, of any size, made in breach of fiduciary duty.[18]

Payment of trustees for serving on the board

7.47 The parliamentary debates on the legislation which became the 2006 Act acknowledged that the issue of payments to trustees was a live debate and should be monitored and reviewed. Lord Hodgson's 2012 review of charity law considered the

---

17 The Commission does, however, regard itself as being able to indicate that it is not intending to pursue restitution, in cases of unauthorised remuneration: Charity Commission operational guidance OG 98 'Power of the Commission to relieve trustees, auditors etc from liability for breach of trust or duty'.
18 Chapter 10, Technical Issues in Charity Law: A Consultation Paper, Law Commission, March 2015.

question of payment of trustees.[19] He acknowledged that 'payment of trustees ... remains a hugely divisive issue in the charity sector'.[20] He recommended, however, that charities with an annual income in excess of £1m should have power to pay their trustees for serving on the board, subject to clear disclosure requirements on the quantum and terms of any remuneration. This recommendation was not supported by the Public Administration Select Committee, and it was not endorsed by Government. Government's view was that 'for the time being at least, and until there is stronger evidence that would support an easing of the general presumption against trustee remuneration, we should retain the status quo'.[21] Government would monitor the number of applications the Commission receives for approval of payment to trustees in individual cases, and the number it grants or refuses.[22]

7.48 Much debate on the issue of payment to trustees fails to recognise the great range in the natures, sizes and needs of charities. While the traditional voluntary principle might continue to work well for smaller community organisations, or grant-making foundations, large-scale service-providing charities may need to operate in a more orthodox commercial way, while still being public benefit organisations. In the authors' view, the general principle against benefit to trustees, with the opportunity for exceptions in the best public benefit interests of charities, has proved to be appropriately flexible law and shows the debate need not be polarised between the traditional principle and complete modern liberality.

---

19 *Trusted and Independent*, paras 4.46–4.52.
20 *Trusted and Independent*, para 4.47.
21 Government Response, p 23.
22 Government Response, p 23.

CHAPTER 8

LAND TRANSACTIONS

OVERVIEW

8.1 The 2011 Act places restrictions on charities (other than exempt charities[1]) that must be complied with before they can enter into any commitment to deal with their land. These restrictions apply in the following circumstances:

- on a disposal; and
- on a mortgage.

They do not apply to the acquisition of land by a charity.

8.2 The restrictions on disposal contained in the 2011 Act previously appeared in s 36 of the 1993 Act, as amended by the 2006 Act.

8.3 The overriding intention of the legislation is the protection of charity assets by ensuring that, before disposing of their property assets, charities take appropriate advice and obtain best value. The charity trustees are custodians of high value assets: the rules protect charity assets by guarding against potential unadvisable disposal at an undervalue. Prior to the 1992 Act Charity Commission consent was required to any disposal of charity land: this was relaxed and replaced with the current regime.

8.4 In a similar vein, the restrictions on mortgaging, which were previously set out in s 38 of the 1993 Act, are intended to protect charity assets by ensuring, again, that charities take appropriate advice before granting lenders or grant providers security over charity property. The regulation avoids the risk that valuable property may be lost through lack of expertise in the transaction.

8.5 In the case of both disposals and mortgaging, the 2011 Act allows for two different methods for compliance with the restrictions in the legislation.

8.6 By far the most common way of proceeding is for the relevant charity to take appropriate advice and obtain a report (as stipulated in the 2011 Act), and effectively self-certify that it has complied with those restrictions.

8.7 The less often used alternative is to apply to the Commission for an order authorising the relevant transaction to proceed.

---

1 See Chapter 5. In its 2015 consultation (see **8.12-8.13**) the Law Commission proposed that exempt charities should be subject to the same requirements as other charities.

8.8 The only circumstance which obliges compliance with one of these alternatives is where the disposal is to a 'connected person' where a Commission order must be obtained (this is considered in more detail below: see **8.30-8.31**).

8.9 This chapter looks at both kinds of property transaction – disposals and mortgages, the way the restrictions in the 2011 Act apply to each, and the alternative ways of complying. It also looks at the exceptions to these requirements.

8.10 As mentioned above, the restrictions on disposal do not apply to acquisitions of land so a charity is free to acquire land without the issues of statutory compliance. However, it is recommended that as best practice charities obtain similar advice to that set out below in relation to the terms of any acquisition. Trustees' general duty of care in relation to the use of charity funds will of course still apply.

8.11 This chapter also covers the statements required in documentation dealing with charity land (see **8.54-8.65**), which may apply to exempt charities, and other miscellaneous provisions relating to charity land.

8.12 In recent years various aspects of the compliance process have been considered and debated. Some want to abolish the regulatory process because of the time and cost to a disposing charity, whilst others feel that it is essential that the sector is regulated if only to retain public confidence, and to ensure best value is obtained. Lord Hodgson's 2012 review of charity law favoured deregulation and the Law Commission, in its 2015 consultation on Technical Issues in Charity Law, made wide-ranging proposals regarding the regulation of charity land transactions.[2] The Law Commission proposed, in particular, that the current detailed requirements regarding the disposal and mortgaging of charity land should be removed and replaced with a simple requirement to take advice. This requirement would apply to all land transactions, including possibly the acquisition of land. The Law Commission also proposed that the strict regime relating to disposals to connected persons should be removed.

8.13 These proposals were not universally welcomed by the sector. For example, there was concern that removing the current requirements would mean the loss of a significant safeguard for charity assets and indeed for charity trustees. Many property-owning charities recognised that the current regime provides an important protection for the vast number of charities owning property but without in house estate teams and property expertise. It therefore remains to be seen whether the proposals will be adopted. At the time of writing the Law Commission is considering the responses to its consultation.

DISPOSALS

8.14 Sections 117–123 of the 2011 Act regulate and set out the restrictions that affect disposals.

8.15 The important first step is to identify what is a disposal, and whether any particular transaction is caught by the 2011 Act. Section 117(1) of the 2011 Act states:

---

2 Chapter 8, Technical Issues in Charity Law, A Consultation Paper, Law Commission, March 2015.

> 'no land held by or in trust for a charity is to be conveyed, transferred, leased or otherwise disposed of'

unless the requirements of the 2011 Act are complied with.

8.16 Clearly all sales – of registered or unregistered land – and the grant of leases, which represent the vast majority of transactions entered into by charities, are caught. But the words 'or otherwise disposed of' catch a number of rather less obvious transactions, which also require compliance with the 2011 Act, such as:

- the surrender of a lease by a charity; or
- the grant of an easement over charity land; or
- the release of a restrictive covenant of which a charity has the benefit.

8.17 It should be noted that a genuine licence (ie not a document that is technically a lease but described with another name), is not a disposal for the purposes of the 2011 Act. True tenancies at will are not considered interests in land and so are also not disposals for the purposes of the 2011 Act.

8.18 More complex transactions, such as the grant of an option or the grant of rights of pre-emption and auction sales of property by a charity, raise rather more difficult questions, as clearly a charity cannot enter into a transaction which commits it to dispose of property without first complying with the 2011 Act.

8.19 Therefore if, by way of an example, an option is intended to commit a charity to dispose – most obviously by a third party serving notice on the charity of its wish to acquire – then the arrangements for compliance with the 2011 Act must have been dealt with before entering into the option.

8.20 In these situations charities should always obtain specialist advice at the earliest opportunity to ensure that the transaction is structured to be compliant.

Disposals not requiring substantive compliance with the 2011 Act

8.21 Although most transactions require compliance, there are some disposals which are specifically excluded from the restrictions of the 2011 Act as follows:

- Disposals which are authorised by some other statute or by a Commission scheme. (The most common example of this is where a charity is also a not-for-profit registered provider. Registered providers are regulated by the Homes and Community Agency, successor to the Housing Corporation. Compliance by the charity with s 172 of the Housing and Regeneration Act 2008 is sufficient and no further compliance with the 2011 Act is required.)
- Disposals for which the authorisation or consent of the Secretary of State is required under the University and College Estates Act 1925.[3]
- Disposals which are made to another charity other than for best value and which are authorised by the trusts of the disposing charity. (In order for this exemption to

---

[3] The Law Commission consulted on whether the complicated regime under the University and College Estates Act 1925 should be repealed and replaced. Chapter 8, Technical Issues in Charity Law, A Consultation Paper, Law Commission, March 2015.

apply, the charity receiving the property must have identical or narrower objects than the disposing charity. The disposal must also be made with an element of gift in furtherance of charitable purposes. If the receiving charity's objects are wider than those of the disposing charity, or if the transaction is at full value, the exemption does not apply and full compliance with the 2011 Act is required.)

- Disposals by way of the grant of a lease to a beneficiary of a charity, other than at best value, which would allow the property to be occupied for the purposes of that charity. (A letting by a housing charity to an individual who was homeless would be an example of this, although note that a letting to a corporate body could also qualify under this exception.)
- Disposals by an exempt charity.
- Disposals by way of a mortgage or other security (see **8.39-8.52**).
- Disposals of an advowson, which is the right to nominate a person to hold ecclesiastical office in a parish.

Disposals requiring substantive compliance with the 2011 Act

8.22 Unless one of the exemptions listed above apply, the restrictions in the 2011 Act must be complied with by either:

- obtaining advice and a report: see **8.23-8.29**; or
- obtaining an order from the Commission.

Where the disposal is to a 'connected person' (see **8.30**) the second method must be used.

Obtaining proper advice and a report (ss 119-120)

8.23 The 2011 Act sets out clearly what advice is needed and the procedures for obtaining it, although the legislation on this point has never been entirely clear on when that advice should be taken. However, it is clear that the advice must be obtained, received, considered and approved by the charity trustees before they enter into any binding commitment to dispose.

8.24 There is a distinction between the level of advice needed for leases for a term of 7 years or less (for which compliance is less prescriptive) and leases for a term of more than 7 years and other dispositions (such as sales of land, the grant of easements, etc) which do not fall within the exceptions listed at **8.21**, which have more detailed requirements for compliance.

8.25 For leases of more than 7 years and other dispositions s 119 provides that the trustees must:

- obtain and consider a written report (which must contain certain prescribed information set out at **8.28** below) on the proposed transaction from a qualified surveyor (defined as a fellow or professional associate of the Royal Institution of Chartered Surveyors) acting exclusively for the charity; and
- advertise the proposed transaction unless the surveyor advises otherwise.

8.26 For leases of less than seven years, s 120 provides that advice must be taken from a person 'who is reasonably believed by the trustees to have the requisite ability and practical experience to provide them with competent advice'. The adviser should consider the terms of the proposed lease and provide advice to the trustees so that they are able to resolve whether the terms of the lease are the best that may reasonably be obtained by the charity. Whilst there is no explicit requirement for the advice to be in writing, practically speaking the charity would be prudent to do this so that it has a record of the advice the trustees have considered.

8.27 In both cases the approval process is the same so that, having taken the requisite advice, the charity trustees must 'decide that they are satisfied ... that the terms on which the disposition is proposed to be made are the best that can reasonably be obtained for the charity'.

8.28 The current requirements for a 'qualified surveyor's report', which is required for all dispositions other than leases of seven years or less, are set out in the Charities (Qualified Surveyors' Reports) Regulations 1992 (see **Appendix 9** of this book).[4] They include:

- a physical description of the property;
- a description of any legal easements and covenants burdening the property;
- whether the property is in good repair, and whether the charity should carry out works to it prior to the sale;
- whether the property would be best divided for sale;
- the applicability or otherwise of VAT to the sale;
- whether, and if so how, the property should be advertised;
- the surveyor's estimate of the value of the property.

8.29 What must be done with the surveyor's report? It is necessary for the charity trustees to consider and approve the surveyor's report prior to exchange of contracts, or before completion where there is no exchange. If this is not done correctly, or if the report is not in the right format, then there is a risk (following *Bayoumi v Women's Total Abstinence Educational Union Ltd*[5]) that the contract for sale will be void or voidable. If a binding contract is not struck, and the charity can only obtain a lower price in a subsequent sale, then a loss has accrued to the charity. This could arguably be attributed to a breach of trust by the trustees, for which they would be personally liable. However, where the trustees had taken proper professional advice, any failure to comply with ss 117 and 119–121 would probably constitute negligence by those advisers, and the loss would be recoverable from them or their insurers.

Charity Commission order (s 117)

8.30 If the proposed transaction involves a 'connected person' it is a requirement of the 2011 Act that an order from the Commission is obtained. A connected person (defined in s 118 of the 2011 Act) is essentially a trustee, officer or employee of the charity, or the spouse or the immediate family of such a person, or a body corporate under their control.

---

4 SI 1992/2980.

5 [2004] 3 All ER 110.

8.31 Even where an order is being sought, professional advice will need to be obtained in terms so far as possible as if an order were not required, in order to demonstrate to the Commission that the disposal is in the best interests of the charity. The Commission will also need to be satisfied that any conflict of interests has been properly managed.

8.32 Whilst this is the only circumstance in which an order must be obtained, there may be other situations where it can usefully be sought. An example might be a necessary low value disposal where the cost and time of obtaining full professional advice would be disproportionate, such as the grant of a long lease at a nominal rent to allow an electricity substation to be constructed on the charity's property.

Disposal of functional land under s 121(1)–(3)

8.33 Land owned by a charity may also be held on trusts which stipulate the use to which the land can be put. The terms of the trust are normally imposed at the time the land was acquired or more often when the land was gifted to the charity. Land restricted in this way is also known as 'specie' or 'designated' land.

8.34 If the land is specie land, the charity needs to give public notice at least one month before a disposal giving notice of its intention to sell, and allowing interested parties to make their own representations on the transaction. The form of the notice and where it should be placed will depend on the property and trust.[6]

8.35 If representations are received, the charity trustees must reasonably consider such representations, but they are not obliged to change any of the terms of the proposed disposal.

8.36 However, if either:

(1) the disposal is a lease for a term of two years or less; or
(2) the property in question is being sold with a view to acquiring replacement land;

there is no requirement to give public notice.

8.37 It is also possible to apply to the Commission to make a disposal exempt from the public notice requirements.

8.38 Note that the disposal of designated land may, depending on the circumstances of how the land is held and in particular, if a specific trust exists to hold the land for certain purposes, entail a change to a charity's objects which may require the Commission's involvement.[7]

MORTGAGES

8.39 Mortgages of charity land are regulated by s 124 of the 2011 Act. Section 124 only applies where the charity is charging its own land, i e where it is the borrower rather than the lender.

---

6 The Law Commission has provisionally proposed that these requirements should be abolished: Chapter 8, Technical Issues in Charity Law, A Consultation Paper, Law Commission, March 2015.

7 See, for example, 12.5.

8.40 Section 124 does not in itself give a charity the power to borrow money or charge its land as security for that borrowing. The charity's constitution must be checked to see whether this power exists. However, even if it does not, s 6 of the Trusts of Land and Appointment of Trustees Act 1996, which gives the trustees of land all the powers of an absolute owner, is likely to be available to unincorporated charities.

8.41 The range of mortgages of land that do not require substantive compliance with s 124 is smaller than for disposals under s 117.

8.42 The following mortgages do not require substantive compliance with s 124:

- mortgages authorised by some other statute or by a Charity Commission Scheme (s 124(9)).
- mortgages by exempt charities (s 124(10)).

Methods of compliance

8.43 As under s 117, the means of compliance are for the charity to either obtain an order from the Commission (s 124(1)), or for the trustees to obtain appropriate advice (s 124(2)). Usually obtaining the appropriate advice would be sufficient. However, where a transaction is particularly complex or the trustees may find it difficult to obtain the advice for any reason, it may be advisable to obtain an order from the Commission.

8.44 Prior to the 2006 Act, the advice process could only be used where the mortgage was by way of security for the repayment of a loan. Mortgages to secure obligations assumed by charities to grant funders always required an order from the Commission, which was felt to be disproportionately time consuming and costly. Changes were introduced in the 2006 Act and s 124 of the 2011 Act now provides that all mortgages of charity land can be sanctioned by way of advice, whether the charge is to secure a 'loan, grant or other obligation'.

Identity of adviser

8.45 Under s 124(8) advice must be obtained from a person who is reasonably believed by the charity trustees to be qualified by ability in and practical experience of financial matters, but who has no financial interest in the making of the loan, grant or other transaction in connection with which the advice is given.

8.46 Section 124(8) also contemplates the adviser being an officer or employee of the charity or a charity trustee. Whilst this may be acceptable for small loans/grants, the authors' view is that best practice for charity trustees is to consider seeking external professional advice from financial or legal professionals in relation to large advances of money (whether by loan or grant) or the assumption of onerous obligations, on the basis that if the advice turns out to be negligent and the charity suffers loss as a result, then the adviser could be sued, and this could afford a method of compensating the charity.

What must the advice cover?

8.47 In the case of a mortgage to secure the repayment of a proposed loan or (since 2006) a grant, the matters which the adviser must cover in the advice given are:

- whether the proposed loan or grant is necessary in order for the charity trustees to be able to pursue the particular course of action in connection with which the loan or grant is sought by them;
- whether the terms of the proposed loan (or grant) are reasonable having regard to the status of the charity as a prospective borrower; and
- the ability of the charity to repay on those terms the sum proposed to be borrowed or received.

8.48 However, where the mortgage is intended to secure other proposed obligations (eg a guarantee of the obligations of a charity's trading company, or the obligations of a charity to the trustees of its pension fund), the requirement is for the adviser to consider whether it is 'reasonable' for the charity trustees to undertake to discharge the obligation, having regard to the charity's purposes (s 124(4) of the 2011 Act).

8.49 One concern which the authors have about advice on a mortgage securing obligations other than a loan or a grant is that in order to give appropriate advice an understanding of the legal issues surrounding a charity's objects and what it can agree to do in furtherance of those is required, whilst the advice relating to a loan or grant covers more easily quantifiable financial criteria.

8.50 However, as set out in s 124(8) of the 2011 Act, the criteria as to what constitutes a suitable adviser are the same for all three categories of loan. We have doubts as to whether a single adviser as envisaged by s 124(8) will necessarily have the skills to give the range of advice required to comply with the requirements under s 124(4) and charities may well feel the need to employ more than one adviser in appropriate circumstances.

Types of charge

8.51 Most charge documents produced by mainstream commercial lenders are drafted as 'all-monies' charges. This means that the charge is intended to secure the obligations of the borrower to the lender at any time both at the date of the mortgage and/or also to cover any other monies that may subsequently be borrowed by the charity.

8.52 Before the passage of the 2006 Act, the Commission's clear view was that a charity could only give an all-monies charge where an order was obtained from the Commission, as the advice that had to be taken could only secure the obligations set out in the loan facility covering the monies actually borrowed and upon which the advice had been taken, and the advice could not cover any future monies borrowed. The 2006 Act changed this, so that s 124(5) permits charities to enter into mortgages that secure the repayment of sums or the discharge of obligations incurred both at and subsequent to the date of the mortgage. However, prior to each assumption of fresh obligations (eg an increase in the amount of a loan facility or of the limit on a secured overdraft) the trustees must take fresh advice (s 124(7)).

SUPPLEMENTARY PROVISIONS RELATING TO DISPOSALS AND MORTGAGES: SS 122, 123, 125 AND 126 OF THE 2011 ACT

8.53 Sections 122, 123, 125 and 126 of the 2011 Act set out, for disposals and mortgages respectively, certain supplemental provisions, particularly relating to statements that have to appear in disposal and charge documents, the protection gained if they do appear, and the consequences if they do not.[8]

Statements to go in disposal documents

8.54 Section 122(1) and (2) of the 2011 Act provide that any contract for the sale or lease or other disposition of land which is held by a charity and any conveyance, transfer, lease or other instrument (eg a deed) effecting a disposal of such land must state:

- that the land is held by or in trust for a charity;
- whether the charity is an exempt charity and whether the disposition is one falling within s 117(3)(a), (b), (c) and (d) (see **8.21**); and
- if it is not an exempt charity and the disposition does not fall within s 117(3)(a), (b), (c) or (d) that the land to be disposed of is land to which the restrictions on disposition contained in ss 117–121 apply.

8.55 At the time of writing the wording to be used is set out in Land Registry Practice Guide 14, 'Charities', which summarises r 180 of the Land Registration Rules 2003.

Statements to go in charge documents

8.56 Sections 125 and 126 provide that any mortgage of land held by or in trust for a charity must state:

- that the land is held by or in trust for a charity;
- whether the charity is an exempt charity or whether the mortgage falls within s 124(9) (see Chapter 5 and **8.42** respectively); and
- if it is not an exempt charity and the mortgage is not within s 124(9) that the mortgage is one to which the restrictions imposed by s 124 apply.

Again, the precise wording to be included is set out in the Land Registry Practice Guide.

Certificates required in documents

8.57 Sections 122(3) and 125(2) also provide that the disposal documents and the charge documents must contain a certificate by the charity trustees that the charity has power under its constitution to enter into the charge, and that the charity trustees have properly complied with s 117 or s 124 as applicable, whether by taking appropriate advice or by obtaining an order of the court or the Commission.

8.58 It is important to note that the certificate is to be given by the charity trustees. Charity trustees are defined in s 177 of the 2011 Act as those persons having the general control and management of the administration of the charity. This raises a particular issue where the charity is a body corporate, as the charity is a separate legal entity to the charity trustees, and according to the Land Registry guidance the individual trustees

8 Note that under s 122 of the 2011 Act when a charity acquires an interest in property, the contract, transfer or other document effecting the acquisition should include a statement indicating the property will be held by or in trust for a charity, and whether that charity is an exempt or non-exempt charity. A restriction will then be entered onto the title register for the property.

therefore also need to be joined in to execute the disposition or charge in order to give the certificate. It is advisable that two of the trustees are delegated to do this pursuant to an authority given under s 333 of the 2011 Act (see **8.66-8.71**).

8.59 Such authority should be given by way of resolution of a meeting of the charity trustees and the authority given may be extended to signing all documents, or, more often, limited to specified trustees signing particular documents.

8.60 The suggested wording of the certificates and descriptions of the charity trustees, depending on the circumstances, are also set out in the Land Registry Practice Guide.

8.61 It should be noted that the charity trustees do not have to give a certificate in an agreement for sale or lease, as this is not a disposal for these purposes. This was one of the points clarified in the case of *Bayoumi v Women's Total Abstinence Educational Union Ltd*.[9]

8.62 The Law Commission has proposed removing all requirements for a certificate of compliance from trustees. This proposal raised a lot of concern from charities and advisers: removing this 'protective' element of the current regime received a largely negative response.

Protection given by the certificates

8.63 Section 122(4), for a disposal, and s 125(3), for a mortgage, provide that so long as the correct certificate is contained in the disposal or mortgage, it is to be conclusively presumed, in favour of a party acquiring an interest in the land (whether under a disposal/charge or subsequently) for money or money's worth, that the facts were as stated in the certificate.

8.64 However, charity trustees should always ensure that they comply properly with the relevant section and do not rely on these provisions, particularly as the *Bayoumi* case[10] clarified that these provisions only apply as from completion. If proper compliance with s 119 has not taken place before exchange of contracts, then the contract appears to be either void or voidable between exchange and completion, leaving the trustees at risk.

8.65 Even where the proper certificate does not appear in the relevant document, s 122(5) and (6) (for a disposal) and s 125(4) and (5) (for a mortgage) protect a party acting in good faith who acquires an interest in the land (whether under the disposal/charge or subsequently) from the consequences of non-compliance.

AUTHORITY TO EXECUTE DOCUMENTS – S 333 OF THE 2011 ACT

8.66 By s 333 of the 2011 Act, the trustees of a charity may, subject to whatever is stated in the constitution of the charity, confer on any two or more trustees a general authority, or an authority limited in such manner as the trustees think fit, to execute in the names and on behalf of all the trustees of the charity assurances or other deeds or

9 [2004] 3 All ER 110.
10 See note 9.

instruments for giving effect to transactions to which the trustees are a party. Any deed or instrument executed under the authority conferred in s 333 shall have the same effect as if executed by all the trustees. This is an extremely useful provision for an unincorporated trust or for unincorporated associations.

8.67 This does not, however, avoid the need where an unincorporated trust or unincorporated association takes an interest in land for all the names of the trustees or committee members to be recited as the persons interested in the land as trustees of the charity (unless the charity's governing document refers to specific property holding trustees), but merely means that the execution of the documents by only two trustees is facilitated.

8.68 Where a document purports to be executed pursuant to s 333, it is to be conclusively presumed, in favour of a party acquiring an interest in or charge over property in good faith for money or money's worth, that it has been duly executed by virtue of that section.

8.69 If an unincorporated charity finds that its property or investment transactions are complicated by the number of trustees, then the charity should consider either incorporation (see **15.10**) or, at the very least, appointing custodian trustees to hold the charity's lands and investments on behalf of the charity. It will be necessary to amend the charity's constitution to allow for the appointment of custodian trustees if the constitution does not so provide. It is also possible to apply to have property vested in the Official Custodian of Charities as trustee of a property (see Chapter 22). Another option for trustees in such a situation would be to incorporate the trustee board under Part 12 of the 2011 Act. It should be noted that whilst this simplifies the holding of title by trustees in the case of an unincorporated charity, it does not change the trustees' liability, which remains personal and unlimited: see **15.69-15.73**.

8.70 The position is different in the case of an incorporated charity. In the case of limited liability companies, any two directors (who are the equivalent of trustees) or one director and the company secretary can usually execute documents on behalf of the company unless the Articles of Association specify differently (in practice, with disposals of charity land it is easiest for two directors/trustee to execute the documents as these individuals can then give the certificate of compliance at the same time: see **8.57-8.62**). There are similar provisions for charitable incorporated organisations, although two trustees will usually be required: see Chapter 14. Equally, in the case of registered cooperatives, community benefit societies, organisations incorporated by Royal Charter or charities created by statute, it is normal (but must be checked in every case) to provide that any two of the members of the executive body (trustees, directors etc) may execute documents on the organisation's behalf.

8.71 Note that it is still prudent for incorporated charities to have a s 333 resolution in place to allow the trustees to delegate the giving of a certificate of compliance on a disposal to two of their number, as this must be given by the trustees: see **8.58**.

CHARITY MERGERS

8.72 The 2006 Act introduced new provisions regarding charity mergers which are now set out in the 2011 Act. Section 310 of the 2011 Act provides that a declaration made by a transferor charity (i e one which is to cease to exist following the merger) that all its property is to vest in the transferee charity shall, if executed as a deed, operate to vest that property without any further document being required. However, this does not apply to leasehold property, where the landlord's consent to assign is required, unless that consent has been obtained prior to the merger date. See Chapter 16 for more details.

8.73 Section 69(1)(c) of the 2011 Act gives the Commission power by order to exercise the same jurisdiction as the courts for 'vesting or transferring property'. It is therefore possible to apply to the Commission for an order which will vest freehold *and* leasehold property regardless of whether the landlord's consent has been obtained. This mechanism has, in the past, been extremely useful for mergers involving a significant number of properties, but in recent years the Commission line has been to refuse to exercise its powers under s 69 in all but exceptional circumstances, leaving merging charities to bear the significant costs of obtaining landlords' consent for the transfer of leasehold properties.

8.74 Whichever procedure is used, a transfer of property will still have to be registered at the Land Registry to be formally completed.

CHARITABLE INCORPORATED ORGANISATIONS

8.75 Provisions regarding the transfer of property to charitable incorporated organisations, or CIOs, on their registration or amalgamation were introduced in the 2006 Act. On the registration of a new CIO, all property held on trust for its purposes becomes vested in the CIO (s 210(2) of the 2011 Act). Sections 239(2) and 244(1) of the 2011 Act contain provisions regarding the transfer of property on the amalgamation of existing CIOs, or a transfer of property between CIOs, respectively. See Chapter 14 for more detail.

STAMP DUTY LAND TAX

8.76 Stamp duty on land transactions was replaced by stamp duty land tax by the Finance Act 2003. Interests in land acquired by charities are exempt from stamp duty land tax provided that they are held for qualifying charitable purposes, namely for the purposes of the charity or as an investment the proceeds of which are applied for charitable purposes.

8.77 The detailed provisions of stamp duty land tax are beyond the scope of this book and specialist advice should be taken.

RENTCHARGES

8.78 A rentcharge is a right to a periodic payment of a sum arising out of land other than under a lease or mortgage. Sections 127 and 128 of the 2011 Act deal with the release of rentcharges by charities, i e where the charity gives up its right to receive the future payment. Provided that the consideration paid to the charity for the release is ten times the annual charge or more, then the restrictions on disposition do not apply to the release. There is also a mechanism for the release of rentcharges set out in the Rentcharges Act 1977. Provided that this is followed, Sections 117, 119–121 and 129(1) do not need to be complied with.

CHAPTER 9

POWERS OF THE CHARITY COMMISSION TO PROTECT AND ASSIST

INTRODUCTION

9.1 The overriding objectives, functions and duties of the Charity Commission are highlighted in Chapter 2. This chapter deals with the Commission's specific powers to protect and assist charities under the 2011 Act. Paragraphs 9.17–9.169 deal with investigating charities' affairs and intervening in how they are run. Paragraphs 9.170–9.203 cover the Commission's powers to support and advise charities and their trustees. Paragraphs 9.204–9.233 explain when charity trustees may be disqualified from acting.

THE COMMISSION'S FOCUS

9.2 The Commission has traditionally had a dual role as regulator and friend to charities, both helping charities and their trustees by providing advice and guidance, and protecting charity funds by investigating and intervening in the way that charities are run. As explained in Chapter 2, the past few years have seen a significant change of focus by the Commission, with far greater priority being given to the investigative and regulatory side of its work than had been the case in earlier years. Political and media comment have enhanced this effect by fomenting a series of public debates relating to charities. This more rigorous approach has resulted in both an increase in the Commission's general regulatory work and the use of its statutory powers. In 2014-15 the Commission exercised its legal powers 1,200 times compared with 790 times in the previous year.[1]

9.3 The priority given to the Commission's investigation and enforcement work has led to a corresponding shift in its approach to the provision of advice and guidance. A raft of valuable generic guidance is available on the Commission's website and a certain level of support is available through its helplines. However, the Commission is now far less likely to provide one-to-one support to charities than in the past. The Commission's Annual Report for 2015 to 2016 states that it 'can rarely offer one-to-one advice'.

---

1 Charity Commission report on its investigations and compliance work in 2014 to 2015, *Tackling abuse and mismanagement*. The Commission exercised its legal powers 216 times in 2012-13 and 188 times in 2011-12.

REFORM

9.4 The Commission's statutory powers have been amended and supplemented over the years. The 2006 Act strengthened the Commission's hand by introducing several new powers, including a power to enter premises and search for documents and a power to give specific directions for the protection of charity property. The Commission was also given a new power to relieve trustees from liability for breach of trust.

9.5 The Charities (Protection and Social Investment) Act 2016 ('the 2016 Act') has introduced more regulatory provisions into the 2011 Act. In 2013, in the wake of Lord Hodgson's 2012 review of charity law, and subsequent reports by the Public Administration Select Committee, the Public Accounts Committee and the National Audit Office,[2] the Commission approached the Government asking for some of its compliance powers to be strengthened to enable it to tackle abuse more effectively. In response, the Cabinet Office published a consultation paper on extending the Commission's statutory powers[3] which led to the publication of a draft Protection of Charities Bill in October 2014.[4] This was scrutinised by a Joint Parliamentary Committee and introduced into Parliament as the Charities (Protection and Social Investment) Bill. The 2016 Act received Royal Assent in March 2016.

9.6 Sections 1 to 12 of the 2016 Act amend the 2011 Act by introducing new and amended provisions dealing with the powers of the Commission to take regulatory action, and with the disqualification of charity trustees. The most significant changes are a new power for the Commission to give official warnings to charities (see **9.32–9.46**) and tighter rules about the disqualification of charity trustees, including a new power for the Commission to disqualify someone from being a charity trustee (see **9.219–9.230**).

9.7 None of the substantive provisions of the 2016 Act came into force immediately, but most were brought into force on 31 July 2016. More provisions will come into force in October and November 2016, with the remaining parts of the 2016 Act likely to take effect in 2017.[5] Further details are given in the relevant parts of this chapter.

9.8 The Law Commission has consulted on some minor changes to the Commission's powers to protect and support charities in its 2015 consultation.[6]

GENERAL POWERS AND DUTIES

9.9 As well as the specific powers explored in this chapter, the Commission has a broad power in s 20 of the 2011 Act (added by the 2006 Act) to do anything which is calculated to facilitate, or is conducive or incidental to, the performance of any of its functions or general duties. But s 20(2) specifically provides that nothing in the 2011 Act authorises the Commission to exercise functions corresponding to those of a charity trustee in relation to a charity or otherwise to be directly involved in a charity's

---

2 See **1.14–1.15**.

3 Consultation on extending the Charity Commission's powers to tackle abuse in charities, Cabinet Office, December 2013.

4 Draft Protection of Charities Bill, Minister for the Cabinet Office, October 2014.

5 The Charities (Protection and Social Investment) Act 2016 (Commencement No. 1 and Transitional Provision) Regulations 2016, SI 2016/815. See also the Bates Wells Braithwaite 'is it in force' page for the 2016 Act at http://www.bwbllp.com/knowledge/2016/08/03/charities-protection-and-social-investment-act-2016-is-it-in-force/ and **1.20**.

6 Technical Issues in Charity Law, A Consultation Paper, Law Commission, March 2015.

administration: the Commission can act as overall supervisor, but should not take direct responsibility for particular charities – the Commission must leave that up to the trustees. (This principle does not, however, restrict the scope of the Commission's powers to give directions for the protection of charities or regarding charity property under ss 84, 84A, 84B and 85 of the 2011 Act: see **9.118–9.125**, **9.126–9.128**, **9.129–9.132** and **9.146–9.152** respectively.)

9.10 In 2015, the Commission was involved in judicial review proceedings in the High Court in relation to action it had taken in response to the funding of a non-charitable organisation by a charity. The scope of the Commission's powers to direct charity trustees, including the scope of its general power to give advice and guidance under s 15 of the 2011 Act (see **9.189–9.190**) was discussed in the proceedings. The principle inherent in s 20(2) was reaffirmed in November 2015 when in an agreed statement the Commission confirmed that it has no power to require trustees to fetter the future exercise of their fiduciary powers under its general power to give advice and guidance.[7]

9.11 It is important for charities to be alert to the Commission's general obligation, under s 16 of the 2011 Act, to exercise its regulatory powers proportionately and consistently (see Chapter 2). Charities should also be aware of the scope to challenge Commission action where they feel the Commission has been too imprecise or heavy-handed (see Chapter 10).

EXEMPT CHARITIES

9.12 Most of the powers described in this chapter apply to exempt charities: details are given in Chapter 5.

REGULATORY ACTION – AN OVERVIEW

9.13 While the Commission has particular statutory powers which allow it to regulate charities, a significant proportion of its regulatory work is taken without recourse to those powers. The Commission uses a range of tools to monitor charities, including desk based research, scrutinising accounts, responding to information from other agencies (for example from the Cifas National Fraud Database) and from whistle-blowing reports,[8] carrying out post-registration monitoring, visiting charities and taking action in relation to serious incidents (see **9.14**). The Commission follows a published Risk Framework when assessing how to respond to regulatory concerns. The Framework identifies the Commission's priority areas: at the time of writing these are fraud and financial abuse, safeguarding, terrorism and other significant breach of trust or non-compliance that impacts significantly on public trust and confidence in charities.[9]

9.14 The Commission expects charity trustees to notify it of any 'serious incidents' which arise in relation to their charity, and has put an increased emphasis on serious

---

7 Order of the High Court dated October 2015 in the case of *R (on the application of Cage Advocacy UK Ltd and Joseph Rowntree Charitable Trust (interested party)) v Charity Commission*.

8 For example, under s 156 of the 2016 Act (see **21.57-21.64**) or from charity workers under the Public Interest Disclosure Act 1998.

9 Charity Commission risk framework, available at www.gov.uk/government/collections/regulatory-work-charity-commission.

incident reporting in recent years.[10] At the time of writing a serious incident is described as one which results in or risks loss or of damage to a charity's assets or property, harm to beneficiaries or harm to a charity's reputation: there is more information in the Commission's guidance *Reporting Serious Incidents – guidance for trustees* which is available on the Commission's website. At the time of writing, trustees of charities with an income of over £25,000 have an obligation to make a declaration in the annual return which they file with the Commission (see **21.87-21.92**) to the effect that that there are no serious incidents or other matters relating to their charity over the previous financial year that they should have brought to the Commission's attention but have not. As a matter of good practice the Commission expects trustees to report a serious incident immediately, if it has resulted or could result in a significant loss of funds or a significant risk to a charity's property, work, beneficiaries or reputation. In a regulatory alert issued in September 2014 the Commission noted:

> 'If trustees fail to report a serious incident and it becomes known to us at a later date, we may consider this to be mismanagement and take regulatory action, particularly if further abuse or damage has arisen following the initial incident.'

However, a decision about whether and when to report a serious incident to the Commission is not completely straightforward. Trustees will need to make a judgement call about whether an incident is sufficiently serious to warrant reporting, and the timing of the report. They may wish to seek professional advice.

9.15 The Commission may provide regulatory guidance to trustees. It may open a compliance case without resorting to its formal statutory powers: in 2015-16 the Commission opened 1,327 operational compliance cases.[11] It may decide to report publicly on such cases: the Commission states that it may do this where there is significant public interest in the issues involved and the outcome or there are lessons that other charities can learn from the case.[12] This has obvious reputational implications for charities involved in these cases, which should seek the opportunity to comment on any report before it is made public.

9.16 The Commission may go further and take enforcement action using its statutory powers. This might involve the Commission directing the application of charity property (see **9.146–9.152**) or removing trustees or employees (see **9.134–9.143**). If the Commission has more serious concerns it may take the significant step of opening a statutory inquiry, which allows it to exercise further protective and remedial powers (see **9.47–9.132**). Fifty-three statutory inquiries were opened in 2015-16 and 103 in 2014-15. The Commission's report on its investigations and compliance case work in 2014-2015 states:[13]

> 'We may open an inquiry where there is a high risk to public trust and confidence in the charity, where there is evidence of misconduct or mismanagement, or where charities' assets, reputation, services or beneficiaries are at a high risk of harm or abuse.'

---

10 In 2015-16, 2,117 serious incidents were reported to the Commission. The figure was 2,129 in 2014-15 and 1,282 in the previous year. Charity Commission Annual Reports 2014-15 and 2015-16.

11 Charity Commission Annual Report 2015-16.

12 Guidance at www.gov.uk/government/collections/charity-commission-reports-decisions-alerts-and-statements and Charity Commission Policy Paper: *How the Charity Commission reports on its regulatory work*, January 2015.

13 *Tackling abuse and mismanagement*, 2014-2015, Annex 1: The Charity Commission's approach to tackling abuse and mismanagement and the Charity Commission Annual Report 2015-16

INFORMATION POWERS

9.17 In order to regulate properly, the Commission needs to be able to find out what charities are doing. Registered charities must file annual reports with the Commission (see Chapter 21), and the Commission has wide powers to obtain information from, and about, charities.

9.18 The Commission can seek information about charities and their activities under s 52 of the 2011 Act. This allows the Commission to make an order requiring a person to provide it with information in his, her or its possession, or documents (or copies or extracts of documents) in his, her or its custody or control which relate to any charity and which are relevant to the discharge of the functions of the Commission or the official custodian (for more information on the official custodian see Chapter 22).

9.19 Orders under s 52 can be appealed to the Charity Tribunal by the person who is required to supply the document or information: in hearing the appeal the Tribunal will simply consider whether the information or documents relate to a charity and whether they are relevant to the functions of the Commission or the official custodian.[14]

9.20 Section 52 also applies to charities registered with the Office of the Scottish Charity Regulator which are managed or controlled wholly or mainly in or from England and Wales.[15]

9.21 The Commission's use of this power has increased significantly in recent years.[16]

9.22 Section 53 of the 2011 Act allows Commission staff to inspect and copy the records or other documents of any court, public registry or records office for any purpose connected with the discharge of the functions of the Commission or the official custodian.

9.23 The Commission and other authorities can exchange information about charities: the provisions dealing with information-sharing, which were changed in some respects by the 2006 Act, are contained in ss 54–59 of the 2011 Act. In the final House of Lords debate on the Bill which became the 2006 Act, the Government Minister, Lord Bassam of Brighton, explained that the information-sharing regime was originally introduced in the 1980s following abuses of charity tax reliefs for personal gain, which were identified by the Revenue. The individuals involved would give different explanations and accounts to the Revenue and to the Commission. Information-sharing enables a joined-up response from the authorities.

9.24 Under s 54 any 'relevant public authority' may disclose information to the Commission for the purpose of enabling or assisting the Commission to discharge any of the Commission's functions. A local authority, for instance, might disclose information to the Commission about unauthorised fundraisers operating in their area. Similarly, under s 56 the Commission may disclose information to any relevant public authority for the purpose of enabling or assisting the authority in question to discharge its

---

14 Section 320 of the 2011 Act and see **10.70**. There are several examples of appeals to the Tribunal in relation to s 52 orders.

15 Section 52(4) of the 2011 Act.

16 The Commission exercised its powers under s 52, 195 times in 2012/13, 516 times in 2013/14 and 422 times in 2014/15. *Tackling abuse and mismanagement*, Charity Commission, 2014-2015.

functions, or if the information is otherwise relevant to the discharge of any of the authority's functions. So the Commission might pass information about fraudulent activity by charity employees to the police.

9.25 A relevant public authority includes:

- any government department (including a Northern Ireland department);
- any local authority;
- any constable; or
- any other body or person discharging functions of a public nature (including a body or person discharging regulatory functions in relation to any description of activities) including, in the case of disclosure by the Commission under s 56, a body or person outside the United Kingdom.

9.26 At the time of writing, the Commission works especially closely with the police.[17]

9.27 The rules in relation to HM Revenue and Customs' (HMRC) disclosure of information to the Commission have always been slightly different from those in relation to other authorities. Under s 55 of the 2011 Act, HMRC can only disclose information to the Commission if it relates to a charity or similar institution (listed in s 55(1)). Under s 57 there is an automatic restriction against onward disclosure of this information: the Commission can only pass it on to another relevant public authority with the consent of HMRC. Failure by the individual concerned to obtain the required consent is an offence.

9.28 Section 59 provides that the powers in ss 54–57 do not override restrictions on the use of personal information and on the use of information contained in communications (such as in phone calls or emails) which are imposed under the Data Protection Act 1998 and Part 1 of the Regulation of Investigatory Powers Act 2000.

9.29 Section 58 deals with information-sharing between the Commission and the principal regulators of exempt charities in carrying out the role of principal regulator (see 5.71-5.72 and see Chapter 5 generally for more information about principal regulators).

9.30 There are penalties for providing false information to the Commission. Under s 60 of the 2011 Act it is an offence knowingly or recklessly to provide the Commission with information which is false or misleading in a material particular. The offence is committed if the information is provided supposedly in compliance with a requirement imposed by or under the 2011 Act (eg the requirement to provide information under s 52) or the person providing the information intends, or could reasonably be expected to know, that the information would be used by the Commission for the purpose of discharging its statutory functions. It is also an offence under s 60 for a person wilfully to alter, suppress, conceal or destroy any document which he, she or it is or is liable to produce to the Commission by or under the 2011 Act. Under s 345 of the 2011 Act no proceedings may be brought under s 60 without the consent of the Director of Public Prosecutions.

---

17 The National Audit Office report, *Follow-up on the Charity Commission*, published January 2015, summary, para 18, notes that 'the Commission's most effective information sharing arrangement is with the police'.

9.31 At the time of writing, the evidence indicates that the Commission is now making far more use of its information-sharing powers than previously. The Commission exchanged information 2,332 times with other public authorities in 2015-16, and 2,131 times in 2014-15. In 2015-16 the Commission requested and was provided with information 922 times compared with 677 times in the previous year.[18] The National Audit Office reported in 2015 that the Commission exchanged more information with HMRC than any other organisation, commenting that: 'The Commission needs a strong relationship with HMRC to support both organisations' interest in combating tax avoidance and fraudulent gift aid claims.'[19] In its 2013 report on the Commission, the National Audit Office had been critical of the information-sharing between the Commission and HMRC which had hindered some of both organisations' investigations.

OFFICIAL WARNINGS

9.32 The 2016 Act introduces a completely new power for the Commission to issue official warnings to charities.[20]

9.33 During the Parliamentary passage of the 2016 Act there were commitments given to consult on guidance relating to warnings by the Commission: at the time of writing the Commission has issued draft guidance for consultation.

9.34 The power to give official warnings was originally proposed in the 2013 Cabinet Office consultation which preceded the 2016 Act.[21] In its response to the consultation, Government stated:

> 'The Government considers that the Commission's current enforcement regime is limited, and in practice is reserved only for the most serious breaches and defaults. The power to issue an official warning would bridge the gap, giving the Commission the ability to apply a more proportionate sanction in less serious cases.'

9.35 The explanatory notes to the 2016 Act state that the power

> 'is intended to be a more reasonable and proportionate way of dealing with breaches of statutory provisions of the Charities Act 2011, breaches of fiduciary duty or other mismanagement where the risks and impact on charitable assets and services are relatively low'.

9.36 Under s 75A the Commission can issue a warning:

- To a trustee 'who it considers has committed a breach of trust or duty or other misconduct or mismanagement in that capacity'; or
- To a charity 'in connection with which it considers a breach of trust or duty or other misconduct or mismanagement has been committed'.

---

18 Charity Commission Annual Report 2015-15. See also the National Audit Office report, *Follow-up on the Charity Commission*, published January 2015.

19 National Audit Office report, *Follow-up on the Charity Commission*, published January 2015, paras 2.11–2.13.

20 Section 1 of the 2016 Act which inserts s 75A into the 2011 Act. This provision will into force on 1 November 2016.

21 See note 3.

The expression 'misconduct or mismanagement' is used elsewhere in the 2011 Act. It has no statutory definition, but the courts and Charity Tribunal have commented on how it should be interpreted: see **9.83**. Failure to follow good practice is not necessarily misconduct or mismanagement: in the Parliamentary debates on the 2016 Act, the Government Minister Rob Wilson MP, in the context of discussions about the warning power, referred to the explanatory notes to the Bill which stated that:

> 'Failure to follow good practice could not automatically be considered to constitute misconduct or mismanagement.'

Mr Wilson agreed that official warnings should not be used to force people to follow good practice.[22]

Notice

9.37 The Commission must give the charity and each of its trustees notice before issuing a warning (except any who cannot be found or who have no known address in the United Kingdom). The notice must specify the grounds for the warning and any action the Commission considers should be taken, or that the Commission is considering taking, to rectify the misconduct or mismanagement which has prompted the proposed issuing of the warning. It must also specify whether the Commission is planning to publish the warning (see **9.40**) and if so, how.

9.38 The notice must also give details of a period during which representations may be made to the Commission about the content of the proposed warning. There were calls for a minimum notice period to be included on the face of the legislation, but these were resisted. However, in the debates on the legislation in the House of Commons, the Government Minister Rob Wilson MP confirmed that:

> 'the Charity Commission has … reassured me that it will normally apply a minimum notice period of 14 days.'[23]

It is expected that this will be confirmed in the Commission's guidance on the warning power.[24]

9.39 The Commission must take into account any representations made in response to the notice within the specified period, but may then issue the warning without further notice (including any changes it thinks are desirable).

Issue and publication

9.40 A warning may be issued in any way the Commission considers appropriate. The Commission may also publish a warning it has issued, again in any way it considers appropriate. When the 2016 Act was debated in Parliament, there were concerns about the scope to publish a warning, in the light of the adverse publicity which a published warning might generate, but the Government Minister, Rob Wilson MP stated it was right that an official warning should be placed in the public domain. However, he did confirm that:

22 26 Jan 2016: Column 208 House of Commons.
23 26 Jan 2016: Column 207 House of Commons.
24 See 9.33.

> 'it should be made clear that when the issue that gave rise to the warning has been addressed, it should be archived after a period'.[25]

Withdrawal and amendments

9.41 Warnings can be withdrawn or amended. The withdrawal or amendment can be published. Notice of any proposed amendments should be given to the charity and its trustees in the same way as a proposed warning. This means that if the issue giving rise to a warning has been addressed, the warning could be amended or withdrawn. In the Parliamentary debates on the legislation, the Government Minister Rob Wilson MP said that:

> 'where the Charity Commission does withdraw a warning it will, as a matter of policy, set out the reasons for doing so when it notifies the recipient of the warning and publicises the withdrawal.'[26]

Sanctions

9.42 Failure to comply with a warning can have serious consequences for the charity. In an amendment to s 76 of the 2011 Act made by s 2(2) of the 2016 Act, a failure to remedy a breach specified in an official warning is one of the triggers which allows the Commission to exercise its temporary protective powers or, when combined with other factors, its permanent protective powers, once a statutory inquiry has been instituted: see **9.79–9.101** and **9.102–9.132** respectively.

9.43 The link between failure to comply with a warning and more significant regulatory action was recommended by the Joint Committee reviewing an early draft of the 2016 Act (see **1.17** and **9.5**), but only if a minimum notice period for warnings was also included, and the warning power was restricted so that it could only be issued in the event of failure to comply with the 2011 Act, or with an order or direction of the Commission. While Government accepted the first part of the Joint Committee's recommendation and duly linked official warnings with the exercise of more significant powers, it did not include the safeguards recommended by the Joint Committee in the legislation.

Concerns

9.44 There is no right to appeal a warning to the Charity Tribunal. In the debates on the 2016 Act in the House of Commons, Government explained that a right of appeal to the Tribunal would be disproportionate and noted that the Commission had said that a right of appeal to the Tribunal would render the power unusable.[27] This means that the only way of challenging a warning is via judicial review which is expensive and time consuming.

9.45 During the passage of the 2016 Act through Parliament, the Government Minister Rob Wilson MP made it clear that the official warning power should not be used to direct to charities. He said:

---

25 26 Jan 2016: Column 207 House of Commons.
26 26 Jan 2016: Column 208 House of Commons.
27 26 Jan 2016: Column 205 House of Commons.

> 'The Government have been consistently clear that the Commission could not use the official warning power to direct charities, and I am happy to reiterate that position again for the record.'

Mr Wilson's remarks are reinforced in the explanatory notes to the 2016 Act which state that 'the official warning does not constitute a power of direction'. This is helpful reassurance. As explained at 9.9, the Commission is not able to act as a trustee, nor be directly involved in a charity's administration, except where this is specifically allowed under ss 84, 84A, 84B and 85, which allow the Commission to issue directions to trustees, subject to express safeguards. The statements in Parliament and the explanatory notes make it clear that the official warning power cannot be used to issue directions, via the back door, thus bypassing the safeguards in ss 84, 84A, 84B and 85.

9.46 However, it is the authors' view that in practice charity trustees and their advisers – and indeed the Commission – will need to make a careful assessment of whether a statement in the notice of a warning about action which the Commission considers should be taken may actually amount to a direction in any particular case. The line will not always be easy to draw, as illustrated by the judicial review proceedings involving the Commission and the Joseph Rowntree Charitable Trust in late 2015 (before the warning power was introduced), when the parties spent the best part of a day in the High Court arguing whether the Commission, in asking the trustees of the charity to give certain assurances, had been issuing a direction or a non-binding request. If a warning does fall on the wrong side of the line, a charity wishing to challenge the warning will need to initiate judicial review proceedings, which may be lengthy and costly, since it may not appeal to the Tribunal. It is regrettable that Mr Wilson's assurance in Parliament was not included on the face of the legislation.

SECTION 46 INQUIRIES

9.47 Section 46 of the 2011 Act allows the Commission to take the significant step of instituting an inquiry into one or more charities. The commencement of a s 46 inquiry has the effect of triggering a range of additional powers.

The scope of the power to institute an inquiry

9.48 The Commission's power is drafted in wide terms. It may 'from time to time institute inquiries with regard to charities or a particular charity or class of charities, either generally or for particular purposes'.

9.49 The Commission does in practice sometimes group charities together for the purposes of undertaking an inquiry: for example in 2013 the Commission opened a class inquiry into charities that had failed to meet their statutory reporting requirements for two or more years in the last five. At the time of writing this inquiry is still ongoing and has expanded to include over 80 charities.

9.50 In recent years, following criticism of the Commission's use of its enforcement powers (see Chapter 2), there has been a significant increase in the number of inquiries opened. In 2015-16 53 charities were placed under inquiry, 103 in 2014-15, 64 in 2013-14 and 15 the year before that.[28]

9.51 The Commission may open a s 46 inquiry into a body entered in the Scottish Charity Register which is managed or controlled wholly or mainly in or from England or Wales, and the powers in ss 47–49 (see **9.61–9.62** and **9.71–9.78**) will apply.[29]

Instituting an inquiry

9.52 The 2011 Act does not impose any pre-conditions on the Commission's discretion to institute an inquiry. For instance, it does not state that the Commission can only open inquiries on reasonable grounds, nor even that the Commission must first have a reasonable suspicion that something is wrong. When the legislation which became the 2006 Act was discussed in Parliament, there was a call for a restriction along these lines to be introduced, but this was resisted by the Government on the grounds that the Commission should act reasonably in any event as a public body and in accordance with its duty to have regard to the principles of best regulatory practice under what is now s 16 of the 2011 Act (see **2.28**).

9.53 In practice, s 46 inquiries are triggered in any number of ways, including a third party complaint about a charity, or an anomaly in a charity's accounts or annual return. The Commission has stated:[30]

> 'In serious cases of abuse and regulatory concern, the commission may open a statutory inquiry. The commission's decision to open an inquiry is not taken lightly, and depends on a careful assessment of a set of factors.'

The Commission applies its Risk Framework[31] before taking a decision to open an inquiry.

9.54 In the Upper Tribunal case of *Regentford Ltd v Charity Commission*,[32] the Upper Tribunal considered the Commission's power to institute inquiries, commenting:[33]

> 'We accept ... that there is no way to identify in advance the "tipping point" at which it becomes reasonable to open a statutory inquiry, and that this question is one of the wide areas of discretion which Parliament has conferred on the Charity Commission in s. 46 of the Act. The Appellant is correct, in our view, to assert that the [Charity Commission] must take care to consider and evaluate all the material provided to it before making its decision, but unless it strays into the arena of ignoring considerations which are mandatory (which include the matters in ss. 14 to 16 of the Act,[34] but may also extend to others depending on the case) or including irrelevant considerations, the extent to which it needs to verify any areas of

[28] Charity Commission Annual Report 2015-16 and *Tackling abuse and mismanagement*, 2014-2015 and 2013–2014.

[29] Section 46(4) of the 2011 Act.

[30] Charity Commission publication CC46: *Statutory Inquiries into Charities: guidance for charities and their advisers*, December 2013.

[31] See **9.13**.

[32] [2014] UKUT 0364 (TCC).

[33] Paragraph 38.

[34] The Commission's objectives, general functions and general duties: see **2.15–2.31**.

legitimate concern before deciding to operate under the auspices of the statutory framework is, we find, properly a matter for its discretion.'

9.55 Given the far-reaching implications that a s 46 inquiry can have, not least because of the disruption an inquiry can cause, even if the Commission does not subsequently exercise any of its other powers, charities should, if possible, cooperate with the Commission from an early stage in order to try to avoid a formal inquiry.

9.56 A decision by the Commission to institute a s 46 inquiry is subject to review by the Tribunal.[35] In determining an application for review, the Tribunal must apply the principles which would be applied by the High Court on an application for judicial review.[36]

9.57 Decisions to open an inquiry have been challenged a number of times before the Tribunal, but at the time of writing, there have been no successful challenges.[37] In 2016 the Court of Appeal refused to allow a charity to seek judicial review of a decision to open an inquiry, on the basis that the correct way to challenge an inquiry was to apply to the Charity Tribunal.[38] The First-tier Tribunal has decided that the Tribunal can hear an application for review of a decision to open an inquiry after the inquiry has been closed.[39]

9.58 Decisions not to institute an inquiry are not subject to challenge before the Tribunal. Thus, a member of the public, who has complained to the Commission about a charity in the hope that the Commission will open an inquiry, will be unable to challenge the Commission in the Tribunal if the Commission decides not to do so.

Notice

9.59 The Commission is not obliged to notify the charity, or the trustees, that an inquiry has been instituted, nor to give reasons for the inquiry. There were calls for an obligation to this effect to be introduced in the 2006 Act, in a bid to make the s 46 inquiry process more transparent, but these were resisted by Government in the light of the Commission's more general obligation to follow best regulatory practice (see **2.28**). As a matter of practice, in most cases the Commission should be expected to inform the charity's trustees about the inquiry, and the reasons for it, at an early stage.

9.60 The Commission's policy at the time of writing is that it will usually release a public statement whenever it opens a statutory inquiry into a charity, and make a note to this effect on the charity's entry in the Register of Charities. The Commission will not release a statement where it considers that this would not be in the public interest, or if the trustees are not aware of the inquiry, or if there would be other adverse implications.[40]

---

[35] See Chapter 10.

[36] Section 321 of the 2011 Act.

[37] See, for example, *Regentford v Charity Commission* [2014] UKUT 0364 (TCC) and *Mountstar (PTC) v Charity Commission* CA/2013/0001 and 0003.

[38] *R (on the application of Watch Tower Bible & Tract Society of Britain) v Charity Commission* [2016] EWCA Civ 154. See also **10.99**.

[39] *Charity Commission v Trustees of the Ethiopian Orthodox Tewahdo Church St Mary of Debre Tsion London* (CRR/2014/0001).

[40] Charity Commission policy paper, *How the Charity Commission reports on its regulatory work*, January 2015.

The inquiry process

9.61 The Commission may conduct the inquiry itself, and usually does so, although it does have power to appoint another person to conduct the inquiry and report back to it. The Commission (or the person appointed to conduct the inquiry) has power under s 47 to direct anyone:

- to provide accounts or written statements, or answer questions in writing, on any matter in question at the inquiry on which he or she has or can reasonably obtain information;
- to provide copies of documents under his, her or its custody or control; and
- to attend in person to give evidence or produce documents.

9.62 The Commission can pay expenses, and no one can be asked to travel more than 10 miles from home unless the expenses are paid or offered. Evidence may be taken on oath and statutory declarations may be required to verify accounts, documents or other information provided.

9.63 The powers automatically conferred on the Commission following institution of a s 46 inquiry are explored below at **9.71–9.132**.

The inquiry report

9.64 Under s 50 of the 2011 Act, the Commission can publish the report of the inquiry, and its results. In practice, the Commission will usually publish inquiry reports on its website, even if it discovers no impropriety. It has stated that it will usually do this within 3 months of concluding the substantive investigation.[41]

9.65 Under s 342 of the 2011 Act a copy of the report, if certified by the Commission to be a true copy, will be admissible in proceedings instituted by the Commission under Part 6 of the 2011 Act (ie ss 61–116) or by the Attorney General. The report is evidence of any fact stated in it and evidence of the opinion of the person conducting the inquiry.

9.66 Given the serious implications of an inquiry report, which can at the very least mean adverse publicity for the charity, the charity will, if possible, want to make sure that it is happy with the report. In most cases, charity trustees are shown a copy of the draft report before publication, and therefore given an opportunity to comment on it, but this is not always the case, and the Commission is not obliged to take any comments on board. Pressure for the 2006 Act to introduce a right for those mentioned in the report to add comments to it prior to publication was resisted by Government, but the Government Minister, Lord Bassam of Brighton, had discussed the issue with the Commission and said at the Bill's Report stage in the House of Lords:[42]

> 'The Commission will ensure that those affected by an inquiry report will have a reasonable time to consider a draft report and make representations about it. That is a guarantee from the Commission.'

---

41 Charity Commission publication CC46: *Statutory Inquiries into Charities: guidance for charities and their advisers*, December 2013.

42 HL Deb, vol 674, col 685 (18 October 2005).

9.67 But this 'guarantee' does not have the force of law, so the Commission is not bound by it. Lord Phillips pointed out in the House of Lords debates on the Bill which became the 2006 Act[43] that it is only the fact of an inquiry that may be challenged before the Tribunal, not its format, so if a report is not as well considered as it might be, the charity has no right of appeal to the Tribunal itself.

9.68 At the time of writing the Commission states that it is committed to 'allow the trustees and other people named in a statement of results of inquiry, to comment on its factual accuracy before it's published'.[44]

9.69 As a matter of practice, all who are given an opportunity to comment on a report prior to publication should use that opportunity to comment on what is written. And anyone affected by a report who does not see it until publication should challenge anything they disagree with as soon as possible.

Confidentiality

9.70 Information disclosed in the course of a s 46 inquiry may, in certain circumstances, be disclosed to third parties, even if it does not appear in the inquiry report. As a public authority, the Commission is subject to the Freedom of Information Act 2000, so information may be disclosed under a freedom of information request, although various exemptions apply.[45]

POWERS EXERCISABLE IN THE COURSE OF A SECTION 46 INQUIRY

Entering premises and seizing documents

9.71 Under s 48 of the 2011 Act, the Commission may enter premises and seize documents in the course of a s 46 inquiry. This power, which was introduced by the 2006 Act, supplements the power to obtain documents in s 52 of the 2011 Act (described at **9.18–9.21**), which does not allow the Commission to enter premises.

9.72 Section 48 allows the Commission to apply to the magistrates' court for a warrant authorising it to enter and search premises. The warrant can be granted if the magistrate is satisfied, on the basis of information given on oath by a member of Commission staff, that there are reasonable grounds for believing:

(a) that a s 46 inquiry has been instituted;

(b) that there are documents or information on certain premises relevant to the inquiry which the Commission could demand under s 52(1); and

(c) that if the Commission issued an order demanding the documents or information, either the order would not be complied with, or the documents or information would be removed, tampered with, concealed or destroyed.

---

43 HL Deb, vol 670, col GC 442 (14 March 2005).

44 Charity Commission publication CC46: *Statutory Inquiries into Charities: guidance for charities and their advisers*, December 2013.

45 The Supreme Court case of *Kennedy v Charity Commission* [2014] UKSC 20 considered the scope of the exemptions.

9.73 The warrant can authorise a named member of Commission staff (and anyone the Commission considers is needed to assist him or her) to enter and search the premises, take possession of documents which appear to fall within **9.72**(b) (and computer disks or electronic storage devices which appear to contain information falling within **9.72**(b)), take steps which appear to be necessary for preserving or preventing interference with the documents or information, take copies of the documents or information and require those on the premises to give an explanation of documents or information or explain where they can be found. It is an offence under s 49 of the 2011 Act to obstruct the exercise of the rights conferred by a warrant.

9.74 Section 49 of the 2011 Act imposes further conditions. The search must be at a reasonable hour and within one month of the date that the warrant is issued. The person making the search must keep a written record, including details of anything taken away, and, under s 49(4), if 'required' to do so, must give a copy of it to the occupier of the premises or someone acting on the occupier's behalf. Section 49 does not give any further details of how the person making the search can be 'required' to hand over a copy of the record, but the Government Minister, Lord Bassam of Brighton, when discussing the relevant section of the 2006 Act in the House of Lords,[46] said, 'if requested to do so [the Commission staff member] must give a copy of the record to the occupier', suggesting that the occupier or his or her representative can simply ask for a copy. This is supported by the explanatory notes to the 2006 Act, which describe what is now s 49(4) of the 2011 Act as providing that the written record 'must be presented on request to the occupier or his representative' and do not refer to a formal procedure. The requirement to make a written record and supply a copy must be complied with before the person conducting the search leaves the premises, unless this is not reasonably practicable.

9.75 Documents and electronic storage devices can be kept for as long as the Commission considers it necessary to retain them for the purposes of its inquiry; the Commission must return original documents where it has copies, unless it considers that it is necessary to hold on to the originals. When the Commission considers that it is no longer necessary to keep documents or devices, it must return them to the person they were seized from, or to any of the charity trustees.

9.76 Section 50 of the Criminal Justice and Police Act 2001 applies to the Commission's power of seizure under s 48(3).[47] This will, in some circumstances, allow the person conducting the search to seize something (such as a computer) if he or she believes that it contains information the Commission is entitled to take, but cannot find that out while on the premises, or if he or she knows it contains such information, but cannot extract it while on the premises.

9.77 These provisions of the 2011 Act allow the Commission to enter a trustee's home and seize anything which looks relevant to the charity, and are therefore potentially extremely invasive. Most occupiers will simply not know that they have a right to ask for a copy of the written record of the search before the person conducting the search leaves, which leaves the process potentially open to abuse, and the Commission open to criticism.

---

46 HL Deb, vol 674, col 399 (12 October 2005).

47 Paragraph 56A, Part 1, Sch 1 to the Criminal Justice and Police Act 2001.

9.78 The Commission has stated that this power 'is not routinely used'.[48] In correspondence with the authors in February 2016, the Commission stated that the power had not been exercised at all during the past 3 years.

Temporary protective powers

9.79 Once the Commission has instituted a s 46 inquiry, the Commission has various powers under ss 76–79 and 83–84B of the 2011 Act to act for the protection of the charity. A distinction is drawn between temporary protective powers, designed to enable the Commission to intervene swiftly to protect assets which it believes to be at risk, and remedial powers which are designed to provide a permanent solution for a charity where the Commission has discovered misconduct or mismanagement.[49]

9.80 A number of temporary protective powers are set out in s 76(3) of the 2011 Act. Under s 76(1) they may be exercised by the Commission if it is satisfied either:

- that there is or has been:
  - (a) a failure to comply with an order or direction of the Commission;
  - (b) a failure to remedy any breach specified in an official warning given under s 75A (see **9.32–9.46**); or
  - (c) any other misconduct or mismanagement in the administration of the charity;

  (s 76(1)(a));

  or
- that it is necessary or desirable to act to protect the property of the charity or to secure the proper application of property for the purposes of the charity (s 76(1)(b)).

9.81 The references to failure to comply with an order or direction and failure to remedy a breach in an official warning were inserted by the 2016 Act.[50] The Commission apparently asked for the reference to breach of an order or direction to be included: in its report following up the 2013 consultation on extending the Commission's powers, the Cabinet Office explained that the Commission was increasingly interpreting non-compliance with an order or direction as misconduct or mismanagement, so that it could use its powers under s 76 and s 79 (see **9.79–9.115**) rather than going down the more onerous route of enforcing its direction in the High Court (see **9.235**). However, this meant that the Commission needed to demonstrate on a case by case basis that the non-compliance amounted to misconduct, and the Commission had been challenged about this in the Tribunal in the past, albeit unsuccessfully.[51] The Cabinet Office said that: 'This proposal will bring clarity for the future (and save Commission resources).'

---

48 Charity Commission publication CC46: *Statutory Inquiries into Charities: guidance for charities and their advisers*, December 2013.

49 These powers, with some adaptations, apply in relation to charities registered with the Office of the Scottish Charity Regulator which are managed or controlled wholly or mainly from England and Wales: s 87 of the 2011 Act, see Chapter 23.

50 Section 2 of the 2016 Act. The reference to failure to comply with an order or direction came into force on 31 July 2016: the reference to an official warning will come into force on 1 November 2016.

51 The case in question was *Nagendram Seevaratnam v Charity Commission and HM Attorney General* (CA/2008/0001).

9.82 The link between failure to comply with a breach specified in an official warning and more significant regulatory action is discussed further at **9.43**.

9.83 Under s 76(2) misconduct or mismanagement extends to spending excessive amounts on services to the charity or administrative costs. There is otherwise no statutory guidance as to what is meant by 'mismanagement' or 'misconduct', but the court has decided that these words should be given their ordinary meaning.[52] The Commission has expressed its view in guidance as to what may constitute misconduct or mismanagement, but the First-tier Tribunal has commented that:

> 'The Commission's guidance may provide illustrations of what might constitute mismanagement and misconduct, but cannot restrict their ordinary meaning.'[53]

As mentioned at **9.36**, the explanatory notes to s 2 of the 2016 Act state that:

> 'Failure to follow good practice could not automatically be considered to constitute misconduct or mismanagement.'

9.84 Under s 76A, which was inserted by the 2016 Act, where the Commission is satisfied that there has been misconduct or mismanagement in relation to a charity, or a breach of a warning, order or direction, (as mentioned in s 76(1)(a)) and that a particular person was responsible for the misconduct or mismanagement, knew of the misconduct or mismanagement and failed to take any reasonable step to oppose it, or contributed to it or facilitated it, the Commission can take account of other conduct by that person when deciding whether or how to exercise its powers under s 76, 79, 84 and 84A, even if that conduct did not relate to the charity which is the subject of the inquiry.[54] In commenting on the legislation which became the 2016 Act, the Charity Law Association working party said that there should be transparency around when the Commission takes other conduct into account in this way, suggesting that this should be made clear in the statement of reasons for an order made under s 86 (see **9.161–9.163**).[55]

9.85 The Commission's powers under s 76(3) are:

(a) to suspend a trustee, officer, agent or employee of the charity for up to 12 months pending consideration being given to their removal;

(b) to appoint additional charity trustees if the Commission considers this to be necessary for the proper administration of the charity;

(c) to vest property of the charity in the official custodian of charities, or order its transfer to the official custodian;

(d) to order a person holding property on behalf of the charity or of any trustee for the charity not to part with that property without the Commission's approval;

(e) to order a debtor of the charity not to make any payment to the charity without the Commission's approval;

---

52 The High Court case of *Scargill v Charity Commissioner* (unreported) 4 September 1998.

53 *Mountstar (PTC) Ltd v Charity Commission* (CA/2013/0001 and 0003), where the First-tier Tribunal considered the terms in the context of s 79 of the 2011 Act: see **9.102–9.115**.

54 Section 3 of the 2016 Act, which came into force on 31 July 2016.

55 Concerns of the Charity Law Association Working Party on the Charities (Protection and Social Investment) Bill, Second reading in the House of Commons.

(f) to restrict the transactions which the charity may enter into without the Commission's approval (eg transactions which exceed a specified value); and

(g) to appoint an interim manager to act as a receiver and manager in respect of the property and affairs of the charity, in accordance with s 78 of the 2011 Act, which is dealt with in more detail at **9.94–9.101**.

9.86 In a change introduced by the 2016 Act, the Commission may extend an order suspending a trustee, officer, agent or employee for a further period of up to 12 months, although the total period of suspension must not be more than 2 years.[56] The explanatory notes to the 2016 Act explain that the Commission had requested this change to allow suspension to continue while awaiting the outcome of a criminal prosecution. The Joint Committee scrutinising the draft legislation recommended that the Commission include statistics in its annual report allowing the effect of extended suspensions to be monitored: the Commission agreed to this.[57]

9.87 The Commission does not need to notify the charity trustees of its intention to exercise the powers, but must usually give notice after the event (see **9.161–9.163**).

9.88 Orders under s 76(3) can be appealed to the Tribunal.

9.89 If the order suspends a person from office, the Commission may also suspend that person from membership of the charity under the power described at **9.116–9.117**.

9.90 Where a trustee is appointed under the power in section 76(3), the Commission may also make an order vesting or transferring property in or to the trustees under s 81 of the 2011 Act.

9.91 The Commission's report *Tackling abuse and mismanagement 2014-15* gives details of how often the Commission's powers under s 76 have been exercised, and shows a sharp increase in use of the powers in the past 3 years.[58]

9.92 Orders made under s 76(3) (except for orders appointing additional trustees) must be reviewed by the Commission at such intervals as it thinks fit, and if it appears to the Commission that a full or part discharge of the order would be appropriate, that must be done.[59] The Commission's stated practice at the time of writing is that a review will usually occur every two months, and when the Commission receives significant new information.[60] A decision to discharge, or not to discharge, an order following a review, can be appealed to the Tribunal, but the Commission cannot be challenged in the Tribunal for failure to carry out a review in the first place.

9.93 Under s 77 it is an offence to contravene an order of the Commission made in relation to the matters mentioned at **9.85**(d), (e) and (f). Section 345 of the 2011 Act provides that proceedings may only be brought with the consent of the Director for

---

56 Section 76(7) of the 2011 Act, introduced by s 2 of the 2016 Act, which came into force on 31 July 2016.

57 Report of the Joint Committee on the Draft Protection of Charities Bill, February 2015.

58 For example, the power under s 76(3)(d) to prevent a person from parting with property was exercised 24 times in 2014-15, 28 times in 2013-14 and only three times in 2012–13. The power under s 76(3)(f) to restrict transactions was exercised once in 2014-15, 15 times in 2013-14 and not at all in 2012–13.

59 Section 76(6) of the 2011 Act.

60 Charity Commission publication CC46: *Statutory Inquiries into Charities: guidance for charities and their advisers*, December 2013.

Public Prosecutions. Conviction does not necessarily preclude the institution of proceedings for breach of trust against a trustee involved.

Interim manager

9.94 The power of the Commission to appoint an interim manager for a charity under s 76(3) of the 2011 Act is built on in s 78. The interim manager is an independent person whose job is to take over the management of the charity from the trustees, with a view to putting the charity back on its feet and sorting out any mismanagement.[61]

9.95 Prior to the 2006 Act an interim manager was known as a 'receiver and manager'. The terminology was changed because there were concerns that this expression implied not only that the appointment was long term, but that winding up of the charity would inevitably follow, which is not the case. The appointment is an interim step only, with the aim of handing management back to trustees in time. Although some charities are wound up following the appointment of an interim manager, this does not always happen.

9.96 The order appointing the interim manager should specify the functions to be discharged by him or her. These may include all or any of the powers of the charity trustees. The order may provide that the interim manager will act to the exclusion of the charity trustees, but need not do so.

9.97 The interim manager is subject to the supervision of the Commission, to whom he or she may turn for advice and the Commission may, in turn, seek directions from the court at the charity's expense. To date the Commission has sought directions from the court on two occasions: once in 2014-15 and once in 2015-16.

9.98 Section 78(8) allows the Minister for the Cabinet Office to make regulations dealing with interim managers: the relevant regulations are the Charities (Receiver and Manager) Regulations 1992[62] (which were made under earlier legislation). These deal with taking security from an interim manager for the proper discharge of their functions, remuneration (to be paid out of a charity's income), the submission of reports to the Commission and removal from office.

9.99 Section 86 of the 2011 Act, which was introduced by the 2006 Act, obliges the Commission, in most cases, to inform the charity (if it is a body corporate) and otherwise each of the trustees of the fact of the appointment, and the reasons for it, as soon as practicable after it has been made (see **9.161–9.163**).

9.100 Although the Commission does have power to pay the interim manager, in practice the costs of doing so, which can be enormous, are invariably met by the charity. Suggestions during the debates on the 2006 Act that the Commission should foot the bill itself were resisted, on the grounds that this would amount to requiring the taxpayer to meet the costs of a charity's mismanagement. Lord Bassam said[63] that:[64]

---

61 Four appointments were made in each of 2015-16 and 2014-15 and six were made in 2013-2014; none were made in the financial year 2012–13. *Tackling abuse and mismanagement*, 2014–15 and Charity Commission Annual Report 2015-16.

62 SI 1992/2355.

63 HL Deb, vol 670, col GC 446 (14 March 2005).

64 In evidence to the Public Accounts Committee in 2013 the then chief executive of the Commission, Sam

'the Government believe in general terms that in most circumstances it would probably be appropriate for [interim] managers to be remunerated from the income of the charities concerned.'

9.101 Prior to the 2006 Act, there were also calls for the Commission to publish details about the appointment of interim managers, including costs. This was not made a statutory requirement, but the debates on the 2006 Act prompted the Commission, as a matter of practice, to publish information about cases where an interim manager has been appointed on its website. Section 46 inquiry reports will also generally include, where relevant, the costs of an interim manager.

Permanent remedial powers

9.102 Once a s 46 inquiry has been instituted, the Commission also has permanent remedial powers to protect the charity's property, set out in s 79.

Scheme for the administration of the charity

9.103 Under s 79(1) and (2), if the Commission is satisfied either:

(a) that there is or has been:
- a failure to comply with an order or direction of the Commission;
- a failure to remedy any breach specified in an official warning given under s 75A (see **9.32–9.46**); or
- any other misconduct or mismanagement in the administration of the charity;

or

(b) that it is necessary or desirable to act to protect the property of the charity or to secure the proper application of property for the purposes of the charity;

(ie, either of the grounds set out in s 76(1): see **9.80**), the Commission may make a scheme for the administration of the charity without the need for an application from the trustees or anyone else.

9.104 This power was amended in two respects by 2016 Act.[65] First, the references to failure to comply with an order or direction and failure to remedy a breach specified in an official warning were inserted: see **9.81**. Second, prior to the 2016 Act the Commission could only make a scheme if it was satisfied that both the condition in **9.103**(a) and the condition in **9.103**(b) had been satisfied. The change means that it will be easier for the Commission to make a scheme under s 79.[66]

9.105 As explained at **9.84**, under s 76A of the 2011 Act, which came into force in July 2016, where the Commission is satisfied that there has been misconduct or mismanagement in relation to a charity, or breach of a warning, order or direction (as

---

Younger, said that in the past year two interim managers funded by the Commission had been appointed. Public Accounts Committee report on The Charity Commission, January 2014.

65 Sections 2(2) and 4 of the 2016 Act, which came into force on 31 July 2016, although the reference to official warnings will not come into force until 1 November 2016: see footnote 50.

66 The Commission did not make any schemes under s 79 in the financial years 2010-2015: *Tackling abuse and mismanagement*, 2014-15.

mentioned in s 76(1)(a)), it may take account of other conduct when deciding whether or how to exercise this power, even if that conduct did not relate to the charity concerned.

9.106 The Commission must generally give notice of its intention to exercise its power under s 79(2) to each charity trustee (see **9.156**). It may also need to give advance notice to any person who is being removed from office and public notice (see **9.157–9.160** and **17.81–17.89**). And the Commission must usually give notice once these powers have been exercised (see **9.161-9.163**).

9.107 Orders under s 79(2) can be appealed to the Charity Tribunal.

Removal of a trustee, officer, agent or employee

9.108 Under s 79(3) and (4), if the Commission is satisfied both:

- that there is or has been:
  - a failure to comply with an order or direction of the Commission;
  - a failure to remedy any breach specified in an official warning given under s 75A (see **9.32–9.46**); or
  - any other misconduct or mismanagement in the administration of the charity;

  and
- that it is necessary or desirable to act to protect the property of the charity or to secure the proper application of property for the purposes of the charity;

(ie *both* of the grounds set out in s 76(1): see **9.80**), the Commission can remove a trustee, officer, agent or employee of the charity who has been responsible for the misconduct or mismanagement, who knew of the misconduct or mismanagement and failed to take any reasonable step to oppose it, or whose conduct contributed to it or facilitated it.

9.109 This power was amended in two respects by 2016 Act.[67] First, as mentioned at **9.81-9.82** the references to failure to comply with an order or direction or to remedy a breach specified in an official warning were inserted. Secondly, the language has been amended slightly, replacing a reference to being 'privy to' misconduct or mismanagement with the reference to knowing of misconduct or mismanagement and failing to oppose it.[68]

9.110 As explained at **9.84**, under s 76A of the 2011 Act, which came into force in July 2016, where the Commission is satisfied that there has been misconduct or mismanagement in relation to a charity, or breach of a warning, order or direction (as mentioned in s 76(1)(a)), it may take account of other conduct when deciding whether or how to exercise this power, even if that conduct did not relate to the charity concerned.

---

[67] Sections 2(2) and 4 of the 2016 Act, which came into force on 31 July 2016.

[68] This change was recommended by the Joint Committee scrutinising the draft Protection of Charities Bill on the basis that the new language is clearer. Report of the Joint Committee on the Draft Protection of Charities Bill, February 2015, para 125.

9.111 The Commission must generally give notice of its intention to exercise its power under s 79(4) to each charity trustee (see **9.156**). It may also need to give advance notice to any person who is being removed from office and public notice (see **9.157–9.160**). And the Commission must usually give notice once these powers have been exercised (see **9.161–9.163**). A trustee removed under s 79(4) is automatically disqualified from acting as a trustee of a charity under s 178 of the 2011 Act (see **9.210(c)**).

9.112 In the 2013 consultation on extending the Commission's powers, it was pointed out that giving prior notice of the Commission's intention to remove a trustee or office holder, under s 89(5) of the 2011 Act, gives them an opportunity to resign from office before they can be removed. This would allow them to go on to serve as trustee of another charity, or even the same charity, as a trustee is only automatically disqualified from acting if they have actually been removed under s 79(4). Section 79(5), which was added by s 4 of the 2016 Act, allows the Commission to proceed to remove a person from an office or employment under s 79(4), having given notice of its intention to make the order under s 82 (see **9.156**) even if the person concerned has stepped down from the office or employment.[69] It might also be possible for the Commission to consider disqualifying the person concerned from acting as a trustee, under its new powers in s 181A of the 2011 Act (see **9.219-9.230**).

9.113 If the Commission has removed a trustee, officer, agent or employee under s 79(4) the Commission has power to suspend him or her from membership, see **9.116**. Where a trustee is removed or appointed under s 79, the Commission may also make an order vesting or transferring property in or to the trustees under s 81 of the 2011 Act.

9.114 Orders under s 79(4) can be appealed to the Charity Tribunal.[70]

9.115 Under s 182 of the 2011 Act the Commission must keep a register of those removed from office under s 79(4), and under earlier legislation: see **9.210**.

Suspension of membership

9.116 Prior to the 2006 Act, there was an anomaly in that while the Commission could remove or suspend trustees, officers and agents of a charity, it had no corresponding power to take away any powers they might have as members of the charity, which would mean that they still had a voice as members, and might, strictly speaking, have a power to effect or influence their reinstatement as trustees or otherwise. Section 83 of the 2011 Act, which was introduced by the 2006 Act, corrected this. Where the Commission suspends a trustee, officer, employee or agent from office under s 76 (see **9.85**) and that person is a member of the charity, it can also suspend them from membership for that period. Where the Commission removes a trustee officer, employee or agent from office or employment under s 79(4) (see **9.108**) and that person is also a member of the charity, it can also terminate their membership and prohibit them from resuming membership without the Commission's consent.[71] There is a presumption in favour of granting consent after 5 years.

---

69 This provision came into force on 31 July 2016.

70 In the case of *Nagendram Seevaratnam v Charity Commission and HM Attorney General* (CA/2008/0001) the First-tier Tribunal allowed the appellant's appeal against the Commission's decision to remove him from the position of trustee, officer and agent of a charity under s 18(2)(i) of the 1993 Act (now s 79(4) of the 2011 Act).

71 Prior to the 2016 Act the Commission's power to terminate membership did not apply to a trustee who had been removed: this was changed by s 4(3) of the 2016 Act, which came into force on 31 July 2016.

9.117 Notice must be given once this power has been exercised (see **9.161–9.163**). Orders under s 83 are subject to appeal to the Tribunal.

Direction to take action expedient in the interests of the charity

9.118 Section 84 of the 2011 Act, which was introduced by the 2006 Act, gives the Commission power to give specific directions to charity trustees or to a charity after a s 46 inquiry has been instituted.

9.119 If, after a s 46 inquiry has commenced, the Commission is satisfied either:

(a) that there is or has been:
- a failure to comply with an order or direction of the Commission;
- a failure to remedy any breach specified in an official warning given under s 75A (see **9.32–9.46**); or
- any other misconduct or mismanagement in the administration of the charity;

or

(b) that it is necessary or desirable to act to protect the property of the charity or to secure the proper application of property for the purposes of the charity;

(ie the same criteria as those which apply to action under the Commission's temporary protective powers under s 76: see **9.80**[72]) it can make an order directing the charity trustees, any trustee for the charity (which might include a custodian trustee), any officer or employee of the charity or (in the case of a corporate charity) the charity itself, to take any action specified in the order which the Commission considers to be expedient in the interests of the charity. The order can require action which would not otherwise be within the powers of the person concerned. It cannot require action which is expressly prohibited by the trusts of the charity, inconsistent with its purposes or prohibited by statute. Where a person or body is directed to do something under a s 84 order, they are protected from allegations that they have acted improperly as far as the charity is concerned (by virtue of s 84(4)), but the contractual and other rights arising in connection with anything done under the authority of an order are unaffected (by virtue of s 84(5)).

9.120 As explained at **9.84**, under s 76A of the 2011 Act, which came into force in July 2016, where the Commission is satisfied that there has been misconduct or mismanagement in relation to a charity, or breach of a warning, order or direction (as mentioned in s 76(1)(a)), it may take account of other conduct when deciding whether or how to exercise this power, even if that conduct did not relate to the charity concerned.

9.121 This power means that, broadly speaking, once a s 46 inquiry has been instituted, the Commission can act as it thinks appropriate. It might, for instance, direct the trustees to wind up some of the charity's projects, or dispose of property belonging to the charity. This power may well save charitable funds, as the Commission may be able to direct the trustees to take action in cases where, before the existence of the power, it might have appointed an interim manager. But the wide discretion given to the Commission prompted concerns that the power may be subject to abuse. When this part of the legislation was under discussion in Parliament, there were attempts in both the

72 As explained at **9.81-9.82** the 2016 Act amended the criteria.

House of Lords and the House of Commons to introduce an element of objectivity into the process, by requiring, for instance, that the Commission could only order action which it 'reasonably believes' to be expedient, or by allowing the Commission only to take action which is 'necessary for the protection of … property'. These attempts failed. In supporting the second of these two amendments Andrew Turner MP argued, in the House of Commons Standing Committee debates, that although s 84 orders are subject to appeal to the Tribunal by the person directed to take action by the order, they would be:[73]

> 'unappealable in practice because the commissioners would have to demonstrate only that they considered it expedient and in the interests of the charity [to act]. Yes, their decision would have to be reasonable and rational, but all they would have to say is "We thought it was expedient". The Tribunal would just say, "Well, you thought it was expedient – sorry, appellant, you've had it".'

At the time of writing there have been three challenges to a s 84 order in the Charity Tribunal. None have proceeded to a substantive hearing, but in the case of *Mckay v Charity Commission*[74] the Commission decided to remove the appellant's name from the order so the appeal was withdrawn.

9.122 The Commission must generally give notice of orders made under s 84 once they have been made (see **9.161–9.163**).

9.123 The Commission has made increasing use of this power in recent years: it was exercised 154 times in 2014-15, 38 times in 2013–14 and not at all in 2012-13.[75]

9.124 In the consultation which preceded the 2016 Act, the Commission called for its powers under s 84 to be exercisable without the need to open a s 46 inquiry, but this was not pursued.[76]

Directions that specified action not be taken

9.125 The Commission has a new power, introduced by the 2016 Act, to issue an order – after a s 46 inquiry has been instituted – directing a charity, charity trustees or an officer or employee of a charity not to take or continue action which the Commission considers would constitute misconduct or mismanagement in the administration of the charity, under s 84A of the 2011 Act.[77] As mentioned at **9.83** there is no statutory definition of misconduct or mismanagement. The order, and the Commission's reasons for making it, must be given to the charity or trustees under s 86: see **9.161–9.163**. The order must be reviewed at least every 6 months.

9.126 In 2013 the Cabinet Office had originally consulted on two related proposals: allowing the Commission to issue directions preventing misconduct or mismanagement or breach of fiduciary duty from taking place; and allowing the Commission to restrict or prevent actions, in both cases after a statutory inquiry had been instigated.

---

[73] HC Standing Committee A, col 159 (11 July 2006).
[74] CA/2013/0010.
[75] *Tackling abuse and mismanagement*: 2014-15.
[76] Consultation on extending the Charity Commission's powers to tackle abuse in charities, Cabinet Office, December 2013. Draft Protection of Charities Bill, Minister for the Cabinet Office, October 2014.
[77] Section 6 of the 2016 Act which came into force on 31 July 2016.

9.127 Prior to the passing of the 2016 Act, the Charity Law Association working party reviewing the legislation asked for clarification that any order under s 84A should not be able to survive the period of an inquiry.

9.128 Directions given under s 84A may be appealed to the Tribunal by any person directed not to take the specified action.

Power to direct winding up

9.129 The 2016 Act introduced a new power for the Commission, after a s 46 inquiry has been instituted, to make a direction which would effect the winding up of the charity, under s 84B of the 2011 Act.[78] Before the power can be exercised the Commission must be satisfied on the following three counts:

(1) Either:

(a) that there is or has been:
- a failure to comply with an order or direction of the Commission;
- a failure to remedy any breach specified in an official warning given under s 75A (see **9.31–9.46**); or
- any other misconduct or mismanagement in the administration of the charity;

or

(b) that it is necessary or desirable to act to protect the property of the charity or to secure the proper application of property for the purposes of the charity;

(ie the same criteria as those which apply to action under the Commission's temporary protective powers under s 76: see **9.80**). As explained at **9.84**, under s 76A of the 2011 Act, where the Commission is satisfied that there has been misconduct or mismanagement in relation to a charity, or breach of a warning, order or direction (as mentioned in s 76(1)(a)), it can take account of other conduct when deciding whether or how to exercise this power, even if that conduct did not relate to the charity concerned;

and

(2) Either:

- that the charity does not operate; or
- that its purposes can be promoted more effectively it if ceases to operate;

and

(3) That exercising the power is expedient in the public interest.

If satisfied on all these counts, the Commission may issue an order directing the trustees, any officer or employee, or the charity (if it is a body corporate) to take any action specified in the order for the purpose of having the charity wound up and dissolved, and any remaining property transferred to a charity with the same purposes. An order can direct a person to take action which might otherwise be beyond their powers (for

---

78 Section 7 of the 2016 Act, which came into force on 31 July 2016.

example by taking action which can usually only be taken by the charity's members), but cannot require action which is prohibited by statute.

9.130 The Commission must give public notice of its intention to make an order. When making the order, it must take account of any representations made within a period specified in the notice. The order cannot be made less than 60 days after public notice has been given, unless the Commission, once it has given notice and duly taken any representations into account, considers that a shorter period is necessary to prevent or reduce misconduct or mismanagement or protect charity property. The Commission must also give copies of the order to the charity or its trustees under s 86: see **9.161–9.163**. Action taken under a s 84B order is treated as properly done, but contractual rights are protected.

9.131 Orders under s 84B may be appealed to the Charity Tribunal by the person directed to act and, where an order directs action which can only be done by the members of the charity, by the members.

9.132 The Commission had requested this power to allow it to force a charity's winding up where there are concerns that the trustees as a whole are not capable of remedying non-compliance or abuse. The Commission estimated that it would only be used in one or two cases per year: the explanatory notes to the 2016 Act state that a winding up following an inquiry would only be appropriate in 'rare' cases.[79]

POWERS INDEPENDENT OF S 46 INQUIRIES

9.133 The more draconian of the Commission's powers may only be exercised after a s 46 inquiry. However, the Commission does have certain powers to act for the protection of charities and their property, even if a s 46 inquiry has not been put in train.

Concurrent jurisdiction with the High Court to deal with trustees, employees and charity property

9.134 Under s 69 of the 2011 Act thc Commission has concurrent jurisdiction with the High Court to take the following action by order:

- to establish a scheme for the administration of a charity (which is dealt with in detail in Chapter 17);
- to appoint, discharge or remove charity trustees;
- to remove charity officers or employees; and
- to vest or transfer property.

9.135 However, these powers cannot generally be exercised by the Commission of its own volition. They may be exercised on the application of the charity or the Attorney General, or as a result of a court order. Where the charity's income is no more than £500 per year the powers may be exercised on the application of a charity trustee, a person interested in the charity or (in the case of a local charity) two or more local residents. Where an order relates to the discharge of a trustee, it may be exercised on the

79 Consultation on extending the Charity Commission's powers to tackle abuse in charities, Cabinet Office, December 2013.

application of the trustee concerned. There is limited scope for the Commission to exercise its scheme-making powers under s 69 without a third party application: see **17.73**.

9.136 Section 70 of the 2011 Act imposes various restrictions on the Commission's scheme making powers: see **17.51-17.54**.

9.137 The Commission must generally give advance notice of its intention to exercise its powers to the charity trustees who are not party to or privy to the application to the Commission (see **9.155**). Orders relating to the appointment, discharge or removal of trustees, officers or employees may also be subject to the notice requirements described at **9.157–9.160**.

9.138 Orders under s 69 are subject to appeal to the Tribunal.[80]

Appointment and removal of trustees

9.139 Under s 80 of the 2011 Act, the Commission may remove trustees and appoint replacements in some circumstances without a prior application from a third party, where there is no ongoing s 46 inquiry. Where a trustee is removed or appointed using this power, the Commission may also make an order vesting in or transferring property to the trustees under s 81 of the 2011 Act. The Commission may also remove a trustee who has been disqualified from acting: see **9.143**.[81]

Removal of trustees

9.140 Under s 80(1) of the 2011 Act the Commission can make an order removing a trustee in the following circumstances:

- where the trustee has had a bankruptcy order (or order sequestrating his or her estate), or arrangement with his or her creditors or the qualifying debts under a debt relief order, discharged within the last 5 years (note that under s 178 of the 2011 Act bankruptcy automatically disqualifies a trustee from acting (see **9.210**));
- where the trustee is a corporation in liquidation;
- where the trustee is incapable of acting because of mental disorder within the meaning of the Mental Health Act 1983;
- where the trustee has not acted and will not declare his or her willingness or unwillingness to act (the legislation gives no indication of the length of time for which a trustee must fail to act before this power can be triggered);
- where the trustee is outside England and Wales or cannot be found, or does not act, and the trustee's absence or failure to act impedes the proper administration of the charity.

9.141 The Commission must generally give notice of its intention to exercise these powers to each charity trustee (see **9.156**). The notice provisions described at **9.157** are also relevant.

---

80 For example, the case of *Anique v Charity Commission* (CA/2014/0016) dealt with an appeal against an order vesting property under s 69(1)(c) of the 2011 Act. The Commission's order was upheld.

81 These powers apply in relation to charities registered with the Office of the Scottish Charity Regulator which are managed or controlled wholly or mainly from England and Wales: s 87 of the 2011 Act, see Chapter 23.

9.142 The exercise of this power is subject to appeal to the Tribunal.

Removal of disqualified trustees

9.143 The 2016 Act has introduced a new power for the Commission to remove a charity trustee, under s 79A of the 2011 Act, if they are disqualified from acting, whether they have been disqualified under the automatic disqualification provisions (see **9.206–9.218**) or by the Commission via a disqualification order (see **9.219–9.230**).[82] A trustee who acts while disqualified commits a criminal offence (see **9.231**) but does not automatically cease to hold office, unless this is covered in the charity's governing document: the Commission now has power to ensure that a trustee does cease to hold office in these circumstances. The Commission must give notice to the trustee concerned (see **9.156**). This power does not allow the Commission to remove a disqualified person from a senior management position: the explanatory notes to the 2016 Act state that this would be for the charity's trustees to enforce, but that their failure to do so could result in the Commission taking action against the trustees. The Commission must keep a register of trustees removed under s 79A, under s 182 of the 2011 Act.

Appointment of trustees

9.144 Under s 80(2) of the 2011 Act the Commission can make an order on its own initiative appointing a charity trustee in the following circumstances:

- as a replacement for a trustee removed by the Commission;
- where there are no trustees, or where there are not enough trustees (including where this is due to absence or incapacity) to make an application to the Commission to appoint additional trustees;
- where there is only one trustee (which is not a corporation aggregate) and the Commission believes it is necessary to increase the number of trustees for the proper administration of the charity;
- where the Commission believes that it is necessary for the proper administration of the charity to have an additional trustee because one of the existing trustees does not act, or cannot be found or is outside England and Wales.

The Commission must generally give notice of its intention to exercise these powers to each charity trustee (see **9.156**). The notice provisions described at **9.158–9.163** will also be relevant.

9.145 The exercise of this power is subject to appeal to the Tribunal.

Power to direct application of charity property

9.146 Section 85 of the 2011 Act, which was introduced by the 2006 Act and amended by the 2016 Act, confers on the Commission power to order a person in possession or control of charity property to apply it in any manner specified in the order.[83] The Commission must be satisfied that the person concerned is unwilling or unable to apply

---

82 Section 5 of the 2016 Act, which came into force on 31 July 2016.

83 This power applies in relation to charities registered with the Office of the Scottish Charity Regulator which are managed or controlled wholly or mainly from England and Wales: s 87 of the 2011 Act, see Chapter 23.

it properly for the purposes of the charity, and that the order is necessary or desirable for the purpose of securing the proper application of the property for the purposes of the charity.

9.147 The order can require action which would not otherwise be within the powers of the person concerned. It cannot require action which is expressly prohibited by the trusts of the charity or prohibited by statute. Where a person is directed to do something under a s 85 order, they are protected from allegations that they have acted improperly as far as the charity is concerned (by virtue of s 85(4)), but the contractual and other rights arising in connection with anything done under the authority of an order are preserved, except in the case of rights held by the charity or its trustees in that capacity (by virtue of s 85(5)).

9.148 An order can be made immediately, without any need for a s 46 inquiry, or prior notice to anyone, although notice must usually be given to the trustees after the event (see **9.161–9.163**).

9.149 The power allows the Commission, for instance, to order a bank holding funds belonging to a charity which has ceased to operate to transfer the funds to another charity.

9.150 While this provision may well save costs, as it allows the Commission to take action without the expense of putting a s 46 inquiry in train, as in the case of ss 84 (see **9.121**) and 84A this must be set against the potential disadvantages of giving the Commission such a wide discretion.

9.151 An order under s 85 may be challenged in the Tribunal by the person directed to act under the order.

9.152 Section 85 was amended slightly by the 2016 Act, which introduced the ability for the Commission to make a direction if a person is 'unable' to apply property properly, as well as being unwilling to do so, and amendments ensuring that compliance with an order does not breach a contractual obligation to the charity.[84] The Commission asked for this change following several cases where financial institutions holding charity property would have been willing to transfer it following a direction from the Commission but were contractually unable to do so. The Commission estimated that this power might be used up to two or three times annually.[85]

NOTICE

9.153 The 2006 Act made some changes to the circumstances in which the Commission must give notice of its exercise of its powers to intervene in a charity's activities. The notice requirements are now largely set out in ss 71, 82, 86 and 89 of the 2011 Act.

9.154 There is some overlap between the requirements set out below.

---

84 Section 8 of the 2016 Act, which came into force on 31 July 2016.

85 Consultation on extending the Charity Commission's powers to tackle abuse in charities, Cabinet Office, December 2013.

Advance notice of s 69 orders

9.155 Under s 71 of the 2011 Act, before it exercises its jurisdiction under s 69 of the Act (see **9.134–9.138**) – except where it is acting under court order – the Commission must give advance notice to each of the charity trustees who are not party or privy to an application requesting the Commission to act, unless they cannot be found or have no known address in the United Kingdom.

Advance notice of orders under s 79, 79A or 80

9.156 Under s 82 of the 2011 Act, before exercising any jurisdiction under s 79 (to remove a trustee, officer, employee or agent, or establish a scheme following institution of a s 46 inquiry), s 79A (to remove a trustee who is disqualified from acting) or s 80 (to remove a trustee or appoint a new trustee of its own motion provided certain conditions are satisfied) – see **9.103–9.115**, **9.143**, **9.140–9.142** and **9.144–9.145** respectively – the Commission must give notice to each charity trustee, except any that cannot be found or have no known address in the United Kingdom.

Advance notice of removal

9.157 Under s 89(5) of the 2011 Act, if the Commission wishes to make an order under the 2011 Act removing a trustee, officer, agent or employee of a charity without his or her consent, it must give them at least 1 month's written notice, unless they cannot be found or have no known address within the United Kingdom. The notice must invite representations to be made within a specified period, and those representations must be taken into account under s 89(6). This requirement does not apply to removal of a disqualified trustee under s 79A (see **9.143**): the explanatory notes to the 2016 Act state that a mechanism for representations is not considered necessary where an already disqualified trustee is being removed.

Advance public notice

9.158 Under s 89(1) of the 2011 Act, if the Commission wishes to make an order appointing, discharging or removing a trustee (except an order relating to the official custodian, an order appointing additional trustees under its temporary protective powers (s 76(3)(b): see **9.85**) or an order removing a disqualified trustee (s 79A: see **9.143**)), it must give advance public notice, inviting representations within a period given in the notice. Under s 89(6) the Commission must take any representations made within that period into account. The Commission can decide when to give the notice.

9.159 The Commission has a broad discretion under s 89(4) to dispense with the requirement to give notice 'if it is satisfied that for any reason compliance with the requirement is unnecessary'.

9.160 These provisions were amended slightly by the 2006 Act: the Commission's discretion to dispense with the public notice requirement is more widely drafted than previously, and the Commission has more flexibility about timescales, in line with the more flexible notice provisions for schemes (see Chapter 17).

Notice – and reasons – after the event

9.161 Section 86 of the 2011 Act obliges the Commission to send copies of various orders under the Act to the charity. This provision was introduced by the 2006 Act: the Government Minister, Lord Bassam of Brighton, explained the reasons behind it in the following terms:[86]

> 'It is the Commission's usual practice to inform the trustees of why it has taken any significant action using its protective powers. The amendment will make that a statutory requirement, subject to certain safeguards.'

9.162 Under s 86, where the Commission makes any order under any of the following provisions of the 2011 Act, it must give copies of the order to the charity (if it is a body corporate) and otherwise to each of the charity trustees as soon as practicable after the order has been made, unless they cannot be found or have no known address in the United Kingdom:

- s 76 (the exercise of temporary protective powers, including the suspension of trustees, following the institution of a s 46 inquiry) (see **9.80–9.101**);
- s 79 (the exercise of permanent protective powers, including the removal of trustees, following the institution of a s 46 inquiry) (see **9.102–9.115**);
- s 80 (the removal or appointment of trustees of the Commission's own motion provided certain conditions are met) (see **9.140–9.142** and **9.144–9.145**);
- s 81 (vesting of property in trustees following a s 76, 79 or 80 order) (see **9.90, 9.113** and **9.139**);
- s 83 (suspending or removing trustees and others from membership following a s 76 or s 79 order) (see **9.116–9.117**);
- s 84 (directing specified action to be taken following the institution of a s 46 inquiry) (see **9.118–9.124**);
- s 84A (directing that certain action not be taken following the institution of a s 46 inquiry) (see **9.125–9.128**);
- s 84B (directing winding up of a charity following a s 46 inquiry) (see **9.129–9.132**); and
- s 85 (directing the application of charity property without the need for a s 46 inquiry) (see **9.146–9.152**).

The copy of the order must be accompanied by a statement of the Commission's reasons for making it.

9.163 There is an exception from this requirement if, and for so long as, the Commission considers that to comply with it would prejudice any inquiry or investigation or would not be in the interests of the charity.

COURT PROCEEDINGS

9.164 Section 114 of the 2011 Act supplements the role of the Commission in dealing directly with abuse by conferring on it powers to initiate court proceedings. The

---

86 HL Deb, vol 674, col 397 (12 October 2005).

Commission has concurrent jurisdiction with the Attorney General to take legal proceedings relating to charities or the property or affairs of charities or, alternatively, to compromise claims with a view to avoiding or ending such proceedings. For example, if the Commission is of the view that a charity has suffered loss as a result of the negligence of the charity trustees, it can initiate proceedings against the trustees, seeking an order that they compensate the charity for the loss, or it can reach agreement with the trustees concerning what recompense the trustees should make to the charity, without instituting proceedings. However, the Commission still needs the Attorney General's consent to institute proceedings and to compromise claims.

CHARITY PROCEEDINGS

9.165 Section 115 of the 2011 Act deals with charity proceedings, which are defined in s 115(8) as proceedings in any court in England or Wales brought under the court's jurisdiction with respect to charities, or the court's jurisdiction with respect to trusts in relation to the administration of a trust for charitable purposes. Charity proceedings can be brought by the charity, any of the trustees, any person interested in the charity, or (in the case of a local charity) two or more local residents. Charity proceedings are proceedings which deal with charity law issues, or internal administration issues: disputes with outsiders are not charity proceedings.[87]

9.166 The court has given some consideration to who will be regarded as interested in the charity for the purposes of s 115. In *Re Hampton Fuel Allotment Charity*[88] the Court of Appeal said that 'a person generally needs to have an interest materially greater than or different from that possessed by ordinary members of the public'. Other cases have considered s 115, including *RSPCA v Attorney General*,[89] which dealt with the charity's policy regarding the exclusion from membership of those it felt were damaging it by seeking to change its anti-hunting policy. The judge referred to the *Hampton Fuel Allotment Charity* case, and held that an annual member and a life member of the RSPCA did have sufficient interest, where the proceedings related to the construction of the charity's membership provisions, but a disappointed applicant for membership did not. In *Rozensweig v NMC Recordings Ltd*[90] a composer was regarded as a person interested in a charity promoting contemporary music on the strength of his relationship with the charity.

9.167 The court cannot deal with charity proceedings unless they have been authorised by Commission order. The purpose of the requirement for authorsation for charity proceedings has been described as:

> 'to prevent charities from frittering away money subject to charitable trusts in pursuing litigation relating to internal disputes'.[91]

The Commission must not, without special reasons, authorise charity proceedings if in its opinion the case can be dealt with by the Commission under other powers in the

---

87 *Muman v Nagasena* [1999] 4 All ER 178.
88 [1989] Ch 484.
89 [2001] 3 All ER 530.
90 [2013] EWHC 3792 (Ch).
91 *Muman v Nagasena* [1999] 4 All ER 178.

2011 Act (apart from s 114). If the Commission refuses to make an order, leave to take proceedings may be sought from a High Court judge in the Chancery Division.[92]

9.168 Where charity trustees are involved in legal proceedings of any nature (even if they are not 'charity proceedings') the trustees may have concerns that they might be personally liable for the cost of the proceedings if they are unsuccessful. It is open to the trustees to protect themselves against this risk by seeking a so-called *Beddoe* order from the court. However, an application for a *Beddoe* order falls within the definition of 'charity proceedings', meaning that it needs to be authorised by the Charity Commission. If the main proceedings involve the Charity Commission itself, the Commission faces an obvious conflict of interest. This issue was considered by the Law Commission in its 2015 consultation. The Law Commission provisionally proposed that in these circumstances, it should be open to the trustees to seek authorisation from either the Charity Commission or the court.[93]

9.169 Section 115 does not apply to proceedings taken by the Attorney General. If the Commission, on receiving an application for its authorisation to charity proceedings, is of the view that it is desirable for those proceedings to be taken by the Attorney General, it must inform him about the proceedings and send him any relevant information.

POWER TO ASSIST CHARITIES

9.170 As mentioned at 9.2, and in Chapter 2, the Commission is both regulator and friend to charities. Its second general function is that of encouraging and facilitating the better administration of charities, which encompasses the provision of advice and guidance.

9.171 The 2011 Act gives the Commission a range of statutory powers to assist trustees: by sanctioning action which the trustees may be unsure about, by advising trustees on their obligations, and by protecting trustees from personal liability where they have acted improperly but honestly.

9.172 As mentioned previously, in recent years the Commission has focused primarily on the regulatory side of its work, and now offers much less one-to-one advice and support to charities than it has done in the past, but it continues to publish a wide range of generic guidance on its website. Increasingly, the Commission is issuing general 'regulatory alerts' to charities about emerging risks.

Sanctioning action by trustees

9.173 Section 105 of the 2011 Act allows the Commission to make orders sanctioning action which appears to the Commission to be expedient in the interests of the charity, even if that action would not otherwise be within the powers of the charity trustees.

9.174 The power is immensely useful, and can be used in a number of situations. For example:

---

[92] As in the case of *Garcha v Charity Commission* [2014] EWHC 2754 (Ch), for example.

[93] Chapter 16, Technical Issues in Charity Law, A Consultation Paper, Law Commission, March 2015.

- A s 105 order may be used to sanction a specific course of action by the charity trustees, such as the remuneration of trustees, or a transaction between the charity and one of its trustees which would otherwise be prohibited because it involves a conflict of interest, but which can be regarded as expedient in the interests of the charity. See, for example, **13.28** and **14.70**.
- The Commission can use a s 105 order to consent the removal of a prohibition on trustee benefit in a charitable company's Articles of Association, where consent is needed because there are not enough independent members to make the change (see **7.21**).[94]
- Section 105 orders are commonly used to sanction particular payments out of charity funds, eg a gratuity to a long-serving employee on his or her retirement. Ordinarily, the trustees would have no power to make such payments, as they are not contractually obliged to pay gratuities, which could therefore be seen as a misuse of charity funds. But the Commission may regard such a payment as being expedient in the interests of the charity, because it demonstrates that the charity is a good employer, which will incentivise other employees and help with recruitment.
- A s 105 order may authorise the transfer of property to another charity.

9.175 There are some restrictions on the Commission's power. It cannot authorise anything expressly prohibited by the charity's constitution, nor (subject to some exceptions listed in s 105) anything which is specifically prohibited by statute. Nor can it change the charity's purposes.

9.176 The Commission's power under s 105 is an enabling power, allowing it to sanction action by the charity trustees, not to take any positive action itself. This means that a s 105 order will be phrased in a way that allows the trustees to do something, for instance to transfer property to another charity, rather than actually effecting the transfer.

9.177 Anything done under the authority of a s 105 order is deemed to be properly done in the exercise of the trustees' powers, so if trustees act on the basis of a s 105 order, they should be protected from any potential breach of trust claim. In the case of a charitable company, a s 105 order may authorise an act even though it involves the breach of a duty imposed on a director of the company under Chapter 2 of Part 10 of the Companies Act 2006 (see **13.28**).

9.178 There is no statutory procedure for applying for a s 105 order.

9.179 A decision not to make an order under s 105 may be appealed to the Tribunal (see Chapter 10).

Ex gratia payments

9.180 Section 105 orders can only permit action which appears to the Commission to be expedient in the interests of the charity. Charity trustees may sometimes feel under a moral obligation to use charity property in a way which is outside their powers (eg by making a payment which they are not contractually obliged to make), but which could

---

94 Charity Commission operational guidance OG 515-2 'The statutory power to pay for services provided by a trustee'.

not be said to be expedient in the interests of the charity. The most common example of this is where a charity has been left a gift by a supporter in his or her will, but it feels that on moral grounds some of that gift should be diverted to friends or relatives of the supporter who may have lost out as a result, say, of a legal technicality or an oversight on the part of the person making the will. If the charity were an individual, it could make the payment if it chose to, but because charity trustees are obliged to act in the best interests of the charity, which would not generally involve giving away funds which a charity has a right to (except to a beneficiary), charities do not have this flexibility. Payments like this are commonly known as ex gratia payments. Although the Commission has no power to make a s 105 order in these circumstances, it can make an order under s 106 of the 2011 Act authorising the charity trustees to make the payment.

9.181 The case of *Re Snowden and Re Henderson*[95] established that ex gratia payments by charities could be authorised by the Attorney General and the court. Section 106 confers the same power on the Commission. The Commission may authorise the trustees of a charity to apply charity property, or waive the charity's entitlement to property, where the trustees would otherwise have no power to take that action but 'in all the circumstances regard themselves as being under a moral obligation to take it'. The exercise of the power is subject to the supervision of the Attorney General and must be exercised in accordance with any directions he may give. The Commission may decide that a case should be referred to the Attorney General for decision. If the Commission refuses to authorise a proposed ex gratia payment, there is a right to resubmit the application to the Attorney General under s 106(6).

9.182 Guidance is available from the Commission[96] on how to make an application to it for authorisation for an ex gratia payment. The application can be made online.

9.183 The Commission accepts that where a payment is small, it may not be cost-effective to apply for authorisation. At the time of writing its operational guidance states that 'where the amount of money involved is relatively small, say, £1,000 or less, the trustees may feel it would not be administratively sensible to apply for authority to make the payment' and confirms that the Commission is unlikely to challenge the payment in these circumstances.[97]

9.184 Following a recommendation from Lord Hodgson in his 2012 review of charity law[98] the Law Commission has considered whether the rules surrounding the making of ex gratia payments should be relaxed. In its 2015 consultation on charity law the Law Commission:[99]

- provisionally proposed that trustees should have a statutory power to make small ex gratia payments without authority from the Charity Commission, Attorney General or the court. A figure of £1,000 or £5,000 was mentioned in the consultation, with power for the Minister to vary it by secondary legislation;
- asked for views on whether a decision to make an ex gratia payment should be capable of being delegated to a member of staff in the charity (under the current rules the decision must be made by the board of trustees itself);

---

95 [1969] 3 WLR 273.
96 For example: 'Ex gratia payments by charities (CC7)'.
97 Charity Commission operational guidance OG 539 'Ex gratia payments by charities', para B4.3.
98 *Trusted and Independent*, Appendix A (i) para 5.
99 Chapter 11, Technical Issues in Charity Law, A Consultation Paper, Law Commission, March 2015.

- provisionally proposed that the Charity Commission, Attorney General and court should be able to authorise ex gratia payments by statutory charities (which is not the case at present).[100]

Formal advice

9.185 There may be circumstances where charity trustees do have power to carry out a particular course of action, but they are not completely certain that what is proposed is legally beyond challenge. For instance, they may be considering making a particular loan, which may be within their investment powers, but have concerns that the Commission might argue that the loan is not necessarily in the best interests of the charity. Section 110 of the 2011 Act can afford comfort to the trustees, as it allows the trustees to apply in writing to the Commission for formal legal advice. A trustee acting in accordance with advice given by the Commission under s 110 is taken to have acted in accordance with the trusts of the charity, unless he or she knew or had reasonable cause to suspect that the Commission was ignorant of material facts, or if a decision of the court or the Tribunal on the matter had been given or was pending. A trustee who acts in accordance with advice given under s 110 is therefore generally protected from a breach of trust claim.

9.186 It is advisable, when seeking advice from the Commission, to refer specifically to s 110 to make it clear that the request is for formal advice, and therefore guarantee protection for the trustees. More general advice, perhaps given over the telephone, will not protect the trustees in the same way.

9.187 Trustees should be aware that they are under no obligation to follow advice given under s 110. There were calls for the 2006 Act to be used as an opportunity for this to be clarified, but these were not taken up. However, as a matter of practice, trustees who do not take account of s 110 advice may subsequently find it more difficult to argue that they have been acting properly.

9.188 The Commission is under no obligation to provide advice under s 110 and in practice may well decline to do so if the matter is contentious. If the Commission does refuse to give formal advice under s 110 on a particular matter, its decision cannot be appealed to the Tribunal (see **10.45**). The authors' experience is that in recent years the Commission has become increasingly reluctant to exercise its power under s 110.

General advice

9.189 Section 15(2) of the 2011 Act confers a more general power on the Commission to give such advice or guidance with respect to the administration of charities as it considers appropriate. This was introduced by the 2006 Act. Advice or guidance may relate to charities generally, any class of charities or any particular charity, and the Commission has flexibility as to how the advice and guidance is given. In practice, the Commission has been issuing general advice to charities through its publications and on its website for many years, even prior to implementation of the 2006 Act.

---

100 *Attorney General v Trustees of the British Museum* [2005] EWHC 1089 (Ch).

9.190 As mentioned at 9.10, the Commission has affirmed, in an agreed statement issued in the context of court proceedings, that it has no power to require trustees to fetter the future exercise of their fiduciary powers under its general power to give advice and guidance.

Power to determine membership

9.191 Under s 111 of the 2011 Act the Commission has power to determine the membership of a charity. This power was introduced by the 2006 Act, because so many charity disputes have their origins in conflicts about membership.

9.192 The power can be exercised if a charity makes an application to the Commission for a determination, or at any time after a s 46 inquiry has been instituted. The Commission can delegate this power to anyone it appoints and may, where relevant, allow the determination to be made by the person conducting the s 46 inquiry.

9.193 While charities should keep up-to-date and accurate records of their members (indeed, charitable companies and charitable incorporated organisations have a statutory obligation to maintain a register of members), this is frequently overlooked in practice. There can be real problems when a charity is not sure exactly who its members are, because the members are likely to have significant powers to make changes to the charity's constitution, and to appoint or remove trustees. This power was welcomed, as it promised to provide a practical way of dealing with difficulties of this kind. In practice, however, the authors' experience is that the Commission has been reluctant to exercise the power. For example, where there is another formal legal mechanism available to determine charity membership, such as under the Companies Act 2006 in the case of charitable companies limited by guarantee, charities have been encouraged to resort to that mechanism before approaching the Commission. In correspondence with the authors in February 2016, the Commission stated that the power had not been exercised at all during the past 3 years.

9.194 The Law Commission, prompted by a recommendation by Lord Hodgson in his 2012 review of charity law, has provisionally proposed that this power should be extended to allow the Commission to determine the identity of a charity's trustees, as well as its members.[101]

Power to relieve from breach of trust

9.195 There may be circumstances where trustees have, strictly speaking, committed a breach of trust, but have acted honestly and reasonably. Prior to the 2006 Act, a trustee wishing to be relieved of liability in those circumstances could make an application to the court, asking that they be relieved, on the basis that they should fairly be excused, under either the Trustee Act 1925 or what is now the Companies Act 2006. However, this was of small comfort to trustees in view of the prohibitive costs of court proceedings.

9.196 The Strategy Unit report which preceded the 2006 Act[102] recommended that charity trustees should be able to apply to the Commission as well as to the court for

---

[101] Chapter 15, Technical Issues In Charity Law, A Consultation Paper, Law Commission, March 2015.

[102] *Private Action, Public Benefit.*

relief from personal liability where they have acted honestly and reasonably, as a result of which what are now ss 191 and 192 of the 2011 Act were introduced.

9.197 Section 191 allows the Commission to grant relief from personal liability to a charity trustee, an auditor of a charity's accounts, or an independent examiner or other person appointed to examine or report on a charity's accounts, for a breach of trust or breach of duty committed in that capacity, where the Commission considers that they have acted honestly and reasonably and ought fairly to be excused for the breach. The relief will be granted by order, and can be in relation to the whole of the liability, or part of it. It only relates to potential breach of trust claims, such as claims which might be brought against trustees for failing to invest or manage charity funds properly, in breach of their duties under charity law. It does not apply to contractual claims brought by third parties, so will not provide comfort to the trustees of unincorporated charities who may be facing claims against their personal property from the charity's creditors.

9.198 This provision is potentially a source of comfort to charity trustees who may be concerned about the risk of personal liability involved in acting as trustee of a charity. In commending the provision to the House of Commons during the passage of the 2006 Act through Parliament, the Government Minister, Hilary Armstrong MP, said that it was 'intended to encourage more people to become or continue as trustees by giving them confidence that they will not be personally penalised for an honest mistake. The fear of having to pay out of one's own pocket to make good an honest mistake can be a real deterrent both to the taking on of a trusteeship and to innovation in the running of a charity'.[103]

9.199 However, the power is not exercised often. In correspondence with the authors in February 2016, the Commission stated that it had not been exercised at all during the past three years.

9.200 The Charity Commission does not consider that its power under s 191 allows it to relieve a trustee from liability to account for a profit made in breach of fiduciary duty, such as where a trustee has received an unauthorised benefit from a charity. The Law Commission has provisionally proposed that the Charity Commission should be given such a power.[104]

9.201 Under s 1157 of the Companies Act 2006 the court has power to grant relief to the officers and auditors of a company for breach of trust or duty. Section 192 of the 2011 Act extends the court's power to all who report on a charity's accounts, whether or not the charities are companies, and to the trustees of charitable incorporated organisations.

9.202 These provisions apply to acts or omissions by trustees and others taking place before, as well as after, the date they came into force.

Dormant bank accounts, documents and solicitor's bills

9.203 The 2011 Act includes several additional powers for the Commission to help charities. Sections 107–109 deal with dormant bank accounts: where charity funds have

---

103 HC Deb, vol 448, col 30 (26 June 2006).

104 See also 7.45-7.46. Chapter 10, Technical Issues in Charity Law, A Consultation Paper, Law Commission, March 2015.

lain dormant for at least five years, and the charity trustees cannot be traced, the Commission may direct that the funds be transferred to other charities. Sections 340 and 341 provide for the Commission to run a facility for the safe keeping of charity documents. Section 112 allows the Commission to refer a solicitor's bill to a charity for assessment by the court, if the Commission is of the view that it contains exorbitant charges.

DISQUALIFICATION OF TRUSTEES

9.204 Under the powers described at **9.108, 9.134** and **9.140**, the Commission can take positive action to remove trustees. The 2011 Act also includes a regime for the disqualification of trustees.

9.205 Sections 178 and 178A of the 2011 Act provide for the automatic disqualification of certain persons from acting as a trustee of a charity. The 2016 Act has introduced a new power for the Commission to actively disqualify trustees.

Automatic disqualification of trustees

9.206 Prior to the 2016 Act, a person was automatically disqualified from acting as a trustee of a charity if they had been convicted of an offence involving dishonesty or deception, and in a number of other situations, including if they were an undischarged bankrupt. The 2016 Act has significantly extended the circumstances in which a person is automatically disqualified from acting as a trustee. However, at the time of writing these changes are not in force: see **9.211**.

Offences

9.207 Under s 178 of the 2011 Act a person is automatically disqualified from acting as a trustee of a charity if:

(a) they have been convicted of any of the offences specified in s 178A; or

(b) they have been convicted of another offence involving dishonesty or deception.

These offences are described as Case A offences. At the time of writing s 178A, which is introduced by s 9 of the 2016 Act, is not in force and it is not expected to come into force until at least April 2017: see **9.211**.[105]

9.208 The offences specified in s 178A are:

- an offence to which Part 4 of the Counter-Terrorism Act 2008 applies (various terrorism offences);
- an offence under ss 13 or 19 of the Terrorism Act 2000 (certain support for proscribed organisations and non-disclosure of information);
- a money laundering offence within the meaning of s 415 of the Proceeds of Crime Act 2002;

---

105 See also *Charities (Protection and Social Investment) Act 2016: Implementation plan*, issued by the Office for Civil Society and Innovation and first published in May 2016.

- various bribery offences under the Bribery Act 2010;
- an offence under s 77 of the 2011 Act, which makes it an offence to contravene various orders made under s 76(3) (see **9.93**); and
- an offence of misconduct in public office, perjury or perverting the course of justice.

Offences which have been superseded by any of these offences are also covered, as are convictions for various ancillary offences such as attempting or inciting the main offences. There is power for the Minister for the Cabinet Office to add or remove offences to or from the list by regulations, which must be approved in Parliament and must be consulted on if they add an offence.

9.209 Importantly, convictions which have been spent under the Rehabilitation of Offenders Act 1974 are not counted. Under the 1974 Act, after a certain period of time convictions may become spent. The period of time varies according to the sentence, and some offences are never spent. Note that the exclusion of spent offences applies only to Case A offences: not to the other circumstances triggering disqualification listed at **9.210**, apart from Case H.[106]

Other circumstances

9.210 A person is also disqualified under s 178 in the following circumstances (note that Cases H to K were introduced by s 9 of the 2016 Act and are not in force at the time of writing):

Case B

(a) he or she has been made bankrupt or sequestration of his or her estate has been awarded and in either case he or she has not been discharged, or he or she is the subject of a bankruptcy restrictions order or an interim order, unless (in the case of charitable companies and CIOs) leave has been granted for him or her to act under s 11 of the Company Directors Disqualification Act 1986;

Case C

(b) he or she has made a composition or arrangement with, or granted a trust deed for, his or her creditors and has not been discharged in respect of it;

Case D

(c) he or she has been removed as trustee, charity trustee, officer, agent or employee of a charity by order of the Commission (under s 79(4) of the 2011 Act (see **9.108-9.115**) or under various now repealed provisions of the Charities Act 1960 or the 1993 Act) or by the High Court, on the ground of any misconduct or mismanagement in the administration of the charity for which he or she was responsible or which he or she knew of and failed to take any reasonable step to

[106] Section 179 of the 2011 Act.

oppose, or which his or her conduct contributed to or facilitated (under s 182 of the 2011 Act the Commission must keep a register, open to the public, of those removed in this way).[107]

This ground is amended by s 9(4) of the 2016 Act: at the time of writing the change is not yet in force. Prior to the change, Case D only applies to a person who has been removed as a trustee or charity trustee;[108]

Case E

(d) he or she has been removed from being concerned in the management or control of any body by the Court of Session in Scotland under various Scottish legislation relating to charities;

Case F

(e) he or she is subject to a disqualification order or disqualification undertaking under the Company Directors Disqualification Act 1986, specified company legislation in Northern Ireland or an order under s 429(2) of the Insolvency Act 1986 (which deals with failure to pay under a county court administration order), unless in certain situations he or she has obtained leave to act (as set out in s 180(2));

Case G

(f) he or she is subject to a moratorium period under a debt relief order or a debt relief restrictions order or interim order under various provisions of the Insolvency Act 1986, unless (in the case of charitable companies and CIOs) leave has been granted for him or her to act under s 11 of the Company Directors Disqualification Act 1986;

Once s 9 of the 2016 Act is brought into force:[109]

Case H

(g) he or she has been found to be in contempt of court for making or causing a false disclosure statement or a false statement in a document verified by a statement of truth, or causing one to be made (although not where the finding of contempt would have been spent under the Rehabilitation of Offenders Act 1974 had it been a conviction for which he or she was dealt with in the same way);

Case I

(h) he or she has been found guilty of disobedience to an order or direction of the Commission on an application to the High Court under s 336(1) of the 2011 Act (see 9.235);

---

107 At the time of writing, the register of removed trustees can be searched via the Commission's website.

108 In addition, s 9(4)(b) of the 2016 Act, which came into force in July 2016, changed a reference to a person being privy to misconduct or mismanagement, to a reference to a person knowing of it and failing to take any reasonable step to oppose it (this change was recommended by the Joint Committee scrutinising the draft Protection of Charities Act, which felt that the new language was clearer: see also 9.109).

109 At the time of writing, s 9 is not expected to come into force until at least April 2017.

Case J

(i) he or she is a designated person under various terrorist asset-freezing regulations; or

Case K

(j) he or she is on the sex offenders register maintained under Part 2 of the Sexual Offences Act 2003. This will apply even where the offence itself is spent under the Rehabilitation of Offenders Act 1974 (see **9.209**).

9.211 During the Parliamentary debates on the 2016 Act, concerns were raised about the impact which the changes to the automatic disqualification provisions would have on ex-offenders. The Government Minister, Rob Wilson MP, committed to producing a report on Government's assessment of the impact of the changes, before they were brought into force. He also committed not to bring the changes into force for 12 months following enactment. Mr Wilson said:

> 'I want to ensure that the disqualification powers in the Bill protect charities from individuals who present a known risk, while at the same time providing for the rehabilitation of offenders and a way back into charity trusteeship or senior management on a case-by-case basis. That strikes me as both fair and proportionate.'[110]

9.212 The disqualification from acting as a trustee applies to all charities, including exempt charities and other unregistered charities. It applies both to the office of managing trustee and to the office of holding trustee.

9.213 Under changes introduced in s 9(6) of the 2016 Act, a person disqualified under s 178 in relation to a charity is also disqualified from holding an office or employment in the charity with senior management functions (although they may be permitted to act if a waiver is in place: see **9.214–9.218**). Section 178(4) includes a definition of senior management function. At the time of writing, these changes are not yet in force.

Waiver

9.214 Disqualification is automatic, but under s 181 of the 2011 Act a person who has been disqualified may apply to the Commission for the disqualification to be waived. The waiver may authorise the person to act as trustee of a particular charity or of a particular class of charities. In relation to a charitable company or CIO, the Commission may not waive the disqualification of a person who is disqualified under various provisions of the Company Directors Disqualification Act 1986 (listed in s 181(5) and (6)) and who has not obtained leave under that Act to act as director of any company or trustee of any CIO.

9.215 Once the provisions of the 2016 Act preventing a trustee disqualified under s 178 from serving in a senior management position in a charity come into force (see **9.213**), it will be possible for a waiver to be limited so that it does not allow the person concerned to serve as a trustee, but does allow them to hold some office or employment with senior management functions in a charity.[111]

---

[110] 26 Jan 2016: column 210 House of Commons.

[111] Section 181(2A), inserted by s 9 of the 2016 Act, which is not in force at the time of writing.

9.216 Section 181(3), which was introduced by the 2006 Act and is amended by the 2016 Act, confers a presumption in favour of granting an application for a waiver under s 181 in certain circumstances. The Commission must grant the application if the disqualification was under the grounds set out in Case D, E or I (see **9.210**)[112] and if five years have passed since he or she was originally disqualified, unless the Commission is satisfied that by reason of any special circumstances the application should be refused. This provision was introduced in a bid to limit the scope for trustees to be subject to a lifetime bar from acting, in line with the ability of bankrupts, in many cases, to act as company directors once they have been discharged from bankruptcy, which will usually be after 12 months.

9.217 At the time of writing, the waiver mechanism is infrequently used. Between 2008 and 2014 the Commission received six waiver applications, all of which were granted.[113]

9.218 Operational guidance available on the Commission's website contains information about waiver, and the circumstances which the Commission will take into account in considering an application for waiver.[114]

Charity Commission power to disqualify trustees

9.219 Prior to the 2016 Act, there was no power for the Commission to disqualify someone from acting as a charity trustee. If the Commission removes a trustee from office under its powers in s 79 of the 2011 Act they are automatically disqualified from being a trustee,[115] but the s 79 power can only be exercised in limited circumstances. In the 2013 Cabinet Office consultation on extending the Commission's regulatory powers, it was reported that there were loopholes in the existing regime that were being exploited. The Cabinet Office believed that these should be addressed by introducing a new power for the Commission to disqualify trustees. The result is s 10 of the 2016 Act, which introduces ss 181A to 181D into the 2011 Act.[116]

9.220 The Commission may make an order disqualifying a person from being a trustee. It may operate in relation to all charities, or just charities specified in the order. A person who has been disqualified in this way is also disqualified from holding a senior management position in the charity, unless the disqualification order provides otherwise.[117]

Preconditions for a disqualification order

9.221 Section 181A(6) and (7) set out the preconditions for an order. The Commission must be satisfied that:

- one or more of the conditions described at **9.222** has been met;
- the person concerned is unfit to be a charity trustee (either generally or in relation to the charities specified in the order); and

---

112 The reference to Case I is included by s 9 of the 2016 Act and is not expected to come into force before April 2017.

113 Evidence from Rob Wilson MP to the Public Bill Committee, Charities (Protection and Social Investment) Bill [Lords] Draft Protection of Charities Bill, Tuesday 5 January 2016, col 69.

114 OG 42 Waiver of disqualification from acting as a charity trustee.

115 See **9.111** and **9.210**.

116 These provisions will come into force on 1 October 2016.

117 Sections 181A(1) to 181A(5) of the 2011 Act.

- making the order is 'desirable in the public interest in order to protect public trust and confidence in charities generally or in the charities or classes of charity specified or described in the order'.

9.222 The Commission must be satisfied that at least one of the following conditions is met in relation to the person to be disqualified before an order can be contemplated:

Condition A

- They have received a caution for an offence within Case A of s 178(1) against a charity or involving the administration of a charity: see **9.207–9.209**;

Condition B

- They have been convicted of an offence outside the United Kingdom in respect of a charity or involving the administration of a charity, where the act giving rise to the offence would have been within Case A of s 178(1) if it had taken place in the United Kingdom (spent convictions are excluded);[118]

Condition C

- They have been found by HMRC not to be a fit and proper person to be manager of a charity, under the Finance Act 2010 (see **4.81**);

Conditions D and E

- They have been a trustee, officer, agent or employee of a charity, or an officer or employee of a corporate charity trustee, at a time when there was misconduct or mismanagement in the administration of the charity (see **9.83**) and the person was concerned was responsible for the misconduct or mismanagement, or they knew of it and failed to take any reasonable step to oppose it, or their conduct contributed to or facilitated it in some way; or

Condition F

- 'any other past or continuing conduct by the person, whether or not in relation to a charity, is damaging or likely to be damaging to public trust and confidence in charities generally', or in the charities mentioned in the order.

Conditions may be amended, added or removed by regulations made by the Minister for the Cabinet Office, which must be approved by Parliament and must be consulted on if they add a condition.

9.223 The scope of this new power has given rise to considerable concerns. The Charity Law Association's working party on the legislation which became the 2016 Act described Condition F as extraordinarily broad and far too subjective.[119] In response to a proposed amendment put forward by the shadow minister for the voluntary and

---

118 Section 181A(11) and (12) contains more detail on the interpretation of this condition.

119 Concerns of the Charity Law Association Working Party on the Charities (Protection and Social Investment) Bill, Second reading in the House of Commons.

community sector and civil society, Anna Turley MP, which would have meant that only 'relevant and serious' conduct could be taken account under Condition F, Government Minister Rob Wilson MP said:

> 'The Charity Commission already considers only conduct that is "relevant and serious". If it were to take account of other conduct, I would expect any resulting disqualification order to be thrown out by the charity tribunal on appeal.'[120]

9.224 At the time of writing the Commission has issued a consultation on its proposed approach to the exercise of the new power.

Notice and suspension

9.225 Under s 181C of the 2011 Act the Commission must give at least one month's notice of its intention to make a disqualification order to the person concerned (unless that person consents to the order), inviting representations. If the person is already a charity trustee the Commission must give notice to their co-trustees, and give public notice inviting representations (unless it is satisfied that it is not necessary to give public notice). Section 181C contains further details about the procedure for giving notice, and taking representations into account.

9.226 Having given notice of its proposal to make a disqualification order to the person concerned, the Commission has power to suspend them from office immediately under section 181B(4). Suspension can last for up to 12 months, and can be extended within that period for a further 12 months, provided the total period of suspension cannot last for more than two years. The order will come to an end before expiry if the Commission goes ahead with a disqualification order (once that order takes effect) or if the Commission decides not to proceed with disqualification after all. In the meantime, suspension orders must be reviewed. If the Commission considers it would be appropriate to discharge a suspension order following a review, it must do so. Sections 181B(9) and (10) deal with procedure while a suspension order is in place, including a specification that a person who has been suspended must not take up an appointment as a charity trustee without the Commission's written approval. Suspension orders can be appealed to the Charity Tribunal by the person who has been suspended. There is also a right of appeal from a decision to discharge, or not to discharge, a suspension order following a review: the appeal can be brought by the person concerned, the charity or other trustees or any other person who is or may be affected by the order.

Making the order and appeals

9.227 Where the Commission makes an order under s 181A in respect of a person it knows or believes to be a charity trustee, as well as serving the order on the person concerned it must also send a copy of the order and a statement of the Commission's reasons for making it to the charity (if it is a corporate charity) or otherwise to all the other trustees. Disqualification orders, once made, can be appealed to the Charity Tribunal by the person to be disqualified. Appeals to the Tribunal must, at the time of writing, be brought within 42 days (see **10.91**). The disqualification order does not take effect until this time period has expired or, if the person concerned decides to appeal,

120 26 Jan 2016: Column 211 House of Commons.

until a decision has been made about the appeal, or the appeal has been withdrawn.[121] If a person has already been suspended under s 181B(4), and the suspension has not expired or been discharged, it seems that the suspension will continue until the disqualification order takes effect.

Duration

9.228 The disqualification order must specify how long disqualification will last, which cannot be longer than 15 years. The period of the order must be 'proportionate', having regard to when convictions become spent, and to the circumstances in which the Commission might grant a waiver in the case of automatic disqualification (see **9.214–9.218**).[122] The consultation paper published by the Commission on its proposed approach to the new power (see **9.224**) sets out the factors the Commission will take into account when deciding on the period of disqualification and it is likely that the Commission's final guidance will do the same.

Variation and discharge

9.229 A person who has been disqualified under s 181A may apply to the Commission for the order to be varied or discharged.[123] A decision not to vary or discharge an order can be appealed to the Charity Tribunal by the person concerned.

Register

9.230 The Commission must keep a register, which must be open to public inspection, of all those disqualified by a s 181A order.[124]

Implications of disqualification

9.231 Under s 183 of the 2011 Act it is an offence, punishable by a term of imprisonment or a fine or both, to act as a trustee (or, under changes introduced by s 9(14) of the 2016 Act, which are not yet in force, to hold a senior management positon in a charity: see **9.213** and **9.220**) while disqualified, except, where the charity is a company or CIO, in the case of the grounds mentioned at Case B, F or G in s 178. Under s 345 of the 2011 Act the proceedings may only be instituted with the consent of the Director of Public Prosecutions.

9.232 Under s 184 of the 2011 Act the Commission may order an individual who has acted as a trustee or senior manager in a charity[125] while disqualified to repay to the charity the whole or part of any sums received by way of remuneration, or expenses, or the value of any benefit received in kind, while so acting.

9.233 Section 184A, which is introduced into the 2011 Act by s 12 of the 2016 Act, makes it a criminal offence for a person who is disqualified as a trustee to have general control or management of a corporate trustee of a charity and take part in decisions

121 Section 181B(3) of the 2011 Act.
122 Sections 181B(1) and (2) of the 2011 Act.
123 Section 181D of the 2011 Act.
124 Section 182 of the 2011 Act, as amended by s 11(5) of the 2016 Act, which is not fully in force at the time of writing.
125 The reference to a senior manager is introduced by s 9 of the 2016 Act: at the time of writing this change is not yet in force: see **9.207**.

relating to the charity's administration. The sanctions set out in s 184 of the 2011 Act (see **9.232**) will also apply to them. At the time of writing, this change is expected to be implemented in April 2017.

HOW THE COMMISSION EXERCISES ITS POWERS

9.234 The Commission can exercise its various powers in a number of ways, including by making a decision, a direction, an order or a scheme.

9.235 Sections 336–339 of the 2011 Act deal with orders and directions of the Commission. Under s 338, directions must be in writing. Orders and directions can include such incidental or supplementary provisions as the Commission thinks expedient for carrying into effect the objects of the order or direction (s 337(1) and 338(2)). Section 339 deals with the service of orders and directions. Under s 336, failure to comply with some orders listed in that section, including orders under ss 52, 84, 84A, 84B and 85,[126] and a Commission order requiring a default under the 2011 Act to be made good, and certain directions, may be treated as contempt of court, if the Commission makes the appropriate application to the High Court.

9.236 Under s 335 of the 2011 Act, if anyone fails to comply with a requirement imposed by or under the 2011 Act, the Commission can issue an order giving them directions designed to remedy the situation (subject to some exceptions set out in s 335(2)). As mentioned at **9.235**, failure to comply with the order may be dealt with as contempt of court.

126 See **9.18-9.21**, **9.118-9.132** and **9.146-9.152** respectively.

CHAPTER 10

CHALLENGING THE CHARITY COMMISSION

INTRODUCTION

10.1 The Commission's wide role and its extensive powers mean that charities can be drastically affected by its decisions. A decision not to register an organisation as a charity, a delay in responding to a charity's queries, or a decision to institute a statutory inquiry, for example, will all affect the organisation and its ability to help its beneficiaries. It is therefore crucial that charities should be able to question how the Commission acts, and challenge how they have been treated.

10.2 Challenges to the Commission fall into two categories: complaints about the Commission's standards of conduct and service, and challenges to the Commission's formal legal decisions.

10.3 Complaints about standards of conduct and service, such as a delay in responding to correspondence, or poor customer service generally, known as maladministration, can be dealt with internally by the Commission and by the Parliamentary and Health Service Ombudsman.

10.4 Challenges to formal legal decisions, such as a decision to register a charity, or to remove an organisation from the register, may be made to the Commission itself and, in many cases, to the Charity Tribunal. The Charity Tribunal was introduced by the 2006 Act: previously the Commission's formal legal decisions could only be challenged via an appeal to the High Court. There may also be scope, in some cases, to challenge the Commission via judicial review proceedings. A detailed discussion of judicial review is outside the scope of this book.

10.5 The process of challenging the Commission is broadly summarised in the flow chart below, and dealt with in more detail in the rest of this chapter.

COMPLAINTS ABOUT MALADMINISTRATION

Internal procedures

10.6 It may be possible to resolve dissatisfaction about the Commission's services through further correspondence with the Commission. If a complainant is still not satisfied, while there is no statutory requirement for the Commission to deal with complaints internally, in practice it has for some time operated an internal complaint and review system.

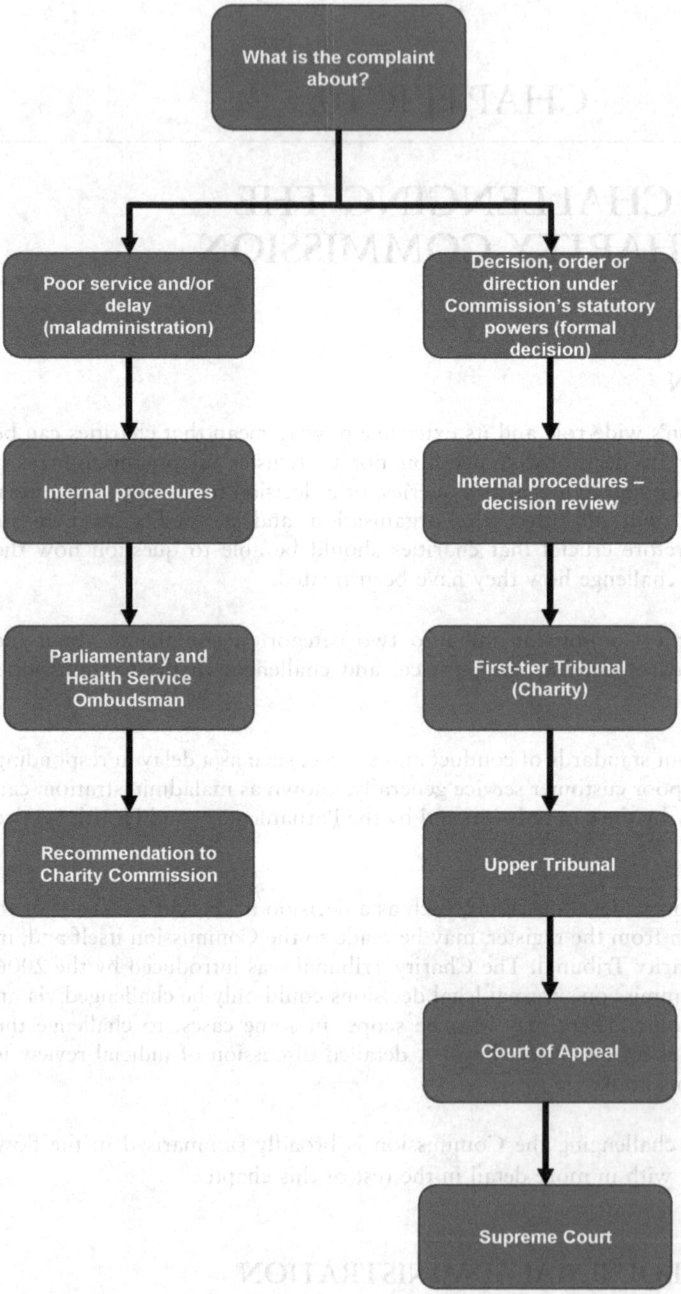

10.7 Where the Commission receives a complaint about a service which it has provided (rather than a decision which it has made), the procedure at the time of writing involves two possible stages:[1]

[1] At the time of writing guidance is available on the Commission's website at www.gov.uk/government/organisations/charity-commission/about/complaints-procedure#complain-about-a-service-weve-provided.

- The first stage focuses on the standard of service received by the complainant and/or issues with the Commission's course of action or the result of a matter that the Commission has been considering. This review will be carried out by an individual more senior than the original case worker, wherever possible.
- If the complainant is unhappy with the outcome of the first stage review a further review can be requested. The second review is carried out by a member of the Commission's Business Assurance Team, which concentrates on how the first review was conducted.

10.8 The result of the second review is final and the only recourse thereafter is a complaint to the Parliamentary and Health Service Ombudsman.

10.9 Previously, if complainants were unhappy with the response of the Commission they had the option to complain to an Independent Complaints Reviewer. However, this avenue was discontinued in the course of the 2012/13 financial year.[2]

The Parliamentary and Health Service Ombudsman

10.10 The only avenue available to those who wish to take a complaint about the Commission's conduct or service (ie not a formal legal decision) further is a complaint to the Parliamentary and Health Service Ombudsman or PHSO.

10.11 The PHSO has statutory power to review the administrative actions of the Commission under the Parliamentary Commissioner Act 1967: it deals with maladministration, such as delay, rather than legal decisions. Complaints to the PHSO must be made via Members of Parliament. At the time of writing, the PHSO expects a complainant to go through the Commission's internal complaints procedures before approaching the PHSO.

10.12 Complaints are reviewed against the Ombudsman's Principles of Good Administration, Good Complaint Handling and Remedy. The PHSO has power to recommend the award of compensation for financial loss or for inconvenience or worry. Although the PHSO has no formal power to enforce its recommendations, in practice they are generally followed. More detail can be found on the PHSO's website.[3]

10.13 During the Parliamentary debates on the legislation which became the 2006 Act, it was clear that the Parliamentary Ombudsman (the equivalent of the PHSO at the time) was used very infrequently to deal with complaints about the Commission. That still appears to be the case, in that in 2014-15 only five complaints about the Commission were assessed by the PHSO and no investigations were upheld.[4] However, in September 2015 the PHSO partly upheld a complaint about the Commission made by the Coal Industry Social Welfare Organisation, finding that the Commission's service was so poor that it amounted to maladministration. The PHSO recommended that the Commission pay in the region of £20,000 to the charity, partly by way of compensation for its costs and partly as a consolatory payment for the impact of the poor service.[5]

---

2 Charity Commission Annual Report 2012/13.

3 www.ombudsman.org.uk.

4 Complaints about UK government departments and agencies, and some UK public organisations 2014-15, Public and Health Service Ombudsman.

5 Report by the Parliamentary Ombudsman to Rt Hon K Barron of an investigation into a complaint made by Coal Industry Social Welfare Organisation, September 2015.

10.14 In 2015 Government consulted on proposals to create a new single public services ombudsman for England which will replace the PHSO. Following the consultation Government has announced that proposals will be developed further and set out in draft legislation.[6]

CHALLENGING FORMAL LEGAL DECISIONS

Internal procedures

10.15 Where possible, charities and their trustees will seek to make their case to the Commission in correspondence leading up to a formal legal decision. Once a formal decision has been made, it can be challenged via the Commission's internal decision review process. Details of the process are available on the Commission's website.[7]

10.16 A decision review may be requested for:

(a) all decisions that can be appealed to or reviewed by the Charity Tribunal: see **10.40-10.43**;
(b) decisions that require the Commission to exercise a formal legal power even if the Charity Tribunal does not have jurisdiction; and
(c) decisions that have a 'significant impact on a charity or its beneficiaries', are likely to be challenged in court or are of 'significant public interest'.

10.17 A decision review is a reconsideration of the Commission's decision. It will be carried out by a member of staff or a member of the Commission's Board: the number of people involved, and their seniority, will vary from case to case. The reviewer will not be the person who made the original decision and will usually be more senior. The outcome of the decision review is final and the only appeal thereafter is to the Charity Tribunal,[8] or to the courts if the decision is not one that can be considered by the Tribunal. The Commission may publish the decision, or a summary of it, on its website.

10.18 A decision review must be requested within three months of the date of notification of the original decision. The Commission will only undertake a decision review outside of the three-month time limit in exceptional circumstances.

Relationship between decision review and applications to the Charity Tribunal

10.19 The Commission's internal decision review process is completely separate from the right to ask the Charity Tribunal to consider a decision. This means that where the decision at issue is one which can also be appealed to or reviewed by the Tribunal, it is not necessary to seek, or wait for the outcome of, a decision review before making an application to the Charity Tribunal. It may also mean considering whether parallel applications to both the Tribunal and the Commission are appropriate. This is because, as explained at **10.21-10.25**, in many cases the time limit for making an application to

---

6 A Public Service Ombudsman, Government Response to Consultation, Cabinet Office, December 2015.

7 At the time of writing the relevant guidance is in Charity Commission leaflet: *Dissatisfied with one of the Charity Commission's decisions: how can we help you?* April 2013. See also the Commission's operational guidance OG 736-1 'Decision Reviews'.

8 But see the commentary at **10.19–10.26** about the Tribunal's time limits.

the Tribunal begins with the Commission's initial decision and *not* a subsequent decision made following a decision review process, so the deadline for applying to the Tribunal may have passed before the decision review is complete.

10.20 Opinions vary about the merits of involving the Tribunal straight away, without asking for an internal decision review at all. Decision review will generally be a cheaper process, and may allow an opportunity for discussions with the Commission which would not be possible in the Tribunal environment. However, the Tribunal's procedures impose obligations on the Commission to disclose documents and information: these do not exist in the internal review process. Alison McKenna, Principal Judge in the First-tier Tribunal (Charity) has expressed the view that a charity may get 'more bang for its buck' if an application is lodged with the Tribunal.[9] There has also been some evidence that in the majority of decision review cases, the Commission stands by its original decision. There may, therefore, be some merit in bypassing the decision review process entirely: each situation will need to be looked at separately. At the time of writing, applications to the Tribunal are free, and generally cost-neutral. Government is, however, proposing to introduce fees for applications to the Tribunal which may deter Tribunal applications.[10]

10.21 It is, in principle, possible to seek a decision review initially and only involve the Tribunal after the decision review process, if the applicant is not satisfied with the result. However, anyone wishing to do so must be aware of the Tribunal's time limits:

(a) First, the time limit for applications to the Tribunal is only 42 days from the issuing or publication of the decision which is the subject of the application.[11] This is shorter than the three-month time limit for requesting a decision review.

(b) Secondly, in many cases the Tribunal's 42-day time limit begins with the Commission's *original* decision, *not* the decision in any subsequent decision review. This means that if a decision review upholds the Commission's original decision, it may no longer be possible to appeal to the Tribunal, as the Tribunal's time limit may have expired, so simultaneous applications for decision review and to the Tribunal may be appropriate.

10.22 For example, in the case of *Muhoro v Charity Commission*[12] the Commission had made an order appointing a corporate trustee of a charity in reliance on ss 80 and 105 of the 2011 Act.[13] The former chair of the charity asked the Commission to review the decision and the Commission upheld the original order. He then sought to appeal the decision to the Tribunal. The First-tier Tribunal decided that because the application was made more than 42 days after the original order, the application was out of time. It ruled that the result of the decision review did not constitute a fresh decision for the purposes of the 42-day time limit. The Tribunal commented:

> 'The [Charity Commission] may offer an internal Decision Review, but this offer has no relationship to the statutory scheme for appealing to the Tribunal .... If a Decision Review offer is accepted, the time limit for applying to the Tribunal may have expired by the time it is completed.'

---

9 Should the Charity Tribunal be Reformed? Alison McKenna, the Charity Law and Practice Review, 2011–12.

10 See **10.90**.

11 See **10.91–10.99** for more detail.

12 CA/2015/0004.

13 See Chapter 9.

In this case, the Tribunal declined to extend the time limit, leaving the appellant without a remedy in the Tribunal (see **10.97**).

10.23 The question of whether a decision review triggers a fresh decision for the purposes of the 42-day time limit varies depending on the nature of the decision and is, regrettably, not straightforward.

10.24 In correspondence with the authors and with the Charity Law Association[14] the Commission has commented as follows:

- Where a decision not to register a charity under s 30 of the 2011 Act[15] is the subject of a decision review, the result of the decision review constitutes a fresh decision which can be appealed to the Tribunal.
- In the case of a decision to make a scheme for a charity under the 2011 Act,[16] the right to appeal to the Tribunal runs from the original decision to make the scheme and not from any subsequent decision review.
- Similarly, where the Commission decides to open a statutory inquiry, the 42-day time limit runs from notice or publication of the original decision to open the inquiry, and is not affected by any subsequent decision to uphold the inquiry following a decision review.[17]

10.25 In cases where the 42-day period runs from the original decision and a decision review does not trigger a fresh, appealable decision, if appellants wish to seek a decision review they would be well advised to also make a protective application to the Tribunal within the 42-day time limit, pending the outcome of the decision review. The Tribunal can be asked to stay the Tribunal proceedings: see **10.103**. However, if proposals to introduce charges for applications to the Tribunal are implemented (see **10.90**), a protective application will, in future, have costs implications.

10.26 Even where a decision review will generate a fresh decision for the purposes of the 42-day period, it may be prudent, when seeking the decision review, to ask the Commission to confirm (within that period) that it is prepared to undertake the review, and that it will be the outcome of the decision review which would be subject to appeal to the Tribunal, rather than the original decision. If the Commission does not provide this reassurance (and possibly in any event) it may be worth considering a protective application to the Tribunal.

The Charity Tribunal

Introduction

10.27 Prior to implementation of the parts of the 2006 Act establishing the Charity Tribunal, those wishing to challenge formal actions taken under the Commission's statutory powers had no avenue of appeal beyond the internal review process, except for the High Court. As court proceedings can be expensive this route was rarely chosen by

14 As reported in Practical Law legal update, Charity Commission provides guidance on giving notice to appeal its decisions, August 2012.
15 See Chapter 4.
16 See Chapters 9 and 17.
17 See also the Commission's guidance *Dissatisfied with one of the Charity Commission's decisions: how can we help you?*

charities. Not only did charities have no cost-effective means of challenging the Commission in such circumstances, which was a particular concern in the light of the Commission's increasing strength as a regulator, but important charity law issues were rarely dealt with by the courts, because it was too expensive to bring cases before a judge.

10.28 The Strategy Unit's 2002 review of charity law, which preceded the 2006 Act, recommended the establishment of a new independent tribunal to enable trustees to challenge the Commission's decisions at a reasonable cost.[18] This resulted in the introduction of a framework under the 2006 Act for the establishment of a new Charity Tribunal.

10.29 The Charity Tribunal became operational in 2008, but was subsequently abolished in 2009 under the Tribunals, Courts and Enforcement Act 2007 which created a unified structure for tribunals in the United Kingdom. Under this legislation, the jurisdiction of the Charity Tribunal was transferred to the General Regulatory Chamber of the First-tier Tribunal and the Tax and Chancery Chamber of the Upper Tribunal.

10.30 The term 'Charity Tribunal' is therefore, strictly speaking, redundant. However, in this book we use 'Charity Tribunal' or 'Tribunal' to refer to the combined jurisdiction of the First-tier and Upper Tribunals in relation to charities.

10.31 The Tribunal has several functions. First, it deals with applications relating to decisions by the Commission to exercise, or not to exercise, a statutory power in relation to a charity. These decisions may be challenged by way of an application for an appeal or a review, depending on the nature of the decision. Secondly, the Tribunal can hear references on matters of charity law by the Attorney General and the Commission: see 10.78-10.82. Finally, the Upper Tribunal can hear applications for judicial review: see 10.38.

The First-tier and Upper Tribunals

10.32 The First-tier and Upper Tribunals are divided into 'Chambers' which share common procedural rules, subject matter and an administrative system.

10.33 In the First-tier Tribunal the charity jurisdiction falls within the General Regulatory Chamber, which is presided over by a president. Cases are heard by one, two, or three members, as determined by the Chamber President, with each member being either a judge or another member who has substantial experience in a charity or not-for-profit organisation.[19] The judges and members of the First-tier Tribunal are appointed by the Senior President of Tribunals.[20] All appointments are made on the recommendation of the Judicial Appointments Commission and are completely independent of the Commission. There is no time limit on how long judges and members of the Tribunal can serve, but they must retire on reaching the age of 70.[21]

10.34 In the Upper Tribunal, charity cases are heard in the Tax and Chancery Chamber.

---

18 *Private Action, Public Benefit, A Review of Charities and the Wider Not-For-Profit Sector* (Strategy Unit, Cabinet Office, September 2002).

19 Practice Statement Composition of Tribunals in relation to matters that fall to be decided by the General Regulatory Chamber on or after 6 March 2015.

20 Schedule 2, Tribunals, Courts and Enforcement Act 2007, as amended by the Crime and Courts Act 2013.

21 Section 26 Judicial Pensions and Retirement Act 1993.

10.35 First-tier Tribunal decisions turn on their own facts and have no precedent value.

10.36 The Upper Tribunal was established as a Superior Court of Record under s 3(5) of the Tribunals, Courts and Enforcement Act 2007. Decisions of the Upper Tribunal have the same authority as those of the High Court. Upper Tribunal decisions create legal precedent, so they are binding on the First-tier Tribunal and on the executive.[22]

10.37 Challenges to the Commission's decisions are generally dealt with by the First-tier Tribunal. However, the Upper Tribunal can also hear 'fast-tracked' cases at first instance.[23] The Upper Tribunal also hears appeals from decisions of the First-tier Tribunal: see **10.110**.

10.38 Applications for judicial review of Commission decisions may be transferred from the Administrative Court to the Upper Tribunal (Tax and Chancery Chamber).[24] This means that where there is a judicial review running alongside an appeal, the two cases can be heard together in the Upper Tribunal.

10.39 The Tribunal case involving the Independent Schools Council provides an example of the Upper Tribunal hearing both a fast-tracked case and an application for judicial review. The Independent Schools Council sought judicial review of the Commission's guidance on public benefit in the Administrative Court: the case was transferred to the Upper Tribunal. The Attorney General made a reference to the First-tier Tribunal seeking a determination on a series of questions about the operation of charity law in relation to independent schools: the reference was transferred to the Upper Tribunal. Both the judicial review application and the reference were case managed together by the Upper Tribunal and were dealt with in a single hearing and judgment.[25]

The Tribunal's jurisdiction

10.40 The Tribunal's main function is to allow challenges to decisions, directions and orders made by the Commission using its statutory powers.

10.41 This means that a potential applicant must establish:

- Is the matter which they wish to challenge a decision, direction or order made by the Commission under its statutory powers?
- If so, is it capable of challenge under the 2011 Act?

Schedule 6 to the 2011 Act includes a detailed Table which sets out in column 1 which decisions, directions or orders are subject to appeal or review, by reference to the section of the 2011 Act containing the power which the Commission has exercised, or failed to exercise.[26] Column 2 of the Table includes details of who, in each case, may bring proceedings and column 3 sets out what action the Tribunal can take.

---

22 *Secretary of State for Justice v RB* [2010] UKUT 454 (AAC).
23 Tribunal Procedure (First-tier Tribunal) (General Regulatory Chamber) Rules 2009, SI 2009/1976, r 19.
24 Section 31A of the Senior Courts Act 1981.
25 *Independent Schools Council v Charity Commission and NCVO* [2011] UKUT 421 (TCC). See Chapter 3 for more information about this case.
26 Sections 319(1) and 321 of the 2011 Act.

10.42 Examples of decisions, directions or orders which can be brought before the Tribunal include:

- a decision to register, or not to register, an organisation as a charity;[27]
- a decision to remove, or not to remove, a charity from the register;
- a direction that a charity must change its name;
- a decision to institute an inquiry under s 46 of the 2011 Act;[28]
- an order appointing an interim manager or removing a trustee, following institution of an inquiry under s 46;[29] and
- a decision to give or withhold consent to proposed regulated alterations of a charitable company's Articles of Association under s 198 of the 2011 Act.[30]

10.43 Rights to appeal to the Tribunal may exist independently of Sch 6.[31]

Gaps in the Tribunal's jurisdiction

10.44 While a great number of the Commission's decisions may be challenged before the Tribunal, there are significant gaps in its jurisdiction.

Powers outside the scope of Schedule 6

10.45 Some statutory powers fall outside the scope of the Table in Sch 6 altogether. For instance, the Commission's new power to give official warnings to charities under s 75A of the 2011 Act cannot be appealed to the Tribunal, despite calls from commentators that it should be possible to appeal this power (see **9.44**). Similarly, the Commission's power to give formal advice to charities under s 110 of the 2011 Act is not mentioned in the Table. This means that if the Commission gives advice which a charity does not like, or declines a charity's request to give formal advice, the charity cannot bring the matter before the Tribunal.

Limited scope to challenge

10.46 In other cases, while a statutory power may be mentioned in Sch 6, it is only the Commission's decision to exercise that power which can be challenged, and a decision *not* to exercise the power cannot. Thus, in the case of *Iain Stowe v Charity Commission*,[32] Mr Stowe complained to the Tribunal about the Commission's failure to remove the trustees of a charity. While an active decision to remove a trustee under s 79 of the 2011 Act can be challenged in the Tribunal,[33] the First-tier Tribunal noted that a

---

27 See, for example, *Full Fact v Charity Commission* (CA/2011/0001); *Uturn UK CIC v Charity Commission* (CA/2011/0006); *Harrogate Fairtrade Shop v Charity Commission* (CA/2013/0009); *Human Dignity Trust v Charity Commission* (CA/2013/0013); *Wilfrid Vernor-Miles & ors v Charity Commission* (CA/2014/0022); *Cambridgeshire Target Shooting Association v Charity Commission* (CA/2015/0002).

28 See, for example, *Mountstar (PTC) Ltd v Charity Commission* (CA/2013/001 and 0003); *Regentford v Charity Commission* (CA/2013/0002) and [2014] UKUT 0364 (TCC).

29 See, for example, *Nagendram Seevaratnam v Charity Commission* (CA/2008/0001); *Mountstar (PTC) Ltd v Charity Commission* (CA/2013/001 and 0003).

30 See, for example, *Alan Bartley v Charity Commission* (CA/2012/0005); *Catholic Care (Diocese of Leeds) v Charity Commission* (CA/2008/0003 and 0004); (CA/2010/007); [2012] UKUT 395 (TCC).

31 Section 57 of the 2006 Act, for example, allows for Commission decisions on public charitable collections to be appealed to the First-tier Tribunal (this provision is not currently in force: see Chapter 18).

32 CA/2013/005.

33 See, for example, *Nagendram Seevaratnam v Charity Commission* (CA/2008/0001).

decision by the Commission *not* to remove a trustee from office does not fall within column 1 of Sch 6: the case therefore fell outside the Tribunal's remit and Mr Stowe's application was struck out.

10.47 In other cases it is only the Commission's refusal to exercise a power which falls within the Tribunal's remit. So in the case of *Morris and Mason v Charity Commission*[34] the Commission had agreed to make orders under what are now ss 105 and 117 of the 2011 Act allowing the charity to use part of its land as a car park. The appellants applied to the Tribunal to quash the orders. The First-tier Tribunal noted that while there is a right to apply for a review of a decision by the Commission not to make an order under ss 105 and 117, there is no right to challenge a positive decision to make an order. The application was struck out.

No exercise of a statutory power

10.48 The first years of the Tribunal's existence, in particular, saw a number of cases which were struck out on the grounds that the Tribunal did not have jurisdiction because the appellants were not challenging the Commission's use of a statutory power. For example, in the cases of *Moss v Charity Commission* and *Cumbers v Charity Commission*[35] the appellants had raised concerns about the governance of a charity and its trustees. The Commission had decided not to exercise its regulatory powers, and the appellants appealed to the Tribunal. The Tribunal said that it had 'been unable to identify a relevant decision order or direction of the [Commission] which falls within column one of the table. Although the [Commission] has attempted to resolve the Appellant's complaints about the charity, it has not exercised any relevant statutory power in doing so'.[36] The applications were struck out.

10.49 Similarly, in the case of *Holland and Piffero v Charity Commission*,[37] the appellants sought to argue that the Commission's failure to intervene in the affairs of a charity, at the appellants' request, constituted a refusal to make an order under what is now s 105 of the 2011 Act. Refusal to make a s 105 order falls within the scope of Sch 6. The relevant statutory power had not been specifically referred to in the correspondence with the Commission. The First-tier Tribunal said that this was not necessarily fatal, but noted that the intervention requested by the appellants was not achievable by such an order. There had not, therefore, been a refusal to make an order, which meant that the Tribunal did not have jurisdiction and the application was struck out.[38]

10.50 Where a matter is not within the scope of Sch 6, applicants will be faced with the prospect of seeking a remedy via judicial review. This is not an attractive option: judicial review is a far more time-consuming, expensive and cumbersome process than an appeal to the Tribunal.

---

34 CA/2010/0001.

35 CA/2010/004 and CA/2010/0005.

36 Paragraph 2.3 of the judgments.

37 CA/2010/0008.

38 See also *The Reverend Sophy Wahab v Charity Commission* (CA/2010/0009); *Basharat Hussain v Charity Commission* (CA/2010/0003); *Poller v Charity Commission* (CA/2010/0002) and *Lennox Patrick Ryan v Charity Commission* (CA/2015/0013) for further examples of cases where the claim has been struck out because the Commission had not made a decision, direction or order which could be challenged in the Tribunal.

10.51 In the cases of *The Reverend Sophy Wahab v Charity Commission*, *Cumbers v Charity Commission* and *Basharat Hussain v Charity Commission*[39] the appellants asked the First-tier Tribunal to transfer their applications to the Administrative Court, so they could proceed as judicial review applications. In the first two cases the requests were turned down but in the third the case was transferred to the Administrative Court.

10.52 The first draft of the legislation which became the 2006 Act[40] had imposed even more severe restrictions on the scope of the Commission actions which could be brought before the Tribunal. In response to concerns about this, the Joint Committee scrutinising the legislation recommended that the Government should aim to add all areas of the Commission's decision-making to the Tribunal's remit, unless there was a strong objection. It also recommended that the Tribunal should be able to hear appeals against all decisions, including 'non-decisions'.[41] As a result, the proposed remit of the Tribunal was expanded significantly, but is still limited. The Government Minister Lord Bassam stated during debates on the legislation which became the 2006 Act that 'the Government have given careful thought to the jurisdiction of the Tribunal and, in response to the Joint Committee's recommendation, have ensured that the Bill reflects as many as possible of the Commission's decisions to exercise, or not to exercise, its statutory powers'.[42]

10.53 However, as the cases mentioned above show, concerns about the narrow scope of the Tribunal's jurisdiction have been borne out in practice. Applicants have been confused and frustrated by the limits on what the Tribunal can do. In the case of *Morris and Mason v Charity Commission*,[43] for example, the First-tier Tribunal recorded that the appellants had 'expressed understandable frustration that the relevant provisions of the … Act do not provide them with a right of appeal to the Tribunal in these particular circumstances'.[44]

Reform?

10.54 Lord Hodgson addressed this issue in his 2012 review of charity law, commenting that the large number of cases struck out for being outside the Tribunal's jurisdiction 'raises the question of whether its jurisdiction is sufficiently well-defined to address the concerns people have about the Commission's work'. He noted that Sch 6 to the 2011 Act 'is seen by the vast majority of contributors to the Review as over-complicated and too narrowly drawn – several specialist charity lawyers complained of difficulty in understanding it'.[45]

10.55 However, Lord Hodgson was concerned that removing Sch 6 altogether and simply allowing the Tribunal to hear appeals against any action or decision of the Commission would open the flood gates to appeals and could undermine the Commission and have an impact on its resources. He recommended that Sch 6 should be abolished but that the right of appeal should be limited to any legal decision of the Commission: any other decision or action of the Commission should be subject to a right of review.[46]

---

39 CA/2010/0009, CA/2010/005 and CA/2010/0003 respectively.
40 Published in May 2004.
41 Report from the Joint Committee on the Draft Charities Bill, HL Paper 167-I HC 660-I, September 2004.
42 HL Deb, vol 669, col GC 333 (23 February 2005).
43 CA/2010/0001.
44 Paragraph 3.2 of the judgment.
45 *Trusted and Independent*, para 7.16.
46 *Trusted and Independent*, paras 7.18 and 7.19.

10.56 Government responded that it supported, in principle, the rationalisation of the appeal rights in Sch 6, provided it could be done in a way which did not expose the Commission to challenges where it decided not to intervene in a charity in accordance with its risk and proportionality framework, and did not create any significant new appeal rights that would add to the Tribunal's case-load. Government committed to work with the Commission, Ministry of Justice and HM Courts and Tribunals Service to explore options. Any proposal would be made through primary legislation and would be subject to a full public consultation.[47]

10.57 In the meantime, in evidence to the Joint Committee reviewing the draft Protection of Charities Bill in early 2015, the principal judge of the First-tier Tribunal (Charity) Alison McKenna made a number of practical observations on the current format of Sch 6. She commented that the average charity trustee does not generally know which section of the 2011 Act has been relied on by the Commission to make the decision which they seek to challenge, with the result that they do not know where to look for it in column 1 of the Table in Sch 6. She said that there could be merit in a system of decision-making by the Commission which allows potential appellants to understand more easily what rights of appeal they may have. She also highlighted the problem of establishing whether the Commission has made a decision, in the context of long-running correspondence: she would favour a system which allows the Commission to signal clearly that it has made a decision which engages rights of appeal.[48]

10.58 The Minister for the Cabinet Office does have power under s 324 of the 2011 Act to amend the Table in Sch 6 by order, subject to the approval of both Houses of Parliament.[49] This power has been exercised to include various decisions relating to the dissolution of charitable incorporated organisations, but to date it has not been used to add other statutory powers to the list.[50]

Who may bring proceedings?

10.59 Column 2 in the Table in Sch 6 to the 2011 Act specifies who can bring proceedings before the Tribunal in any particular case.[51] This generally includes the charity trustees, the charity itself (if it is a body corporate) and any other person who is or may be affected by the decision.

10.60 Other categories of claimant exist in particular circumstances. For example:

- a decision to institute a statutory inquiry under s 46 of the 2011 Act may be challenged by 'the persons who have control or management of the institution';[52]
- an order removing a trustee under s 79(4) of the 2011 Act may be challenged by the person who has been removed;[53]

---

47 Government Response, p 34.

48 House of Lords, House of Common, Joint Committee on the Draft Protection of Charities Bill 25 February 2015, HL Paper 108, HC 813, Appendix 5.

49 Section 349 of the 2011 Act.

50 Charitable Incorporated Organisations (Consequential Amendments) Order 2012, SI 2012/3014.

51 Section 319(2)(b) and 321(2)(b) of the 2011 Act.

52 The case of *Jennings v Charity Commission* (CA/2014/0017) was a challenge to a s 46 inquiry. The appellant argued that he was regarded as a de facto trustee of the charity by the Commission, but his application failed as the Tribunal ruled that he did not have control or management of the charity at the time the inquiry was opened.

53 As in the case of *Nagendram Seevaratman v Charity Commission and Attorney General* (CA/2008/0001).

- an order under s 84 of the 2011 Act directing a person to take specified action may be challenged by the person directed to take the action;[54]
- an order under s 52 of the 2011 Act requiring a person to supply information or a document may be challenged by the person who is the subject of the order;[55] and
- a creditor of a CIO may object to the Commission's decision to approve a transfer of the CIO's undertaking to another CIO under s 240(1) of the 2011 Act.

Persons affected

10.61 The ability of 'any other person who is or may be affected' by a decision or order to challenge the Commission in the Tribunal has given rise to a number of questions over the years, not least how this should be interpreted in any particular case. The issue has now been considered by the Upper Tribunal in the case of *Nicholson v Charity Commission*.[56]

10.62 In this case the Upper Tribunal decided that Mr Nicholson, who was seeking to challenge the Commission's decision not to remove three charities from the register, was not a person affected by the decision, so he did not have standing to challenge it. In coming to this conclusion, the Tribunal said that it was clear that the category of persons 'affected by' a decision in each case:

> 'is not prone to a definitive definition. It is fact sensitive and must be considered in each case in the light of all the relevant circumstances'.

The Tribunal analysed the wording of the legislation, commenting:

> 'It is necessary … to focus solely upon the particular decision and to determine whether in all the circumstances it has had an effect upon the particular person in question …. [I]n order to be affected by the decision, first the decision itself must relate to the person in some way. Secondly, the person's legal rights must have been impinged or affected by the decision and to be a person who "may" be affected, there must be an identifiable impact on the person's legal rights which is likely to occur …'

and

> 'In context … "affected by the decision" should be construed to connote circumstances in which the decision in question has a direct, or the potential for a direct, effect upon a person's legal rights.'

The Tribunal decided that the fact that the Commission has sent its decision to a person (as had happened in this case: the Commission's decision had been addressed to Mr Nicholson) does not of itself mean that they are 'affected by' the decision.[57] Mr Nicholson was 'merely an interested taxpayer who criticises the Commission'.

10.63 The *Nicholson* decision was based on an interpretation of the expression 'any other person who is or may be affected' in relation to a challenge to a decision not to

---

54 See, for example, *Mckay v Charity Commission* (CA/2013/0010).

55 For example, *JJ Goldstein & Co v Charity Commission* (CA/2013/0004); *J Kaur, G Kaur and E Giles v Charity Commission* (CA/2014/0008); *Atherton v Charity Commission* (CA/2014/0019) and *Shakespeare v Charity Commission* (CA/2014/0020).

56 [2016] UKUT 0198 (TCC).

57 In coming to this conclusion, the Upper Tribunal decided that an earlier contradictory decision of the First-tier Tribunal in the case of *Lasper v Charity Commission* was wrong: see 4.94.

remove a charity from the register. However, the Upper Tribunal's analysis will prove useful when assessing whether a person is 'affected by' other decisions of the Commission.

10.64 A case in the First-tier Tribunal involving the charity the Dove Trust[58] (which predates the Upper Tribunal decision in the *Nicholson* case) is an interesting example of the complexities of the question of who has standing in the Tribunal. Mr Colman, a former trustee of the charity the Dove Trust, sought to challenge the Commission's decisions, made under s 76(6) of the 2011 Act, not to review its orders under s 76(3) of the 2011 Act appointing an interim manager for the charity and freezing charity bank accounts. Mr Colman had been a trustee at the time the original orders were made, but by the time the Commission had issued final decisions not to discharge those orders under s 76(6), Mr Colman had resigned. While decisions under s 76(6) may be challenged by a trustee of the charity, Mr Colman was no longer a trustee by the time that these decisions were made. Mr Colman sought to argue that he had standing to make the challenge on the basis that he was a person affected by the orders, but the First-tier Tribunal did not agree, concluding that he had 'no interest in the ... Commission's decision greater than that of an ordinary member of the public'.[59] In the event, permission was granted for Mr Colman to be removed as the appellant and two of the other trustees were substituted in his place.[60]

10.65 Lord Hodgson was not concerned by the breadth of the term 'persons affected', and recommended that persons 'affected' by the Commission's action or inaction should have standing to appeal or seek a review.[61] It is not clear why the wider category of 'persons who may be affected', which currently also applies, was not included in his recommendation. Government agreed to consider his proposals, along with the proposals to widen the scope of the Tribunal's jurisdiction: see **10.55**.

10.66 Kenneth Dibble, head of legal services at the Commission, was reported as suggesting at a public meeting of the Commission in 2013 that those who are 'affected' by a decision should be replaced with those who are 'interested' in an attempt to weed out frivolous cases, for example, those where people use the First-tier Tribunal to further arguments that they have with the charity and not with the Commission itself. The principal judge of the First-tier Tribunal (Charity), Alison McKenna, noted in November 2013 that the questions raised by third party applications might be described as a somewhat neglected issue in the debate about reform of the Tribunal. She pointed out that applications from 'persons who are or may be affected' had formed a not inconsiderable proportion of the Tribunal's work so far. As well as giving rise to questions about who may or may not be a 'person affected' in a particular case, this issue also raises questions about case management, costs and remedies, and how to balance the rights and interests of the charity (which may have originally sought the decision made by the Commission) with those of the applicant who seeks to overturn it on appeal.[62] The narrow analysis in the Upper Tribunal's judgment in the 2016 *Nicholson* case may address these concerns.

---

58 *Colman v Charity Commission* (CA/2014/0001 and 0002).

59 CA/2014/0001 and CA/2014/002, para 18, ruling on preliminary issue dated 17 April 2014.

60 *Gunn and Naghshineh v Charity Commission* (CA/2014/0001 and 0002).

61 *Trusted and Independent*, para 7.19.

62 McKenna, 'Applications to the First-tier Tribunal (Charity) by "persons affected" by the Charity Commission's decision' (2013-14) 16 *The Charity Law & Practice Review* 147.

10.67 The Attorney General, acting as the protector of charity on behalf of the Crown, may bring a case in relation to any decision, direction or order listed in the Table.[63] This was a significant consideration in the *Nicholson* case: it was noted that the Attorney General is in a position to bring an appeal in the public interest. The Attorney General has a non-adversarial role, representing charity generally, rather than the parties to the dispute. (See also **10.115-10.118**.)

How can the Tribunal deal with an application?

10.68 Most of the decisions, directions and orders listed in Sch 6 may be challenged by means of an appeal. However, a number of decisions are subject to review rather than appeal.

10.69 Appeals involve substantive re-hearings. The Tribunal must consider afresh the original action by the Commission, and can take account of evidence which was not available to the Commission at the time.[64] Appeals are de novo proceedings so that the Tribunal effectively steps into the Commission's shoes and retakes the decision under appeal.

10.70 Appeals against orders to produce information or documents under s 52 of the 2011 Act (see **9.18**) are a special case: the Tribunal cannot consider the order generally, but only the narrow issue of whether the information or documents can properly be called for under s 52.[65]

10.71 A small number of matters are not subject to appeal, but to review. These include a decision to institute an inquiry under s 46 of the 2011 Act and decisions not to make orders under ss 105 (authorising dealings with charity property), 117 (consent to disposition of land) and 124 (consent to mortgage).[66] This means that the Tribunal will not reconsider the matter, but will review the Commission's decision-making process, applying the principles which are used on judicial review, namely whether the Commission acted lawfully within its powers, fairly and proportionately, and whether a body in the Commission's shoes, acting reasonably, could have come to the same decision. There are several examples of the Tribunal reviewing decisions to open a s 46 inquiry (see Chapter 9), including the decision of the Upper Tribunal in *Regentford v Charity Commission*. In that case the Upper Tribunal commented on the process:[67]

> 'We accept … that, when exercising its review jurisdiction, the FTT is not required in every case to test, in a formulaic manner, the Charity Commission's decision against the "classic" grounds for judicial review. We agree that the FTT's role is to consider whether the decision to open the inquiry was one that no reasonable decision maker could have made at the time it did so, and that this will include consideration of a range of fact-sensitive issues, depending on the facts in the case and the nature of the challenge made to the Charity Commission's decision.'

---

63 Sections 319(2)(a) and 321(2)(a) of the 2011 Act.

64 Section 319 of the 2011 Act.

65 Section 320 of the 2011 Act. See, for example, *Atherton v Charity Commission* (CA/2014/0019) and *Shakespeare v Charity Commission* (CA/2014/0020). However, see **10.99** for details of a case where a charity was granted permission to seek judicial review of an order made under s 52.

66 Sections 321 and 322 of the 2011 Act.

67 [2014] UKUT 0364 (TCC), para 37.

10.72 Alison McKenna, the principal judge of the First-tier Tribunal (Charity) has pointed out that the distinction between appeals and reviews is confusing for users of the Tribunal: she would favour an approach which makes this distinction clearer.[68]

10.73 Column 3 of the Table in Sch 6 to the 2011 Act specifies what action the Tribunal is able to take if it allows the application made to it. Alternatives include quashing the Commission's original action, remitting the matter back to the Commission (with or without a direction to determine the matter in a particular way), and substituting its own rulings.

10.74 For example, if the Tribunal allows an appeal by an organisation against a decision not to register it as a charity, the Tribunal can quash the original decision. It can also decide to remit the decision back to the Commission, either generally or for determination in accordance with a finding or direction from the Tribunal, or it may simply direct the Commission to add the organisation to the register.

10.75 In the case of applications for review, if the application is allowed, the Tribunal can take the action listed in the Table, which can involve quashing the original decision but will not, in most of these cases, include substituting its own decision.

10.76 As explained at **10.127–10.128**, although the Tribunal has power to make costs orders in certain cases, it has no power to award compensation.

10.77 Following a recommendation in Lord Hodgson's review of charity law,[69] in its 2015 consultation the Law Commission invited views on whether the Tribunal should have power to suspend the effects of a Commission decision pending the determination of a case. The Law Commission has also asked for views on whether decisions of the Commission should only take effect after a certain period of time, acknowledging that this would be complicated and controversial.[70]

References – general questions of law

10.78 The 2011 Act includes a power for the Commission itself (with the Attorney General's consent), and for the Attorney General, to refer questions of charity law to the Tribunal.[71] The Attorney General and Commission (if not already parties), and, if the Tribunal agrees, the charity trustees of any charity likely to be affected by the Tribunal's decision (and the charity itself if a corporate body) and any other person likely to be affected, may be a party to the proceedings. This provision was introduced into the legislation which became the 2006 Act in the House of Lords with the intention of ensuring that important questions may be resolved by the Tribunal without any particular charity needing to find the funds to bring a case.

10.79 Sections 327–330 of the 2011 Act contain procedural rules in relation to a reference, dealing with what action the Commission may take while a reference is in progress and subsequently, the suspension of time limits during a reference, and rights of appeal in respect of matters determined on references.

---

68 House of Lords, House of Common, Joint Committee on the Draft Protection of Charities Bill 25 February 2015, HL Paper 108, HC 813, Appendix 5.

69 *Trusted and Independent*, Appendix A, para 15.

70 Paragraphs 16.65-16.86, Technical Issues in Charity Law, A Consultation Paper, Law Commission, March 2015.

71 Sections 325 and 326 of the 2011 Act.

10.80 To date, the Attorney General has made two references to the Tribunal. The first concerned various hypothetical questions on the impact of charity law on independent schools and the second the effects of the 2006 Act on charities whose purpose is to relieve poverty.[72] Both were referred to the Upper Tribunal, which is consistent with idea that a reference should give clarity to the law, as decisions of the Upper Tribunal have precedent value.

10.81 It has been suggested that the Attorney General should give some indication of when he might exercise this power. For instance, the Attorney General could publish a policy statement describing in broad terms the situations in which he might exercise his power and providing charities with information about how to petition him.[73]

10.82 In his review of charity law, Lord Hodgson recommended that the Commission should be able to make references without the consent of the Attorney General. The Law Commission has asked for views on this proposal in its 2015 consultation. The Law Commission also considered the powers exercisable by the Tribunal when it determines a reference, expressing the provisional view that the Tribunal's ability to determine references is satisfactory, but inviting comments on whether the Tribunal should have power to award remedies in reference proceedings.[74] Lord Hodgson also said that there should be better guidance on the procedures for intervention in reference proceedings.

Procedure in the Charity Tribunal

10.83 Charity cases in the First-tier Tribunal are managed under the Tribunal Procedure (First-tier Tribunal) (General Regulatory Chamber) Rules 2009 (as amended) ('the 2009 Rules').[75] In the Upper Tribunal they are managed under the Tribunal Procedure (Upper Tribunal) Rules 2008.[76] The rules have been designed to enable generic case management across the jurisdictions in each of the Chambers which means that apart from a few bespoke provisions they are not specific to charities.

10.84 Tribunal rules are made by the Tribunals Procedure Committee (TPC), which was established under the Tribunals, Courts and Enforcement Act 2007. Rules made by the Tribunal Procedure Committee must be submitted to the Lord Chancellor who has the power to allow or disallow the rules that have been made by the TPC. The Lord Chancellor also has the power to require the TPC to make rules. The rules are laid before Parliament so that they are finalised as statutory instruments.

10.85 The Lord Chancellor also has power to make rules under s 316(2) of the 2011 Act: at the time of writing there are no rules made under this power in existence.

10.86 As mentioned at **10.83**, the 2009 Rules govern the practice and procedure to be followed in the First-tier Tribunal in the General Regulatory Chamber. Parts 1 and 2 cover issues such as the overriding objective (see **10.108**), the Tribunal's case

---

72 *Independent Schools Council v Charity Commission* [2011] UKUT 421 (TCC) and *Her Majesty's Attorney General v Charity Commission* [2012] UKUT 420 (TCC).

73 This was suggested by Alison McKenna, principal judge of the First-tier Tribunal (Charity), in her lecture 'Strike outs, Transfers and Elevations: Is the Charity Tribunal Fit for Purpose' delivered to the Charity Law and Policy Unit, Liverpool University Law School on 18 November 2010.

74 Paragraphs 16.87-16.102, Technical Issues in Charity Law, A Consultation Paper, Law Commission, March 2015.

75 SI 2009/1976.

76 SI 2008/2698.

management powers, the giving of directions, the power to strike out a party's case, the addition, substitution and removal of parties, the service of documents and rules about representatives, evidence, submissions, witnesses and costs. Part 3 contains provisions for the charity jurisdiction relating to starting proceedings and the procedure up to and including the making and notification of Tribunal decisions. Part 4 contains provisions about correcting, setting aside, reviewing and appealing Tribunal decisions.

Making an application

10.87 Under the 2009 Rules,[77] proceedings are initiated by filing a notice of appeal with the Tribunal. The notice of appeal, together with guidance notes, is available on the HM Courts and Tribunals Service website.[78]

10.88 It is not necessary for a party to exhaust the Commission's internal review process prior to making an application to the Tribunal. The merits of making an application to the Tribunal without first seeking a review by the Commission, or making simultaneous applications to the Commission and Tribunal, are considered at **10.19-10.26**.

10.89 Charities are not required to obtain the consent of the court or the Commission before appealing to the Tribunal, unlike in the case of 'charity proceedings' (see **9.165–9.167**). Nor is the Tribunal's consent required. In its 2015 consultation on charity law, the Law Commission asked for views on whether charities should be required to seek prior authorisation from the Charity Commission or the Tribunal before commencing proceedings in the Tribunal, but its own view was that such authorisation should not be required.[79]

10.90 At the time of writing, there is no fee for filing an application with the Tribunal. However, the Ministry of Justice has decided to introduce fees in the First-tier Tribunal (General Regulatory Chamber) and in the Upper Tribunal (Tax and Chancery) in relation to appeals from the First-tier Tribunal. The proposals were set out in a 2015 consultation paper, and despite considerable opposition (see **10.135**), in December 2015 Government announced that it intended to proceed with its proposals and would introduce fees by way of statutory instrument when Parliamentary time allows. At the time of writing the proposal is for an initial issue fee of £100 in the First-tier Tribunal, with a further £500 fee to bring the case to an oral hearing. There will be similar fees in the Upper Tribunal, including a fee of £100 to seek permission to appeal from decisions of the First-tier Tribunal, a fee of £100 to bring an appeal and a £2,000 hearing fee.[80]

Time limits

10.91 The notice of appeal must be received by the Tribunal no later than 42 days after the Commission's decision was (a) sent to the appellant or, (b) (if the appellant was not

---

77 Rule 26.

78 At the time of writing the link is http://hmctsformfinder.justice.gov.uk/HMCTS/FormFinder.do (choose 'Charity Tribunal' under 'Available Types').

79 Paragraphs 16.35-16.41, Technical Issues in Charity Law, A Consultation Paper, Law Commission, March 2015. The Law Commission did suggest that the Tribunal should be allowed to make *Beddoes* orders, which would allow charity trustees to seek comfort in respect of costs in Tribunal proceedings: see **10.131**.

80 *Court and Tribunal Fees, The Government response to consultation on enhanced fees for divorce proceedings, possession claims, and general applications in civil proceedings and Consultation on further fees proposals*, Ministry of Justice, August 2015 and *Court and Tribunal Fees, The Government response to consultation on further fees proposals*, Ministry of Justice, December 2015.

the subject of the decision) published, although the First-tier Tribunal has the power to extend the time allowed and to allow appeals made out of time to proceed, under its general case management powers.[81] A number of cases have dealt with exactly when the 42-day period begins, and extensions of time.

10.92 The case of *Stephen Hunt v Charity Commission*[82] involved a dispute about when the 42-day period starts. In that case, the Annuity Helpline had applied for registration as a CIO and the application had been turned down by the Commission under s 208 of the 2011 Act (see Chapter 14). The Commission's decision was emailed to Mr Hunt, who was the named contact for the application, and several days later it was published on the Commission's website. Mr Hunt appealed to the Tribunal. The Commission argued that the appeal was made out of time, because it was made more than 42 days after the decision was sent to Mr Hunt. The First-tier Tribunal disagreed, ruling that Annuity Helpline was the subject of the decision, not Mr Hunt. This meant that the 42-day period for Mr Hunt to appeal only started to run from the date the decision was published on the Commission's website, so Mr Hunt's application was in time. However, the Upper Tribunal overturned the decision of the First-tier Tribunal, deciding that as one of the applicants for registration of the CIO, Mr Hunt was in fact the subject of the decision, so his appeal was out of time. The Upper Tribunal also said that in this case the decision had been 'published' to Mr Hunt, for the purpose of the time limits, when the email informing him of the decision was sent and received.

10.93 In the case of *The Steadfast Trust v Charity Commission*[83], the Commission had emailed its decision to the appellant charity, but stated that the decision did not take effect until some weeks later. The charity did not actually receive the Commission's email for some time as a result of a change of an email address and delayed access to its emails. The First-tier Tribunal held that notwithstanding the delayed effect of the decision and late receipt of the email the 42-day period started to run on the date on which the Commission's email was sent, so the application to the Tribunal was out of time (but see **10.95**).

10.94 However, the First-tier Tribunal has been willing to relax the strict time limits. At the time of writing, in deciding whether to grant an extension of time the Tribunal will as a general rule consider (a) what the purpose of the time limit is, (b) how long the delay was, (c) whether there is a good explanation for the delay, (d) what consequences granting a time extension will have for the parties, and (e) what consequences refusing a time extension will have for the parties, under the principles in the Upper Tribunal decision in *Data Select Ltd v HMRC.*[84]

10.95 For example, in the *Steadfast Trust* case mentioned at **10.93** the application was allowed to proceed even though it was out of time. The Tribunal found that the period of delay was short (23 days) and there were good reasons for the overall delay.

10.96 Similarly, in the case of *Mckay*, the Tribunal gave leave for an appeal to proceed notwithstanding that it was filed 7 days after the time limit for bringing the appeal expired.[85] One of the factors taken into account by the Tribunal was the lay appellant's difficulty in understanding the time limits for bringing the appeal. The appellant had

---

81 Rules 26 and 5 of the 2009 Rules.
82 CA/2015/0008 and [2016] UKUT 210 (TCC).
83 CA/2015/0003.
84 [2012] UKUT 187 (TCC).
85 See *Ronald McKay v Charity Commission* (CA/2013/0010).

thought that because he had requested a review of the Commission's direction under the internal review process the 42-day period would start on the date on which he asked for the internal review rather than the date on which the direction was first sent to him.

10.97 However, there was a different result in the case of *Muhoro*, mentioned at 10.22. Here, in circumstances where the appeal to the Tribunal had not been lodged until after the result of an internal decision review by the Commission, the First-tier Tribunal decided not to allow an extension of the time limit. In that case the delay was around 90 days, the time limits had been explained by the Commission when it notified the appellant of its original decision and the appellant had had legal representation throughout. The First-tier Tribunal commented, in its judgment, that:

> 'The purpose of the time limit for initiating proceedings in charity cases is to allow charities a reasonably generous amount of time in which to decide whether to make an application to the Tribunal whilst balancing against that consideration the [Charity Commission]'s wish to carry out its statutory duties as swiftly as possible.'

10.98 The case of *Nicholson*[86] is a further example of the Tribunal refusing to extend the time limits. In that case, six applicants had appealed the Commission's decision not to remove three charities from the register. Two further applicants were later joined to the appeal and a further three applicants subsequently sought to join the appeal some two-and-a-half months out of time. The Tribunal refused permission to the three applicants to join the appeal because 'it would not be fair and just to allow [the] appeals to proceed out of time'.[87] The Tribunal noted that the applicants raised the same issues as had already been made by others in the proceedings and there would be no significant impact if the Tribunal refused permission.

10.99 A further example of a case where the time limit was not extended is the case of *Watchtower Bible and Tract Society of Britain v Charity Commission*.[88] This case concerned an appeal against an order under s 52 of the 2011 Act, and an application for a review of a decision to open a statutory inquiry. The notice of appeal was out of time, because the charity had first made an application to the Administrative Court for judicial review of the decisions, which was refused.[89] The First-tier Tribunal refused to allow an extension of time. The judge said:

> '... the statutory framework does not envisage that a charity would bring proceedings in the Administrative Court and then in the Tribunal, in successive challenges to the same decision of the [Charity Commission]. It seems to me that the Charity's litigation strategy in this case risks undermining the balance struck by Parliament's carefully considered scheme by elongating unreasonably the period of time in which the [Charity Commission] will be delayed from carrying out its inquiry pending determination of a challenge to its decision.'

---

86 *John Nicholson & ors v Charity Commission* (CA/2014/0004).

87 Paragraph 12, May 2014 judgment.

88 CA/2014/0023 and CRR/2015/0001.

89 The charity was then granted permission to appeal from the Administrative Court to the Court of Appeal. The Court of Appeal refused to allow the charity to seek judicial review of the decision to open an inquiry, on the basis that the correct way to challenge an inquiry was to appeal to the Charity Tribunal (at the time of writing the charity is appealing the decision to the Supreme Court). The Court of Appeal allowed the application to seek judicial review of the Commission's decision to make a s 52 order to proceed. *R (on the application of Watch Tower Bible & Tract Society of Britain) v Charity Commission* [2016] EWCA Civ 154.

The Tribunal noted that the charity should have made an application to the Tribunal in time and then applied for a stay of proceedings pending a decision of the Administrative Court.

10.100 In his 2012 review of charity law, Lord Hodgson noted that the 42-day time limit was considered to be 'too short ... which allows trustees limited time to make decisions and fails to reflect the reality that many trustee meeting cycles operate on a quarterly basis' and 'renders interaction with the Charity Commission's own Internal Decision Review process very difficult'.[90] He recommended that the time limit be extended to four months.[91] Government drew this recommendation to the Tribunal Procedure Committee, which has responsibility for the rules of procedure in the Tribunal.[92]

10.101 The Commission must file its response within 28 days, providing a list of the documents which it relied on when reaching the decision which is the subject of the application, and any other documents which the Commission considers could adversely affect its case or support the applicant's case.[93] The appellant may, if it wishes, file a reply within 28 days:[94] if it does so the Commission has 14 days to file further material.[95]

Case management

10.102 The First-tier Tribunal may regulate its own procedure using its case management powers.[96] This may involve a directions hearing dealing with the exchange and filing of evidence, an oral hearing, a review of the papers without a hearing and, if the case is settled, a consent order or the withdrawal of an application.

10.103 The First-tier Tribunal may stay proceedings. This is illustrated by the case of *Besley & ors and Armstrong & ors v Charity Commission*,[97] which involved an appeal against the Commission's refusal to register a Plymouth Brethren meeting hall known as the Preston Down Trust. The time limits were repeatedly extended, and the Tribunal granted a stay to the proceedings, with the consent of the parties, to see whether the issues could be resolved outside the Tribunal process. The Preston Down Trust was ultimately registered, and the case was withdrawn.[98]

10.104 The First-tier Tribunal may strike out proceedings.[99] It must do so if it lacks jurisdiction, as illustrated by the cases mentioned at **10.46-10.49**, and may also do so if it considers there is no reasonable prospect of the case succeeding. For example, the cases of *Atherton v Charity Commission* and *Shakespeare v Charity Commission*[100] both dealt with appeals against order to produce information under s 52 of the 2011 Act. The matters which the Tribunal can take into account when considering such an appeal are limited to whether the information can be properly called for (see **10.70**). In

90 *Trusted and Independent*, para 7.22.
91 *Trusted and Independent*, ch 7, recommendation 6.
92 Government Response, p 35.
93 Rule 27 of the 2009 Rules.
94 Rule 28 of the 2009 Rules.
95 Rule 29 of the 2009 Rules.
96 Rule 5 of the 2009 Rules.
97 CA/2012/003 and 0003b.
98 See **3.128–3.129**.
99 Rule 8 of the 2009 Rules.
100 CA/2014/0019 and CA/2014/0020 respectively.

both cases the First-tier Tribunal decided that the appellant's prospect of success was 'fanciful' rather than 'realistic' and the appeals were struck out.

10.105 The First-tier Tribunal may allow additional parties to join the proceedings and remove and substitute parties.[101] It may also allow, or request, any person who is not a party to proceedings to attend and take part in a hearing or to make written representations in relation to a particular issue (known as intervention).[102] For example, in the case of *Human Dignity Trust v Charity Commission* (CA/2013/0013) the First-tier Tribunal allowed two third party organisations to intervene in the proceedings on the basis that their intervention would help the Tribunal to make its decision.

10.106 Hearings are usually in public: a final hearing is usually heard by a panel of three including a judge and lay members. Some procedural hearings may be heard by a judge only.

10.107 The First-tier Tribunal aims to complete each case in less than 30 weeks.

10.108 The overriding objective of the 2009 Rules is to enable the First-tier Tribunal to deal with cases fairly and justly. This may include avoiding unnecessary formality and seeking flexibility in the proceedings. Parties must help the Tribunal to further this overriding objective and cooperate with the Tribunal generally. The expectation, therefore, is that the environment of the proceedings will not be adversarial.

10.109 All decisions of the First-tier Tribunal and the register of cases are available on the Tribunal's website.[103]

Appeals from decisions of the First-tier Tribunal

10.110 Following the Tribunals, Courts and Enforcement Act 2007, appeals from the First-tier Tribunal are heard by the Upper Tribunal.[104] Any party to a case has a right of appeal, as do the Commission and the Attorney General.[105] Most appeals must be on a point of law, but where the appeal is against a decision determining a question referred to the Tribunal by the Commission or the Attorney General, the Upper Tribunal will reconsider the question which was referred to the Tribunal, and may take into account evidence which was not available to the Tribunal.[106] The right to appeal may only be exercised with the permission of the First-tier Tribunal or the Upper Tribunal.

The Upper Tribunal

10.111 Applications are made to the First-tier Tribunal in the first instance.[107] However, as mentioned at **10.37**, the First-tier Tribunal may refer cases to the Upper Tribunal for determination. The Upper Tribunal also hears appeals from decisions of the First-tier Tribunal, and certain applications for judicial review: see **10.110** and **10.38**.

---

101 Rule 9 of the 2009 Rules. See for example *Gunn and Naghshineh v Charity Commission* (CA/2014/0001 and 0002) which involved the substitution of the original party to the proceedings: see 10.64.

102 Rule 33 of the 2009 Rules.

103 www.charity.tribunals.gov.uk/decisions.htm.

104 Section 11 of the Tribunals, Courts and Enforcement Act 2007.

105 Section 317(1) of the 2011 Act.

106 Section 317(2) of the 2011 Act.

107 Section 315 of the 2011 Act.

10.112 As mentioned at **10.34**, charity cases are dealt with by the Tax and Chancery Chamber of the Upper Tribunal. Procedure is governed by the Tribunal Procedure (Upper Tribunal) Rules 2008.[108] The overriding objective of these rules is the same as the overriding objective of the 2009 Rules in the First-tier Tribunal (see **10.108**).

10.113 Decisions of the Upper Tribunal are available on its website (and may be accompanied by a summary of the decision).[109]

10.114 There is a right of appeal from decisions of the Upper Tribunal to the Court of Appeal on any point of law arising from the decision. The permission of the Upper Tribunal, or the Court of Appeal itself, must be given.[110]

The Attorney General

10.115 The potential breadth of the Attorney General's role in charity cases is great. As well as having a right to make references to the Tribunal (see **10.78**) and to initiate appeals and reviews of the decisions, directions or orders in the Sch 6 Table (see **10.67** and **10.110**), he may also be joined as a party to any proceedings before the First-tier or Upper Tribunal, or to any onward appeal from the First-tier Tribunal to the Upper Tribunal, or from the Upper Tribunal, whether or not he was a party to the original proceedings. The Attorney General can also be asked to 'assist' the Tribunal with any question arising in the proceedings, without participating in the whole case.

10.116 Under s 318 of the 2011 Act the Attorney General has a right to intervene in any case before the Tribunal, or on an appeal from the Tribunal. The Tribunal or relevant appellate body, on its own initiative, or on the application of any party to proceedings before it, can send the relevant papers to the Attorney General, but his right to intervene is not limited to cases where papers have been sent. In the House of Commons debates on the legislation which became the 2006 Act, Government Minister, Ed Miliband MP explained that:[111]

> 'those powers for the Attorney-General to intervene do not mean that he represents either party in the dispute, but that he is supposed to have a non-adversarial role, essentially as a friend of the court, in representing the interests of the beneficiary.'

10.117 For example, in the case of *Regentford*, which considered the Commission's decision to open an inquiry under s 46 of the 2011 Act, the Upper Tribunal invited the Attorney General to intervene: his counsel made a number of submissions to the Tribunal.[112]

10.118 The Attorney General's involvement may save costs. His role was referred to in a letter from the then Attorney General, Lord Goldsmith QC, to Lord Phillips of Sudbury given in evidence before the Joint Committee which examined the draft Bill which ultimately became the 2006 Act:[113]

---

108 SI 2008/2698.
109 www.tribunals.gov.uk/financeandtax/Decisions.htm#cha.
110 Section 13 Tribunals, Courts and Enforcement Act 2007.
111 HC Standing Committee A, col 148 (6 July 2006).
112 *Regentford Ltd v Charity Commission and Attorney General* [2014] UKUT 0364 (TCC).
113 Written evidence item 7 (DCH 362) accompanying the Joint Committee report (September 2004).

> 'The Commission ... has indicated that, either at the request of the Tribunal or at my own request, I would be a party to cases demonstrating a clear public interest in the review of the relevant law. I would therefore be in a position to argue the case fully before the Tribunal, thus relieving the applicant of a degree of the burden of the costs of legal representation.'

Whilst there is potential for the Attorney General's role to be broad, the frequency with which his powers will be exercised is relatively uncertain and some certainty on this would be welcome.

Costs in Tribunal proceedings

10.119 At the time of writing, there is no fee to pay to lodge a Notice of Application with the Tribunal, although as mentioned at **10.90** this is due to change. However, the parties may of course incur the cost of legal representation.

10.120 Unlike in regular court cases dealing with commercial disputes where the court has full discretion to order that one party should pay the other's costs, the Tribunal is, in general, a costs neutral environment, meaning that each party bears their own costs.

10.121 There are, however, some situations in which the Tribunal does have power to order that one of the parties must pay the other's costs.

10.122 First, the Tribunal may make an order in respect of costs if it considers that any party has acted 'unreasonably in bringing, defending or conducting the proceedings'.[114] Thus, if either the Commission or another party to the proceedings acts unreasonably in the course of the proceedings before the Tribunal, it might be ordered to pay the other party's costs as well as its own.

10.123 This is a risk for a charity bringing a case to the Tribunal, as if the Tribunal decides that its conduct in the proceedings is unreasonable, the charity could be penalised in costs. Having said that, to date no costs awards have been made under these powers, although they (and the power to award wasted costs mentioned below) were alluded to in the case of *Augustine Housing Trust v Charity Commission*.[115] The foreword to NCVO's guide to the Charity Tribunal (see **10.133**), which was written by the Principal Judge of the First-tier Tribunal (Charity) stresses that there is no risk of costs being awarded against a charity simply because it loses a case in the Tribunal.

10.124 Secondly, the Tribunal may make an order for wasted costs against a party's representative where the costs result from any improper, unreasonable or negligent act or omission on the part of the representative, under s 29(4) of the Tribunals, Courts and Enforcement Act 2007.

10.125 Thirdly, if the Tribunal considers that the decision, direction or order of the Commission which is the subject of the proceedings was unreasonable in the first place, it can order the Commission to pay all or part of the other party's costs.[116] But if the Tribunal decides that the Commission may have taken an incorrect decision, but did not

---

[114] Rule 10 of the 2009 Rules and Rule 10 of the 2008 Rules.
[115] CRR/2014/0004, Directions dated 24 July 2014.
[116] Rule 10 of the 2009 Rules and Rule 10 of the 2008 Rules.

act unreasonably, there is no power for it to order the Commission to pay the charity's costs. The charity may have won, but it may still have suffered financially through paying for the Tribunal proceedings.

10.126 At the time of writing, there have been no costs orders against the Commission using this power. However, in the case of *Nagendram Seevaratnam v Charity Commission*,[117] which was one of the earliest cases heard by the Tribunal, various considerations, including the proportionality of the decision, the reasonableness of the Commission's actions and the consistency of the Commission's approach prompted the First-tier Tribunal to invite representations on whether it should exercise this power to award costs against the Commission. The Tribunal said that the power to award costs arose where the order which had been challenged was unreasonable (rather than the Commission's conduct leading up to the making of the order). It adopted the ordinary meaning of 'unreasonable' (i e not in accordance with reason, irrational) rather than the administrative law definition of the word (or *Wednesbury* unreasonableness). In the event, the Tribunal ultimately concluded that the Commission's order was not unreasonable and declined to award costs against it.[118]

Compensation

10.127 Although it may make awards in relation to the costs of proceedings before it, the Tribunal has no power to order that an applicant should be compensated for loss it has suffered as a result of a Commission decision.

10.128 For example, a charity which has been wrongly removed from the register may be able to show that it has suffered considerable financial loss, resulting, for instance, from the withdrawal of funding. But even if it is successful in appealing the decision to remove it from the register in front of the Tribunal, the Tribunal can only order the Commission to reimburse it for the costs of the proceedings before it, and then only in limited circumstances, and cannot make any award to take account of other financial losses.

Accessibility of the Tribunal

10.129 One of the main objectives behind the establishment of the Tribunal was to introduce a low cost, accessible forum for delivering justice and challenging the Commission on points of law.

10.130 However the ability of the Tribunal to meet this objective has come under criticism. The 2013 report of the Public Administration Select Committee[119] noted that Lord Hodgson had suggested in his 2012 review that the Tribunal had not succeeded its objective to reduce both the costs, compared to the High Court process, and the adversarial nature of the process. This was highlighted by the presence of eight QCs on the Independent Schools Council's case. Indeed, William Shawcross, the chair of the Charity Commission, has stated that 'the Tribunal is turning out to be more expensive than I think Parliament envisaged in the 2006 Act', and the Charity Law Association reported that a lower number of people have used the Tribunal than expected, and that

---

117 CA/2008/0001.

118 CA/2008/0001. Costs ruling dated 10 December 2009.

119 The role of the Charity Commission and 'public benefit': Post-legislative scrutiny of the Charities Act 2006, Third Report of Session 2013-14, HC 76 incorporating HC 574-i-vi, Session 2012-13, Public Administration Select Committee.

many of those who have used it have found it 'slow and expensive'.[120] Such comments and observations led the PASC report to conclude that the Tribunal had 'failed in its objective to reduce the cost of disputes'.[121]

10.131 In its response to the PASC report, Government emphasised that it is 'up to the parties in any proceedings before the Tribunal, including both charities and individual beneficiaries, to make their own choices about whether to incur the cost of legal representation'.[122] The Government did however note that the Tribunal Procedure Committee was reviewing the suggestion published in the Report on 'Costs in Tribunals'[123] concerning the power for the Tribunal to make prospective costs orders in charity cases, which would enable trustees of a charity, if they chose to incur legal costs, to obtain authority to recover those costs out of the charity's funds. The Law Commission, in its 2015 consultation on charity law issues, has provisionally proposed that the Tribunal should have power to make *Beddoe* orders in respect of proceedings before it, which would give the trustees of a charity involved in the proceedings an advance assurance that their costs would be paid from the charity's funds.[124]

10.132 The foreword to NCVO's guide to the Charity Tribunal (see **10.133**), written by the Principal Judge of the First-tier Tribunal (Charity), stresses that it is not necessary to be legally represented, and that the Tribunal is always happy to assist anyone who chooses to represent themselves. This willingness to assist applicants and flexible approach is evident from many of the Tribunal's judgments.

10.133 Contributors to Lord Hodgson's review were critical of the complexity of Tribunal proceedings, noting that guidance on how the Tribunal works and ways of accessing it was neither sufficient nor widely available. Guidance from the NCVO, which has been mentioned above, is now available, and at the time of writing is accessible via the Tribunal's website.[125]

10.134 Feedback to Lord Hodgson's review indicated that there was scope for the Tribunal to assist litigants and the efficient administration of justice by making more frequent and robust use of its case management powers, although there was some evidence that the Tribunal was already adopting a more inquisitorial, fact-finding approach. Lord Hodgson recommended that the Tribunal should consider whether there were further ways in which it could use its case management powers to simplify proceedings, make them less adversarial and dispose of cases rapidly.[126] Government agreed to draw Lord Hodgson's recommendation to the Tribunal Procedure Committee.[127]

10.135 The recent proposals to introduce fees for applications to the Tribunal (see **10.90**) will, in the authors' view, serve as a new obstacle to accessibility to the Tribunal. The Charity Law Association working group commenting on the proposals argued that they would 'be a significant disincentive to some charity litigants, and would have a material adverse effect on the flow of charity cases being brought'. The working group's

---

120 See the Public Administration Select Committee Report, referred to at note 119, section 6 for references.
121 PASC Report, para 101.
122 Government Response, p 14.
123 'Costs in Tribunals', 2011.
124 Paragraphs 16.42-16.64, Technical Issues in Charity Law, A Consultation Paper, Law Commission, March 2015.
125 www.gov.uk/appeal-against-a-charity-commission-decision-about-your-charity.
126 *Trusted and Independent*, paras 7.20–7.21 and chapter 7, recommendation 9.
127 Government Response, p 36.

view was that the introduction of fees would be likely to reduce the number of charity cases coming before the Tribunal and it said:

> 'This will work directly against the objectives for which the [Tribunal] was established, namely to be an accessible low-cost forum for challenging decisions of the Charity Commission and to stimulate the development of charity law.'[128]

Conclusion

10.136 The establishment of the Tribunal was one of the most significant changes introduced by the 2006 Act. There is no doubt that the Tribunal has helped charities, trustees and other concerned parties which have been unjustly treated and, more generally, it has been an effective catalyst for the Commission to improve its functions and the manner it makes decisions 'thereby enhancing access to justice'.[129]

10.137 The Tribunal has also begun to develop charity law.[130] However, concerns about the Tribunal remain. The limited and complex nature of the Tribunal's jurisdiction has meant that it is difficult to understand whether the Tribunal can review a matter or hear an appeal, and there have been several cases where appellants have been frustrated by the Tribunal's lack of jurisdiction. The Tribunal has had to dedicate time to considering the extent of its jurisdiction. The proposed introduction of fees in the Tribunal is, in the authors' view, a step towards discouraging appropriate challenge to the Tribunal when the current need is more in the opposite direction. Ultimately the accountability of the Commission and the progressive development of charity law will be served by general accessibility to the Tribunal.

10.138 The Public Administration Select Committee May 2013 report was critical of what it termed 'the … Commission's reliance on the Charity Tribunal to resolve contentious areas of the law'. It said that this 'amounts to an abdication of responsibility by the … Commission, and an expensive, time-consuming and unjust way to test the law'. More particularly, the Committee said that the 'policy for determining questions of public benefit has proved disastrous in terms of the time and commitment of the … Commission and the charities involved'. The PASC recommended that the Commission should 'devise informal dispute resolution procedures and should not use the tribunal system as a means of determining the law, except as a last resort'.[131]

10.139 It is worth observing in this context that charity law is essentially permissive and charity law principles should be properly and progressively interpreted, for example to take account of social developments, as reaffirmed in the progressive definition of

---

128 Charity Law Association working party report, Ministry of Justice consultation, Introduction of Fees to the General Regulatory Chamber and Upper Tier Tax and Chancery Chamber, September 2015.

129 See Thomas, *Analysis: The charity tribunal – has it been a success?*, Third Sector, 5 November 2013 and Morris, *The First-tier Tribunal (Charity): enhanced access to justice for charities or a case of David versus Goliath*, CJQ 2010 491.

130 See, for example, *The Independent Schools Council v Charity Commission* [2011] UKUT 421 (TCC) and *Her Majesty's Attorney General v Charity Commission* [2012] UKUT 420 (TCC) which dealt with public benefit; and *Regentford Ltd v Charity Commission and Attorney General* [2014] UKUT 0364 (TCC), which sets out the principles to be applied by the Commission when deciding whether to open an inquiry under s 46 of the 2011 Act.

131 The role of the Charity Commission and 'public benefit': Post-legislative scrutiny of the Charities Act 2006, Third Report of Session 2013-14, HC 76 incorporating HC 574-i-vi, Session 2012-13.

charitable purposes introduced by the 2006 Act. This should be recognised as a facilitative guiding principle, which has served charity law very well without voluminous case law.

10.140 Notwithstanding concerns about the Tribunal, those appellants who have been successful in challenging the Commission before the Tribunal are undoubtedly grateful for its existence. Charity lawyers are able to rely on Upper Tribunal judgments in areas where, hitherto, there may have been doubt. Statistics show that the number of applications to the Tribunal is on the increase.[132] Whatever its shortcomings, the Charity Tribunal affords applicants far more of a chance of access to justice than was the case in the past.

[132] House of Lords, House of Common, Joint Committee on the Draft Protection of Charities Bill 25 February 2015, HL Paper 108, HC 813, Appendix 5.

CHAPTER 11

CHARITY INVESTMENTS

INTRODUCTION

11.1 The powers and duties of charity trustees in relation to investment by charities are affected by both the 2011 Act (as amended by the 2016 Act) and the Trustee Act 2000 ('the 2000 Act').

11.2 The 2000 Act confers wide statutory investment powers on the trustees of unincorporated charities, subject to overriding duties to act prudently, to have regard to certain investment considerations, and to take advice. The 2000 Act does not apply to charitable companies, except where they hold property on charitable trust, but the provisions of the 2000 Act provide a reasonable analogy for the general duty of trustees to act reasonably and prudently in relation to investment powers. Some of the provisions of the 2000 Act apply to charitable incorporated organisations.[1]

11.3 Prior to 2016 the 2011 Act contained limited provisions relating to charity investment. One of the most significant implications of the 2016 Act was the introduction of a new statutory power for trustees to carry out 'social investment', which is investment which is not only aimed at achieving a financial return, but also to further the charity's objects: see **11.54-11.61**.

11.4 All charity trustees should be aware of the Commission's attitude to investment by charities: at the time of writing its most recent guidance is 'Charities and investment matters: a guide for trustees' (CC14). This guidance was last updated in 2011 but the Commission issued a supplement to CC14 in July 2016 regarding the new statutory power to make social investments (see **11.54-11.61**) and has indicated that it will undertake a full review of CC14 in 2017, which may include amendments as a result of the publication of the Christopher McCall opinion mentioned at **11.45-11.46**.

CHARITY POWERS AND DUTIES IN RELATION TO INVESTMENT

What powers do charity trustees have?

11.5 The first port of call for charity trustees in determining their investment powers is the charity's constitution. A well-drafted constitution should contain a power to invest, and ancillary powers to delegate to investment managers and to put investments in the name of nominees. If these powers do not appear, a charity may well wish to change its constitution to include them.

---

1 Regulation 33 of the Charitable Incorporated Organisations (General) Regulations 2012.

11.6 However, the trustees of unincorporated charities also have statutory powers to invest and to appoint investment managers and nominees, under the 2000 Act. The trustees of charitable incorporated organisations, or CIOs, have statutory powers to appoint investment managers and nominees.

Powers of investment

11.7 The trustees of unincorporated charities benefit from a statutory power under the 2000 Act to make any kind of investment they could make if they were absolutely entitled to the charity's assets. This power is subject to any restrictions or exclusions in the charity's constitution, except where the constitution is dated before 3 August 1961.[2]

11.8 The statutory power essentially gives the trustees free reign, subject to the scope of the term 'investment' and to their duties to act prudently, to take appropriate criteria into account, and to take advice (see **11.28-11.39**).

11.9 The statutory power does not apply to charitable companies, except where they hold property on trust. However, charitable companies will generally have express powers to invest set out in their Articles of Association, sometimes with specific reference to the 2000 Act.[3] The Commission expects the trustees of charitable companies to comply with similar duties of prudence when managing investments (see **11.29**).

11.10 Any charity whose constitution contains investment powers which pre-date the 2000 Act may wish to consider whether a review of those powers would be appropriate, particularly if they impose restrictions on the nature of the property the trustees may invest in.

11.11 Prior to 2011, the Commission's guidance on investment by charities was clear that it did not regard art or commodities, such as gold or vintage wine, as investments. This was on the basis that there is no prospect of an income return, but only the hope of a profit once the item is sold, making the transaction more akin to trading than investing. The Commission's 2011 guidance and the accompanying 'Legal underpinning' document took a less rigid approach. The Commission accepted case law demonstrating that buying commodities is capable of being investment rather than trading, whilst maintaining that often this will not be the case. This may depend on the intentions underpinning the transaction, with a purchase made on a short-term basis for the purpose of making a profit on the item's sale likely to be trading and not investment.

11.12 The Commission's pre-2011 guidance took a similar approach to derivatives: acquiring and disposing of these was also regarded as trading activity and not as investment, except where ancillary to an investment transaction, for example where derivatives are used to reduce the charity's exposure when planning to sell investments in the future. The Commission's 2011 guidance again took a more flexible approach, recognising that derivatives can constitute proper investments in their own right, depending on the nature of the product and the basis on which the investment is made. In particular, the Commission expressed the view that derivatives should not constitute more than a small proportion of a large investment fund.

---

[2] Trustees of unincorporated charities also have a statutory power to make social investments: see **11.54–11.61**.

[3] Charitable companies also have a statutory power to make social investments: see **11.54–11.61**.

11.13 The Commission also accepts that hedge funds are a possible investment for a charity.

11.14 Charities which wish to purchase assets which the Commission may not regard as investments could be well advised to consider changing their constitutions to make it clear that they have power to invest in those assets. But charities should be alert to the potential tax consequences of investing in this way (see **11.40**) as well as to their overriding duty to act prudently.

11.15 Charities which acquire such assets other than by purchasing them, for example where they are left valuable paintings in a supporter's will, should consider whether retention of them is consistent with their investment duties and the charity's investment policy. However, this may not be relevant where the item is used for the charity's purposes, such as a gift of a painting for a charitable art gallery's collection.

11.16 The power of investment in the 2000 Act does not include land, but the 2000 Act does include a separate power to purchase land in the United Kingdom as an investment, or in order to further the objects of the charity.[4]

11.17 Most of the powers conferred by the 2000 Act do not generally apply to the trustees of common investment funds and common deposit funds.

Investment managers

11.18 The trustees of unincorporated charities have a statutory power under the 2000 Act to delegate any function relating to the investment of the charity's assets. This allows them to appoint an investment manager to take responsibility for investing the charity's funds. Where land is held as an investment, the trustees are able to delegate the management of the land.

11.19 These provisions of the 2000 Act do not apply to charitable companies, except where property is held by charitable companies on trust, and not as part of their corporate property. However, well-drafted Articles of Association for a charitable company will include express powers to appoint investment managers: often the provisions of the 2000 Act are specifically referred to.

11.20 The statutory powers do apply, with some adaptations, to charitable incorporated organisations.[5]

11.21 The 2000 Act imposes some conditions. These apply to the trustees of unincorporated charities where the investment manager is appointed under the statutory powers. Some also apply where managers are appointed under powers in the charity's constitution. For corporate charities, compliance with similar conditions may be a constitutional requirement, and will generally be regarded as consistent with good practice.

- The agreement with the investment manager must be in writing, or at least there must be written evidence of it, such as a note of what has been agreed.

---

4 Note that special rules apply where a charity disposes of land: see Chapter 8.

5 The Charitable Incorporated Organisations (General) Regulations 2012, reg 33.

- The trustees must prepare a written policy statement, which sets out how the manager's functions should be exercised. This must ensure that the manager's functions are exercised in the best interests of the charity. The agreement with the manager must oblige the manager to ensure that the statement is complied with. The policy statement, and the manager's compliance with it, must be kept under review by the trustees.
- If, as is likely, the manager is to be paid, the agreement must make this clear, and the level of payment must be reasonable in the circumstances. (Trustees acting as investment managers will only be entitled to payment in limited circumstances: see Chapter 7 for more on the rules about remuneration of trustees.)
- Terms of the arrangement allowing the manager to appoint a substitute, restricting the liability of the manager (or substitute) and allowing the manager to act even if there might be a conflict of interest are only allowed if the trustees are satisfied that they are 'reasonably necessary'. In practice, this means that if these terms are included in standard agreements produced by the investment manager, if the charity trustees cannot negotiate for their removal they must be happy that the terms are standard in the market and they could not appoint a similar manager on more favourable terms.

The power is subject to any restriction or exclusion imposed by the constitution, but such cases will be rare.

11.22 Where the 2000 Act applies, the arrangements with investment managers must be reviewed regularly. This requirement applies even where the manager is appointed using powers in the constitution, unless it is inconsistent with the terms of the constitution. In practice, a regular review of the arrangements is consistent with the charity trustees' normal duties of prudence, regardless of a charity's legal form.

Nominees and custodians

11.23 Again, a well-drafted constitution should contain powers for the trustees to put investments in the name of nominees, and to make use of custodians for holding charity assets. In the absence of an express power, the 2000 Act includes statutory powers for the trustees of unincorporated charities to appoint a nominee or custodian in relation to such of the assets of the charity as they determine. These provisions of the 2000 Act do not apply to charitable companies, except where they hold property on trust, but express powers are often conferred by the Articles of Association, possibly with a reference to the 2000 Act. The statutory powers do apply, with some adaptations, to the trustees of charitable incorporated organisations.[6]

11.24 There are some restrictions on the appointment of nominees and custodians under the statutory powers. (Note that the restrictions relating to the agreement with the nominee or custodian also appear to apply to appointments under powers in the charity's constitution.)

- A nominee or custodian must be a person who carries on the business of acting as nominee or custodian, or a company controlled by the trustees, or a solicitors' nominee company.

---

6 The Charitable Incorporated Organisations (General) Regulations 2012, reg 33.

- Provided the condition above is satisfied, a nominee or custodian can be a trustee (if it is a trust corporation), or two trustees acting jointly.
- A nominee or custodian may be a person also appointed as an agent to the trustees, such as an investment manager.
- An appointment must be in writing or evidenced in writing.
- Certain terms should only be included in the agreement with the nominee or custodian if they are 'reasonably necessary', namely any term permitting substitutions, restricting liability or allowing the nominee or custodian to act despite a conflict of interest. As in the case of investment managers, in practice this means that these terms should only be accepted in the standard terms of business of a corporate nominee or custodian if the trustees cannot negotiate for their removal and are satisfied that they are indeed market standard terms and they could not appoint a similar person on more favourable terms.
- If the nominee is to be remunerated, this must be included in the terms of appointment, and the level of remuneration must be reasonable. (As in the case of investment managers, if the nominee or custodian is a trustee, see Chapter 7 in relation to the remuneration of trustees generally.)

11.25 It is a term of the 2000 Act that trustees of an unincorporated charity which is not an exempt charity must have regard to Commission guidance when selecting a nominee or custodian for appointment under the powers in that Act. At the time of writing, the statutory guidance appears in Commission publication CC42: 'Appointing Nominees and Custodians' (February 2001). The Commission recommends that all charity trustees bear the guidance in mind when appointing nominees or custodians, regardless of the charity's legal form, even where making the appointment using powers in the charity's constitution, rather than the statutory powers. The guidance covers: considering whether the use of a nominee or custodian rather than direct control of the assets is appropriate in each case, assessing the risks involved, and the terms of the arrangement.

11.26 The arrangements which trustees of unincorporated charities make with nominees and custodians must be reviewed regularly, whether appointed under the statutory powers or powers in the constitution itself unless, in the latter case, the constitution provides otherwise. In practice, a regular review of the arrangements is consistent with the charity trustees' normal duties of prudence, regardless of the charity's legal form.

11.27 The statutory powers are subject to any restriction or exclusion in the charity's constitution. They do not apply to a trust with a custodian trustee nor in relation to any assets vested in the official custodian (for more information on the official custodian see Chapter 22).

What duties do charity trustees have?

Statutory duty of care

11.28 The trustees of unincorporated charities are subject to a general duty of care, set out in the 2000 Act, in relation to investment.

11.29 As mentioned previously, the 2000 Act does not apply to charitable companies, except where they hold property on trust. Nonetheless, the Commission's view is that trustees of charitable companies would be well advised to comply with all duties imposed by the 2000 Act in any event, as they are acting in a similar fiduciary capacity and so are likely to have comparable duties under the general law.

11.30 The trustees of CIOs have a general duty of care by virtue of s 221 of the 2011 Act, which is in similar terms to the duty in the 2000 Act.[7]

11.31 The general duty of care under the 2000 Act is a duty to exercise such care and skill as is reasonable in the circumstances, having regard in particular:

(a) to any special knowledge or experience that the trustee has or holds him or herself out as having; and
(b) if the trustee acts as trustee in the course of a business or profession, to any special knowledge or experience that it is reasonable to expect of a person acting in the course of that kind of business or profession.

11.32 This means that a trustee who works with investments, for instance, will have a higher standard of care imposed on him or her when it comes to making investment decisions for the charity.

11.33 The statutory duty of care under the 2000 Act will apply to the following decisions of the trustees, unless it appears from the constitution that it is not meant to apply:

- the exercise of any power of investment, including a power in the constitution;
- reviewing the charity's investments (see **11.39**);
- considering the standard investment criteria (see **11.34**) when reviewing investments;
- obtaining and considering advice (see **11.36-11.37**);
- the acquisition and management of land under any power, including a power in the constitution;
- the appointment of agents, nominees and custodians (and decisions about their terms of appointment, including preparing a policy statement in respect of investments) under any power, including a power in the constitution;
- the review of arrangements with agents, nominees and custodians required under the 2000 Act;
- the exercise of any power to compound liabilities, including any power granted in the constitution; and
- the exercise of any power to insure, including any power in the constitution.

Standard investment criteria

11.34 Where the 2000 Act applies, when exercising any power of investment (whether in the constitution or conferred by the 2000 Act), apart from a power to make social investments (see **11.59**), and when reviewing the trust investments, the trustees must have regard to the so-called 'standard investment criteria' in the 2000 Act. These are:

---

7 See Chapter 14.

(a) the suitability to the trust of investments of the same kind as any particular investment proposed to be made or retained and of that particular investment as an investment of that kind; and

(b) the need for diversification of investments of the trust, in so far as is appropriate to the circumstances of the trust.

11.35 It will generally be good practice for all charity trustees to have regard to these criteria. At the time of writing, the Commission's guidance on investment by charity trustees makes it clear that this will include considering risk issues, the importance in the case of permanent endowment of balancing the furtherance of charitable purposes in both the present and future, and the duty to take account of any other relevant issues (which might include, for example, any ethical investment policy (see **11.42-11.47**)).[8]

Advice

11.36 Under the 2000 Act, before exercising any power of investment, whether in the Act or in the constitution, (apart from a power to make social investments: see **11.59**) and when reviewing the investments of the charity, a trustee of an unincorporated charity must obtain and consider proper advice about the way in which, having regard to the standard investment criteria, the investment power should be exercised or the investments varied. Proper advice is the advice of a person who is reasonably believed by the trustee to be qualified to give it, by his ability in and practical experience of financial and other matters relating to the proposed investment.

11.37 There is an exception from this rule where the trustee 'reasonably concludes that in all the circumstances it is unnecessary or inappropriate to do so'. This gives the trustees some flexibility, perhaps where they consider that they have appropriate investment experience themselves, or where it would not be cost effective to seek advice.

11.38 Even where the 2000 Act does not strictly apply, it will generally be prudent for charities to consider whether to obtain investment advice.

Review

11.39 The 2000 Act requires trustees to review the investments of the charity from time to time and consider whether they should be varied, having regard to the standard investment criteria. This is a prudent exercise for all charity trustees.

Tax considerations

11.40 Some investments may be regarded as 'non-charitable expenditure' by HM Revenue & Customs (HMRC), if they are not 'approved charitable investments' under s 511 of the Corporation Tax Act 2010 (in relation to incorporated charities) and s 558 of the Income Tax Act 2007 (in relation to unincorporated charities). Investments of a type listed in those sections, which include (for example) shares listed on a recognised stock exchange, have no tax implications. Investments which are not of a type listed in those sections, such as private equity and hedge fund investments, may affect the tax reliefs to which the charity would otherwise be entitled if an officer of HMRC is not satisfied, on a claim, that the investment is made for the benefit of the charity and not

8 CC14 'Charities and Investment Matters: A Guide for Trustees' (2011).

for the avoidance of tax. Where charity trustees are adopting a reasonably diligent approach to investment, there should not generally be any tax issues, but trustees should nonetheless be alert to the tax rules.

THE NATURE OF INVESTMENT

11.41 The Commission has recognised that charities can invest in a number of ways to achieve their charitable aims.[9]

- 'Financial investment' is intended to yield the best risk-adjusted financial return for the charity.
- Even where a charity engages in financial investment, it may be appropriate and in the best interests of the charity to take ethical considerations into account: see **11.42-11.47**.
- 'Programme-related investment' is activity which is intended to directly further the charity's aims, rather than necessarily seeking the best financial return: see **11.48-11.50**.
- 'Mixed-motive investment', as its name suggests, has elements of both financial and programme related investment: it is intended both to further the charity's aims and to generate a reasonable financial return in so doing: see **11.51-11.53**.

Ethical investment

11.42 Trustees of charities are often concerned about whether they have scope, or indeed obligations, to invest the charity's funds ethically. The law on ethical investment is set out in *Harries (Bishop of Oxford) v Church Commissioners*[10] (often known as the *Bishop of Oxford* case), and was not amended or clarified by the 2006 Act or the 2000 Act. Some regard this as an omission: Martin Horwood MP expressed disappointment in the final House of Commons debate on the 2006 Act that the legislation 'still fails to protect trustees from liability in respect of pursuing ethical investment policies, which strikes me as entirely laudable'.[11]

11.43 The basic rule from the *Bishop of Oxford* case is that the trustees' powers of investment must be used to further the charity's purposes. Where property is held by trustees for the purpose of generating money (ie as a financial investment) then, on the face of it, the purposes of the charity will normally be best served by seeking the maximum investment return which is consistent with commercial prudence.

11.44 There are three cases where trustees are able to allow their financial investment strategy to be governed by considerations other than the level of investment return:

- charities can avoid investing in a business which would conflict with the aims of the charity. Thus, an environmental protection charity might feel it inappropriate to invest in a business which pollutes the environment;
- charities can avoid investments that might hamper their work. For instance, some investments may alienate the charity's beneficiaries or supporters, although the

9 CC14 'Charities and Investment Matters: A Guide for Trustees' (2011).

10 [1992] 1 WLR 1241.

11 HC Deb, vol 450, col 1623 (25 October 2006).

trustees must always balance the difficulties which this might involve with any corresponding financial risk of poorly performing investments; and

- trustees can accommodate the views of those who consider the investment to be inappropriate on moral grounds, but only if this does not involve 'a risk of significant financial detriment'.

11.45 In November 2015, following instructions from the authors, Christopher McCall QC published a written legal opinion on the subject of ethically questionable investments, particularly in relation to 'carbon intensive investments' including fossil fuels such as coal, oil and gas. His opinion raises the prospect that a wide range of different charities may be legally required to re-evaluate their approach to carbon intensive investments. This conclusion is based on the principles recognised in the *Bishop of Oxford* case (as summarised above), but the opinion also notes that the *Bishop of Oxford* case predates modern concerns about global warming and climate change.

11.46 The key conclusions from Christopher McCall's opinion are:

- where it is clear that the investment conflicts with the objects of the charity, trustees of charities must divest from carbon intensive investments regardless of the financial consequences;
- investment in carbon intensive investments may in many cases be 'irreconcilable' with the intent by charities with a wide range of different missions, such as missions relating to the environment, poverty, health or other purposes relating to matters where carbon intensive assets and the consequences of dangerous climate change are of particular concern;
- where the presence of a conflict is subject to opinion, trustees should seek financial advice and if there is no material risk of financial detriment in not including such investments in the portfolio, trustees can invest in accordance with the ethical principles of the trust;
- where the work of the charity may be impeded by the investment (known as a 'latent conflict') an ethical approach to investment may be justified if it does not otherwise result in financial detriment; and
- given the potential magnitude of financial risks associated with investment in 'stranded assets' all fiduciaries – and not just charity investors – 'must be ready to consider, with the benefit of advice, the extent to which the risks associated with carbon intensive assets may be currently underappreciated and not fully priced into the market'.[12]

11.47 The Statement of Recommended Practice for Charities requires the trustees' annual report, in the case of a charity subject to a statutory audit requirement, to include, where material financial investments are held by a charity, a statement of the charity's investment policy and objectives, including the extent (if any) to which social, environmental or ethical considerations are taken into account.[13]

---

12 The authors have shared the opinion with the Charity Commission and requested that it issues guidance on the issue of ethical investment for the benefit of the charitable sector as a whole.

13 SORP 2015 FRS 102: see Chapter 21.

Programme-related investment

11.48 'Programme-related investment' is where charities actually carry out their charitable purposes through investment activities. It is therefore different to ethical investment. Although programme-related investment activity may generate a financial return for the charity, the primary motivation for it is not financial, but the furtherance of the charity's objects. Examples include lending money, at a favourable rate of interest, to a project which helps the charity's beneficiaries, or buying shares in a company which only employs people that the charity is set up to help, eg those with disabilities.

11.49 Neither the Commission nor HMRC regard this as investment in the conventional sense, which means that the investment principles described earlier in this chapter do not apply. The trustees must, however, act appropriately when making programme-related investments. Other charity law rules and restrictions do apply; for instance, the general duties of trustees and the requirement to act within the particular charitable purposes of the relevant charity and the provisions of its own constitution, including any limitations on its powers and the use of its charitable assets.

11.50 The Commission's guidance at the time of writing[14] sets out the Commission's view that consideration of the nature of any private benefit generated by the investment is of particular importance. The Commission takes the view that some private benefit is acceptable if the trustees are satisfied that it is necessary in the circumstances, reasonable in amount and in the interests of the charity.

Mixed-motive investment

11.51 For some time, the Commission has expressly recognised the principle of 'mixed-motive investment'.[15] This categorisation will apply to investments made in part to further a charity's objects and in part for a financial return.

11.52 When pursuing a mixed-motive investment the trustees will need to be satisfied that it is in the best interests of the charity even though it may not be entirely justifiable as a financial or programme-related investment alone. This will be the case where the investment can be justified by the combination of the anticipated financial return and the contribution the funded activities will make to the charity's aims.

11.53 The trustees should apply the same decision-making criteria as when making both financial and programme-related investments and also consider whether any private benefit arising from the mixed-motive investment is acceptable taking into account the contribution the funded activities make to the objects of the charity. They should have a clear concept, without this necessarily being scientific, as to how they are balancing the financial and programme-related investment elements of the investment.

Social investment

11.54 The terms of reference of Lord Hodgson's 2012 review included measures to facilitate social investment by, and into charities. Lord Hodgson concluded that charity

---

14 CC14 'Charities and Investment Matters: A Guide for Trustees' (2011).

15 CC14 'Charities and Investment Matters: A Guide for Trustees' (2011).

law, whilst it does not actively prohibit social investment, is not set up to support it. He set out 12 specific recommendations to integrate social investment into the legal and regulatory framework, including:

- a statutory clarification of the investment responsibilities of charity trustees and an express statutory power for charity trustees to engage in social investment;
- a statutory power for charities to invest permanent endowment in social investments, subject to certain conditions;
- a clarification that private benefit in the context of social investment should be 'proportionate' and need not be merely 'incidental';
- the development of a standard social investment vehicle to allow funding from different sources to be invested in the same product; and
- setting up a tax pre-clearance procedure in relation to social investment.[16]

11.55 Following a consultation exercise, in September 2014 the Law Commission published its recommendations on proposed reform of charity trustees' duties in respect of social investment, building on Lord Hodgson's proposals. The Law Commission expressed the view that charities could combine their powers to invest and their powers to spend charity funds to make a social investment, but acknowledged that not all lawyers agree.[17] It recommended the introduction of a new express statutory power for charity trustees to make social investments, to ensure that uncertainty over their legal duties does not dissuade trustees from making social investments that would achieve their charity's objects. The Law Commission also recommended that HM Treasury should review and seek to amend tax legislation to reflect the new statutory power and should introduce a prior clearance procedure for social investments.

11.56 The 2016 Act duly introduced new ss 292A-292C into the 2011 Act, and made some consequential amendments to the 2000 Act (these provisions came into force on 31 July 2016). Section 292B gives incorporated charities, and the trustees of unincorporated charities, (with some exceptions: see 11.58) power to make social investments. This statutory power will supplement powers that charities may already have to make social investments.

11.57 Section 292A defines social investment as a use of funds or other property (or a commitment in relation to a third party liability, such as a guarantee) which:

> '… is carried out with a view to both–
>
> (a) directly furthering the charity's purposes; and
> (b) achieving a financial return for the charity.'

Section 292A includes more detail about the meaning of 'financial return'. A social investment can be made by a charity by either (a) direct application or use of funds or property or (b) taking on a commitment in relation to the liability of another person (such as a guarantee) that puts the charity's funds or other property at risk of being applied (both methods are defined in s 292A(4) as being 'relevant acts'). A financial return is achieved under (a) if its outcome is better for the charity in financial terms than expending the whole of the funds or other property in question. A financial return is

16 *Trusted and Independent*, ch 9.
17 Social Investment by Charities, Law Commission's recommendations, September 2014, para 1.12.

achieved under (b) if the liability (eg the guarantee) is not called upon or is called upon without resulting in the expenditure of the whole of the funds or other property at risk.

11.58 It is clear that the statutory power is in addition to any other powers which the charity or the trustees may have[18] There are, however, some restrictions on the power:

- it does not apply in relation to Royal Charter charities or charities established by, or whose purposes and functions are set out in, legislation;
- it may be restricted or excluded under the charity's constitution; and
- it does not allow social investment of permanent endowment, unless the trustees expect that making the social investment will not contravene any restrictions on spending the permanent endowment.

11.59 When exercising the power, any duties to have regard to standard investment criteria or to take advice which might otherwise apply under the 2000 Act (see **11.34-11.38**) do not apply. However, when making any social investments, whether or not under the statutory power, the trustees must:

(a) consider whether in all the circumstances they should obtain any advice about the proposed social investment;

(b) obtain and consider any advice they decide ought to be obtained; and

(c) satisfy themselves that it is in the interests of the charity to make the social investment, having regard to the benefit they expect to achieve for the charity (by directly furthering the charity's purposes and achieving a financial return).

This obligation may not be excluded or restricted by the charity's constitution.

11.60 The trustees are under an obligation to review the social investments from time to time. At that stage they must consider whether they should obtain any advice about the social investments (or any particular social investment), and if they do, obtain and consider the advice. This obligation may not be excluded by the constitution.

11.61 The new statutory power has been welcomed by the sector. At the reading of the legislation which became the 2016 Act in the House of Commons, the government spokesman Matthew Hancock MP highlighted the growing importance of social investment for charities:

> 'On the new social investment power, the Bill will help charities that want to get involved in this exciting new area of finance for charities. We are committed to growing social investment as a sustainable source of finance for charities and other social ventures. The UK is a world leader in this respect, and the social investment power will help charities to play a bigger role.'[19]

---

[18] Section 292B(3)(b) of the 2011 Act.

[19] HC Deb, col 233 (26 January 2016).

COMMON INVESTMENT SCHEMES AND COMMON DEPOSIT FUNDS

11.62 Sections 96–104 of the 2011 Act allow the Commission to make schemes to set up common investment funds and common deposit funds for charities. Common investment funds are collective investment schemes, under which charities can transfer property into a common fund which is invested under the control of the trustees of the fund. They are only open to charities. Common investment funds are charities in their own right and are registered with the Commission. Common deposit funds are similar arrangements, allowing the pooling of cash rather than investments.

11.63 Prior to the 2006 Act, only charities in England and Wales could invest in common deposit funds and common investment funds. The 2006 Act changed the position by allowing Scottish and Northern Irish charities (defined in ss 97–104 of the 2011 Act) to participate, if the trustees of the fund so wish. Organisations established in the EEA which are recognised as charities by HMRC (see **4.81**) may also be allowed to participate, under changes introduced in 2013.

11.64 Under transitional provisions in Sch 9 of the 2011 Act, at the time of writing common deposit funds and common investment schemes which only admit exempt charities are also exempt charities in their own right (see Chapter 5).

11.65 At the time of writing, a new type of investment fund for charities is being developed: the charity authorised investment fund. The Commission can create such a scheme under ss 96–104 of the 2011 Act. Similarly to common investment funds, charity authorised investment funds will be charities in their own right and subject to oversight from the Commission to the extent they are subject to charity law. However, they will differ from common investment funds as they will also be regulated by the Financial Conduct Authority as authorised funds under the Financial Services and Markets Act 2000.

CHAPTER 12

PERMANENT ENDOWMENT

INTRODUCTION

12.1 Permanent endowment is property held by a charity on the basis that the trustees have power to spend the income which the property produces, but not the underlying capital funds. The capital must be preserved indefinitely.

12.2 Permanent endowment can provide charities with an important degree of security, since the charity's property should be available for the benefit of future generations. However, it can be inflexible. As explained in this chapter, over the years the law has been changed to give the trustees of permanent endowment more flexibility around the use of their funds. The 2011 Act allows the capital of permanent endowment to be spent in certain circumstances, and also allows trustees to decide that their permanent endowment should be invested without regard to the strict rules on the distinction between capital and income, under a so-called 'total return' approach.

12.3 Permanent endowment typically falls into one of two categories.

Investment permanent endowment

12.4 Permanent endowment can consist of investment property which generates an income for the charity, such as shares which generate dividends or land which produces rent. The income can be spent on the charity's purposes. The underlying investments may be sold in order to purchase more investments, but the sale proceeds, including any capital growth generated on a sale, cannot be used for the charity's purposes but must be retained to generate income for the future. The Commission refers to this type of permanent endowment as 'investment permanent endowment'.

Functional permanent endowment

12.5 Alternatively, permanent endowment may consist of an asset, such as land, which does not produce an income, but is used directly by the charity to further its purposes. Village halls, recreation grounds and historic buildings, or indeed significant works of art, may be held in this way, for example. The Commission describes this type of permanent endowment as 'functional permanent endowment'. Often functional permanent endowment is held on particular charitable trusts, which may be so specific that they can only be fulfilled by retaining the original property, meaning that it cannot be sold without altering the charity's purposes.[1]

---

1 *Oldham MBC v Attorney General* [1993] 2 All ER 432.

Identifying permanent endowment

12.6 It can sometimes be surprisingly difficult to identify whether a charity's property is permanent endowment or not. Often a detailed analysis of the history of the funds is required. In the authors' experience it is not uncommon for unrestricted property to be wrongly designated as permanent endowment, or vice versa, over a considerable period.

12.7 The 2011 Act provides that:[2]

> 'A charity is to be treated for the purposes of this Act as having a permanent endowment unless all property held for the purposes of the charity may be expended for those purposes without distinction between-
>
> (a) capital; and
> (b) income;
>
> and in this Act "permanent endowment" means, in relation to any charity, property held subject to a restriction on its being expended for the purposes of the charity.'

12.8 This suggests that unless there is evidence that when the property in question was given to the charity the donor definitely intended the charity to be able to spend the capital as well as the income, the property will be treated as permanent endowment. During the passage of the 2006 Act through the House of Lords, there was some enthusiasm for reversing this presumption so that property would only be treated as permanent endowment if there was an express stipulation at the time of the gift to charity that only the income could be used for the purposes of the charity, but the Government resisted the proposal.

12.9 However, at the time of writing the Commission's approach to identifying permanent endowment is more in line with the flexible approach suggested in the House of Lords. Its operational guidance states:[3]

> 'If there is nothing [in the governing document] to indicate that there is a restriction on spending capital we will usually agree that it can be spent on the charity's purposes. It is not necessary for there to be a clear power to spend capital in order to support the view that the charity's assets are all expendable and consequently not subject to a permanent endowment restriction. However, if a power to spend income is given but the governing document does not mention capital, that is an indication of the charity having permanent endowment.'

12.10 The Commission accepts that it may be necessary to look at evidence over and above the governing document when seeking to establish the status of a charity's funds.

12.11 Note that there is a significant distinction between 'expendable endowment' and 'permanent endowment'. Expendable endowment is capital (and treated as such in the charity's accounts) but the trustees have power to decide to spend it.[4]

---

2 Section 353(3) of the 2011 Act.
3 OG 545-1 Identifying and Spending Permanent Endowment.
4 See, eg, Charities SORP (FRS 102).

SPENDING PERMANENT ENDOWMENT

12.12 There are a number of situations in which a charity's trustees may be able to spend permanent endowment:

- under specific statutory powers to spend permanent endowment in ss 281–292 of the 2011 Act which specifically deal with the release of restrictions over permanent endowment (see **12.13-12.52**);
- by obtaining authority from the Commission under s 105 of the 2011 Act, generally in circumstances where the permanent endowment spent will ultimately be replaced (see **12.53-12.57**); and
- if they have adopted a total return approach to investment under the 2011 Act, by taking advantage of powers in the Charities (Total Return) Regulations 2013 to spend a limited amount of the permanent endowment and replace it over time (see **12.58-12.83**).

SPECIFIC STATUTORY POWERS

12.13 Prior to the 2006 Act, the 1993 Act contained some powers for charities with an income of less than £1,000 per year to spend their permanent endowment, but these were clearly available to a limited number of charities only and were subject to strict conditions, including obtaining prior Commission consent and giving public notice.

12.14 When the Strategy Unit conducted its review of charity law in 2002, it recognised the difficulties which permanent endowment can cause and recommended that the rules be relaxed. However, it highlighted that those donors who specifically intend to create a permanent endowment 'should not have their intention overturned lightly or on slender grounds'.[5] As a result, the 2006 Act significantly extended the circumstances in which permanent endowment can be spent. Smaller charities may spend their permanent endowment without the Commission's involvement, and larger charities also have power to spend their permanent endowment in some circumstances, provided the Commission consents.

12.15 The statutory powers for trustees to spend the capital of permanent endowment property are set out in ss 281–286 of the 2011 Act (and ss 287–292 in the case of special trusts).

12.16 The powers in ss 281 and 282 only apply to the 'available endowment fund of a charity which is not a company or other body corporate', ie to unincorporated charities. However, the Commission takes the view that a charitable company cannot hold permanent endowment as part of its corporate property.[6] This means that a charitable company will hold its permanent endowment on a separate charitable trust, of which it acts as trustee, so the statutory powers in ss 281 and 282 will apply to that trust. The trust may be linked to the main charity for accounting and other purposes under s 12 of

---

5 *Private Action, Public Benefit, A Review of Charities and the Wider Not-For-Profit Sector* (Strategy Unit, Cabinet Office, September 2002), para 4.66.

6 See, eg, Charity Commission publication CC12, 'Managing a charity's finances' (January 2016), para 3.3.

the 2011 Act.[7] An attempt during the 2006 Act's passage through the House of Lords to change the law to allow incorporated vehicles to hold permanent endowment directly failed.

12.17 There has been some debate about whether the statutory powers apply to permanent endowment funds held by Royal Charter bodies. In the 2005 House of Lords debates on the legislation which became the 2006 Act, the Government spokesman Lord Bassam said that Royal Charter bodies hold all their property on a trust, which suggested that the statutory powers would not apply to their permanent endowment funds.[8] However, in the 2011 Ministry of Justice paper summarising responses to the consultation on the Trusts (Capital and Income) Bill the Commission's view is cited as being that Royal Charter bodies can hold their property as beneficial owner, but would hold an endowment on trust. This corresponds with the authors' practical experience of the Commission's approach, which is to allow Royal Charter bodies to take advantage of the statutory powers in relation to their permanent endowment. Nevertheless the matter is not free from doubt. Lord Hodgson recommended that the Law Commission consider taking steps to clarify whether property is held by Royal Charter bodies on trust, or as corporate property for charitable purposes, to make administration and transactions easier (particularly as regards permanent endowment).[9] In its 2015 consultation, the Law Commission considered this point, expressing the view that the language in the legislation caused unnecessary uncertainty, and provisionally proposed that ss 281 and 282 should be amended to make it clear that they apply to permanent endowment held by an incorporated charity.[10]

12.18 Where a charity, whether incorporated or unincorporated, holds more than one permanent endowment fund, each fund must be treated separately by the trustees for the purposes of exercising their powers. However, the income thresholds set out in ss 281 and 282 apply differently depending on whether the charity is incorporated or unincorporated: see **12.25**.

12.19 The powers apply to any land held as permanent endowment. Earlier drafts of the legislation which became the 2006 Act excluded land held on trusts stipulating that it must be used for the purposes (or any particular purposes) of the charity, but the exclusion was removed by an eleventh hour amendment in the House of Commons.

12.20 However, restrictions may apply in any event if land, or indeed any other asset held as permanent endowment, is functional permanent endowment (see **12.5**). As explained below, the powers in ss 281 and 282 can only be exercised where the trustees are of the view that the purposes which apply to the permanent endowment fund could be carried out more effectively if the capital is spent. The Commission points out that where the fund consists of functional land, for example, which must be used for a particular charitable purpose, it is difficult to see how that purpose could be carried out more effectively if all of the land was disposed of.[11] Spending the capital would involve a change to the charity's purposes: the Commission might need to make a scheme changing the purposes under its cy-près jurisdiction (see Chapter 17).

---

7 See **4.12**.

8 Hansard 16 March 2005, col GC 549.

9 *Trusted and Independent: Giving Charity Back to Charities*, Appendix A.

10 Paragraphs 9.52–9.57, Technical Issues in Charity Law, A Consultation Paper, Law Commission, March 2015.

11 Charity Commission operational guidance OG 545-1 'Identifying and Spending Permanent Endowment'.

12.21 Note also that before selling any land the trustees need to comply with their obligations regarding sale of land in the 2011 Act (see Chapter 8).

12.22 The procedures which apply to spending permanent endowment using the statutory powers differ depending on whether the fund is regarded as a small or large fund.

SMALL FUND

What is a small fund?

12.23 Section 281 of the 2011 Act gives trustees of smaller permanent endowment funds powers to spend the permanent endowment without involving the Commission. A permanent endowment fund is a small fund if:

- the charity's gross income, in the last financial year, was £1,000 or less; or
- the fund has a market value of £10,000 or less (as recorded in its accounts for the last financial year, or if none, the value determined by a special valuation carried out for this purpose).

12.24 This means that where a charity's annual income was £1,000 or less in the last financial year, even if its permanent endowment fund is worth, say, £15,000, the permanent endowment fund will be treated as a small fund for the purposes of these rules. Similarly, if a charity has a total income of over £1,000, if its permanent endowment fund is not worth more than £10,000, it will also be regarded as small for these purposes.

12.25 Where the permanent endowment fund is held by an unincorporated charity, it is the capital value of the fund, but the gross income of the charity as a whole which is relevant when considering whether these thresholds have been exceeded, since the legislation refers to the market value of the 'endowment fund' but the gross income of 'the charity'.[12] Where the permanent endowment is held by an incorporated charity, it is, again, the capital value of the fund which is relevant, but in this situation it is the income of the fund, rather than the charity as a whole which is relevant. This is because the permanent endowment fund will be regarded as a separate 'charity' from the incorporated charity (see **12.16**).

12.26 The Minister for the Cabinet Office can alter the thresholds by order.[13]

12.27 A fund will also be treated as a small fund if, regardless of its size and the size of the endowment it wishes to spend, the endowment was not given by just one individual or institution, or several individuals or institutions with a common purpose (see **12.33**).

---

[12] Section 282(1)(b) of the 2011 Act. The position may be different where the permanent endowment fund constitutes a special trust.

[13] See s 285 and see **12.34** for proposals for reform of the thresholds.

What must the trustees do?

12.28 The trustees must satisfy themselves that the purposes which apply to the permanent endowment fund in question could be carried out more effectively if the capital as well as the income could be spent.

12.29 The trustees can then resolve that all or part of the fund should be free from the restriction on spending the capital. There is no need to seek the Commission's consent, and the resolution may take effect immediately, or from a future date specified in the resolution. If the fund is registered as a charity (including a linked charity: see **4.12**), in the authors' view a copy of the resolution should be sent to the Commission once it has been passed as the resolution will effect a change in the charity's trusts.[14] If the entire fund is spent following the resolution, the trustees must inform the Commission so that it may be removed from the register.[15]

LARGER FUNDS

What is a larger fund?

12.30 The trustees of larger permanent endowment funds may also resolve to spend the fund, but must involve the Commission.[16]

12.31 A permanent endowment fund is a larger fund for these purposes if:

- the gross income of the charity in the last financial year was over £1,000; and
- the market value of the fund (as recorded in its accounts for the last financial year, or if none, the value determined by a special valuation carried out for this purpose) is over £10,000.

If only one of these conditions is met, the fund will be a small fund and the rules set out at **12.23-12.29** will apply.

12.32 As mentioned at **12.25**, the property which is taken into account when considering whether the income threshold is met can vary depending on whether the permanent endowment is held by an unincorporated charity, or an incorporated charity.

12.33 In addition, the fund will only be a large fund if the capital of the fund consists entirely of property given by a particular individual (whether under a will or during their lifetime), or a particular institution, or by two or more individuals or institutions in pursuit of a common purpose. Permanent endowment will usually be 'entirely given' in this way, but an example of where the fund is not 'entirely given' includes where the trustees have created their own permanent endowment using a power in the governing document. In this situation the fund will be treated as small, regardless of its size.

12.34 Lord Hodgson recommended that the thresholds should be revised, in line with his other threshold changes, which were not supported by Government (see **4.21**). He acknowledged that the Law Commission would need to consult on where the right

---

14 Section 35(3) of the 2011 Act.
15 Section 35(3)(a) of the 2011 Act. See Chapter 4.
16 Sections 282–284 of the 2011 Act.

balance lies, but suggested a significant increase, perhaps assets of £100,000 and income of £10,000. In its 2015 consultation, the Law Commission commented that it could see the attraction of increasing the thresholds, and invited views on the nature of any increase, and the rationale for it.[17]

What must the trustees do?

12.35 The trustees must satisfy themselves that the purposes which apply to the permanent endowment fund in question could be carried out more effectively if the capital as well as the income could be spent.[18]

12.36 The trustees can then resolve that the permanent endowment fund, or a portion of it, should be free from the restriction on spending the capital.[19]

12.37 A copy of the resolution must be sent to the Commission, together with a statement of the trustees' reasons for passing it.[20] At the time of writing, the trustees can inform the Commission via an online application form available on the Commission's website.

What can the Commission do?

12.38 The Commission has power, on receipt of a copy of the resolution, to direct the trustees to give public notice of it, in the manner specified in the direction. The Commission must then take account of any representations by persons appearing to the Commission to be interested in the charity which are made to it within 28 days of the public notice being given.[21] It is the authors' experience that it is rare for the Commission to ask for public notice.

12.39 The Commission can also direct the trustees to provide it with additional information or explanations about the circumstances in and by reference to which they have decided to act. The Commission can ask for information about the trustees' compliance with any obligations imposed on them by or under ss 282 or 283 of the 2011 Act in connection with the resolution (see **12.35-12.39**).[22]

12.40 Whether or not it exercises its powers to direct that public notice be given, or to ask for more information, the Commission must consider whether to concur with the trustees' decision. The following factors are relevant:

- The Commission must take into account any evidence available to it as to the wishes of the individuals or institutions who contributed the funds to the charity.
- The Commission must take into account any changes in the circumstances relating to the charity since the funds were given to it, including in particular its financial position, the needs of its beneficiaries, and the social, economic and legal environment which it operates in.

---

17 Paragraphs 9.58–9.60, Technical Issues in Charity Law, A Consultation Paper, Law Commission, March 2015.
18 Section 282(3) of the 2011 Act.
19 Section 282(2) of the 2011 Act.
20 Section 282(4) of the 2011 Act.
21 Section 283 of the 2011 Act.
22 Section 283 of the 2011 Act.

- The Commission may only concur with the trustees' decision if it is satisfied that:
  - implementing the trustees' resolution would accord with the spirit of the original gift; and
  - that the trustees have complied with the obligations imposed on them by or under ss 282 or 283 in connection with the resolution.[23]

12.41 At the time of writing, the Commission's operational guidance states:[24]

'We should expect that in most cases:

- the trustees with their knowledge of the charity will be in the best position to decide that the resolution meets [the relevant] criteria; and
- we can concur with the resolution without the need to publish notices or ask for more information where the trustees use the web based application form which will normally give us all the information we need to make the decision.

However, there will be cases where we will not agree with the trustees' decision. This is more likely to occur in cases where the charity has been established more recently where, unlike older charities, the value or (sic) the endowment may not have had the chance to decline or the purpose of the charity can still be delivered within the spirit of the gift.'

12.42 Within three months of receiving the copy of the resolution (or, in a case where public notice must be given, three months of the date on which public notice is given) the Commission must notify the trustees whether or not it concurs with their decision. If it does, the resolution that the capital may be spent will take effect immediately.[25] When the Commission concurs with a resolution, it will record this on the Register of Charities.[26]

12.43 If the Commission decides not to concur with the resolution, the charity trustees and any other person who is or may be affected by the decision may appeal to the Tribunal.[27]

12.44 Lord Hodgson recommended that the Law Commission should give consideration to reducing this 3-month period to 60 days, in line with the statutory procedure for small charities wishing to change their purposes or transfer property (see Chapter 15), with a power for the Commission to extend its deadline for objection if it considers there to be good reason for doing so.[28] The Law Commission invited views on this in its 2015 consultation.[29]

12.45 If the Commission does not notify the trustees of its decision within the 3-month period, the trustees are entitled to act as though the Commission had concurred with their decision.[30] In these circumstances, the trustees would be well advised to confirm the date on which the Commission received a copy of their resolution before they act on it.

---

23 Section 284 of the 2011 Act.
24 OG 545-1 Identifying and Spending Permanent Endowment.
25 Section 284 of the 2011 Act.
26 OG 545-1 Identifying and Spending Permanent Endowment.
27 Section 319 and Sch 6 of the 2011 Act.
28 *Trusted and Independent*, Appendix A.
29 Paragraphs 9.61–9.63, Technical Issues in Charity Law, A Consultation Paper, Law Commission, March 2015.
30 Section 284(5) of the 2011 Act.

12.46 The Commission's operational guidance includes more information about the issues which it will consider when deciding whether to concur with a resolution, to ask for additional information or to require the trustees to publish information about the proposals.[31]

12.47 During the passage of the 2006 Act through Parliament, this part of the Act came under criticism for not giving sufficient respect to the views of the donor. Amendments were sought which would require at least three-quarters of the trustees to approve the resolution, and which would ensure that these powers could not be exercised for at least 100 years after the gift. The Government resisted these proposals, pointing out that the Commission does have to take the views of the donor into account, which would 'guard against' a situation where trustees could decide to spend capital the day after the charity was founded.[32] The explanatory notes to the 2006 Act stated that the Commission's involvement is 'meant to ensure ... that the intentions of the donor or donors in making the gift are treated with due consideration'. The Commission's operational guidance confirms that it may refuse to concur with the trustees' resolution in the case of 'a relatively new charity on the basis that circumstances may not have changed very much since the charity's inception and the donor's wishes may still be carried out using the income from the endowment'.[33] However, there may be situations where permanent endowment funds which have been established relatively recently may not generate enough income to be viable, particularly where they have been made under the terms of a will which was executed some time before the testator's death. The authors' experience is that the Commission will generally expect the trustees to have held the fund for at least a year before passing a resolution under s 282, in order to make an accurate assessment of its income.

SPECIAL TRUSTS

12.48 Section 288 of the 2011 Act allows the trustees of a so-called 'special trust' to spend permanent endowment, under procedures which are the same as those set out in ss 281–284.

12.49 A 'special trust' is defined in s 287 as 'property which (a) is held and administered by or on behalf of a charity for any special purposes of the charity, and (b) is so held and administered on separate trusts relating only to that property'. Sections 288–291 only apply where the Commission has directed that the special trust should be treated as a distinct charity under s 12(1) of the 2011 Act for the purposes of ss 288–292. Under s 12(1) the Commission can direct that a special trust should be treated as part of the main charity, or as a distinct charity.[34]

12.50 The trustees of the special trust can resolve that any permanent endowment property which they hold should be freed from the restriction on spending the capital, provided they are satisfied that the purposes which apply to the permanent endowment property in question could be carried out more effectively if the capital as well as the income could be spent.[35] Where the market value of the fund in question is more than

31 OG 545-1 Identifying and Spending Permanent Endowment.
32 HL Deb, vol 670, col GC 535 (16 March 2005).
33 OG 545-1 Identifying and Spending Permanent Endowment.
34 See **4.12**.
35 Sections 288 and 289 of the 2011 Act.

£10,000[36] and the capital consists entirely of property given by a particular individual (whether under a will or during their lifetime), or a particular institution, or by two or more individuals or institutions in pursuit of a common purpose, the trustees must comply with a procedure which is essentially the same as that set out at **12.30-12.46**.[37] There is a similar right of appeal to the Tribunal if the Commission decides not to concur with the resolution.[38] Note that the income of the charity is not relevant here, in contrast to the position under s 282.

12.51 In the authors' experience this power is rarely, if ever used. The requirement that the Commission should have directed that the special trust in question be treated as a separate charity under s 12(1) of the 2011 Act may mean that it is unlikely to be used as, in the authors' experience, s 12(1) is usually used to link charities rather than to treat them separately. At the time of writing, the Commission's operational guidance suggests that trustees wishing to make use of the s 288 and 289 powers may, in practice, be better advised to use the s 281 and 282 powers, as this avoids the need to apply for a direction under s 12(1).[39]

12.52 The Law Commission, in its 2015 consultation, recommended that ss 288 and 289 should be repealed. It commented that any permanent endowment which is a special trust would fall within the definition of 'available endowment fund' in ss 281 and 282 in any event. The Law Commission was not aware that these powers have ever been used, and said that their continuing existence causes confusion.[40]

EXPENDITURE AND REPLACEMENT OF PERMANENT ENDOWMENT

12.53 There may be circumstances where the statutory powers to spend permanent endowment under ss 281 and 282 are not available or appropriate. In these circumstances, the Commission may be prepared to authorise the trustees to spend permanent endowment using its powers of authorisation under s 105 of the 2011 Act.[41] This is generally on the basis that it is replaced over time from the charity's income. Section 105(6) of the 2011 Act specifically allows the directions given under a s 105 order to include directions for charging expenditure to capital and for requiring it to be recouped out of income within a specified period.

12.54 The Commission must be happy that the proposal is expedient in the interests of the charity. Replacement of the permanent endowment will generally be on a pound-for-pound basis, and the replacement term will be specified in the order. In some circumstances, the Commission may be prepared to waive repayment.

12.55 The Commission will not make an order where it would override an express prohibition in the relevant governing document. However, a scheme could be used to override a prohibition in the governing document, or to change the charity's purposes

36 The Minister for the Cabinet Office may alter this figure by order under s 292 of the 2011 Act.
37 Section 289 of the 2011 Act.
38 Section 319 and Sch 6 of the 2011 Act.
39 OG 545-1 Identifying and Spending Permanent Endowment.
40 Paragraphs 9.50 and 9.51, Technical Issues in Charity Law, A Consultation Paper, Law Commission, March 2015.
41 See **9.173–9.179**.

where the expenditure of the permanent endowment might involve a change of purpose, such as in the case of the disposal of functional permanent endowment.

12.56 More detail about the Commission's approach can be found in its operational guidance.[42]

12.57 Where trustees have adopted a total return approach to investment without the Commission's involvement under the new powers in ss 104A and 104B of the 2011 Act (see **12.58-12.83**) they have an automatic power to spend and replace up to 10% of the permanent endowment fund (see **12.76**).

TOTAL RETURN

12.58 One of the implications of permanent endowment is that the trustees, when managing an investment portfolio of permanent endowment funds, are bound by rigid rules which make a strict distinction between what is income return, which they can spend, and what is capital growth, which they cannot. This can mean that in a year when income yields are low, but capital growth is high, the trustees may only be able make limited provision for their beneficiaries in the short term, which can be frustrating. It can also make for an inflexible approach to investment management: since the trustees are under a duty to balance the needs of present and future beneficiaries, the strict distinction between income and capital yields means that they must invest in a way which balances the income return with the capital growth. This does not necessarily allow for the highest overall return.

12.59 In recognition of this, in 2001 the Commission adopted a policy of allowing permanently endowed charities to apply to it for permission to adopt a 'total return' approach to investment. Under a total return approach, although the trustees are still under a duty to take account of the needs of current and future beneficiaries in an even-handed way, in relation to investment returns they are not constrained by the strict legal rules determining what is income and what is capital growth, which gives scope for more flexibility. Prior to January 2014, charities wishing to adopt a total return approach were required to seek an order to this effect from the Commission under s 105 of the 2011 Act (see **12.53–12.56**).[43]

12.60 The scope for trustees to use this approach was significantly extended in January 2014 when changes to the 2011 Act introduced a power for trustees to resolve to adopt a total return approach to investment of their permanent endowment without involving the Commission.[44] The Charities (Total Return) Regulations 2013 ('the Total Return Regulations'), made by the Commission under the new provisions of the 2011 Act, provide a framework for this new power.[45] The Total Return Regulations are reproduced at **Appendix 11** of this book.

12.61 It is important to note that under the Total Return Regulations, the trustees have an overriding duty to exercise their powers 'in such a way as not to prejudice the ability

42 OG 545-2 Expenditure and Replacement of Permanent Endowment.

43 It is worth mentioning that a number of commentators, including the Charity Law Association, doubted the Commission's strict legal ability to adopt this policy.

44 Sections 104A and 104B were added to the 2011 Act by the Trusts (Capital and Income) Act 2013 with effect from 1 January 2014.

45 The regulations were made under s 104B of the 2011 Act and came into force on 1 January 2014.

of the charity to further its purposes now and in the future'.[46] This duty ensures that if a total return approach is adopted, the spirit of the permanent endowment must be maintained. The Commission specifically acknowledges in its guidance that the Total Return Regulations 'preserve the principle of permanent endowment and the right of donors and settlors to establish a charity with a permanent endowment'.[47] The Commission's guidance states: 'The total return approach is not just about spending resources which under the standard rules would be capital gains. It can also be about retaining resources ... for the protection of the interests of future beneficiaries.'[48]

12.62 The adoption of a total return approach under the new rules involves a series of steps.

Preliminary considerations

12.63 The trustees must obtain and consider proper advice about how the powers should be exercised, unless they reasonably conclude that in all the circumstances it is unnecessary or inappropriate to do so. Proper advice is the advice of someone reasonably believed by the trustees to be qualified to give it by their ability in and practical experience of investment and relevant matters.[49]

12.64 The legislation is ambiguous as to whether the trustees should obtain advice before passing a resolution to adopt a total return approach, or only once they are considering how to deal with the permanent endowment on an ongoing basis, after a total return approach has been adopted. It is the authors' view that the trustees should take appropriate advice at both stages (unless, in line with the Total Return Regulations, they reasonably conclude it is unnecessary or inappropriate).

The resolution

12.65 Next, the trustees must resolve that all or part of their permanent endowment should be invested without the need to maintain a balance between capital and income returns, and accordingly that it should be freed from the restrictions with respect to expenditure of capital that apply to it.[50]

12.66 The trustees, in passing the resolution, must be satisfied that is in the interests of the charity for the framework set out in the Total Return Regulations to apply to the fund in place of the usual permanent endowment regime. Once the resolution has been passed, the framework in the Total Return Regulations will apply.[51]

Valuation of the funds

12.67 In order to operate the total return approach, the relevant permanent endowment fund must be divided between the assets representing the value of the original endowment when it was made and any additions of capital such as further gifts into the

---

46 Regulation 6(2).

47 Charity Commission Guidance, Total Return Investment for Permanently Endowed Charities (2013), para C3.

48 Charity Commission Guidance, Total Return Investment for Permanently Endowed Charities (2013), para F3.

49 Regulation 6(3).

50 Section 104A(2) of the 2011 Act.

51 Sections 104A(3) and 104A(4) of the 2011 Act.

fund (known as the trust for investment, or investment fund) and the assets representing return on the endowment, including both any unspent income plus any capital gain, since that date (which becomes known as the unapplied total return). This division will be the starting point for the new treatment of the funds described below (see **12.70-12.75**).

12.68 The trustees must therefore identify a value for the investment fund, either on the date on which the fund was established, or a subsequent date decided on by the trustees. The date, the value of the investment fund on that date, and the value of the unapplied total return since that date must be recorded. While the Commission recognises that 'trustees won't be expected to carry out an elaborate tracing exercise here', it recommends that trustees take legal and accountancy advice when making their decision.[52]

12.69 Once this division has been made, the trustees cannot change it, except by revoking the resolution, as to which see **12.81**.

The total return approach

12.70 Once the resolution has been passed, and the values of the investment fund and unapplied total return arising from it have been established, the permanent endowment is treated in the following way.

12.71 The investment fund, or trust for investment, continues to be invested over time, and cannot be spent.

12.72 The trustees must decide how to treat the return from the investment fund (known as the unapplied total return). This will comprise the unapplied total return at the date of the resolution and investment return which arises going forward and is added to the unapplied total return. The investment return includes interest, dividends and rent and other income, and the capital gain resulting from the disposal or revaluation of assets, less any capital losses arising on the disposal or revaluation of assets.[53] Unrealised capital gains or losses are therefore taken into account.

12.73 Subject to the overriding duty mentioned at **12.61**, and to the duty to obtain advice mentioned at **12.63**, any part of the unapplied total return may be allocated to an 'income fund' (also known as the trust for application). This must be used for the charity's beneficiaries within a reasonable period.[54]

12.74 The trustees may also decide to accumulate part of the unapplied total return as part of the trust for investment.[55] This cannot then be spent. There is a cap on how much of the unapplied total return can be dealt with in this way, based on the inflationary increase in the value of the investment fund. The cap is set at the increase in value of the investment fund (not taking into account any unapplied total return) by reference to the rise in either the Retail Price Index or the Consumer Prices Index (or any

---

52 Charity Commission Guidance, Total Return Investment for Permanently Endowed Charities (2013), para D6.

53 Regulation 2.

54 Regulation 2.

55 Regulation 3(3).

similar index), since the last time unapplied total return was accumulated (or, if there has been no such accumulation, since the date from which the investment fund was initially valued: see **12.67-12.68**).[56]

12.75 Any unapplied total return which is not allocated to the income fund or accumulated as part of the investment fund must be invested in the same way as the property held within the trust for investment.[57] The Commission will expect the trustees to justify the balance of funds remaining as unapplied total return, and to have a policy for determining how the unapplied total return should be treated.[58]

Expenditure and replacement of the investment fund

12.76 The Total Return Regulations go beyond the allocation of investment returns, by giving trustees who have passed a s 104A(2) resolution a power to spend part of the investment fund, provided they recoup the expenditure over time. They may allocate up to 10% of the investment fund (or trust for investment) to the income fund (or trust for application), provided it is repaid on a pound-for-pound basis over a period to be reasonably determined by the trustees. The 10% is calculated by reference to the value of the investment fund (excluding any unapplied total return) on the date of the first such allocation which has not yet been recouped.[59]

Duties of the trustees

12.77 The trustees must comply with the overriding duty mentioned at **12.61** when making the initial division between the investment fund and the unapplied total return, and when deciding how to deal with the unapplied total return on an ongoing basis.

12.78 The trustees must also exercise such care and skill as is relevant in the circumstances, having regard to any special knowledge or experience the particular trustee has or holds themselves out as having and, if the trustee acts as such in the course of a business or profession, to any special knowledge or experience it is reasonable to expect someone in that business or profession to have.[60]

Reporting

12.79 The trustees' annual report must contain details of the policy adopted by the trustees in making the initial division between the investment fund and the unapplied total return, and the date from which the trust for investment was valued (unless it was the date on which the charity was established). They must explain the consideration and policies relevant to the trustees' determination of how the unapplied total return was divided between the investment fund and the income fund in the year. Where any part of the investment fund has been allocated to the income fund (see **12.76**), the trustees must also explain the consideration and policies relevant to that decision. They must identify

---

56 Regulation 5.
57 Regulation 3(4).
58 Charity Commission Guidance, Total Return Investment for Permanently Endowed Charities (2013), para E1.
59 Regulation 4.
60 Regulation 6(1).

who gave the advice mentioned at **12.63** above.[61] If no annual report is required, all this information should appear in the notes to the accounts.[62]

Pre-existing total return orders

12.80 Where charities are operating under a total return order issued by the Commission prior to the commencement of ss 104A and 104B and the Total Return Regulations, that order continues to apply, but may be overridden by a new s 104A(2) resolution, provided the trustees continue to comply with any directions as to recoupment of capital which form part of the original order.[63]

Revocation

12.81 The Regulations contemplate that trustees may change their mind about adopting a total return approach, by allowing for revocation of a s 104A(2) resolution, although the Commission warns that 'this will be difficult and not to be undertaken lightly'.[64] The trustees must consider how much of the unapplied total return should be added to the investment fund: this amount is capped. The balance will be treated as expendable endowment (see **12.11**). If there is a negative unapplied total return, the trustees must make arrangements for this, plus an additional amount to take account of inflation, to be repaid to the fund over a period of not more than 10 years.[65]

General

12.82 The Commission is obliged to publish a review of the Total Return Regulations by 1 January 2019.[66]

12.83 More detail about the rules is set out in the Charity Commission Guidance.[67]

REFORM

12.84 At the time of writing, several aspects of the rules on permanent endowment are under review. As mentioned earlier in this chapter (see **12.17** and **12.34**):

- In his 2012 review of charity law, Lord Hodgson suggested a review of the thresholds and time limits which apply to the statutory powers to spend permanent endowment. This is now under way following the Law Commission's 2015 consultation.
- Lord Hodgson recommended that the basis on which Royal Charter bodies hold their permanent endowment should be clarified: the Law Commission has simply proposed that the statutory powers to spend permanent endowment should be amended to make it clear that they apply to permanent endowment held by corporate charities.

---

61 Regulation 6(4).
62 Regulation 6(4).
63 Regulation 7.
64 Charity Commission Guidance, Total Return Investment for Permanently Endowed Charities (2013), section H.
65 Regulation 8.
66 Regulation 9.
67 Total Return Investment for Permanently Endowed Charities (2013).

12.85 Lord Hodgson also recommended that the Law Commission review the issue of the availability of permanent endowment funds to a charity's creditors.[68] The Law Commission's 2015 consultation paper contained an extensive analysis of the position of charitable trusts in insolvency, including permanent endowment, proposing that the Commission's guidance on insolvency should be clarified in a number of respects.[69]

12.86 As mentioned at **16.14**, the Law Commission has proposed that the regime for transferring permanent endowment between charities on a merger should be simplified.

12.87 Lord Hodgson recommended that the Government should introduce a legal power for non-functional permanent endowment to be invested in mixed purpose investments (see Chapter 11), with the requirement that capital levels must be restored within a reasonable period.[70] Government welcomed the recommendation and the Law Commission's consultation paper on social investment considered the issue.[71] The Law Commission concluded, however, that no such power was necessary, expressing the view that 'charity trustees already have the power to use permanent endowment to make social investments which are anticipated to produce a positive financial return'.[72] The new statutory power to make social investment introduced into the 2011 Act by the 2016 Act (see **11.54–11.61**) does not, therefore, allow social investment of permanent endowment, unless the trustees expect that making the social investment will not contravene any restrictions on spending the permanent endowment.

12.88 However, the Law Commission's 2015 consultation paper did put forward more radical suggestions for a completely new regime, which it suggested might be called 'preserved endowment', which would run parallel to the existing permanent endowment regime.[73] Under the proposals, trustees would have power to spend the capital of the 'preserved endowment' fund provided that they sought to ensure that the real value of the fund was maintained in the long term. This would mean that there would be no difficulty in making a loss-making investment, which might be appropriate in the context of social investment, so long as the fund maintained its value over the long term. The Law Commission's consultation expressed the view that under the existing permanent endowment rules, trustees are obliged simply to maintain the actual value of the fund on a pound-for-pound basis, rather than the real value of the fund after taking account of inflation, although it did acknowledge that in practice trustees will seek to maintain the fund's real value given their duty to act even-handedly between present and future beneficiaries. The 'preserved endowment' regime would oblige the trustees to seek to ensure the real value was maintained over time.

12.89 The Law Commission invited comments on the suggestion and thoughts on how a new regime might operate. It conceded that a new regime would not be simple to devise, suggesting that if there is enthusiasm for a new regime, it may well be some time before it was implemented.

---

68 *Trusted and Independent*, Appendix A.
69 Chapter 13, Technical Issues in Charity Law, A Consultation Paper, Law Commission, March 2015.
70 *Trusted and Independent*, ch 9, recommendation 3.
71 Social Investment by Charities, Law Commission consultation paper 216, April 2014, ch 5.
72 Paragraph 5.30.
73 Paragraphs 9.69–9.82, Technical Issues in Charity Law, A Consultation Paper, Law Commission, March 2015.

CHAPTER 13

REGULATION OF CHARITABLE COMPANIES

OVERVIEW

13.1 Charitable companies are regulated under both company law and charity law. This raises particular issues, including:

(a) requirements for charitable companies to disclose their charitable status on their stationery and other documents: see **13.2-13.8**;

(b) a requirement for the Charity Commission's prior consent to changes to a charitable company's Articles of Association which are material to charity law: see **13.9-13.17**;

(c) a requirement for Commission consent to transactions between a charitable company and its trustees raising potential conflict of interest: see **13.18-13.24**;

(d) a power for the Commission and the Attorney General to wind up or reinstate charitable companies: see **13.29-13.31**;

(e) control of the names that can be used by charitable companies: see **6.6–6.11**; and

(g) particular (though broadly similar) requirements for accounting and reporting (see Chapter 21).

The directors of charitable companies are regarded as directors under company law, and as charity trustees under charity law.

DISCLOSURE OF CHARITABLE STATUS

13.2 Section 194 of the 2011 Act requires a charitable company which does not include the word 'charity' or 'charitable' in its name to state that it is a charity in every description of document or communication in which it is required by regulations made under s 82 of the Companies Act 2006[1] to state its registered name, and in all conveyances purporting to be executed by the company. It is usual practice for registered charities to comply by stating their registered charity numbers.

13.3 This means that unless the word 'charity' or 'charitable' appears in its name, a charitable company must state that it is a charity on its conveyances and on:

(a) its business letters, notices and other official publications;

---

1 At the time of writing these are the Company, Limited Liability Partnership and Business (Names and Trading Disclosures) Regulations 2015, SI 2015/17.

(b) its bills of exchange, promissory notes, endorsements and order forms;
(c) cheques purporting to be signed by or on behalf of the company;
(d) orders for money, goods or services purporting to be signed by or on behalf of the company;
(e) its bills of parcels, invoices and other demands for payment, receipts and letters of credit;
(f) its applications for licences to carry on a trade or activity;
(g) all other forms of its business correspondence and documentation; and
(h) its websites.

13.4 Failure to make the statements required under s 194 has civil and criminal law consequences. The charity's ability to bring legal proceedings attempting to enforce rights arising out of a non-compliant contract or conveyance may be affected, under s 195. Under s 196 failure to comply with s 194 without reasonable excuse means that the company, and every officer of the company (which can include a shadow director), commits an offence, and may be liable on summary conviction to a fine (with daily default fines for continued contravention). However the authors are not aware of any prosecutions being made under s 196.

13.5 Section 194 is concerned with charitable status rather than registered charity status. It applies to all charitable companies, whether registered or not and regardless of income. Registered charitable companies with income over £10,000 must also comply with the rules on disclosure of registered charity status set out in s 39 of the 2011 Act, which are described in detail at **4.72–4.79**.

13.6 Note that, where relevant, registered charitable companies must comply with both s 39 and s 194. For example, the word 'charity' on a cheque issued by a charitable company which is a registered charity is not sufficient. The words 'registered charity' are necessary to comply with both statutory provisions. A practical way to ensure compliance is for a registered charity to state its registered charity number on the cheque.

13.7 Section 194 also requires a charitable company which does not include the word 'charity' or 'charitable' in its name to state the fact that it is a charity, in legible characters, in every location in which it is required by regulations under s 82 of the Companies Act 2006 to state its registered name.[2] This means that the statement must be made at the company's registered office, in any other location where the company keeps company records available for inspection in accordance with a requirement of company law and in locations where the company carries on business.[3] Under s 196 there are potential criminal law consequences if a charity fails to comply: see **13.4**.

13.8 Company law also imposes other disclosure requirements on charitable companies.[4] These include:

---

2 At the time of writing these are the Company, Limited Liability Partnership and Business (Names and Trading Disclosures) Regulations 2015, SI 2015/17.

3 Regulations 21 and 22 of the Company, Limited Liability Partnership and Business (Names and Trading Disclosures) Regulations 2015, SI 2015/17. There are various exceptions from disclosure under regs 21 and 22.

4 Part 6 of the Company, Limited Liability Partnership and Business (Names and Trading Disclosures) Regulations 2015, SI 2015/17.

- A requirement for the company to display its registered name (meaning the name it is registered under at Companies House) at its registered office, the place where its records are available for inspection and other business locations.
- The company must display its registered name on the documents and communications mentioned at **13.3**(a) to (h).
- The following details must be disclosed on the company's business letters, order forms and websites:
  - the part of the United Kingdom in which the company is registered under the Companies Acts;
  - the company's registered number (meaning the number with which the company is registered at Companies House);
  - the address of the company's registered office (meaning its registered office under company law).

  The fact that it is a limited company must also be stated on these documents and websites.

AMENDMENTS TO ARTICLES OF ASSOCIATION

Regulated alterations

13.9 Charitable companies have a statutory power to amend their Articles of Association by special resolution of the members.[5] However, under s 198 of the 2011 Act certain changes which are material to charity law require the prior written consent of the Commission. These changes are known as 'regulated alterations'. Regulated alterations are ineffective without this consent.[6]

13.10 Section 198 applies to all charitable companies, including charitable companies not registered with the Commission, such as exempt charities.

13.11 'Regulated alterations'[7] are:

(a) any amendment of the Articles of Association adding, removing or altering a statement of the company's objects (s 198(2)(a));[8]

(b) any alteration of any provision of the Articles of Association directing the application of property of the company on its dissolution (s 198(2)(b)); and

(c) any alteration of any provision of the Articles of Association where the alteration would provide authorisation for any benefit to be obtained by directors or members of the company or persons connected with them (s 198(2)(c)).

Prior to the Companies Act 2006, provisions dealing with the objects, benefits to trustees and dissolution were contained in a charitable company's Memorandum of

---

5 Section 21 of the Companies Act 2006. Under s 22 of the Companies Act 2006 a company's Articles may also impose more restrictive conditions or procedures on amending the Articles, known as provision for 'entrenchment'.

6 Section 198(1) of the 2011 Act.

7 Section 198(2) of the 2011 Act.

8 See, for example, the case of *Catholic Care (Diocese of Leeds)*, in which the Commission refused to provide its consent for the charity to amend its objects clause so as to permit it to refuse to offer its adoption services to same-sex couples: the case was considered by both the First-tier Tribunal (*Catholic Care (Diocese of Leeds) v Charity Commission* (CA/2010/0007)) and by the Upper Tribunal (*Catholic Care (Diocese of Leeds) v Charity Commission* [2012] UKUT 395 (TCC)).

Association, rather than in its Articles of Association. Under s 28 of the Companies Act 2006 all provisions in the Memorandum of Association are treated as provisions of the Articles. This means that s 198 of the 2011 Act equally applies to relevant changes to the Memorandum of Association of older companies.

Trustee benefit

13.12 Changes to the Articles which would allow a trustee or a person connected to a trustee to obtain any benefit which would be authorised under the statutory power to remunerate trustees and persons connected to them for services needed by and provided to relevant charities (subject to appropriate safeguards)[9] are not regulated alterations and therefore do not need prior Commission consent. This is because 'benefit' in s 198(2)(c) is defined in s 199 as a direct or indirect benefit of any nature, but does not include remuneration which may be authorised by s 185. If payments are permitted under s 185, changes to the Articles are not necessary, but charities may wish to amend their Articles so that the powers available under statute are clear from the face of the governing document. Note, however, that there are restrictions on the application of the statutory power, including where there is a prohibition in the governing document: see 7.20-7.22 for more details.

13.13 The definition of a person connected to a trustee or member for the purposes of s 198(2)(c) is set out in s 200, which in turn cross refers to ss 350 and 352 of the 2011 Act.

Non-substantive changes

13.14 When a charitable company established prior to the coming into force of the Companies Act 2006 first changes its constitution, it is common for the provisions of the Memorandum of Association to be incorporated into the Articles of Association so that going forward the charity has only one governing document. Another alternative, which may be used in cases where none of the provisions contained in the Memorandum are being amended, is to annex the Memorandum to the Articles as a Schedule.

13.15 Changes of formatting along these lines may mean changes to the numbering of provisions dealing with the objects, benefits to trustees and dissolution, and changes to those provisions to reflect changes to the numbering of other provisions of the Articles. This can give rise to questions about whether such changes are regulated alterations. At the time of writing, the position is as follows:[10]

- Objects and dissolution clauses – The Commission's view is that renumbering of these clauses and changes to them to reflect changes to the numbering of other provisions of the Articles are not regulated alterations.
- Trustee benefit clauses – It is the authors' view that renumbering of clauses dealing with trustee benefit, and changes to those clauses to reflect renumbering of other Articles, are not regulated alterations so long as they do not have the effect of authorising any additional benefit to trustees, members or persons connected with them.

---

9 Section 185 of the 2011 Act: see Chapter 7.

10 Operational guidance OG 518 'Alterations to Governing Documents: Charitable Companies'.

Procedure

13.16 Note that the Commission's written consent must be obtained *before* the special resolution to effect the amendment is passed. Details of the proposed changes should be sent to the Commission seeking its approval. At the time of writing, the Commission asks for consent to be sought via an online application form. The Commission's operational guidance, OG 518 'Alterations to Governing Documents: Charitable Companies', currently gives an indication of the criteria that the Commission will apply when assessing an application. The fundamental question is whether the alteration is in the best interests of the charity.

13.17 In addition to the usual Companies House filing requirements, evidence of any required Commission consent must be sent to Companies House when filing a copy of the special resolution: failure to comply is a criminal offence.[11]

CHARITY COMMISSION CONSENT TO TRANSACTIONS

13.18 Under the Companies Act 2006, certain transactions between a company and its directors require the approval of the company's members.[12] These include directors' long-term service contracts (s 188 of the Companies Act 2006), substantial property transactions (s 190 of the Companies Act 2006), loans to directors (s 197 of the Companies Act 2006) and payments to directors for loss of office (s 217 of the Companies Act 2006). Under s 201 of the 2011 Act, in the case of a charitable company, some of those transactions, listed in s 201(2), also require the prior written consent of the Commission.

13.19 The general rules on restricting benefits to charity trustees mean that charitable companies are unlikely to be caught by these provisions very often. However, s 190 of the Companies Act 2006, which deals with substantial property transactions, may well apply where a charitable company is involved in any restructuring. If it does apply, the Commission's prior written consent will be needed under s 201 of the 2011 Act.

13.20 Section 190(1) of the Companies Act 2006 provides that the members of a company must approve any

> 'arrangement under which-
>
> (a) a director of the company or of its holding company, or a person connected with such a director, acquires or is to acquire from the company (directly or indirectly) a substantial non-cash asset, or
>
> (b) the company acquires or is to acquire a substantial non-cash asset (directly or indirectly) from such a director or a person so connected'

An asset is a substantial non-cash asset in relation to a company if its value exceeds 10% of the company's asset value and is more than £5,000, or if its value exceeds £100,000.[13] (Sections 252–255 of the Companies Act 2006 deal with the definition of a person connected with a director.)

---

11 Section 198(3)–(5) of the 2011 Act and s 30 of the Companies Act 2006.

12 Part 10, Chapter 4 of the Companies Act 2006.

13 Section 191 of the Companies Act 2006.

13.21 The Commission's view[14] is that s 190 can apply where an unincorporated charity – a charitable trust or a charitable unincorporated association – transfers assets to a charitable company, and one or more of the trustees of the unincorporated charity are also directors of the charitable company. This is a relatively common scenario. Unincorporated charities which wish to 'convert' to charitable companies, under a process often called 'incorporation' or 'reconstitution', typically do so by transferring their assets to a new charitable company, whose directors are the trustees of the unincorporated charity. Section 190 may also apply in a range of merger situations involving charitable companies (including circumstances where all the charities involved in the merger are companies).

13.22 In all these situations the charitable company will need to consider whether s 190 applies, depending on the nature and value of the assets to be transferred. If it is of the view that s 190 is relevant, it will need to seek the prior written approval of the Commission, and subsequently seek the approval of the members of the company.[15]

13.23 The Commission has expressed the view that the giving of approval under s 201 can also authorise any trustee conflicts of interest arising in relation to the transaction.[16]

13.24 The relevant provisions of the Companies Act 2006[17] make some exceptions to the requirement for member approval where the company is a wholly owned subsidiary of another body corporate. However, s 202 of the 2011 Act requires that the Commission's prior written approval should still be obtained in these circumstances.

CAPACITY

13.25 What was previously s 65 of the 1993 Act has now been included in s 42 of the Companies Act 2006. These provisions exclude charities from the relaxation of the ultra vires rule, which enables other companies in certain circumstances to undertake activities otherwise unauthorised by the company's Articles of Association. There is, however, protection for a person who gave full consideration and without knowing that the transaction was beyond the powers of the charitable company or who did not know that the company was a charity.

13.26 Section 41 of the Companies Act 2006 allows a company to affirm certain transactions between a company and its directors, or persons connected to the directors: in the case of charitable companies the prior written consent of the Commission is required in these circumstances.[18]

---

14 The Commission's view has not been tested in the courts. It was expressed only relatively recently (in 2012) and some practitioners do not agree. The authors consider the Commission's view that s 190 consent is required in the circumstances to be unhelpful, since it is introducing a requirement for a purely technical consent. The company law requirement is, in reality, focused on conflict of interest in the context of purely financial interest, which in most cases does not apply on the reconstitution of a charity or a merger.

15 The authors' experience is that seeking the approval of the Commission is a relatively straightforward process.

16 Letter from Charity Commission to the Charity Law Association, 9 September 2013.

17 Part 10, Chapter 4 of the Companies Act 2006.

18 Section 42(4) of the Companies Act 2006.

DUTIES OF COMPANY DIRECTORS AND COMMISSION'S POWER TO AUTHORISE ACTIONS

13.27 Part 2 of Chapter 10 of the Companies Act 2006 imposes a range of duties on directors of a company. A detailed analysis of those duties is outside the scope of this book, but they include duties to exercise reasonable care and to avoid conflicts of interest. These apply to the trustees of a charitable company as well as their general duties under charity law. The usual company law duties are modified in some respects in relation to charitable companies under s 181 of the Companies Act 2006.

13.28 Section 105 of the 2011 Act, which allows the Commission to authorise action which is expedient in the interests of the charity (see **9.173–9.179**), specifically provides in s 105(9) that the Commission may authorise the actions of the trustees of a charitable company even if those actions involve the breach of a duty imposed by Part 2 of Chapter 10 of the Companies Act 2006. In practice the authors are aware that the Commission has used s 105 to authorise trustees to take actions that would otherwise place them in breach of their duty under the Companies Act 2006 to avoid a conflict of interest.

WINDING UP

13.29 Section 113 of the 2011 Act confers on the Attorney General the power to apply to the court to wind up a charitable company under the Insolvency Act 1986. The Commission may also do so if it has instituted an inquiry into the charity concerned under s 46 (see Chapter 9) and is satisfied that there has been failure to comply with an order or direction of the Commission, failure to remedy a breach specified in an official warning given under s 75A, or any other mismanagement or misconduct, or that action should be taken to protect the charity or to ensure that its property is applied for the purposes of the charity.[19]

13.30 Under s 203 of the 2011 Act the Commission may apply to the court to have a charitable company which has been wound up or struck off the register of companies (held at Companies House) restored to that register.

13.31 The powers of the Commission under ss 113 and 203 are exercisable only with the agreement of the Attorney General.

AUDITORS' DUTIES

13.32 Section 159 of the 2011 Act, which was introduced by the 2006 Act, ensures that auditors' duties to report matters to the Commission also apply to where the charity in question is a charitable company.[20]

---

[19] Section 113 cross-refers to the preconditions set out in s 76(1) of the 2011 Act: at the time of writing not all of these are in force (see **9.80–9.81**).

[20] See **21.57–21.64**.

CHAPTER 14

CHARITABLE INCORPORATED ORGANISATIONS

INTRODUCTION

14.1 One of the most significant changes brought about by the 2006 Act was the creation of a new incorporated legal form designed especially for charities, the charitable incorporated organisation, or CIO.

14.2 The idea of a new incorporated legal form for charities had been under discussion for many years. The proposal was contained in the Department for Trade and Industry's 2001 Company Law Review and was developed by an Advisory Group set up by the Charity Commission. The 2002 review of charity law by the Strategy Unit, *Private Action, Public Benefit* noted that there was 'an incomplete menu of organisational forms for the full range of activity undertaken by charities and the wider not-for-profit sector'[1] and recommended the introduction of the charitable incorporated organisation to address this.

14.3 The report noted that the charitable company limited by guarantee, which was then the legal form of choice for most charities wishing to take advantage of an incorporated legal form, faces ongoing double regulation by both Companies House and the Charity Commission. Charitable companies have to comply with a corporate governance regime which is not tailored to fit the trustee governance structure. As board members are both directors for the purposes of company law and trustees under charity law, confusion can arise as to how these two sets of duties interrelate. The report therefore recommended that the CIO should be an incorporated legal form with limited liability for the members of the organisation, regulated by the Charity Commission alone, with various recommended key features.

14.4 The framework for the CIO, reflecting the recommendations of the Strategy Unit, was duly included in the 2006 Act. However, the implementation of the relevant provisions took several years. The bulk of the provisions of the 2011 Act dealing with CIOs were finally brought into force on 2 January 2013[2] and the first CIOs were registered with the Commission on this date.

14.5 Initially, the Commission staggered the registration of CIOs. New charities were only able to register as CIOs if their income exceeded £5,000. Existing unincorporated charities wishing to set up CIOs as successor bodies[3] were initially only able to do so if their income exceeded £250,000: this threshold was gradually reduced during the course

---

1 *Private Action, Public Benefit*, para 3.3.

2 Charities Act 2011 (Commencement No 1) Order 2012, SI 2012/3011.

3 See **14.228–14.239**.

of 2013. By 1 January 2014 it was possible to register a CIO, whether as a completely new charity or as a successor to an existing unincorporated charity, regardless of the level of its income.

14.6 While there are advantages and disadvantages to the new legal form, which are explored in more detail at **14.9-14.19**, the CIO has undoubtedly proved popular. In the period April 2015 to April 2016 over 35% of new charity registration applications were for CIOs.[4]

14.7 Not all of the provisions of the 2011 Act dealing with CIOs have been implemented. At the time of writing, the provisions of the 2011 Act allowing existing charitable companies and registered societies to convert to a CIO from an existing charitable company are not yet in force, although a consultation on regulations allowing charitable companies and community interest companies to become CIOs was issued in the spring of 2016: see **14.210–14.225**.

14.8 A review of the impact of CIOs is expected in 2016: see **14.244**.

ADVANTAGES AND DISADVANTAGES OF THE CIO

14.9 During the second reading of the legislation which became the 2006 Act in the House of Lords, Baroness Barker of Anagach in Highland welcomed the CIO in the following terms:[5]

> 'Up until now in the charity world we have had unincorporated associations, which are rather like battered old slippers; they are very comfortable but not quite what we want. We have had companies limited by guarantees, which are rather like clogs; they are very hard-working and durable but they do not fit exactly with what we need them to do. Now we have CIOs, which some of us are led to believe will be the high-performance, all-terrain shoe that we need in order to do our business.'

14.10 The CIO has undoubtedly proved popular, but it is not for everyone. Any organisation considering the CIO as an option for their legal structure will need to consider its features carefully, and compare them with the other legal forms available to charities. There are some clear advantages, such as the benefits of limited liability which come with incorporated status, and some disadvantages, such as the more significant degree of regulation of CIOs as compared with charitable trusts and unincorporated organisations. Some of the CIO's features, such as the less extensive statutory rights for members as compared with a company limited by guarantee, may be regarded as an advantage by some, but as a disadvantage by others. This section sets out what are regarded as the main pros and cons of the CIO.

Advantages

14.11 The main advantage of the CIO is that it is incorporated.

---

4 Charity Commission Annual Report 2015–2016.
5 HL Deb, vol 672, col 817 (7 June 2005).

14.12 An unincorporated charity is technically comprised of the individual trustees acting collectively. It therefore has no legal identity of its own. An incorporated charity, by contrast, does have its own legal identity.

14.13 It is conceptually clearer and administratively more convenient for an organisation to have its own legal identity, so it is the organisation itself that acts, not, technically, individual trustees on behalf of the organisation. This is increasingly significant the larger the charity gets and the more it assumes legal obligations.

14.14 For example, the employer of employees in an unincorporated organisation is, technically, the group of individual trustees collectively. Similarly, the individual trustees are lessees under a lease and contracting parties under a contract. The risks and liabilities involved in running the charity's activities are taken on by the charity trustees themselves. While the trustees can use the charity's assets to meet the liabilities properly incurred in running the charity, if the charity's assets are not sufficient to cover its debts and liabilities, the trustees' personal assets are at risk.

14.15 There are further potential complications when the trustees of an unincorporated charity change. The original contracting trustees who cease to be trustees need to pass on the responsibility to the new trustees. So, for example where individual trustees are registered as the proprietors of charity land, the registered information can become out of date and problems can arise when title needs to be dealt with by the named ex-trustee owners at a later date.

14.16 All of these issues are resolved by operating through a corporate charity like a CIO.[6] Trustees are therefore increasingly concerned to establish new incorporated charities in the first place, or convert existing unincorporated charities into incorporated charities.

14.17 CIOs enjoy the benefits of an incorporated form but, unlike other incorporated legal forms (such as companies or community benefit societies), they are governed by charity law alone and do not need to comply with the additional legislative and regulatory framework imposed by company or registered society law.

14.18 The other main advantages of the CIO include:

- Single registration with, and regulation by, the Commission. This is the same as for unincorporated charities, but charitable companies must also register and file information with Companies House.
- Less onerous accounting requirements, with small CIOs preparing only receipts and payments accounts and larger CIOs preparing accruals accounts. All charitable companies, by contrast, are required to prepare accruals accounts compliant with company law. See Chapter 21.
- Lower costs, because the Commission (unlike the Registrar of Companies) does not charge for registration and filing certain information.[7]

---

6 Note, however, that trustees of incorporated charities are not immune from personal liability. The rules on fraudulent and wrongful trading which apply to charitable companies also apply to CIOs: see **14.199**. Trustees of incorporated charities can be liable for some criminal offences and civil penalties, for breach of trust or duty, and under any personal guarantees they may give.

7 There have been discussions about introducing charging for charity registration and filing: see Chapters 2 and 4.

- A proportionate enforcement regime which does not impose strict liability on the trustees for administrative offences.
- The CIO is the only bespoke vehicle for charities. There are, for example, codified duties for trustees and members which specifically reflect the charitable nature of a CIO: see **14.58-14.59** and **14.74**.
- Unlike a charitable company, a CIO is not required to comply with company law. However, the lack of an extensive body of law supporting the legal form is sometimes seen as a disadvantage.
- A flexible membership regime allowing, for instance, more flexibility than company law regarding the rights of members and methods of communication with members: see **14.33** and **14.75**. Again, this is not always seen as an advantage.
- The ability to register with the Commission even where the charity's income does not exceed £5,000: since the existence of a CIO depends on its registration with the Commission, CIOs must register regardless of the level of their income. This may not always be viewed as an advantage.
- Scope for the constitution to include provision for decision-making by consensus: see **14.82** and **14.96**. This may be particularly attractive to some faith-based groups.
- Narrower public access to the charity's register of members than is the case for charitable companies: see **14.110**.
- Charitable companies are required to keep a register of 'people with significant control' over the company: there is no such requirement for CIOs.
- A simplified regime for the transfer of permanent endowment when setting up a CIO as a successor to an unincorporated charity: see **14.236**.

Disadvantages

14.19 While the take up of the new legal form has been enthusiastic (see 14.6), a number of factors mean that the CIO will not always be the most suitable choice. Particular disadvantages include:

- The fact that the CIO is still very new, whereas charitable companies are supported by a well-established framework of company law. It may take some time before CIOs are well recognised outside the charity sector.
- There is no public register of charges for CIOs. By contrast, where a charitable company grants a charge over its assets, that charge is registered with Companies House and the details of the charge are publicly available. This gives security to lenders. As explained in more detail at **14.114-14.116**, there is no corresponding public register of charges for CIOs. This can deter possible lenders, and may inhibit the CIO's ability to borrow money.
- The registration process may be an issue. A CIO's corporate identity is dependent on recognition of its charitable status and the CIO is only established once it is registered with the Commission. A charitable company, by contrast, can start to operate as soon as it is registered with the Registrar of Companies, which can be achieved in a day: the company will subsequently seek charitable registration with the Commission. This means that there will inevitably be a delay before a CIO can start to operate, particularly if there any concerns about the organisation's charitable status.

- Similarly, when a CIO is removed from the register of charities, whether because it is no longer charitable, or for some other reason, it ceases to exist: this is not the case with a charitable company.
- Constitutional amendments only take effect when they are registered with the Commission: see **14.148**.
- A CIO, like a charitable company, must have both trustees and members (although they may be the same people): see **14.26-14.29**. This is not the case for charitable trusts.
- The rules on conflicts of interest are more restrictive than is the case for charitable companies: see **14.60-14.70**.
- The majorities for written resolutions of the members of CIOs are higher than is the case for charitable companies: see **14.99**.
- In some circumstances, creditors have fewer rights on the dissolution of a CIO than they do in relation to a charitable company, which may affect a CIO's relationship with third parties: see **14.206**.
- Companies limited by guarantee will, in due course, be able to convert to CIO status: see **14.210-14.224**. There is, at present, no legislative regime allowing for CIOs to convert to charitable companies.
- CIOs are more heavily regulated than other charities in some respects. For example, all CIOs must register with the Commission, regardless of their income: other charities, if required to register, generally need only do so once their income exceeds £5,000: see Chapter 4. CIOs are subject to more stringent requirements than unincorporated charities in terms of filing with the Commission. There are also time limits for filing some information with the Commission which do not apply to other charities: see, for example, **14.148**.
- Broadly speaking, CIOs are less straightforward to run than unincorporated charities.
- Some may adopt a 'wait and see' attitude to CIOs, preferring to wait until the legal form is more well-established and grey areas have been ironed out.
- It is interesting to note that while there is no formal restriction on the size of CIO, the Cabinet Office impact assessment which accompanied the Charitable Incorporated Organisations (General) Regulations 2012 (see **14.21**) assumed that the target market for CIOs was charities with incomes of between £10,000 and £500,000.

STATUTORY FRAMEWORK

14.20 The basic statutory framework for CIOs is set out in Part 11 (ss 204–250) of the 2011 Act 2011. This is supplemented by detailed regulations made by the Minister for the Cabinet Office under the 2011 Act. The regulations were made following a detailed consultation by the Cabinet Office in 2008.[8]

14.21 The Charitable Incorporated Organisations (General) Regulations 2012[9] ('the General Regulations'; see **Appendix 5** of this book) cover matters concerned with the

---

8 See http://webarchive.nationalarchives.gov.uk/20100304103842/http:/www.cabinetoffice.gov.uk/third_sector/consultations/completed_consultations/cio.aspx.

9 SI 2012/3012.

formation and running of CIOs such as requirements for the content of constitutions, registration procedures and rules for meetings and communications.

14.22 The Charitable Incorporated Organisations (Insolvency and Dissolution) Regulations 2012[10] ('the Dissolution Regulations'; see **Appendix 6** of this book) include detailed provisions for the dissolution of CIOs and the application of parts of the Insolvency Act 1986 to CIOs, with a schedule of modifications.

14.23 The Charitable Incorporated Organisations (Consequential Amendments) Order 2012[11] applies the Company Directors Disqualification Act 1986 to the charity trustees of CIOs and adds a number of Commission decisions concerning CIOs to the schedule of decisions which can be the subject of appeal or application to the Charity Tribunal.

14.24 Further regulations will deal with the conversion of existing charitable companies to CIOs: see 14.210-14.224.

KEY FEATURES OF CIOS

14.25 Section 205 of the Act sets out the nature of CIOs by providing that a CIO shall:

- be a body corporate;
- have a constitution;
- have a principal office, which must be in England or Wales; and
- have one or more members.

14.26 This means that, like companies limited by guarantee, CIOs have a two-tier structure with both members and trustees.

14.27 The 2002 Strategy Unit report had recommended, by contrast, that the CIO be available in both member and non-member forms, so that it could have single-tier governance. This recommendation was echoed by extensive lobbying while the 2006 Act was passing through Parliament. But these calls were not heeded.

14.28 The two-tier structure of the CIO means that CIOs retain one aspect of company structure which frequently causes confusion to organisations which lack a membership body separate from the trustees. It is not unusual for charitable companies to operate as if the trustees were the only members of the charity even when their Articles of Association actually provide otherwise. This can lead to the charity falling foul of company law requirements concerning admission of members, holding general meetings and passing members' resolutions, consequently invalidating trustees' appointments and decisions they have made.

14.29 Having said that, s 206(6) of the 2011 Act does make it clear that trustees may, but need not be, members of the CIO, and vice versa, and that the members and trustees may, but need not be, identical. This is reinforced by the Commission's publication of two separate model constitutions for CIOs, a foundation model where the only members

---

10 SI 2012/3013.
11 SI 2012/3014.

are the trustees, and an association model where there is a wider membership: see **14.38**. The General Regulations recognise the distinction between the two models.[12] Where a foundation model is adopted, it is crucial that the trustees/members are aware of what decisions they must make in their capacity as trustees and what decisions (such as resolutions to amend the constitution) must be made in their capacity as members.

14.30 The members are either not liable to contribute to the assets of the CIO on a winding up, or have limited liability: see **14.32**.

THE CONSTITUTION

What must be in the constitution?

14.31 Sections 206(1) and (2) of the 2011 Act and reg 13 of the General Regulations set out the matters to be provided for in a CIO's constitution.

14.32 A CIO's constitution is required to state:[13]

- its name;
- its purposes;
- whether its principal office is in England or in Wales;
- whether or not its members are liable to contribute to its assets if it is wound up, and (if they are) up to what amount; and
- the names of the persons who are to be the first charity trustees.

14.33 The constitution must also include provisions covering the following:[14]

Members

- who is eligible for membership;
- how a person becomes a member;
- how a member retires from membership;
- other circumstances in which, and method by which, membership may or must be terminated;
- the holding of members' meetings (called general meetings), and in particular:
  - the procedure for calling meetings;
  - the appointment of a chair for such meetings;
  - representation of any member which is a body corporate at such meetings;
  - the quorum;
  - if the members have the right to demand a poll, the exercise of that right and the manner in which a poll is to be conducted;
  - if the constitution permits members to appoint a proxy, provision about the way in which the appointment is made, the rights of the proxy and the termination of such an appointment;

---

12 Regulation 26(2) of the General Regulations requires a foundation CIO to maintain a register of trustees only, without the need for a register of members.

13 Section 206(1) of the 2011 Act and reg 13(1) of the General Regulations.

14 Sections 206(2) and 223(3) of the 2011 Act and regs 13(2) to (14) of the General Regulations.

- procedures for postal voting, if permitted;
- procedures for voting at meetings otherwise than by voting on resolutions, if permitted;
- if the members have different voting rights, the rights attached to each class of member;

- procedures for decisions by members outside general meetings, if permitted, which would include decisions by written resolution;
- if members are to be treated, as a result of becoming members, to have agreed to receive communications from the CIO by electronic means, a statement to this effect, and the circumstances in which members will receive communications by electronic means;
- if a CIO is to communicate with its members by website, details of the circumstances in which a website may be used;

Trustees

- the appointment of trustees and any conditions of eligibility for appointment;
- how a charity trustee retires from office;
- the other circumstances in which charity trustees will cease to hold office, in particular, if the CIO's constitution permits the members to remove a charity trustee from office, the circumstances in which this may occur, and the procedures for doing so;
- the holding of trustees' meetings, in particular:
  - the procedure for calling meetings;
  - the appointment of a chair of such meetings;
  - the quorum;
  - if the trustees are to have a right to call a poll, details of the exercise of that right and the manner in which the poll is to be conducted;
- subject to compliance with s 222 of the 2011 Act and reg 36 of the General Regulations (which deal with personal benefit and payments: see **14.60-14.70**), the extent to which a trustee may benefit personally from any arrangement or transaction entered into by the CIO;
- procedures for voting at trustees' meetings otherwise than by voting on resolutions, if this is to be permitted;
- procedures for making decisions otherwise than at trustees' meetings, if this is to be permitted, which would include decisions by written resolution or by email;
- if the constitution requires more than one trustee to be in office for its business to be discharged, the minimum number of trustees that is required must be specified;

Other

- if a CIO is to have a common seal, provision about the use of the seal; and
- directions about the application of the property of the CIO on dissolution.

This list highlights significant differences between CIOs and charitable companies. Charitable companies are governed by company law, which gives members rights to appoint proxies, to demand polls, to make decisions by written resolution and to remove trustees from the board.[15] A CIO's constitution may of course be drafted to include similar rights,[16] but they do not apply automatically. Similarly, company law generally requires the express agreement of each member to the receipt of electronic communications from the company: CIOs may include deeming provisions in the constitution to the effect that members are automatically treated as having agreed to receive electronic communications from the CIO. Some charities may be attracted by the relative flexibility of the CIO.

14.34 A CIO's constitution must not include any restriction of its powers under s 216 of the 2011 Act (see **14.76**) which would deprive it of the ability to dispose of its property.[17] If the members are liable to make a contribution to the CIO's assets on a winding up, the constitution binds the CIO and its members to the same extent as if it were a contract.[18]

14.35 The constitution may include provision for entrenchment, so that specified provisions of the constitution may be amended or repealed by resolution of its members only if specified conditions are met, or specified procedures are complied with that are more restrictive than those under s 224(2) of the 2011 Act (which deals with amendment of the constitution by the members: see **14.140-14.151**). Provision for entrenchment may only be made in the constitution proposed in the charity registration application or by an amendment of the constitution approved by all members. Provision for entrenchment does not prevent amendment of the CIO's constitution by all members or by order of the court or the Commission.[19]

14.36 The constitution must provide for such other matters, and comply with such requirements, as are specified in regulations made by the Minister for the Cabinet Office.[20] Many of the requirements listed above are set out in the General Regulations: it is clearly open to the Minister to amend or add to them.

14.37 The constitution must be in English, unless the principal office is in Wales, in which case the constitution may be in English or Welsh.[21]

Foundation vs association structure

14.38 While the requirement for a CIO to have both members and trustees means that the CIO is a two tier structure, it is specifically contemplated that the members and trustees may be identical (see **14.29**). A CIO may therefore adopt a structure in which the members and the charity trustees are the same people. This is known as a 'foundation CIO', while a CIO with a wider body of members is known as an 'association CIO'. The Commission has published two model constitutions: both a foundation model and an association model: see **14.40-14.42**. It is important, when using the foundation structure for the trustees/members to understand which capacity they are acting in when taking any decision.

---

15 Sections 324, 321, 288 and 168 of the Companies Act 2006.
16 Many of these rights are included in the Commission's model association CIO constitution: see **14.40-14.43**.
17 Regulation 14 of the General Regulations.
18 Section 217(2) of the 2011 Act.
19 Regulation 15 of the General Regulations.
20 Sections 206(3) and 247 of the 2011 Act.
21 Section 206(4) of the 2011 Act.

14.39 The Commission has reported that it receives significantly more applications for registration of foundation CIOs than for association CIOs.

Model constitutions

14.40 Section 206(5) of the 2011 Act provides that a CIO's constitution must be in the form specified in regulations made by the Commission or as near to that form as the circumstances admit. This provision relates to the form rather than the content of the constitution and follows the company law position as discussed in the case of *Gaiman & Ors v National Association for Mental Health*.[22] The Commission has made regulations containing two model constitutions: a foundation model for CIOs whose only voting members are the charity trustees, and an association model for CIOs with voting members other than the charity trustees. Template versions of the model constitutions are available on the Commission's website.[23]

14.41 The Commission recommends the use of one of the model constitutions when establishing a CIO. The models satisfy the requirements of the 2011 Act and the General Regulations, and registration using a model constitution is invariably quicker than using a bespoke constitution. However, in practice the Commission does accept constitutions that depart from the models, provided they cover all the matters which are required by the 2011 Act and the General Regulations. In the authors' experience, in these cases the Commission finds it helpful if the applicants also include a track change version of the constitution, showing the differences between the bespoke constitution and the Commission's model, and/or a note showing which provisions of the constitution cover the matters required by the legislation.

14.42 The model constitutions are not currently available in a word format. This means that from a practical perspective, if applicants wish to make changes to the Commission's models, they must either print a hard copy of the model from the Commission's website, and make manuscript changes, or retype the model from scratch and make appropriate alterations. The Commission has indicated in the past that an interactive version of the models may be made available, but this has not yet been forthcoming.

14.43 The Commission has approved a number of model CIO constitutions for umbrella bodies with member charities wishing to adopt the CIO form: these are not available on the Commission's website.

REGISTRATION OF A CIO

14.44 Sections 207–210 of the 2011 Act and regs 5–8 of the General Regulations deal with CIO registration. Regulation 6 amends ss 29–38 of the 2011 Act in their application to CIOs (see **Appendix** 7 of this book). Decisions to register, or not to register, a CIO may be appealed to the Charity Tribunal.

---

22 1969 G 4145.

23 www.gov.uk/government/publications/setting-up-a-charity-model-governing-documents.

Application for registration

14.45 Registration is by application to the Commission with a copy of the proposed constitution of the CIO, together with such other documents or information prescribed by regulations made by the Minister for the Cabinet Office or as the Commission may require.[24] The application is made online in the same way as any other charity application (see Chapter 4). The only difference is that CIOs are not required in their application to prove that they have an income in excess of £5,000.

14.46 Where the proposed constitution includes a provision for entrenchment (see 14.36) this fact must be included in the application for registration.[25]

14.47 Regulation 7 of the General Regulations permits the Commission to require the contents of any document to be in standard form, produced in a manner that can be scanned or copied, and authenticated by a particular person or persons of a particular description by any specified means. The Commission may also specify the means of submission, eg by post or electronically, and if in electronic form may specify the hardware or software to be used. Any such requirements must be published in such manner as the Commission thinks fit. Where applications are made electronically, the applicants are treated as having agreed to accept a response in electronic form, to the email address used or given in the application (subject to any limitations specified when that address was provided).

14.48 In practice the Commission has specified that it will only accept applications for CIO registration in electronic form.

14.49 The Commission must refuse an application for registration if it is not satisfied that the CIO would be a charity at the time of registration, or if the proposed constitution does not comply with the requirements of s 206 or other requirements set out in the General Regulations or any other regulations made under s 206, which deal with the required contents of a CIO's constitution.[26] An exempt charity may not be registered as a CIO.[27]

14.50 The Commission may refuse an application if the proposed name of the CIO is the same as, or too like, the name of any other charity (whether registered or not), or if the name meets any of the other criteria which permit the Commission to direct a charity to change its name (see Chapter 6).[28]

Implications of registration

14.51 Once the Commission grants an application to register a CIO, it must register the CIO in the register of charities, giving its date of registration and a note to the effect that it is constituted as a CIO, as well as the particulars and information which would generally be included in the register for any charity. A copy of the register entry must be sent to the CIO at its principal office.[29]

---

24 Section 207 of the 2011 Act.
25 Regulation 8 of the General Regulations.
26 Section 208(1) of the 2011 Act.
27 Regulation 5 of the 2011 Regulations.
28 Section 208(2) of the 2011 Act.
29 Section 209 of the 2011 Act and s 29 of the 2011 Act as amended by reg 6 of the General Regulations.

14.52 The CIO becomes a body corporate by virtue of its registration.[30] In the same way as any other charity, registration means that it is conclusively presumed to be a charity.[31]

14.53 Those who made the application for registration are the first members of the CIO.[32] Any property vested in the applicant(s) on trust for charitable purposes vests in the CIO on its registration.[33] It appears that this provision may override the need for the formalities usually required for the transfer of some types of property (such as land or shares) to take effect. However, it is not clear how the vesting would be evidenced for the purposes of re-registering freehold or (where applicable) leasehold property. Neither does the legislation deal with the position where property is mortgaged or, in the case of leasehold property, requires the landlord's consent for assignment. Note that any liabilities which the applicants have taken on do not automatically transfer to the new CIO, so they may need to seek a contractual indemnity from the CIO once it is registered to cover these liabilities.

14.54 Once registered, the trustees must notify the Commission of any changes in the particulars of the CIO entered in the register of charities within 28 days and supply the Commission with particulars of the change.[34] For other registered charities there is no such time limit: this provision is in line with the higher disclosure requirements for CIOs. The CIO's register entry will be open to public inspection, in the same way as any other charity, as will a copy of its constitution.[35]

14.55 Any person who is or may be affected by the registration of a CIO may object to its registration or apply to the Commission for its removal.[36]

CHARITY TRUSTEES

Eligibility

14.56 The minimum age for charity trustees of a CIO is set at 16.[37] The minimum age was the subject of consultation in 2008 and opinion was evenly divided between a minimum of 16 and 18 years. The Government opted for 16 years on the grounds that this struck the right balance between wanting to encourage young people to become involved in running charities, whilst recognising that charities need to be administered by people who are able to understand and manage the responsibilities of charity trusteeship.

14.57 A person who is disqualified from being a charity trustee under s 178 of the 2011 Act or under the General Regulations may not be appointed as a trustee of a CIO.[38] The provisions of the 2011 Act which apply to disqualification of trustees generally apply to CIOs: see **9.204–9.233**. The Company Directors Disqualification Act 1986 also applies to CIOs. This means that a court may make an order under the 1986 Act disqualifying

30 Section 210(1) of the 2011 Act.
31 Section 37 of the 2011 Act: see 4.80.
32 Section 210(1)(c) of the 2011 Act.
33 Section 210(2) of the 2011 Act.
34 Section 35 of the 2011 Act as amended by reg 6 of the General Regulations.
35 Section 38 of the 2011 Act as amended by reg 6 of the General Regulations. See also **4.7–4.8**.
36 Section 36 of the 2011 Act as amended by reg 6 of the General Regulations.
37 Regulation 31(1)–(4) of the General Regulations.
38 Regulation 31(5) of the General Regulations.

a person from being a charity trustee of a CIO (or acting as a receiver of a CIO's property or from being involved in the promotion, formation or management of a CIO) without the leave of the court.[39]

14.58 The 2011 Act imposes a statutory duty of care on the trustees of a CIO. Each trustee must exercise the powers and perform the functions that they have in the capacity of trustee in the way that they decide, in good faith, would be most likely to further the purposes of the CIO.[40]

14.59 In the performance of their functions as trustee, each charity trustee of a CIO must exercise such care and skill as is reasonable in the circumstances, having regard in particular to any special knowledge or experience that the charity trustee has or purports to have. If the charity trustee is acting in the course of a business or profession the duty takes into account the special knowledge or experience that it is reasonable to expect of a person acting in that kind of business or profession.[41] Regulations may permit the statutory duty in s 221(2) to be disapplied or modified in the constitution of a CIO.[42] However, this was the subject of consultation in 2008 and the overwhelming majority of responses thought that it should not be possible for a constitution to replace the duty of care in the 2011 Act with a lesser duty, on the grounds that the higher duty is necessary if the CIO is to command confidence as a legal structure. Some responses also considered that the charity sector should promote the highest standards of governance in order to promote public confidence. These views have been followed and the General Regulations include no power to modify the statutory duty of care in a CIO's constitution.

Trustee benefits and conflicts of interest

14.60 Restrictions on benefits to charity trustees and the management of conflicts of interest are covered in s 222 of the 2011 Act and in regs 34 and 36 of the General Regulations. While the provisions are at first sight less complex than the equivalent company law requirements, it is the authors' experience that they can, in some circumstances, be less flexible.

14.61 A trustee of a CIO may not accept benefits from third parties obtained by reason of being a trustee. This duty is not infringed if the benefit cannot reasonably be regarded as likely to give rise to a conflict of interest.[43]

14.62 The CIO's constitution is likely to include restrictions on the benefits which trustees may receive from the CIO. The Commission's model constitutions for CIOs, for example, prohibit the trustees, or persons connected to them, from:

- buying or receiving goods or services from the CIO on terms preferential to those applicable to members of the public;
- selling goods, services or any interest in land to the CIO;
- being employed by, or receiving any remuneration from, the CIO; and

---

39 Section 22F of the Company Directors Disqualification Act 1986, as amended by the Charitable Incorporated Organisations (Consequential Amendments) Order 2012, SI 2012/3014.

40 Section 221(1) of the 2011 Act.

41 Section 221(2) of the 2011 Act.

42 Section 222(3) and (4) of the 2011 Act.

43 Regulation 34 of the General Regulations.

- receiving any other financial benefit from the CIO;

except for in a range of fairly standard circumstances.

14.63 The trustees of a CIO have a statutory right to expenses: under s 222(3) of the 2011 Act a trustee of a CIO may be reimbursed by the CIO, or may pay out of the CIO's funds, expenses 'properly incurred' by them in the performance of their functions as trustee.

14.64 Where a trustee is permitted to benefit, the procedures regarding conflicts of interest set out in s 222 of the 2011 Act and reg 36 of the General Regulations must be followed.

14.65 Under s 222 of the 2011 Act, where the CIO is contemplating a transaction or arrangement from which a trustee may derive some personal benefit, the trustee must, before the transaction or arrangement is entered into, disclose to all the other trustees any material interest (direct or indirect) which the trustee has in the transaction or arrangement, or in a person or body party to it. Failure to do so means that the trustee may not benefit personally from the transaction or arrangement. It is not clear exactly how trustees are expected to make disclosure to all of the trustees. The Commission's model constitutions adopt a pragmatic approach, requiring that a trustee should declare the nature and extent of any interest, direct or indirect, in a proposed – or existing – transaction or arrangement 'which has not previously been declared'.[44] This would allow for disclosure to be made via a register of trustees' interests.

14.66 In addition, under reg 36 of the General Regulations, a trustee of a CIO who would benefit personally, whether directly or indirectly, from a transaction or arrangement which the CIO proposes to enter into must not take part in the making of the decision whether or not to enter into the transaction or arrangement and must not be counted in the quorum necessary for making the decision. This applies to both trustees' decisions and to members' decisions. This requirement does not, however, apply where the proposed transaction or arrangement cannot reasonably be regarded as likely to give rise to a conflict of interest. The Commission's model CIO constitutions include a similar (but arguably not identical) requirement for trustees to absent themselves from any discussions of the trustees 'in which it is possible that a conflict of interest will arise between his or her duty to act solely in the interests of the CIO and any personal interest (including but not limited to any financial interest)'.[45]

14.67 These restrictions apply in addition to any other restrictions in the constitution or otherwise, such as the restrictions on a trustee acting in relation to any decision to remunerate the trustee or a person connected to them under the statutory power in s 185 of the 2011 Act (see Chapter 7).

14.68 Regardless of any legal obligation, advance disclosure of interests and not voting in the relevant decision-making process is, at the very least, good governance practice regardless of the legal form of the charity. A well-drafted constitution should always include procedures for dealing with conflicts of interest, in a manner appropriate to the individual charity. (There are similar, but not identical, duties on trustees of charitable companies to avoid conflicts of interest under company law.)

---

44 Clause 7 of the model foundation and association constitutions, August 2014 versions.

45 Clause 7 of the model foundation and association constitutions, August 2014 versions.

14.69 However, the authors have concerns that the conflicts of interest procedures imposed by the General Regulations, in particular, may be unduly restrictive in some circumstances. There will be some situations where all the trustees share an interest, such as decisions regarding taking out trustee indemnity insurance which will benefit the whole trustee body, decisions varying benefits or services to beneficiaries where all the trustees are beneficiaries, and the adoption of a trustee expenses policy. It may be possible to argue that the situation in question 'cannot reasonably be regarded as likely to give rise to a conflict of interest' within the meaning of reg 36(3). If it is not possible to make this argument, the conflict of interest will need to be dealt with in another way, perhaps by seeking an order from the Commission under s 105 of the 2011 Act[46] authorising the trustees of the CIO to enter into the proposed arrangement notwithstanding the conflict. Regulation 36(4) specifically provides that nothing in reg 36 affects the power of the Commission to authorise dealings under s 105.

14.70 The conflict of interest issue is likely to arise where an unincorporated charity transfers its undertaking to a new CIO which has been established as a successor to the unincorporated charity: see **14.228-14.239**. It is typical, in these situations, for the new CIO to give an indemnity to the trustees of the unincorporated charity undertaking to meet any proper liabilities of the unincorporated charity trustees which arise after the transfer of the undertaking. Under reg 36, any trustees of the new CIO who are also trustees of the unincorporated charity will be unable to participate in a decision to enter into the indemnity, which may well mean that there are not enough 'unconflicted' trustees (or members, in the case of a members' resolution) to approve the indemnity on behalf of the CIO. In these circumstances the Commission should be asked to authorise the proposed indemnity by way of an order under s 105 of the 2011 Act. The authors' experience is that the Commission is, in principle, willing to grant s 105 orders in this situation.

Validity of trustee's acts

14.71 Regulation 32 of the General Regulations confirms that the acts of any person acting as a trustee are valid even if later it is discovered there had been a defect in their appointment, they are disqualified or they had ceased to hold office. This could be a very useful provision, particularly where, as is quite often the case, there is a technical flaw in the appointment of charity trustees.

14.72 Regulation 32 also provides that the acts of a trustee will be valid even if it is later discovered that they were not entitled to vote on the matter in question, or, where a decision is taken by consensus (see **14.82**), they were not entitled to take part in the relevant decision. However, this only applies in favour of the CIO, and any third party (other than the CIO or the trustee concerned) to an agreement or transaction entered into as a consequence of the trustee voting or taking part in a decision when they were not permitted to do so.

14.73 Clause 20 of the Commission's model CIO constitution also includes saving provisions which preserve the validity of a trustees' decision notwithstanding certain technical problems.

---

[46] See Chapter 9.

MEMBERS

14.74 Section 220 of the 2011 Act imposes a specific duty on each member of a CIO to exercise the powers which they have in that capacity in the way that they decide 'in good faith, would be most likely to further the purposes of the CIO'. This statutory duty is unique to CIOs: legal opinion varies on whether there is a similar duty in the case of charitable companies, but in the case of CIOs the matter is put beyond doubt.

14.75 As mentioned at **14.33**, members have very few statutory rights when compared to the rights of members of charitable companies. This was considered in the 2008 consultation on the legislative framework for CIOs. Two-thirds of the respondents thought that members' rights, if any, should be left to provision in the constitution. One reason for this was that prescribing rights in the regulations could hinder the proper administration of CIOs as it could lead to minority interests taking control of the CIO. The other third of the respondents argued that members of a CIO should have the same guaranteed rights as company members under company law, including the right to call a general meeting, the right to demand a poll, the right to vote by proxy and the right to remove a trustee. The majority view was accepted by the Government so that CIOs wanting to include members' rights similar to those under company law will need to ensure that these specific provisions are included in the constitution.

RUNNING A CIO

Powers of the CIO

14.76 Subject to anything in its constitution, a CIO may do anything which is calculated to further its purposes or is conducive or incidental to doing so.[47] As mentioned at **14.34**, a CIO's constitution must not include any restriction of this power that would deprive it of its ability to dispose of its property.[48]

Exercise of powers by trustees

14.77 The CIO's charity trustees are to manage the affairs of the CIO and may for that purpose exercise all the powers of the CIO.[49]

Capacity

14.78 A CIO must operate in accordance with its constitution.[50] Section 218 of the 2011 Act includes protection for innocent third parties dealing with a CIO or its trustees in circumstances where the CIO lacks constitutional capacity, or where the trustees have constitutional limitations on their powers. This does not, however absolve the trustees from their duty to act within their constitution and in accordance with any constitutional limitations on their powers, nor does it affect any liability incurred by them for acting beyond their constitutional powers.[51]

---

47 Section 216(1) of the 2011 Act.
48 Regulation 14 of the General Regulations.
49 Section 216(2) of the 2011 Act.
50 Section 217(1) of the 2011 Act.
51 Section 219 of the 2011 Act.

Agents, nominees and custodians

14.79 The provisions of the Trustee Act 2000 which relate to the appointment and remuneration of agents, nominees and custodians (see Chapter 11) are applied to CIOs with various modifications, under reg 33 of the General Regulations. This means that the trustees of a CIO have power to appoint and pay agents, investment managers, nominees and custodians in a similar manner to trustees of unincorporated charities.

Trustees' decision-making

14.80 As mentioned above, the CIO's constitution must include various provisions regarding the holding of trustees' meetings: see **14.33**. However, provided the areas specified by the 2011 Act and the General Regulations are covered in the constitution, there is little statutory regulation of how trustees' meetings are called and held, and how trustees make their decisions.

Notice of trustees' meetings

14.81 The General Regulations[52] contain provisions regarding the manner of communication with the CIO which will apply to communications with trustees and may therefore affect the manner of giving notice of trustees' meetings: see **14.117-14.129**.

Decisions without voting

14.82 It is clear from reg 13(13) of the General Regulations that it is possible for the constitution to provide that decisions will be taken at a trustees' meeting otherwise than by voting on resolutions. This will allow the constitution to include procedures allowing decisions to be taken by consensus, which may be attractive to some charities. The alternative decision-making process must be specified in the constitution.

Decisions outside meetings

14.83 If the trustees are to be permitted to make decisions outside meetings, this must be specified in the constitution.[53] This is restrictive: for most other types of charity it will usually be possible for the trustees to make unanimous decisions outside meetings even if the governing document is silent. The Commission's model constitutions for CIOs allow trustees to take unanimous decisions by means of a resolution in writing or in electronic form.[54] Minutes of trustees' meetings and a record of decisions made otherwise than in meetings must be kept for at least 6 years from the date of the meeting or decision, respectively.[55]

---

52 Regulations 49–59 and Sch 3.

53 Regulation 13(14) of the General Regulations.

54 Clause 17 of the model association constitution and clause 13 of the model foundation constitution, August 2014.

55 Regulation 37 of the General Regulations.

Conflicts of interest

14.84 In the event of a conflict of interest which affects a matter to be decided on by the trustees, the procedures mentioned above (see **14.60-14.70**) must be followed, as well as any additional restrictions imposed by the constitution.

Record keeping

14.85 Minutes of a trustees' meeting can be evidence of the proceedings at the meeting if they purport to be authenticated by the chair of that meeting or the next meeting. Where minutes have been made, the meeting is treated as having been duly held and convened, the proceedings at the meeting are treated as having taken place, and all appointments made at the meeting are treated as valid, until the contrary is proved.[56] There are similar provisions in relation to records of decisions made otherwise than at meetings.[57]

Members' decision-making

14.86 As mentioned at **14.33**, the 2011 Act and the General Regulations require a CIO's constitution to include various provisions regarding the holding of members' meetings (also called general meetings). While the rules which apply to CIOs are far less prescriptive about the holding of members' meetings than is the case under company law, the following should be noted.

Members' rights to call a meeting

14.87 If the CIO wishes its members to have rights to call members' meetings these rights must be included in the constitution (although there is a statutory right for members to ask the Commission to call a meeting: see **14.97**). The Commission's model association constitution includes rights for 10% (and 5% in some circumstances) of the members to oblige the trustees to call a members' meeting.

Notice periods

14.88 While there is no generic minimum notice period for members' meetings, in practice many of the resolutions which might be passed at a members' meeting do require that a minimum period of notice be given. Where a resolution is to be tabled which deals with amendment of the constitution (see **14.140-14.151**), amalgamation (see **14.153-14.163**) or the transfer the CIO's undertaking to another CIO (see **14.164-14.170**), or an application to the Commission for dissolution (see **14.177-14.183**) not less than 14 days' notice must be given to all members entitled to vote at the meeting and the charity trustees. (Where the constitution permits members to make decisions otherwise than by voting, notice must be given to all members entitled to take part in the decision, and the trustees.)[58] The day of the meeting and the day on which notice is given are not counted when calculating the notice period. The constitution may include a longer notice period. Shorter notice is acceptable with the consent of a qualifying majority, which is a majority in number of the members with rights to attend and vote at the meeting, representing 90% of the voting rights, or such

---

56 Regulation 38 of the General Regulations.
57 Regulation 39 of the General Regulations.
58 Regulation 35 of the General Regulations and reg 6 of the Dissolution Regulations.

higher percentage as may be specified in the CIO's constitution, up to 95%. Where the constitution permits decision making at a meeting other than by resolution, all the members entitled to attend and take part in decisions at the meeting must agree to shorter notice.[59] The provisions of the General Regulations regarding communications with the CIO may affect the giving of notice of members' meetings: see **14.117-14.129**.

Contents of the notice

14.89 For resolutions which amend the constitution, or deal with amalgamation or the transfer of the CIO's undertaking to another CIO, or with an application to the Commission for dissolution, the notice must contain particulars of the resolution that is to be proposed.[60] The constitution may include more stringent requirements.

Proxies and poll voting

14.90 If the CIO wishes its members to have rights to appoint proxies to represent them at members' meetings and to demand a poll vote at members' meetings, these rights must be included in the constitution. The Commission's model association constitution includes rights for 10% of the members to demand a poll. Both of the Commission's model constitutions include optional provisions allowing members to appoint proxies.

Voting majorities

14.91 Resolutions which amend the constitution, or which deal with amalgamation or the transfer of the CIO's undertaking to another CIO, or an application to the Commission for dissolution of the CIO, must be passed by a 75% majority of those voting at the meeting.[61]

Postal voting

14.92 The General Regulations envisage that members may cast their votes at members' meetings by post, but if this is to be permitted the constitution must include provision about the circumstances in which, and the way in which, such votes may be given. The Commission's model constitutions include optional wording which allows for votes to be cast by post, and by email.[62] Where the 2011 Act and the Dissolution Regulations require a resolution to be passed by a 75% majority, this includes 'those voting … by post, if voting that way is permitted'.[63] The Commission has expressed the view, in correspondence with the authors, that voting by post in this context includes voting by email.

Class rights

14.93 It is possible for different classes of member to have different voting rights, but this must be provided for in the constitution.[64]

---

59 Regulation 35 of the General Regulations and reg 6 of the Dissolution Regulations.

60 Regulation 35 of the General Regulations and reg 6 of the Dissolution Regulations.

61 Section 224 of the 2011 Act (amendment), s 235 of the 2011 Act (amalgamation), s 240 of the 2011 Act (transfer of undertaking) and reg 6 of the Dissolution Regulations (dissolution).

62 Appendix, Charity Commission model foundation and association constitutions, August 2014.

63 Section 224 of the 2011 Act (amendment), s 235 of the 2011 Act (amalgamation), s 240 of the 2011 Act (transfer of undertaking) and reg 6 of the Dissolution Regulations (dissolution).

64 Regulation 13(9) of the General Regulations.

Conflicts of interest

14.94 Trustees who are also members may be prevented from taking part in some decisions if they have a personal interest: see **14.60-14.70**.

Annual General Meeting

14.95 There is no statutory requirement for an annual members' meeting (or AGM) although for association CIOs the Commission strongly recommends including a constitutional requirement for an AGM: there is a constitutional requirement for an AGM in the Commission's model association CIO constitution.[65]

Decisions without voting

14.96 CIOs may include provisions in their constitution allowing the members to make decisions at general meetings otherwise than by voting on resolutions.[66] This can allow for decision-making by consensus and may be useful for charities, including some religious charities, where decision-making by consensus is the norm.

Charity Commission power to order a meeting

14.97 Where it is impracticable to call or conduct a meeting in accordance with the constitution, the Commission or the court may order that a meeting be called, held and conducted in any manner they think fit.[67] This power may be exercised on the initiative of the court or Commission, on the application of a trustee of the CIO, or on the application of a member entitled to vote or take part in decisions at the meeting. Where an order is made, ancillary directions may also be made including a direction that one member present at a meeting shall constitute a quorum. This provision could, potentially, be useful in many situations, including the case where there is a stalemate and the quorum stated in the constitution cannot be achieved to amend the constitution.

Decisions outside meetings

14.98 If the members are to be permitted to make decisions otherwise than at a meeting, for example by written or email resolution, this must be provided for in the constitution.[68] This, is different to the position under company law, which gives members a statutory right to pass written resolutions, even if the Articles of Association are silent. The Commission's model CIO constitutions allow for written resolutions of the members.[69]

14.99 Where resolutions which deal with amendments to amend the CIO's constitution, amalgamation, transfer of a CIO's undertaking, or dissolution by the Commission are passed otherwise than at a general meeting, for example in writing, they must be unanimous.[70] This means that a higher majority is required for written resolutions dealing with these issues than is the case where they are put to a general meeting. The

---

65 Clause 11, and accompanying notes, Charity Commission model association constitution, August 2014.
66 Regulation 13(7) of the General Regulations.
67 Regulation 40 of the General Regulations.
68 Regulation 13(8) of the General Regulations.
69 Charity Commission model CIO constitutions, August 2014.
70 Section 224 of the 2011 Act (amendment), s 235 of the 2011 Act (amalgamation), s 240 of the 2011 Act (transfer of undertaking) and reg 6 of the Dissolution Regulations (dissolution).

position is different for charitable companies, where the majorities required for members' resolutions are the same, regardless of whether the resolution is approved at a meeting or in writing. Lord Hodgson, in his 2012 review of charity law, recommended that this discrepancy should be eliminated in relation to resolutions to make amendments to the constitution or to transfer assets.[71]

Record keeping

14.100 Every CIO must keep minutes of all proceedings of general meetings, copies of all resolutions passed otherwise than at general meetings and details of decisions made by a sole member.[72] The records must be kept for at least 6 years from the date of the meeting, resolution or decision and must be available for inspection by any member of the CIO without charge either at the principal office or another address decided on by the trustees. A member can call for a copy on payment of such fee as the trustees may reasonably require in respect of the costs of complying with the request.[73] The minutes of a general meeting are evidence of the proceedings of the meeting if they purport to be signed by the chair of that meeting or of the following meeting. Where there is a record of the proceedings of the meeting then, unless the contrary is proved, the meeting is treated as duly held and convened, all proceedings are treated as having taken place and all appointments made at the meeting are treated as valid. The record of a resolution passed otherwise than at a general meeting, or a decision made otherwise than by resolution is evidence of the passing of that resolution or the making of that decision if purported to be signed by a charity trustee of the CIO.[74] Similar provisions apply to decisions, resolutions and meetings of a class of members.[75]

14.101 These records may be kept in hard copy or electronic form and may be arranged in such manner as the charity trustees think fit, provided that if the records are kept in electronic form they must be capable of being reproduced in hard copy.[76]

REGISTERS

14.102 CIOs are required to keep various registers and allow them to be inspected in certain circumstances.

Register of members

14.103 Association CIOs are required to keep a register of members. Foundation CIOs, whose constitution provides that the same persons are to be its members and its charity trustees, do not need to keep a register of members.[77]

14.104 The register of members must include the member's name, a service address, the date membership was registered and ends and a statement of their class, if the CIO has more than one class of member. A service address is an address at which the service of documents can be effected by physical delivery, and at which the delivery of documents

71 *Trusted and Independent*, Appendix A.
72 Regulations 41 and 43 of the General Regulations.
73 Regulation 44 of the General Regulations.
74 Regulation 42 of the General Regulations.
75 Regulation 45 of the General Regulations.
76 Regulation 46 of the General Regulations.
77 Regulation 26 of the General Regulations.

can be recorded by obtaining an acknowledgement of delivery. The service address may be specified as 'the principal office of the CIO'. The ability to specify a service address means that the member's residential address need not be included in the register, which addresses a matter of concern for some charities. Where there are more than 50 members, the register must be kept as an index. If the CIO only has one member a statement to this effect must be included in the register and if additional members are later admitted, then the date when it ceased to be a single member CIO must be recorded. Entries relating to former members may be removed 10 years after they ceased to be members.[78]

14.105 The Commission may, by order, require the trustees to amend the register of members where it has made a determination of membership under s 111 of the 2011 Act (see **9.191–9.194**).[79]

14.106 The court is also given the power to order rectification of the register of members on application by someone aggrieved by the entry or omission of their name from the register, or by default or delay in recording that they are no longer a member, or by a member, the CIO or the Commission.[80]

Register of trustees

14.107 All CIOs are obliged to keep a register of charity trustees.[81] This must include the trustee's name, a service address (which is an address at which service can be effected by physical delivery, and delivery can be acknowledged), the date of registration as a trustee and the date on which they ceased to be a trustee. Where the trustee is an individual, former names used for business purposes in the last 20 years must also be included[82] and the service address may be 'the principal office of the CIO'. As is the case for members, this can help preserve trustee privacy. Where the trustee is a body corporate, its service address must be its registered or principal office and its 'company registration information' must be included. For companies within the European Economic Area, this essentially means details of the register on which it is registered and registration number and, for non-EEA companies, it means its legal form, governing law and (if relevant) the register where it is registered and its registration number.[83] If a foundation CIO has more than one class of member, the register of trustees must include a statement of the class of member to which each trustee belongs.[84] The register of trustees must include details of any person who has been appointed as interim manager of the CIO under s 76 of the 2011 Act (see **9.94–9.101**).[85]

Updating the registers

14.108 Alterations to the registers of members or trustees must be made within 28 days of the relevant event.[86]

78 Regulation 2 and Sch 1, Part 1 of the General Regulations.
79 Regulation 27 of the General Regulations.
80 Regulation 28 of the General Regulations.
81 Regulation 26 of the General Regulations.
82 Paragraph 11 of Sch 1 to the General Regulations.
83 Paragraph 4(5) of Sch 1 to the General Regulations.
84 Schedule 1, Part 2 of the General Regulations.
85 Paragraph 4(4) of Sch 1 to the General Regulations.
86 Paragraph 5 of Sch 1 to the General Regulations.

Access to the registers

14.109 The registers must be available for inspection at the principal office, or any other address decided on by the trustees.

14.110 Access to the register of members is limited to members and trustees of the CIO where they seek access 'for the purposes of carrying out [their] duties as a charity trustee or member of the CIO' or they wish to see the register entry relating to themselves. They are entitled to ask for copies of the register, or relevant part of it: there is no fee. An early draft of the regulations which became the General Regulations had followed the company law position and given the public rights of access to the register of members with criminal sanctions for non-compliance, but this changed following objections at consultation stage as the Government accepted that it was not necessary or appropriate to adopt the company law requirements for CIOs.[87] Where the constitution provides that some or all of the CIO's members are liable to contribute to its assets if it is wound up (see **14.32**), where the CIO has been or is in the course of being wound up, a person may inspect or seek a copy of the register of members (or relevant part of it) if the request is made for the purposes of recovering a member's contribution. In these circumstances the CIO may charge such fee as the trustees may reasonably require in respect of the costs of complying with the request.[88]

14.111 The register of trustees is open for public inspection and anyone is entitled to obtain a copy of all or part of the register.[89] However, a request for information relating to a serving or former trustee may be refused if the person in question is affected by a dispensation under regs 40 and 41 of the Charities (Accounts and Reports) Regulations 2008, under which the Commission may dispense with the requirement to give details of a trustee's name or the charity's principal address in the charity's annual report, if disclosure could lead to that person being placed in any personal danger: see **21.72**.[90]

14.112 Where a member or trustee of the CIO makes the request to inspect or have a copy of the register of trustees for the purposes of carrying out their duties as a member or trustee, or their request is to see or have a copy of their own register entry, there is no fee. In other circumstances, the CIO may ask for payment of such fee as the trustees may reasonably require in respect of the costs of complying with the request.[91]

Pending alterations

14.113 Where anyone asks to inspect either register, or seeks a copy of the register or an extract, the CIO must confirm when the register, or the relevant part of it, was last updated and whether there are any pending alterations.[92]

Register of charges

14.114 The parts of the General Regulations which deal with the registers of members and trustees are made under s 246 of the 2011 Act, which allows the Minister to make

---

87 Paragraphs 6 and 7 of Sch 1 to the General Regulations.
88 Paragraph 7 of Sch 1 to the General Regulations.
89 Paragraph 8 of Sch 1 to the General Regulations.
90 Paragraph 9 of Sch 1 to the General Regulations.
91 Paragraph 8 of Sch 1 to the General Regulations.
92 Regulation 10 of Sch 1 to the General Regulations.

regulations about a number of matters, including 'the maintenance of registers of members and of charity trustees'. Section 246 also provides that regulations made under it may make provision about 'the maintenance of other registers (for example, a register of charges over the CIO's assets)'. An earlier draft of the regulations which became the General Regulations included a requirement for CIOs to maintain a register of charges and for notification of charges to the Commission. This was the subject of consultation in 2008 and the overwhelming majority supported this proposal. The main concern expressed was how the Commission would make information available in relation to charges over CIO property and some suggested that an online publicly searchable register of charges similar to that operated by Companies House would be required. However, for reasons possibly concerned with cost, the final General Regulations included no requirements, either for the maintenance of a register of charges or for notification of charges to the Commission.

14.115 Although the model CIO constitutions include a power for CIOs to borrow money and charge the whole or part of their property, the lack of any public disclosure of charges is likely to make it very difficult in practice to create a floating charge over the CIO's property or issue debentures. However, the lack of a public register of charges may not deter lenders where the borrowing can be secured over land owned by the CIO by a charge registered at the Land Registry. In the absence of any suitable land, borrowing will be considered on a case-by-case basis.

14.116 In his 2012 review of charity law, Lord Hodgson rejected calls for a register of charges on the grounds that whereas the lack of a public register may discourage some large organisations likely to have floating charges from becoming CIOs, the issue is far less important for smaller organisations as mortgages over property will still be registered with the Land Registry and noted in the charity's accounts and thus accessible to potential lenders.[93]

COMMUNICATIONS

14.117 Regulations 49–59 and Schs 2 and 3 of the General Regulations set out detailed provisions for communication to and from a CIO. These provisions apply for the purposes of any 'charity law provision' that authorises or requires documents or information to be sent or supplied by or to a CIO. 'Charity law provision' means any provision of the 2011 Act, the General Regulations, the Dissolution Regulations and the provisions of the CIO's constitution.[94] It does not include provisions of the Insolvency Act 1986, which will be relevant in relation to dissolution of a CIO under that Act: see **14.196-14.197**.

14.118 The so-called CIO communications provisions have effect subject to any requirements imposed or contrary provision made by or under any Act. Significantly, they also have effect subject to any contrary provision in a CIO's constitution, so far as it concerns communications between the CIO and its members or the CIO and its trustees. However, provision is not regarded as contrary to the CIO communications provisions simply because it expressly authorises documents or information to be sent or supplied in a certain way.[95]

93 *Trusted and Independent*, para 10.27.
94 Regulation 59 of the General Regulations.
95 Regulation 49 of the General Regulations.

Communications to a CIO

14.119 Documents or information to be sent or supplied to a CIO must be sent or supplied in accordance with Sch 2 of the General Regulations. Schedule 2 allows documents and information to be sent or supplied:

(a) in hard copy, by hand or post to an address specified by the CIO for the purpose, or to the CIO's principal office;

(b) in electronic form, if the CIO has agreed (generally or specifically) that the document or information may be sent or supplied in that form (and has not revoked that agreement) or if the CIO is treated as having so agreed under reg 51 of the General Regulations. Regulation 51 provides that where a CIO sends or supplies documents or information to any person in electronic form, it is treated as having agreed to accept a response in electronic form. The electronic address that can be used is an electronic address specified for the purpose (generally or specifically) by the CIO, or where reg 51 applies, the response can be sent to the electronic address used by the CIO to send the original communication, or any electronic address supplied in the communication itself (subject to any limitations specified when providing that address).

Schedule 2 also deals with the supply of documents and information in electronic form by hand or by post, for example where an electronic document is sent by physical delivery of a CD or memory stick rather than by email.

14.120 The effect of reg 51 and Sch 2 is that if a CIO emails its members, it is deemed to have agreed that any responses to that communication may be returned by email to the email address used to send the original communication.

14.121 The Commission's model CIO constitutions include optional wording dealing with electronic communications which covers authentication of electronic communications sent to a CIO.

Communications by a CIO

14.122 Documents or information sent or supplied by a CIO must be sent or supplied in accordance with the provisions of Sch 3 to the General Regulations.[96] This will apply to communications with members and trustees, and to any communications with another CIO.[97]

14.123 Documents or information sent or supplied by a CIO may be sent:

(a) in hard copy by hand, by handing the communication to the intended recipient;

(b) in hard copy by hand or post to an address specified for the purpose by the intended recipient, or in the case of a trustee or member of the CIO to the address shown for them in the relevant register of trustees or members, or in the case of another CIO its principal office. If none of these addresses can be obtained, the CIO can use the last address known to the CIO;

---

96 Regulation 50(2) of the General Regulations.

97 Regulation 50(3), para 1 of Sch 2 and para 1 of Sch 3 to the General Regulations.

(c) in electronic form where the recipient has agreed (generally or specifically) that the document or information may be sent or supplied in that form and the person has not revoked that agreement. The communication may be sent electronically to an address specified for the purpose (generally or specifically) by the intended recipient. Schedule 3 also provides for the sending of electronic documents by hand or post, for example where the information is on a CD or memory stick.

Regulation 13(10) is helpful here. It provides that:

> 'If the members of a CIO are to be treated, as a result of becoming members, as having agreed to receive communications from the CIO by electronic means, the constitution must include (a) a statement to this effect; and (b) provision setting out, as a result of the deemed agreement, the circumstances in which its members will receive communications by electronic means from the CIO'.

The effect of this is that a CIO's constitution can provide, for example, that all members supplying an email address to the CIO can be taken as having agreed that the CIO may communicate with them by email to that address, unless the member indicates otherwise. The Commission's model constitutions include optional wording which is intended to have this effect.

The Commission's optional wording also includes communications with trustees: they too will be deemed to have agreed that the CIO can communicate with them by email if they have supplied an email address to the CIO. The Commission has expressed the view, in correspondence with the authors in 2013, that:

> 'there is nothing stopping a CIO from extending [the deemed consent provisions referred to in reg 13(10)] to others such as any charity trustees who are not members of the CIO. This is what the model constitution has done'.

This mechanism is extremely helpful, and much more flexible than the corresponding provisions in company law, which do not allow for deemed consent to communication by email;

(d) by means of a website, to a person who has agreed (generally or specifically) that the communication may be sent in that way, and has not revoked that agreement, or who is treated as having agreed to such communication under para 10 of Sch 3. Paragraph 10 includes a mechanism allowing a CIO to ask its members to agree to receiving communications via a website: if there is no response within 28 days the member can be treated as having agreed to this form of communication (subject to some exceptions specified in para 10(4)). This mechanism is only available where the members have resolved that the CIO may send or supply documents or information to members via website, or where the CIO's constitution contains provision to that effect. This is similar to provisions allowing deemed consent to website communications under company law.

Interestingly, reg 13(11) of the General Regulations provides that:

> 'If a CIO is to communicate with its members by means of a website, the constitution must make provision as to the circumstances in which a website may be used as a means of communication with its members'.

This is in apparent contradiction with Sch 3, which appears to allow website communication, subject to the necessary consents, even if it is not provided for in the constitution. In the authors' view, CIOs wishing to take advantage of website communication would be well advised to put the matter beyond doubt by stating in their constitution that website communication is permissible: both of the Commission's model constitutions include optional wording to this effect.[98]

Where a CIO communicates via a website, Sch 3 contains various requirements regarding the format of the communication, notifying the intended recipients that the document or information is available on the website, and how long the documents or information must remain available.[99]

14.124 Under reg 52 of the General Regulations, where a member has received a document or information otherwise than in hard copy, they have a right to require that it be sent to them in hard copy free of charge within 21 days.

14.125 Regulation 53 of the General Regulations deals with the time of receipt of documents or information sent by a CIO.

14.126 Where a communication is sent by post or electronically it is treated as being received 48 hours after being sent. Weekends and bank holidays (including Christmas Day and Good Friday) are not counted. This means that where notice of a members' meeting, for example, is sent out by email on a Friday, it is not deemed to be received until the following Tuesday (the period will be longer if there are bank holidays). CIOs should be aware of this when calculating when to send out notices and other information.

14.127 Regulation 53 also deals with the time of receipt of website communications.

14.128 Regulation 53 has effect subject to any contrary provision agreed between the CIO and the intended recipient and, as mentioned at **14.118** above, reg 53 is also subject to any contrary provision in the constitution, in the case of communications between a CIO and its members and/or trustees.[100] CIOs may, therefore, want to include different provisions in their constitutions for communications with members and trustees.

14.129 Regulations 54–58 of the General Regulations deal with communications with the Commission. The Commission may specify that documents or information must be sent electronically. The scope for the Commission to impose requirements as to the form of documents submitted to it mirrors what the Commission may specify in relation to the submission of documents in an application for CIO registration: see **14.47**.

MAKING AND EXECUTING CONTRACTS AND DEEDS

14.130 The provisions for the making and execution of contracts, documents and deeds by a CIO are similar to those for a company. A CIO contract may be made by the CIO, by writing under its common seal, or on behalf of a CIO by a person acting under its authority, express or implied.[101]

14.131 A document is executed by a CIO either by affixing its common seal (as mentioned at **14.33** if a CIO is to have a common seal its constitution must include provisions about the use of the seal) or by the signature of two or more of its trustees, or

---

98 Charity Commission Model CIO Constitutions, August 2014.
99 Paragraphs 11 to 13 of Sch 1 to the General Regulations.
100 Regulation 49(3)(b) of the General Regulations.
101 Regulation 19 of the General Regulations.

one, if a single trustee CIO.[102] If a document is executed in this way and also expressed on its face to be a deed then it will be treated as a deed on delivery.[103] A CIO may, by deed, authorise a person to act as its attorney to execute deeds or other documents on its behalf.[104] Regulations 23 and 24 of the General Regulations deal with use of a seal by a CIO and apply various company law offences. Regulation 25 of the General Regulations deals with bills of exchange and promissory notes.

SERVICE OF DOCUMENTS

14.132 Regulations 47 and 48 of the General Regulations set out rules for the service of documents on a CIO, its trustees and any interim manager.

DISCLOSURE

14.133 Sections 211 and 212 of the Act require similar disclosure of the name and status of a CIO as is required for a charitable company limited by guarantee: see Chapter 13.

14.134 The CIO's name must appear in legible characters in every description of document or communication in which a charitable company would be required by regulations under s 82 of the Companies Act 2006 to state its registered name[105] and in all conveyances purported to be executed by the CIO.[106] This means that the CIO's name must appear in conveyances and in:

(a) its business letters, notices and other official publications;
(b) its bills of exchange, promissory notes, endorsements and order forms;
(c) cheques purporting to be signed by or on behalf of the CIO;
(d) orders for money, goods or services purporting to be signed by or on behalf of the CIO;
(e) its bills of parcels, invoices and other demands for payment, receipts and letters of credit;
(f) its applications for licences to carry on a trade or activity;
(g) all other forms of its business correspondence and documentation; and
(h) its websites.

14.135 If the name of a CIO does not include 'charitable incorporated organisation' or 'CIO' (or their Welsh equivalents, if the CIO's constitution is in Welsh), then the fact that it is a CIO must also be stated in the documents mentioned above. The statement must be in English, unless the rest of the document is wholly in Welsh, in which case the statement may be in Welsh.[107]

---

[102] Regulation 20 of the General Regulations.
[103] Regulation 21 of the General Regulations.
[104] Regulation 22 of the General Regulations.
[105] At the time of writing these are the Company, Limited Liability Partnership and Business (Names and Trading Disclosures) Regulations 2015, SI 2015/17.
[106] Section 211 of the 2011 Act.
[107] Section 212 of the 2011 Act.

14.136 The CIO's name must also appear in legible characters in every location in which a charitable company would be required by regulations under s 82 of the Companies Act 2006 to state its registered name.[108] The relevant regulations refer to the company's registered office, any other location where the company keeps company records available for inspection in accordance with a requirement of company law and other locations (except any primarily used for living accommodation) where it carries on business. It seems, therefore, that a CIO should display its name at its principal office, and any other place where it carries on business (except living accommodation) or where the trustees have decided that its registers should be made available for inspection (see **14.109**). In the circumstances described at **14.135**, the fact that the CIO is a CIO must also be stated at the relevant location.

14.137 Under s 214 of the 2011 Act breach of s 211 or 212 without reasonable excuse is an offence on the part of each trustee. It is also an offence for any other person to sign or authorise the signature of a document which fails to comply with the disclosure requirements, or otherwise commit or authorise the offending act or omission. Under s 215 it is an offence to hold out a body as being a CIO when it is not one. On conviction, a fine not exceeding level 3 on the standard scale is payable,[109] with a daily default fine for continued contravention in the case of a s 211 offence. There are also potential civil consequences for failure to make the appropriate disclosure.[110]

14.138 See also **4.72–4.78** in relation to charity stationery and other documents.

ACCOUNTING AND REPORTING

14.139 CIOs are required to keep accounting records and prepare accounts and reports and annual returns in accordance with charity law. This means that they must:

(a) keep accounting records and preserve them for 6 years: see **21.14–21.17**;

(b) prepare annual accounts. Where the CIO's annual income for the relevant financial year exceeds £250,000, accounts must be prepared on the accruals basis, in compliance with SORP and the relevant accounting regulations: see **21.23–21.27**. If the CIO has an annual income of £250,000 or less, it may choose to prepare receipts and payments accounts and a statement of assets and liabilities: see **21.28**. Where a CIO elects to prepare receipts and payments accounts instead of accruals accounts, it must provide, with the statement of assets and liabilities, particulars of any guarantee given by the CIO, where any potential liability is outstanding at the date of the statement, and particulars of any debt outstanding which is owed by the CIO and secured by an express charge on any of the CIO's assets;[111]

(c) have the accounts audited or independently examined, depending on the CIO's income and/or assets: see **21.33–21.44**;

(d) prepare a trustees' annual report: see **21.68–21.74**;

---

[108] See note 105.

[109] Currently £1,000.

[110] See s 213 of the 2011 Act.

[111] Regulation 62 of the General Regulations.

(e) file the accounts, auditor's or examiner's report (if any) and trustees' annual report with the Commission within 10 months of the end of their financial year, regardless of the CIO's level of income: see **21.76–21.79** and **21.81**;[112]

(f) submit an annual return to the Commission, regardless of the CIO's level of income, within 10 months of the end of the financial year: see **21.87–21.92**.[113]

AMENDING THE CONSTITUTION

14.140 Amending a CIO's constitution requires a members' resolution which must be passed by a 75% majority of those voting at a general meeting (including proxy or postal votes, if permitted) or unanimously if passed otherwise than at a general meeting.[114]

14.141 Where the resolution is proposed at a general meeting, at least 14 clear days' notice of the meeting must be given to the members entitled to vote, and to the trustees. The constitution may include more restrictive provisions. See **14.88-14.89** and **14.96** for more detail about the required content of the notice, the scope for short notice and the position where the constitution permits members to make decisions otherwise than by voting.[115]

14.142 Where the constitution contains provision for entrenchment (see **14.35**), any amendment to the entrenched provisions must comply with the relevant conditions or procedures.

14.143 Section 224(3) of the 2011 Act and reg 16 of the General Regulations deal with the date on which a resolution amending the constitution is passed. If passed at a meeting, this is the date of the meeting. If passed otherwise than at a meeting, the date of passing is the date on which the last member agreed to it, although the constitution may provide that it should be treated as having been passed on a later date.

Restrictions on amendment

14.144 A CIO may not amend its constitution in such a way that it would cease to be a charity.[116]

14.145 Some alterations to the constitution require the prior written consent of the Commission. A resolution containing an amendment which would make a so-called 'regulated alteration' to a CIO's constitution is ineffective, to that extent, unless the Commission has given its prior written consent to the amendment.[117] This requirement is similar to the requirement for charitable companies to obtain the Commission's prior written consent to certain proposed alterations to their Articles of Association, under s 198 of the 2011 Act: see Chapter 13. A 'regulated alteration' for a CIO is:

---

112 Registered charities which are not CIOs only need to file the annual report and accompanying documents with the Commission if their income exceeds £25,000.

113 Registered charities which are not CIOs only need to file an annual return with the Commission if their income exceeds £10,000.

114 Section 224 of the 2011 Act. Lord Hodgson recommended a change in the law to allow a 75% majority of the members to pass a resolution outside a meeting: see **14.99**.

115 See also reg 35 of the General Regulations.

116 Section 225 of the 2011 Act.

117 Section 226 of the 2011 Act.

(a) any alteration of the CIO's purposes;

(b) any alteration of any provision of the CIO's constitution directing the application of property of the CIO on its dissolution; and

(c) any alteration of any provision of the CIO's constitution where the alteration would provide authorisation for any benefit to be obtained by charity trustees or members of the CIO or persons connected with them. The definitions of 'benefit' and 'connected person' are in ss 248 and 249. As is the case for charitable companies (see **13.12-13.13**) 'benefit' does not include any remuneration which may be authorised under s 185 (see Chapter 7).

14.146 Failure to obtain the Commission's prior consent is not necessarily fatal: the Commission may still register the amendment under s 227(4) and (5) of the 2011 Act: see **14.149**(b).

14.147 A member of a CIO is not bound by an amendment to the constitution increasing the member's liability to contribute to the CIO's assets on a winding up which is made after they become a member, unless the member agrees in writing.[118]

Registration of amendments

14.148 Resolutions changing a CIO's constitution and the amended constitution (and any other documents or information required by the Commission) must be filed with the Commission within 15 days of the date on which the resolution is passed: see **14.143**.[119] Changes do not take effect until they are registered by the Commission.[120] This delay to amendments to a governing document is unique to CIOs: in most other situations amendments to a charity's governing document will take effect immediately.[121]

14.149 The Commission has some powers and obligations to refuse to register amendments:[122]

(a) the Commission must refuse to register an amendment if:

 (i) in the Commission's view, the CIO had no power to make it (for example, because the effect of making it would be that the CIO ceased to be a charity, or that the CIO or its constitution did not comply with any requirement imposed by or virtue of the 2011 Act or any other enactment). This means that when making amendments to its constitution, a CIO must ensure that the amended constitution will still comply with the requirements of the 2011 Act and the General Regulations outlined at **14.31-14.37**;

 (ii) the amendment changes the CIO's name, and the Commission could have refused to register a new CIO with the proposed name under s 208(2) of the 2011 Act (which it may do if the name is too like another charity's name, misleading or offensive: see **14.50**). The Commission may therefore effectively block a proposed name change: it does not have power to do this in the case of other charities: see Chapter 6;

---

118 Regulation 18 of the General Regulations.

119 Section 227(1) of the 2011 Act.

120 Section 227(2) of the 2011 Act.

121 Although changes to a charitable company's objects do not take effect until noted in the Companies House register, s 31(2) Companies Act 2006.

122 Section 227(3)–(6) of the 2011 Act.

(b) the Commission has discretion to refuse to register an amendment if the proposed alteration is a regulated alteration, and the Commission's prior written consent has not been obtained. But the Commission may, if it wishes, decide to register the amendment anyway.

14.150 In his 2012 review of charity law, Lord Hodgson recommended that constitutional changes to CIOs should take effect immediately, provided any necessary prior approval from the Commission has been obtained.[123] The CIO would need to notify the Commission of the changes. This would reduce the current uncertainty about when changes to the constitution will take effect and would mean that the Commission would not effectively review 'regulated alterations' twice: once before the resolution is passed and then again afterwards. This would bring CIOs more into line with charitable companies.

14.151 Where the CIO's constitution provides for entrenchment, when the CIO notifies the Commission of any changes it must also include a statement of compliance, certifying that the amendment is in accordance with the provision for entrenchment. The Commission may then rely on this as sufficient evidence of the matters stated in it.[124]

MERGER

14.152 The 2011 Act contains provisions dealing with the merger of CIOs. They facilitate the amalgamation of two or more CIOs into a new single CIO, and the transfer of one CIO's undertaking to another CIO.

Amalgamation of two or more CIOs into one new CIO

14.153 Sections 235–239 of the 2011 Act deal with the amalgamation of two or more CIOs ('the old CIOs') into a newly incorporated successor CIO ('the new CIO'). This mechanism could be used in order to facilitate a merger where the parties wish to create a new entity to take on the old charities' operations after the merger, with the old charities ceasing to exist.

14.154 The procedure is similar to that for a new CIO registration, but with the old CIOs as applicants. The old CIOs must provide the Commission with a copy of the proposed constitution of the new CIO, and any other documents or information required by the Commission.[125] Where the proposed new constitution includes provision for entrenchment, this must be specified in the application.[126]

14.155 The old CIOs must also each submit a copy of resolutions passed by their respective members approving the proposed amalgamation and adopting the proposed constitution of the new CIO. The resolutions require a majority of 75% of those voting at a general meeting of the relevant CIO (including postal and proxy votes, if permitted by the CIO's constitution), or unanimity if they are passed in any way other than at a

123 *Trusted and Independent*, Appendix A, para 32.
124 Regulation 17 of the General Regulations.
125 Section 235(2)(b) allows the Minister for the Cabinet Office to make regulations requiring additional documents and information to be supplied to the Commission: at the time of writing apart from reg 9 of the General Regulations (see note 126) no such regulations have been made.
126 Regulation 9 of the General Regulations.

general meeting (for example by written resolution).[127] Where the resolution is passed at a meeting, 14 clear days' notice is required, with provision for short notice if a sufficient majority of the members agree.[128] Where the resolution is passed at a meeting, it is passed on the date of the meeting. Where the resolution is not passed at a meeting (for example by written resolution), it is passed on the date on which the constitution treats it as being passed (the date may not be later than the date on which the last member agreed to it).[129] It is therefore important for CIO constitutions to address this issue: at the time of writing the Commission's model CIO constitutions do not specifically cover it.

14.156 The old CIOs must give notice of the proposed amalgamation in a way that the trustees consider will make it most likely to come to the attention of those who would be affected by it. The notice must invite those who consider that they would be affected to make written representations to the Commission concerning the proposed amalgamation by a date determined by the Commission and specified in the notice. This means that in practice, the old CIOs will need to be in communication with the Commission about the proposals before public notice is given, so that the Commission can suggest a date to include. The old CIOs must send a copy of the final notice to the Commission.[130]

14.157 The Commission must refuse the application to amalgamate if:

- it is not satisfied that the new CIO would be a charity at the time it would be registered;
- the proposed constitution does not comply with the requirements of s 206 or regulations made under s 206: see **14.31-14.37**; or
- the Commission considers that there is a serious risk that the new CIO would be unable to pursue its purposes properly.[131]

14.158 The Commission may also refuse an application if it is not satisfied that the equivalent provisions in the constitution of the new CIO are the same (or substantially the same) as those in the constitutions of each of the old CIOs concerning:

- the purposes of the CIO;
- the application of the property of the CIO on its dissolution; and
- authorisation for any benefit to be obtained by any of the trustees or members of the CIO or persons connected with them.[132]

14.159 Sections 248 and 249, which cross refer to ss 350–352, apply when interpreting 'benefit' and 'connected persons'.

---

127 Section 235 of the 2011 Act. Lord Hodgson recommended a change in the law to allow a 75% majority of the members to pass a resolution to transfer assets outside a meeting: see **14.99**. If this change is made in future, it may also apply to resolutions approving an amalgamation.

128 Regulation 35 of the General Regulations: see **14.88-14.89** for more detail about the notice required.

129 Section 235 of the 2011 Act. The 2011 Act also envisages that regulations made about CIOs might set a longstop date for the passing of a written resolution, but at the time of writing no such date is included in the General Regulations.

130 Section 236 of the 2011 Act.

131 Section 237(1) and (2) of the 2011 Act.

132 Section 237(4)–(6) of the 2011 Act.

14.160 The Commission may also refuse the application if the proposed name of the new CIO is the same as or too like another charity's name, misleading or offensive, in the same way that it may refuse registration of a CIO because of its name:[133] see **14.50**.

14.161 On granting an application, the Commission must enter the new CIO in the register of charities. The register entry will include a note to the effect that the CIO was formed following amalgamation of the old CIOs.[134] The new CIO becomes a body corporate, with the members of the old CIOs as its first members. All property, rights and liabilities of each of the old CIOs vest in the new CIO and the old CIOs are dissolved. Gifts to any of the old CIOs will automatically take effect as gifts to the new CIO.[135] It is conceivable, however, that legacies to the old CIOs which are expressed to fail if the old CIO ceases to exist may not be effective: see Chapter 16 for a fuller discussion of this.

14.162 Note that this type of merger of CIOs falls outside the definition of 'relevant charity merger' and so the provisions in the 2011 Act relating to the register of mergers cannot be used.[136]

14.163 The General Regulations contain provisions dealing with the transfer and retention of accounting records on amalgamation.[137]

Transfer of undertaking between CIOs

14.164 Sections 240–244 contain provisions facilitating the transfer of all of a CIO's property, rights and liabilities to another CIO. This mechanism allows for a merger in which one of the merging charities ('the transferee CIO') continues to exist, and takes on the assets and liabilities of the other charity or charities ('the transferor CIO(s)'). The transferor CIO or CIOs are automatically dissolved.

14.165 The transferor CIO must first resolve that all its property, rights and liabilities should be transferred to the CIO named in the resolution. The transferee CIO must also pass a resolution agreeing to the transfer. Both resolutions require a majority of 75% of those voting at a general meeting of the CIO (including postal and proxy votes, if permitted by the CIO's constitution) or unanimity if they are passed in any way other than at a general meeting (for example by written resolution).[138] Where the resolution is passed at a meeting, 14 clear days' notice is required, although an appropriate majority may consent to short notice: see **14.88**.[139] As in the case of resolutions to amalgamate, if the resolution is passed at a meeting, it is passed on the date of the meeting. If the resolution is not passed at a meeting (eg by way of written resolution), it is passed on the date on which the constitution, or regulations under s 223 of the 2011 Act, treat it as being passed (the date may not be later than the date on which the last member agreed to it).[140] Since there are no regulations to this effect at the time of writing, the date of passing of a relevant written resolution should, therefore, be specified in the

---

[133] Section 237(3) of the 2011 Act.
[134] Section 238 of the 2011 Act.
[135] Section 239 of the 2011 Act.
[136] Section 314 of the 2011 Act.
[137] Regulations 10 and 11 of the General Regulations.
[138] Section 240 of the 2011 Act. Lord Hodgson recommended a change in the law to allow a 75% majority of the members to pass a resolution outside a meeting: see **14.99**.
[139] Regulation 35 of the General Regulations. See also **14.89** for more on the content of the notice.
[140] Section 240(4) of the 2011 Act.

constitution. The resolution of the transferor does not, however, actually take effect until it has been confirmed by the Commission: see 14.167.

14.166 The transferor CIO must send both resolutions to the Commission.[141] The Commission may then require the transferor CIO to give public notice of its resolution. If it does so, it must take into account any representations made within 28 days by persons appearing to the Commission to be interested in the transferor CIO.[142]

14.167 The resolution to transfer does not take effect until it has been confirmed by the Commission.[143] The Commission must refuse to confirm the resolution if it considers there is a serious risk that the transferee CIO would be unable properly to pursue the purposes of the transferor CIO. As with amalgamations, the Commission may refuse to confirm the resolution if it is not satisfied that certain provisions in the transferee CIO's constitution regarding purposes, the application of property on dissolution and trustee and member benefit are the same or substantially the same as the equivalent provisions in the transferor CIO's constitution: see **14.158**.[144]

14.168 If the Commission approves the transfer, it may confirm the resolution. If the Commission does not notify the transferor CIO of the confirmation or refusal of a resolution within 6 months from the date when both the resolutions are received by the Commission, or if the Commission has requested public notice, 6 months from when such public notice is given, the resolution is treated as confirmed. The Commission may extend the deadline by up to six months by giving notice within the initial 6-month period setting out the reasons for the extension.[145]

14.169 When the resolution is confirmed (or is treated as confirmed), all the property, rights and liabilities of the transferor CIO are transferred to the transferee CIO, and the transferor CIO is dissolved. Gifts to the transferor CIO after this date will automatically take effect as gifts to the transferee CIO:[146] as mentioned at **14.161** this will not necessarily apply to legacies which are expressed to fail if the recipient charity ceases to exist.

14.170 This type of CIO merger also falls outside the definition of 'relevant charity merger' and so the provisions in the 2011 Act relating to the register of mergers cannot be used.[147]

Comment

14.171 These provisions only apply where all the entities involved are CIOs. They do not appear to be compulsory, meaning that it should be possible for CIOs to transfer assets and liabilities to another CIO without invoking the statutory regime, should they wish to do so.

14.172 CIOs considering whether or not to take advantage of these procedures will need to consider which would be more appropriate for their circumstances.

141 Section 240(2) of the 2011 Act.
142 Section 241 of the 2011 Act.
143 Section 240(5) of the 2011 Act.
144 Section 242 of the 2011 Act.
145 Section 243 of the 2011 Act.
146 Section 244 of the 2011 Act.
147 Section 314 of the 2011 Act.

Amalgamation involves the creation of a completely new CIO, whereas the transfer route allows one CIO to take on the operations of the other party or parties. Amalgamation orchestrates an automatic transfer of membership of all the merging CIOs to the new CIO, which is not the case with the transfer mechanism.

14.173 The automatic transfer of assets and liabilities will undoubtedly save paperwork. However, this could cause problems if one CIO is wary of taking on all the liabilities of another: as with any merger careful due diligence will be required. The practicalities of the merger process will not be eliminated entirely: for example where there is a transfer of operations to a new legal entity, employees will need to be consulted under TUPE, and other third parties will need to be notified. There may be changes of name and charity number. Public notice may be required: this is not usually necessary where other legal entities merge. For some charities, it will be a concern that it is not possible for the 'old' CIOs to continue to exist, even as shell charities, for the purpose of receiving legacies.

14.174 In addition, the process of merger under these provisions may be hard to manage, because a crucial aspect of the timing of the merger will be taken out of the charities' control. Two charitable companies merging into a new charitable company can contractually agree the date that the transfer will take effect (often to coincide with their financial year end), having first arranged for the new company to be registered with the Commission. Where two CIOs which wish to merge using these procedures, the merger or amalgamation only takes effect upon the Commission granting the application (or, in the case of a transfer, if it is treated as confirmed). It may be difficult to reconcile the timing of this legal process with handling the practical and administrative aspects of a merger.

WINDING UP, INSOLVENCY AND DISSOLUTION

14.175 Under s 245 of the 2011 Act, the Minister for the Cabinet Office may make provision about the winding up, insolvency and dissolution of CIOs, and their revival and restoration to the register. The Charitable Incorporated Organisations (Insolvency and Dissolution) Regulations ('the Dissolution Regulations'; see **Appendix 6** of this book) therefore set out procedures for the dissolution and winding up of CIOs in different situations.

Dissolution by the Commission

14.176 Part 3 of the Dissolution Regulations establishes a regime for the dissolution of CIOs by the Commission. This allows the Commission to dissolve the CIO on the application of the CIO, or on its own initiative in certain circumstances.

Application by the CIO

14.177 A CIO may apply to the Commission for dissolution under Part 3 of the Dissolution Regulations. The application must be made on behalf of the CIO by at least a majority of the charity trustees and contain:

- a copy of a resolution of the members to make an application for dissolution: see **14.178**;

- a declaration by or on behalf of the trustees that any debts and other liabilities of the CIO have been settled or otherwise provided for in full; and
- a statement made by or on behalf of the trustees setting out how the property vested in or held on trust for the CIO has been or is to be applied on dissolution in accordance with its constitution.[148]

14.178 The resolution to make an application for dissolution must be passed at a members' meeting, of which 14 days' notice has been given (excluding the day of the meeting and the day on which notice is given), and must be passed by a 75% majority of those voting (including postal and proxy votes if permitted). The notice must contain particulars of the proposed resolution. Shorter notice is possible if it is agreed to by a majority in number of the members with a right to attend and vote at the meeting representing 90% (or a higher majority up to 95%, if this is specified in the constitution) of the total voting rights at that meeting of all the members. If the constitution permits decision-making at a meeting other than by resolution, shorter notice is possible if all the members with the right to attend the meeting and take part in decisions agree, and the decision must be taken with no expression of dissent. If the constitution allows decision-making outside a meeting, for example by written resolution, all the members must approve the resolution:[149] the resolution is treated as having been passed on the date on which the last member agreed to it, unless the constitution provides for a later date.[150]

14.179 The Commission must publish notice of the application for dissolution in any manner it thinks fit. The CIO must not be dissolved until 3 months after the notice and in the absence of any objection showing why dissolution should not take place.[151]

14.180 The trustees must not apply for dissolution if:

- any debts or liabilities have not been settled or provided for in full;
- any decision required to give effect to the constitutional directions about the application of the CIO's property on dissolution has not been taken;
- a voluntary arrangement has been made under Part 1 of the Insolvency Act 1986 ('the 1986 Act');
- the CIO is in administration under Part 2 of the 1986 Act;
- an interim moratorium is in effect under para 44 of Sch B1 to the 1986 Act;
- the CIO is being wound up under Part 4 of the 1986 Act whether voluntarily or by the court, or a petition for winding up by the court has been presented and not finally dealt with or withdrawn; or
- a receiver, manager or interim manager has been appointed.

It is an offence for a charity trustee to apply for dissolution in any of these circumstances.[152]

---

[148] Regulation 5 of the Dissolution Regulations.

[149] Lord Hodgson recommended a change in the law to allow a 75% majority of the members to pass a resolution to transfer assets outside a meeting: see **14.99**. If this change is made in future, a similar change may also be made to the majority required for resolutions to make an application for dissolution outside a meeting.

[150] Regulation 6 of the Dissolution Regulations.

[151] Regulation 7 of the Dissolution Regulations.

[152] Regulations 8 and 9 of the Dissolution Regulations.

14.181 Once an application has been made the CIO must not engage in any activity except one necessary or expedient for proceeding with the application, giving effect to any decision made under the provisions of the constitution dealing with the application of property on dissolution, or complying with a statutory requirement. It must not incur any debts or other liabilities.[153] If property is received after the application, the trustees must notify the Commission and either withdraw the application or tell the Commission how that property has been or will be applied in accordance with the provisions in the constitution about the application of property on dissolution.[154]

14.182 The trustees making the application must give notice of the application within seven days to every member and employee and any other trustees, giving the date of the application and the names of the trustees making it. Failure to do so is an offence.[155] Regulation 13 of the Dissolution Regulations contains supplementary provisions around how notice is given.

14.183 The charity trustees must notify the Commission and withdraw the application if before it is finally dealt with:

- an application is made to the court for an administration order under para 12 of Sch B1 to the 1986 Act;
- an administrator is appointed under para 14 or 22 of Sch B1 to the 1986 Act, or a copy of notice of intention to appoint such an administrator is filed with the court;
- any circumstances arise in which the CIO may be voluntarily wound up under s 84(1) of the 1986 Act;
- a petition is presented for the winding up of the CIO under Part 4 of the 1986 Act;
- a receiver, manager or interim manager of the CIO's property is appointed; or
- the CIO incurs any liability.

It is a criminal offence for a charity trustee to fail to withdraw the application in any of these circumstances.[156]

Dissolution without an application from the CIO

14.184 There are three circumstances in which the Commission must dissolve a CIO without an application from the charity trustees. (Note that s 34 of the 2011 Act, which obliges the Commission to remove charities from the register in certain circumstances, does not apply to CIOs.[157])

No longer operating

14.185 The Commission must dissolve a CIO if it has reasonable cause to believe it is no longer operating. Regulation 16 of the Dissolution Regulations sets out the procedures that the Commission must take to confirm whether the CIO is in fact operating and then requires the Commission to publish notice of its intention to dissolve. After 3 months from the date of the notice, the Commission must dissolve the

153 Regulation 10 of the Dissolution Regulations.
154 Regulation 11 of the Dissolution Regulations.
155 Regulation 12 of the Dissolution Regulations.
156 Regulation 14 of the Dissolution Regulations.
157 Regulation 6(3) of the General Regulations.

CIO by removing it from the register unless it is satisfied that the CIO is in fact operating, or will be operating within a reasonable period of time.

No longer a charity

14.186 Under reg 17 of the Dissolution Regulations the Commission must dissolve a CIO if it no longer considers it to be a charity. If the Commission is to take this action it must first publish notice of its intention to dissolve the CIO after three months unless cause is shown to the contrary. If cause is not shown to the contrary the Commission must dissolve the CIO by removing it from the register.

Winding up of CIO

14.187 Under reg 18 of the Dissolution Regulations the Commission must also dissolve a CIO if it is being wound up and the Commission has reasonable cause to believe that no liquidator is acting or that the affairs of the CIO have been fully wound up, and the returns required to be made by the liquidator have not been made for a period of 6 months. The Commission must first publish a notice of intention to dissolve, and if no cause is shown to the contrary, must then dissolve the CIO after three months by removing it from the register.

14.188 Regulation 19 of the Dissolution Regulations contains more detailed provisions about giving notice under regs 16–18. There is, notably, no statutory obligation for the Commission to notify third parties, such as creditors, funders or the Land Registry, of its intention to dissolve a CIO. The authors have suggested to the Commission that it would be helpful for a single page on the Commission's website to list all pending CIO dissolutions.

Effect of dissolution

14.189 The date of dissolution is the date on which the CIO is removed from the register. The Commission must publish a notice giving the date of dissolution.[158]

14.190 The liabilities of the CIO's trustees and members are unaffected by dissolution and the court continues to have power to wind up the CIO.[159] It is not completely clear what the effect of this provision is, but it is the authors' view that it does not necessarily offer any comfort to creditors.

14.191 On the dissolution of a CIO by the Commission under the provisions described at **14.176-14.188**, all its property vests in the Official Custodian (see Chapter 22), other than property held on trust for any other person or for any special purposes, and property which will be transferred on dissolution in accordance with the provisions in the constitution about the application of property on dissolution. The Official Custodian holds the property of the dissolved CIO on trust for its charitable purposes.[160]

14.192 The Commission may by order specify the charitable purposes, charity or charities for which the Official Custodian holds the property on trust. The order must not be made until at least 3 months after the date of dissolution. The Commission must

---

158 Regulations 20 and 21 of the Dissolution Regulations.

159 Regulation 22 of the Dissolution Regulations.

160 Regulation 23 of the Dissolution Regulations.

have regard to the provisions in the constitution about the application of property on dissolution, the desirability of applying the property for charitable purposes close to the CIO's purposes immediately before dissolution and the need for the property to be applied for charitable purposes which are suitable and effective in the light of current social and economic circumstances. Publicity must be given in the same manner as for schemes (see Chapter 17), unless the Commission decides that this is unnecessary.[161] Where the Commission has made an order to this effect, it may make another order vesting the CIO's property in one or more charities.[162]

14.193 Regulations 27–32 of the Dissolution Regulations include detailed provisions covering the disclaimer of assets of a dissolved CIO held by the Official Custodian.

14.194 The following decisions of the Commission relating to the dissolution of CIOs may be appealed to the Charity Tribunal:

- a decision to grant or not to grant an application for dissolution by a CIO;
- a decision to dissolve a CIO which it has reasonable cause to believe is not in operation;
- a decision to dissolve a CIO which it no longer considers to be a charity; and
- a decision to dissolve a CIO which is being wound up.

14.195 The list of persons who may make the application varies depending on the nature of the application, but may include the CIO, the trustees, any creditor, the liquidator and any other person who is or may be affected by the decision. There are also rights to appeal orders by the Commission specifying the purposes for which the property of a dissolved CIO should be held, and vesting property held by the Official Custodian.[163]

Winding up and dissolution under the Insolvency Act 1986

14.196 Regulation 3 and the Schedule to the Dissolution Regulations provide an alternative regime for the dissolution of a CIO. They apply the provisions of the Insolvency Act 1986 ('the 1986 Act'), with modifications, to make a CIO subject to the same insolvency and dissolution procedures as a registered company. The Schedule sets out general modifications which relate mainly to terminology, such as the substitution of charity trustees for directors. It also sets out a table of specific modifications to relevant sections of the 1986 Act. Most of these modifications are minor, for example the deletion of references to Scotland, but some modifications are necessary to reflect the requirements of charity law, for example that the interests of the charity must always come before the interests of members.

14.197 The relevant provisions of the 1986 Act, as amended, provide for voluntary arrangements, administration, administrative receivership, members' voluntary liquidation, creditors' voluntary liquidation and compulsory liquidation. The final stage of the liquidation procedures involves an application to the Commission to dissolve the CIO.

---

161 Regulation 25 of the Dissolution Regulations.
162 Regulation 26 of the Dissolution Regulations.
163 Schedule 6 to the 2011 Act.

14.198 In order to assist with a clear understanding of the insolvency provisions, Government prepared an informal consolidation of the amendments to the 1986 Act as at November 2012. This set out all the provisions of the 1986 Act (on that date) as they apply to CIOs and may be a useful resource.[164]

Fraudulent and wrongful trading

14.199 The provisions of the Companies Act 2006 and the 1986 Act which relate to fraudulent and wrongful trading are applied to CIOs. Fraudulent trading, involving carrying on a business fraudulently or with the intent to defraud creditors, gives rise to criminal liability on the part of the trustees[165] as well as personal liability to contribute to the CIO's assets. Wrongful trading, which can arise where the trustees continue to allow the CIO to trade even though they knew or should have known that insolvent liquidation was unavoidable, can render the trustees personally liable to contribute to the CIO's assets.

Restoration to the register

14.200 Both the Commission and the court have power to restore a dissolved CIO to the register in certain circumstances.

14.201 The Commission may restore a CIO which has been removed from the register on the grounds that it was thought not to be operating (under reg 16) or there was no liquidator acting (under reg 18): see **14.185** and **14.187** respectively. The Commission may do this on its own initiative, or on the application of anyone who was a trustee immediately before the dissolution. Restoration is not possible where the Commission has already made an order vesting all the CIO's property in another charity, unless all appeal rights in connection with the order have been exhausted, any appeal in connection with the order has been discontinued, or the period for any appeal has expired. There is a 6-year time limit for such restorations.[166]

14.202 There is no power for the Commission to restore a CIO which has been dissolved on the application of the CIO itself (under regs 4–14: see **14.177–14.183**) nor a CIO which has been dissolved on the grounds it is no longer a charity (under reg 17: see **14.186**).[167]

14.203 Decisions by the Commission to restore or not restore a CIO to the register may be appealed to the Charity Tribunal by the trustees (or former trustees) and any other person who is or may be affected by the decision.[168] If a decision to restore a CIO to the register is appealed, the register entry is maintained in suspense while the appeal is pending.[169]

14.204 The court may restore a dissolved CIO to the register where the CIO has been dissolved under Chapter 9 of Part 4 of the 1986 Act or para 84(6) of Sch B1 to the 1986

---

164 At the time of writing, the informal consolidation is available at www.gov.uk/government/publications/charitable-incorporated-organisation-secondary-legislation-before-parliament.

165 Section 993 of the Companies Act 2006 as applied to CIOs by reg 60 of the General Regulations.

166 Regulation 33 of the Dissolution Regulations.

167 So far as the authors are aware, the court has no power to restore a CIO dissolved under regs 4–14 or 17 either.

168 Schedule 6 to the 2011 Act.

169 Section 36 of the 2011 Act, as amended by reg 6 of the General Regulations.

Act (as they apply to CIOs). This includes a members' or creditors' winding up where the liquidator has sent a final account to the Commission, early dissolution on the application of the official receiver and dissolution once the winding up of a CIO is complete. The list of those who can make an application to the court is wider than those who can make an application to the Commission under reg 33.[170] The application must generally be made within 6 years of dissolution.[171]

14.205 Where a CIO is restored to the register the Commission must publish notice of restoration.[172] The effect of restoration is that the CIO is treated for all purposes as if it had not been dissolved.[173] On the date of restoration all the property of the CIO vested in the Official Custodian vests in the CIO.[174] There is no mechanism for property which was transferred to third parties to be returned to the CIO.

Comment

14.206 In the authors' view, there are some aspects of the dissolution regime for CIOs which cause concern. For example, there is scope for a CIO to be dissolved by the Commission within a relatively short time scale, and in some situations neither the Commission nor the court have the power to restore the CIO to the register. This may well give rise to concerns on the part of creditors, or potential creditors, particularly in the absence of a statutory requirement for the Commission to notify known creditors of a pending dissolution. These are issues which could usefully be addressed on any review of the legislation.

14.207 The procedure for dissolution where a CIO has ceased to be a charity gives rise to a number of questions, including how the timing of this would fit in with an appeal to the Tribunal. In this case the CIO may still be operating and although the assets will vest in the Official Custodian on dissolution and be transferred to another charity or charities, there is no provision for dealing with any liabilities including claims of employees.

CONVERSION TO A CIO

14.208 The legislation provides a framework for charitable companies, registered societies and community interest companies to convert to CIO status by means of a relatively simple resolution.

14.209 Where an unincorporated charity wishes to become a CIO, there is no 'conversion' process. The unincorporated charity must form a new CIO and transfer its undertaking to the new CIO. There are, however, mechanisms in the legislation which facilitate this: see **14.228-14.239**.

---

170 Regulation 34 of the Dissolution Regulations.
171 Regulation 35 of the Dissolution Regulations.
172 Regulation 38 of the Dissolution Regulations.
173 Regulation 39 of the Dissolution Regulations.
174 Regulation 40 of the Dissolution Regulations.

Conversion from a charitable company or registered society

14.210 Sections 228–230 of the 2011 Act provide a framework for charitable companies, cooperatives and community benefit societies to convert into a CIO. At the time of writing, these provisions are not yet in force. However, in April 2016 Government stated that it intended to bring the provisions relating to the conversion of charitable companies into force from October 2016 and published draft regulations for consultation under s 246 which allows the Minister for the Cabinet Office to make regulations dealing with conversion. At the time of writing, Government's response to the consultation is awaited.

14.211 The Act allows charitable companies and charitable 'registered societies',[175] to apply to the Commission to be converted into a CIO, and for the CIO's registration as a charity. To convert, a company or registered society with a share capital must not have any shares which are not fully paid up, nor must it be an exempt charity.[176] As explained in Chapter 5, at the time of writing all charitable community benefit and cooperative societies are exempt charities, although this is due to change.

14.212 The company or registered society which is seeking to convert to a CIO will need to supply the Commission with:

- a copy of a resolution of the company or registered society that it be converted into a CIO;
- a copy of the proposed constitution of the CIO;
- a copy of a resolution of the company or registered society adopting the proposed constitution of the CIO; and
- such other documents or information as the Commission may require.

The resolutions of the company or registered society must be either special resolutions or unanimous members' written resolutions.[177]

14.213 Regulations may prescribe what other documents or information must be submitted to the Commission.

14.214 When a charitable company limited by guarantee converts into a CIO and the liability of each member to contribute to its assets on a winding up is £10 or less, the guarantee is extinguished on the conversion into a CIO. However, if the members' liability is to contribute is more than £10 each, the new CIO's constitution must provide for the members to contribute to the assets of the CIO if it is wound up. The constitution must state the amount up to which they are liable, which must not be less than their liability to contribute to the assets of the company.[178]

14.215 The Commission must notify the appropriate registrar (the Registrar of Companies and in the case of registered societies, the Financial Conduct Authority and (where appropriate) the Prudential Regulation Authority) and such other persons as it thinks appropriate of any application for conversion and must consult them about

---

175 As defined in the Co-operative and Community Benefit Societies Act 2014.
176 Sections 228 and 229 of the 2011 Act.
177 Sections 228 and 229 of the 2011 Act.
178 Section 228(6)–(8) of the 2011 Act.

whether the application should be granted.[179] The company does not, therefore, need to file its resolution to convert to a CIO with Companies House.[180]

14.216 A framework for the Commission's consideration of applications for conversion to CIO status is set out in s 231. The basis on which an application for conversion may or must be refused is the same as for refusing an application for registration of a new CIO (see **14.49-14.50**), with two additions:

- the Commission must also refuse an application for conversion by a company limited by guarantee if the constitution does not comply with the requirements outlined at **14.214** concerning the members' liability to contribute to the assets on a winding up; and
- the Commission may refuse an application for conversion if, having considered representations from those whom it has consulted, it considers that it would not be appropriate to grant the application.

14.217 Regulations may make provision about circumstances in which it would not be appropriate to grant an application for conversion. The draft regulations issued for consultation in April 2016 (see **14.210**) refer to outstanding filings with Companies House or the Charity Commission. The Commission must notify the appropriate registrar if it refuses an application for conversion.[181]

14.218 Sections 232 and 233 set out the procedures to be followed when a charity successfully applies for conversion. If the Commission grants the application, it must enter the CIO in the register of charities, including a note of the name of the company or registered society, and send the appropriate registrar a copy of:

- each of the resolutions of the converting company or registered society; and
- the entry in the register of charities relating to the CIO.

14.219 The registrar must register the documents which have been sent to it, cancel the registration of the company or registered society in the relevant register and notify the Commission that this has been done. Upon cancellation of the relevant registration, the company or registered society is converted into a CIO, with the constitution and name set out in the application for conversion. The first members are the members of the converting company or registered society immediately before the moment of conversion.

14.220 If the converting company or registered society had share capital, the shares are cancelled on the conversion into a CIO and no former shareholder has any right in respect of cancelled shares. This does not affect any rights accrued before the shares are cancelled.

14.221 The registration of the CIO with the Commission is provisional until the registration of the company or registered society has been cancelled. Once the Commission has been notified of the cancellation, the entry relating to the new CIO's registration in the register must include a note that it is constituted as a CIO and the date when this happened. The Commission must send a copy of the register entry to the CIO at its principal office.

---

179 Section 230 of the 2011 Act.
180 Section 228(5) of the 2011 Act.
181 Section 231 of the 2011 Act.

14.222 Section 233(4) provides that the conversion of a charitable company or registered society does not affect any liability to which the company or registered society was subject by virtue of its being a charitable company or registered society. The Government Minister, Lord Bassam of Brighton, explained during the parliamentary debates on the legislation which became the 2006 Act that 'the process of conversion will not interrupt the legal personality of the entity',[182] so its liabilities will be unaffected by the conversion. Section 233(4) is intended to cover liabilities which are specific to the charity's previous corporate status as a company or registered society, such as penalties for late filing of accounts, and to ensure these are not wiped out by the conversion.

14.223 Conversion means that the company or registered society will transmogrify to CIO status without any interruption in its legal personality. It is submitted that there would be no transfer of employees for the purposes of Transfer of Undertakings (Protection of Employment) Regulations 2006, that registrations with external bodies (such as the Information Commissioner or Ofsted) would be unaffected and the conversion should not affect the charity's pension arrangements. Similarly, there should be no disruption of Gift Aid declarations benefiting the charity. At the time of writing, it is not yet completely clear whether an incorporated charity converting to CIO status will retain the same charity number.

14.224 However, banks and suppliers should be notified of the change of status. The charity will need a new letterhead disclosing its CIO status (see **14.134-14.135**) (and banks may issue new cheque books for the same reason). Undoubtedly it will take a while for banks and other suppliers to become familiar with the CIO form and what conversion means, but the practical changes required should be minimal.

Conversion from a community interest company

14.225 Section 234 authorises regulations by the Minister for the Cabinet Office to provide for the conversion of community interest companies into CIOs. In April 2016 Government issued draft regulations to this effect for consultation, suggesting that from October 2017 it would be possible for community interest companies to convert to CIOs.

Conversion from other legal forms

14.226 There is no mechanism for charities which are established by Act of Parliament or Royal Charter to convert to being a CIO. However it is suggested that such a charity could apply to become a company registered under the Companies Act 2006 and immediately convert into a CIO using the power in s 228.

Conversion from CIO status

14.227 One of the recommendations in Lord Hodgson's 2012 review of charity law was the need for a conversion process for CIOs to become charitable companies limited by guarantee.[183] As it is likely that CIOs will be most suitable for small and medium sized charities they may grow to a point when the company format will be more suitable, particularly if they want to take on more finance which is made difficult by the

---

[182] HL Deb, vol 674, col 700 (18 October 2005).
[183] *Trusted and Independent*, para 10.28.

lack of a public register of charges. Government was supportive of this recommendation, but noted that primary legislation would be needed.[184]

'INCORPORATION' – TRANSFER OF UNDERTAKING FROM AN UNINCORPORATED CHARITY TO A CIO

14.228 The CIO is proving attractive as a legal form not only for new charities, but also for existing unincorporated charities. However, an existing unincorporated charity cannot convert into a CIO simply by passing a resolution to do so. A new CIO has to be registered with the Commission and the undertaking of the unincorporated charity must then be transferred to the new CIO. The mechanism is essentially the same as for the transfer of the undertaking of an unincorporated charity to a successor charitable company, although there are some provisions in the legislation which may facilitate the process where the successor charity is a CIO.

14.229 The first step will be to apply to the Commission for registration of a new CIO. The application should state that the CIO will be a successor to an existing unincorporated charity. Once the application has been approved, the assets and liabilities can be transferred.

Approving the transfer

14.230 Any so-called 'incorporation' process requires a resolution of the unincorporated charity approving the transfer of the unincorporated charity's undertaking to the new incorporated successor charity. This will often be achieved using powers in the unincorporated charity's governing document. However, where the powers in the governing document are inadequate, the trustees may be able to approve the transfer using powers in the 2011 Act.

14.231 Section 268 of the 2011 Act contains a statutory power for the trustees of an unincorporated charity to transfer all of the charity's property to one or more different charities (see Chapter 15). This generally only applies to charities with an annual income of £10,000 or less, but where the transfer is to one or more CIOs, the statutory power applies regardless of the size of the transferring charity.[185] The trustees may resolve that all the property of the charity should be transferred to the CIO (or CIOs) specified in the resolution. They must be satisfied that it is expedient in the interests of furthering the purposes for which the property is held by the unincorporated charity for the property to be transferred in accordance with the resolution, and that the purposes (or any of the purposes) of any CIO to which the property is to be transferred under the resolution are substantially similar to the purposes (or any of the purposes) of the unincorporated charity. The resolution must be approved by at least two-thirds of the trustees who vote on the resolution.[186]

14.232 A copy of the resolution must be sent to the Commission, with a statement of the trustees' reasons for passing it. The Commission may then direct public notice of the resolution, and ask for further information. If the Commission does not object to the resolution, it takes effect after 60 days. (See **15.21-15.45** for more detail.)

---

184 Government Response, p 45.
185 Section 267(2) of the 2011 Act.
186 Section 268 of the 2011 Act.

14.233 The statutory power can be used where the unincorporated charity holds permanent endowment (see **15.46–15.56**). It cannot be used where the unincorporated charity holds 'designated land' (see **15.25**). Note that the statutory power does not relate to the transfer of liabilities to the CIO so the issue of liabilities needs to be addressed separately.

14.234 As mentioned at **14.70**, it is very likely that any resolution of the CIO to accept the assets and/or liabilities of the unincorporated charity will involve a conflict of interest for those trustees of the CIO who are also trustees of the unincorporated charity. Since trustees with a conflict of interest are unable to take part in the relevant decision, if there are not enough unconflicted trustees (or members) to approve the transfer, the Commission will need to be asked to give its approval by way of an order under s 105 of the 2011 Act (see Chapter 9).

Effecting the transfer

14.235 The property of the unincorporated charity will need to be transferred to the new CIO. The method of transfer will depend on the nature of the property of the unincorporated charity, but it is likely that one of the following methods will be used:

- the trustees of the unincorporated charity may enter into a deed of transfer with the new CIO;
- where the resolution to transfer takes effect under s 268 of the 2011 Act, the Commission may be asked to make an order vesting property of the unincorporated charity in the CIO;[187] and
- the unincorporated charity may make a pre-merger vesting declaration under s 310 of the 2011 Act.

14.236 Section 310 of the 2011 Act applies to charity mergers, and allows for the transfer of one charity's property to another by means of a deed (see Chapter 16). Section 310 has been adapted, in its application to the transfer of property to a CIO, by reg 61 of the General Regulations (see **Appendix** 7 of this book). The key changes are that where the transferring charity (in this case the unincorporated charity) holds permanent endowment or property on special trusts, the receiving CIO will hold that property on the same trusts as the transferring charity, and:

(a) the CIO will be treated as a trust corporation in relation to that property for the purposes of the enactments set out in para 3 of Sch 7 to the 2011 Act.[188] The most significant effect of this is that the CIO will be able to give good receipt on any sale of land comprised in the permanent endowment or special trust, without needing to take any other steps to be treated as a trust corporation (see Chapter 15 for more detail on trust corporations);

(b) the permanent endowment or special trust fund will be linked with the CIO itself for the purposes of Parts 4 and 8 of the 2011 Act, which deal with registration and accounting. This means that there is no need to make a separate application to the Commission for the fund to be linked to the CIO (see **4.12** for more on linking charities).

---

187 Section 272(4) of the 2011 Act.

188 Regulation 61(4) of the General Regulations.

14.237 Note, however, that certain types of property, including leasehold property, cannot be transferred by pre-merger vesting declaration.[189] Note also that the pre-merger vesting declaration route is only available where the transfer is part of a 'relevant charity merger' (as defined in s 306 of the 2011 Act: see **16.4-16.8**), which means that the arrangement must be registered on the Commission's register of mergers and as part of the arrangement the unincorporated charity must cease to exist. This could create potential problems for unincorporated charities which expect to receive legacy income: see Chapter 16.

14.238 Whichever route is chosen, it is likely that further steps will be required to effect a full transfer of the unincorporated charity's undertaking to the CIO. The trustees of the unincorporated charity may want an indemnity from the CIO for any properly-incurred liabilities of the unincorporated charity which arise after the transfer. Any employees will need to transfer under the TUPE Regulations (triggering a requirement for consultation). If the charity is a member of a defined benefit multi-employer pension scheme, the transfer will almost certainly be regarded as a 'cessation event' triggering obligations under pensions' legislation. The charity should liaise with HMRC Charities to confirm whether it may still benefit from Gift Aid declarations benefiting the charity and will need to liaise with banks, funders and suppliers to inform them of the transfer and seek to assign or novate contracts, where necessary. A new bank account may be needed. It is also likely that the new CIO will have to re-register with external bodies, as these registrations are unlikely to be transferable.

14.239 Once the transfer has taken place, the unincorporated charity may be wound up, and the Commission should be notified.[190]

THE FUTURE

14.240 When commenting on the legislation which became the 2006 Act, Baroness Scotland of Asthal hailed the CIO as 'a significant deregulatory measure',[191] because it allows charities to receive the benefits of incorporation without having to deal with dual regulation by both Companies House and the Commission. CIOs have, indeed, proved very popular, but as the CIO is a completely new legal structure, there are inevitably some uncertainties and grey areas which will need to be resolved over time. The existence and operation of the CIO form is still not necessarily widely understood and may need to be explained to funders and institutional lenders so that CIOs do not experience difficulty opening bank accounts and accessing funding. It may take some time for the CIO to be recognised beyond the charity sector and to build up the necessary confidence in the new legal structure.

Future reform

14.241 Lord Hodgson was unable to comment very fully on CIOs, as his review of charity law took place before the Commission had begun to register CIOs. He did, however, make a number of recommendations:

[189] Section 310(3) of the 2011 Act.
[190] See Chapter 4.
[191] HL Deb, vol 672, col 785 (7 June 2005).

(1) It should be possible for a CIO to convert to charitable company status: see **14.227**.

(2) The discrepancy between the majorities required to pass resolutions to amend constitutions and transfer assets at a meeting (75 per cent majority) and outside a meeting (unanimity) should be eliminated, in line with similar provisions in company law: see **14.99**.

(3) Changes to a CIO's constitution should take effect immediately, although 'regulated alterations' would need to be approved in advance: see **14.150**.

14.242 Lord Hodgson rejected the call for a public register of charges: see **14.116**.

14.243 Around the time of the 2006 Act, Government indicated that it would consider whether other forms of incorporation should still be available for charities once CIOs had been introduced. There has been no recent discussion of this proposal, so it is hoped that the CIO will simply co-exist alongside the other incorporated legal forms. In the authors' view, while the CIO is a welcome alternative vehicle for charities, flexibility is more appropriate.

14.244 Lord Hodgson recommended that the impact of CIOs should be assessed three years after implementation: this was endorsed by Government, so a review can be expected before the end of 2016.[192]

---

[192] *Trusted and Independent*, ch 10, recommendation 3.

CHAPTER 15

UNINCORPORATED CHARITIES

INTRODUCTION

15.1 The vast majority of charities are unincorporated. While unincorporated status is often perceived as being less formal than incorporated status, which may make it attractive to smaller charities, it has some disadvantages.

15.2 There are two types of unincorporated charity: charitable trusts and charitable unincorporated associations. Where an unincorporated charity has been established intentionally, it should have a properly drafted constitution: a charitable trust might be constituted by a trust deed or a will, for example, and an unincorporated association might have a set of rules. It is possible for an unincorporated charity to be created inadvertently: a charitable trust might arise where assets are held on trust for charitable purposes, and a charitable unincorporated association could be created where a group of people come together for charitable purposes. The scope for unincorporated charities to come into existence in a relatively informal way means that in some circumstances there can be a lack of understanding and organisation around their operation. This is compounded by the absence of a comprehensive statutory framework for unincorporated charities.

15.3 A significant feature of unincorporated status is that an unincorporated charity is technically comprised of the individual trustees, acting collectively. It has no separate legal identity of its own. The charity's property is held by the trustees, and the commitments involved in running the charity are assumed by the trustees themselves. The trustees, personally and collectively, are the employer of charity employees, for example. The trustees, personally and collectively, enter into contracts and hold the charity's assets, including land, subject to the use of nominees.

15.4 This means that when the trustees of the charity change, responsibility must be passed to the new trustees, which can give rise to complications.

15.5 A further concern is potential personal liability for the trustees. The trustees are formally personally and collectively responsible for the liabilities of the unincorporated charity. They are able to use the charity's funds to meet those liabilities, but their responsibility for the liabilities continues even once the charity's funds are exhausted, which leaves them vulnerable to unlimited personal liability in those circumstances. Disadvantaged creditors may wish to take advantage of this by seeking redress from the trustees personally.

15.6 By contrast, an incorporated charity has its own legal personality, so its property is unaffected by any changes in the identity of the individual trustees, and incorporated status generally confers limited liability on the trustees.

15.7 A further difference between incorporated and unincorporated charities is that since there is no comprehensive statutory framework for unincorporated organisations, the mechanism for changing the governing document of an unincorporated charity is, generally speaking, far less straightforward than is the case with an incorporated charity. Charitable companies and charitable incorporated organisations, for example, have statutory powers to change their governing document, although some changes require the involvement of the Commission (see **13.9-13.17** and **14.145**). The position of unincorporated charities is more complicated. In some cases, the governing document of an unincorporated charity will contain a power for the trustees or members of the charity to make amendments. However, this is not always the case, and such powers may be limited. The 2011 Act does contain various statutory powers for the trustees of unincorporated charities to amend their governing documents, but while they were significantly extended by the 2006 Act, they are not completely comprehensive. The statutory powers are described in detail in this chapter.

15.8 The 2011 Act also includes a mechanism for the incorporation of the trustee body, and various miscellaneous administrative provisions, which may be of assistance to unincorporated charities (see **15.69-15.73** and **15.77-15.80**).

15.9 In his 2012 review of charity law, Lord Hodgson considered whether limited liability should be made available to the trustees of unincorporated charities. At the time, there had been some discussion about introducing this in Scotland.[1] He decided against it, but recommended that there should be better promotion of user-friendly practical guidance on the legal position. One of the factors in Lord Hodgson's decision was the scope for unincorporated charities to adopt the new legal form, the charitable incorporated organisation, which does confer limited liability on the trustees (see Chapter 14).[2]

15.10 It is increasingly common for charities to be incorporated, particularly given the availability of the charitable incorporated organisation (or CIO): see Chapter 14. New charities can be incorporated from the outset, or existing charities may wish to reconstitute by transferring their assets and liabilities to a new incorporated charity, under a process often referred to as 'incorporation'.

STATUTORY POWERS FOR TRUSTEES OF UNINCORPORATED CHARITIES

15.11 Prior to the 2006 Act, the trustees of some smaller unincorporated charities had certain statutory powers to resolve to transfer property to other charities and to amend their objects and administrative powers. Certain conditions had to be met, including giving public notice, and informing the Commission, which had powers to object to the trustees' resolution. The 2002 Strategy Unit report recommended a package of measures to facilitate the administrative running of charities, including extending these powers to larger charities, and removing the requirement for the Commission's involvement in some circumstances.[3] The result was the statutory powers now set out in ss 267–280 of the 2011 Act.

1 Report on Unincorporated Associations, Scottish Law Commission No 217, 2009.

2 *Trusted and Independent: Giving Charity Back to Charities*, para 4.37.

3 *Private Action, Public Benefit*, recommendation 6.

POWER TO MODIFY A CHARITY'S POWERS OR PROCEDURES

15.12 Section 280 of the 2011 Act allows the trustees of any unincorporated charity to modify their administrative powers and procedures. This power was introduced in the 2006 Act and has made life easier for a great many unincorporated charities. It is not uncommon for older unincorporated charities to find themselves hampered by inadequate administrative powers: prior to the 2006 Act, unless the constitution contained a power for the trustees to make amendments, or unless the charity was small, the trustees had to apply to the Commission for changes or additions, no matter how minor, to be made by scheme.

15.13 The power in s 280 applies to all unincorporated charities, regardless of size. It allows the trustees to modify any provision in the trusts of the charity 'relating to any of the powers exercisable by the charity trustees in the administration of the charity'[4] or 'regulating the procedure to be followed in any respect in connection with its administration'.[5]

15.14 The trustees simply need to pass a resolution making the changes. If the charity is an unincorporated association with a body of members who are distinct from the trustees, the resolution must also be approved at a general meeting, either by a majority of not less than two-thirds of the members entitled to attend and vote at the meeting who vote on the resolution, or by a decision taken without a vote and without any expression of dissent in response to the question put to the meeting. The two-thirds majority requirement reflects the usual procedure for changing the constitution of an unincorporated association, but the rules also allow for circumstances where a charity traditionally makes decisions by mutual agreement without a vote.

15.15 There is no need to consult the Commission, which means that the change to the powers or provisions can take effect from the date specified in the trustees' resolution or, if later, the date of any necessary members' resolution. However, in line with s 35(3) of the 2011 Act, which requires details of any change in a registered charity's constitution to be sent to the Commission, if the charity is registered with the Commission the trustees should send a copy of the resolution or resolutions to the Commission once they have been passed.[6]

15.16 The Commission has taken a relatively broad view of the scope of this power. It accepts that it can be used to alter powers to change a charity's name, to borrow or invest and to cooperate with other charities, and to alter procedures relating to membership, the appointment of trustees and the management of meetings. It can be used to introduce totally new provisions. The Commission is also of the view that the power can be used to change provisions giving third parties rights to nominate trustees, provided the third party has ceased to exist or has given consent to the change.

15.17 The s 280 power can be used even if the governing document already contains a power of amendment. Indeed, where the governing document includes a power of amendment which is subject to the Commission's approval, the Commission positively encourages trustees to use the s 280 power instead, as it does not require the Commission's involvement.

---

4 Section 280(2)(a) of the 2011 Act.

5 Section 280(2)(b) of the 2011 Act.

6 See 4.70.

15.18 The Commission has stated that the power cannot be used to alter a charity's purposes (or to give the trustees a power to change the purposes), to spend capital held as permanent endowment or to authorise payment to the trustees.[7]

15.19 More details on the Commission's approach to the power can be found in its publications and operational guidance.[8]

15.20 The Law Commission has expressed concern that the wording of s 280 is uncertain. In its 2015 consultation[9] the Law Commission notes, for example, despite the Charity Commission's published views on s 280, that changes to trustee benefit provisions and permanent endowment may in fact fall within the scope of the current wording, but changes to third party powers to appoint trustees may not. The Law Commission commented that s 280 might benefit from reform to clarify its scope.

POWER TO TRANSFER PROPERTY

15.21 Section 268 of the 2011 Act allows the trustees of smaller unincorporated charities to transfer all of the charity's property to one or more different charities, where there is no such power in the charity's governing document.

15.22 For example, a long-established charity set up to help with education in a particular area may have spent most of its funds, and the trustees may decide that it would be more efficient for what is left to be transferred to a larger local charity which can use them for its ongoing work. If the constitution does not contain the powers the trustees need to make the transfer, they may be able to rely on s 268.

When does the power apply?

15.23 The power only applies to unincorporated charities whose gross income in the previous financial year was £10,000 or less. (The Minister for the Cabinet Office has power under s 285 to make an order changing this figure.) However, the £10,000 limit does not apply where the transfer is to one or more charitable incorporated organisations.[10] In his 2012 review, Lord Hodgson recommended that the threshold should be increased to £25,000.[11]

15.24 Section 268 will apply where an incorporated charity acts as trustee of a separate unincorporated charitable trust, which is not uncommon. In this case it is the income of the separate unincorporated charity which is relevant for the purposes of the income threshold, rather than the income of the main incorporated charity.

15.25 The power does not apply to charities which hold so-called 'designated land', which is land held on trusts which stipulate that it must be used for the purposes, or any particular purposes, of the charity.[12]

---

7 Charity Commission publication CC36 *Changing your Charity's Governing Document* and operational guidance OG 519 'Unincorporated Charities: Changes to Governing Documents and Transfer of Property'.

8 See, eg, CC36 *Changing your Charity's Governing Document* and operational guidance OG 519 'Unincorporated Charities: Changes to Governing Documents and Transfer of Property'.

9 Chapter 6, Technical Issues in Charity Law, A Consultation Paper, Law Commission, March 2015.

10 See **14.231**.

11 *Trusted and Independent*, Appendix A, para 26.

12 Section 267(1) of the 2011 Act.

15.26 The Law Commission, in its 2015 consultation,[13] asked for views on whether the scope of s 268 should be expanded in a number of ways, including by increasing the financial thresholds, allowing the power to apply to designated land, and reducing the need for the Charity Commission to be involved.

What must the trustees do?

15.27 First, the trustees must satisfy themselves that:

(a) it is expedient in the interests of furthering the purposes for which the property is held by the charity for it to be transferred in the way which is proposed; and

(b) the purposes, or any of the purposes, of any charity which is to receive the property are substantially similar to the purposes, or any of the purposes, of the transferring charity.[14]

15.28 The Commission's operational guidance, at the time of writing, states that in considering whether the purposes of the transferring and receiving charities are 'substantially similar':

> 'we need to be flexible in our approach ... but ensure that:
>
> – where current beneficiaries exist they are not deprived of their access to the charity's services without a compelling reason; and
> – property is not transferred for purposes completely unrelated to the original purpose.'[15]

15.29 Since not all of the purposes of the transferring and receiving charities need to be substantially similar, a charity whose objects are to work with children in Lincolnshire and Leicestershire, could, for example, resolve to transfer its funds to a charity whose objects are to work with children in Lincolnshire alone.

15.30 The trustees should then resolve to approve the transfer. The transfer can be to one or more charities. Where the transfer is to more than one charity, the resolution should specify how the property will be divided between them. The resolution must deal with all the charity's property: the power only caters for transferring all the property of the charity, not part of it.[16]

15.31 The resolution must be passed by a majority of not less than two-thirds of the trustees who vote on the resolution.[17] If the charity has a membership, there is no need for them to approve the resolution, but the Commission encourages consultation with the membership.[18]

---

13 Paragraphs 12.46–12.50, Technical Issues in Charity Law, A Consultation Paper, Law Commission, March 2015.

14 Section 268(3) of the 2011 Act.

15 Operational guidance OG 519 'Unincorporated Charities: Changes to Governing Documents and Transfer of Property'.

16 Section 268(1) of the 2011 Act.

17 Section 268(4) of the 2011 Act.

18 Operational guidance OG 519 'Unincorporated Charities: Changes to Governing Documents and Transfer of Property'.

15.32 The trustees must send a copy of the resolution to the Commission, with a statement of their reasons for passing it.[19] Trustees are encouraged to do this via the Commission's website.

When does the resolution take effect?

15.33 If the Commission does not take any of the actions described at **15.34-15.40** (which include power to object to the resolution), the resolution will automatically take effect at the end of the period of 60 days beginning with the date on which the Commission receives a copy of the resolution.[20]

15.34 The Commission has power, on receipt of a copy of the resolution, to direct the trustees to give public notice of the resolution, in the manner it specifies in the direction. The Commission must then take account of any representations made to it by persons appearing to the Commission to be interested in the charity which are made to the Commission within 28 days of the public notice being given.[21] The authors' experience is that it is rare for the Commission to ask for public notice.

15.35 If the Commission makes a direction along these lines, the 60-day period will be suspended as from the date on which the direction is given to the trustees until the end of the period of 42 days beginning with the date on which the public notice is given, under s 271.

15.36 Under s 269 the Commission can also direct the trustees to provide it with additional information or explanations about the circumstances in and by reference to which the trustees have decided to act. And the Commission can ask for information about the trustees' compliance with any obligations imposed on them by or under ss 268 or 269 in connection with the resolution, which might include a direction to give public notice.

15.37 In these circumstances, the 60-day period will be suspended as from the date on which the Commission directs the trustees to provide the information or explanations until the date on which the information or explanations are provided to the Commission, under s 271. Again, the authors' experience is that it is rare for the Commission to ask for additional information in this way.

15.38 If the 60-day period is suspended for more than 120 days in the circumstances described at **15.35** or **15.37**, the resolution will be treated as if it had never been passed, under s 271(6) and (7). Trustees should therefore ensure that they respond in good time to directions from the Commission to give public notice, or to supply information.

15.39 The resolution will not take effect at all if the Commission objects to it. The Commission can do so within the 60-day period before the resolution is due to take effect, or the extended period if the circumstances described at **15.35** or **15.37** apply. The Commission can object on procedural grounds, on the basis that any obligation imposed by or under s 268 or 269 has not been complied with, or on the merits of the

---

[19] Section 268(5) of the 2011 Act.
[20] Section 270 of the 2011 Act.
[21] Section 269 of the 2011 Act.

proposals. If the Commission objects, the charity trustees and any other person who is or may be affected by the decision may appeal to the Tribunal.[22]

15.40 The Commission's operational guidance gives more information about when the Commission is likely to object to a resolution, and when it may ask for more information or for public notice to be given.[23]

15.41 The authors' practical experience is that the Commission will generally respond to the filing of a resolution well within the time limits, giving the charity details of the date on which the resolution will take effect.

What happens once the resolution takes effect?

15.42 The trustees must arrange the transfer of the property, on a date after the resolution takes effect, which must be agreed with the trustees of the recipient charity or charities. Under s 272 the trustees of the recipient charity or charities must secure, so far as is reasonably practicable, that the property is held for such of its purposes as are substantially similar to those of the transferring charity, unless the recipient trustees consider that this would not result in a suitable and effective method of applying the property. The property will be subject to any restrictions on expenditure to which it was subject when it was the property of the original charity.[24]

15.43 The Commission can, at the request of the charity trustees of the recipient charity, make orders vesting any of the property of the original charity in the recipient charity or its trustees or nominees. This might be useful, for instance, to avoid the costs of obtaining the landlord's consent for transfers of leasehold property. However, the authors' experience is that the Commission is unwilling to exercise its power if there is an alternative method of transfer.

15.44 It would also be possible to register the transfer as a merger and therefore take advantage of the pre-merger vesting declaration procedure which can allow a transfer of the property via a simple document without the Commission's involvement (see Chapter 16).

15.45 If the transferring charity is registered with the Commission, it will cease to exist after the transfer so the trustees will need to notify the Commission under s 35(3) of the 2011 Act (see **4.98**).

What about permanent endowment?

15.46 Sections 268–272 apply in the way described above to smaller charities which do not have any permanent endowment property.[25] The regime for smaller charities which do hold permanent endowment is slightly different, and is set out in ss 273 and 274 of the 2011 Act.

---

22 Section 319 and Sch 6 of the 2011 Act.

23 Operational guidance OG 519 'Unincorporated Charities: Changes to Governing Documents and Transfer of Property'.

24 Section 272(2)(b) of the 2011 Act.

25 See Chapter 12 for more detail on permanent endowment.

15.47 If a charity holds both permanent endowment property and non-permanent endowment property (described as 'unrestricted property'), both must be dealt with in the transfer resolution made under s 268. The rules which apply to the unrestricted property are the same as those described above, but the rules which apply to the permanent endowment are slightly different, as described at **15.50-15.56.**

15.48 Where all the charity's property is permanent endowment, while the trustees may make a resolution under s 268, the regime is adapted, as described at **15.50-15.56.**

15.49 The adaptations which are made to ss 268-272 in relation to permanent endowment do not affect those provisions in so far as they relate to the majority required for the resolution, notifying the Commission, the Commission's powers on receipt of the resolution and the timescale.

15.50 Where the transfer includes permanent endowment property, before making the resolution under s 268, instead of satisfying themselves that the purposes, or any of the purposes, of any charity which is to receive the permanent endowment property are substantially similar to the purposes, or any of the purposes, of the transferring charity (see **15.27**(b)), the trustees must satisfy themselves as follows:

(a) if the transfer of permanent endowment is to one charity only, that the charity has purposes which are substantially similar to *all* of the purposes of the transferring charity; and
(b) if the transfer of permanent endowment is to more than one charity, that those charities, taken together, have purposes which are substantially similar to *all* of the purposes of the transferring charity, and that each of the proposed recipient charities has purposes which are substantially similar to one or more of the purposes of the transferring charity.[26]

15.51 This means, taking the example given at **15.29**, that a charity whose objects are to work with children in Lincolnshire and Leicestershire could only resolve to transfer its permanent endowment to a charity whose objects include working with children in both Lincolnshire and Leicestershire, or to two or more charities whose objects, taken together, include working with children in both counties: for example, where one works with children in Lincolnshire and another with children in Leicestershire.

15.52 Where the transfer is to be to more than one charity, the property must be divided between them in a way which takes account of any guidance on the subject given by the Commission, which may take such form and be given in such manner as the Commission thinks appropriate.[27]

15.53 The Commission may ask for information about the trustees' compliance with these additional obligations and may object to the resolution if the trustees do not comply.[28]

15.54 The charity trustees of the recipient charity or charities must secure, so far as is reasonably practicable, that the property transferred to them is held for such of their charity's purposes as are substantially similar to those of the transferring charity, unless

---

26 Section 274(3) and (4) of the 2011 Act.
27 Sections 274(5) and (8) of the 2011 Act.
28 Section 274(6) of the 2011 Act.

they consider that this would not result in a suitable and effective way of applying the property, and in doing so they must ensure that the application of the property takes account of any relevant guidance given by the Commission. The Commission has discretion about the form of guidance and the manner in which it is given.[29]

15.55 The property will continue to be permanent endowment after the transfer. The Commission's guidance includes a reminder that if the recipient charity is a charitable company, it cannot hold the permanent endowment as part of its corporate property, but must hold it on a separate trust of which the company is a trustee.[30]

15.56 In its 2015 consultation,[31] the Law Commission commented that there is 'no clear rationale' for the more onerous condition described at **15.50**, and provisionally proposed that it should be removed.

POWER TO CHANGE A CHARITY'S PURPOSES

15.57 Section 275 of the 2011 Act gives the charity trustees of smaller unincorporated charities power to replace all or any of the charity's purposes with other charitable purposes by means of a simple resolution.

15.58 For example, the trustees of a charity established to provide grants to children in need living in a particular town may feel that their pool of beneficiaries has dwindled over time to the extent that it would be better for their purposes to be expanded to encompass other towns in the region. While there may be scope to ask the Commission to make a cy-près scheme for the charity (see Chapter 17), s 275, if it applies, provides a simpler mechanism and gives more latitude to the trustees in choosing new purposes.

15.59 The Commission is of the view that this power can be used not only to change a charity's main purposes but also its purposes on dissolution.[32]

When does the power apply?

15.60 The power only applies to unincorporated charities whose gross income in the previous financial year was £10,000 or less. (The Minister of the Cabinet Office has power under s 285 to make an order changing this figure.) Where an incorporated charity holds property on separate unincorporated charitable trusts (as in **15.24**), the threshold relates to the income of the unincorporated charity.

15.61 The power does not apply to charities which hold so-called 'designated land', which is land held on trusts which stipulate that it must be used for the purposes, or any particular purposes of the charity.

15.62 In his 2012 review, Lord Hodgson recommended that the income threshold should be increased from £10,000 to £25,000[33] and in its 2015 consultation the Law

---

29 Sections 274(7) and (8) of the 2011 Act.

30 Operational guidance OG 519 'Unincorporated Charities: Changes to Governing Documents and Transfer of Property'.

31 Paragraphs 12.51–12.54, Technical Issues in Charity Law, A Consultation Paper, Law Commission, March 2015.

32 OG 519 *Unincorporated Charities: Changes to Governing Documents and Transfer of Property*.

33 *Trusted and Independent*, Appendix A, para 26.

Commission provisionally proposed that s 275 should be extended to charities with a larger income, and to charities with designated land.[34]

What must the trustees do?

15.63 The trustees must be satisfied that:

(a) it is expedient in the interests of the charity for the purposes in question to be replaced; and

(b) so far as is reasonably practicable, the new purposes consist of or include purposes which are similar in character to those which are to be replaced.[35]

15.64 The Commission, at the time of writing, accepts that 'the trustees, with their knowledge of the situation in which the charity operates, are in the best position to decide what is "reasonably practical"'. It states that 'trustees … need to be flexible and imaginative in considering what is "similar in character" to the existing purposes'. When considering s 275 resolutions (see **15.66-15.67**) the Commission's starting point for whether the new purposes are similar in character may be its guidance on cy-près applications, although s 275 allows for a wider application than the cy-près regime. It will be alert to situations where existing beneficiaries are unreasonably deprived or excluded from the benefits of the charity.[36]

15.65 The trustees should then pass a resolution resolving to modify the trusts of the charity by replacing all or any of its purposes with other purposes specified in the resolution. The resolution must be passed by a majority of not less than two-thirds of the trustees who vote on it.[37]

15.66 The trustees must send a copy of the resolution to the Commission, with a statement of their reasons for passing it.[38]

When does the resolution take effect?

15.67 The rules about when the resolution will take effect, what directions the Commission can give in response to the resolution, and how the Commission can object to the resolution, are the same as those which apply in relation to the power to transfer property under s 268, which are set out at **15.33-15.41**.[39]

What happens once the resolution takes effect?

15.68 As soon as the resolution takes effect, the trusts of the charity will be taken to have been modified in accordance with the resolution, so the new purposes will apply.[40]

---

34 Paragraphs 5.21–5.23, Technical Issues in Charity Law, A Consultation Paper, Law Commission, March 2015.

35 Section 275(4) of the 2011 Act.

36 Operational guidance OG 519 'Unincorporated Charities: Changes to Governing Documents and Transfer of Property'. See also **17.11–17.41** on cy-près schemes.

37 Section 275(2) and 275(5) of the 2011 Act.

38 Section 275(6) of the 2011 Act.

39 Sections 276–278 of the 2011 Act.

40 Section 279 of the 2011 Act.

INCORPORATION OF CHARITY TRUSTEES

15.69 One of the disadvantages of unincorporated status is that each time there is a change in the identity of the trustees, the charity's property may need to be transferred to the new trustees, although there are exceptions, such as where the charity's property is held by the Official Custodian (see Chapter 22), via separate 'holding trustees' or in the name of nominees. Any contracts should, strictly, be novated into the names of the new trustees.

15.70 Sections 251–266 of the 2011 Act provide a mechanism for overcoming this problem by allowing for the incorporation of the board of trustees of an unincorporated charity. This is different to so-called 'incorporation', where the undertaking of an unincorporated charity is wound up and its property transferred to a successor incorporated charity. Under the 2011 Act procedure it is the board of trustees, rather than the charity itself, which becomes incorporated.

15.71 The trustees can apply to the Commission for a certificate of incorporation of the trustee body. Once the certificate is granted, all the charity's property, including land, is vested in the incorporated trustees. Further formalities, such as registering the transfer at the Land Registry, may also be required in order to effect the transfer.

15.72 Significantly, incorporation under this mechanism does not confer limited liability on the trustees. It does not diminish the personal liability of the trustees of the charity in any way: they will remain potentially liable to the charity's creditors, should the charity run out of funds. Where the charity trustees have concerns about their personal liability, they may wish to consider incorporation of the charity itself as a charitable company or CIO.

15.73 At the time of writing, the Commission has published operational guidance on incorporation of charity trustees.[41]

TRUST CORPORATIONS

15.74 Some unincorporated charities have a corporate trustee: while the charity itself is unincorporated, the trustee is an incorporated body, such as a company. The directors of the company acting as trustee have limited liability, unlike the trustees of a charity whose board has been incorporated under the 2011 Act (see **15.69-15.73**).

15.75 However, it is not always possible for trust property to be held effectively by a corporate trustee, unless the trustee qualifies as a 'trust corporation'. In particular, where land held in trust is sold, the proceeds of sale must be paid to either two trustees or a trust corporation. The purchaser will not generally obtain good receipt if the proceeds of sale are paid to just one corporate trustee, which is not a trust corporation.[42] In addition, a sole corporate trustee which is not a trust corporation may be unable to give a proper discharge to an outgoing trustee.[43]

15.76 There are a number of ways of qualifying as a trust corporation. For instance, a body authorised to act as a custodian trustee under the Public Trustee Rules 1912, which

---

41 OG 50 *Incorporation of Charity Trustees.*

42 See, eg, the Law of Property Act 1925.

43 Section 37 of the Trustee Act 1925.

includes a corporation authorised by the Lord Chancellor to act as a trust corporation in relation to any charitable trust (via an application to the Ministry for Justice), is a trust corporation for the purposes of the relevant legislation. In relation to the relevant legislation a trust corporation also includes a corporation appointed by the Commission to be a trustee under the 2011 Act, by virtue of Sch 7, para 3. It may therefore be helpful for an unincorporated charity with a sole corporate trustee to seek a scheme from the Commission to appoint the trustee: this ensures that the trustee qualifies as a trust corporation for the purposes of that particular trust. If a charitable incorporated organisation acts as trustee of an unincorporated charity, thanks to a pre-merger vesting declaration made under s 310 of the 2011 Act, as modified in its application to CIOs, the CIO is treated as a trust corporation for the purposes of the legislation mentioned in Sch 7, para 3.[44]

ADMINISTRATION

15.77 The 2011 Act also includes several additional provisions which may help with the administration of an unincorporated charity.

15.78 Section 334 contains a mechanism for vesting property in new or continuing charity trustees by a memorandum executed as a deed, where the trustees are changed by resolution at a trustees' meeting. This may be helpful when the trustees of an unincorporated charity change.

15.79 Section 332 deals with giving notice to charity trustees, members or subscribers, providing that notice may be given by post to the address which appears in the list of trustees, members or subscribers currently in use by the charity: if this mechanism is used for notice of an election or a meeting which is required by the charity's trusts, the notice only needs to be given if the intended recipient's address is in the United Kingdom.

15.80 Section 333, which is dealt with in detail in Chapter 8, allows the trustees to give any two of their number authority to sign documents on their behalf. This is very useful in facilitating the execution of documents by the trustees of an unincorporated charity.

---

44 Regulation 61(4) of the Charitable Incorporated Organisations (General) Regulations 2012, SI 2012/3012. See 14.236.

CHAPTER 16

MERGERS

OVERVIEW

16.1 Sections 305 to 314 of the 2011 Act, which were introduced by the 2006 Act, are designed to facilitate charity mergers. They include measures to simplify the legal formalities needed to transfer certain types of property. They also aim to preserve post-merger gifts to original transferring charities, where a merger is recorded in a register of charity mergers, kept by the Commission. While useful for some mergers, these provisions do however have several limitations:

- they do not apply to all types of charity merger, but only to mergers falling within the definition of 'relevant charity merger' (see **16.4–16.8**);
- they do not cover all types of charity property (see **16.12–16.17**);
- for more complex mergers, these provisions cannot be relied upon solely as the means of effecting a merger (see **16.38–16.47**); and
- due to a problem unforeseen by the parliamentary draftsmen, registration of a merger does not currently preserve all legacies to the original charities (see **16.31-16.32**).

The 2011 Act also contains specific provisions which may apply where a merger involves two or more CIOs: see Chapter 14.

16.2 In his 2012 review of charity law, Lord Hodgson made a number of recommendations designed to improve the impact of the merger provisions in the 2011 Act.[1] These have since been considered by the Law Commission, which has made some proposals for reform.[2] Those proposals are highlighted in this chapter.

16.3 Lord Hodgson also recommended that where a merger involves an unincorporated charity transferring its undertaking to a successor incorporated charity (known as incorporation or reconstitution), both the Commission and Her Majesty's Revenue and Customs (HMRC) should allow the successor incorporated charity to use the same registration number as the predecessor unincorporated charity.[3]

---

1 *Trusted and Independent: Giving Charity Back to Charities.*
2 Technical Issues in Charity Law: A Consultation Paper, Law Commission, March 2015.
3 *Trusted and Independent*, para 10.7.

WHAT IS A 'RELEVANT CHARITY MERGER'?

16.4 As mentioned above, these provisions of the 2011 Act only apply to 'relevant charity mergers'. 'Relevant charity merger' has a fairly narrow definition (s 306(1) of the 2011 Act). It means either:

> '(a) a merger of two or more charities in connection with which one of them ("the transferee") has transferred to it all the property of the other or others, each of which ("a transferor") ceases to exist, or is to cease to exist, on or after the transfer of its property to the transferee; or
>
> (b) a merger of two or more charities ("transferors") in connection with which both or all of them cease to exist, or are to cease to exist, on or after the transfer of all of their property to a new charity ("the transferee").'

16.5 Note the requirement for the transferring charity to 'cease to exist'. For charities which are companies limited by guarantee, this would be the point when the company is struck off the register of companies. For unincorporated charities there is a less obvious date at which they 'cease to exist'. The authors' view is that, generally, a charitable trust will cease to exist at the point that it has no assets, while an unincorporated association will cease to exist if its trustees or members have taken deliberate and precise actions which are equivalent to dissolving a charity.

16.6 In practice there may be compelling reasons why it would not be in the best interests of the merging parties for one or other of the original charities to cease to exist. Particularly, if there could be potential legacies (see **16.31-16.32**) or, say, if the transferring charity has a lease which contains an absolute prohibition on assignment (in which case the transferring charity may need to be kept in existence so the premises can continue to be used, usually by granting an underlease to the receiving charity, although see the proposals for reform mentioned at **16.14**).

16.7 Where the transferring charity owns a mix of permanent endowment and other assets, the transfer of the non-permanent endowment assets will fall within the definition of 'relevant charity merger', provided the charity's trusts do not contain a power to dissolve.[4] In this scenario, the transferor can remain in existence post 'merger' to hold the permanent endowment.

16.8 Note also:

- only mergers of charities which are subject to the jurisdiction of the High Court can be 'relevant charity mergers'. This means if the merger involves a charity established in any other jurisdiction, including Scotland and Northern Ireland, it cannot be a relevant charity merger;
- mergers involving charitable incorporated organisations which are effected under the provisions of the 2011 Act dealing with amalgamation of CIOs or transfer of undertaking between CIOs (see Chapter 14) will not qualify as a relevant charity merger[5].

This table sets out some key examples of what is and is not a relevant charity merger:

---

4 Section 306(2) and (3) of the 2011 Act .

5 Section 314 of the 2011 Act.

Relevant charity merger	Not a relevant charity merger
Transfer of the assets of Charity A to Charity B and then Charity A ceases to exist (but see exception in next column for certain CIO mergers).	Transfer of the assets of Charity A to Charity B (where Charity A and Charity B are both charitable incorporated organisations and the transfer is effected using the provisions of the 2011 Act which relate to the merger of CIOs).
Transfer of the assets of Charity A to Charity B, the renaming of the receiving charity as Charity C with revised governing document and the dissolution of Charity A.	Transfer of the assets of Charity A to Charity B with Charity A remaining as a 'shell' charity.
Charity A and Charity B transfer their assets to Charity C and then cease to exist (but see exception in next column for certain CIO mergers).	Transfer of the assets of Charity A and Charity B to a new charity where Charity A, Charity B and the new charity are all charitable incorporated organisations and the transfer is effected using the provisions of the 2011 Act which relate to the merger of CIOs. Charity A and Charity B transfer their assets to Charity C and remain as 'shell' charities.
Charity A retains permanent endowment property and transfers all other property to Charity B – Charity A continues to exist post-merger. (NB: this is not a relevant charity merger if Charity A's trusts contain provision for dissolution of the charity.)	Charity A becomes corporate trustee of Charity B.
Charities A and B retain their permanent endowment property and transfer all other property to Charity C – Charities A and B continue to exist post-merger. (NB this is not a relevant charity merger if Charity A's or Charity B's trusts contain provision for dissolution of the charity.)	Charity A and Charity B become subsidiaries of a new Charity C
	A number of charities are consolidated or given common administration under a Scheme.
	A merger involves a charity established in Scotland or Northern Ireland.

WHAT IS THE SIGNIFICANCE OF BEING A 'RELEVANT CHARITY MERGER'?

16.9 There are three main consequences:

- the transferring charity can make a vesting declaration (see **16.10–16.22**);
- the Commission will, if notified, include the merger in its register of mergers – any merger that is not a relevant charity merger cannot be noted in the register (see **16.23–16.27**); and

- once the merger is recorded in the register of mergers, most subsequent gifts to the transferring charity take effect as gifts to the receiving charity (see **16.29–16.34**).

VESTING DECLARATION

16.10 A vesting declaration (also referred in the 2011 Act as a 'pre-merger vesting declaration') has the effect of transferring the legal title to a wide range of property in just one document without the need for any other formalities.[6] In the Parliamentary debates on the 2006 Act, which introduced these provisions, Lord Phillips of Sudbury described it as an 'extraordinary … thing. No conveyances; no transfer documents … Whoomp. It happens overnight, by magic'.[7]

16.11 The transfer of property takes place on the date specified in the declaration, except in the case of registered land, where the vesting declaration will have to be registered at the Land Registry to complete the transfer of the property. Note that the vesting declaration will trigger first registration for previously unregistered land.

16.12 Not all property can be transferred under a vesting declaration and there are some grey areas:

Property which can be transferred under a vesting declaration	**Property which cannot be transferred under a vesting declaration**	**Grey areas**
Petty cash.	Any land held by the transferor as security for money subject to the trusts of the transferor (other than land held on trust for securing debentures or debenture stock).[8]	Debts.
Cash held in bank accounts (although whether banks will in practice allow a receiving charity to be recorded as the new owner of existing accounts of the transferring charity will probably be a matter for internal bank policy).	A lease containing a prohibition on assignment without consent of the landlord where the landlord's consent has not been obtained before the transfer date (but see **16.14**).	A lease containing an absolute prohibition on transfer (but see **16.14**). Land owned by the transferor and subject to a charge or mortgage (see **16.13**).
Office furniture, equipment and stock.	Freehold or leasehold land which is subject to any covenant against assignment where the relevant consent has not been obtained before the transfer date.	Right to use personal data held under the Data Protection Act 1998.
Vehicles.	Shares.	

6 Section 310 of the 2011 Act.
7 HL Deb, vol 672, col 794 (7 June 2005).
8 This wording appears in s 310(3)(a). In September 2012, in correspondence shared with the Charity Law Association, the Commission confirmed its interpretation of s 310(3)(a) as meaning a pre-merger vesting declaration does not operate to transfer a mortgage (i e where the trustees have advanced money secured by way of mortgage). Mortgages granted in favour of the transferor are therefore excluded and must be transferred separately. See **16.13** for the effect of vesting declarations in relation to land (owned by the transferor) which is mortgaged in favour of a third party.

Property which can be transferred under a vesting declaration	Property which cannot be transferred under a vesting declaration	Grey areas
Unmortgaged freehold land which is not subject to any covenant against assignment or, if there is such a covenant, the consent has been obtained before the transfer date.	Other stock, annuity or other property which is only transferable in books kept by a company or other body.	
Unmortgaged leases, provided there is no prohibition on assignment without consent of the landlord or, if there is such a prohibition, the consent has been obtained before the transfer date.	Other property which is only transferable under any enactment.	
	Property held on permanent endowment, except where the receiving charity is a CIO (see 14.236), but see 16.14.	

16.13 The effect of vesting declarations in relation to land owned by the transferor but subject to a mortgage or charge is complex. Although such land is not specifically excluded from the scope of a vesting declaration under s 310, the authors' view is that a vesting declaration is likely to take effect only as a transfer in equity of the land. This is because, in most cases, there will be a restriction on the title in favour of the mortgagee, meaning it is not possible to register the vesting of the land without the consent of the mortgagee. The solution in practice is to exclude land owned by the transferor and subject to a mortgage or charge from a vesting declaration – this also avoids the risk the transferor could breach its mortgage and/or underlying loan covenants.

16.14 The Law Commission has proposed that the exception relating to the transfer of leases containing a prohibition against assignment without the landlord's consent (where that consent has not been obtained) should be removed. The Law Commission acknowledged the uncertainty over whether there is also an exception for leases containing an absolute prohibition against assignment but expressed the provisional view that there should be no such exception. The Law Commission has also provisionally proposed that the exception relating to permanent endowment should be removed.[9]

16.15 Importantly, vesting declarations do not transfer many types of important contracts, eg funding contracts, employment contracts, software licences and other intellectual property licences.[10] Therefore, in many mergers, these contracts will need to be assigned or novated separately.

16.16 Vesting declarations do not transfer liabilities: see **16.39-16.42.**

16.17 Note also that vesting declarations do not have the effect of transferring to the receiving charity the benefit of any registrations with external bodies, for example the Care Quality Commission. The receiving charity will need to ensure it has arranged its own registration with any relevant bodies prior to merger.

---

9 Chapter 12, Technical Issues in Charity Law: A Consultation Paper, Law Commission, March 2015.

10 In the debates in the House of Lords on the legislation which became the 2006 Act, which introduced these provisions, the Government Minister, Lord Bassam of Brighton, expressed the clear view that the merger provisions did not apply to liabilities such as contractual obligations.

16.18 The requirements for a vesting declaration to take effect are:

- it must be made by deed;
- it must be made by the charity trustees of the transferring charity; and
- there must be a declaration to the effect that all of the transferring charity's property is to vest in the receiving charity on a date specified in the declaration.

16.19 If a vesting declaration is made, the trustees of the receiving charity must notify the Commission of the merger once the transfer has taken place. Note that although the obligation to make the declaration is on the trustees of the transferring charity, it is the trustees of the receiving charity who have the obligation to notify the Commission. The authors' view is that a vesting declaration is valid and takes effect even if the necessary notification is not made to the Commission. The wording of s 310 suggests that the vesting declaration takes effect before the obligation to notify arises. So it is difficult to see how its validity is dependent on the notification. The clause was amended during the third reading of the legislation in the House of Lords to make notification obligatory where there has been a vesting declaration, but the debates did not specifically address the issue of whether the declaration is valid only if notification is made to the Commission.

Other consequences of a vesting declaration

16.20 Vesting declarations may have consequences for other aspects of the transferring charity's activities. For example, it is likely that a vesting declaration would trigger an automatic transfer of any employees of the transferring charity to the receiving charity under the Transfer of Undertakings (Protection of Employment) Regulations 2006.

16.21 There will no doubt be other areas affected, one of which may be a charity's pension scheme. Some schemes (particularly defined benefit multi-employer schemes) are drafted so as to be affected by a 'cessation event', and a vesting declaration may well be treated as a cessation event in relation to the transferring charity's pension scheme.

16.22 The provisions of the 2011 Act which relate to vesting declarations are adapted in their application to the transfer of property to a CIO: see **14.236** for details.

REGISTER OF MERGERS AND NOTIFICATION

16.23 The Commission maintains a Register of Mergers which can be accessed online via the Commission's website.[11] The Commission is only obliged to record in the register 'relevant charity mergers' (see **16.4-16.8**) which are notified to it using the correct procedure.[12]

16.24 Each entry in the register must specify[13] the date(s) on which transfer(s) of property took place and where a vesting declaration was made, the date the declaration was made and the date on which it took effect. The Commission has decided that, in addition, the register will also contain the date the merger was registered and the names and registered numbers (if any) of the transferor and transferee charities.

---

[11] Sections 305 and 309 of the 2011 Act.

[12] Section 305(2) of the 2011 Act.

[13] Section 308 of the 2011 Act.

16.25 Whether or not a merger has to be notified to the Commission for recording in the register depends on whether a vesting declaration has been made – if it has, the merger must be registered; otherwise registration is optional. The timing of notification also varies (see the table below).

	Notification where no vesting declaration	**Notification where a vesting declaration has been made**
Obligation to notify	No – notification is optional.	Yes – notification is obligatory.
Timing	Any time after the last transfer of property has been made.	When the last transfer of property has been made.
Notification to include	(a) The transfer or transfers of property involved in the merger and the date or dates on which it or they took place; (b) a statement from the charity trustees that appropriate arrangements have been made with respect to the discharge of any liabilities of the transferor(s).	(a) The transfer or transfers of property involved in the merger and the date or dates on which it or they took place; (b) a statement from the charity trustees that appropriate arrangements have been made with respect to the discharge of any liabilities of the transferor(s); (c) the fact that a vesting declaration has been made; (d) the date of the declaration itself and the date on which the vesting of title under the declaration took place.

16.26 The Commission is willing to register mergers which took place prior to the relevant sections of the 2006 Act coming into force. The authors' view is that this is consistent with the legislation, because the Commission's duty to keep the register applies to mergers that took place before the relevant provisions came into force (as well as those occurring after that date) and there is no time limit for notifying a merger.

16.27 To cover situations where a transferee charity wishes to ensure that there is no gap between a charity ceasing to exist[14] and the date of registration of the merger, the Commission will accept a 'conditional notification', ie advance notification of a merger. When completing the form to notify the merger to the Commission, the date of the transfer of property to the transferee and the date the merger is to be registered should be recorded as the same date. The conditional notification will become an effective notification on the date the property is transferred and will then be registered. The Commission advises that the date specified must allow the Commission sufficient time (at least 2 weeks) to register the merger.[15]

---

14 See **16.5**.

15 Charity Commission Operational Guidance OG 60 'Register of Charity Mergers: ss 305–314 of the Charities Act 2011'.

Register of mergers and mergers which are not 'relevant charity mergers'

16.28 The Commission is not obliged to record mergers which are not 'relevant charity mergers' in the Register of Mergers, but it could do so (in theory). In the authors' view, it would be helpful for the Commission to include all kinds of mergers on the register, regardless of the technical law, to provide relevant information to the public. This could be helpful, for example, where a legacy has been left to a charity which no longer exists and a search is being made for the successor charity.

POST-MERGER GIFTS TO TRANSFERRING CHARITY

16.29 One of the main proposed benefits of the charity merger provisions was that they would help preserve legacies. The first part of s 311 states:

> '(1) This section applies where a relevant charity merger is registered in the register of charity mergers.
>
> (2) Any gift which–
>
> (a) is expressed as a gift to the transferor, and
> (b) takes effect on or after the date of registration of the merger,
>
> takes effect as a gift to the transferee, unless it is an excluded gift.'

16.30 The explanatory notes to the 2006 Act (in which these provisions were first introduced) state:

> 'Section [311] deals with a gift to a charity where the gift takes effect after the date of registration of a merger affecting the charity. In the example of a merger in which charity A transfers all its property to charity B then ceases to exist, there might later be gifts – such as legacies under wills written before the merger – which fall due to charity A after it has ceased to exist. Subsection (2) provides that such a gift takes effect as if the gift had originally been made to charity B rather than charity A.'

16.31 However, in practice, s 311 does not save all legacies. It has been held not to apply where a testator has specifically described what should happen to the legacy if the recipient charity is no longer in existence. In *Berry & anor v IBS-STL (UK) Ltd (in liquidation) & anor*,[16] the High Court considered whether s 311 acted to preserve the share of a residuary estate left to an unincorporated charity, the International Bible Society (IBS), which was no longer in existence at the time of the testator's death. Since the date of the will and the testator's death, IBS had gone through an incorporation process (transferring its assets to a new charitable company) which had been recorded in the register of mergers. In this case, the will made specific provision that:

> 'IF any charity or charitable organisation which I have named as a beneficiary in this Will is found never to have existed or to have ceased to exist or to have become amalgamated with another organisation or to have changed its name before my death then the gift contained in this Will for such charity or charitable organisation shall be transferred to whatever

---

16 [2012] EWHC 666 (Ch).

charitable institution or institutions and if more than one in whatever proportions as my Trustees shall in their absolute discretion think fit and

I EXPRESS THE WISH but without imposing any obligation on my Trustees that the gift be given to such charitable institution or institutions whose purpose is as close as possible to those of the charity or charitable organisation named by me in this Will.'

16.32 The judge concluded that as the will expressly dealt with what should happen if a named beneficiary charity had ceased to exist, s 311 did not preserve the legacy for the newly incorporated charity.

16.33 It is worth noting that it is relatively common for wills to include a provision along these lines. The issue in this case has been identified as one of the problems with the legislation; for a proposed solution, see **16.36**.

16.34 Note, there is a statutory exclusion to the automatic transfer of gifts to the transferee charity which applies where the transferring charity had both permanent endowment and other property (unrestricted property), and there was no provision for dissolution of the transferring charity: see **16.7**. In that situation, any gift which is intended to be held on the same trusts as the permanent endowment will take effect as a gift to the transferring charity, rather than a gift to the transferee.[17]

To register or not to register?

16.35 As a result of the uncertainty surrounding preservation of legacies on a merger, charities with any significant expectation of legacy income should consider carefully whether to go down the route of registering the merger. A safer option is for the transferor charity to remain in existence (so as to receive any post-merger legacies). Administration can be simplified by applying for the transferor and transferee charity to be linked by uniting direction under s 12 of the 2011 Act.[18] Note, however, that there can be some practical issues to consider. For example, the transferring charity should retain at least a small amount of property in order to ensure its continuing existence. The transferring charity should also retain its original name as a change of name can affect some legacies.

16.36 The Law Commission, in response to a recommendation in Lord Hodgson's 2012 review of charity law, considered how the difficulties surrounding legacies and mergers might be addressed. It provisionally proposed that the legislation should be amended so that when considering whether a gift has been made to a transferring charity which takes effect after the merger, for the purposes of s 311(2) the transferring charity should be deemed to have continued to exist, despite the merger. This would ensure that a gift in a will would not lapse simply because the original beneficiary charity had merged with another charity, unless the testator had specifically provided that the gift was conditional on the charity not having merged. The authors, in their response to the consultation, expressed the concern that this proposal may go too far. However, some change to the current position would be appropriate, in order to avoid the current practice of retaining a shell charity purely for the purpose of receiving legacies.[19]

---

17 Section 311(3) of the 2011 Act.

18 See **4.12**.

19 Chapter 12, Technical Issues in Charity Law: A Consultation Paper, Law Commission, March 2015.

16.37 If registering, it is advisable to register as soon as possible after the date of the merger (or apply for conditional registration – see **16.27**). Otherwise, any gift which crystallises in the period between merging and registration will not be preserved.

PROBLEM AREAS

16.38 As mentioned at **16.1**, the provisions described above do not apply to all charity mergers. So, in each case there should be a careful analysis of whether the merger qualifies as a relevant charity merger and, if so, what property, if any, can transfer under a vesting declaration. Even then, any charity with contractual obligations and liabilities should consider whether to have separate merger documentation dealing with the transfer of the contractual liabilities. It would be a rare merger where relying on the vesting declaration alone would be sufficient. Some particular concerns are set out below.

Liabilities – continuing exposure of trustees of the transferring charity

16.39 It is usual, and technically necessary, in a merger for the receiving charity to give an indemnity to the trustees of the transferring charity, so that if they are later pursued for some debt or liability of the transferring charity, they can call on the receiving charity to indemnify them. This can be particularly important where the transferring charity is unincorporated and the potential liability of the transferring trustees is direct.

16.40 The disadvantage of only using a vesting declaration to transfer property is that the trustees of the transferring charity would not get such an indemnity. As mentioned at **16.16**, liabilities do not transfer under a vesting declaration.

16.41 Although several parties, including the Charity Law Association, made submissions in relation to the legislation which became the 2006 Act to the effect that, following merger, the trustees of the transferring charity should not be held liable for pre-merger liabilities, this did not find its way into the final legislation. In 2015 the Law Commission considered whether an automatic transfer of liabilities would be appropriate, as is the case in relation to mergers under the provisions of the 2011 Act relating to CIOs (see **14.161** and **14.169**), but decided that it would not.[20]

16.42 In practice, the way to resolve the problem of pre-merger liabilities is by the receiving charity entering into a separate deed of indemnity in favour of the trustees of the transferring charity.

Creditors of the transferring charity

16.43 One effect of the vesting declaration is that if for any reason there are any outstanding creditors of the transferring charity after the merger, they would be left 'high and dry' with no charity assets to claim against once the vesting declaration had taken effect. The position is particularly difficult for creditors of a corporate charity. As Lord Phillips of Sudbury put it in debates on the Bill leading to the 2006 Act:[21]

---

20 Chapter 12, Technical Issues in Charity Law: A Consultation Paper, Law Commission, March 2015.

21 HL Deb, vol 673, col 1080 (12 July 2005).

> 'in the case of corporate charities, creditors who were left in the lurch would be faced with what can only be described as an assault course in trying to get back their entitlements. They would be in the position of having to ask for the corporate charity, the affairs of which had been wound up, to be reinstated. They would then have to trace the assets and the former directors to see whether there was a prospect of recovering their entitlements.'

16.44 The position is not so dire for creditors of unincorporated charities, as the trustees will remain jointly and severally liable to creditors by virtue of trust law.

16.45 One step taken by Parliament to address these concerns was to put an obligation on the transferring trustees, when notifying a merger to the Commission, to make a statement of the appropriate arrangements that have been made to discharge the liabilities of the transferring charity.[22] But the 2011 Act does not create any remedy for a creditor prejudiced by the trustees' failure to do this correctly.

16.46 In this situation, the creditor's only recourse would be to see if it can bring a claim against individual trustees of the transferring charity – this will only be possible if the trustee can be shown to have some personal liability for the obligation to the creditor which, in the case of a corporate charity, would not automatically be the case and, indeed, would be highly unlikely.

16.47 The situation is further complicated where permanent endowment is involved. The transferring charity will continue to exist to hold the permanent endowment, and there may be scope for any outstanding creditors to make a claim against the retained permanent endowment. In the debates on the legislation which became the 2006 Act, Lord Bassam of Brighton, the Government spokesperson, conceded 'there is a question about whether the new charity formed from the transfer is liable and whether the funds of that charity should be used before recourse is made to the residual permanent endowment charity'.[23] It is not clear however on what basis he thought a creditor could trace his claim against the new charity.

OTHER PROVISIONS RELEVANT TO MERGERS

16.48 Other useful sections of the 2011 Act are:

- s 268, which gives trustees of certain small charities power to transfer the property of the charity to one or more charities. See Chapter 15 for more details;[24]
- ss 62 and 67, which deal with when and how charity assets can be applied cy-près via a scheme: see Chapter 17 for more details;
- s 201 which has the effect that the Commission's prior written consent is needed for some mergers (see **13.18-13.23** for a full discussion);
- ss 235 and 240 which set out procedures for amalgamation of CIOs and transfer of a CIO's undertaking to another CIO (see Chapter 14).

---

22 See **16.25**.

23 HL Deb, vol 674, col 712 (18 October 2005).

24 In its consultation on charity law, the Law Commission asked for views on whether the scope of s 268 should be expanded, including by making it available to incorporated charities. Technical Issues in Charity Law: A Consultation Paper, Law Commission, March 2015.

16.49 The Commission has published a range of guidance on its website for charities considering merger, including, at the time of writing:

- operational guidance OG 60 'Register of charity mergers: sections 305-314 of the Charities Act 2011';
- CC34 Collaborative working and mergers: an introduction;
- Making Mergers Work: Helping you Succeed;
- How to merge or link charities;
- Choosing to Collaborate: Helping you Succeed; and
- Checklist for Mergers.

CHAPTER 17

SCHEMES

WHAT IS A SCHEME?

17.1 A scheme is a device which can be used by the Charity Commission or the court to alter the terms on which charitable property is held. There is, in principle, a variety of ways in which a scheme can be used, but charities are most likely to encounter schemes where they are used to alter the governing document of an unincorporated charity, particularly the objects, or to save charitable gifts where the purposes for which the gift was originally made have failed.

17.2 The 2011 Act gives the Charity Commission jurisdiction to make schemes, sets out the conditions which apply to so-called cy-près schemes and includes a special regime for schemes dealing with the proceeds of failed charitable appeals. These provisions are described in more detail in this chapter.

17.3 In recent years, the authors have seen a significant decline in the Commission's use of its scheme-making powers. There are three main reasons for this.

17.4 First, as explained in Chapter 15, the 2006 Act introduced significant new powers for the trustees of unincorporated charities to make changes to their governing documents without the Commission's involvement. Section 280 of the 2011 Act, for example, allows the trustees of an unincorporated charity to make changes to its administrative powers and procedures even if there is no such power in the charity's governing document. Section 275 allows smaller unincorporated charities to change their purposes. There is therefore now far less demand for the Commission's scheme-making powers by unincorporated charities in these circumstances.

17.5 Secondly, in the past few years it has been the Commission's stated policy that it will only make a scheme to alter a charity's governing document where there is no other option available to the trustees (for example where there is no express power of amendment in the charity's governing document or s 280 of the 2011 Act is not available).[1] This is in line with the Commission's intention to ensure that its resources are used in the most efficient, effective and economic way.[2]

17.6 Thirdly, if what the charity wishes to do can be achieved by means of an order, the Commission will assist the charity by order using its order making powers under the 2011 Act,[3] rather than by making a scheme.

---

1 Charity Commission operational guidance OG 500 'Schemes', last updated June 2015, overview.

2 See Chapter 2.

3 See Chapter 9.

17.7 At the time of writing the Commission's operational guidance states that the Commission will be prepared to consider making a scheme amending a charity's governing document if the trustees are unable to make the amendments themselves and the proposed amendments:

- alter the charity's objects;
- alter a specific provision in a charity's governing document (eg remove a prohibition);
- affect designated property, ie property held for the specific purposes of a charity;
- alter a charity's dissolution provisions;
- remove third party rights, against the wishes of the third party; or
- change the purposes of a fundraising appeal where this has failed.[4]

JURISDICTION TO MAKE SCHEMES

17.8 The Commission's scheme-making jurisdiction is set out in s 69 of the 2011 Act. The High Court has an inherent jurisdiction to direct a scheme in respect of any charitable trust: under s 69(1)(a) the Commission may by order exercise the same jurisdiction and powers for the purposes of establishing a scheme for the administration of a charity. Sections 69(1)(b) and (c) also give the Commission concurrent jurisdiction with the High Court to take various action in relation to trustees, employees and charity property: these are discussed in Chapter 9.

17.9 The Commission's scheme–making powers were extended by the 2006 Act which broadened the Commission's powers in relation to cy-près schemes, introduced new measures to facilitate the cy-près application of charitable property from a failed appeal and relaxed the publicity requirements for schemes.

AMENDMENT OF GOVERNING DOCUMENTS BY SCHEME

17.10 The most common schemes made by the Commission are cy-près schemes, which alter the purposes for which charity property is applied, and administrative schemes, which amend the terms on which charity property is held in some other way.

Cy-près schemes

17.11 'Cy-près' is a Norman French word meaning 'as near as'. The doctrine of cy-près has developed over several centuries to allow assets dedicated to charity to be directed to alternative, but similar, charitable purposes if they cannot be used for their original purpose. The principles established by the courts have been modified by statute over the years, most recently by the 2006 Act, which extended the powers of the court and Commission to make cy-près schemes.

17.12 Cy-près schemes can be made to change a charity's objects. While charitable companies and charitable incorporated organisations have statutory powers to change their governing documents,[5] the objects of unincorporated charities may only be altered

---

4 Charity Commission operational guidance OG 500 'Schemes', last updated June 2015, charts.

5 See Chapters 13 and 14 respectively.

if there is power in the governing document, or using the limited powers under s 275 of the 2011 Act, which only apply to small charities.[6] If there is no power in the governing document, and s 275 does not apply, a scheme will be needed.

17.13 The making of a cy-près scheme is a two stage process. First, the Commission or the court must be satisfied that a so-called 'cy-près' occasion has arisen. The Commission's or court's power to make a scheme must then be exercised in accordance with s 67 of the 2011 Act.

Has a cy-près occasion arisen?

17.14 A charity's purposes may only be altered by a cy-près scheme if a cy-près occasion, falling within the circumstances described in s 62(1)(a)–(e) of the 2011 Act, has arisen.

17.15 These circumstances are as follows:

- *The purposes have already been fulfilled, or can no longer be carried out*

  'where the original purposes, in whole or in part

  (i) have been as far as may be fulfilled, or
  (ii) cannot be carried out, or not according to the directions given and to the spirit of the gift' (s 62(1)(a));

- *Not all of the property can be used for the purposes*

  'where the original purposes provide a use for part only of the property available by virtue of the gift' (s 62(1)(b));

- *It would be more effective to combine the property with other property*

  'where

  (i) the property available by virtue of the gift, and
  (ii) other property applicable for similar purposes,

  can be more effectively used in conjunction, and to that end can suitably, regard being had to the appropriate considerations, be made applicable to common purposes' (s 62(1)(c));

- *Changes to an area or a group of people mean that the purposes are no longer appropriate*

  'where the original purposes were laid down by reference to

  (i) an area which then was but has ceased to be a unit for some other purpose, or
  (ii) a class of persons or an area which has for any reason since ceased to be suitable, regard being had to the appropriate considerations, or to be practical in administering the gift' (s 62(1)(d));

---

[6] See Chapter 15.

- ***The original purposes have been provided for, are no longer charitable or are no longer suitable and effective***

> 'where the original purposes, in whole or in part, have, since they were laid down
>
> (i) been adequately provided for by other means,
> (ii) ceased, as being useless or harmful to the community or for other reasons, to be in law charitable, or
> (iii) ceased in any other way to provide a suitable and effective method of using the property available by virtue of the gift, regard being had to the appropriate considerations' (s 62(1)(e)).

The ground mentioned in s 62(1)(e)(iii) is, in the authors' experience, most commonly relied on. The reference to the 'appropriate considerations' was introduced by the 2006 Act in place of a reference to 'the spirit of the gift': see **17.18-17.19**.

17.16 Any one of those subsections can be relied upon as the basis for a cy-près occasion.[7]

17.17 A number of the terms used in s 62(1) are defined further in s 62, and have been considered by the courts and the Charity Tribunal.[8]

Appropriate considerations

17.18 Section 62(1)(c), (d) and (e) all require that regard should be had to 'the appropriate considerations'. This is defined in s 62(2) as '(a) (on the one hand) the spirit of the gift concerned, and (b) (on the other) the social and economic circumstances prevailing at the time of the proposed alteration of the original purposes.'

17.19 The requirement to have regard to the prevailing social and economic circumstances, as well as the spirit of the gift, was introduced by the 2006 Act. During the passage of that legislation through the House of Lords, Baroness Scotland of Asthal explained that:[9]

> 'by also allowing the social and economic circumstances within which a charity operates to be taken into account when changing charitable purposes, the Bill will help more effective use to be made of charitable resources.'

Original purposes

17.20 Under s 62(4), in cases where the charity's objects have been altered since it was established, 'original purposes' means the charity's current purposes.

---

7 Decision of the First-tier Tribunal (Charity) in *Aliss and Hesketh v Charity Commission, Lytham Schools Trustee Ltd and The United Church Schools Trust* (CA/2011/0007) ('the *Lytham Schools* case'), decision dated 12 March 2012, para 9.

8 As explained in Chapter 10, decisions of the First-tier Tribunal do not have precedent value, but decisions of the Upper Tribunal create legally binding precedent.

9 Hansard, HL Deb, col 887 (20 January 2005).

Spirit of the gift

17.21 In determining the spirit of the gift the Commission should look not only at the purposes expressed in the original gift, but also any relevant evidence as to the circumstances in which the gift was made.[10]

Prevailing social and economic circumstances

17.22 In the *Lytham Schools* case, the First-tier Tribunal, when considering the social and economic circumstances prevailing at the time of the scheme, adopted a broad view. It considered a wide range of circumstances, not simply those which affected the current and future financial position of the charities concerned.[11]

Examples of cy-près occasions

17.23 The following cases provide useful examples of the application of s 62.

Section 62(1)(c) – combination of charitable property

17.24 The *Lytham Schools* case[12] involved a scheme which effected the merger of two charitable schools. The two charities concerned both provided for the advancement of education, but had beneficiaries situated in different geographical areas.

17.25 The First-tier Tribunal was clear that the purposes of the two charities concerned need only be 'similar', not identical, and that differences in the manner of the implementation of purposes (in this case, the different styles, content and ethos of the education provided by the two charities) and in the beneficiary class did not make their underlying charitable purposes dissimilar. The Tribunal said that in assessing whether the charities had similar purposes it was appropriate to take account of the full range of potential charitable purposes set out in s 3 of the 2011 Act (see Chapter 3).

17.26 In assessing whether a charity's property could be used more effectively in conjunction with other charitable property, effectiveness should be assessed by reference to the purposes of the charity in respect of which the scheme is sought. In this case, would the proposed merger of the two schools be more effective in advancing education for the public benefit?

17.27 It was appropriate, when considering whether property could be used more effectively, to consider more than the wording of the new objects: since s 62(1)(c) refers to the 'use' of the property, the existing and potential future use of a charity's property must be considered in coming to a view on whether the circumstances in s 62(1)(c) apply.

Section 62(1)(e)(iii) – purposes no longer suitable and effective

17.28 In the case of *White v Williams*,[13] where a schism had developed between members of a Christian congregation, the court decided that a cy-près occasion had

---

10 *Varsani v Jesani* [1999] Ch 219; *White v Williams* [2010] EWHC 940 (Ch); and *Ground, Pople, Lemieux & Lawrence v Charity Commission and Guildford Diocesan Board of Finance* (CA/2011/0004) ('the *Dunsfold School* case').

11 See note 7: decision dated 17 May 2012.

12 See note 7.

13 [2010] EWHC 940 (Ch).

arisen under s 62(1)(e)(iii). A similar decision had been reached in the case of *Varsani v Jesani*,[14] which involved a schism between the adherents of a Hindu religious sect: this case pre-dated the changes to s 62(1)(e)(iii) in the 2006 Act (see 17.15). In *Varsani v Jesani*, the Court of Appeal also helpfully clarified that it is not necessary to show that the existing purposes have failed, in the sense that they have become impossible or impractical to carry out, in order for a cy-près occasion to arise.

17.29 In the *Dunsfold School* case,[15] which dealt with a challenge by local residents to a Charity Commission scheme made in relation to a school site which had been unused for several years, the parties before the First-tier Tribunal accepted that these were circumstances where the original purposes for which the site had been given had ceased to provide a suitable and effective method of using the property available, within the meaning of s 62(1)(e)(iii).

17.30 The *Bath Recreation Ground* case[16] concerned a scheme for land near to the centre of Bath. There was disagreement about whether a cy-près occasion had arisen: on appeal the Upper Tribunal decided that there was no cy-près occasion. However, the Upper Tribunal did express the view in its judgment that a cy-près occasion may arise as a result of a breach of trust.

The terms of the scheme

17.31 Once it has been established that a cy-près occasion has arisen, the provisions of s 67 of the 2011 Act apply.

17.32 Prior to the 2006 Act, when making a cy-près scheme, the Commission was required to draft new charitable purposes that were as close as reasonably possible to the existing purposes. The position was altered by the introduction of what is now s 67 of the 2011 Act.

17.33 Section 67(1) provides that the power of the court or Commission to make schemes for the application of property cy-près must be exercised in accordance with s 67.

17.34 Under s 67(2), the Commission, or the court, may make a scheme providing for the property to be applied for such charitable purposes, and by or on trust for such other charity (where the scheme provides for the transfer of property to another charity), as it considers appropriate, having regard to the matters set out in s 67(3).

17.35 Under s 67(3), the Commission or court must have regard to:

(a) the spirit of the original gift (s 67(3)(a));
(b) the desirability of securing that the property is applied for charitable purposes which are close to the original purposes (s 67(3)(b)); and
(c) the need for the relevant charity to have purposes which are suitable and effective in the light of current social and economic circumstances (s 67(3)(c)).

---

14 See note 10.

15 *Ground, Pople, Lemieux & Lawrence v Charity Commission and Guildford Diocesan Board of Finance* (CA/2011/0004).

16 *Sparrow, Carne and Websper v Charity Commission and The Trustees of the Bath Recreation Ground* (CA/2013/0006, 0007 and 0008), [2015] UKUT 0420 (TCC).

17.36 Section 67(2) 'confers wide discretion on the Commission … in permitting it to make a scheme providing for the property to be applied "as it considers appropriate" having regard to the matters in' s 67(3).[17]

17.37 The court has decided that the principles which apply to determining 'the spirit of the gift' in s 62 apply equally to s 67.[18]

17.38 In the case of the transfer of charitable property by scheme to another charity, s 67(4) permits the scheme to impose an express duty on the charity trustees of the recipient charity to apply the property transferred for purposes which are, so far as is reasonably practicable, similar in character to the original purposes. As the explanatory notes to the 2006 Act, which introduced this provision into the legislation, stated:

> 'This is to cover cases where the original purposes are still useful but the court or the Commission believes that the property can be more effectively used in conjunction with other property.'

Examples of cy-près schemes

17.39 The First-tier Tribunal considered the application of s 67 in the *Dunsfold School* case.[19] The Commission had argued that, all things being equal, one should look for the application of assets closest to the original purpose and work outwards. The Tribunal, noting that s 67(3)(b) refers to the desirability of securing new charitable purposes which are 'close' to the original purposes, rather than 'closest' to those purposes, could see the sense in this argument, but made it clear that this is not an express statutory requirement.

17.40 The Tribunal confirmed that the need for the charity to have purposes which are suitable and effective in the light of current social and economic circumstances has equal weight to the other considerations in s 67(3), which are not set out in any order of priority. In this case, however, where the charity's property had stood empty for some years, it seemed right to give this consideration more prominence than one otherwise might.

17.41 The Tribunal noted that since the Commission's decision to seal the scheme had not specifically referred to the matters set out in s 67(3)(c), the Tribunal could not be satisfied that it had all the relevant considerations in mind when making its decision.

Administrative schemes

17.42 The Commission's jurisdiction to make schemes is not restricted to making changes to a charity's objects by means of a cy-près scheme.

17.43 For example, in the case of *In re JW Laing Trust*[20] the court decided that although a direction that a charity's property should be distributed within a certain time did not form part of the charity's purposes, so could not be altered under the cy-près regime, the court did have power to alter that administrative provision under its inherent

---

17 The *Dunsfold School* case (see note 10), decision dated 6 December 2011, para 5.5.
18 *White v Williams* (see note 10).
19 See **17.29**.
20 [1984] 1 All ER 50.

jurisdiction. In considering what changes were expedient to regulate the administration of the charity, the court would take all the circumstances of the charity into account. The Commission has the same powers.[21]

17.44 Cases before the Charity Tribunal provide examples of administrative schemes made by the Commission. In a case dealing with land at Central Park, Dartford ('the *Dartford Central Park* case'),[22] the Tribunal approved a scheme including a new framework for the administration of the charity, including powers of investment and a reference to a code of conduct under which potential conflicts of interest might be managed going forward. A case involving the Llanfair Waterdine Charities[23] concerned a scheme removing the prohibition on benefits to trustees from the charity's governing document. In *Bartley v Charity Commission*,[24] the Commission had made an administrative scheme which appointed a corporate trustee to two charitable trusts and transferred legal title to the trust property to that trustee.

17.45 Other situations where the Commission's scheme-making powers might be invoked include the removal of third party rights against the wishes of a third party, or alteration of a charity's dissolution provisions. As mentioned at **15.76**, the Commission may also be asked to appoint a corporate trustee by way of scheme, in order to ensure that the trustee becomes a trust corporation for the purposes of various statutory provisions.

Changes to the objects

17.46 The Commission's approach at the time of writing seems to be that it will only be prepared to make an amendment to a charity's objects by scheme if a cy-près occasion has arisen.[25] In the past, the Commission has been willing to make a scheme to change the objects in the absence of a cy-près occasion: in the *Dartford Central Park* case,[26] the Commission argued that it had merely 'restated' the objects 'using a modern formulation.'[27]

CY-PRÈS – OTHER ISSUES

Income

17.47 The Commission may authorise trustees to apply small amounts of income which cannot be effectively applied for a charity's purposes cy-près without the need for a scheme, subject to minimum thresholds.[28] In the authors' experience this is rarely used.

---

21 This was confirmed in the First-tier Tribunal's 27 March 2014 decision in the *Bath Recreation Ground* case, para 36 (CA/2013/0006, 0007 and 0008).
22 *Maidment and Lennox Ryan v Charity Commission* (CA/2009/0001 and 0002).
23 *Thomas v Charity Commission* (CA/2012/0001).
24 CA/2013/0016.
25 OG 500 'Schemes', para B2, last updated June 2015, which states that this is on resource grounds.
26 See **17.44**.
27 Decision dated 16 November 2009, para 5.6.
28 Section 75 of the 2011 Act.

Failed gifts to charity

17.48 While many of the cy-près schemes dealt with by the Commission concern changes to the objects of an existing charity, it is also possible for the Commission or the court to make a scheme under the cy-près regime in order to secure a gift to charity which has failed from the outset. Examples might include where an appeal for a particular charitable project fails: this is dealt with in more detail at **17.55-17.70**. Another example is where a legacy is made to a charity which has ceased to exist by the time the testator dies.

17.49 It is only possible to make a cy-près scheme where a gift to charity has failed from the outset (technically known as 'initial failure') if the donor had a 'general charitable intention', ie an overriding intention to make a gift to charity. There are a number of cases which clarify when there is general charitable intent.[29]

Reform

17.50 In its 2015 consultation paper,[30] the Law Commission considered whether it would be appropriate for charity trustees, as well as the Charity Commission, to have power to make cy-près schemes, following a recommendation by Lord Hodgson.[31] The Law Commission expressed the view that the power to make cy-près schemes is one for the Charity Commission, rather than charity trustees, but suggested that the existing statutory power for the trustees of smaller unincorporated charities to change their objects could usefully be extended (see **15.62**).

RESTRICTIONS ON THE COMMISSION'S JURISDICTION

17.51 Section 70 of the 2011 Act imposes various restrictions on the Commission's jurisdiction to make schemes.

17.52 Section 70(1) prohibits the Commission from exercising its jurisdiction under s 69 to determine the title to property or any question as to the existence or extent of any charge or trust. In the *Dunsfold School* case,[32] the First-tier Tribunal reiterated that neither the Commission, nor the Tribunal on appeal, had power to rule on the question of which of two documents established the charitable trusts on which the property was held.

17.53 Section 70(8) prohibits the Commission from exercising its jurisdiction in any case which by reason of its contentious character or because it involves special questions of law or of fact would, in the opinion of the Commission, be more fit to be adjudicated by the court (unless the case is one which has been referred to it by the court). In the *Lytham Schools* case,[33] the appealing parties argued that the objections to the proposed scheme should have led the Commission to conclude that it was so controversial that

---

29 See, for example, *Re Broadbent (deceased); Imperial Cancer Research Fund & ors v Bradley & anor* [2001] EWCA Civ 714 and *Kings v Bultitude* [2010] EWHC 1795 (Ch).

30 Paragraphs 5.24–5.31, Technical Issues in Charity Law, A Consultation Paper, Law Commission, March 2015.

31 *Trusted and Independent*, Appendix A.

32 See **17.29**.

33 See **17.22** and **17.24–17.27**.

under s 70(8) a scheme was inappropriate. In the *Bartley* case,[34] the appellant made the same argument, but the First-tier Tribunal decided that s 70(8) did not apply, commenting that 'The mere fact that a proposed scheme is opposed by some respondents to consultation is insufficient to oust the Commission's jurisdiction under s 69 of the Act.'

17.54 The Commission's approach to the degree of consultation and publicity which will be required before a scheme can be made (see **17.75** and **17.84**) reflects the need to establish whether the proposals are likely to be contentious. In the *Bartley* case mentioned in the preceding paragraph, the draft scheme which was issued for consultation was altered by the Commission before it was finalised: the First-tier Tribunal noted that 'Had the Commission wished to proceed with a scheme in the form of the original consultation draft, then Mr Bartley's concerns … may well have been such that the matter would have been more fit to be adjudicated on by the court.' In cases involving the cy-près application of charity legacies, it is the authors' experience that the Commission will be unwilling to make a scheme to resolve any difficulties with the gift (such as where the legacy is left to charity for a purpose that cannot be fulfilled) unless those who would be entitled to the legacy if it failed have agreed to the scheme being made.

FAILED CHARITY APPEALS

17.55 There are two contrasting sets of circumstances in which charitable appeals can give rise to problems.

17.56 The first is where an appeal for a particular project exceeds its target. For instance, a healthcare charity may launch an appeal for the purpose of purchasing some expensive equipment. If the appeal raises more than is needed to buy the equipment, how does the charity deal with the surplus funds?

17.57 The second is where the appeal fails to reach its target. In the example given above, if insufficient funds are raised, the equipment cannot be purchased. What should the charity do with the funds which it has raised?

17.58 Both of these problems can be avoided if the appeal literature is appropriately drafted. The simplest approach is to appeal for funds for the charity's general purposes, but giving examples as to how the funds raised might be used. Alternatively, the literature can make it clear that while funds are being raised for a particular purpose, if the appeal target is not met – or surplus funds are raised – the funds which cannot be used for the specified purpose will be used for the charity's general purposes.

17.59 In the authors' experience, most charities do use appropriate wording in their appeal literature, meaning that in practice charitable appeals rarely fail in this way. However, an appeal does fail, the cy-près rules may provide a solution.[35]

---

34 See **17.44**.

35 Special rules apply to National Health Service charities under s 222 of the National Health Service Act 2006: in the case of both surplus funds and failed appeals the trustees can apply the funds to similar purposes of the charity.

Surplus funds

17.60 If an appeal for a particular purpose exceeds its target, and raises more than is needed for the specific purpose of the appeal, the funds cannot be returned to the donors. Since the purposes for which they were raised cannot be fulfilled, the Commission can be asked to make a cy-près scheme so that the excess funds can be used in a way which is similar to the purposes of the appeal. Sections 62 and 67 of the 2011 Act will apply, and the principles discussed above are relevant. In these circumstances it is generally assumed that each donor had a 'general charitable intention' (see **17.49**), so there is no need for this to be proved in individual cases.[36]

17.61 If the fund is small, the trustees may be able to take advantage of the powers in s 275 of the 2011 Act to change the purposes for which it is held (see Chapter 15) without the need to apply for a cy-près scheme.[37]

Failure to reach an appeal target

17.62 If insufficient funds are raised to fulfil the purposes of the appeal, the Commission cannot usually exercise its jurisdiction to make a cy-près scheme. As mentioned at **17.49**, the cy-près rules require that the donor should have had a 'general charitable intention': in these circumstances it is unlikely that such an intention can be assumed. On the face of it, the funds raised belong to the donor (as there is a resulting trust in their favour) and would need to be returned. This can give rise to particular problems where donors cannot be traced.

17.63 However, ss 63–66 of the 2011 Act contain provisions which may help in these situations. These provisions were extended significantly by the 2006 Act.

17.64 Section 63(1) extends the circumstances in which the cy-près rules apply. It provides that in certain circumstances, where property is given for specific charitable purposes which fail, it may be applicable cy-près as if given for charitable purposes generally. Those circumstances are:

(a) where the property belongs to a donor who cannot be identified or found after the trustees have published advertisements and made inquiries in the form and for the period prescribed in the Charities (Failed Appeals) Regulations 2008 (which were made by the Commission under what is now s 66) (s 63(1)(a)) (see **Appendix 12** of this book);

(b) where the property belongs to a donor who has executed a disclaimer in the form prescribed by the Charities (Failed Appeals) Regulations 2008 (s 63(1)(b)); or

(c) where the donor is presumed to be unidentifiable under s 64 (see **17.65**).

Donor presumed unidentifiable

17.65 Under s 64(1) of the 2011 Act, the proceeds of cash collections made by means of collecting boxes, or similar methods which mean that individual gifts cannot separately be identified, and the proceeds of lotteries, competitions, entertainments, sales or similar

---

36 This is the current approach of the Commission: OG 53 Charitable Appeals: Avoiding and Dealing with Failure, A, paras 1.4 and 2.4.

37 Charity Commission operational guidance, OG 53 'Charitable Appeals: Avoiding and Dealing with Failure', A, para 2.4.

fundraising activities, are presumed to belong to donors who cannot be identified. Under s 64(2) the court and (since the 2006 Act) the Commission can direct by order that property should be treated as belonging to unidentifiable donors (without the need to advertise or to make any inquiries) if it appears to the court or Commission:

- that it would be unreasonable to incur expense in seeking to have the property returned (in view of the amounts likely to be returned); or
- that it would be unreasonable for the donors to expect the return of their property, in view of the nature, circumstances and amounts of the gifts, and the lapse of time since they were made.

Rights to reclaim donations

17.66 Donors who cannot be identified or found under s 63(1)(a) (see **17.64**(a)), but not those deemed unidentifiable under s 64 (see **17.65**), have a right to reclaim their donations (less expenses properly incurred by the trustees in respect of the claims) within 6 months of the date of a scheme.[38] Section 63(4) enables the Commission to direct charity trustees to set aside a specific amount to meet such claims. Under s 63(6) and (7), if the amount set aside is insufficient to meet the claims, the Commission may authorise the trustees to reduce proportionately the amount paid to each claimant and to deduct expenses properly incurred by the trustees in dealing with claims. This ensures that neither the expenses nor any shortfall become the personal liability of the trustees, but are deducted from the donors' funds.

Alternative mechanism – s 65

17.67 Section 65, which was introduced by the 2006 Act, provides a supplementary mechanism under which donors may be treated as if they had executed a written disclaimer under s 63(1)(b) (see **17.64**(b)) even where they have not done so. If a statement giving notice of alternative general charitable application in the event of failure[39] accompanies any 'solicitation' made in the course of an appeal, then, if the appeal fails, the property given for the failed appeal can be applied cy-près under s 63, as if the donor had made a disclaimer under s 63(1)(b). There is an exception for property given by a donor who has made a 'relevant declaration' (as described in s 65(3)) and who reclaims the donation at the time of failure.[40] If donors have made a relevant declaration, attempts are made to find them, and either they cannot be found or they waive return of their donation, such donations can also be applied cy-près under s 63. Sections 65(4), (5) and (6) and the Charities (Failed Appeals) Regulations 2008 deal with the procedure to be followed where the purposes have failed and where the donor has made a relevant declaration.

17.68 During the passage of the 2006 Act through the House of Commons concern was expressed that securing complicated declarations as a matter of course would be impractical and might jeopardise potential donations. Despite these concerns, the relevant provisions of the Act were not changed, but even the Commission acknowledges the complications inherent in the s 65 machinery. Its operational guidance on avoiding and dealing with the failure of charitable appeals reads: 'We anticipate that

---

38 Section 63(4) and (5) of the 2011 Act.

39 Section 65(2)(b) specifies the nature of the statement required.

40 If the donation is to be returned to the donor, s 65(5) provides that the value of the donation to be returned is to be its value at the date the donation was made and not the date when the purposes fail.

in most cases it will still be simpler for charities to word their appeals in such a way that if the primary purpose of the appeal failed, funds would automatically become applicable for other purposes without involving the Commission or going back to donors' (see the approach recommended at **17.58**). This coincides with the authors' experience, which is that s 65 is used rarely, if at all. However, the Commission's view is that there may still be a place for the s 65 mechanism, 'for example in the case of substantial donations where the donor wants to retain some control over how the funds are used, or if trustees are concerned that some donors might object to having their donations applied for other purposes'. However, the Commission recommends that the provisions of s 65 should only be used in preference to recommended good practice where the trustees have decided that there are good reasons for doing so.[41]

17.69 Section 65, in contrast to s 63, applies whether or not consideration is received in return for the property given. So a 'solicitation' under s 65 could include, for example, promotion of a concert held in aid of a particular charitable cause where a proportion of the price of a ticket is to go to the charitable cause, or the promotion of a product by a commercial participator, in which a proportion of the price of the product will go to a particular charitable cause.

Reform

17.70 The Law Commission, in its 2015 consultation, analysed ss 63 and 66 in some detail, concluding that the mechanism in s 63(1)(a) requiring advertisements and inquiries was cumbersome, and the procedures under s 63(1)(b) requiring a disclaimer or declaration appeared unrealistic.[42] The Law Commission invited views on whether the regime should be changed.

APPLYING FOR A SCHEME

17.71 Except in exceptional circumstances (see **17.73**), the Charity Commission cannot make a scheme under s 69 of the 2011 Act on its own initiative, but only in pursuance of an order of the court or on an application made under s 70. Most applications are made by the charity, but this may not be possible if, for example, the trustees disagree among themselves or with the Commission over the need for a scheme, or if there are insufficient trustees to make a valid decision.

17.72 The Commission may make a scheme or order under s 69:

(a) on the application of the charity;[43]

(b) in pursuance of a court order;[44]

(c) on the application of the Attorney-General;[45] or

(d) if the gross income of the charity does not exceed £500 per year, on the application of:

---

41 OG 53, para 5.3.

42 Technical Issues in Charity Law, A Consultation Paper, Law Commission, para 7.31.

43 Section 70(2)(a) of the 2011 Act.

44 Section 70(2)(b) of the 2011 Act.

45 Section 70(2)(c) of the 2011 Act. Note that s 70(2)(c) applies in relation to exempt charities, by virtue of the 2006 Act, but not in relation to those exempt charities whose future status is undecided at the time of writing: see Chapter 5 for more detail.

(i) any one or more of the charity trustees;
(ii) any person interested in the charity, eg a potential beneficiary; or
(iii) any two or more of the inhabitants of the area of benefit of the charity, if the charity is a local charity.[46]

The sum of £500 may be varied by order of the Minister for the Cabinet Office under s 72, either to take account of inflation or to bring more charities within the scope of this provision. Gross income includes income from special trusts.[47]

17.73 If the Commission is satisfied that the charity trustees ought, in the interests of the charity, to apply for a scheme, but have unreasonably refused or neglected to do so and the Commission has given the trustees an opportunity to make representations to it, the Commission may proceed to establish a scheme on its own initiative without an application being made to it.[48] The Commission may only alter a charity's purposes in this way if the charity was established at least 40 years ago. This process is not available in relation to exempt charities.

17.74 If charity trustees are willing to apply for a scheme, but are prevented from doing so because of a vacancy in their number, or the absence or incapacity of any of them, the Commission may establish a scheme on the application of however many of the charity trustees as it thinks appropriate under s 70(6). This avoids the need for the Commission to make a preliminary order to appoint trustees to comply with the requirements of the trusts of the charity, and then to invite those trustees to apply for a scheme to alter the trusts of the charity: the appointment of trustees and the alteration of the trusts can be dealt with in one document.[49]

17.75 While there is a statutory requirement for the Commission to consider whether it should give public notice of its intention to make a scheme (see **17.81-17.84**), there is no corresponding requirement for the trustees to consult interested parties before making an application to the Commission. However, in practice the Commission now expects the trustees to have carried out some form of consultation on their proposals in most cases. The Commission's operational guidance[50] makes it clear that the Commission will 'usually expect the trustees to have carried out a genuine and appropriate consultation exercise to take into account the views of the charity's stakeholders about the proposals and properly inform their own decision as to whether a scheme is required', before they will make a decision about whether a scheme should be made. The Commission's policy is that consultation should be carried out in all but exceptional cases, which might include circumstances where there are no surviving beneficiaries, or where changes are being made only in order to comply with legislation. The Commission is not prescriptive about the form of the consultation, recognising that this will vary depending on the circumstances. Any consultation should be designed to seek the views of those who would be affected by, or those who might have a particular interest in, the changes proposed.

---

[46] Section 70(3) of the 2011 Act. A 'local charity' is defined in s 293 of the 2011 Act. Note that s 70(3) applies in relation to exempt charities, by virtue of the 2006 Act, but not in relation to those exempt charities whose future status is undecided at the time of writing: see Chapter 5 for more detail.

[47] Section 353(1) of the 2011 Act.

[48] Section 70(4) and (5) of the 2011 Act.

[49] The Commission's operational guidance states that there must be at least one serving trustee before this power can be used, meaning that if there are no trustees at all, a new trustee or trustees may first need to be appointed by order. OG 500 'Schemes', para E5.

[50] OG 500 'Schemes', para B4.2.

17.76 As mentioned at 17.53, the Commission cannot make a scheme in a case which is so contentious that the Commission thinks the scheme should be made by the court: evidence of a consultation exercise, and the responses to it, will help the Commission decide whether a case is contentious. A further driver behind the introduction of this non-statutory requirement is likely to be the Commission's wish to avoid subsequent challenges to schemes. The Commission's operational guidance comments that the process:

> 'helps to ensure that the trustees have properly established the case for making the changes in the interests of the charity and for showing that the criteria have been met before we commit staff time and resources to proceeding'.

17.77 The authors have some concerns about the requirement for early consultation. Under s 61 of the 2011 Act, charity trustees are obliged to apply for a cy-près scheme once a cy-près occasion has arisen, and it is usually the trustees who are best placed to make a decision about whether the circumstances which give rise to a cy-près occasion have occurred. Early consultation amongst stakeholders can give rise to misunderstandings about a charity's current objects and proposed changes to them, since this is a technically difficult area. Moreover, if the Commission is not satisfied with the scope of any consultation carried out prior to the application for a scheme, the trustees run the risk that they will need to carry out the exercise again, meaning wasted time and money.

17.78 The Commission's operational guidance contains more information about the procedure for making an application.[51]

17.79 The Commission imposes no charge for making a scheme. In his July 2012 review of charity law, Lord Hodgson suggested that consideration should be given to imposing fees in these situations, arguing that 'it seems an inappropriate use of scarce resources for the Commission to spend not-insignificant sums (on occasions, amounting to thousands of pounds) on work that will in most cases only benefit single, or at best a handful of, charities'.[52] In its September 2013 response to Lord Hodgson's review, Government indicated that this is a complex and sensitive issue: it said there were no immediate plans to introduce charging and there would be a proper consultation with the sector before any decision was made along these lines.[53]

PUBLICITY

Notice to trustees

17.80 The Commission must give notice of its intention to establish a scheme for a charity under s 69 of the 2011 Act to every trustee of the charity unless he or she is party or privy to the application or cannot be found or has no known address in the UK.[54] In practice, when applying for the scheme the Commission requires a declaration to the effect that the charity has formally made a decision to apply for the scheme (with details

---

51 OG 500 'Schemes'.

52 *Trusted and Independent*, para 5.11 and ch 6, recommendation 19. See also Chapter 2 for more discussion of charging by the Commission.

53 Government Response, pages 9 and 33.

54 Section 71 of the 2011 Act. There is an exception where the court has ordered the Commission to make the scheme.

of the date that the meeting was held), that the meeting was quorate and that all the trustees are aware that the application is being made.

Wider publicity

17.81 Section 88 deals with wider publicity relating to schemes made under the 2011 Act. Under s 88(1) the Commission must comply with the publicity requirements set out in s 88(2) before making any scheme, unless it decides under s 88(4) that any of those requirements should not apply.

17.82 Section 88(2) requires the Commission to give public notice of its proposals, inviting representations to be made to it within a period specified in the notice. In the case of a scheme relating to certain local charities, a draft of the scheme must be communicated to certain local representatives.[55]

17.83 However, s 88(4), which was introduced by the 2006 Act, gives the Commission discretion to decide whether publication of its proposals to make a scheme is necessary and, if the Commission decides publication is necessary, discretion over time limits.

17.84 The Commission's approach to the publicity requirement is set out in its operational guidance.[56] At the time of writing, the Commission's policy is as follows:

- Where the scheme will change the use of community assets, give a power to dispose of designated property (see **17.7**) or involve the displacement of beneficiaries, it will generally require public notice, primarily because cases of this kind can often be contentious.
- Other cases will be considered on a case-by-case basis. Relevant factors might include a significant level of public interest, whether the scheme will materially affect designated property, whether the scheme will materially affect the charity's objects or whether the Commission is aware of opposition to the scheme.

17.85 As mentioned at **17.53-17.54**, the Commission cannot make a scheme in circumstances which are so contentious that the Commission thinks that the court should be involved: publicity will help the Commission to establish whether the case is a contentious one.

17.86 Under s 88(8) of the 2011 Act, the Commission has discretion about the contents of the notice and the manner in which publicity is given. If the Commission decides that public notice is necessary, it is its stated practice to post a copy of the draft scheme on its website, regardless of any other publicity.[57]

17.87 In the First-tier Tribunal decision in the *Bath Recreation Ground* case the First-tier Tribunal considered whether the Commission had complied with the statutory requirements regarding publication of the scheme.[58]

---

55 'Local charity' is defined in s 293 of the 2011 Act. The Commission may also be required to consult with other bodies under different legislation, or memoranda of understanding. For example, the Homes and Communities Agency or Welsh Assembly Government must be consulted in relation to amendments to the objects of registered social housing providers.

56 OG 500 'Schemes', para B10.5.

57 OG 500 'Schemes', para B10.6.

58 See 17.30.

17.88 The Commission must take account of any representations made to it within the period specified in the notice and may proceed with the proposals with or without modification.[59]

17.89 Once a scheme has been established, a copy of the order establishing the scheme must be available for one month after the order is published at the Commission's office and, in the case of some local charities, at some convenient place in the area of the charity, unless the Commission considers local publication unnecessary.[60] In practice, the Commission's practice is to post the scheme on its website for a 3-month period after it has been made.[61]

APPEALS

17.90 A Charity Commission order making a scheme under s 69(1) can be appealed to the Charity Tribunal.[62] The application may be made by the trustees or by any other person who is or may be affected by the order. In determining the appeal the Tribunal must consider the order afresh, and may take into account evidence which was not available to the Commission. The Tribunal has power to quash the order in whole or in part and (if appropriate) remit it to the Commission, to substitute any other order which could have been made by the Commission, and to add anything which could have been contained in an order made by the Commission.

17.91 At the time of writing, there have been six decisions by the Tribunal in relation to Charity Commission schemes. It is interesting to note that in five of those cases the appeals were brought by 'persons affected' by the scheme, and five cases the appeals were at least partially successful.

OTHER SCHEME-MAKING POWERS

17.92 There are specific powers for the court to make schemes enlarging certain geographical areas of benefit referred to in charitable objects under s 62(5) and (6) and Sch 4 of the 2011 Act.

17.93 The 2011 Act also includes special provisions in relation to schemes for charities governed by a Royal Charter (s 68) and charities governed by Act of Parliament (s 73). Lord Hodgson recommended that the need for a scheme under s 68 where objects are being changed on a cy-près basis should be clarified, as should the circumstances in which the Commission would exercise its powers under s 73.[63] The Law Commission's March 2015 consultation considered, in some detail, possible reforms to the means by which the governing documents of charitable Royal Charter bodies and charities with statutory governing documents are amended.[64]

17.94 The Commission has power under s 79 of the 2011 Act to make a scheme after opening a formal statutory inquiry into a charity, provided it is satisfied that there has

---

59 Section 88(5) of the 2011 Act.

60 Section 88(6) and (7) of the 2011 Act. 'Local charity' is defined in s 293 of the 2011 Act.

61 OG 500 'Schemes', para B10.10.

62 Section 319 and Sch 6 of the 2011 Act.

63 *Trusted and Independent*, Appendix A.

64 Technical Issues in Charity Law, A Consultation Paper, Law Commission, March 2015, ch 3 and 4.

been misconduct or mismanagement (or a breach of an order, direction or official warning) or that charity property needs protecting: see Chapter 9 for more details.

17.95 The Commission may make and bring into effect schemes for the establishment of common investment funds and common deposit funds.[65]

17.96 The Commission also has scheme-making powers under various other legislation including the Reverter of Sites Act 1987,[66] the Commons Act 1899 and the Coal Industry Act 1987.

---

[65] Sections 96 and 100 of the 2011 Act: see Chapter 11.
[66] See Chapter 22.

CHAPTER 18

CONTROL OF FUNDRAISING: GENERAL

INTRODUCTION

18.1 Charity legislation deals with the regulation of fundraising in the following ways:

- The Charities Act 1992 ('the 1992 Act') imposes restrictions on the relationships between charities and professional fundraisers, which are explored in detail in Chapter 19.
- The 1992 Act imposes similar restrictions on relationships between charities and businesses (so called 'commercial participators') which are not fundraising businesses, but which represent that they are making donations to charities. These provisions are explained in Chapter 20.
- Larger charities are obliged to include information about fundraising standards in their annual trustees' report: see **18.21** and **21.71**.
- The 1992 Act includes various miscellaneous provisions relating to unauthorised fundraising and representations about a charity's status: see **18.26-18.32**.
- While, at the time of writing, charity fundraising is subject to a system of self-regulation, rather than being subject to statutory regulation, the 1992 Act includes reserve powers for Government to introduce a statutory backdrop to self-regulation of fundraising or to give the Charity Commission specific powers to regulate fundraising. The current system, and the powers in the 1992 Act, are summarised in this Chapter.
- The 2006 Act includes a framework for regulation of public charitable collections (also known as house to house and street collections). However, at the time of writing, these provisions seem unlikely ever to be brought into force. The background is explained further at **18.22-18.25**.

18.2 As explained in Chapter 1, the provisions of the 1992 Act were not consolidated into the 2011 Act. Government insisted that since the 1992 Act deals not only with charitable fundraising but also with fundraising for philanthropic and benevolent purposes, it was beyond the scope of the consolidation exercise. The authors, and many others in the sector, regard this as illogical and disappointing.

18.3 At the time of writing, fundraising practices in the sector are under intense scrutiny. In 2015 a series of press stories about certain fundraising methods used by charities and fundraising businesses provoked a strong reaction from the public and prompted a range of initiatives by Government and sector bodies, as explained in more detail below. New provisions were introduced into the Charities (Protection and Social Investment) Act 2016 ('the 2016 Act'), which was making its way through Parliament at the time, designed to improve fundraising practices: see **18.8**, **18.21**, **19.54** and **20.41**.

REGULATION OF FUNDRAISING

Background

18.4 The Strategy Unit report which preceded the 2006 Act[1] reported that there was 'a view that fundraising is under-regulated'. It concluded that this should be addressed by a self-regulatory scheme set up and run by the sector. A system of statutory regulation should only be introduced if self-regulation was not successful. The Office for the Third Sector (now the Office for Civil Society and Innovation) and the Scottish Executive duly gave start-up funding to the Fundraising Standards Board (FRSB), to put in place a mechanism for the self-regulation of fundraising in the charity sector: see **18.17-18.20** for more detail.

18.5 The 2006 Act itself also introduced a so-called 'reserve power' into the 1992 Act for Government to control fundraising: see **18.12-18.14**. It was not intended that this power would be exercised during the first years following the implementation of the 2006 Act but that it should be a backdrop if self-regulation failed.

18.6 Lord Hodgson considered the regulation of fundraising in his 2012 review. While he made a number of recommendations designed to improve the current system, his conclusion was that Government should review the progress of self-regulation in five years' time and leave the option of exercising its reserve power to regulate this area open for the future.[2]

18.7 However, the issue of fundraising regulation raised its head again following a number of media stories about fundraising in 2015. Government asked the chief executive of the National Council for Voluntary Organisations, Sir Stuart Etherington, to lead a review into the effectiveness of the current self-regulatory system for fundraising. The results of the review were published in September 2015.[3] The review made a number of recommendations, including the establishment of a new single regulator, the Fundraising Regulator, with accountability to Parliament. The regulator would be funded by the sector. It would have jurisdiction over all fundraising organisations and would have a wide range of sanctioning powers, although it would not be able to fine charities. Government endorsed all the recommendations of the Etherington Review.

18.8 In the meantime, the 2016 Act introduced further provisions which bolster the scope for Government to introduce a system of statutory regulation of fundraising, should self-regulation fail. The scope for the Minister for the Cabinet Office to make regulations about fundraising in s 64A of the 1992 Act (see **18.12-18.14**) is supplemented by new ss 64B and 64C (see **18.15-18.16**).

18.9 It is clear that self-regulation of fundraising will be kept under close review. At the third reading of the Bill which became the 2016 Act in the House of Commons, the Government spokesman Matthew Hancock MP commented that:

---

1 *Private Action, Public Benefit*, 2002.

2 *Trusted and Independent*, ch 8, recommendation (i)8.

3 Regulating Fundraising for the Future: Trust in Charities, Confidence in Fundraising Regulation, September 2015.

> 'It really is the last chance for self-regulation … I do not want to have to resort to statutory regulation, but we will if we must. We now have the reserve powers to do so in case they are needed.'[4]

18.10 One additional recommendation of the Etherington Review was that the Charity Commission should play a limited 'last resort' role in the regulation of fundraising, stepping in to regulate charities if poor fundraising practices are evidence of wider trustee governance failures.

Statutory powers

18.11 Section 64 of the 1992 Act gives the Minister for the Cabinet Office power to make 'such regulations as appear to him to be necessary or desirable' for any purposes connected with Part II of the 1992 Act. It was under this provision that the Secretary of State made the Charitable Institutions (Fund-Raising) Regulations 1994, the content of which is described in Chapters 19 and 20.

18.12 Section 64A of the 1992 Act, which was introduced by the 2006 Act, is a 'reserve' power to control fundraising by charitable institutions. The reserve power covers 'fundraising' both for specific charities and also for general charitable, benevolent or philanthropic purposes. Section 64A(1) gives the Minister for the Cabinet Office power to make such regulations as appear to him to be necessary or desirable for or in connection with regulating charity fundraising. This includes controls over fundraising where it is carried out by a charity itself (except where the funds are raised through primary purpose trading), and where it is carried out by third parties for charities.

18.13 Section 64A(3) refers in particular to imposing good practice requirements and s 64A(4) goes on to define this as meaning requirements to ensure that fundraising:

- does not unreasonably intrude on privacy;
- does not involve unreasonably persistent approaches for donations;
- does not result in undue pressure being used to procure donations; and
- does not involve making false or misleading representations on a number of specified matters.

18.14 However the power under s 64A(1) clearly goes wider than merely imposing these good practice requirements.

18.15 Section 64B of the 1992 Act was introduced by the 2016 Act (and came into force on 31 July 2016). It effectively provides a statutory backdrop to a non-statutory fundraising regulator by making it absolutely clear that regulations made under s 64A may require charities to do the following:

- to comply with requirements imposed by a regulator;
- to have regard to guidance issued by a regulator;
- to be registered with a regulator for the purpose of its regulation of charity fundraising; and

---

4 HC Deb, col 232 (26 January 2016).

- to pay fees to a regulator (the regulations or the regulator itself may determine the amount of the fees).

These provisions only apply to a regulator whose principal function is charity fundraising. They do not apply where the regulator is maintained out of money provided by Parliament.

18.16 Section 64C of the 1992 Act was also introduced by the 2016 Act (and came into force on 31 July 2016). It makes it clear that regulations under s 64A may confer functions on the Charity Commission, and may allow for the Commission to appoint a third party to exercise its powers in this respect. It is also clear that the Commission may charge fees in relation to the regulation of fundraising, even where it regulates institutions which are not charities.

'Self-regulation' of fundraising

18.17 For the period from 2007 to 2016, the self-regulation regime for charitable fundraising in the UK comprised the following:

- the Fundraising Standards Board (FRSB) which adjudicated complaints about member charities and fundraising businesses;
- the Public Fundraising Association (PFRA) which aimed specifically to regulate non-cash face-to-face fundraising undertaken by its members; and
- central to the self-regulatory regime was the Code of Fundraising Practice which was set by the Institute of Fundraising (IoF).

18.18 Over the summer of 2016, the landscape of fundraising self-regulation changed significantly:

- In July 2016, a new Fundraising Regulator opened its doors for business. It regulates fundraising in England and Wales and also any fundraising carried out in Scotland by charities headquartered in England and Wales. Full details of how it deals with complaints and its 'remedial action against poor practice' can be found on its website www.fundraisingregulator.org.uk.
- The Code of Fundraising Practice and the PFRA rule books were transferred from the IOF and the PFRA to the Fundraising Regulator.
- As of July 2016, the IoF and the PFRA are underway with a plan to merge which is expected to complete by autumn 2016.
- The FRSB will be closing down sometime in autumn 2016 when it has completed all outstanding investigations.
- A new Independent Panel linked to the Office of the Scottish Charity Regulator has been set up in Scotland to regulate charities registered with the Office of the Scottish Charity Regulator.[5]
- Decisions on arrangements for fundraising regulation in Northern Ireland are expected to be taken in the autumn of 2016.

---

5 https://fundraisingcomplaints.scot.

Other sector initiatives at the time of going to press included a working party developing a Fundraising Preference Service and a working party preparing recommendations on collecting and using donor data.

The Code of Fundraising Practice

18.19 In 1983, the Institute of Fundraising (IoF)[6] was founded by a committed group of fundraisers getting together to tackle fundraising issues. Over the years the IoF produced a range of Codes of fundraising practice covering a variety of types of fundraising. In 2012, these Codes were unified in a single Code of Fundraising Practice which in summer 2016 was transferred to the Fundraising Regulator.

18.20 The Code is drafted to contain:

- obligations drafted as 'must*'s – ie with an asterisk – this is where there is a corresponding legal obligation;
- obligations drafted as 'must's – this is where there is no legal requirement but the Fundraising Regulator is treating the issue as a professional standard to be met by fundraising organisations.

The Code sets compliance standards for England, Wales, Scotland and Northern Ireland. Decisions on changes to the Code are made by the Fundraising Regulator's Standards Committee. The IoF now publishes supporting guidance on areas covered by the Code.

FUNDRAISING STANDARDS INFORMATION

18.21 Under s 162A of the 2011 Act, which was introduced in the 2016 Act, and will come into force on 1 November 2016, charities which are required to have their accounts audited must include a statement covering various aspects of fundraising in their trustees' annual report: see **21.71**. This was one of the measures in the 2016 Act designed to improve fundraising standards. When introducing it into the legislation in the House of Lords, the Government Minister Lord Bridges of Headley said that:

> 'the point is to require the leadership of a charity to take responsibility for their fundraising practice and set it out for all to see.'[7]

PUBLIC CHARITABLE COLLECTIONS

18.22 At the time of writing, street and house to house collections, which are collectively known as public charitable collections, are regulated by a patchwork of legislation comprising s 5 of the Police, Factories, etc (Miscellaneous Provisions) Act 1916 and the House to House Collections Act 1939 (both amended by the Local Government Act 1972). The current framework has been variously described as restrictive, inconsistent, complex, illogical, fragmented and outdated.

18.23 There have been two attempts to modernise the legislation. The 1992 Act, when it was first enacted, included a regime for the regulation of public charitable collections,

---

6 www.institute-of-fundraising.org.uk.
7 HL Deb, col 929 (20 July 2015).

but this was never brought into force. The Government commented, in its response to the 2002 Strategy Unit report,[8] that this was because the licensing scheme in the 1992 Act 'was believed by charities to have flaws in the detail of its procedures which would have made the scheme unworkable overall.'

18.24 The 2006 Act repealed the relevant provisions of the 1992 Act and introduced another regime for the regulation of public charitable collections, set out in ss 45-66 of the 2006 Act. However, Charity Commission concerns about the costs associated with the Commission's central role in the 2006 Act regime have meant it has never been brought into force.

18.25 The relevant provisions of the 2006 Act are reproduced in **Appendix 2** of this book for reference. Given that it seems highly unlikely these provisions will ever be implemented, this book does not include any detailed commentary on the 2006 Act public collections regime.[9] In practice, for non-cash face to face public collections, many local authorities work with the PFRA (and from autumn 2016, the IoF) to put in place Site Management Agreements which set controls on where and when fundraising can take place.

MISCELLANEOUS CONTROLS

Right of charitable institutions to prevent unauthorised fundraising

18.26 The 1992 Act provides a statutory right for charitable institutions[10] to prevent unauthorised fundraising. Under s 62(1), where the court (ie the High Court or county court) is satisfied that any person has been, or is, either soliciting money or other property for the benefit of a charitable institution or representing that charitable contributions are to be given, and that unless restrained he is likely to do further acts of that nature, if the court is satisfied as to one or more of the matters set out in s 62(2), it may grant an injunction restraining the unauthorised fundraising.

18.27 The charitable institution has to establish, to the court's satisfaction, one or more of the following under s 62(2):

(a) that the person in question is using methods of fundraising to which the institution objects;

(b) that that person is not a fit and proper person to raise funds for the institution; and/or

(c) in the case where it is represented that charitable contributions (as defined in s 58(1)[11]) are to be given, that the institution does not wish to be associated with the particular promotional or other fundraising venture in which that person is engaged.

18.28 Before the charitable institution can obtain an injunction, it must have given not less than 28 days' notice in writing to the person in question (s 62(3) of the 1992 Act).

---

8 *Private Action, Public Benefit*, 2002.

9 A detailed explanation of ss 45-66 of the 2006 Act appeared in the earlier edition of this book: *Charities, The New Law 2006: A Practical Guide to the Charities Acts*.

10 See **19.13-19.15** for more on the meaning of 'charitable institution'.

11 See **20.15**.

The notice must request him to cease forthwith and state that if he does not comply with the notice the institution will make an application for an injunction. The notice must also specify the circumstances which gave rise to the serving of the notice and the grounds on which an application under s 62 is to be made (reg 4 of Charitable Institutions (Fund-Raising) Regulations 1994). Service of the notice can be effected by complying with s 76 of the 1992 Act.

18.29 To help charitable institutions which may be plagued by unauthorised fundraisers, where a charitable institution has given the 28-day notice under s 62(3), but the person, having initially complied with the notice, subsequently begins to carry on the same activities, the charitable institution can immediately apply for an injunction without having to serve a further notice. This only applies if the application for the injunction is made not more than 12 months after the date of service of the relevant notice upon the fundraiser.

18.30 It is likely that a charity may also have a claim against any unauthorised fundraiser for trademark infringement or under the laws of passing off. This is in addition to the statutory right provided by way of s 62 of the 1992 Act.

Representations regarding status

18.31 Section 63 of the 1992 Act makes it a criminal offence for a person who is representing that an institution is a registered charity to solicit money or other property for the benefit of that institution when it is not a registered charity. Not all charities are registered charities: see Chapters 4 and 5.

18.32 An unlimited fine can be imposed under this section.

CHAPTER 19

CONTROL OF FUNDRAISING: PROFESSIONAL FUNDRAISERS

GENERAL BACKGROUND

19.1 The 1992 Act contains provisions regulating fundraising by paid fundraisers and commercial businesses. These have been amended by:

- the 2006 Act, which amended s 60 and inserted new ss 60A and 60B;
- the Charities Acts 1992 and 1993 (Substitution of Sums) Order 2009[1] which increased a number of the financial thresholds; and
- the 2016 Act, which amended s 59.[2]

However these provisions, along with other provisions of the 1992 Act, were not consolidated into the 2011 Act.

19.2 The Government's rationale for not consolidating the 1992 Act provisions into the 2011 Act was as follows:[3]

> 'The fundraising provisions go much wider, covering fundraising for charitable, philanthropic and benevolent purposes, and professional fundraisers and commercial companies undertaking charity promotions. They are therefore beyond the scope of a Bill to consolidate the law relating to charities.'

Many lawyers in the sector did not agree, including the Charity Law Association which commented that the reason for not consolidating the 1992 Act 'does not pass the common sense test.' These sections therefore remain separate to the vast majority of charity legislation which is in the 2011 Act.

19.3 As a general comment, the provisions of the 1992 Act (and the Regulations made under it) are often now a poor fit with the diverse and innovative means by which charities now raise funds, particularly in the online environment. As a result it can be difficult to determine how they apply in practice to fundraising arrangements.

BACKGROUND TO THE 1992 ACT

19.4 The 1992 Act introduced, for the first time, specific obligations on certain individuals and businesses who were fundraising for charities in return for payment in

1 SI 2009/508.
2 At the time of writing this amendment is not yet in force, but it will come into force on 1 November 2016.
3 Parliamentary Briefing Note: Charities Bill, HL Deb (9 December 2011).

some form. These obligations are set out in Part II of the 1992 Act, which covers ss 58–64C. The key terms introduced were 'professional fundraiser' and 'commercial participator' (which is dealt with in more detail in Chapter 20). There are also related regulations, The Charitable Institutions (Fund-Raising) Regulations 1994[4] ('the 1994 Regulations'), which are reproduced at **Appendix 10** of this book.

19.5 In the lead-up to the 2006 Act, there was discussion about whether the 1992 Act provisions went far enough to set a standard of transparency that the public might expect. The Strategy Unit report which preceded the 2006 Act[5] recommended changes to those parts of the 1992 Act relating to commercial participators. The Government in its response agreed with the suggestion to make changes and went further by proposing equivalent amendments in relation to professional fundraisers as well. Sections 67 and 68 of the 2006 Act (which are still in force) therefore made some refinements to the existing provisions, and they introduced an important change affecting other paid fundraisers, particularly employees of charities.

19.6 Concerns about fundraising practices (see Chapter 18) and in particular media coverage of some fundraising techniques prompted a further amendment to the 1992 Act, made by s 14 of the 2016 Act, which is designed to ensure that fundraising agreements refer to appropriate fundraising standards (see **19.54** and **20.41**).

19.7 Note that the 1992 Act (as amended) only applies (save in certain very limited cases) to England and Wales. See **19.102–19.110** in relation to Scotland and Northern Ireland.

CODES OF PRACTICE AND GUIDANCE

19.8 The most relevant guidance is that published by the Cabinet Office:

- 'Charitable Fundraising: Guidance on Part 2 of the Charities Act 1992'.[6] This was published in December 2008 ('the 2008 Guidance'); and
- 'Guidance for employees and paid officers or trustees of a charity required to make a solicitation statement', April 2008.

At the time of going to press, both are only accessible via the Government archive website.[7]

19.9 In his 2012 review of charity law, Lord Hodgson recommended that the Government should work with the Institute of Fundraising, Fundraising Standards Board and other specialists to produce simple guidance on solicitation statements for professional fundraisers and commercial participators.[8] In September 2013 the Government accepted this recommendation and said it would 'work with the charity

4 SI 1994/3024.
5 *Private Action, Public Benefit.*
6 This replaced earlier Home Office Guidance 'Charitable Fundraising: Professional and Commercial Involvement' (February 1995).
7 www.nationalarchives.gov.uk/webarchive.
8 *Trusted and Independent*, Chapter 8, recommendation 9.

sector and other partners to develop simple guidance on solicitation statements.'[9] However at the time of going to press, no updated guidance had been published.

19.10 The Charity Commission has also published guidance which contains some commentary and Commission best practice recommendations about relationships with professional fundraisers. The latest version is 'CC20 Charity Fundraising: A Guide to Trustee Duties' published in June 2016. The previous version of CC20 may also be useful to refer to its content about professional fundraisers.

19.11 The Code of Fundraising Practice (see **18.19-18.20**) covers a number of professional fundraiser scenarios. In addition to setting out the strict legal requirements, the Code 'outlines the standards expected of all charitable fundraising organisations across the UK.'[10]

WHEN DOES PART II OF THE 1992 ACT APPLY?

19.12 Part II of the 1992 Act (as amended by the 2006 Act) applies to:

- 'charitable institutions' as defined by the 1992 Act (see **19.13-19.19**);
- 'professional fundraisers' as defined by the 1992 Act (see **19.20-19.49**);
- 'commercial participators' as defined by the 1992 Act (see Chapter 20);
- paid individuals carrying out a public charitable collection (see **19.89**); and
- paid officers, employees or trustees of a charitable institution or company connected with a charitable institution who act as collectors (see **19.85-19.88**).

WHAT IS A CHARITABLE INSTITUTION?

19.13 Section 58(1) defines a 'charitable institution' as:

> 'a charity or an institution (other than a charity) which is established for charitable, benevolent or philanthropic purposes.'

This wording follows the House to House Collections Act 1939. The definition includes registered charities, charities which are exempt from registration, such as universities (see Chapter 5) and charities which are excepted from registration as charities (see Chapter 4).

19.14 Section 58(4) of the 1992 Act provides that 'charitable purposes' has the same meaning as in s 2(1) of the 2011 Act, namely a purpose which falls within the scope of s 3(1) of the 2011 Act and is for the public benefit (see Chapter 3). An organisation established under the laws of another country (eg France) could qualify as an institution established for charitable purposes provided it has purposes which are charitable under s 2(1) of the 2011 Act.

---

9 See p 39 of the Government Response to Lord Hodgson's review at www.gov.uk/government/uploads/system/uploads/attachment_data/file/237077/Response-charities-legal-framework.pdf.

10 See www.fundraisingregulator.co.uk.

19.15 However, there is a very important and clear distinction between the two phrases 'charitable purposes' and 'charitable institution' under the 1992 Act. When coupled with 'purposes', 'charitable' means charitable under the 2011 Act. But when 'charitable' is joined with 'institution' under the 1992 Act it means something much wider: it encompasses 'benevolent and philanthropic purposes' as well.

Benevolent

19.16 'Benevolent' is defined in the *Online Oxford English Dictionary* as 'Desirous of the good of others, of a kindly disposition, charitable, generous'. There is however a dearth of reported cases on the meaning of 'benevolent'. In 1891, Lord Branwen distinguished 'benevolent' and 'charitable' in *Income Tax Commissioners v Pemsel*:[11]

> 'I think there is some fund for providing oysters at one of the Inns of Court for the Benchers. This, however benevolent, would hardly be called charitable.'

Philanthropic

19.17 In *Re Macduff*,[12] concerning a person the Shakespearian connections of whose name hardly evoke philanthropy, Stirling J said (at 481):

> '"Philanthropic" is no doubt a word of narrower meaning than "benevolent". An act may be benevolent if it indicates goodwill to a particular individual only; whereas an act cannot be said to be philanthropic unless it indicates goodwill to mankind at large. Still, it seems to me that "philanthropic" is wide enough to comprise purposes not technically charitable.'

On appeal, Lindley LJ put no definite meaning on the word, but observed:

> 'All I can say is that a philanthropic purpose must be a purpose which indicates goodwill towards mankind in general.'

19.18 More recent legal discussions of the word 'philanthropic' can be found in VAT cases as, under VAT legislation, supplies to its members by a body which has objects which are in the public domain and are of a 'philanthropic nature' are VAT exempt. In the leading case of *Rotary International v Customs and Excise Commissioners*[13] the tribunal concluded that the rotary's objects were philanthropic because they were 'redolent of a desire to promote the well-being of mankind by serving one's fellow'. By contrast, there have been several subsequent VAT tribunal decisions where organisations have been unsuccessful in attempts to have their aims recognised as philanthropic. See, for example, the decisions of the *Camping and Caravanning Club*,[14] *Newport County AFC Social Club Ltd*,[15] *The Worshipful Company of Painter Stainers*[16] and, more recently in 2014, the *United Grand Lodge of England (Freemasons)*.[17]

19.19 The term 'philanthropic' should be wide enough to cover the non-charitable work of Amnesty International or charitable-type organisations established in other

---

11 [1891] AC 531.
12 [1896] 2 Ch 481.
13 [1991] VATTR 177 at 183E.
14 Decision No 20679, 4 and 5 February 2008.
15 Decision No V19807, 12 October 2006.
16 Decision No V20668, 6 May 2008.
17 Decision No TC03302, 3 February 2014.

jurisdictions concerned with mankind, eg Médecins sans Frontières, which, if not charitable under English law (see Chapter 3), should fall within the definition of 'philanthropic'. But is the phrase wide enough to include organisations such as Greenpeace or Friends of the Earth, who are primarily dedicated to preserving the environment or wildlife (rather than 'mankind')? In a 2001 case (again relating to VAT legislation)[18] it was agreed by all parties that a body whose activities are primarily directed at wildlife (rather than human beings) should not on those grounds be excluded from being philanthropic. In concluding that the nature of the trust is philanthropic, the VAT tribunal stated (at [77]):

> 'its aims can fairly be said to fall within the ambit of the promotion and well-being of mankind. Its activities are primarily directed at wildlife (which includes game of all species) and they serve to benefit the general community.'

WHAT IS A PROFESSIONAL FUNDRAISER?

19.20 There are two tests for identifying a professional fundraiser.

Test one

19.21 Any person (apart from a charitable institution) who carries on a fundraising business is a professional fundraiser. A fundraising business is defined in s 58(1) of the 1992 Act as 'any business carried on for gain and wholly or primarily engaged in soliciting or otherwise procuring money or other property for charitable, benevolent or philanthropic purposes'.

19.22 For the purposes of determining whether a business is a fundraising business 'wholly or primarily' engaged in procuring money for such purposes, presumably one must consider the overall activities of that business in the course of its financial year.

19.23 The words 'otherwise procuring' are important but vague – it helps slightly that when the draft Bill preceding the 1992 Act was considered, the Government made it clear in the House of Lords that in its view these words have a very limited meaning. As Viscount Astor said:[19]

> 'The expression "procuring" is used in preference to "obtaining" in order to make clear that the fundraiser in question must actively achieve the obtaining of funds for charitable purposes and not simply be a passive recipient by accident.'

Test two

19.24 The second test is 'any other person who for reward solicits money or other property for the benefit of a charitable institution'. Under this test, the person who is paid for soliciting money or other property for a charitable institution will be a professional fundraiser (even if he does not carry on a fundraising business), because he will be soliciting for reward (but see the exemptions for remuneration below certain

---

[18] *The Game Conservancy Trust 17394* [2001] 17 October.

[19] HL Deb, vol 535, col 1202–3 (18 February 1992).

levels at **19.37-19.40**). Equally, the business which is paid to carry on fundraising activities for charitable institutions but which does not do this 'wholly or primarily' will be caught under this test.

'Solicits'

19.25 Note that 'solicits' has quite a wide meaning. It includes:

- speaking directly to the person being solicited;
- a statement published in any newspaper, film, radio or television programme;
- under s 58(6)(b), situations where something is given in return for the donation; and
- under s 58(7) of the 1992 Act, a fundraiser will also be treated as 'soliciting' if he is responsible for receiving money on behalf of a charity, even if the fundraiser did not make the corresponding appeal.

19.26 What about 'prospecting' or two-step fundraising, where a paid fundraiser asks donors to support a charity by providing their names and addresses to the charity, so that the charity itself can contact them later to solicit donations? The 2008 Guidance states: 'In our view, a request only for contact details, such as name, address and telephone number, would not be a solicitation of money or other property for the purposes of part 2 of the 1992 Act.'

'For reward'

19.27 Does 'for reward' include where the fundraiser is not paid but gains some other benefit? For example, participants in a marathon where the charity purchased the place for them, or participants in an overseas bike ride where the charity pays the travel and accommodation costs. Although there have been no cases on this, the consensus in the sector is that they would be treated as fundraising 'for reward' and therefore fall within the second test. But again, see the exemption for remuneration below certain levels at **19.37-19.40**.

19.28 Also, what if the fundraiser is paid, but not by the charity? In relation to some charity events, there is sometimes a 'middle man' who arranges corporate sponsors, and it is the sponsors who pay the middle man's fee. The authors' view is that technically the middleman is a professional fundraiser.

19.29 There is potential for clarification of what 'reward' means. The Charity Law Association, in its submission to Lord Hodgson's 2012 review of charity law, made the point that although the definition of professional fundraiser uses the word 'reward', elsewhere in the 1992 Act and the 1994 Regulations, reference is made to 'remuneration *or expenses*.' Arguably, therefore it is not clear whether 'reward' in the definition of 'professional fundraiser' is intended to include both remuneration *and* expenses or, as the term 'reward' might suggest, remuneration only. Lord Hodgson agreed that this should be clarified, recommending: 'This is a small point that could be addressed by defining 'reward' in guidance.'[20]

---

20 *Trusted and Independent*, Appendix A, recommendation 24.

Exemptions from the definition of professional fundraiser

19.30 Sections 58(2) and (3) of the 1992 Act set out some specific exemptions from the definition of 'professional fundraiser'. These are:

(a) charitable institutions (see **19.31-19.32**);
(b) companies connected with charitable institutions (see **19.33-19.36**);
(c) people paid below certain limits (see **19.37–19.40**);
(d) collectors (see **19.41**); and
(e) celebrities (see **19.42-19.43**).

Exemption for charitable institutions

19.31 Charities fundraising for themselves are not professional fundraisers, nor are they if they fundraise on behalf of another charity, for example the BBC's Children In Need Appeal (which is itself a registered charity). Charity trustees or employees are not professional fundraisers, but note the obligation on charity employees and trustees to make disclosure statements in certain situations (see **19.85-19.88**).

19.32 There is some suggestion in Government guidance that where Charity A fundraises for Charity B, Charity A should, as a matter of good practice, follow the requirements that apply to professional fundraisers. See **19.35** for more details.

Exemption for companies connected with a charitable institution

19.33 As a general rule, a charity's trading company will not be a professional fundraiser (s 58(2)(a) of the 1992 Act). The test is whether the company is 'connected' with a charitable institution. A company is 'connected with' a charitable institution if one or more charitable institutions is or are entitled (whether directly or through one or more nominees) to exercise, or control the exercise of, the whole of the voting power at any general meeting of the company (s 58(5) of the 1992 Act).

19.34 What if a charity's trading subsidiary is paid to fundraise for another charity? The Charity Commission has taken the view in the past[21] that in those circumstances the trading subsidiary is a professional fundraiser. However, an analysis of the 1992 Act suggests this might not be correct – the exemption for companies connected with charities set out in s 58(2) does not require there to be any link between the company and the charity for which it is fundraising.

19.35 On a separate but linked point, the Commission has stated in the course of several statutory inquiry reports (and most recently in the 2016 version of CC20) its view that where a charity uses a wholly owned trading subsidiary for fundraising, both the charity and the trading subsidiary should as a matter of good practice treat the arrangements as being regulated by Part II of the 1992 Act, and have a written agreement in place and make the appropriate solicitation statements.[22] This is consistent with the 2008 Guidance which states (at para 3.5.3):

---

21 See 2010 Charity Commission Inquiry Report 'Dedicate Ltd and Raise a Smile Ltd'.
22 See section 5.4, CC20 Charity Fundraising: A Guide to Trustee Duties and 2012 Charity Commission Inquiry Report, 'The Needy Children International Foundation'.

'Whilst regard has to be had to the different circumstances where a charitable institution or its connected company undertakes direct fund-raising compared with fund-raising undertaken by professional fund-raisers or commercial participators, the Office of the Third Sector and (in relation to charities) the Charity Commission strongly recommend, as a matter of good practice and in so far as they are applicable, that these bodies follow the requirements that apply in relation to professional fund-raisers and commercial participators.'

19.36 Following increased scrutiny of charity fundraising arrangements in 2015-16, including the Charity Commission's report into Age UK,[23] there has been an increased emphasis in the media and from the Commission on transparency in fundraising arrangements. Therefore while the authors do not agree that the 1992 Act definition of 'professional fundraiser' catches charity trading subsidiaries, the authors' view is that, if it can be done easily, as part of a fundraising campaign, it is a good idea to include a short statement explaining that the trading subsidiary is wholly owned by a charity.

Exemption for people paid below certain levels

19.37 When the Bill leading up to the 1992 Act was first published there was considerable concern that the definition of 'professional fundraiser' was so wide that it would include people who collected money for charity and were paid expenses and a nominal fee. The Government addressed this concern in s 58(3) of the 1992 Act, which now provides that a person is not a professional fundraiser if he/she does not receive more than £10 per day or £1,000 per year by way of remuneration in connection with soliciting money or other property.[24] Examples of fundraisers falling within this exemption include:

- someone paid £10 per day or less for 'rattling a tin' in the street; or
- someone paid £900 for organising an annual garden fete to raise money for a charity.

19.38 Note that the fundraiser can in addition be paid reimbursement for properly incurred expenses, for example a street collector can be reimbursed lunch expenses each day, yet still stay within the exemption. Similarly, the fete organiser can be paid additional expenses incurred in setting up the fete and still stay within the exemption.

19.39 The wording of the exemption may cover some individuals taking part in charity-sponsored events, provided the value of the 'remuneration' they receive is not more than £1,000 a year. So, for example, if they take part in a sponsored event like the London to Paris bike ride with the charity paying their travel costs, then, provided the value of the travel costs (which is a benefit to them) is £1,000 or less, they are not a professional fundraiser. If, however, they did two events in one year, they could be a professional fundraiser for the second event if the combined value of the travel costs takes them over the £1,000 limit.

19.40 What if a person is paid less than £10 per day but more than £1,000 per year? It appears they still fall within the low paid collector exception though it is not clear this is what Parliament intended. The Charity Law Association submission to Lord Hodgson's 2012 review of charity law suggested an amendment to the legislation to clarify the

---

[23] Charity Commission Case Report, Age UK, April 2016.

[24] These are the figures as from 1 April 2009: Charities Acts 1992 and 1993 (Substitution of Sums) Order 2009, SI 2009/508.

position and Lord Hodgson agreed, recommending both that this should be tidied up and that the thresholds for this exception should be reviewed.[25]

Exemption for collectors

19.41 If a professional fundraiser uses paid collectors or agents to solicit funds for a charitable institution, those collectors or agents are not themselves 'professional fundraisers'. They are, in effect, sheltered by the professional fundraiser, who contracts their services (s 58(2)(c) of the 1992 Act). The 1992 Act does provide that where the paid collector is carrying out a public collection, there is a separate obligation to make a solicitation statement, but these provisions are not yet in force, and it currently seems unlikely that they will ever be brought into force.[26]

Exemption for appeals by celebrities

19.42 The first draft of the Bill leading up to the 1992 Act caused concern that celebrities employed by professional fundraisers or charitable institutions to make appeals on radio and television would be caught in the net of the professional fundraiser definition. The Bill was amended.

19.43 Section 58(2)(d) of the 1992 Act excludes from its definition of professional fundraiser for the purposes of s 58(1):

> 'any person who in the course of a relevant programme, that is to say a radio or television programme in the course of which a fundraising venture is undertaken by:
>
> (i) a charitable institution; or
> (ii) a company connected with such an institution,
>
> makes any solicitation at the instance of that institution or company.'

Hence, even if a celebrity is paid to make an appeal on behalf of a charity, he will not be a professional fundraiser.

Applying the test in practice

19.44 In practice, there are some situations where it is clear whether a person is or is not a professional fundraiser. For example, see the table below. There are, however other situations where it is less clear, in which case the 2008 Guidance may be helpful as it examines a number of scenarios potentially involving professional fundraisers; see particularly Section 2.2 and Appendix A.

---

25 *Trusted and Independent*, Appendix A, recommendation 35.
26 See 19.89 and 18.24-18.25.

Examples of professional fundraisers

Not a professional fundraiser	Professional fundraiser
Consultant who advises charity 'behind the scenes' on a fundraising strategy.	Consultant who implements a fundraising strategy which includes the consultant asking for donations.
Company which sends out fundraising text messages from the charity and asks for donations to be sent to the charity.	Agency which is paid to get donors to sign up for direct debit donations.
Telemarketing agency which recruits people to sell raffle tickets on behalf of a charity.	Participant in one or more sponsored events whose participation costs are paid by the charity and exceed £1,000 in one year.
Telemarketing agency which aims to set up appointments for fundraisers to visit individuals at home to sign up direct debit schemes.	Direct mail company which sends out a fundraising letter which is in the charity's name and asks for donations to be sent to the direct mail company.
Volunteer who rings round to get prizes for a raffle and whose telephone expenses are reimbursed.	Volunteer who hosts 12 dinner parties a year to raise funds and who charges the charity a nominal fee of £100 per dinner party.

Grey areas

19.45 There are a number of grey areas, particularly as there are now methods of fundraising not even envisaged at the time of the 1992 Act, such as online and text message fundraising. The grey areas include the following:

Secondees

19.46 A secondee to a charity fundraising department (from eg a bank or agency) may fall within the definition of professional fundraiser if he or she solicits donations. This is because they are being paid, yet do not necessarily fall within the exemption for charity employees. See also **19.84-19.89**, which discusses the obligation on other paid fundraisers to make a different kind of statement.

Telephone fundraising agencies

19.47 Telephone fundraising potentially raises a number of problems. The 2008 Guidance gives the following examples:

> 'Incoming telephone services; if a company answers telephone calls, simply to record credit card details for people who have decided to make a donation, eg in response to an appeal by direct mail or newspaper or television advertisement, and the donations are credited direct to the institutions' (not the company's) bank account, the company may not be a professional fundraiser. However, the distinction is a narrow one and care is needed; if, for example, the operator repeats or explains details about the appeal, even in response to a request for clarification from the caller, this may well amount to professional fundraising, and operators must therefore be able to recognise this distinction and respond appropriately in each case.

Where incoming telephone services are provided by automated (eg computer-based) answering equipment owned by a service provider and rented to an institution, then even when a solicitation is made by a person whose voice is recorded provided that person is from the charitable institution, the service provider may not be regarded as a professional fundraiser.'

Facilitating donations

19.48 Many fundraising campaigns now involve third parties who facilitate the giving of donations – for example online giving sites and phone companies facilitating donations by text message. In some cases, the business facilitating the giving of the donation is paid to do so. Does this make it a professional fundraiser? The key is whether s 58(7) of the 1992 Act is triggered. At the time of going to press, neither the 2008 Guidance nor guidance from the Commission comment on this difficult area. In each case, it will require a careful analysis of whether the business in question falls within 'Test one' (ie carries on a fundraising business) or falls within 'Test two' (ie soliciting money or other property for reward) where the effect of s 58(7) needs to be considered. See also **20.27** for discussion of when these businesses might fall within the definition of 'commercial participator'.

Add-on services

19.49 What if a business which is paid to provide non-fundraising services to the charity offers, as part of the service, to ask for donations? For example, a catalogue fulfilment company which at the end of every call or website order asks the customer to round-up the amount due, donating the extra to the charity. Whether the business is a professional fundraiser will require careful analysis of whether the business is a fundraising business or whether the asking for donations is something the business is doing 'for reward'.

WHAT ARE THE CONSEQUENCES OF BEING A PROFESSIONAL FUNDRAISER?

19.50 There are three main consequences of being a professional fundraiser:

- the professional fundraiser must have a written agreement with the charity for which it is fundraising which must meet certain minimum requirements; (s 59 of the 1992 Act) – see **19.51–19.57**;
- the professional fundraiser must make a statement each time it makes a solicitation (s 60 of the 1992 Act) – see **19.62-19.81**; and
- the professional fundraiser must pass money or other property to the charity within certain minimum deadlines (reg 6 of the 1994 Regulations) – see **19.82–19.83**.

It is clear in the 1992 Act that these are all obligations on the professional fundraiser and the Act itself does not put any obligation on the charity to ensure that they are observed. However, the Commission has on occasions stated that it regards a charity's trustees as being under an obligation to ensure compliance with the 1992 Act.[27] The

[27] For example, see 2014 Charity Commission Operational Compliance Report, Wildlife Rescue Sanctuaries and 2016 Charity Commission Case Report, Our Local Heroes Foundation.

authors would not put it as strongly as the trustees being under an obligation to ensure compliance, but think it is reasonable for charity trustees, who should have awareness of the legislation in this area, to take reasonable and proper steps to ensure that there is transparency and clarity in relation to the contractual relationship between the charity and the fundraiser. In practice, any charity entering into arrangements which are not compliant with the 1992 Act is likely to be in breach of a standard set in the Code of Fundraising Practice.[28]

SECTION 59 AGREEMENT

Minimum requirements

19.51 Section 59(1) of the 1992 Act says:

> 'it shall be unlawful for a professional fundraiser to solicit money or other property for the benefit of a charitable institution unless he does so in accordance with an agreement with the institution satisfying the prescribed requirements.'

19.52 The prescribed requirements are laid down in s 59(7)-(8) and in the 1994 Regulations.[29] Regulation 2 provides that the agreement between the charitable institution and a professional fundraiser shall be in writing and shall be signed by or on behalf of the charitable institution and the professional fundraiser. It must cover some specific terms.

19.53 A professional fundraiser agreement has to specify:

(a) the name and address of each of the parties to the agreement;

(b) the date on which the agreement was signed by or on behalf of those parties;

(c) the period for which the agreement is to subsist;

(d) any terms relating to termination of the agreement prior to the date on which the period expires;

(e) any terms relating to the variation of the agreement during that period;

(f) a statement of its principal objectives and the methods to be used in pursuit of those objectives;

(g) if there is more than one charitable institution party to the agreement, provision as to the manner in which the proportion in which the institutions which are so party are respectively to benefit under the agreement is to be determined;

(h) provision as to the amount by way of remuneration or expenses which the professional fundraiser is to be entitled to receive in respect of things done by him in pursuance of the agreement and the manner in which that amount is to be determined;

(i) any voluntary scheme for regulating fundraising, or any voluntary standard of fundraising, that the professional fundraiser undertakes to be bound by for the purposes of the agreement;

(j) how the professional fundraiser is to protect vulnerable people and other members of the public from:

---

28 Paragraph 4(2)(b) Code of Fundraising Practice. See **18.19-18.20**.

29 SI 1994/3024.

- unreasonable intrusion on a person's privacy;
- unreasonably persistent fundraising;
- placing undue pressure on a person to donate;

in the course of, or in connection with, the activities to which the agreement relates; and

(k) arrangements enabling the charity to monitor compliance with the requirement in s 59(1) by reference to the agreement.

19.54 The requirements mentioned at **19.53**(i)-(k) were introduced by the 2016 Act largely in response to media and Parliamentary concerns about certain fundraising techniques (see **18.3**). These new requirements come into force on 1 November 2016. At the time of writing it is not clear to what extent they will apply to agreements made before that date. In the debates on the 2016 Act in the House of Lords, the Government Minister Lord Bridges of Headley commented that the requirements would allow both charities and the fundraisers to be clear and upfront about what would be done in the charity's name, and about their respective responsibilities.[30]

19.55 The terms 'unreasonable intrusion', 'unreasonably persistent' and 'undue pressure' are not defined, and the Parliamentary debates on the 2016 Act shed little light on what Parliament intended should be caught by these terms. During the House of Lords debates on 20 July 2015, in response to a question from Lady Barker about who decides what is unreasonable, Lord Bridges of Headley said:

> 'In the first instance, the charity itself decides in setting the terms of its fundraising agreement, but ultimately the Charity Commission can intervene, using its existing powers, if the charity is not doing enough. That said – and this is an important point – the Charity Commission has already committed to updating its fundraising guidance later this year and will take these new requirements into account when it does so.'[31]

The Charity Commission guidance CC20 (June 2016 version) does not include any commentary on these terms. In the absence of specific guidance or case law, the Code of Fundraising Practice (and the Public Fundraising Regulatory Association Rule Books)[32] set some practical boundaries around times of day to fundraise, locations, frequency and number of asks. Although it is worth noting that in 2015 the Fundraising Standards Board criticised a provision in the Code of Fundraising Practice which states that a telephone fundraiser must not ask for a donation more than three times in a call, as potentially permitting 'undue pressure'. The FRSB expressed the view that 'a third ask, when a donor has already said no twice, can constitute undue pressure'.[33]

19.56 As mentioned at **18.21** and **21.71**, charities which are required to have their accounts audited must include in their trustees' annual report certain key information about the charity's dealing with professional fundraisers.

19.57 In addition to these requirements reg 5 provides that a professional fundraiser who is party to an agreement under s 59:

---

30 Hansard, col 929 (20 July 2015).
31 Hansard, col 934 (20 July 2015).
32 See Chapter 18.
33 FRSB Adjudication, Listen Ltd, December 2015.

> 'shall, on request and at all reasonable times, make available to any charitable institution which is a party to that agreement any books, documents or other records (however kept) which relate to that institution and are kept for the purposes of the agreement.'

By reg 5(2), the records have to be kept in legible form.

Recommended additional safeguards

19.58 The requirements laid down by the 1994 Regulations are the legal minimum. Charitable institutions may well want to build on the requirements set out in the Regulations to protect themselves on other issues. For example:

- making sure all the commercial terms of the contract are clearly described, eg targets, KPIs, costs, invoicing, payment, rights to any refunds;
- imposing a penal rate of interest on the professional fundraiser should it delay making payments due to the charitable institution under the fundraising agreement;
- being clear who owns copyright in artwork or any copy produced by the professional fundraiser;
- stating the position on the ownership of data and database rights in lists of names generated by the professional fundraiser and dealing in detail with all necessary data protection safeguards;
- including duties of confidentiality;
- including a restriction on the professional fundraiser undertaking any work of a similar nature for any organisation which operates within the same or a similar field of activity as the charitable institution for the duration of the agreement;
- in addition to detailed termination provisions, including rights to suspend the contract and provisions dealing with consequences of suspension and termination;
- being clear what the governing law of the contract is; and
- if the charity is required to have its accounts audited, a requirement to provide the charity with the information needed for the trustees' annual report (see **21.71**), including any failure by the professional fundraiser to comply with any voluntary scheme or standard; and the number of complaints received by the professional fundraiser.

The Commission advises that trustees should ensure that no legal document is signed unless they are satisfied that the terms are in the charity's best interests.[34]

19.59 There is no legal requirement for a s 59 agreement to be signed by a trustee but in some charities it may be good practice for this to happen.

Failure to comply with s 59

19.60 If a professional fundraiser does not have a s 59 compliant agreement in place, the professional fundraiser can only enforce its arrangements with the charity (such as for payment) if it obtains a court order allowing it to do so.

---

34 CC20 'Charity Fundraising: A Guide to Trustee Duties', June 2016 version.

19.61 Charities are given the right to apply to court for an injunction to prevent any person soliciting money without having entered into a s 59 agreement. The court in question is either the High Court or a county court. In injunction cases, either court could be used.

SECTION 60 STATEMENT

19.62 Section 60(1), which was amended by the 2006 Act, requires that where a professional fundraiser solicits money or other property for the benefit of one or more particular charitable institutions, the solicitation shall be accompanied by a statement clearly indicating:

(a) the name or names of the institutions concerned (eg 'XYZ charity');
(b) if there is more than one institution concerned, the proportions in which the institutions are respectively to benefit (eg 'XYZ charity 50%, ABC charity 50%'); and
(c) the method by which the fundraiser's remuneration in connection with the appeal is to be determined and the 'notifiable amount' of the remuneration (see **19.68**).

19.63 Where an appeal is for general charitable purposes (as opposed to for named charities) there is an obligation under s 60(2) to make a similar statement.

19.64 There are two situations where the general requirements are varied:

- s 60(4) – for solicitation statements as part of TV and radio appeals which include an announcement that payment can be made by debit or credit card, the s 60 statement must also include details of the donor's right to a refund – see **19.93**.
- s 60(5) – for solicitation statements made verbally but not in the presence of the donor (eg by telephone) and where the donor gives £100 or more, there is an additional requirement to give the donor a follow up written statement. This must be given to the donor within seven days of the payment being made and must include:
  - a written version of the solicitation statement; and
  - details of the donor's right to a refund/cancel – see **19.94**.

Section 60(6) contains detailed provisions for determining when the payment is treated as being paid, thereby triggering the seven-day period for making the written statement.

19.65 Failure to comply with s 60(1) or (2) is a criminal offence for the professional fundraiser – see **19.98–19.101**.

How detailed does the statement need to be?

19.66 Before the 2006 Act, there was great debate and uncertainty about how detailed the statement needed to be. The 2006 Act introduced changes requiring more detail to be disclosed but there are still some grey areas.

19.67 Looking at s 60(1)(c), there are several separate requirements. First, there is an obligation to disclose the *method* by which the fundraiser's remuneration is determined.

Then, there is an additional requirement to disclose the 'notifiable amount'. Finally, both must be disclosed in relation to 'the appeal'.

19.68 'Notifiable amount' is defined in s 60(3A) of the 1992 Act as a reference:

> '(a) to the actual amount of the remuneration or sum, if that is known at the time when the statement is made; and
> (b) otherwise to the estimated amount of the remuneration or sum, calculated as accurately as is reasonably possible in the circumstances.'

19.69 'The appeal' is defined in s 60(10) of the 1992 Act as 'in relation to any solicitation by a professional fundraiser: the campaign or other fundraising venture in the course of which the solicitation is made'.

19.70 Therefore, it is not enough for the fundraiser to state how much they are being paid per solicitation. Under s 60(1)(c) the requirement is to state 'the method by which the fundraiser's remuneration *in connection with the appeal* is to be determined and the notifiable amount of that remuneration' (emphasis added). So, the notifiable amount must relate to the entire appeal. Initially there was some concern among professional fundraisers that disclosing the total amount they were being paid for an appeal could put donors off. In practice it seems that has not proved as big an issue as anticipated.

Cabinet Office guidance on wording of solicitation statements

19.71 The 2008 Guidance sets out lengthy and complex guidance on how fundraising statements should be worded, with Annex B setting out a range of example statements.

19.72 Many in the sector, including Lord Hodgson in his 2012 review of charity law, have asked for simpler guidance to be issued by government. At the time of going to press, simpler guidance has been promised but not published – see **19.9**.

19.73 As explained below, the authors agree with some but not all of the 2008 Guidance.

Estimated amounts

19.74 The 2008 Guidance states that where the figure to be used in a statement is an estimate, strictly speaking there is no legal requirement to make clear in the statement that it is an estimate. The authors agree with this analysis. However, the 2008 Guidance also says that as well as stating an overall estimated amount, the description of the fundraising method must include a notifiable amount, for example £x per day: the authors do not agree with this.

19.75 The Cabinet Office also suggests that where estimates are used, particularly for a long appeal, the professional fundraiser should review the estimated figure at regular intervals to ensure it remains 'calculated as accurately as is reasonably possible in the circumstances'. The authors agree with this suggestion.

What is the 'appeal'?

19.76 The 2008 Guidance says that the solicitation statement can reflect the fact that some campaigns are limited 'geographically, regionally, in time or theme-based'. This means the amount in a statement need not be the total amount the charity will pay the professional fundraiser but can instead be limited to the amount to be paid for that particular 'appeal'.

When and where should the statement be made?

19.77 The 2006 Act made no change to the law relating to when and where statements should be made. The guiding principle remains that whenever a solicitation is made, a s 60(1) or (2) statement has to accompany it. For example:

- if a professional fundraiser organises a street collection, the collector will have to display the statement;
- if a professional fundraiser arranges a charity ball, the tickets will have to bear the statement; and
- if a professional fundraiser arranges a telephone appeal, the statement will have to be given during each call.

19.78 With any oral appeal, there is an issue about how soon the s 60 statement should be made. Should it be the first thing the person says, or is it acceptable for them to make sure the statement is made at some point during the conversation?

19.79 The 2008 Guidance states at para 2.9 that the solicitation must be made 'prior to the donation being given'. At Annex B several of the example statements include wording to the effect 'Before I ask you to sign ...', which reinforces the Cabinet Office view that the solicitation must precede the donation.

19.80 There are no known reported court cases on this, but the Commission has commented in inquiry reports on a similar issue for commercial participator arrangements (see **20.79**). Following the Commission's line of thinking in the commercial participator cases, it may be possible to argue it is sufficient if the statement is made as close in time as possible after the solicitation for the charity. It does however remain a grey area.

19.81 Remember as well that in some circumstances, an oral statement must be followed up by a written statement – see **19.64**.

TRANSMISSION OF MONEY AND OTHER PROPERTY BY THE PROFESSIONAL FUNDRAISER

19.82 All professional fundraisers, whether they have an agreement in place or not, are required, unless they have a reasonable excuse, to pay over any money or any negotiable instrument received by them to the account of the charitable institution as soon as is reasonably practicable after receipt, and in any event not later than the expiration of 28 days after that receipt, unless another period has been agreed with the institution.[35] Payment has to be made to the charitable institution itself, or into an account in the name of the institution.

---

[35] 1994 Regulations, reg 6.

19.83 If the professional fundraiser receives property other than money, then it has to be dealt with in accordance with any instructions given for that purpose by the charitable institution. Pending the handing over of any property it has to be kept securely by the professional fundraiser.

STATEMENTS BY OTHER PERSONS

19.84 The 1992 Act also imposes a requirement to make a statement on an additional category of 'paid' fundraisers who would otherwise fall outside the definition of professional fundraiser. This additional category was added by the 2006 Act.

19.85 Paid employees or paid officers of a charity or its connected trading subsidiary, or paid trustees of a charity who collect in the course of a public collection have various obligations under s 60A(4)–(10) of the 1992 Act. If they make a solicitation for a particular charity, they have to make a statement indicating:

(a) the name or names of the institution(s) which will benefit and, if more than one, the proportions in which they will benefit;
(b) the fact that they are an officer, employee or trustee of the institution; and
(c) the fact that they are receiving remuneration as an officer, employee, trustee or for acting as a collector.

They do not have to state the amount of their remuneration.

19.86 If they make a solicitation for general charitable, benevolent or philanthropic purposes (as opposed to a specific named charity), then they have to make a similar statement that they are being paid for those general purposes.

19.87 There is a similar 'lower paid' exception if the person receives not more than £10 per day or £1,000 per year or a lump sum which is not more than £1,000. In any of these cases, there is no obligation to make a statement.

19.88 In April 2008 the Cabinet Office published 'Guidance for employees and paid officers or trustees of a charity required to make a solicitation statement' (see **19.8**). This fairly short guidance, though helpfully including three example statements, does not shed much light on when the requirement to make a statement kicks in (and elements of the contents are now out of date as the guidance does not reflect subsequent changes to the 'lower paid' exception thresholds). Specifically, many charities feel that if staff choose to take part in a public collection outside their work hours, then there should be no requirement to make a statement. The Charity Law Association submission to Lord Hodgson's 2012 review of charity law included a recommendation that this guidance should be updated and expanded. But while Government has committed to update its other 2008 Guidance on the 1992 Act, there have been no indications that this guidance will be updated.

19.89 The 2006 Act made amendments to the 1992 Act which would require paid individuals carrying out a public charitable collection to make a statement equivalent to a s 60 statement in some circumstances. However, at the time of going to press, those provisions are not in force and it currently seems unlikely that they will ever be brought into force: see **18.24-18.25**.

FAILURE TO COMPLY WITH S 60

19.90 One consequence of a professional fundraiser failing to make the necessary s 60 statement is that technically the professional fundraiser commits a criminal offence. See **19.98-19.101**. The charity for which the professional fundraiser was fundraising does not commit an offence.

19.91 Given the current lack of appetite for prosecutions (see **19.98**), the more likely consequence of failing to make the necessary s 60 statement is that the professional fundraiser, the charity or both face censure from one of the sector regulatory bodies, the national press and/or sector press, with knock-on damage to reputation. The Fundraising Standards Board carried out a number of adjudications where a charity's failure to monitor compliance by a professional fundraiser was examined.[36] The Charity Commission has historically shied away from regulating professional fundraisers but it has commented in one case[37] that charities should do the following:

- build into the arrangements an obligation on the professional fundraiser to make the necessary s 60 statement;
- include an obligation on the professional fundraiser to train its fundraisers on the timing and wording of the s 60 statement; and
- carry out regular review meetings with the professional fundraiser and check at those meetings that s 60 statements are being made.

The June 2016 version of CC20 'Charity Fundraising: A Guide to Trustee Duties' reinforces this in broader terms (see section 5.3). One of the challenges facing charities now is what level of monitoring of professional fundraisers they should carry out to protect the charity and satisfy the Fundraising Regulator and/or Charity Commission. In practice, concerns about compliance with the 1992 Act have taken a backseat to concerns about use of donor data, and high pressure fundraising techniques. More rarely, and only in more extreme cases, the Insolvency Service has taken action to wind up fundraising companies and (in one case that the authors are aware of) a charity, on public interest grounds pursuant to s 124A of the Insolvency Act 1986.[38] The Insolvency Service can also take action to ban individuals from acting as company directors.

THE RIGHT TO CANCEL/REFUND

19.92 The 1992 Act sets out limited specific rights for donors to cancel a donation or receive a refund.

Payments made in response to radio or TV appeals – s 61(1)

19.93 Where, in response to a radio or TV appeal, a donor makes a payment of £100 or more using a credit or debit card, he can cancel within 7 days of the date of the solicitation, and any monies paid must be refunded by the fundraiser.

---

36 See December 2012 FRSB decision TAG Campaigns and July 2016 FRSB decision Fundraising Initiatives Ltd.

37 Charity Commission Operational Case Report, Marie Curie Cancer Care, December 2013.

38 See 2012 Charity Commission Inquiry Report 'The Needy Children International Foundation' and see 20.79.

Donations as a result of verbal solicitations – s 61(2)

19.94 Where, in response to a verbal solicitation, a donor donates £100 or more (or enters into an agreement under which he is potentially liable to pay £100 or more), he is entitled to a refund or to cancel the agreement. The 7 days runs from the date the donor receives the written statement which the professional fundraiser is required to send under s 60(5) – see **19.64**. This mainly applies to telephone fundraising as it does not apply where the solicitation is made verbally in person or as part of a radio or TV programme.

How must a donor notify his wish for a refund/cancellation?

19.95 There is no 'magic wording' the donor has to use but the donor must put something in writing. Under s 61(1) and (2) the donor must serve on the relevant fundraiser a notice in writing which 'however expressed, indicates the donor's intention to cancel the payment'. Note that sending notice by email may not be sufficient – s 76 of the 1992 Act (which sets out detailed provisions about how documents can be validly served) does not allow for service by email.

How much refund?

19.96 Section 61(4) of the 1992 Act allows the fundraiser to deduct 'administrative expenses reasonably incurred' in connection with making the refund. In the debates on the Bill which became the 1992 Act Viscount Astor explained:[39]

> '"administrative expenses" is intended to cover the direct costs of refunding the payment, for costs such as staff time, postage, bank charges and so forth. It will also cover the costs of dealing with any notice of cancellation of an agreement to make payment.'

CHARITY REPORTING REQUIREMENT IN RELATION TO PROFESSIONAL FUNDRAISERS

19.97 As mentioned at **19.56** and **21.71**, charities which are required to have their accounts audited must include details about their arrangements with professional fundraisers in their annual reports.

OFFENCES AND ENFORCEMENT

19.98 Although technically Part II of the 1992 Act provides for a number of criminal offences (see the table below), in practice neither the authors nor the Charity Commission are aware of a single prosecution under this part of the 1992 Act. Even, for example, where the Fundraising Standards Board made a clear finding in one case that s 60 statements had not been made, there was no follow-up criminal prosecution.[40] The situation is much the same as enforcement (or lack of it) against commercial participators (see **20.79**).

---

39 HL Deb, vol 535, col 1215 (18 February 1992).

40 See Fundraising Standards Board decision, December 2012, TAG Campaigns.

19.99

Offences	
Professional fundraiser fails to give the statements required under s 60(1), (2), (4) and (5) when collecting for specific charities.	Unlimited fine.
Paid officer, employee or trustee fails to make the statement required under s 60A.	Unlimited fine.
Collector fails to make the statement required under s 60A.	Unlimited fine.
Professional fundraiser breaches reg 5(1) (allowing access to its records); reg 6(2) (passing money on to the charity); reg 7(2) (failing to make a statement when collecting for general charitable purposes).	Fine not exceeding level 2 on the standard scale (which as of July 2016 is £500).

19.100 It is a defence for a person charged with any offence under s 60 or 60A 'to prove that he took all reasonable precautions and exercised all due diligence to avoid the commission of the offence' (s 60(8)). This is similar to a phrase used in the Trade Descriptions Act 1968, s 24. It shifts the burden of proof from the prosecution, who would, under normal rules of criminal law, have to prove that the defendant had mens rea and committed the offence, onto the defendant, who has to show that he took all reasonable precautions etc. That is a heavy burden. In one case under the Trade Descriptions Act 1968, *Tesco Supermarkets v Nattrass*,[41] the House of Lords ruled that the defendants had exercised all due diligence by devising a proper system for the operation of their supermarket and by securing its implementation as far as was reasonably practicable.

19.101 Section 60(9) contains a sting. It provides that where there is a breach of s 60 which is due to the act or default of some other person, that other person shall be guilty of the offence. The same defence of having taken all reasonable precautions etc can be pleaded. The subsection is principally designed to allow charges to be brought against employees who break the requirements of the Act, in breach, for example, of their employer's rule book. Note that s 75 of the 1992 Act which relates to offences committed by corporate bodies (see **20.77-20.78**) also applies to professional fundraisers).

SCOTLAND

19.102 Scottish law also now regulates the activities of 'professional fundraisers', but not to exactly the same extent as the law of England and Wales. There are similarities and differences.

19.103 The relevant law is set out in the Charities and Trustee Investment (Scotland) Act 2005 and the Charities and Benevolent Fundraising (Scotland) Regulations 2009 ('the 2009 Regulations').

---

[41] [1971] 2 All ER 127.

19.104 The fundraising controls protect all 'benevolent' bodies, which means a body (including a charity) established for charitable, benevolent or philanthropic purposes.

19.105 The main definition of 'professional fundraiser' (see s 79 of the Charities and Trustee Investment (Scotland) Act 2005) is pretty much identical to the definition in the 1992 Act. Although in principle the Act provides an exemption for fundraisers paid below certain amounts per day or year, it leaves the threshold to be set out in regulations, which has not yet been done. (The 2009 Regulations do not cover this.)

19.106 It is unlawful for a professional fundraiser to solicit on behalf of a benevolent body unless they do so in accordance with a written agreement with the body which satisfies certain minimum requirements. Again the regulations in which these minimum requirements will be set out have not been published at the time of writing, so whether they will be the same as or different to the law in England and Wales is not clear.

19.107 Failure to have the appropriate agreement means the professional fundraiser cannot enforce payment unless it obtains an order of the sheriff.

19.108 There is no requirement in the main legislation for professional fundraisers to make a statement when soliciting – that is set out in the 2009 Regulations. Two notable differences from the position in England and Wales are as follows:

- If a professional fundraiser or commercial participator makes the solicitation statement orally, they must also state that the details of the remuneration/amount going to the charity are available in writing if the person wants to see them (if made by telephone, the information must be sent in writing if the person requests it).
- The definition of notifiable amount is slightly different in Scotland so far as using an estimated amount is concerned. In England and Wales, the notifiable amount, if an estimate, must be calculated 'as reasonably as possible in the circumstances'. By contrast, the 2009 Regulations just refer to 'the estimated amount' so there appears to be no similar requirement to calculate it 'reasonably'.

Scottish Guidance

19.109 The Office of the Scottish Charity Regulator has issued guidance on complying with the Regulations – 'Benevolent Fundraising: A Guide to the Charities and Benevolent Fundraising (Scotland) Regulations 2009'.[42]

NORTHERN IRELAND

19.110 The Charities Act (Northern Ireland) 2008 includes provisions regulating professional fundraisers and commercial participators but at the time of writing these are not yet in force.

---

42 Available on the OSCR website at www.oscr.org.uk.

CHAPTER 20

CONTROL OF FUNDRAISING: COMMERCIAL PARTICIPATORS

INTRODUCTION

20.1 The 1992 Act contains a number of controls on fundraising for charitable institutions. In addition to those controls placed on professional fundraisers (see Chapter 19), the 1992 Act also aims to regulate the actions of those who encourage the purchase of goods or services on the grounds that a charitable institution will benefit from that purchase, known as commercial participators. A commercial participator will be required to enter into an agreement with the relevant charitable institution (see **20.37-20.41**) and will also need to make a statement, containing certain specified information, to any potential purchasers (see **20.51-20.65**).

20.2 Although the 1992 Act was amended by the 2006 Act, and again by the 2016 Act, there has not been a full review of the legislation (or the regulations made under it) since it was originally brought in. This means that the legislation can result in uncertainties and unexpected results, particularly with regard to new developments in online fundraising.

20.3 As mentioned at **19.1-19.2**, the provisions of the 1992 Act were not consolidated into the 2011 Act. The rationale for this was that the provisions of the 1992 Act cover fundraising for charitable, philanthropic and benevolent purposes and are therefore beyond the scope of legislation to consolidate the law relating to charities. The authors, in common with many in the sector, consider that it would have been far more appropriate for the legislation to be consolidated.

Background to the 1992 Act

20.4 Originating in the recommendations set out in the Woodfield Report of 1988, the intention behind the 1992 Act was to ensure that potential purchasers of commercial participators' goods or services were given a fair indication of the extent to which charitable institutions or charitable purposes would benefit from the transaction before they made their decision whether or not to purchase. Before the 1992 Act, the conduct of any such fundraising arrangements – often known as cause-related marketing – was considered solely in the light of the charity law duties placed on the trustees of the relevant charity, whereas the 1992 Act, for the first time, imposed obligations directly on those that were deemed to be commercial participators. These are set out in Part II of the 1992 Act and introduced the phrase 'commercial participator' to the voluntary sector dictionary.

20.5 The 1992 Act provides that whenever goods or services are advertised or offered for sale, with an indication that some part of the proceeds is to be devoted to charity, there should be specified:

(a) the charity or charities that are to benefit; and

(b) the manner in which the sums they are to receive will be calculated.

20.6 After the 1992 Act came into force, it was criticised for appearing to allow very general statements to be made to the public. In particular, the Strategy Unit report published ahead of the 2006 Act[1] found that the statements about the extent to which a particular cause benefited were insufficiently specific, leading to a perceived lack of transparency. The Government accepted the proposals presented in the Strategy Unit report to provide for a more specific statement to be required. As a result, the 2006 Act made a number of amendments to the 1992 Act, which came into force on 1 April 2008.

20.7 In 2015, parliamentary concern about some fundraising techniques reported in the media prompted a further amendment to the 1992 Act by the 2016 Act: see **20.41**.

Guidance on the 1992 Act

20.8 The Cabinet Office has historically issued guidance on Part II of the 1992 Act, accompanied by examples of statements which it considers to be fully compliant with the legislation. At the time of going to print, the most recently published Cabinet Office guidance is 'Charitable Fundraising: Guidance on Part 2 of the Charities Act 1992' dated December 2008 ('the 2008 Guidance'), although this is now only available via the Government archive website.[2] However, Government committed to producing simplified guidance as part of its response to Lord Hodgson's review 2012 of charity law,[3] but at the time of writing new guidance has yet to be produced.

20.9 The Code of Fundraising Practice (see **18.19-18.20**) includes fundraising standards in relation to commercial participators and solicitation statements. The Charity Commission sets out both the legal requirements and what it considers to be good practice in relation to charity arrangements with commercial participators in its guidance 'Charity Fundraising: A Guide to Trustee Duties' (CC20) (June 2016 version). (The previous version of CC20 (May 2011) may also be useful to refer to for its more detailed commentary on commercial participator arrangements.)

WHAT IS A COMMERCIAL PARTICIPATOR?

20.10 A 'commercial participator' is, in essence, someone who encourages purchases of goods or services on the grounds that some of the proceeds will go to a charitable institution, or that a donation will be made to a charitable institution.

---

1 Prime Minister's Strategy Unit, *Private Action, Public Benefit*, September 2002.

2 http://webarchive.nationalarchives.gov.uk/20081230001423/http:/www.cabinetoffice.gov.uk/media/110668/amended%20guidance%20final.pdf.

3 Page 39 of the Government Responses to: (1) The Public Administration Select Committee's Third Report of 2013-14: The role of the Charity Commission and 'public benefit': Post-legislative scrutiny of the Charities Act 2006 and (2) Lord Hodgson's statutory review of the Charities Act 2006: Trusted and Independent, giving charity back to charities, September 2013.

20.11 Section 58(1) defines a commercial participator as:

> 'in relation to any charitable institution ... any person ... who–
>
> (a) carries on for gain a business other than a fund-raising business, but
> (b) in the course of that business, engages in any promotional venture in the course of which it is represented that charitable contributions are to be given to or applied for the benefit of the institution.'

20.12 A number of the expressions used in this definition are also defined in the 1992 Act. The definition of 'a charitable institution' and the definition of 'a fundraising business' have been considered (see **19.13–19.15** and **19.21–19.23**, respectively).

20.13 'Promotional venture' is defined by s 58(1) of the 1992 Act as 'any advertising or sales campaign or any other venture undertaken for promotional purposes'. 'Venture' has not, apparently, been defined in any statute or, remarkably, considered in any judgment. The Online Oxford English Dictionary defines a venture as: 'an enterprise of a business nature in which there is considerable risk of loss as well as chance of gain; a commercial speculation'.

20.14 'Represent' is defined by s 58(6) of the 1992 Act as meaning to represent:

> '... in any manner whatever, whether expressly or impliedly and whether done ... by speaking directly ... or ... by means of a statement published in any newspaper, film or radio or television programme, ... or otherwise ...'

20.15 'Charitable contributions' is defined by s 58(1) of the 1992 Act as meaning:

> 'in relation to any representation made by any commercial participator or other person ...—
>
> (a) the whole or part of—
>   (i) the consideration given for goods or services sold or supplied by him, or
>   (ii) any proceeds (other than such consideration) of a promotional venture undertaken by him, or
> (b) sums given by him by way of donation in connection with the sale or supply of any such goods or services (whether the amount of such sums is determined by reference to the value of any such goods or services or otherwise).'

20.16 'Services' is defined by s 58(9) of the 1992 Act as including:

> 'facilities, and in particular—
>
> (a) access to any premises or event;
> (b) membership of any organisation;
> (c) the provision of advertising space; and
> (d) the provision of any financial facilities;
>
> and references to the supply of services shall be construed accordingly.'

20.17 In debate at the committee stage of the Bill which became the 1992 Act, Viscount Astor, referring to the definition of commercial participator, stated:

> 'It is a wide definition drafted to ensure that a broad range of types of facility or service that may be offered by a person acting as a commercial participator are encompassed within the Bill.'[4]

EXEMPTIONS FROM THE DEFINITION OF COMMERCIAL PARTICIPATOR

Companies controlled by charitable institutions

20.18 Following an amendment to the 1992 Act by the Deregulation and Contracting Out Act 1994, the controls on commercial participators were further aligned with those on professional fundraisers by excluding 'a company connected with the institution' from the definition of a commercial participator. A company will be connected to an institution if one or more charitable institutions can exercise, or control the exercise of, the whole of the voting power at any general meeting of the company (s 58(5) of the 1992 Act). In a slight departure from the exclusion applying to professional fundraisers (see **19.33-19.34**), for the commercial participator exception the company must be connected to the particular charitable institution in relation to which the representation is made.

20.19 This means that if a trading company is wholly owned by charity A, all statements concerning charitable contributions made by that trading company to charity A are technically excluded from the scope of the controls in the 1992 Act. However, if the trading company is wholly owned by charity A but carries on activities for the benefit of charities B, C and D and makes representations concerning payments to charities B, C and D, then that trading company is a commercial participator in respect of its dealings with charities B, C and D because it is not a company 'connected' (as defined in s 58(5) of the 1992 Act) with charities B, C or D. This is supported by the Government in the 2008 Guidance, however the 2008 Guidance also goes a step further and states that for companies connected to a charitable institution:[5]

> '...even if the company is not required to comply with the requirements of Part 2, we would as a matter of good practice and of setting a good example, strongly recommend connected companies wherever possible to operate on a similar basis.'

The 2008 Guidance gives the example of a trading subsidiary making a statement in a charity shop by way of a notice at the till saying all profits are covenanted to the charity. The June 2016 version of the Charity Commission's guidance CC20 makes similar recommendations.[6]

20.20 Following increased scrutiny of charity fundraising arrangements in 2015-16, including the Charity Commission's report into Age UK,[7] there has been an increased emphasis in the media and from the Commission on transparency in fundraising arrangements with commercial partners. Therefore while the authors do not agree that the 1992 Act definition of 'commercial participator' catches a charity's wholly owned trading subsidiary, the authors' view is that, if it can be done easily, it is a good idea to

4 Public Bill Committee, Fifth Sitting, col 221 (11 December 1992).

5 Charitable Fundraising: Guidance on Part 2 of the Charities Act 1992, Annex A, Example 6.

6 See para 5.4 of CC20 'Charity Fundraising: A Guide to Trustee Duties'.

7 Charity Commission Case Report, Age UK, April 2016.

include a short statement explaining that the trading subsidiary is wholly owned by a charity as part of any fundraising carried out by the subsidiary for the charity.

Other exemptions

20.21 A person who represents that charitable contributions will be given for general charitable purposes, rather than to a specific charitable institution or institutions, will not be a commercial participator. They may, however, have to comply with certain other regulations, which are discussed further at paragraph 20.73–20.76.

20.22 By virtue of the definitions of 'commercial participator' and 'professional fundraiser' (s 58(1) of the 1992 Act), a person cannot be a commercial participator if they are a professional fundraiser (and vice versa).

20.23 There is currently no low value exemption to the definition of a commercial participator. As a result, a person may be a commercial participator and have to comply with the consequential requirements, even if they will only be donating £1 to the charitable institution. This was raised as a potential issue by the Charity Law Association, particularly for larger charities, in its submission to Lord Hodgson's 2012 review of charity law, however it was not included in Lord Hodgson's final recommendations. It would require primary legislation to amend the 1992 Act to provide for any such exemption.

EXAMPLES OF COMMERCIAL PARTICIPATORS

20.24 The 2008 Guidance provides a number of examples of arrangements involving commercial participators (see particularly para 3.2 and Appendix A). The paragraphs below deal with some common commercial participator arrangements as well as some grey areas. Note, even if you reach the conclusion that technically a commercial partner does not fall within the definition of 'commercial participator', the Charity Commission recommends in some situations that the charity takes steps to ensure transparency around the arrangements:[8]

> 'You should have effective systems in place so that, where products or services are sold through or in the name of the charity, the nature of the commercial partnership and the fee or commission received by the charity is clear and transparent.'

Broadcast appeals

20.25 At the time that the 1992 Act was originally proposed, much concern was expressed in the House of Lords' debates about broadcast appeals, where all the contributions go to the charitable institution on whose behalf the broadcast appeal is made. The appeals use building societies and credit card companies, which provide facilities for the receipt of donations and charge for their services. Are they commercial participators? Viscount Astor confirmed:[9]

---

8 Section 5.4, CC20, 'Charity Fundraising: A Guide to Trustee Duties' (June 2016 version) and Charity Commission Case Report, Age UK, April 2016.

9 Public Bill Committee, Fifth Sitting, col 222 (11 December 1992).

> 'the definition … of commercial participator [is] not intended to include commercial organisations providing services for broadcast appeals as part of their normal business.'

This clearly accords with the definition of commercial participator, which requires the participator to be engaged in a 'promotional venture' in the course of which it is represented that charitable contributions will be given. If a bank charges a charity for running pledge lines during a broadcast appeal, it is not engaging in a 'promotional venture' (as defined in s 58(1) of the 1992 Act).

20.26 On a separate but linked point, if a representation is made by a commercial participator as part of a broadcast appeal by radio or television programme and announces that payments in response to that representation may be made by debit or credit card, then the representation must include details of the donor's right to a refund of any payment of £100 or more under s 61(1) of the 1992 Act (s 60(4) of the 1992 Act): see 20.62.

Facilitating donations – online platforms

20.27 In the online environment, the 1992 Act can be a poor fit with the diverse and innovative means by which charities raise funds. Working out whether certain online 'fundraising' platforms or digital campaigns fall within the definition of either commercial participator or professional fundraiser can be difficult and there are grey areas. If the business behind the website/campaign is a fundraising business (as defined in s 58 of the 1992 Act) it will not, by definition, be a commercial participator. This is because of limb (a) of the definition of commercial participator. But if the business does not fall within the definition of fundraising business, then it will be a commercial participator if it is engaging in a 'promotional venture' in the course of which it is represented that money will be given to one or more charities. See 19.48 for discussion of when websites facilitating donations are caught within the definition of professional fundraiser.

Producer/retailer distinction

20.28 Suppose the manufacturer or producer of goods initiates the principal agreement with the charitable institution and then supplies the products to many different retailers. The items in question will bear the charitable institution's logo; does this make the retailer an implied commercial participator, given the breadth of the definition 'to represent' contained in s 58(5) of the 1992 Act? If the answer to this question were yes, the legislation would then require that the retailer had an agreement with the relevant charity. For example, Sainsbury's would need to have an agreement with every charity with which one of its suppliers has agreed to a cause-related marketing arrangement. This cannot be the intention of the legislation. The 2008 Guidance states that this area requires particularly careful consideration, but does not provide a blanket exemption that a retailer in such a situation could never be a commercial participator. Instead the 2008 Guidance states that the situation is:[10]

> 'likely to vary with individual circumstances … it may be helpful to ensure that any statement included on the product clearly identifies the producer (as opposed to the retailer) as the person having the relationship with the institution, to avoid drawing the retailer in, unnecessarily, as an additional commercial participator'.

---

[10] Charitable Fundraising: Guidance on Part 2 of the Charities Act 1992, Appendix A, Example 7.

In practice it is likely that any statement will identify the producer rather than the retailer, allowing the argument that the retailer is not making a representation, only the producer is doing so and so only the producer is a commercial participator. For example, if Flora has a deal with British Heart Foundation to give 10p per carton of margarine and makes such representation on its cartons which are then sold by Sainsbury's, only Flora and not Sainsbury's is the commercial participator. The position would be different if the product being sold was a Sainsbury's own brand product.

Christmas cards

20.29 The analysis at **20.28** often applies to Christmas cards which state they are 'sold in aid of XYZ Charity'. A common scenario is that XYZ Charity will establish a trading company, XYZ Trading Limited, to carry out the sale of Christmas cards. XYZ Charity will have licensed XYZ Trading Limited to use XYZ Charity's name on the card. XYZ Trading Limited will then sell the cards to a wholesaler, making a profit on the transaction. XYZ Trading Limited will, by Gift Aid, donate its profits to XYZ Charity. The wholesaler will supply the cards to a retailer, who will then sell the cards to the public. In this scenario it is arguable that neither the wholesaler nor the retailer are commercial participators, as the representation is made by XYZ Trading Limited. XYZ Trading Limited is not a commercial participator because it is controlled by XYZ Charity (see **20.18-20.20**). However the 2008 Guidance states at Appendix A, Example 8, that even if Christmas cards are sold directly to the public by a connected company, 'it is recommended that a similar statement to that required under Part II is made, for reasons of consistency, clarity and transparency'.

20.30 This is to be distinguished from the position where the retailer itself pays for the production costs of the cards and agrees to pay the charitable institution a percentage of its profits on the sales of the cards, in which case the retailer would be most likely to be a commercial participator.

Use of a charitable institution's logo

20.31 A potential area of uncertainty is where a charitable institution's logo appears on a product but no express statement is made that the charitable institution will benefit from the sale of that product. For example, if the logo of a large health charity were to appear on a packet of breakfast cereal, the logo alone may be sufficient to constitute an implied representation that charitable contributions were being made to the charitable institution, even without an express statement. (A slightly different scenario was the subject of a Charity Commission case report in April 2016 relating to Age UK and a commercial partnership with E.ON.) Parties entering into any such arrangement would need to consider the likely interpretation by the public of the inclusion of the logo, particularly if the logo is being placed on a product that is unrelated to the work of the charitable institution. See also **20.24** for Charity Commission recommendations where products or services are sold through or in the name of a charity, even if they fall short of being a commercial participator agreement.

Charity of the year arrangements and similar

20.32 A corporate entity will not necessarily be a commercial participator in relation to a charitable institution that it has named as its charity of the year. Whether or not it is a commercial participator is likely to depend on how, and to what extent, it is publicising the arrangement and whether this amounts to a 'promotional venture'. A similar analysis may be necessary in relation to a corporate sponsor that donates to a charity and then publicises these donations on their website. Again see **20.24** for Charity Commission recommendations which may apply even if these arrangements do not technically trigger the 'commercial participator' obligations.

Affinity cards

20.33 Historically, affinity cards have been a popular way for financial institutions to work with charities, and although they are less common today, there are still many schemes available on the market. Under this type of arrangement, banks issue credit cards dedicated to a particular charity and donate a percentage of the customer's monthly payments to a charity. Clearly, in this situation, the bank is:

(a) engaging in a business (banking) which is not a fundraising business; but
(b) in the course of that, is engaging in a promotional venture in which it is representing that a percentage of the consideration paid for the services provided by the bank will go to a charitable institution.

Hence, the bank is a commercial participator. This is made clear by s 58(9)(d) of the 1992 Act, where the definition of 'services' includes 'the provision of any financial facilities'.

Other examples of commercial participators

20.34 Other examples of commercial participators include the following.

(a) The maker of a product who prints a charity's logo on the product and states:

> '1p will go to XYZ charity for each packet sold.'

(b) The organiser of an event who represents that money from the event will be donated to a charitable institution.
(c) A travel company which offers to pay one per cent of the price of a holiday to a named charitable institution.

WHAT ARE THE CONSEQUENCES OF BEING A COMMERCIAL PARTICIPATOR?

20.35 Two main requirements are placed on a person who is deemed to be a commercial participator:

- the commercial participator must have entered into a written agreement, which meets certain minimum requirements, with the charitable institution, or institutions, in relation to which it is making the relevant representation (s 59 of the 1992 Act) – see **20.37-20.41**; and
- the representation itself must be accompanied by a statement that satisfies the requirements of s 60(3) of the 1992 Act – see **20.51-20.65**.

The obligations under the 1992 Act fall directly on the commercial participator and the charitable institution is not required under the 1992 Act to ensure that the commercial participator is observing the requirements. The exception to this is that, under s 60(9) of the 1992 Act, if a breach of any of ss 60(1)-(5) of the 1992 Act is due to the act or default of some other person, that person shall be guilty of an offence. Therefore if, for example, the charitable institution provided the commercial participator with any incorrect information, which led to the commercial participator failing to satisfy the statement requirements of s 60(3), the charitable institution itself could also be liable.

20.36 Notwithstanding the above, the Commission has increasingly moved to a position of expecting charities to take steps to monitor and ensure compliance by commercial participators, and has publicly criticised trustees for failing to ensure that the relevant legal requirements were met.[11] See also the commentary on the likely implications of failing to comply with the legislation at **19.50** and **19.91**.

SECTION 59 AGREEMENTS

20.37 Section 59(2) of the 1992 Act states that it is unlawful for a commercial participator to represent that charitable contributions are to be given to a charitable institution 'unless he does so in accordance with an agreement with the institution satisfying the prescribed requirements'.

Minimum legal requirements

20.38 The prescribed requirements are set out in s 59(7)-(8) and in the Charitable Institutions (Fund-Raising) Regulations 1994 (SI 1994/3024) ('the 1994 Regulations') which are reproduced at Appendix 10 of this book. Regulation 3 states that the agreement between a charitable institution and commercial participator required by s 59(2) of the 1992 Act has to be in writing and has to be signed by or on behalf of the charitable institution and the commercial participator.

20.39 The agreement has to specify:

(a) the name and address of each of the parties to the agreement;
(b) the date on which the agreement was signed by or on behalf of each of those parties;
(c) the period for which the agreement is to subsist;
(d) any terms relating to the termination of the agreement prior to the date on which that period expires; and
(e) any terms relating to the variation of the agreement during that period.

20.40 The agreement must also:

(a) contain a statement of its principal objectives and the methods to be used in pursuit of those objectives;
(b) contain provision as to the manner in which are to be determined:

---

11 Charity Commission, Operational Compliance Report, Wildlife Rescue Sanctuaries (1118457), published 29 January 2014.

(i) if there is more than one charitable institution party to the agreement, the proportion in which the institutions which are so party are respectively to benefit under the agreement; and
(ii) the proportion of the consideration given for goods or services sold or supplied by the commercial participator or of any other proceeds of a promotional venture undertaken by him, which is to be given to or applied for the benefit of the charitable institution; or
(iii) the sums by way of donations by the commercial participator in connection with the sale or supply of any goods or services sold or supplied by him which are to be so given or applied;

as the case may require; and

(c) contain provision as to any amount by way of remuneration or expenses which the commercial participator is to be entitled to receive in respect of things done by him in pursuance of the agreement and the manner in which any such amount is to be determined;

(d) specify any voluntary scheme for regulating fundraising, or any voluntary standard of fundraising, that the commercial participator undertakes to be bound by for the purposes of the agreement;

(e) specify how the commercial participator is to protect vulnerable people and other members of the public from:
- unreasonable intrusion on a person's privacy;
- unreasonably persistent fundraising;
- placing undue pressure on a person to donate;

in the course of, or in connection with, the activities to which the agreement relates;

(f) specify arrangements enabling the charity to monitor compliance with s 59(2) by reference to the agreement.

20.41 The requirements mentioned at 20.40(d)-(f) were introduced into the 1992 Act by the 2016 Act largely in response to media and Parliamentary concerns about certain fundraising techniques (see **18.3**). At the time of writing, these new requirements are not yet in force but they will come into force on 1 November 2016. At the time of writing it is not clear to what extent they will apply to agreements made before that date. In the debates on the 2016 Act in the House of Lords, the Government Minister Lord Bridges of Headley commented that the requirements would allow both charities and fundraisers to be clear and upfront about what would be done in the charity's name, and about their respective responsibilities.[12] While it is of course possible the actions of a commercial participator could amount to an 'unreasonable intrusion', be 'unreasonably persistent' or constitute 'undue pressure', it is difficult to immediately see these sorts of problems arising from a classic 5p per can of beans promotion. Where there are more likely to be problems are where a charity shares its membership list say with a corporate, so that the corporate can market directly to the charity's supporters. For commentary on how the terms 'unreasonable intrusion', 'unreasonably persistent' and 'undue pressure' are likely to be interpreted, see **19.55**.

20.42 The list above is the legal minimum and there are likely to be many other aspects of the relationship which should be included in the agreement.

---

12 Hansard, HL Deb, col 929 (20 July 2015).

20.43 As mentioned at 18.21 and 21.71, charities which are required to have their accounts audited must include in their trustees' annual report certain key information about the charity's dealings with commercial participators.

Recommended additional safeguards

20.44 Although the protection afforded by the 1994 Regulations for charitable institutions contracting with commercial participators is considerable, nonetheless charitable institutions should also consider whether or not there are other clauses that should be inserted in such a contract to safeguard their best interests.

20.45 In addition to the requirements laid down by the 1994 Regulations, a charity would usually seek clauses such as:

(a) a warranty by the commercial participator that neither it nor any of its associated companies will at any time during the duration of the agreement do anything which could bring the reputation of the charity into disrepute;

(b) a termination clause allowing the charity to terminate the agreement (and particularly any licence of the charity's name and logo) immediately, should, in its opinion, its name be brought into disrepute or if the commercial participator is in material breach of any of the terms of the agreement;

(c) a term relating to what happens to stock bearing the charity's logo in the event of early termination of the agreement due to its breach by the commercial participator;

(d) strict controls on the use of the charity's name and logo and recognition of its copyright and any other intellectual property; and

(e) if the charity's income is above the audit threshold, a requirement to provide the charity with the information needed for the trustees' annual report (see **20.71**) including:
   (i) any failure by the commercial participator to comply with any voluntary scheme or standard; and
   (ii) the number of complaints received by the commercial participator.

20.46 A charity might also wish to seek other clauses such as:

(a) a warranty that the price of the commercial participator's goods or services will remain competitive in the marketplace;

(b) an agreement that the commercial participator will not enter into a similar arrangement with any other organisation operating in the same field as the charity for the duration of the agreement;

(c) an indemnity in respect of any losses or damage suffered by the charity as a result of any action by the commercial participator; and

(d) an obligation on the commercial participator to segregate moneys due to the charitable institution in a separate bank account, preferably marked with the name of the charity so that, should the commercial participator go into liquidation, the moneys in the account will be deemed to be trust moneys and not part of the general assets of the commercial participator available for distribution to the general body of its creditors.

20.47 The Charity Commission also advises that 'proper' due diligence checks are carried out on a proposed commercial participator, looking at its 'solvency, integrity and reputation' and whether the arrangement is consistent with the charity's values.[13]

Tax and VAT treatment of commercial participator agreements

20.48 Consideration will need to be given to the potential tax treatment of any payments made by a commercial participator to a charitable institution. It is possible that these may be treated by HMRC as taxable profits, in which case corporation or income tax (depending on how the charity is constituted) could be levied on such profits. Any such payments may also be subject to VAT. Such tax considerations may influence the structure of the agreement with the commercial participator, which may include making the charity's trading subsidiary a party to the agreement, and specific tax advice should be taken in respect of this.

Consequences of failure to comply with s 59

20.49 If a commercial participator seeks to represent that charitable contributions are to be given to a charitable institution without the benefit of a s 59 agreement complying with the prescribed requirements, or there is an agreement but it does not satisfy those requirements, then any such agreement is unenforceable by the commercial participator without the approval of the High Court or county court. In addition, if the agreement provides for the commercial participator to receive remuneration or expenses, under s 59(5) these will not be payable under a defective agreement until the agreement satisfies the prescribed requirements or a court orders that the commercial participator may be paid.

20.50 This provision is rarely of much use to charitable institutions because money will normally pass from the commercial participator to the charitable institution (eg '5p per bottle of water sold goes to XYZ Charity') rather than vice versa. In this scenario, sales have been made by the commercial participator with a proportion of sales income being forwarded to the charity. It is only where moneys are going from the charitable institution to the commercial participator that the charitable institution could refuse to pay until the court has ordered it to do so or the agreement has been rectified so as to ensure that it complies with the prescribed requirements. It is therefore difficult to envisage commercial circumstances where this provision could be of much use to charitable institutions. It should be noted that a defective agreement is only unenforceable against the charitable institution; in the scenario above, the commercial participator could not refuse to pay the 5p per bottle on the basis that the agreement was defective.

SECTION 60 STATEMENTS

20.51 Section 60(3) of the 1992 Act makes similar provisions, in terms of statements to be made by commercial participators, as s 60(1) and (2) makes for professional fundraisers (see **19.62-19.81**).

20.52 Section 60(3) (as amended by the 2006 Act) provides that where any representation is made by a commercial participator to the effect that charitable

---

13 Section 5.3, CC20, 'Charity Fundraising: A Guide to Trustee Duties' (June 2016 version).

contributions are to be given to or applied for the benefit of one or more particular charitable institutions the representation shall be accompanied by a statement clearly indicating:

> '(a) the name or names of the institution or institutions concerned;
> (b) if there is more than one institution concerned, the proportions in which the institutions are respectively to benefit; and
> (c) the notifiable amount of whichever of the following sums is applicable in the circumstances—
> (i) the sum representing so much of the consideration given for goods or services sold or supplied by him as is to be given to or applied for the benefit of the institution or institutions concerned,
> (ii) the sum representing so much of any other proceeds of a promotional venture undertaken by him as is to be so given or applied, or
> (iii) the sum of the donations by him in connection with the sale or supply of any such goods or services which are to be so given or supplied.'

What is the 'notifiable amount'?

20.53 In response to concerns that the statements made in relation to representations were not sufficiently informative as to allow the public to make an informed judgement of the benefits to a charitable institution, the 2006 Act introduced the concept of a 'notifiable amount'. Since this amendment came into force on 1 April 2008, commercial participators have had to include in their statements the notifiable amount of charitable contributions to be given to or applied for the benefit of those institutions. Section 60(3A) (inserted by the 2006 Act) provides that the reference to 'notifiable amount' is a reference:

> '(a) to the actual amount of the remuneration or sum, if that is known at the time when the statement is made; and
> (b) otherwise to the estimated amount of the remuneration or sum, calculated as accurately as is reasonably possible in the circumstances.'

20.54 The result of sections 60(3) and 60(3A) of the 1992 Act mean that a commercial participator is obliged to state either:

- the amount of the price paid for each product or service by the public, which will be given to the charitable institution (which may be expressed as a percentage of the overall price or a precise amount);
- the actual amount that he intends to give to the charity; or
- if the actual amount is not known at the time, an estimate, to be calculated accurately (insofar as that is reasonably possible), of such amount.

This ensures that commercial participators are transparent about their dealings with charities. For example, a statement such as '20% of the profit made on sale of this item' would not be sufficient. A commercial participator would need to estimate their profit and then put that figure in the statement. Similarly, if a company wished to donate 10% of their total profits for a particular month, the statement would need to include an estimate of the amount that will be actually donated at the end of the month.

20.55 Where an estimated figure is used, the 2008 Guidance is silent as to whether a commercial participator should make it clear that the figure used is an estimate. The Guidance is also silent as to whether commercial participators should keep estimated figures under review. (By comparison, the 2008 Guidance covers both these points in relation to professional fundraisers: see **19.74-19.75**.)

Trading subsidiaries

20.56 For tax reasons, payments from a commercial participator to a charity are often routed all or in part via the charity's trading subsidiary. In such situations, it is not clear how the s 60 statement should be worded. Neither the 1992 Act nor the 2008 Guidance offer any direction on this.[14] For example, does the statement need to mention that payment is being made via the trading subsidiary? And if the statement does mention the trading subsidiary, is it enough to state how much is paid to the subsidiary or does the statement need to say how much the charity will actually receive?

20.57 The requirement in s 60(3) is phrased as a requirement to state how much 'is to be given or applied for the benefit of the institution or institutions concerned'. The authors' view is therefore that:

- there is no requirement to mention that money is being routed through a trading subsidiary; and
- a statement along the lines 'Charity will receive Xp from the sale of each tin of beans' is compliant provided the charity will actually receive that amount from the trading subsidiary.

In some cases, a trading subsidiary will pass all money straight through to the charity, but in others, the charity is likely to receive only a proportion of what was paid to the subsidiary so the amount in the statement needs to be adjusted accordingly. Any person involved in calculating the amount to include in such a statement should be aware of the, in theory, potential criminal liability under s 60(9) – see **20.35** although neither the authors nor the Commission are aware of any prosecutions of this kind.

20.58 Statements that are more commonly seen in practice take the form of 'Xp per item is paid to XYZ Trading Limited which gives all its taxable profits to XYZ a registered charity'. There must be an argument as to whether or not a payment made to a trading company is, to quote s 60(3)(c)(i), 'given to or applied for the benefit of the institution or institutions concerned'. The best argument is that the payment being made to the trading company is 'applied' for the benefit of the institution, since the trading company gives its profits to the charity. However:

- so far as the authors are aware, there is no Cabinet Office or Charity Commission commentary on this interpretation; and
- when drafting any statement along these lines, consideration needs to be given to whether the trading subsidiary does in fact pay all its taxable profits each year to the charity.[15]

These two options are perhaps the best compromise that can be made in order to comply with the spirit of the 1992 Act (as amended by the 2006 Act) and to ensure that the charity's affairs are structured in the most tax-efficient manner.

---

14 Although the 2008 Guidance does include one example statement which mentions a charity's trading subsidiary, this is in relation to a different scenario – see **20.29** above.

15 Under company law a trading subsidiary may not pay more than its accounting profits to its parent charity each year. Accounting profits may be lower than taxable profits.

Examples of a s 60(3) statement

20.59 The sample statements below are all examples of types of statement that could be used in order to comply with s 60(3) of the 1992 Act. Provided that the requirements are complied with, there is no restriction on the commercial participator including any further information in their statement.

In a shop

20.60 The statement should take the form:

> Five per cent of the purchase price of this bottle will be donated to XYZ charity.

or

> In respect of each bottle sold, five pence will be donated to XYZ charity.

Each of these statements mirror the example statements included at Annex B of the 2008 Guidance.

A statement made on radio or TV

20.61 In a broadcast concerning the sale of goods (eg a lawnmower), the statement should take the form:

> Five per cent of the price you pay for your lawnmower will be donated to XYZ charity. If you pay for goods which cost more than £100 by credit or debit card you have the right to cancel your purchase within seven days of this broadcast.

or

> ABC Company will donate 10% of all profits made on the sale of lawnmowers this bank holiday Saturday, Sunday and Monday to XYZ charity. This is expected to be at least £Y. If you pay for goods which cost more than £100 by credit or debit card you have the right to cancel your purchase within seven days of this broadcast.

Each of these statements mirror the example statements included at Annex B of the 2008 Guidance.

20.62 Both sample statements reflect the fact that under s 61(1) of the 1992 Act a donation of £100 or more made by credit or debit card in response to a s 60(3) representation made in the course of a radio or telephone programme can be cancelled by the donor within seven days, and under s 60(4) full details of this right must be included in the s 60(3) statement. Note that under s 61(4)(b) where goods have been purchased, any right to cancel and have a refund under s 61(1) is conditional upon restitution being made by the purchaser of the goods in question.

Telephone sales

20.63 If a representation under s 60(3) is made by telephone, the commercial participator is obliged, within seven days of any payment of £100 or more to the commercial participator, to give any person making a payment in response to the representation a written s 60(3) statement. Under s 61(2) if a donor makes, or agrees to make, a payment of £100 or more in response to a telephone representation, the donor has a right to a refund, or to cancel the agreement. The s 60(3) statement must give details of this right, under s 60(4). The right to a refund or to cancel the agreement arises within seven days of the statement.

A statement regarding more than one charitable institution

20.64 If charitable contributions are to be made to more than one charitable institution, the statement should take the form:

> ABC Company will donate 20% of the profit from this promotional venture to XYZ Charity and FGH Charity in equal proportion. The total donation to both of these charities is expected to be £Y.

This statement mirrors an example statement included at Annex B of the 2008 Guidance.

A statement with varying notifiable amounts

20.65 The 2008 Guidance recognises that it may be commercially reasonable for a commercial participator to make varying donations to the charity depending on how many items are sold or services are bought. A statement in relation to such a situation should take the form:

> ABC Company will donate 10p to XYZ Charity as a result of this promotion for the first 10,000 bags of popcorn sold, and a further 5p for each additional bag of popcorn sold.

This statement mirrors an example statement included at Annex B of the 2008 Guidance.

CRIMINAL SANCTIONS FOR BREACH OF S 60

20.66 Just as the professional fundraiser who breaches s 60(1)–(5) commits a criminal offence, so also does the commercial participator, with scope for an unlimited fine. The same points concerning the criminal sanctions for breaching s 60 which apply to professional fundraisers also apply to commercial participators (see **19.98-19.101**).

20.67 It should be noted that although the criminal sanctions largely fall on the commercial participator, others can be caught too – under s 60(9) anyone whose act or default leads to another committing the offence of non-compliance also commits an offence. See **20.35** and **20.57** for how this could lead (in theory) to criminal liability for anyone who, say, provides a commercial participator with incorrect figures to include in the commercial participator statement.

20.68 Note, however, that there has been little, if any, enforcement of these provisions: see 20.79.

FURTHER REQUIREMENTS UNDER THE 1994 REGULATIONS AND THE 2011 ACT

20.69 Under reg 5, a commercial participator must, on request and at all reasonable times, make available to any charitable institution which is a party to an agreement with that commercial participator any books, documents or other records, however kept, which relate to the institution and are kept for the purposes of the agreement. These records have to be kept in legible form. If a charity's trading subsidiary is also made a party to the agreement, a clause should be inserted into that agreement expressly providing that the trading subsidiary will have the benefit of reg 5.

20.70 Under reg 6, any money due to the charitable institution from a commercial participator has to be paid over as soon as is reasonably practicable after its receipt 'unless he has a reasonable excuse' and 'in any event not later than the expiration of 28 days after that receipt or such other period as may be agreed with the institution'. Payment has to be made to the charitable institution or into a bank account controlled by it. If payments are to be made to the charity's trading subsidiary instead of the charity due to tax considerations (see **20.48**), then this may be a problem as those moneys will usually be held until virtually the year end before profits (if any) are paid out by Gift Aid to the charity. In order to protect the commercial participator, it is suggested that the agreement between the trading company and the commercial participator should make it clear that the charity accepts that payments will be made by the commercial participator to the trading company and that the profits of the trading company are only paid up at certain specified intervals.

20.71 Breaches of regs 5 and 6 are criminal offences which give rise to a maximum fine not exceeding level two on the standard scale. At the time of writing this is set at £500 per offence.

20.72 As mentioned at **20.43** and **21.71**, charities which are required to have their accounts audited must include details about their arrangements with commercial participators in their annual reports.[16]

QUASI-COMMERCIAL PARTICIPATORS

20.73 A person is not a commercial participator if they seek to sell goods or services coupled with the inducement that part of the proceeds will go to a general charitable cause, even if they make representations to that end, eg 'to relieve poverty in the Third World'. This is different from the position in relation to professional fundraisers (see **19.63**).

20.74 However, the 1994 Regulations provide for some controls over such activities. Regulation 7 applies to 'any person who carries on for gain a business other than a fund-raising business' and who 'engages in any promotional venture in the course of which it is represented that charitable contributions are to be applied for charitable, benevolent or philanthropic purposes of any description (rather than for the benefit of one or more particular charitable institutions)'. In this book, such persons are called quasi-commercial participators.

---

[16] Section 162A of the 2011 Act, as amended by the 2016 Act.

20.75 For example, the owner of a pizza restaurant states '£1 per pizza will be sent to the victims of the Tsunami'. In these circumstances, by reg 7(2), as amended by The Charitable Institutions (Fund-Raising) (Amendment) Regulations 2009, which introduced the concept of a notifiable amount in line with the 2006 Act, the quasi-commercial participator has to ensure that the representation is accompanied by a statement clearly indicating:

(a) the fact that charitable contributions are to be applied for those purposes and not for the benefit of any particular charitable institution;

(b) the notifiable amount of whichever of the following sums is applicable in the circumstances:
   (i) the sum representing so much of the consideration given for goods or services sold or supplied by him as is to be applied for those purposes;
   (ii) the sum representing so much of any other proceeds of a promotional venture undertaken by him as is to be so applied; or
   (iii) the sum of the donations by him in connection with the sale or supply of any such goods or services which are to be so applied, and

(c) the method by which it is to be determined how the charitable contributions referred to in the representation are to be distributed between different charitable institutions.

Here 'notifiable amount' is a reference:

(i) to the actual amount of the sum, if that is known at the time when the statement is made; and

(ii) otherwise to the estimated amount of the sum, calculated as accurately as is reasonably possible in the circumstances.

20.76 An appropriate statement would be:

> £1 per pizza sold will be applied for the benefit of children in Bosnia and not for the benefit of a particular charitable institution. The proprietor of the restaurant will decide which charitable institutions will be supported.

Breach of reg 7(2) is a criminal offence but, as this is laid down by statutory instrument and not by primary legislation, the maximum fine must not exceed level two on the standard scale which is set at £500 at the time of writing.

SECTION 75

20.77 Under s 75 where any offence under the 1992 Act (ie those areas dealt with in Chapters 19 and 20) is committed by a body corporate and is proved to have been committed with the consent or connivance of, or to be attributable to any neglect on the part of, any director, manager, secretary or other similar officer of the body corporate, or any person who was purporting to act in any such capacity, he as well as the body corporate shall be guilty of that offence and shall be liable to be proceeded against and be punished accordingly.

20.78 This means that if, for example, a company which was a commercial participator acted in breach of Part II, then possibly the directors of that company could also be made personally liable under s 75.

ENFORCEMENT

20.79 Instances of enforcement action taken against commercial participators are rare. Neither the authors nor the Charity Commission are aware of any prosecutions of commercial participators under the 1992 Act for failure to make the correct solicitation statement, nor were there any FRSB adjudications against commercial participators. There have however been a few rare instances of action taken by the Commission and Government departments in relation to commercial participators. For example:

- In 2004, a Charity Commission inquiry examined the charity Childwatch's relationship with the commercial participator Yellow Partnership Limited ('YPL'). YPL's business model was to sell advertising space in planners and other publications, representing that a proportion of the money would go to Childwatch. The inquiry considered in particular the solicitation statement read out during telephone calls made by YPL staff. The Commission concluded that YPL failed to comply with the requirements in s 60(3), to give specific information to their customers on what proportion of payments made would go to the charity. There were also issues surrounding the timing of the statement which was read out at the end of the call after the contract was made. Following the inquiry, YPL changed the timing of the statement and Childwatch negotiated a new agreement with them.
- In 2010, the Insolvency Service also took action against YPL. It obtained court orders banning the three directors responsible for running YPL from acting as company directors for a period of 8 years. The Insolvency Service's public interest unit decided that the directors (as individuals – see **20.77-20.78**) had breached the 1992 Act by failing to inform customers of the proportion of the fee which would be donated to charity, to the extent that some customers believed that the companies were themselves charities, and that the full fee was therefore a donation to charity.
- In an earlier case in 2002, the then Department for Trade and Industry petitioned for the winding up of a company carrying out misleading fundraising practices.[17] The court agreed to wind up two companies which were essentially operating commercial participator arrangements in which the average return for the charities was around 3.7%. The companies were ringing businesses asking them to support named charities by paying for advertising in publications such as diaries and wall planners. The judge held that the scripts were likely to mislead advertisers, that the directors of the company were aware of that, and that that was sufficiently contrary to the public interest to require the companies to be wound up.
- More recently, in April 2016, the Charity Commission published a case report about a commercial partnership between Age UK and E.ON. The relationship was not categorised by the Commission as being that of a commercial participator but nevertheless the Commission made a number of recommendations around transparency (see **20.24**).

---

17 The *Re Derek Colins Associates* case [2002] All ER (D) 474.

It remains to be seen whether the new Fundraising Regulator (see Chapter 18) will have within its remit taking action against commercial participators. At this stage it seems more likely that charities which fail to ensure proper arrangements are in place with commercial participators could find themselves on the receiving end of regulatory action from the Charity Commission.

SCOTLAND

20.80 The 1992 Act only applies to activities in England and Wales. Part 2 of the Charities and Trustee Investment (Scotland) Act 2005 outlines the requirements in relation to professional fundraisers and commercial participators in Scotland. Requirements for certain types of fundraising for charitable or benevolent purposes in Scotland are set out in the Charities and Benevolent Fundraising (Scotland) Regulations 2009 ('the Scottish Regulations'). The Office of the Scottish Charity Regulator has issued guidance on complying with the Regulations.[18]

20.81 The Scottish Regulations largely mirror the system of regulation in England and Wales for 'commercial participators'. Three significant differences in Scotland are:

- If a commercial participator makes the solicitation statement orally, they must also state that the details of the remuneration/amount going to the charity is available in writing if the person wants to see it (if made by telephone, the information must be sent in writing if the person requests it).
- The definition of notifiable amount is slightly different in Scotland when dealing with an estimated amount. In England and Wales, the 1992 Act (as amended by the 2006 Act) requires an estimated amount to be calculated 'as reasonably as possible in the circumstances'. By contrast, the Scottish Regulations just refer to 'the estimated amount' so there appears to be no similar requirement to calculate it 'reasonably'.
- A commercial participator has to pass on funds to the charitable institution or benevolent body as soon as reasonably practicable and in any event within 28 days of receipt. There is no exception where there is a reasonable excuse and the parties cannot contract out of the requirement.

NORTHERN IRELAND

20.82 The Charities Act (Northern Ireland) 2008 includes provisions similar to those which apply in England and Wales; however, at the time of writing, these are not in force. In the meantime, existing Northern Ireland legislation applying to public collections, house-to-house collections, gaming and lotteries may apply.

THE FUTURE – LORD HODGSON'S REVIEW

20.83 The existing law in relation to commercial participators fell within the scope of Lord Hodgson's 2012 review of charity law. In his report,[19] Lord Hodgson found that no significant change to the law was required however, simpler guidance about how to

---

18 www.oscr.org.uk.

19 *Trusted and Independent*, ch 8, recommendations (i)(9).

comply with the various legal requirements was needed. In its response to Lord Hodgson's review,[20] the Government accepted this recommendation and said that it would work with the charity sector and other partners to develop simple guidance. As mentioned at 20.8, at the time of writing no new guidance has been issued.

20.84 Lord Hodgson also picked up some technical amendments suggested by the Charity Law Association, being:

- the reference in s 60 to 'donations' should be replaced with 'payments'[21] and
- Regulation 6 of the 1994 Regulations should be amended to make it clear that references there to payment to the charitable institution include payment to a connected company of the charitable institution where this is agreed with that institution.[22]

However, as mentioned at 20.23, disappointingly he did not pick up the Charity Law Association's suggestion that there should be a low value exemption for commercial participators (below which it would not be necessary to comply with various requirements) to correspond with the exemption which exists for professional fundraisers.

---

20 Government Responses to: (1) The Public Administration Select Committee's Third Report of 2013-14: The role of the Charity Commission and 'public benefit': Post-legislative scrutiny of the Charities Act 2006 and (2) Lord Hodgson's statutory review of the Charities Act 2006: Trusted and Independent, Giving charity back to charities, September 2013.

21 *Trusted and Independent*, Appendix A, recommendation 36.

22 *Trusted and Independent*, Appendix A, recommendation 37.

CHAPTER 21

CHARITY ACCOUNTS

INTRODUCTION

21.1 The rules on charity accounting and reporting have changed significantly over the years. Radical changes were introduced by the 1992 Act in order to improve the quality of charity accounts and to establish systems for supplying information to the Commission on a regular basis. Further amendments were made by the 2006 Act, including more rigorous obligations regarding group accounting and an increase in the audit threshold, which was increased again in 2015. In 2009 differences in thresholds for charitable companies and other types of charity were largely eliminated, meaning that for the most part a single proportionate regime now applies to registered charities, with different requirements according to size and particular circumstances.

21.2 The legislative framework for charity accounting is set out in Part 8 of the 2011 Act, although much of the detail regarding the content of accounts and reports, and examination of accounts, is left to regulations.

21.3 Charity accounting is also significantly influenced by the Statement of Recommended Practice, known as the charity SORP, issued by the Charity Commission and OSCR under the authority of the Financial Reporting Council. The SORP, which sets out detailed requirements and guidelines regarding the format and content of the accounts and trustees' annual report, is binding on charities which prepare accruals accounts (see **21.23-21.27**).

21.4 For financial years commencing before 1 January 2015 the 2005 SORP applied. Two new SORPs, SORP 2015 FRSSE (for smaller charities) and SORP 2015 FRS 102 were introduced for financial years commencing on or after 1 January 2015. For financial years commencing on or after 1 January 2016 the SORP 2015 FRSSE has been withdrawn, and changes have been made to the SORP 2015 FRS 102. These reflect changes to audit thresholds and changes to the body of accounting standards and guidance published by the UK Accounting Standards Board, known as the Generally Accepted Accounting Practice in the UK, or UK GAAP.[1] In the course of 2016 the Commission and OSCR published an invitation to suggest improvements to the SORP. Certain types of charity (eg housing associations) may be obliged to follow a more specific SORP (such as the Housing SORP).

21.5 The detailed requirements of the SORP are outside the scope of this book: for more information see www.gov.uk/government/organisations/charity-commission and www.charitysorp.org.

---

1 For more information see www.charitysorp.org.

21.6 At the time of writing, the main regulations which affect charity accounting are the Charities (Accounts and Reports) Regulations 2008 (SI 2008/629) ('the 2008 Regulations'). It had been expected that the 2008 Regulations would be replaced in the course of 2015, not least because they refer to the 2005 SORP, which has now been replaced, but at the time of writing no new regulations had been issued.[2] This chapter therefore includes references to the relevant provisions of the 2008 Regulations.

21.7 Lord Hodgson's 2012 review of charity law considered charity accounting, reporting and audit procedures. He concluded that the current thresholds should remain unchanged, subject to a recommendation that the audit threshold should be increased, which was subsequently implemented.[3] Another recommendation was that thought should be given to the costs, benefits and logistics of introducing fines for the late filing of accounts and annual returns with the Commission.[4]

21.8 This chapter explores the regime for charity accounting and reporting set out in the 2011 Act, including:

- the keeping and preservation of accounting records;
- the requirements to prepare annual reports and accounts and to have them audited or examined;
- the rules on filing reports and accounts with the Commission;
- the obligation to file annual returns with the Commission; and
- the particular rules which apply to group accounts.

The requirements vary depending on the legal form of the charity, its size, and whether or not it is registered with the Commission. Summary tables setting out the thresholds and requirements for charities which do not need group accounts appear at the end of this chapter.

21.9 This chapter deals mainly with the accounting and reporting requirements under charity law, and obligations to file documents and information with the Commission. Depending on their legal form and the nature of their work, charities may be subject to additional requirements, including obligations to file information with different regulators. Charitable companies, for example, must file reports, accounts and confirmation statements with Companies House. Charitable community benefit societies (which are, at the time of writing, exempt charities) are subject to requirements to file accounts and annual returns with the Financial Conduct Authority. Other exempt charities are generally subject to specific requirements: for example academy trusts are subject to strict financial and audit requirements under the Academies Financial Handbook, imposed via their funding agreement with Government.

21.10 Note that different requirements apply to charities in Scotland and Northern Ireland: see Chapter 23.

---

2 It likely that new regulations will be issued for consultation before they take effect. The Commission has issued guidance for charities, auditors and independent examiners on how to deal with inconsistencies between the 2008 Regulations and the requirements reflected in the 2015 SORPs. At the time of writing the guidance is *Charity Reporting and Accounting: The Essentials March 2015, section 8*.

3 See **21.35-21.38**.

4 *Trusted and Independent*, ch 6, recommendation 17. Government Response, p 33.

DEFINITIONS

21.11 Many of the accounting and reporting obligations refer to a charity's 'financial year'. References to a 'financial year' in the 2011 Act are to be interpreted in accordance with regulations made under s 132(3) (see **21.23–21.24**: at the time of writing the detail appears in reg 3 of the 2008 Regulations). In the case of charitable companies, 'financial year' is interpreted in accordance with s 390 of the Companies Act 2006.[5] Financial years are determined by reference to the charity's accounting reference date: the relevant provisions of the 2008 Regulations and the Companies Act 2006 set out how the accounting reference date may be determined and adjusted.

21.12 The term 'gross income', which is also used throughout the relevant provisions of the 2011 Act, is defined in s 353(1) of the 2011 Act: '"gross income", in relation to a charity, means its gross recorded income from all sources including special trusts'.

ACCOUNTING RECORDS

21.13 All charities are required to keep and preserve accounting records.

Charities other than charitable companies and exempt charities

21.14 The requirements for all charities other than charitable companies and exempt charities are set out in ss 130 and 131 of the 2011 Act.

21.15 Section 130 requires charity trustees to ensure that accounting records are kept which are sufficient to show and explain all the charity's transactions, and which are such as to:

(a) disclose at any time, with reasonable accuracy, the financial position of the charity at that time; and

(b) enable the trustees to ensure that any statements of accounts required by the 2011 Act comply with the statutory requirements.

The records must contain entries showing from day to day all sums received and expended, and the matters in respect of which the receipt and expenditure took place and must contain a record of the charity's assets and liabilities.

21.16 Charities do not need to update their accounting records daily, but the records should be sufficiently detailed, showing transactions on a daily basis, to enable accounts to be drawn up to reveal the financial position of the charity on any particular date in the past.

21.17 Under s 131, accounting records must be preserved for at least 6 years from the end of the financial year in which they are made. If a charity ceases to exist within the 6-year period, the last charity trustees must preserve the records, unless the Commission gives its written consent to the destruction of the records or to their being disposed of in some other way.

---

5 Section 353(1) of the 2011 Act.

Charitable companies

21.18 While ss 130 and 131 of the 2011 Act do not apply to charitable companies, charitable companies are subject to similar requirements to keep and preserve accounting records under ss 386–389 of the Companies Act 2006. Private companies – which includes charitable companies – are only required to preserve records for a 3-year period.[6] This discrepancy is not easy to justify and in the authors' view charitable companies would be well advised to keep records for 6 years.

Exempt charities

21.19 Under s 136 exempt charities are required to keep 'proper books of account' with respect to the affairs of the charity. The books of account must be preserved for a period of at least 6 years (although the Commission may consent to the records being destroyed or otherwise disposed of if the charity ceases to exist).

Group charities

21.20 Where a charity is part of a group, there may be additional obligations regarding accounting records: see **21.130-21.131**.

PREPARATION OF ANNUAL ACCOUNTS

21.21 All charities are required to keep annual accounts.

Charities other than charitable companies and exempt charities

21.22 Sections 132 to 134 of the 2011 Act deal with the requirements for all charities other than charitable companies and exempt charities.

Accruals accounts

21.23 Section 132 obliges the trustees of a charity whose income in the relevant financial year exceeds £250,000[7] to prepare a statement of accounts which complies in form and content with requirements set out in regulations made by the Minister for the Cabinet Office.

21.24 Sections 132(2)–(4) set the parameters for what the regulations can cover. They may, in particular, require the accounts to be prepared in accordance with specified methods and principles, and provide what information must be included in the notes to the accounts. At the time of writing the relevant regulations are contained in Part 2 of the 2008 Regulations. The basic requirement is for:[8]

(a) a statement of financial activities (SOFA) showing the total incoming resources, the application of the resources and the movement in total resources of the charity in the relevant financial year; and

---

6 Section 388 of the Companies Act 2006.

7 The Minister for the Cabinet Office has power to alter this figure by order, under s 174.

8 Regulation 8 of the 2008 Regulations.

(b) a balance sheet showing the state of affairs of the charity at the end of the financial year.

These are generally known as accruals accounts.

21.25 The statement of financial activities must give a true and fair view of the incoming resources and application of the resources in the relevant financial year; the balance sheet must give a true and fair view of the state of affairs of the charity at the end of the relevant financial year. The statement of accounts must be prepared in accordance with the methods and principles set out in the Charities SORP.[9]

21.26 There are different requirements under the 2008 Regulations for common deposit funds and common investment funds: see **11.62–11.65**. There are also different rules for certain housing charities, educational charities and formerly exempt charities, which are simply required to prepare an income and expenditure account giving a true and fair view of the charity's income and expenditure for the year, and a balance sheet giving a true and fair view of the state of affairs at the end of the year: the Charities SORP does not apply. However, these charities may of course be subject to additional requirements by virtue of the regulatory or legislative regime which applies to them.

21.27 Regulations under s 132 may not impose any requirement to disclose the identities of recipients of grants or the amounts of individual grants in situations where the charity is a trust and the settlor or his or her spouse or civil partner are still alive.[10]

Receipts and payments accounts

21.28 Under s 133, charities with a gross income which does not exceed £250,000[11] in a financial year may elect to prepare simplified accounts in the form of a receipts and payments account and a statement of assets and liabilities if they choose. They are not obliged to comply with the relevant requirements in the regulations made under s 132, which means that they are not bound by the SORP. Note, however that this option is not available to a parent charity which is obliged to prepare group accounts: see **21.114**.[12]

Charitable companies

21.29 Charitable companies are required to prepare accounts under the regime set out in Part 15 of the Companies Act 2006. Company accounts are prepared on the accruals basis: charitable companies must follow the requirements of the SORP in order to give a 'true and fair view' as required by the Companies Act 2006.

Exempt charities

21.30 Exempt charities are likely to be required to produce periodical statements of account under their own legal frameworks or the requirements of their principal

---

9 See **21.3**. As mentioned at **21.6**, at the time of writing the reference in the 2008 Regulations is to the 2005 SORP, In its guidance *Charity reporting and accounting: the essentials March 2015* the Commission has expressed the view that notwithstanding this it is possible to apply either SORP 2015 FRS 102 or FRSSE in preference to the old SORP: presumably the same would apply to the amended SORP 2015 FRS 102 for financial years commencing on or after 1 January 2016.

10 Section 132(4) of the 2011 Act.

11 The Minister for the Cabinet Office has power to alter this figure by order under s 174.

12 Section 138(3) of the 2011 Act.

regulator. For example, academy trusts are obliged to comply with the Academies Financial Handbook, which includes obligations to follow the SORP, under their funding agreement with Government. Exempt charities which are companies must follow the rules which apply to charitable companies.

21.31 If, however, there is no such requirement, exempt charities must, in any event, prepare consecutive statements of account consisting of an income and expenditure account relating to a period of not more than 15 months, and a balance sheet relating to the end of that period.[13]

Preservation of accounts

21.32 Charities preparing accounts under s 132 or 133 must keep the statement of accounts for at least 6 years from the end of the financial year to which it relates. If the charity ceases to exist within the 6-year period, the last trustees must comply with this obligation, unless the Commission gives its written consent to the accounts being destroyed or disposed of.[14] There is a similar requirement for statements of account relating to an exempt charity under s 136.[15]

AUDIT AND INDEPENDENT EXAMINATION OF ACCOUNTS

21.33 Sections 144 and 145 of the 2011 Act set out the requirements for charities to have their accounts audited or examined by an independent examiner. They require charities whose gross income for the year exceeds £25,000 to have their accounts audited or independently examined.

21.34 The following categories of charity fall outside the scope of ss 144 and 145:

(a) NHS charities: see **21.47**;

(b) charitable companies which require an audit under Part 16 of the Companies Act 2006: see **21.45-21.46**;

(c) exempt charities: see **21.48**; and

(d) unregistered charities with an annual income of £5,000 or less: see **21.49**.

Audit under s 144

21.35 Under s 144 of the 2011 Act, a charity's accounts must be audited if in the relevant financial year:

(a) the charity's gross income exceeds £1 million;[16] or

(b) the charity's gross income exceeds the threshold at which accruals accounts are required under ss 132 and 133 (see **21.23-21.28**), namely £250,000, and the aggregate value of its assets at the end of the year exceeds £3.26 million.[17]

---

13 Section 136(2) of the 2011 Act.

14 Section 134 of the 2011 Act.

15 Section 136(3) of the 2011 Act.

16 For financial years ending before 31 March 2015, the income threshold was £500,000: see **21.37**. The Minister for the Cabinet Office has power to alter the threshold under s 174 of the 2011 Act.

17 The Minister for the Cabinet Office has power to alter these thresholds under s 174 of the 2011 Act.

If a charity is the parent charity in a group whose accounts must be audited, the parent charity's own accounts must also be audited, even if it falls below these thresholds: see **21.118**.[18]

21.36 The audit must be carried out by a person who is a member of a body specified in regulations made by the Minister of the Cabinet Office under s 154 of the 2011 Act (which deals with the making of regulations relating to audits and examinations), who is eligible under the rules of that body for appointment as auditor of the charity, or by a person eligible for appointment as a statutory auditor under Part 42 of the Companies Act 2006[19]. At the time of writing, no regulations to this effect have been made under s 154, so the auditor must be someone eligible to act under company law.

21.37 For financial years ending prior to 31 March 2015, the income threshold for charity audits was £500,000. In his 2012 review of charity law, Lord Hodgson had recommended an increase in the threshold to £1 million:[20] this recommendation was implemented following consultation.[21]

21.38 Lord Hodgson had also recommended that the asset threshold for an audit should be removed completely.[22] In 2014-2015 Government consulted on an increase in the asset threshold to £5 million and an increase in the income component of the asset threshold to £500,000. Government had expressed reservations about the increase in the asset threshold to £5 million and following the consultation this was not taken forward. While there was support amongst respondents to the consultation for the increase in the income component to £500,000, it was not possible to achieve this by secondary legislation without also increasing the threshold for accruals accounts under ss 132 and 133. Government did not wish to do this. However, Government expressed the hope of revisiting a change in the income component if an opportunity arose to reconfigure the asset threshold in primary legislation.[23]

Independent examination under s 145

21.39 Under s 145 of the 2011 Act, a charity whose income exceeds £25,000[24] which is not required to have an audit under s 144, and which does not fall within the categories set out at **21.34** must have its accounts examined by an independent examiner, or elect to have a full audit.

21.40 If the group accounts of a parent charity are to be examined, then the parent charity's own accounts must also be examined or audited under s 145(1), whether or not this would otherwise have been the case: see **21.124** (s 152(8)).

21.41 An independent examiner is defined as 'an independent person who is reasonably believed by the trustees to have the requisite ability and practical experience to carry out

18 Section 151(5) of the 2011 Act.

19 Section 144(2) of the 2011 Act.

20 *Trusted and Independent*, ch 6, recommendation 14.

21 The Charities Act 2011 (Accounts and Audit) Order 2015, SI 2015/321.

22 *Trusted and Independent*, ch 6, recommendation 14.

23 Government Response to the Consultation on Charity Audit and Independent Examination, Cabinet Office, February 2015.

24 The Minister for the Cabinet Office has power to change this threshold by order, under s 174.

a competent examination of the accounts' (s 145(1)(a)). However, where the charity's income exceeds £250,000,[25] the independent examiner must also be:

(i) a member of:-
- (a) the Institute of Chartered Accountants in England and Wales;
- (b) the Institute of Chartered Accountants of Scotland;
- (c) the Institute of Chartered Accountants in Ireland;
- (d) the Association of Chartered Certified Accountants;
- (e) the Association of Authorised Public Accountants;
- (f) the Association of Accounting Technicians;
- (g) the Association of International Accountants;
- (h) the Chartered Institute of Management Accountants;
- (i) the Institute of Chartered Secretaries and Administrators;
- (j) the Chartered Institute of Public Finance and Accountancy;
- (k) the Institute of Financial Accountants;[26] or
- (l) the Certified Public Accountants Association;[27] or

(ii) a Fellow of the Association of Charity Independent Examiners.

The Minister for the Cabinet Office may amend this list by order, under s 145(6).[28]

21.42 The Charity Commission may give guidance to trustees in connection with the selection of an independent examiner, and may give such directions as it thinks appropriate with respect to the carrying out of an independent examination. The guidance and directions may be general, or in respect of a particular charity.[29]

21.43 The Commission has published guidance on independent examiners: Independent examination of charity accounts: trustees (CC31). At the time of writing, s 4 contains the Commission's guidance on selecting an independent examiner. The Commission has also issued directions to independent examiners: these are set out in the Commission's guidance Independent examination of charity accounts: examiners (CC32) alongside more general guidance for independent examiners. At the time of writing the Commission is consulting on revised directions and changes to CC32.

Dispensation by the Commission

21.44 Section 154 allows the Minister for the Cabinet Office to make regulations allowing the Commission to dispense with the requirements for an audit or independent examination under ss 144 or 145 in circumstances specified in the regulations. At the time of writing, the 2008 Regulations allow the Commission to issue such a dispensation where, broadly speaking, the accounts are audited or examined under requirements similar to those set out in the 2011 Act. In exceptional circumstances, the Commission may allow examination by an independent examiner rather than a full audit.[30]

---

25 The Minister for the Cabinet Office has power to change this threshold by order, under s 174.
26 For financial years ending on or after 31 March 2015.
27 For financial years ending on or after 31 March 2015.
28 The two bodies listed at (i)(k) and (i)(l) were added under the Charities Act 2011 (Accounts and Audit) Order 2015, SI 2015/321.
29 Section 145(5) of the 2011 Act.
30 Regulation 34 of the 2008 Regulations.

Charitable companies

21.45 The requirements of ss 144 and 145 do not apply to a charitable company whose accounts are required to be audited under Part 16 of the Companies Act 2006. The Companies Act 2006 requires an audit unless an exemption applies: there are a number of exemptions from audit which may be relevant to charitable companies, including an exemption for 'small companies', namely those that meet two of the following three criteria:

- a turnover of not more than £10.2m (for financial years beginning on or after 1 January 2016; prior to that the turnover threshold was £6.5m);
- gross assets of not more than £5.1m (for financial years beginning on or after 1 January 2016; prior to that the assets threshold was £3.26m); and
- average number of employees for the year is not more than 50.[31]

21.46 Where a charitable company claims exemption from audit under the Companies Act 2006, ss 144–145 will apply, meaning that:

- if the company exceeds the audit thresholds under s 144 of the 2011 Act (see **21.35**), an audit will be required under the 2011 Act;
- if the company falls within the thresholds for independent examination under s 145 (see **21.39**), an independent examination will be required; or
- if the company falls below the £25,000 threshold for independent examination under s 145, no independent scrutiny of the accounts is required.

NHS charities

21.47 There are slightly different provisions under ss 148–150 of the 2011 Act for the audit or examination of English and Welsh NHS charity accounts.

Exempt, excepted and unregistered charities

21.48 Exempt charities are not required to have their accounts audited or independently examined under the 2011 Act,[32] but may be subject to a requirement to this effect under another regime. So, for example, exempt charities which are charitable companies may be required to have their accounts audited under company law. Academy trusts are subject to audit requirements under the Academies Financial Handbook, through their funding agreement with Government.

21.49 Charities which are not registered with the Commission because their annual income does not exceed £5,000 are not required to have their accounts audited or independently examined,[33] unless required to do so under their constitution, or by a funder. However, charities which are not registered with the Commission because they are excepted from registration under s 30(2)(b) or (c) of the 2011 Act, such as certain religious or armed forces charities with income which does not exceed £100,000 (see

---

31 See sections 475, 477 and 382 of the Companies Act 2006 for more detail about qualifying for the small company exemption. A statement by the directors to the effect that the company is entitled to the exemption must appear in the balance sheet.

32 Section 160 of the 2011 Act.

33 Section 161 of the 2011 Act.

4.25–4.40), do fall within the scope of ss 144 and 145. They therefore require an audit or independent examination if their annual income exceeds £25,000.

Constitutional requirement

21.50 If there is a constitutional requirement for an independent examination or an audit which is more stringent than what would otherwise be required under the legislation, the constitution will prevail. Funders may also impose requirements in relation to the scrutiny of accounts.

Commission's power to order audit

21.51 Under s 146 of the 2011 Act the Commission may make an order requiring that a charity's accounts be audited. The Commission may exercise this power if it appears that the statutory requirement under s 144 or 145 for the accounts to be audited or examined has not been complied with within 10 months of the end of the relevant financial year.[34] The auditor must be a person appointed by the Commission.

21.52 The costs of the audit, including the auditor's remuneration, can be recovered from the trustees, who are personally liable, jointly and severally. The expenses can only be met from the funds of the charity if the Commission is of the view that it is not practical to seek recovery of the expenses from the trustees.

21.53 The Commission may also order the audit of accounts of a charity which does not meet the audit threshold if the Commission is of the view that an audit is desirable.[35] In this case, if the trustees appoint an auditor in compliance with the Commission's order, the costs of the audit may be met from the funds of the charity.

21.54 Section 146 does not apply to NHS charities, exempt charities, or unregistered charities with income which does not exceed £5,000.

21.55 In the case of charitable companies (other than exempt charities) whose accounts are required to be audited in accordance with Part 16 of the Companies Act 2006, the Commission may order an investigation and audit under s 147 of the 2011 Act. The expenses of the audit must be met by the Commission. Section 147(3) sets out the rights and obligations of the auditor.

Rights and duties of auditors and independent examiners

21.56 Under s 154 of the 2011 Act, the Minister for the Cabinet Office may make regulations which, among other things, cover auditor's duties, independent examiners' reports and auditors' and examiners' rights of access to records and information. At the time of writing these matters are dealt with in Part 4 of the 2008 Regulations. Under s 155, the Commission can issue directions if a person fails to give access or information to an auditor, examiner or independent examiner in compliance with such regulations.

21.57 As well as these detailed duties, s 156 of the 2011 Act imposes obligations on auditors and independent examiners and on the examiners of NHS charity accounts to report various matters to the Commission. These were introduced by the 2006 Act.

---

34 Section 146(1)(a) of the 2011 Act.
35 Section 146(1)(b) of the 2011 Act.

(a) An auditor, examiner or independent examiner *must* make an immediate written report to the Commission if they become aware of a matter which relates to the activities or affairs of the charity (or an institution or body connected to it) and which they have reasonable cause to believe is likely to be of material significance for the purpose of Commission's exercise of its functions under ss 46, 47 and 50 (inquiries by the Commission: see **9.47–9.70**) or ss 76 and 79–82 (powers to act for the protection of charities: see **9.79–9.115**, **9.139–9.145** and **9.156**) of the 2011 Act.

(b) Such a person *may* make a report to the Commission if they become aware of any matter which does not appear to them to be one that they are required to report under para (a) above, but which they have reasonable cause to believe is likely to be relevant for the purposes of the exercise by the Commission of any of its functions.

21.58 The duties apply not just to information about the charity but also about any 'connected institution or body', which is defined in s 157 as an institution which is controlled by, or a body corporate in which a substantial interest is held by, a charity or any one or more of the charity trustees acting as such. Sections 351 and 352 of the 2011 Act apply for the purposes of interpreting this provision.

21.59 The duty or power to report is not affected if the person concerned ceases to act in the capacity of auditor or examiner.[36]

21.60 Any auditor, examiner or independent examiner reporting in compliance with s 156 is protected from contravening any other duties (eg the duty of confidentiality to its client) under s 156(6).

21.61 If a person is appointed to audit or report on the accounts of an exempt charity that person is under the duties and powers in s 156, but the report must be made to the charity's principal regulator.[37]

21.62 Auditors of charitable companies appointed under the Companies Act 2006 are also subject to the duties and powers in s 156.[38]

21.63 The Commission's guidance, Guidance for auditors and independent examiners, comments on the duty and contains a list of situations which the Commission will always consider to be of material significance and hence reportable. At the time of writing revised guidance is under consultation.

21.64 The Commission dealt with 143 whistle-blowing enquiries in the year 2015-16, up from 114 in the previous year.[39]

---

36 Section 156(5) of the 2011 Act.

37 Section 160(2). The duty does not apply in the case of exempt charities whose status remains undecided (see Chapter 5), by virtue of para 22 of Sch 9 to the 2011 Act.

38 Section 159 of the 2011 Act.

39 Charity Commission Annual Report 2015–16. These figures include whistle-blowing reports from several sources; approximately a third of cases in 2015–16 came through auditors and independent examiners.

Liability of auditors and examiners

21.65 Under s 191 of the 2011 Act, which was introduced by the 2006 Act, the Commission has power to make an order relieving an auditor or examiner from personal liability for a breach of trust or breach of duty (other than a personal contractual liability). The Commission must be satisfied that the person acted honestly and reasonably and ought fairly to be excused for the breach of duty or trust.

21.66 Under s 192 of the 2011 Act the court's power under s 1157 of the Companies Act 2006 to relieve the auditor of a company from liability if they have acted honestly and reasonably and ought fairly to be excused also applies to auditors or examiners of charity accounts where the charities are not companies.

Filing with the Charity Commission

21.67 Where an annual report is filed with the Commission (see **21.76-21.84**) the accounts and any auditor's or examiner's report must be attached.

TRUSTEES' ANNUAL REPORT

21.68 The trustees of every registered charity must prepare an annual report in respect of each financial year of the charity.[40] Depending on the income level of the charity, there are different requirements as to what should be in the report and whether the report must be filed with the Commission.

Content of annual report

21.69 The content of the annual report must comply with regulations made by the Minister for the Cabinet Office.[41] At the time of writing the relevant requirements are set out in Part 5 of the 2008 Regulations.

21.70 The requirements may differ depending on the size of the charity. For example, under the 2008 Regulations, a charity which is not required to have its accounts audited must include a brief summary setting out 'the main activities undertaken by the charity to further its charitable purposes for the public benefit; and … the main achievements of the charity during the year'. Where an audit is required, the report must include 'a review of the significant activities undertaken by the charity … to further its charitable purposes for the public benefit or to generate resources to be used to further its purposes', including a range of specified information.[42]

21.71 Under s 162A of the 2011 Act, which was introduced in the 2016 Act, charities which are required to have their accounts audited must also include a statement about the following in their trustees' annual report:

- The charity's approach to fundraising, and in particular whether a professional fundraiser or commercial participator was used.[43]

---

[40] Section 162 of the 2011 Act, subject to ss 167 and 168.

[41] Section 162(1) of the 2011 Act.

[42] Regulation 40(2)(b)(i) and (ii). See also Chapter 3. There are different requirements for investment funds and for parent charities in a group.

[43] See Chapters 19 and 20 for more on professional fundraisers and commercial participators.

- Whether the charity or anyone fundraising on its behalf has agreed to any voluntary fundraising schemes or standards, including the relevant details, and details of any failure to comply. The Code of Fundraising Practice and any registration scheme run by the Fundraising Regulator (see Chapter 18) are obvious examples.
- Whether and how the charity monitored fundraising activities carried out on its behalf.
- How many complaints the charity or anyone acting on its behalf has received about fundraising.
- What the charity has done to protect vulnerable people and others from unreasonable intrusion on a person's privacy, unreasonably persistent approaches or undue pressure to give, in connection with fundraising for the charity.

This provision was one of the measures in the 2016 Act designed to improve fundraising standards (see Chapter 18). It will come into force on 1 November 2016 and will apply for financial years beginning on or after that day, although charities may choose to include a statement along these lines for earlier financial years.

21.72 The regulations may allow the Commission to dispense with certain prescribed requirements. For example, the Commission may dispense with the requirement to disclose the names of trustees or the principal address of the charity where disclosure could put that person in personal danger,[44] for example in the case of a women's refuge.

21.73 SORP 2005, SORP FRSEE and SORP FRS102 (including SORP FRS102 as amended for financial years beginning on or after 1 January 2016) all contain sections on the trustees' annual report.

21.74 Where a parent charity prepares group accounts, its trustees' annual report must include a report on the activities of the subsidiary undertakings: see **21.127** (s 166).

21.75 There are additional requirements for:

- charitable companies, which must also comply with Part 15, Chapter 5 of the Companies Act 2006, and regulations made under those provisions, which deal with the content of company directors' reports. In practice, charitable companies will prepare one single report which covers the requirements of charity and company law; and
- charities subject to a more specialised SORP.

Filing the annual report with the Commission

21.76 All registered charities with a gross income of more than £25,000[45] and all charitable incorporated organisations (regardless of their gross income) must file their annual report with the Commission within 10 months of the end of the financial year. The Commission may extend that period 'for any special reason' in the case of a particular report.[46]

---

44 Section 162(2) of the 2011 Act and regs 40(4) and 41(4) of the 2008 Regulations.

45 The Minister for the Cabinet Office has power to change this threshold by order, under s 174 of the 2011 Act.

46 Sections 163(1) and (3) of the 2011 Act, subject to ss 167 and 168.

21.77 Registered charities which have a gross income of £25,000 or less are only obliged to file their annual report with the Commission on request (unless they are charitable incorporated organisations). If the request is made within 7 months of the year end, the report must be sent to the Commission within 10 months of the year end. Otherwise, the report must be filed within 3 months of the request. The Commission may allow a longer period.[47]

21.78 Failure to comply with these requirements is an offence: see **21.98-21.102**.

21.79 If the charity is a parent charity in a group whose aggregate gross income exceeds £25,000, the annual report must be sent to the Commission: see **21.128** (s 166(4)).

21.80 Where charities are obliged to prepare an annual report under legislation other than the 2011 Act, this may need to be filed with the relevant regulator. Charitable companies, for example, must file the directors' report prepared under the Companies Act 2006 with Companies House within 9 months of the end of the relevant accounting reference period.[48]

Filing accounts with the annual report

21.81 Any annual report filed with the Commission must have the charity's accounts for the relevant year attached to it. Where the accounts have been audited or examined, a copy of any auditor's or examiner's report must also be attached. Charitable companies must attach to their annual report a copy of the accounts prepared under Part 15 of the Companies Act 2006 together with the auditor's or examiner's report.[49] Failure to comply is an offence: see **21.98-21.102**.

Exempt, unregistered and excepted charities

21.82 Exempt charities are under no legal obligation to prepare an annual report under the 2011 Act, although the Commission considers it good practice to do so.[50] As mentioned at **21.80** they may of course be required by other legislation to prepare a similar report.

21.83 Unregistered charities whose income does not exceed £5,000 are under no legal obligation to prepare an annual report.[51]

21.84 Excepted charities with income of over £5,000, but not more than £100,000, which are not registered with the Commission do not generally need to prepare annual reports. However, the Commission regards preparation of an annual report as good practice.[52] The Commission also has power under s 168(3) of the 2011 Act to request that an annual report be prepared for such a charity in respect of any specified financial year: if an excepted charity receives such a request they must prepare a report which complies with the regulations made under s 162: see **21.69-21.72**. The report must be accompanied by the accounts and the relevant auditor's or examiner's report, and must

47 Section 163(2) of the 2011 Act.
48 Part 15, Chapter 10, Companies Act 2006.
49 Section 164 of the 2011 Act.
50 Section 167 of the 2011 Act and Charity Commission publication Charity Reporting and Accounting: The Essentials, March 2015.
51 Section 168(1) of the 2011 Act.
52 Charity Commission publication Charity Reporting and Accounting: The Essentials, March 2015.

be filed within the time limits set out at **21.76**. If the charity in question is a parent charity, the group accounts and relevant auditor's or examiner's report must also be attached.[53]

Preservation of the annual report

21.85 Under s 165 of the 2011 Act, any annual report sent to the Commission under s 163 (see **21.76-21.79**), together with the documents attached to it, must be kept by the Commission for such period as the Commission thinks fit.

21.86 If the trustees have prepared an annual report under s 162 but have not been required to send it to the Commission, they must keep a copy for 6 years from the end of the relevant financial year. If the charity ceases to exist, the report must be kept by the last charity trustees, unless the Commission consents to the destruction or disposal of the records.[54]

ANNUAL RETURN

21.87 All registered charities whose gross income for the financial year exceeds £10,000[55] and all charitable incorporated organisations (or CIOs), regardless of their income, must complete an annual return in relation to the relevant financial year and return it to the Commission.[56] The time scale for sending the annual return mirrors that for sending annual reports to the Commission, ie within 10 months of the end of the financial year to which the return relates.[57] Failure to comply is an offence: see **21.98-21.102**.

21.88 The content of the annual return is prescribed by regulations made by the Commission.[58] At the time of writing charities whose income exceeds £500,000 are required to submit a more detailed financial analysis.

21.89 Registered charities with income of £10,000 or below are not required to complete an annual return, unless they are CIOs. However, they do need to make sure that the details held by the Commission are correct, and to notify the Commission of any change in their particulars under s 35(3) of the 2011 Act (see **4.70**). Smaller charities can do this by filing a simplified version of the annual return form via the Commisson's website.

21.90 The Commission has power under s 169(4) of the 2011 Act to waive the need to prepare an annual return in the case of a particular charity or class of charities, either generally or in respect of a particular financial year.

21.91 Since they are not registered, exempt charities and excepted charities which fall below the registration threshold for excepted charities[59] are not obliged to complete annual returns.

---

53 Sections 168(2)–(8) of the 2011 Act. See Chapter 4 for more on excepted charities.
54 Section 165 of the 2011 Act.
55 The Minister for the Cabinet Office has power to change this figure by order, under s 174 of the 2011 Act.
56 Section 169 of the 2011 Act.
57 Sections 169(3) and 163(1) of the 2011 Act.
58 Section 169(1) of the 2011 Act.
59 See 4.33.

21.92 Lord Hodgson recommended, in his review of charity law, that Government should work with the Commission to develop a fair and proportionate system of charging for filing annual returns with the Commission (as well as charging for registration: see **4.67–4.69**).[60] Government responded that there were no plans to introduce charging, and that any such plans would be subject to full consultation with the sector.[61] See Chapter 2 for more discussion of charging by the Commission.

PUBLIC ACCESS TO ANNUAL REPORT AND ACCOUNTS

21.93 As mentioned at **21.85**, under s 165 of the 2011 Act, any annual report sent to the Commission under s 163 (see **21.68-21.85**), together with the documents attached to it, which might include the accounts and auditor's or examiner's report (see **21.81**), must be kept by the Commission for such period as the Commission thinks fit.

21.94 The Commission must allow public inspection of these documents at all reasonable times while they are kept by the Commission or during such shorter period as the Commission may specify.[62]

21.95 Where the trustees have prepared an annual report (either in accordance with the requirement under s 162, see **21.68**, or, in the case of an excepted charity, where they have been required to do so by the Commission under s 168(3), see **21.84**) the trustees must supply a copy of the most recent annual report to anyone who makes a written request, subject to payment of any reasonable fee for the costs of complying. The trustees must comply within 2 months of the date of the request.[63]

21.96 All charities, including exempt charities and charitable companies, must supply their most recent accounts to anyone who makes a written request, on payment of any reasonable fee for the costs of complying. The charity must comply with the request within 2 months.[64] Section 172 of the 2011 Act identifies which accounts are 'the most recent accounts' of a charity.

21.97 It is an offence for a trustee to fail to comply with such a request to supply the report or accounts.

OFFENCES AND SANCTIONS

21.98 Section 173 of the 2011 Act makes it a criminal offence for a charity trustee to fail to comply with various requirements of the legislation relating to reports and accounts. A charity trustee commits an offence if the charity fails to comply with:

(1) the requirement under s 163 to transmit an annual report and, where appropriate, accompanying documents, to the Commission;

(2) the requirement under s 169 for registered charities to transmit an annual return to the Commission; or

---

60 *Trusted and Independent*, ch 6, recommendation 18.
61 Government Response p 33.
62 Section 170 of the 2011 Act.
63 Sections 171 of the 2011 Act.
64 Section 172 of the 2011 Act.

(3) the requirements under s 171 and 172 to supply a member of the public with a copy of the charity's annual report and accounts.

21.99 It is a defence to prove that the trustee took all reasonable steps for securing that the requirement in question would be complied with in time. It would be less easy to establish a reasonable excuse if no steps had been taken to prepare the documents in the first place.

21.100 Under s 173(4), the punishment is either:

(a) a fine not exceeding level 4 on the standard scale (which is £2,500 at the time of writing); or

(b) for continued contravention, a daily default fine not exceeding 10% of level 4 on the standard scale for as long as the person concerned remains a trustee of the charity.

Proceedings cannot be issued without the consent of the Director of Public Prosecutions.[65]

21.101 The authors are not aware of any prosecutions having been made for these offences. However, failure to file documents with the Commission on time can have adverse consequences. In the case of registered charities, failure to file the annual return and/or accounts on time is publicised on the Commission's website. Late filing may also trigger further investigation by the Commission. In 2013, the Commission instigated a class inquiry, using its powers under the 2011 Act,[66] into charities which had failed to file their annual documents with the Commission for two or more years in the past five, and met certain additional criteria. At the time of writing, the inquiry is still ongoing: more charities have been added over the course of the inquiry.

21.102 In his 2012 review of charity law, Lord Hodgson recommended that thought should be given to the costs, benefits and logistics of introducing fines for the late filing of accounts and annual returns with the Commission: Government agreed to explore the scope for this with the Commission.[67] See Chapter 2 for more discussion of the question of charging by the Commission.

GROUP ACCOUNTS

21.103 One of the main changes orchestrated by the 2006 Act was the introduction of new rules on charity group accounting. These are now set out in Part 8 of the 2011 Act, particularly ss 137–142 (the preparation and preservation of group accounts) and ss 151–153 (audit or examination of group accounts), supplemented by the 2008 Regulations.

21.104 The provisions of the 2011 Act dealing with group accounts do not apply in the case of exempt charities.[68]

---

65 Section 345 of the 2011 Act.

66 See Chapter 9.

67 *Trusted and Independent*, ch 6, recommendation 17. Government Response p 33.

68 Sections 143 and 160(1) and (3) of the 2011 Act.

Definitions

21.105 A group means a 'parent charity' and one or more 'subsidiary undertakings'.[69]

21.106 A charity is a parent charity if it is to be treated as a 'parent undertaking' in relation to one or more other undertakings in accordance with the provisions of s 1162 of, and Sch 7 to, the Companies Act 2006.[70]

21.107 It is worth setting out in full s 1162(2) of the Companies Act 2006 which states:

> 'An undertaking is a parent undertaking in relation to another undertaking, a subsidiary undertaking, if:
>
> (a) it holds a majority of the voting rights in the undertaking, or
> (b) it is a member of the undertaking and has the right to appoint or remove a majority of its board of directors, or
> (c) it has the right to exercise a dominant influence over the undertaking—
>   (i) by virtue of provisions contained in the undertaking's articles, or
>   (ii) by virtue of a control contract, or
> (d) it is a member of the undertaking and controls alone, pursuant to an agreement with other shareholders or members, a majority of the voting rights in the undertaking.'

21.108 The remainder of s 1162 and Sch 7 of the Companies Act 2006 explain further the meanings of some of the terms used.

21.109 The most common parent/subsidiary relationships for charities are where Charity A (parent) is the sole shareholder of a trading company (subsidiary), or where Charity A (parent) is the sole member of Charity B (subsidiary).

21.110 Section 1162 and Sch 7 of the Companies Act 2006 also apply for the purposes of identifying a subsidiary undertaking.[71] However, the following are not necessarily subsidiary undertakings:[72]

- any special trusts of a charity;
- any institution which, by virtue of a direction under s 12(1) of the 2011 Act is to be treated as forming part of a charity for the purposes of Part 8 of the 2011 Act, which deals with charity accounts, reports and returns (see **4.12**); and
- any charity to which a direction under s 12(2) of the 2011 Act applies, namely that two or more charities with the same trustees are to be treated as a single charity, for the purposes of Part 8 of the 2011 Act (see **4.12**).

Who is obliged to prepare group accounts?

21.111 The trustees of any charity which, at the end of a financial year, falls within the definition of 'parent charity' (see **21.106-21.108**) must prepare group accounts for that year under s 138(2) of the 2011 Act. There are four exceptions:

---

69 Section 141(5) of the 2011 Act.
70 Section 141(2) of the 2011 Act.
71 Section 141(3) of the 2011 Act.
72 Section 141(4) of the 2011 Act.

- if the aggregate gross income of the group for that year does not exceed a threshold set out in regulations made by the Minister for the Cabinet Office under s 139(2) of the 2011 Act. For financial years ending on or after 31 March 2015 the threshold is £1m. This was increased from £500,000 in line with the increase in the audit threshold (see **21.37**).[73] The term 'aggregate gross income' may be defined in regulations made by the Minister for the Cabinet Office under s 175: at the time of writing the definition is set out in reg 9 of the 2008 Regulations;
- if the parent charity is a company which is required to prepare consolidated accounts under s 399 of the Companies Act 2006;[74]
- if the parent charity is itself a subsidiary of another charity;[75] or
- if all of a parent charity's subsidiary undertakings fall within a category which the Minister for the Cabinet Office has prescribed must or may be excluded from group accounts required to be prepared, in regulations made under s 139(3) of the 2011 Act. These include circumstances where the information needed for preparing the group accounts cannot be obtained without disproportionate expense or delay.[76]

What are group accounts?

21.112 Group accounts are consolidated accounts relating to the group and prepared in compliance with regulations made by the Minister for the Cabinet Office under s 142 of the 2011 Act.[77]

21.113 Group accounts must always be a full statement of accounts – the option of preparing simplified accounts on a receipts and payments basis is not available.

21.114 Where parent charities are required to prepare group accounts, they must also prepare individual accounts on the accruals basis rather than on the receipts and payments basis, regardless of the level of their income (see **21.23-21.28**).[78]

Audit and examination of group accounts

21.115 Group accounts prepared under s 138(2) of the 2011 Act must be audited where:

(a) either:
  (i) the aggregate gross income of the group in that year exceeds the 'relevant income threshold' (s 151(1)(a) of the 2011 Act); or
  (ii) the aggregate value of the assets of the group exceeds the 'relevant assets threshold' and the aggregate gross income of the group in that year exceeds the 'relevant income threshold' (s 151(1)(b) of the 2011 Act).

The 'relevant assets threshold' and 'relevant income threshold' may be prescribed in regulations made by the Minister for the Cabinet Office under s 176 of the 2011 Act. For financial years ending on or after 31 March 2015, the

---

73 Regulations 2 and 3 of the Charities Act 2011 (Group Accounts) Regulations 2015, SI 2015/322.
74 Section 138(1)(b) of the 2011 Act.
75 Section 139(1) of the 2011 Act.
76 At the time of writing the relevant provisions are set out in the 2008 Regulations, reg 19.
77 Section 142(1) of the 2011 Act. At the time of writing, the requirements are set out in regs 12–17 of the 2008 Regulations.
78 Section 138(3)(a) of the 2011 Act.

relevant income threshold for the purposes of s 151(1)(a) is £1m. This was increased from £500,000 in line with the increase in the audit threshold for individual charity accounts (see **21.37**).[79] No relevant thresholds have been prescribed for the purposes of s 151(1)(b); or

(b) the parent charity's own accounts would be subject to an audit.[80]

Since the income threshold for an audit of group accounts under s 151(1)(a) is currently the same as the threshold at which group accounts must be prepared, and there are currently no set thresholds for group accounts under s 151(1)(b), at the time of writing where group accounts are prepared in line with the statutory requirement, they will always need to be audited.

21.116 The auditor must be a person within s 144(2) of the 2011 Act (see **21.36**), with variations in the case of English and Welsh National Health Service charities.[81]

21.117 The Commission has power under s 153 of the 2011 Act to require group accounts to be audited in some circumstances: the conditions are similar to those which apply in the case of individual charities (see **21.51-21.54**). Where the Commission appoints an auditor, it may recover the expenses of any such audit from the charity trustees or the funds of the parent charity.

21.118 If group accounts are required to be audited because the group exceeds the thresholds in s 151(1), the parent charity's own accounts must also be audited, even if it would not otherwise require an audit.[82]

21.119 Section 152 sets out a framework for independent examination of group accounts where the audit threshold is not reached. Section 152 will apply where group accounts must be prepared under s 138(2) (see **21.111**), and an audit is not required under s 151. However since, as mentioned at **21.115**, the threshold for preparing group accounts coincides with the audit threshold for group accounts, it appears that s 152 currently has limited practical effect. This may well continue to be the case: in its response to the consultation on increasing audit thresholds and group accounting thresholds in 2014–2015, Government expressed the view that an audit is more suited to the complexity of group accounts than independent examination.[83] However, it is possible that some trustees of groups which fall below the thresholds may wish to prepare group accounts on a voluntary basis, and may opt to have those accounts independently examined (see **21.123**).

21.120 Section 152 provides that the trustees of any parent charity required to produce group accounts which is not required to have its accounts audited under s 151 must, if the aggregate gross group income exceeds £25,000 (which is the threshold for independent examination of individual accounts under s 145(1): see **21.39**) elect either:

- for the group accounts to be audited; or
- for the accounts of the group to be examined by an independent examiner.

---

79 Regulations 4 and 5 of the Charities Act 2011 (Group Accounts) Regulations 2015, SI 2015/322.
80 Section 151(2) of the 2011 Act.
81 Section 151(4) of the 2011 Act.
82 Section 151(5) of the 2011 Act.
83 The Government response to the Consultation on Charity Audit and Independent Examination, Cabinet Office, February 2015.

21.121 If the trustees opt for independent examination, as is the case for individual accounts, where the aggregate gross group income exceeds £250,000 (which is the level set out in s 145(3)) the examiner must be a member of one of the bodies listed in s 145(4) (see **21.41**(i)), or a Fellow of the Association of Charity Independent Examiners: s 152(4).

21.122 For English and Welsh National Health Service charities there are special rules regarding examination and audit of group accounts (see s 152(6) and (7)).

21.123 As is the case for individual accounts (see **21.42**), the Commission may give guidance in connection with the selection of an independent examiner, and may give such directions as it thinks appropriate with respect to the carrying out of an independent examination. This may be general, or in respect of a particular charity (s 152(5)). At the time of writing, no directions have been given, but the Commission is consulting on whether it would be appropriate to produce guidance to this effect.[84]

21.124 If the group accounts of a parent charity are to be examined or audited under s 152(2), then the parent charity's own accounts must also be examined or audited under s 145(1), whether or not it this would otherwise have been the case (s 152(8)).

Duties of auditors/examiners of group accounts

21.125 The duties and powers of auditors and examiners of charity accounts to report certain matters to the Commission (see **21.56-21.64**) also apply in relation to the audit or examination of group accounts.[85]

21.126 Similarly, the Minister for the Cabinet Office may make regulations dealing with the duties and rights of auditors and examiners of group accounts under s 154, and their rights to access records and request information can be the subject of directions from the Commission under s 155. At the time of writing the duties of an auditor of group accounts are set out in reg 30 of the 2008 Regulations.

Annual reports

21.127 Where a parent charity prepares group accounts, the annual report of the charity trustees of the parent charity must include such a report on the activities of the subsidiary undertakings, and such other information relating to any of those undertakings, as may be prescribed by regulations made by the Minister for the Cabinet Office under s 166. The regulations may allow the Commission to dispense with any requirement for information in the case of a particular subsidiary undertaking, or a class of subsidiary undertakings. At the time of writing the requirements are set out in reg 41 of the 2008 Regulations.

21.128 If the aggregate gross income of the group in a financial year exceeds £25,000, which is the threshold for sending annual reports for individual charities to the

---

[84] Charity Commission Guidance Independent Examination of Charity Accounts: Independent Examiners (CC32), para 3.6, March 2012.

[85] Section 158 of the 2011 Act.

Commission under s 163 (see **21.76**), the parent charity must send the annual report to the Commission.[86] The group accounts and the auditor's or examiner's report must be attached.[87]

21.129 Where an excepted charity is required by the Commission to prepare an annual report and send it to the Commission under s 168(3)–(5) of the 2011 Act (see **21.84**), if it is a parent charity which is required to produce group accounts, the group accounts and the auditor's or examiner's report must also be sent to the Commission alongside the annual report.[88]

Accounting records

21.130 Both parent charities and subsidiary undertakings must ensure that accounting records kept under the 2011 Act and, where relevant, s 386 of the Companies Act 2006 (see **21.15-21.18**) are such as to enable the trustees of the parent charity to ensure that, where group accounts are prepared, they comply with the requirements set out in regulations made under s 142: see **21.112**.

21.131 Where a subsidiary would not usually be obliged to keep accounting records under s 130(1), or under s 386 of the Companies Act 2006, being part of the group does not change that, but the trustees of the parent charity must take reasonable steps to make sure the undertaking keeps such records as to enable the parent to prepare the necessary group accounts (s 137(3) and (4)).

Preservation of group accounts

21.132 The trustees of a parent charity must keep accounts for at least 6 years from the end of the financial year to which they relate, although the Commission may make concessions in the case of a charity which has ceased to exist.[89]

Public inspection of annual reports and accounts

21.133 Where a person requests a copy of a charity's most recent accounts under s 172 of the 2011 Act (see **21.96**), if the charity has prepared group accounts, a copy of the most recent group accounts must be supplied.[90]

Offences

21.134 As is the case with individual accounts (see **21.98**) the trustees may be guilty of an offence under s 173 if a charity which has prepared group accounts fails to file the group accounts (together with auditor's or examiner's report) with the annual report. It is also an offence to fail to supply copies of group accounts under s 172(3). The penalty is a fine of up to level 4 on the standard scale, or a daily default fine of up to 10% of level 4 of the standard scale: see **21.100**.

---

86 Section 166(4) of the 2011 Act.
87 Section 166(5) of the 2011 Act.
88 Section 168(6)–(8) of the 2011 Act.
89 Section 140 of the 2011 Act.
90 Section 172(3) of the 2011 Act.

Summary of accounting and reporting requirements for individual charities[91]

Type of charity	**Requirement to prepare annual accounts**	**Requirement for audit or independent examination[92]**	**Requirement for trustees' annual report under the 2011 Act**	**Requirement for annual return to be filed with the Commission**
All charities other than charitable companies and exempt charities	Yes	Charities with income over £1m: audit required	All trustees of registered charities required to prepare an annual report. If (a) the charity is a CIO or (b) the charity's income exceeds £25,000: requirement to file the annual report, together with the accounts and the auditor's or examiner's report with the Commission	If (a) the charity is a CIO or (b) the charity's income exceeds £10,000 and the charity is registered with the Commission: annual return must be completed and filed with the Commission
	Charities with income over £250,000 required to prepare accruals accounts and to comply with SORP	Charities with income over £250,000 and assets over £3.26m: audit required		
		Charities with income over £250,000 but no more than £1m with assets of £3.26m or less: independent examination required, or may opt for audit		
	Charities with income of up to £250,000 may opt to prepare receipts and payments accounts	Charities with income over £25,000 but no more than £250,000: independent examination required, or may opt for audit		
		Charities with income of £25,000 or less: no audit or independent examination required		

91 If the charity's constitution imposes more stringent requirements, they will prevail. This table does not deal with charities in a group.

92 There are special provisions for NHS charities. Note also that the charity's constitution may include more stringent requirements: if this is the case the constitution will prevail (see **21.50**).

Charitable companies	Yes: accruals accounts are required under Part 15 of the Companies Act 2006	Audit is required under Part 15 Companies Act, unless exempt from audit (for example small companies may claim exemption if two of the following criteria apply: (a) turnover of not more than £10.2m;[93] (b) assets of not more than £5.1m;[94] (c) average number of employees not more than 50) If no audit is required under the Companies Act, the rules which apply to other types of charity (other than exempt charities) apply (see above)	All trustees of registered charities required to prepare an annual report. If the charity's turnover exceeds £25,000: requirement to file the annual report, together with the accounts and the auditor's or examiner's report with the Commission	If the charity's income exceeds £10,000 and the charity is registered with the Commission: annual return must be completed and filed with the Commission
Exempt charities	Yes	No requirement under 2011 Act but may be required under another regime	No requirement under 2011 Act but may be required under another regime	No

93 For financial years beginning on or after 1 January 2016: prior to that the figure was £6.5m.
94 For financial years beginning on or after 1 January 2016: prior to that the figure was £3.26m.

CHAPTER 22

MISCELLANEOUS

INTRODUCTION

22.1 This chapter deals with various miscellaneous provisions of the 2006 and 2011 Acts which are not covered elsewhere in this book.

THE OFFICIAL CUSTODIAN FOR CHARITIES

22.2 The official custodian for charities is dealt with in s 21 and Sch 2 to the 2011 Act. The role of the official custodian is to act as trustee for charities in the cases provided for by the 2011 Act. These include holding land on behalf of charities and, less commonly, holding charity investments following an order of the court under ss 90 and 91 or an order of the Commission under s 76. The official custodian also acts as custodian of the property of a dissolved CIO, following its dissolution under Part 3 of the Charitable Incorporated Organisations (Insolvency and Dissolution) Regulations 2012 (see Chapter 14).

22.3 A charity which wishes to avail itself of the official custodian's land holding service can make an application to the Commission. The service is useful to unincorporated charities: title to the land can remain in the name of the official custodian despite changes in the identity of the charity trustees. The official custodian has no power to manage the land, nor any liabilities in respect of it; these continue to be the responsibility of the charity trustees. The official custodian makes no charge for the service.

REVERTER OF SITES ACT 1987

22.4 Under various nineteenth-century legislation, land could be given for charitable purposes, for example as a school, on the basis that once it ceased to be used for the purposes for which it was given, it would revert to the original donor or their successors. Under the Reverter of Sites Act 1987, when this happens, the land will be held on a statutory trust for sale for the benefit of the successors of the original landowner, under which the trustees have powers to manage, repair and sell it. Under ss 92–95 of the 2011 Act, if reverter occurs when the land is in the name of the official custodian, the Commission can make an order discharging him and transferring title into the names of the charity trustees. Section 95 makes it clear that, once a trust for sale has arisen under the 1987 legislation, the powers of management and liabilities under the trust for sale fall on the charity trustees, and not on the official custodian, even before an order for his discharge is made.

22.5 Sections 92–95 will not be relevant where, as is sometimes the case (eg because the successors to the original landowners cannot be traced), an application is made to the Commission under the 1987 legislation for the property to continue to be held on charitable trusts.

LOCAL CHARITIES

22.6 Sections 293–304 of the 2011 Act deal with local and parochial charities. In ss 293 and 303 of the 2011 Act respectively, local charities are defined as charities directed wholly or mainly towards work in a particular area, and parochial charities are defined, broadly speaking, as charities whose benefits are confined to the inhabitants of one or more particular parishes or Welsh communities. Local authorities may maintain public lists of local charities, and may carry out reviews into the workings of groups of certain local charities, with the consent of the charity trustees. Local authorities may work together with local charities which provide similar or complementary activities to them, in order to ensure that those activities are properly coordinated. Sections 298–302 confer various powers on the trustees of parochial charities to transfer property to the parish or community council and to appoint trustees in certain circumstances, with the Commission's consent.

22.7 Under s 88 of the 2011 Act, before making a scheme relating to a local charity in a parish or in a community in Wales, a draft must be sent to the parish or community council (unless it is an ecclesiastical charity).

SUPPLEMENTARY PROVISIONS OF THE 2011 ACT

22.8 Part 18 of the 2011 Act contains various general provisions which have not been covered elsewhere in this book.

22.9 Section 343 deals with evidence of documents issued by the Commission, providing that evidence of a Commission order, certificate or other document may come in the form of a copy certified by an authorised member of the Commission's staff.

22.10 Section 346 deals with offences under the 2011 Act, and provides that where a body corporate commits an offence, its officers and managers may also be prosecuted in some circumstances.

22.11 Sections 347–349 deal with orders and regulations made by the Minister for the Cabinet Office, setting out how the powers to make orders and regulations can be exercised, and in what circumstances they can be annulled by Parliament.

22.12 Schedule 9 to the 2011 Act deals with the various provisions of the 2011 Act which were not brought into force in March 2012, which is when the bulk of the 2011 Act became law. Schedule 9 is necessary because not all of the provisions of the 1993 Act were in force when the 1993 Act was consolidated into the 2011 Act. Schedule 9 includes an appropriate transitional regime.

FINANCIAL ASSISTANCE TO CHARITABLE, BENEVOLENT OR PHILANTHROPIC INSTITUTIONS

22.13 Section 70 of the 2006 Act, which was not consolidated into the 2011 Act, confers power on the Secretary of State or the Minister for the Cabinet Office to give financial assistance to any charitable, benevolent or philanthropic institution in respect of any of its activities which directly or indirectly benefit the whole or any part of England. Financial assistance may be given in any form, including by way of grant or loan, and on such terms and conditions as the relevant Minister considers appropriate.

22.14 A report on how this power has been exercised must be made to Parliament annually.

22.15 Section 71 contains similar provisions in relation to Wales.

CHAPTER 23

SCOTLAND AND NORTHERN IRELAND

INTRODUCTION

23.1 The 2011 Act deals, for the most part, with charities which are governed by the law of England and Wales. However, there are some provisions of the 2011 Act which do affect charities established in Scotland and Northern Ireland.

23.2 Charities in Scotland and Northern Ireland are also subject to their own local regulatory frameworks. In Scotland, regulation and registration of charities are dealt with by the Office of the Scottish Charity Regulator, or OSCR, which, amongst other things, maintains the 'Scottish Charity Register'. The charity regulator in Northern Ireland is the Charity Commission for Northern Ireland.

23.3 This chapter deals with the provisions of the 2011 Act which apply to charities in Scotland and Northern Ireland. It also outlines, in brief, the framework for charity regulation in Scotland and Northern Ireland. A fuller discussion of the rules in Scotland and Northern Ireland is beyond the scope of this book.

SCOTLAND

The application of the Charities Act 2011

23.4 There are a number of provisions of the 2011 Act which extend to Scotland. The most significant of these are:

- The basic definitions of 'charity' and 'charitable purposes' in the 2011 Act apply in Scottish legislation in relation to matters reserved from devolution, under ss 7 and 356 of the 2011 Act.
- The powers of the Commission under ss 46–49 of the 2011 Act to institute inquiries and to obtain evidence and search warrants for the purposes of such inquiries apply to bodies registered on the Scottish Charity Register but managed or controlled wholly or mainly in or from England or Wales.[1]
- The Commission's powers to order disclosure of information or documents relating to a charity under s 52 of the 2011 Act also apply to a body registered on the Scottish Charity Register which is managed or controlled wholly or mainly in or from England or Wales.[2]
- The provisions in ss 54–59 of the 2011 Act, which relate to information sharing between the Commission and other public authorities, extend to the whole of the

---

1 Section 46(4) of the 2011 Act.

2 Section 52(4) of the 2011 Act.

United Kingdom.[3] Under s 55 HMRC may disclose information to the Commission if it relates to a body entered in the Scottish Charity Register which is managed or controlled wholly or mainly in or from England or Wales.

- The Commission's powers to act for the protection of charities under ss 76–82 of the 2011 Act as amended by the 2016 Act (except for the power in s 79(2) to make a scheme for the administration of a charity) apply in relation to any body which is registered on the Scottish Charity Register and managed or controlled wholly or mainly in or from England or Wales. The Commission's powers to direct specified action to be taken or not taken, to wind up charities and to direct the application of charity property under ss 84-86 of the 2011 Act also apply in these circumstances.[4]
- Under s 87(2)–(4) of the 2011 Act, where a body registered on the Scottish Charity Register is managed or controlled wholly or mainly in or from Scotland, but a person in England and Wales holds any property on behalf of the body or any person concerned in its management or control, the Commission has power to make a freezing order in relation to that property. The Commission must be satisfied, on the basis of information supplied to it by the Office of the Scottish Charity Regulator, that there has been misconduct or mismanagement in the administration of the body, and that the order is necessary or desirable to protect the property or to secure its proper application for the purposes of the body.
- Under s 87(5)–(8) of the 2011 Act the Commission can, in similar circumstances, order a person holding such property to transfer it to another similar charity (whether Scottish, or English and Welsh), appoint a person to transfer the property, or make a vesting order in respect of it.
- Sections 97, 101 and 104 of the 2011 Act provide for Scottish charities to participate in common investment schemes and common deposit schemes with the proviso that the Scottish charity must be recognised by HMRC as being entitled to charitable tax relief.
- If a person has been removed from office by the court under the Charities and Trustee Investment (Scotland) Act 2005 or earlier legislation they are not eligible to serve as a charity trustee in England and Wales under s 178 of the 2011 Act.

Scottish regulation

23.5 The main source of regulation of charities in Scotland is the Charities and Trustee Investment (Scotland) Act 2005 ('the 2005 Scotland Act'). The 2005 Scotland Act established the Office of the Scottish Charity Regulator, or OSCR.[5] OSCR is the regulator of charities in Scotland, with responsibility for maintaining the Scottish Charity Register.

23.6 The Charity Commission and OSCR have issued a Memorandum of Understanding setting out how they cooperate on cross-border issues, including, where appropriate, carrying out joint case operations or joint inquiries.

---

3 Section 356 of the 2011 Act.
4 Section 87(1) of the 2011 Act.
5 www.oscr.org.uk.

English and Welsh charities

23.7 Significantly, English and Welsh charities which wish to represent themselves as charities in Scotland, and have a certain level of activity in Scotland, are obliged to register with OSCR, even if they are already registered with the Charity Commission in England and Wales. Triggers for registration in Scotland include the following:[6]

- where the charity is managed or controlled wholly or mainly within Scotland. Relevant issues will be where the office of the charity is, where the administration of the charity takes place or where the charity trustees meet on a regular basis;
- where the charity occupies land or premises in Scotland. Simply owning an investment property does not count;
- where the charity carries out activities in any office, shop or similar premises in Scotland. 'Similar premises' is taken to mean a place of business, that is, a place in which commercial activity and/or the activities of the charity are carried out. When assessing whether a charity carries out activities in Scotland, the following will be relevant:
  - Are the activities in Scotland significant to the charity relative to its activities elsewhere?
  - Are they of a frequent or ongoing nature?
  - Is the overall impact of the activities significant?

Note that there is no minimum income threshold for registration in Scotland.

23.8 Where an English and Welsh charity is obliged to register with OSCR, it must satisfy the Scottish statutory charity test. This means that its purposes must be recognised as charitable under Scottish law, which may mean that a change to its legal objects is required.

The implications of registration in Scotland

23.9 Once registered with OSCR, an English and Welsh charity must comply with the Scottish regulatory regime, as well as the regime in England and Wales. This includes the following:

Reporting

23.10 Any charity registered with OSCR has to submit an annual return, together with an information return containing details about its Scottish activities, and a copy of its annual accounts, within 9 months of the year end. Separate Scottish accounts are not required for cross-border charities, but OSCR expects some narrative in the trustees' report about activities in Scotland. The accounts must comply with the requirements of the Scottish accounting regulations: note that the requirements for external scrutiny of accounts are more stringent in Scotland.

---

6 This is based on s 14 of the 2005 Scotland Act and on guidance in OSCR's publication, *Seeking Charitable Status in Scotland, Guidance for England and Wales charities on registration with the Office of the Scottish Charity Regulator*, at the time of writing.

Publicity

23.11 The Charities References in Documents (Scotland) Regulations 2007[7] contain rules about the disclosure of information on various documents. A charity registered on the Scottish Charity Register must disclose its registered and working name and Scottish charity number and (if the name does not include the word charity or charitable) state that it is a charity, on a wide range of documents, including business letters and emails, advertisements and campaign documents.

Consents

23.12 Any charity registered in Scotland must seek OSCR's prior consent, at least 42 days in advance, if it wishes to:

- change its name;
- amend its constitution in relation to its purposes;
- merge or amalgamate with another body;
- wind up or dissolve; or
- apply to the court in relation to any of the above.

23.13 Charities registered in both England and Wales and Scotland will therefore, in some cases, such as a proposed change of name, need to seek prior consent from OSCR in circumstances where they do not need prior consent from the Charity Commission. In some cases, the consent of both regulators will be needed.

23.14 Certain other changes, such as change of address of principal office, must be notified to OSCR within 3 months of the change. Again, cross-border charities will need to comply with these requirements, as well as any requirement to notify the Charity Commission of the change.

Remuneration of trustees and conflicts of interest

23.15 Charities which are registered with OSCR are subject to the provisions of the 2005 Scotland Act in relation to the remuneration of trustees and conflicts of interest at trustee level. These are similar, but not identical, to the rules which apply in England and Wales.

Fundraising in Scotland

23.16 The 2005 Scotland Act and the Charities and Benevolent Fundraising (Scotland) Regulations 2009[8] include restrictions on third party fundraising in Scotland without proper agreements in place with the benefiting body. These are similar to provisions under the 1992 Act and relevant regulations in England and Wales. The 2009 Regulations require professional fundraisers and commercial participators to make public statements when soliciting funds or making representations.

---

7 SSI 2007/203.
8 SSI 2009/121.

23.17 Any charity organising a public collection in Scotland (irrespective of whether that charity is registered in Scotland) must comply with the relevant Scottish licensing scheme.

23.18 The self-regulatory schemes developed by the Institute of Fundraising and the Fundraising Standards Board applied in Scotland, and the Professional Fundraising Association also operated in Scotland, but this will change following the reform of the self-regulatory fundraising regime in England and Wales (see Chapter 18).

NORTHERN IRELAND

The application of the Charities Act 2011

23.19 The following provisions of the 2011 Act are specifically stated to have effect in Northern Ireland:

- The basic definitions of 'charity' and 'charitable purposes' apply in Northern Ireland for the purposes of the matters reserved from devolution, such as taxes, under ss 8 and 356 of the 2011 Act.
- The provisions in ss 54–59 of the 2011 Act, which relate to information sharing between the Commission and other public authorities, extend to the whole of the United Kingdom.[9] Section 54(3)(a) specifically contemplates the exchange of information between the Commission and Northern Ireland Government departments. Under s 72 of the 2006 Act and the Charities (Disclosure of Revenue and Customs Information to the Charity Commission for Northern Ireland) Regulations 2010,[10] HMRC is authorised to disclose Revenue and Customs information to the Charity Commission for Northern Ireland in relation to certain charitable, benevolent or tax-exempt organisations, including organisations recognised as charitable under the law of Northern Ireland (with some exceptions).
- Sections 68(3) and (4) of the 2011 Act deal with the amendment of Royal Charters where a scheme is made with respect to a body corporate under Northern Ireland legislation or the jurisdiction of the courts of Northern Ireland relating to charities.
- Sections 97, 101 and 104 of the 2011 Act provide for Northern Ireland charities to participate in common investment schemes and common deposit schemes with the proviso that the Northern Ireland charity must be recognised as a charity under the laws of Northern Ireland and recognised by HMRC as being entitled to charitable tax relief.
- A person who is subject to a disqualification order under certain company legislation in Northern Ireland is disqualified from acting as a charity trustee under s 178 of the 2011 Act.

Northern Ireland regulation

23.20 Northern Ireland now has its own charity legislation, the Charities Act (Northern Ireland) 2008 ('the 2008 Northern Ireland Act'), and its own charity regulator, the Charity Commission for Northern Ireland or CCNI. CCNI was established in March

9 Section 356 of the 2011 Act.
10 SI 2010/1219.

2009 to deliver the legislative requirements of the 2008 Northern Ireland Act, and certain functions of the Department for Social Development in Northern Ireland were transferred to CCNI in 2013.

English and Welsh charities

23.21 In December 2013, CCNI began the process of registering charities in Northern Ireland. At the time of writing, registration is taking place in stages, with the first phase relating to organisations which:

- have exclusively charitable purposes;
- are governed by the law of Northern Ireland; and
- have control and direction over their governance and resources.

23.22 Charities which are registered in England and Wales and have operations in Northern Ireland are not, at the time of writing, required to register with CCNI, unless their activities in Northern Ireland are carried on by a branch which might fall within the first phase of registration: this could be the case if they are separately constituted and pass the third limb of the test in terms of autonomy.

23.23 However, as is the case in Scotland, the reach of the 2008 Northern Ireland Act extends beyond organisations which are charities under the law of Northern Ireland. Organisations which are not charities under the law of Northern Ireland but which operate for charitable purposes in or from Northern Ireland are dealt with under s 167 of the 2008 Northern Ireland Act. Section 167 is not in force at the time of writing, and there is as yet no guidance on the precise scope of 'operate for charitable purposes'. However, it is clear that once the legislation does come into force English and Welsh charities which have activities in Northern Ireland will be affected.

23.24 Section 167 sets out a requirement for so-called 's 167 institutions' to prepare a financial statement and a statement of activities relating to their operations for charitable purposes in or from Northern Ireland, on an annual basis. Section 167 also contemplates that the Department for Social Development will make further provision in relation to s 167 institutions, including a requirement for CCNI to keep a register of them. A requirement for s 167 institutions to register in Northern Ireland is therefore a distinct possibility.

23.25 Having said that, it is expected that s 167 institutions will be subject to less onerous registration and reporting requirements than charities governed by the law of Northern Ireland. In particular, it is hoped that they will not need to change their objects to ensure that they are charitable under the law of Northern Ireland, in contrast to the position in Scotland. Note, however, that unlike in Scotland, the legislation in Northern Ireland does not appear to require any particular level of activity before s 167 applies.

23.26 At the time of writing, the authors' understanding is that English charities are not likely to be called forward to register with CCNI until 2017 at the earliest.

Fundraising in Northern Ireland

23.27 The 2008 Northern Ireland Act includes provisions similar those in the 1992 Act relating to professional fundraisers and commercial participators, but at the time of writing these are not in force.

23.28 Any charity carrying out a public collection in Northern Ireland must comply with the Northern Ireland collections regime. The Institute of Fundraising and Fundraising Standards Board operated in Northern Ireland but it is yet to be seen how the new self-regulatory regime in England and Wales will impact on Northern Ireland.

APPENDIX 1

CHARITIES ACT 2011

PART 1
MEANING OF 'CHARITY' AND 'CHARITABLE PURPOSE'

Chapter 1
General

Charity

1 Meaning of 'charity'

(1) For the purposes of the law of England and Wales, 'charity' means an institution which –

(a) is established for charitable purposes only, and
(b) falls to be subject to the control of the High Court in the exercise of its jurisdiction with respect to charities.

(2) The definition of 'charity' in subsection (1) does not apply for the purposes of an enactment if a different definition of that term applies for those purposes by virtue of that or any other enactment.

Charitable purpose

2 Meaning of 'charitable purpose'

(1) For the purposes of the law of England and Wales, a charitable purpose is a purpose which –

(a) falls within section 3(1), and
(b) is for the public benefit (see section 4).

(2) Any reference in any enactment or document (in whatever terms) –

(a) to charitable purposes, or
(b) to institutions having purposes that are charitable under the law relating to charities in England and Wales,

is to be read in accordance with subsection (1).

(3) Subsection (2) does not apply where the context otherwise requires.

(4) This section is subject to section 11 (which makes special provision for Chapter 2 of this Part onwards).

3 Descriptions of purposes

(1) A purpose falls within this subsection if it falls within any of the following descriptions of purposes –

(a) the prevention or relief of poverty;
(b) the advancement of education;
(c) the advancement of religion;
(d) the advancement of health or the saving of lives;
(e) the advancement of citizenship or community development;
(f) the advancement of the arts, culture, heritage or science;
(g) the advancement of amateur sport;
(h) the advancement of human rights, conflict resolution or reconciliation or the promotion of religious or racial harmony or equality and diversity;
(i) the advancement of environmental protection or improvement;
(j) the relief of those in need because of youth, age, ill-health, disability, financial hardship or other disadvantage;
(k) the advancement of animal welfare;
(l) the promotion of the efficiency of the armed forces of the Crown or of the efficiency of the police, fire and rescue services or ambulance services;
(m) any other purposes –
  (i) that are not within paragraphs (a) to (l) but are recognised as charitable purposes by virtue of section 5 (recreational and similar trusts, etc) or under the old law,
  (ii) that may reasonably be regarded as analogous to, or within the spirit of, any purposes falling within any of paragraphs (a) to (l) or sub-paragraph (i), or
  (iii) that may reasonably be regarded as analogous to, or within the spirit of, any purposes which have been recognised, under the law relating to charities in England and Wales, as falling within sub-paragraph (ii) or this sub-paragraph.

(2) In subsection (1) –

(a) in paragraph (c), 'religion' includes –
  (i) a religion which involves belief in more than one god, and
  (ii) a religion which does not involve belief in a god,
(b) in paragraph (d), 'the advancement of health' includes the prevention or relief of sickness, disease or human suffering,
(c) paragraph (e) includes –
  (i) rural or urban regeneration, and
  (ii) the promotion of civic responsibility, volunteering, the voluntary sector or the effectiveness or efficiency of charities,
(d) in paragraph (g), 'sport' means sports or games which promote health by involving physical or mental skill or exertion,
(e) paragraph (j) includes relief given by the provision of accommodation or care to the persons mentioned in that paragraph, and
(f) in paragraph (l), 'fire and rescue services' means services provided by fire and rescue authorities under Part 2 of the Fire and Rescue Services Act 2004.

(3) Where any of the terms used in any of paragraphs (a) to (l) of subsection (1), or in subsection (2), has a particular meaning under the law relating to charities in England and Wales, the term is to be taken as having the same meaning where it appears in that provision.

(4) In subsection (1)(m)(i), 'the old law' means the law relating to charities in England and Wales as in force immediately before 1 April 2008.

4 The public benefit requirement

(1) In this Act 'the public benefit requirement' means the requirement in section 2(1)(b) that a purpose falling within section 3(1) must be for the public benefit if it is to be a charitable purpose.

(2) In determining whether the public benefit requirement is satisfied in relation to any purpose falling within section 3(1), it is not to be presumed that a purpose of a particular description is for the public benefit.

(3) In this Chapter any reference to the public benefit is a reference to the public benefit as that term is understood for the purposes of the law relating to charities in England and Wales.

(4) Subsection (3) is subject to subsection (2).

Recreational trusts and registered sports clubs

5 Recreational and similar trusts, etc

(1) It is charitable (and is to be treated as always having been charitable) to provide, or assist in the provision of, facilities for –

(a) recreation, or
(b) other leisure-time occupation,

if the facilities are provided in the interests of social welfare.

(2) The requirement that the facilities are provided in the interests of social welfare cannot be satisfied if the basic conditions are not met.

(3) The basic conditions are –

(a) that the facilities are provided with the object of improving the conditions of life for the persons for whom the facilities are primarily intended, and
(b) that –
   (i) those persons have need of the facilities because of their youth, age, infirmity or disability, poverty, or social and economic circumstances, or
   (ii) the facilities are to be available to members of the public at large or to male, or to female, members of the public at large.

(4) Subsection (1) applies in particular to –

(a) the provision of facilities at village halls, community centres and women's institutes, and
(b) the provision and maintenance of grounds and buildings to be used for purposes of recreation or leisure-time occupation,

and extends to the provision of facilities for those purposes by the organising of any activity.

But this is subject to the requirement that the facilities are provided in the interests of social welfare.

(5) Nothing in this section is to be treated as derogating from the public benefit requirement.

6 Registered sports clubs

(1) A registered sports club established for charitable purposes is to be treated as not being so established, and accordingly cannot be a charity.

(2) In subsection (1), 'registered sports club' means a registered club within the meaning of Chapter 9 of Part 13 of the Corporation Tax Act 2010 (community amateur sports clubs).

Supplementary

7 Application of this Chapter in relation to Scotland

(1) This Chapter affects the law of Scotland only in so far as it affects the construction of references to –

(a) charities, or
(b) charitable purposes,

in enactments which relate to matters falling within Section A1 of Part 2 of Schedule 5 to the Scotland Act 1998 (reserved matters: fiscal policy etc).

(2) In so far as this Chapter affects the law of Scotland –

(a) references in sections 1(1) and 2(1) to the law of England and Wales are to be read as references to the law of Scotland, and
(b) the reference in section 1(1) to the High Court is to be read as a reference to the Court of Session.

8 Application of this Chapter in relation to Northern Ireland

(1) This Chapter affects the law of Northern Ireland only in so far as it affects the construction of references to –

(a) charities, or
(b) charitable purposes,

in enactments which relate to matters falling within paragraph 9 of Schedule 2 to the Northern Ireland Act 1998 (excepted matters: taxes and duties).

(2) In so far as this Chapter affects the law of Northern Ireland –

(a) references in sections 1(1) and 2(1) to the law of England and Wales are to be read as references to the law of Northern Ireland, and
(b) the reference in section 1(1) to the High Court is to be read as a reference to the High Court in Northern Ireland.

9 Interpretation

(1) In this Chapter 'enactment' includes –

(a) any provision of subordinate legislation (within the meaning of the Interpretation Act 1978), and
(b) a provision of a Measure of the Church Assembly or of the General Synod of the Church of England,

and references to enactments include enactments whenever passed or made.

(2) In section 2(2) the reference to a document includes a document whenever made.

(3) In this Act 'institution' means an institution whether incorporated or not, and includes a trust or undertaking.

(4) Subsections (1) to (3) apply except where the context otherwise requires.

Chapter 2
Special Provision for this Act

10 Ecclesiastical corporations etc not charities in certain contexts

(1) In the rest of this Act, 'charity', except in so far as the context otherwise requires, has the meaning given by section 1(1).

(2) But in the rest of this Act (apart from Chapter 3 of Part 17) 'charity' is not applicable to –

(a) any ecclesiastical corporation in respect of the corporate property of the corporation, except a corporation aggregate having some purposes which are not ecclesiastical in respect of its corporate property held for those purposes,

(b) any Diocesan Board of Finance, or any subsidiary of such a Board, in respect of the diocesan glebe land of the diocese, or

(c) any trust of property for purposes for which the property has been consecrated.

(3) 'Ecclesiastical corporation' means any corporation in the Church of England, whether sole or aggregate, which is established for spiritual purposes.

(4) 'Diocesan Board of Finance', 'subsidiary' and 'diocesan glebe land' have the same meaning as in the Endowments and Glebe Measure 1976.

11 Charitable purposes

In the rest of this Act, 'charitable purposes' means, except in so far as the context otherwise requires, purposes which are exclusively charitable purposes (as defined by section 2(1)).

12 Direction as to what is (or is not) a separate charity

(1) The Commission (see section 13) may direct that for all or any of the purposes of this Act an institution established for any special purposes of or in connection with a charity (being charitable purposes) is to be treated –

(a) as forming part of that charity, or

(b) as forming a distinct charity.

(2) The Commission may direct that for all or any of the purposes of this Act two or more charities having the same charity trustees are to be treated as a single charity.

PART 2
THE CHARITY COMMISSION AND THE OFFICIAL CUSTODIAN FOR CHARITIES

The Commission

13 The Charity Commission

(1) There continues to be a body corporate known as the Charity Commission for England and Wales (in this Act referred to as 'the Commission').

(2) In Welsh the Commission is known as 'Comisiwn Elusennau Cymru a Lloegr'.

(3) The functions of the Commission are performed on behalf of the Crown.

(4) In the exercise of its functions the Commission is not subject to the direction or control of any Minister of the Crown or of another government department.

(5) But subsection (4) does not affect –

- (a) any provision made by or under any enactment;
- (b) any administrative controls exercised over the Commission's expenditure by the Treasury.

(6) Schedule 1 contains provisions relating to the Commission.

14 The Commission's objectives

The Commission has the following objectives –

1 The public confidence objective

The public confidence objective is to increase public trust and confidence in charities.

2 The public benefit objective

The public benefit objective is to promote awareness and understanding of the operation of the public benefit requirement.

3 The compliance objective

The compliance objective is to promote compliance by charity trustees with their legal obligations in exercising control and management of the administration of their charities.

4 The charitable resources objective

The charitable resources objective is to promote the effective use of charitable resources.

5 The accountability objective

The accountability objective is to enhance the accountability of charities to donors, beneficiaries and the general public.

15 The Commission's general functions

(1) The Commission has the following general functions –

1. Determining whether institutions are or are not charities.
2. Encouraging and facilitating the better administration of charities.
3. Identifying and investigating apparent misconduct or mismanagement in the administration of charities and taking remedial or protective action in connection with misconduct or mismanagement in the administration of charities.
4. Determining whether public collections certificates should be issued, and remain in force, in respect of public charitable collections.
5. Obtaining, evaluating and disseminating information in connection with the performance of any of the Commission's functions or meeting any of its objectives.
6. Giving information or advice, or making proposals, to any Minister of the Crown on matters relating to any of the Commission's functions or meeting any of its objectives.

(2) The Commission may, in connection with its second general function, give such advice or guidance with respect to the administration of charities as it considers appropriate.

(3) Any advice or guidance so given may relate to –

(a) charities generally,
(b) any class of charities, or
(c) any particular charity,

and may take such form, and be given in such manner, as the Commission considers appropriate.

(4) The Commission's fifth general function includes (among other things) the maintenance of an accurate and up-to-date register of charities under sections 29 (the register) and 34 (removal of charities from register).

(5) The Commission's sixth general function includes (among other things) complying, so far as is reasonably practicable, with any request made by a Minister of the Crown for information or advice on any matter relating to any of its functions.

(6) In this section 'public charitable collection' and 'public collections certificate' have the same meaning as in Chapter 1 of Part 3 of the Charities Act 2006.

16 The Commission's general duties

The Commission has the following general duties –

1 So far as is reasonably practicable the Commission must, in performing its functions, act in a way –

(a) which is compatible with its objectives, and
(b) which it considers most appropriate for the purpose of meeting those objectives.

2 So far as is reasonably practicable the Commission must, in performing its functions, act in a way which is compatible with the encouragement of –

(a) all forms of charitable giving, and
(b) voluntary participation in charity work.

3 In performing its functions the Commission must have regard to the need to use its resources in the most efficient, effective and economic way.

4 In performing its functions the Commission must, so far as relevant, have regard to the principles of best regulatory practice (including the principles under which regulatory activities should be proportionate, accountable, consistent, transparent and targeted only at cases in which action is needed).

5 In performing its functions the Commission must, in appropriate cases, have regard to the desirability of facilitating innovation by or on behalf of charities.

6 In managing its affairs the Commission must have regard to such generally accepted principles of good corporate governance as it is reasonable to regard as applicable to it.

17 Guidance as to operation of public benefit requirement

(1) The Commission must issue guidance in pursuance of its public benefit objective (see paragraph 2 of section 14).

(2) The Commission may from time to time revise any guidance issued under this section.

(3) The Commission must carry out such public and other consultation as it considers appropriate –

(a) before issuing any guidance under this section, or
(b) (unless it considers that it is unnecessary to do so) before revising any guidance under this section.

(4) The Commission must publish any guidance issued or revised under this section in such manner as it considers appropriate.

(5) The charity trustees of a charity must have regard to any such guidance when exercising any powers or duties to which the guidance is relevant.

18 Supply by Commission of copies of documents

The Commission must, at the request of any person, provide that person with copies of, or extracts from, any document in the Commission's possession which is for the time being open to or available for inspection under any provision of this Act.

19 Fees and other amounts payable to Commission

(1) The Minister may by regulations require the payment to the Commission of such fees as may be prescribed by the regulations in respect of –

(a) the discharge by the Commission of such functions under the enactments relating to charities as may be so prescribed;
(b) the inspection of the register of charities or of other material kept by the Commission under those enactments, or the provision of copies of or extracts from documents so kept.

(2) Regulations under this section may –

(a) confer, or provide for the conferring of, exemptions from liability to pay a prescribed fee;
(b) provide for the remission or refunding of a prescribed fee (in whole or in part) in circumstances prescribed by the regulations.

(3) The Commission may impose charges of such amounts as it considers reasonable in respect of the supply of any publications produced by it.

(4) Any fees and other payments received by the Commission by virtue of this section are to be paid into the Consolidated Fund.

20 Incidental powers

(1) The Commission may do anything which is calculated to facilitate, or is conducive or incidental to, the performance of any of its functions or general duties.

(2) But nothing in this Act authorises the Commission –

(a) to exercise functions corresponding to those of a charity trustee in relation to a charity, or
(b) otherwise to be directly involved in the administration of a charity.

(3) Subsection (2) does not affect the operation of section 84[, 84A][, 84B] or 85 (power of Commission to direct specified action to be taken or to direct application of charity property).

NOTES

Sub-s (3) amended by the Charities (Protection and Social Investment) Act 2016, ss 6(1), (3), 7(1), (3).

The official custodian

21 The official custodian for charities

(1) There continues to be an officer known as the official custodian for charities (in this Act referred to as 'the official custodian').

(2) The official custodian's function is to act as trustee for charities in the cases provided for by this Act.

(3) The official custodian is such individual as the Commission may from time to time designate.

(4) The official custodian's duties must be performed in accordance with such general or special directions as may be given by the Commission.

(5) Schedule 2 contains provisions relating to the official custodian.

PART 3
EXEMPT CHARITIES AND THE PRINCIPAL REGULATOR

Exempt charities

22 Meaning of 'exempt charity' and Sch 3

(1) In this Act 'exempt charity' means any institution, so far as it is a charity, that is within Schedule 3.

(2) Subsection (1) is subject to any other enactment by virtue of which a charity is an exempt charity.

23 Power to amend Sch 3 so as to add or remove exempt charities

(1) The Minister may by order make such amendments of Schedule 3 as the Minister considers appropriate for securing –

(a) that (so far as they are charities) institutions of a particular description become or (as the case may be) cease to be exempt charities, or
(b) that (so far as it is a charity) a particular institution becomes or (as the case may be) ceases to be an exempt charity.

(2) An order under subsection (1) may be made only if the Minister is satisfied that the order is desirable in the interests of ensuring appropriate or effective regulation of the charities or charity concerned in connection with compliance by the charity trustees of the charities or charity with their legal obligations in exercising control and management of the administration of the charities or charity.

(3) The Minister may by order make such amendments or other modifications of any enactment as the Minister considers appropriate in connection with –

(a) charities of a particular description becoming, or ceasing to be, exempt charities, or
(b) a particular charity becoming, or ceasing to be, an exempt charity,

as a result of provision made under subsection (1).

(4) In subsection (3), 'enactment' includes –

(a) any provision of subordinate legislation (within the meaning of the Interpretation Act 1978), and
(b) a provision of a Measure of the Church Assembly or of the General Synod of the Church of England,

and references to enactments include enactments whenever passed or made.

24 Power to remove defunct institutions from Sch 3

The Minister may by order make such amendments of Schedule 3 as the Minister considers appropriate for removing from that Schedule an institution that has ceased to exist.

The principal regulator

25 Meaning of 'the principal regulator'

In this Act 'the principal regulator', in relation to an exempt charity, means such body or Minister of the Crown as is prescribed as its principal regulator by regulations made by the Minister.

26 General duty of principal regulator in relation to exempt charity

(1) This section applies to any body or Minister of the Crown who is the principal regulator in relation to an exempt charity.

(2) The body or Minister must do all that the body or Minister reasonably can to meet the compliance objective in relation to the charity.

(3) The compliance objective is to promote compliance by the charity trustees with their legal obligations in exercising control and management of the administration of the charity.

27 Power to make amendments in connection with s 26

(1) Regulations under section 25 may make such amendments or other modifications of any enactment as the Minister considers appropriate for the purpose of facilitating, or otherwise in connection with, the discharge by a principal regulator of the duty under section 26(2).

(2) In subsection (1), 'enactment' includes –

(a) any provision of subordinate legislation (within the meaning of the Interpretation Act 1978), and
(b) a provision of a Measure of the Church Assembly or of the General Synod of the Church of England,

and references to enactments include enactments whenever passed or made.

28 Commission to consult principal regulator

Before exercising in relation to an exempt charity any specific power exercisable by it in relation to the charity, the Commission must consult the charity's principal regulator.

PART 4
REGISTRATION AND NAMES OF CHARITIES

The register

29 The register

(1) There continues to be a register of charities, to be kept by the Commission in such manner as it thinks fit.

(2) The register must contain –

(a) the name of every charity registered in accordance with section 30, and
(b) such other particulars of, and such other information relating to, every such charity as the Commission thinks fit.

(3) In this Act, except in so far as the context otherwise requires, 'the register means' the register of charities kept under this section and 'registered' is to be read accordingly.

Charities required to be registered

30 Charities required to be registered: general

(1) Every charity must be registered in the register unless subsection (2) applies to it.

(2) The following are not required to be registered –

(a) an exempt charity (see section 22 and Schedule 3),
(b) a charity which for the time being –
    (i) is permanently or temporarily excepted by order of the Commission, and
    (ii) complies with any conditions of the exception,
  and whose gross income does not exceed £100,000,
(c) a charity which for the time being –
    (i) is, or is of a description, permanently or temporarily excepted by regulations made by the Minister, and
    (ii) complies with any conditions of the exception,
  and whose gross income does not exceed £100,000, and
(d) a charity whose gross income does not exceed £5,000.

(3) A charity within –

(a) subsection (2)(b) or (c), or
(b) subsection (2)(d),

must, if it so requests, be registered in the register.

(4) In this section any reference to a charity's gross income is to be read, in relation to a particular time –

(a) as a reference to the charity's gross income in its financial year immediately preceding that time, or

(b) if the Commission so determines, as a reference to the amount which the Commission estimates to be the likely amount of the charity's gross income in such financial year of the charity as is specified in the determination.

31 Restrictions on extending the range of excepted charities etc

(1) No order may be made under section 30(2)(b) so as to except any charity that was not excepted immediately before 31 January 2009.

(2) Subject to subsection (3), no regulations may be made under section 30(2)(c) so as to except any charity or description of charities that was not excepted immediately before 31 January 2009.

(3) Such regulations must be made under section 30(2)(c) as are necessary to secure that any institution ceasing to be an exempt charity by virtue of an order made under section 23 is excepted under section 30(2)(c) (subject to compliance with any conditions of the exception and the financial limit mentioned in section 30(2)(c)).

(4) Subsection (1) does not prevent an order which –

(a) was in force immediately before 31 January 2009, and
(b) has effect (by virtue of paragraph 4 of Schedule 8) as if made under section 30(2)(b),

from being varied or revoked.

(5) Subsection (2) does not prevent regulations which –

(a) were in force immediately before 31 January 2009, and
(b) have effect (by virtue of paragraph 4 of Schedule 8) as if made under section 30(2)(c),

from being varied or revoked.

32 Power to alter sums specified in s 30(2)

(1) The Minister may by order amend –

(a) section 30(2)(b) and (c), or
(b) section 30(2)(d),

by substituting a different sum for the sum for the time being specified there.

(2) The Minister may only make an order under subsection (1) –

(a) so far as it amends section 30(2)(b) and (c), if the Minister considers it expedient to do so with a view to reducing the scope of the exceptions provided by section 30(2)(b) and (c);
(b) so far as it amends section 30(2)(d), if the Minister considers it expedient to do so –
    (i) in consequence of changes in the value of money, or
    (ii) with a view to extending the scope of the exception provided by section 30(2)(d).

(3) No order may be made by the Minister under subsection (1)(a) unless a copy of a report under section 73 of the Charities Act 2006 has been laid before Parliament in accordance with that section.

33 Power to repeal provisions relating to excepted charities

The following provisions –

(a) section 30(2)(b) and (c) and (3)(a),
(b) section 31,
(c) section 32(1)(a), (2)(a) and (3), and
(d) this section,

cease to have effect on such day as the Minister may by order appoint for the purposes of this section.

Removal of charities from register

34 Removal of charities from register

(1) The Commission must remove from the register –

(a) any institution which it no longer considers is a charity, and
(b) any charity which has ceased to exist or does not operate.

(2) If the removal of an institution under subsection (1)(a) is due to any change in its trusts, the removal takes effect from the date of the change.

(3) A charity which is for the time being registered under section 30(3) (voluntary registration) must be removed from the register if it so requests.

Registration: duties of trustees and claims and objections

35 Duties of trustees in connection with registration

(1) If a charity required to be registered by virtue of section 30(1) is not registered, the charity trustees must –

(a) apply to the Commission for the charity to be registered, and
(b) supply the Commission with the required documents and information.

(2) The required documents and information are –

(a) copies of the charity's trusts or (if they are not set out in any extant document) particulars of them,
(b) such other documents or information as may be prescribed by regulations made by the Minister, and
(c) such other documents or information as the Commission may require for the purposes of the application.

(3) If an institution is for the time being registered, the charity trustees (or the last charity trustees) must –

(a) notify the Commission if the institution ceases to exist, or if there is any change in its trusts or in the particulars of it entered in the register, and
(b) so far as appropriate, supply the Commission with particulars of any such change and copies of any new trusts or alterations of the trusts.

(4) Nothing in subsection (3) requires a person –

(a) to supply the Commission with copies of schemes for the administration of a charity made otherwise than by the court,

(b) to notify the Commission of any change made with respect to a registered charity by such a scheme, or
(c) if the person refers the Commission to a document or copy already in the Commission's possession, to supply a further copy of the document.

36 Claims and objections to registration

(1) A person who is or may be affected by the registration of an institution as a charity may, on the ground that it is not a charity –

(a) object to its being entered by the Commission in the register, or
(b) apply to the Commission for it to be removed from the register.

(2) Provision may be made by regulations made by the Minister as to the manner in which any such objection or application is to be made, prosecuted or dealt with.

(3) Subsection (4) applies if there is an appeal to the Tribunal against any decision of the Commission –

(a) to enter an institution in the register, or
(b) not to remove an institution from the register.

(4) Until the Commission is satisfied whether the decision of the Commission is or is not to stand, the entry in the register –

(a) is to be maintained, but
(b) is in suspense and must be marked to indicate that it is in suspense.

(5) Any question affecting the registration or removal from the register of an institution –

(a) may be considered afresh by the Commission, even though it has been determined by a decision on appeal under Chapter 2 of Part 17 (appeals and applications to Tribunal), and
(b) is not concluded by that decision, if it appears to the Commission that –
    (i) there has been a change of circumstances, or
    (ii) the decision is inconsistent with a later judicial decision.

Effect of registration and right to inspect register

37 Effect of registration

(1) An institution is, for all purposes other than rectification of the register, conclusively presumed to be or to have been a charity at any time when it is or was on the register.

(2) For the purposes of subsection (1) an institution is to be treated as not being on the register during any period when the entry relating to it is in suspense under section 36(4).

38 Right to inspect register

(1) The register (including the entries cancelled when institutions are removed from the register) must be open to public inspection at all reasonable times.

(2) If any information contained in the register is not in documentary form, subsection (1) is to be read as requiring the information to be available for public inspection in legible form at all reasonable times.

(3) If the Commission so determines, subsection (1) does not apply to any particular information contained in the register that is specified in the determination.

(4) Copies (or particulars) of the trusts of any registered charity as supplied to the Commission under section 35 (duties of trustees in connection with registration) must, so long as the charity remains on the register –

(a) be kept by the Commission, and
(b) be open to public inspection at all reasonable times.

(5) If a copy of a document relating to a registered charity –

(a) is not required to be supplied to the Commission as the result of section 35(4), but
(b) is in the Commission's possession,

a copy of the document must be open to inspection under subsection (4) as if supplied to the Commission under section 35.

Disclosure of registered charity status

39 Statement required to be made in official publications etc

(1) This section applies to a registered charity if its gross income in its last financial year exceeded £10,000.

(2) If this section applies to a registered charity, the fact that it is a registered charity must be stated in legible characters –

(a) in all notices, advertisements and other documents issued by or on behalf of the charity and soliciting money or other property for the benefit of the charity,
(b) in all bills of exchange, promissory notes, endorsements, cheques and orders for money or goods purporting to be signed on behalf of the charity, and
(c) in all bills rendered by it and in all its invoices, receipts and letters of credit.

(3) The statement required by subsection (2) must be in English, except that, in the case of a document which is otherwise wholly in Welsh, the statement may be in Welsh if it consists of or includes 'elusen cofrestredig' (the Welsh equivalent of 'registered charity').

(4) Subsection (2)(a) has effect –

(a) whether the solicitation is express or implied, and
(b) whether or not the money or other property is to be given for any consideration.

40 Power to alter sum specified in s 39(1)

The Minister may by order amend section 39(1) by substituting a different sum for the sum for the time being specified there.

41 Offences

(1) It is an offence for a person, in the case of a registered charity to which section 39 applies, to issue or authorise the issue of any document falling within section 39(2)(a) or (c) which does not contain the statement required by section 39(2).

(2) It is an offence for a person, in the case of a registered charity to which section 39 applies, to sign any document falling within section 39(2)(b) which does not contain the statement required by section 39(2).

(3) A person guilty of an offence under subsection (1) or (2) is liable on summary conviction to a fine not exceeding level 3 on the standard scale.

Power to require charity's name to be changed

42 Power to require name to be changed

(1) If this subsection applies to a charity, the Commission may give a direction requiring the name of the charity to be changed, within such period as is specified in the direction, to such other name as the charity trustees may determine with the approval of the Commission.

(2) Subsection (1) applies to a charity if –

(a) it is a registered charity and its name ('the registered name') –
 (i) is the same as, or
 (ii) is in the opinion of the Commission too like,
 the name, at the time when the registered name was entered in the register in respect of the charity, of any other charity (whether registered or not),
(b) the name of the charity is in the opinion of the Commission likely to mislead the public as to the true nature of –
 (i) the purposes of the charity as set out in its trusts, or
 (ii) the activities which the charity carries on under its trusts in pursuit of those purposes,
(c) the name of the charity includes any word or expression for the time being specified in regulations made by the Minister and the inclusion in its name of that word or expression is in the opinion of the Commission likely to mislead the public in any respect as to the status of the charity,
(d) the name of the charity is in the opinion of the Commission likely to give the impression that the charity is connected in some way with Her Majesty's Government or any local authority, or with any other body of persons or any individual, when it is not so connected, or
(e) the name of the charity is in the opinion of the Commission offensive.

(3) Any direction given by virtue of subsection (2)(a) must be given within 12 months of the time when the registered name was entered in the register in respect of the charity.

(4) In subsection (2) any reference to the name of a charity is, in relation to a registered charity, a reference to the name by which it is registered.

(5) Any direction given under this section with respect to a charity must be given to the charity trustees.

43 Duty of charity trustees on receiving direction under s 42

(1) On receiving a direction under section 42 the charity trustees must give effect to it regardless of anything in the trusts of the charity.

(2) If the name of any charity is changed by virtue of section 42, the charity trustees must without delay notify the Commission of –

(a) the charity's new name, and
(b) the date on which the change occurred.

(3) Subsection (2) does not affect section 35(3) (duty of charity trustees to notify changes in registered particulars).

44 Change of name not to affect existing rights and obligations etc

A change of name by a charity by virtue of section 42 does not affect any rights or obligations of the charity; and any legal proceedings that might have been continued or commenced by or against it in its former name may be continued or commenced by or against it in its new name.

45 Change of name where charity is a company

(1) In relation to a charitable company, any reference in section 42 or 43 to the charity trustees of a charity is to be read as a reference to the directors of the company.

(2) Subsections (3) to (5) apply if a direction is given under section 42 with respect to a charitable company.

(3) The direction is to be treated as requiring the name of the company to be changed by resolution of the directors of the company.

(4) Where a resolution of the directors is passed in accordance with subsection (3), the company must give notice of the change to the registrar of companies.

(5) Where the name of the company is changed in compliance with the direction, the registrar of companies must –

- (a) if satisfied that the new name complies with the requirements of Part 5 of the Companies Act 2006, enter the new name on the register of companies in place of the former name, and
- (b) issue a certificate of incorporation altered to meet the circumstances of the case;

and the change of name has effect from the date on which the altered certificate is issued.

PART 5
INFORMATION POWERS

Inquiries instituted by Commission

46 General power to institute inquiries

(1) The Commission may from time to time institute inquiries with regard to charities or a particular charity or class of charities, either generally or for particular purposes.

(2) But no such inquiry is to extend to any exempt charity except where this has been requested by its principal regulator.

(3) The Commission may –

- (a) conduct such an inquiry itself, or
- (b) appoint a person to conduct it and make a report to the Commission.

(4) This section and sections 47 to 49 (obtaining evidence and search warrants) have effect in relation to a body entered in the Scottish Charity Register which is managed or controlled wholly or mainly in or from England or Wales as they have effect in relation to a charity.

47 Obtaining evidence etc for purposes of inquiry

(1) In this section 'inquiry' means an inquiry under section 46.

(2) For the purposes of an inquiry, the Commission, or a person appointed by the Commission to conduct it, may direct any person –

(a) if a matter in question at the inquiry is one on which the person has or can reasonably obtain information –
  (i) to provide accounts and statements in writing with respect to the matter, or to return answers in writing to any questions or inquiries addressed to the person on the matter, and
  (ii) to verify any such accounts, statements or answers by statutory declaration;

(b) to provide copies of documents which are in the custody or under the control of the person and which relate to any matter in question at the inquiry, and to verify any such copies by statutory declaration;

(c) to attend at a specified time and place and give evidence or produce any such documents.

But this is subject to the provisions of this section.

(3) For the purposes of an inquiry –

(a) evidence may be taken on oath, and the person conducting the inquiry may for that purpose administer oaths, or

(b) the person conducting the inquiry may instead of administering an oath require the person examined to make and subscribe a declaration of the truth of the matters about which that person is examined.

(4) The Commission may pay to any person attending to give evidence or produce documents for the purpose of an inquiry the necessary expenses of doing so.

(5) A direction under subsection (2)(c) may not require a person to go more than 10 miles from the person's place of residence unless those expenses are paid or tendered to the person.

48 Power to obtain search warrant for purposes of inquiry

(1) A justice of the peace may issue a warrant under this section if satisfied, on information given on oath by a member of the Commission's staff, that there are reasonable grounds for believing that each of the conditions in subsection (2) is satisfied.

(2) The conditions are –

(a) that an inquiry has been instituted under section 46,

(b) that there is on the premises to be specified in the warrant any document or information relevant to that inquiry which the Commission could require to be produced or provided under section 52(1), and

(c) that, if the Commission were to make an order requiring the document or information to be so produced or provided –
  (i) the order would not be complied with, or
  (ii) the document or information would be removed, tampered with, concealed or destroyed.

(3) A warrant under this section is a warrant authorising the member of the Commission's staff who is named in it ('P') –

(a) to enter and search the premises specified in it;
(b) to take such other persons with P as the Commission considers are needed to assist P in doing anything that P is authorised to do under the warrant;
(c) to take possession of any documents which appear to fall within subsection (2)(b), or to take any other steps which appear to be necessary for preserving, or preventing interference with, any such documents;
(d) to take possession of any computer disk or other electronic storage device which appears to contain information falling within subsection (2)(b), or information contained in a document so falling, or to take any other steps which appear to be necessary for preserving, or preventing interference with, any such information;
(e) to take copies of, or extracts from, any documents or information falling within paragraph (c) or (d);
(f) to require any person on the premises to provide an explanation of any such document or information or to state where any such documents or information may be found;
(g) to require any such person to give P such assistance as P may reasonably require for the taking of copies or extracts as mentioned in paragraph (e).

49 Execution of search warrant

(1) Entry and search under a warrant under section 48 must be at a reasonable hour and within one month of the date of its issue.

(2) The member of the Commission's staff who is authorised under such a warrant ('P') must, if required to do so, produce –

(a) the warrant, and
(b) documentary evidence that P is a member of the Commission's staff,

for inspection by the occupier of the premises or anyone acting on the occupier's behalf.

(3) P must make a written record of –

(a) the date and time of P's entry on the premises,
(b) the number of persons (if any) who accompanied P on to the premises and the names of any such persons,
(c) the period for which P (and any such persons) remained on the premises,
(d) what P (and any such persons) did while on the premises, and
(e) any document or device of which P took possession while there.

(4) If required to do so, P must give a copy of the record to the occupier of the premises or someone acting on the occupier's behalf.

(5) Unless it is not reasonably practicable to do so, P must before leaving the premises comply with –

(a) the requirements of subsection (3), and
(b) any requirement made under subsection (4) before P leaves the premises.

(6) Where possession of any document or device is taken under section 48 –

(a) the document may be retained for so long as the Commission considers that it is necessary to retain it (rather than a copy of it) for the purposes of the relevant inquiry under section 46, or
(b) the device may be retained for so long as the Commission considers that it is necessary to retain it for the purposes of that inquiry,

as the case may be.

(7) Once it appears to the Commission that the retention of any document or device has ceased to be so necessary, it must arrange for the document or device to be returned as soon as is reasonably practicable –

(a) to the person from whose possession it was taken, or
(b) to any of the charity trustees of the charity to which it belonged or related.

For the purposes of this subsection as it has effect by virtue of section 46(4), the reference in paragraph (b) to the charity trustees of the charity is to be read as a reference to the persons having the general control and management of the administration of the body entered in the Scottish Charity Register.

(8) It is an offence for a person intentionally to obstruct the exercise of any rights conferred by a warrant under section 48.

(9) A person guilty of an offence under subsection (8) is liable on summary conviction –

(a) to imprisonment for a term not exceeding 51 weeks, or
(b) to a fine not exceeding level 5 on the standard scale,

or to both.

50 Publication of results of inquiries

(1) This section applies where an inquiry has been held under section 46.

(2) The Commission may –

(a) cause the report of the person conducting the inquiry, or such other statement of the results of the inquiry as the Commission thinks fit, to be printed and published, or
(b) publish any such report or statement in some other way which is calculated in the Commission's opinion to bring it to the attention of persons who may wish to make representations to the Commission about the action to be taken.

51 Contributions by local authorities to inquiries into local charities

(1) A council may contribute to the expenses of the Commission in connection with inquiries under section 46 into local charities in the council's area.

(2) In subsection (1) 'council' means –

(a) a district council;
(b) a county council;
(c) a county borough council;
(d) a London borough council;
(e) the Common Council of the City of London.

Power to call for documents and search records

52 Power to call for documents

(1) The Commission may by order –

(a) require any person to provide the Commission with any information which is in that person's possession and which –
(i) relates to any charity, and

(ii) is relevant to the discharge of the functions of the Commission or of the official custodian;

(b) require any person who has custody or control of any document which relates to any charity and is relevant to the discharge of the functions of the Commission or of the official custodian –

(i) to provide the Commission with a copy of or extract from the document, or

(ii) to transmit the document itself to the Commission for its inspection (unless the document forms part of the records or other documents of a court or of a public or local authority).

(2) The Commission is entitled without payment to keep any copy or extract provided to it under subsection (1).

(3) If a document transmitted to the Commission under subsection (1) for it to inspect –

(a) relates only to one or more charities, and

(b) is not held by any person entitled as trustee or otherwise to the custody of it,

the Commission may keep it or may deliver it to the charity trustees or to any other person who may be so entitled.

(4) This section has effect in relation to any body entered in the Scottish Charity Register which is managed or controlled wholly or mainly in or from England or Wales as it has effect in relation to a charity.

53 Power to search records

(1) Any member of the staff of the Commission, if so authorised by it, is entitled without payment to inspect and take copies of or extracts from the records or other documents of –

(a) any court, or

(b) any public registry or office of records,

for any purpose connected with the discharge of the functions of the Commission or of the official custodian.

(2) The reference in subsection (1) to a member of the staff of the Commission includes the official custodian even if not a member of the staff of the Commission.

(3) The rights conferred by subsection (1), in relation to information recorded otherwise than in legible form, include the right to require the information to be made available in legible form –

(a) for inspection, or

(b) for a copy or extract to be made of or from it.

Disclosure of information

54 Disclosure to Commission: general

(1) A relevant public authority may disclose information to the Commission if the disclosure is made for the purpose of enabling or assisting the Commission to discharge any of its functions.

(2) Subsection (1) is subject to section 55.

(3) In this section 'relevant public authority' means –

(a) any government department (including a Northern Ireland department),
(b) any local authority,
(c) any constable, and
(d) any other body or person discharging functions of a public nature (including a body or person discharging regulatory functions in relation to any description of activities).

55 Disclosure to Commission: Revenue and Customs information

(1) Revenue and Customs information may be disclosed under section 54(1) only if it relates to an institution, undertaking or body falling within one (or more) of the following paragraphs –

(a) a charity;
(b) an institution which is established for charitable, benevolent or philanthropic purposes;
(c) an institution by or in respect of which a claim for tax exemption has at any time been made;
(d) a subsidiary undertaking of a charity;
(e) a body entered in the Scottish Charity Register which is managed or controlled wholly or mainly in or from England or Wales.

(2) In subsection (1)(d) 'subsidiary undertaking of a charity' means an undertaking (as defined by section 1161(1) of the Companies Act 2006) in relation to which –

(a) a charity is (or is to be treated as) a parent undertaking in accordance with the provisions of section 1162 of, and Schedule 7 to, the Companies Act 2006, or
(b) two or more charities would, if they were a single charity, be (or be treated as) a parent undertaking in accordance with those provisions.

(3) For the purposes of the references to a parent undertaking –

(a) in subsection (2), and
(b) in section 1162 of, and Schedule 7 to, the Companies Act 2006 as they apply for the purposes of subsection (2),

'undertaking' includes a charity which is not an undertaking as defined by section 1161(1) of that Act.

(4) In this section 'Revenue and Customs' information means information held as mentioned in section 18(1) of the Commissioners for Revenue and Customs Act 2005.

(5) For the purposes of subsection (1)(c), 'claim for tax exemption means' –

(a) a claim for exemption under section 505(1) of the Income and Corporation Taxes Act 1988,
(b) a claim for exemption under Part 10 of the Income Tax Act 2007, or
(c) a claim for exemption under Part 11 of the Corporation Tax Act 2010, if it is not –
    (i) a claim for exemption under section 475, 476 or 477 (reliefs for eligible bodies and scientific research organisations), or
    (ii) a claim made by virtue of section 490 or 491 (application of exemptions to eligible bodies and scientific research organisations).

56 Disclosure by Commission: general

(1) The Commission may disclose to any relevant public authority any information received by the Commission in connection with any of the Commission's functions if –

(a) the disclosure is made for the purpose of enabling or assisting the relevant public authority to discharge any of its functions, or
(b) the information so disclosed is otherwise relevant to the discharge of any of the functions of the relevant public authority.

(2) Subsection (1) is subject to subsection (3) and section 57(1) and (2).

(3) In the case of information disclosed to the Commission under section 54(1), the Commission's power to disclose the information under subsection (1) is exercisable subject to any express restriction subject to which the information was disclosed to the Commission.

(4) In this section 'relevant public authority' has the same meaning as in section 54, except that it also includes any body or person within section 54(3)(d) in a country or territory outside the United Kingdom.

57 Disclosure by Commission: Revenue and Customs information

(1) Section 56(3) does not apply in relation to Revenue and Customs information disclosed to the Commission under section 54(1).

(2) But any such information may not be further disclosed (whether under section 56(1) or otherwise) except with the consent of the Commissioners for Her Majesty's Revenue and Customs.

(3) It is an offence for a responsible person to disclose information in contravention of subsection (2).

(4) A person guilty of an offence under subsection (3) is liable –

(a) on summary conviction, to imprisonment for a term not exceeding 12 months or to a fine not exceeding the statutory maximum, or both;
(b) on conviction on indictment, to imprisonment for a term not exceeding 2 years or to a fine, or both.

(5) It is a defence, where a responsible person is charged with an offence under subsection (3) of disclosing information, to prove that that person reasonably believed –

(a) that the disclosure was lawful, or
(b) that the information had already and lawfully been made available to the public.

(6) In the application of this section to Northern Ireland, the reference to 12 months in subsection (4) is to be read as a reference to 6 months.

(7) In this section 'Revenue and Customs information' means information held as mentioned in section 18(1) of the Commissioners for Revenue and Customs Act 2005.

(8) In this section 'responsible person' means a person who is or was –

(a) a member of the Commission,
(b) a member of the staff of the Commission,
(c) a person acting on behalf of –
    (i) the Commission, or
    (ii) a member of the staff of the Commission, or

(d) a member of a committee established by the Commission.

58 Disclosure to and by principal regulators of exempt charities

(1) Sections 54 to 57 apply with the modifications in subsections (2) to (4) in relation to the disclosure of information to or by the principal regulator of an exempt charity.

(2) References in those sections to the Commission or to any of its functions are to be read as references to the principal regulator of an exempt charity or to any of the functions of that body or person as principal regulator in relation to the charity.

(3) Section 55 has effect as if for subsections (1) and (2) there were substituted –

'(1) Revenue and Customs information may be disclosed under section 54(1) only if it relates to –

(a) the exempt charity in relation to which the principal regulator has functions as such, or
(b) a subsidiary undertaking of the exempt charity.

(2) In subsection (1)(b) 'subsidiary undertaking of the exempt charity' means an undertaking (as defined by section 1161(1) of the Companies Act 2006) in relation to which –

(a) the exempt charity is (or is to be treated as) a parent undertaking in accordance with the provisions of section 1162 of, and Schedule 7 to, the Companies Act 2006, or
(b) the exempt charity and one or more other charities would, if they were a single charity, be (or be treated as) a parent undertaking in accordance with those provisions.'

(4) Section 57 has effect as if for the definition of 'responsible person' in subsection (8) there were substituted a definition specified by regulations under section 25 ('meaning of principal regulator').

(5) Regulations under section 25 may also make such amendments or other modifications of any enactment as the Minister considers appropriate for securing that any disclosure provisions that would otherwise apply in relation to the principal regulator of an exempt charity do not apply in relation to that body or person as principal regulator.

(6) In subsection (5) 'disclosure provisions' means provisions having effect for authorising, or otherwise in connection with, the disclosure of information by or to the principal regulator concerned.

(7) In subsection (5) 'enactment' includes –

(a) any provision of subordinate legislation (within the meaning of the Interpretation Act 1978), and
(b) a provision of a Measure of the Church Assembly or of the General Synod of the Church of England,

and references to enactments include enactments whenever passed or made.

59 Disclosure: supplementary

Nothing in sections 54 to 57 (or in those sections as applied by section 58(1) to (4)) authorises the making of a disclosure which –

(a) contravenes the Data Protection Act 1998, or
(b) is prohibited by Part 1 of the Regulation of Investigatory Powers Act 2000.

Supply of false or misleading information to Commission etc

60 Supply of false or misleading information to Commission etc

(1) It is an offence for a person knowingly or recklessly to provide the Commission with information which is false or misleading in a material particular if the information is provided –

(a) in purported compliance with a requirement imposed by or under this Act, or
(b) otherwise than as mentioned in paragraph (a) but in circumstances in which the person providing the information –
  (i) intends, or
  (ii) could reasonably be expected to know,

that it would be used by the Commission for the purpose of discharging its functions under this Act.

(2) It is an offence for a person wilfully to alter, suppress, conceal or destroy any document which the person is or is liable to be required, by or under this Act, to produce to the Commission.

(3) A person guilty of an offence under this section is liable –

(a) on summary conviction, to a fine not exceeding the statutory maximum;
(b) on conviction on indictment, to imprisonment for a term not exceeding 2 years or to a fine, or both.

(4) In this section references to the Commission include references to any person conducting an inquiry under section 46.

PART 6
CY-PRÈS POWERS AND ASSISTANCE AND SUPERVISION OF CHARITIES BY COURT AND COMMISSION

Cy-près powers and variation of charters

61 Duty of trustees in relation to application of property cy-près

It is hereby declared that a trust for charitable purposes places a trustee under a duty, where the case permits and requires the property or some part of it to be applied cy-près, to secure its effective use for charity by taking steps to enable it to be so applied.

62 Occasions for applying property cy-près

(1) Subject to subsection (3), the circumstances in which the original purposes of a charitable gift can be altered to allow the property given or part of it to be applied cy-près are –

(a) where the original purposes, in whole or in part –
  (i) have been as far as may be fulfilled, or
  (ii) cannot be carried out, or not according to the directions given and to the spirit of the gift,
(b) where the original purposes provide a use for part only of the property available by virtue of the gift,
(c) where –
  (i) the property available by virtue of the gift, and
  (ii) other property applicable for similar purposes,

can be more effectively used in conjunction, and to that end can suitably, regard being had to the appropriate considerations, be made applicable to common purposes,

(d) where the original purposes were laid down by reference to –

(i) an area which then was but has since ceased to be a unit for some other purpose, or

(ii) a class of persons or an area which has for any reason since ceased to be suitable, regard being had to the appropriate considerations, or to be practical in administering the gift, or

(e) where the original purposes, in whole or in part, have, since they were laid down –

(i) been adequately provided for by other means,

(ii) ceased, as being useless or harmful to the community or for other reasons, to be in law charitable, or

(iii) ceased in any other way to provide a suitable and effective method of using the property available by virtue of the gift, regard being had to the appropriate considerations.

(2) In subsection (1) the 'appropriate considerations' means –

(a) (on the one hand) the spirit of the gift concerned, and

(b) (on the other) the social and economic circumstances prevailing at the time of the proposed alteration of the original purposes.

(3) Subsection (1) does not affect the conditions which must be satisfied in order that property given for charitable purposes may be applied cy-près except in so far as those conditions require a failure of the original purposes.

(4) References in subsections (1) to (3) to the original purposes of a gift are to be read, where the application of the property given has been altered or regulated by a scheme or otherwise, as referring to the purposes for which the property is for the time being applicable.

(5) The court may by scheme made under the court's jurisdiction with respect to charities, in any case where the purposes for which the property is held are laid down by reference to any such area as is mentioned in column 1 in Schedule 4, provide for enlarging the area to any such area as is mentioned in column 2 in the same entry in that Schedule.

(6) Subsection (5) does not affect the power to make schemes in circumstances falling within subsection (1).

63 Application cy-près: donor unknown or disclaiming

(1) Property given for specific charitable purposes which fail is applicable cy-près as if given for charitable purposes generally, if it belongs –

(a) to a donor who after –

(i) the prescribed advertisements and inquiries have been published and made, and

(ii) the prescribed period beginning with the publication of those advertisements has ended,

cannot be identified or cannot be found, or

(b) to a donor who has executed a disclaimer in the prescribed form of the right to have the property returned.

(2) Where the prescribed advertisements and inquiries have been published and made by or on behalf of trustees with respect to any such property, the trustees are not liable to any person in respect of the property if no claim by that person to be interested in it is received by them before the end of the period mentioned in subsection (1)(a)(ii).

(3) Where property is applied cy-près by virtue of this section, all the donor's interest in it is treated as having been relinquished when the gift was made.

(4) But where property is so applied as belonging to donors who cannot be identified or cannot be found, and is not so applied by virtue of section 64 (donors treated as unidentifiable) –

- (a) the scheme must specify the total amount of that property,
- (b) the donor of any part of that amount is entitled, on making a claim within the time limit, to recover from the charity for which the property is applied a sum equal to that part, less any expenses properly incurred by the charity trustees after the scheme's date in connection with claims relating to the donor's gift, and
- (c) the scheme may include directions as to the provision to be made for meeting any claims made in accordance with paragraph (b).

(5) For the purposes of subsection (4)(b) –

- (a) a claim is made within the time limit only if it is made no later than 6 months after the date on which the scheme is made, and
- (b) the 'scheme's date' means the date on which the scheme is made.

(6) Subsection (7) applies if –

- (a) any sum is, in accordance with any directions included in the scheme under subsection (4)(c), set aside for meeting claims made in accordance with subsection (4)(b), but
- (b) the aggregate amount of any such claims actually made exceeds the relevant amount;

and for this purpose the 'relevant amount' means the amount of the sum so set aside after deduction of any expenses properly incurred by the charity trustees in connection with claims relating to the donors' gifts.

(7) If the Commission so directs, each of the donors in question is entitled only to such proportion of the relevant amount as the amount of the donor's claim bears to the aggregate amount referred to in subsection (6)(b).

64 Donors treated as unidentifiable

(1) For the purposes of section 63 property is conclusively presumed (without any advertisement or inquiry) to belong to donors who cannot be identified, in so far as it consists of –

- (a) the proceeds of cash collections made –
  - (i) by means of collecting boxes, or
  - (ii) by other means not adapted for distinguishing one gift from another, or
- (b) the proceeds of any lottery, competition, entertainment, sale or similar money-raising activity, after allowing for property given to provide prizes or articles for sale or otherwise to enable the activity to be undertaken.

(2) The court or the Commission may by order direct that property not falling within subsection (1) is for the purposes of section 63 to be treated (without any advertisement or inquiry) as belonging to donors who cannot be identified if it appears to the court or the Commission –

(a) that it would be unreasonable, having regard to the amounts likely to be returned to the donors, to incur expense with a view to returning the property, or

(b) that it would be unreasonable, having regard to the nature, circumstances and amounts of the gifts, and to the lapse of time since the gifts were made, for the donors to expect the property to be returned.

65 Donors treated as disclaiming

(1) This section applies to property given –

(a) for specific charitable purposes, and
(b) in response to a solicitation within subsection (2).

(2) A solicitation is within this subsection if –

(a) it is made for specific charitable purposes, and
(b) it is accompanied by a statement to the effect that property given in response to it will, in the event of those purposes failing, be applicable cy-près as if given for charitable purposes generally, unless the donor makes a relevant declaration at the time of making the gift.

(3) A relevant declaration is a declaration in writing by the donor to the effect that, in the event of the specific charitable purposes failing, the donor wishes to be given the opportunity by the trustees holding the property to request the return of the property in question (or a sum equal to its value at the time of the making of the gift).

(4) Subsections (5) and (6) apply if –

(a) a person has given property as mentioned in subsection (1),
(b) the specific charitable purposes fail, and
(c) the donor has made a relevant declaration.

(5) The trustees holding the property must take the prescribed steps for the purpose of –

(a) informing the donor of the failure of the purposes,
(b) enquiring whether the donor wishes to request the return of the property (or a sum equal to its value), and
(c) if within the prescribed period the donor makes such a request, returning the property (or such a sum) to the donor.

(6) If those trustees have taken all appropriate prescribed steps but –

(a) they have failed to find the donor, or
(b) the donor does not within the prescribed period request the return of the property (or a sum equal to its value),

section 63(1) applies to the property as if it belonged to a donor within section 63(1)(b) (application of property where donor has disclaimed right to return of property).

(7) If –

(a) a person has given property as mentioned in subsection (1),
(b) the specific charitable purposes fail, and

(c) the donor has not made a relevant declaration,

section 63(1) similarly applies to the property as if it belonged to a donor within section 63(1)(b).

(8) For the purposes of this section –

(a) 'solicitation' means a solicitation made in any manner and however communicated to the persons to whom it is addressed,
(b) it is irrelevant whether any consideration is or is to be given in return for the property in question, and
(c) where any appeal consists of –
   (i) solicitations that are accompanied by statements within subsection (2)(b), and
   (ii) solicitations that are not so accompanied,

a person giving property as a result of the appeal is to be presumed, unless the contrary is proved, to have responded to the former solicitations and not the latter.

66 Unknown and disclaiming donors: supplementary

(1) For the purposes of sections 63 and 65, charitable purposes are to be treated as failing if any difficulty in applying property to those purposes makes that property or the part not applicable cy-près available to be returned to the donors.

(2) In sections 63 to 65 and this section –

(a) references to a donor include persons claiming through or under the original donor, and
(b) references to property given include the property for the time being representing the property originally given or property derived from it.

(3) Subsection (2) applies except in so far as the context otherwise requires.

(4) In sections 63 and 65 'prescribed' means prescribed by regulations made by the Commission.

(5) Any such regulations are to be published by the Commission in such manner as it thinks fit.

(6) Any such regulations may, as respects the advertisements which are to be published for the purposes of section 63(1)(a), make provision as to the form and content of such advertisements as well as the manner in which they are to be published.

67 Cy-près schemes

(1) The power of the court or the Commission to make schemes for the application of property cy-près must be exercised in accordance with this section.

(2) Where any property given for charitable purposes is applicable cy-près, the court or the Commission may make a scheme providing for the property to be applied –

(a) for such charitable purposes, and
(b) (if the scheme provides for the property to be transferred to another charity) by or on trust for such other charity,

as it considers appropriate, having regard to the matters set out in subsection (3).

(3) The matters are –

(a) the spirit of the original gift,
(b) the desirability of securing that the property is applied for charitable purposes which are close to the original purposes, and
(c) the need for the relevant charity to have purposes which are suitable and effective in the light of current social and economic circumstances.

The 'relevant charity' means the charity by or on behalf of which the property is to be applied under the scheme.

(4) If a scheme provides for the property to be transferred to another charity, the scheme may impose on the charity trustees of that charity a duty to secure that the property is applied for purposes which are, so far as is reasonably practicable, similar in character to the original purposes.

(5) In this section references to property given include the property for the time being representing the property originally given or property derived from it.

(6) In this section references to the transfer of property to a charity are references to its transfer –

(a) to the charity,
(b) to the charity trustees,
(c) to any trustee for the charity, or
(d) to a person nominated by the charity trustees to hold it in trust for the charity,

as the scheme may provide.

(7) In this section references to the original purposes of a gift are to be read, where the application of the property given has been altered or regulated by a scheme or otherwise, as referring to the purposes for which the property is for the time being applicable.

68 Charities governed by charter, or by or under statute

(1) Subsection (2) applies where a Royal charter establishing or regulating a body corporate is amendable by the grant and acceptance of a further charter.

(2) A scheme relating to the body corporate or to the administration of property held by the body (including a scheme for the cy-près application of any such property) –

(a) may be made by the court under the court's jurisdiction with respect to charities even though the scheme cannot take effect without the alteration of the charter, but
(b) must be so framed that the scheme, or such part of it as cannot take effect without the alteration of the charter, does not purport to come into operation unless or until Her Majesty thinks fit to amend the charter in such manner as will permit the scheme or that part of it to have effect.

(3) Subsection (4) applies where, under –

(a) the court's jurisdiction with respect to charities or the corresponding jurisdiction of a court in Northern Ireland, or
(b) powers conferred by this Act or by any Northern Ireland legislation relating to charities,

a scheme is made with respect to a body corporate and it appears to Her Majesty expedient, having regard to the scheme, to amend any Royal charter relating to that body.

(4) Her Majesty may, on the application of the body corporate, amend the charter accordingly by Order in Council in any way in which the charter could be amended by the grant and acceptance of a further charter; and any such Order in Council may be revoked or varied in the same manner as the charter it amends.

(5) The jurisdiction of the court with respect to charities is not excluded or restricted in the case of a charity of a description mentioned in Schedule 5 by the operation of the enactments or instruments there mentioned in relation to that description.

(6) A scheme established for a charity of a description mentioned in Schedule 5 –

(a) may modify or supersede in relation to it the provision made by any such enactment or instrument as if made by a scheme of the court, and
(b) may also make any such provision as is authorised by that Schedule.

Powers of Commission to make schemes etc

69 Commission's concurrent jurisdiction with High Court for certain purposes

(1) The Commission may by order exercise the same jurisdiction and powers as are exercisable by the High Court in charity proceedings for the following purposes –

(a) establishing a scheme for the administration of a charity;
(b) appointing, discharging or removing a charity trustee or trustee for a charity, or removing an officer or employee;
(c) vesting or transferring property, or requiring or entitling any person to call for or make any transfer of property or any payment.

(2) Subsection (1) is subject to the provisions of this Act.

(3) If the court directs a scheme for the administration of a charity to be established –

(a) the court may by order refer the matter to the Commission for it to prepare or settle a scheme in accordance with such directions (if any) as the court sees fit to give, and
(b) any such order may provide for the scheme to be put into effect by order of the Commission as if prepared under subsection (1) and without any further order of the court.

70 Restrictions on Commission's concurrent jurisdiction

(1) The Commission does not have jurisdiction under section 69 to try or determine –

(a) the title at law or in equity to any property as between –
 (i) a charity or trustee for a charity, and
 (ii) a person holding or claiming the property or an interest in it adversely to the charity, or
(b) any question as to the existence or extent of any charge or trust.

(2) Subject to the following subsections, the Commission must not exercise its jurisdiction under section 69 as respects any charity except –

(a) on the application of the charity,
(b) on an order of the court under section 69(3), or
(c) on the application of the Attorney General.

(3) In the case of a charity whose gross income does not exceed £500 a year, the Commission may exercise its jurisdiction under section 69 on the application of –

(a) any one or more of the charity trustees,
(b) any person interested in the charity, or
(c) any two or more inhabitants of the area of the charity if it is a local charity.

(4) Subsection (5) applies where in the case of a charity, other than an exempt charity, the Commission –

(a) is satisfied that the charity trustees –
  (i) ought in the interests of the charity to apply for a scheme, but
  (ii) have unreasonably refused or neglected to do so, and
(b) has given the charity trustees an opportunity to make representations to it.

(5) The Commission –

(a) may proceed as if an application for a scheme had been made by the charity, but
(b) may not, where it acts by virtue of this subsection, alter the purposes of a charity unless 40 years have elapsed from the date of the charity's foundation.

(6) Where –

(a) a charity cannot apply to the Commission for a scheme because of any vacancy among the charity trustees or the absence or incapacity of any of them, but
(b) such an application is made by such number of the charity trustees as the Commission considers appropriate in the circumstances of the case,

the Commission may nevertheless proceed as if the application were an application made by the charity.

(7) The Commission may on the application of any charity trustee or trustee for a charity exercise its jurisdiction under section 69 for the purpose of discharging the applicant from trusteeship.

(8) The Commission must not exercise its jurisdiction under section 69 in any case (not referred to it by order of the court) which –

(a) because of its contentious character, or any special question of law or of fact which it may involve, or
(b) for other reasons,

the Commission may consider more fit to be adjudicated on by the court.

71 Exercise of Commission's concurrent jurisdiction: notice

(1) Before exercising any jurisdiction under section 69 otherwise than on an order of the court, the Commission must give notice of its intention to do so to each of the charity trustees except any –

(a) that cannot be found or has no known address in the United Kingdom, or
(b) who is party or privy to an application for the exercise of the jurisdiction.

(2) Any such notice –

(a) may be given by post, and
(b) if given by post, may be addressed to the recipient's last known address in the United Kingdom.

72 Power to alter sum specified in s 70(3)

If the Minister thinks it expedient to do so –

(a) in consequence of changes in the value of money, or
(b) with a view to increasing the number of charities in respect of which the Commission may exercise its jurisdiction under section 69 in accordance with section 70(3),

the Minister may by order amend section 70(3) by substituting a different sum for the sum for the time being specified there.

73 Powers to make schemes altering provision made by Acts, etc

(1) If it appears to the Commission that a scheme should be established for the administration of a charity, but also –

(a) that it is necessary or desirable for the scheme –
   (i) to alter the provision made by an Act establishing or regulating the charity, or
   (ii) to make any other provision which goes or might go beyond the powers exercisable by the Commission apart from this section, or
(b) that it is for any reason proper for the scheme to be subject to parliamentary review,

the Commission may (subject to subsection (7)) settle a scheme accordingly with a view to its being given effect under this section.

(2) A scheme settled by the Commission under this section may be given effect by order of the Minister.

(3) Subject to subsections (4) and (6), an order under subsection (2) is subject to annulment in pursuance of a resolution of either House of Parliament.

(4) In the case of a scheme which goes beyond the powers exercisable apart from this section in altering a statutory provision contained in or having effect under any public general Act, no order may be made unless a draft of the order has been laid before and approved by a resolution of each House of Parliament.

(5) Subject to subsection (6), any provision of a scheme brought into effect under this section may be modified or superseded by the court or the Commission as if it were a scheme brought into effect by order of the Commission under section 69.

(6) Where subsection (4) applies to a scheme, the order giving effect to it –

(a) may direct that the scheme must not be modified or superseded by a scheme brought into effect otherwise than under this section, and
(b) may also direct that subsection (4) is to apply to any scheme modifying or superseding the scheme to which the order gives effect.

(7) The Commission must not proceed under this section without the same application, and the same notice to the charity trustees, as would be required if the Commission was proceeding (without an order of the court) under section 69.

(8) But on any application for a scheme, or in a case where it acts by virtue of section 70(5) or (6), the Commission may proceed under this section or section 69 as appears to it appropriate.

74 Restriction on expenditure on promoting Bills

(1) No expenditure incurred in preparing or promoting a Bill in Parliament is to be defrayed without the consent of the court or the Commission out of any money applicable for the purposes of a charity.

(2) Subsection (1) applies regardless of anything in the trusts of a charity.

75 Further powers to alter application of charitable property

(1) Subsection (2) applies where the Commission is satisfied that –

(a) the whole of the income of a charity cannot in existing circumstances be effectively applied for the purposes of the charity,
(b) if those circumstances continue, a scheme might be made for applying the surplus cy-près, and
(c) it is for any reason not yet desirable to make such a scheme.

(2) The Commission may by order authorise the charity trustees at their discretion (but subject to any conditions imposed by the order) to apply any accrued or accruing income for any purposes for which it might be made applicable by such a scheme.

(3) Any application of accrued or accruing income authorised by an order under subsection (2) is to be treated as being within the purposes of the charity.

(4) An order under subsection (2) must not extend –

(a) to more than £300 out of income accrued before the date of the order,
(b) to income accruing more than 3 years after that date, or
(c) to more than £100 out of the income accruing in any of those 3 years.

Powers of Commission to act for protection of charities etc

[75A Official warnings by the Commission

(1) The Commission may issue a warning –

(a) to a charity trustee or trustee for a charity who it considers has committed a breach of trust or duty or other misconduct or mismanagement in that capacity, or
(b) to a charity in connection with which it considers a breach of trust or duty or other misconduct or mismanagement has been committed.

(2) The Commission –

(a) may publish a warning it has issued;
(b) may issue or publish a warning in any way it considers appropriate.

(3) Before issuing a warning under this section, the Commission must give notice of its intention to do so to the charity, and each charity trustee or trustee for the charity, except any who cannot be found or who has no known address in the United Kingdom.

(4) Any such notice –

(a) may be given by post, and
(b) if given by post, may be addressed to the recipient's last known address in the United Kingdom.

(5) The notice must specify –

(a) the power under subsection (1) to give the warning, and the grounds for the warning;
(b) any action that the Commission considers should be taken, or that the Commission is considering taking, to rectify the misconduct or mismanagement referred to in subsection (1);
(c) whether and, if so, how the Commission proposes to publish the warning;
(d) a period within which representations may be made to the Commission about the content of the proposed warning.

(6) Where the Commission gives notice under subsection (3) of its intention to issue a warning –

(a) it must take into account any representations made to it within the period specified in the notice, and
(b) it may (without further notice) issue the warning either without modifications or with such modifications as it thinks desirable.

(7) The Commission may vary or withdraw a warning under this section.

(8) Subsection (2) applies to the variation or withdrawal of a warning as it applies to a warning.

(9) Subsections (3) to (6) apply to the variation of a warning as they apply to a warning, except that –

(a) in subsection (5)(a) references to the warning are to be read as references to the warning as varied, and
(b) the matter to be specified under subsection (5)(b) is any change as a result of the variation in the action previously proposed by the Commission.]

NOTES

Inserted by the Charities (Protection and Social Investment) Act 2016, s 1 as from 1 November 2016.

76 Suspension of trustees etc and appointment of interim managers

(1) Subsection (3) applies where, at any time after it has instituted an inquiry under section 46 with respect to any charity, the Commission is satisfied –

(a) that there is or has been *any* [a failure to comply with an order or direction of the Commission, a failure to remedy any breach specified in a warning under section 75A, or any other] misconduct or mismanagement in the administration of the charity, or
(b) that it is necessary or desirable to act for the purpose of –
   (i) protecting the property of the charity, or
   (ii) securing a proper application for the purposes of the charity of that property or of property coming to the charity.

(2) The reference in subsection (1) to misconduct or mismanagement extends (regardless of anything in the trusts of the charity) to the employment –

(a) for the remuneration or reward of persons acting in the affairs of the charity, or
(b) for other administrative purposes,

of sums which are excessive in relation to the property which is or is likely to be applied or applicable for the purposes of the charity.

(3) The Commission may of its own motion do one or more of the following –

(a) by order suspend any person who is a trustee, charity trustee, officer, agent or employee of the charity from office or employment pending consideration being given to the person's removal (whether under section 79 or 80 or otherwise);

(b) by order appoint such number of additional charity trustees as it considers necessary for the proper administration of the charity;

(c) by order –

  (i) vest any property held by or in trust for the charity in the official custodian,

  (ii) require the persons in whom any such property is vested to transfer it to the official custodian, or

  (iii) appoint any person to transfer any such property to the official custodian;

(d) order any person who holds any property on behalf of the charity, or of any trustee for it, not to part with the property without the approval of the Commission;

(e) order any debtor of the charity not to make any payment in or towards the discharge of the debtor's liability to the charity without the approval of the Commission;

(f) by order restrict (regardless of anything in the trusts of the charity) the transactions which may be entered into, or the nature or amount of the payments which may be made, in the administration of the charity without the approval of the Commission;

(g) by order appoint (in accordance with section 78) an interim manager, to act as receiver and manager in respect of the property and affairs of the charity.

(4) The Commission may not make an order under subsection (3)(a) so as to suspend a person from office or employment for a period of more than 12 months[, subject to any extension under subsection (7)].

(5) But any order under subsection (3)(a) made in the case of any person ('P') may make provision, as respects the period of P's suspension for matters arising out of it, and in particular –

(a) for enabling any person to execute any instrument in P's name or otherwise act for P, and

(b) in the case of a charity trustee, for adjusting any rules governing the proceedings of the charity trustees to take account of the reduction in the number capable of acting.

This does not affect the generality of section 337(1) and (2).

(6) The Commission –

(a) must, at such intervals as it thinks fit, review any order made by it under paragraph (a), or any of paragraphs (c) to (g), of subsection (3), and

(b) if on any such review it appears to the Commission that it would be appropriate to discharge the order in whole or in part, must so discharge it (whether subject to any savings or other transitional provisions or not).

[(7) At any time before the expiry of an order under paragraph (a) of subsection (3) the Commission may extend or further extend the suspension by an order under that paragraph, provided that –

(a) the order does not extend the suspension for a period of more than 12 months, and

(b) the total period of suspension is not more than 2 years.]

NOTES

Sub-s (1) amended by the Charities (Protection and Social Investment) Act 2016, s 2(1), (2) partly as from 31 July 2016 and fully as from 1 November 2016.

Sub-s (4) amended by the Charities (Protection and Social Investment) Act 2016, s 2(1), (3).

Sub-s (7) inserted by the Charities (Protection and Social Investment) Act 2016, s 2(1), (4).

[76A Exercise of powers where section 76(1)(a) applies

(1) This section applies to any power under this Part which is exercisable in cases where the Commission is satisfied as mentioned in section 76(1)(a) in relation to a charity (misconduct or mismanagement), with or without any other condition.

(2) If in such a case the Commission is also satisfied –

(a) that a particular person has been responsible for the misconduct or mismanagement,
(b) that a particular person knew of the misconduct or mismanagement and failed to take any reasonable step to oppose it, or
(c) that a particular person's conduct contributed to it or facilitated it,

the Commission may take into account the matters mentioned in subsection (3) in deciding whether or how to exercise the power.

(3) Those matters are –

(a) the conduct of that person in relation to any other charity;
(b) any other conduct of that person that appears to the Commission to be damaging or likely to be damaging to public trust and confidence in charities generally or particular charities or classes of charity.]

NOTES

Inserted by the Charities (Protection and Social Investment) Act 2016, s 3.

77 Offence of contravening certain orders under s 76

(1) It is an offence for a person to contravene an order under –

(a) section 76(3)(d) (order prohibiting person from parting with property),
(b) section 76(3)(e) (order prohibiting debtor of charity from discharging liability), or
(c) section 76(3)(f) (order restricting transactions or payments).

(2) A person guilty of an offence under subsection (1) is liable on summary conviction to a fine not exceeding level 5 on the standard scale.

(3) This section is not to be treated as precluding the bringing of proceedings for breach of trust against any charity trustee or trustee for a charity in respect of a contravention of an order under section 76(3)(d) or (f) (whether or not proceedings in respect of the contravention are brought against the trustee under this section).

78 Interim managers: supplementary

(1) The Commission may under section 76(3)(g) appoint to be interim manager in respect of a charity such person (other than a member of its staff) as it thinks fit.

(2) An order made by the Commission under section 76(3)(g) may make provision with respect to the functions to be discharged by the interim manager appointed by the order.

This does not affect the generality of section 337(1) and (2).

(3) Those functions are to be discharged by the interim manager under the supervision of the Commission.

(4) In connection with the discharge of those functions, an order under section 76(3)(g) may provide –

(a) for the interim manager appointed by the order to have such powers and duties of the charity trustees of the charity concerned (whether arising under this Act or otherwise) as are specified in the order;
(b) for any powers or duties specified by virtue of paragraph (a) to be exercisable or performed by the interim manager to the exclusion of those trustees.

(5) Where a person has been appointed interim manager by any such order –

(a) section 110 (power to give advice and guidance) applies to the interim manager and the interim manager's functions as it applies to a charity trustee of the charity concerned and to the charity trustee's duties as such, and
(b) the Commission may apply to the High Court for directions in relation to any particular matter arising in connection with the discharge of those functions.

(6) The High Court may on an application under subsection (5)(b) –

(a) give such directions, or
(b) make such orders declaring the rights of any persons (whether before the court or not),

as it thinks just.

(7) The costs of an application under subsection (5)(b) must be paid by the charity concerned.

(8) Regulations made by the Minister may make provision with respect to –

(a) the appointment and removal of persons appointed in accordance with this section;
(b) the remuneration of such persons out of the income of the charities concerned;
(c) the making of reports to the Commission by such persons.

(9) Regulations under subsection (8) may, in particular, authorise the Commission –

(a) to require security for the due discharge of the functions of a person so appointed to be given by that person;
(b) to determine the amount of such a person's remuneration;
(c) to disallow any amount of remuneration in such circumstances as are prescribed by the regulations.

[79 Removal of trustee or officer etc for protective etc purposes

(1) Subsection (2) applies where, at any time after it has instituted an inquiry under section 46 with respect to any charity, the Commission is satisfied either as mentioned in section 76(1)(a) (misconduct or mismanagement) or as mentioned in section 76(1)(b) (need to protect property etc).

(2) The Commission may of its own motion by order establish a scheme for the administration of the charity.

(3) Subsection (4) applies where, at any time after it has instituted an inquiry under section 46 with respect to any charity, the Commission is satisfied both as mentioned in section 76(1)(a) (misconduct or mismanagement) and as mentioned in section 76(1)(b) (need to protect property etc).

(4) Whether or not it acts under subsection (2), the Commission may of its own motion by order remove any trustee, charity trustee, officer, agent or employee of the charity –

(a) who has been responsible for the misconduct or mismanagement,
(b) who knew of the misconduct or mismanagement and failed to take any reasonable step to oppose it, or
(c) whose conduct contributed to it or facilitated it.

(5) Where the Commission has given notice under section 82 of its intention to make an order under subsection (4) removing a person from an office or employment, the Commission may proceed to make the order even though the person has ceased to hold the office or employment.

(6) Where an order is made relying on subsection (5) –

(a) section 81(1) (power to make supplementary provision) and Case D in section 178(1) (disqualification) apply as if the person was removed by the order, but
(b) the order does not affect the time when the person ceased to hold the office or employment.]

NOTES

Substituted by the Charities (Protection and Social Investment) Act 2016, s 4(1), (2).

[79A Removal of disqualified trustee

The Commission may remove a charity trustee or trustee for a charity by order made of its own motion if the person is disqualified from being a charity trustee or trustee for a charity (generally or in relation to the charity concerned) –

(a) by virtue of section 178, or
(b) by an order under section 181A.]

NOTES

Inserted by the Charities (Protection and Social Investment) Act 2016, s 5(1), (2).

80 Other powers to remove or appoint charity trustees

(1) The Commission may remove a charity trustee by order made of its own motion if –

(a) within the last 5 years, the trustee –
  (i) having previously been [made] bankrupt, has been discharged, or
  (ii) having previously made a composition or arrangement with, or granted a trust deed for, creditors, has been discharged in respect of it; [or
  (iii) having previously been the subject of a debt relief order, has been discharged from all the qualifying debts under the debt relief order;]
(b) the trustee is a corporation in liquidation;
(c) the trustee is incapable of acting because of mental disorder within the meaning of the Mental Health Act 1983;
(d) the trustee has not acted, and will not make a declaration of willingness or unwillingness to act;
(e) the trustee –

(i) is outside England and Wales or cannot be found, or
(ii) does not act,

and the trustee's absence or failure to act impedes the proper administration of the charity.

(2) The Commission may by order made of its own motion appoint a person to be a charity trustee –

(a) in place of a charity trustee removed by the Commission under section 79 or subsection (1) or otherwise;
(b) if there are no charity trustees, or if because of vacancies in their number or the absence or incapacity of any of their number the charity cannot apply for the appointment;
(c) if there is a single charity trustee who is not a corporation aggregate and the Commission is of opinion that it is necessary to increase the number for the proper administration of the charity;
(d) if the Commission is of opinion that it is necessary for the proper administration of the charity to have an additional charity trustee because one of the existing charity trustees who ought nevertheless to remain a charity trustee –
    (i) is outside England and Wales or cannot be found, or
    (ii) does not act.

(3) In subsection (1)(a)(i), the reference to the trustee having been [made] bankrupt includes a reference to the trustee's estate having been sequestrated.

(4) This section does not apply in relation to an exempt charity except at a time after the Commission has instituted an inquiry under section 46 with respect to it.

NOTES

Sub-s (1)(a) amended by SI 2012/2404, art 3(2), Sch 2, para 62(1), (2); SI 2016/481, reg 2(1), Sch 1, Pt 1, para 17(1), (2).

Sub-s (3) amended by SI 2016/481, reg 2(1), Sch 1, Pt 1, para 17(1), (2).

81 Removal or appointment of charity trustees etc: supplementary

(1) The powers of the Commission under sections 76, 79 and 80 to remove or appoint charity trustees of its own motion include power to make any such order with respect to the vesting in or transfer to the charity trustees of any property as the Commission could make on the removal or appointment of a charity trustee by it under section 69 (Commission's concurrent jurisdiction with High Court for certain purposes).

(2) Any order under any of those sections or this section –

(a) for the removal or appointment of a charity trustee or trustee for a charity, or
(b) for the vesting or transfer of any property,

has the same effect as an order made under section 69.

(3) Subsection (1) does not apply in relation to an exempt charity except at a time after the Commission has instituted an inquiry under section 46 with respect to it.

82 Removal of trustees etc: notice

(1) Before exercising any jurisdiction by virtue of section 79[, 79A] or 80, the Commission must give notice of its intention to do so to each of the charity trustees, except any that cannot be found or has no known address in the United Kingdom.

(2) Any such notice –

(a) may be given by post, and
(b) if given by post, may be addressed to the recipient's last known address in the United Kingdom.

NOTES

Sub-s (1) amended by the Charities (Protection and Social Investment) Act 2016, s 5(1), (3).

83 Power to suspend or remove trustees etc from membership of charity

(1) Subsection (2) applies where –

(a) the Commission makes an order under section 76(3) suspending from office or employment a person who is a trustee, charity trustee, officer, agent or employee of a charity, and
(b) the person is a member of the charity.

(2) The Commission may also make an order suspending the person's membership of the charity for the period for which the person is suspended from office or employment.

(3) Subsection (4) applies where –

(a) the Commission makes an order under section [79(4)] removing from office or employment a person who is [a trustee, charity trustee, officer,] agent or employee of a charity, and
(b) the person is a member of the charity.

(4) The Commission may also make an order –

(a) terminating the person's membership of the charity, and
(b) prohibiting the person from resuming membership of the charity without the Commission's consent.

(5) If an application for the Commission's consent under subsection (4)(b) is made 5 years or more after the order was made, the Commission must grant the application unless satisfied that, because of any special circumstances, it should be refused.

NOTES

Sub-s (3)(a) amended by the Charities (Protection and Social Investment) Act 2016, s 4(1), (3)(a), (b).

84 Power to direct specified action to be taken

(1) This section applies where, at any time after the Commission has instituted an inquiry under section 46 with respect to any charity, it is satisfied either as mentioned in section 76(1)(a) (misconduct or mismanagement etc) or as mentioned in section 76(1)(b) (need to protect property etc).

(2) The Commission may by order direct –

(a) the charity trustees,
(b) any trustee for the charity,
(c) any officer or employee of the charity, or
(d) (if a body corporate) the charity itself,

to take any action specified in the order which the Commission considers to be expedient in the interests of the charity.

(3) An order under this section –

(a) may require action to be taken whether or not it would otherwise be within the powers exercisable by the person or persons concerned, or by the charity, in relation to the administration of the charity or to its property, but
(b) may not require any action to be taken which is prohibited by any Act or expressly prohibited by the trusts of the charity or is inconsistent with its purposes.

(4) Anything done by a person or body under the authority of an order under this section is to be treated as properly done in the exercise of the powers mentioned in subsection (3)(a).

(5) Subsection (4) does not affect any contractual or other rights arising in connection with anything which has been done under the authority of such an order.

[84A Power to direct specified action not to be taken

(1) This section applies where, at any time after the Commission has instituted an inquiry under section 46 with respect to any charity, the Commission considers that any action, if taken or continued by a person listed in section 84(2), would constitute misconduct or mismanagement in the administration of the charity.

(2) The Commission may make an order specifying the action and directing the person not to take it or continue it.

(3) While an order under this section is in force, the Commission must review it at intervals of not more than 6 months.]

NOTES

Inserted by the Charities (Protection and Social Investment) Act 2016, s 6(1), (2).

[84B Power to direct winding up

(1) This section applies where the conditions in section 84(1) are met for that section to apply, but the Commission is satisfied –

(a) that the charity does not operate, or
(b) that its purposes can be promoted more effectively if it ceases to operate,

and that exercising the power in subsection (2) is expedient in the public interest.

(2) The Commission may by order direct –

(a) the charity trustees,
(b) any trustee for the charity,
(c) any officer or employee of the charity, or
(d) (if a body corporate) the charity itself,

to take any action specified in the order for the purpose of having the charity wound up and dissolved, and any remaining property transferred to a charity with the same purposes.

(3) An order under this section –

(a) may require action to be taken whether or not it would otherwise be within the powers exercisable by the person or persons concerned, or by the charity, in relation to the winding up and dissolution of the charity or to its property, and

(b) in particular, may require the person or persons concerned to do anything for the purpose of having the charity wound up and dissolved and its property transferred that could otherwise only be done by the members of the charity or any of them,

but may not require any action to be taken which is prohibited by any Act.

(4) Before making an order under this section the Commission must give public notice of its intention to make the order, inviting representations to be made to it within a period specified in the notice.

(5) The Commission –

(a) must take into account any representations made to it within the period specified in the notice, and
(b) may make the order (without further notice) either without modifications or with such modifications as it thinks desirable.

(6) An order under this section may not be made less than 60 days after the first day on which public notice under subsection (4) is given, unless the Commission is satisfied after complying with subsections (4) and (5) that it is necessary to make the order to prevent or reduce misconduct or mismanagement in the administration of the charity or to protect the property of the charity or property that may come to the charity.

(7) Anything done by a person or body under the authority of an order under this section is to be treated as properly done in the exercise of the powers mentioned in subsection (3)(a).

(8) Subsection (7) does not affect any contractual or other rights arising in connection with anything which has been done under the authority of such an order.]

NOTES

Inserted by the Charities (Protection and Social Investment) Act 2016, s 7(1), (2).

85 Power to direct application of charity property

(1) This section applies where the Commission is satisfied –

(a) that a person or persons in possession or control of any property held by or on trust for a charity is or are unwilling [or unable] to apply it properly for the purposes of the charity, and
(b) that it is necessary or desirable to make an order under this section for the purpose of securing a proper application of that property for the purposes of the charity.

(2) The Commission may by order direct the person or persons concerned to apply the property in such manner as is specified in the order.

(3) An order under this section –

(a) may require action to be taken whether or not it would otherwise be within the powers exercisable by the person or persons concerned in relation to the property, but
(b) may not require any action to be taken which is prohibited by any Act or expressly prohibited by the trusts of the charity.

(4) Anything done by a person under the authority of an order under this section is to be treated as properly done in the exercise of the powers mentioned in subsection (3)(a).

(5) Subsection (4) does not affect any contractual or other rights arising in connection with anything which has been done under the authority of such an order.

[(6) Subsection (5) does not apply to rights of the charity or of a charity trustee or trustee for the charity in that capacity.]

NOTES

Sub-s (1) amended by the Charities (Protection and Social Investment) Act 2016, s 8(1), (2).

Sub-s (6) inserted by the Charities (Protection and Social Investment) Act 2016, s 8(1), (3).

86 Copy of certain orders, and reasons, to be sent to charity

(1) Where the Commission makes an order under a provision mentioned in subsection (2) it must send the documents mentioned in subsection (3) –

(a) to the charity concerned (if a body corporate), or
(b) (if not) to each of the charity trustees.

(2) The provisions are –

section 76 (suspension of trustees etc and appointment of interim managers);
section 79 (removal of trustee or officer etc for protective etc purposes);
section 80 (other powers to remove or appoint charity trustees);
section 81 (removal or appointment of charity trustees etc: supplementary);
section 83 (power to suspend or remove trustees etc from membership of charity);
section 84 (power to direct specified action to be taken);
section 85 (power to direct application of charity property).
[section 84A (power to direct specified action not to be taken);]
[section 84B (power to direct winding up);]

(3) The documents are –

(a) a copy of the order, and
(b) a statement of the Commission's reasons for making it.

(4) The documents must be sent to the charity or charity trustees as soon as practicable after the making of the order.

(5) The Commission need not comply with subsection (4) in relation to the documents, or (as the case may be) the statement of its reasons, if it considers that to do so –

(a) would prejudice any inquiry or investigation, or
(b) would not be in the interests of the charity;

but, once the Commission considers that this is no longer the case, it must send the documents, or (as the case may be) the statement, to the charity or charity trustees as soon as practicable.

(6) Nothing in this section requires any document to be sent to a person who –

(a) cannot be found, or
(b) has no known address in the United Kingdom.

(7) Any documents required to be sent to a person under this section may be sent to, or otherwise served on, the person in the same way as an order made by the Commission under this Act could be served on the person in accordance with section 339.

NOTES

Sub-s (2) amended by the Charities (Protection and Social Investment) Act 2016, ss 6(1), (4), 7(1), (4).

87 Supervision by Commission of certain Scottish charities

(1) Sections 76 to 82 (except section [79(1) and (2)]) and sections 84 to 86 have effect in relation to any body which –

(a) is entered in the Scottish Charity Register, and
(b) is managed or controlled wholly or mainly in or from England or Wales,

as they have effect in relation to a charity.

(2) Subsection (3) applies where –

(a) a body entered in the Scottish Charity Register is managed or controlled wholly or mainly in or from Scotland, but
(b) any person in England and Wales holds any property on behalf of the body or of any person concerned in its management or control.

(3) If the Commission is satisfied, on the basis of such information as may be supplied to it by the Scottish Charity Regulator, as to the matters mentioned in subsection (4), it may make an order requiring the person holding the property not to part with it without the Commission's approval.

(4) The matters are –

(a) that there has been any misconduct or mismanagement in the administration of the body, and
(b) that it is necessary or desirable to make an order under subsection (3) for the purpose of protecting the property of the body or securing a proper application of such property for the purposes of the body.

(5) Subsection (6) applies where –

(a) any person in England and Wales holds any property on behalf of a body entered in the Scottish Charity Register or of any person concerned in the management or control of such a body, and
(b) the Commission is satisfied (whether on the basis of such information as may be supplied to it by the Scottish Charity Regulator or otherwise) –
    (i) that there has been any misconduct or mismanagement in the administration of the body, and
    (ii) that it is necessary or desirable to make an order under subsection (6) for the purpose of protecting the property of the body or securing a proper application of such property for the purposes of the body.

(6) The Commission may by order –

(a) vest the property in such body or charity as is specified in the order in accordance with subsections (7) and (8),
(b) require any persons in whom the property is vested to transfer it to any such body or charity, or
(c) appoint any person to transfer the property to any such body or charity.

(7) The Commission may specify in an order under subsection (6) –

(a) such other body entered in the Scottish Charity Register, or
(b) such charity,

as it considers appropriate, if the purposes of the body or charity are, in the opinion of the Commission, as similar in character to those of the body referred to in subsection (5)(a) as is reasonably practicable.

(8) But the Commission must not so specify any body or charity unless it has received from –

(a) the persons concerned in the management or control of the body, or
(b) (as the case may be) the charity trustees of the charity,

written confirmation that they are willing to accept the property.

NOTES

Sub-s (1) amended by the Charities (Protection and Social Investment) Act 2016, s 4(1), (4).

Publicity relating to schemes and orders

88 Publicity relating to schemes

(1) The Commission may not –

(a) make any order under this Act to establish a scheme for the administration of a charity, or
(b) submit such a scheme to the court or the Minister for an order giving it effect,

unless, before doing so, the Commission has complied with the publicity requirements in subsection (2).
This is subject to any disapplication of those requirements under subsection (4).

(2) The publicity requirements are –

(a) that the Commission must give public notice of its proposals, inviting representations to be made to it within a period specified in the notice, and
(b) that, in the case of a scheme relating to a local charity (other than an ecclesiastical charity) in a parish, or in a community in Wales, the Commission must communicate a draft of the scheme to –
   (i) the parish council or, if the parish has no council, the chairman of the parish meeting, or
   (ii) the community council or, if the community has no council, the county council or county borough council.

(3) The time when any such notice is given or any such communication takes place is to be decided by the Commission.

(4) The Commission may determine that either or both of the publicity requirements is or are not to apply in relation to a particular scheme if it is satisfied that –

(a) because of the nature of the scheme, or
(b) for any other reason,

compliance with the requirement or requirements is unnecessary.

(5) Where the Commission gives public notice of any proposals under this section –

(a) it must take into account any representations made to it within the period specified in the notice, and
(b) it may (without further notice) proceed with the proposals either without modifications or with such modifications as it thinks desirable.

(6) Where the Commission makes an order under this Act to establish a scheme for the administration of a charity, a copy of the order must be available, for at least a month after the order is published, for public inspection at all reasonable times –

(a) at the Commission's office, and
(b) if the charity is a local charity, at some convenient place in the area of the charity.

(7) Subsection (6)(b) does not apply if the Commission is satisfied that for any reason it is unnecessary for a copy of the scheme to be available locally.

(8) Any public notice of any proposals which is to be given under this section –

(a) is to contain such particulars of the proposals, or such directions for obtaining information about them, as the Commission thinks sufficient and appropriate, and
(b) is to be given in such manner as the Commission thinks sufficient and appropriate.

89 Publicity for orders relating to trustees or other individuals

(1) The Commission may not make any order under this Act to appoint, discharge or remove a charity trustee or trustee for a charity, other than –

(a) an order relating to the official custodian, or
(b) an order under section 76(3)(b) (appointment of additional charity trustees), [or
(c) an order under section 79A (removal of disqualified trustee),]

unless, before doing so, the Commission has complied with the publicity requirement in subsection (2).

This is subject to any disapplication of that requirement under subsection (4).

(2) The publicity requirement is that the Commission must give public notice of its proposals, inviting representations to be made to it within a period specified in the notice.

(3) The time when any such notice is given is to be decided by the Commission.

(4) The Commission may determine that the publicity requirement is not to apply in relation to a particular order if it is satisfied that for any reason compliance with the requirement is unnecessary.

(5) Before the Commission makes an order under this Act[, other than an order under section 79A,] to remove a person who is –

(a) a charity trustee or trustee for a charity, or
(b) an officer, agent or employee of a charity,

without the person's consent, the Commission must give the person not less than one month's notice of its proposals, inviting representations to be made to it within a period specified in the notice.

This does not apply if the person cannot be found or has no known address in the United Kingdom.

(6) Where the Commission gives notice of any proposals under this section –

(a) it must take into account any representations made to it within the period specified in the notice, and
(b) it may (without further notice) proceed with the proposals either without modifications or with such modifications as it thinks desirable.

(7) Any notice of any proposals which is to be given under this section –

(a) is to contain such particulars of the proposals, or such directions for obtaining information about them, as the Commission thinks sufficient and appropriate, and

(b) (in the case of a public notice) is to be given in such manner as the Commission thinks sufficient and appropriate.

(8) Any notice to be given under subsection (5) –

(a) may be given by post, and

(b) if given by post, may be addressed to the recipient's last known address in the United Kingdom.

NOTES

Sub-s (1)(c) inserted, together with word 'or' immediately preceding it, by the Charities (Protection and Social Investment) Act 2016, s 5(1), (4).

Sub-s (5) amended by the Charities (Protection and Social Investment) Act 2016, s 5(1), (5).

Property vested in official custodian

90 Entrusting charity property to official custodian, and termination of trust

(1) The court may by order –

(a) vest in the official custodian any land held by or in trust for a charity,

(b) authorise or require the persons in whom any such land is vested to transfer it to the official custodian, or

(c) appoint any person to transfer any such land to the official custodian.

(2) But subsection (1) does not apply to any interest in land by way of mortgage or other security.

(3) Where property is vested in the official custodian in trust for a charity, the court may make an order discharging the official custodian from the trusteeship as respects all or any of that property.

(4) Where –

(a) the official custodian is discharged from the trusteeship of any property, or

(b) the trusts on which the official custodian holds any property come to an end,

the court may make such vesting orders and give such directions as may seem to the court to be necessary or expedient in consequence.

(5) No person is liable for any loss occasioned by –

(a) acting in conformity with an order under this section, or

(b) giving effect to anything done in pursuance of such an order.

(6) No person is excused from –

(a) acting in conformity with an order under this section, or

(b) giving effect to anything done in pursuance of such an order,

because the order has been in any respect improperly obtained.

91 Supplementary provisions as to property vested in official custodian

(1) Subject to the provisions of this Act, where property is vested in the official custodian in trust for a charity, the official custodian –

(a) must not exercise any powers of management, but
(b) as trustee of any property –
  (i) has all the same powers, duties and liabilities,
  (ii) is entitled to the same rights and immunities, and
  (iii) is subject to the control and orders of the court in the same way,

as a corporation appointed custodian trustee under section 4 of the Public Trustee Act 1906.

(2) Subsection (1) does not confer on the official custodian a power to charge fees.

(3) Subject to subsection (4), where any land is vested in the official custodian in trust for a charity, the charity trustees may, in the name and on behalf of the official custodian, execute and do all assurances and things which they could properly execute or do in their own name and on their own behalf if the land were vested in them.

(4) If any land is so vested in the official custodian by virtue of an order under section 76(3)(c), the power conferred on the charity trustees by subsection (3) is not exercisable by them in relation to any transaction affecting the land, unless the transaction is authorised by order of the court or of the Commission.

(5) Where any land is vested in the official custodian in trust for a charity –

(a) the charity trustees have the same power to make obligations entered into by them binding on the land as if it were vested in them, and
(b) any covenant, agreement or condition which is enforceable by or against the official custodian because the land is vested in the official custodian is enforceable by or against the charity trustees as if the land were vested in them.

(6) In relation to a corporate charity, subsections (3) to (5) apply with the substitution of references to the charity for references to the charity trustees.

(7) Subsections (3) to (5) do not authorise any charity trustees or charity to impose any personal liability on the official custodian.

(8) Where the official custodian is entitled as trustee for a charity to the custody of securities or documents of title relating to the trust property, the official custodian may permit them to be in the possession or under the control of the charity trustees without incurring any liability by doing so.

Official custodian and Reverter of Sites Act 1987

92 Divestment of official custodian where 1987 Act due to operate

(1) Subsection (2) applies where –

(a) any land is vested in the official custodian in trust for a charity, and
(b) it appears to the Commission that section 1 of the 1987 Act (right of reverter replaced by trust) will, or is likely to, operate in relation to the land at a particular time or in particular circumstances.

(2) The jurisdiction which, under section 69, is exercisable by the Commission for the purpose of discharging a trustee for a charity may, at any time before section 1 of the 1987 Act operates in relation to the land, be exercised by the Commission of its own motion for the purpose of –

(a) making an order discharging the official custodian from the trusteeship of the land, and
(b) making such vesting orders and giving such directions as appear to the Commission to be necessary or expedient in consequence.

(3) In this section and sections 93 to 95 –

(a) 'the 1987 Act' means the Reverter of Sites Act 1987, and
(b) any reference to section 1 of the 1987 Act operating in relation to any land is a reference to a trust arising in relation to the land under that section.

93 Divestment of official custodian where 1987 Act has operated

(1) Subsection (2) applies where –

(a) section 1 of the 1987 Act has operated in relation to any land which, immediately before the time when that section so operated, was vested in the official custodian in trust for a charity, and
(b) the land remains vested in the official custodian but on the trust arising under that section.

(2) The court or the Commission (of its own motion) may –

(a) make an order discharging the official custodian from the trusteeship of the land, and
(b) (subject to sections 94 and 95) make such vesting orders and give such directions as appear to it to be necessary or expedient in consequence.

94 Vesting of land in relevant charity trustees following divestment

(1) Subsection (2) applies where an order discharging the official custodian from the trusteeship of any land –

(a) is made by –
  (i) the court under section 90(3), or
  (ii) the Commission under section 69,
  on the ground that section 1 of the 1987 Act will, or is likely to, operate in relation to the land, or
(b) is made by the court or the Commission under section 93.

(2) The persons in whom the land is to be vested on the discharge of the official custodian are the relevant charity trustees, unless the court or (as the case may be) the Commission is satisfied that it would be appropriate for it to be vested in some other persons.

(3) In subsection (2) the 'relevant charity' trustees means –

(a) in relation to an order made as mentioned in subsection (1)(a), the charity trustees of the charity in trust for which the land is vested in the official custodian immediately before the time when the order takes effect, or
(b) in relation to an order made under section 93, the charity trustees of the charity in trust for which the land was vested in the official custodian immediately before the time when section 1 of the 1987 Act operated in relation to the land.

95 Supplementary provisions in connection with 1987 Act

(1) Subsection (2) applies where –

(a) section 1 of the 1987 Act has operated in relation to any such land as is mentioned in section 93(1)(a), and
(b) the land remains vested in the official custodian as mentioned in section 93(1)(b).

(2) Subject to subsection (3) –

(a) all the powers, duties and liabilities that would, apart from this section, be those of the official custodian as trustee of the land are instead to be those of the charity trustees of the charity concerned, and
(b) those trustees may, in the name and on behalf of the official custodian, execute and do all assurances and things which they could properly execute or do in their own name and on their own behalf if the land were vested in them.

(3) Subsection (2) is not to be treated as requiring or authorising those trustees to sell the land at a time when it remains vested in the official custodian.

(4) Where –

(a) the official custodian has been discharged from the trusteeship of any land by an order under section 93, and
(b) the land has, in accordance with section 94, been vested in the charity trustees concerned or (as the case may be) in any persons other than those trustees,

the land is to be held by those trustees, or (as the case may be) by those persons, as trustees on the terms of the trust arising under section 1 of the 1987 Act.

(5) The official custodian is not liable to any person in respect of any loss or misapplication of any land vested in the official custodian in accordance with section 1 of the 1987 Act unless it is occasioned by or through any wilful neglect or default of –

(a) the official custodian, or
(b) any person acting for the official custodian.

(6) But the Consolidated Fund is liable to make good to any person any sums for which the official custodian may be liable because of any such neglect or default.

Establishment of common investment or deposit funds

96 Power to make common investment schemes

(1) The court or the Commission may by order make and bring into effect schemes for the establishment of common investment funds under trusts which provide –

(a) for property transferred to the fund by or on behalf of a charity participating in the scheme to be invested under the control of trustees appointed to manage the fund, and
(b) for the participating charities to be entitled (subject to the provisions of the scheme) to the capital and income of the fund in shares determined by reference to the amount or value of the property transferred to it by or on behalf of each of them and to the value of the fund at the time of the transfers.

(2) In this section and sections 97 to 99 'common investment scheme' means a scheme under subsection (1).

(3) The court or the Commission may make a common investment scheme on the application of any two or more charities.

97 Bodies which may participate in common investment schemes

(1) A common investment scheme –

- (a) may be made in terms admitting any charity to participate, or
- (b) may restrict the right to participate in any manner.

(2) A common investment scheme may provide for appropriate bodies to be admitted to participate in the scheme (in addition to the participating charities) to such extent as the trustees appointed to manage the fund may determine.

(3) In this section 'appropriate body' means –

- (a) a Scottish recognised body; . . .
- (b) a Northern Ireland charity; [or
- (c) any body of persons or trust that –
  - (i) is established in an EEA state other than the United Kingdom, and
  - (ii) is a charity as defined by paragraph 1 of Schedule 6 to the Finance Act 2010],

and, in the application of the relevant provisions in relation to a scheme which contains provisions authorised by subsection (2), 'charity' includes an appropriate body.

(4) The relevant provisions are –

- (a) section 96(1) (power to make common investment schemes),
- (b) section 98 (provisions which may be included in common investment schemes),
- (c) section 99(1) (provisions relating to rights of participating charity etc), and
- (d) (in relation only to a Northern Ireland charity) section 99(2) (power to participate in common investment schemes).

NOTES

Sub-s (3)(a) amended by SI 2013/1773, reg 80, Sch 1, Pt 2, para 44(a); sub-s (3)(c) inserted, together with word '; or' immediately preceding it, by SI 2013/1773, reg 80, Sch 1, Pt 2, para 44(b).

98 Provisions which may be included in common investment schemes

(1) A common investment scheme may make provision for, and for all matters connected with, the establishment, investment, management and winding up of the common investment fund, and may in particular include provision –

- (a) for remunerating persons appointed trustees to hold or manage the fund or any part of it, with or without provision authorising a person to receive the remuneration even though the person is also a charity trustee of or trustee for a participating charity;
- (b) for restricting the size of the fund, and for regulating as to time, amount or otherwise the right to transfer property to or withdraw it from the fund, and for enabling sums to be advanced out of the fund by way of loan to a participating charity pending the withdrawal of property from the fund by the charity;
- (c) for enabling income to be withheld from distribution with a view to avoiding fluctuations in the amounts distributed, and generally for regulating distributions of income;

(d) for enabling money to be borrowed temporarily for the purpose of meeting payments to be made out of the funds;
(e) for enabling questions arising under the scheme as to the right of a charity to participate, or as to the rights of participating charities, or as to any other matter, to be conclusively determined by the decision of the trustees managing the fund or in any other manner;
(f) for regulating the accounts and information to be supplied to participating charities.

(2) A common investment scheme, in addition to the provision for property to be transferred to the fund on the basis that the charity is to be entitled to a share in the capital and income of the fund, may include provision for enabling sums to be deposited by or on behalf of a charity on the basis that (subject to the provisions of the scheme) the charity is to be entitled –

(a) to repayment of the sums deposited, and
(b) to interest on them at a rate determined by or under the scheme.

(3) Where a scheme makes any such provision it must also provide for excluding from the amount of capital and income to be shared between charities participating otherwise than by way of deposit such amounts (not exceeding the amounts properly attributable to the making of deposits) as are from time to time reasonably required in respect of the liabilities of the fund –

(a) for the repayment of deposits, and
(b) for the interest on deposits,

including amounts required by way of reserve.

99 Further provisions relating to common investment schemes and funds

(1) Except in so far as a common investment scheme provides to the contrary –

(a) the rights under it of a participating charity are not capable of being assigned or charged;
(b) a trustee or other person concerned in the management of the common investment fund is not required or entitled to take account of any trust or other equity affecting a participating charity or its property or rights.

(2) The powers of investment of every charity include power to participate in common investment schemes unless the power is excluded by a provision specifically referring to common investment schemes in the trusts of the charity.

(3) A common investment fund is to be treated for all purposes as being a charity.

(4) Subsection (3) applies not only to common investment funds established under section 96, but also to any similar fund established for the exclusive benefit of charities by or under any enactment relating to any particular charities or class of charities.

100 Power to make common deposit schemes

(1) The court or the Commission may by order make and bring into effect schemes for the establishment of common deposit funds under trusts which provide –

(a) for sums to be deposited by or on behalf of a charity participating in the scheme and invested under the control of trustees appointed to manage the fund, and

(b) for any such charity to be entitled (subject to the provisions of the scheme) to repayment of any sums so deposited and to interest on them at a rate determined under the scheme.

(2) In this section and sections 101 to 103 'common deposit scheme' means a scheme under subsection (1).

(3) The court or the Commission may make a common deposit scheme on the application of any two or more charities.

101 Bodies which may participate in common deposit schemes

(1) A common deposit scheme –

(a) may be made in terms admitting any charity to participate, or
(b) may restrict the right to participate in any manner.

(2) A common deposit scheme may provide for appropriate bodies to be admitted to participate in the scheme (in addition to the participating charities) to such extent as the trustees appointed to manage the fund may determine.

(3) In this section 'appropriate body' means –

(a) a Scottish recognised body;. . .
(b) a Northern Ireland charity; [or
(c) any body of persons or trust that–
  (i) is established in an EEA state other than the United Kingdom, and
  (ii) is a charity as defined by paragraph 1 of Schedule 6 to the Finance Act 2010],

and, in the application of the relevant provisions in relation to a scheme which contains provisions authorised by subsection (2), 'charity' includes an appropriate body.

(4) The relevant provisions are –

(a) section 100(1) (power to make common deposit schemes),
(b) section 102 (provisions which may be included in common deposit schemes),
(c) section 103(1) (provisions relating to rights of participating charity etc), and
(d) (in relation only to a Northern Ireland charity) section 103(2) (power to participate in common deposit schemes).

NOTES

Sub-s (3))a) amended by SI 2013/1773, reg 80, Sch 1, Pt 2, para 44(a); sub-s (3)(c) inserted, together with word '; or' immediately preceding it, by SI 2013/1773, reg 80, Sch 1, Pt 2, para 44(b).

102 Provisions which may be included in common deposit schemes

A common deposit scheme may make provision for, and for all matters connected with, the establishment, investment, management and winding up of the common deposit fund, and may in particular include provision –

(a) for remunerating persons appointed trustees to hold or manage the fund or any part of it, with or without provision authorising a person to receive the remuneration even though the person is also a charity trustee of or trustee for a participating charity;
(b) for regulating as to time, amount or otherwise the right to repayment of sums deposited in the fund;

(c) for authorising a part of the income for any year to be credited to a reserve account maintained for the purpose of counteracting any losses accruing to the fund, and generally for regulating the manner in which the rate of interest on deposits is to be determined from time to time;
(d) for enabling money to be borrowed temporarily for the purpose of meeting payments to be made out of the funds;
(e) for enabling questions arising under the scheme as to the right of a charity to participate, or as to the rights of participating charities, or as to any other matter, to be conclusively determined by the decision of the trustees managing the fund or in any other manner;
(f) for regulating the accounts and information to be supplied to participating charities.

103 Further provisions relating to common deposit schemes and funds

(1) Except in so far as a common deposit scheme provides to the contrary –

(a) the rights under it of a participating charity are not capable of being assigned or charged;
(b) a trustee or other person concerned in the management of the common deposit fund is not required or entitled to take account of any trust or other equity affecting a participating charity or its property or rights.

(2) The powers of investment of every charity include power to participate in common deposit schemes unless the power is excluded by a provision specifically referring to common deposit schemes in the trusts of the charity.

(3) A common deposit fund is to be treated for all purposes as being a charity.

(4) Subsection (3) applies not only to common deposit funds established under section 100, but also to any similar fund established for the exclusive benefit of charities by or under any enactment relating to any particular charities or class of charities.

104 Meaning of 'Scottish recognised body' and 'Northern Ireland charity'

(1) In sections 97 and 101 'Scottish recognised body' means a body –

(a) established under the law of Scotland, or
(b) managed or controlled wholly or mainly in or from Scotland,

to which HMRC have given intimation, which has not subsequently been withdrawn, that tax relief is due in respect of income of the body which is applicable and applied to charitable purposes only.

(2) In sections 97 and 101 'Northern Ireland charity' means an institution –

(a) which is a charity under the law of Northern Ireland, and
(b) to which HMRC have given intimation, which has not subsequently been withdrawn, that tax relief is due in respect of income of the institution which is applicable and applied to charitable purposes only.

(3) For the purposes of this section –

'HMRC' means the Commissioners for Her Majesty's Revenue and Customs;
'tax relief' means relief under –
(a) Part 10 of the Income Tax Act 2007, or

(b) any provision of Part 11 of the Corporation Tax Act 2010 other than sections 480 (exemption for profits of small-scale trades) and 481 (exemption from charges under provisions to which section 1173 applies).

[Total return investment

104A Investment of endowment fund on total return basis

(1) This section applies to any available endowment fund of a charity.

(2) If the condition in subsection (3) is met in relation to the charity, the charity trustees may resolve that the fund, or a portion of it –

(a) should be invested without the need to maintain a balance between capital and income returns, and

(b) accordingly, should be freed from the restrictions with respect to expenditure of capital that apply to it.

(3) The condition is that the charity trustees are satisfied that it is in the interests of the charity that regulations under section 104B(1)(b) should apply in place of the restrictions mentioned in subsection (2)(b).

(4) While a resolution under subsection (2) has effect, the regulations apply in place of the restrictions.

(5) In this section 'available endowment fund', in relation to a charity, means –

(a) the whole of the charity's permanent endowment if it is all subject to the same trusts, or

(b) any part of its permanent endowment which is subject to any particular trusts that are different from those to which any other part is subject.]

NOTES

Inserted, in relation to England and Wales, by the Trusts (Capital and Income) Act 2013, s 4.

[104B Total return investment: regulations

(1) The Commission may by regulations make provision about –

(a) resolutions under section 104A(2),

(b) the investment of a relevant fund without the need to maintain a balance between capital and income returns, and expenditure from such a fund, and

(c) the steps that must be taken by charity trustees in respect of a fund, or portion of a fund, in the event of a resolution under section 104A(2) ceasing to have effect in respect of the fund or portion.

(2) Regulations under subsection (1)(a) may, in particular –

(a) specify steps that must be taken by charity trustees before passing a resolution under section 104A(2),

(b) make provision about the variation and revocation of such a resolution,

(c) require charity trustees to notify the Commission of the passing, variation or revocation of such a resolution, and

(d) specify circumstances in which such a resolution is to cease to have effect.

(3) Regulations under subsection (1)(b) may, in particular –

(a) make provision requiring a relevant fund to be invested, and the returns from that investment to be allocated, in such a way as to maintain (so far as practicable) the long-term capital value of the fund,
(b) make provision about the taking of advice by charity trustees in connection with the investment of, and expenditure from, a relevant fund,
(c) confer on the charity trustees of a relevant fund a power (subject to such restrictions as may be specified in the regulations) to accumulate income,
(d) make provision about expenditure from a relevant fund (including by imposing limits on expenditure and specifying circumstances in which expenditure requires the Commission's consent), and
(e) require charity trustees to report to the Commission on the investment of, and expenditure from, a relevant fund.

(4) A power to accumulate income conferred by regulations under subsection (1)(b) or (c) is not subject to section 14(3) of the Perpetuities and Accumulations Act 2009 (which provides for certain powers to accumulate income to cease to have effect after 21 years).

(5) Any regulations made by the Commission under this section must be published by the Commission in such manner as it thinks fit.

(6) In this section 'relevant fund' means a fund, or portion of a fund, in respect of which a resolution under section 104A(2) has effect, and includes the returns from the investment of the fund or portion.]

NOTES

Inserted, in relation to England and Wales, by the Trusts (Capital and Income) Act 2013, s 4.

Power to authorise dealings with charity property, ex gratia payments etc

105 Power to authorise dealings with charity property etc

(1) Subject to the provisions of this section, where it appears to the Commission that any action proposed or contemplated in the administration of a charity is expedient in the interests of the charity, the Commission may by order sanction that action, whether or not it would otherwise be within the powers exercisable by the charity trustees in the administration of the charity.

(2) Anything done under the authority of an order under this section is to be treated as properly done in the exercise of those powers.

(3) An order under this section –

(a) may be made so as to authorise a particular transaction, compromise or the like, or a particular application of property, or so as to give a more general authority, and
(b) may authorise a charity to use common premises, or employ a common staff, or otherwise combine for any purpose of administration, with any other charity.

Paragraph (b) does not affect the generality of subsection (1).

(4) An order under this section may give directions –

(a) as to the manner in which any expenditure is to be borne, and
(b) as to other matters connected with or arising out of the action authorised by the order.

(5) Where anything is done in pursuance of an authority given by an order under this section, any directions given in connection with that authority –

(a) are binding on the charity trustees for the time being as if contained in the trusts of the charity, but
(b) may on the application of the charity be modified or superseded by a further order.

(6) The directions which may be given by an order under this section in particular include directions –

(a) for meeting any expenditure out of a specified fund,
(b) for charging any expenditure to capital or to income,
(c) for requiring expenditure charged to capital to be recouped out of income within a specified period,
(d) for restricting the costs to be incurred at the expense of the charity, or
(e) for the investment of money arising from any transaction.

This does not affect the generality of subsection (4).

(7) An order under this section may authorise any act even though –

(a) it is prohibited by the Ecclesiastical Leases Act 1836, or
(b) the trusts of the charity provide for the act to be done by or under the authority of the court.

(8) But an order under this section may not –

(a) authorise the doing of any act expressly prohibited by any Act other than the Ecclesiastical Leases Act 1836, or by the trusts of the charity, or
(b) extend or alter the purposes of the charity.

(9) In the case of a charitable company, an order under this section may authorise an act even though it involves the breach of a duty imposed on a director of the company under Chapter 2 of Part 10 of the Companies Act 2006 (general duties of directors).

(10) An order under this section does not confer any authority in relation to a building which has been consecrated and of which the use or disposal is regulated, and can be further regulated, by a scheme having effect or treated as having effect under or by virtue of the Mission and Pastoral Measure 2011.

(11) The reference in subsection (10) to a building is to be treated as including –

(a) part of a building, and
(b) any land which under such a scheme is to be used or disposed of with a building to which the scheme applies.

106 Power to authorise ex gratia payments etc

(1) Subject to subsection (5), the Commission may by order exercise the same power as is exercisable by the Attorney General to authorise the charity trustees of a charity to take any action falling within subsection (2)(a) or (b) in a case where the charity trustees –

(a) (apart from this section) have no power to take the action, but
(b) in all the circumstances regard themselves as being under a moral obligation to take it.

(2) The actions are –

(a) making any application of property of the charity, or
(b) waiving to any extent, on behalf of the charity, its entitlement to receive any property.

(3) The power conferred on the Commission by subsection (1) is exercisable by the Commission under the supervision of, and in accordance with such directions as may be given by, the Attorney General.

(4) Any such directions may in particular require the Commission, in such circumstances as are specified in the directions –

(a) to refrain from exercising the power conferred by subsection (1), or
(b) to consult the Attorney General before exercising it.

(5) Where –

(a) an application is made to the Commission for it to exercise the power conferred by subsection (1) in a case where it is not precluded from doing so by any such directions, but
(b) the Commission considers that it would nevertheless be desirable for the application to be entertained by the Attorney General rather than by the Commission,

the Commission must refer the application to the Attorney General.

(6) It is hereby declared that where –

(a) an application is made to the Commission as mentioned in subsection (5)(a), and
(b) the Commission determines the application by refusing to authorise charity trustees to take any action falling within subsection (2)(a) or (b),

that refusal does not preclude the Attorney General, on an application subsequently made to the Attorney General by the charity trustees, from authorising them to take that action.

Power to give directions about dormant bank accounts of charities

107 Power to direct transfer of credits in dormant bank accounts

(1) The Commission may give a direction under subsection (2) where –

(a) it is informed by a relevant institution –
   (i) that it holds one or more accounts in the name of or on behalf of a particular charity ('the relevant charity'), and
   (ii) that the account, or (if it so holds two or more accounts) each of the accounts, is dormant, and
(b) it is unable, after making reasonable inquiries, to locate that charity or any of its trustees.

(2) A direction under this subsection is a direction which –

(a) requires the institution concerned to transfer the amount, or (as the case may be) the aggregate amount, standing to the credit of the relevant charity in the account or accounts in question to such other charity as is specified in the direction in accordance with subsection (3), or

(b) requires the institution concerned to transfer to each of two or more other charities so specified in the direction such part of that amount or aggregate amount as is there specified in relation to that charity.

(3) The Commission –

(a) may specify in a direction under subsection (2) such other charity or charities as it considers appropriate, having regard, in a case where the purposes of the relevant charity are known to the Commission, to those purposes and to the purposes of the other charity or charities, but

(b) must not so specify any charity unless it has received from the charity trustees written confirmation that those trustees are willing to accept the amount proposed to be transferred to the charity.

(4) Any amount received by a charity by virtue of this section is to be received by the charity on terms that –

(a) it is to be held and applied by the charity for the purposes of the charity, but

(b) as property of the charity, it is nevertheless subject to any restrictions on expenditure to which it was subject as property of the relevant charity.

(5) The receipt of any charity trustees or trustee for a charity in respect of any amount received from a relevant institution by virtue of this section is a complete discharge of the institution in respect of that amount.

108 Accounts which cease to be dormant before transfer

(1) This section applies where –

(a) the Commission has been informed as mentioned in section 107(1)(a) by any relevant institution, and

(b) before any transfer is made by the institution in pursuance of a direction under section 107(2), the institution has, by reason of any circumstances, cause to believe that the account, or (as the case may be) any of the accounts, held by it in the name of or on behalf of the relevant charity is no longer dormant.

(2) The institution must without delay notify those circumstances in writing to the Commission.

(3) If it appears to the Commission that the account or accounts in question is or are no longer dormant, it must revoke any direction under section 107(2) which has previously been given by it to the institution with respect to the relevant charity.

109 Dormant bank accounts: supplementary

(1) No obligation as to secrecy or other restriction on disclosure (however imposed) precludes a relevant institution from disclosing any information to the Commission for the purpose of enabling the Commission to discharge its functions under sections 107 and 108.

(2) For the purposes of sections 107 and 108 and this section, an account is dormant if no transaction, other than –

(a) a transaction consisting in a payment into the account, or

(b) a transaction which the institution holding the account has itself caused to be effected, has been effected in relation to the account within the period of 5 years immediately preceding the date when the Commission is informed as mentioned in section 107(1)(a).

(3) For the purposes of sections 107 and 108 and this section, 'a relevant institution' means –

(a) the Bank of England,
(b) a person who has permission under [Part 4A] of the Financial Services and Markets Act 2000 to accept deposits,
(c) an EEA firm of the kind mentioned in paragraph 5(b) of Schedule 3 to that Act which has permission under paragraph 15 of that Schedule (as a result of qualifying for authorisation under paragraph 12(1) of that Schedule) to accept deposits, or
(d) such other person who may lawfully accept deposits in the United Kingdom as may be prescribed by the Minister.

(4) In subsection (3), paragraphs (b) to (d) are to be read with –

(a) section 22 of the Financial Services and Markets Act 2000,
(b) any relevant order under that section, and
(c) Schedule 2 to that Act.

(5) For the purposes of sections 107 and 108, references to the transfer of any amount to a charity are references to its transfer –

(a) to the charity trustees, or
(b) to any trustee for the charity,

as the charity trustees may determine (and any reference to any amount received by a charity is to be read accordingly).

(6) For the purpose of determining the matters in respect of which any of the powers conferred by sections 46 to 53 (inquiries and searches) may be exercised it is to be assumed that the Commission has no functions under section 107 or 108 in relation to accounts to which this subsection applies.

(This has the result that, for example, a relevant institution is not, in connection with the Commission's functions under sections 107 and 108, required under section 47(2)(a) to provide any statements, or answer any questions or inquiries, with respect to any such accounts held by the institution.)

(7) Subsection (6) applies to accounts which –

(a) are dormant accounts by virtue of subsection (2), but
(b) would not be dormant accounts if subsection (2)(a) were omitted.

NOTES

Sub-s (3)(b) amended by the Financial Services Act 2012, s 114(1), Sch 18, Pt 2, para 136.

Additional powers of Commission

110 Power to give advice

(1) The Commission may, on the written application of any charity trustee or trustee for a charity, give the applicant its opinion or advice in relation to any matter –

(a) relating to the performance of any duties of the applicant, as such a trustee, in relation to the charity concerned, or
(b) otherwise relating to the proper administration of the charity.

(2) A person ('P') who –

(a) is a charity trustee or trustee for a charity, and
(b) acts in accordance with any opinion or advice given by the Commission under subsection (1) (whether to P or another trustee),

is to be treated, as regards P's responsibility for so acting, as having acted in accordance with P's trust.

(3) But subsection (2) does not apply to P if, when so acting –

(a) P knows or has reasonable cause to suspect that the opinion or advice was given in ignorance of material facts, or
(b) a decision of the court or the Tribunal has been obtained on the matter or proceedings are pending to obtain one.

111 Power to determine membership of charity

(1) The Commission may –

(a) on the application of a charity, or
(b) at any time after the institution of an inquiry under section 46 with respect to a charity,

determine who are the members of the charity.

(2) The Commission's power under subsection (1) may also be exercised by a person appointed by the Commission for the purpose.

(3) In a case within subsection (1)(b) the Commission may, if it thinks fit, so appoint the person appointed to conduct the inquiry.

112 Power to order assessment of solicitor's bill

(1) The Commission may order that a solicitor's bill of costs for business done for a charity, or for charity trustees or trustees for a charity, is to be assessed, together with the costs of the assessment –

(a) by a costs officer in such division of the High Court as may be specified in the order, or
(b) by the costs officer of any other court having jurisdiction to order the assessment of the bill.

(2) On any order under this section for the assessment of a solicitor's bill –

(a) the assessment is to proceed,
(b) the costs officer has the same powers and duties, and
(c) the costs of the assessment are to be borne,

as if the order had been made, on the application of the person chargeable with the bill, by the court in which the costs are assessed.

(3) No order under this section for the assessment of a solicitor's bill is to be made after payment of the bill, unless the Commission is of opinion that it contains exorbitant charges.

(4) No order under this section is to be made in any case where the solicitor's costs are not subject to assessment on an order of the High Court because of –

(a) an agreement as to the solicitor's remuneration, or

(b) the lapse of time since payment of the bill.

Legal proceedings relating to charities

113 Petitions for winding up charities under Insolvency Act

(1) This section applies where a charity may be wound up by the High Court under the Insolvency Act 1986.

(2) A petition for the charity to be wound up under the 1986 Act by any court in England or Wales having jurisdiction may be presented by the Attorney General, as well as by any person authorised by that Act.

(3) Such a petition may also be presented by the Commission if, at any time after it has instituted an inquiry under section 46 with respect to the charity, it is satisfied either as mentioned in section 76(1)(a) (misconduct or mismanagement etc) or as mentioned in section 76(1)(b) (need to protect property etc).

(4) The power exercisable by the Commission by virtue of this section is exercisable –

(a) by the Commission of its own motion, but
(b) only with the agreement of the Attorney General on each occasion.

114 Proceedings by the Commission

(1) Subject to subsection (2), the Commission may exercise the same powers with respect to –

(a) the taking of legal proceedings with reference to charities or the property or affairs of charities, or
(b) the compromise of claims with a view to avoiding or ending such proceedings,

as are exercisable by the Attorney General acting ex officio.

(2) Subsection (1) does not apply to the power of the Attorney General under section 113(2) to present a petition for the winding up of a charity.

(3) The practice and procedure to be followed in relation to any proceedings taken by the Commission under subsection (1) are the same in all respects (and in particular as regards costs) as if they were proceedings taken by the Attorney General acting ex officio.

(4) No rule of law or practice is to be treated as requiring the Attorney General to be a party to any such proceedings.

(5) The powers exercisable by the Commission by virtue of this section are exercisable –

(a) by the Commission of its own motion, but
(b) only with the agreement of the Attorney General on each occasion.

115 Proceedings by other persons

(1) Charity proceedings may be taken with reference to a charity by –

(a) the charity,
(b) any of the charity trustees,
(c) any person interested in the charity, or
(d) if it is a local charity, any two or more inhabitants of the area of the charity,

but not by any other person.

(2) Subject to the following provisions of this section, no charity proceedings relating to a charity are to be entertained or proceeded with in any court unless the taking of the proceedings is authorised by order of the Commission.

(3) The Commission must not, without special reasons, authorise the taking of charity proceedings where in its opinion the case can be dealt with by the Commission under the powers of this Act other than those conferred by section 114.

(4) This section does not require an order for the taking of proceedings –

(a) in a pending cause or matter, or
(b) for the bringing of any appeal.

(5) Where subsections (1) to (4) require the taking of charity proceedings to be authorised by an order of the Commission, the proceedings may nevertheless be entertained or proceeded with if, after the order had been applied for and refused, leave to take the proceedings was obtained from one of the judges of the High Court attached to the Chancery Division.

(6) Nothing in subsections (1) to (5) applies –

(a) to the taking of proceedings by the Attorney General, with or without a relator, or
(b) to the taking of proceedings by the Commission in accordance with section 114.

(7) If it appears to the Commission, on an application for an order under this section or otherwise, that it is desirable –

(a) for legal proceedings to be taken with reference to any charity or its property or affairs, and
(b) for the proceedings to be taken by the Attorney General,

the Commission must so inform the Attorney General and send the Attorney General such statements and particulars as the Commission thinks necessary to explain the matter.

(8) In this section 'charity proceedings' means proceedings in any court in England or Wales brought under –

(a) the court's jurisdiction with respect to charities, or
(b) the court's jurisdiction with respect to trusts in relation to the administration of a trust for charitable purposes.

Supplementary

116 Effect of provisions relating to vesting or transfer of property

No vesting or transfer of any property in pursuance of any provision of this Part operates as a breach of a covenant or condition against alienation or gives rise to a forfeiture.

PART 7
CHARITY LAND

Restrictions on dispositions of land in England and Wales

117 Restrictions on dispositions of land: general

(1) No land held by or in trust for a charity is to be conveyed, transferred, leased or otherwise disposed of without an order of –

(a) the court, or
(b) the Commission.

But this is subject to the following provisions of this section, sections 119 to 121 (further provisions about restrictions on dispositions) and section 127 (release of charity rentcharges).

(2) Subsection (1) does not apply to a disposition of such land if –

(a) the disposition is made to a person who is not –
 (i) a connected person (as defined in section 118), or
 (ii) a trustee for, or nominee of, a connected person, and
(b) the requirements of –
 (i) section 119(1) (dispositions other than certain leases), or
 (ii) section 120(2) (leases which are for 7 years or less etc),
 have been complied with in relation to it.

(3) The restrictions on disposition imposed by this section and sections 119 to 121 apply regardless of anything in the trusts of a charity; but nothing in this section or sections 119 to 121 applies to –

(a) any disposition for which general or special authority is expressly given (without the authority being made subject to the sanction of an order of the court) by –
 (i) any statutory provision contained in or having effect under an Act, or
 (ii) any scheme legally established,
(b) any disposition for which the authorisation or consent of the Secretary of State is required under the Universities and College Estates Act 1925,
(c) any disposition of land held by or in trust for a charity which –
 (i) is made to another charity otherwise than for the best price that can reasonably be obtained, and
 (ii) is authorised to be so made by the trusts of the first-mentioned charity, or
(d) the granting, by or on behalf of a charity and in accordance with its trusts, of a lease to any beneficiary under those trusts where the lease –
 (i) is granted otherwise than for the best rent that can reasonably be obtained, and
 (ii) is intended to enable the demised premises to be occupied for the purposes, or any particular purposes, of the charity.

(4) Nothing in this section or sections 119 to 121 applies to –

(a) any disposition of land held by or in trust for an exempt charity,
(b) any disposition of land by way of mortgage or other security, or
(c) any disposition of an advowson.

118 Meaning of 'connected person' in s 117(2)

(1) In section 117(2) 'connected person', in relation to a charity, means any person who falls within subsection (2) –

(a) at the time of the disposition in question, or
(b) at the time of any contract for the disposition in question.

(2) The persons are –

(a) a charity trustee or trustee for the charity,
(b) a person who is the donor of any land to the charity (whether the gift was made on or after the establishment of the charity),
(c) a child, parent, grandchild, grandparent, brother or sister of any such trustee or donor,
(d) an officer, agent or employee of the charity,
(e) the spouse or civil partner of any person falling within any of paragraphs (a) to (d),
(f) a person carrying on business in partnership with any person falling within any of paragraphs (a) to (e),
(g) an institution which is controlled –
  (i) by any person falling within any of paragraphs (a) to (f), or
  (ii) by two or more such persons taken together, or
(h) a body corporate in which –
  (i) any connected person falling within any of paragraphs (a) to (g) has a substantial interest, or
  (ii) two or more such persons, taken together, have a substantial interest.

(3) Sections 350 to 352 (meaning of child, spouse and civil partner, controlled institution and substantial interest) apply for the purposes of subsection (2).

119 Requirements for dispositions other than certain leases

(1) The requirements mentioned in section 117(2)(b) are that the charity trustees must, before entering into an agreement for the sale, or (as the case may be) for a lease or other disposition, of the land –

(a) obtain and consider a written report on the proposed disposition from a qualified surveyor instructed by the trustees and acting exclusively for the charity,
(b) advertise the proposed disposition for such period and in such manner as is advised in the surveyor's report (unless it advises that it would not be in the best interests of the charity to advertise the proposed disposition), and
(c) decide that they are satisfied, having considered the surveyor's report, that the terms on which the disposition is proposed to be made are the best that can reasonably be obtained for the charity.

(2) Subsection (1) does not apply where the proposed disposition is the granting of such a lease as is mentioned in section 120(1).

(3) For the purposes of subsection (1) a qualified surveyor is a person who –

(a) is a fellow or professional associate of the Royal Institution of Chartered Surveyors or satisfies such other requirement or requirements as may be prescribed by regulations made by the Minister, and

(b) is reasonably believed by the charity trustees to have ability in, and experience of, the valuation of land of the particular kind, and in the particular area, in question.

(4) Any report prepared for the purposes of subsection (1) must contain such information, and deal with such matters, as may be prescribed by regulations made by the Minister.

120 Requirements for leases which are for 7 years or less etc

(1) Subsection (2) applies where the proposed disposition is the granting of a lease for a term ending not more than 7 years after it is granted (other than one granted wholly or partly in consideration of a fine).

(2) The requirements mentioned in section 117(2)(b) are that the charity trustees must, before entering into an agreement for the lease –

(a) obtain and consider the advice on the proposed disposition of a person who is reasonably believed by the trustees to have the requisite ability and practical experience to provide them with competent advice on the proposed disposition, and
(b) decide that they are satisfied, having considered that person's advice, that the terms on which the disposition is proposed to be made are the best that can reasonably be obtained for the charity.

121 Additional restrictions where land held for stipulated purposes

(1) Subsection (2) applies where –

(a) any land is held by or in trust for a charity, and
(b) the trusts on which it is so held stipulate that it is to be used for the purposes, or any particular purposes, of the charity.

(2) The land must not be conveyed, transferred, leased or otherwise disposed of unless the charity trustees have before the relevant time –

(a) given public notice of the proposed disposition, inviting representations to be made to them within a time specified in the notice, which must be not less than one month from the date of the notice, and
(b) taken into consideration any representations made to them within that time about the proposed disposition.

(3) Subsection (2) –

(a) is subject to subsections (5) and (6), and
(b) does not affect the operation of sections 117 to 120.

(4) In subsection (2) the 'relevant time' means –

(a) where the charity trustees enter into an agreement for the sale, or (as the case may be) for the lease or other disposition, the time when they enter into that agreement, and
(b) in any other case, the time of the disposition.

(5) Subsection (2) does not apply to any such disposition of land as is there mentioned if –

(a) the disposition is to be effected with a view to acquiring by way of replacement other property which is to be held on the trusts referred to in subsection (1)(b), or

(b) the disposition is the granting of a lease for a term ending not more than 2 years after it is granted (other than one granted wholly or partly in consideration of a fine).

(6) The Commission may, if the condition in subsection (7) is met, direct –

(a) that subsection (2) is not to apply to dispositions of land held by or in trust for a charity or class of charities (whether generally or only in the case of a specified class of dispositions or land, or otherwise as may be provided in the direction), or

(b) that subsection (2) is not to apply to a particular disposition of land held by or in trust for a charity.

(7) The condition is that the Commission, on an application made to it in writing by or behalf of the charity or charities in question, is satisfied that it would be in the interests of the charity or charities for the Commission to give the direction.

122 Instruments concerning dispositions of land: required statements, etc

(1) Subsection (2) applies to any of the following instruments –

(a) a contract for the sale, or for a lease or other disposition, of land which is held by or in trust for a charity, and

(b) a conveyance, transfer, lease or other instrument effecting a disposition of such land.

(2) An instrument to which this subsection applies must state –

(a) that the land is held by or in trust for a charity,

(b) whether the charity is an exempt charity and whether the disposition is one falling within section 117(3)(a), (b), (c) or (d), and

(c) if it is not an exempt charity and the disposition is not one falling within section 117(3)(a), (b), (c) or (d), that the land is land to which the restrictions on disposition imposed by sections 117 to 121 apply.

(3) Where any land held by or in trust for a charity is conveyed, transferred, leased or otherwise disposed of by a disposition to which section 117(1) or (2) applies, the charity trustees must certify in the instrument by which the disposition is effected –

(a) (where section 117(1) applies) that the disposition has been sanctioned by an order of the court or of the Commission (as the case may be), or

(b) (where section 117(2) applies) that the charity trustees have power under the trusts of the charity to effect the disposition and have complied with sections 117 to 121 so far as applicable to it.

(4) Where subsection (3) has been complied with in relation to any disposition of land, then in favour of a person who (whether under the disposition or afterwards) acquires an interest in the land for money or money's worth, it is conclusively presumed that the facts were as stated in the certificate.

(5) Subsection (6) applies where –

(a) any land held by or in trust for a charity is conveyed, transferred, leased or otherwise disposed of by a disposition to which section 117(1) or (2) applies, but

(b) subsection (3) has not been complied with in relation to the disposition.

(6) In favour of a person who (whether under the disposition or afterwards) in good faith acquires an interest in the land for money or money's worth, the disposition is valid whether or not –

(a) the disposition has been sanctioned by an order of the court or of the Commission, or
(b) the charity trustees have power under the trusts of the charity to effect the disposition and have complied with sections 117 to 121 so far as applicable to it.

(7) Subsection (8) applies to any of the following instruments –

(a) a contract for the sale, or for a lease or other disposition, of land which will, as a result of the disposition, be held by or in trust for a charity, and
(b) a conveyance, transfer, lease or other instrument effecting a disposition of such land.

(8) An instrument to which this subsection applies must state –

(a) that the land will, as a result of the disposition, be held by or in trust for a charity,
(b) whether the charity is an exempt charity, and
(c) if it is not an exempt charity, that the restrictions on disposition imposed by sections 117 to 121 will apply to the land (subject to section 117(3)).

(9) In this section and section 123 references to a disposition of land do not include references to –

(a) a disposition of land by way of mortgage or other security,
(b) any disposition of an advowson, or
(c) any release of a rentcharge falling within section 127(1).

123 Charity land and land registration

(1) Where the disposition to be effected by any such instrument as is mentioned in section 122(1)(b) or (7)(b) will be –

(a) a registrable disposition, or
(b) a disposition which triggers the requirement of registration,

the statement which, by virtue of section 122(2) or (8), is to be contained in the instrument must be in such form as may be prescribed by land registration rules.

(2) Where the registrar approves an application for registration of –

(a) a disposition of registered land, or
(b) a person's title under a disposition of unregistered land,

and the instrument effecting the disposition contains a statement complying with section 122(8) and subsection (1), the registrar must enter in the register a restriction reflecting the limitation under sections 117 to 121 on subsequent disposal.

(3) Where –

(a) any such restriction is entered in the register in respect of any land, and
(b) the charity by or in trust for which the land is held becomes an exempt charity,

the charity trustees must apply to the registrar for the removal of the entry.

(4) On receiving any application duly made under subsection (3) the registrar must remove the entry.

(5) Where –

(a) any registered land is held by or in trust for an exempt charity and the charity ceases to be an exempt charity, or

(b) any registered land becomes, as a result of a declaration of trust by the registered proprietor, land held in trust for a charity (other than an exempt charity),

the charity trustees must apply to the registrar for such a restriction as is mentioned in subsection (2) to be entered in the register in respect of the land.

(6) On receiving any application duly made under subsection (5) the registrar must enter such a restriction in the register in respect of the land.

Restrictions on mortgages of land in England and Wales

124 Restrictions on mortgages

(1) Subject to subsection (2), no mortgage of land held by or in trust for a charity is to be granted without an order of –

(a) the court, or

(b) the Commission.

(2) Subsection (1) does not apply to a mortgage of any such land if the charity trustees have, before executing the mortgage, obtained and considered proper advice, given to them in writing, on the relevant matters or matter mentioned in subsection (3) or (4) (as the case may be).

(3) In the case of a mortgage to secure the repayment of a proposed loan or grant, the relevant matters are –

(a) whether the loan or grant is necessary in order for the charity trustees to be able to pursue the particular course of action in connection with which they are seeking the loan or grant,

(b) whether the terms of the loan or grant are reasonable having regard to the status of the charity as the prospective recipient of the loan or grant, and

(c) the ability of the charity to repay on those terms the sum proposed to be paid by way of loan or grant.

(4) In the case of a mortgage to secure the discharge of any other proposed obligation, the relevant matter is whether it is reasonable for the charity trustees to undertake to discharge the obligation, having regard to the charity's purposes.

(5) Subsection (3) or (as the case may be) subsection (4) applies in relation to such a mortgage as is mentioned in that subsection whether the mortgage –

(a) would only have effect to secure the repayment of the proposed loan or grant or the discharge of the proposed obligation, or

(b) would also have effect to secure the repayment of sums paid by way of loan or grant, or the discharge of other obligations undertaken, after the date of its execution.

(6) Subsection (7) applies where –

(a) the charity trustees of a charity have executed a mortgage of land held by or in trust for a charity in accordance with subsection (2), and
(b) the mortgage has effect to secure the repayment of sums paid by way of loan or grant, or the discharge of other obligations undertaken, after the date of its execution.

(7) In such a case, the charity trustees must not after that date enter into any transaction involving –

(a) the payment of any such sums, or
(b) the undertaking of any such obligations,

unless they have, before entering into the transaction, obtained and considered proper advice, given to them in writing, on the matters or matter mentioned in subsection (3)(a) to (c) or (4) (as the case may be).

(8) For the purposes of this section proper advice is the advice of a person –

(a) who is reasonably believed by the charity trustees to be qualified by ability in and practical experience of financial matters, and
(b) who has no financial interest in relation to the loan, grant or other transaction in connection with which the advice is given;

and such advice may constitute proper advice for those purposes even though the person giving it does so in the course of employment as an officer or employee of the charity or of the charity trustees.

(9) This section applies regardless of anything in the trusts of a charity; but nothing in this section applies to any mortgage –

(a) for which general or special authority is given as mentioned in section 117(3)(a), or
(b) for which the authorisation or consent of the Secretary of State is required as mentioned in section 117(3)(b).

(10) Nothing in this section applies to an exempt charity.

125 Mortgages: required statements, etc

(1) Any mortgage of land held by or in trust for a charity must state –

(a) that the land is held by or in trust for a charity,
(b) whether the charity is an exempt charity and whether the mortgage is one falling within section 124(9), and
(c) if it is not an exempt charity and the mortgage is not one falling within section 124(9), that the mortgage is one to which the restrictions imposed by section 124 apply.

(2) Where section 124(1) or (2) applies to any mortgage of land held by or in trust for a charity, the charity trustees must certify in the mortgage –

(a) (where section 124(1) applies) that the mortgage has been sanctioned by an order of the court or of the Commission (as the case may be), or
(b) (where section 124(2) applies) that the charity trustees have power under the trusts of the charity to grant the mortgage, and have obtained and considered such advice as is mentioned in section 124(2).

(3) Where subsection (2) has been complied with in relation to any mortgage, then in favour of a person who (whether under the mortgage or afterwards) acquires an interest in the land in question for money or money's worth, it is conclusively presumed that the facts were as stated in the certificate.

(4) Subsection (5) applies where –

(a) section 124(1) or (2) applies to any mortgage of land held by or in trust for a charity, but

(b) subsection (2) has not been complied with in relation to the mortgage.

(5) In favour of a person who (whether under the mortgage or afterwards) in good faith acquires an interest in the land for money or money's worth, the mortgage is valid whether or not –

(a) the mortgage has been sanctioned by an order of the court or of the Commission, or

(b) the charity trustees have power under the trusts of the charity to grant the mortgage and have obtained and considered such advice as is mentioned in section 124(2).

(6) Where section 124(7) applies to any mortgage of land held by or in trust for a charity, the charity trustees must certify in relation to any transaction falling within section 124(7) that they have obtained and considered such advice as is mentioned in section 124(7).

(7) Where subsection (6) has been complied with in relation to any transaction, then, in favour of a person who (whether under the mortgage or afterwards) has acquired or acquires an interest in the land for money or money's worth, it is conclusively presumed that the facts were as stated in the certificate.

126 Mortgages of charity land and land registration

(1) Where the mortgage referred to in section 125(1) will be a registrable disposition, the statement required by section 125(1) must be in such form as may be prescribed by land registration rules.

(2) Where any such mortgage will be one to which section 4(1)(g) of the Land Registration Act 2002 applies –

(a) the statement required by section 125(1) must be in such form as may be prescribed by land registration rules, and

(b) if the charity is not an exempt charity, the mortgage must also contain a statement, in such form as may be prescribed by land registration rules, that the restrictions on disposition imposed by sections 117 to 121 apply to the land (subject to section 117(3)).

(3) Where –

(a) the registrar approves an application for registration of a person's title to land in connection with such a mortgage as is mentioned in subsection (2),

(b) the mortgage contains statements complying with section 125(1) and subsection (2), and

(c) the charity is not an exempt charity,

the registrar must enter in the register a restriction reflecting the limitation under sections 117 to 121 on subsequent disposal.

(4) Subsections (3) and (4) of section 123 (removal of entry) apply in relation to any restriction entered under subsection (3) as they apply in relation to any restriction entered under section 123(2).

Release of charity rentcharges

127 Release of charity rentcharges

(1) Section 117(1) does not apply to the release by a charity of a rentcharge which it is entitled to receive if the release is given in consideration of the payment of an amount which is not less than 10 times the annual amount of the rentcharge.

(2) Where a charity which is entitled to receive a rentcharge releases it in consideration of the payment of an amount not exceeding £1,000, any costs incurred by the charity in connection with proving its title to the rentcharge are recoverable by the charity from the person or persons in whose favour the rentcharge is being released.

(3) Neither section 117(1) nor subsection (2) of this section applies where a rentcharge which a charity is entitled to receive is redeemed under sections 8 to 10 of the Rentcharges Act 1977.

128 Power to alter sum specified in s 127(2)

The Minister may by order amend section 127(2) by substituting a different sum for the sum for the time being specified there.

Interpretation

129 Interpretation

(1) In sections 117 to 126 'land' means land in England and Wales.

(2) In sections 124 to 126 'mortgage' includes a charge.

(3) Sections 123 and 126 are to be construed as one with the Land Registration Act 2002.

PART 8

CHARITY ACCOUNTS, REPORTS AND RETURNS

Chapter 1
Individual Accounts

130 Accounting records

(1) The charity trustees of a charity must ensure that accounting records are kept in respect of the charity which are sufficient to show and explain all the charity's transactions, and which are such as to –

(a) disclose at any time, with reasonable accuracy, the financial position of the charity at that time, and

(b) enable the trustees to ensure that, where any statements of accounts are prepared by them under section 132(1), those statements of accounts comply with the requirements of regulations under section 132(1).

(2) The accounting records must in particular contain –

(a) entries showing from day to day all sums of money received and expended by the charity, and the matters in respect of which the receipt and expenditure takes place, and
(b) a record of the assets and liabilities of the charity.

131 Preservation of accounting records

(1) The charity trustees of a charity must preserve any accounting records made for the purposes of section 130 in respect of the charity for at least 6 years from the end of the financial year of the charity in which they are made.

(2) Subsection (3) applies if a charity ceases to exist within the period of 6 years mentioned in subsection (1) as it applies to any accounting records.

(3) The obligation to preserve the accounting records in accordance with subsection (1) must continue to be discharged by the last charity trustees of the charity, unless the Commission consents in writing to the records being destroyed or otherwise disposed of.

132 Preparation of statement of accounts

(1) The charity trustees of a charity must (subject to section 133) prepare in respect of each financial year of the charity a statement of accounts complying with such requirements as to its form and contents as may be prescribed by regulations made by the Minister.

(2) Regulations under subsection (1) may in particular make provision –

(a) for any such statement to be prepared in accordance with such methods and principles as are specified or referred to in the regulations;
(b) as to any information to be provided by way of notes to the accounts.

(3) Regulations under subsection (1) may also make provision for determining the financial years of a charity for the purposes of this Act and any regulations made under it.

(4) But regulations under subsection (1) may not impose on the charity trustees of a charity that is a charitable trust created by any person ('the settlor') any requirement to disclose, in any statement of accounts prepared by them under subsection (1) –

(a) the identities of recipients of grants made out of the funds of the charity, or
(b) the amounts of any individual grants so made,

if the disclosure would fall to be made at a time when the settlor or any spouse or civil partner of the settlor was still alive.

133 Account and statement an option for lower-income charities

If a charity's gross income in any financial year does not exceed £250,000, the charity trustees may, in respect of that year, elect to prepare –

(a) a receipts and payments account, and
(b) a statement of assets and liabilities,

instead of a statement of accounts under section 132(1).

134 Preservation of statement of accounts or account and statement

(1) The charity trustees of a charity must preserve –

(a) any statement of accounts prepared by them under section 132(1), or
(b) any account and statement prepared by them under section 133,

for at least 6 years from the end of the financial year to which any such statement relates or (as the case may be) to which any such account and statement relate.

(2) Subsection (3) applies if a charity ceases to exist within the period of 6 years mentioned in subsection (1) as it applies to any statement of accounts or account and statement.

(3) The obligation to preserve the statement or account and statement in accordance with subsection (1) must continue to be discharged by the last charity trustees of the charity, unless the Commission consents in writing to the statement or account and statement being destroyed or otherwise disposed of.

135 Charitable companies

Nothing in sections 130 to 134 (preparation and preservation of individual accounts) applies to a charitable company.

136 Exempt charities

(1) Nothing in sections 130 to 134 (preparation and preservation of individual accounts) applies to an exempt charity.

(2) But the charity trustees of an exempt charity –

(a) must keep proper books of account with respect to the affairs of the charity, and
(b) if not required by or under the authority of any other Act to prepare periodical statements of account must prepare consecutive statements of account consisting on each occasion of –
 (i) an income and expenditure account relating to a period of not more than 15 months, and
 (ii) a balance sheet relating to the end of that period.

(3) The books of accounts and statements of account relating to an exempt charity must be preserved for a period of at least 6 years unless –

(a) the charity ceases to exist, and
(b) the Commission consents in writing to their being destroyed or otherwise disposed of.

Chapter 2
Group Accounts

137 Accounting records

(1) The charity trustees of a parent charity or of any charity which is a subsidiary undertaking must ensure that the accounting records kept in respect of the charity under –

(a) section 130(1) (individual accounts: accounting records), or
(b) (as the case may be) section 386 of the Companies Act 2006 (duty to keep accounting records),

are such as to enable the charity trustees of the parent charity to ensure that, where any group accounts are prepared by them under section 138(2), those accounts comply with the requirements of regulations under section 142.

(2) The duty in subsection (1) is in addition to the duty to ensure that the accounting records comply with the requirements of –

- (a) section 130(1), or
- (b) section 386 of the Companies Act 2006.

(3) Subsection (4) applies if a parent charity has a subsidiary undertaking in relation to which the requirements of –

- (a) section 130(1), or
- (b) section 386 of the Companies Act 2006,

do not apply.

(4) The charity trustees of the parent charity must take reasonable steps to secure that the undertaking keeps such accounting records as to enable the trustees to ensure that, where any group accounts are prepared by them under section 138(2), those accounts comply with the requirements of regulations under section 142.

138 Preparation of group accounts

(1) This section applies in relation to a financial year of a charity if –

- (a) the charity is a parent charity at the end of that year, and
- (b) (where it is a company) it is not required to prepare consolidated accounts for that year under section 399 of the Companies Act 2006 (duty to prepare group accounts), whether or not such accounts are in fact prepared.

(2) The charity trustees of the parent charity must prepare group accounts in respect of that year.

(3) If the requirement in subsection (2) applies to the charity trustees of a parent charity (other than a parent charity which is a company) in relation to a financial year –

- (a) that requirement so applies in addition to the requirement in section 132(1) (statement of accounts), and
- (b) the option of preparing the documents mentioned in section 133 (account and statement) is not available in relation to that year (whatever the amount of the charity's gross income for that year).

(4) If –

- (a) the requirement in subsection (2) applies to the charity trustees of a parent charity in relation to a financial year, and
- (b) the charity is a company,

that requirement so applies in addition to the requirement in section 394 of the Companies Act 2006 (duty to prepare individual accounts).

(5) Subsection (2) is subject to section 139.

139 Exceptions to requirement to prepare group accounts

(1) The requirement in section 138(2) does not apply to the charity trustees of a parent charity in relation to a financial year if at the end of that year it is itself a subsidiary undertaking in relation to another charity.

(2) The requirement in section 138(2) does not apply to the charity trustees of a parent charity in relation to a financial year if the aggregate gross income of the group for that year does not exceed such sum as is specified in regulations made by the Minister.

(3) Regulations made by the Minister may prescribe circumstances in which a subsidiary undertaking may or (as the case may be) must be excluded from group accounts required to be prepared under section 138(2) for a financial year.

(4) Where, by virtue of such regulations, each of the subsidiary undertakings which are members of a group is –

(a) permitted to be excluded from any such group accounts for a financial year, or
(b) required to be so excluded,

the requirement in section 138(2) does not apply to the charity trustees of the parent charity in relation to that year.

140 Preservation of group accounts

(1) The charity trustees of a charity must preserve any group accounts prepared by them under section 138(2) for at least 6 years from the end of the financial year to which the accounts relate.

(2) Subsection (3) applies if a charity ceases to exist within the period of 6 years mentioned in subsection (1) as it applies to any group accounts.

(3) The obligation to preserve the accounts in accordance with subsection (1) must continue to be discharged by the last charity trustees of the charity, unless the Commission consents in writing to the accounts being destroyed or otherwise disposed of.

141 'Parent charity', 'subsidiary undertaking' and 'group'

(1) This section applies for the purposes of this Part.

(2) A charity is a parent charity if it is (or is to be treated as) a parent undertaking in relation to one or more other undertakings in accordance with the provisions of section 1162 of, and Schedule 7 to, the Companies Act 2006.

(3) Each undertaking in relation to which a parent charity is (or is to be treated as) a parent undertaking in accordance with those provisions is a subsidiary undertaking in relation to the parent charity.

(4) But subsection (3) does not have the result that any of the following is a subsidiary undertaking –

(a) any special trusts of a charity,
(b) any institution which, by virtue of a direction under section 12(1), is to be treated as forming part of a charity for the purposes of this Part, or
(c) any charity to which a direction under section 12(2) applies for the purposes of this Part.

(5) 'The group', in relation to a parent charity, means that charity and its subsidiary undertaking or undertakings, and any reference to the members of the group is to be read accordingly.

(6) For the purposes of this section and the operation for those purposes of section 1162 of, and Schedule 7 to, the Companies Act 2006 'undertaking' means –

(a) an undertaking as defined by section 1161(1) of the 2006 Act, or
(b) a charity which is not an undertaking as so defined.

142 'Group accounts'

(1) For the purposes of this Part, 'group accounts' means consolidated accounts –

(a) relating to the group, and
(b) complying with such requirements as to their form and contents as may be prescribed by regulations made by the Minister.

(2) Regulations under subsection (1) may in particular make provision –

(a) for any such accounts to be prepared in accordance with such methods and principles as are specified or referred to in the regulations;
(b) for dealing with cases where the financial years of the members of the group do not all coincide;
(c) as to any information to be provided by way of notes to the accounts.

(3) Regulations under subsection (1) may also make provision –

(a) for determining the financial years of subsidiary undertakings for the purposes of this Part;
(b) for imposing on the charity trustees of a parent charity requirements with respect to securing that such financial years coincide with that of the charity.

143 Exempt charities

Nothing in sections 137 to 142 (preparation and preservation of group accounts) applies to an exempt charity.

Chapter 3
Audit or Examination of Accounts

Audit or examination of individual accounts

144 Audit of accounts of larger charities

(1) Subsection (2) applies to a financial year of a charity if –

(a) the charity's gross income in that year exceeds [£1 million], or
(b) the charity's gross income in that year exceeds the accounts threshold and at the end of the year the aggregate value of its assets (before deduction of liabilities) exceeds £3.26 million.

'The accounts threshold' means the sum for the time being specified in section 133 (account and statement an option for lower-income charities).

(2) If this subsection applies to a financial year of a charity, the accounts of the charity for that year must be audited by a person who –

(a) is eligible for appointment as a statutory auditor under Part 42 of the Companies Act 2006, or
(b) is a member of a body for the time being specified in regulations under section 154 and is under the rules of that body eligible for appointment as auditor of the charity.

NOTES

Sub-s (1)(a) amended by SI 2015/321, arts 2, 3.

145 Examination of accounts an option for lower-income charities

(1) If section 144(2) does not apply to a financial year of a charity but its gross income in that year exceeds £25,000, the accounts of the charity for that year must, at the election of the charity trustees, be –

(a) examined by an independent examiner, that is, an independent person who is reasonably believed by the trustees to have the requisite ability and practical experience to carry out a competent examination of the accounts, or
(b) audited by a person within section 144(2)(a) or (b).

(2) Subsection (1) is subject to –

(a) subsection (3), and
(b) any order under section 146(1).

(3) If subsection (1) applies to the accounts of a charity for a year and the charity's gross income in that year exceeds £250,000, a person qualifies as an independent examiner for the purposes of subsection (1)(a) if (and only if) the person is independent and –

(a) a member of one of the bodies listed in subsection (4), or
(b) a Fellow of the Association of Charity Independent Examiners.

(4) The bodies referred to in subsection (3)(a) are –

(a) the Institute of Chartered Accountants in England and Wales;
(b) the Institute of Chartered Accountants of Scotland;
(c) the Institute of Chartered Accountants in Ireland;
(d) the Association of Chartered Certified Accountants;
(e) the Association of Authorised Public Accountants;
(f) the Association of Accounting Technicians;
(g) the Association of International Accountants;
(h) the Chartered Institute of Management Accountants;
(i) the Institute of Chartered Secretaries and Administrators;
(j) the Chartered Institute of Public Finance and Accountancy;
[(k) the Institute of Financial Accountants;
(l) the Certified Public Accountants Association.]

(5) The Commission may –

(a) give guidance to charity trustees in connection with the selection of a person for appointment as an independent examiner;
(b) give such directions as it thinks appropriate with respect to the carrying out of an examination in pursuance of subsection (1)(a);

and any such guidance or directions may either be of general application or apply to a particular charity only.

(6) The Minister may by order –

(a) amend subsection (3) by adding or removing a description of person to or from the list in that subsection or by varying any entry for the time being included in that list;
(b) amend subsection (4) by adding or removing a body to or from the list in that subsection or by varying any entry for the time being included in that list.

NOTES

Sub-s (4)(k), (l) inserted by SI 2015/321, arts 2, 4.

146 Commission's powers to order audit

(1) The Commission may by order require the accounts of a charity for a financial year to be audited by a person within section 144(2)(a) or (b) if it appears to the Commission that –

(a) section 144(2), or (as the case may be) section 145(1), has not been complied with in relation to that year within 10 months from the end of that year, or

(b) although section 144(2) does not apply to that year, it would nevertheless be desirable for the accounts of the charity for that year to be audited by a person within section 144(2)(a) or (b).

(2) If the Commission makes an order under subsection (1) with respect to a charity, the auditor must be a person appointed by the Commission unless –

(a) the order is made by virtue of subsection (1)(b), and

(b) the charity trustees themselves appoint an auditor in accordance with the order.

(3) The expenses of any audit carried out by an auditor appointed by the Commission under subsection (2), including the auditor's remuneration, are recoverable by the Commission –

(a) from the charity trustees of the charity concerned, who are personally liable, jointly and severally, for those expenses, or

(b) to the extent that it appears to the Commission not to be practical to seek recovery of those expenses in accordance with paragraph (a), from the funds of the charity.

147 Accounts required to be audited under Companies Act

(1) Nothing in sections 144 to 146 applies in relation to the accounts of a charitable company for a financial year if those accounts are required to be audited in accordance with Part 16 of the Companies Act 2006 ('Part 16' accounts).

(2) In the case of a charitable company, the Commission may by order require that the condition and Part 16 accounts of the company for such period as the Commission thinks fit are to be investigated and audited by an auditor who –

(a) is eligible for appointment as a statutory auditor under Part 42 of the Companies Act 2006, and

(b) is appointed by the Commission.

(3) An auditor acting under subsection (2) –

(a) has a right of access to all books, accounts and documents relating to the company which are in the possession or control of the charity trustees or to which the charity trustees have access;

(b) is entitled to require from any charity trustee, past or present, and from any past or present officer or employee of the company such information and explanation as the auditor thinks necessary for the performance of the auditor's duties;

(c) must at the conclusion or during the progress of the audit make such reports to the Commission about the audit or about the accounts or affairs of the company as the auditor thinks the case requires, and must send a copy of any such report to the charity trustees.

(4) The expenses of any audit under subsection (2) including the remuneration of the auditor, are to be paid by the Commission.

(5) If any person fails to afford an auditor any facility to which the auditor is entitled under subsection (3), the Commission may by order give to that person or to the charity trustees for the time being such directions as the Commission thinks appropriate for securing that the default is made good.

148 NHS charities: general

Nothing in sections 144 to 146 applies in relation to a financial year of a charity where, at any time in the year, it is –

(a) an English NHS charity (as defined in section 149), or
(b) a Welsh NHS charity (as defined in section 150).

149 Audit or examination of English NHS charity accounts

(1) This section applies in relation to a financial year of a charity where, at any time in the year, it is an English NHS charity.

(2) If section 144(1)(a) or (b) is satisfied in relation to that financial year of the charity, the accounts of the charity for that year must be audited by *a person appointed by the Audit Commission* [a person who –

(a) is eligible for appointment as a statutory auditor under Part 42 of the Companies Act 2006,
(b) is eligible for appointment as a local auditor (see Part 4 of the Local Audit and Accountability Act 2014), or
(c) is a member of a body for the time being specified in regulations under section 154 and is under the rules of that body eligible for appointment as auditor of the charity].

(3) In any other case, the accounts of the charity for that financial year must, at the election of *the Audit Commission* [the charity trustees], be –

(a) audited by *a person appointed by the Audit Commission* [a person who is within subsection (2)(a), (b) or (c)], or
(b) examined by *a person so appointed* [a person who is qualified to be an independent examiner].

[(3A) For the purposes of subsection (3)(b), a person is qualified to be an independent examiner if (and only if) –

(a) the person is independent,
(b) the charity trustees reasonably believe that the person has the requisite ability and practical experience to carry out a competent examination of the accounts, and
(c) the person –
    (i) falls within a description of person for the time being included in the list in section 145(3), or

(ii) is eligible for appointment as a local auditor (see Part 4 of the Local Audit and Accountability Act 2014).]

(4) Section 3 of the Audit Commission Act 1998 applies in relation to any appointment under subsection (2) or (3)(a).

(5) The Charity Commission may give such directions as it thinks appropriate with respect to the carrying out of an examination in pursuance of subsection (3)(b); and any such directions may either be of general application or apply to a particular charity only.

[(5) The Commission may –

(a) give guidance to charity trustees of an English NHS charity in connection with the selection of a person for appointment as an independent examiner;

(b) give such directions as it thinks appropriate with respect to the carrying out of an examination in pursuance of subsection (3)(b);

and any such guidance or directions may either be of general application or apply to a particular charity only.]

(6) The Comptroller and Auditor General may at any time examine and inspect –

(a) the accounts of the charity for the financial year,
(b) any records relating to those accounts, and
(c) any report of a person appointed under subsection (2) or (3) to audit or examine those accounts.

(7) In this section, 'English NHS charity' means a charitable trust, the trustees of which are –

(a) ...
(b) ...
[(ba) the National Health Service Commissioning Board,
(bb) a clinical commissioning group,
(bc) *trustees for the National Health Service Commissioning Board appointed in pursuance of paragraph 11 of Schedule A1 to the National Health Service Act 2006, or*
(bd) *trustees for a clinical commissioning group appointed in pursuance of paragraph 15 of Schedule 1A to that Act,*]
(c) *a National Health Service trust all or most of whose hospitals, establishments and facilities are situated in England,*
(d) *trustees appointed in pursuance of paragraph 10 of Schedule 4 to the National Health Service Act 2006 for a National Health Service trust falling within paragraph (c),*
(e) *special trustees appointed in pursuance of section 29(1) of the National Health Service Reorganisation Act 1973, section 95(1) of the National Health Service Act 1977 and section 212(1) of the National Health Service Act 2006 for such a National Health Service trust, or*
(f) ....

(8) In this Chapter 'the Audit Commission' means the Audit Commission for Local Authorities and the National Health Service in England.

NOTES

Sub-s (2) words in italics repealed and subsequent words in square brackets substituted by the Local Audit and Accountability Act 2014, s 45, Sch 12, para 119(1), (2) as from 1 April 2017.

Sub-s (3): words in italics repealed and subsequent words in square brackets substituted by the Local Audit and Accountability Act 2014, s 45, Sch 12, para 119(1), (3) as from 1 April 2017.

Sub-s (3A) inserted by the Local Audit and Accountability Act 2014, s 45, Sch 12, para 119(1), (4) as from 1 April 2017.

Sub-s (4) repealed by the Local Audit and Accountability Act 2014, s 45, Sch 12, para 119(1), (5) as from 1 April 2017.

Sub-s (5) substituted by the Local Audit and Accountability Act 2014, s 45, Sch 12, para 119(1), (6) as from 1 April 2017.

Sub-s (7)(a), (b) repealed by the Health and Social Care Act 2012, s 55(2), Sch 5, para 184(a), (b).

Sub-s (7)(ba)-(bd) inserted by the Health and Social Care Act 2012, s 55(2), Sch 5, para 184(c).

Sub-s (7)(bc), (bd) repealed by the NHS (Charitable Trusts Etc) Act 2016, s 1(9), Sch 1, para 15 as from a date to be appointed.

Sub-s (7)(c)-(e) repealed by the Health and Social Care Act 2012, s 179(6), Sch 14, Pt 2, paras 117, 118.

Sub-s (7)(f) repealed by the Health and Social Care Act 2012, s 55(2), Sch 5, para 184(d).

Sub-s (8) repealed by the Local Audit and Accountability Act 2014, s 45, Sch 12, para 119(1), (7) as from 1 April 2017.

150 Audit or examination of Welsh NHS charity accounts

(1) This section applies in relation to a financial year of a charity where, at any time in the year, it is a Welsh NHS charity.

(2) If section 144(1)(a) or (b) is satisfied in relation to that financial year of the charity, the accounts of the charity for that year must be audited by the Auditor General for Wales.

(3) In any other case, the accounts of the charity for that financial year must, at the election of the Auditor General for Wales, be audited or examined by the Auditor General for Wales.

(4) In this section 'Welsh NHS charity' means a charitable trust, the trustees of which are –

(a) a Local Health Board,

(b) a National Health Service trust *all or most of whose hospitals, establishments and facilities are situated in Wales*,

(c) trustees appointed in pursuance of paragraph 10 of Schedule 3 to the National Health Service (Wales) Act 2006 for a National Health Service trust *falling within paragraph (b)*, or

(d) special trustees appointed in pursuance of section 29(1) of the National Health Service Reorganisation Act 1973, section 95(1) of the National Health Service Act 1977 and section 160(1) of the National Health Service (Wales) Act 2006 for *such* a National Health Service trust.

(5) References in this Act to an auditor or an examiner have effect in relation to this section as references to the Auditor General for Wales acting under this section as an auditor or examiner.

NOTES

Sub-s (4) words in italics repealed by the Health and Social Care Act 2012, s 179(6), Sch 14, Pt 2, paras 117, 119(a)-(c) from a date to be appointed.

Audit or examination of group accounts

151 Audit of accounts of larger groups

(1) This section applies where group accounts are prepared for a financial year of a parent charity under section 138(2) and –

(a) the aggregate gross income of the group in that year exceeds the relevant income threshold (see section 176(1)), or
(b) the aggregate gross income of the group in that year exceeds the relevant income threshold and at the end of the year the aggregate value of the assets of the group (before deduction of liabilities) exceeds the relevant assets threshold (see section 176(2)).

(2) This section also applies where –

(a) group accounts are prepared for a financial year of a parent charity under section 138(2), and
(b) the appropriate audit provision applies in relation to the parent charity's own accounts for that year.

(3) In this section 'the appropriate audit provision', in relation to a financial year of a parent charity, means –

(a) (subject to paragraph (b), (c) or (d)) section 144(2) (audit of accounts of larger charities);
(b) if section 149 (audit or examination of English NHS charity accounts) applies in relation to that year, section 149(2);
(c) if section 150 (audit or examination of Welsh NHS charity accounts) applies in relation to that year, section 150(2);
(d) if the parent charity is a company –
 (i) section 144(2), or
 (ii) (as the case may be) Part 16 of the Companies Act 2006.

(4) If this section applies in relation to a financial year of a parent charity by virtue of subsection (1) or (2), the group accounts for that year must be audited –

(a) (subject to paragraph (b) or (c)) by a person within section 144(2)(a) or (b);
(b) if section 149 applies in relation to that year, by *a person appointed by the Audit Commission* [a person, appointed by the charity trustees of the parent charity, who is within section 149(2)(a), (b) or (c)];
(c) if section 150 applies in relation to that year, by the Auditor General for Wales.

(5) If this section applies in relation to a financial year of a parent charity by virtue of subsection (1) –

(a) (subject to paragraph (b)) the appropriate audit provision applies in relation to the parent charity's own accounts for that year (whether or not it would otherwise so apply);
(b) if the parent charity is a company and its own accounts for that year are not required to be audited in accordance with Part 16 of the Companies Act 2006, section 144(2) applies in relation to those accounts (whether or not it would otherwise so apply).

(6) *Subsections (4) and (6) of section 149* [Section 149(6) applies] apply in relation to any appointment under subsection (4)(b) as *they apply* [it applies] in relation to an appointment under section 149(2).

(7) References in this Act to an auditor have effect in relation to subsection (4)(c) as references to the Auditor General for Wales acting under subsection (4)(c) as an auditor.

NOTES

Sub-s (4)(b): words in italics repealed and subsequent words in square brackets substituted by the Local Audit and Accountability Act 2014, s 45, Sch 12, para 120(1), (2) as from 1 April 2017.

Sub-s (6): words in italics repealed and subsequent words in square brackets substituted by the Local Audit and Accountability Act 2014, s 45, Sch 12, para 120(1), (3)(a), (b) as from 1 April 2017.

152 Examination of accounts an option for smaller groups

(1) This section applies if –

(a) group accounts are prepared for a financial year of a parent charity under section 138(2), and

(b) section 151 (audit of accounts of larger groups) does not apply in relation to that year.

(2) If –

(a) this section applies in relation to a financial year of a parent charity,

(b) the aggregate gross income of the group in that year exceeds the sum specified in section 145(1), and

(c) subsection (6) or (7) (NHS charity: group accounts) does not apply in relation to it,

the group accounts for that year must, at the election of the charity trustees of the parent charity, be examined by an independent examiner (as defined in section 145(1)(a)) or audited by a person within section 144(2)(a) or (b).

(3) Subsection (2) is subject to –

(a) subsection (4), and

(b) any order under section 153(1).

(4) If subsection (2) applies to the group accounts for a year and the aggregate gross income of the group in that year exceeds the sum specified in section 145(3), a person qualifies as an independent examiner for the purposes of subsection (2) if (and only if) the person is independent and meets the requirements of section 145(3)(a) or (b).

(5) The Commission may –

(a) give guidance to charity trustees of a parent charity in connection with the selection of a person for appointment as an independent examiner;

(b) give such directions as it thinks appropriate with respect to the carrying out of an examination in pursuance of subsection (2);

and any such guidance or directions may either be of general application or apply to a particular charity only.

(6) If –

(a) this section applies in relation to a financial year of a parent charity, and

(b) section 149 (audit or examination of English NHS charity accounts) also applies in relation to that year,

the group accounts for that year must at the election of *the Audit Commission be audited by a person appointed by the Audit Commission or examined by a person so appointed* [the charity trustees of the parent charity be audited by a person, appointed by those trustees, who is within section 149(2)(a), (b) or (c); or examined by a person, appointed by those trustees, who is qualified to be an independent examiner].

Subsections *(4) to (6)* [(3A), (5) and (6)] of section 149 apply for the purposes of this subsection as they apply for the purposes of section 149(3)[; except that in subsection (3A)(b) of that section the reference to 'the charity trustees' is to be read as a reference to 'the charity trustees of the parent charity'].

(7) If –

(a) this section applies in relation to a financial year of a parent charity, and
(b) section 150 (audit or examination of Welsh NHS charity accounts) also applies in relation to that year,

the group accounts for that year must, at the election of the Auditor General for Wales, be audited or examined by the Auditor General for Wales.

References in this Act to an auditor or an examiner have effect in relation to this subsection as references to the Auditor General for Wales acting under this subsection as an auditor or examiner.

(8) If the group accounts for a financial year of a parent charity are to be examined or audited in accordance with subsection (2), section 145(1) applies in relation to the parent charity's own accounts for that year (whether or not it would otherwise so apply).

(9) Nothing in subsection (6) or (7) affects the operation of section 149(3) to (6) or (as the case may be) section 150(3) in relation to the parent charity's own accounts for the financial year in question.

NOTES

Sub-s (6) words in italics repealed and subsequent words in square brackets substituted or inserted by the Local Audit and Accountability Act 2014, s 45, Sch 12, para 121(1), (2)(a)-(c) as from 1 April 2017.

153 Commission's powers to order audit of group accounts

(1) The Commission may by order require the group accounts of a parent charity for a financial year to be audited by a person within section 144(2)(a) or (b) if it appears to the Commission that –

(a) section 151(4)(a), or (as the case may be) section 152(2), has not been complied with in relation to that year within 10 months from the end of that year, or
(b) although section 151(4)(a) does not apply to that year, it would nevertheless be desirable for the group accounts for that year to be audited by a person within section 144(2)(a) or (b).

But this subsection does not apply if section 149 or 150 (audit or examination of NHS charity accounts) applies in relation to the parent charity for that year.

(2) If the Commission makes an order under subsection (1) with respect to group accounts, the auditor must be a person appointed by the Commission unless –

(a) the order is made by virtue of subsection (1)(b), and
(b) the charity trustees of the parent charity themselves appoint an auditor in accordance with the order.

(3) The expenses of any audit carried out by an auditor appointed by the Commission under subsection (2), including the auditor's remuneration, are recoverable by the Commission –

(a) from the charity trustees of the parent charity, who are personally liable, jointly and severally, for those expenses, or

(b) to the extent that it appears to the Commission not to be practical to seek recovery of those expenses in accordance with paragraph (a), from the funds of the parent charity.

Regulations relating to audits and examinations

154 Regulations relating to audits and examinations

(1) The Minister may by regulations make provision –

(a) specifying one or more bodies for the purposes of section 144(2)(b);

[(aa) specifying one or more bodies for the purposes of section 149(2)(c);]

(b) with respect to the duties of an auditor carrying out an audit of individual or group accounts, including provision with respect to the making by the auditor of a report on –

(i) the statement of accounts prepared for the financial year in question under section 132(1),

(ii) the account and statement so prepared under section 133,

(iii) the accounts so prepared under section 394 of the Companies Act 2006 (duty to prepare individual accounts), or

(iv) group accounts so prepared under section 138(2),

as the case may be;

(c) with respect to the making of a report in respect of an examination of individual or group accounts by the independent examiner or examiner who has carried out the examination;

(d) conferring on an auditor or on an independent examiner or examiner a right of access with respect to books, documents and other records (however kept) which relate to –

(i) the charity (if the audit or examination is of individual accounts), or

(ii) any member of the group (if the audit or examination is of group accounts);

(e) entitling an auditor or an independent examiner or examiner to require information and explanations from –

(i) past or present charity trustees or trustees for, or past or present officers or employees of, the charity (if the audit or examination is of individual accounts), or

(ii) past or present charity trustees or trustees for, or past or present officers or employees of, any member of the group (if the audit or examination is of group accounts);

(f) enabling the Commission, in circumstances specified in the regulations, to dispense with the requirements of section 144(2), 145(1), 151(4)(a) or 152(2) –

(i) in the case of a particular charity, or

(ii) in the case of any particular financial year of a charity.

(2) Regulations under subsection (1)(e) may in particular make, in relation to audits or examinations of group accounts, provision corresponding or similar to any provision

made by section 499 or 500 of the Companies Act 2006 in connection with the rights exercisable by an auditor of a company in relation to a subsidiary undertaking of the company.

(3) In this section –

'audit of individual or group accounts' means an audit under –
- (a) section 144, 145, 146, 149 or 150 (individual accounts), or
- (b) section 151, 152 or 153 (group accounts);

'examination of individual or group accounts' means an examination under –
- (a) section 145, 149 or 150 (individual accounts), or
- (b) section 152 (group accounts);

and the references in this section and section 155 to an audit or examination of individual accounts and to an audit or examination of group accounts are to be read accordingly.

NOTES

Sub-s (1)(aa) inserted by the Local Audit and Accountability Act 2014, s 45, Sch 12, para 122 as from 1 April 2017.

155 Power of Commission to direct compliance with certain regulations

If any person fails to afford an auditor or an independent examiner or examiner any facility to which the auditor, independent examiner or examiner is entitled by virtue of section 154(1)(d) or (e), the Commission, for securing that the default is made good, may by order give such directions as it thinks appropriate –

- (a) to that person,
- (b) if the audit or examination is of individual accounts, to the charity trustees for the time being of the charity concerned, or
- (c) if the audit or examination is of group accounts, to the charity trustees for the time being of such member of the group as the Commission thinks appropriate.

Duty of auditors etc to report matters to Commission

156 Duty of auditors etc to report matters to Commission

(1) This section applies to a person ('P') who –

- (a) is acting as an auditor or independent examiner appointed by or in relation to a charity under sections 144 to 146 (audit or examination of individual accounts),
- (b) is acting as an auditor or examiner appointed under section 149(2) or (3) (audit or examination of English NHS charity accounts), or
- (c) is the Auditor General for Wales acting under section 150(2) or (3) (audit or examination of Welsh NHS charity accounts).

(2) If, in the course of acting in the capacity mentioned in subsection (1), P becomes aware of a matter –

- (a) which relates to the activities or affairs of the charity or of any connected institution or body, and
- (b) which P has reasonable cause to believe is likely to be of material significance for the purposes of the exercise by the Commission of its functions under the provisions mentioned in subsection (3),

P must immediately make a written report on the matter to the Commission.

(3) The provisions are –

(a) sections 46, 47 and 50 (inquiries by Commission);
(b) sections 76 and 79 to 82 (Commission's powers to act for protection of charities).

(4) If, in the course of acting in the capacity mentioned in subsection (1), P becomes aware of any matter –

(a) which does not appear to P to be one that P is required to report under subsection (2), but
(b) which P has reasonable cause to believe is likely to be relevant for the purposes of the exercise by the Commission of any of its functions,

P may make a report on the matter to the Commission.

(5) Where the duty or power under subsection (2) or (4) has arisen in relation to P when acting in the capacity mentioned in subsection (1), the duty or power is not affected by P's subsequently ceasing to act in that capacity.

(6) Where P makes a report as required or authorised by subsection (2) or (4), no duty to which P is subject is to be regarded as contravened merely because of any information or opinion contained in the report.

157 Meaning of 'connected institution or body' in s 156(2)

(1) In section 156(2) 'connected institution or body', in relation to a charity, means –

(a) an institution which is controlled by, or
(b) a body corporate in which a substantial interest is held by,

the charity or any one or more of the charity trustees acting as such.

(2) Sections 351 and 352 (meaning of controlled institution and substantial interest) apply for the purposes of subsection (1).

158 Application of duty in relation to auditors etc of group accounts

(1) Subsections (2) to (6) of section 156 (duty of auditors etc of individual accounts to report matters to Commission) apply in relation to a person appointed to audit, or report on, any group accounts under sections 151 to 153 as they apply in relation to the person referred to in section 156 as 'P'.

(2) In section 156(2)(a), as it applies in accordance with subsection (1), the reference to the charity or any connected institution or body is to be read as a reference to the parent charity or any of its subsidiary undertakings.

159 Application of duty in relation to Companies Act auditors

(1) Sections 156(2) to (6) and 157 (duty of auditors etc of individual accounts to report matters to Commission) apply in relation to a person acting as a Companies Act auditor of a charitable company as they apply in relation to the person referred to in section 156 as 'P', but reading any reference to P's acting in the capacity mentioned in section 156(1) as a reference to the person acting as a Companies Act auditor.

(2) In subsection (1), 'Companies Act auditor' means an auditor appointed under Chapter 2 of Part 16 of the Companies Act 2006 (appointment of auditors).

Exempt and excepted charities

160 Exempt charities

(1) Nothing in sections 144 to 155 (audit or examination of accounts) applies to an exempt charity.

(2) Sections 156(2) to (6) and 157 (duty of auditors etc of individual accounts to report matters to Commission) apply in relation to a person appointed to audit, or report on, the accounts of an exempt charity which is not a company as they apply in relation to the person referred to in section 156 as 'P', but reading –

(a) any reference to P's acting in the capacity mentioned in section 156(1) as a reference to the person acting as a person so appointed, and
(b) any reference to the Commission or to any of its functions as a reference to the charity's principal regulator or to any of the latter's functions as principal regulator in relation to the charity.

(3) Nothing in section 158 (duty of auditors etc in relation to group accounts) applies to an exempt charity.

161 Excepted charities

(1) Nothing in sections 144 to 146 (audit or examination of individual accounts) applies to any charity which –

(a) falls within section 30(2)(d) (whether or not it also falls within section 30(2)(b) or (c)), and
(b) is not registered.

(2) Except in accordance with subsections (3) and (4), nothing in –

(a) section 154 or 155 (regulations relating to audits and examinations), or
(b) section 156 or 157 (duty of auditors etc to report matters to Commission),

applies to a charity mentioned in subsection (1).

(3) Sections 154 to 157 apply to a charity mentioned in subsection (1) which is also –

(a) an English NHS charity (as defined in section 149), or
(b) a Welsh NHS charity (as defined in section 150).

(4) Sections 156 and 157 apply in accordance with section 160(2) to a charity mentioned in subsection (1) which is also an exempt charity.

Chapter 4
Annual Reports and Returns and Public Access to Accounts etc

Annual reports etc

162 Charity trustees to prepare annual reports

(1) The charity trustees of a charity must prepare in respect of each financial year of the charity an annual report containing –

(a) such a report by the trustees on the activities of the charity during that year, and
(b) such other information relating to the charity or to its trustees or officers,

as may be prescribed by regulations made by the Minister.

(2) Regulations under subsection (1) may in particular make provision –

(a) for any such report as is mentioned in subsection (1)(a) to be prepared in accordance with such principles as are specified or referred to in the regulations;

(b) enabling the Commission to dispense with any requirement prescribed by virtue of subsection (1)(b) –

(i) in the case of a particular charity or a particular class of charities, or

(ii) in the case of a particular financial year of a charity or of any class of charities.

[162A Annual reports: fund-raising standards information

(1) If section 144(2) applies to a financial year of a charity, the annual report in respect of that year must include a statement of each of the following for that year –

(a) he approach taken by the charity to activities by the charity or by any person on behalf of the charity for the purpose of fund-raising, and in particular whether a professional fund-raiser or commercial participator carried on any of those activities;

(b) whether the charity or any person acting on behalf of the charity was subject to an undertaking to be bound by any voluntary scheme for regulating fund-raising, or any voluntary standard of fund-raising, in respect of activities on behalf of the charity, and, if so, what scheme or standard;

(c) any failure to comply with a scheme or standard mentioned under paragraph (b);

(d) whether the charity monitored activities carried on by any person on behalf of the charity for the purpose of fund-raising, and, if so, how it did so;

(e) the number of complaints received by the charity or a person acting on its behalf about activities by the charity or by a person on behalf of the charity for the purpose of fund-raising;

(f) what the charity has done to protect vulnerable people and other members of the public from behaviour within subsection (2) in the course of, or in connection with, such activities.

(2) The behaviour within this subsection is –

(a) unreasonable intrusion on a person's privacy;

(b) unreasonably persistent approaches for the purpose of soliciting or otherwise procuring money or other property on behalf of the charity;

(c) placing undue pressure on a person to give money or other property.

(3) In this section –

(a) 'commercial participator' and 'professional fund-raiser' have the meaning given by section 58 of the Charities Act 1992 (control of fund-raising: interpretation));

(b) 'fund-raising' means soliciting or otherwise procuring money or other property for charitable purposes.

(4) Section 58(6) and (7) of the Charities Act 1992 (references to soliciting money etc) apply for the purposes of this section as they apply for the purposes of Part 2 of that Act.]

NOTES

Inserted by the Charities (Protection and Social Investment) Act 2016, s 13(4) as from 1 November 2016.

163 Transmission of annual reports to Commission in certain cases

(1) Where a charity's gross income in any financial year exceeds £25,000, a copy of the annual report required to be prepared under section 162 in respect of that year must be transmitted to the Commission by the charity trustees within –

(a) 10 months from the end of that year, or

(b) such longer period as the Commission may for any special reason allow in the case of that report.

(2) Where a charity's gross income in any financial year does not exceed £25,000, a copy of the annual report required to be prepared under section 162 in respect of that year must, if the Commission so requests, be transmitted to it by the charity trustees –

(a) in the case of a request made before the end of 7 months from the end of the financial year to which the report relates, within 10 months from the end of that year, and

(b) in the case of a request not so made, within 3 months from the date of the request,

or, in either case, within such longer period as the Commission may for any special reason allow in the case of that report.

(3) In the case of a charity which is constituted as a CIO –

(a) the requirement imposed by subsection (1) applies whatever the charity's gross income is, and

(b) subsection (2) does not apply.

164 Documents to be transmitted with annual report

(1) Subject to subsection (3), any copy of an annual report transmitted to the Commission under section 163 must have attached to it –

(a) a copy of the statement of accounts prepared for the financial year in question under section 132(1), or

(b) (as the case may be) a copy of the account and statement so prepared under section 133,

and a copy of the relevant auditor's or examiner's report.

(2) In subsection (1), 'the relevant auditor's or examiner's report' means –

(a) if the accounts of the charity for that year have been audited under section 144, 145, 146, 149 or 150, the report made by the auditor on that statement of accounts or (as the case may be) on that account and statement;

(b) if the accounts of the charity for that year have been examined under section 145, 149 or 150, the report made by the person carrying out the examination.

(3) Subsections (1) and (2) do not apply to a charitable company, and any copy of an annual report transmitted by the charity trustees of a charitable company under section 163 must have attached to it –

(a) a copy of the company's annual accounts prepared for the financial year in question under Part 15 of the Companies Act 2006, and

(b) a copy of the relevant auditor's or examiner's report.

(4) In subsection (3), 'the relevant auditor's or examiner's report' means –

(a) if the accounts of the company for that year have been audited under Part 16 of the Companies Act 2006, the report made by the auditor on those accounts;
(b) if the accounts of the company for that year have been audited under section 144, 145 or 146, the report made by the auditor on those accounts;
(c) if the accounts of the company for that year have been examined under section 145, the report made by the person carrying out the examination.

165 Preservation of annual reports etc

(1) Any copy of an annual report transmitted to the Commission under section 163, together with the documents attached to it, is to be kept by the Commission for such period as it thinks fit.

(2) The charity trustees of a charity must preserve for at least 6 years from the end of the financial year to which it relates an annual report prepared by them under section 162(1) if they have not been required to transmit a copy of it to the Commission.

(3) Subsection (4) applies if a charity ceases to exist within the period of 6 years mentioned in subsection (2) as it applies to any annual report.

(4) The obligation to preserve the annual report in accordance with subsection (2) must continue to be discharged by the last charity trustees of the charity, unless the Commission consents in writing to the annual report being destroyed or otherwise disposed of.

166 Annual reports and group accounts

(1) This section applies where group accounts are prepared for a financial year of a parent charity under section 138(2).

(2) The annual report prepared by the charity trustees of the parent charity in respect of that year under section 162 must include –

(a) such a report by the trustees on the activities of the charity's subsidiary undertakings during that year, and
(b) such other information relating to any of those undertakings,

as may be prescribed by regulations made by the Minister.

(3) Regulations under subsection (2) may in particular make provision –

(a) for any such report as is mentioned in subsection (2)(a) to be prepared in accordance with such principles as are specified or referred to in the regulations;
(b) enabling the Commission to dispense with any requirement prescribed by virtue of subsection (2)(b) in the case of –
    (i) a particular subsidiary undertaking, or
    (ii) a particular class of subsidiary undertakings.

(4) Section 163 (transmission of annual report to Commission in certain cases) applies in relation to the annual report referred to in subsection (2) as if any reference to the charity's gross income in the financial year in question were a reference to the aggregate gross income of the group in that year.

(5) When transmitted to the Commission in accordance with subsection (4), the copy of the annual report must have attached to it both a copy of the group accounts prepared for that year under section 138(2) and –

(a) a copy of the report made by the auditor on those accounts, or
(b) if those accounts have been examined under section 152, a copy of the report made by the person carrying out the examination.

(6) The requirements in this section are in addition to those in sections 162 to 165.

167 Exempt charities

Nothing in sections 162 to 166 (annual reports etc) applies to any exempt charity.

168 Excepted charities

(1) Nothing in sections 162 to 165 (annual reports etc) applies to any charity which –

(a) falls within section 30(2)(d) (whether or not it also falls within section 30(2)(b) or (c)), and
(b) is not registered.

(2) Except in accordance with subsection (5), nothing in sections 162 to 165 applies to any charity which –

(a) falls within section 30(2)(b) or (c) but does not fall within section 30(2)(d), and
(b) is not registered.

(3) If requested to do so by the Commission, the charity trustees of any such charity as is mentioned in subsection (2) must prepare an annual report in respect of such financial year of the charity as is specified in the Commission's request.

(4) Any report prepared und er subsection (3) must contain –

(a) such a report by the charity trustees on the activities of the charity during the year in question, and
(b) such other information relating to the charity or to its trustees or officers,

as may be prescribed by regulations made under section 162(1) in relation to annual reports prepared under section 162(1).

(5) The following provisions apply in relation to any report required to be prepared under subsection (3) as if it were an annual report required to be prepared under section 162(1) –

(a) section 163(1) (transmission of annual report in certain cases), with the omission of the words preceding 'a copy of the annual report', and
(b) sections 164 (documents to be transmitted with annual report) and 165(1) (preservation of annual reports etc).

(6) Subsections (7) and (8) apply where –

(a) a charity is required to prepare an annual report in respect of a financial year by virtue of subsection (3),
(b) the charity is a parent charity at the end of the year, and
(c) group accounts are prepared for that year under section 138(2) by the charity trustees of the charity.

(7) When transmitted to the Commission in accordance with subsection (5), the copy of the annual report must have attached to it both a copy of the group accounts and –

(a) a copy of the report made by the auditor on those accounts, or
(b) if those accounts have been examined under section 152, a copy of the report made by the person carrying out the examination.

(8) The requirement in subsection (7) is in addition to that in subsection (4).

Annual returns

169 Annual returns by registered charities

(1) Subject to subsection (2), every registered charity must prepare in respect of each of its financial years an annual return in such form, and containing such information, as may be prescribed by regulations made by the Commission.

(2) Subsection (1) does not apply in relation to any financial year of a charity in which the charity's gross income does not exceed £10,000 (but this subsection does not apply if the charity is constituted as a CIO).

(3) Any such return must be transmitted to the Commission by the date by which the charity trustees are, by virtue of section 163(1), required to transmit to the Commission the annual report required to be prepared in respect of the financial year in question.

(4) The Commission may dispense with the requirements of subsection (1) –

(a) in the case of a particular charity or a particular class of charities, or
(b) in the case of a particular financial year of a charity or of any class of charities.

Availability of documents to public

170 Public inspection of annual reports etc kept by Commission

Any document kept by the Commission in pursuance of section 165(1) (preservation of annual reports etc) must be open to public inspection at all reasonable times –

(a) during the period for which it is so kept, or
(b) if the Commission so determines, during such lesser period as it may specify.

171 Supply by charity trustees of copy of most recent annual report

(1) This section applies if an annual report has been prepared in respect of any financial year of a charity in pursuance of section 162(1) or 168(3).

(2) If the charity trustees of a charity –

(a) are requested in writing by any person to provide that person with a copy of its most recent annual report, and
(b) are paid by that person such reasonable fee (if any) as they may require in respect of the costs of complying with the request,

they must comply with the request within the period of 2 months beginning with the date on which it is made.

(3) The reference in subsection (2) to a charity's most recent annual report is a reference to the annual report prepared in pursuance of section 162(1) or 168(3) in respect of the last financial year of the charity in respect of which an annual report has been so prepared.

172 Supply by charity trustees of copy of most recent accounts

(1) If the charity trustees of a charity –

(a) are requested in writing by any person to provide that person with a copy of the charity's most recent accounts, and
(b) are paid by that person such reasonable fee (if any) as they may require in respect of the costs of complying with the request,

they must comply with the request within the period of 2 months beginning with the date on which it is made.

(2) The reference in subsection (1) to a charity's most recent accounts is –

(a) in the case of a charity other than one falling within paragraph (b) or (c), a reference to –
   (i) the statement of accounts prepared in pursuance of section 132(1), or
   (ii) the account and statement prepared in pursuance of section 133,
   in respect of the last financial year of the charity in respect of which a statement of accounts or account and statement has or have been so prepared;
(b) in the case of a charitable company, a reference to the most recent annual accounts of the company prepared under Part 16 of the Companies Act 2006 in relation to which any of the following conditions is satisfied –
   (i) they have been audited,
   (ii) they have been examined by an independent examiner under section 145(1)(a), or
   (iii) they relate to a year in respect of which the company is exempt from audit under Part 16 of the Companies Act 2006 and neither section 144(2) nor section 145(1) applied to them, and
(c) in the case of an exempt charity, a reference to the accounts of the charity most recently audited in pursuance of any statutory or other requirement or, if its accounts are not required to be audited, the accounts most recently prepared in respect of the charity.

(3) In subsection (1), the reference to a charity's most recent accounts includes, in relation to a charity whose charity trustees have prepared any group accounts under section 138(2), the group accounts most recently prepared by them.

Offences

173 Offences of failing to supply certain documents

(1) If any requirement within subsection (2) is not complied with, each person who immediately before the specified date for compliance was a charity trustee of the charity is guilty of an offence.

(2) A requirement is within this subsection if it is imposed –

(a) by section 163 or by virtue of section 166(4) (requirements to transmit annual report to Commission), taken with sections 164, 166(5) and 168(7) (documents to be supplied with annual report), as applicable,
(b) by section 169(3) (requirement to transmit annual return to Commission),
(c) by section 171(2) (supply by charity trustees of copy of most recent annual report), or
(d) by section 172(1) or by virtue of section 172(3) (supply by charity trustees of copy of most recent accounts);

and in subsection (1) 'the specified date for compliance' means the date for compliance specified in the section in question.

(3) It is a defence, where a person is charged with an offence under subsection (1), to prove that the person took all reasonable steps for securing that the requirement in question would be complied with in time.

(4) A person guilty of an offence under subsection (1) is liable on summary conviction to –

(a) a fine not exceeding level 4 on the standard scale, and
(b) for continued contravention, a daily default fine not exceeding 10% of level 4 on the standard scale for so long as the person in question remains a charity trustee of the charity.

Chapter 5
Powers to Set Financial Thresholds

174 Powers to alter certain sums specified in this Part

(1) The Minister may by order amend any provision listed in subsection (2) –

(a) by substituting a different sum for the sum for the time being specified in that provision, or
(b) if the provision specifies more than one sum, by substituting a different sum for any sum specified in that provision.

(2) The provisions are –

section 133 (gross income in connection with option to prepare account and statement instead of statement of accounts);
section 144(1)(a) or (b) (gross income and value of assets in connection with requirements as to audit of larger charities);
section 145(1) (gross income in connection with option to have accounts examined instead of audited);
section 145(3) (gross income in connection with requirements as to qualifications of independent examiner);
section 163(1) or (2) (gross income in connection with requirements to transmit annual report to Commission);
section 169(2) (gross income in connection with requirement to prepare annual return).

175 Aggregate gross income of group

The Minister may by regulations make provision for determining for the purposes of this Part the amount of the aggregate gross income for a financial year of a group consisting of a parent charity and its subsidiary undertaking or undertakings.

176 Larger groups: 'relevant income threshold' and 'relevant assets threshold'

(1) The reference to the relevant income threshold in paragraph (a) or (b) of section 151(1) is a reference to the sum prescribed as the relevant income threshold for the purposes of that paragraph.

(2) The reference to the relevant assets threshold in paragraph (b) of section 151(1) is a reference to the sum prescribed as the relevant assets threshold for the purposes of that paragraph.

(3) 'Prescribed' means prescribed by regulations made by the Minister.

PART 9
CHARITY TRUSTEES, TRUSTEES AND AUDITORS ETC

Meaning of 'charity trustees'

177 Meaning of 'charity trustees'

In this Act, except in so far as the context otherwise requires, 'charity trustees' means the persons having the general control and management of the administration of a charity.

Disqualification of charity trustees and trustees

178 Persons disqualified from being charity trustees or trustees of a charity

(1) A person ('P') is disqualified from being a charity trustee or trustee for a charity in the following cases –

Case A

P has been convicted *of any offence involving dishonesty or deception* [of –
(a) an offence specified in section 178A;
(b) an offence, not specified in section 178A, that involves dishonesty or deception].

Case B

P has been [made] bankrupt or sequestration of P's estate has been awarded and (in either case) –
(a) P has not been discharged, or
(b) P is the subject of a bankruptcy restrictions order or an interim order.

Case C

P has made a composition or arrangement with, or granted a trust deed for, creditors and has not been discharged in respect of it.

Case D

P has been removed *from the office of charity trustee or trustee for a charity* [as a trustee, charity trustee, officer, agent or employee of a charity] by an order made –
(a) by the Commission under section [79(4)] or by the Commission or the Commissioners under a relevant earlier enactment (as defined by section 179(5)), or
(b) by the High Court,
on the ground of any misconduct or mismanagement in the administration of the charity for which P was responsible or [which P knew of and failed to take any reasonable step to oppose,] or which P's conduct contributed to or facilitated.

Case E

P has been removed, under section 34(5)(e) of the Charities and Trustee Investment (Scotland) Act 2005 (asp 10) (powers of the Court of Session) or the relevant earlier legislation (as defined by section 179(6)), from being concerned in the management or control of any body.

Case F

P is subject to –

(a) a disqualification order or disqualification undertaking under the Company Directors Disqualification Act 1986 or the Company Directors Disqualification (Northern Ireland) Order 2002 (SI 2002/3150 (N.I.4)), or

(b) an order made under section 429(2) of the Insolvency Act 1986 (disabilities on revocation of county court administration order).

[*Case G*

P is subject to –

(a) a moratorium period under a debt relief order under Part 7A of the Insolvency Act 1986; or

(b) a debt relief restrictions order or interim order under Schedule 4ZB to that Act.]

[*Case H*

P has been found to be in contempt of court under Civil Procedure Rules for –

(a) making a false disclosure statement, or causing one to be made, or

(b) making a false statement in a document verified by a statement of truth, or causing one to be made.

Case I

P has been found guilty of disobedience to an order or direction of the Commission on an application to the High Court under section 336(1).

Case J

P is a designated person for the purposes of –

(a) Part 1 of the Terrorist Asset-Freezing etc Act 2010, or

(b) the Al-Qaida (Asset-Freezing) Regulations 2011.

Case K

P is subject to the notification requirements of Part 2 of the Sexual Offences Act 2003.]

(2) Subsection (1) is subject to sections 179 to 181.

[(3) While a person is disqualified under this section in relation to a charity, the person is also disqualified from holding an office or employment in the charity with senior management functions.

(4) A function of an office or employment held by a person '(A)' is a senior management function if –

(a) it relates to the management of the charity, and A is not responsible for it to another officer or employee (other than a charity trustee or trustee for the charity), or

(b) it involves control over money and the only officer or employee (other than a charity trustee or trustee for the charity) to whom A is responsible for it is a person with senior management functions other than ones involving control over money.]

NOTES

Sub-s (1), in Case A words in italics repealed and subsequent words in square brackets substituted by the Charities (Protection and Social Investment) Act 2016, s 9(1), (3) as from a date to be appointed; Case B amended by SI 2016/481, reg 2(1), Sch 1, Pt 1, para 17(1), (3); in Case D words in italics repealed and subsequent words in first pair of square brackets substituted by the Charities (Protection and Social Investment) Act 2016, s 9(1),

(4)(a) as from a date to be appointed, reference in second pair of square brackets substituted by the Charities (Protection and Social Investment) Act 2016, s 4(1), (5); words in third pair of square brackets substituted by the Charities (Protection and Social Investment) Act 2016, s 9(1), (4)(b); Case G inserted by SI 2012/2404, art 3(2), Sch 2, para 62(1), (3); Cases H-K inserted by the Charities (Protection and Social Investment) Act 2016, s 9(1), (5) as from a date to be appointed.

Sub-ss (3), (4) inserted by the Charities (Protection and Social Investment) Act 2016, s 9(1), (6) as from a date to be appointed.

[178A Case A: specified offences

(1) The following offences are specified for the purposes of Case A –

1 An offence to which Part 4 of the Counter-Terrorism Act 2008 applies (see sections 41 to 43 of that Act).

2 An offence under section 13 or 19 of the Terrorism Act 2000 (wearing of uniform etc, and failure to disclose information).

3 A money laundering offence within the meaning of section 415 of the Proceeds of Crime Act 2002.

4 An offence under any of the following provisions of the Bribery Act 2010 –

(a) section 1 (bribing another person),

(b) section 2 (offences relating to being bribed),

(c) section 6 (bribery of foreign public officials),

(d) section 7 (failure of commercial organisations to prevent bribery).

5 An offence under section 77 of this Act.

6 An offence of –

(a) misconduct in public office,

(b) perjury,

(c) perverting the course of justice.

(2) An offence which has been superseded (directly or indirectly) by an offence specified in subsection (1) is also specified for the purposes of Case A.

(3) In relation to an offence specified in subsection (1) or (2), the following offences are also specified for the purposes of Case A –

(a) an offence of attempt, conspiracy or incitement to commit the offence;
(b) an offence of aiding, abetting, counselling or procuring the commission of the offence;
(c) an offence under Part 2 of the Serious Crime Act 2007 (encouraging or assisting) in relation to the offence.

(4) The Minister may amend this section by regulations to add or remove an offence.]

NOTES

Inserted by the Charities (Protection and Social Investment) Act 2016, s 9(1), (7) as from a date to be appointed.

179 Disqualification: pre-commencement events etc

(1) Case A –

(a) applies whether the conviction occurred before or after the commencement of section 178(1) [or section 178A or any amendment of that section], but
(b) does not apply in relation to any conviction which is a spent conviction for the purposes of the Rehabilitation of Offenders Act 1974.

(2) Case B applies whether the [making bankrupt] or the sequestration or the making of a bankruptcy restrictions order or an interim order occurred before or after the commencement of section 178(1).

(3) Case C applies whether the composition or arrangement was made, or the trust deed was granted, before or after the commencement of section 178(1).

(4) Cases D to F apply in relation to orders made and removals effected before or after the commencement of section 178(1).

(5) In Case D –

(a) 'the Commissioners' means the Charity Commissioners for England and Wales, and
(b) 'relevant earlier enactment' means –
 (i) section 18(2)(i) of the Charities Act 1993 (power to act for protection of charities),
 (ii) section 20(1A)(i) of the Charities Act 1960, or
 (iii) section 20(1)(i) of the 1960 Act (as in force before the commencement of section 8 of the Charities Act 1992).

(6) In Case E, 'the relevant earlier legislation' means section 7 of the Law Reform (Miscellaneous Provisions) (Scotland) Act 1990 (powers of Court of Session to deal with management of charities).

[(7) Case H does not apply in relation to a finding of contempt which, if it had been a conviction for which P was dealt with in the same way, would be a spent conviction for the purposes of the Rehabilitation of Offenders Act 1974.]

NOTES

Sub-s (1) amended by the Charities (Protection and Social Investment) Act 2016, s 9(1), (8), (9) as from a date to be appointed.

Sub-s (2) amended by SI 2016/481, reg 2(1), Sch 1, Pt 1, para 17(1), (4).

Sub-s (7) inserted by the Charities (Protection and Social Investment) Act 2016, s 9(1), (8), (10) as from a date to be appointed.

180 Disqualification: exceptions in relation to charitable companies

(1) Where (apart from this subsection) a person ('P') is disqualified under Case B [or G] from being a charity trustee or trustee for a charitable company [or a CIO], P is not so disqualified if leave has been granted under section 11 of the Company Directors Disqualification Act 1986 (undischarged bankrupts) for P to act as director of the company [or charity trustee of the CIO (as the case may be)].

(2) Similarly, a person ('P') is not disqualified under Case F from being a charity trustee or trustee for a charitable company [or a CIO] if, in a case set out in the first column of the table, leave has been granted as mentioned in the second column for P to act as director of the company [or charity trustee of the CIO (as the case may be)] –

P is subject to a disqualification order or disqualification undertaking under the Company Directors Disqualification Act 1986.	Leave has been granted for the purposes of section 1(1)(a) or 1A(1)(a) of the 1986 Act.
P is subject to a disqualification order or disqualification undertaking under the Company Directors Disqualification (Northern Ireland) Order 2002 (SI 2002/3150 (NI 4)).	Leave has been granted by the High Court in Northern Ireland.
P is subject to an order under section 429(2) of the Insolvency Act 1986.	Leave has been granted by the court which made the order.

NOTES

Sub-s (1) amended by SI 2012/2404, art 3(2), Sch 2, para 62(1), (4), SI 2012/3014, art 5(a).

Sub-s (2) amended by SI 2012/3014, art 5(b).

181 Power to waive disqualification

(1) This section applies where a person ('P') is disqualified under section 178(1).

(2) The Commission may, if P makes an application under this subsection, waive P's disqualification –

(a) generally, or
(b) in relation to a particular charity or a particular class of charities.

[(2A) A waiver under subsection (2) –

(a) may relate to the whole of P's disqualification or only to disqualification under section 178(3);
(b) in relation to disqualification under section 178(3) may relate to a particular office or employment or to any office or employment of a particular description.]

(3) If –

(a) P is disqualified under Case D *or E*[, E or I] and makes an application under subsection (2) 5 years or more after the date on which the disqualification took effect, and
(b) the Commission is not prevented from granting the application by subsection (5),

the Commission must grant the application unless satisfied that, because of any special circumstances, it should be refused.

(4) Any waiver under subsection (2) must be notified in writing to P.

(5) No waiver may be granted under subsection (2) in relation to any charitable company [or CIO] if –

(a) P is for the time being prohibited from acting as director of the company [or charity trustee of the CIO (as the case may be)], by virtue of –
  (i) a disqualification order or disqualification undertaking under the Company Directors Disqualification Act 1986, or
  (ii) a provision of the 1986 Act mentioned in subsection (6), and

(b) leave has not been granted for P to act as [director of any company or charity trustee of any CIO].

(6) The provisions of the 1986 Act are –

section 11(1) (undischarged bankrupts);
section 12(2) (failure to pay under county court administration order);
section 12A (Northern Irish disqualification orders);
section 12B (Northern Irish disqualification undertakings).

NOTES

Sub-s (2A) inserted by the Charities (Protection and Social Investment) Act 2016, s 9(1), (11), (12) as from a date to be appointed.

Sub-s (3)(a) words in italics repealed and subsequent words in square brackets substituted by the Charities (Protection and Social Investment) Act 2016, s 9(1), (11), (13) as from a date to be appointed.

Sub-s (5) amended by SI 2012/3014, art 6(a)-(c).

[181A Disqualification orders

(1) The Commission may by order disqualify a person from being a charity trustee or trustee for a charity.

(2) The order may disqualify a person –

(a) in relation to all charities, or
(b) in relation to such charities or classes of charity as may be specified or described in the order.

(3) While a person is disqualified by virtue of an order under this section in relation to a charity, the person is also disqualified, subject to subsection (5), from holding an office or employment in the charity with senior management functions.

(4) A function of an office or employment held by a person ('A') is a senior management function if –

(a) it relates to the management of the charity, and A is not responsible for it to another officer or employee (other than a charity trustee or trustee for the charity), or
(b) it involves control over money and the only officer or employee (other than a charity trustee or trustee for the charity) to whom A is responsible for it is a person with senior management functions other than ones involving control over money.

(5) An order under this section may provide for subsection (3) not to apply –

(a) generally, or
(b) in relation to a particular office or employment or to any office or employment of a particular description.

(6) The Commission may make an order disqualifying a person under this section only if it is satisfied that –

(a) one or more of the conditions listed in subsection (7) are met in relation to the person,
(b) the person is unfit to be a charity trustee or trustee for a charity (either generally or in relation to the charities or classes of charity specified or described in the order), and

(c) making the order is desirable in the public interest in order to protect public trust and confidence in charities generally or in the charities or classes of charity specified or described in the order.

(7) These are the conditions –

A that the person has been cautioned for a disqualifying offence against a charity or involving the administration of a charity.

B that –

(a) under the law of a country or territory outside the United Kingdom the person has been convicted in respect of an offence against a charity or involving the administration of a charity, and

(b) the act which constituted the offence would have constituted a disqualifying offence if it had been done in any part of the United Kingdom.

C that the person has been found by Her Majesty's Revenue and Customs not to be a fit and proper person to be a manager of a body or trust, for the purposes of paragraph 4 of Schedule 6 to the Finance Act 2010 (definition of charity for tax purposes), and the finding has not been overturned.

D that the person was a trustee, charity trustee, officer, agent or employee of a charity at a time when there was misconduct or mismanagement in the administration of the charity, and –

(a) the person was responsible for the misconduct or mismanagement,

(b) the person knew of the misconduct or mismanagement and failed to take any reasonable step to oppose it, or

(c) the person's conduct contributed to or facilitated the misconduct or mismanagement.

E that the person was an officer or employee of a body corporate at a time when the body was a trustee or charity trustee for a charity and when there was misconduct or mismanagement by it in the administration of the charity, and –

(a) the person was responsible for the misconduct or mismanagement,

(b) the person knew of the misconduct or mismanagement and failed to take any reasonable step to oppose it, or

(c) the person's conduct contributed to or facilitated the misconduct or mismanagement.

F that any other past or continuing conduct by the person, whether or not in relation to a charity, is damaging or likely to be damaging to public trust and confidence in charities generally or in the charities or classes of charity specified or described in the order.

(8) The Minister may amend this section by regulations to add or remove a condition.

(9) In this section 'disqualifying offence' means an offence within Case A in section 178(1).

(10) Conditions A and B apply whether the caution or conviction occurred before or after the commencement of this section.

(11) Condition B does not apply in relation to a conviction which is spent under the law of the country or territory concerned.

(12) For the purposes of condition B –

(a) an act punishable under the law of a country or territory outside the United Kingdom constitutes an offence under that law, however it is described in that law, and

(b) 'charity' means an institution that is a charity under the law of any part of the United Kingdom or that is established under the law of another country or territory principally for charitable, benevolent or philanthropic purposes.]

NOTES

Inserted by the Charities (Protection and Social Investment) Act 2016, s 10(1), (2) as from 1 October 2016.

[181B Duration of disqualification, and suspension pending disqualification

(1) An order under section 181A must specify the period for which the person is disqualified.

(2) The period –

(a) must be not more than 15 years beginning with the day on which the order takes effect, and

(b) must be proportionate, having regard in particular to the time when a conviction becomes spent or, where condition B applies, would become spent if it were a conviction for the relevant disqualifying offence, and to circumstances in which the Commission may or must grant a waiver under section 181 where a person is disqualified under section 178.

(3) An order takes effect –

(a) at the end of the time specified by Tribunal Procedure Rules for starting proceedings for an appeal against the order, if no proceedings are started within that time, or

(b) (subject to the decision on the appeal) when any proceedings started within that time are withdrawn or finally determined.

(4) The Commission may by order suspend a person from being a charity trustee or trustee for a charity if it has given notice under section 181C(1)(a) of its proposal to make an order under section 181A in respect of the person.

(5) The Commission may not make an order under subsection (4) so as to suspend a person for a period of more than 12 months, but at any time before the expiry of an order the Commission may extend or further extend the suspension by a further order under that subsection, provided that –

(a) the order does not extend the suspension for a period of more than 12 months, and

(b) the total period of suspension is not more than 2 years.

(6) An order under subsection (4) ceases to have effect –

(a) if the Commission notifies the person that it will not proceed with its proposal, on the notification being given;

(b) if the Commission makes the order under section 181A, on the order taking effect;

or, if earlier, at the end of the period specified in accordance with subsection (5).

(7) The Commission must review any order under subsection (4), at such intervals as it thinks fit.

(8) If on a review it appears to the Commission that it would be appropriate to discharge an order under subsection (4) in whole or in part, the Commission must do so (whether subject to any savings or other transitional provisions or not).

(9) An order under subsection (4) made in the case of any person ('P') may make provision, as respects the period of P's suspension, for matters arising out of it, and in particular –

(a) for enabling any person to execute any instrument in P's name or otherwise act for P, and
(b) in the case of a charity trustee, for adjusting any rules governing the proceedings of the charity trustees to take account of the reduction in the number capable of acting.

This does not affect the generality of section 337(1) and (2).

(10) While an order under subsection (4) is in force suspending a person from being a charity trustee or trustee for a charity, the person must not take up any appointment as a charity trustee or trustee for any other charity without the written approval of the Commission.]

NOTES

Inserted by the Charities (Protection and Social Investment) Act 2016, s 10(1), (2) as from 1 October 2016.

[181C Disqualification orders: procedure

(1) Before making an order in respect of a person under section 181A without the person's consent the Commission must –

(a) give the person not less than one month's notice of its proposals, and
(b) invite representations to be made to it within a period specified in the notice.

(2) Before making an order under section 181A in respect of a person who the Commission knows or believes to be a charity trustee or trustee for a charity, the Commission must also –

(a) give notice of its proposals to each of the charity trustees of the charity in question;
(b) comply with the publicity requirement, unless the Commission is satisfied that for any reason compliance with the requirement is unnecessary.

(3) The publicity requirement is that the Commission must give public notice of its proposals, inviting representations to be made to it within a period specified in the notice.

(4) The time when any such notice is given is to be decided by the Commission.

(5) Any notice of any proposals which is to be given under this section is to contain such particulars of the proposals, or such directions for obtaining information about them, as the Commission thinks sufficient and appropriate.

(6) Where the Commission gives notice of any proposals under this section –

(a) it must take into account any representations made to it within the period specified in the notice, and
(b) it may (without further notice) proceed with the proposals either without modifications or with such modifications as it thinks desirable;

but a notice under subsection (2)(a) need not specify a period for the purposes of paragraph (a) if the charity came to the Commission's knowledge or belief after the expiry of the period specified for the purposes of subsection (1)(b).

(7) A notice under subsection (1) or (2)(a) –

(a) may be given by post, and
(b) if given by post, may be addressed to the recipient's last known address in the United Kingdom.

(8) A notice under subsection (2)(b) is to be given in such manner as the Commission thinks sufficient and appropriate.

(9) Where the Commission makes an order under section 181A in respect of a person it knows or believes to be a charity trustee or trustee for a charity it must (as well as serving it on that person) send a copy of the order and a statement of the Commission's reasons for making it –

(a) to the charity in question (if a body corporate), or
(b) (if not) to each of the charity trustees of the charity in question.

(10) Nothing in this section requires the Commission to give notice, or send a document, to a person who cannot be found or has no known address in the United Kingdom.

(11) Any documents required to be sent to a person under this section may be sent to, or otherwise served on, the person in the same way as an order made by the Commission under this Act could be served on the person in accordance with section 339.]

NOTES

Inserted by the Charities (Protection and Social Investment) Act 2016, s 10(1), (2) as from 1 October 2016.

[181D Disqualification orders: variation and revocation

A person in respect of whom an order under section 181A is in force may at any time apply to the Commission for an order varying or discharging that order.]

NOTES

Inserted by the Charities (Protection and Social Investment) Act 2016, s 10(1), (2) as from 1 October 2016.

182 Records of persons removed from office

(1) For the purposes of sections 178 to *181* [181A] the Commission must keep, in such manner as it thinks fit, a register of [the following.]

[(1A) The register must include] all persons who have been removed from office as mentioned in Case D –

(a) by an order of the Commission or the Commissioners made before or after the commencement of section 178(1), or
(b) by an order of the High Court made after the commencement of section 45(1) of the Charities Act 1992;

and, where any person is so removed from office by an order of the High Court, the court must notify the Commission of the person's removal.

[(1B) The register must include all persons who have been disqualified by an order of the Commission under section 181A.

(1C) The register must include all persons who have been removed from office by an order of the Commission under section 79A (removal of disqualified trustee).]

(2) The entries in the register kept under subsection (1) must be available for public inspection in legible form at all reasonable times.

(3) In this section 'the Commissioners' means the Charity Commissioners for England and Wales.

NOTES

Sub-s (1): reference in italics repealed and subsequent reference or words in square brackets substituted or inserted, by the Charities (Protection and Social Investment) Act 2016, s 11(1), (2) as from a date to be appointed.

Sub-s (1A) renumbered as such and amended by the Charities (Protection and Social Investment) Act 2016, s 11(1), (3), (4) as from a date to be appointed.

Sub-s (1B) inserted by the Charities (Protection and Social Investment) Act 2016, s 11(1), (5) as from 1 October 2016.

Sub-s (1C) inserted by the Charities (Protection and Social Investment) Act 2016, s 11(1), (5).

183 Criminal consequences of acting while disqualified

(1) Subject to subsection (2), it is an offence for any person to act as a charity trustee or trustee for a charity [or to hold an office or employment] while disqualified from being such a trustee [or from holding that office or employment] by virtue of section 178 [or an order under section 181A].

(2) Subsection (1) does not apply if –

(a) the charity concerned is a company [or a CIO], and
(b) the disqualified person is disqualified by virtue only of Case B[, F or G] [in section 178].

(3) A person guilty of an offence under subsection (1) is liable –

(a) on summary conviction, to imprisonment for a term not exceeding 12 months or to a fine not exceeding the statutory maximum, or both;
(b) on conviction on indictment, to imprisonment for a term not exceeding 2 years or to a fine, or both.

NOTES

Sub-s (1) amended by the Charities (Protection and Social Investment) Act 2016, ss 9(1), (14)(a), (b), 10(1), (3)(a) partly as from 1 October 2016 and fully as from a date to be appointed.

Sub-s (2) amended by SI 2012/2404, art 3(2), Sch 2, para 62(1), (5); SI 2012/3014, art 7; the Charities (Protection and Social Investment) Act 2016, s 10(1), (3)(b) as from 1 October 2016.

184 Civil consequences of acting while disqualified

(1) Any acts done as charity trustee or trustee for a charity [or as officer or employee of a charity] by a person disqualified from being such a trustee [or from holding that office or employment] by virtue of section 178 [or an order under section 181A] are not invalid merely because of that disqualification.

(2) Subsection (3) applies if the Commission is satisfied that any person –

(a) has acted as charity trustee or trustee for a charity [or as officer or employee of a charity] while disqualified from being such a trustee [or from holding that office or employment] by virtue of section 178 [or an order under section 181A], and
(b) while so acting, has received from the charity any sums by way of remuneration or expenses, or any benefit in kind, in connection with acting as charity trustee or trustee for the charity [or holding the office or employment].

(3) The Commission may by order direct the person –
(a) to repay to the charity the whole or part of any such sums, or
(b) (as the case may be) to pay to the charity the whole or part of the monetary value (as determined by the Commission) of any such benefit.

(4) Subsection (3) does not apply to any sums received by way of remuneration or expenses in respect of any time when the person concerned was not disqualified from being a charity trustee or trustee for the charity.

NOTES

Sub-s (1) amended by the Charities (Protection and Social Investment) Act 2016, ss 9(1), (15), (16)(a), (b), 10(1), (4)(a) partly as from 1 October 2016 and fully as from a date to be appointed.

Sub-s (2) amended by the Charities (Protection and Social Investment) Act 2016, ss 9(1), (15), (16)(a), (b), (17) 10(1), (4)(b) partly as from 1 October 2016 and fully as from a date to be appointed.

[184A Sections 183 and 184: participation in corporate decisions

(1) For the purposes of sections 183 and 184, a person who is not a charity trustee or trustee for a charity is treated as acting as one if that person –

(a) is an officer of a body corporate which is a charity trustee or trustee for a charity, and
(b) takes part in that capacity in any decision relating to the administration of the charity.

(2) In subsection (1) 'officer' includes any of the persons having general control and management of the administration of the body.]

NOTES

Inserted by the Charities (Protection and Social Investment) Act 2016, s 12 as from a date to be appointed.

Remuneration of charity trustees and trustees etc

185 Remuneration of charity trustees or trustees etc providing services to charity

(1) This section applies to remuneration for services provided by a person ('P') to or on behalf of a charity where –

(a) P is a charity trustee or trustee for the charity, or
(b) P is connected with a charity trustee or trustee for the charity and the remuneration might result in that trustee obtaining any benefit.

This is subject to subsection (3).

(2) If Conditions A to D are met in relation to remuneration within subsection (1), P is entitled to receive the remuneration out of the funds of the charity.

Condition A

Condition A is that the amount or maximum amount of the remuneration –

(a) is set out in an agreement in writing between the charity or its charity trustees (as the case may be) and P under which P is to provide the services in question to or on behalf of the charity, and

(b) does not exceed what is reasonable in the circumstances for the provision by P of the services in question.

Condition B

Condition B is that, before entering into that agreement, the charity trustees decided that they were satisfied that it would be in the best interests of the charity for the services to be provided by P to or on behalf of the charity for the amount or maximum amount of remuneration set out in the agreement.

Condition C

Condition C is that if immediately after the agreement is entered into there is, in the case of the charity, more than one person who is a charity trustee and is –

(a) a person in respect of whom an agreement within Condition A is in force,

(b) a person who is entitled to receive remuneration out of the funds of the charity otherwise than by virtue of such an agreement, or

(c) a person connected with a person falling within paragraph (a) or (b),

the total number of them constitute a minority of the persons for the time being holding office as charity trustees of the charity.

Condition D

Condition D is that the trusts of the charity do not contain any express provision that prohibits P from receiving the remuneration.

(3) Nothing in this section applies to –

(a) any remuneration for services provided by a person in the person's capacity as a charity trustee or trustee for a charity or under a contract of employment, or

(b) any remuneration not within paragraph (a) which a person is entitled to receive out of the funds of a charity by virtue of –

(i) any provision contained in the trusts of the charity;

(ii) any order of the court or the Commission;

(iii) any statutory provision contained in or having effect under an Act other than this section.

(4) Before entering into an agreement within Condition A the charity trustees must have regard to any guidance given by the Commission concerning the making of such agreements.

(5) The duty of care in section 1(1) of the Trustee Act 2000 applies to a charity trustee when making such a decision as is mentioned in Condition B.

(6) For the purposes of Condition C an agreement within Condition A is in force so long as any obligations under the agreement have not been fully discharged by a party to it.

(7) Sections 187 and 188 (interpretation) apply for the purposes of this section.

186 Disqualification of charity trustee or trustee receiving remuneration under s 185

(1) This section applies to any charity trustee or trustee for a charity –

(a) who is or would be entitled to remuneration under an agreement or proposed agreement within Condition A, or
(b) who is connected with a person who is or would be so entitled.

(2) The charity trustee or trustee for a charity is disqualified from acting as such in relation to any decision or other matter connected with the agreement.

(3) But if an act is done by a person who is disqualified from doing it by virtue of subsection (2), the act is not invalid merely because of that disqualification.

(4) If the Commission is satisfied –

(a) that a person ('P') has done any act which P was disqualified from doing by virtue of subsection (2), and
(b) that P or a person connected with P has received or is to receive from the charity any remuneration under the agreement in question,

it may make an order under subsection (5) or (6) (as appropriate).

(5) An order under this subsection is one requiring P –

(a) to reimburse to the charity the whole or part of the remuneration received as mentioned in subsection (4)(b);
(b) to the extent that the remuneration consists of a benefit in kind, to reimburse to the charity the whole or part of the monetary value (as determined by the Commission) of the benefit in kind.

(6) An order under this subsection is one directing that P or (as the case may be) the connected person is not to be paid the whole or part of the remuneration mentioned in subsection (4)(b).

(7) If the Commission makes an order under subsection (5) or (6), P or (as the case may be) the connected person accordingly ceases to have any entitlement under the agreement to so much of the remuneration (or its monetary value) as the order requires P to reimburse to the charity or (as the case may be) as it directs is not to be paid to P.

(8) Sections 187 and 188 (interpretation) apply for the purposes of this section.

187 Meaning of 'benefit', 'remuneration', 'services' etc

In sections 185 and 186 –

'benefit' means a direct or indirect benefit of any nature;
'maximum amount', in relation to remuneration, means the maximum amount of the remuneration whether specified in or ascertainable under the terms of the agreement in question;
'remuneration' includes any benefit in kind (and 'amount' accordingly includes monetary value);
'services', in the context of remuneration for services, includes goods that are supplied in connection with the provision of services.

188 Meaning of 'connected person'

(1) For the purposes of sections 185 and 186, the following persons are connected with a charity trustee or trustee for a charity –

(a) a child, parent, grandchild, grandparent, brother or sister of the trustee;
(b) the spouse or civil partner of the trustee or of any person falling within paragraph (a);

(c) a person carrying on business in partnership with the trustee or with any person falling within paragraph (a) or (b);

(d) an institution which is controlled –

(i) by the trustee or by any person falling within paragraph (a), (b) or (c), or

(ii) by two or more persons falling within sub-paragraph (i), when taken together.

(e) a body corporate in which –

(i) the trustee or any connected person falling within any of paragraphs (a) to (c) has a substantial interest, or

(ii) two or more persons falling within sub-paragraph (i), when taken together, have a substantial interest.

(2) Sections 350 to 352 (meaning of child, spouse and civil partner, controlled institution and substantial interest) apply for the purposes of subsection (1).

Indemnity insurance for charity trustees and trustees

189 Indemnity insurance for charity trustees and trustees

(1) The charity trustees of a charity may arrange for the purchase, out of the funds of the charity, of insurance designed to indemnify the charity trustees or any trustees for the charity against any personal liability in respect of –

(a) any breach of trust or breach of duty committed by them in their capacity as charity trustees or trustees for the charity, or

(b) any negligence, default, breach of duty or breach of trust committed by them in their capacity as directors or officers of –

(i) the charity (if it is a body corporate), or

(ii) any body corporate carrying on any activities on behalf of the charity.

(2) But the terms of such insurance must be so framed as to exclude the provision of any indemnity for a person ('P') in respect of –

(a) any liability incurred by P to pay –

(i) a fine imposed in criminal proceedings, or

(ii) a sum payable to a regulatory authority by way of a penalty in respect of non-compliance with any requirement of a regulatory nature (however arising),

(b) any liability incurred by P in defending any criminal proceedings in which P is convicted of an offence arising out of any fraud or dishonesty, or wilful or reckless misconduct, by P, or

(c) any liability incurred by P to the charity that arises out of any conduct –

(i) which P knew (or must reasonably be assumed to have known) was not in the interests of the charity, or

(ii) in the case of which P did not care whether it was in the best interests of the charity or not.

(3) For the purposes of subsection (2)(b) –

(a) the reference to any such conviction is a reference to one that has become final,

(b) a conviction becomes final –

(i) if not appealed against, at the end of the period for bringing an appeal, or

(ii) if appealed against, at the time when the appeal (or any further appeal) is disposed of, and

(c) an appeal is disposed of –

(i) if it is determined and the period for bringing any further appeal has ended, or
(ii) if it is abandoned or otherwise ceases to have effect.

(4) The charity trustees of a charity may not purchase insurance under this section unless they decide that they are satisfied that it is in the best interests of the charity for them to do so.

(5) The duty of care in section 1(1) of the Trustee Act 2000 applies to a charity trustee when making such a decision.

(6) This section –

(a) does not authorise the purchase of any insurance whose purchase is expressly prohibited by the trusts of the charity, but
(b) has effect despite any provision prohibiting the charity trustees or trustees for the charity receiving any personal benefit out of the funds of the charity.

190 Power to amend s 189

The Minister may by order make such amendments of section 189(2) and (3) as the Minister considers appropriate.

Powers to relieve trustees and auditors etc from liability

191 Commission's power to relieve trustees and auditors etc from liability

(1) This section applies to a person ('P') who is or has been –

(a) a charity trustee or trustee for a charity,
(b) a person appointed to audit a charity's accounts (whether appointed under an enactment or otherwise), or
(c) an independent examiner or other person appointed to examine or report on a charity's accounts (whether appointed under an enactment or otherwise).

(2) If the Commission considers –

(a) that P is or may be personally liable for a breach of trust or breach of duty committed in P's capacity as a person within subsection (1)(a), (b) or (c), but
(b) that P has acted honestly and reasonably and ought fairly to be excused for the breach of trust or duty,

the Commission may make an order relieving P wholly or partly from any such liability.

(3) An order under subsection (2) may grant the relief on such terms as the Commission thinks fit.

(4) Subsection (2) does not apply in relation to any personal contractual liability of a charity trustee or trustee for a charity.

(5) For the purposes of this section and section 192 –

(a) subsection (1)(b) is to be read as including a reference to the Auditor General for Wales acting as auditor under Part 8, and
(b) subsection (1)(c) is to be read as including a reference to the Auditor General for Wales acting as examiner under Part 8;

and in subsection (1)(b) and (c) any reference to a charity's accounts is to be read as including any group accounts prepared by the charity trustees of a charity.

(6) This section does not affect the operation of –

(a) section 61 of the Trustee Act 1925 (power of court to grant relief to trustees),
(b) section 1157 of the Companies Act 2006 (power of court to grant relief to officers or auditors of companies), or
(c) section 192 (which extends section 1157 to auditors etc of charities which are not companies).

192 Court's power to grant relief to apply to all auditors etc of charities which are not companies

(1) Section 1157 of the Companies Act 2006 (power of court to grant relief to officers or auditors of companies) has effect in relation to a person to whom this section applies as it has effect in relation to a person employed as an auditor by a company.

(2) This section applies to –

(a) a person acting in a capacity within section 191(1)(b) or (c) in a case where, apart from this section, section 1157 of the 2006 Act would not apply in relation to that person as a person so acting, and
(b) a charity trustee of a CIO.

PART 10
CHARITABLE COMPANIES ETC

Introductory

193 Meaning of 'charitable company'

In this Act 'charitable company' means a charity which is a company.

Disclosure of charitable status by companies

194 Requirement to disclose charitable status

(1) Where a charitable company's name does not include the word 'charity' or 'charitable', the fact that the company is a charity must be stated in legible characters –

(a) in every location, and in every description of document or communication, in which it is required by regulations under section 82 of the Companies Act 2006 to state its registered name, and
(b) in all conveyances purporting to be executed by the company.

(2) Where a company's name includes the word 'elusen' or 'elusennol' (the Welsh equivalents of 'charity' and 'charitable'), subsection (1) does not apply in relation to any document that is wholly in Welsh.

(3) The statement required by subsection (1) must be in English, except that, in the case of a document that is otherwise wholly in Welsh, the statement may be in Welsh if it consists of or includes the word 'elusen' or 'elusennol'.

(4) In subsection (1)(b) 'conveyance' means any instrument creating, transferring, varying or extinguishing an interest in land.

195 Civil consequences of failure to make required disclosure

(1) This section applies to any legal proceedings brought by a charitable company to which section 194 applies to enforce a right arising out of a contract or conveyance in connection with which there was a failure to comply with that section.

(2) The proceedings must be dismissed if it is shown that the defendant to the proceedings –

(a) has a claim against the company arising out of the contract or conveyance that the defendant has been unable to pursue because of the company's failure to comply with section 194, or

(b) has suffered some financial loss in connection with the contract or conveyance because of the company's failure to comply with that section,

unless the court before which the proceedings are brought is satisfied that it is just and equitable to permit the proceedings to continue.

(3) This section does not affect the right of any person to enforce such rights as that person may have against another in any proceedings brought by the other.

196 Criminal consequences of failure to make required disclosure

(1) Where a charitable company fails, without reasonable excuse, to comply with section 194, an offence is committed by –

(a) the company, and

(b) every officer of the company who is in default.

(2) For this purpose a shadow director of the company is treated as an officer of the company if the failure is to comply with section 194(1)(a) and that person would be treated as an officer of the company for the purposes of the corresponding requirement of regulations under section 82 of the Companies Act 2006.

(3) A person guilty of such an offence is liable on summary conviction to a fine not exceeding level 3 on the standard scale and, for continued contravention, a daily default fine not exceeding 10% of level 3 on the standard scale.

(4) Expressions used in this section have the same meaning as in section 84 of the Companies Act 2006 (criminal consequences of failure to disclose company's registered name).

Restrictions on alteration of objects

197 Alteration of objects by bodies corporate and charitable status

(1) Subsection (2) applies where a charity –

(a) is a company or other body corporate, and

(b) has power to alter the instruments establishing or regulating it as a body corporate.

(2) No exercise of the power which has the effect of the body ceasing to be a charity is valid so as to affect the application of –

(a) any property acquired under any disposition or agreement previously made otherwise than for full consideration in money or money's worth, or any property representing property so acquired,

(b) any property representing income which has accrued before the alteration is made, or
(c) the income from any such property.

198 Alteration of objects by companies and Commission's consent

(1) Any regulated alteration by a charitable company –

(a) requires the prior written consent of the Commission, and
(b) is ineffective if such consent has not been obtained.

(2) The following are regulated alterations –

(a) an amendment of the company's articles of association adding, removing or altering a statement of the company's objects,
(b) any alteration of any provision of its articles of association directing the application of property of the company on its dissolution, and
(c) any alteration of any provision of its articles of association where the alteration would provide authorisation for any benefit to be obtained by directors or members of the company or persons connected with them.

(3) Where a company that has made a regulated alteration in accordance with subsection (1) is required –

(a) by section 26 of the Companies Act 2006 to send to the registrar of companies a copy of its articles as amended,
(b) by section 30 of that Act to forward to the registrar a copy of the special resolution effecting the alteration, or
(c) by section 31 of that Act to give notice to the registrar of the amendment,

the copy or notice must be accompanied by a copy of the Commission's consent.

(4) If more than one of those provisions applies and they are complied with at different times, the company need not send a further copy of the Commission's consent if a copy was sent on an earlier occasion.

(5) Subsections (2) to (4) of section 30 of that Act (offence of failing to comply with section 30) apply in relation to a failure to comply with subsection (3) as in relation to a failure to comply with that section.

199 Meaning of 'benefit' in s 198(2)

For the purposes of section 198(2)(c) 'benefit' means a direct or indirect benefit of any nature, except that it does not include any remuneration (within the meaning of section 185) whose receipt may be authorised under that section.

200 Meaning of 'connected person' in s 198(2)

(1) For the purposes of section 198(2)(c), the following persons are connected with a director or member of a charitable company –

(a) a child, parent, grandchild, grandparent, brother or sister of the director or member;
(b) the spouse or civil partner of the director or member or of any person falling within paragraph (a);
(c) a person carrying on business in partnership with the director or member or with any person falling within paragraph (a) or (b);
(d) an institution which is controlled –

(i) by the director or member or by any person falling within paragraph (a), (b) or (c), or
(ii) by two or more persons falling within sub-paragraph (i), when taken together.

(e) a body corporate in which –
(i) the director or member or any connected person falling within any of paragraphs (a) to (c) has a substantial interest, or
(ii) two or more persons falling within sub-paragraph (i), when taken together, have a substantial interest.

(2) Sections 350 to 352 (meaning of child, spouse, civil partner, controlled institution and substantial interest) apply for the purposes of subsection (1).

Acts requiring Commission consent

201 Consent of Commission required for approval etc by members of charitable companies

(1) In the case of a charitable company, each of the following is ineffective without the prior written consent of the Commission –

(a) any approval given by the members of the company under any provision of Chapter 4 of Part 10 of the Companies Act 2006 (transactions with directors requiring approval by members) listed in subsection (2), and
(b) any affirmation given by members of the company under section 196 or 214 of the 2006 Act (affirmation of unapproved property transactions and loans).

(2) The provisions of the 2006 Act are –

(a) section 188 (directors' long-term service contracts);
(b) section 190 (substantial property transactions with directors etc);
(c) section 197, 198 or 200 (loans and quasi-loans to directors etc);
(d) section 201 (credit transactions for benefit of directors etc);
(e) section 203 (related arrangements);
(f) section 217 (payments to directors for loss of office);
(g) section 218 (payments to directors for loss of office: transfer of undertaking etc).

202 Consent of Commission required for certain acts of charitable company

(1) A charitable company may not do an act to which this section applies without the prior written consent of the Commission.

(2) This section applies to an act that –

(a) does not require approval under a listed provision of Chapter 4 of Part 10 of the Companies Act 2006 (transactions with directors) by the members of the company, but
(b) would require such approval but for an exemption in the provision in question that disapplies the need for approval on the part of the members of a body corporate which is a wholly-owned subsidiary of another body corporate.

(3) The reference to a listed provision is a reference to a provision listed in section 201(2).

(4) If a company acts in contravention of this section, the exemption referred to in subsection (2)(b) is to be treated as being of no effect in relation to the act.

Restoration of charitable company to register

203 Application for restoration of charitable company to register

(1) The Commission may make an application under section 1029 of the Companies Act 2006 (application to court for restoration to the register of companies) to restore a charitable company to the register of companies.

(2) The power exercisable by the Commission by virtue of this section is exercisable –

(a) by the Commission of its own motion, but
(b) only with the agreement of the Attorney General on each occasion.

PART 11
CHARITABLE INCORPORATED ORGANISATIONS (CIOS)

Chapter 1
General

Nature and constitution

204 Meaning of 'CIO'

In this Act 'CIO' means charitable incorporated organisation.

205 Nature

(1) A CIO is a body corporate.

(2) A CIO must have –

(a) a constitution;
(b) a principal office, which must be in England or in Wales;
(c) one or more members.

(3) The members may be –

(a) not liable to contribute to the assets of the CIO if it is wound up, or
(b) liable to do so up to a maximum amount each.

206 Constitution

(1) A CIO's constitution must state –

(a) its name,
(b) its purposes,
(c) whether its principal office is in England or in Wales, and
(d) whether or not its members are liable to contribute to its assets if it is wound up, and (if they are) up to what amount.

(2) A CIO's constitution must make provision –

(a) about who is eligible for membership, and how a person becomes a member,
(b) about the appointment of one or more persons who are to be charity trustees of the CIO, and about any conditions of eligibility for appointment, and
(c) containing directions about the application of property of the CIO on its dissolution.

(3) A CIO's constitution must also provide for such other matters, and comply with such requirements, as are specified in CIO regulations.

(4) A CIO's constitution –

(a) must be in English if its principal office is in England;
(b) may be in English or in Welsh if its principal office is in Wales.

(5) A CIO's constitution must be in the form specified in regulations made by the Commission, or as near to that form as the circumstances admit.

(6) Subject to anything in a CIO's constitution –

(a) a charity trustee of the CIO may, but need not, be a member of it,
(b) a member of the CIO may, but need not, be one of its charity trustees, and
(c) those who are members of the CIO and those who are its charity trustees may, but need not, be identical.

Formation and registration of CIO

207 Application for CIO to be constituted and registered

(1) Any one or more persons ('the applicants') may apply to the Commission for a CIO to be constituted and for its registration as a charity.

(2) The applicants must supply the Commission with –

(a) a copy of the proposed constitution of the CIO,
(b) such other documents or information as may be prescribed by CIO regulations, and
(c) such other documents or information as the Commission may require for the purposes of the application.

208 Cases where application must or may be refused

(1) The Commission must refuse an application under section 207 if –

(a) it is not satisfied that the CIO would be a charity at the time it would be registered, or
(b) the CIO's proposed constitution does not comply with one or more of the requirements of section 206 (constitution of CIOs) and any regulations made under that section.

(2) The Commission may refuse such an application if –

(a) the proposed name of the CIO –
    (i) is the same as, or
    (ii) is in the opinion of the Commission too like,
    the name of any other charity (whether registered or not), or
(b) the Commission is of the opinion referred to in any of paragraphs (b) to (e) of section 42(2) (power to require charity's name to be changed) in relation to the proposed name of the CIO (reading paragraph (b) as referring to the proposed purposes of the CIO and to the activities which it is proposed it should carry on).

209 Registration of CIO

(1) If the Commission grants an application under section 207 it must register the CIO to which the application relates as a charity in the register of charities.

(2) The entry relating to the charity's registration in the register of charities must include –

(a) the date of the charity's registration, and
(b) a note saying that it is constituted as a CIO.

(3) A copy of the entry in the register must be sent to the charity at the principal office of the CIO.

210 Effect of registration of CIO

(1) Upon the registration of the CIO in the register of charities, it becomes by virtue of the registration a body corporate –

(a) whose constitution is that proposed in the application,
(b) whose name is that specified in the constitution, and
(c) whose first member is, or first members are, the applicants referred to in section 207.

(2) All property for the time being vested in the applicants (or, if more than one, any of them) on trust for the charitable purposes of the CIO (when incorporated) by virtue of this subsection becomes vested in the CIO upon its registration.

Name and status

211 Name

(1) The name of a CIO must appear in legible characters –

(a) in every location, and in every description of document or communication, in which a charitable company would be required by regulations under section 82 of the Companies Act 2006 to state its registered name, and
(b) in all conveyances purporting to be executed by the CIO.

(2) In subsection (1)(b), 'conveyance' means any instrument creating, transferring, varying or extinguishing an interest in land.

212 Status

(1) Subsection (3) applies if the name of a CIO does not include –

(a) 'charitable incorporated organisation',
(b) 'CIO', with or without full stops after each letter, or
(c) a Welsh equivalent mentioned in subsection (2) (but this option applies only if the CIO's constitution is in Welsh),

and it is irrelevant, in any such case, whether or not capital letters are used.

(2) The Welsh equivalents referred to in subsection (1)(c) are –

(a) 'sefydliad elusennol corfforedig', or
(b) 'SEC', with or without full stops after each letter.

(3) If this subsection applies, the fact that a CIO is a CIO must be stated in legible characters in all the locations, documents, communications and conveyances mentioned in section 211(1).

(4) The statement required by subsection (3) must be in English, except that in the case of a document which is otherwise wholly in Welsh, the statement may be in Welsh.

213 Civil consequences of failure to disclose name or status

(1) This section applies to any legal proceedings brought by a CIO to enforce a right arising out of a contract or conveyance in connection with which there was a failure to comply with section 211 or 212.

(2) The proceedings must be dismissed if it is shown that the defendant to the proceedings –

(a) has a claim against the CIO arising out of the contract or conveyance that the defendant has been unable to pursue because of the failure to comply with section 211 or 212, or

(b) has suffered some financial loss in connection with the contract or conveyance because of the failure to comply with section 211 or 212,

unless the court before which the proceedings are brought is satisfied that it is just and equitable to permit the proceedings to continue.

(3) This section does not affect the right of any person to enforce such rights as that person may have against another in any proceedings brought by the other.

214 Offence of failing to disclose name or status

(1) In the case of failure, without reasonable excuse, to comply with section 211 or 212 an offence is committed by –

(a) every charity trustee of the CIO who is in default, and

(b) any other person who on the CIO's behalf –

(i) signs or authorises the signing of the offending document, communication or conveyance, or

(ii) otherwise commits or authorises the offending act or omission.

(2) A person guilty of an offence under subsection (1) is liable on summary conviction to a fine not exceeding level 3 on the standard scale and, for continued contravention, a daily default fine not exceeding 10% of level 3 on the standard scale.

(3) The reference in subsection (1) to a charity trustee being in default, and the reference in subsection (2) to a daily default fine, have the same meaning as in the Companies Acts (see sections 1121 to 1123 and 1125 of the Companies Act 2006).

215 Offence of holding out that a body is a CIO

(1) It is an offence for a person (in whatever way) to hold any body out as being a CIO when it is not.

(2) It is a defence where a person is charged with an offence under subsection (1) to prove that the person believed on reasonable grounds that the body was a CIO.

(3) A person guilty of an offence under subsection (1) is liable on summary conviction to a fine not exceeding level 3 on the standard scale.

Chapter 2
Powers, Capacity and Procedure etc

216 Powers of CIO

(1) Subject to anything in its constitution, a CIO may do anything which is calculated to further its purposes or is conducive or incidental to doing so.

(2) The CIO's charity trustees are to manage the affairs of the CIO and may for that purpose exercise all the powers of the CIO.

217 Constitutional requirements

(1) A CIO must use and apply its property in furtherance of its purposes and in accordance with its constitution.

(2) If the CIO is one whose members are liable to contribute to its assets if it is wound up, its constitution binds the CIO and its members for the time being to the same extent as if its provisions were contained in a contract –

(a) to which the CIO and each of its members was a party, and
(b) which contained obligations on the part of the CIO and each member to observe all the provisions of the constitution.

(3) Money payable by a member to the CIO under the constitution is a debt due from that member to the CIO, and is of the nature of an ordinary contract debt.

218 Third parties

(1) Subject to subsection (3), the validity of an act done (or purportedly done) by a CIO is not to be called into question on the ground that the CIO lacked constitutional capacity.

(2) Subject to subsection (3), the power of the charity trustees of a CIO to act so as to bind the CIO (or authorise others to do so) is not to be called into question on the ground of any constitutional limitations on their powers.

(3) Subsections (1) and (2) apply only in favour of a person who gives full consideration in money or money's worth in relation to the act in question, and does not know –

(a) in a subsection (1) case, that the act is beyond the CIO's constitutional capacity, or
(b) in a subsection (2) case, that the act is beyond the constitutional powers of its charity trustees,

and (in addition) subsection (2) applies only if the person dealt with the CIO in good faith (which the person is presumed to have done unless the contrary is proved).

(4) A party to an arrangement or transaction with a CIO is not bound to inquire –

(a) whether it is within the CIO's constitutional capacity, or
(b) as to any constitutional limitations on the powers of its charity trustees to bind the CIO or authorise others to do so.

(5) If a CIO purports to transfer or grant an interest in property, the fact –

(a) that the act was beyond its constitutional capacity, or
(b) that its charity trustees in connection with the act exceeded their constitutional powers,

does not affect the title of a person who subsequently acquires the property or any interest in it for full consideration without actual notice of any such circumstances affecting the validity of the CIO's act.

(6) In any proceedings arising out of subsections (1) to (3), the burden of proving that a person knew that an act –

(a) was beyond the CIO's constitutional capacity, or
(b) was beyond the constitutional powers of its charity trustees,

lies on the person making that allegation.

(7) In this section and section 219 –

(a) references to a CIO's lack of constitutional capacity are to lack of capacity because of anything in its constitution, and
(b) references to constitutional limitations on the powers of a CIO's charity trustees are to limitations on their powers under its constitution, including limitations deriving from a resolution of the CIO in general meeting, or from an agreement between the CIO's members, and the references to constitutional powers are to be read accordingly.

219 Limits to s 218

(1) Nothing in section 218 prevents a person from bringing proceedings to restrain the doing of an act which would be –

(a) beyond the CIO's constitutional capacity, or
(b) beyond the constitutional powers of the CIO's charity trustees.

(2) But no such proceedings may be brought in respect of an act to be done in fulfilment of a legal obligation arising from a previous act of the CIO.

(3) Subsection (2) does not prevent the Commission from exercising any of its powers.

(4) Nothing in section 218(2) affects any liability incurred by the CIO's charity trustees (or any one of them) for acting beyond their (or that charity trustee's) constitutional powers.

(5) Nothing in section 218 absolves the CIO's charity trustees from their duty to act within the CIO's constitution and in accordance with any constitutional limitations on their powers.

220 Duty of CIO members

Each member of a CIO must exercise the powers that the member has in that capacity in the way that the member decides, in good faith, would be most likely to further the purposes of the CIO.

221 Duties of charity trustees

(1) Each charity trustee of a CIO must exercise the powers and perform the functions that the charity trustee has in that capacity in the way that the charity trustee decides, in good faith, would be most likely to further the purposes of the CIO.

(2) Each charity trustee of a CIO must in the performance of functions in that capacity exercise such care and skill as is reasonable in the circumstances, having regard in particular –

(a) to any special knowledge or experience that the charity trustee has or purports to have, and
(b) if the charity trustee acts as such in the course of a business or profession, to any special knowledge or experience that it is reasonable to expect of a person acting in the course of that kind of business or profession.

But this is subject to any provision of a CIO's constitution permitted by virtue of regulations made under subsection (3).

(3) CIO regulations may permit a CIO's constitution to provide that the duty in subsection (2) –

(a) does not apply, or
(b) does not apply in so far as is specified in the constitution.

(4) Regulations under subsection (3) may provide for limits on the extent to which, or the cases in which, a CIO's constitution may disapply the duty in subsection (2).

222 Personal benefit and payments

(1) A charity trustee of a CIO may not benefit personally from an arrangement or transaction entered into by the CIO if, before the arrangement or transaction was entered into, the charity trustee did not disclose to all the charity trustees of the CIO any material interest (whether direct or indirect) which the charity trustee had in it or in any other person or body party to it.

(2) Nothing in subsection (1) confers authority for a charity trustee of a CIO to benefit personally from any arrangement or transaction entered into by the CIO.

(3) A charity trustee of a CIO –

(a) is entitled to be reimbursed by the CIO, or
(b) may pay out of the CIO's funds,

expenses properly incurred by the charity trustee in the performance of that charity trustee's functions as such.

223 Regulations about procedure of CIOs

(1) CIO regulations may make provision about the procedure of CIOs.

(2) Subject to –

(a) any such regulations,
(b) any other requirement imposed by or by virtue of this Act or any other enactment, and
(c) anything in the CIO's constitution,

a CIO may regulate its own procedure.

(3) But a CIO's procedure must include provision for the holding of a general meeting of its members, and the regulations referred to in subsection (1) may in particular make provision about such meetings.

Chapter 3
Amendment of Constitution

224 Amendment of constitution and procedure

(1) A CIO may by resolution of its members amend its constitution (and a single resolution may provide for more than one amendment).

(2) Such a resolution must be passed –

(a) by a 75% majority of those voting at a general meeting of the CIO (including those voting by proxy or by post, if voting that way is permitted), or
(b) unanimously by the CIO's members, otherwise than at a general meeting.

(3) The date of passing of such a resolution is –

(a) the date of the general meeting at which it was passed, or
(b) if it was passed otherwise than at a general meeting, the date on which provision in the CIO's constitution or in regulations made under section 223 treats it as having been passed (but that date may not be earlier than that on which the last member agreed to it).

225 Amendment of constitution and charitable status

The power of a CIO to amend its constitution is not exercisable in any way which would result in the CIO's ceasing to be a charity.

226 Amendment of constitution and Commission's consent

(1) Subject to section 227(5), a resolution containing an amendment which would make any regulated alteration is to that extent ineffective unless the prior written consent of the Commission has been obtained to the making of the amendment.

(2) The following are regulated alterations –

(a) any alteration of the CIO's purposes,
(b) any alteration of any provision of the CIO's constitution directing the application of property of the CIO on its dissolution, and
(c) any alteration of any provision of the CIO's constitution where the alteration would provide authorisation for any benefit to be obtained by charity trustees or members of the CIO or persons connected with them.

(3) Sections 248 (meaning of 'benefit') and 249 (meaning of 'connected person') apply for the purposes of this section.

227 Registration and coming into effect of amendments

(1) A CIO must send to the Commission a copy of a resolution containing an amendment to its constitution, together with –

(a) a copy of the constitution as amended, and
(b) such other documents and information as the Commission may require,

by the end of the period of 15 days beginning with the date of passing of the resolution (see section 224(3)).

(2) An amendment to a CIO's constitution does not take effect until it has been registered.

(3) The Commission must refuse to register an amendment if –

(a) in the opinion of the Commission the CIO had no power to make it (for example, because the effect of making it would be that the CIO ceased to be a charity, or that the CIO or its constitution did not comply with any requirement imposed by or by virtue of this Act or any other enactment), or
(b) the amendment would change the name of the CIO, and the Commission could have refused an application under section 207 for the constitution and registration of a CIO with the name specified in the amendment on a ground set out in section 208(2).

(4) The Commission may refuse to register an amendment if –

(a) the amendment would make a regulated alteration, and
(b) the consent referred to in section 226(1) had not been obtained.

(5) But if the Commission does register such an amendment, section 226(1) does not apply.

Chapter 4
Conversion, Amalgamation and Transfer

Conversion of certain bodies to CIO

228 Application for conversion by charitable company

(1) A charitable company may apply to the Commission to be converted into a CIO, and for the CIO's registration as a charity, in accordance with this section.

(2) But such an application may not be made by –

(a) a company having a share capital if any of the shares are not fully paid up, or
(b) an exempt charity.

(3) The company must supply the Commission with –

(a) a copy of a resolution of the company that it be converted into a CIO,
(b) a copy of the proposed constitution of the CIO,
(c) a copy of a resolution of the company adopting the proposed constitution of the CIO,
(d) such other documents or information as may be prescribed by CIO regulations, and
(e) such other documents or information as the Commission may require for the purposes of the application.

(4) The resolution referred to in subsection (3)(a) must be –

(a) a special resolution of the company, or
(b) a unanimous written resolution signed by or on behalf of all the members of the company who would be entitled to vote on a special resolution.

(5) Chapter 3 of Part 3 of the Companies Act 2006 (resolutions and agreements affecting a company's constitution) does not apply to such a resolution.

(6) In the case of a company limited by guarantee which makes an application under this section (whether or not it also has a share capital), the proposed constitution of the CIO must (unless subsection (8) applies) provide –

(a) for the CIO's members to be liable to contribute to its assets if it is wound up, and
(b) for the amount up to which they are so liable.

(7) That amount must not be less than the amount up to which they were liable to contribute to the assets of the company if it was wound up.

(8) If the amount each member of the company is liable to contribute to its assets on its winding up is £10 or less –

(a) the guarantee is extinguished on the conversion of the company into a CIO, and
(b) the requirements of subsections (6) and (7) do not apply.

229 Application for conversion by registered society

(1) A charity which is a registered society may apply to the Commission to be converted into a CIO, and for the CIO's registration as a charity, in accordance with this section.

'Registered society' has the same meaning as in [the Co-operative and Community Benefit Societies Act 2014].

(2) But such an application may not be made by –

(a) a registered society having a share capital if any of the shares are not fully paid up, or
(b) an exempt charity.

(3) The registered society must supply the Commission with –

(a) a copy of a resolution of the registered society that it be converted into a CIO,
(b) a copy of the proposed constitution of the CIO,
(c) a copy of a resolution of the registered society adopting the proposed constitution of the CIO,
(d) such other documents or information as may be prescribed by CIO regulations, and
(e) such other documents or information as the Commission may require for the purposes of the application.

(4) The resolution referred to in subsection (3)(a) must be –

(a) a special resolution of the registered society, or
(b) a unanimous written resolution signed by or on behalf of all the members of the registered society who would be entitled to vote on a special resolution.

(5) In subsection (4), 'special resolution' has the meaning given in [section 113 of the Co-operative and Community Benefit Societies 2014].

NOTES

Sub-s (1) amended by the Co-operative and Community Benefit Societies Act 2014, s 151(1), Sch 4, Pt 2, paras 181, 182(1), (2).

Sub-s (5) amended by the Co-operative and Community Benefit Societies Act 2014, s 151(1), Sch 4, Pt 2, paras 181, 182(1), (3)

230 Commission to consult appropriate registrar and others

(1) The Commission must notify the following of an application for conversion –

(a) the appropriate registrar, and

(b) such other persons (if any) as the Commission thinks appropriate in the particular case,

and must consult those notified about whether the application should be granted.

(2) In subsection (1) and sections 231 to 233, 'the appropriate registrar' means –

(a) in the case of an application by a charitable company, the registrar of companies;
(b) in the case of an application by a registered society, the [Financial Conduct Authority and, if the society is a PRA-authorised person within the meaning of section 2B of the Financial Services and Markets Act 2000, the Prudential Regulation Authority].

(3) In this section and sections 231 to 233, 'application for conversion' means an application under section 228 or 229.

NOTES

Sub-s (2) amended by SI 2013/496, art 2(c), Sch 11, para 11.

231 Cases where application must or may be refused

(1) The Commission must refuse an application for conversion if –

(a) it is not satisfied that the CIO would be a charity at the time it would be registered,
(b) the CIO's proposed constitution does not comply with one or more of the requirements of section 206 (constitution of CIOs) and any regulations made under that section, or
(c) in the case of an application for conversion made by a company limited by guarantee, the CIO's proposed constitution does not comply with the requirements of section 228(6) and (7).

(2) The Commission may refuse an application for conversion if –

(a) the proposed name of the CIO –
  (i) is the same as, or
  (ii) is in the opinion of the Commission too like,
  the name of any other charity (whether registered or not),
(b) the Commission is of the opinion referred to in any of paragraphs (b) to (e) of section 42(2) (power to require charity's name to be changed) in relation to the proposed name of the CIO (reading paragraph (b) as referring to the proposed purposes of the CIO and to the activities which it is proposed it should carry on), or
(c) having considered any representations received from those whom it has consulted under section 230(1), the Commission considers (having regard to any regulations made under subsection (3)) that it would not be appropriate to grant the application.

(3) CIO regulations may make provision about circumstances in which it would not be appropriate to grant an application for conversion.

(4) If the Commission refuses an application for conversion, it must so notify the appropriate registrar.

232 Provisional and final registration of converting body

(1) If the Commission grants an application for conversion, it must –

(a) register the CIO to which the application related in the register of charities, and
(b) send to the appropriate registrar a copy of –
 (i) each of the relevant resolutions of the converting company or registered society, and
 (ii) the entry in the register relating to the CIO.

(2) In subsection (1)(b), the 'relevant resolutions' means –

(a) in the case of a converting company, the resolutions referred to in section 228(3)(a) and (c), and
(b) in the case of a converting society, the resolutions referred to in section 229(3)(a) and (c).

(3) The registration of the CIO in the register is provisional only until the appropriate registrar cancels the registration of the company or society as required by subsection (4)(b).

(4) The appropriate registrar must –

(a) register the documents sent under subsection (1)(b), and
(b) cancel the registration of the company in the register of companies, or of the society in the mutual societies register,

and must notify the Commission that this action has been taken.

(5) The entry relating to the charity's registration in the register must include –

(a) a note that it is constituted as a CIO,
(b) the date on which it became so constituted, and
(c) a note of the name of the company or society which was converted into the CIO.

(6) But the matters mentioned in subsections (5)(a) and (b) are to be included only when the appropriate registrar has notified the Commission as required by subsection (4).

(7) A copy of the entry in the register must be sent to the charity at the principal office of the CIO.

233 Effect of registration becoming final

(1) Upon the cancellation by the appropriate registrar of the registration of the company or of the registered society, the company or society is converted into a CIO, a body corporate –

(a) whose constitution is that proposed in the application for conversion,
(b) whose name is that specified in the constitution, and
(c) whose first members are the members of the converting company or society immediately before the moment of conversion.

(2) If the converting company or society had a share capital –

(a) upon the conversion of the company or society all the shares are by virtue of this subsection cancelled, and
(b) no former holder of any cancelled share has any right in respect of it after its cancellation.

(3) Subsection (2) does not affect any right which accrued in respect of a share before its cancellation.

(4) The conversion of a company or society into a CIO does not affect, in particular, any liability to which the company or society was subject by virtue of its being a charitable company or registered society.

234 Conversion of community interest company

(1) CIO regulations may make provision for –

(a) the conversion of a community interest company into a CIO, and
(b) the CIO's registration as a charity.

(2) The regulations may, in particular, apply, or apply with modifications specified in the regulations, or disapply, anything in –

(a) sections 53 to 55 of the Companies (Audit, Investigations and Community Enterprise) Act 2004, or
(b) sections 228 to 233.

Amalgamation of CIOs

235 Application for amalgamation of CIOs

(1) Any two or more CIOs ('the old CIOs') may, in accordance with this section, apply to the Commission to be amalgamated, and for the incorporation and registration as a charity of a new CIO ('the new CIO') as their successor.

(2) The old CIOs must supply the Commission with –

(a) a copy of the proposed constitution of the new CIO,
(b) such other documents or information as may be prescribed by CIO regulations, and
(c) such other documents or information as the Commission may require for the purposes of the application.

(3) In addition to the documents and information referred to in subsection (2), the old CIOs must supply the Commission with –

(a) a copy of a resolution of each of the old CIOs approving the proposed amalgamation, and
(b) a copy of a resolution of each of the old CIOs adopting the proposed constitution of the new CIO.

(4) The resolutions referred to in subsection (3) must have been passed –

(a) by a 75% majority of those voting at a general meeting of the CIO (including those voting by proxy or by post, if voting that way is permitted), or
(b) unanimously by the CIO's members, otherwise than at a general meeting.

(5) The date of passing of such a resolution is –

(a) the date of the general meeting at which it was passed, or
(b) if it was passed otherwise than at a general meeting, the date on which provision in the CIO's constitution or in regulations made under section 223 treats it as having been passed (but that date may not be earlier than that on which the last member agreed to it).

236 Notice of application for amalgamation

(1) Each old CIO must –

(a) give notice of the proposed amalgamation in the way (or ways) that in the opinion of its charity trustees will make it most likely to come to the attention of those who would be affected by the amalgamation, and
(b) send a copy of the notice to the Commission.

(2) The notice must invite any persons who consider that they would be affected by the proposed amalgamation to make written representations to the Commission no later than a date determined by the Commission and specified in the notice.

237 Cases where application must or may be refused

(1) The Commission must refuse an application for amalgamation if –

(a) it is not satisfied that the new CIO would be a charity at the time it would be registered, or
(b) the new CIO's proposed constitution does not comply with one or more of the requirements of section 206 and any regulations made under that section.

(2) In addition to being required to refuse it on one of the grounds mentioned in subsection (1), the Commission must refuse an application for amalgamation if it considers that there is a serious risk that the new CIO would be unable properly to pursue its purposes.

(3) The Commission may refuse an application for amalgamation if –

(a) the proposed name of the new CIO –
 (i) is the same as, or
 (ii) is in the opinion of the Commission too like,
 the name of any other charity (whether registered or not), or
(b) the Commission is of the opinion referred to in any of paragraphs (b) to (e) of section 42(2) (power to require charity's name to be changed) in relation to the proposed name of the new CIO (reading paragraph (b) as referring to the proposed purposes of the new CIO and to the activities which it is proposed it should carry on).

(4) The Commission may refuse an application for amalgamation if it is not satisfied that the provision in the constitution of the new CIO about the matters mentioned in subsection (5) is –

(a) the same, or
(b) substantially the same,

as the provision about those matters in the constitutions of each of the old CIOs.

(5) The matters are –

(a) the purposes of the CIO,
(b) the application of property of the CIO on its dissolution, and
(c) authorisation for any benefit to be obtained by charity trustees or members of the CIO or persons connected with them.

(6) Sections 248 (meaning of 'benefit') and 249 (meaning of 'connected person') apply for the purposes of this section.

(7) In this section and sections 238 and 239, 'application for amalgamation' means an application under section 235.

238 Registration of amalgamated CIO

(1) If the Commission grants an application for amalgamation, it must register the new CIO in the register of charities.

(2) The entry relating to the registration in the register of the charity constituted as the new CIO must include –

(a) a note that it is constituted as a CIO,
(b) the date of the charity's registration, and
(c) a note that the CIO was formed following amalgamation, and of the name of each of the old CIOs.

(3) A copy of the entry in the register must be sent to the charity at the principal office of the new CIO.

239 Effect of registration

(1) Upon the registration of the new CIO it becomes by virtue of the registration a body corporate –

(a) whose constitution is that proposed in the application for amalgamation,
(b) whose name is that specified in the constitution, and
(c) whose first members are the members of the old CIOs immediately before the new CIO was registered.

(2) Upon the registration of the new CIO –

(a) all the property, rights and liabilities of each of the old CIOs become by virtue of this subsection the property, rights and liabilities of the new CIO, and
(b) each of the old CIOs is dissolved.

(3) Any gift which –

(a) is expressed as a gift to one of the old CIOs, and
(b) takes effect on or after the date of registration of the new CIO,

takes effect as a gift to the new CIO.

Transfer of CIO's undertaking to another CIO

240 Resolutions about transfer of CIO's undertaking to another CIO

(1) A CIO may resolve that all its property, rights and liabilities should be transferred to another CIO specified in the resolution.

(2) Where a CIO has passed such a resolution, it must send to the Commission –

(a) a copy of the resolution, and
(b) a copy of a resolution of the transferee CIO agreeing to the transfer to it.

(3) The resolutions referred to in subsections (1) and (2)(b) must have been passed –

(a) by a 75% majority of those voting at a general meeting of the CIO (including those voting by proxy or by post, if voting that way is permitted), or
(b) unanimously by the CIO's members, otherwise than at a general meeting.

(4) The date of passing of such a resolution is –

(a) the date of the general meeting at which it was passed, or

(b) if it was passed otherwise than at a general meeting, the date on which provision in the CIO's constitution or in regulations made under section 223 treats it as having been passed (but that date may not be earlier than that on which the last member agreed to it).

(5) The resolution of the transferor CIO does not take effect until confirmed by the Commission.

241 Notice of transfer of CIO's undertaking to another CIO

Having received the copy resolutions referred to in section 240(2), the Commission –

(a) may direct the transferor CIO to give public notice of its resolution in such manner as is specified in the direction, and
(b) if it gives such a direction, must take into account any representations made to it by persons appearing to it to be interested in the transferor CIO, where those representations are made to it within the period of 28 days beginning with the date when public notice of the resolution is given by the transferor CIO.

242 Cases where confirmation of resolution must or may be refused

(1) The Commission must refuse to confirm the resolution of the transferor CIO if it considers that there is a serious risk that the transferee CIO would be unable properly to pursue the purposes of the transferor CIO.

(2) The Commission may refuse to confirm the resolution if it is not satisfied that the provision in the constitution of the transferee CIO about the matters mentioned in subsection (3) is –

(a) the same, or
(b) substantially the same,

as the provision about those matters in the constitution of the transferor CIO.

(3) The matters are –

(a) the purposes of the CIO,
(b) the application of property of the CIO on its dissolution, and
(c) authorisation for any benefit to be obtained by charity trustees or members of the CIO or persons connected with them.

(4) Sections 248 (meaning of 'benefit') and 249 (meaning of 'connected person') apply for the purposes of this section.

243 Confirmation of resolution

(1) If the Commission does not notify the transferor CIO within the relevant period that it is either confirming or refusing to confirm the transferor CIO's resolution, the resolution is to be treated as confirmed by the Commission on the day after the end of that period.

(2) Subject to subsection (3), 'the relevant period' means –

(a) if the Commission directs the transferor CIO under section 241 to give public notice of its resolution, the period of 6 months beginning with the date when that notice is given, or

(b) otherwise, the period of 6 months beginning with the date when both of the copy resolutions referred to in section 240(2) have been received by the Commission.

(3) The Commission may at any time within the period of 6 months mentioned in subsection (2)(a) or (b) give the transferor CIO a notice extending the relevant period by such period (not exceeding 6 months) as is specified in the notice.

(4) A notice under subsection (3) must set out the Commission's reasons for the extension.

244 Effect of confirmation of resolution

(1) If the resolution of the transferor CIO is confirmed (or treated as confirmed) by the Commission –

(a) all the property, rights and liabilities of the transferor CIO become by virtue of this subsection the property, rights and liabilities of the transferee CIO in accordance with the resolution, and
(b) the transferor CIO is dissolved.

(2) Any gift which –

(a) is expressed as a gift to the transferor CIO, and
(b) takes effect on or after the date on which the resolution is confirmed (or treated as confirmed),

takes effect as a gift to the transferee CIO.

Chapter 5
Supplementary

245 Regulations about winding up, insolvency and dissolution

(1) CIO regulations may make provision about –

(a) the winding up of CIOs,
(b) their insolvency,
(c) their dissolution, and
(d) their revival and restoration to the register following dissolution.

(2) The regulations may, in particular, make provision –

(a) about the transfer on the dissolution of a CIO of its property and rights (including property and rights held on trust for the CIO) to the official custodian or another person or body;
(b) requiring any person in whose name any stocks, funds or securities are standing in trust for a CIO to transfer them into the name of the official custodian or another person or body;
(c) about the disclaiming, by the official custodian or other transferee of a CIO's property, of title to any of that property;
(d) about the application of a CIO's property cy-près;
(e) about circumstances in which charity trustees may be personally liable for contributions to the assets of a CIO or for its debts;
(f) about the reversal on a CIO's revival of anything done on its dissolution.

(3) The regulations may –

(a) apply any enactment which would not otherwise apply, either without modification or with modifications specified in the regulations,
(b) disapply, or modify (in ways specified in the regulations) the application of, any enactment which would otherwise apply.

(4) In subsection (3), 'enactment' includes a provision of subordinate legislation within the meaning of the Interpretation Act 1978.

246 Power to make further provision about CIOs

(1) CIO regulations may make further provision about applications for registration of CIOs, the administration of CIOs, the conversion of charitable companies, registered societies and community interest companies into CIOs, the amalgamation of CIOs, and in relation to CIOs generally.

(2) The regulations may, in particular, make provision about –

(a) the execution of deeds and documents;
(b) the electronic communication of messages or documents relevant to a CIO or to any dealing with the Commission in relation to one;
(c) the maintenance of registers of members and of charity trustees;
(d) the maintenance of other registers (for example, a register of charges over the CIO's assets).

(3) The regulations may –

(a) apply any enactment which would not otherwise apply, either without modification or with modifications specified in the regulations,
(b) disapply, or modify (in ways specified in the regulations) the application of, any enactment which would otherwise apply.

(4) The regulations may, in relation to charities constituted as CIOs –

(a) disapply any of sections 29 to 38 (registration of charities),
(b) modify the application of any of those sections in ways specified in the regulations.

(5) In subsection (3), 'enactment' includes a provision of subordinate legislation within the meaning of the Interpretation Act 1978.

247 Meaning of 'CIO regulations'

In this Part 'CIO regulations' means regulations made by the Minister.

248 Meaning of 'benefit'

(1) This section applies for the purposes of sections 226(2)(c), 237(5)(c) and 242(3)(c) (cases where Commission may refuse to consent to amendment of constitution, to grant an application for amalgamation or to confirm a resolution transferring a CIO's undertaking).

(2) 'Benefit' means a direct or indirect benefit of any nature, except that it does not include any remuneration (within the meaning of section 185) whose receipt may be authorised under that section.

249 Meaning of 'connected person'

(1) This section applies for the purposes of sections 226(2)(c), 237(5)(c) and 242(3)(c).

(2) The following persons are connected with a charity trustee or member of a CIO –

(a) a child, parent, grandchild, grandparent, brother or sister of the trustee or member;

(b) the spouse or civil partner of the trustee or member or of any person falling within paragraph (a);

(c) a person carrying on business in partnership with the trustee or member or with any person falling within paragraph (a) or (b);

(d) an institution which is controlled –

(i) by the trustee or member or by any person falling within paragraph (a), (b) or (c), or

(ii) by two or more persons falling within sub-paragraph (i), when taken together.

(e) a body corporate in which –

(i) the trustee or member or any connected person falling within any of paragraphs (a) to (c) has a substantial interest, or

(ii) two or more persons falling within sub-paragraph (i), when taken together, have a substantial interest.

(3) Sections 350 to 352 (meaning of child, spouse, civil partner, controlled institution and substantial interest) apply for the purposes of subsection (2).

250 Effect of provisions relating to vesting or transfer of property

No vesting or transfer of any property in pursuance of any provision of this Part operates as a breach of a covenant or condition against alienation or gives rise to a forfeiture.

PART 12
INCORPORATION OF CHARITY TRUSTEES

General

251 Incorporation of charity trustees

(1) The Commission may grant a certificate of incorporation of the charity trustees of a charity as a body corporate if –

(a) the charity trustees of the charity, in accordance with section 256, apply to the Commission for such a certificate, and

(b) the Commission considers that the incorporation of the charity trustees would be in the interests of the charity.

(2) Such a certificate is subject to such conditions or directions as the Commission thinks fit to insert in it.

(3) But the Commission must not grant such a certificate if the charity –

(a) appears to the Commission to be required to be registered in accordance with section 30, but

(b) is not so registered.

(4) On the grant of such a certificate –

(a) the charity trustees of the charity become a body corporate by such name as is specified in the certificate, and
(b) any rights or liabilities of those trustees in connection with any property vesting in the body under section 252 become rights or liabilities of that body.

Paragraph (b) does not affect the operation of section 254 (liability of charity trustees not affected by incorporation).

(5) After their incorporation the charity trustees –

(a) may sue and be sued in their corporate name, and
(b) have the same powers, and are subject to the same restrictions and limitations, as respects the holding, acquisition and disposal of property for or in connection with the purposes of the charity as they had or were subject to while unincorporated;

and any relevant legal proceedings that might have been continued or commenced by or against the charity trustees may be continued or commenced by or against them in their corporate name.

(6) In subsection (5) 'relevant legal proceedings' means legal proceedings in connection with any property vesting in the incorporated body under section 252.

(7) An incorporated body need not have a common seal.

252 Estate to vest in incorporated body

(1) The certificate of incorporation vests in the incorporated body all real and personal estate, of whatever nature or tenure, belonging to or held by any person or persons in trust for the relevant charity.

(2) On the vesting of all real and personal estate under subsection (1), any person or persons in whose name or names any stocks, funds or securities are standing in trust for the relevant charity must transfer them into the name of the incorporated body.

(3) Subsections (1) and (2) do not apply to property vested in the official custodian.

253 Gifts to take effect as gifts to incorporated body

(1) After the incorporation under this Part of the charity trustees of any charity, every relevant donation, gift and disposition of property made –

(a) to or in favour of the charity, or the charity trustees of the charity, or
(b) otherwise for the purposes of the charity,

takes effect as if made to or in favour of the incorporated body or otherwise for the same purposes.

(2) For the purposes of subsection (1), a donation, gift or disposition of property is a relevant one if (whether of real or personal property and whether made by deed, will or otherwise) –

(a) it was lawfully made before the incorporation but has not actually taken effect, or
(b) it is lawfully made after the incorporation.

254 Liability of charity trustees not affected by incorporation

After a certificate of incorporation has been granted under this Part, all charity trustees of the charity are, despite their incorporation –

(a) chargeable for such property as comes into their hands, and
(b) answerable and accountable for their own acts, receipts, neglects, and defaults, and for the due administration of the charity and its property,

in the same manner and to the same extent as if no such incorporation had been effected.

255 Charity trustees bound by conditions in certificate etc

(1) All conditions and directions inserted in any certificate of incorporation are binding upon and must be performed or observed by the charity trustees as trusts of the charity.

(2) Section 336 (enforcement of orders of Commission) applies to any charity trustee who fails to perform or observe any such condition or direction as it applies to a person guilty of disobedience to any such order of the Commission as is mentioned in that section.

Application procedure

256 Applications for incorporation

(1) Every application to the Commission for a certificate of incorporation under this Part must be –

(a) in writing and signed by the charity trustees of the charity concerned, and
(b) accompanied by such documents or information as the Commission may require for the purpose of the application.

(2) The Commission may require –

(a) any statement contained in any such application, or
(b) any document or information supplied under subsection (1)(b),

to be verified in such manner as it may specify.

257 Requirement to be met before certificate is granted

Before a certificate of incorporation is granted under this Part, charity trustees of the charity must have been effectually appointed to the satisfaction of the Commission.

258 Certificate conclusive as to compliance with incorporation requirements etc

(1) A certificate of incorporation granted under this Part is conclusive evidence that all the preliminary requirements for incorporation under this Part have been complied with.

(2) The date of incorporation mentioned in the certificate is to be treated as being the date at which incorporation has taken place.

Administration etc of charity whose charity trustees are incorporated

259 Filling up of vacancies in charity trustees

(1) This section applies where a certificate of incorporation is granted under this Part.

(2) Vacancies in the number of the charity trustees of the charity must from time to time be filled up so far as required by the constitution or settlement of the charity, or by any conditions or directions in the certificate –

(a) by such legal means as would have been available for the appointment of new charity trustees of the charity if no certificate of incorporation had been granted, or
(b) otherwise as required by such conditions or directions.

260 Execution of documents by incorporated body: general

(1) This section and section 261 have effect as respects the execution of documents by an incorporated body.

(2) If an incorporated body has a common seal, a document may be executed by the body by the affixing of its common seal.

(3) Whether or not it has a common seal, a document may be executed by an incorporated body by being –

(a) signed by a majority of the charity trustees of the relevant charity and expressed (in whatever form of words) to be executed by the body, or
(b) executed in pursuance of an authority given under section 261(1).

(4) A document duly executed by an incorporated body which makes it clear on its face that it is intended by the person or persons making it to be a deed has effect, upon delivery, as a deed; and it is presumed, unless a contrary intention is proved, to be delivered upon its being so executed.

(5) In favour of a purchaser a document is to be treated as having been duly executed by an incorporated body if it purports to be signed by –

(a) a majority of the charity trustees of the relevant charity, or
(b) such of the charity trustees of the relevant charity as are authorised by the charity trustees of that charity to execute it in the name and on behalf of the body,

and, if the document makes it clear on its face that it is intended by the person or persons making it to be a deed, it is to be treated as having been delivered upon its being executed.

(6) For the purposes of subsection (5) 'purchaser' –

(a) means a purchaser in good faith for valuable consideration, and
(b) includes a lessee, mortgagee or other person who for valuable consideration acquires an interest in property.

261 Conferral of authority to execute documents

(1) For the purposes of section 260(3)(b) the charity trustees of the relevant charity in the case of an incorporated body may, subject to the trusts of the charity, confer on any two or more of their number –

(a) a general authority, or
(b) an authority limited in such manner as the charity trustees think fit,

to execute in the name and on behalf of the body documents for giving effect to transactions to which the body is a party.

(2) An authority under subsection (1) –

(a) suffices for any document if it is given in writing or by resolution of a meeting of the charity trustees of the relevant charity, despite the want of any formality that would be required in giving an authority apart from that subsection;
(b) may be given so as to make the powers conferred exercisable by any of the charity trustees, or may be restricted to named persons or in any other way;
(c) subject to any such restriction, and until it is revoked, has effect, despite any change in the charity trustees of the relevant charity, as a continuing authority given by the charity trustees from time to time of the charity and exercisable by such charity trustees.

(3) In any authority under subsection (1) to execute a document in the name and on behalf of an incorporated body there is, unless the contrary intention appears, implied authority also to execute it for the body in the name and on behalf of the official custodian or of any other person, in any case in which the charity trustees could do so.

Commission's powers to amend certificate or dissolve body

262 Amendment of certificate of incorporation

(1) The Commission may amend a certificate of incorporation –

(a) on the application of the incorporated body to which it relates, or
(b) of its own motion.

(2) Before making any such amendment of its own motion, the Commission must by notice in writing –

(a) inform the charity trustees of the relevant charity of its proposals, and
(b) invite those charity trustees to make representations to it within a time specified in the notice.

(3) The time so specified must be not less than one month from the date of the notice.

(4) The Commission –

(a) must take into consideration any representations made by those charity trustees within the time so specified, and
(b) may then (without further notice) proceed with its proposals either without modification or with such modifications as appear to it to be desirable.

(5) The Commission may amend a certificate of incorporation by –

(a) making an order specifying the amendment, or
(b) issuing a new certificate of incorporation taking account of the amendment.

263 Dissolution of incorporated body

(1) The Commission may of its own motion make an order dissolving an incorporated body from such date as is specified in the order, if the Commission is satisfied –

(a) that the body has no assets or does not operate,
(b) that the relevant charity has ceased to exist,
(c) that the institution previously constituting, or treated by the Commission as constituting, the relevant charity has ceased to be, or (as the case may be) was not at the time of the body's incorporation, a charity, or
(d) that the purposes of the relevant charity –

(i) have been achieved so far as is possible, or
(ii) are in practice incapable of being achieved.

(2) The Commission may make an order dissolving an incorporated body from such date as is specified in the order, if the Commission is satisfied, on the application of the charity trustees of the relevant charity, that it would be in the interests of the charity for the body to be dissolved.

(3) Subject to subsection (4), an order made under this section with respect to an incorporated body has the effect of vesting in the charity trustees of the relevant charity, in trust for that charity, all property for the time being vested –

(a) in the body, or
(b) in any other person (apart from the official custodian),

in trust for that charity.

(4) If the Commission so directs in the order –

(a) all or any specified part of that property, instead of vesting in the charity trustees of the relevant charity, vests in –
 (i) a specified person as trustee for, or nominee of, that charity, or
 (ii) such persons (other than the charity trustees of the relevant charity) as may be specified;
(b) any specified investments, or any specified class or description of investments, held by any person in trust for the relevant charity are to be transferred to –
 (i) the charity trustees of that charity, or
 (ii) any such person or persons as is or are mentioned in paragraph (a)(i) or (ii).

For this purpose 'specified' means specified by the Commission in the order.

(5) Where an order to which this subsection applies is made with respect to an incorporated body –

(a) any rights or liabilities of the body become rights or liabilities of the charity trustees of the relevant charity, and
(b) any legal proceedings that might have been continued or commenced by or against the body may be continued or commenced by or against those trustees.

(6) Subsection (5) applies to any order under this section by virtue of which –

(a) any property vested as mentioned in subsection (3) is vested –
 (i) in the charity trustees of the relevant charity, or
 (ii) in any person as trustee for, or nominee of, that charity, or
(b) any investments held by any person in trust for the relevant charity are required to be transferred –
 (i) to the charity trustees of that charity, or
 (ii) to any person as trustee for, or nominee of, that charity.

Supplementary

264 Records of applications and certificates

(1) The Commission must keep a record of all applications for, and certificates of, incorporation under this Part.

(2) Documents sent to the Commission under this Part are to be kept by the Commission for such period as it thinks fit.

(3) Documents kept under this section are to be open to public inspection at all reasonable times.

(4) Any person who is provided with a copy or extract of any document kept under this section may require it to be certified by a certificate signed by a member of the staff of the Commission.

265 Meaning of 'incorporated body' and 'relevant charity'

In this Part –

'incorporated body' means a body incorporated under section 251;

'the relevant charity', in relation to an incorporated body, means the charity the charity trustees of which have been incorporated as that body.

266 Effect of provisions relating to vesting or transfer of property

No vesting or transfer of any property in pursuance of any provision of this Part operates as a breach of a covenant or condition against alienation or gives rise to a forfeiture.

PART 13
UNINCORPORATED CHARITIES

Power to transfer all property of unincorporated charity

267 Introduction

(1) Section 268 (resolution to transfer all property) applies to a charity if –

(a) (subject to subsection (2)) its gross income in its last financial year did not exceed £10,000,

(b) it does not hold any designated land, and

(c) it is not a company or other body corporate.

'Designated land' means land held on trusts which stipulate that it is to be used for the purposes, or any particular purposes, of the charity.

(2) Subsection (1)(a) does not apply in relation to a resolution by the charity trustees of a charity –

(a) to transfer all its property to a CIO, or

(b) to divide its property between two or more CIOs.

(3) Where a charity has a permanent endowment, sections 268 to 272 have effect in accordance with sections 273 and 274.

(4) In sections 268 to 274 references to the transfer of property to a charity are references to its transfer –

(a) to the charity,

(b) to the charity trustees,

(c) to any trustee for the charity, or

(d) to a person nominated by the charity trustees to hold it in trust for the charity, as the charity trustees may determine.

268 Resolution to transfer all property

(1) The charity trustees of a charity to which this section applies (see section 267) may resolve for the purposes of this section –

(a) that all the property of the charity should be transferred to another charity specified in the resolution, or

(b) that all the property of the charity should be transferred to two or more charities specified in the resolution in accordance with such division of the property between them as is so specified.

(2) Any charity so specified may be either a registered charity or a charity which is not required to be registered.

(3) But the charity trustees of a charity ('the transferor charity') do not have power to pass a resolution under subsection (1) unless they are satisfied –

(a) that it is expedient in the interests of furthering the purposes for which the property is held by the transferor charity for the property to be transferred in accordance with the resolution, and

(b) that the purposes (or any of the purposes) of any charity to which property is to be transferred under the resolution are substantially similar to the purposes (or any of the purposes) of the transferor charity.

(4) Any resolution under subsection (1) must be passed by a majority of not less than two-thirds of the charity trustees who vote on the resolution.

(5) Where charity trustees have passed a resolution under subsection (1), they must send a copy of it to the Commission, together with a statement of their reasons for passing it.

269 Notice of, and information about, resolution to transfer property

(1) Having received the copy of the resolution under section 268(5), the Commission –

(a) may direct the charity trustees to give public notice of the resolution in such manner as is specified in the direction, and

(b) if it gives such a direction, must take into account any representations made to it –

(i) by persons appearing to it to be interested in the charity, and

(ii) within the period of 28 days beginning with the date when public notice of the resolution is given by the charity trustees.

(2) The Commission may also direct the charity trustees to provide the Commission with additional information or explanations relating to –

(a) the circumstances in and by reference to which they have decided to act under section 268, or

(b) their compliance with any obligation imposed on them by or under section 268 or this section in connection with the resolution.

270 General rule as to when s 268 resolution takes effect

Subject to section 271, a resolution under section 268(1) takes effect at the end of the period of 60 days beginning with the date on which the copy of it was received by the Commission.

271 S 268 resolution not to take effect or to take effect at later date

(1) A resolution does not take effect under section 270 if before the end of –

(a) the 60-day period, or
(b) that period as modified by subsection (4) or (5),

the Commission notifies the charity trustees in writing that it objects to the resolution, either on procedural grounds or on the merits of the proposals contained in the resolution.

(2) 'The 60-day period' means the period of 60 days mentioned in section 270.

(3) 'On procedural grounds' means on the grounds that any obligation imposed on the charity trustees by or under section 268 or 269 has not been complied with in connection with the resolution.

(4) If under section 269(1) the Commission directs the charity trustees to give public notice of a resolution, the running of the 60-day period is suspended by virtue of this subsection –

(a) as from the date on which the direction is given to the charity trustees, and
(b) until the end of the period of 42 days beginning with the date on which public notice of the resolution is given by the charity trustees.

(5) If under section 269(2) the Commission directs the charity trustees to provide any information or explanations, the running of the 60-day period is suspended by virtue of this subsection –

(a) as from the date on which the direction is given to the charity trustees, and
(b) until the date on which the information or explanations is or are provided to the Commission.

(6) Subsection (7) applies once the period of time, or the total period of time, during which the 60-day period is suspended by virtue of either or both of subsections (4) and (5) exceeds 120 days.

(7) At that point the resolution (if not previously objected to by the Commission) is to be treated as if it had never been passed.

272 Transfer of property in accordance with s 268 resolution

(1) Subsection (2) applies where a resolution under section 268(1) has taken effect.

(2) The charity trustees must arrange for all the property of the transferor charity to be transferred in accordance with the resolution, and on terms that any property so transferred –

(a) is to be held by the charity to which it is transferred ('the transferee charity') in accordance with subsection (3), but
(b) when so held is nevertheless to be subject to any restrictions on expenditure to which it was subject as property of the transferor charity;

and the charity trustees must arrange for the property to be so transferred by such date after the resolution takes effect as they agree with the charity trustees of the transferee charity or charities concerned.

(3) The charity trustees of any charity to which property is transferred under this section must secure, so far as is reasonably practicable, that the property is applied for such of its purposes as are substantially similar to those of the transferor charity.

But this requirement does not apply if those charity trustees consider that complying with it would not result in a suitable and effective method of applying the property.

(4) For the purpose of enabling any property to be transferred to a charity under this section, the Commission may, at the request of the charity trustees of that charity, make orders vesting any property of the transferor charity –

(a) in the transferee charity, in its charity trustees or in any trustee for that charity, or

(b) in any other person nominated by those charity trustees to hold property in trust for that charity.

273 Transfer where charity has permanent endowment: general

(1) This section and section 274 provide for the operation of sections 268 to 272 where a charity within section 267(1) has a permanent endowment (whether or not the charity's trusts contain provision for the termination of the charity).

(2) If the charity has both a permanent endowment and other property ('unrestricted property') –

(a) a resolution under section 268(1) must relate to both its permanent endowment and its unrestricted property, and
(b) sections 268 to 272 apply –
 (i) in relation to its unrestricted property, as if references in those sections to all or any of the property of the charity were references to all or any of its unrestricted property, and
 (ii) in relation to its permanent endowment, in accordance with section 274.

(3) If all of the property of the charity is comprised in its permanent endowment, sections 268 to 272 apply in relation to its permanent endowment in accordance with section 274.

274 Requirements relating to permanent endowment

(1) Sections 268 to 272 apply in relation to the permanent endowment of the charity (as mentioned in section 273(2)(b)(ii) and (3)) with the following modifications.

(2) References in sections 268 to 272 to all or any of the property of the charity are references to all or any of the property comprised in its permanent endowment.

(3) If the property comprised in its permanent endowment is to be transferred to a single charity, the charity trustees must (instead of being satisfied as mentioned in section 268(3)(b)) be satisfied that the proposed transferee charity has purposes which are substantially similar to all of the purposes of the transferor charity.

(4) If the property comprised in its permanent endowment is to be transferred to two or more charities, the charity trustees must (instead of being satisfied as mentioned in section 268(3)(b)) be satisfied –

(a) that the proposed transferee charities, taken together, have purposes which are substantially similar to all of the purposes of the transferor charity, and
(b) that each of the proposed transferee charities has purposes which are substantially similar to one or more of the purposes of the transferor charity.

(5) In the case of a transfer to which subsection (4) applies, the resolution under section 268(1) must provide for the property comprised in the permanent endowment of

the charity to be divided between the transferee charities in such a way as to take account of such guidance as may be given by the Commission for the purposes of this section.

(6) For the purposes of sections 268 to 272, the references in sections 269(2)(b) and 271(3) to any obligation imposed on the charity trustees by or under section 268 or 269 includes a reference to any obligation imposed on them by virtue of any of subsections (3) to (5).

(7) The requirement in section 272(3) applies in the case of every such transfer, and in complying with that requirement the charity trustees of a transferee charity must secure that the application of property transferred to the charity takes account of such guidance as may be given by the Commission for the purposes of this section.

(8) Any guidance given by the Commission for the purposes of this section may take such form and be given in such manner as the Commission considers appropriate.

Powers to alter purposes or powers etc of unincorporated charity

275 Resolution to replace purposes of unincorporated charity

(1) This section applies to a charity if –

- (a) its gross income in its last financial year did not exceed £10,000,
- (b) it does not hold any designated land, and
- (c) it is not a company or other body corporate.

'Designated land' means land held on trusts which stipulate that it is to be used for the purposes, or any particular purposes, of the charity.

(2) The charity trustees of such a charity may resolve for the purposes of this section that the trusts of the charity should be modified by replacing all or any of the purposes of the charity with other purposes specified in the resolution.

(3) The other purposes so specified must be charitable purposes.

(4) But the charity trustees of a charity do not have power to pass a resolution under subsection (2) unless they are satisfied –

- (a) that it is expedient in the interests of the charity for the purposes in question to be replaced, and
- (b) that, so far as is reasonably practicable, the new purposes consist of or include purposes that are similar in character to those that are to be replaced.

(5) Any resolution under subsection (2) must be passed by a majority of not less than two-thirds of the charity trustees who vote on the resolution.

(6) Where charity trustees have passed a resolution under subsection (2), they must send a copy of it to the Commission, together with a statement of their reasons for passing it.

276 Notice of, and information about, s 275 resolution

(1) Having received the copy of the resolution under section 275(6), the Commission –

- (a) may direct the charity trustees to give public notice of the resolution in such manner as is specified in the direction, and
- (b) if it gives such a direction, must take into account any representations made to it –
    - (i) by persons appearing to it to be interested in the charity, and

(ii) within the period of 28 days beginning with the date when public notice of the resolution is given by the charity trustees.

(2) The Commission may also direct the charity trustees to provide the Commission with additional information or explanations relating to –

(a) the circumstances in and by reference to which they have decided to act under section 275, or

(b) their compliance with any obligation imposed on them by or under section 275 or this section in connection with the resolution.

277 General rule as to when s 275 resolution takes effect

Subject to section 278, a resolution under section 275(2) takes effect at the end of the period of 60 days beginning with the date on which the copy of it was received by the Commission.

278 S 275 resolution not to take effect or to take effect at a later date

(1) A resolution does not take effect under section 277 if before the end of –

(a) the 60-day period, or

(b) that period as modified by subsection (4) or (5),

the Commission notifies the charity trustees in writing that it objects to the resolution, either on procedural grounds or on the merits of the proposals contained in the resolution.

(2) 'The 60-day period' means the period of 60 days mentioned in section 277.

(3) 'On procedural grounds' means on the grounds that any obligation imposed on the charity trustees by or under section 275 or 276 has not been complied with in connection with the resolution.

(4) If under section 276(1) the Commission directs the charity trustees to give public notice of a resolution, the running of the 60-day period is suspended by virtue of this subsection –

(a) as from the date on which the direction is given to the charity trustees, and

(b) until the end of the period of 42 days beginning with the date on which public notice of the resolution is given by the charity trustees.

(5) If under section 276(2) the Commission directs the charity trustees to provide any information or explanations, the running of the 60-day period is suspended by virtue of this subsection –

(a) as from the date on which the direction is given to the charity trustees, and

(b) until the date on which the information or explanations is or are provided to the Commission.

(6) Subsection (7) applies once the period of time, or the total period of time, during which the 60-day period is suspended by virtue of either or both of subsections (4) and (5) exceeds 120 days.

(7) At that point the resolution (if not previously objected to by the Commission) is to be treated as if it had never been passed.

279 Replacement of purposes in accordance with s 275

As from the time when a resolution takes effect under section 277, the trusts of the charity concerned are to be taken to have been modified in accordance with the terms of the resolution.

280 Power to modify powers or procedures of unincorporated charity

(1) This section applies to any charity which is not a company or other body corporate.

(2) The charity trustees of such a charity may resolve for the purposes of this section that any provision of the trusts of the charity –

(a) relating to any of the powers exercisable by the charity trustees in the administration of the charity, or

(b) regulating the procedure to be followed in any respect in connection with its administration,

should be modified in such manner as is specified in the resolution.

(3) Subsection (4) applies if the charity is an unincorporated association with a body of members distinct from the charity trustees.

(4) Any resolution of the charity trustees under subsection (2) must be approved by a further resolution which is passed at a general meeting of the body –

(a) by a majority of not less than two-thirds of the members entitled to attend and vote at the meeting who vote on the resolution, or

(b) by a decision taken without a vote and without any expression of dissent in response to the question put to the meeting.

(5) Where –

(a) the charity trustees have passed a resolution under subsection (2), and

(b) (if subsection (4) applies) a further resolution has been passed under that subsection,

the trusts of the charity are to be taken to have been modified in accordance with the terms of the resolution.

(6) The trusts are to be taken to have been so modified as from –

(a) such date as is specified for this purpose in the resolution under subsection (2), or

(b) (if later) the date when any such further resolution was passed under subsection (4).

Powers of unincorporated charities to spend capital

281 Power of unincorporated charities to spend capital: general

(1) This section applies to any available endowment fund of a charity which is not a company or other body corporate.

(2) But this section does not apply to a fund if sections 282 to 284 (power to spend larger fund given for particular purpose) apply to it.

(3) If the condition in subsection (4) is met in relation to the charity, the charity trustees may resolve for the purposes of this section that the fund, or a portion of it, ought to be freed from the restrictions with respect to expenditure of capital that apply to it.

(4) The condition is that the charity trustees are satisfied that the purposes set out in the trusts to which the fund is subject could be carried out more effectively if the capital of the fund, or the relevant portion of the capital, could be expended as well as income accruing to it, rather than just such income.

(5) Once the charity trustees have passed a resolution under subsection (3), the fund or portion may by virtue of this section be expended in carrying out the purposes set out in the trusts to which the fund is subject without regard to the restrictions mentioned in that subsection.

(6) The fund or portion may be so expended as from such date as is specified for this purpose in the resolution.

(7) In this section 'available endowment fund', in relation to a charity, means –

(a) the whole of the charity's permanent endowment if it is all subject to the same trusts, or

(b) any part of its permanent endowment which is subject to any particular trusts that are different from those to which any other part is subject.

282 Resolution to spend larger fund given for particular purpose

(1) This section applies to any available endowment fund of a charity which is not a company or other body corporate if –

(a) the capital of the fund consists entirely of property given –

(i) by a particular individual,

(ii) by a particular institution (by way of grant or otherwise), or

(iii) by two or more individuals or institutions in pursuit of a common purpose, and

(b) the charity's gross income in its last financial year exceeded £1,000 and the market value of the endowment fund exceeds £10,000.

(2) If the condition in subsection (3) is met in relation to the charity, the charity trustees may resolve for the purposes of this section that the fund, or a portion of it, ought to be freed from the restrictions with respect to expenditure of capital that apply to it.

(3) The condition is that the charity trustees are satisfied that the purposes set out in the trusts to which the fund is subject could be carried out more effectively if the capital of the fund, or the relevant portion of the capital, could be expended as well as income accruing to it, rather than just such income.

(4) The charity trustees –

(a) must send a copy of any resolution under subsection (2) to the Commission, together with a statement of their reasons for passing it, and

(b) may not implement the resolution except in accordance with sections 283 and 284.

(5) In this section –

'available endowment fund' has the same meaning as in section 281;

'market value', in relation to an endowment fund, means –

(a) the market value of the fund as recorded in the accounts for the last financial year of the relevant charity, or

(b) if no such value was so recorded, the current market value of the fund as determined on a valuation carried out for the purpose.

(6) In subsection (1), the reference to the giving of property by an individual includes the individual's giving it by will.

283 Notice of, and information about, s 282 resolution

(1) Having received the copy of the resolution under section 282(4), the Commission may –

(a) direct the charity trustees to give public notice of the resolution in such manner as is specified in the direction, and
(b) if it gives such a direction, must take into account any representations made to it –
  (i) by persons appearing to it to be interested in the charity, and
  (ii) within the period of 28 days beginning with the date when public notice of the resolution is given by the charity trustees.

(2) The Commission may also direct the charity trustees to provide the Commission with additional information or explanations relating to –

(a) the circumstances in and by reference to which they have decided to act under section 282, or
(b) their compliance with any obligation imposed on them by or under section 282 or this section in connection with the resolution.

284 When and how s 282 resolution takes effect

(1) When considering whether to concur with the resolution under section 282(2), the Commission must take into account –

(a) any evidence available to it as to the wishes of the donor or donors mentioned in section 282(1)(a), and
(b) any changes in the circumstances relating to the charity since the making of the gift or gifts (including, in particular, its financial position, the needs of its beneficiaries, and the social, economic and legal environment in which it operates).

(2) The Commission must not concur with the resolution unless it is satisfied –

(a) that its implementation would accord with the spirit of the gift or gifts mentioned in section 282(1)(a) (even though it would be inconsistent with the restrictions mentioned in section 282(2)), and
(b) that the charity trustees have complied with the obligations imposed on them by or under section 282 or 283 in connection with the resolution.

(3) Before the end of the period of 3 months beginning with the relevant date, the Commission must notify the charity trustees in writing –

(a) that the Commission concurs with the resolution, or
(b) that it does not concur with it.

(4) In subsection (3) 'the relevant date' means –

(a) if the Commission directs the charity trustees under section 283(1) to give public notice of the resolution, the date when that notice is given, and
(b) otherwise, the date on which the Commission receives the copy of the resolution in accordance with section 282(4).

(5) Where –

(a) the charity trustees are notified by the Commission that it concurs with the resolution, or
(b) the period of 3 months mentioned in subsection (3) has elapsed without the Commission notifying them that it does not concur with the resolution,

the fund or portion may, by virtue of this section, be expended in carrying out the purposes set out in the trusts to which the fund is subject without regard to the restrictions mentioned in section 282(2).

Supplementary

285 Power to alter sums specified in this Part

(1) The Minister may by order amend any provision listed in subsection (2) –

(a) by substituting a different sum for the sum for the time being specified in that provision, or
(b) if the provision specifies more than one sum, by substituting a different sum for any sum specified in that provision.

(2) The provisions are –

section 267(1) (income level for purposes of resolution to transfer property of unincorporated charity);
section 275(1) (income level for purposes of resolution to replace purposes of unincorporated charity);
section 282(1) (income level and market value of fund for purposes of resolution to spend larger fund given for particular purpose).

286 Effect of provisions relating to vesting or transfer of property

No vesting or transfer of any property in pursuance of any provision of this Part operates as a breach of a covenant or condition against alienation or gives rise to a forfeiture.

PART 14
SPECIAL TRUSTS

287 Meaning of 'special trust'

(1) In this Act, 'special trust' means property which –

(a) is held and administered by or on behalf of a charity for any special purposes of the charity, and
(b) is so held and administered on separate trusts relating only to that property.

(2) But a special trust does not, by itself, constitute a charity for the purposes of Part 8 (charity accounts, reports and returns).

288 Power to spend capital subject to special trusts: general

(1) This section applies to any available endowment fund of a special trust which, as the result of a direction under section 12(1), is to be treated as a separate charity ('the relevant charity') for the purposes of this section and sections 289 to 292.

(2) But this section does not apply to such a fund if sections 289 to 291 (power to spend capital subject to special trusts: larger fund) apply in relation to it.

(3) If the condition in subsection (4) is met in relation to the relevant charity, the charity trustees may resolve for the purposes of this section that the fund, or a portion of it, ought to be freed from the restrictions with respect to expenditure of capital that apply to it.

(4) The condition is that the charity trustees are satisfied that the purposes set out in the trusts to which the fund is subject could be carried out more effectively if the capital of the fund, or the relevant portion of the capital, could be expended as well as income accruing to it, rather than just such income.

(5) Once the charity trustees have passed a resolution under subsection (3), the fund or portion may, by virtue of this section, be expended in carrying out the purposes set out in the trusts to which the fund is subject without regard to the restrictions mentioned in that subsection.

(6) The fund or portion may be so expended as from such date as is specified for this purpose in the resolution.

(7) In this section, 'available endowment fund' has the same meaning as in section 281 (power of unincorporated charities to spend capital: general).

289 Resolution to spend capital subject to special trusts: larger fund

(1) This section applies to a fund within section 288(1) if –

- (a) the capital of the fund consists entirely of property given –
  - (i) by a particular individual,
  - (ii) by a particular institution (by way of grant or otherwise), or
  - (iii) by two or more individuals or institutions in pursuit of a common purpose, and
- (b) the market value of the fund exceeds £10,000.

(2) If the condition in subsection (3) is met in relation to the relevant charity, the charity trustees may resolve for the purposes of this section that the fund, or a portion of it, ought to be freed from the restrictions with respect to expenditure of capital that apply to it.

(3) The condition is that the charity trustees are satisfied that the purposes set out in the trusts to which the fund is subject could be carried out more effectively if the capital of the fund, or the relevant portion of the capital, could be expended as well as income accruing to it, rather than just such income.

(4) The charity trustees –

- (a) must send a copy of any resolution under subsection (2) to the Commission, together with a statement of their reasons for passing it, and
- (b) may not implement the resolution except in accordance with sections 290 and 291.

(5) In this section, 'market value' has the same meaning as in section 282 (resolution to spend larger fund for given for particular purpose).

(6) In subsection (1), the reference to the giving of property by an individual includes the individual's giving it by will.

290 Notice of, and information about, s 289 resolution

(1) Having received the copy of the resolution under section 289(4), the Commission may –

(a) direct the charity trustees to give public notice of the resolution in such manner as is specified in the direction, and

(b) if it gives such a direction, must take into account any representations made to it –

(i) by persons appearing to it to be interested in the relevant charity, and

(ii) within the period of 28 days beginning with the date when public notice of the resolution is given by the charity trustees.

(2) The Commission may also direct the charity trustees to provide the Commission with additional information or explanations relating to –

(a) the circumstances in and by reference to which they have decided to act under section 289, or

(b) their compliance with any obligation imposed on them by or under section 289 or this section in connection with the resolution.

291 When and how s 289 resolution takes effect

(1) When considering whether to concur with the resolution under section 289(2), the Commission must take into account –

(a) any evidence available to it as to the wishes of the donor or donors mentioned in section 289(1)(a), and

(b) any changes in the circumstances relating to the relevant charity since the making of the gift or gifts (including, in particular, its financial position, the needs of its beneficiaries, and the social, economic and legal environment in which it operates).

(2) The Commission must not concur with the resolution unless it is satisfied –

(a) that its implementation would accord with the spirit of the gift or gifts mentioned in section 289(1)(a) (even though it would be inconsistent with the restrictions mentioned in section 289(2)), and

(b) that the charity trustees have complied with the obligations imposed on them by or under section 289 or 290 in connection with the resolution.

(3) Before the end of the period of 3 months beginning with the relevant date, the Commission must notify the charity trustees in writing –

(a) that the Commission concurs with the resolution, or

(b) that it does not concur with it.

(4) In subsection (3) 'the relevant date' means –

(a) if the Commission directs the charity trustees under section 290(1) to give public notice of the resolution, the date when that notice is given, and

(b) otherwise, the date on which the Commission receives the copy of the resolution in accordance with section 289(4).

(5) Where –

(a) the charity trustees are notified by the Commission that it concurs with the resolution, or

(b) the period of 3 months mentioned in subsection (3) has elapsed without the Commission notifying them that it does not concur with the resolution,

the fund or portion may, by virtue of this section, be expended in carrying out the purposes set out in the trusts to which the fund is subject without regard to the restrictions mentioned in section 289(2).

(6) The fund or portion may be so expended as from such date as is specified for this purpose in the resolution.

292 Power to alter sum specified in s 289

The Minister may by order amend section 289(1) (market value of fund for purposes of resolution to spend capital subject to special trusts: larger fund) by substituting a different sum for the sum for the time being specified there.

[PART 14A
SOCIAL INVESTMENTS

292A Meaning of 'social investment'

(1) This section applies for the purposes of this Part.

(2) A social investment is made when a relevant act of a charity is carried out with a view to both –

(a) directly furthering the charity's purposes; and
(b) achieving a financial return for the charity.

(3) References to an act of a charity are, in the case of an unincorporated charity, to an act of the charity trustees.

(4) A relevant act of a charity is –

(a) an application or use of funds or other property; or
(b) taking on a commitment in relation to a liability of another person (such as a guarantee) that puts the charity's funds or other property at risk of being applied or used.

(5) An act mentioned in subsection (4)(a) is to be regarded as achieving a financial return if its outcome is better for the charity in financial terms than expending the whole of the funds or other property in question.

(6) A commitment mentioned in subsection (4)(b) is to be regarded as achieving a financial return if –

(a) it is not called upon; or
(b) it is called upon without resulting in the expenditure of the whole of the funds or other property put at risk.

(7) The fact that a relevant act may also have results other than those mentioned in subsection (2)(a) and (b) does not prevent the carrying out of that act being regarded as the making of a social investment.

(8) The fact that carrying out a relevant act of a charity is regarded as the making of a social investment for the purposes of this Part does not of itself make the act an investment for any other purpose.]

NOTES

Inserted by the Charities (Protection and Social Investment) Act 2016, s 15(1).

[292B General power to make social investments

(1) An incorporated charity has, and the charity trustees of an unincorporated charity have, power to make social investments.

(2) The power conferred by this section may not be used to make a social investment involving –

(a) the application or use of permanent endowment, or
(b) taking on a commitment mentioned in section 292A(4)(b) that puts permanent endowment at risk of being applied or used,

unless the charity trustees expect that making the social investment will not contravene any restriction with respect to expenditure that applies to the permanent endowment in question.

(3) The power conferred by this section –

(a) may be restricted or excluded by the trusts of the charity;
(b) is (subject to paragraph (a)) in addition to any other power to make social investments that the charity or charity trustees may have.

(4) This section and section 292C do not apply in relation to –

(a) charities established by, or whose purposes and functions are set out in, legislation;
(b) charities established by Royal Charter;

but they apply in relation to all other charities, whether established before or after this section comes into force.

(5) In subsection (4) 'legislation' means –

(a) an Act of Parliament or an Act or Measure of the National Assembly for Wales; or
(b) subordinate legislation (within the meaning of the Interpretation Act 1978) made under such an Act or Measure.]

NOTES

Inserted by the Charities (Protection and Social Investment) Act 2016, s 15(1).

[292C Charity trustees' duties in relation to social investments

(1) This section applies in relation to social investments that are made after section 292B comes into force, whether or not made by the exercise of the power conferred by section 292B.

(2) The charity trustees of a charity must, before exercising a power to make a social investment –

(a) consider whether in all the circumstances any advice about the proposed social investment ought to be obtained;
(b) obtain and consider any advice they conclude ought to be obtained; and
(c) satisfy themselves that it is in the interests of the charity to make the social investment, having regard to the benefit they expect it to achieve for the charity (by directly furthering the charity's purposes and achieving a financial return).

(3) The charity trustees of a charity must from time to time review the charity's social investments.

(4) When carrying out a review the charity trustees must –

(a) consider whether any advice about the social investments (or any particular social investment) ought to be obtained; and
(b) obtain and consider any advice they conclude ought to be obtained.

(5) The duties under this section may not be restricted or excluded by the charity's trusts.

(6) In the case of an unincorporated charity, the duties under this section apply in relation to relevant social investments in place of any duties under sections 4 and 5 of the Trustee Act 2000 that would otherwise apply.

(7) In subsection (6) 'relevant social investments' means social investments that are investments for the purposes of Part 2 of the Trustee Act 2000.]

NOTES

Inserted by the Charities (Protection and Social Investment) Act 2016, s 15(1).

PART 15
LOCAL CHARITIES

Indexes and reviews etc

293 Meaning of 'local charity'

In this Act, except in so far as the context otherwise requires, 'local charity' means, in relation to any area, a charity established for purposes which are –

(a) by their nature, or
(b) by the trusts of the charity,

directed wholly or mainly to the benefit of that area or of part of it.

294 Local authority's index of local charities

(1) A council may maintain an index of local charities or of any class of local charities in the council's area, and may publish information contained in the index, or summaries or extracts taken from it.

(2) A council proposing to establish or maintaining under this section an index of local charities or of any class of local charities must, on request, be supplied by the Commission free of charge –

(a) with copies of such entries in the register of charities as are relevant to the index, or
(b) with particulars of any changes in the entries of which copies have been supplied before;

and the Commission may arrange that it will without further request supply a council with particulars of any such changes.

(3) An index maintained under this section must be open to public inspection at all reasonable times.

295 Reviews of local charities by local authority

(1) A council may –

(a) subject to the following provisions of this section, initiate, and carry out in co-operation with the charity trustees, a review of the working of any group of local charities with the same or similar purposes in the council's area, and

(b) make to the Commission such report on the review and such recommendations arising from it as the council, after consultation with the trustees, think fit.

(2) A council having power to initiate reviews under this section may –

(a) co-operate with other persons in any review by them of the working of local charities in the council's area (with or without other charities), or

(b) join with other persons in initiating and carrying out such a review.

(3) No review initiated by a council under this section is to extend –

(a) to any charity without the consent of the charity trustees, or

(b) to any ecclesiastical charity.

(4) No review initiated under this section by a district council is to extend to the working in any county of a local charity established for purposes similar or complementary to any services provided by county councils unless the review so extends with the consent of the council of that county.

(5) Subsection (4) does not apply in relation to Wales.

296 S 294 and s 295: supplementary

(1) In sections 294 and 295 and this section 'council' means –

(a) a district council,
(b) a county council,
(c) a county borough council,
(d) a London borough council, or
(e) the Common Council of the City of London.

(2) A council may employ any voluntary organisation as their agent for the purposes of sections 294 and 295, on such terms and within such limits (if any) or in such cases as they may agree.

(3) In subsection (2), 'voluntary organisation' means any body –

(a) whose activities are carried on otherwise than for profit, and
(b) which is not a public or local authority.

(4) A joint board discharging any of a council's functions has the same powers under sections 294 and 295 and this section as the council as respects local charities in the council's area which are established for purposes similar or complementary to any services provided by the board.

297 Co-operation between charities, and between charities and local authorities

(1) Any local council and any joint board discharging any functions of a local council –

(a) may make, with any charity established for purposes similar or complementary to services provided by the council or board, arrangements for co-ordinating –
(i) the activities of the council or board, and
(ii) those of the charity,

in the interests of persons who may benefit from those services or from the charity, and

(b) is at liberty to disclose to any such charity in the interests of those persons any information obtained in connection with the services provided by the council or board, whether or not arrangements have been made with the charity under this subsection.

(2) In subsection (1), 'local council' means –

(a) in relation to England –
  (i) a district council,
  (ii) a county council,
  (iii) a London borough council,
  (iv) a parish council,
  (v) the Common Council of the City of London, or
  (vi) the Council of the Isles of Scilly, and

(b) in relation to Wales –
  (i) a county council,
  (ii) a county borough council, or
  (iii) a community council.

(3) Charity trustees may, regardless of anything in the trusts of the charity, by virtue of this subsection do all or any of the following things, if it appears to them likely to promote or make more effective the work of the charity –

(a) they may co-operate in any review undertaken under section 295 or otherwise of the working of charities or any class of charities;

(b) they may make arrangements with an authority acting under subsection (1) or with another charity for co-ordinating their activities and those of the authority or of the other charity;

(c) they may publish information of other charities with a view to bringing them to the notice of those for whose benefit they are intended.

(4) Charity trustees may defray the expense of acting under subsection (3) out of any income or money applicable as income of the charity.

Parochial charities

298 Transfer of property to parish or community council or its appointees

(1) This section applies where trustees hold any property –

(a) for the purposes of a public recreation ground, or of allotments (whether under inclosure Acts or otherwise), for the benefit of inhabitants of a parish having a parish council or (in Wales) community having a community council, or

(b) for other charitable purposes connected with such a parish or community;

and it applies to property held for any public purposes as it applies to property held for charitable purposes.

But it does not apply where trustees hold property for an ecclesiastical charity.

(2) The trustees may, with the approval of the Commission and with the consent of the parish or community council, transfer the property to –

(a) the parish or community council, or

(b) persons appointed by the parish or community council;

and the council or their appointees must hold the property on the same trusts and subject to the same conditions as the trustees did.

299 Local authorities' power to appoint representative trustees

(1) This section applies where a parochial charity in a parish or (in Wales) a community is not –

(a) an ecclesiastical charity, or
(b) a charity founded within the preceding 40 years.

(2) If the charity trustees do not include persons –

(a) elected by the local government electors or inhabitants of the parish or community, or
(b) appointed by the parish council or parish meeting or (in Wales) by the community council or the county council or (as the case may be) county borough council,

the parish council or parish meeting or the community council or the county council or county borough council may appoint additional charity trustees, to such number as the Commission may allow.

(3) If there is a sole charity trustee not elected or appointed as mentioned in subsection (2), the number of the charity trustees may, with the approval of the Commission, be increased to 3, of whom –

(a) one may be nominated by the person holding the office of the sole trustee, and
(b) one may be nominated by the parish council or parish meeting or by the community council or the county council or county borough council.

300 Powers of appointment deriving from pre-1894 powers

(1) Subsection (2) applies where, under the trusts of a charity other than an ecclesiastical charity –

(a) the inhabitants of a rural parish (whether in vestry or not), or
(b) a select vestry,

were formerly (in 1894) entitled to appoint charity trustees for, or trustees or beneficiaries of, the charity.

(2) The appointment is to be made –

(a) in a parish having a parish council or (in Wales) a community having a community council, by the parish or community council, or in the case of beneficiaries, by persons appointed by the parish or community council;
(b) in a parish not having a parish council or (in Wales) a community not having a community council, by the parish meeting or by the county council or (as the case may be) county borough council.

(3) Subsection (4) applies where –

(a) overseers as such, or
(b) except in the case of an ecclesiastical charity, churchwardens as such,

were formerly (in 1894) charity trustees of or trustees for a parochial charity in a rural parish, either alone or jointly with other persons.

(4) Instead of the former overseer or church warden trustees there are to be trustees (to a number not greater than that of the former overseer or churchwarden trustees) appointed –

(a) by the parish council or, if there is no parish council, by the parish meeting, or
(b) by the community council or, if there is no community council, by the county council or (as the case may be) county borough council.

(5) In this section 'formerly (in 1894)' relates to the period immediately before the passing of the Local Government Act 1894 and 'former' is to be read accordingly.

301 Powers of appointment deriving from pre-1927 powers

(1) Subsection (2) applies where, outside Greater London (other than the outer London boroughs), overseers of a parish as such were formerly (in 1927) charity trustees of or trustees for any charity, either alone or jointly with other persons.

(2) Instead of the former overseer trustees there are to be trustees (to a number not greater than that of the former overseer trustees) appointed –

(a) by the parish council or, if there is no parish council, by the parish meeting, or
(b) (in Wales) by the community council or, if there is no community council, by the county council or (as the case may be) county borough council.

(3) In the case of an urban parish existing immediately before the passing of the Local Government Act 1972 which after 1st April 1974 is not comprised in a parish, the power of appointment under subsection (2) is exercisable by the district council.

(4) In this section 'formerly (in 1927)' relates to the period immediately before 1 April 1927 and 'former is to be read accordingly.

302 Term of office of trustees appointed under s 299 to s 301

(1) Any appointment of a charity trustee or trustee for a charity which is made by virtue of sections 299 to 301 must be for a term of 4 years, and a retiring trustee is eligible for re-appointment.

But this is subject to subsections (2) and (3).

(2) On an appointment under section 299, where –

(a) no previous appointments have been made by virtue of –
  (i) section 299, or
  (ii) the corresponding provision of the Local Government Act 1894, the Charities Act 1960 or the Charities Act 1993, and
(b) more than one trustee is appointed,

half of those appointed (or as nearly as may be) must be appointed for a term of 2 years.

(3) An appointment made to fill a casual vacancy must be for the remainder of the term of the previous appointment.

303 S 298 to s 302: supplementary

(1) In sections 299 and 300, 'parochial charity' means, in relation to any parish or (in Wales) community, a charity the benefits of which are, or the separate distribution of the benefits of which is, confined to inhabitants of –

(a) the parish or community,

(b) a single ancient ecclesiastical parish which included that parish or community or part of it, or
(c) an area consisting of that parish or community with not more than 4 neighbouring parishes or communities.

(2) Sections 298 to 302 do not affect the trusteeship, control or management of any foundation or voluntary school within the meaning of the School Standards and Framework Act 1998.

(3) Sections 298 to 302 –

(a) do not apply to the Isles of Scilly, and
(b) have effect subject to any order (including any future order) made under any enactment relating to local government with respect to local government areas or the powers of local authorities.

Supplementary

304 Effect of provisions relating to vesting or transfer of property

No vesting or transfer of any property in pursuance of any provision of this Part operates as a breach of a covenant or condition against alienation or gives rise to a forfeiture.

PART 16
CHARITY MERGERS

Registration

305 Register of charity mergers

(1) There continues to be a register of charity mergers, to be kept by the Commission in such manner as it thinks fit and maintained by it.

(2) The register must contain an entry in respect of every relevant charity merger which is notified to the Commission in accordance with section 307 and such procedures as it may determine.

306 Meaning of 'relevant charity merger' etc

(1) In this Part 'relevant charity merger' means –

(a) a merger of two or more charities in connection with which one of them ('the transferee') has transferred to it all the property of the other or others, each of which ('a transferor') ceases to exist, or is to cease to exist, on or after the transfer of its property to the transferee, or
(b) a merger of two or more charities ('transferors') in connection with which both or all of them cease to exist, or are to cease to exist, on or after the transfer of all of their property to a new charity ('the transferee').

(2) In the case of a merger involving the transfer of property of any charity –

(a) which has both a permanent endowment and other property ('unrestricted property'), and
(b) whose trusts do not contain provision for the termination of the charity,

subsection (1)(a) or (b) applies subject to the modifications in subsection (3).

(3) The modifications in relation to any such charity are –

(a) the reference to all of its property is to be treated as a reference to all of its unrestricted property, and
(b) any reference to its ceasing to exist is to be treated as omitted.

(4) In this section and sections 307 and 308 –

(a) any reference to a transfer of property includes a transfer effected by a vesting declaration, and
(b) 'vesting declaration' means a declaration to which section 310(2) applies.

307 Notification of charity mergers

(1) A notification under section 305(2) may be given in respect of a relevant charity merger at any time after –

(a) the transfer of property involved in the merger has taken place, or
(b) (if more than one transfer of property is so involved) the last of those transfers has taken place.

(2) If a vesting declaration is made in connection with a relevant charity merger, a notification under section 305(2) must be given in respect of the merger once the transfer, or the last of the transfers, mentioned in subsection (1) has taken place.

(3) A notification under section 305(2) is to be given by the charity trustees of the transferee and must –

(a) specify the transfer or transfers of property involved in the merger and the date or dates on which it or they took place,
(b) include a statement that appropriate arrangements have been made with respect to the discharge of any liabilities of the transferor charity or charities, and
(c) in the case of a notification required by subsection (2), set out the matters mentioned in subsection (4).

(4) The matters are –

(a) the fact that the vesting declaration in question has been made,
(b) the date when the declaration was made, and
(c) the date on which the vesting of title under the declaration took place by virtue of section 310(2).

308 Details to be entered in register of charity mergers

(1) Subsection (2) applies to the entry to be made in the register of charity mergers in respect of a relevant charity merger, as required by section 305(2).

(2) The entry must –

(a) specify the date when the transfer or transfers of property involved in the merger took place,
(b) if a vesting declaration was made in connection with the merger, set out the matters mentioned in section 307(4), and
(c) contain such other particulars of the merger as the Commission thinks fit.

309 Right to inspect register of charity mergers

(1) The register of charity mergers must be open to public inspection at all reasonable times.

(2) Where any information contained in the register is not in documentary form, subsection (1) is to be read as requiring the information to be available for public inspection in legible form at all reasonable times.

Vesting declarations and effect of merger on certain gifts

310 Pre-merger vesting declarations

(1) Subsection (2) applies to a declaration which –

(a) is made by deed for the purposes of this section by the charity trustees of the transferor,
(b) is made in connection with a relevant charity merger, and
(c) is to the effect that (subject to subsections (3) and (4)) all of the transferor's property is to vest in the transferee on such date as is specified in the declaration ('the specified date').

(2) The declaration operates on the specified date to vest the legal title to all of the transferor's property in the transferee, without the need for any further document transferring it.

This is subject to subsections (3) and (4).

(3) Subsection (2) does not apply to –

(a) any land held by the transferor as security for money subject to the trusts of the transferor (other than land held on trust for securing debentures or debenture stock),
(b) any land held by the transferor under a lease or agreement which contains any covenant (however described) against assignment of the transferor's interest without the consent of some other person, unless that consent has been obtained before the specified date, or
(c) any shares, stock, annuity or other property which is only transferable in books kept by a company or other body or in a manner directed by or under any enactment.

(4) In its application to registered land within the meaning of the Land Registration Act 2002, subsection (2) is subject to section 27 of that Act (dispositions required to be registered).

311 Effect of registering charity merger on gifts to transferor

(1) This section applies where a relevant charity merger is registered in the register of charity mergers.

(2) Any gift which –

(a) is expressed as a gift to the transferor, and
(b) takes effect on or after the date of registration of the merger,

takes effect as a gift to the transferee, unless it is an excluded gift.

(3) A gift is an excluded gift if –

(a) the transferor is a charity within section 306(2), and
(b) the gift is intended to be held subject to the trusts on which the whole or part of the charity's permanent endowment is held.

312 'Transferor' and 'transferee' etc in s 310 and s 311

(1) In sections 310 and 311 –

(a) any reference to the transferor, in relation to a relevant charity merger, is a reference to the transferor (or one of the transferors) within the meaning of section 306, and
(b) any reference to all of the transferor's property, where the transferor is a charity within section 306(2), is a reference to all of the transferor's unrestricted property (within the meaning of section 306(2)(a)).

(2) In sections 310 and 311, any reference to the transferee, in relation to a relevant charity merger, is a reference to –

(a) the transferee (within the meaning of section 306), if it is a company or other body corporate, and
(b) otherwise, the charity trustees of the transferee (within the meaning of section 306).

Supplementary

313 Effect of provisions relating to vesting or transfer of property

No vesting or transfer of any property in pursuance of any provision of this Part operates as a breach of a covenant or condition against alienation or gives rise to a forfeiture.

314 Exception for CIOs

Nothing in this Part applies in a case where section 235 (amalgamation of CIOs) or 240 (transfer of CIO's undertaking to another CIO) applies.

PART 17
THE TRIBUNAL

Chapter 1
General

315 The Tribunal

(1) In this Act, 'the Tribunal' in relation to any appeal, application or reference, means –

(a) the Upper Tribunal, in any case where it is determined by or under Tribunal Procedure Rules that the Upper Tribunal is to hear the appeal, application or reference, or
(b) the First-tier Tribunal, in any other case.

(2) The Tribunal has jurisdiction to hear and determine –

(a) such appeals and applications as may be made to the Tribunal in accordance with Chapter 2, or any other enactment, in respect of decisions, orders or directions of the Commission, and

(b) such matters as may be referred to the Tribunal in accordance with Chapter 3 by the Commission or the Attorney General.

(3) Such appeals, applications and matters are to be heard and determined by the Tribunal in accordance with Chapters 2 and 3, or any such enactment, taken with –

(a) rules made under section 316(2), and
(b) Tribunal Procedure Rules.

316 Rules relating to appeals, applications or references

(1) This section applies in relation to appeals, applications or references to the Tribunal which are mentioned in section 315(2).

(2) The Lord Chancellor may make rules –

(a) specifying steps which must be taken before appeals, applications or references are made to the Tribunal (and the period within which any such steps must be taken);
(b) requiring the Commission to inform persons of their right to appeal or apply to the Tribunal following a final decision, direction or order of the Commission.

(3) Tribunal Procedure Rules may make any other provision regulating the exercise of rights to appeal or to apply to the Tribunal and matters relating to the making of references to it.

(4) Rules under subsection (2) or (3) may confer a discretion on –

(a) the Tribunal, or
(b) any other person.

(5) Rules of the Lord Chancellor under this section –

(a) are to be made by statutory instrument, and
(b) are subject to annulment in pursuance of a resolution of either House of Parliament.

(6) Rules of the Lord Chancellor under this section may make –

(a) different provision for different cases, and
(b) such supplemental, incidental, consequential or transitional provision or savings as the Lord Chancellor considers appropriate.

317 Appeal from Tribunal

(1) For the purposes of sections 11(2)and 13(2) of the Tribunals, Courts and Enforcement Act 2007, the Commission and the Attorney General are to be treated as parties to cases before the Tribunal in respect of any such appeal, application or reference as is mentioned in section 315(2).

(2) In the case of an appeal under section 11 or 13 of the Tribunals, Courts and Enforcement Act 2007 against a decision of the Tribunal which determines a question referred to it by the Commission or the Attorney General, the tribunal or court hearing the appeal –

(a) must consider afresh the question referred to the Tribunal, and
(b) may take into account evidence which was not available to the Tribunal.

318 Intervention by Attorney General

(1) This section applies to any proceedings –

(a) before the Tribunal, or
(b) on an appeal from the Tribunal,

to which the Attorney General is not a party.

(2) The appropriate body may at any stage of the proceedings direct that all the necessary papers in the proceedings be sent to the Attorney General.

(3) A direction under subsection (2) may be made by the appropriate body –

(a) of its own motion, or
(b) on the application of any party to the proceedings.

(4) The Attorney General may –

(a) intervene in the proceedings in such manner as the Attorney General thinks necessary or expedient, and
(b) argue before the appropriate body any question in relation to the proceedings which the appropriate body considers it necessary to have fully argued.

(5) Subsection (4) applies whether or not a direction is given under subsection (2).

(6) In this section the 'appropriate body' means the Tribunal or, in the case of an appeal from the Tribunal, the tribunal or court hearing the appeal.

Chapter 2
Appeals and Applications to Tribunal

319 Appeals: general

(1) Except in the case of a reviewable matter (see section 322) an appeal may be brought to the Tribunal against any decision, direction or order mentioned in column 1 of Schedule 6.

(2) Such an appeal may be brought by –

(a) the Attorney General, or
(b) any person specified in the corresponding entry in column 2 of Schedule 6.

(3) The Commission is to be the respondent to such an appeal.

(4) In determining such an appeal the Tribunal –

(a) must consider afresh the decision, direction or order appealed against, and
(b) may take into account evidence which was not available to the Commission.

(5) The Tribunal may –

(a) dismiss the appeal, or
(b) if it allows the appeal, exercise any power specified in the corresponding entry in column 3 of Schedule 6.

320 Appeals: orders under s 52

(1) Section 319(4)(a) does not apply in relation to an appeal against an order made under section 52 (power to call for documents).

(2) On such an appeal the Tribunal must consider whether the information or document in question –

(a) relates to a charity;
(b) is relevant to the discharge of the functions of the Commission or the official custodian.

(3) The Tribunal may allow such an appeal only if it is satisfied that the information or document in question does not fall within subsection (2)(a) or (b).

321 Reviews

(1) An application may be made to the Tribunal for the review of a reviewable matter.

(2) Such an application may be made by –

(a) the Attorney General, or
(b) any person mentioned in the entry in column 2 of Schedule 6 which corresponds to the entry in column 1 which relates to the reviewable matter.

(3) The Commission is to be the respondent to such an application.

(4) In determining such an application the Tribunal must apply the principles which would be applied by the High Court on an application for judicial review.

(5) The Tribunal may –

(a) dismiss the application, or
(b) if it allows the application, exercise any power mentioned in the entry in column 3 of Schedule 6 which corresponds to the entry in column 1 which relates to the reviewable matter.

322 Reviewable matters

(1) In this Chapter references to reviewable matters are to –

(a) decisions to which subsection (2) applies, and
(b) orders to which subsection (3) applies.

(2) This subsection applies to decisions of the Commission –

(a) to institute an inquiry under section 46 with regard to a particular institution;
(b) to institute an inquiry under section 46 with regard to a class of institutions;
(c) not to make a common investment scheme under section 96;
(d) not to make a common deposit scheme under section 100;
(e) not to make an order under section 105 (power to authorise dealings with charity property etc) in relation to a charity;
(f) not to make an order under section 117 (restrictions on dispositions of land) in relation to land held by or in trust for a charity;
(g) not to make an order under section 124 (restrictions on mortgages) in relation to a mortgage of land held by or in trust for a charity.

(3) This subsection applies to an order made by the Commission under section 147(2) (investigation and audit) in relation to a charitable company.

323 Remission of matters to Commission

References in column 3 of Schedule 6 to the power to remit a matter to the Commission are to the power to remit the matter –

(a) generally, or
(b) for determination in accordance with a finding made or direction given by the Tribunal.

324 Power to amend provisions relating to appeals and applications to Tribunal

(1) The Minister may by order –

(a) amend or otherwise modify an entry in Schedule 6,
(b) add an entry to Schedule 6, or
(c) remove an entry from Schedule 6.

(2) An order under subsection (1) may make such amendments, repeals or other modifications of –

(a) sections 319 to 323, or
(b) an enactment which applies this Chapter and Schedule 6,

as the Minister considers appropriate in consequence of any change in Schedule 6 made by the order.

(3) Subsections (1) and (2) apply (with the necessary modifications) in relation to section 57 of the Charities Act 2006 as if –

(a) that section were contained in this Chapter, and
(b) the reference in subsection (2) to sections 319 to 323 included a reference to any other provision relating to appeals to the Tribunal which is contained in Chapter 1 of Part 3 of the Charities Act 2006.

Chapter 3
References to Tribunal

325 References by Commission

(1) A question which –

(a) has arisen in connection with the exercise by the Commission of any of its functions, and
(b) involves either the operation of charity law in any respect or its application to a particular state of affairs,

may be referred to the Tribunal by the Commission if the Commission considers it desirable to refer the question to the Tribunal.

(2) The Commission may make such a reference only with the consent of the Attorney General.

(3) The Commission is to be a party to proceedings before the Tribunal on the reference.

(4) The following are entitled to be parties to proceedings before the Tribunal on the reference –

(a) the Attorney General, and
(b) with the Tribunal's permission –
  (i) the charity trustees of any charity which is likely to be affected by the Tribunal's decision on the reference,
  (ii) any such charity which is a body corporate, and
  (iii) any other person who is likely to be so affected.

326 References by Attorney General

(1) A question which involves –

(a) the operation of charity law in any respect, or
(b) the application of charity law to a particular state of affairs,

may be referred to the Tribunal by the Attorney General if the Attorney General considers it desirable to refer the question to the Tribunal.

(2) The Attorney General is to be a party to proceedings before the Tribunal on the reference.

(3) The following are entitled to be parties to proceedings before the Tribunal on the reference –

(a) the Commission, and
(b) with the Tribunal's permission –
  (i) the charity trustees of any charity which is likely to be affected by the Tribunal's decision on the reference,
  (ii) any such charity which is a body corporate, and
  (iii) any other person who is likely to be so affected.

327 Powers of Commission in relation to matters referred to Tribunal

(1) This section applies where a question which involves the application of charity law to a particular state of affairs has been referred to the Tribunal under section 325 or 326.

(2) The Commission must not take any steps in reliance on any view as to the application of charity law to that state of affairs until –

(a) proceedings on the reference (including any proceedings on appeal) have been concluded, and
(b) any period during which an appeal (or further appeal) may ordinarily be made has ended.

(3) Where –

(a) paragraphs (a) and (b) of subsection (2) are satisfied, and
(b) the question has been decided in proceedings on the reference,

the Commission must give effect to that decision when dealing with the particular state of affairs to which the reference related.

328 Suspension of time limits while reference is in progress

(1) Subsection (2) applies if –

(a) section 327(2) prevents the Commission from taking any steps which it would otherwise be permitted or required to take, and
(b) the steps in question may be taken only during a period specified in an enactment ('the specified period').

(2) The running of the specified period is suspended for the period which –

(a) begins with the date on which the question is referred to the Tribunal, and
(b) ends with the date on which paragraphs (a) and (b) of section 327(2) are satisfied.

(3) Nothing in –

- (a) this section, or
- (b) section 271 or 278 (suspension of period during which Commission may object to resolution of unincorporated charity),

prevents the specified period being suspended concurrently by virtue of subsection (2) and any of the provisions of sections 271 and 278.

329 Agreement for Commission to act while reference is in progress

(1) Section 327(2) does not apply in relation to any steps taken by the Commission with the agreement of –

- (a) the persons who are parties to the proceedings on the reference at the time when those steps are taken, and
- (b) (if not within paragraph (a)) the charity trustees of any charity which –
  - (i) is likely to be directly affected by the taking of those steps, and
  - (ii) is not a party to the proceedings at that time.

(2) The Commission may take those steps despite the suspension in accordance with section 328(2) of any period during which it would otherwise be permitted or required to take them.

(3) Section 327(3) does not require the Commission to give effect to a decision as to the application of charity law to a particular state of affairs to the extent that the decision is inconsistent with any steps already taken by the Commission in relation to that state of affairs in accordance with this section.

330 Appeals and applications in respect of matters determined on references

(1) No appeal or application may be made to the Tribunal by a person to whom subsection (2) applies in respect of an order or decision made, or direction given, by the Commission in accordance with section 327(3).

(2) This subsection applies to a person who was at any stage a party to the proceedings in which the question referred to the Tribunal was decided.

(3) Any enactment (including one contained in this Act) which provides for an appeal or application to be made to the Tribunal has effect subject to subsection (1).

331 Interpretation

(1) In this Chapter –

'charity law' means –

- (a) any enactment contained in, or made under, this Act or the Charities Act 2006,
- (b) any other enactment specified in regulations made by the Minister, and
- (c) any rule of law which relates to charities, and

'enactment' includes an enactment comprised in subordinate legislation (within the meaning of the Interpretation Act 1978), and includes an enactment whenever passed or made.

(2) The exclusions contained in section 10(2) (ecclesiastical corporations etc) do not have effect for the purposes of this Chapter.

PART 18
MISCELLANEOUS AND SUPPLEMENTARY

Administrative provisions about charities

332 Manner of giving notice of charity meetings, etc

(1) All notices which are required or authorised by the trusts of a charity to be given to a charity trustee, member or subscriber –

(a) may be sent by post, and
(b) if sent by post, may be addressed to any address given as the address of the charity trustee, member or subscriber in the list of such persons for the time being in use at the office or principal office of the charity.

(2) Subsections (3) and (4) apply where a notice is required by the trusts of the charity to be given to a charity trustee, member or subscriber.

(3) If the notice is given by post, it is to be treated as having been given by the time at which the letter containing it would be delivered in the ordinary course of post.

(4) If the notice is a notice of any meeting or election, the notice need not be given to any charity trustee, member or subscriber who, in the list mentioned in subsection (1)(b), has no address in the United Kingdom.

333 Conferral of authority to execute documents

(1) Charity trustees may, subject to the trusts of the charity, confer on any two or more of their body –

(a) a general authority, or
(b) an authority limited in such manner as the charity trustees think fit,

to execute in the names and on behalf of the charity trustees documents for giving effect to transactions to which the charity trustees are a party.

(2) Any document executed in pursuance of an authority under subsection (1) is of the same effect as if executed by the whole body.

(3) An authority under subsection (1) –

(a) suffices for any document if it is given in writing or by resolution of a meeting of the charity trustees, despite the want of any formality that would be required in giving an authority apart from that subsection;
(b) may be given so as to make the powers conferred exercisable by any of the charity trustees, or may be restricted to named persons or in any other way;
(c) subject to any such restriction, and until it is revoked, has effect, despite any change in the charity trustees, as a continuing authority given by the charity trustees from time to time of the charity and exercisable by such charity trustees.

(4) In any authority under this section to execute a document in the names and on behalf of charity trustees there is, unless the contrary intention appears, implied authority also to execute it for them in the name and on behalf of the official custodian or of any other person, in any case in which the charity trustees could do so.

(5) Where a document purports to be executed in pursuance of this section, then in favour of a person who (then or afterwards) in good faith acquires for money or money's worth –

(a) an interest in or charge on property, or
(b) the benefit of any covenant or agreement expressed to be entered into by the charity trustees,

it is conclusively presumed to have been duly executed by virtue of this section.

(6) The powers conferred by this section are in addition to and not in derogation of any other powers.

334 Transfer and evidence of title to property vested in trustees

(1) Subsection (2) applies where, under the trusts of a charity, trustees of property held for the purposes of the charity may be appointed or discharged by resolution of a meeting of the charity trustees, members or other persons.

(2) A memorandum declaring a trustee to have been so appointed or discharged is sufficient evidence of that fact if the memorandum –

(a) is signed either at the meeting by the person presiding or in some other manner directed by the meeting, and
(b) is attested by two persons present at the meeting.

(3) A memorandum evidencing the appointment or discharge of a trustee under subsection (2), if executed as a deed, has the same operation under section 40 of the Trustee Act 1925 (vesting declarations as respects trust property in deeds appointing or discharging trustees) as if the appointment or discharge were effected by the deed.

(4) For the purposes of this section, where a document purports to have been signed and attested as mentioned in subsection (2), then on proof (whether by evidence or as a matter of presumption) of the signature the document is presumed to have been so signed and attested, unless the contrary is shown.

(5) This section applies to a memorandum made at any time, except that subsection (3) applies only to those made on or after 1 January 1961.

(6) This section applies in relation to any institution to which the Literary and Scientific Institutions Act 1854 applies as it applies in relation to a charity.

(7) No vesting or transfer of any property in pursuance of any provision of this section operates as a breach of a covenant or condition against alienation or gives rise to a forfeiture.

Enforcement powers of Commission etc

335 Enforcement of requirements by order of Commission

(1) If a person fails to comply with any requirement imposed by or under this Act then (subject to subsection (2)) the Commission may by order give that person such directions as it considers appropriate for securing that the default is made good.

(2) Subsection (1) does not apply to any such requirement if –

(a) a person who fails to comply with, or is persistently in default in relation to, the requirement is liable to any criminal penalty, or
(b) the requirement is imposed by –

(i) an order of the Commission to which section 336 applies, or
(ii) a direction of the Commission to which section 336 applies by virtue of section 338(2).

336 Enforcement of orders of Commission

(1) A person guilty of disobedience to an order mentioned in subsection (2) may on the application of the Commission to the High Court be dealt with as for disobedience to an order of the High Court.

(2) The orders are –

(a) an order of the Commission under –
section 52(1) (power to call for documents),
section 84 (power to direct specified action to be taken),
[section 84A (power to direct specified action not to be taken),]
[section 84B (power to direct winding up),]
section 85 (power to direct application of charity property),
section 87 (supervision of certain Scottish charities),
section 155 (power to direct compliance with regulations giving auditors etc access to information etc),
section 184 (civil consequences of acting while disqualified),
section 186 (disqualification of charity trustee or trustee receiving remuneration under section 185),
section 263 (dissolution of incorporated body),
(b) an order of the Commission under –
section 69 (concurrent jurisdiction with High Court for certain purposes), or
any of sections 76 and 79 to 81 (powers to act for protection of charities etc),
requiring a transfer of property or payment to be called for or made, or
(c) an order of the Commission requiring a default under this Act to be made good.

NOTES

Sub-s (2) amended by the Charities (Protection and Social Investment) Act 2016, ss 6(1), (4), 7(1), (4).

337 Other provisions as to orders of Commission

(1) Any order made by the Commission under this Act may include such incidental or supplementary provisions as the Commission thinks expedient for carrying into effect the objects of the order.

(2) Where the Commission exercises any jurisdiction to make an order under this Act on an application or reference to it, it may insert any such provisions in the order even though the application or reference does not propose their insertion.

(3) Where the Commission makes an order under this Act, the Commission –

(a) may itself give such public notice as it thinks fit of the making or contents of the order, or
(b) may require it to be given by –
(i) any person on whose application the order is made, or
(ii) any charity affected by the order.

(4) The Commission may, with or without any application or reference to it, discharge an order in whole or in part, and subject or not to any savings or other transitional provisions, if –

(a) it made the order under any provision of this Act other than section 263 (dissolution of incorporated body), and
(b) at any time within 12 months after it made the order, it is satisfied that the order was made by mistake or on misrepresentation or otherwise than in conformity with this Act.

(5) Except for the purposes of subsection (4) or an appeal under this Act, an order made by the Commission under this Act –

(a) is to be treated as having been duly and formally made, and
(b) is not to be called in question on the ground only of irregularity or informality,

but (subject to any further order) has effect according to its tenor.

(6) Any order made by the Commission under any provision of this Act may be varied or revoked by a subsequent order so made and may include transitional provisions or savings.

338 Directions of the Commission or person conducting inquiry

(1) Any direction given by the Commission under any provision of this Act –

(a) may be varied or revoked by a further direction given under that provision, and
(b) must be given in writing.

(2) Sections 336 (enforcement of orders) and 337(1) to (3) and (5) (other provisions as to orders) apply to any such directions as they apply to an order of the Commission.

(3) In subsection (1) the reference to the Commission includes, in relation to a direction under section 47(2) (obtaining evidence etc for the purposes of an inquiry), a reference to any person conducting an inquiry under section 46.

(4) Nothing in this section is to be read as applying to any directions contained in an order made by the Commission under section 335(1) (directions for securing that default is made good).

339 Service of orders and directions

(1) This section applies to any order or direction made or given by the Commission under this Act.

(2) Any such order or direction may be served on a person (other than a body corporate) by –

(a) delivering it to that person,
(b) leaving it at that person's last known address in the United Kingdom, or
(c) sending it by post to that person at that address.

(3) Any such order or direction may be served on a body corporate by delivering it or sending it by post –

(a) to the registered or principal office of the body in the United Kingdom, or
(b) if it has no such office in the United Kingdom, to any place in the United Kingdom where it carries on business or conducts its activities (as the case may be).

(4) Any such order or direction may also be served on a person (including a body corporate) by sending it by post to that person at an address notified by that person to the Commission for the purposes of this subsection.

(5) In this section any reference to the Commission includes, in relation to a direction under section 47(2) (obtaining evidence etc for the purposes of an inquiry), a reference to any person conducting an inquiry under section 46.

Documents and evidence etc

340 Enrolment and deposit of documents etc

(1) The Commission may provide books in which any deed, will or other document relating to a charity may be enrolled.

(2) The Commission may accept for safe keeping any document of or relating to a charity, and the charity trustees or other persons having the custody of documents of or relating to a charity (including a charity which has ceased to exist) may with the consent of the Commission deposit them with the Commission for safe keeping, except in the case of documents required by some other enactment to be kept elsewhere.

(3) Regulations made by the Minister may make provision for such documents deposited with the Commission under this section as may be prescribed by the regulations to be destroyed or otherwise disposed of after such period or in such circumstances as may be so prescribed.

(4) Subsection (3) applies to any document –

(a) transmitted to the Commission under section 52, and
(b) kept by the Commission under section 52(3),

as if the document had been deposited with the Commission for safe keeping under this section.

(5) Subsections (3) and (4) apply (with any necessary adaptations) to documents enrolled by, deposited with or transmitted to the Charity Commissioners for England and Wales under corresponding previous enactments, including in particular the Charitable Trusts Act 1853 to 1939.

341 Evidence of documents received by Commission etc

(1) Subsection (2) applies where a document is enrolled by the Commission or is for the time being deposited with the Commission under section 340.

(2) Evidence of the document's contents may be given by means of a copy certified by any member of the staff of the Commission generally or specially authorised by the Commission to act for this purpose.

(3) A document purporting to be such a copy is to be received in evidence without proof –

(a) of the official position, authority or handwriting of the person certifying it, or
(b) of the original document being enrolled or deposited.

(4) Subsections (2) and (3) apply to any document –

(a) transmitted to the Commission under section 52, and
(b) kept by the Commission under section 52(3),

as if the document had been deposited with the Commission for safe keeping under section 340.

(5) Subsections (2) to (4) apply (with any necessary adaptations) to documents enrolled by, deposited with or transmitted to the Charity Commissioners for England and Wales under corresponding previous enactments, including in particular the Charitable Trusts Act 1853 to 1939.

342 Report of inquiry to be evidence in certain proceedings

(1) A copy of the report of the person conducting an inquiry under section 46, if certified by the Commission to be a true copy, is admissible in any proceedings to which this section applies –

(a) as evidence of any fact stated in the report, and
(b) as evidence of the opinion of that person as to any matter referred to in it.

(2) This section applies to –

(a) any legal proceedings instituted by the Commission under Part 6, and
(b) any legal proceedings instituted by the Attorney General in respect of a charity.

(3) A document purporting to be a certificate issued for the purposes of subsection (1) is to be –

(a) received in evidence, and
(b) treated as such a certificate,

unless the contrary is proved.

343 Evidence of documents issued by Commission etc

(1) Evidence of any order, certificate or other document issued by the Commission may be given by means of a copy retained by it, or taken from a copy so retained, if the copy is certified to be a true copy by any member of the staff of the Commission generally or specially authorised by the Commission to act for this purpose.

(2) Evidence of an entry in any register kept by the Commission may be given by means of a copy of the entry, if the copy is certified to be a true copy by any member of the staff of the Commission generally or specially authorised by the Commission to act for this purpose.

(3) A document purporting to be such a copy as is mentioned in subsection (1) or (2) is to be received in evidence without proof of the official position, authority or handwriting of the person certifying it.

(4) Subsections (1) and (3) apply to any order, certificate or other document issued by the Charity Commissioners for England and Wales as they apply to any order, certificate or other document issued by the Commission.

344 Other miscellaneous provisions as to evidence

(1) Subsection (2) applies to proceedings to recover or compel payment of any rentcharge or other periodical payment claimed by or on behalf of a charity out of land or of the rents, profits or other income of land, otherwise than as rent incident to a reversion.

(2) If it is shown in any proceedings to which this subsection applies that the rentcharge or other periodical payment has at any time been paid for 12 consecutive years to or for the benefit of the charity –

(a) that is prima facie evidence of the perpetual liability to it of the land or income, and
(b) no proof of its origin is necessary.

(3) In any proceedings, the following documents are admissible as evidence of the documents and facts stated in them –

(a) the printed copies of the reports of the Commissioners for enquiring concerning charities, 1818 to 1837, who were appointed under the Act 58 Geo. 3 c 91 and subsequent Acts, and
(b) the printed copies of the reports which were made for various counties and county boroughs to the Charity Commissioners by their assistant commissioners and presented to the House of Commons as returns to orders of various dates beginning with 8 December 1890, and ending with 9 September 1909.

Offences

345 Restriction on institution of proceedings for certain offences

(1) No proceedings for an offence to which this section applies are to be instituted except by or with the consent of the Director of Public Prosecutions.

(2) This section applies to any offence under –

(a) section 41 (offences in connection with statements required in official publications etc),
(b) section 60 (supply of false or misleading information to Commission etc),
(c) section 77(1) (offence of contravening certain orders made for protection of charities),
(d) section 173 (offences of failing to supply certain documents), or
(e) section 183(1) (criminal consequences of acting while disqualified).

346 Offences by bodies corporate

(1) If an offence under this Act –

(a) is committed by a body corporate, and
(b) is proved to have been committed with the consent or connivance of, or to be attributable to any neglect on the part of, an officer of the body corporate,

the officer as well as the body corporate is guilty of the offence and liable to be proceeded against and punished accordingly.

(2) In this section, 'officer', in relation to a body corporate, means –

(a) any director, manager, secretary or other similar officer of the body corporate, or
(b) any person who was purporting to act in any such capacity,

and, in relation to a body corporate whose affairs are managed by its members, 'director' means a member of the body corporate.

Regulations and orders

347 Regulations and orders: general

(1) Any power of the Minister to make any regulations or order under this Act is exercisable by statutory instrument.

(2) Subject to sections 348(1) and 349(1), regulations or orders of the Minister under this Act are subject to annulment in pursuance of a resolution of either House of Parliament.

(3) Any regulations of the Minister or the Commission and any order of the Minister under this Act may make –

(a) different provision for different cases or descriptions of case or different purposes or areas, and
(b) such supplemental, incidental, consequential, transitory or transitional provision or savings as the Minister or, as the case may be, the Commission considers appropriate.

(4) Nothing in this section applies to an order under paragraph 29 of Schedule 9 (transitory modifications).

348 Regulations subject to affirmative procedure etc

(1) Section 347(2) (negative procedure) does not apply to –

(a) regulations under section 19 (fees and other amounts payable to Commission) which require the payment of a fee in respect of any matter for which no fee was previously payable;
(b) regulations under section 25 (meaning of 'principal regulator') which amend any provision of an Act;
[(ba) regulations under section 178A(4) (offences specified for automatic disqualification of charity trustees);]
[(bb) regulations under section 181A(8) (conditions for disqualification by order);]
(c) regulations under section 245 (regulations about winding up, insolvency and dissolution of CIOs).

(2) No regulations within subsection (1)(a)[, (ba)][, (bb)] or (c) may be made unless a draft of the regulations has been laid before and approved by a resolution of each House of Parliament.

(3) No regulations within subsection (1)(b) may be made (whether alone or with other provisions) unless a draft of the regulations has been laid before and approved by a resolution of each House of Parliament.

(4) Before making any regulations under –

[(za) section 178A(4), if the regulations add an offence,]
[(zb) section 181A(8), if the regulations add a condition,]
(a) Part 8 (charity accounts, reports and returns), or
(b) section 245 or 246 (certain powers to make regulations about CIOs),

the Minister must consult such persons or bodies of persons as the Minister considers appropriate.

NOTES

Sub-s (1) amended by the Charities (Protection and Social Investment) Act 2016, ss 9(1), (18), (19), 10(1), (6) partly as from 1 October 2016 and fully as from a date to be appointed.

Sub-s (2) amended by the Charities (Protection and Social Investment) Act 2016, ss 9(1), (18), (20), 10(1), (7) partly as from 1 October 2016 and fully as from a date to be appointed.

Sub-s (4) amended by the Charities (Protection and Social Investment) Act 2016, s 9(1), (18), (21), 10(1), (8) partly as from 1 October 2016 and fully as from a date to be appointed.

349 Orders subject to affirmative procedure etc

(1) Section 347(2) (negative procedure) does not apply to –

(a) an order under section 23 (power to amend Schedule 3 so as to add or remove exempt charities);

(b) an order under section 73(2) (powers to make schemes altering provision made by Acts etc);

(c) an order under section 190 (power to amend provisions relating to indemnity insurance for charity trustees and trustees);

(d) an order under section 324 (power to amend provisions relating to appeals and applications to Tribunal).

(2) No order within subsection (1)(a) may be made (whether alone or with other provisions) unless a draft of the order has been laid before and approved by a resolution of each House of Parliament.

(3) No order within subsection (1)(c) or (d) may be made unless a draft of the order has been laid before and approved by a resolution of each House of Parliament.

(4) If a draft of an instrument containing an order under section 23 would, apart from this subsection, be treated for the purposes of the Standing Orders of either House of Parliament as a hybrid instrument, it is to proceed in that House as if it were not such an instrument.

Interpretation

350 Connected person: child, spouse and civil partner

(1) In sections 118(2)(c), 188(1)(a), 200(1)(a) and 249(2)(a), 'child' includes a stepchild and an illegitimate child.

(2) For the purposes of sections 118(2)(e), 188(1)(b), 200(1)(b) and 249(2)(b) –

(a) a person living with another as that person's husband or wife is to be treated as that person's spouse;

(b) where two people of the same sex are not civil partners but live together as if they were, each of them is to be treated as the civil partner of the other.

351 Connected person: controlled institution

For the purposes of sections 118(2)(g), 157(1)(a), 188(1)(d), 200(1)(d) and 249(2)(d), a person controls an institution if the person is able to secure that the affairs of the institution are conducted in accordance with the person's wishes.

352 Connected person: substantial interest in body corporate

(1) For the purposes of sections 118(2)(h), 157(1)(b), 188(1)(e), 200(1)(e) and 249(2)(e), any such connected person as is there mentioned has a substantial interest in a body corporate if the person or institution in question –

(a) is interested in shares comprised in the equity share capital of that body of a nominal value of more than one-fifth of that share capital, or

(b) is entitled to exercise, or control the exercise of, more than one-fifth of the voting power at any general meeting of that body.

(2) The rules set out in Schedule 1 to the Companies Act 2006 (rules for interpretation of certain provisions of that Act) apply for the purposes of subsection (1) as they apply for the purposes of section 254 of that Act ('connected persons' etc).

(3) In this section 'equity share capital' and 'share' have the same meaning as in that Act.

353 Minor definitions

(1) In this Act, except in so far as the context otherwise requires –

'company' means a company registered under the Companies Act 2006 in England and Wales or Scotland;

'the court' means –

(a) the High Court, and

(b) within the limits of its jurisdiction, any other court in England and Wales having a jurisdiction in respect of charities concurrent (within any limit of area or amount) with that of the High Court,

and includes any judge or officer of the court exercising the jurisdiction of the court;

'ecclesiastical charity' has the same meaning as in the Local Government Act 1894;

'financial year' –

(a) in relation to a charitable company, is to be construed in accordance with section 390 of the Companies Act 2006, and

(b) in relation to any other charity, is to be construed in accordance with regulations made by virtue of section 132(3);

but this is subject to any provision of regulations made by virtue of section 142(3) (financial years of subsidiary undertakings);

'gross income', in relation to a charity, means its gross recorded income from all sources including special trusts;

'independent examiner', in relation to a charity, means such a person as is mentioned in section 145(1)(a);

'members', in relation to a charity with a body of members distinct from the charity trustees, means any of those members;

'the Minister' means the Minister for the Cabinet Office;

'trusts' –

(a) in relation to a charity, means the provisions establishing it as a charity and regulating its purposes and administration, whether those provisions take effect by way of trust or not, and

(b) in relation to other institutions has a corresponding meaning.

(2) In this Act, except in so far as the context otherwise requires, 'document' includes information recorded in any form, and, in relation to information recorded otherwise than in legible form –

(a) any reference to its production is to be read as a reference to the provision of a copy of it in legible form, and
(b) any reference to the provision of a copy of, or extract from, it is accordingly to be read as a reference to the provision of a copy of, or extract from, it in legible form.

(3) A charity is to be treated for the purposes of this Act as having a permanent endowment unless all property held for the purposes of the charity may be expended for those purposes without distinction between –
(a) capital, and
(b) income;

and in this Act 'permanent endowment' means, in relation to any charity, property held subject to a restriction on its being expended for the purposes of the charity.

PART 19
FINAL PROVISIONS

354 Amendments etc

(1) Schedule 7 contains consequential amendments.

(2) Schedule 8 contains transitional provisions and savings.

(3) Schedule 9 contains transitory modifications.

(4) Schedule 10 contains repeals and revocations.

355 Commencement

This Act comes into force at the end of the period of 3 months beginning with the day on which it is passed.

356 Extent

(1) Subject to subsections (2) to (7), this Act extends to England and Wales only.

(2) Chapter 1 of Part 1 (meaning of 'charity' and 'charitable' purpose: general) –
(a) extends also to Scotland, but affects the law of Scotland only so far as mentioned in section 7;
(b) extends also to Northern Ireland, but affects the law of Northern Ireland only so far as mentioned in section 8.

(3) In Part 5 (information powers), sections 54 to 59 (disclosure of information to and by Commission) extend to the whole of the United Kingdom.

(4) In Part 6 (application of property cy-près etc) –
(a) section 68(3) and (4) (amendment of Royal charters by Order in Council where body corporate the subject of a scheme), and
(b) sections 96 to 104 (common investment or deposit funds),

extend also to Northern Ireland.

(5) Paragraph 2 of Schedule 7 (construction of references in enactments and documents to Charity Commissioners for England and Wales) extends also to Scotland and Northern Ireland.

(6) Subject to any provision made by Schedule 7, any amendment, repeal or revocation made by Schedule 7 or 10 has the same extent as the enactment or provision to which it relates.

(7) In Part 2 of Schedule 8 (transitionals and savings: recreational etc purposes) –

(a) paragraphs 9 to 12 extend also to Scotland but paragraphs 10 and 12 affect the law of Scotland only so far as mentioned in those paragraphs;
(b) paragraphs 9 to 11 and 13 extend also to Northern Ireland but paragraphs 10 and 13 affect the law of Northern Ireland only so far as mentioned in those paragraphs.

357 Index of defined expressions

Schedule 11 lists the places where some of the expressions used in this Act are defined or otherwise explained.

358 Short title

This Act may be cited as the Charities Act 2011.

SCHEDULE 1
The Charity Commission

Section 13

Membership

1 (1) The Commission is to consist of –

(a) a person appointed by the Minister to chair the Commission, and
(b) at least 4, but not more than 8, other members appointed by the Minister.

(2) The Minister must exercise the power in sub-paragraph (1) so as to secure that –

(a) the knowledge and experience of the members of the Commission (taken together) includes knowledge and experience of the matters mentioned in sub-paragraph (3),
(b) at least two members have a 7 year general qualification within the meaning of section 71 of the Courts and Legal Services Act 1990, and
(c) at least one member –
   (i) knows about conditions in Wales, and
   (ii) has been appointed following consultation with the Welsh Ministers.

(3) The matters are –

(a) the law relating to charities,
(b) charity accounts and the financing of charities, and
(c) the operation and regulation of charities of different sizes and descriptions.

(4) In sub-paragraph (2)(c) 'member' does not include the person appointed to chair the Commission.

Terms of appointment and remuneration

2 The members of the Commission hold and vacate office as such in accordance with the terms of their respective appointments.

3 (1) An appointment of a person to hold office as a member of the Commission must be for a term of no more than 3 years.

(2) A person holding office as a member of the Commission –

(a) may resign that office by giving notice in writing to the Minister, and
(b) may be removed from office by the Minister on the ground of incapacity or misbehaviour.

(3) Before removing a member of the Commission the Minister must consult –

(a) the Commission, and
(b) if the member was appointed following consultation with the Welsh Ministers, the Welsh Ministers.

(4) No person may hold office as a member of the Commission for more than 10 years in total.

(5) For the purposes of sub-paragraph (4), time spent holding office as a Charity Commissioner for England and Wales counts as time spent holding office as a member of the Commission.

4 (1) The Commission must pay to its members such remuneration, and such other allowances, as may be determined by the Minister.

(2) The Commission must, if required to do so by the Minister –

(a) pay such pension, allowances or gratuities as may be determined by the Minister to or in respect of a person who is or has been a member of the Commission, or
(b) make such payments as may be so determined towards provision for the payment of a pension, allowances or gratuities to or in respect of such a person.

(3) Sub-paragraph (4) applies if the Minister determines that there are special circumstances which make it right for a person ceasing to hold office as a member of the Commission to receive compensation.

(4) The Commission must pay to the person a sum by way of compensation of such amount as may be determined by the Minister.

Staff

5 (1) The Commission –

(a) must appoint a chief executive, and
(b) may appoint such other staff as it may determine.

(2) The terms and conditions of service of persons appointed under sub-paragraph (1) are to be such as the Commission may determine with the approval of the Minister for the Civil Service.

Committees

6 (1) The Commission may establish committees and any committee of the Commission may establish sub-committees.

(2) The members of a committee of the Commission may include persons who are not members of the Commission (and the members of a sub-committee may include persons who are not members of the committee or of the Commission).

Procedure etc

7 (1) The Commission may regulate its own procedure (including quorum).

(2) The validity of anything done by the Commission is not affected by –

(a) a vacancy among its members, or
(b) a defect in the appointment of a member.

Performance of functions

8 Anything authorised or required to be done by the Commission may be done by –

(a) any member or member of staff of the Commission who is authorised for that purpose by the Commission, whether generally or specially;
(b) any committee of the Commission which has been so authorised.

Evidence

9 The Documentary Evidence Act 1868 has effect as if –

(a) the Commission were mentioned in the first column of the Schedule to that Act,
(b) any member or member of staff of the Commission authorised to act on behalf of the Commission were specified in the second column of that Schedule in connection with the Commission, and
(c) the regulations referred to in that Act included any document issued by or under the authority of the Commission.

Execution of documents

10 (1) A document is executed by the Commission by the fixing of its common seal to the document.

(2) But the fixing of that seal to a document must be authenticated by the signature of –

(a) any member of the Commission, or
(b) any member of its staff,

who is authorised for the purpose by the Commission.

(3) A document which is expressed (in whatever form of words) to be executed by the Commission and is signed by –

(a) any member of the Commission, or
(b) any member of its staff,

who is authorised for the purpose by the Commission has the same effect as if executed in accordance with sub-paragraphs (1) and (2).

(4) A document executed by the Commission which makes it clear on its face that it is intended to be a deed has effect, upon delivery, as a deed; and it is to be presumed (unless a contrary intention is proved) to be delivered upon its being executed.

(5) In favour of a purchaser a document is to be treated as having been duly executed by the Commission if it purports to be signed on its behalf by –

(a) any member of the Commission, or
(b) any member of its staff;

and, if it makes it clear on its face that it is intended to be a deed, it is to be treated as having been delivered upon its being executed.

(6) For the purposes of this paragraph –

'authorised' means authorised whether generally or specially, and
'purchaser' –
(a) means a purchaser in good faith for valuable consideration, and
(b) includes a lessee, mortgagee or other person who for valuable consideration acquired an interest in property.

Annual report

11 (1) As soon as practicable after the end of each financial year the Commission must publish a report on –

(a) the discharge of its functions,
(b) the extent to which, in its opinion, its objectives (see section 14) have been met,
(c) the performance of its general duties (see section 16), and
(d) the management of its affairs,

during that year.

(2) The Commission must lay a copy of each such report before Parliament.

(3) 'Financial year' means the 12 months ending with 31 March in any year.

Annual public meeting

12 (1) The Commission must hold a public meeting ('the annual meeting') for the purpose of enabling a report under paragraph 11 to be considered.
(2) The annual meeting must be held within the period of 3 months beginning with the day on which the report is published.

(3) The Commission must organise the annual meeting so as to allow –

(a) a general discussion of the contents of the report which is being considered, and
(b) a reasonable opportunity for those attending the meeting to put questions to the Commission about matters to which the report relates.

(4) But subject to sub-paragraph (3) the annual meeting is to be organised and conducted in such a way as the Commission considers appropriate.

(5) The Commission must –

(a) take such steps as are reasonable in the circumstances to ensure that notice of the annual meeting is given to every registered charity, and
(b) publish notice of the annual meeting in the way appearing to it to be best calculated to bring it to the attention of members of the public.

(6) Each such notice must –

(a) give details of the time and place at which the meeting is to be held,
(b) set out the proposed agenda for the meeting,
(c) indicate the proposed duration of the meeting, and
(d) give details of the Commission's arrangements for enabling persons to attend.

(7) If the Commission proposes to alter any of the arrangements which have been included in notices given or published under sub-paragraph (5) it must –

(a) give reasonable notice of the alteration, and
(b) publish the notice in the way appearing to it to be best calculated to bring it to the attention of registered charities and members of the public.

SCHEDULE 2
The Official Custodian

Section 21

Status and official seal

1 The official custodian is a corporation sole whose official seal is to be officially and judicially noticed.

Expenses

2 The expenses of the official custodian (except those reimbursed to, or recovered by, the official custodian as trustee for any charity) are to be defrayed by the Commission.

Performance of functions and liability for loss or misapplication of property

3 Anything which is required to or may be done by, to or before the official custodian may be done by, to or before any member of the staff of the Commission generally or specially authorised by it to act for the official custodian during a vacancy in the official custodian's office or otherwise.

4 (1) The official custodian is not liable as trustee for any charity in respect of any loss or of the misapplication of any property unless it is occasioned by or through the wilful neglect or default of –

(a) the official custodian, or
(b) any person acting for the official custodian.

(2) But the Consolidated Fund is liable to make good to a charity any sums for which the official custodian may be liable because of any such neglect or default.

Accounts

5 The official custodian must –

(a) keep such books of account and such records in relation to them as may be directed by the Treasury, and
(b) prepare accounts, in such form, in such manner and at such times as may be directed by the Treasury.

6 The Comptroller and Auditor General must –

(a) examine, certify and report on the accounts so prepared, and
(b) send a copy of the certified accounts and the report to the Commission.

7 The Commission must publish and lay before Parliament a copy of the documents sent to it under paragraph 6(b).

SCHEDULE 3
Exempt Charities

Section 22

Institutions with an exemption from the Charitable Trusts Acts 1853 to 1939

1 (1) Any institution which, if the Charities Act 1960 had not been passed, would be exempted from the powers and jurisdiction, under the Charitable Trusts Acts 1853 to 1939, of –

(a) the Charity Commissioners for England and Wales, or
(b) the Minister of Education,

(apart from any power of the Commissioners or Minister to apply those Acts in whole or in part to charities otherwise exempt) by the terms of any enactment not contained in the Charitable Trusts Acts 1853 to 1939 other than section 9 of the Places of Worship Registration Act 1855.

(2) Sub-paragraph (1) does not include –

(a) any Investment Fund or Deposit Fund within the meaning of the Church Funds Investment Measure 1958,
(b) any investment fund or deposit fund within the meaning of the Methodist Church Funds Act 1960, or
(c) the representative body of the Welsh Church or property administered by it.

Educational institutions

2 The universities of Oxford, Cambridge, London, Durham, Newcastle and Manchester.

3 King's College London and Queen Mary and Westfield College in the University of London.

4 (1) Any of the following, if Her Majesty declares it by Order in Council to be an exempt charity for the purposes of this Act –

(a) a university in England,
(b) a university college in England, or
(c) an institution which is connected with a university in England or a university college in England.

(2) Sub-paragraph (1) does not include –

(a) any college in the university of Oxford;
(b) any college or hall in the university of Cambridge or Durham;
(c) any students' union.

(3) For the purposes of this paragraph –

(a) a university or university college is in England if its activities are carried on, or principally carried on, in England;
(b) the Open University is to be treated as a university in England.

5 (1) An English higher education corporation.

(2) For the purposes of this paragraph a higher education corporation is an English higher education corporation if the activities of the institution conducted by that corporation are carried on, or principally carried on, in England.

6 (1) A successor company to a higher education corporation at a time when the institution conducted by the company is eligible, by virtue of an order made under section 129 of the 1988 Act, to receive support from funds administered by the Higher Education Funding Council for England.

(2) In this paragraph 'the 1988 Act' means the Education Reform Act 1988 and 'successor company to a higher education corporation' has the meaning given by section 129(5) of the 1988 Act.

7 A further education corporation.

8 A qualifying Academy proprietor (as defined in section 12(2) of the Academies Act 2010).

9 The governing body of any foundation, voluntary or foundation special school.

10 Any foundation body established under section 21 of the School Standards and Framework Act 1998.

11 A sixth form college corporation (within the meaning of the Further and Higher Education Act 1992).

Museums, galleries etc

12 The Board of Trustees of the Victoria and Albert Museum.

13 The Board of Trustees of the Science Museum.

14 The Board of Trustees of the Armouries.

15 The Board of Trustees of the Royal Botanic Gardens, Kew.

16 The Board of Trustees of the National Museums and Galleries on Merseyside.

17 The trustees of the British Museum.

18 The trustees of the Natural History Museum.

19 The Board of Trustees of the National Gallery.

20 The Board of Trustees of the Tate Gallery.

21 The Board of Trustees of the National Portrait Gallery.

22 The Board of Trustees of the Wallace Collection.

23 The Trustees of the Imperial War Museum.

24 The Trustees of the National Maritime Museum.

25 The British Library Board.

Housing

26 Any registered society within the meaning of [the Co-operative and Community Benefit Societies Act 2014], if the society is also a non-profit registered provider of social housing.

27 Any registered society within the meaning of [the Co-operative and Community Benefit Societies Act 2014], if the society is also registered in the register of social landlords under Part 1 of the Housing Act 1996.

Connected institutions

28 (1) Any institution which –

(a) is administered by or on behalf of an institution included in any of paragraphs 1 to 8 and 11 to 25, and
(b) is established for the general purposes of, or for any special purpose of or in connection with, the institution mentioned in paragraph (a).

(2) Sub-paragraph (1) does not include –

(a) any college in the university of Oxford which is administered by or on behalf of that university;
(b) any college or hall in the university of Cambridge or Durham which is administered by or on behalf of that university;
(c) any student's union.

(3) Any institution which –

(a) is administered by or on behalf of a body included in paragraph 9 or 10, and
(b) is established for the general purposes of, or for any special purpose of or in connection with, that body or any foundation, voluntary or foundation special school or schools.

NOTES

Paras 26, 27 amended by the Co-operative and Community Benefit Societies Act 2014, s 151(1), Sch 4, Pt 2, paras 181, 183(1)–(3).

SCHEDULE 4
Enlargement of Areas of Local Charities

Section 62

1 Existing area	*2 Permitted enlargement*

1 Greater London	Any area which includes Greater London
2 Any area in Greater London and not in, or partly in, the City of London	(i) Any area in Greater London and not in, or partly in, the City of London; (ii) the area of Greater London exclusive of the City of London; (iii) any area which includes the area of Greater London, exclusive of the City of London; (iv) any area partly in Greater London and partly in any adjacent parish or parishes (civil or ecclesiastical), and not partly in the City of London.
3 A district	Any area which includes the district
4 A Welsh county or county borough	Any area which includes the county or county borough.
5 Any area in a district	(i) Any area in the district; (ii) the district; (iii) any area which includes the district; (iv) any area partly in the district and partly in any adjacent district or in any adjacent Welsh county or county borough.
6 Any area in a Welsh county or county borough	(i) Any area in the county or county borough; (ii) the county or county borough; (iii) any area which includes the county or county borough; (iv) any area partly in the county or county borough and partly in any adjacent Welsh county or county borough or in any adjacent district.
7 A parish (civil or ecclesiastical), or two or more parishes, or an area in a parish, or partly in each of two or more parishes.	Any area not extending beyond the parish or parishes which – (i) includes, or include, the area in column 1, or (ii) is, or are, adjacent to the area in column 1.
8 in Wales, a community, or two or more communities, or an area in a community, or partly in each of two or more communities.	Any area not extending beyond the community or communities which – (i) includes, or include, the area in column 1, or (ii) is, or are, adjacent to the area in column 1.

SCHEDULE 5
Court's Jurisdiction over Certain Charities Governed by or under Statute

Section 68

1 The court may by virtue of section 68(5) and (6) exercise its jurisdiction with respect to charities in relation to –

(a) charities established or regulated by any provision of the Seamen's Fund Winding-up Act 1851 repealed by the Charities Act 1960;
(b) charities established or regulated by schemes under the Endowed Schools Act 1869 to 1948, or section 75 of the Elementary Education Act 1870 or by schemes given effect under section 2 of the Education Act 1973 or section 554 of the Education Act 1996;
(c) fuel allotments, that is, land which, by any enactment relating to inclosure or any instrument having effect under such an enactment, is vested in trustees upon trust that the land or the rents and profits of the land are to be used for the purpose of providing poor persons with fuel;
(d) charities established or regulated by any provision of the Municipal Corporations Act 1883 repealed by the Charities Act 1960 or by any scheme having effect under any such provision;
(e) charities regulated by schemes under the London Government Act 1899;
(f) charities established or regulated by orders or regulations under section 2 of the Regimental Charitable Funds Act 1935;
(g) charities regulated by sections 298 to 302 or by any such order as is mentioned in section 303.

2 Regardless of anything in section 19 of the Commons Act 1876 a scheme for the administration of a fuel allotment (within the meaning of paragraph 1(c)) may provide –

(a) for the sale or letting of the allotment or any part of it, for the discharge of the land sold or let from any restrictions as to the use of it imposed by or under any enactment relating to inclosure and for the application of the sums payable to the trustees of the allotment in respect of the sale or lease,
(b) for the exchange of the allotment or any part of it for other land, for the discharge from any such restrictions of the land given in exchange by the trustees of the allotment, and for the application of any money payable to those trustees for equality of exchange, or
(c) for the use of the allotment or any part of it for any purposes specified in the scheme.

Schedule 6
Appeals and Applications to Tribunal

Sections 319, 321, 323 and 324

1 Decision, direction or order	*2 Appellants/applicants (see sections 319(2)(b) and 321(2)(b))*	*3 Tribunal powers if appeal or application allowed*
Decision of the Commission not to give a direction under section 12(1) or (2) in relation to an institution or a charity.	The persons are the trustees of the institution or charity concerned.	Power to quash the decision and (if appropriate) remit the matter to the Commission.
Decision of the Commission under section 30 or 34 – (a) to enter or not to enter an institution in the register of charities, or (b) to remove or not to remove an institution from the register.	The persons are – (a) the persons who are or claim to be the charity trustees of the institution, (b) (if a body corporate) the institution itself, and (c) any other person who is or may be affected by the decision.	Power to quash the decision and (if appropriate) – (a) remit the matter to the Commission; (b) direct the Commission to rectify the register.
Decision of the Commission not to make a determination under section 38(3) in relation to particular information contained in the register.	The persons are – (a) the charity trustees of the charity to which the information relates, (b) (if a body corporate) the charity itself, and (c) any other person who is or may be affected by the decision.	Power to quash the decision and (if appropriate) remit the matter to the Commission.
Direction given by the Commission under section 42 requiring the name of a charity to be changed.	The persons are – (a) the charity trustees of the charity to which the direction relates, (b) (if a body corporate) the charity itself, and (c) any other person who is or may be affected by the direction.	Power to – (a) quash the direction and (if appropriate) remit the matter to the Commission; (b) substitute for the direction any other direction which could have been given by the Commission.
Decision of the Commission to institute an inquiry under section 46 with regard to a particular institution.	The persons are – (a) the persons who have control or management of the institution, and (b) (if a body corporate) the institution itself.	Power to direct the Commission to end the inquiry.

1 Decision, direction or order	*2 Appellants/applicants (see sections 319(2)(b) and 321(2)(b))*	*3 Tribunal powers if appeal or application allowed*
Decision of the Commission to institute an inquiry under section 46 with regard to a class of institutions.	The persons are – (a) the persons who have control or management of any institution which is a member of the class of institutions, and (b) (if a body corporate) any such institution.	Power to – (a) direct the Commission that the inquiry should not consider a particular institution; (b) direct the Commission to end the inquiry.
Order made by the Commission under section 52 requiring a person to supply information or a document.	The persons are any person who is required to supply the information or document.	Power to – (a) quash the order; (b) substitute for all or part of the order any other order which could have been made by the Commission.
Order made by the Commission under section 69(1) (including such an order made by virtue of section 92(2)).	The persons are – (a) in a section 69(1)(a) case, the charity trustees of the charity to which the order relates or (if a body corporate) the charity itself, (b) in a section 69(1)(b) case, any person discharged or removed by the order, and (c) any other person who is or may be affected by the order.	Power to – (a) quash the order in whole or in part and (if appropriate) remit the matter to the Commission; (b) substitute for all or part of the order any other order which could have been made by the Commission; (c) add to the order anything which could have been contained in an order made by the Commission.
Order made by the Commission under section 76(3) in relation to a charity.	The persons are – (a) the charity trustees of the charity, (b) (if a body corporate) the charity itself, (c) in a section 76(3)(a) case, any person suspended by the order, and (d) any other person who is or may be affected by the order.	Power to – (a) quash the order in whole or in part and (if appropriate) remit the matter to the Commission; (b) substitute for all or part of the order any other order which could have been made by the Commission; (c) add to the order anything which could have been contained in an order made by the Commission.

1 Decision, direction or order	*2 Appellants/applicants (see sections 319(2)(b) and 321(2)(b))*	*3 Tribunal powers if appeal or application allowed*
Decision of the Commission – (a) to discharge an order following a review under section 76(6), or (b) not to discharge an order following such a review.	The persons are – (a) the charity trustees of the charity to which the order relates, (b) (if a body corporate) the charity itself, (c) if the order in question was made under section 76(3)(a), any person suspended by it, and (d) any other person who is or may be affected by the order.	Power to – (a) quash the decision and (if appropriate) remit the matter to the Commission; (b) make the discharge of the order subject to savings or other transitional provisions; (c) remove any savings or other transitional provisions to which the discharge of the order was subject; (d) discharge the order in whole or in part (whether subject to any savings or other transitional provisions or not).
Order made by the Commission under section 79(2) [or (4)] in relation to a charity.	The persons are – (a) the charity trustees of the charity, (b) (if a body corporate) the charity itself, (c) in a section [79(4)] case, any person removed by the order, and (d) any other person who is or may be affected by the order.	Power to – (a) quash the order in whole or in part and (if appropriate) remit the matter to the Commission; (b) substitute for all or part of the order any other order which could have been made by the Commission; (c) add to the order anything which could have been contained in an order made by the Commission.
Order made by the Commission under section 80(1) removing a charity trustee.	The persons are – (a) the charity trustee, (b) the remaining charity trustees of the charity of which that trustee was a charity trustee, (c) (if a body corporate) the charity itself, and (d) any other person who is or may be affected by the order.	Power to – (a) quash the order in whole or in part and (if appropriate) remit the matter to the Commission; (b) substitute for all or part of the order any other order which could have been made by the Commission; (c) add to the order anything which could have been contained in an order made by the Commission.

1 Decision, direction or order	*2 Appellants/applicants (see sections 319(2)(b) and 321(2)(b))*	*3 Tribunal powers if appeal or application allowed*
Order made by the Commission under section 80(2) appointing a charity trustee.	The persons are – (a) the other charity trustees of the charity, (b) (if a body corporate) the charity itself, and (c) any other person who is or may be affected by the order.	Power to – (a) quash the order in whole or in part and (if appropriate) remit the matter to the Commission; (b) substitute for all or part of the order any other order which could have been made by the Commission; (c) add to the order anything which could have been contained in an order made by the Commission.
Order made by the Commission under section 83(2) which suspends a person's membership of a charity.	The persons are – (a) the person whose membership is suspended by the order, and (b) any other person who is or may be affected by the order.	Power to quash the order and (if appropriate) remit the matter to the Commission.
Order made by the Commission under section 84(2) which directs a person to take action specified in the order.	The persons are any person who is directed by the order to take the specified action.	Power to quash the order and (if appropriate) remit the matter to the Commission.
[Order made by the Commission under section 84A(2) which directs a person not to take action specified in the order.	The persons are any person who is directed by the order not to take the specified action.	Power to quash the order and (if appropriate) remit the matter to the Commission.]
[Order made by the Commission under section 84B(2) which directs a person to take action specified in the order.	The persons are any person who is directed by the order to take the specified action.	Power to quash the order and (if appropriate) remit the matter to the Commission.
Order made by the Commission under section 84B(2) which directs a person to do anything that could otherwise only be done by the members of the charity or any of them.	The persons are the member or members concerned.	Power to quash the order and (if appropriate) remit the matter to the Commission.]

1 Decision, direction or order	*2 Appellants/applicants (see sections 319(2)(b) and 321(2)(b))*	*3 Tribunal powers if appeal or application allowed*
Order made by the Commission under section 85(2) which directs a person to apply property in a specified manner.	The persons are any person who is directed by the order to apply the property in the specified manner.	Power to quash the order and (if appropriate) remit the matter to the Commission.
Order made by the Commission under section 87(3) in relation to a person holding property on behalf of a body entered in the Scottish Charity Register or of any person concerned in its management or control.	The persons are – (a) the person holding the property in question, and (b) any other person who is or may be affected by the order.	Power to quash the order and (if appropriate) remit the matter to the Commission.
Order made by the Commission under section 93(2) in relation to any land vested in the official custodian in trust for a charity.	The persons are – (a) the charity trustees of the charity, (b) (if a body corporate) the charity itself, and (c) any other person who is or may be affected by the order.	Power to – (a) quash the order and (if appropriate) remit the matter to the Commission; (b) substitute for the order any other order which could have been made by the Commission; (c) add to the order anything which could have been contained in an order made by the Commission.
Decision of the Commission not to make a common investment scheme under section 96.	The persons are – (a) the charity trustees of a charity which applied to the Commission for the scheme, (b) (if a body corporate) the charity itself, and (c) any other person who is or may be affected by the decision.	Power to quash the decision and (if appropriate) remit the matter to the Commission.
Decision of the Commission not to make a common deposit scheme under section 100.	The persons are – (a) the charity trustees of a charity which applied to the Commission for the scheme, (b) (if a body corporate) the charity itself, and (c) any other person who is or may be affected by the decision.	Power to quash the decision and (if appropriate) remit the matter to the Commission.

1 Decision, direction or order	*2 Appellants/applicants (see sections 319(2)(b) and 321(2)(b))*	*3 Tribunal powers if appeal or application allowed*
Decision by the Commission not to make an order under section 105 in relation to a charity.	The persons are – (a) the charity trustees of the charity, and (b) (if a body corporate) the charity itself.	Power to quash the decision and (if appropriate) remit the matter to the Commission.
Direction given by the Commission under section 107 in relation to an account held in the name of or on behalf of a charity.	The persons are – (a) the charity trustees of the charity, (b) (if a body corporate) the charity itself, and (c) any other person who is or may be affected by the order.	Power to – (a) quash the direction and (if appropriate) remit the matter to the Commission; (b) substitute for the direction any other direction which could have been given by the Commission; (c) add to the direction anything which could have been contained in a direction given by the Commission.
Order made by the Commission under section 112 for the assessment of a solicitor's bill.	The persons are – (a) the solicitor, (b) any person for whom the work was done by the solicitor, and (c) any other person who is or may be affected by the order.	Power to – (a) quash the order; (b) substitute for the order any other order which could have been made by the Commission; (c) add to the order anything which could have been contained in an order made by the Commission.
Decision of the Commission not to make an order under section 117 in relation to land held by or in trust for a charity.	The persons are – (a) the charity trustees of the charity, (b) (if a body corporate) the charity itself, and (c) any other person who is or may be affected by the decision.	Power to quash the decision and (if appropriate) remit the matter to the Commission.
Decision of the Commission not to make an order under section 124 in relation to a mortgage of land held by or in trust for a charity.	The persons are – (a) the charity trustees of the charity, (b) (if a body corporate) the charity itself, and (c) any other person who is or may be affected by the decision.	Power to quash the decision and (if appropriate) remit the matter to the Commission

1 Decision, direction or order	*2 Appellants/applicants (see sections 319(2)(b) and 321(2)(b))*	*3 Tribunal powers if appeal or application allowed*
Order made by the Commission under section 146(1) requiring the accounts of a charity to be audited.	The persons are – (a) the charity trustees of the charity, (b) (if a body corporate) the charity itself, and (c) any other person who is or may be affected by the order.	Power to – (a) quash the order; (b) substitute for the order any other order which could have been made by the Commission; (c) add to the order anything which could have been contained in an order made by the Commission.
Order made by the Commission under section 147(2) in relation to a charitable company.	The persons are – (a) the directors of the company, (b) the company itself, and (c) any other person who is or may be affected by the order.	Power to – (a) quash the order and (if appropriate) remit the matter to the Commission; (b) substitute for the order any other order which could have been made by the Commission; (c) add to the order anything which could have been contained in an order made by the Commission.
Order made by the Commission under section 147(5) in relation to a charitable company, or a decision of the Commission not to make such an order in relation to a charitable company.	The persons are – (a) the charity trustees of the company, (b) the company itself, (c) in the case of a decision not to make an order, the auditor, and (d) any other person who is or may be affected by the order or the decision.	Power to – (a) quash the order or decision and (if appropriate) remit the matter to the Commission; (b) substitute for the order any other order of a kind the Commission could have made; (c) make any order which the Commission could have made.
Order made by the Commission under section 153(1) requiring the group accounts of a parent charity to be audited.	The persons are – (a) the charity trustees of the parent charity, (b) (if a body corporate) the parent charity itself, and (c) any other person who is or may be affected by the order.	Power to – (a) quash the order; (b) substitute for the order any other order which could have been made by the Commission; (c) add to the order anything which could have been contained in an order made by the Commission.

1 Decision, direction or order	*2 Appellants/applicants (see sections 319(2)(b) and 321(2)(b))*	*3 Tribunal powers if appeal or application allowed*
Order made by the Commission under section 155 in relation to a charity, or a decision of the Commission not to make such an order in relation to a charity.	The persons are – (a) the charity trustees of the charity, (b) (if a body corporate) the charity itself, (c) in the case of a decision not to make an order, the auditor, independent examiner or examiner, and (d) any other person who is or may be affected by the order or the decision.	Power to – (a) quash the order or decision and (if appropriate) remit the matter to the Commission; (b) substitute for the order any other order of a kind the Commission could have made; (c) make any order which the Commission could have made.
Order made by the Commission under section 155 in relation to a member of a group, or a decision of the Commission not to make such an order in relation to a member of a group.	The persons are – (a) the charity trustees of the member of the group, (b) (if a body corporate) the member of the group itself, (c) in the case of a decision not to make an order, the auditor, independent examiner or examiner, and (d) any other person who is or may be affected by the order or the decision.	Power to – (a) quash the order or decision and (if appropriate) remit the matter to the Commission; (b) substitute for the order any other order of a kind the Commission could have made; (c) make any order which the Commission could have made.
Decision of the Commission under section 168(3) to request charity trustees to prepare an annual report for a charity.	The persons are – (a) the charity trustees, and (b) (if a body corporate) the charity itself.	Power to quash the decision and (if appropriate) remit the matter to the Commission.
Decision of the Commission not to dispense with the requirements of section 169(1) in relation to a charity or class of charities.	The persons are the charity trustees of any charity affected by the decision.	Power to quash the decision and (if appropriate) remit the matter to the Commission.

1 Decision, direction or order	*2 Appellants/applicants (see sections 319(2)(b) and 321(2)(b))*	*3 Tribunal powers if appeal or application allowed*
Decision of the Commission under section 181(2) to waive, or not to waive, a person's disqualification.	The persons are – (a) the person who applied for the waiver, and (b) any other person who is or may be affected by the decision.	Power to – (a) quash the decision and (if appropriate) remit the matter to the Commission; (b) substitute for the decision any other decision of a kind which could have been made by the Commission.
[Order made by the Commission under section 181A.	The persons are the person who is the subject of the order.	Power to – (a) quash the order in whole or in part and (if appropriate) remit the matter to the Commission; (b) substitute for all or part of the order any other order which could have been made by the Commission; (c) add to the order anything which could have been contained in an order made by the Commission.
Order made by the Commission under section 181B(4).	The persons are the person who is the subject of the order.	Power to – (a) quash the order in whole or in part and (if appropriate) remit the matter to the Commission; (b) substitute for all or part of the order any other order which could have been made by the Commission; (c) add to the order anything which could have been contained in an order made by the Commission.

1 Decision, direction or order	*2 Appellants/applicants (see sections 319(2)(b) and 321(2)(b))*	*3 Tribunal powers if appeal or application allowed*
Decision of the Commission – (a) to discharge an order following a review under section 181B(7), or (b) not to discharge an order following such a review.	The persons are – (a) the person who is the subject of the order, (b) the charity trustees of the charity to which the order relates, (c) (if a body corporate) the charity itself, and (d) any other person who is or may be affected by the order.	Power to – (a) quash the decision and (if appropriate) remit the matter to the Commission; (b) make the discharge of the order subject to savings or other transitional provisions; (c) remove any savings or other transitional provisions to which the discharge of the order was subject; (d) discharge the order in whole or in part (whether subject to any savings or other transitional provisions or not).
Decision of the Commission under section 181D not to revoke or vary an order under section 181A.	The persons are the person who is the subject of the order.	Power to – (a) quash the decision and (if appropriate) remit the matter to the Commission; (b) substitute for the decision any other decision of a kind which could have been made by the Commission.]
Order made by the Commission under section 184(3) in relation to a person who has acted as charity trustee or trustee for a charity.	The persons are – (a) the person subject to the order, and (b) any other person who is or may be affected by the order.	Power to – (a) quash the order and (if appropriate) remit the matter to the Commission; (b) substitute for the order any other order which could have been made by the Commission.
Order made by the Commission under section 186(5) or (6) requiring a trustee or connected person to repay, or not to receive, remuneration.	The persons are – (a) the trustee or connected person, (b) the other charity trustees of the charity concerned, and (c) any other person who is or may be affected by the order.	Power to – (a) quash the order and (if appropriate) remit the matter to the Commission; (b) substitute for the order any other order which could have been made by the Commission.

1 Decision, direction or order	*2 Appellants/applicants (see sections 319(2)(b) and 321(2)(b))*	*3 Tribunal powers if appeal or application allowed*
Decision of the Commission to give, or withhold, consent under section 198(1) or 201(1) in relation to a charitable company.	The persons are – (a) the charity trustees of the company, (b) the company itself, and (c) any other person who is or may be affected by the decision.	Power to quash the decision and (if appropriate) remit the matter to the Commission.
Decision of the Commission to grant an application under section 207 for the constitution of a CIO and its registration as a charity.	The persons are any person (other than the persons who made the application) who is or may be affected by the decision.	Power to quash the decision and (if appropriate) – (a) remit the matter to the Commission; (b) direct the Commission to rectify the register of charities.
Decision of the Commission under section 208 to refuse an application for the constitution of a CIO and its registration as a charity.	The persons are – (a) the persons who made the application, and (b) any other person who is or may be affected by the decision.	Power to – (a) quash the decision and (if appropriate) remit the matter to the Commission; (b) direct the Commission to grant the application.
Decision of the Commission under section 227 to refuse to register an amendment to the constitution of a CIO.	The persons are – (a) the CIO, (b) the charity trustees of the CIO, and (c) any other person who is or may be affected by the decision.	Power to quash the decision and (if appropriate) – (a) remit the matter to the Commission; (b) direct the Commission to register the amendment.
Decision of the Commission under section 231 to refuse an application for the conversion of a charitable company or a registered society into a CIO and the CIO's registration as a charity.	The persons are – (a) the charity which made the application, (b) the charity trustees of the charity, and (c) any other person who is or may be affected by the decision.	Power to – (a) quash the decision and (if appropriate) remit the matter to the Commission; (b) direct the Commission to grant the application.

1 Decision, direction or order	*2 Appellants/applicants (see sections 319(2)(b) and 321(2)(b))*	*3 Tribunal powers if appeal or application allowed*
Decision of the Commission to grant an application under section 235 for the amalgamation of two or more CIOs and the incorporation and registration as a charity of a new CIO as their successor.	The persons are any creditor of any of the CIOs being amalgamated.	Power to quash the decision and (if appropriate) remit the matter to the Commission.
Decision of the Commission under section 237 to refuse an application for the amalgamation of two or more CIOs and the incorporation and registration as a charity of a new CIO as their successor.	The persons are – (a) the CIOs which applied for the amalgamation, (b) the charity trustees of the CIOs, and (c) any other person who is or may be affected by the decision.	Power to – (a) quash the decision and (if appropriate) remit the matter to the Commission; (b) direct the Commission to grant the application.
Decision of the Commission to confirm a resolution passed by a CIO under section 240(1).	The persons are any creditor of the CIO.	Power to quash the decision and (if appropriate) remit the matter to the Commission.
Decision of the Commission under section 242 to refuse to confirm a resolution passed by a CIO.	The persons are – (a) the CIO, (b) the charity trustees of the CIO, and (c) any other person who is or may be affected by the decision.	Power to – (a) quash the decision and (if appropriate) remit the matter to the Commission; (b) direct the Commission to confirm the resolution.
[Decision of the Commission under regulations made by virtue of section 245 to grant an application for the dissolution of a CIO.	The persons are – (a) the CIO, (b) he charity trustees of the CIO, or the persons who were or claim to have been the charity trustees of the CIO immediately before it was dissolved, (c) any creditor of the CIO, and (d) any other person who is or may be affected by the decision.	Power to quash the decision and (if appropriate) remit the matter to the Commission.

1 Decision, direction or order	*2 Appellants/applicants (see sections 319(2)(b) and 321(2)(b))*	*3 Tribunal powers if appeal or application allowed*
Decision of the Commission under regulations made by virtue of section 245 not to grant an application for the dissolution of a CIO.	The persons are – (a) the CIO, (b) the charity trustees of the CIO, and (c) any other person who is or may be affected by the decision.	Power to – (a) quash the decision and (if appropriate) remit the matter to the Commission, (b) direct the Commission to grant the application.
Decision of the Commission under regulations made by virtue of section 245 to dissolve a CIO which it has reasonable cause to believe is not in operation.	The persons are – (a) the persons who were or claim to have been the charity trustees of the CIO immediately before it was dissolved, (b) any creditor of the CIO, and (c) any other person who is or may be affected by the decision.	Power to quash the decision and (if appropriate) remit the matter to the Commission.
Decision of the Commission under regulations made by virtue of section 245 to dissolve a CIO it no longer considers to be a charity.	The persons are – (a) the persons who were or claim to have been the charity trustees of the CIO immediately before it was dissolved, (b) any creditor of the CIO, and (c) any other person who is or may be affected by the decision.	Power to quash the decision and (if appropriate) remit the matter to the Commission.
Decision of the Commission under regulations made by virtue of section 245 to dissolve a CIO which is being wound up.	The persons are – (a) the persons who were or claim to have been the charity trustees of the CIO immediately before it was dissolved, (b) the liquidator of the CIO (if any), (c) any creditor of the CIO, and (d) any other person who is or may be affected by the decision.	Power to quash the decision and (if appropriate) remit the matter to the Commission.

1 Decision, direction or order	*2 Appellants/applicants (see sections 319(2)(b) and 321(2)(b))*	*3 Tribunal powers if appeal or application allowed*
Order made by the Commission under regulations made by virtue of section 245 specifying the charitable purposes, charity or charities for which the official custodian holds on trust the property of a CIO which has been dissolved.	The persons are – (a) the persons who were or claim to have been the charity trustees of the CIO immediately before it was dissolved, and (b) any other person who is or may be affected by the order.	Power to – (a) quash the order in whole or in part and (if appropriate) remit the matter to the Commission, (b) substitute for all or part of the order any other order which could have been made by the Commission, (c) add to the order anything which could have been included in an order made by the Commission.
Order made by the Commission under regulations made by virtue of section 245 vesting property held by the official custodian in a charity or charities.	The persons are – (a) the persons who were or claim to have been the charity trustees of the CIO immediately before it was dissolved, and (b) any other person who is or may be affected by the order.	Power to – (a) quash the order in whole or in part and (if appropriate) remit the matter to the Commission, (b) substitute for all or part of the order any other order which could have been made by the Commission, (c) add to the order anything which could have been included in an order made by the Commission.
Decision of the Commission under regulations made by virtue of section 245 to restore or not to restore a CIO to the register.	The persons are – (a) the persons who were or claim to have been the charity trustees of the CIO immediately before it was dissolved, and (b) any other person who is or may be affected by the decision.	Power to quash the decision and (if appropriate) – (a) remit the matter to the Commission, (b) direct the Commission to rectify the register.]
Decision of the Commission – (a) to grant a certificate of incorporation under section 251(1) to the charity trustees of a charity, or (b) not to grant such a certificate.	The persons are – (a) the charity trustees of the charity, and (b) any other person who is or may be affected by the decision.	Power to quash – (a) the decision; (b) any conditions or directions inserted in the certificate;

1 Decision, direction or order	*2 Appellants/applicants (see sections 319(2)(b) and 321(2)(b))*	*3 Tribunal powers if appeal or application allowed*
Decision of the Commission to amend a certificate of incorporation under section 262(5).	The persons are – (a) the charity trustees of the charity, and (b) any other person who is or may be affected by the amended certificate of incorporation.	Power to quash the decision and (if appropriate) remit the matter to the Commission.
Decision of the Commission not to amend a certificate of incorporation under section 262(5).	The persons are – (a) the charity trustees of the charity, and (b) any other person who is or may be affected by the decision not to amend the certificate of incorporation.	Power to – (a) quash the decision and (if appropriate) remit the matter to the Commission; (b) make any order the Commission could have made under section 262(5).
Order of the Commission under section 263(1) or (2) which dissolves an incorporated body.	The persons are – (a) the charity trustees of the charity, and (b) any other person who is or may be affected by the order.	Power to – (a) quash the order and (if appropriate) remit the matter to the Commission; (b) substitute for the order any other order which could have been made by the Commission; (c) add to the order anything which could have been contained in an order made by the Commission.
Decision of the Commission to notify charity trustees under section 271(1) that it objects to a resolution of the charity trustees under section 268(1).	The persons are – (a) the charity trustees, and (b) any other person who is or may be affected by the decision.	Power to quash the decision.
Decision of the Commission to notify charity trustees under section 278(1) that it objects to a resolution of the charity trustees under section 275(2).	The persons are – (a) the charity trustees, and (b) any other person who is or may be affected by the decision.	Power to quash the decision.
Decision of the Commission not to concur under section 284 with a resolution of charity trustees under section 282(2).	The persons are – (a) the charity trustees, and (b) any other person who is or may be affected by the decision.	Power to quash the decision and (if appropriate) remit the matter to the Commission.

1 Decision, direction or order	*2 Appellants/applicants (see sections 319(2)(b) and 321(2)(b))*	*3 Tribunal powers if appeal or application allowed*
Decision of the Commission not to concur under section 291 with a resolution of charity trustees under section 289(2).	The persons are – (a) the charity trustees, (b) (if a body corporate) the charity itself, and (c) any other person who is or may be affected by the decision.	Power to quash the decision and (if appropriate) remit the matter to the Commission.
Decision of the Commission to withhold approval for the transfer of property from trustees to a parish or community council under section 298(2).	The persons are – (a) the trustees, (b) the parish or community council, and (c) any other person who is or may be affected by the decision.	Power to quash the decision and (if appropriate) remit the matter to the Commission.
Decision of the Commission to give or withhold consent under section 42(4) of the Companies Act 2006.	The persons are – (a) the charity trustees of the charitable company, (b) the company itself, and (c) any other person who is or may be affected by the decision.	Power to quash the decision and (if appropriate) remit the matter to the Commission.

NOTES

Entry relating to 'Order made by the Commission under section 79(2) or (4) in relation to a charity.' amended by the Charities (Protection and Social Investment) Act 2016, s 4(1), (6)(a), (b).

Entry relating to 'Order made by the Commission under section 84A(2) which directs a person not to take action specified in the order.' inserted by the Charities (Protection and Social Investment) Act 2016, s 6(1), (5).

Entry relating to 'Order made by the Commission under section 84B(2) which directs a person to take action specified in the order.' and entry relating to 'Order made by the Commission under section 84B(2) which directs a person to do anything that could otherwise only be done by the members of the charity or any of them.' inserted by the Charities (Protection and Social Investment) Act 2016, s 7(1), (5).

Entries from entry relating to 'Order made by the Commission under section 181A.' to entry relating to 'Decision of the Commission under section 181D not to revoke or vary an order under section 181A.' inserted by the Charities (Protection and Social Investment) Act 2016, s 10(1), (9) as from 1 October 2016.

Entries from entry relating to 'Decision of the Commission under regulations made by virtue of section 245 to grant an application for the dissolution of a CIO.' to entry relating to 'Decision of the Commission under regulations made by virtue of section 245 to restore or not to restore a CIO to the register.' inserted by SI 2012/3014, art 8.

SCHEDULE 7
Consequential Amendments

Section 354

PART 1
GENERAL AMENDMENTS

References to the Charitable Uses Act 1601 (c 4)

1 A reference in any enactment or document to a charity within the meaning of the Charitable Uses Act 1601 or the preamble to it is to continue to be construed as a reference to a charity as defined by section 1(1).

References to the Charity Commissioners for England and Wales

2 (1) Any enactment or document is to continue to have effect, so far as necessary in consequence of the transfer effected by section 6(4) of the Charities Act 2006, as if any reference to –

(a) the Charity Commissioners for England and Wales, or
(b) any Charity Commissioner for England and Wales,

were a reference to the Charity Commission for England and Wales.

(2) In sub-paragraph (1) 'enactment' includes –

(a) any provision of subordinate legislation (within the meaning of the Interpretation Act 1978),
(b) a provision of a Measure of the Church Assembly or of the General Synod of the Church of England, and
(c) any provision made by or under an Act of the Scottish Parliament or Northern Ireland legislation.

Application of certain enactments to trust corporations

3 (1) In the definition of 'trust corporation' contained in the provisions listed in sub-paragraph (2) the reference to a corporation appointed by the court in any particular case to be a trustee includes a reference to a corporation appointed by the Commission under this Act to be a trustee.

(2) The provisions are –

(a) section 117(1)(xxx) of the Settled Land Act 1925,
(b) paragraph (18) of section 68(1) of the Trustee Act 1925,
(c) section 205(1)(xxviii) of the Law of Property Act 1925,
(d) section 55(1)(xxvi) of the Administration of Estates Act 1925, and
(e) section 128 of the Senior Courts Act 1981 (c 54).

(3) This paragraph is to be treated as always having had effect.

(4) In sub-paragraph (2), the reference to section 128 of the Senior Courts Act 1981 is to be read –

(a) in relation to any time before 1 January 1982, as a reference to section 175(1) of the Supreme Court of Judicature (Consolidation) Act 1925, and

(b) in relation to any time on or after that date but before the day on which paragraph 1(2) of Schedule 11 to the Constitutional Reform Act 2005 came into force, as a reference to section 128 of the Supreme Court Act 1981 (c 54).

PART 2
PARTICULAR AMENDMENTS

Literary and Scientific Institutions Act 1854 (c 112)

4 (1) In section 6, for 'except with the consent of the Charity Commission or in accordance with such provisions of section 36(2) to (8) of the Charities Act 1993 as are applicable' substitute 'except with the consent of the Charity Commission or in accordance with such provisions of sections 117(2) and 119 to 121 of the Charities Act 2011 as are applicable'.

(2) This paragraph does not extend to Northern Ireland.

Places of Worship Registration Act 1855 (c 81)

5 (1) In section 9(1) –

(a) for 'shall, so far as it is a charity, be treated for the purposes of section 3A(4)(b) of the Charities Act 1993 (institutions to be excepted from registration under that Act) as if that provision applied to it' substitute 'is, so far as it is a charity, to be treated for the purposes of section 31(3) of the Charities Act 2011 (institutions required to be excepted from registration under that Act) as if that provision applied to it', and

(b) paragraph (b) continues to have effect with the substitution, for 'Charity Commissioners' of 'Charity Commission'.

(2) For section 9(2) substitute –

> '(2) Section 337 of the 2011 Act (provisions as to orders under that Act) applies to any order under subsection (1)(b) as it applies to orders under that Act.'

Places of Worship Sites Amendment Act 1882 (c 21)

6 In section 1(d) for 'except with the consent of the Charity Commission or in accordance with such provisions of section 36(2) to (8) of the Charities Act 1993 as are applicable' substitute 'except with the consent of the Charity Commission or in accordance with such provisions of sections 117(2) and 119 to 121 of the Charities Act 2011 as are applicable'.

Technical and Industrial Institutions Act 1892 (c 29)

7 In section 9(1), for 'with the consent of the Charity Commission or in accordance with such provisions of section 36(2) to (8) of the Charities Act 1993 as are applicable' substitute 'with the consent of the Charity Commission or in accordance with such provisions of sections 117(2) and 119 to 121 of the Charities Act 2011 as are applicable'.

Open Spaces Act 1906 (c 25)

8 (1) In section 4(1A)(b), for 'section 36(2) to (8) of the Charities Act 1993' substitute 'sections 117(2) and 119 to 121 of the Charities Act 2011'.

(2) For section 4(4) substitute –

> '(4) Section 337 of the Charities Act 2011 (provisions as to orders under that Act) applies to any order of the Charity Commission under this section as it applies to orders made by it under that Act.'

(3) This paragraph does not extend to Northern Ireland.

New Parishes Measure 1943 (No 1)

9 (1) For section 14(1)(b) substitute –

> '(b) any trustees for charitable purposes but (except in the case of an exempt charity within the meaning of the Charities Act 2011) only –
> (i) with the sanction of an order of the Charity Commission, or
> (ii) in accordance with such provisions of sections 117(2) and 119 to 121 of the Charities Act 2011 as are applicable;.'

(2) For section 14(4) substitute –

> '(4) Section 337 of the Charities Act 2011 (provisions as to orders under that Act) applies to any order under subsection (1)(b) as it applies to orders under that Act.'

10 In section 31, for 'the Charities Act 1993' substitute 'section 10 of the Charities Act 2011'.

London County Council (General Powers) Act 1947 (c xlvi)

11 For section 6(3) substitute –

> '(3) In relation to any disposition of land falling within section 117(1) of the Charities Act 2011, the Council or the borough council may, instead of acting with the sanction of an order of the court or of the Charity Commission, make the disposition in accordance with such provisions of sections 117(2) and 119 to 121 of that Act as are applicable.'

London County Council (General Powers) Act 1955 (c xxix)

12 For section 34(3) substitute –

> '(3) In relation to any disposition of land falling within section 117(1) of the Charities Act 2011, the Council may, instead of acting with the sanction of an order of the court or of the Charity Commission, make the disposition in accordance with such provisions of sections 117(2) and 119 to 121 of that Act as are applicable.'

Incumbents and Churchwardens (Trusts) Measure 1964 (No 2)

13 In section 1, in the definition of 'permanent trusts' for 'section 96(3) of the Charities Act 1993' substitute 'section 353(3) of the Charities Act 2011'.

14 . . .

Leasehold Reform Act 1967 (c 88)

15 In section 23(4), for 'section 36 of the Charities Act 1993' substitute 'sections 117 to 121 of the Charities Act 2011.'

16 . . .

Redundant Churches and other Religious Buildings Act 1969 (c 22)

17 (1) In section 4, for subsections (6) to (8A) substitute –

'(6) The Charity Commission may, on the application of the acquirer of the relevant premises, by order establish a scheme under section 69 of the Charities Act 2011 (Commission's concurrent jurisdiction with the High Court for certain purposes) making provision for the restoration of the relevant premises, or part of them, to use as a place of public worship.

(7) The Charity Commission may so establish any such scheme notwithstanding –

(a) anything in section 70(2) of that Act, or
(b) that the relevant charity has ceased to exist;

and if the relevant charity has ceased to exist, any such scheme may provide for the constitution of a charity by or in trust for which the relevant premises are to be held on the restoration of those premises, or part of them, to use as a place of public worship.

(8) The Charity Commission has the same jurisdiction and powers in relation to the establishment of a scheme under subsection (2) above as it has under the provisions of sections 69 to 71 of the Charities Act 2011 (except section 70(4) and (5)) in relation to the establishment of a scheme for the administration of a charity; and section 88 of that Act (publicity relating to schemes) accordingly has effect in relation to the establishment of a scheme under subsection (2) above as it has effect in relation to the establishment of a scheme for the administration of a charity.

(8A) Chapter 2 of Part 17 of, and Schedule 6 to, the Charities Act 2011 (appeals and applications to Tribunal) apply in relation to an order made by virtue of subsection (8) above as they apply in relation to an order made under section 69(1) of that Act.'

(2) In section 4(13), for the definition of 'charity' substitute –

'"charity" has the meaning given by section 10 of the Charities Act 2011'.

(3) In section 4(13), for the definition of 'the court' substitute –

'"the court" has the same meaning as in the Charities Act 2011;'.

18 In section 7, for subsection (2) substitute –

'(2) Nothing in this Act affects –

(a) any power of the court (within the meaning of the Charities Act 2011) or the Charity Commission to establish a scheme for the administration of a charity, or
(b) the power of the Charity Commission under section 105 of that Act to authorise dealings with trust property.'

Sharing of Church Buildings Act 1969 (c 38)

19 In section 2(4), for 'the Charities Act 1993' substitute 'the Charities Act 2011'.

20 (1) In section 8(1), for 'the Charities Act 1993' substitute 'the Charities Act 2011'.

(2) In section 8(2), for 'section 96(2) of the Charities Act 1993' substitute 'section 10(2) to (4) of the Charities Act 2011'.

(3) In section 8(3), for 'Section 36 of the Charities Act 1993 (restrictions on dispositions of charity land)' substitute 'Sections 117 to 121 of the Charities Act 2011 (restrictions on dispositions of charity land)'.

Synodical Government Measure 1969 (No 2)

21 (1) Amend Schedule 3 as follows.

(2) In Rule 46A(a), for 'section 72(1) of the Charities Act 1993 and the disqualification is not for the time being subject to a general waiver by the Charity Commission under subsection (4) of that section or to a waiver by it under that subsection' substitute 'section 178 of the Charities Act 2011 and the disqualification is not for the time being subject to a general waiver by the Charity Commission under section 181 of that Act or to a waiver by it under that section'.

(3) In Rule 54(1) –

(a) in the definition of 'auditor', for 'section 43(2) of the Charities Act 1993' substitute 'section 144(2) of the Charities Act 2011', and

(b) in the definition of 'independent examiner', for 'Section 43(3)(a) of the Charities Act 1993' substitute 'section 145(1)(a) of the Charities Act 2011'.

(4) In Section 4 of Appendix I, in Note 3, for 'section 72(1) of the Charities Act 1993 and the disqualification is not for the time being subject to a general waiver by the Charity Commission under subsection (4) of that section or to a waiver by it under that subsection' substitute 'section 178 of the Charities Act 2011 and the disqualification is not for the time being subject to a general waiver by the Charity Commission under section 181 of that Act or to a waiver by it under that section'.

(5) In Section 6 of Appendix I, in the Note, for 'section 72(1) of the Charities Act 1993 and the disqualification is not for the time being subject to a general waiver by the Charity Commission under subsection (4) of that section or to a waiver by it under that subsection' substitute 'section 178 of the Charities Act 2011 and the disqualification is not for the time being subject to a general waiver by the Charity Commission under section 181 of that Act or to a waiver by it under that section'.

(6) In Appendix II, in paragraph 16, 'the Charity Commission for an order for directions pursuant to section 44(2) of the Charities Act 1993' substitute 'the Charity Commission for an order for directions pursuant to section 155 of the Charities Act 2011'.

Local Government Act 1972 (c 70)

22 In section 11(3)(c), for 'section 79 of the Charities Act 1993 (parochial charities)' substitute 'sections 298 to 303 of the Charities Act 2011 (parochial charities)'.

23 In section 27F(6), for 'section 79 of the Charities Act 1993 (parochial charities)' substitute 'sections 298 to 303 of the Charities Act 2011 (parochial charities)'.

24 In section 27H(6), for 'section 79 of the Charities Act 1993 (parochial charities)' substitute 'sections 298 to 303 of the Charities Act 2011 (parochial charities)'.

25 In section 29(6), for 'section 79 of the Charities Act 1993 (parochial charities)' substitute 'sections 298 to 303 of the Charities Act 2011 (parochial charities)'.

26 In section 127(4) for 'the Charities Act 1993' substitute 'the Charities Act 2011'.

27 In section 131(3) –

(a) for 'section 36 of the Charities Act 1993 (restrictions on disposition of charity land)' substitute 'sections 117 to 121 of the Charities Act 2011 (restrictions on dispositions of charity land)', and

(b) for 'section 36(9)(a) of that Act (certain statutorily authorised transactions not to require the sanction of the Charity Commission)' substitute 'section 117(3)(a) (certain statutorily authorised dispositions not to require the sanction of the Charity Commission)'.

28 In Schedule 12A, for paragraphs 8(f) and 19(f) substitute –

'(f) the Charities Act 2011'.

Consumer Credit Act 1974 (c 39)

29 In section 189(1), in the definition of 'charity', for 'the Charities Act 1993' substitute 'the Charities Act 2011'.

Friendly Societies Act 1974 (c 46)

30 In section 32A(6), for 'as defined by section 1(1) of the Charities Act 2006', substitute 'as defined by section 1(1) of the Charities Act 2011,'.

House of Commons Disqualification Act 1975 (c 24)

31 Part 2 of Schedule 1 continues to include, at the appropriate place –

'The Charity Commission'.

Northern Ireland Assembly Disqualification Act 1975 (c 25)

32 Part 2 of Schedule 1 continues to include, at the appropriate place –

'The Charity Commission'.

Theatres Trust Act 1976 (c 27)

33 In section 2(2)(d), for 'sections 36 and 38 of the Charities Act 1993' substitute 'sections 117 to 121 and 124 of the Charities Act 2011'.

Endowments and Glebe Measure 1976 (No 4)

34 In section 11(2), for 'the Charity Commission or in accordance with such provisions of section 36(2) to (8) of the Charities Act 1993 as are applicable' substitute 'the Charity Commission or in accordance with such provisions of sections 117(2) and 119 to 121 of the Charities Act 2011 as are applicable'.

Interpretation Act 1978 (c 30)

35 In Schedule 1, for the definition of 'Charity Commission' substitute –

> '"Charity Commission" means the Charity Commission for England and Wales (see section 13 of the Charities Act 2011)'.

Ancient Monuments and Archaeological Areas Act 1979 (c 46)

36 In section 49(3), for 'the Charities Act 1993' substitute 'the Charities Act 2011'.

Disused Burial Grounds (Amendment) Act 1981 (c 18)

37 For section 6 substitute –

> **'6 Saving for Charity Commission**
>
> Nothing in this Act affects the charitable jurisdiction of the High Court or the Charity Commission and in particular, in the absence of appropriate provisions in the governing instrument of the charity concerning –
>
> (a) the future use of the said land, or
> (b) the application of the proceeds of sale of the whole or any part of it,
>
> it is under section 61 of the Charities Act 2011 the duty of the church or religious body owning the land or other trustees of the said land to make an application for the appropriate relief by way of a scheme'.

Pastoral Measure 1983 (No 1)

38 For section 55(1) substitute –

> '(1) The power of the court (as defined by the Charities Act 2011) to make schemes under its jurisdiction with respect to charities, and the power of the Charity Commission to make schemes under that Act, extend to the making of schemes with respect to consecrated chapels belonging to charities which are no longer needed for the purposes of the charity, and section 10(2)(c) of that Act shall not be taken as preventing the making of any such scheme'.

39 In section 63(3), for 'the Charities Act 1993' substitute 'the Charities Act 2011'.

40 In section 87(1), in the definition of 'charity', for 'section 96 of the Charities Act 1993' substitute 'section 10 of the Charities Act 2011'.

41 (1) Amend Schedule 3 as follows.

(2) In paragraph 11(6) –

(a) for 'section 16 of the Charities Act 1993' substitute 'section 69 of the Charities Act 2011', and
(b) for 'that section' substitute 'sections 69 to 71 of that Act'.

(3) In paragraph 16(1)(e) for 'section 16 of the Charities Act 1993' substitute 'section 69 of the Charities Act 2011'.

Greater London Council (General Powers) Act 1984 (c xxvii)

42 In section 10(2)(n), for 'the Charities Act 1993' substitute 'the Charities Act 2011'.

Housing Act 1985 (c 68)

43 In section 6A(5), for 'in accordance with section 3A of the Charities Act 1993' substitute 'in accordance with section 30 of the Charities Act 2011'.

44 In section 525, in the definition of 'charity trustees', for' the Charities Act 1993' substitute 'the Charities Act 2011'.

Housing Associations Act 1985 (c 69)

45 In section 10(1), for 'sections 36 and 38 of the Charities Act 1993' substitute 'sections 117 to 121 and 124 of the Charities Act 2011'.

46 In section 35(2)(c), for 'section 36 of the Charities Act 1993 (restrictions on dispositions of charity land)' substitute 'sections 117 to 121 of the Charities Act 2011 (restrictions on dispositions of charity land)'.

Coal Industry Act 1987 (c 3)

47 (1) In section 5(7), for 'the Charities Act 1993' substitute 'the Charities Act 2011'.

(2) For section 5(8) to (8B) substitute –

> '(8) Sections 70(1), 71, 73(1) to (6), 74, 88 and 89 of the Charities Act 2011 apply in relation to the powers of the Commission and the making of schemes under this section as they apply in relation to its powers and the making of schemes under that Act and sections 337 and 339 of that Act apply to orders and decisions under this section as they apply to orders and decisions under that Act.
>
> (8A) The Commission must not proceed under section 73 of that Act (as applied by subsection (8)) without the same application and notice to the trustees of the trust in question, as would be required if the Commission was proceeding under subsection (1); but on any application made with a view to a scheme under subsection (1) the Commission may proceed under that subsection or under section 73 of that Act (as so applied) as appears to it appropriate.
>
> (8B) Chapter 2 of Part 17 of, and Schedule 6 to, the Charities Act 2011 (appeals and applications to Tribunal) apply in relation to an order made under this section as they apply in relation to an order made under section 69(1) of that Act.'

Reverter of Sites Act 1987 (c 15)

48 For section 4(2) and (4) substitute –

> '(2) Chapter 2 of Part 17 of, and Schedule 6 to, the Charities Act 2011 (appeals and applications to Tribunal) apply in relation to an order made under section 2 above as they apply in relation to an order made under section 69(1) of that Act, except that the persons who may bring an appeal against an order made under section 2 above are –
>
> (a) the Attorney General;
> (b) the trustees of the trust established under the order;
> (c) a beneficiary of, or the trustees of, the trust in respect of which the application for the order had been made;
> (d) any person interested in the purposes for which the last-mentioned trustees or any of their predecessors held the relevant land before the cesser of use in consequence of which the trust arose under section 1 above;
> (e) any two or more inhabitants of the locality where that land is situated;

(f) any other person who is or may be affected by the order.

(4) Sections 337 and 339 of the Charities Act 2011 (supplemental provisions with respect to orders) apply in relation to orders under section 2 above as they apply in relation to orders under that Act.'

Education Reform Act 1988 (c 40)

49 In section 124(2)(fa), for '(within the meaning of section 69A of the Charities Act 1993)' substitute '(within the meaning of Part 11 of the Charities Act 2011)'.

50 For section 125A substitute –

'125A Charitable status of a higher education corporation

A higher education corporation shall be a charity and –

(a) an English higher education corporation is, in accordance with Schedule 3 to the Charities Act 2011, an exempt charity for the purposes of that Act, and
(b) a Welsh higher education corporation is, in accordance with regulations made in compliance with section 31(3) of that Act, excepted from registration under that Act.'

51 In section 128(5), for '"charitable purposes" has the same meaning as in the Charities Act 1993' substitute '"charitable purposes" has the meaning given by section 11 of the Charities Act 2011'.

Copyright, Designs and Patents Act 1988 (c 48)

52 In Schedule 6, in paragraph 7(3), for 'the Charities Act 1993' substitute 'the Charities Act 2011'.

Imperial College Act 1988 (c xxiv)

53 In section 10, for '"the Commissioners" and "the court" have the same meanings as in the Charities Act 1993' substitute the '"Commission" and the "court" have the same meanings as in the Charities Act 2011'.

54 (1) In section 17(1), for 'section 22 of the Charities Act 1960' substitute 'section 96 of the Charities Act 2011'.

(2) In section 17(2) –

(a) for 'the Commissioners' substitute 'the Commission', and
(b) for 'the said section 22' substitute 'section 96 of the 2011 Act'.

Courts and Legal Services Act 1990 (c 41)

55 In Schedule 11, for the entry beginning 'Member of the Charity Commission' substitute –

'Member of the Charity Commission appointed as provided in Schedule 1 to the Charities Act 2011'.

London Local Authorities Act 1991 (c xiii)

56 In section 4, in paragraph (d) of the definition of 'establishment for special treatment' for 'in accordance with section 3A of the Charities Act 1993 or is not required to be registered (by virtue of subsection (2) of that section)' substitute 'in accordance with section 30 of the Charities Act 2011 or is not required to be registered (by virtue of subsection (2) of that section)'.

Further and Higher Education Act 1992 (c 13)

57 In section 19(4)(bc), for '(within the meaning of section 69A of the Charities Act 1993)' substitute '(within the meaning of Part 11 of the Charities Act 2011)'.

58 For section 22A substitute –

> **'22A Charitable status of a further education corporation**
>
> A further education corporation shall be a charity (and, in accordance with Schedule 3 to the Charities Act 2011, is an exempt charity for the purposes of that Act).'

59 In section 27(5), for '"charitable purposes" has the same meaning as in the Charities Act 1993' substitute '"charitable purposes" has the meaning given by section 11 of the Charities Act 2011'.

60 In section 33F(6)(d), for '(within the meaning of section 69A of the Charities Act 1993)' substitute '(within the meaning of Part 11 of the Charities Act 2011)'.

61 In section 33M, for '(and, as a result of its inclusion in Schedule 2 to the Charities Act 1993, is an exempt charity for the purposes of that Act)' substitute '(and, as a result of its inclusion in Schedule 3 to the Charities Act 2011, is an exempt charity for the purposes of that Act)'.

62 In section 33N(10), for '"charitable purposes" has the same meaning as in the Charities Act 1993' substitute '"charitable purposes" has the meaning given by section 11 of the Charities Act 2011'.

63 In section 69 –

(a) in subsection (1A), for 'section 13 of the Charities Act 2006)' substitute 'section 25 of the Charities Act 2011)', and

(b) in subsection (1B), for 'section 10A of the Charities Act 1993' substitute 'section 56 or 57 of that Act'.

64 In section 79A –

(a) for 'section 13 of the Charities Act 2006)' substitute 'section 25 of the Charities Act 2011)', and

(b) for 'subsection (2) of that section' substitute 'section 26(2) of that Act'.

Charities Act 1992 (c 41)

65 (1) In section 58(1), in the definition of 'company' for 'section 97 of the Charities Act 1993' substitute 'section '353 of the Charities Act 2011'.

(2) In section 58(4), for 'as defined by section 2(1) of the Charities Act 2006' substitute 'as defined by section 2(1) of the Charities Act 2011'.

66 In section 63(2), for 'section 3 of the Charities Act 1993' substitute section 29 of the Charities Act 2011'.

Leasehold Reform, Housing and Urban Development Act 1993 (c 28)

67

In section 93(6)(a), for 'section 36 of the Charities Act 1993' substitute 'sections 117 to 121 of the Charities Act 2011'.

Environment Act 1995 (c 25)

68 In Schedule 9, in paragraph 15, for 'Sections 76 to 78 of the Charities Act 1993' substitute 'Sections 294 to 297 of the Charities Act 2011'.

Reserve Forces Act 1996 (c 14)

69 (1) In Schedule 5, in paragraph 2, in the definition of 'charity', for 'as it has under section 1(1) of the Charities Act 2006' substitute 'as it has under section 1(1) of the Charities Act 2011'.

(2) In paragraph 5 of that Schedule, for sub-paragraphs (2) and (3) substitute –

'(2) An application under this paragraph –

(a) may be made at any time within the period of 6 months beginning with the day on which the warrant comes into force; and

(b) is subject to subsections (2) to (5) of section 115 of the Charities Act 2011 (proceedings not to be begun without the consent of the Charity Commission or leave of a judge of the High Court),

and for the purposes of subsection (5) of that section an application for an order of the Commission authorising proceedings under this paragraph is deemed to be refused if it is not granted during the period of one month beginning with the day on which the application is received by the Commission.

(3) In this paragraph the 'court' has the same meaning as in the Charities Act 2011.

(3) For paragraph 6 substitute –

'6 In any case where –

(a) the Secretary of State requests the Charity Commission to make provision with respect to any charitable property which is held for the purposes of a unit of a reserve force that has been or is to be disbanded, or

(b) an order is made under paragraph 4 or 5 excluding any charitable property so held from the operation of paragraph 3(1),

the Commission may, regardless of anything in section 70(2) of the Charities Act 2011 (limit on jurisdiction to make schemes etc for the protection of charities), exercise its jurisdiction under section 69 with respect to the property to which the request or order relates.'

Trusts of Land and Appointment of Trustees Act 1996 (c 47)

70 In Schedule 1, in paragraph 4(2) –

(a) in paragraph (a), for 'section 37(1) nor section 39(1) of the Charities Act 1993' substitute 'section 122(2) nor section 125(1) of the Charities Act 2011', and

(b) in paragraph (b), for 'section 37(2) nor section 39(2)' substitute 'section 122(3) nor section 125(2)'.

Housing Act 1996 (c 52)

71 In section 58, for subsection (1) substitute –

(1) In this Part –

(a) 'trusts', in relation to a charity, has the same meaning as in the Charities Act 2011 and 'trustee' means a charitable trustee within the meaning of that Act, and

(b) 'registered charity' means a charity which is registered in accordance with section 30 of that Act.'

72 (1) Amend Schedule 1 as follows.

(2) In paragraph 4(2)(d), for 'section 72 of the Charities Act 1993' substitute 'section 178 of the Charities Act 2011'.

(3) For paragraph 18(4) substitute –

'(4) The charity must appoint a qualified auditor ('the auditor') to audit the accounts prepared in accordance with sub-paragraph (3) in respect of each period of account in which –

(a) the charity's gross income arising in connection with its housing activities exceeds the sum for the time being specified in section 144(1)(a) of the Charities Act 2011, or

(b) the charity's gross income arising in that connection exceeds the accounts threshold and at the end of that period the aggregate value of its assets (before deduction of liabilities) in respect of its housing activities exceeds the sum for the time being specified in section 144(1)(b) of that Act;

and in this sub-paragraph 'gross income' and 'accounts threshold' have the same meanings as in section 144 of that Act.'

(4) In paragraph 18A(2)(b), for 'the Charities Act 1993' substitute 'the Charities Act 2011'.

Housing Grants, Construction and Regeneration Act 1996 (c 53)

73 In section 95(6), for 'but otherwise has the same meaning as in the Charities Act 1993' substitute 'but otherwise has the same meaning as it has under section 10 of the Charities Act 2011'.

Education Act 1996 (c 56)

74 In section 537C –

(a) in subsection (1)(a), for 'section 13 of the Charities Act 2006)' substitute 'section 25 of the Charities Act 2011)', and

(b) in subsection (2), for 'section 10A of the Charities Act 1993' substitute 'section 56 or 57 of the Charities Act 2011'.

School Standards and Framework Act 1998 (c 31)

75 (1) In section 23, for subsection (1A) substitute –

'(1A) Any body to which subsection (1)(a) or (b) applies is, as a result of its inclusion in Schedule 3 to the Charities Act 2011, an exempt charity for the purposes of that Act.'

(2) In subsection (3), for', and is an institution to which section 3A(4)(b) of the Charities Act 1993 applies' substitute 'and is an institution which is to be treated for the purposes of section 31(3) of the Charities Act 2011 as if that provision applied to it.'

(3) For subsection (4)(a) substitute –

'(a) institution has the same meaning as in the Charities Act 2011;'.

76 In section 23A(10), in the definitions of 'charity trustee' and 'institution', for 'the Charities Act 1993' substitute 'the Charities Act 2011'.

77 In section 23B(2), for 'section 18 of the Charities Act 1993' substitute 'section 76 or sections 79 to 81 of the Charities Act 2011'.

78 In Schedule 1, for paragraph 10 substitute –

'10 An Education Action Forum shall be a charity and is an institution which is to be treated for the purposes of section 31(3) of the Charities Act 2011 (institutions required to be excepted from registration under that Act) as if that provision applied to it.'

79 In Schedule 22, in paragraph 8A(2)(c), for 'removed under subsection (4) of section 3 of the Charities Act 1993 from the register of charities kept under that section,' substitute 'removed under section 34 of the Charities Act 2011 from the register of charities kept under section 29 of that Act,'.

National Institutions Measure 1998 (No 1)

80 (1) In section 3(1), for 'Part VI of the Charities Act 1993' substitute 'Part 8 of the Charities Act 2011'.

(2) In section 3(2), for 'under subsection (2) of section 43 of that Act to carry out an audit under that subsection' substitute 'under subsection (2) of section 144 of that Act to carry out an audit under that subsection'.

(3) In section 3(3), for 'Part VI, to have been appointed in pursuance of the said section 43' substitute 'Part 8, to have been appointed in pursuance of the said section 144'.

Finance Act 1999 (c 16)

81 In Schedule 19, in paragraph 15 –

(a) in sub-paragraph (a), for 'or section 24 of the Charities Act 1993,' substitute ', section 24 of the Charities Act 1993 or section 96 of the Charities Act 2011,' and

(b) in sub-paragraph (b), for 'or section 25 of the Charities Act 1993' substitute ', section 25 of the Charities Act 1993 or section 100 of the Charities Act 2011'.

Cathedrals Measure 1999 (No 1)

82 In section 4(4), for 'section 72(1) of the Charities Act 1993' substitute 'section 178 of the Charities Act 2011'.

83 In section 15(1), in paragraph (iii) of the proviso, for 'section 36 of the Charities Act 1993,' substitute 'sections 117 to 121 of the Charities Act 2011,'.

84 In section 27(1), for 'section 43 of the Charities Act 1993' substitute 'section 144 of the Charities Act 2011'.

85 In section 34, for 'same meaning as in the Charities Act 1993' substitute 'meaning given by section 10 of the Charities Act 2011'.

Financial Services and Markets Act 2000 (c 8)

86 In Schedule 11A, in paragraph 7(2)(a), for the words from 'within the meaning of – to '(ii)' substitute

' –

(i) as defined by section 1(1) of the Charities Act 2011, or
(ii) within the meaning of'.

87 In Schedule 11B, in paragraph 12(4)(b), for 'or section 24 or 25 of the Charities Act 1993 (c 10)' substitute 'section 24 or 25 of the Charities Act 1993 or section 96 or 100 of the Charities Act 2011'.

Learning and Skills Act 2000 (c 21)

88 In section 143(6)(d), for 'the Charities Act 1993) substitute 'the Charities Act 2011)'.

Trustee Act 2000 (c 29)

89 In section 38 –

(a) in paragraph (a), for 'section 24 of the Charities Act 1993' substitute 'section 96 of the Charities Act 2011', and
(b) in paragraph (b), for 'section 25' substitute 'section 100'.

90 In section 39(1) –

(a) in the definition of 'charitable purposes', for 'has the same meaning as in the Charities Act 1993' substitute 'has the meaning given by section 11 of the Charities Act 2011', and
(b) in the definition of 'exempt charity' for 'the Charities Act 1993' substitute 'the Charities Act 2011'.

Criminal Justice and Court Services Act 2000 (c 43)

91 In section 42(1), for '"charity trustee" has the same meaning as in the Charities Act 1993' substitute '"charity trustee" has the same meaning as in the Charities Act 2011'.

Criminal Justice and Police Act 2001 (c 16)

92 In Part 1 of Schedule 1, for paragraph 56A and its heading substitute –

> **'56A Charities Act 2011**
>
> The power of seizure conferred by section 48(3) of the Charities Act 2011 (seizure of material for the purposes of an inquiry under section 46 of that Act).'

Churchwardens Measure 2001 (No 1)

93 In section 2(1), for 'under section 72(1) of the Charities Act 1993 (c 10) and the disqualification is not for the time being subject to a general waiver by the Charity Commission under subsection (4) of that section or to a waiver by it under that subsection' substitute 'under section 178 of the Charities Act 2011 and the disqualification is not for the time being subject to a general waiver by the Charity Commission under section 181 of that Act or to a waiver by it under that section'.

Land Registration Act 2002 (c 9)

94 In section 4(1)(aa), for 'section 83 of the Charities Act 1993' substitute 'section 334 of the Charities Act 2011'.

Licensing Act 2003 (c 17)

95 In section 16(3), omit the definition of 'charity'.

96 In Schedule 2, for paragraph 5(4) substitute –

> '(4) In sub-paragraph (1)(d) 'registered charity' means –
>
> (a) a charity which is registered in accordance with section 30 of the Charities Act 2011, or
>
> (b) a charity which by virtue of subsection (2) of that section is not required to be so registered.'

Higher Education Act 2004 (c 8)

97 In section 40 –

(a) in subsection (1A), for 'section 13 of the Charities Act 2006)' substitute 'section 25 of the Charities Act 2011)',

(b) in subsection (1B), for 'section 10A of the Charities Act 1993' substitute 'section 56 or 57 of the Charities Act 2011', and

(c) in subsection (3) for 'section 13 of the Charities Act 2006)' substitute 'section 25 of the Charities Act 2011)'.

Companies (Audit, Investigations and Community Enterprise) Act 2004 (c 27)

98 In section 54C(3), for '"exempt charity" has the same meaning as in the Charities Act 1993 (see section 96 of that Act)' substitute 'exempt charity has the same meaning as in the Charities Act 2011 (see section 22 of that Act).'

99 In section 63(1), in the definition of 'English charity' for 'as defined by section 1(1) of the Charities Act 2006' substitute 'as defined by section 1(1) of the Charities Act 2011'.

100 In Schedule 3, for paragraph 4 substitute –

> '4 The person appointed to chair the Charity Commission may make available to the Regulator, to assist in the exercise of the Regulator's functions –
>
> (a) any other member of the Commission appointed under paragraph 1(1) of Schedule 1 to the Charities Act 2011, or
>
> (b) any member of staff of the Commission appointed under paragraph 5(1) of that Schedule.'

Pensions Act 2004 (c 35)

101 In Schedule 3, for the entry relating to the Charity Commission substitute –

'The Charity Commission	Functions under the Charities Act 2006 or the Charities Act 2011.'

102 In Schedule 8, for the entry relating to the Charity Commission substitute –

'The Charity Commission	Functions under the Charities Act 2006 or the Charities Act 2011.'

Serious Organised Crime and Police Act 2005 (c 15)

103 In section 146(3)(b), for 'charity trustee (within the meaning of the Charities Act 1993 (c 10))' substitute 'charity trustee (within the meaning of the Charities Act 2011)'.

Education Act 2005 (c 18)

104 In section 92(5), for 'section 13 of the Charities Act 2006)' substitute 'section 25 of the Charities Act 2011)'.

Gambling Act 2005 (c 19)

105 In section 19(2)(a), for 'purposes which are exclusively charitable according to the law of England and Wales' substitute 'purposes which are exclusively charitable purposes (as defined by section 2 of the Charities Act 2011)'.

Charities and Trustee Investment (Scotland) Act 2005 (asp 10)

106 In section 36(1), for paragraphs (a) and (b) substitute –

> '(a) which is registered as a charity in England and Wales in accordance with section 30 of the Charities Act 2011, or
>
> (b) which, by virtue of subsection (2) of that section, is not required to register as a charity under that section.'

107 In section 69(2)(d)(i), after 'Wales under' insert 'section 79(2)(a) of the Charities Act 2011 or' and for '18(2)(i) of that Act' substitute '18(2)(i) of the 1993 Act'.

108 In section 96(3), for 'sections 24 and 25 of the Charities Act 1993 (c 10)' substitute 'sections 96 and 100 of the Charities Act 2011'.

Natural Environment and Rural Communities Act 2006 (c 16)

109 In section 81(2)(h), for 'section 13 of the Charities Act 2006)' substitute 'section 25 of the Charities Act 2011)'.

Education and Inspections Act 2006 (c 40)

110 In Schedule 2, in paragraph 10(2)(b), for 'charity trustee (within the meaning of the Charities Act 1993 (c 10))' substitute 'charity trustee (within the meaning of the Charities Act 2011)'.

National Health Service Act 2006 (c 41)

111 In section 217(5), for 'the court (as defined in the Charities Act 1993 (c 10))' substitute 'the court (as defined in the Charities Act 2011)'.

National Health Service (Wales) Act 2006 (c 42)

112 In section 165(5), for 'the court (as defined in the Charities Act 1993 (c 10))' substitute 'the court (as defined in the Charities Act 2011)'.

Companies Act 2006 (c 46)

113 In section 21(2)(a), for 'section 64 of the Charities Act 1993 (c 10)' substitute 'sections 197 and 198 of the Charities Act 2011'.

114 In section 31(4)(a), for 'section 64 of the Charities Act 1993 (c 10)' substitute 'sections 197 and 198 of the Charities Act 2011'.

115 In –

(a) section 1140(2)(c)(ii), and
(b) section 1154(1)(b) and (2)(b),

for 'section 18 of the Charities Act 1993 (c 10)' substitute 'section 76 of the Charities Act 2011'.

116 In Schedule 1, in paragraph 6(4)(b) for 'or section 24 or 25 of the Charities Act 1993 (c 10),' substitute ', section 24 or 25 of the Charities Act 1993 or section 96 or 100 of the Charities Act 2011,'.

Safeguarding Vulnerable Groups Act 2006 (c 47)

117 In Schedule 4, in –

(a) paragraph 4(7) and
(b) paragraph 8(6),

for '"charity trustee" has the same meaning as in the Charities Act 1993 (c 10)' substitute '"charity trustee" has the same meaning as in the Charities Act 2011'.

Charities Act 2006 (c 50)

118 In section 54(2), for 'section 9 of the 1993 Act' substitute 'section 52 of the Charities Act 2011'.

119 In section 72(3), for 'section 10(2) to (4) of the 1993 Act' substitute 'section 55 of the Charities Act 2011'.

120 (1) In section 73(5)(b), for 'the appointed day (within the meaning of section 10 of this Act)' substitute '31 January 2009'.

(2) After section 73(5) insert –

> '(6) This section has effect, in relation to any time occurring on or after the commencement of the Charities Act 2011 as if –
>
> (a) the reference in subsection (1) to the operation of this Act included (in relation to provisions of this Act repealed and re-enacted by the 2011 Act) a reference to the operation of the 2011 Act,
> (b) the reference in subsection (2)(a) to the effect of the Act included (in relation to provisions of this Act repealed and re-enacted by the 2011 Act) a reference to the effect of the 2011 Act, and
> (c) the reference in subsection (5)(a) to paragraph (b) or (c) of section 3A(2) of the 1993 Act (as amended by section 9 of this Act) were a reference to paragraph (b) or (c) of section 30(2) of the 2011 Act.'

121 (1) In section 74(4), omit –

(a) paragraphs (a) and (b), and
(b) in paragraph (e), '76 or'.

(2) In section 74(5), omit '(a), (b),'.

(3) Omit section 74(6).

122 Omit section 76.

123 (1) In section 78(2) –

(a) omit paragraph (a);
(b) in paragraph (b), for '(in accordance with section 2(6)) the meaning given by section 2(1)' substitute '(in accordance with section 2(2) of the Charities Act 2011) the meaning given by section 2(1) of that Act';
(c) in paragraph (c), for 'the 1993 Act' substitute 'that Act';
(d) omit the words following paragraph (c).

(2) Omit section 78(3).

(3) In section 78(4)(c), omit '6(5) or'.

124 In section 79(1), omit –

(a) paragraph (a), and
(b) in paragraph (g), the words from 'paragraph 104' to 'paragraph 174(d)'.

125 In section 80 –

(a) omit subsections (3)(a), (b) and (d) (but not the 'and' following it), (4), (5)(a) to (c) and (e) (but not the 'and' following it), (6) and (8),
(b) in subsections (3)(e) and (5)(f), for '76' substitute '77', and
(c) in subsection (9) –
  (i) omit 'also' and paragraph (a) (together with the 'or' following it), and
  (ii) in paragraph (b), for 'those' substitute 'the amendments'.

Income Tax Act 2007 (c 3)

126 (1) Amend section 558 as follows.

(2) Under the heading 'Type 2,' for 'or' preceding paragraph (c) substitute –

'(bb) section 96 of the Charities Act 2011, or'.

(3) Under the heading 'Type 3', omit 'or' preceding paragraph (b) and at the end of paragraph (b) insert –

'or
(c) section 100 of the Charities Act 2011.'

Legal Services Act 2007 (c 29)

127 In section 194(9)(a), for 'in accordance with section 3A of the Charities Act 1993 (c 10)', substitute 'in accordance with section 30 of the Charities Act 2011,'.

Dioceses, Pastoral and Mission Measure 2007 (No 1)

128 In section 62(1), in the definition of 'charity', for section '78(2) of the Charities Act 2006 (c 50)' substitute 'section 10 of the Charities Act 2011'.

129 In Schedule 2, in paragraph 13(2), for 'charity trustee within the meaning of the Charities Act 1993 (1993 c 10)' substitute 'charity trustee within the meaning of the Charities Act 2011'.

Regulatory Enforcement and Sanctions Act 2008 (c 13)

130 In Schedule 3, omit 'Charities Act 1993 (c 10), sections 76 to 78' and after the entry relating to the Charities Act 2006 insert 'Charities Act 2011, sections 294 to 297'.

Housing and Regeneration Act 2008 (c 17)

131 In section 135(6), for 'sections 41 to 45 of the Charities Act 1993 (c 10) (charity accounts)' substitute 'Part 8 of the Charities Act 2011'.

132 In section 136 –

(a) in subsection (4), 'for section 43(1)(a) of the Charities Act 1993' substitute section 144(1)(a) of the Charities Act 2011',
(b) in subsection (5)(a), for 'section 43(1) of the Charities Act 1993', substitute 'section 144(1) of the Charities Act 2011,',
(c) in subsection (5)(b), for 'section 43(1)(b),' substitute 'section 144(1)(b),' and
(d) in subsection (6), for 'section 43 of the Charities Act 1993 (c 10)' substitute 'section 144 of the Charities Act 2011'.

133 In section 138(3)(a), for 'the Charities Act 1993' substitute the 'Charities Act 2011'.

134 In section 266(6), for 'section 72 of the Charities Act 1993 (c 10)' substitute 'section 178 of the Charities Act 2011'.

135 In section 275 –

(a) in the definition of 'non-registrable charity', for 'section 3A of the Charities Act 1993 (c 10),', substitute 'section 30 of the Charities Act 2011,', and
(b) in the definition of 'registered charity', for 'the Charities Act 1993 (c 10)', substitute 'the Charities Act 2011,'.

Planning Act 2008 (c 29)

136 (1) Amend section 210 as follows.

(2) In subsection (1)(b), for 'section 2 of the Charities Act 2006 (c 50)' substitute 'section 2 of the Charities Act 2011'.

(3) In subsection (4) –

(a) in paragraph (a), for 'section 3 of the Charities Act 1993 (c 10)', substitute 'section 29 of the Charities Act 2011,', and
(b) in paragraph (b), for 'section 1(1) of the Charities Act 2006 but is not required to be registered in the register kept under section 3 of the Charities Act 1993' substitute 'section 1(1) of the Charities Act 2011 but is not required to be registered in the register kept under section 29 of that Act'.

(4) In subsection (5), for 'section 2(2) of the Charities Act 2006;' substitute 'section 3(1) of the Charities Act 2011;'.

Charities Act (Northern Ireland) 2008 (c 12 (NI))

137 In section 56(1)(a), for under 'section 3 of the Charities Act 1993 (c 10), or which, by virtue of section 3A(2) of that Act, is not required to register as a charity under that section' substitute 'in the register kept under section 29 of the Charities Act 2011, or which, by virtue of section 30(2) of that Act, is not required to be registered in that register'.

138 In section 86(1)(e) –

(a) in sub-paragraph (i), after 'under' insert 'section 79(2)(a) of the Charities Act 2011 or', and
(b) in sub-paragraph (ii), for 'that provision' substitute 'section 18(2)(i) of the 1993 Act'.

Apprenticeships, Skills, Children and Learning Act 2009 (c 22)

139 In section 71A(1), for 'section 13 of the Charities Act 2006)' substitute 'section 25 of the Charities Act 2011)'.

140 In Schedule 3, in paragraph 19(4)(c), for '(within the meaning of section 69A of the Charities Act 1993 (c 10))' substitute (within the meaning of Part 11 of the Charities Act 2011)'.

141 In Schedule 4, in paragraph 9(4)(c), for '(within the meaning of section 69A of the Charities Act 1993 (c 10))' substitute '(within the meaning of Part 11 of the Charities Act 2011)'.

Corporation Tax Act 2010 (c 4)

142 (1) Amend section 511 as follows.

(2) Under the heading 'Type 2', for 'or' preceding paragraph (c) substitute –

'(bb) section 96 of the Charities Act 2011, or'.

(3) Under the heading 'Type 3', omit 'or' preceding paragraph (b) and at the end of paragraph (b) insert –

'or

(c) section 100 of the Charities Act 2011.'

Finance Act 2010 (c 13)

143 (1) Amend Schedule 6 as follows.

(2) In paragraph 1(4) –

(a) for 'see section 2 of the Charities Act 2006' substitute 'see section 2 of the Charities Act 2011', and

(b) in paragraph (b), for '(see section 80(3) to (6) of that Act)' substitute '(see sections 7 and 8 of that Act)'.

(3) In paragraph 3(1)(a), for 'within the meaning of the Charities Act 1993' substitute 'within the meaning of section 10 of the Charities Act 2011'.

(4) In paragraph 3(2), for 'section 3 of the Charities Act 1993' substitute 'section 29 of the Charities Act 2011'.

Equality Act 2010 (c 15)

144 In section 194(3)(a), for 'section 1(1) of the Charities Act 2006' substitute 'section 1(1) of the Charities Act 2011'.

Church of England (Miscellaneous Provisions) Measure 2010 (No 1)

145 In section 10(1), for' section 96(2) of the Charities Act 1993 (c 10)' substitute 'section 10 of the Charities Act 2011'.

Mission and Pastoral Measure 2011 (No 3)

146 For section 67(1) substitute –

'(1) The power of the court (as defined by the Charities Act 2011) to make schemes under its jurisdiction with respect to charities, and the power of the Charity Commission to make schemes under that Act, shall extend to the making of schemes with respect to consecrated chapels belonging to charities which are no longer needed for the purposes of the charity, and section 10(2)(c) of that Act shall not be taken as preventing the making of any such scheme.'

147 In section 77(3), for 'the Charities Act 1993' substitute 'the Charities Act 2011'.

148 In section 106(1), in the definition of 'charity', for 'section 78(2) of the Charities Act 2006 (c 50)' substitute 'section 10 of the Charities Act 2011'.

149 (1) Amend Schedule 3 as follows.

(2) In paragraph 9(6) –

(a) for 'section 16 of the Charities Act 1993' substitute 'section 69 of the Charities Act 2011', and

(b) for 'that section' substitute 'sections 69 to 71 of that Act'.

(3) In paragraph 14(1)(e) for 'section 16 of the Charities Act 1993' substitute 'section 69 of the Charities Act 2011'.

NOTES

Paras 14, 16 repealed by the Co-operative and Community Benefit Societies Act 2014 s 151(4), Sch 7.

SCHEDULE 8
Transitionals and Savings

Section 354

PART 1
GENERAL

Continuity of the law

1 The repeal and re-enactment of provisions by this Act does not affect the continuity of the law.

2 A reference, express or implied, in this Act, another enactment or an instrument or document, to a provision of this Act is, subject to its context, to be read as being or including a reference to the corresponding provision repealed by this Act, in relation to times, circumstances or purposes in relation to which the repealed provision had effect.

3 (1) A reference, express or implied, in any enactment, instrument or document to a provision repealed by this Act is, subject to its context, to be read as being or including a reference to the corresponding provision of this Act, in relation to times, circumstances or purposes in relation to which that provision has effect.

(2) Where a power conferred by an Act is expressed to be exercisable in relation to enactments contained in Acts passed before or in the same Session as the Act conferring the power, the power is also exercisable in relation to provisions of this Act that reproduce such enactments.

(3) The powers in –

(a) section 75(4) and (5) of the Charities Act 2006 (to make supplementary and consequential provision etc), and

(b) section 77 of that Act (to make amendments in consequence of, or in connection with, changes to the provisions of company law relating to the accounts of charitable companies etc),

are, so far as they were exercisable in relation to any provision repealed and re-enacted by this Act, exercisable in relation to the corresponding provision of this Act.

(4) Sub-paragraphs (2) and (3) do not affect the generality of sub-paragraph (1).

4 Anything done, or having effect as if done, under (or for the purposes of or in reliance on) a provision repealed by this Act, and in force or effective immediately before the commencement of this Act, has effect after that commencement as if done under (or for the purposes of or in reliance on) the corresponding provision of this Act.

5 Paragraphs 1 to 4 have effect in place of section 17(2) of the Interpretation Act 1978; but nothing in this Schedule affects any other provision of that Act.

EFFECT OF OLD TRANSITIONALS AND SAVINGS

6 The repeals made by this Act do not affect the operation of any transitional provision or saving relating to the coming into force of a provision reproduced in this Act in so far as the transitional provision or saving is not specifically reproduced in this Act but remains capable of having effect in relation to the corresponding provision of this Act or otherwise.

7 (1) The repeal by this Act of an enactment previously repealed subject to savings does not affect the continued operation of those savings.

(2) The repeal by this Act of a saving on the previous repeal of an enactment does not affect the operation of the saving in so far as it is not specifically reproduced in this Act but remains capable of having effect.

Use of existing forms etc

8 Any reference to an enactment repealed by this Act which is contained in a document made, served or issued after the commencement of the repeal is, subject to its context, to be read as being or including a reference to the corresponding provision of this Act.

PART 2
RECREATIONAL ETC PURPOSES

General

9 In this Part of this Schedule 'the 1958 Act' means the Recreational Charities Act 1958.

10 (1) Where section 2 of the 1958 Act applied to any trusts immediately before the day on which section 5(3) of the Charities Act 2006 came into force, the repeal by this Act of paragraph 2 of Schedule 10 to the 2006 Act does not prevent the trusts from continuing to be charitable if they constitute a charity in accordance with section 1(1) of this Act.

(2) Sub-paragraph (1) –

(a) affects the law of Scotland only so far as it affects the construction of references to charities or charitable purposes in enactments which relate to matters falling within Section A1 of Part 2 of Schedule 5 to the Scotland Act 1998 (reserved matters: fiscal policy etc);
(b) affects the law of Northern Ireland only so far as it affects the construction of references to charities or charitable purposes in enactments which relate to matters falling within paragraph 9 of Schedule 2 to the Northern Ireland Act 1998 (excepted matters: taxes and duties).

11 The repeal by this Act of subsections (2) and (3) of section 3 of the 1958 Act does not affect any saving in either of those subsections which is capable of having continuing effect.

Scotland

12 Sections 1 and 2 of the 1958 Act as in force before the commencement of section 5 of the Charities Act 2006 continue to have effect in relation to the law of Scotland so far as they affect the construction of any references to charities or charitable purposes which –

(a) are to be construed in accordance with the law of England and Wales, but
(b) are not contained in enactments relating to matters falling within Section A1 of Part 2 of Schedule 5 to the Scotland Act 1998 (reserved matters: fiscal policy etc).

Northern Ireland

13 Sections 1 and 2 of the 1958 Act as in force before the commencement of section 5 of the Charities Act 2006 continue to have effect in relation to the law of Northern Ireland so far as they affect the construction of any references to charities or charitable purposes which –

(a) are to be construed in accordance with the law of England and Wales, but
(b) are not contained in enactments relating to matters falling within paragraph 9 of Schedule 2 to the Northern Ireland Act 1998 (excepted matters: taxes and duties).

PART 3
MISCELLANEOUS

Regulations relating to fees

14 Despite the revocation by this Act of the Charities (Pre-consolidation Amendments) Order 2011 (SI 2011/1396), regulations having effect as if made under section 19 continue to have effect as if any reference to the furnishing of a document were a reference to the provision of the document.

Exempt charities

15 (1) Despite the repeal by this Act of section 11(13) of the Charities Act 2006 (power to make amendments or modifications of enactments in connection with changes in exempt charities), the Minister may by order make such amendments or other modifications of any enactment as the Minister considers appropriate in connection with –

(a) charities of a particular description becoming, or ceasing to be, exempt charities, or
(b) a particular charity becoming, or ceasing to be, an exempt charity,

as a result of provision made by or under section 11 of the 2006 Act.

(2) In sub-paragraph (1) 'enactment' includes –

(a) any provision of subordinate legislation (within the meaning of the Interpretation Act 1978), and
(b) a provision of a Measure of the Church Assembly or of the General Synod of the Church of England;

and references to enactments include enactments whenever passed or made.

16 The repeal and re-enactment by this Act of –

(a) section 11(13) of the Charities Act 2006 (power to make amendments or modifications of enactments in connection with changes in exempt charities), and
(b) section 13(5) of that Act (power to make amendments or modifications of enactments in connection with principal regulator regulations),

is not to be treated as preventing any amendment or modification being made of an enactment contained in this Act which re-enacts an enactment of which an amendment or modification could have been made under section 11(13) or 13(5).

Application cy-près: donors unknown or disclaiming or treated as disclaiming

17 Sections 63, 64 and 67 apply to property given for charitable purposes whether before or on or after the commencement of this Act.

Official custodian as successor to official trustee of charity lands and official trustees of charity funds

18 (1) Despite the repeal by this Act of paragraph 26 of Schedule 10 to the Charities Act 2006, the official custodian for charities is to continue to be treated as the successor for all purposes both of the official trustee of charity lands and of the official trustees of charitable funds as if –

(a) the functions of the official trustee or trustees had been functions of the official custodian, and
(b) the official trustee or trustees had been, and had discharged the functions of the official trustee or trustees as, holder of the office of the official custodian.

(2) Despite the repeal of paragraph 26 of that Schedule (and without affecting the generality of sub-paragraph (1)) –

(a) any property which immediately before the commencement of that repeal was, by virtue of paragraph 26(2) of that Schedule, held by the official custodian continues to be so held, as if vested in the official custodian under section 90, and

(b) any enactment or document referring to the official trustee or trustees mentioned above continues to have effect, so far as the context permits, as if the official custodian had been mentioned instead.

Savings for consequential amendments

19 (1) The repeal by this Act of paragraph 23(a) of Schedule 10 to the Charities Act 2006 (saving for consequential amendment made by the Charities Act 1960) does not affect the amendment made by Schedule 6 to the Charities Act 1960 in section 9 of the Places of Worship Registration Act 1855.

(2) The repeal by this Act of paragraph 23(d) of Schedule 10 to the Charities Act 2006 (saving for consequential amendment made by the Charities Act 1960) does not affect the amendment made by Schedule 6 to the Charities Act 1960 in section 31 of the New Parishes Measure 1943.

(3) The repeal by this Act of paragraph 30 of Schedule 6 to the Charities Act 1993 does not affect the amendments made by that paragraph in –

(a) section 90(4) of the Local Government Act 1985, or
(b) section 192(11) of the Education Reform Act 1988.

Universities of Durham and Newcastle-upon-Tyne Act 1963

20 Despite the revocation by this Act of the Charities (Pre-consolidation Amendments) Order 2011 (SI 2011/1396), the Universities of Durham and Newcastle-upon-Tyne Act 1963 continues to have effect as if Schedule 7 to the Charities Act 1993 (repeals) had never referred to section 10 of the 1963 Act.

SCHEDULE 9
Transitory Modifications

Section 354

Commission's general functions –public charitable collections

1 (1) Sub-paragraph (2) applies if Chapter 1 of Part 3 of the 2006 Act (public charitable collections) has not been brought into force before the commencement of this Act.

(2) Section 15 (the Commission's general functions) has effect until the appointed day as if –

(a) paragraph 4 of section 15(1), and
(b) section 15(6),

were omitted.

(3) 'The appointed day' means the day on which Chapter 1 of Part 3 of the 2006 Act is brought into force by virtue of an order made under section 79 of that Act.

'Exempt charity' and common investment and deposit funds

2 (1) Sub-paragraph (2) applies if –

(a) section 11(10) of the 2006 Act (amendment of section 24(8) of the 1993 Act), and
(b) paragraph 173(3)(a) of Schedule 8 to the 2006 Act (amendment of definition of 'exempt charity' in section 96(1) of the 1993 Act),

have not been brought into force before the commencement of this Act.

(2) Subsection (3) of –

(a) section 99 (further provisions relating to common investment schemes and funds), and
(b) section 103 (further provisions relating to common deposit schemes and funds),

has effect until the relevant commencement date as if at the end of the subsection there were inserted' ; and if the scheme admits only exempt charities, the fund is an exempt charity for the purposes of this Act'.

'Exempt charity' and 'church funds'

3 (1) Sub-paragraph (2) applies if section 11(9) of the 2006 Act (removing certain exempt charities from Schedule 2 to the 1993 Act), so far as relating to –

(a) an Investment Fund or Deposit Fund within the meaning of the Church Funds Investment Measure 1958, or
(b) an investment fund or deposit fund within the meaning of the Methodist Church Funds Act 1960,

has not been brought into force before the commencement of this Act.

(2) Schedule 3 (exempt charities) has effect until the relevant commencement date as if paragraphs (a) and (b) of paragraph 1(2) were omitted.

'Exempt charity' and registered societies etc

4 (1) Sub-paragraph (2) applies if section 11(8) of the 2006 Act (changing the exemption under paragraph (y) of Schedule 2 to the 1993 Act) has not been brought into force before the commencement of this Act.

(2) Schedule 3 (exempt charities) has effect until the relevant commencement date as if, in paragraph 27, for 'if the society is also registered in the register of social landlords under Part 1 of the Housing Act 1996' there were substituted 'and any registered society or branch within the meaning of the Friendly Societies Act 1974'.

5 . . .

Power to amend enactments in connection with changes in exempt charities

6 (1) Sub-paragraph (2) applies if paragraph 2, 3 or 4 applies in relation to charities of a particular description or to a particular charity.

(2) In relation to those charities or that charity, section 23 has effect as if for subsection (3) there were substituted –

'(3) The Minister may by order make such amendments or other modifications of any enactment as the Minister considers appropriate in connection with –

(a) charities of a particular description ceasing to be exempt charities on the relevant commencement date, or
(b) a particular charity ceasing to be an exempt charity on the relevant commencement date.'

Exempt charities and the principal regulator

7 (1) Sub-paragraph (2) applies if, in relation to charities of a particular description or a particular charity –

(a) section 13(1) to (3) of the 2006 Act (general duty of principal regulator), and
(b) section 86A of the 1993 Act (duty of Commission to consult principal regulator),

have not been brought into before the commencement of this Act.

(2) In relation to those charities or that charity, Part 3 has effect until the relevant commencement date as if –

(a) section 26 (general duty of principal regulator), and
(b) section 28 (duty of Commission to consult principal regulator),

were omitted.

Voluntary registration

8 (1) Sub-paragraph (2) applies if section 3A(6) of the 1993 Act (voluntary registration) has not been brought into force before the commencement of this Act.

(2) Part 4 (registration and names of charities) has effect until the relevant commencement date with the omission of section 30(3) (but subject to the modifications specified in the Charities Act 2006 (Commencement No 5, Transitional and Transitory Provisions and Savings) Order 2008 (SI 2008/3267) as it has effect in accordance with Part 1 of Schedule 8).

Regulations to secure that any institution ceasing to be an exempt charity on the relevant commencement date is excepted

9 (1) Sub-paragraph (2) applies if paragraph 2, 3 or 4 applies and, on the date which is the relevant commencement date in relation to that paragraph, an institution ceases to be an exempt charity.

(2) In relation to that institution, section 31 has effect as if for subsection (3) there were substituted –

> '(3) Such regulations must be made under section 30(2)(c) as are necessary to secure that the institution is excepted under section 30(2)(c) (subject to compliance with any conditions of the exception and the financial limit mentioned in section 30(2)(c)).'

Change of name and exempt charities

10 (1) Sub-paragraph (2) applies if, in relation to charities of a particular description or a particular charity, paragraph 1 of Schedule 5 to the 2006 Act (removal of exception for exempt charities from power to require charity's name to be changed) has not been brought into before the commencement of this Act.

(2) In relation to those charities or that charity, section 42 (power to require name to be changed) has effect until the relevant commencement date as if at the end there were inserted –

> '(6) Nothing in this section applies to an exempt charity.'

Power to institute inquiries and exempt charities

11 (1) Sub-paragraph (2) applies if, in relation to charities of a particular description or a particular charity, paragraph 2 of Schedule 5 to the 2006 Act (restriction of exclusion of exempt charities from power to institute inquiries) has not been brought into force before the commencement of this Act.

(2) In relation to those charities or that charity, section 46 (general power to institute inquiries) has effect until the relevant commencement date as if, in subsection (2), 'except where this has been requested by its principal regulator' were omitted.

Maximum term of imprisonment for offence under section 49(8)

12 In relation to an offence committed before the commencement of section 281(5) of the Criminal Justice Act 2003 (alteration of penalties for summary offences), the reference to 51 weeks in section 49(9) is to be read as a reference to 3 months.

Power to call for documents etc and exempt charities

13 (1) Sub-paragraph (2) applies if, in relation to charities of a particular description or a particular charity, paragraph 3 of Schedule 5 to the 2006 Act (removal of exclusion of exempt charities from power to call for documents etc) has not been brought into force before the commencement of this Act.

(2) In relation to those charities or that charity, section 52 (power to call for documents) has effect until the relevant commencement date with the insertion after subsection (1) of –

> '(1A) No person properly having the custody of documents relating only to an exempt charity is required under subsection (1) to transmit to the Commission any of those documents, or to provide any copy of or extract from any of them.'

Maximum term of imprisonment for offence under section 57(3)

14 In relation to an offence committed before the commencement of section 154(1) of the Criminal Justice Act 2003 (general limit on the magistrates' court's power to impose imprisonment) the reference to 12 months in section 57(4) is to be read as a reference to 6 months.

Exempt charities and disclosure to and by principal regulator

15 (1) Sub-paragraph (2) applies if, in relation to charities of a particular description or a particular charity, the main provisions of section 10B of the 1993 Act (disclosure to and by principal regulators of exempt charities) have not been brought into force before the commencement of this Act.

(2) In relation to those charities or that charity, this Act has effect until the relevant commencement date as if section 58 (disclosure to and by principal regulators of exempt charities), except in so far as it confers power to make regulations, were omitted.

(3) In sub-paragraph (1), 'the main provisions of section 10B of the 1993 Act' means section 10B except in so far as it confers power to make regulations.

Exempt charities and Commission's concurrent jurisdiction with High Court

16 (1) Sub-paragraph (2) applies if, in relation to charities of a particular description or a particular charity, paragraph 4 of Schedule 5 to the 2006 Act (removal of exclusion of exempt charities from Commission's concurrent jurisdiction) has not been brought into force before the commencement of this Act.

(2) In relation to those charities or that charity, section 70 (restrictions on Commission's concurrent jurisdiction) has effect until the relevant commencement date as if –

(a) at the beginning of subsection (2)(c) there were inserted 'in the case of a charity other than an exempt charity', and

(b) in subsection (3), 'after In the case of a charity' there were inserted 'which is not an exempt charity and'.

Exempt charities and restriction on expenditure on promoting Bills

17 (1) Sub-paragraph (2) applies if, in relation to charities of a particular description or a particular charity, paragraph 5 of Schedule 5 to the 2006 Act (restriction on expenditure on promoting Bills to apply to exempt charities) has not been brought into force before the commencement of this Act.

(2) In relation to those charities or that charity, section 74 (restriction on expenditure on promoting Bills) has effect until the relevant commencement date as if, at the end of subsection (2), there were inserted 'but does not apply in the case of an exempt charity'.

Exempt charities and power to act for protection of charities

18 (1) Sub-paragraph (2) applies if, in relation to charities of a particular description or a particular charity, paragraph 6 of Schedule 5 to the 2006 Act (restriction of exception for exempt charities from Commission's powers to act for protection of charities) has not been brought into force before the commencement of this Act.

(2) In relation to those charities or that charity, Part 6 (cy-près powers etc) has effect as if sections 80(4) and 81(3) were omitted and after section 82 there were inserted –

> **'82A Exempt charities**
>
> Sections 76 to 82 (powers to act for protection of charities) do not apply to an exempt charity.'

Reference to Mission and Pastoral Measure 2011

19 (1) Sub-paragraph (2) applies if the Mission and Pastoral Measure 2011 has not been brought into force before the commencement of this Act.

(2) In the application of section 105(10) before the commencement of the 2011 Measure the reference to the Mission and Pastoral Measure 2011 is to be read as a reference to the Pastoral Measure 1983.

Exempt charities and power to give directions about dormant bank accounts

20 (1) Sub-paragraph (2) applies if, in relation to charities of a particular description or a particular charity, paragraph 7 of Schedule 5 to the 2006 Act (removal of exclusion of exempt charities from power to give directions about dormant accounts) has not been brought into force before the commencement of this Act.

(2) In relation to those charities or that charity, section 107 (power to direct transfer of credits in dormant bank accounts) has effect until the relevant commencement date as if after subsection (5) there were inserted –

> '(6) Subsection (1) does not apply to any account held in the name of or on behalf of an exempt charity.'

Exempt charities and Commission's consent to proceedings etc

21 (1) Sub-paragraph (2) applies if, in relation to charities of a particular description or a particular charity, paragraph 8 of Schedule 5 to the 2006 Act (proceedings relating to exempt charity must be authorised by Commission etc) has not been brought into force before the commencement of this Act.

(2) In relation to those charities or that charity, section 115 (proceedings by persons other than the Commission) has effect until the relevant commencement date as if –

(a) in subsection (2), after 'relating to a charity', and
(b) in subsection (7)(a), after 'with reference to any charity',

there were inserted '(other than an exempt charity)'.

Exempt charities and duty of auditors etc to report matters to Commission

22 (1) Sub-paragraph (2) applies if, in relation to charities of a particular description or a particular charity, section 29(2) of the 2006 Act (amendments of section 46 of the 1993 Act about application to exempt charities of duty of auditors etc to report matters to Commission) has not been brought into force before the commencement of this Act.

(2) In relation to those charities or that charity, section 160 (audit or examination of accounts: exempt charities) has effect until the relevant commencement date as if –

(a) in subsection (1) (provision corresponding to section 46(1)), for 'sections 144 to 155 (audit or examination of accounts)' there were substituted 'sections 144 to 157 (audit or examination of accounts and duty of auditors etc to report matters to Commission)', and
(b) subsection (2) (provision corresponding to section 46(2A) and (2B)) were omitted.

(3) Sub-paragraph (4) applies if, in relation to charities of a particular description or a particular charity, section 46(3A) of the 1993 Act (application to certain excepted charities which are also exempt charities of duty of auditors etc to report matters to Commission) has not been brought into force before the commencement of this Act.

(4) In relation to those charities or that charity, section 161 (audit or examination of accounts: excepted charities) has effect until the relevant commencement date as if subsection (4) (provision corresponding to section 46(3A)) were omitted.

(5) Sub-paragraph (6) applies if –

(a) sub-paragraph (2) applies and, on the date which is the relevant commencement date in relation to that sub-paragraph, section 160 applies without the modifications in that sub-paragraph, or
(b) sub-paragraph (4) applies and, on the date which is the relevant commencement date in relation to that sub-paragraph, section 161 applies without the modifications in that sub-paragraph.

(6) Section 160(2) or (as the case may be) 161(4) applies in relation to matters ('pre-commencement matters') of which a person became aware at any time falling –

(a) before the relevant commencement date, and
(b) during a financial year ending on or after that date,

as well as in relation to matters of which the person becomes aware on or after that date.

(7) Any duty imposed by virtue of sub-paragraph (6) must be complied with in relation to any such pre-commencement matters as soon as practicable after the relevant commencement date.

Disqualification and references to section 429(2) of Insolvency Act 1986

23 (1) This paragraph applies if paragraph 7 of Schedule 16 to the Tribunals, Courts and Enforcement Act 2007 (administration orders: consequential amendments) has not been brought into force before the commencement of this Act.

(2) Section 178(1) has effect until the relevant commencement date as if in Case F for 'section 429(2) of the Insolvency Act 1986 (disabilities on revocation of county court administration order)' there were substituted 'section 429(2)(b) of the Insolvency Act 1986 (failure to pay under county court administration order)'.

(3) Section 180(2) has effect until the relevant commencement date as if for 'section 429(2) of the Insolvency Act 1986' there were substituted 'section 429(2)(b) of the Insolvency Act 1986'.

Maximum term of imprisonment for offence under section 183(1)

24 In relation to an offence committed before the commencement of section 154(1) of the Criminal Justice Act 2003 (general limit on the magistrates' court's power to impose imprisonment) the reference to 12 months in section 183(3)(a) is to be read as a reference to 6 months.

Exempt charities and power to order disqualified trustee to repay sums

25 (1) Sub-paragraph (2) applies if, in relation to charities of a particular description or a particular charity, paragraph 9 of Schedule 5 to the 2006 Act (Commission to have power to order disqualified charity trustee or trustee to repay sums to exempt charity) has not been brought into force before the commencement of this Act.

(2) In relation to those charities or that charity, section 184 (civil consequences of acting while disqualified) has effect until the relevant commencement date as if in subsection (2)(a), after for 'a charity', there were inserted '(other than an exempt charity)'.

CIOs

26 (1) Sub-paragraph (2) applies if any provision of the 1993 Act relating to CIOs –

(a) has not been brought into force before the commencement of this Act, or

(b) has not been brought into force for all purposes or for all areas before the commencement of this Act;

and in sub-paragraph (2) 'excluded purpose or area' means any purpose or area in relation to which that provision of the 1993 Act has not been brought into force.

(2) This Act has effect until the relevant commencement date as if the provision of this Act corresponding to that provision of the 1993 Act –

(a) were omitted, or

(b) were omitted in relation to the excluded purpose or area.

(3) For the purposes of this paragraph, the provisions of the 1993 Act relating to CIOs, and the corresponding provisions of this Act, are –

provision of the 1993 Act	corresponding provision of this Act
section 45(3B)	section 163(3)
in section 48(1A), '(but this subsection does not apply if the charity is constituted as a CIO)'	in section 169(2), '(but this subsection does not apply if the charity is constituted as a CIO)'
any provision of Part 8A, including Schedule 5B but excluding section 69O	the corresponding provision of Part 11
section 69O	section 267(2)
section 73E(2)(b)	section 192(2)(b)
section 75C(11)	section 314
in section 97(1), the definition of 'CIO'	section 204
paragraph 1 of Schedule 1C in relation to a decision of the Commission under a provision of Part 8A or Schedule 5B mentioned in column 1 of the Table in Schedule 1C	section 319 in relation to a decision of the Commission under a provision of Part 11 mentioned in column 1 of Schedule 6.

27 . . .

28 . . .

Meaning of the 'relevant commencement date'

29 (1) Subject to sub-paragraph (2), in this Schedule 'the relevant commencement date' means such day as the appropriate authority may by order appoint.

(2) If, in the case of a provision referred to in any paragraph above which has not been brought into force before the commencement of this Act, an order has been made before the commencement of this Act appointing a day for the coming into force of that provision, 'the relevant commencement date' in relation to that provision means that appointed day.

(3) 'The appropriate authority' means –

(a) in relation to paragraph 23 (disqualification and references to section 429(2) of Insolvency Act 1986), the Lord Chancellor;
(b) otherwise, the Minister.

(4) An order made in relation to paragraph 23 may make different provision for different purposes.

(5) An order made in relation to any other paragraph of this Schedule may –

(a) appoint different days for different purposes or different areas;
(b) make such provision as the Minister considers necessary or expedient for transitory, transitional or saving purposes in connection with the coming into force of the order.

(6) Any power to make an order under this paragraph is exercisable by statutory instrument.

References to Acts

30 In this Schedule –

'the 1993 Act' means the Charities Act 1993;
'the 2006 Act' means the Charities Act 2006.

NOTES

Paras 5, 27, 28 repealed by the Co-operative and Community Benefit Societies Act 2014 s 151(4), Sch 7.

SCHEDULE 10
Repeals and Revocations

Section 354

Short title or title	Extent of repeal or revocation
Recreational Charities Act 1958 (c 17)	The whole Act.
Charities Act 1992 (c 41)	In Schedule 6, paragraphs 1, 3 to 8, 13(1) and (3) and 14 to 16.
Charities Act 1993 (c 10)	The whole Act.
Welsh Language Act 1993 (c 38)	Sections 32 and 33.
Local Government (Wales) Act 1994 (c 19)	In Schedule 16, paragraph 101.
Deregulation and Contracting Out Act 1994 (c 40)	Section 29(1) to (6).
	Section 30.
	In Schedule 11, paragraph 12.
Charities (Amendment) Act 1995 (c 48)	The whole Act.
Trusts of Land and Appointment of Trustees Act 1996 (c 47)	In Schedule 3, paragraph 26.
Education Act 1996 (c 56)	In Schedule 37, paragraphs 119 and 121.

Education Act 1997 (c 44)	In Schedule 7, paragraph 7.
Bank of England Act 1998 (c 11)	In Schedule 5, paragraph 42.
School Standards and Framework Act 1998 (c 31)	In Schedule 30, paragraph 49.
Insolvency Act 2000 (c 39)	In Schedule 4, paragraph 18.
Land Registration Act 2002 (c 9)	In Schedule 11, paragraph 29.
Licensing Act 2003 (c 17)	In section 16(3), the definition of 'charity'.
Civil Partnership Act 2004 (c 33)	In Schedule 21, paragraph 38.
	In Schedule 27, paragraph 147.
National Health Service (Consequential Provisions) Act 2006 (c 43)	In Schedule 1, paragraphs 160 to 162.
Companies Act 2006 (c 46)	Section 181(4).
	Section 226.
Charities Act 2006 (c 50)	Sections 1 to 9 and 11 to 44.
	In section 74, in subsection (4), paragraphs (a) and (b) and in paragraph (e) '76 or', in subsection (5) '(a), (b)', and subsection (6).
	Section 76.
	In section 78, in subsection (2), paragraph (a) and the words following paragraph (c), subsection (3) and, in subsection (4)(c), '6(5) or'.
	In section 79(1), paragraph (a) and in paragraph (g) the words from 'paragraph 104' to 'paragraph 174(d)'.
	In section 80 subsections (3)(a), (b) and (d) (but not the 'and' following it), (4), (5)(a) to (c) and (e) (but not the 'and' following it), (6) and (8) and in subsection (9) 'also' and paragraph (a) (together with the 'or' following it).
	Schedules 1, 2 and 4 to 7.
	In Schedule 8, paragraphs 1, 2, 6, 8, 13(4), 30, 33(3), 37(3), 39, 50 to 52, 54, 55, 57, 59, 61, 65, 69, 73, 77(3), 80(5)(d) (together with the 'and' preceding it), (6) to (8), 83(3) and (4), 85 to 88, 90(4), 96 to 178, 180, 181(4) and (5), 191, 192(4), 193 to 195, 198, 199, 204 to 207, 210(b) (together with the 'and' following it) and (c) and 212.

	In Schedule 10, paragraphs 1 to 14, 17 to 20, 23(a), (b) and (d) (together with the 'or' preceding it), 24 and 26.
Income Tax Act 2007 (c 3)	In section 558, under the heading 'Type 3', the word 'or' preceding paragraph (b).
	In Schedule 1, paragraph 353.
Tribunals, Courts and Enforcement Act 2007 (c 15)	In Schedule 16, paragraph 7.
Further Education and Training Act 2007 (c 25)	In Schedule 1, paragraph 8.
Local Government and Public Involvement in Health Act 2007 (c 28)	In Schedule 9, paragraph 1(2)(i).
Regulatory Enforcement and Sanctions Act 2008 (c 13)	In Schedule 3, 'Charities Act 1993 (c 10), sections 76 to 78'.
Apprenticeships, Skills, Children and Learning Act 2009 (c 22)	In Schedule 12, paragraph 8.
Corporation Tax Act 2010 (c 4)	In section 511, under the heading 'Type 3', the word 'or' preceding paragraph (b).
	In Schedule 1, paragraphs 273 to 275 and 491 to 493.
Academies Act 2010 (c 32)	Section 12(4).
Church of England (Miscellaneous Provisions) Measure 2000 (No 1)	Section 11.
Companies Act 1985 (Audit Exemption) Regulations 1994 (SI 1994/1935)	In Schedule 1, paragraphs 6 and 7.
Charities Act 1993 (Substitution of Sums) Order 1995 (SI 1995/2696)	The whole Order.
Financial Services and Markets Act 2000 (Consequential Amendments and Repeals) Order 2001 (SI 2001/3649)	Article 339.
Insolvency Act 2000 (Company Directors Disqualification Undertakings) Order 2004 (SI 2004/1941)	In the Schedule, paragraph 5.
Regulatory Reform (National Health Service Charitable and Non-Charitable Trust Accounts and Audit) Order 2005 (SI 2005/1074)	Article 3.
Qualifications, Curriculum and Assessment Authority for Wales (Transfer of Functions to the National Assembly for Wales and Abolition) Order 2005 (SI 2005/3239 (W 244))	In Schedule 1, paragraph 4.

Charities and Trustee Investment (Scotland) Act 2005 (Consequential Provisions and Modifications) Order 2006 (SI 2006/242 (S.2))	In the Schedule, paragraph 6.
Enterprise Act 2002 (Disqualification from Office: General) Order 2006 (SI 2006/1722)	In Schedule 2, paragraph 4.
Transfer of Functions (Third Sector, Communities and Equality) Order 2006 (SI 2006/2951)	In the Schedule, paragraph 4.
Companies Act 2006 (Commencement No 3, Consequential Amendments, Transitional Provisions and Savings) Order 2007 (SI 2007/2194)	In Schedule 4, paragraphs 78 to 82.
Charities Act 2006 (Charitable Companies Audit and Group Accounts Provisions) Order 2008 (SI 2008/527)	The whole Order.
Companies Act 2006 (Consequential Amendments etc) Order 2008 (SI 2008/948)	In Schedule 1, paragraphs 1(rr), 17 and 192. In Schedule 3, paragraphs 7 to 12.
Charities Acts 1992 and 1993 (Substitution of Sums) Order 2009 (SI 2009/508)	Articles 7 to 11.
Transfer of Functions of the Charity Tribunal Order 2009 (SI 2009/1834)	In Schedule 1, paragraphs 6 to 15.
Companies Act 2006 (Consequential Amendments, Transitional Provisions and Savings) Order 2009 (SI 2009/1941)	In Schedule 1, paragraph 139.
Legal Services Act 2007 (Consequential Amendments) Order 2009 (SI 2009/3348)	Article 4.
Charities Act 2006 (Changes in Exempt Charities) Order 2010 (SI 2010/500)	Article 2. In Schedule 1, paragraphs 3 and 4.
Income Tax Act 2007 (Amendment) Order 2010 (SI 2010/588)	Article 4.
Housing and Regeneration Act 2008 (Consequential Provisions) Order 2010 (SI 2010/866)	In Schedule 2, paragraph 78.
Charities (Pre-consolidation Amendments) Order 2011 (SI 2011/1396)	The whole Order.
Charities Act 2006 (Changes in Exempt Charities) Order 2011 (SI 2011/1725)	Article 2. In the Schedule, paragraphs 1 to 4.

SCHEDULE 11
Index of Defined Expressions

Section 357

the register	section 29(3)
registered	section 29(3)
the relevant charity, in relation to an incorporated body (in Part 12)	section 265
the relevant charity, in relation to power to spend capital subject to special trust (in Part 14)	section 288(1)
relevant charity merger (in Part 16)	section 306(1)
the relevant commencement date (in Schedule 9)	Schedule 9, paragraph 29
relevant institution (in sections 107 to 109)	section 109(3)
remit (in column 3 of Schedule 6)	section 323
remuneration (in sections 185 and 186)	section 187
reviewable matter (in Chapter 2 of Part 17)	section 322
Scottish recognised body (in sections 97 and 101)	section 104(1)
services (in sections 185 and 186)	section 187
special trust	section 287
spouse (in sections 118(2)(e), 188(1)(b), 200(1)(b) and 249(2)(b))	section 350(2)
subsidiary undertaking, in relation to a parent charity (in Part 8)	section 141(3) and (4)
substantial interest in a body corporate (in sections 118(2)(h), 157(1)(b), 188(1)(e), 200(1)(e) and 249(2)(e))	section 352
transfer of property (in sections 268 to 274)	section 267(4)
transfer of property (in sections 306 to 308)	section 306(4)(a)
transferee and transferor (in Part 16)	sections 306(1) and 312
transferor's property, all of (in Part 16)	sections 306(3)(a) and 312(1)(b)
the Tribunal	section 315(1)
trusts, in relation to a charity and other institutions	section 353(1)
undertaking (for certain specified purposes)	sections 55(3) and 141(6)
vesting declaration (in sections 306 to 308)	section 306(4)(b)
the 1958 Act (in Part 2 of Schedule 8)	Schedule 8, paragraph 9
the 1987 Act, and references to section 1 of the 1987 Act operating (in sections 92 to 95)	section 92(3)
the 1993 Act (in Schedule 9)	Schedule 9, paragraph 30
the 2006 Act (in Schedule 9)	Schedule 9, paragraph 30

APPENDIX 2

CHARITIES ACT 2006

…

PART 3
FUNDING FOR CHARITABLE, BENEVOLENT OR PHILANTHROPIC INSTITUTIONS

Chapter 1
Public Charitable Collections
Preliminary

45 Regulation of public charitable collections

(1) This Chapter regulates public charitable collections, which are of the following two types—

(a) collections in a public place; and
(b) door to door collections.

(2) For the purposes of this Chapter—

(a) 'public charitable collection' means (subject to section 46) a charitable appeal which is made—
 (i) in any public place, or
 (ii) by means of visits to houses or business premises (or both);
(b) 'charitable appeal' means an appeal to members of the public which is—
 (i) an appeal to them to give money or other property, or
 (ii) an appeal falling within subsection (4),
 (or both) and which is made in association with a representation that the whole or any part of its proceeds is to be applied for charitable, benevolent or philanthropic purposes;
(c) a 'collection in a public place' is a public charitable collection that is made in a public place, as mentioned in paragraph (a)(i);
(d) a 'door to door collection' is a public charitable collection that is made by means of visits to houses or business premises (or both), as mentioned in paragraph (a)(ii).

(3) For the purposes of subsection (2)(b)—

(a) the reference to the giving of money is to doing so by whatever means; and
(b) it does not matter whether the giving of money or other property is for consideration or otherwise.

(4) An appeal falls within this subsection if it consists in or includes—

(a) the making of an offer to sell goods or to supply services, or
(b) the exposing of goods for sale,

to members of the public.

(5) In this section—

'business premises' means any premises used for business or other commercial purposes;
'house' includes any part of a building constituting a separate dwelling;
'public place' means—

- (a) any highway, and
- (b) (subject to subsection (6)) any other place to which, at any time when the appeal is made, members of the public have or are permitted to have access and which either—
  - (i) is not within a building, or
  - (ii) if within a building, is a public area within any station, airport or shopping precinct or any other similar public area.

(6) In subsection (5), paragraph (b) of the definition of 'public place' does not include—

- (a) any place to which members of the public are permitted to have access only if any payment or ticket required as a condition of access has been made or purchased; or
- (b) any place to which members of the public are permitted to have access only by virtue of permission given for the purposes of the appeal in question.

46 Charitable appeals that are not public charitable collections

(1) A charitable appeal is not a public charitable collection if the appeal—

- (a) is made in the course of a public meeting; or
- (b) is made—
  - (i) on land within a churchyard or burial ground contiguous or adjacent to a place of public worship, or
  - (ii) on other land occupied for the purposes of a place of public worship and contiguous or adjacent to it,

  where the land is enclosed or substantially enclosed (whether by any wall or building or otherwise); or
- (c) is made on land to which members of the public have access only—
  - (i) by virtue of the express or implied permission of the occupier of the land, or
  - (ii) by virtue of any enactment,

  and the occupier is the promoter of the collection; or
- (d) is an appeal to members of the public to give money or other property by placing it in an unattended receptacle.

(2) For the purposes of subsection (1)(c) 'the occupier', in relation to unoccupied land, means the person entitled to occupy it.

(3) For the purposes of subsection (1)(d) a receptacle is unattended if it is not in the possession or custody of a person acting as a collector.

47 Other definitions for purposes of this Chapter

(1) In this Chapter—

'charitable, benevolent or philanthropic institution' means—

- (a) a charity, or

(b) an institution (other than a charity) which is established for charitable, benevolent, or philanthropic purposes;

'collector', in relation to a public charitable collection, means any person by whom the appeal in question is made (whether made by him alone or with others and whether made by him for remuneration or otherwise);

'local authority' means a unitary authority, the council of a district so far as it is not a unitary authority, the council of a London borough or of a Welsh county or county borough, the Common Council of the City of London or the Council of the Isles of Scilly;

'prescribed' means prescribed by regulations under section 63;

'proceeds', in relation to a public charitable collection, means all money or other property given (whether for consideration or otherwise) in response to the charitable appeal in question;

'promoter', in relation to a public charitable collection, means—

(a) a person who (whether alone or with others and whether for remuneration or otherwise) organises or controls the conduct of the charitable appeal in question, or

(b) where there is no person acting as mentioned in paragraph (a), any person who acts as a collector in respect of the collection,

and associated expressions are to be construed accordingly;

'public collections certificate' means a certificate issued by the Commission under section 52.

(2) In subsection (1) 'unitary authority' means—

(a) the council of a county so far as it is the council for an area for which there are no district councils;

(b) the council of any district comprised in an area for which there is no county council.

(3) The functions exercisable under this Chapter by a local authority are to be exercisable—

(a) as respects the Inner Temple, by its Sub-Treasurer, and

(b) as respects the Middle Temple, by its Under Treasurer;

and references in this Chapter to a local authority or to the area of a local authority are to be construed accordingly.

Restrictions on conducting collections

48 Restrictions on conducting collections in a public place

(1) A collection in a public place must not be conducted unless—

(a) the promoters of the collection hold a public collections certificate in force under section 52 in respect of the collection, and

(b) the collection is conducted in accordance with a permit issued under section 59 by the local authority in whose area it is conducted.

(2) Subsection (1) does not apply to a public charitable collection which is an exempt collection by virtue of section 50 (local, short-term collections).

(3) Where—

(a) a collection in a public place is conducted in contravention of subsection (1), and

(b) the circumstances of the case do not fall within section 50(6),

every promoter of the collection is guilty of an offence and liable on summary conviction to a fine not exceeding level 5 on the standard scale.

49 Restrictions on conducting door to door collections

(1) A door to door collection must not be conducted unless the promoters of the collection—

(a) hold a public collections certificate in force under section 52 in respect of the collection, and
(b) have within the prescribed period falling before the day (or the first of the days) on which the collection takes place—
  (i) notified the local authority in whose area the collection is to be conducted of the matters mentioned in subsection (3), and
  (ii) provided that authority with a copy of the certificate mentioned in paragraph (a).

(2) Subsection (1) does not apply to a door to door collection which is an exempt collection by virtue of section 50 (local, short-term collections).

(3) The matters referred to in subsection (1)(b)(i) are—

(a) the purpose for which the proceeds of the appeal are to be applied;
(b) the prescribed particulars of when the collection is to be conducted;
(c) the locality within which the collection is to be conducted; and
(d) such other matters as may be prescribed.

(4) Where—

(a) a door to door collection is conducted in contravention of subsection (1), and
(b) the circumstances of the case do not fall within section 50(6),

every promoter of the collection is guilty of an offence and liable on summary conviction to a fine not exceeding level 5 on the standard scale.

This is subject to subsection (5).

(5) Where—

(a) a door to door collection is conducted in contravention of subsection (1),
(b) the appeal is for goods only, and
(c) the circumstances of the case do not fall within section 50(6),

every promoter of the collection is guilty of an offence and liable on summary conviction to a fine not exceeding level 3 on the standard scale.

(6) In subsection (5) 'goods' includes all personal chattels other than things in action and money.

50 Exemption for local, short-term collections

(1) A public charitable collection is an exempt collection if—

(a) it is a local, short-term collection (see subsection (2)), and
(b) the promoters notify the local authority in whose area it is to be conducted of the matters mentioned in subsection (3) within the prescribed period falling before the day (or the first of the days) on which the collection takes place,

unless, within the prescribed period beginning with the date when they are so notified, the local authority serve a notice under subsection (4) on the promoters.

(2) A public charitable collection is a local, short term collection if—

(a) the appeal is local in character; and
(b) the duration of the appeal does not exceed the prescribed period of time.

(3) The matters referred to in subsection (1)(b) are—

(a) the purpose for which the proceeds of the appeal are to be applied;
(b) the date or dates on which the collection is to be conducted;
(c) the place at which, or the locality within which, the collection is to be conducted; and
(d) such other matters as may be prescribed.

(4) Where it appears to the local authority—

(a) that the collection is not a local, short-term collection, or
(b) that the promoters or any of them have or has on any occasion—
    (i) breached any provision of regulations made under section 63, or
    (ii) been convicted of an offence within section 53(2)(a)(i) to (v),

they must serve on the promoters written notice of their decision to that effect and the reasons for their decision.

(5) That notice must also state the right of appeal conferred by section 62(1) and the time within which such an appeal must be brought.

(6) Where—

(a) a collection in a public place is conducted otherwise than in accordance with section 48(1) or a door to door collection is conducted otherwise than in accordance with section 49(1), and
(b) the collection is a local, short term collection but the promoters do not notify the local authority as mentioned in subsection (1)(b),

every promoter of the collection is guilty of an offence and liable on summary conviction to a fine not exceeding level 3 on the standard scale.

Public collections certificates

51 Applications for certificates

(1) A person or persons proposing to promote public charitable collections (other than exempt collections) may apply to the Charity Commission for a public collections certificate in respect of those collections.

(2) The application must be made—

(a) within the specified period falling before the first of the collections is to commence, or
(b) before such later date as the Commission may allow in the case of that application.

(3) The application must—

(a) be made in such form as may be specified,
(b) specify the period for which the certificate is sought (which must be no more than 5 years), and

(c) contain such other information as may be specified.

(4) An application under this section may be made for a public collections certificate in respect of a single collection; and the references in this Chapter, in the context of such certificates, to public charitable collections are to be read accordingly.

(5) In subsections (2) and (3) 'specified' means specified in regulations made by the Commission after consulting such persons or bodies of persons as it considers appropriate.

(6) Regulations under subsection (5)—

(a) must be published in such manner as the Commission considers appropriate,
(b) may make different provision for different cases or descriptions of case, and
(c) may make such incidental, supplementary, consequential or transitional provision as the Commission considers appropriate.

(7) In this section 'exempt collection' means a public charitable collection which is an exempt collection by virtue of section 50.

52 Determination of applications and issue of certificates

(1) On receiving an application for a public collections certificate made in accordance with section 51, the Commission may make such inquiries (whether under section 54 or otherwise) as it thinks fit.

(2) The Commission must, after making any such inquiries, determine the application by either—

(a) issuing a public collections certificate in respect of the collections, or
(b) refusing the application on one or more of the grounds specified in section 53(1).

(3) A public collections certificate—

(a) must specify such matters as may be prescribed, and
(b) shall (subject to section 56) be in force for—
 (i) the period specified in the application in accordance with section 51(3)(b), or
 (ii) such shorter period as the Commission thinks fit.

(4) The Commission may, at the time of issuing a public collections certificate, attach to it such conditions as it thinks fit.

(5) Conditions attached under subsection (4) may include conditions prescribed for the purposes of that subsection.

(6) The Commission must secure that the terms of any conditions attached under subsection (4) are consistent with the provisions of any regulations under section 63 (whether or not prescribing conditions for the purposes of that subsection).

(7) Where the Commission—

(a) refuses to issue a certificate, or
(b) attaches any condition to it,

it must serve on the applicant written notice of its decision and the reasons for its decision.

(8) That notice must also state the right of appeal conferred by section 57(1) and the time within which such an appeal must be brought.

53 Grounds for refusing to issue a certificate

(1) The grounds on which the Commission may refuse an application for a public collections certificate are—

(a) that the applicant has been convicted of a relevant offence;

(b) where the applicant is a person other than a charitable, benevolent or philanthropic institution for whose benefit the collections are proposed to be conducted, that the Commission is not satisfied that the applicant is authorised (whether by any such institution or by any person acting on behalf of any such institution) to promote the collections;

(c) that it appears to the Commission that the applicant, in promoting any other collection authorised under this Chapter or under section 119 of the 1982 Act, failed to exercise the required due diligence;

(d) that the Commission is not satisfied that the applicant will exercise the required due diligence in promoting the proposed collections;

(e) that it appears to the Commission that the amount likely to be applied for charitable, benevolent or philanthropic purposes in consequence of the proposed collections would be inadequate, having regard to the likely amount of the proceeds of the collections;

(f) that it appears to the Commission that the applicant or any other person would be likely to receive an amount by way of remuneration in connection with the collections that would be excessive, having regard to all the circumstances;

(g) that the applicant has failed to provide information—

(i) required for the purposes of the application for the certificate or a previous application, or

(ii) in response to a request under section 54(1);

(h) that it appears to the Commission that information so provided to it by the applicant is false or misleading in a material particular;

(i) that it appears to the Commission that the applicant or any person authorised by him—

(i) has breached any conditions attached to a previous public collections certificate, or

(ii) has persistently breached any conditions attached to a permit issued under section 59;

(j) that it appears to the Commission that the applicant or any person authorised by him has on any occasion breached any provision of regulations made under section 63(1)(b).

(2) For the purposes of subsection (1)—

(a) a 'relevant offence' is—

(i) an offence under section 5 of the 1916 Act;

(ii) an offence under the 1939 Act;

(iii) an offence under section 119 of the 1982 Act or regulations made under it;

(iv) an offence under this Chapter;

(v) an offence involving dishonesty; or

(vi) an offence of a kind the commission of which would, in the opinion of the Commission, be likely to be facilitated by the issuing to the applicant of a public collections certificate; and

(b) the 'required due diligence' is due diligence—
  (i) to secure that persons authorised by the applicant to act as collectors for the purposes of the collection were (or will be) fit and proper persons;
  (ii) to secure that such persons complied (or will comply) with the provisions of regulations under section 63(1)(b) of this Act or (as the case may be) section 119 of the 1982 Act; or
  (iii) to prevent badges or certificates of authority being obtained by persons other than those the applicant had so authorised.

(3) Where an application for a certificate is made by more than one person, any reference to the applicant in subsection (1) or (2) is to be construed as a reference to any of the applicants.

(4) Subject to subsections (5) and (6), the reference in subsection (2)(b)(iii) to badges or certificates of authority is a reference to badges or certificates of authority in a form prescribed by regulations under section 63(1)(b) of this Act or (as the case may be) under section 119 of the 1982 Act.

(5) Subsection (2)(b) applies to the conduct of the applicant (or any of the applicants) in relation to any public charitable collection authorised—

(a) under regulations made under section 5 of the 1916 Act (collection of money or sale of articles in a street or other public place), or
(b) under the 1939 Act (collection of money or other property by means of visits from house to house),

as it applies to his conduct in relation to a collection authorised under this Chapter, but subject to the modifications set out in subsection (6).

(6) The modifications are—

(a) in the case of a collection authorised under regulations made under the 1916 Act—
  (i) the reference in subsection (2)(b)(ii) to regulations under section 63(1)(b) of this Act is to be construed as a reference to the regulations under which the collection in question was authorised, and
  (ii) the reference in subsection (2)(b)(iii) to badges or certificates of authority is to be construed as a reference to any written authority provided to a collector pursuant to those regulations; and
(b) in the case of a collection authorised under the 1939 Act—
  (i) the reference in subsection (2)(b)(ii) to regulations under section 63(1)(b) of this Act is to be construed as a reference to regulations under section 4 of that Act, and
  (ii) the reference in subsection (2)(b)(iii) to badges or certificates of authority is to be construed as a reference to badges or certificates of authority in a form prescribed by such regulations.

(7) In subsections (1)(c) and (5) a reference to a collection authorised under this Chapter is a reference to a public charitable collection that—

(a) is conducted in accordance with section 48 or section 49 (as the case may be), or
(b) is an exempt collection by virtue of section 50.

(8) In this section—

'the 1916 Act' means the Police, Factories, &c. (Miscellaneous Provisions) Act 1916 (c 31);

'the 1939 Act' means the House to House Collections Act 1939 (c 44); and
'the 1982 Act' means the Civic Government (Scotland) Act 1982 (c 45).

54 Power to call for information and documents

(1) The Commission may request—

(a) any applicant for a public collections certificate, or
(b) any person to whom such a certificate has been issued,

to provide it with any information in his possession, or document in his custody or under this control, which is relevant to the exercise of any of its functions under this Chapter.

(2) Nothing in this section affects the power conferred on the Commission by [section 52 of the Charities Act 2011].

NOTE

Sub-s (2): words in square brackets substituted by the Charities Act 2011, s 354(1), Sch 7, Pt 2, para 118.

55 Transfer of certificate between trustees of unincorporated charity

(1) One or more individuals to whom a public collections certificate has been issued ('the holders') may apply to the Commission for a direction that the certificate be transferred to one or more other individuals ('the recipients').

(2) An application under subsection (1) must—

(a) be in such form as may be specified, and
(b) contain such information as may be specified.

(3) The Commission may direct that the certificate be transferred if it is satisfied that—

(a) each of the holders is or was a trustee of a charity which is not a body corporate;
(b) each of the recipients is a trustee of that charity and consents to the transfer; and
(c) the charity trustees consent to the transfer.

(4) Where the Commission refuses to direct that a certificate be transferred, it must serve on the holders written notice of—

(a) its decision, and
(b) the reasons for its decision.

(5) That notice must also state the right of appeal conferred by section 57(2) and the time within which such an appeal must be brought.

(6) Subsections (5) and (6) of section 51 apply for the purposes of subsection (2) of this section as they apply for the purposes of subsection (3) of that section.

(7) Except as provided by this section, a public collections certificate is not transferable.

56 Withdrawal or variation etc of certificates

(1) Where subsection (2), (3) or (4) applies, the Commission may—

(a) withdraw a public collections certificate,
(b) suspend such a certificate,

(c) attach any condition (or further condition) to such a certificate, or
(d) vary any existing condition of such a certificate.

(2) This subsection applies where the Commission—

(a) has reason to believe there has been a change in the circumstances which prevailed at the time when it issued the certificate, and
(b) is of the opinion that, if the application for the certificate had been made in the new circumstances, it would not have issued the certificate or would have issued it subject to different or additional conditions.

(3) This subsection applies where—

(a) the holder of a certificate has unreasonably refused to provide any information or document in response to a request under section 54(1), or
(b) the Commission has reason to believe that information provided to it by the holder of a certificate (or, where there is more than one holder, by any of them) for the purposes of the application for the certificate, or in response to such a request, was false or misleading in a material particular.

(4) This subsection applies where the Commission has reason to believe that there has been or is likely to be a breach of any condition of a certificate, or that a breach of such a condition is continuing.

(5) Any condition imposed at any time by the Commission under subsection (1) (whether by attaching a new condition to the certificate or by varying an existing condition) must be one that it would be appropriate for the Commission to attach to the certificate under section 52(4) if the holder was applying for it in the circumstances prevailing at that time.

(6) The exercise by the Commission of the power conferred by paragraph (b), (c) or (d) of subsection (1) on one occasion does not prevent it from exercising any of the powers conferred by that subsection on a subsequent occasion; and on any subsequent occasion the reference in subsection (2)(a) to the time when the Commission issued the certificate is a reference to the time when it last exercised any of those powers.

(7) Where the Commission—

(a) withdraws or suspends a certificate,
(b) attaches a condition to a certificate, or
(c) varies an existing condition of a certificate,

it must serve on the holder written notice of its decision and the reasons for its decision.

(8) That notice must also state the right of appeal conferred by section 57(3) and the time within which such an appeal must be brought.

(9) If the Commission—

(a) considers that the interests of the public require a decision by it under this section to have immediate effect, and
(b) includes a statement to that effect and the reasons for it in the notice served under subsection (7),

the decision takes effect when that notice is served on the holder.

(10) In any other case the certificate shall continue to have effect as if it had not been withdrawn or suspended or (as the case may be) as if the condition had not been attached or varied—

(a) until the time for bringing an appeal under section 57(3) has expired, or
(b) if such an appeal is duly brought, until the determination or abandonment of the appeal.

(11) A certificate suspended under this section shall (subject to any appeal and any withdrawal of the certificate) remain suspended until—

(a) such time as the Commission may by notice direct that the certificate is again in force, or
(b) the end of the period of six months beginning with the date on which the suspension takes effect,

whichever is the sooner.

57 Appeals against decisions of the Commission

(1) A person who has duly applied to the Commission for a public collections certificate may appeal to the [Tribunal] against a decision of the Commission under section 52—

(a) to refuse to issue the certificate, or
(b) to attach any condition to it.

(2) A person to whom a public collections certificate has been issued may appeal to the Tribunal against a decision of the Commission not to direct that the certificate be transferred under section 55.

(3) A person to whom a public collections certificate has been issued may appeal to the Tribunal against a decision of the Commission under section 56—

(a) to withdraw or suspend the certificate,
(b) to attach a condition to the certificate, or
(c) to vary an existing condition of the certificate.

(4) The Attorney General may appeal to the Tribunal against a decision of the Commission—

(a) to issue, or to refuse to issue, a certificate,
(b) to attach, or not to attach, any condition to a certificate (whether under section 52 or section 56),
(c) to direct, or not to direct, that a certificate be transferred under section 55,
(d) to withdraw or suspend, or not to withdraw or suspend, a certificate, or
(e) to vary, or not to vary, an existing condition of a certificate.

(5) In determining an appeal under this section, the Tribunal—

(a) must consider afresh the decision appealed against, and
(b) may take into account evidence which was not available to the Commission.

(6) On an appeal under this section, the Tribunal may—

(a) dismiss the appeal,
(b) quash the decision, or
(c) substitute for the decision another decision of a kind that the Commission could have made;

and in any case the Tribunal may give such directions as it thinks fit, having regard to the provisions of this Chapter and of regulations under section 63.

(7) If the Tribunal quashes the decision, it may remit the matter to the Commission (either generally or for determination in accordance with a finding made or direction given by the Tribunal).

[(8) In this section 'the Tribunal', in relation to any appeal under this section, means –

(a) the Upper Tribunal, in any case where it is determined by or under Tribunal Procedure Rules that the Upper Tribunal is to hear the appeal; or
(b) the First-tier Tribunal, in any other case.]

NOTE

Sub-s (1): word 'Tribunal' in square brackets substituted by SI 2009/1834, art 4(1), Sch 1, para 17(a).

Sub-s (8): inserted by SI 2009/1834, art 4(1), Sch 1, para 17(b).

Permits

58 Applications for permits to conduct collections in public places

(1) A person or persons proposing to promote a collection in a public place (other than an exempt collection) in the area of a local authority may apply to the authority for a permit to conduct that collection.

(2) The application must be made within the prescribed period falling before the day (or the first of the days) on which the collection is to take place, except as provided in subsection (4).

(3) The application must—

(a) specify the date or dates in respect of which it is desired that the permit, if issued, should have effect (which, in the case of two or more dates, must not span a period of more than 12 months);
(b) be accompanied by a copy of the public collections certificate in force under section 52 in respect of the proposed collection; and
(c) contain such information as may be prescribed.

(4) Where an application ('the certificate application') has been made in accordance with section 51 for a public collections certificate in respect of the collection and either—

(a) the certificate application has not been determined by the end of the period mentioned in subsection (2) above, or
(b) the certificate application has been determined by the issue of such a certificate but at a time when there is insufficient time remaining for the application mentioned in subsection (2) ('the permit application') to be made by the end of that period,

the permit application must be made as early as practicable before the day (or the first of the days) on which the collection is to take place.

(5) In this section 'exempt collection' means a collection in a public place which is an exempt collection by virtue of section 50.

59 Determination of applications and issue of permits

(1) On receiving an application made in accordance with section 58 for a permit in respect of a collection in a public place, a local authority must determine the application within the prescribed period by either—

(a) issuing a permit in respect of the collection, or
(b) refusing the application on the ground specified in section 60(1).

(2) Where a local authority issue such a permit, it shall (subject to section 61) have effect in respect of the date or dates specified in the application in accordance with section 58(3)(a).

(3) At the time of issuing a permit under this section, a local authority may attach to it such conditions within paragraphs (a) to (d) below as they think fit, having regard to the local circumstances of the collection—

(a) conditions specifying the day of the week, date, time or frequency of the collection;
(b) conditions specifying the locality or localities within their area in which the collection may be conducted;
(c) conditions regulating the manner in which the collection is to be conducted;
(d) such other conditions as may be prescribed for the purposes of this subsection.

(4) A local authority must secure that the terms of any conditions attached under subsection (3) are consistent with the provisions of any regulations under section 63 (whether or not prescribing conditions for the purposes of that subsection).

(5) Where a local authority—

(a) refuse to issue a permit, or
(b) attach any condition to it,

they must serve on the applicant written notice of their decision and the reasons for their decision.

(6) That notice must also state the right of appeal conferred by section 62(2) and the time within which such an appeal must be brought.

60 Refusal of permits

(1) The only ground on which a local authority may refuse an application for a permit to conduct a collection in a public place is that it appears to them that the collection would cause undue inconvenience to members of the public by reason of—

(a) the day or the week or date on or in which,
(b) the time at which,
(c) the frequency with which, or
(d) the locality or localities in which,

it is proposed to be conducted.

(2) In making a decision under subsection (1), a local authority may have regard to the fact (where it is the case) that the collection is proposed to be conducted—

(a) wholly or partly in a locality in which another collection in a public place is already authorised to be conducted under this Chapter, and
(b) on a day on which that other collection is already so authorised, or on the day falling immediately before, or immediately after, any such day.

(3) A local authority must not, however, have regard to the matters mentioned in subsection (2) if it appears to them—

(a) that the proposed collection would be conducted only in one location, which is on land to which members of the public would have access only—

(i) by virtue of the express or implied permission of the occupier of the land, or
(ii) by virtue of any enactment, and

(b) that the occupier of the land consents to that collection being conducted there;

and for this purpose 'the occupier', in relation to unoccupied land, means the person entitled to occupy it.

(4) In this section a reference to a collection in a public place authorised under this Chapter is a reference to a collection in a public place that—

(a) is conducted in accordance with section 48, or
(b) is an exempt collection by virtue of section 50.

61 Withdrawal or variation etc of permits

(1) Where subsection (2), (3) or (4) applies, a local authority who have issued a permit under section 59 may—

(a) withdraw the permit,
(b) attach any condition (or further condition) to the permit, or
(c) vary any existing condition of the permit.

(2) This subsection applies where the local authority—

(a) have reason to believe that there has been a change in the circumstances which prevailed at the time when they issued the permit, and
(b) are of the opinion that, if the application for the permit had been made in the new circumstances, they would not have issued the permit or would have issued it subject to different or additional conditions.

(3) This subsection applies where the local authority have reason to believe that any information provided to them by the holder of a permit (or, where there is more than one holder, by any of them) for the purposes of the application for the permit was false or misleading in a material particular.

(4) This subsection applies where the local authority have reason to believe that there has been or is likely to be a breach of any condition of a permit issued by them, or that a breach of such a condition is continuing.

(5) Any condition imposed at any time by a local authority under subsection (1) (whether by attaching a new condition to the permit or by varying an existing condition) must be one that it would be appropriate for the authority to attach to the permit under section 59(3) if the holder was applying for it in the circumstances prevailing at that time.

(6) The exercise by a local authority of the power conferred by paragraph (b) or (c) of subsection (1) on one occasion does not prevent them from exercising any of the powers conferred by that subsection on a subsequent occasion; and on any subsequent occasion the reference in subsection (2)(a) to the time when the local authority issued the permit is a reference to the time when they last exercised any of those powers.

(7) Where under this section a local authority—

(a) withdraw a permit,
(b) attach a condition to a permit, or
(c) vary an existing condition of a permit,

they must serve on the holder written notice of their decision and the reasons for their decision.

(8) That notice must also state the right of appeal conferred by section 62(3) and the time within which such an appeal must be brought.

(9) Where a local authority withdraw a permit under this section, they must send a copy of their decision and the reasons for it to the Commission.

(10) Where a local authority under this section withdraw a permit, attach any condition to a permit, or vary an existing condition of a permit, the permit shall continue to have effect as if it had not been withdrawn or (as the case may be) as if the condition had not been attached or varied—

- (a) until the time for bringing an appeal under section 62(3) has expired, or
- (b) if such an appeal is duly brought, until the determination or abandonment of the appeal.

62 Appeals against decisions of local authority

(1) A person who, in relation to a public charitable collection, has duly notified a local authority of the matters mentioned in section 50(3) may appeal to a magistrates' court against a decision of the local authority under section 50(4)—

- (a) that the collection is not a local, short-term collection, or
- (b) that the promoters or any of them has breached any such provision, or been convicted of any such offence, as is mentioned in paragraph (b) of that subsection.

(2) A person who has duly applied to a local authority for a permit to conduct a collection in a public place in the authority's area may appeal to a magistrates' court against a decision of the authority under section 59—

- (a) to refuse to issue a permit, or
- (b) to attach any condition to it.

(3) A person to whom a permit has been issued may appeal to a magistrates' court against a decision of the local authority under section 61—

- (a) to withdraw the permit,
- (b) to attach a condition to the permit, or
- (c) to vary an existing condition of the permit.

(4) An appeal under subsection (1), (2) or (3) shall be by way of complaint for an order, and the Magistrates' Courts Act 1980 (c 43) shall apply to the proceedings.

(5) Any such appeal shall be brought within 14 days of the date of service on the person in question of the relevant notice under section 50(4), section 59(5) or (as the case may be) section 61(7); and for the purposes of this section an appeal shall be taken to be brought when the complaint is made.

(6) An appeal against the decision of a magistrates' court on an appeal under subsection (1), (2) or (3) may be brought to the Crown Court.

(7) On an appeal to a magistrates' court or the Crown Court under this section, the court may confirm, vary or reverse the local authority's decision and generally give such directions as it thinks fit, having regard to the provisions of this Chapter and of any regulations under section 63.

(8) On an appeal against a decision of a local authority under section 50(4), directions under subsection (7) may include a direction that the collection may be conducted—

(a) on the date or dates notified in accordance with section 50(3)(b), or
(b) on such other date or dates as may be specified in the direction;

and if so conducted the collection is to be regarded as one that is an exempt collection by virtue of section 50.

(9) It shall be the duty of the local authority to comply with any directions given by the court under subsection (7); but the authority need not comply with any directions given by a magistrates' court—

(a) until the time for bringing an appeal under subsection (6) has expired, or
(b) if such an appeal is duly brought, until the determination or abandonment of the appeal.

Supplementary

63 Regulations

(1) The Minister may make regulations—

(a) prescribing the matters which a local authority are to take into account in determining whether a collection is local in character for the purposes of section 50(2)(a);
(b) for the purpose of regulating the conduct of public charitable collections;
(c) prescribing anything falling to be prescribed by virtue of any provision of this Chapter.

(2) The matters which may be prescribed by regulations under subsection (1)(a) include—

(a) the extent of the area within which the appeal is to be conducted;
(b) whether the appeal forms part of a series of appeals;
(c) the number of collectors making the appeal and whether they are acting for remuneration or otherwise;
(d) the financial resources (of any description) of any charitable, benevolent or philanthropic institution for whose benefit the appeal is to be conducted;
(e) where the promoters live or have any place of business.

(3) Regulations under subsection (1)(b) may make provision—

(a) about the keeping and publication of accounts;
(b) for the prevention of annoyance to members of the public;
(c) with respect to the use by collectors of badges and certificates of authority, or badges incorporating such certificates, including, in particular, provision—
  (i) prescribing the form of such badges and certificates;
  (ii) requiring a collector, on request, to permit his badge, or any certificate of authority held by him of the purposes of the collection, to be inspected by a constable or a duly authorised officer of a local authority, or by an occupier of any premises visited by him in the course of the collection;
(d) for prohibiting persons under a prescribed age from acting as collectors, and prohibiting others from causing them so to act.

(4) Nothing in subsection (2) or (3) prejudices the generality of subsection (1)(a) or (b).

(5) Regulations under this section may provide that any failure to comply with a specified provision of the regulations is to be an offence punishable on summary conviction by a fine not exceeding level 2 on the standard scale.

(6) Before making regulations under this section the Minister must consult such persons or bodies of persons as he considers appropriate.

64 Offences

(1) A person commits an offence if, in connection with any charitable appeal, he displays or uses—

(a) a prescribed badge or prescribed certificate of authority which is not for the time being held by him for the purposes of the appeal pursuant to regulations under section 63, or

(b) any badge or article, or any certificate or other document, so nearly resembling a prescribed badge or (as the case may be) a prescribed certificate of authority as to be likely to deceive a member of the public.

(2) A person commits an offence if—

(a) for the purposes of an application made under section 51 or section 58, or

(b) for the purposes of section 49 or section 50,

he knowingly or recklessly furnishes any information which is false or misleading in a material particular.

(3) A person guilty of an offence under this section is liable on summary conviction to a fine not exceeding level 5 on the standard scale.

(4) In subsection (1) 'prescribed badge' and 'prescribed certificate of authority' mean respectively a badge and a certificate of authority in such form as may be prescribed.

65 Offences by bodies corporate

(1) Where any offence under this Chapter or any regulations made under it—

(a) is committed by a body corporate, and

(b) is proved to have been committed with the consent or connivance of, or to be attributable to any neglect on the part of, any director, manager, secretary or other similar officer of the body corporate, or any person who was purporting to act in any such capacity,

he as well as the body corporate shall be guilty of that offence and shall be liable to be proceeded against and punished accordingly.

(2) In subsection (1) 'director', in relation to a body corporate whose affairs are managed by its members, means a member of the body corporate.

66 Service of documents

(1) This section applies to any notice required to be served under this Chapter.

(2) A notice to which this section applies may be served on a person (other than a body corporate)—

(a) by delivering it to that person;

(b) by leaving it at his last known address in the United Kingdom; or

(c) by sending it by post to him at that address.

(3) A notice to which this section applies may be served on a body corporate by delivering it or sending it by post—

(a) to the registered or principal office of the body in the United Kingdom, or
(b) if it has no such office in the United Kingdom, to any place in the United Kingdom where it carries on business or conducts its activities (as the case may be).

(4) A notice to which this section applies may also be served on a person (including a body corporate) by sending it by post to that person at an address notified by that person for the purposes of this subsection to the person or persons by whom it is required to be served.

CHAPTER 2
FUND-RAISING

67 Statements indicating benefits for charitable institutions and fund-raisers

(1) Section 60 of the Charities Act 1992 (c 41) (fund-raisers required to indicate institutions benefiting and arrangements for remuneration) is amended as follows.

(2) In subsection (1) (statements by professional fund-raisers raising money for particular charitable institutions), for paragraph (c) substitute—

'(c) the method by which the fund-raiser's remuneration in connection with the appeal is to be determined and the notifiable amount of that remuneration.'

(3) In subsection (2) (statements by professional fund-raisers raising money for charitable purposes etc), for paragraph (c) substitute—

'(c) the method by which his remuneration in connection with the appeal is to be determined and the notifiable amount of that remuneration.'

(4) In subsection (3) (statements by commercial participators raising money for particular charitable institutions), for paragraph (c) substitute—

'(c) the notifiable amount of whichever of the following sums is applicable in the circumstances—
(i) the sum representing so much of the consideration given for goods or services sold or supplied by him as is to be given to or applied for the benefit of the institution or institutions concerned,
(ii) the sum representing so much of any other proceeds of a promotional venture undertaken by him as is to be so given or applied, or
(iii) the sum of the donations by him in connection with the sale or supply of any such goods or services which are to be so given or supplied.'

(5) After subsection (3) insert—

'(3A) In subsections (1) to (3) a reference to the "notifiable amount" of any remuneration or other sum is a reference—

(a) to the actual amount of the remuneration or sum, if that is known at the time when the statement is made; and
(b) otherwise to the estimated amount of the remuneration or sum, calculated as accurately as is reasonably possible in the circumstances.'

68 Statements indicating benefits for charitable institutions and collectors

After section 60 of the 1992 Act insert—

'60A Other persons making appeals required to indicate institutions benefiting and arrangements for remuneration

(1) Subsections (1) and (2) of section 60 apply to a person acting for reward as a collector in respect of a public charitable collection as they apply to a professional fund-raiser.

(2) But those subsections do not so apply to a person excluded by virtue of—

(a) subsection (3) below, or
(b) section 60B(1) (exclusion of lower-paid collectors).

(3) Those subsections do not so apply to a person if—

(a) section 60(1) or (2) applies apart from subsection (1) (by virtue of the exception in section 58(2)(c) for persons treated as promoters), or
(b) subsection (4) or (5) applies,

in relation to his acting for reward as a collector in respect of the collection mentioned in subsection (1) above.

(4) Where a person within subsection (6) solicits money or other property for the benefit of one or more particular charitable institutions, the solicitation shall be accompanied by a statement clearly indicating—

(a) the name or names of the institution or institutions for whose benefit the solicitation is being made;
(b) if there is more than one such institution, the proportions in which the institutions are respectively to benefit;
(c) the fact that he is an officer, employee or trustee of the institution or company mentioned in subsection (6); and
(d) the fact that he is receiving remuneration as an officer, employee or trustee or (as the case may be) for acting as a collector.

(5) Where a person within subsection (6) solicits money or other property for charitable, benevolent or philanthropic purposes of any description (rather than for the benefit of one or more particular charitable institutions), the solicitation shall be accompanied by a statement clearly indicating—

(a) the fact that he is soliciting money or other property for those purposes and not for the benefit of any particular charitable institution or institutions;
(b) the method by which it is to be determined how the proceeds of the appeal are to be distributed between different charitable institutions;
(c) the fact that he is an officer, employee or trustee of the institution or company mentioned in subsection (6); and
(d) the fact that he is receiving remuneration as an officer, employee or trustee or (as the case may be) for acting as a collector.

(6) A person is within this subsection if—

(a) he is an officer or employee of a charitable institution or a company connected with any such institution, or a trustee of any such institution,
(b) he is acting as a collector in that capacity, and

(c) he receives remuneration either in his capacity as officer, employee or trustee or for acting as a collector.

(7) But a person is not within subsection (6) if he is excluded by virtue of section 60B(4).

(8) Where any requirement of—

(a) subsection (1) or (2) of section 60, as it applies by virtue of subsection (1) above, or
(b) subsection (4) or (5) above,

is not complied with in relation to any solicitation, the collector concerned shall be guilty of an offence and liable on summary conviction to a fine not exceeding level 5 on the standard scale.

(9) Section 60(8) and (9) apply in relation to an offence under subsection (8) above as they apply in relation to an offence under section 60(7).

(10) In this section—

"the appeal", in relation to any solicitation by a collector, means the campaign or other fund-raising venture in the course of which the solicitation is made;
"collector" has the meaning given by section 47(1) of the Charities Act 2006;
"public charitable collection" has the meaning given by section 45 of that Act.

60B Exclusion of lower-paid collectors from provisions of section 60A

(1) Section 60(1) and (2) do not apply (by virtue of section 60A(1)) to a person who is under the earnings limit in subsection (2) below.

(2) A person is under the earnings limit in this subsection if he does not receive—

(a) more than—
(i) £5 per day, or
(ii) £500 per year,

by way of remuneration for acting as a collector in relation to relevant collections, or
(b) more than £500 by way of remuneration for acting as a collector in relation to the collection mentioned in section 60A(1).

(3) In subsection (2) "relevant collections" means public charitable collections conducted for the benefit of—

(a) the charitable institution or institutions, or
(b) the charitable, benevolent or philanthropic purposes,

for whose benefit the collection mentioned in section 60A(1) is conducted.

(4) A person is not within section 60A(6) if he is under the earnings limit in subsection (5) below.

(5) A person is under the earnings limit in this subsection if the remuneration received by him as mentioned in section 60A(6)(c)—

(a) is not more than—
(i) £5 per day, or
(ii) £500 per year, or

(b) if a lump sum, is not more than £500.

(6) The Minister may by order amend subsections (2) and (5) by substituting a different sum for any sum for the time being specified there.'

69 Reserve power to control fund-raising by charitable institutions

After section 64 of the 1992 Act insert—

'64A Reserve power to control fund-raising by charitable institutions

(1) The Minister may make such regulations as appear to him to be necessary or desirable for or in connection with regulating charity fund-raising.

(2) In this section "charity fund-raising" means activities which are carried on by—

(a) charitable institutions,
(b) persons managing charitable institutions, or
(c) persons or companies connected with such institutions,

and involve soliciting or otherwise procuring funds for the benefit of such institutions or companies connected with them, or for general charitable, benevolent or philanthropic purposes.

But "activities" does not include primary purpose trading.

(3) Regulations under this section may, in particular, impose a good practice requirement on the persons managing charitable institutions in circumstances where—

(a) those institutions,
(b) the persons managing them, or
(c) persons or companies connected with such institutions,

are engaged in charity fund-raising.

(4) A "good practice requirement" is a requirement to take all reasonable steps to ensure that the fund-raising is carried out in such a way that—

(a) it does not unreasonably intrude on the privacy of those from whom funds are being solicited or procured;
(b) it does not involve the making of unreasonably persistent approaches to persons to donate funds;
(c) it does not result in undue pressure being placed on persons to donate funds;
(d) it does not involve the making of any false or misleading representation about any of the matters mentioned in subsection (5).

(5) The matters are—

(a) the extent or urgency of any need for funds on the part of any charitable institution or company connected with such an institution;
(b) any use to which funds donated in response to the fund-raising are to be put by such an institution or company;
(c) the activities, achievements or finances of such an institution or company.

(6) Regulations under this section may provide that a person who persistently fails, without reasonable excuse, to comply with any specified requirement of the regulations is to be guilty of an offence and liable on summary conviction to a fine not exceeding level 2 on the standard scale.

(7) For the purposes of this section—

(a) "funds" means money or other property;
(b) "general charitable, benevolent or philanthropic purposes" means charitable, benevolent or philanthropic purposes other than those associated with one or more particular institutions;
(c) the persons "managing" a charitable institution are the charity trustees or other persons having the general control and management of the administration of the institution; and
(d) a person is "connected" with a charitable institution if he is an employee or agent of—
(i) the institution,
(ii) the persons managing it, or
(iii) a company connected with it,

or he is a volunteer acting on behalf of the institution or such a company.

(8) In this section "primary purpose trading", in relation to a charitable institution, means any trade carried on by the institution or a company connected with it where—

(a) the trade is carried on in the course of the actual carrying out of a primary purpose of the institution; or
(b) the work in connection with the trade is mainly carried out by beneficiaries of the institution.'

Chapter 3
Financial Assistance

70 Power of relevant Minister to give financial assistance to charitable, benevolent or philanthropic institutions

(1) A relevant Minister may give financial assistance to any charitable, benevolent or philanthropic institution in respect of any of the institution's activities which directly or indirectly benefit the whole or any part of England (whether or not they also benefit any other area).

(2) Financial assistance under subsection (1) may be given in any form and, in particular, may be given by way of—

(a) grants,
(b) loans,
(c) guarantees, or
(d) incurring expenditure for the benefit of the person assisted.

(3) Financial assistance under subsection (1) may be given on such terms and conditions as the relevant Minister considers appropriate.

(4) Those terms and conditions may, in particular, include provision as to—

(a) the purposes for which the assistance may be used;
(b) circumstances in which the assistance is to be repaid, or otherwise made good, to the relevant Minister, and the manner in which that is to be done;
(c) the making of reports to the relevant Minister regarding the uses to which the assistance has been put;
(d) the keeping, and making available for inspection, of accounts and other records;

(e) the carrying out of examinations by the Comptroller and Auditor General into the economy, efficiency and effectiveness with which the assistance has been used;

(f) the giving by the institution of financial assistance in any form to other persons on such terms and conditions as the institution or the relevant Minister considers appropriate.

(5) A person receiving assistance under this section must comply with the terms and conditions on which it is given, and compliance may be enforced by the relevant Minister.

(6) A relevant Minister may make arrangements for—

(a) assistance under subsection (1) to be given, or

(b) any other of his functions under this section to be exercised,

by some other person.

(7) Arrangements under subsection (6) may make provision for the functions concerned to be so exercised—

(a) either wholly or to such extent as may be specified in the arrangements, and

(b) either generally or in such cases or circumstances as may be so specified,

but do not prevent the functions concerned from being exercised by a relevant Minister.

(8) As soon as possible after 31 March in each year, a relevant Minister must make a report on any exercise by him of any powers under this section during the period of 12 months ending on that day.

(9) The relevant Minister must lay a copy of the report before each House of Parliament.

(10) In this section 'charitable, benevolent or philanthropic institution' means—

(a) a charity, or

(b) an institution (other than a charity) which is established for charitable, benevolent or philanthropic purposes.

(11) In this section 'relevant Minister' means the Secretary of State [or the Minister for the Cabinet Office].

NOTE

Sub-s (11): words 'or the Minister for the Cabinet Office' in square brackets substituted by SI 2010/1839, arts 3(2)(b), 7, Schedule, para 15.

71 Power of National Assembly for Wales to give financial assistance to charitable, benevolent or philanthropic institutions

(1) The National Assembly for Wales may give financial assistance to any charitable, benevolent or philanthropic institution in respect of any of the institution's activities which directly or indirectly benefit the whole or any part of Wales (whether or not they also benefit any other area).

(2) Financial assistance under subsection (1) may be given in any form and, in particular, may be given by way of—

(a) grants,

(b) loans,

(c) guarantees, or

(d) incurring expenditure for the benefit of the person assisted.

(3) Financial assistance under subsection (1) may be given on such terms and conditions as the Assembly considers appropriate.

(4) Those terms and conditions may, in particular, include provision as to—

(a) the purposes for which the assistance may be used;
(b) circumstances in which the assistance is to be repaid, or otherwise made good, to the Assembly, and the manner in which that is to be done;
(c) the making of reports to the Assembly regarding the uses to which the assistance has been put;
(d) the keeping, and making available for inspection, of accounts and other records;
(e) the carrying out of examinations by the Auditor General for Wales into the economy, efficiency and effectiveness with which the assistance has been used;
(f) the giving by the institution of financial assistance in any form to other persons on such terms and conditions as the institution or the Assembly considers appropriate.

(5) A person receiving assistance under this section must comply with the terms and conditions on which it is given, and compliance may be enforced by the Assembly.

(6) The Assembly may make arrangements for—

(a) assistance under subsection (1) to be given, or
(b) any other of its functions under this section to be exercised,

by some other person.

(7) Arrangements under subsection (6) may make provision for the functions concerned to be so exercised—

(a) either wholly or to such extent as may be specified in the arrangements, and
(b) either generally or in such cases or circumstances as may be so specified,

but do not prevent the functions concerned from being exercised by the Assembly.

(8) After 31 March in each year, the Assembly must publish a report on the exercise of powers under this section during the period of 12 months ending on that day.

(9) In this section 'charitable, benevolent or philanthropic institution' means—

(a) a charity, or
(b) an institution (other than a charity) which is established for charitable, benevolent or philanthropic purposes.

PART 4
MISCELLANEOUS AND GENERAL

MISCELLANEOUS

72 Disclosure of information to and by Northern Ireland regulator

(1) This section applies if a body (referred to in this section as 'the Northern Ireland regulator') is established to exercise functions in Northern Ireland which are similar in nature to the functions exercised in England and Wales by the Charity Commission.

(2) The Minister may by regulations authorise relevant public authorities to disclose information to the Northern Ireland regulator for the purpose of enabling or assisting the Northern Ireland regulator to discharge any of its functions.

(3) If the regulations authorise the disclosure of Revenue and Customs information, they must contain provision in relation to that disclosure which corresponds to the provision made in relation to the disclosure of such information by [section 55 of the Charities Act 2011] . . ..

(4) In the case of information disclosed to the Northern Ireland regulator pursuant to regulations made under this section, any power of the Northern Ireland regulator to disclose the information is exercisable subject to any express restriction subject to which the information was disclosed to the Northern Ireland regulator.

(5) Subsection (4) does not apply in relation to Revenue and Customs information disclosed to the Northern Ireland regulator pursuant to regulations made under this section; but any such information may not be further disclosed except with the consent of the Commissioners for Her Majesty's Revenue and Customs.

(6) Any person specified, or of a description specified, in regulations made under this section who discloses information in contravention of subsection (5) is guilty of an offence and liable–

(a) on summary conviction, to imprisonment for a term not exceeding 12 months or to a fine not exceeding the statutory maximum, or both;
(b) on conviction on indictment, to imprisonment for a term not exceeding two years or to a fine, or both.

(7) It is a defence for a person charged with an offence under subsection (5) of disclosing information to prove that he reasonably believed–

(a) that the disclosure was lawful, or
(b) that the information had already and lawfully been made available to the public.

(8) In the application of this section to Scotland or Northern Ireland, the reference to 12 months in subsection (6) is to be read as a reference to 6 months.

(9) In this section –

'relevant public authority' means

(a) any government department (other than a Northern Ireland department),
(b) any local authority in England, Wales or Scotland,
(c) any person who is a constable in England and Wales or Scotland,
(d) any other body or person discharging functions of a public nature (including a body or person discharging regulatory functions in relation to any description of activities), except a body or person whose functions are exercisable only or mainly in or as regards Northern Ireland and relate only or mainly to transferred matters;

'Revenue and Customs information' means information held as mentioned in section 18(1) of the Commissioners for Revenue and Customs Act 2005 (c 11);

'transferred matter' has the same meaning as in the Northern Ireland Act 1998 (c 47).

NOTES

Sub-s (3): words in square brackets substituted by the Charities Act 2011, s 354(1), Sch 7, Pt 2, para 119.

Sub-s (3): words omitted repealed by the Corporation Tax Act 2010, s 1177, Sch 1, Pt 2, paras 491, 493.

73 Report on operation of this Act

(1) The Minister must, before the end of the period of five years beginning with the day on which this Act is passed, appoint a person to review generally the operation of this Act.

(2) The review must address, in particular, the following matters–

(a) the effect of the Act on–
  (i) excepted charities,
  (ii) public confidence in charities,
  (iii) the level of charitable donations, and
  (iv) the willingness of individuals to volunteer,

(b) the status of the Charity Commission as a government department, and

(c) any other matters the Minister considers appropriate.

(3) After the person appointed under subsection (1) has completed his review, he must compile a report of his conclusions.

(4) The Minister must lay before Parliament a copy of the report mentioned in subsection (3).

(5) For the purposes of this section a charity is an excepted charity if–

(a) it falls within paragraph (b) or (c) of section 3A(2) of the 1993 Act (as amended by section 9 of this Act), or

(b) it does not fall within either of those paragraphs but, immediately before [31 January 2009], it fell within section 3(5)(b) or (5B)(b) of the 1993 Act.

[(6) This section has effect, in relation to any time occurring on or after the commencement of the Charities Act 2011 as if–

(a) the reference in subsection (1) to the operation of this Act included (in relation to provisions of this Act repealed and re-enacted by the 2011 Act) a reference to the operation of the 2011 Act,

(b) the reference in subsection (2)(a) to the effect of the Act included (in relation to provisions of this Act repealed and re-enacted by the 2011 Act) a reference to the effect of the 2011 Act, and

(c) the reference in subsection (5)(a) to paragraph (b) or (c) of section 3A(2) of the 1993 Act (as amended by section 9 of this Act) were a reference to paragraph (b) or (c) of section 30(2) of the 2011 Act.]

NOTES

Sub-s (5): in para (b) words '31 January 2009' in square brackets substituted by the Charities Act 2011, s 354(1), Sch 7, Pt 2, para 120(1).

Sub-s (6): inserted by the Charities Act 2011, s 354(1), Sch 7, Pt 2, para 120(2).

General

74 Orders and regulations

(1) Any power of a relevant Minister to make an order or regulations under this Act is exercisable by statutory instrument.

(2) Any such power –

(a) may be exercised so as to make different provision for different cases or descriptions of case or different purposes or areas, and

(b) includes power to make such incidental, supplementary, consequential, transitory, transitional or saving provision as the relevant Minister considers appropriate.

(3) Subject to subsection (4), orders or regulations made by a relevant Minister under this Act are to be subject to annulment in pursuance of a resolution of either House of Parliament.

(4) Subsection (3) does not apply to –

(a) . . .
(b) . . .
(c) any regulations under section 72,
(d) any order under section 75(4) which amends or repeals any provision of an Act or an Act of the Scottish Parliament,
(e) any order under section . . . 77, or
(f) any order under section 79(2).

(5) No order or regulations within subsection (4). . . (c), (d) or (e) may be made by a relevant Minister (whether alone or with other provisions) unless a draft of the order or regulations has been laid before, and approved by resolution of, each House of Parliament.

(6) . . .

(7) In this section 'relevant Minister' means the Secretary of State or the Minister for the Cabinet Office.

NOTES

Sub-s (4): paras (a), (b) repealed by the Charities Act 2011, s 354(1), (4), Sch 7, Pt 2, para 121(1)(a), Sch 10.

Sub-s (4): in para (e) words omitted repealed by the Charities Act 2011, s 354(1), (4), Sch 7, Pt 2, para 121(1)(b), Sch 10.

Sub-s (5): reference omitted repealed by the Charities Act 2011, s 354(1), (4), Sch 7, Pt 2, para 121(2), Sch 10.

Sub-s (6): repealed by the Charities Act 2011, s 354(1), (4), Sch 7, Pt 2, para 121(3), Sch 10.

75 Amendments, repeals, revocations and transitional provisions

(1) Schedule 8 contains minor and consequential amendments.

(2) Schedule 9 makes provision for the repeal and revocation of enactments (including enactments which are spent).

(3) Schedule 10 contains transitional provisions and savings.

(4) A relevant Minister may by order make–

(a) such supplementary, incidental or consequential provision, or
(b) such transitory, transitional or saving provision,

as he considers appropriate for the general purposes, or any particular purposes, of this Act or in consequence of, or for giving full effect to, any provision made by this Act.

(5) An order under subsection (4) may amend, repeal, revoke or otherwise modify any enactment (including an enactment restating, with or without modifications, an enactment amended by this Act).

(6) In this section 'relevant Minister' means the Secretary of State or the Minister for the Cabinet Office.

76 [*repealed*]

. . .

NOTES

Repealed by the Charities Act 2011, s 354(1), (4), Sch 7, Pt 2, para 122, Sch 10.

77 Amendments reflecting changes in company law audit provisions

(1) The Minister may by order make such amendments of the 1993 Act or this Act as he considers appropriate –

(a) in consequence of, or in connection with, any changes made or to be made by any enactment to the provisions of company law relating to the accounts of charitable companies or to the auditing of, or preparation of reports in respect of, such accounts;

(b) for the purposes of, or in connection with, applying provisions of Schedule 5A to the 1993 Act (group accounts) to charitable companies that are not required to produce group accounts under company law.

(2) In this section –

'accounts' includes group accounts;
'amendments' includes repeals and modifications;
'charitable companies' means companies which are charities;
'company law' means the enactments relating to companies.

78 Interpretation

(1) In this Act–

'the 1992 Act' means the Charities Act 1992 (c 41);
'the 1993 Act' means the Charities Act 1993 (c 10).

(2) In this Act –

(a) . . .

(b) 'charitable purposes' has [(in accordance with section 2(2) of the Charities Act 2011) the meaning given by section 2(1) of that Act]; and

(c) 'charity trustees' has the same meaning as in [that Act];

. . .

(3) . . .

(4) In this Act 'enactment' includes–

(a) any provision of subordinate legislation (within the meaning of the Interpretation Act 1978 (c 30)),

(b) a provision of a Measure of the Church Assembly or of the General Synod of the Church of England, and

(c) (in the context of section . . . 75(5)) any provision made by or under an Act of the Scottish Parliament or Northern Ireland legislation,

and references to enactments include enactments passed or made after the passing of this Act.

(5) In this Act 'institution' means an institution whether incorporated or not, and includes a trust or undertaking.

(6) In this Act 'the Minister' means the Minister for the Cabinet Office.

(7) Subsections (2) to (5) apply except where the context otherwise requires.

NOTES

Sub-s (2): para (a) repealed by the Charities Act 2011, s 354(1), (4), Sch 7, Pt 2, para 123(1)(a), Sch 10.

Sub-s (2): in para (b) words from '(in accordance with' to 'of that Act' in square brackets substituted by the Charities Act 2011, s 354(1), Sch 7, Pt 2, para 123(1)(b).

Sub-s (2): in para (c) words 'that Act' in square brackets substituted by the Charities Act 2011, s 354(1), Sch 7, Pt 2, para 123(1)(c).

Sub-s (2): final words omitted repealed by the Charities Act 2011, s 354(1), (4), Sch 7, Pt 2, para 123(1)(d), Sch 10.

Sub-s (3): repealed by the Charities Act 2011, s 354(1), Sch 7, Pt 2, para 123(2).

Sub-s (4): in para (c) words omitted repealed by the Charities Act 2011, s 354(1), (4), Sch 7, Pt 2, para 123(3), Sch 10.

79 Commencement

(1) The following provisions come into force on the day on which this Act is passed–

(a) . . .
(b) section 74,
(c) section 75(4) and (5),
(d) section 78,
(e) section 77,
(f) this section and section 80, and
(g) the following provisions of Schedule 8 –
paragraph 90(2),
. . .
and section 75(1) so far as relating to those provisions.

(2) Otherwise, this Act comes into force on such day as the Minister may by order appoint.

(3) An order under subsection (2)–

(a) may appoint different days for different purposes or different areas;
(b) make such provision as the Minister considers necessary or expedient for transitory, transitional or saving purposes in connection with the coming into force of any provision of this Act.

NOTES

Sub-s (1): para (a) repealed by the Charities Act 2011, s 354(1), (4), Sch 7, Pt 2, para 124(a), Sch 10.

Sub-s (1): in sub-para (g) words omitted repealed by the Charities Act 2011, s 354(1), (4), Sch 7, Pt 2, para 124(b), Sch 10.

80 Short title and extent

(1) This Act may be cited as the Charities Act 2006.

(2) Subject to subsections (3) to (7), this Act extends to England and Wales only.

(3) The following provisions extend also to Scotland–

(a) . . .

(b) . . .
(c) sections 72 and 74,
(d) . . . and
(e) section 75(4) and (5), sections [77] to 79 and this section.

(4) . . .

(5) The following provisions extend also to Northern Ireland–

(a) . . .
(b) . . .
(c) . . .
(d) sections 72 and 74,
(e) . . . and
(f) section 75(4) and (5), sections [77] to 79 and this section.

(6) [*repealed*]

(7) Any amendment, repeal or revocation made by this Act has the same extent as the enactment to which it relates.

(8) [*repealed*]

(9) Subsection (7) [. . .] does not apply to –

(a) [*repealed*]
(b) [the amendments] made by Schedule 8 in the Police, Factories, &c. (Miscellaneous Provisions) Act 1916 (c 31), or
(c) the repeal made in that Act by Schedule 9,

which extend to England and Wales only.

NOTES

Sub-s (3): paras (a), (b) repealed by the Charities Act 2011, s 354(1), (4), Sch 7, Pt 2, para 125(a), Sch 10.

Sub-s (3): para (d) repealed by the Charities Act 2011, s 354(1), (4), Sch 7, Pt 2, para 125(a), Sch 10.

Sub-s (3): in para (e) reference to '77' in square brackets substituted by the Charities Act 2011, s 354(1), Sch 7, Pt 2, para 125(b).

Sub-s (4): repealed by the Charities Act 2011, s 354(1), (4), Sch 7, Pt 2, para 125(a), Sch 10.

Sub-s (5): paras (a)-(c) repealed by the Charities Act 2011, s 354(1), (4), Sch 7, Pt 2, para 125(a), Sch 10.

Sub-s (5): para (e) repealed by the Charities Act 2011, s 354(1), (4), Sch 7, Pt 2, para 125(a), Sch 10.

Sub-s (5): in para (f) reference to '77' in square brackets substituted by the Charities Act 2011, s 354(1), Sch 7, Pt 2, para 125(b).

Sub-s (6): repealed by the Charities Act 2011, s 354(1), (4), Sch 7, Pt 2, para 125(a), Sch 10.

Sub-s (8): repealed by the Charities Act 2011, s 354(1), (4), Sch 7, Pt 2, para 125(a), Sch 10.

Sub-s (9): word omitted repealed by the Charities Act 2011, s 354(1), (4), Sch 7, Pt 2, para 125(c)(i), Sch 10.

Sub-s (9): para (a) repealed by the Charities Act 2011, s 354(1), (4), Sch 7, Pt 2, para 125(c)(i), Sch 10.

Sub-s (9): in para (b) words 'the amendments' in square brackets substituted by the Charities Act 2011, s 354(1), Sch 7, Pt 2, para 125(c)(ii).

Schedules

Schedules 8, 9 and 10 remain in force but are not reproduced here.

APPENDIX 3

CHARITIES (PROTECTION AND SOCIAL INVESTMENT) ACT 2016

1 Official warnings by the Commission

Before section 76 of the Charities Act 2011, after the heading 'Powers of Commission to act for protection of charities etc' insert–

'75A Official warnings by the Commission

(1) The Commission may issue a warning–

(a) to a charity trustee or trustee for a charity who it considers has committed a breach of trust or duty or other misconduct or mismanagement in that capacity, or

(b) to a charity in connection with which it considers a breach of trust or duty or other misconduct or mismanagement has been committed.

(2) The Commission–

(a) may publish a warning it has issued;

(b) may issue or publish a warning in any way it considers appropriate.

(3) Before issuing a warning under this section, the Commission must give notice of its intention to do so to the charity, and each charity trustee or trustee for the charity, except any who cannot be found or who has no known address in the United Kingdom.

(4) Any such notice–

(a) may be given by post, and

(b) if given by post, may be addressed to the recipient's last known address in the United Kingdom.

(5) The notice must specify–

(a) the power under subsection (1) to give the warning, and the grounds for the warning;

(b) any action that the Commission considers should be taken, or that the Commission is considering taking, to rectify the misconduct or mismanagement referred to in subsection (1);

(c) whether and, if so, how the Commission proposes to publish the warning;

(d) a period within which representations may be made to the Commission about the content of the proposed warning.

(6) Where the Commission gives notice under subsection (3) of its intention to issue a warning–

(a) it must take into account any representations made to it within the period specified in the notice, and

(b) it may (without further notice) issue the warning either without modifications or with such modifications as it thinks desirable.

(7) The Commission may vary or withdraw a warning under this section.

(8) Subsection (2) applies to the variation or withdrawal of a warning as it applies to a warning.

(9) Subsections (3) to (6) apply to the variation of a warning as they apply to a warning, except that–

(a) in subsection (5)(a) references to the warning are to be read as references to the warning as varied, and
(b) the matter to be specified under subsection (5)(b) is any change as a result of the variation in the action previously proposed by the Commission.'

2 Investigations and power to suspend

(1) Section 76 of the Charities Act 2011 (suspension of trustees etc and appointment of interim managers) is amended as follows.

(2) In subsection (1)(a), for 'any' substitute 'a failure to comply with an order or direction of the Commission, a failure to remedy any breach specified in a warning under section 75A, or any other'.

(3) In subsection (4), at the end insert ', subject to any extension under subsection (7)'.

(4) At the end add–

'(7) At any time before the expiry of an order under paragraph (a) of subsection (3) the Commission may extend or further extend the suspension by an order under that paragraph, provided that–

(a) the order does not extend the suspension for a period of more than 12 months, and
(b) the total period of suspension is not more than 2 years.'

3 Range of conduct to be considered when exercising powers

After section 76 of the Charities Act 2011 insert–

'76A Exercise of powers where section 76(1)(a) applies

(1) This section applies to any power under this Part which is exercisable in cases where the Commission is satisfied as mentioned in section 76(1)(a) in relation to a charity (misconduct or mismanagement), with or without any other condition.

(2) If in such a case the Commission is also satisfied–

(a) that a particular person has been responsible for the misconduct or mismanagement,
(b) that a particular person knew of the misconduct or mismanagement and failed to take any reasonable step to oppose it, or
(c) that a particular person's conduct contributed to it or facilitated it,

the Commission may take into account the matters mentioned in subsection (3) in deciding whether or how to exercise the power.

(3) Those matters are–

(a) the conduct of that person in relation to any other charity;
(b) any other conduct of that person that appears to the Commission to be damaging or likely to be damaging to public trust and confidence in charities generally or particular charities or classes of charity.'

4 Power to remove trustees etc following an inquiry

(1) The Charities Act 2011 is amended as follows.

(2) For section 79 (Commission's power to remove trustees etc following an inquiry) substitute–

'79 Removal of trustee or officer etc for protective etc purposes

(1) Subsection (2) applies where, at any time after it has instituted an inquiry under section 46 with respect to any charity, the Commission is satisfied either as mentioned in section 76(1)(a) (misconduct or mismanagement) or as mentioned in section 76(1)(b) (need to protect property etc).

(2) The Commission may of its own motion by order establish a scheme for the administration of the charity.

(3) Subsection (4) applies where, at any time after it has instituted an inquiry under section 46 with respect to any charity, the Commission is satisfied both as mentioned in section 76(1)(a) (misconduct or mismanagement) and as mentioned in section 76(1)(b) (need to protect property etc).

(4) Whether or not it acts under subsection (2), the Commission may of its own motion by order remove any trustee, charity trustee, officer, agent or employee of the charity–

(a) who has been responsible for the misconduct or mismanagement,
(b) who knew of the misconduct or mismanagement and failed to take any reasonable step to oppose it, or
(c) whose conduct contributed to it or facilitated it.

(5) Where the Commission has given notice under section 82 of its intention to make an order under subsection (4) removing a person from an office or employment, the Commission may proceed to make the order even though the person has ceased to hold the office or employment.

(6) Where an order is made relying on subsection (5)–

(a) section 81(1) (power to make supplementary provision) and Case D in section 178(1) (disqualification) apply as if the person was removed by the order, but
(b) the order does not affect the time when the person ceased to hold the office or employment.'

(3) In section 83(3) (power to suspend or remove trustees etc from membership of charity)–

(a) for '79(2)' substitute '79(4)';
(b) for 'an officer,' substitute 'a trustee, charity trustee, officer,'.

(4) In section 87(1) (supervision by Commission of certain Scottish charities), for '79(2)(b)' substitute '79(1) and (2)'.

(5) In section 178(1) (automatic disqualification of charity trustees), in Case D for '79(2)(a)' substitute '79(4)'.

(6) In Schedule 6 (appeals to tribunals), in the entry relating to an order made by the Commission under section 79(2) in relation to a charity–

(a) in column 1, after '79(2)' insert 'or (4)';
(b) in column 2, for '79(2)(a)' substitute '79(4)'.

5 Power to remove disqualified trustee

(1) The Charities Act 2011 is amended as follows.

(2) After section 79 insert–

'79A Removal of disqualified trustee

The Commission may remove a charity trustee or trustee for a charity by order made of its own motion if the person is disqualified from being a charity trustee or trustee for a charity (generally or in relation to the charity concerned)–

(a) by virtue of section 178, or
(b) by an order under section 181A.'

(3) In section 82(1) (removal of trustees etc: notice), after '79' insert ', 79A'.

(4) In section 89(1) (orders relating to trustees etc: exceptions to publicity requirement), after paragraph (b) insert, 'or

(c) an order under section 79A (removal of disqualified trustee),'.

(5) In section 89(5) (notice inviting representations on order to remove), after 'an order under this Act' insert ', other than an order under section 79A,'.

6 Power to direct specified action not to be taken

(1) The Charities Act 2011 is amended as follows.

(2) After section 84 insert–

'84A Power to direct specified action not to be taken

(1) This section applies where, at any time after the Commission has instituted an inquiry under section 46 with respect to any charity, the Commission considers that any action, if taken or continued by a person listed in section 84(2), would constitute misconduct or mismanagement in the administration of the charity.

(2) The Commission may make an order specifying the action and directing the person not to take it or continue it.

(3) While an order under this section is in force, the Commission must review it at intervals of not more than 6 months.'

(3) In section 20 (incidental powers), in subsection (3) after '84' insert ', 84A'.

(4) In section 86(2) (copy of certain orders, and reasons, to be sent to charity) and section 336(2)(a) (enforcement of orders of Commission) insert in the appropriate place–

'section 84A (power to direct specified action not to be taken),'.

(5) In Schedule 6 (appeals and applications to Tribunal), insert in the appropriate place–

'Order made by the Commission under section 84A(2) which directs a person not to take action specified in the order.	The persons are any person who is directed by the order not to take the specified action.	Power to quash the order and (if appropriate) remit the matter to the Commission.'

7 Power to direct winding up

(1) The Charities Act 2011 is amended as follows.

(2) Before section 85 insert–

'84B Power to direct winding up

(1) This section applies where the conditions in section 84(1) are met for that section to apply, but the Commission is satisfied–

(a) that the charity does not operate, or
(b) that its purposes can be promoted more effectively if it ceases to operate,

and that exercising the power in subsection (2) is expedient in the public interest.

(2) The Commission may by order direct–

(a) the charity trustees,
(b) any trustee for the charity,
(c) any officer or employee of the charity, or
(d) (if a body corporate) the charity itself,

to take any action specified in the order for the purpose of having the charity wound up and dissolved, and any remaining property transferred to a charity with the same purposes.

(3) An order under this section–

(a) may require action to be taken whether or not it would otherwise be within the powers exercisable by the person or persons concerned, or by the charity, in relation to the winding up and dissolution of the charity or to its property, and
(b) in particular, may require the person or persons concerned to do anything for the purpose of having the charity wound up and dissolved and its property transferred that could otherwise only be done by the members of the charity or any of them,

but may not require any action to be taken which is prohibited by any Act.

(4) Before making an order under this section the Commission must give public notice of its intention to make the order, inviting representations to be made to it within a period specified in the notice.

(5) The Commission–

(a) must take into account any representations made to it within the period specified in the notice, and
(b) may make the order (without further notice) either without modifications or with such modifications as it thinks desirable.

(6) An order under this section may not be made less than 60 days after the first day on which public notice under subsection (4) is given, unless the Commission is satisfied after complying with subsections (4) and (5) that it is necessary to make

the order to prevent or reduce misconduct or mismanagement in the administration of the charity or to protect the property of the charity or property that may come to the charity.

(7) Anything done by a person or body under the authority of an order under this section is to be treated as properly done in the exercise of the powers mentioned in subsection (3)(a).

(8) Subsection (7) does not affect any contractual or other rights arising in connection with anything which has been done under the authority of such an order.'

(3) In section 20 (incidental powers), in subsection (3) before 'or 85' insert ', 84B'.

(4) In section 86(2) (copy of certain orders, and reasons, to be sent to charity) and section 336(2)(a) (enforcement of orders of Commission) insert in the appropriate place–

'section 84B (power to direct winding up),'.

(5) In Schedule 6 (appeals and applications to Tribunal), insert in the appropriate place–

'Order made by the Commission under section 84B(2) which directs a person to take action specified in the order.	The persons are any person who is directed by the order to take the specified action.	Power to quash the order and (if appropriate) remit the matter to the Commission.
Order made by the Commission under section 84B(2) which directs a person to do anything that could otherwise only be done by the members of the charity or any of them.	The persons are the member or members concerned.	Power to quash the order and (if appropriate) remit the matter to the Commission.'

8 Power to direct property to be applied to another charity

(1) Section 85 of the Charities Act 2011 (power to direct application of charity property where person is unwilling) is amended as follows.

(2) In subsection (1)(a), after 'unwilling' insert 'or unable'.

(3) After subsection (5) insert–

'(6) Subsection (5) does not apply to rights of the charity or of a charity trustee or trustee for the charity in that capacity.'

9 Automatic disqualification from being a trustee

(1) The Charities Act 2011 is amended as follows.

(2) Section 178 (persons disqualified from being charity trustees or trustees for a charity) is amended as follows.

(3) In subsection (1), in Case A, for 'of any offence involving dishonesty or deception.' substitute 'of–

(a) an offence specified in section 178A;
(b) an offence, not specified in section 178A, that involves dishonesty or deception.'

(4) In Case D–

(a) for 'from the office of charity trustee or trustee for a charity' substitute 'as a trustee, charity trustee, officer, agent or employee of a charity';
(b) for 'to which P was privy,' substitute 'which P knew of and failed to take any reasonable step to oppose,'.

(5) At the end of subsection (1) insert–

'Case H

P has been found to be in contempt of court under Civil Procedure Rules for–

(a) making a false disclosure statement, or causing one to be made, or
(b) making a false statement in a document verified by a statement of truth, or causing one to be made.

Case I

P has been found guilty of disobedience to an order or direction of the Commission on an application to the High Court under section 336(1).

Case J

P is a designated person for the purposes of–

(a) Part 1 of the Terrorist Asset-Freezing etc Act 2010, or
(b) the Al-Qaida (Asset-Freezing) Regulations 2011.

Case K

P is subject to the notification requirements of Part 2 of the Sexual Offences Act 2003.'

(6) After subsection (2) insert–

'(3) While a person is disqualified under this section in relation to a charity, the person is also disqualified from holding an office or employment in the charity with senior management functions.

(4) A function of an office or employment held by a person '(A)' is a senior management function if–

(a) it relates to the management of the charity, and A is not responsible for it to another officer or employee (other than a charity trustee or trustee for the charity), or
(b) it involves control over money and the only officer or employee (other than a charity trustee or trustee for the charity) to whom A is responsible for it is a person with senior management functions other than ones involving control over money.'

(7) After section 178 insert–

'178A Case A: specified offences

(1) The following offences are specified for the purposes of Case A–

1 An offence to which Part 4 of the Counter-Terrorism Act 2008 applies (see sections 41 to 43 of that Act).

2 An offence under section 13 or 19 of the Terrorism Act 2000 (wearing of uniform etc, and failure to disclose information).

3 A money laundering offence within the meaning of section 415 of the Proceeds of Crime Act 2002.

4 An offence under any of the following provisions of the Bribery Act 2010–
(a) section 1 (bribing another person),
(b) section 2 (offences relating to being bribed),
(c) section 6 (bribery of foreign public officials),
(d) section 7 (failure of commercial organisations to prevent bribery).

5 An offence under section 77 of this Act.

6 An offence of–
(a) misconduct in public office,
(b) perjury,
(c) perverting the course of justice.

(2) An offence which has been superseded (directly or indirectly) by an offence specified in subsection (1) is also specified for the purposes of Case A.

(3) In relation to an offence specified in subsection (1) or (2), the following offences are also specified for the purposes of Case A–

(a) an offence of attempt, conspiracy or incitement to commit the offence;
(b) an offence of aiding, abetting, counselling or procuring the commission of the offence;
(c) an offence under Part 2 of the Serious Crime Act 2007 (encouraging or assisting) in relation to the offence.

(4) The Minister may amend this section by regulations to add or remove an offence.'

(8) Section 179 (disqualification: pre-commencement events etc) is amended as follows.

(9) In subsection (1), after '178(1)' insert 'or section 178A or any amendment of that section'.

(10) At the end add–

'(7) Case H does not apply in relation to a finding of contempt which, if it had been a conviction for which P was dealt with in the same way, would be a spent conviction for the purposes of the Rehabilitation of Offenders Act 1974.'

(11) Section 181 (waiver of disqualification) is amended as follows.

(12) After subsection (2) insert–

'(2A) A waiver under subsection (2)–

(a) may relate to the whole of P's disqualification or only to disqualification under section 178(3);
(b) in relation to disqualification under section 178(3) may relate to a particular office or employment or to any office or employment of a particular description.'

(13) In subsection (3) (presumption for waiver after 5 years) for 'or E' substitute ', E or I'.

(14) In section 183 (criminal consequences of acting while disqualified), in subsection (1)–

(a) after 'for a charity' insert 'or to hold an office or employment';
(b) after 'such a trustee' insert 'or from holding that office or employment'.

(15) Section 184 (civil consequences of acting while disqualified) is amended as follows.

(16) In subsections (1) and (2)(a)–

(a) after 'for a charity' insert 'or as officer or employee of a charity', and
(b) after 'such a trustee' insert 'or from holding that office or employment'.

(17) In subsection (2)(b) after 'for the charity' insert 'or holding the office or employment'.

(18) Section 348 (regulations subject to affirmative procedure etc) is amended as follows.

(19) In subsection (1), after paragraph (b) insert–

'(ba) regulations under section 178A(4) (offences specified for automatic disqualification of charity trustees);'.

(20) In subsection (2) after '(1)(a)' insert ', (ba)'.

(21) In subsection (4) after 'regulations under–' insert–

'(za) section 178A(4), if the regulations add an offence,'.

10 Power to disqualify from being a trustee

(1) The Charities Act 2011 is amended as follows.

(2) After section 181 insert–

'181A Disqualification orders

(1) The Commission may by order disqualify a person from being a charity trustee or trustee for a charity.

(2) The order may disqualify a person–

(a) in relation to all charities, or
(b) in relation to such charities or classes of charity as may be specified or described in the order.

(3) While a person is disqualified by virtue of an order under this section in relation to a charity, the person is also disqualified, subject to subsection (5), from holding an office or employment in the charity with senior management functions.

(4) A function of an office or employment held by a person ('A') is a senior management function if–

(a) it relates to the management of the charity, and A is not responsible for it to another officer or employee (other than a charity trustee or trustee for the charity), or
(b) it involves control over money and the only officer or employee (other than a charity trustee or trustee for the charity) to whom A is responsible for it is a person with senior management functions other than ones involving control over money.

(5) An order under this section may provide for subsection (3) not to apply–

(a) generally, or
(b) in relation to a particular office or employment or to any office or employment of a particular description.

(6) The Commission may make an order disqualifying a person under this section only if it is satisfied that–

(a) one or more of the conditions listed in subsection (7) are met in relation to the person,
(b) the person is unfit to be a charity trustee or trustee for a charity (either generally or in relation to the charities or classes of charity specified or described in the order), and
(c) making the order is desirable in the public interest in order to protect public trust and confidence in charities generally or in the charities or classes of charity specified or described in the order.

(7) These are the conditions–

A that the person has been cautioned for a disqualifying offence against a charity or involving the administration of a charity.

B that–
(a) under the law of a country or territory outside the United Kingdom the person has been convicted in respect of an offence against a charity or involving the administration of a charity, and
(b) the act which constituted the offence would have constituted a disqualifying offence if it had been done in any part of the United Kingdom.

C that the person has been found by Her Majesty's Revenue and Customs not to be a fit and proper person to be a manager of a body or trust, for the purposes of paragraph 4 of Schedule 6 to the Finance Act 2010 (definition of charity for tax purposes), and the finding has not been overturned.

D that the person was a trustee, charity trustee, officer, agent or employee of a charity at a time when there was misconduct or mismanagement in the administration of the charity, and–
(a) the person was responsible for the misconduct or mismanagement,
(b) the person knew of the misconduct or mismanagement and failed to take any reasonable step to oppose it, or
(c) the person's conduct contributed to or facilitated the misconduct or mismanagement.

E that the person was an officer or employee of a body corporate at a time when the body was a trustee or charity trustee for a charity and when there was misconduct or mismanagement by it in the administration of the charity, and–
(a) the person was responsible for the misconduct or mismanagement,
(b) the person knew of the misconduct or mismanagement and failed to take any reasonable step to oppose it, or
(c) the person's conduct contributed to or facilitated the misconduct or mismanagement.

F that any other past or continuing conduct by the person, whether or not in relation to a charity, is damaging or likely to be damaging to public trust and confidence in charities generally or in the charities or classes of charity specified or described in the order.

(8) The Minister may amend this section by regulations to add or remove a condition.

(9) In this section 'disqualifying offence' means an offence within Case A in section 178(1).

(10) Conditions A and B apply whether the caution or conviction occurred before or after the commencement of this section.

(11) Condition B does not apply in relation to a conviction which is spent under the law of the country or territory concerned.

(12) For the purposes of condition B–

(a) an act punishable under the law of a country or territory outside the United Kingdom constitutes an offence under that law, however it is described in that law, and

(b) 'charity' means an institution that is a charity under the law of any part of the United Kingdom or that is established under the law of another country or territory principally for charitable, benevolent or philanthropic purposes.

181B Duration of disqualification, and suspension pending disqualification

(1) An order under section 181A must specify the period for which the person is disqualified.

(2) The period–

(a) must be not more than 15 years beginning with the day on which the order takes effect, and

(b) must be proportionate, having regard in particular to the time when a conviction becomes spent or, where condition B applies, would become spent if it were a conviction for the relevant disqualifying offence, and to circumstances in which the Commission may or must grant a waiver under section 181 where a person is disqualified under section 178.

(3) An order takes effect–

(a) at the end of the time specified by Tribunal Procedure Rules for starting proceedings for an appeal against the order, if no proceedings are started within that time, or

(b) (subject to the decision on the appeal) when any proceedings started within that time are withdrawn or finally determined.

(4) The Commission may by order suspend a person from being a charity trustee or trustee for a charity if it has given notice under section 181C(1)(a) of its proposal to make an order under section 181A in respect of the person.

(5) The Commission may not make an order under subsection (4) so as to suspend a person for a period of more than 12 months, but at any time before the expiry of an order the Commission may extend or further extend the suspension by a further order under that subsection, provided that–

(a) the order does not extend the suspension for a period of more than 12 months, and

(b) the total period of suspension is not more than 2 years.

(6) An order under subsection (4) ceases to have effect–

(a) if the Commission notifies the person that it will not proceed with its proposal, on the notification being given;

(b) if the Commission makes the order under section 181A, on the order taking effect;

or, if earlier, at the end of the period specified in accordance with subsection (5).

(7) The Commission must review any order under subsection (4), at such intervals as it thinks fit.

(8) If on a review it appears to the Commission that it would be appropriate to discharge an order under subsection (4) in whole or in part, the Commission must do so (whether subject to any savings or other transitional provisions or not).

(9) An order under subsection (4) made in the case of any person ('P') may make provision, as respects the period of P's suspension, for matters arising out of it, and in particular–

(a) for enabling any person to execute any instrument in P's name or otherwise act for P, and

(b) in the case of a charity trustee, for adjusting any rules governing the proceedings of the charity trustees to take account of the reduction in the number capable of acting.

This does not affect the generality of section 337(1) and (2).

(10) While an order under subsection (4) is in force suspending a person from being a charity trustee or trustee for a charity, the person must not take up any appointment as a charity trustee or trustee for any other charity without the written approval of the Commission.

181C Disqualification orders: procedure

(1) Before making an order in respect of a person under section 181A without the person's consent the Commission must–

(a) give the person not less than one month's notice of its proposals, and

(b) invite representations to be made to it within a period specified in the notice.

(2) Before making an order under section 181A in respect of a person who the Commission knows or believes to be a charity trustee or trustee for a charity, the Commission must also–

(a) give notice of its proposals to each of the charity trustees of the charity in question;

(b) comply with the publicity requirement, unless the Commission is satisfied that for any reason compliance with the requirement is unnecessary.

(3) The publicity requirement is that the Commission must give public notice of its proposals, inviting representations to be made to it within a period specified in the notice.

(4) The time when any such notice is given is to be decided by the Commission.

(5) Any notice of any proposals which is to be given under this section is to contain such particulars of the proposals, or such directions for obtaining information about them, as the Commission thinks sufficient and appropriate.

(6) Where the Commission gives notice of any proposals under this section–

(a) it must take into account any representations made to it within the period specified in the notice, and
(b) it may (without further notice) proceed with the proposals either without modifications or with such modifications as it thinks desirable;

but a notice under subsection (2)(a) need not specify a period for the purposes of paragraph (a) if the charity came to the Commission's knowledge or belief after the expiry of the period specified for the purposes of subsection (1)(b).

(7) A notice under subsection (1) or (2)(a)–

(a) may be given by post, and
(b) if given by post, may be addressed to the recipient's last known address in the United Kingdom.

(8) A notice under subsection (2)(b) is to be given in such manner as the Commission thinks sufficient and appropriate.

(9) Where the Commission makes an order under section 181A in respect of a person it knows or believes to be a charity trustee or trustee for a charity it must (as well as serving it on that person) send a copy of the order and a statement of the Commission's reasons for making it–

(a) to the charity in question (if a body corporate), or
(b) (if not) to each of the charity trustees of the charity in question.

(10) Nothing in this section requires the Commission to give notice, or send a document, to a person who cannot be found or has no known address in the United Kingdom.

(11) Any documents required to be sent to a person under this section may be sent to, or otherwise served on, the person in the same way as an order made by the Commission under this Act could be served on the person in accordance with section 339.

181D Disqualification orders: variation and revocation

A person in respect of whom an order under section 181A is in force may at any time apply to the Commission for an order varying or discharging that order.'

(3) In section 183 (criminal consequences of acting while disqualified)–

(a) in subsection (1), after 'section 178' insert 'or an order under section 181A';
(b) in subsection (2)(b), after 'G' insert 'in section 178'.

(4) In section 184 (civil consequences of acting while disqualified)–

(a) in subsection (1), after 'section 178' insert 'or an order under section 181A';
(b) in subsection (2)(a), after 'section 178' insert 'or an order under section 181A.'

(5) Section 348 (regulations subject to affirmative procedure etc) is amended as follows.

(6) In subsection (1), before paragraph (c) insert–

'(ba) regulations under section 181A(8) (conditions for disqualification by order);'.

(7) In subsection (2) before 'or (c)' insert ', (bb)'.

(8) In subsection (4) before paragraph (a) insert–

'(zb) section 181A(8), if the regulations add a condition,'.

(9) In Schedule 6 (appeals and applications to tribunal), after the entry relating to a decision of the Commission under section 181(2) to waive, or not waive, a person's disqualification insert–

'Order made by the Commission under section 181A.	The persons are the person who is the subject of the order.	Power to– (a) quash the order in whole or in part and (if appropriate) remit the matter to the Commission; (b) substitute for all or part of the order any other order which could have been made by the Commission; (c) add to the order anything which could have been contained in an order made by the Commission.
Order made by the Commission under section 181B(4).	The persons are the person who is the subject of the order.	Power to– (a) quash the order in whole or in part and (if appropriate) remit the matter to the Commission; (b) substitute for all or part of the order any other order which could have been made by the Commission; (c) add to the order anything which could have been contained in an order made by the Commission.

Decision of the Commission– (a) to discharge an order following a review under section 181B(7), or (b) not to discharge an order following such a review.	The persons are– (a) the person who is the subject of the order, (b) the charity trustees of the charity to which the order relates, (c) (if a body corporate) the charity itself, and (d) any other person who is or may be affected by the order.	Power to– (a) quash the decision and (if appropriate) remit the matter to the Commission; (b) make the discharge of the order subject to savings or other transitional provisions; (c) remove any savings or other transitional provisions to which the discharge of the order was subject; (d) discharge the order in whole or in part (whether subject to any savings or other transitional provisions or not).
Decision of the Commission under section 181D not to revoke or vary an order under section 181A.	The persons are the person who is the subject of the order.	Power to– (a) quash the decision and (if appropriate) remit the matter to the Commission; (b) substitute for the decision any other decision of a kind which could have been made by the Commission.'

11 Records of disqualification and removal

(1) Section 182 of the Charities Act 2011 (records of persons removed from office) is amended as follows.

(2) In subsection (1)–

(a) for '181' substitute '181A';
(b) after 'a register of' insert, 'the following.'

(3) The words in subsection (1) from 'all persons' to the end become subsection (1A).

(4) At the beginning of that subsection insert–

'(1A) The register must include'.

(5) After subsection (1A) insert–

'(1B) The register must include all persons who have been disqualified by an order of the Commission under section 181A.

(1C) The register must include all persons who have been removed from office by an order of the Commission under section 79A (removal of disqualified trustee).'

12 Participation in corporate decisions while disqualified

In the Charities Act 2011, after section 184 insert–

'184A Sections 183 and 184: participation in corporate decisions

(1) For the purposes of sections 183 and 184, a person who is not a charity trustee or trustee for a charity is treated as acting as one if that person–

(a) is an officer of a body corporate which is a charity trustee or trustee for a charity, and
(b) takes part in that capacity in any decision relating to the administration of the charity.

(2) In subsection (1) 'officer' includes any of the persons having general control and management of the administration of the body.'

13 Fund-raising

(1) Section 59 of the Charities Act 1992 (prohibition on certain fund-raising without agreement in prescribed form), is amended as follows.

(2) In subsection (6) for 'such requirements' substitute 'the requirement in subsection (7) and such other requirements (including any requirements supplementing subsections (7) and (8))'.

(3) After that subsection insert–

'(7) The requirement in this subsection is that the agreement must specify all of the following–

(a) any voluntary scheme for regulating fund-raising, or any voluntary standard of fund-raising, that the professional fund-raiser or commercial participator undertakes to be bound by for the purposes of the agreement;
(b) how the professional fund-raiser or commercial participator is to protect vulnerable people and other members of the public from behaviour within subsection (8) in the course of, or in connection with, the activities to which the agreement relates;
(c) arrangements enabling the charitable institution to monitor compliance with subsection (1) or (2) by reference to the agreement.

(8) The behaviour mentioned in subsection (7)(b) is–

(a) unreasonable intrusion on a person's privacy;
(b) unreasonably persistent approaches for the purpose of soliciting or otherwise procuring money or other property;
(c) placing undue pressure on a person to give money or other property.'

(4) In the Charities Act 2011, after section 162 insert–

'162A Annual reports: fund-raising standards information

(1) If section 144(2) applies to a financial year of a charity, the annual report in respect of that year must include a statement of each of the following for that year–

(a) the approach taken by the charity to activities by the charity or by any person on behalf of the charity for the purpose of fund-raising, and in particular whether a professional fund-raiser or commercial participator carried on any of those activities;
(b) whether the charity or any person acting on behalf of the charity was subject to an undertaking to be bound by any voluntary scheme for regulating fund-raising, or any voluntary standard of fund-raising, in respect of activities on behalf of the charity, and, if so, what scheme or standard;
(c) any failure to comply with a scheme or standard mentioned under paragraph (b);

(d) whether the charity monitored activities carried on by any person on behalf of the charity for the purpose of fund-raising, and, if so, how it did so;
(e) the number of complaints received by the charity or a person acting on its behalf about activities by the charity or by a person on behalf of the charity for the purpose of fund-raising;
(f) what the charity has done to protect vulnerable people and other members of the public from behaviour within subsection (2) in the course of, or in connection with, such activities.

(2) The behaviour within this subsection is–

(a) unreasonable intrusion on a person's privacy;
(b) unreasonably persistent approaches for the purpose of soliciting or otherwise procuring money or other property on behalf of the charity;
(c) placing undue pressure on a person to give money or other property.

(3) In this section–

(a) 'commercial participator' and 'professional fund-raiser' have the meaning given by section 58 of the Charities Act 1992 (control of fund-raising: interpretation));
(b) 'fund-raising' means soliciting or otherwise procuring money or other property for charitable purposes.

(4) Section 58(6) and (7) of the Charities Act 1992 (references to soliciting money etc) apply for the purposes of this section as they apply for the purposes of Part 2 of that Act.'

14 Reserve powers to control fund-raising

(1) The Charities Act 1992 is amended as follows.

(2) In Part 2, after section 64A (reserve power to control fund-raising by charitable institutions) insert–

'64B Reserve power in relation to fund-raising regulators

(1) Regulations under section 64A may, in particular, impose on charitable institutions requirements to do any of the following–

(a) to comply with requirements imposed by a regulator;
(b) to have regard to guidance issued by a regulator;
(c) to pay fees to a regulator of an amount determined by the regulations or determined by the regulator in accordance with the regulations;
(d) to be registered with a regulator for the purpose of its regulation of charity fund-raising.

(2) 'Regulator' means a body specified in the regulations as a regulator for the purposes of this section.

(3) A body may be specified as a regulator for the purposes of this section only if the regulation of charity fund-raising appears to the Minister to be a principal function of the body.

(4) A body maintained out of money provided by Parliament may not be specified as a regulator (and this section does not confer power by regulations to establish a body to act as regulator).'

(3) In Part 2, after section 64B insert–

'64C Reserve power to confer additional powers on Charity Commission

(1) In the case of charity fund-raising which–

(a) is carried on by a charity, a person managing a charity or a person or company connected with a charity, or

(b) involves soliciting or otherwise procuring funds for the benefit of a charity or a company connected with a charity, or for charitable purposes,

regulations under section 64A may, in particular, make provision conferring functions on the Charity Commission, including provision applying or reproducing, with or without modification, any provision of the Charities Act 2011.

(2) The regulations may provide for a power that is exercisable by the Commission by virtue of the regulations to be exercisable by a person appointed by the Commission for the purpose.

(3) Where regulations by virtue of this section apply in relation to charity fund-raising by institutions that are not charities, section 19 of the Charities Act 2011 (fees and other amounts payable to Commission) applies in relation to the regulations as it applies in relation to the enactments relating to charities (but that is without prejudice to the application of other provisions by virtue of this section or section 77(3)).'

(4) In section 64A(2) after 'this section' insert 'and sections 64B and 64C'.

(5) In section 77(4) (regulations and orders) at the end insert 'and, in the case of regulations made by virtue of section 64B or 64C, shall in particular consult the Charity Commission.'

15 Power to make social investments

(1) In the Charities Act 2011, after section 292 insert–

'Part 14A

Social Investments

292A Meaning of 'social investment'

(1) This section applies for the purposes of this Part.

(2) A social investment is made when a relevant act of a charity is carried out with a view to both–

(a) directly furthering the charity's purposes; and
(b) achieving a financial return for the charity.

(3) References to an act of a charity are, in the case of an unincorporated charity, to an act of the charity trustees.

(4) A relevant act of a charity is–

(a) an application or use of funds or other property; or

(b) taking on a commitment in relation to a liability of another person (such as a guarantee) that puts the charity's funds or other property at risk of being applied or used.

(5) An act mentioned in subsection (4)(a) is to be regarded as achieving a financial return if its outcome is better for the charity in financial terms than expending the whole of the funds or other property in question.

(6) A commitment mentioned in subsection (4)(b) is to be regarded as achieving a financial return if–

(a) it is not called upon; or
(b) it is called upon without resulting in the expenditure of the whole of the funds or other property put at risk.

(7) The fact that a relevant act may also have results other than those mentioned in subsection (2)(a) and (b) does not prevent the carrying out of that act being regarded as the making of a social investment.

(8) The fact that carrying out a relevant act of a charity is regarded as the making of a social investment for the purposes of this Part does not of itself make the act an investment for any other purpose.

292B General power to make social investments

(1) An incorporated charity has, and the charity trustees of an unincorporated charity have, power to make social investments.

(2) The power conferred by this section may not be used to make a social investment involving–

(a) the application or use of permanent endowment, or
(b) taking on a commitment mentioned in section 292A(4)(b) that puts permanent endowment at risk of being applied or used,

unless the charity trustees expect that making the social investment will not contravene any restriction with respect to expenditure that applies to the permanent endowment in question.

(3) The power conferred by this section–

(a) may be restricted or excluded by the trusts of the charity;
(b) is (subject to paragraph (a)) in addition to any other power to make social investments that the charity or charity trustees may have.

(4) This section and section 292C do not apply in relation to–

(a) charities established by, or whose purposes and functions are set out in, legislation;
(b) charities established by Royal Charter;

but they apply in relation to all other charities, whether established before or after this section comes into force.

(5) In subsection (4) 'legislation' means–

(a) an Act of Parliament or an Act or Measure of the National Assembly for Wales; or
(b) subordinate legislation (within the meaning of the Interpretation Act 1978) made under such an Act or Measure.

292C Charity trustees' duties in relation to social investments

(1) This section applies in relation to social investments that are made after section 292B comes into force, whether or not made by the exercise of the power conferred by section 292B.

(2) The charity trustees of a charity must, before exercising a power to make a social investment–

(a) consider whether in all the circumstances any advice about the proposed social investment ought to be obtained;
(b) obtain and consider any advice they conclude ought to be obtained; and
(c) satisfy themselves that it is in the interests of the charity to make the social investment, having regard to the benefit they expect it to achieve for the charity (by directly furthering the charity's purposes and achieving a financial return).

(3) The charity trustees of a charity must from time to time review the charity's social investments.

(4) When carrying out a review the charity trustees must–

(a) consider whether any advice about the social investments (or any particular social investment) ought to be obtained; and
(b) obtain and consider any advice they conclude ought to be obtained.

(5) The duties under this section may not be restricted or excluded by the charity's trusts.

(6) In the case of an unincorporated charity, the duties under this section apply in relation to relevant social investments in place of any duties under sections 4 and 5 of the Trustee Act 2000 that would otherwise apply.

(7) In subsection (6) 'relevant social investments' means social investments that are investments for the purposes of Part 2 of the Trustee Act 2000.'

(2) The Trustee Act 2000 is amended as follows.

(3) In section 4 (standard investment criteria), after subsection (3) insert–

'(4) This section has effect subject to section 292C(6) of the Charities Act 2011 (which disapplies the duties under this section in cases where they would otherwise apply in relation to a social investment within the meaning of Part 14A of that Act).'

(4) In section 5 (advice), after subsection (4) insert–

'(5) This section has effect subject to section 292C(6) of the Charities Act 2011 (which disapplies the duties under this section in cases where they would otherwise apply in relation to a social investment within the meaning of Part 14A of that Act).'

16 Reviews of the operation of this Act

(1) The Minister for the Cabinet Office must carry out reviews of the operation of this Act including, on each review, how the Act affects–

(a) public confidence in charities,
(b) the level of charitable donations, and
(c) people's willingness to volunteer.

(2) After each review the Minister must publish a report of the review and lay a copy before Parliament.

(3) The reports must be published not more than 5 years apart.

(4) The first review must begin within 3 years after this Act is passed, and the report of that review must be published within 4 years after this Act is passed.

17 Short title, extent and commencement

(1) This Act may be cited as the Charities (Protection and Social Investment) Act 2016.

(2) This Act extends to England and Wales only.

(3) This section and section 16 come into force on the day on which this Act is passed.

(4) The other provisions of this Act come into force on whatever day the Minister for the Cabinet Office appoints by regulations made by statutory instrument.

(5) The regulations–

(a) may appoint different days for different purposes;
(b) may make transitional, transitory or saving provision.

APPENDIX 4

CHARITIES ACT 1992

PART II

CONTROL OF FUND-RAISING FOR CHARITABLE INSTITUTIONS

Preliminary

58 Interpretation of Part II

(1) In this Part –

"charitable contributions", in relation to any representation made by any commercial participator or other person, means –

(a) the whole or part of –

(i) the consideration given for goods or services sold or supplied by him, or

(ii) any proceeds (other than such consideration) of a promotional venture undertaken by him, or

(b) sums given by him by way of donation in connection with the sale or supply of any such goods or services (whether the amount of such sums is determined by reference to the value of any such goods or services or otherwise);

"charitable institution" means a charity or an institution (other than a charity) which is established for charitable, benevolent or philanthropic purposes;

. . .

"commercial participator", in relation to any charitable institution, means any person [(apart from a company connected with the institution)] who –

(a) carries on for gain a business other than a fund-raising business, but

(b) in the course of that business, engages in any promotional venture in the course of which it is represented that charitable contributions are to be given to or applied for the benefit of the institution;

"company" has the meaning given by section [section 353 of the Charities Act 2011];

"the court" means the High Court or [the county court];

"credit card" means a card which is a credit-token within the meaning of the Consumer Credit Act 1974;

"debit card" means a card the use of which by its holder to make a payment results in a current account of his at a bank, or at any other institution providing banking services, being debited with the payment;

"fund-raising business" means any business carried on for gain and wholly or primarily engaged in soliciting or otherwise procuring money or other property for charitable, benevolent or philanthropic purposes;

"institution" includes any trust or undertaking;

["the Minister" means the Minister for the Cabinet Office;]

"professional fund-raiser" means –

(a) any person (apart from a charitable institution [or a company connected with such an institution]) who carries on a fund-raising business, or

(b) any other person (apart from a person excluded by virtue of subsection (2) or (3)) who for reward solicits money or other property for the benefit of a charitable institution, if he does so otherwise than in the course of any fund-raising venture undertaken by a person falling within paragraph (a) above;

"promotional venture" means any advertising or sales campaign or any other venture undertaken for promotional purposes;

"radio or television programme" includes any item included in a programme service within the meaning of the Broadcasting Act 1990.

(2) In subsection (1), paragraph (b) of the definition of "professional fund-raiser" does not apply to any of the following, namely –

(a) any charitable institution or any company connected with any such institution;
(b) any officer or employee of any such institution or company, or any trustee of any such institution, acting (in each case) in his capacity as such;
(c) any person acting as a collector in respect of a public charitable collection (apart from a person who is [a promoter of such a collection as defined in section 47(1) of the Charities Act 2006]);
(d) any person who in the course of a relevant programme, that is to say a radio or television programme in the course of which a fund-raising venture is undertaken by –
  (i) a charitable institution, or
  (ii) a company connected with such an institution,

makes any solicitation at the instance of that institution or company; or

(e) any commercial participator;

and for this purpose "collector" and "public charitable collection" have the same meaning as in [Chapter 1 of Part 3 of the Charities Act 2006].

(3) In addition, paragraph (b) of the definition of "professional fund-raiser" does not apply to a person if he does not receive –

(a) more than –
  (i) [£10] per day, or
  (ii) [£1,000] per year,

  by way of remuneration in connection with soliciting money or other property for the benefit of the charitable institution referred to in that paragraph; or
(b) more than [£1,000] by way of remuneration in connection with any fund-raising venture in the course of which he solicits money or other property for the benefit of that institution.

(4) In this Part any reference to charitable purposes, where occurring in the context of a reference to charitable, benevolent or philanthropic purposes, is a reference to charitable purposes [as defined by section 2(1) of the Charities Act 2011].

(5) For the purposes of this Part a company is connected with a charitable institution if –

(a) the institution, or
(b) the institution and one or more other charitable institutions, taken together,

is or are entitled (whether directly or through one or more nominees) to exercise, or control the exercise of, the whole of the voting power at any general meeting of the company.

(6) In this Part –

(a) "represent" and "solicit" mean respectively represent and solicit in any manner whatever, whether expressly or impliedly and whether done –
(i) by speaking directly to the person or persons to whom the representation or solicitation is addressed (whether when in his or their presence or not), or
(ii) by means of a statement published in any newspaper, film or radio or television programme,
or otherwise, and references to a representation or solicitation shall be construed accordingly; and
(b) any reference to soliciting or otherwise procuring money or other property is a reference to soliciting or otherwise procuring money or other property whether any consideration is, or is to be, given in return for the money or other property or not.

(7) Where –

(a) any solicitation of money or other property for the benefit of a charitable institution is made in accordance with arrangements between any person and that institution, and
(b) under those arrangements that person will be responsible for receiving on behalf of the institution money or other property given in response to the solicitation,

then (if he would not be so regarded apart from this subsection) that person shall be regarded for the purposes of this Part as soliciting money or other property for the benefit of the institution.

(8) Where any fund-raising venture is undertaken by a professional fund-raiser in the course of a radio or television programme, any solicitation which is made by a person in the course of the programme at the instance of the fund-raiser shall be regarded for the purposes of this Part as made by the fund-raiser and not by that person (and shall be so regarded whether or not the solicitation is made by that person for any reward).

(9) In this Part "services" includes facilities, and in particular –

(a) access to any premises or event;
(b) membership of any organisation;
(c) the provision of advertising space; and
(d) the provision of any financial facilities;

and references to the supply of services shall be construed accordingly.

(10) The [Minister] may by order amend subsection (3) by substituting a different sum for any sum for the time being specified there.

NOTE

Sub-s (1): amended by Deregulation and Contracting Out Act 1994, s 25; Charities Act 2006, s 75(1), Sch 8, paras 89, 90(1), (2); Charities Act 2011, s 354(1), Sch 7, Pt 2, para 65(1); SI 2011/1396, art 2, Schedule, Pt 4, para 40(1), (2)(c); Crime and Courts Act 2013, s 17(5), Sch 9, Pt 3, para 52(1)(b), (2).

Sub-s (2): amended by Charities Act 2006, s 75(1), Sch 8, paras 89, 90(1), (3)(a)–(b).

Sub-s (3): amended by SI 2009/508, arts 2, 3(a), (b) and (c).

Sub-s (4): amended by Charities Act 2011, s 354(1), Sch 7, Pt 2, para 65(2).

Sub-s (10): amended by SI 2006/2951, art 6, Schedule, para 3(a).

Control of fund-raising

59 Prohibition on professional fund-raiser etc raising funds for charitable institution without an agreement in prescribed form

(1) It shall be unlawful for a professional fund-raiser to solicit money or other property for the benefit of a charitable institution unless he does so in accordance with an agreement with the institution satisfying the prescribed requirements.

(2) It shall be unlawful for a commercial participator to represent that charitable contributions are to be given to or applied for the benefit of a charitable institution unless he does so in accordance with an agreement with the institution satisfying the prescribed requirements.

(3) Where on the application of a charitable institution the court is satisfied –

- (a) that any person has contravened or is contravening subsection (1) or (2) in relation to the institution, and
- (b) that, unless restrained, any such contravention is likely to continue or be repeated,

the court may grant an injunction restraining the contravention; and compliance with subsection (1) or (2) shall not be enforceable otherwise than in accordance with this subsection.

(4) Where –

- (a) a charitable institution makes any agreement with a professional fund-raiser or a commercial participator by virtue of which –
  - (i) the professional fund-raiser is authorised to solicit money or other property for the benefit of the institution, or
  - (ii) the commercial participator is authorised to represent that charitable contributions are to be given to or applied for the benefit of the institution,

as the case may be, but

- (b) the agreement does not satisfy the prescribed requirements in any respect,

the agreement shall not be enforceable against the institution except to such extent (if any) as may be provided by an order of the court.

(5) A professional fund-raiser or commercial participator who is a party to such an agreement as is mentioned in subsection (4)(a) shall not be entitled to receive any amount by way of remuneration or expenses in respect of anything done by him in pursuance of the agreement unless –

- (a) he is so entitled under any provision of the agreement, and
- (b) either –
  - (i) the agreement satisfies the prescribed requirements, or
  - (ii) any such provision has effect by virtue of an order of the court under subsection (4).

(6) In this section "the prescribed requirements" means [the requirement in subsection (7) and such other requirements (including any requirements supplementing subsections (7) and (8))] as are prescribed by regulations made by virtue of section 64(2)(a).

[(7) The requirement in this subsection is that the agreement must specify all of the following –

(a) any voluntary scheme for regulating fund-raising, or any voluntary standard of fund-raising, that the professional fund-raiser or commercial participator undertakes to be bound by for the purposes of the agreement;
(b) how the professional fund-raiser or commercial participator is to protect vulnerable people and other members of the public from behaviour within subsection (8) in the course of, or in connection with, the activities to which the agreement relates;
(c) arrangements enabling the charitable institution to monitor compliance with subsection (1) or (2) by reference to the agreement.]

[(8) The behaviour mentioned in subsection (7)(b) is –

(a) unreasonable intrusion on a person's privacy;
(b) unreasonably persistent approaches for the purpose of soliciting or otherwise procuring money or other property;
(c) placing undue pressure on a person to give money or other property.]

NOTE

Sub-s (6) amended by Charities (Protection and Social Investment) Act 2016; s 13 from 1 November 2016.

Sub-s (7) inserted by Charities (Protection and Social Investment) Act 2016; s 13 from 1 November 2016.

Sub-s (8) inserted by Charities (Protection and Social Investment) Act 2016; s 13 from 1 November 2016.

60 Professional fund-raisers etc required to indicate institutions benefiting and arrangements for remuneration

(1) Where a professional fund-raiser solicits money or other property for the benefit of one or more particular charitable institutions, the solicitation shall be accompanied by a statement clearly indicating –

(a) the name or names of the institution or institutions concerned;
(b) if there is more than one institution concerned, the proportions in which the institutions are respectively to benefit; and
[(c) the method by which the fund-raiser's remuneration in connection with the appeal is to be determined and the notifiable amount of that remuneration].

(2) Where a professional fund-raiser solicits money or other property for charitable, benevolent or philanthropic purposes of any description (rather than for the benefit of one or more particular charitable institutions), the solicitation shall be accompanied by a statement clearly indicating –

(a) the fact that he is soliciting money or other property for those purposes and not for the benefit of any particular charitable institution or institutions;
(b) the method by which it is to be determined how the proceeds of the appeal are to be distributed between different charitable institutions; and
[(c) the method by which his remuneration in connection with the appeal is to be determined and the notifiable amount of that remuneration].

(3) Where any representation is made by a commercial participator to the effect that charitable contributions are to be given to or applied for the benefit of one or more particular charitable institutions, the representation shall be accompanied by a statement clearly indicating –

(a) the name or names of the institution or institutions concerned;
(b) if there is more than one institution concerned, the proportions in which the institutions are respectively to benefit; and

[(c) the notifiable amount of whichever of the following sums is applicable in the circumstances –
(i) the sum representing so much of the consideration given for goods or services sold or supplied by him as is to be given to or applied for the benefit of the institution or institutions concerned,
(ii) the sum representing so much of any other proceeds of a promotional venture undertaken by him as is to be so given or applied, or
(iii) the sum of the donations by him in connection with the sale or supply of any such goods or services which are to be so given or supplied].

[(3A) In subsections (1) to (3) a reference to the "notifiable amount" of any remuneration or other sum is a reference –

(a) to the actual amount of the remuneration or sum, if that is known at the time when the statement is made; and
(b) otherwise to the estimated amount of the remuneration or sum, calculated as accurately as is reasonably possible in the circumstances.]

(4) If any such solicitation or representation as is mentioned in any of subsections (1) to (3) is made –

(a) in the course of a radio or television programme, and
(b) in association with an announcement to the effect that payment may be made, in response to the solicitation or representation, by means of a credit or debit card,

the statement required by virtue of subsection (1), (2) or (3) (as the case may be) shall include full details of the right to have refunded under section 61(1) any payment of [£100] or more which is so made.

(5) If any such solicitation or representation as is mentioned in any of subsections (1) to (3) is made orally but is not made –

(a) by speaking directly to the particular person or persons to whom it is addressed and in his or their presence, or
(b) in the course of any radio or television programme,

the professional fund-raiser or commercial participator concerned shall, within seven days of any payment of [£100] or more being made to him in response to the solicitation or representation, give to the person making the payment a written statement –

(i) of the matters specified in paragraphs (a) to (c) of that subsection; and
(ii) including full details of the right to cancel under section 61(2) an agreement made in response to the solicitation or representation, and the right to have refunded under section 61(2) or (3) any payment of [£100] or more made in response thereto.

(6) In subsection (5) above the reference to the making of a payment is a reference to the making of a payment of whatever nature and by whatever means, including a payment made by means of a credit card or a debit card; and for the purposes of that subsection –

(a) where the person making any such payment makes it in person, it shall be regarded as made at the time when it is so made;
(b) where the person making any such payment sends it by post, it shall be regarded as made at the time when it is posted; and

(c) where the person making any such payment makes it by giving, by telephone or by means of any other [electronic communications apparatus], authority for an account to be debited with the payment, it shall be regarded as made at the time when any such authority is given.

(7) Where any requirement of subsections (1) to (5) is not complied with in relation to any solicitation or representation, the professional fund-raiser or commercial participator concerned shall be guilty of an offence and liable on summary conviction to a fine not exceeding the fifth level on the standard scale.

(8) It shall be a defence for a person charged with any such offence to prove that he took all reasonable precautions and exercised all due diligence to avoid the commission of the offence.

(9) Where the commission by any person of an offence under subsection (7) is due to the act or default of some other person, that other person shall be guilty of the offence; and a person may be charged with and convicted of the offence by virtue of this subsection whether or not proceedings are taken against the first-mentioned person.

(10) In this section –

"the appeal", in relation to any solicitation by a professional fund- raiser, means the campaign or other fund-raising venture in the course of which the solicitation is made;

...

NOTE

Sub-s (1): amended by Charities Act 2006, s 67(1), (2).

Sub-s (2): amended by Charities Act 2006, s 67(1), (3).

Sub-s (3): amended by Charities Act 2006, s 67(1), (4).

Sub-s (3A): inserted by Charities Act 2006, s 67(1), (5).

Sub-s (4): amended by SI 2009/508, arts 2, 4.

Sub-s (5): amended by SI 2009/508, arts 2, 4.

Sub-s (6): amended by Communications Act 2003, s 406(1), Sch 17, para 118.

Sub-s (10): amended by Communications Act 2003, s 406(7), Sch 19(1).

[60A Other persons making appeals required to indicate institutions benefiting and arrangements for remuneration]

[(1) Subsections (1) and (2) of section 60 apply to a person acting for reward as a collector in respect of a public charitable collection as they apply to a professional fund-raiser.

(2) But those subsections do not so apply to a person excluded by virtue of –

(a) subsection (3) below, or
(b) section 60B(1) (exclusion of lower-paid collectors).

(3) Those subsections do not so apply to a person if –

(a) section 60(1) or (2) applies apart from subsection (1) (by virtue of the exception in section 58(2)(c) for persons treated as promoters), or
(b) subsection (4) or (5) applies,

in relation to his acting for reward as a collector in respect of the collection mentioned in subsection (1) above.

(4) Where a person within subsection (6) solicits money or other property for the benefit of one or more particular charitable institutions, the solicitation shall be accompanied by a statement clearly indicating –

(a) the name or names of the institution or institutions for whose benefit the solicitation is being made;
(b) if there is more than one such institution, the proportions in which the institutions are respectively to benefit;
(c) the fact that he is an officer, employee or trustee of the institution or company mentioned in subsection (6); and
(d) the fact that he is receiving remuneration as an officer, employee or trustee or (as the case may be) for acting as a collector.

(5) Where a person within subsection (6) solicits money or other property for charitable, benevolent or philanthropic purposes of any description (rather than for the benefit of one or more particular charitable institutions), the solicitation shall be accompanied by a statement clearly indicating –

(a) the fact that he is soliciting money or other property for those purposes and not for the benefit of any particular charitable institution or institutions;
(b) the method by which it is to be determined how the proceeds of the appeal are to be distributed between different charitable institutions;
(c) the fact that he is an officer, employee or trustee of the institution or company mentioned in subsection (6); and
(d) the fact that he is receiving remuneration as an officer, employee or trustee or (as the case may be) for acting as a collector.

(6) A person is within this subsection if –

(a) he is an officer or employee of a charitable institution or a company connected with any such institution, or a trustee of any such institution,
(b) he is acting as a collector in that capacity, and
(c) he receives remuneration either in his capacity as officer, employee or trustee or for acting as a collector.

(7) But a person is not within subsection (6) if he is excluded by virtue of section 60B(4).

(8) Where any requirement of –

(a) subsection (1) or (2) of section 60, as it applies by virtue of subsection (1) above, or
(b) subsection (4) or (5) above,

is not complied with in relation to any solicitation, the collector concerned shall be guilty of an offence and liable on summary conviction to a fine not exceeding level 5 on the standard scale.

(9) Section 60(8) and (9) apply in relation to an offence under subsection (8) above as they apply in relation to an offence under section 60(7).

(10) In this section –

"the appeal", in relation to any solicitation by a collector, means the campaign or other fund-raising venture in the course of which the solicitation is made;

"collector" has the meaning given by section 47(1) of the Charities Act 2006;
"public charitable collection" has the meaning given by section 45 of that Act.]

NOTE

Inserted by Charities Act 2006, s 68. Sub-ss (1)–(3) and 8(a) are not in force at the time of writing.

[60B Exclusion of lower-paid collectors from provisions of section 60A]

[(1) Section 60(1) and (2) do not apply (by virtue of section 60A(1)) to a person who is under the earnings limit in subsection (2) below.

(2) A person is under the earnings limit in this subsection if he does not receive –

(a) more than –
 (i) [£10] per day, or
 (ii) [£1,000] per year,

by way of remuneration for acting as a collector in relation to relevant collections, or

(b) more than [£1,000] by way of remuneration for acting as a collector in relation to the collection mentioned in section 60A(1).

(3) In subsection (2) "relevant collections" means public charitable collections conducted for the benefit of –

(a) the charitable institution or institutions, or
(b) the charitable, benevolent or philanthropic purposes,

for whose benefit the collection mentioned in section 60A(1) is conducted.

(4) A person is not within section 60A(6) if he is under the earnings limit in subsection (5) below.

(5) A person is under the earnings limit in this subsection if the remuneration received by him as mentioned in section 60A(6)(c) –

(a) is not more than –
 (i) [£10] per day, or
 (ii) [£1,000] per year, or
(b) if a lump sum, is not more than [£1,000].

(6) The Minister may by order amend subsections (2) and (5) by substituting a different sum for any sum for the time being specified there.]

NOTE

Inserted by the Charities Act 2006, s 68. Sub-ss (1)–(3) are not in force at the time of writing.

Sub-s (2): amended by SI 2009/508, arts 2, 5(a)–(c).

Sub-s (5): amended by SI 2009/508, arts 2, 5(a)–(c).

61 Cancellation of payments and agreements made in response to appeals

(1) Where –

(a) a person ("the donor"), in response to any such solicitation or representation as is mentioned in any of subsections (1) to (3) of section 60 which is made in the course of a radio or television programme, makes any payment of [£100] or more to the relevant fund-raiser by means of a credit card or a debit card, but

(b) before the end of the period of seven days beginning with the date of the solicitation or representation, the donor serves on the relevant fund-raiser a notice in writing which, however expressed, indicates the donor's intention to cancel the payment,

the donor shall (subject to subsection (4) below) be entitled to have the payment refunded to him forthwith by the relevant fund-raiser.

(2) Where –

(a) a person ("the donor"), in response to any solicitation or representation falling within subsection (5) of section 60, enters into an agreement with the relevant fund-raiser under which the donor is, or may be, liable to make any payment or payments to the relevant fund-raiser, and the amount or aggregate amount which the donor is, or may be, liable to pay to him under the agreement is [£100] or more, but
(b) before the end of the period of seven days beginning with the date when he is given any such written statement as is referred to in that subsection, the donor serves on the relevant fund-raiser a notice in writing which, however expressed, indicates the donor's intention to cancel the agreement,

the notice shall operate, as from the time when it is so served, to cancel the agreement and any liability of any person other than the donor in connection with the making of any such payment or payments, and the donor shall (subject to subsection (4) below) be entitled to have any payment of [£100] or more made by him under the agreement refunded to him forthwith by the relevant fund-raiser.

(3) Where, in response to any solicitation or representation falling within subsection (5) of section 60, a person ("the donor") –

(a) makes any payment of [£100] or more to the relevant fund-raiser, but
(b) does not enter into any such agreement as is mentioned in subsection (2) above,

then, if before the end of the period of seven days beginning with the date when the donor is given any such written statement as is referred to in subsection (5) of that section, the donor serves on the relevant fund-raiser a notice in writing which, however expressed, indicates the donor's intention to cancel the payment, the donor shall (subject to subsection (4) below) be entitled to have the payment refunded to him forthwith by the relevant fund-raiser.

(4) The right of any person to have a payment refunded to him under any of subsections (1) to (3) above –

(a) is a right to have refunded to him the amount of the payment less any administrative expenses reasonably incurred by the relevant fund-raiser in connection with –
    (i) the making of the refund, or
    (ii) (in the case of a refund under subsection (2)) dealing with the notice of cancellation served by that person; and
(b) shall, in the case of a payment for goods already received, be conditional upon restitution being made by him of the goods in question.

(5) Nothing in subsections (1) to (3) above has effect in relation to any payment made or to be made in respect of services which have been supplied at the time when the relevant notice is served.

(6) In this section any reference to the making of a payment is a reference to the making of a payment of whatever nature and (in the case of subsection (2) or (3)) a

payment made by whatever means, including a payment made by means of a credit card or a debit card; and subsection (6) of section 60 shall have effect for determining when a payment is made for the purposes of this section as it has effect for determining when a payment is made for the purposes of subsection (5) of that section.

(7) In this section "the relevant fund-raiser", in relation to any solicitation or representation, means the professional fund-raiser or commercial participator by whom it is made.

(8) The [Minister] may by order –

(a) amend any provision of this section by substituting a different sum for the sum for the time being specified there; and
(b) make such consequential amendments in section 60 as he considers appropriate.

NOTE

Sub-s (1): amended by SI 2009/508, arts 2, 6(a).

Sub-s (2): amended by SI 2009/508, arts 2, 6(b).

Sub-s (3): amended by SI 2009/508, arts 2, 6(c).

Sub-s (8): amended by SI 2006/2951, art 6, Schedule, para 3(b).

62 Right of charitable institution to prevent unauthorised fund-raising

(1) Where on the application of any charitable institution –

(a) the court is satisfied that any person has done or is doing either of the following, namely –
 (i) soliciting money or other property for the benefit of the institution, or
 (ii) representing that charitable contributions are to be given to or applied for the benefit of the institution,

and that, unless restrained, he is likely to do further acts of that nature, and

(b) the court is also satisfied as to one or more of the matters specified in subsection (2),

then (subject to subsection (3)) the court may grant an injunction restraining the doing of any such acts.

(2) The matters referred to in subsection (1)(b) are –

(a) that the person in question is using methods of fund-raising to which the institution objects;
(b) that that person is not a fit and proper person to raise funds for the institution; and
(c) where the conduct complained of is the making of such representations as are mentioned in subsection (1)(a)(ii), that the institution does not wish to be associated with the particular promotional or other fund-raising venture in which that person is engaged.

(3) The power to grant an injunction under subsection (1) shall not be exercisable on the application of a charitable institution unless the institution has, not less than 28 days before making the application, served on the person in question a notice in writing –

(a) requesting him to cease forthwith –
 (i) soliciting money or other property for the benefit of the institution, or

(ii) representing that charitable contributions are to be given to or applied for the benefit of the institution,

as the case may be; and

(b) stating that, if he does not comply with the notice, the institution will make an application under this section for an injunction.

(4) Where –

(a) a charitable institution has served on any person a notice under subsection (3) ("the relevant notice") and that person has complied with the notice, but
(b) that person has subsequently begun to carry on activities which are the same, or substantially the same, as those in respect of which the relevant notice was served,

the institution shall not, in connection with an application made by it under this section in respect of the activities carried on by that person, be required by virtue of that subsection to serve a further notice on him, if the application is made not more than 12 months after the date of service of the relevant notice.

(5) This section shall not have the effect of authorising a charitable institution to make an application under this section in respect of anything done by a professional fund-raiser or commercial participator in relation to the institution.

63 False statements relating to institutions which are not registered charities

(1) Where –

(a) a person solicits money or other property for the benefit of an institution in association with a representation that the institution is a registered charity, and
(b) the institution is not such a charity,

he shall be guilty of an offence and liable on summary conviction to a fine not exceeding the fifth level on the standard scale.

[(1A) In any proceedings for an offence under subsection (1), it shall be a defence for the accused to prove that he believed on reasonable grounds that the institution was a registered charity.]

(2) In [this section] "registered charity" means a charity which is for the time being registered in the register of charities kept under [section 29 of the Charities Act 2011].

NOTE

Sub-s (1A): inserted by Deregulation and Contracting Out Act 1994, s 26(2).

Sub-s (2): amended by Deregulation and Contracting Out Act 1994, s 26(3); Charities Act 2011, s 354(1), Sch 7, Pt 2, para 66.

Supplementary

64 Regulations about fund-raising

(1) The [Minister] may make such regulations as appear to him to be necessary or desirable for any purposes connected with any of the preceding provisions of this Part.

(2) Without prejudice to the generality of subsection (1), any such regulations may –

(a) prescribe the form and content of –
(i) agreements made for the purposes of section 59, and

(ii) notices served under section 62(3);

(b) require professional fund-raisers or commercial participators who are parties to such agreements with charitable institutions to make available to the institutions books, documents or other records (however kept) which relate to the institutions;

(c) specify the manner in which money or other property acquired by professional fund-raisers or commercial participators for the benefit of, or otherwise falling to be given to or applied by such persons for the benefit of, charitable institutions is to be transmitted to such institutions;

(d) provide for any provisions of section 60 or 61 having effect in relation to solicitations or representations made in the course of radio or television programmes to have effect, subject to any modifications specified in the regulations, in relation to solicitations or representations made in the course of such programmes –

(i) by charitable institutions, or

(ii) by companies connected with such institutions,

and, in that connection, provide for any other provisions of this Part to have effect for the purposes of the regulations subject to any modifications so specified;

(e) make other provision regulating the raising of funds for charitable, benevolent or philanthropic purposes (whether by professional fund-raisers or commercial participators or otherwise).

(3) In subsection (2)(c) the reference to such money or other property as is there mentioned includes a reference to money or other property which, in the case of a professional fund-raiser or commercial participator –

(a) has been acquired by him otherwise than in accordance with an agreement with a charitable institution, but

(b) by reason of any solicitation or representation in consequence of which it has been acquired, is held by him on trust for such an institution.

(4) Regulations under this section may provide that any failure to comply with a specified provision of the regulations shall be an offence punishable on summary conviction by a fine not exceeding the second level on the standard scale.

NOTE

Sub-s (1): amended by SI 2006/2951, art 6, Sch, para 3(c).

[64A Reserve power to control fund-raising by charitable institutions]

[(1) The Minister may make such regulations as appear to him to be necessary or desirable for or in connection with regulating charity fund-raising.

(2) In this section [and sections 64B and 64C] "charity fund-raising" means activities which are carried on by –

(a) charitable institutions,

(b) persons managing charitable institutions, or

(c) persons or companies connected with such institutions,

and involve soliciting or otherwise procuring funds for the benefit of such institutions or companies connected with them, or for general charitable, benevolent or philanthropic purposes.

But "activities" does not include primary purpose trading.

(3) Regulations under this section may, in particular, impose a good practice requirement on the persons managing charitable institutions in circumstances where –

(a) those institutions,
(b) the persons managing them, or
(c) persons or companies connected with such institutions,

are engaged in charity fund-raising.

(4) A "good practice requirement" is a requirement to take all reasonable steps to ensure that the fund-raising is carried out in such a way that –

(a) it does not unreasonably intrude on the privacy of those from whom funds are being solicited or procured;
(b) it does not involve the making of unreasonably persistent approaches to persons to donate funds;
(c) it does not result in undue pressure being placed on persons to donate funds;
(d) it does not involve the making of any false or misleading representation about any of the matters mentioned in subsection (5).

(5) The matters are –

(a) the extent or urgency of any need for funds on the part of any charitable institution or company connected with such an institution;
(b) any use to which funds donated in response to the fund-raising are to be put by such an institution or company;
(c) the activities, achievements or finances of such an institution or company.

(6) Regulations under this section may provide that a person who persistently fails, without reasonable excuse, to comply with any specified requirement of the regulations is to be guilty of an offence and liable on summary conviction to a fine not exceeding level 2 on the standard scale.

(7) For the purposes of this section –

(a) "funds" means money or other property;
(b) "general charitable, benevolent or philanthropic purposes" means charitable, benevolent or philanthropic purposes other than those associated with one or more particular institutions;
(c) the persons "managing" a charitable institution are the charity trustees or other persons having the general control and management of the administration of the institution; and
(d) a person is "connected" with a charitable institution if he is an employee or agent of –
   (i) the institution,
   (ii) the persons managing it, or
   (iii) a company connected with it,

or he is a volunteer acting on behalf of the institution or such a company.

(8) In this section "primary purpose trading", in relation to a charitable institution, means any trade carried on by the institution or a company connected with it where –

(a) the trade is carried on in the course of the actual carrying out of a primary purpose of the institution; or
(b) the work in connection with the trade is mainly carried out by beneficiaries of the institution.]

NOTE

Inserted by Charities Act 2006, s 69.

Sub-s (2) amended by Charities (Protection and Social Investment) Act 2016, s 14(1), (4).

[64B Reserve power in relation to fund-raising regulators

(1) Regulations under section 64A may, in particular, impose on charitable institutions requirements to do any of the following—

(a) to comply with requirements imposed by a regulator;
(b) to have regard to guidance issued by a regulator;
(c) to pay fees to a regulator of an amount determined by the regulations or determined by the regulator in accordance with the regulations;
(d) to be registered with a regulator for the purpose of its regulation of charity fund-raising.

(2) "Regulator" means a body specified in the regulations as a regulator for the purposes of this section.

(3) A body may be specified as a regulator for the purposes of this section only if the regulation of charity fund-raising appears to the Minister to be a principal function of the body.

(4) A body maintained out of money provided by Parliament may not be specified as a regulator (and this section does not confer power by regulations to establish a body to act as regulator).]

NOTE

Section inserted by Charities (Protection and Social Investment) Act 2016, s 14(1), (2).

[64C Reserve power to confer additional powers on Charity Commission

(1) In the case of charity fund-raising which—

(a) is carried on by a charity, a person managing a charity or a person or company connected with a charity, or
(b) involves soliciting or otherwise procuring funds for the benefit of a charity or a company connected with a charity, or for charitable purposes,

regulations under section 64A may, in particular, make provision conferring functions on the Charity Commission, including provision applying or reproducing, with or without modification, any provision of the Charities Act 2011.

(2) The regulations may provide for a power that is exercisable by the Commission by virtue of the regulations to be exercisable by a person appointed by the Commission for the purpose.

(3) Where regulations by virtue of this section apply in relation to charity fund-raising by institutions that are not charities, section 19 of the Charities Act 2011 (fees and other amounts payable to Commission) applies in relation to the regulations as it applies in relation to the enactments relating to charities (but that is without prejudice to the application of other provisions by virtue of this section or section 77(3)).]

NOTE

Section inserted by Charities (Protection and Social Investment) Act 2016, s 14(1), (3).

[. . .]

PART IV
GENERAL

75 Offences by bodies corporate

Where any offence –

(a) under this Act or any regulations made under it, or
(b) . . .

is committed by a body corporate and is proved to have been committed with the consent or connivance of, or to be attributable to any neglect on the part of, any director, manager, secretary or other similar officer of the body corporate, or any person who was purporting to act in any such capacity, he as well as the body corporate shall be guilty of that offence and shall be liable to be proceeded against and punished accordingly.

In relation to a body corporate whose affairs are managed by its members, "director" means a member of the body corporate.

NOTE

Amended by Charities Act 1993, s 98(2), Sch 7.

76 Service of documents

(1) This section applies to –

(a) . . .
(b) any notice or other document required or authorised to be given or served under Part II of this Act; . . .
(c) . . ..

(2) A document to which this section applies may be served on or given to a person (other than a body corporate) –

(a) by delivering it to that person;
(b) by leaving it at his last known address in the United Kingdom; or
(c) by sending it by post to him at that address.

(3) A document to which this section applies may be served on or given to a body corporate by delivering it or sending it by post –

(a) to the registered or principal office of the body in the United Kingdom, or
(b) if it has no such office in the United Kingdom, to any place in the United Kingdom where it carries on business or conducts its activities (as the case may be).

(4) Any such document may also be served on or given to a person (including a body corporate) by sending it by post to that person at an address notified by that person for the purposes of this subsection to the person or persons by whom it is required or authorised to be served or given.

NOTE

Sub-s (1): amended by Charities Act 1993, s 98(2), Sch 7; Charities Act 2006, s 75(1), (2), Sch 8, paras 89, 92, Sch 9.

77 Regulations and orders

(1) Any regulations or order of the [Minister] under this Act –

(a) shall be made by statutory instrument; and
(b) (subject to [subsections (2) and (2A)]) shall be subject to annulment in pursuance of a resolution of either House of Parliament.

(2) Subsection (1)(b) does not apply –

(a)-(c) [. . .] ; or
(d) to an order under section 79(2).

[(2A) Subsection (1)(b) does not apply to regulations under section 64A, and no such regulations may be made unless a draft of the statutory instrument containing the regulations has been laid before, and approved by a resolution of, each House of Parliament.]

(3) Any regulations or order of the [Minister] under this Act may make –

(a) different provision for different cases; and
(b) such supplemental, incidental, consequential or transitional provision or savings as the [Minister] considers appropriate.

(4) Before making any regulations under section [. . .] 64 [or 64A] . . . the [Minister] shall consult such persons or bodies of persons as he considers appropriate [and, in the case of regulations made by virtue of section 64B or 64C, shall in particular consult the Charity Commission].

NOTE

Sub-s (1): amended by SI 2006/2951, art 6, Schedule, para 3(e); Charities Act 2006, s 75(1), Sch 8, paras 89, 93(1), (2).

Sub-s (2): amended by Charities Act 1993, s 98(2), Sch 7.

Sub-s (2A): inserted by Charities Act 2006, s 75(1), Sch 8, paras 89, 93(1), (3).

Sub-s (3): amended by SI 2006/2951, art 6, Schedule, para 3(e).

Sub-s (4): amended by Charities Act 1993, s 98(2), Sch 7; Charities Act 2006, s 75(1), Sch 8, paras 89, 93(1), (4)(a), (b), Sch 9; SI 2006/2951, art 6, Schedule, para 3(e); Charities (Protection and Social Investment) Act 2016, s 14(1), (5).

78 Minor and consequential amendments and repeals

(1) The enactments mentioned in Schedule 6 to this Act shall have effect subject to the amendments there specified (which are either minor amendments or amendments consequential on the provisions of this Act).

(2) The enactments mentioned in Schedule 7 to this Act (which include some that are already spent or are no longer of practical utility) are hereby repealed to the extent specified in the third column of that Schedule.

79 Short title, commencement and extent

(1) This Act may be cited as the Charities Act 1992.

(2) This Act shall come into force on such day as the [Minister] may by order appoint; and different days may be so appointed for different provisions or for different purposes.

(3) Subject to subsections (4) to (6) below, this Act extends only to England and Wales.

(4), (5) . . .

(6) The amendments in Schedule 6, and *(subject to subsection (7))* the repeals in Schedule 7, have the same extent as the enactments to which they refer, and section 78 extends accordingly.

(7) *The repeal in Schedule 7 of the Police, Factories, &c (Miscellaneous Provisions) Act 1916 does not extend to Northern Ireland.*

NOTE

Sub-s (2): amended by SI 2006/2951, art 6, Schedule, para 3(f).

Sub-ss (4), (5): repealed by Charities Act 1993, s 98(2), Sch 7;

Sub-s (6): words in italics repealed by Charities Act 2006, s 75(1), (2), Sch 8, paras 89, 94(a), Sch 9 from a date to be appointed.

Sub-s (7): words in italics repealed by Charities Act 2006, s 75(1), (2), Sch 8, paras 89, 94(b), Sch 9 from a date to be appointed.

Schedules

Schedules 6 and 7 remain in force but are not reproduced here.

APPENDIX 5

CHARITABLE INCORPORATED ORGANISATIONS (GENERAL) REGULATIONS 2012

SI 2012/3012

The Minister for the Cabinet Office makes the following Regulations in exercise of the powers conferred by sections 30(2)(c), 42(2)(c), 206(3), 207(2)(b), 223, 246 and 347(3) of the Charities Act 2011.

In accordance with section 348(4) of that Act the Minister has consulted such persons and bodies of persons as he considers appropriate.

1 General

1 CITATION AND COMMENCEMENT

These Regulations may be cited as the Charitable Incorporated Organisations (General) Regulations 2012 and come into force on 2nd January 2013.

2 INTERPRETATION: GENERAL

In these Regulations–

"the 2011 Act" means the Charities Act 2011;
"application for registration" means an application to be constituted and registered under section 207 of the 2011 Act;
"association CIO" means a CIO which is not a foundation CIO;
"enactment" has the meaning given by section 245(4) of the 2011 Act;
"foundation CIO" means a CIO whose constitution provides that the same persons are to be its members and its charity trustees;
"provision for entrenchment" has the meaning given by regulation 15;
"service address" means, in relation to a person, an address at which–

(a) the service of documents can be effected by physical delivery; and
(b) the delivery of documents is capable of being recorded by the obtaining of an acknowledgment of delivery.

3 INTERPRETATION: BODIES CORPORATE AND ASSOCIATED BODIES CORPORATE

For the purposes of these Regulations–

(a) "body corporate" includes a body incorporated outside the United Kingdom but does not include–
 (i) a corporation sole; or

(ii) a partnership that, whether or not a legal person, is not regarded as a body corporate under the law by which it is governed;

(b) bodies corporate are associated if–

(i) one is a subsidiary of the other; or

(ii) both are subsidiaries of the same body corporate,

and for these purposes "subsidiary" has the meaning given by section 1159 of, and Schedule 6 to, the Companies Act 2006 with the substitution, in relation to CIOs, of references to charity trustees for references to directors.

4 INTERPRETATION: HARD COPY, ELECTRONIC FORM AND RELATED EXPRESSIONS

(1) The following provisions apply for the purposes of these Regulations.

(2) A document or information is sent or supplied in hard copy form if it is sent or supplied in a paper copy or similar form capable of being read and references to "hard copy" in these Regulations have a corresponding meaning.

(3) A document or information is sent or supplied in electronic form if it is sent or supplied–

(a) by electronic means (for example, by e-mail or fax); or

(b) by any other means whilst in electronic form (for example, sending a disk by post).

(4) A document or information is sent or supplied by electronic means if it is–

(a) sent initially and received at its destination by means of electronic equipment for the processing (which expression includes digital compression) or storage of data; and

(b) entirely transmitted, conveyed and received by wire, by radio, by optical means or by other electromagnetic means,

and references to "electronic means" in these Regulations have a corresponding meaning.

(5) A document or information authorised or required to be sent or supplied in electronic form must be sent or supplied in a form, and by a means, that the sender or supplier reasonably considers will enable the recipient–

(a) to read it; and

(b) to retain a copy of it.

(6) For the purposes of this regulation, a document or information can be read only if–

(a) it can be read with the naked eye; or

(b) to the extent that it consists of images (for example, photographs, pictures, maps, plans or drawings), it can be seen with the naked eye.

(7) The provisions of this regulation apply whether the provision of these Regulations in question uses the words "sent" or "supplied" or uses other words (such as "deliver", "provide" "produce", "transmit" or, in the case of notice, "give") to refer to the sending or supplying of a document or information.

UK Parliament SIs 2010-Present/2012/3001-3050/Charitable Incorporated Organisations (General) Regulations 2012 (SI 2012/3012)/Part 2 Registration/5 CIO not to be exempt

2 Registration

5 CIO NOT TO BE EXEMPT

No application may be made for a CIO to be constituted and registered where the resulting charity would be an exempt charity.

6 APPLICATION OF REGISTRATION PROVISIONS IN 2011 ACT

(1) In their application to CIOs the following provisions of the 2011 Act are to be read subject to the modifications specified.

(2) In section 29 of that Act (the register)–

(a) in subsection (2)(a) for "charity registered in accordance with section 30" substitute "CIO";

(b) in subsection (2)(b) before "such other particulars" insert " in addition to any particulars and information required to be included by any other provision of this Act or of regulations made under it,".

(3) Sections 30 to 34 of that Act do not apply.

(4) In section 35 of that Act (duties of trustees in connection with registration)–

(a) subsections (1) and (2) do not apply;

(b) for subsection (3) substitute–

"(3) The charity trustees of a CIO must within 28 days–

(a) notify the Commission if there is any change in the particulars of the CIO entered in the register; and

(b) so far as appropriate, supply the Commission with particulars of any such change.".

(5) In section 36 of that Act (claims and objections to registration–

(a) in subsection (1) for "registration of an institution as a charity" substitute "registration of a CIO";

(b) in subsection (3)(b) after "an institution from the register" insert–

", or

(c) to restore a CIO to the register".

(6) In section 38 of that Act (right to inspect register) for subsection (4) substitute–

"(4) Copies of the constitution of any CIO as supplied to the Commission must, so long as the CIO remains on the register–

(a) be kept by the Commission, and

(b) be open to public inspection at all reasonable times.".

7 APPLICATIONS FOR REGISTRATION: COMMUNICATIONS WITH COMMISSION

(1) This regulation applies in relation to any requirement for applicants to send documents or information to the Commission under section 207 of the 2011 Act (application for CIO to be constituted and registered).

(2) The Commission may–

(a) require the contents of the document to be in a standard form;

(b) require the document to be produced in the manner the Commission considers fit for the purpose of enabling that document to be scanned or copied;

(c) require the document to be authenticated by a particular person or persons of a particular description;
(d) where a requirement is imposed under sub-paragraph (c), specify the means of authentication;
(e) specify the means to be used for sending the document to the Commission (for example by post or by electronic means);
(f) where the document is to be sent by electronic means, specify–
    (i) the hardware or software to be used; and
    (ii) the requirements as to the technical specifications including protocol, security, anti-virus protection and encryption.

(3) Any requirements imposed by the Commission under this regulation–

(a) must not be inconsistent with requirements imposed by any enactment as to the form, authentication or manner of sending the document concerned; and
(b) must be published by the Commission in such manner as it thinks fit.

(4) Where a document or information is sent or supplied by the applicants by electronic means, it may only be sent or supplied to an address specified for the purpose by the Commission.

(5) If the applicants send or supply a document or information to the Commission in electronic form–

(a) the applicants are treated as having agreed to accept a response in electronic form; and
(b) where the document or information is sent or supplied by the applicants by electronic means from an electronic address, or the applicants have given such an address in the document or information (subject to any limitations specified when providing that address), the applicants are treated as having agreed to the response being sent by electronic means to that address.

8 APPLICATIONS FOR REGISTRATION: INFORMATION TO BE INCLUDED

In a case where one or more persons makes an application for registration and the proposed constitution of the CIO includes provision for entrenchment, the applicants must specify that fact in the application.

9 APPLICATIONS FOR AMALGAMATION: INFORMATION TO BE INCLUDED

In a case where two or more CIOs make an application for amalgamation and the proposed constitution of the new CIO includes provision for entrenchment, the old CIOs must specify that fact in the application.

10 TRANSFER OF ACCOUNTING RECORDS ON AMALGAMATION

(1) The charity trustees of each old CIO must, on registration of the new CIO, transfer the relevant accounting records to the charity trustees of the new CIO.

(2) In paragraph (1) "relevant accounting records" means the accounting records which the charity trustees of the old CIO were, immediately before the registration of the new CIO, under a duty to preserve under section 131 of the 2011 Act (preservation of accounting records).

(3) On transfer of the records in accordance with paragraph (1), the charity trustees of the old CIO shall be treated as having discharged their duty under section 131.

11 RETENTION OF ACCOUNTING RECORDS AFTER AMALGAMATION

(1) The charity trustees of a new CIO must preserve the records transferred to it under regulation 10 for at least 6 years from the end of the financial year in which the records were made ("the retention period").

(2) Subject to paragraph (3), where a new CIO is dissolved within the retention period, the obligation to preserve those records in accordance with this regulation is to continue to be discharged by the persons who were the charity trustees of the new CIO immediately before its dissolution.

(3) Paragraph (2) does not apply if the Commission consents in writing to the records being destroyed or otherwise disposed of.

12 INTERPRETATION

In this Part–

"new CIO" and "old CIO" have the meanings given by section 235(1) of the 2011 Act (application for amalgamation of CIOs); and

"application for amalgamation" means an application under section 235 of the 2011 Act.

3 Constitution

13 MATTERS TO BE PROVIDED FOR IN CONSTITUTION

(1) A CIO's constitution must state the names of the persons who are to be the first charity trustees of the CIO.

(2) In addition to the provision required by section 206(2) of the 2011 Act, a CIO's constitution must make–

- (a) the standard charity trustee provisions; and
- (b) the standard member provisions.

(3) In this regulation–

"standard charity trustee provisions" means provision about–

- (a) how a charity trustee of the CIO retires from office;
- (b) the other circumstances in which a charity trustee of the CIO will cease to hold office and in particular, if the CIO's constitution permits its members to remove a charity trustee from office, the circumstances in which a charity trustee may be removed from office and the procedure for doing so;
- (c) the holding of meetings of the charity trustees of the CIO and in particular–
  - (i) the procedure for calling such meetings;
  - (ii) the appointment of a chair of such meetings;
  - (iii) the quorum for such meetings;
  - (iv) if the charity trustees of the CIO are to have the right to demand a poll, the exercise of that right and the manner in which the poll is to be conducted; and
- (d) subject to compliance with section 222 of the 2011 Act and regulation 36, the extent to which a charity trustee of the CIO may, if at all, benefit personally from any arrangement or transaction entered into by the CIO.

"standard member provisions" means provision about–

(a) how a member retires from membership of the CIO;
(b) the other circumstances in which, and method by which, a member's membership of the CIO may or must be terminated; and
(c) the holding of general meetings of its members and in particular–
  (i) the procedure for calling such meetings;
  (ii) the appointment of a chair of such meetings;
  (iii) the representation at such meetings of any body corporate who is a member of the CIO;
  (iv) the quorum for such meetings; and
  (v) if the members of the CIO are to have the right to demand a poll, the exercise of that right and the manner in which a poll is to be conducted.

(4) If the CIO is to have a common seal, the constitution must make provision about the use of the seal.

(5) If a CIO's constitution permits its members to appoint a proxy, the constitution must make provision about–

(a) the way in which a member makes such an appointment;
(b) the rights of the proxy; and
(c) the termination of such an appointment.

(6) If a CIO's constitution permits its members to vote by post, the constitution must make provision about the circumstances in which, and the way in which, such votes may be given.

(7) If a CIO's constitution permits its members to make decisions at a general meeting otherwise than by voting on resolutions, the constitution must make provision as to the alternative process by which the members may make decisions at a general meeting.

(8) If a CIO's constitution permits its members to make decisions otherwise than at a general meeting, the constitution must make provision as to the alternative process by which the members may make decisions otherwise than at a general meeting.

(9) If the members of a CIO are to have different voting rights, the constitution must state the voting rights which are to attach to each class of member.

(10) If the members of a CIO are to be treated, as a result of becoming members, as having agreed to receive communications from the CIO by electronic means, the constitution must include–

(a) a statement to this effect; and
(b) provision setting out, as a result of the deemed agreement, the circumstances in which its members will receive communications by electronic means from the CIO.

(11 If a CIO is to communicate with its members by means of a website, the constitution must make provision as to the circumstances in which a website may be used as a means of communication with its members.

(12) If a CIO's constitution requires more than one charity trustee to be in office for the business of the CIO to be discharged, the constitution must make provision indicating the minimum number of charity trustees that are to be in office to enable its business to be discharged.

(13) If a CIO's constitution is to permit its charity trustees to make decisions at a meeting otherwise than by voting on resolutions, the constitution must make provision as to the alternative process by which the charity trustees may make decisions at a meeting.

(14) If a CIO's constitution is to permit its charity trustees to make decisions otherwise than at a meeting, the constitution must make provision as to the alternative process by which the charity trustees may make decisions otherwise than at a meeting.

14 CONSTITUTION NOT TO RESTRICT ABILITY TO DISPOSE OF PROPERTY

A CIO's constitution must not include any restriction of the power in section 216 of the 2011 Act (powers of CIO) that would deprive the CIO of its ability to dispose of its property.

15 PROVISION FOR ENTRENCHMENT

(1) A CIO's constitution may contain provision ("provision for entrenchment") to the effect that specified provisions of the constitution may be amended or repealed by resolution of its members only if specified conditions are met, or specified procedures are complied with, that are more restrictive than those applied by section 224(2) of the 2011 Act (amendment of constitution by resolution of members).

(2) Provision for entrenchment may only be made–

- (a) in the constitution proposed in the application for registration; or
- (b) by an amendment of the constitution agreed to by all of the members of the CIO.

(3) Provision for entrenchment does not prevent amendment of the CIO's constitution–

- (a) by agreement of all of the members of the CIO; or
- (b) by order of the court or by the Commission.

(4) Nothing in this regulation affects–

- (a) any power of a court or the Commission to alter a CIO's constitution; or
- (b) the operation of sections 225 to 227 of the 2011 Act (amendment of constitution, Commission's consent and coming into effect of amendments).

16 DATE OF RESOLUTION AMENDING CONSTITUTION

(1) Subject to paragraph (2), if a resolution under section 224 of the 2011 Act to amend a CIO's constitution is passed otherwise than at a general meeting it is treated as having been passed on the date on which the last member agreed to it.

(2) Paragraph (1) does not apply if a provision in the CIO's constitution treats such a resolution as having been passed on a date later than the date on which the last member agreed to it.

17 PROVISION FOR ENTRENCHMENT: STATEMENT OF COMPLIANCE

(1) This regulation applies where a CIO's constitution contains provision for entrenchment.

(2) If the CIO amends its constitution, it must send a statement of compliance to the Commission with the documents that it is required to send to the Commission by section 227(1) of the 2011 Act.

(3) The Commission may rely on the statement of compliance as sufficient evidence of the matters stated in it.

(4) In this regulation "statement of compliance" means a statement certifying that the amendment has been made in accordance with the provision for entrenchment.

18 EFFECT OF AMENDMENT OF CONSTITUTION ON MEMBERS

(1) A member of a CIO ("M") is not bound by an amendment to its constitution after the date on which M became a member, if that amendment increases in any way M's liability to contribute to the CIO's assets if it is wound up.

(2) Paragraph (1) does not apply if M agrees in writing, either before or after the amendment is made, to be bound by the amendment.

4 CIO Capacity and Related Matters

19 CIO CONTRACTS

(1) A contract may be made–

- (a) by a CIO, by writing under its common seal; or
- (b) on behalf of a CIO, by a person acting under its authority, express or implied.

(2) Any formalities required by law in the case of a contract made by an individual also apply, unless a contrary intention appears, to a contract made by or on behalf of a CIO.

20 EXECUTION OF DOCUMENTS

(1) A document is executed by a CIO–

- (a) by the affixing of its common seal; or
- (b) whether or not the CIO has a common seal, in accordance with paragraph (2).

(2) A document is validly executed by a CIO if it is signed–

- (a) where the CIO has more than one charity trustee, by at least two of the CIO's charity trustees; or
- (b) where the CIO has only one charity trustee, by that charity trustee.

(3) A document–

- (a) signed in accordance with paragraph (2); and
- (b) expressed, in whatever words, to be executed by the CIO,

has the same effect as if executed under the common seal of the CIO.

(4) In favour of a purchaser a document is to be treated as duly executed by a CIO if it purports to be signed in accordance with paragraph (2).

(5) For the purposes of paragraph (4), "purchaser" means a purchaser in good faith for valuable consideration and includes a lessee, mortgagee or other person who for valuable consideration acquires an interest in property.

(6) References in this regulation to a document being (or purporting to be) signed by a charity trustee are to be read, in a case where a body corporate is a charity trustee, as references to the document being (or purporting to be) signed by an individual authorised by the body corporate to sign on its behalf.

21 EXECUTION OF DEEDS

(1) A document–

(a) executed by a CIO in accordance with regulation 20; and
(b) which makes clear on its face that it is intended by the person or persons making it to be a deed,

has effect, upon delivery, as a deed.

(2) For the purposes of paragraph (1) a document is presumed, unless the contrary intention is proved, to be delivered upon its being executed.

(3) In favour of a purchaser–

(a) if a document is treated as duly executed under regulation 20 and
(b) the document makes clear on its face that it is intended by the person or persons making it to be a deed,

the document is treated as having been delivered upon its being executed.

(4) In paragraph (3) "purchaser" has the meaning given by regulation 20(5).

22 EXECUTION OF DEEDS OR OTHER DOCUMENTS BY ATTORNEY

(1) A CIO may, by instrument executed as a deed, empower a person, either generally or in respect of specified matters, as its attorney to execute deeds or other documents on its behalf.

(2) A deed or other document so executed, whether in the United Kingdom or elsewhere, has effect as if executed by the CIO.

23 COMMON SEAL

(1) A CIO may have a common seal but need not have one.

(2) A CIO which has a common seal must have its name engraved in legible characters on the seal.

(3) Subsections (3) and (5) of section 45 of the Companies Act 2006 (offence of failure to comply with requirements in relation to common seal) apply in relation to a failure by a CIO to comply with paragraph (2) as they apply in relation to a failure by a company to comply with subsection (2) of that section; and, in its application by virtue of this paragraph, subsection (3) of that section has effect as if paragraph (a) were omitted.

(4) Subsections (4) and (5) of that section (offence of using etc a seal which does not satisfy the necessary requirements) apply to the use, or authorisation of the use, of a seal of a CIO which does not comply with paragraph (2) as they apply to the use, or authorisation of the use, of a seal of a company which does not comply with subsection (2) of that section.

(5) The following provisions of Part 36 of the Companies Act 2006 (offences under the Companies Acts) apply in relation to an offence under that Act committed by virtue of this regulation as they apply to an offence under the Companies Acts–

(a) section 1121 (liability of officer in default);
(b) section 1122 (liability of company as officer in default);
(c) section 1127 (summary proceedings: venue);
(d) section 1128 (summary proceedings: time limit for proceedings);
(e) section 1129 (legal professional privilege); and

(f) section 1132 (production and inspection of documents where offence suspected).

(6) In their application to CIOs the provisions of the Companies Act 2006 mentioned in this regulation have effect as if–

(a) for references to a company there were substituted references to a CIO;
(b) for references to an officer of a company there were substituted references to a charity trustee of a CIO;
(c) provisions relating only to Scotland or Northern Ireland were omitted;
(d) references to the Secretary of State were omitted.

(7) In its application to CIOs section 1121 has effect as if subsection (2) were omitted.

(8) In its application to CIOs section 1122 has effect as if the following were substituted–

"(1) Where a company is an officer of a CIO, it does not commit an offence as a charity trustee in default unless one of its officers is in default.
(2) Where any such offence is committed by a company the officer in question also commits the offence and is liable to be proceeded against and punished accordingly.
(3) In this section–

"in default" has the meaning given by section 1121;
"officer" includes any director, manager or secretary.".

(9) In its application to CIOs section 1132(3)(b) has effect as if for "the secretary of the company, or such other officer of it" there were substituted "such charity trustee of the CIO".

24 OFFICIAL SEAL FOR USE ABROAD

(1) A CIO that has a common seal may have an official seal for use outside the United Kingdom.

(2) The official seal must be a facsimile of the CIO's common seal, with the addition on its face of the place or places where it is to be used.

(3) The official seal when duly affixed to a document has the same effect as the CIO's common seal.

(4) A CIO having an official seal may, by writing under its common seal, authorise any person ap-pointed for the purpose to affix the official seal to any deed or other document to which the CIO is a party.

25 BILLS OF EXCHANGE AND PROMISSORY NOTES

A bill of exchange or promissory note is deemed to have been made, accepted or endorsed on behalf of a CIO if made, accepted or endorsed in the name of, or by or on behalf of or on account of the CIO by a person acting under its authority.

5 Registers of Members and Charity Trustees

26 REQUIREMENT TO KEEP REGISTERS

(1) Every association CIO must keep a register of members in accordance with Part 1 of Schedule 1 and a register of charity trustees in accordance with Part 2 of Schedule 1.

(2) Every foundation CIO must keep a register of charity trustees (who are also the members of the CIO) in accordance with Part 2 of Schedule 1.

(3) Part 3 of Schedule 1 makes further provision about maintenance of and access to a CIO's register or registers.

(4) If a CIO fails to comply with a requirement imposed by Schedule 1 the Commission may, by order, give the charity trustees of the CIO such directions as it considers appropriate for securing that the default is made good.

(5) Sections 336 and 337 of the 2011 Act (enforcement of and other provisions as to orders of the Commission) apply to an order made under paragraph (4) as they apply to an order made under section 52(1) of that Act (power to call for documents).

(6) No order may be made under section 335 of the 2011 Act in respect of a CIO's failure to comply with any requirement imposed by Schedule 1.

(7) In regulations 27 to 30 a reference to a CIO's register of members is, in the case of a foundation CIO, a reference to its register of charity trustees kept in accordance with Part 2 of Schedule 1.

27 POWER OF COMMISSION TO ORDER RECTIFICATION OF REGISTER OF MEMBERS

(1) Where–

(a) the Commission, or a person appointed by the Commission, makes a determination under section 111 of the 2011 Act (power to determine membership of a charity); and

(b) the determination reveals the membership of a CIO to be different from the membership specified in its register of members,

the Commission may, by order, require the CIO, or the charity trustees of the CIO, to rectify the register.

(2) Sections 336 and 337 of the 2011 Act (enforcement of and other provisions as to orders of the Commission) apply to an order made under paragraph (1) as they apply to an order made under section 52(1) of that Act (power to call for documents).

28 POWER OF COURT TO ORDER RECTIFICATION OF REGISTER OF MEMBERS

(1) If–

(a) the name of any person is, without sufficient cause, entered in or omitted from a CIO's register of members; or

(b) default is made or unnecessary delay takes place in entering in the register the fact that any person has ceased to be a member,

a relevant person may apply to the court for the rectification of the register.

(2) The court may either–

(a) refuse the application; or

(b) order the rectification of the register and payment by the CIO of any damages sustained by a party aggrieved.

(3) On such an application the court may decide the title of persons who are parties to the application to have their names entered in or omitted from the register, whether the question arises–

(a) between members;
(b) between members and the CIO;
(c) between members and the Commission; or
(d) between the CIO and the Commission.

(4) On such an application the court may also decide any question necessary or expedient to be decided for rectification of the register.

(5) For the purposes of paragraph (3) references to members of a CIO include references to alleged members of a CIO.

(6) In this regulation "relevant person" means–

(a) the person aggrieved by the entry, omission, default or delay;
(b) a member of the CIO;
(c) the CIO; or
(d) the Commission.

29 REGISTER OF MEMBERS TO BE EVIDENCE

A CIO's register of members is to be prima facie evidence of any matters which are by these Regulations required to be inserted in it.

30 TIME LIMIT FOR CLAIMS ARISING FROM ENTRY IN REGISTER OF MEMBERS

(1) Liability incurred by a CIO from–

(a) the making or deletion of an entry in its register of members; or
(b) a failure to make or delete such an entry,

is not enforceable more than 10 years after the date on which the entry was made or deleted or, as the case may be, the failure first occurred.

(2) This is without prejudice to any lesser period of limitation.

6 Charity Trustees: Appointment, Powers and Duties

31 ELIGIBILITY FOR APPOINTMENT AS CHARITY TRUSTEE

(1) Only a person who has attained the age of 16 years is eligible to be appointed as a charity trustee of a CIO.

(2) Paragraph (1) does not affect the validity of an appointment that is not to take effect until the person appointed attains that age.

(3) Where the office of charity trustee of a CIO is held by a corporation sole, or otherwise by virtue of another office, the appointment to that other office of a person ("A") who has not attained the age of 16 years is not effective also to make A a charity trustee of the CIO until A attains the age of 16 years.

(4) Subject to paragraph (5), in any case where the operation of paragraph (3) means there is not a sufficient number of charity trustees to conduct the business of the relevant CIO in accordance with its constitution, the CIO may appoint such other person as it considers fit to act as charity trustee until A attains the age of 16 years.

(5) A CIO may not appoint any person to act as charity trustee under paragraph (4) if that person is disqualified from being a charity trustee by–

(a) any provision of these Regulations; or
(b) section 178 of the 2011 Act.

(6) An appointment of a charity trustee made in contravention of this regulation is void.

(7) Nothing in this regulation affects the liability of a person ("A") under any provision of these Regulations or the 2011 Act if A purports to act as a charity trustee of a CIO although A could not, by virtue of this regulation, be appointed as such a charity trustee.

32 VALIDITY OF ACTS OF CHARITY TRUSTEE

(1) Subject to paragraph (2), the acts of a person ("A") as a charity trustee of a CIO are valid even if it is afterwards discovered that–

(a) there was a defect in A's appointment;
(b) A was disqualified from holding office;
(c) A had ceased to hold office;
(d) A was not entitled to vote on the matter in question; or
(e) where the CIO's constitution permits the charity trustees to make decisions otherwise than by voting, A was not entitled to take part in the decision on the matter in question.

(2) Paragraph (1)(d) and (e) apply only in favour of (as the case may be)–

(a) the CIO; and
(b) any party, other than A or the CIO, to an agreement or transaction entered into as a consequence of–
  (i) A voting on a matter on which A was not entitled to vote; or
  (ii) where the constitution permits the charity trustees to make decisions otherwise than by voting, A taking part in a decision in which A was not entitled to take part.

(3) This regulation does not affect the application of sections 183 and 184 of the 2011 Act (criminal and civil consequences of acting while disqualified).

33 DELEGATION AND APPOINTMENT OF NOMINEES ETC BY CHARITY TRUSTEES

(1) The provisions of the Trustee Act 2000 ("the 2000 Act") specified in paragraph (2) apply in relation to a CIO as they apply to a charitable trust but with the modifications specified in paragraph (3).

(2) The provisions of the 2000 Act which apply are–

(a) Part 4 (agents, nominees and custodians) other than sections 11(2), 12(3), 13(3) to (5), 18, 25(2) and 27; and
(b) section 32 (remuneration of agents, nominees and custodians).

(3) The modifications are–

(a) any reference to a charitable trust or a trust is to be read as a reference to a CIO;
(b) any reference to the trustees of a trust or to the trustees is to be read as a reference to the charity trustees of a CIO;

(c) any reference to property or assets subject to the trust, or of the trust, is to be read as a reference to the property or assets of a CIO;
(d) any reference to the acquisition of property which is to be subject to the trust is to be read as a reference to the acquisition of property by a CIO;
(e) any reference to the trust instrument is to be read as a reference to CIO's constitution;
(f) any reference to a provision of the 2000 Act is to be read as a reference to a provision of that Act as it applies in relation to CIOs;
(g) any reference to trust funds is to be read as a reference to the funds of a CIO;
(h) any reference to section 12(3), 13(5) or 18 is omitted;
(i) in sections 14(1) and 20(1) the reference to sections 29 to 32 is to be read as a reference to section 32;
(j) in sections 14(3)(b) and 20(3)(b) the words "or any beneficiary" are omitted;
(k) in sections 16(3) and 17(4) references to a CIO having a custodian trustee are omitted;
(l) any reference to the duty of care applicable to a trustee under paragraph 3 of Schedule 1 to the 2000 Act is to be read as a reference to the duty of care in section 221(2) of the 2011 Act (duties of charity trustees);
(m) the reference in section 11(3)(d) to any other function prescribed by an order made by the Secretary of State is to be read as a reference to any function prescribed by an order made by the Secretary of State under that provision in relation to a charitable trust and any such order applies in relation to a CIO in so far as it applies to a charity which is not an exempt charity with appropriate modifications;
(n) in section 19(4) the words "which is not an exempt charity" are omitted;
(o) in section 25(1) the words "subject to subsection (2)" are omitted.

34 DUTY NOT TO ACCEPT BENEFITS FROM THIRD PARTIES

(1) A charity trustee ("T") of a CIO must not accept a benefit from a third party conferred by reason of–

(a) T being a charity trustee; or
(b) T doing (or not doing) anything as a charity trustee.

(2) Benefits received by T from a person by whom T's services (as charity trustee or otherwise) are provided to the CIO are not regarded as conferred by a third party.

(3) This duty is not infringed if the acceptance of the benefit cannot reasonably be regarded as likely to give rise to a conflict of interest.

(4) In this regulation "third party" means a person other than the CIO, an associated body corporate, or a person acting on behalf of the CIO or an associated body corporate.

7 Meetings and Procedure

35 NOTICE OF RESOLUTIONS TO BE PROPOSED AT A GENERAL MEETING

(1) Subject to paragraph (3) and any more restrictive provision included in the CIO's constitution, where a resolution to which this regulation applies is to be proposed at a general meeting of a CIO–

(a) notice of not less than 14 days of the general meeting must be given by the person calling the meeting to–

(i) all members of the CIO entitled to vote at the meeting or, where the CIO's constitution permits the members to make decisions otherwise than by voting, all members entitled to take part in the decision to be made at the meeting; and

(ii) any charity trustee of the CIO who is not also a member entitled to vote at the meeting or, where the CIO's constitution permits the members to make decisions otherwise than by voting, who is not also a member entitled to take part in the decision to be made at the meeting;

(b) the notice referred to in sub-paragraph (a) must contain particulars of the resolution that is to be proposed at that meeting.

(2) This regulation applies to a resolution under section 224 (amendment of constitution and procedure) or 235 (application for amalgamation of CIOs) or 240 (resolutions about transfer of CIO's undertaking to another CIO) of the 2011 Act.

(3) For the purpose of calculating the period of notice to be given under paragraph (1)(a) the following are to be excluded–

(a) the day of the meeting; and

(b) the day on which notice is given.

(4) If a qualifying majority agrees, a resolution which is to be proposed at a general meeting may be passed without the requirements of paragraph (1) being satisfied.

(5) In this regulation–

"qualifying majority" means–

(a) in relation to a CIO whose members take decisions by voting, a majority in number of the members having a right to attend and vote at the meeting, who together represent not less than the requisite percentage of the total voting rights at that meeting of all the members;

(b) in relation to a CIO where the CIO's constitution permits the members to make decisions otherwise than by voting, all of the members having the right to attend the meeting and take part in the decisions to be made at the meeting;

"requisite percentage" means 90% or such higher percentage (not exceeding 95%) as may be specified in the CIO's constitution for the purposes of this regulation.

36 CHARITY TRUSTEE WITH PERSONAL INTEREST IN DECISION

(1) A charity trustee of a CIO who would benefit personally, whether directly or indirectly, from a transaction or arrangement into which the CIO proposes to enter–

(a) must not take part in the making of any decision whether or not to enter into that transaction or arrangement; and

(b) must not be counted in the quorum necessary for the discharge of that business.

(2) Paragraph (1)(a) applies to any decision whether of the charity trustees of the CIO or its members.

(3) The restrictions in paragraph (1) do not apply where the transaction or arrangement to be entered into by the CIO cannot reasonably be regarded as likely to give rise to a conflict of interest.

(4) Nothing in this regulation affects the power of the Commission to authorise dealings with charity property etc under section 105 of the 2011 Act.

37 RECORDS TO BE KEPT OF CHARITY TRUSTEES' DECISIONS

(1) Every CIO must–

(a) cause minutes of all proceedings at meetings of its charity trustees to be recorded; and

(b) if decisions are made by its charity trustees otherwise than in meetings, must cause the decisions made to be recorded.

(2) The records must be kept for at least 6 years from–

(a) in the case of minutes of meetings, the date of the meeting;

(b) in the case of decisions made otherwise in meetings, the date on which the decision was made.

38 CHARITY TRUSTEE MINUTES AS EVIDENCE

(1) Minutes of a meeting of a CIO's charity trustees are evidence of the proceedings at the meeting if they purport to be authenticated by–

(a) the chair of that meeting; or

(b) the chair of the next charity trustees' meeting.

(2) Where minutes have been made of the proceedings of a meeting of the charity trustees, then, until the contrary is proved–

(a) the meeting is treated as having been duly held and convened;

(b) all proceedings at the meeting are treated as having duly taken place; and

(c) all appointments made at the meeting are treated as valid.

39 CHARITY TRUSTEE DECISION RECORDS AS EVIDENCE

(1) Records of decisions made by a CIO's charity trustees otherwise than in meetings are evidence of those decisions if they purport to be authenticated by–

(a) in the case of a CIO having more than one charity trustee, any one of those trustees who was not prevented by these Regulations or otherwise by the CIO's constitution from taking part in the relevant decision;

(b) in the case of a CIO having only one charity trustee, by that charity trustee.

(2) Where a decision of the charity trustees made otherwise than in a meeting has been recorded, then, until the contrary is proved–

(a) the decision is treated as having been duly made in accordance with the provisions of the CIO's constitution; and

(b) where the decision was that an appointment should be made, that appointment is treated as valid.

40 POWER OF COURT OR COMMISSION TO ORDER MEETING

(1) This regulation applies if for any reason it is impracticable–

(a) to call a meeting of the CIO in any manner in which meetings of that CIO may be called; or

(b to conduct the meeting in the manner prescribed by the CIO's constitution.

(2) The court or the Commission may order a meeting to be called, held and conducted in any such manner as the court or the Commission, as the case may be, thinks fit.

(3) Where the court or the Commission makes an order under paragraph (2), the court or the Com-mission, as the case may be, may give such ancillary or consequential directions as it thinks expedient.

(4) Directions under paragraph (3) may include a direction that one member of the CIO present at the meeting be treated as constituting a quorum.

(5) The power in paragraph (2) is exercisable by the court or the Commission–

- (a) of its own motion; or
- (b) on the application of a charity trustee of the CIO; or
- (c) on the application of a member of the CIO who–
  - (i) would be entitled to vote at the meeting; or
  - (ii) where the constitution permits the members to make decisions otherwise than by voting, would be entitled to take part in decisions made at the meeting.

(6) A meeting called, held and conducted in accordance with an order made under this regulation is treated for all purposes as being a meeting of the CIO duly called, held and conducted.

41 RECORDS TO BE KEPT OF MEMBERS' DECISIONS

(1) Every CIO must keep records comprising–

- (a) minutes of all proceedings of general meetings;
- (b) copies of the resolutions of members passed otherwise than at general meetings;
- (c) copies of decisions of members made otherwise than by resolution; and
- (d) details provided to the CIO in accordance with regulation 43.

(2) The records must be kept for at least 6 years from the date of the meeting, resolution or decision, as the case may be.

42 RECORDS AS EVIDENCE OF MEMBERS' DECISIONS

(1) Minutes of proceedings of a general meeting are evidence of the proceedings at the meeting if they purport to be signed by–

- (a) the chair of that meeting; or
- (b) the chair of the next general meeting.

(2) Where there is a record of proceedings of a general meeting of the members of a CIO then, until the contrary is proved–

- (a) the meeting is treated as having been duly held and convened;
- (b) all proceedings at the meeting are treated as having duly taken place; and
- (c) all appointments made at the meeting are treated as valid.

(3) The record of a resolution of the members passed otherwise than at a general meeting is evidence of the passing of the resolution if they purport to be signed by a charity trustee of the CIO.

(4) The record of a decision of the members made otherwise than by resolution is evidence of the making of the decision if they purport to be signed by a charity trustee of the CIO.

43 RECORDS OF DECISIONS BY SOLE MEMBER

(1) This regulation applies to a CIO that has only one member.

(2) Where the member takes any decision that–

(a) may be taken by the members of the CIO in general meeting; and
(b) has effect as if agreed by the CIO in general meeting,

the member must provide the CIO with details of that decision.

(3) Paragraph (2) does not apply if the member takes the relevant decision by way of a written resolution.

44 INSPECTION OF RECORDS OF DECISIONS AND MEETINGS

(1) The records referred to in regulation 41 relating to the previous 6 years must be kept available for inspection at–

(a) the CIO's principal office as it appears on the register of charities; or
(b) where the charity trustees pass a resolution to that effect, any other address specified in the resolution.

(2) The records must be open to inspection by any member of the CIO without charge.

(3) Any member may require a copy of the records on payment of such fee, if any, as the charity trustees of the CIO may reasonably require in respect of the costs of complying with the request.

45 RECORDS OF RESOLUTIONS AND MEETINGS OF CLASSES OF MEMBERS

Regulations 41 to 44 apply, with any necessary modifications, to the resolutions, decisions and meetings of a class of members of a CIO as they apply in relation to resolutions and decisions of members generally and to general meetings.

46 CIO RECORDS

(1) CIO records–

(a) may be kept in hard copy or electronic form; and
(b) may be arranged in such manner as the charity trustees of the CIO think fit,

provided the information in question is adequately recorded for future reference.

(2) Where the records are kept in electronic form, they must be capable of being reproduced in hard copy form.

(3) In this regulation "CIO records" means any register, minutes or other document required by these Regulations to be kept by a CIO.

8 Service of Documents

47 SERVICE OF DOCUMENTS ON CIO

A document may be served on a CIO by leaving it at, or sending it by post to, the CIO's principal office as it appears on the register of charities.

48 SERVICE OF DOCUMENTS ON CHARITY TRUSTEES ETC

(1) A document may be served on a person to whom this regulation applies by leaving it at, or sending it by post to, the person's registered service address.

(2) This regulation applies to–

(a) a charity trustee of the CIO; and
(b) an interim manager for the CIO.

(3) This regulation is restricted to service for purposes–

(a) arising out of or in connection with the appointment or position mentioned in paragraph (2); or
(b) in connection with the CIO.

(4) Nothing in this regulation is to be regarded as preventing the Commission from serving a document on an individual at the individual's last address known to the Commission.

(5) For the purposes of this regulation–

(a) "interim manager" means an interim manager appointed under section 76 of the 2011 Act;
(b) "registered service address" means, in relation to a charity trustee or an interim manager of a CIO, the service address appearing in the entry for that person in the CIO's register of charity trustees.

(6) If a registered service address is changed after a person ("A") inspected, or obtained a copy of, the relevant entry in the relevant register, A may validly serve a document at the previous registered service address until the end of the period of 14 days starting with the day on which A inspected, or obtained a copy of, as the case may be, that entry.

(7) For the purposes of paragraph (6) "previous registered service address" means, in relation to a person, the service address which appeared in the entry relating to that person in the relevant register on the day on which A inspected, or obtained a copy of, that entry.

9 Communications Provisions

49 THE CIO COMMUNICATIONS PROVISIONS

(1) The provisions of this Part ("the CIO communications provisions") have effect for the purposes of any charity law provision that authorises or requires documents or information to be sent or supplied by or to a CIO.

(2) The CIO communications provisions apply whether the charity law provision in question uses the words "sent" or "supplied" or uses other words (such as "deliver", "provide", "produce", "transmit" or, in the case of notice, "give") to refer to the sending or supplying of a document or information.

(3) The CIO communications provisions have effect subject to–

(a) any requirements imposed or contrary provision made by or under any Act; or
(b) any contrary provision (so far as it concerns communications between the CIO and its members or the CIO and its charity trustees) in a CIO's constitution.

(4) For the purposes of paragraph (3), provision is not to be regarded as contrary to the CIO communications provisions by reason only of the fact that it expressly authorises a document or information to be sent or supplied in hard copy form, in electronic form or by means of a website.

50 SENDING OR SUPPLYING DOCUMENTS OR INFORMATION

(1) Documents or information to be sent or supplied to a CIO must be sent or supplied in accordance with the provisions of Schedule 2.

(2) Documents or information to be sent or supplied by a CIO must be sent or supplied in accordance with the provisions of Schedule 3.

(3) The provisions referred to in Schedule 3 apply (and those referred to in Schedule 2 do not apply) in relation to a document or information that is to be sent or supplied by one CIO to another.

51 CIO'S IMPLIED AGREEMENT TO RECEIVE INFORMATION IN ELECTRONIC FORM

(1) If a CIO sends or supplies documents or information to another person in electronic form–

- (a) the CIO is treated as having agreed to accept a response in electronic form; and
- (b) where the document or information is sent or supplied by the CIO by electronic means from an electronic address, or the CIO has given such an address in the document or information (subject to any limitations specified when providing that address), the CIO is treated as having agreed to the response being sent by electronic means to that address.

(2) In this regulation "electronic address" means any address or number used for the purpose of sending or receiving documents or information by electronic means.

52 MEMBER'S RIGHT TO HARD COPY

(1) Where a member of a CIO ("M") has received a document or information from the CIO otherwise than in hard copy form, M is entitled to require the CIO to send M a version of the document or information in hard copy form.

(2) The CIO–

- (a) must send the document or information in hard copy form within 21 days of receipt of M's re-quest; and
- (b) may not make a charge for providing the document or information in that form.

53 INFORMATION SENT BY CIO: TIME OF RECEIPT

(1) This regulation applies in relation to documents or information sent or supplied by a CIO.

(2) Where–

- (a) the document or information is sent by post (whether in hard copy or electronic form) to an address in the United Kingdom, and
- (b) the CIO is able to show that it was properly addressed, prepaid and posted,

it is treated as having been received by the intended recipient 48 hours after it was posted.

(3) For the purposes of paragraph (2) a document or information is properly addressed if it is ad-dressed in accordance with paragraph 4 of Schedule 3.

(4) Where–

- (a) the document or information is sent or supplied by electronic means; and
- (b) the CIO is able to show that it was properly addressed,

it is treated as having been received by the intended recipient 48 hours after it was sent.

(5) For the purposes of paragraph (4) a document or information is properly addressed if it is ad-dressed in accordance with paragraph 7 of Schedule 3.

(6) Where the document or information is sent or supplied by means of a website, it is treated as having been received by the intended recipient–

- (a) when the material is first made available on the website; or
- (b) if later, when the intended recipient received (or is treated as having received) notice of the fact that the material is available on the website.

(7) In calculating a period of hours for the purposes of this regulation, no account is to be taken of any part of a day that is–

- (a) a Saturday or Sunday;
- (b) Christmas Day;
- (c) Good Friday; or
- (d) a bank holiday under the Banking and Financial Dealings Act 1971 in England and Wales.

(8) This regulation has effect subject to any contrary provision agreed between the CIO and the in-tended recipient.

54 COMMISSION'S REQUIREMENTS AS TO FORM ETC OF DOCUMENT

(1) Where a document or information is required or authorised to be sent or supplied by a CIO to the Commission, the Commission may–

- (a) require the contents of the document or information to be in a standard form;
- (b) require the document or information to be produced in the manner the Commission considers fit for the purpose of enabling it to be scanned or copied;
- (c) require the document or information to be authenticated by a particular person or persons of a particular description;
- (d) where a requirement is imposed under sub-paragraph (c), specify the means of authentication;
- (e) specify the means to be used for sending the document or information to the Commission (for example by post or by electronic means);
- (f) where the document or information is to be sent by electronic means, specify–
  - (i) the hardware or software to be used; and
  - (ii) the requirements as to the technical specifications including protocol, security, anti-virus protection and encryption.

(2) Any requirements imposed by the Commission under this regulation–

(a) must not be inconsistent with requirements imposed by any enactment as to the form, authentication or manner of sending the document or information concerned; and
(b) must be published by the Commission in such manner as it thinks fit.

55 AGREEMENT WITH COMMISSION TO SEND BY ELECTRONIC MEANS

(1) The Commission may agree with a CIO that documents or information relating to the CIO which are required or authorised to be sent or supplied by the CIO to the Commission–

(a) will be sent or supplied by electronic means, except as provided for in the agreement; and
(b) will conform to such requirements as may be specified in the agreement or specified by the Commission in accordance with the agreement.

(2) An agreement under this regulation may relate to all or any description of document or information to be sent or supplied to the Commission.

(3) Documents or information in relation to which an agreement is in force under this regulation must be sent or supplied to the Commission in accordance with that agreement.

56 REQUIREMENTS FOR PROPER DELIVERY TO COMMISSION

(1) A document or information sent or supplied by a CIO to the Commission is not properly delivered unless–

(a) any applicable requirements specified by the Commission under regulation 54 are met; and
(b) any applicable requirements under an agreement made under regulation 55 are met.

(2) Subject to regulation 57, a document or information that is not properly delivered to the Com-mission is treated for the purposes of the provision requiring or authorising it to be sent or supplied to the Commission as not having been so sent or supplied.

57 COMMISSION'S POWER TO ACCEPT DOCUMENT NOT PROPERLY DELIVERED

(1) The Commission may–

(a) accept; and
(b in any relevant case, issue a certificate of notification in relation to,

a document or information that does not comply with the requirements for proper delivery in regulation 56.

(2) No objection may be taken to the legal consequences of a document or information being accepted by the Commission under this regulation on the grounds that the requirements for proper delivery were not met.

(3) The acceptance by the Commission of a document or information under this regulation does not affect–

(a) the continuing obligation to comply with the requirements for proper delivery; and

(b) subject to paragraph (4), any liability for failure to comply with those requirements.

(4) For the purposes of any qualifying provision the period after the document or information is accepted does not count as a period during which there is a default in complying with the requirements for delivery.

(5) In this regulation "qualifying provision" means a provision which imposes a daily default fine for failure to send or supply the document or information.

58 REPLACEMENT OF DOCUMENT NOT PROPERLY DELIVERED TO COMMISSION

(1) The Commission may accept a replacement for a document or information previously sent or supplied to it that did not comply with the requirements for proper delivery in regulation 56.

(2) A replacement must not be accepted by the Commission unless it is satisfied that it is sent or transmitted by–

(a) the person by whom the original document or information was sent or supplied; or
(b) the CIO to which the original document or information relates,

and that it complies with the requirements for proper delivery.

59 INTERPRETATION OF THE CIO COMMUNICATIONS PROVISIONS

(1) In the CIO communications provisions–

"address" includes a number or address used for the purpose of sending or receiving documents or information by electronic means;
"charity law provision" means any provision of–

(a) the 2011 Act;
(b) these Regulations;
(c) the Charitable Incorporated Organisations (Insolvency and Dissolution) Regulations 2012 ("the Dissolution Regulations"); or
(d) a CIO's constitution;

but not the provisions of the Insolvency Act 1986 and subordinate legislation as applied in relation to CIOs by the Dissolution Regulations;

"document" includes summons, notice, order or other legal process and registers.

(2) References in the CIO communications provisions to documents or information being sent or supplied by or to a CIO include references to documents or information being sent or supplied by or to the charity trustees of a CIO acting on behalf of the CIO.

10 Supplementary Provisions

60 FRAUDULENT TRADING

(1) Section 993 of the Companies Act 2006 (offence of fraudulent trading) applies in relation to any activity of a CIO as it applies in relation to any business of a company.

(2) The following provisions of Part 36 of the Companies Act 2006 (offences under the Companies Acts) apply in relation to an offence under that Act committed by virtue of this regulation as they apply to an offence under the Companies Acts–

(a) section 1127 (summary proceedings: venue);
(b) section 1128 (summary proceedings: time limit for proceedings);
(c) section 1129 (legal professional privilege);
(d) section 1131 (imprisonment on summary conviction in England and Wales: transitory provision); and
(e) section 1132 (production and inspection of documents where offence suspected).

(3) In their application to CIOs the provisions of the Companies Act 2006 mentioned in this regulation have effect as if–

(a) for references to a company there were substituted references to a CIO;
(b) for references to an officer of a company there were substituted references to a charity trustee of a CIO;
(c) provisions relating only to Scotland or Northern Ireland were omitted;
(d) references to the Secretary of State were omitted.

(4) In its application to CIOs section 1132(3)(b) has effect as if for "the secretary of the company, or such other officer of it" there were substituted "such charity trustee of the CIO".

61 PRE-MERGER VESTING DECLARATIONS

(1) Sections 310 (pre-merger vesting declarations) and 312 ("transferor" and "transferee" etc in s.310 and s.311) of the 2011 Act apply in relation to a relevant charity merger under Part 16 of that Act where the transferee is a CIO with the following modifications.

(2) In section 310–

(a) in subsection (1)(c) after "property" insert "including any permanent endowment or other property held on special trust which is specified in the declaration ("specified trust property")";
(b) in subsection (2)–
  (i) after "property" insert "including specified trust property";
  (ii) at the end of the subsection insert a new sentence "The transferee shall hold specified trust property on the same trusts, so far as is reasonably practicable, on which the property was held immediately before the merger.";
(c) after subsection (4) insert–

"(5) Where specified trust property vests in the transferee by virtue of subsection (2), unless the Commission directs otherwise the specified trust property and the transferee are to be treated as a single charity for the purposes of Parts 4 and 8 of this Act.".

(3) In section 312 in subsection (1) omit the words from "and (b)" to the end of the subsection.

(4) Where a CIO holds specified trust property as trustee by virtue of section 310 as modified by this regulation, the CIO is to be treated for the purposes of the provisions identified in paragraph 3 of Schedule 7 to the 2011 Act (application of certain enactments to trust corporations) as if it were a corporation appointed by the court to be trustee.

62 NOTES TO CIO'S ACCOUNTS AND STATEMENT

(1) This regulation applies where a CIO elects under section 133 of the 2011 Act to prepare a receipts and payments account and a statement of assets and liabilities, instead of a statement of accounts.

(2) The following information must be provided by way of notes to the statement of assets and liabilities–

(a) particulars of any guarantee given by the CIO, where any potential liability under the guarantee is outstanding at the date of the statement; and
(b) particulars of any debt outstanding at the date of the statement which is owed by the CIO and which is secured by an express charge on any of the assets of the CIO.

11 Consequential Amendments to Secondary Legislation

63 CONSEQUENTIAL AMENDMENTS TO SECONDARY LEGISLATION

The consequential amendments in Schedule 4 have effect.

Schedule 1
Registers

Regulation 26

1 REGISTER OF MEMBERS

1

(1) In a register of members there must be entered for each member of the CIO–

(a) the name of the member;
(b) a service address of the member;
(c) the date on which the person was registered as a member;
(d) if the CIO has more than one class of member, a statement of the class to which the member belongs; and
(e) the date on which the person ceased to be a member.

(2) For the purpose of sub-paragraph (1)(b) "The principal office of the CIO" may be entered as the service address.

(3) Every CIO having more than 50 members must keep the register in such a form as to constitute in itself an index.

SINGLE MEMBER CIO

2

(1) If a CIO has only one member there must be entered in the register, with the entry in the register relating to the sole member, a statement that the CIO has only one member.

(2) If the number of members of a CIO falls to one there must be entered in the register, with the entry in the register relating to the sole member, the date on which the CIO became a CIO having only one member.

(3) If the number of members of a CIO increases from one to two or more members there must be entered in the register, with the entry in the register relating to the sole member, the date on which the CIO ceased to be a CIO having only one member.

REMOVAL OF ENTRIES RELATING TO FORMER MEMBERS AFTER 10 YEARS

3

An entry relating to a former member of a CIO may be removed from the register of members after the expiration of 10 years from the date on which that person ceased to be a member.

2 REGISTER OF CHARITY TRUSTEES

4

(1) In a register of charity trustees there must be entered for each charity trustee of the CIO–

- (a) the name of the charity trustee, including in respect of an individual any former name or names;
- (b) a service address of the charity trustee;
- (c) the date on which the person was registered as a charity trustee;
- (d) if the CIO (being a foundation CIO) has more than one class of member, a statement of the class to which the charity trustee belongs;
- (e) the date on which the person ceased to be a charity trustee.

(2) If the charity trustee is an individual "The principal office of the CIO" may be entered as the service address.

(3) If the charity trustee is a body corporate–

- (a) the service address entered in the register must be the registered or principal office of the body corporate;
- (b) company registration information for the body corporate must be entered in the register.

(4) If a person has been appointed interim manager of the CIO, there must be entered in the register–

- (a) a statement that such a manager has been appointed under section 76 of the 2011 Act (suspension of trustees etc and appointment of interim managers); and
- (b) the interim manager particulars.

(5) In this paragraph–

"company registration information" means–

- (a) in the case of an EEA company to which the First Company Law Directive (68/151/EEC) applies, particulars of–
  - (i) the register in which the company file mentioned in Article 3 of that Directive is kept (including details of the relevant state); and
  - (ii) the registration number in that register;
- (b) in the case of a body corporate which is not an EEA company mentioned in paragraph (a), particulars of–

- (i) the legal form of the company or body corporate and the law by which it is governed; and
- (ii) if applicable, the register in which it is entered (including details of the state) and its registration number in that register;

"EEA company" means a company governed by the law of an EEA state;

"interim manager particulars" means, in relation to a person appointed as interim manager under section 76 of the 2011 Act–

- (a) the person's name;
- (b) where the person appointed is a body corporate, the name of the individual responsible for dealing with all matters arising from the body corporate's appointment as interim manager;
- (c) the person's service address; and
- (d) the date on which the person was appointed as interim manager.

3 MAINTENANCE OF AND ACCESS TO REGISTERS UPDATING REGISTERS

5

The CIO must make an alteration to the register of members or register of charity trustees within 28 days of the date on which the event necessitating the alteration occurs.

REGISTERS TO BE KEPT AVAILABLE FOR INSPECTION

6

A CIO must keep a register maintained in accordance with this Schedule available for inspection at its principal office as it appears on the register of charities or, where the charity trustees pass a resolution to that effect, at any other address specified in the resolution.

MEMBERS REGISTER: RIGHTS OF ACCESS

7

(1) A member or charity trustee of the CIO is entitled on request to inspect or to be provided with a copy of all or part of the register of members where–

- (a) the request is made for the purposes of carrying out the requester's duties as a charity trustee or member of the CIO; or
- (b) the request is to inspect or to be provided with a copy of the entry in the register which is made for the requester.

(2) No other person is entitled to inspect or to be provided with a copy of the register kept by a CIO except as provided in sub-paragraph (3).

(3) A person is entitled on request to inspect or to be provided with a copy of all or part of the register of members if–

- (a) in accordance with its constitution, some or all of the members of the CIO are liable to contribute to its assets if it is wound up;
- (b) the CIO has been or is in the course of being wound up; and
- (c) the request is made for the purposes of recovering a member's contribution.

(4) For the purposes of sub-paragraph (3), if not all of its members are liable to contribute to its assets if it is wound up, the entitlement is limited to those entries on the register that relate to members who are so liable.

(5) Where a CIO makes the register available for inspection or provides a copy in response to a request other than under sub-paragraph (1) it may require payment of such fee as the charity trustees may reasonably require in respect of the costs of complying with the request.

TRUSTEES REGISTER: RIGHTS OF ACCESS

8

(1) Any person is entitled on request to inspect or to be provided with a copy of all or part of the register of charity trustees kept by the CIO.

(2) Where a CIO makes the register available for inspection or provides a copy in response to a request other than under sub-paragraph (3), it may require payment of such fee as the charity trustees may reasonably require in respect of the costs of complying with the request.

(3) A member or charity trustee of the CIO is entitled to inspect or to be provided with a copy of all or part of the register without payment of a fee where–

- (a) the request is made for the purposes of carrying out the requester's duties as a charity trustee or member of the CIO; or
- (b) the request is to inspect or to be provided with a copy of the entry in the register which is made for the requester.

INFORMATION RELATING TO CHARITY TRUSTEES: GROUNDS FOR REFUSAL

9

A CIO may refuse a request under paragraph 8 in relation to any entry in the register relating to a person who is or was a charity trustee if that person is affected by a dispensation from any reporting requirements under regulations 40 and 41 of the Charities (Accounts and Reports) Regulations 2008.

INFORMATION AS TO STATE OF REGISTER

10

(1) When a person inspects a CIO's register of members or register of charity trustees or is provided with a copy of the register or part of it, the CIO must provide that person with the information specified in sub-paragraph (2).

(2) The information to be provided is–

- (a) the most recent date (if any) on which alterations were made to the register or to the relevant part of it; and
- (b) confirmation either–
  - (i) that there are no further alterations to be made to the register or to the relevant part of it; or
  - (ii) if there are alterations to be made but which have not yet been made, that there are alterations to be made.

4 INTERPRETATION
NAMES AND FORMER NAMES

11

(1) For the purposes of paragraphs 1 and 4 of this Schedule–

"name" means, in relation to an individual, the individual's forename and surname;
"former name" means a name by which an individual was formerly known for business purposes but does not include–

(a) in the case of a peer or an individual normally known by a British title, a name by which the person was known previous to the adoption of or succession to the title;
(b) in the case of any person, a name that–
(i) was changed or disused before the person attained the age of 16 years; or
(ii) has been changed or disused for 20 years or more.

(2) Despite paragraph (1), in the case of a peer or an individual usually known by a title, the title may be stated instead of or in addition to the peer or individual's forename and surname.

Schedule 2
Documents and information sent or supplied to a CIO

Regulation 50

APPLICATION OF THIS SCHEDULE

1

This Schedule applies to documents or information sent or supplied to a CIO but not to documents or information sent or supplied by one CIO to another.

COMMUNICATIONS IN HARD COPY FORM: INTRODUCTION

2

A document or information is validly sent or supplied to a CIO if it is sent or supplied in hard copy form in accordance with this Schedule.

METHOD OF COMMUNICATION IN HARD COPY FORM

3

(1) A document or information in hard copy form may be sent or supplied by hand or by post to an address in accordance with paragraph 4.

(2) For the purposes of this Schedule, a person sends a document or information by post if the person posts a prepaid envelope containing the document or information.

ADDRESS FOR COMMUNICATIONS IN HARD COPY FORM

4

A document or information in hard copy form may be sent or supplied–

(a) to an address specified by the CIO for the purpose;
(b) to the CIO's principal office as it appears on the register of charities.

COMMUNICATIONS IN ELECTRONIC FORM: INTRODUCTION

5

A document or information is validly sent or supplied to a CIO if it is sent or supplied in electronic form in accordance with this Schedule.

CONDITIONS FOR USE OF COMMUNICATIONS IN ELECTRONIC FORM

6

A document or information may only be sent or supplied to a CIO in electronic form if–

(a) the CIO has agreed (generally or specifically) that the document or information may be sent or supplied in that form and the CIO has not revoked that agreement; or
(b) the CIO is treated by regulation 51 as having so agreed.

ADDRESS FOR COMMUNICATIONS IN ELECTRONIC FORM

7

(1) Where a document or information is sent or supplied in electronic form by electronic means, it may only be sent or supplied to an address–

(a) specified for the purpose (generally or specifically) by the CIO; or
(b) treated by regulation 51 as being so specified.

(2) Where a document or information is sent or supplied in electronic form by hand or by post, it must be sent or supplied to an address to which, if it were in hard copy form, it could be validly sent in accordance with paragraphs 3 and 4.

Schedule 3
Communications by a CIO

Regulation 50

APPLICATION OF THIS SCHEDULE

1

This Schedule applies to documents or information sent or supplied by a CIO, including documents or information sent or supplied by one CIO to another.

COMMUNICATIONS IN HARD COPY FORM: INTRODUCTION

2

A document or information is validly sent or supplied by a CIO if it is sent or supplied in hard copy form in accordance with this Schedule.

METHOD OF COMMUNICATION IN HARD COPY FORM

3

(1) A document or information in hard copy form must be–

(a) handed to the intended recipient; or
(b) sent or supplied by hand or by post to an address in accordance with paragraph 4.

(2) For the purposes of this Schedule, a person sends a document or information by post if the person posts a prepaid envelope containing the document or information.

ADDRESS FOR COMMUNICATIONS IN HARD COPY FORM

4

(1) A document or information in hard copy form may be sent or supplied by the CIO–

(a) to an address specified for the purpose by the intended recipient;
(b) to a person in their capacity as a member of the CIO at that person's address as shown in the CIO's register of members;
(c) to a person in their capacity as a charity trustee of the CIO at that person's address as shown in the CIO's register of charity trustees;
(d) to another CIO at its principal office as it appears on the register of charities.

(2) Where the CIO is unable to obtain an address falling within sub-paragraph (1), the document or information may be sent or supplied to the intended recipient's last address known to the CIO.

COMMUNICATIONS IN ELECTRONIC FORM: INTRODUCTION

5

A document or information is validly sent or supplied by a CIO if it is sent in electronic form in accordance with this Schedule.

CONDITIONS FOR USE OF COMMUNICATIONS IN ELECTRONIC FORM

6

A document or information may only be sent or supplied by a CIO in electronic form to a person who has agreed (generally or specifically) that the document or information may be sent or supplied in that form and the person has not revoked that agreement.

ADDRESS FOR COMMUNICATIONS IN ELECTRONIC FORM

7

(1) Where a document or information is sent or supplied in electronic form by electronic means, it may only be sent or supplied to an address specified for the purpose (generally or specifically) by the intended recipient.

(2) Where a document or information is sent or supplied in electronic form by hand or by post, it must be–

(a) handed to the intended recipient; or

(b) sent or supplied to an address to which, if it were in hard copy form, it could be validly sent in accordance with paragraphs 3 and 4.

COMMUNICATIONS BY MEANS OF A WEBSITE: INTRODUCTION

8

A document or information is validly sent or supplied by a CIO if it is made available on a website in accordance with this Schedule.

AGREEMENT TO USE OF WEBSITE

9

A document or information may only be sent or supplied by the CIO to a person ("A") by being made available on a website if A–

(a) has agreed (generally or specifically) that the document or information may be sent or supplied in that manner, and has not revoked that agreement; or
(b) is treated as having so agreed under paragraph 10.

IMPLICIT AGREEMENT OF MEMBERS TO USE OF WEBSITE

10

(1) This paragraph applies to a document or information to be sent or supplied by a CIO to a person in their capacity as a member of the CIO.

(2) To the extent that–

(a) the members of the CIO have resolved that the CIO may send or supply documents or information to members by making them available on a website; or
(b) the CIO's constitution contains provision to that effect,

a person in relation to whom the conditions in sub-paragraph (3) are met is treated as having agreed that documents or information may be sent or supplied to them in that manner.

(3) The conditions are–

(a) the person ("M") has been asked individually by the CIO to agree that the CIO may send or supply documents or information generally, or the documents or information in question, to M by means of a website; and
(b) the CIO has not received a response from M within the period of 28 days starting with the date on which the CIO's request was sent.

(4) M is not treated as having agreed if the CIO's request–

(a) did not state clearly what the effect of a failure to respond would be; or
(b) was sent less than 12 months after a previous request made to M for the purpose of this paragraph in respect of the same or a similar class of documents or information.

AVAILABILITY OF DOCUMENT OR INFORMATION ON WEBSITE

11

(1) A document or information authorised or required to be sent or supplied by a CIO by means of a website must be made available in a form, and by a means, that the CIO reasonably considers will enable the intended recipient–

(a) to read it; and
(b) to retain a copy of it.

(2) For this purpose a document or information can only be read if–

(a) it can be read with the naked eye; or
(b) to the extent that it consists of images (for example photographs, pictures, maps, plans or drawings) it can be seen with the naked eye.

NOTIFICATION OF AVAILABILITY ON WEBSITE

12

(1) The CIO must notify the intended recipient of–

(a the presence of the document or information on the website;
(b) the address of the website;
(c) the place on the website where it may be accessed; and
(d) how to access the document or information.

(2) The document or information is treated as having been sent or supplied–

(a) on the date on which the notification required by this paragraph is sent; or
(b) if later, the date on which the document or information first appears on the website after the notification is sent.

PERIOD OF AVAILABILITY OF WEBSITE

13

(1) The CIO must make the document or information available throughout–

(a) any period specified by any applicable charity law provision; or
(b) if no such period is specified, the period of 28 days starting on the date on which the notification required under paragraph 12 is sent to the person in question.

(2) For the purposes of this paragraph, a failure to make a document or information available on a website throughout the period mentioned in sub-paragraph (1) is to be disregarded if–

(a) it is made available on the website for part of that period; and
(b) the failure to make it available throughout that period is wholly attributable to circumstances that it would not be reasonable to expect the CIO to prevent or avoid.

Schedule 4
Consequential amendments

Regulation 63

AMENDMENT OF THE CHARITIES (EXCEPTION FROM REGISTRATION AND ACCOUNTS) REGULATIONS 1965

1

After sub-paragraph (c) of regulation 2 of the Charities (Exception from Registration and Accounts) Regulations 1965 insert–

"or
(d) a charitable incorporated organisation.".

AMENDMENT OF THE CHARITIES (EXCEPTION OF UNIVERSITIES FROM REGISTRATION) REGULATIONS 1966

2

In regulation 2 of the Charities (Exception of Universities from Registration) Regulations 1966, after "Charities Act 1960" insert "or a charitable incorporated organisation".

AMENDMENT OF THE CHARITIES (MISLEADING NAMES) REGULATIONS 1992

3

In the Schedule to the Charities (Misleading Names) Regulations 1992–

(a) after "Building society" insert "Charitable incorporated organisation"; and
(b) after "Royalty" insert "Sefydliad elusennol corfforedig".

AMENDMENT OF THE CHARITIES (EXCEPTION FROM REGISTRATION) REGULATIONS 1996

4

(1) The Charities (Exception from Registration) Regulations 1996 are amended as follows.

(2) In regulation 4–

(a) at the start of paragraph (2), insert "Subject to paragraph (4),"; and
(b) after paragraph (3), insert–
"(4) This regulation shall not apply to a charity which is constituted as a charitable incorporated organisation.".

(3) In regulation 5–

(a) at the start of paragraph (2), insert "Subject to paragraph (3),"; and
(b) after paragraph (2), insert–
"(3) This regulation shall not apply to a charity which is constituted as a charitable incorporated organisation.".

AMENDMENT OF THE CHARITIES (EXCEPTION FROM REGISTRATION) REGULATIONS 2008

5

(1) The Charities (Exception from Registration) Regulations 2008 are amended as follows.

(2 In regulation 2–

(a) at the start of paragraph (2), insert "Subject to paragraph (4),"; and

(b) after paragraph (3), insert–

> "(4) This regulation does not apply to a charity which is constituted as a charitable incorporated organisation.".

AMENDMENT OF THE CHARITIES (EXCEPTION FROM REGISTRATION) REGULATIONS 2010

6

(1) The Charities (Exception from Registration) Regulations 2010 are amended as follows.

(2) In regulation 2 after "Subject to" insert "regulation 4 and to".

(3) In regulation 3 after "Subject to" insert "regulation 4 and to".

(4) After regulation 3 insert–

> "(4) These Regulations do not apply to a charity which is constituted as a charitable incorporated organisation.".

APPENDIX 6

CHARITABLE INCORPORATED ORGANISATIONS (INSOLVENCY AND DISSOLUTIONS) REGULATIONS 2012

SI 2012/2013

Coming into force in accordance with regulation 1

The Minister for the Cabinet Office makes the following Regulations in exercise of the powers conferred by sections 245 and 347(3) of the Charities Act 2011.

In accordance with section 348(4) of that Act the Minister has consulted such persons and bodies of persons as the Minister considers appropriate.

A draft of these Regulations has been approved by a resolution of each House of Parliament pursuant to section 348(2) of that Act.

1 General

1 CITATION AND COMMENCEMENT

These Regulations may be cited as the Charitable Incorporated Organisations (Insolvency and Dissolu-tion) Regulations 2012 and come into force on the twenty eighth day after the day on which they are made.

2 INTERPRETATION: GENERAL

(1) In these Regulations–

"the 1986 Act" means the Insolvency Act 1986;
"the 2011 Act" means the Charities Act 2011;
"constitutional directions" means the directions included in the CIO's constitution in accordance with section 206(2)(c) of the 2011 Act.

(2) For the purposes of these Regulations "body corporate" includes a body incorporated outside the United Kingdom but does not include–

(a) a corporation sole; or
(b) a partnership that, whether or not a legal person, is not regarded as a body corporate under the law by which it is governed.

2 Application of the Insolvency Act 1986

3 APPLICATION OF THE INSOLVENCY ACT 1986 TO CIOS

The Schedule (which makes provision concerning the application to CIOs of the 1986 Act and subordinate legislation made under that Act) has effect.

3 Dissolution Otherwise than Under the Insolvency Act 1986

4 DISSOLUTION BY COMMISSION ON APPLICATION OF CIO

(1) The Commission may, on the application of a CIO, dissolve the CIO by removing it from the register.

(2) Such an application is referred to in this Part as an application for dissolution and must be made in accordance with regulation 5.

5 APPLICATION FOR DISSOLUTION

An application for dissolution–

(a) must be made on the CIO's behalf by the charity trustees or by a majority of them; and

(b) must contain–

  (i) a copy of the resolution passed in accordance with the procedure prescribed in regulation 6;

  (ii) declaration, made by or on behalf of the charity trustees of the CIO, that any debts and other liabilities of the CIO have been settled or otherwise provided for in full; and

  (iii) a statement, made by or on behalf of the charity trustees of the CIO, setting out the way in which any property vested in, or held on trust for, the CIO has been or is to be applied on dissolution in accordance with its constitutional directions.

6 DISSOLUTION RESOLUTION

(1) The resolution to make an application for dissolution ("a dissolution resolution") must be passed by the members–

(a) at a general meeting of the CIO–

  (i) by a 75% majority of those voting (including those voting by proxy or by post, if voting that way is permitted); or

  (ii) where the CIO's constitution permits the members to make decisions otherwise than by voting, by a decision taken without a vote and without any expression of dissent in response to the question put to the meeting; or

(b) unanimously, otherwise than at a general meeting.

(2) Subject to paragraph (4), where a dissolution resolution is to be proposed at a general meeting of a CIO the person calling the meeting must give notice of not less than 14 days to–

(a) all members of the CIO entitled to vote at the meeting or, where the CIO's constitution permits the members to make decisions otherwise than by voting, all members entitled to take part in the decision to be made as to whether to pass the resolution at the meeting; and

(b) any charity trustee of the CIO who is not also a member of the CIO entitled to vote at the meeting or, where the CIO's constitution permits the members to make decisions otherwise than by voting, who is not also a member entitled to take part in the decision to be made as to whether to pass the resolution at that meeting;

and the notice must contain particulars of the dissolution resolution that is to be proposed.

(3) For the purpose of calculating the period of notice to be given under paragraph (2) the following are to be excluded–

(a) the day of the meeting; and
(b) the day on which notice is given.

(4) If a qualifying majority agrees, a dissolution resolution which is to be proposed at a general meeting may be passed without the notice provisions in paragraph (2) being satisfied.

(5) Where a dissolution resolution is passed otherwise than at a general meeting it is treated as hav-ing been passed on the date on which the last member agreed to it, unless the CIO's constitution pro-vides that it is to be treated as having been passed on a later date.

(6) In this regulation–

"qualifying majority" means–

(a) in relation to a CIO whose members take decisions by voting, a majority in number of the members having a right to attend and vote at the meeting, who together represent not less than the requisite percentage of the total voting rights at that meeting of all the members;
(b) in relation to a CIO where the CIO's constitution permits the members to make decisions otherwise than by voting, all of the members having the right to attend the meeting and take part in the decisions to be made at the meeting;

"requisite percentage" means 90% or such higher percentage (not exceeding 95%) as may be speci-fied in the CIO's constitution for the purposes of this regulation.

7 NOTICE TO BE GIVEN BEFORE DISSOLUTION

(1) The Commission must not dissolve a CIO under regulation 4 until 3 months after the publication by the Commission, in such manner as it thinks fit, of a notice stating that it has received an application for dissolution from the CIO.

(2) The Commission must not dissolve the CIO if, within the period mentioned in sub-paragraph (1), any person has shown cause why the Commission should not dissolve the CIO.

8 APPLICATION NOT TO BE MADE IF CIO PROCEDURES NOT COMPLETED

(1) The charity trustees must not make an application for dissolution if–

(a) the CIO has any debts or other liabilities which have not been settled or otherwise provided for in full; or
(b) any decision which must be taken for the purpose of giving effect to the constitutional directions has not been taken.

(2) Subsections (5) to (7) of section 1004 of the Companies Act 2006 (offence of applying for a company to be struck off in contravention of requirements of that section) apply in relation to an application by a charity trustee in contravention of paragraph (1) as they apply in relation to an application in contravention of that section.

(3) Section 1004(6) of that Act, in its application by virtue of paragraph (2), has effect as if for "that he did not know, and could not reasonably have known, of the existence of the facts that led to the contravention" there were substituted—

"(a) if the CIO had outstanding debts or other liabilities at the time the application was made, that the accused reasonably believed all of the CIO's debts or other liabilities had been settled in full or otherwise provided for;

(b) if a decision required to be taken for the purpose of the constitutional directions had not been taken, that the accused reasonably believed the necessary decision had been properly taken.".

9 APPLICATION NOT TO BE MADE IF OTHER PROCEDURES NOT COMPLETED

(1) The charity trustees must not make an application for dissolution if–

(a) a voluntary arrangement in relation to the CIO has been proposed under Part 1 of the 1986 Act and the matter has not been finally concluded;

(b) the CIO is in administration under Part 2 of that Act;

(c) an interim moratorium is in effect in relation to the CIO under paragraph 44 of Schedule B1 to that Act;

(d) the CIO is being wound up under Part 4 of that Act, whether voluntarily or by the court, or a petition under that Part for the winding up of the CIO by the court has been presented and not been finally dealt with or withdrawn;

(e) a receiver, manager or interim manager of the CIO's property has been appointed.

(2) For the purposes of paragraph (1)(a), the matter is finally concluded if–

(a) no meetings are to be summoned under section 3 of the 1986 Act;

(b) meetings summoned under that section fail to approve the arrangement;

(c) an arrangement approved by meetings summoned under that section, or in consequence of a direction under section 6(4)(b) of that Act, has been fully implemented; or

(d) the court makes an order under section 6(5) of that Act revoking approval given at previous meetings and, if the court gives any directions under section 6(6) of that Act, the CIO has done what-ever it is required to do under those directions.

(3) Subsections (4) to (6) of section 1005 of the Companies Act 2006 (offence of applying for a company to be struck off in contravention of requirements of that section) apply in relation to an application by a charity trustee in contravention of paragraph (1) as they apply in relation to an application in contravention of that section.

10 RESTRICTIONS FOLLOWING APPLICATION FOR DISSOLUTION

In any case where an application for dissolution has been made, the CIO must not–

(a) engage in any activity except one which is necessary or expedient for the purposes of–

(i) proceeding with the application;

(ii) giving effect to any decision made under the constitutional directions; or

(iii) complying with any statutory requirement; or

(b) otherwise incur any debts or other liabilities.

11 PROPERTY RECEIVED AFTER MAKING APPLICATION FOR DISSOLUTION

If property is received by the CIO after the date on which the application for dissolution was made, the charity trustees must give notice to the Commission and either–

(a) withdraw the application; or
(b) send to the Commission a statement, made by or on behalf of the charity trustees of the CIO, setting out the way in which the property has been or is to be applied on dissolution in accordance with its constitutional directions.

12 TRUSTEES TO GIVE NOTICE OF APPLICATION FOR DISSOLUTION

(1) The charity trustees who make an application for dissolution on behalf of a CIO must secure that, within 7 days beginning with the day on which the application is made, notice of it is given to every person who at any time on that day is–

(a) a member of the CIO;
(b) an employee of the CIO; or
(c) a charity trustee of the CIO.

(2) Paragraph (1) does not require notice to be given to any charity trustee who is party to the application.

(3) The notice must state–

(a) the date on which the application for dissolution is made;
(b) the names of the charity trustees making the application.

(4) The duty imposed by this regulation ceases to apply if the application is withdrawn before the end of the period for giving notice.

(5) Subsections (4) to (7) of section 1006 of the Companies Act 2006 (offence of failing to comply with duty to provide copy of striking off application in respect of a company to members, employees etc) apply in relation to a failure by a charity trustee to perform the duty imposed by paragraph (1) as they apply in relation to a failure to perform the duty imposed by that section.

(6) Section 1006(7) of that Act, in its application by virtue of paragraph (5), has effect as if paragraph (b)(ii) were omitted.

13 NOTICE OF APPLICATION FOR DISSOLUTION: HOW TO BE GIVEN

(1) The following provisions have effect for the purposes of regulation 12.

(2) Notice of an application for dissolution is treated as being given to a person ("P") if it is–

(a) delivered to P;
(b) left at P's proper address; or
(c) sent by post to P at that address.

(3) For the purposes of paragraph (2) above and section 7 (service of documents by post) of the Interpretation Act 1978 as it applies in relation to that paragraph, the proper address of a person is–

(a) in the case of a body corporate incorporated in the United Kingdom, its registered or principal office;
(b) in the case of a body corporate incorporated outside the United Kingdom–

(i) if it has a place of business in the United Kingdom, its principal office in the United Kingdom; or
(ii) if it does not have a place of business in the United Kingdom, its registered or principal office;

(c) in the case of an individual, that individual's last known address.

14 CIRCUMSTANCES IN WHICH APPLICATION MUST BE WITHDRAWN

(1) This regulation applies if an application for dissolution has been made and before it is finally dealt with or withdrawn–

(a) an application to the court for an administration order in respect of the CIO is made under paragraph 12 of Schedule B1 to the 1986 Act;
(b) an administrator is appointed in respect of the CIO under paragraph 14 or 22 of Schedule B1 to that Act or a copy of notice of intention to appoint an administrator of the CIO under either of those provisions is filed with the court;
(c) there arise any of the circumstances in which, under section 84(1) of that Act, the CIO may be voluntarily wound up;
(d) a petition is presented for the winding up of the CIO by the court under Part 4 of that Act;
(e) a receiver, manager or interim manager of the CIO's property is appointed; or
(f) the CIO incurs any liability contrary to regulation 10.(2) A person who, at the end of the day on which any of the events mentioned in paragraph (1) oc-curs, is a charity trustee of the CIO must immediately notify the Commission that the event has occurred and withdraw the CIO's application.

(3) Subsections (5) to (7) of section 1009 of the Companies Act 2006 (offence of failing to withdraw striking off application in respect of a company) apply in relation to a failure by a charity trustee to per-form the duty imposed by paragraph (2) as they apply in relation to a failure to perform the duty imposed by that section.

(4) Section 1009(6) of that Act, in its application by virtue of paragraph (3), has effect as if for "the company had made an application under section 1003" there were substituted "an application for the dissolution of the CIO had been made under regulation 5 of the Charitable Incorporated Organisations (Insolvency and Dissolution) Regulations 2012".

15 OFFENCES UNDER THE COMPANIES ACTS

(1) The following provisions of Part 36 of the Companies Act 2006 (offences under the Companies Act) apply to an offence under that Act committed by virtue of regulation 8, 9, 12 or 14 as they apply to an offence under the Companies Acts–

(a) section 1127 (summary proceedings: venue);
(b) section 1128 (summary proceedings: time limit for proceedings);
(c) section 1129 (legal professional privilege);
(d) section 1131 (imprisonment on summary conviction in England and Wales: transitory provision); and
(e) section 1132 (production and inspection of documents where offence suspected).

(2) In their application to CIOs those sections have effect as if–

(a) for references to a company there were substituted references to a CIO;

(b) for references to an officer of a company there were substituted references to a charity trustee of a CIO;

(c) provisions relating only to Scotland or Northern Ireland were omitted;

(d) references to the Secretary of State were omitted.

(3) In its application to CIOs section 1132(3)(b) has effect as if for "the secretary of the company, or such other officer of it" there were substituted "such charity trustee of the CIO".

16 DISSOLUTION OF CIO WHICH IS NOT IN OPERATION

(1) If the Commission has reasonable cause to believe that a CIO is not in operation it must send the CIO a letter inquiring whether the CIO is in operation.

(2) If it does not receive an answer within 1 month after the date of the letter the Commission must, no later than 2 months after the date of the letter, send the CIO a second letter inquiring whether the CIO is in operation.

(3) The second letter must refer to the first letter and state that, if an answer is not received to either letter within 1 month after the date of the second letter, the Commission will publish notice of its intention to dissolve the CIO.

(4) If the Commission–

(a) receives an answer to either letter to the effect that the CIO is not in operation; or

(b) has, after 1 month beginning with the date of the second letter, not received any answer to either letter;

the Commission must publish, in such manner as it thinks fit, notice of its intention to dissolve the CIO after 3 months from the date of the notice unless it is shown that the CIO is in operation or will be in operation within a reasonable period of time.

(5) The Commission must send the CIO a copy of the notice published under paragraph (4).

(6) No earlier than 3 months after the publication of the notice of intention the Commission must dissolve the CIO by removing it from the register, unless it is satisfied that–

(a) the CIO is in operation; or

(b) the CIO will be in operation within a reasonable period of time.

(7) In this regulation the date of a letter is the date on which it is sent.

17 DISSOLUTION OF CIO WHICH IS NO LONGER A CHARITY

(1) If the Commission no longer considers a CIO to be a charity it must publish, in such manner as it thinks fit, notice of its intention to dissolve the CIO after 3 months beginning with the date of the notice unless cause is shown to the contrary.

(2) The Commission must send the CIO a copy of the notice published under paragraph (1).

(3) No earlier than 3 months after the publication of the notice of intention the Commission must, unless cause has been shown to the contrary, dissolve the CIO by removing it from the register.

18 DISSOLUTION OF CIO WHICH IS BEING WOUND UP

(1) If a CIO is being wound up and–

- (a) the Commission has reasonable cause to believe that no liquidator is acting or that the affairs of the CIO are fully wound up; and
- (b) the returns required to be made by the liquidator have not been made for a period of 6 consecutive months,

the Commission must publish, in such manner as it thinks fit, notice of its intention to dissolve the CIO after 3 months beginning with the date of the notice unless cause is shown to the contrary.

(2) The Commission must send the CIO and the liquidator (if any) a copy of the notice published under paragraph (1).

(3) No earlier than 3 months after the publication of the notice of intention the Commission must, unless cause has been shown to the contrary, dissolve the CIO by removing it from the register.

19 PROCEDURE FOR DISSOLUTION: DELIVERY OF LETTERS AND NOTICES

(1) This regulation applies for the purpose of determining the manner of delivery of letters and no-tices to be sent under regulation 16, 17 or 18.

(2) The letter or notice must be sent to the CIO at its principal office as it appears on the register of charities.

(3) If the Commission has reasonable grounds to believe that sending the letter or notice to the CIO's principal office as it appears on the register of charities is unlikely to bring it to the attention of the charity trustees, the Commission must also send it to any other address the Commission has for the CIO.

(4) If the Commission has reasonable grounds to believe that sending the letter or notice to any other address it has for the CIO is unlikely to bring it to the attention of the charity trustees, the Commission must also send it to each charity trustee of the CIO for whom the Commission has an address.

(5) If there are no charity trustees for whom the Commission has an address, the Commission must also send the letter or notice to any member of the CIO for whom the Commission has an address.

(6) A notice to be sent to a liquidator may be addressed to the liquidator at the liquidator's last known place of business.

(7) The Commission may send a letter (other than a letter under regulation 16(3)) or notice by electronic means to an electronic address if the intended recipient has agreed that the Commission may send documents or other information by electronic means to that address.

(8) In this regulation "electronic means" has the meaning given by regulation 4 of the Charitable Incorporated Organisations (General) Regulations 2012.

20 DATE OF DISSOLUTION

If the Commission removes a CIO from the register under this Part, it is dissolved on the date on which it is removed.

21 NOTICE TO BE GIVEN OF DISSOLUTION

(1) If the Commission dissolves a CIO under this Part the Commission must publish a notice stating the date on which the CIO was dissolved.

(2) The notice under paragraph (1) must be published by the Commission in the same manner as any notice published in relation to the CIO under regulation 7, 16, 17 or 18 (as the case may be).

22 LIABILITIES AND POWERS UNAFFECTED BY DISSOLUTION

Despite the dissolution of a CIO under this Part–

(a) the liability (if any) of every charity trustee and member of the CIO continues and may be en-forced as if the CIO had not been dissolved; and
(b) the court continues to have the power to wind up the CIO.

4 Application of Property on Dissolution Under Part 3

23 VESTING OF PROPERTY TO OFFICIAL CUSTODIAN ON DISSOLUTION

(1) On the dissolution of a CIO under Part 3, all relevant property vests in the official custodian.

(2) For the purposes of this regulation "relevant property" includes any property and rights whatsoever (including leasehold property) vested in or held on trust for the CIO immediately before its dissolution.

(3) But "relevant property" does not include–

(a) any property held by the CIO on trust for any other person;
(b) any property held by the CIO on trust for any special purposes of the CIO;
(c) any property vested in or held on trust for the CIO if–
 (i) the CIO, or the charity trustees (as the case may be) had, before its dissolution, complied with the constitutional directions in respect of that property; but
 (ii) in accordance with those directions, the transfer or other disposition of that property would only take effect on the dissolution of the CIO.

(4) Subject to regulation 25, any property which vests in the official custodian under this regulation is held by the official custodian on trust for the charitable purposes of the CIO immediately before its dissolution.

24 DISPOSAL OF PROPERTY VESTED IN OFFICIAL CUSTODIAN

The official custodian may not dispose of any property which vests in him under regulation 23 otherwise than–

(a) in accordance with an order of the Commission under regulation 26; or
(b) by disclaiming title to it under regulation 27.

25 POWER OF COMMISSION TO SPECIFY CHARITABLE PURPOSES ETC

(1) The Commission may by order specify the charitable purposes, charity or charities (as the case may be) for which the official custodian holds the property of a CIO on trust.

(2) In determining what charitable purposes, charity or charities to specify the Commission must have regard to–

(a) the constitutional directions included in the CIO's constitution immediately before its dissolution;
(b) the desirability of securing that the property of the CIO is applied for charitable purposes which are close to the charitable purposes of the CIO immediately before its dissolution; and
(c) the need for the property to be applied for charitable purposes which are suitable and effective in the light of current social and economic circumstances.

(3) The Commission may not make an order under this regulation until 3 months after the date on which the CIO was dissolved.

(4) Section 88 of the 2011 Act (publicity relating to schemes) applies to an order under this regulation as it applies to an order under that Act to establish a scheme for the administration of a charity.

(5) The Commission may determine that either or both of the publicity requirements in section 88(2) of the 2011 Act is or are not to apply if it is satisfied that compliance with the requirement or requirements is unnecessary in a particular case.

26 POWER OF COMMISSION TO MAKE VESTING ORDER

(1) Where property is held by the official custodian in accordance with an order made under regulation 25, the Commission may by order make provision for the vesting of all or any of that property–

(a) in a charity or, in such shares as it considers appropriate, in any two or more of the charities specified in the order made under regulation 25; or
(b) in a charity or, in such shares as it considers appropriate, in any two or more charities which, in the Commission's view, further the charitable purposes specified in the order made under regulation 25.

(2) An order under this regulation may be made at the same time as an order under regulation 25.

(3) Any order made under paragraph (1) may give such directions as the Commission thinks necessary or expedient in consequence of the provision made by the order.

(4) A person acting in conformity with an order made under this regulation, or giving effect to any-thing done in pursuance of such an order, is not liable for any loss occasioned by so acting.

(5) A person is not excused from acting in conformity with an order made under this regulation by reason of the order having been in any respect improperly obtained.

27 DISCLAIMER OF PROPERTY BY OFFICIAL CUSTODIAN

(1) Where property vests in the official custodian under regulation 23 the official custodian may by notice disclaim title to any or all of that property.

(2) A notice for the purposes of this regulation–

(a) may be in such form as the official custodian thinks fit; but
(b) must be signed by, or on behalf of, the official custodian.

(3) The official custodian may disclaim property under this regulation whether or not the Commission has made an order under regulation 25.

(4) The right to disclaim property under this regulation may be waived by or on behalf of the official custodian by an express waiver or by the official custodian taking possession of the property.

(5) A notice of disclaimer is not effective unless it is signed within 3 years after–

(a) the date on which the fact that the property may have vested in the official custodian under regulation 23 first comes to the notice of the official custodian; or

(b) if ownership of the property is not established at that date, the end of the period reasonably necessary for the official custodian to establish ownership of the property.

(6) If an application in writing is made to the official custodian by a person interested in the property requiring the official custodian to decide whether or not to disclaim, a notice of disclaimer is not effective unless it is signed within 12 months after the application is made or such further period as may be al-lowed by the court.

(7) The official custodian must within 14 days after signing a notice of disclaimer–

(a) send a copy of it to–

  (i) the Commission; and

  (ii) any person who has given notice to the official custodian claiming to be interested in the property; and

(b) publish it in such manner as the official custodian thinks fit having regard in particular to the manner in which the Commission published any notice relating to the CIO under any provision of Part 3 of these Regulations.

28 EFFECT OF A DISCLAIMER BY OFFICIAL CUSTODIAN

(1) Where any property is disclaimed, it is treated as not having vested in the official custodian un-der regulation 23.

(2) A disclaimer operates so as to terminate, from the date the notice of disclaimer is signed, the rights, interests and liabilities of the CIO in or in respect of the disclaimed property.

(3) A disclaimer does not, except so far as is necessary for the purpose of releasing the CIO from any liability, affect the rights or liabilities of any other person.

29 DISCLAIMER OF LEASEHOLDS

(1) A disclaimer of property of a leasehold character does not take effect unless a copy of the no-tice under regulation 27 has been served (so far as the official custodian is aware of their addresses) on every person claiming under the CIO as underlessee or mortgagee and either–

(a) no application under regulation 30 is made with respect to that property within 14 days of the day on which the copy of the notice was served; or

(b) where such an application has been made, the court directs that the disclaimer shall take effect.

(2) If the court directs that the disclaimer shall take effect, it may make such order as it thinks fit with respect to fixtures, tenant's improvements and other matters arising out of the lease.

30 POWER OF COURT TO MAKE VESTING ORDER

(1) The court may make an order under paragraph (2), on such terms as it thinks fit, on the application of a person who–

(a) claims an interest in the disclaimed property; or
(b) is under a liability in respect of the disclaimed property that is not discharged by the dis-claimer.

(2) An order under this paragraph is an order to vest the disclaimed property in, or require its delivery to–

(a) a person entitled to it (or a trustee for such a person); or
(b) a person subject to a liability as is mentioned in paragraph (1)(b) (or a trustee for such a per-son).

(3) An order under paragraph (2)(b) may only be made where it appears to the court that it would be just to do so for the purpose of compensating the person subject to the liability in respect of the dis-claimed property.

(4) On an order being made, the property comprised in it vests in the person named in the order without conveyance, assignment or transfer.

31 PROTECTION OF PERSONS HOLDING UNDER A LEASE

(1) The court must not make an order under regulation 30 vesting property of a leasehold nature in a person ("P") claiming under the CIO as underlessee or mortgagee except on terms making P–

(a) subject to the same liabilities and obligations as those to which the CIO was subject under the lease; or
(b) if the court thinks fit, subject to the same liabilities and obligations as if the lease had been assigned to P.

(2) Where the order relates to only part of the property comprised in the lease, paragraph (1) applies as if the lease had comprised only the property comprised in the order.

(3) A person claiming under the CIO as underlessee or mortgagee who declines to accept a vesting order on such terms is excluded from all interest in the property.

(4) If there is no person claiming under the CIO as underlessee or mortgagee who is willing to accept an order on such terms, the court may vest the CIO's estate or interest in the property in any person who is liable (whether personally or in a representative character, and whether alone or jointly with the CIO) to perform the lessee's covenants in the lease.

(5) The court may vest that estate and interest in such person freed and discharged from all estates, incumbrances and interests created by the CIO.

32 LAND SUBJECT TO RENTCHARGE

Where, in consequence of the disclaimer, land that is subject to a rentcharge vests in any person ("P"), neither P nor P's successors in title are subject to any personal liability in respect of sums becoming due under the rentcharge, except sums becoming due after P, or some person claiming under or through P, has taken possession or control of the land or has entered into occupation of it.

5 Restoration of a CIO to the Register

33 RESTORATION BY COMMISSION

(1) The Commission may restore to the register any CIO which it removed from the register under regulation 16 or 18.

(2) The Commission may restore a CIO under this regulation of its own motion or on the application of any person who was a charity trustee of the CIO immediately before its dissolution.

(3) Where the Commission has made an order under regulation 26 vesting in a charity or charities all of the property which is or was held on trust by the official custodian under regulation 23, the Commission must not restore the CIO to the register unless–

(a) all appeal rights in connection with that order have been exhausted;
(b) any appeal brought in connection with that order has been discontinued before it was finally determined; or
(c) the period within which any appeal, or any subsequent appeal, may have been made has expired.

(4) The Commission must not restore the CIO to the register after the end of the period of 6 years from the date of dissolution.

34 RESTORATION BY THE COURT

(1) On an application under this regulation the court may, if it considers it just to do so, order that a CIO is restored to the register.

(2) An application may be made to restore a CIO–

(a) that has been dissolved under Chapter 9 of Part 4 of the 1986 Act, as it applies to CIOs; or
(b) that is treated as having been dissolved under paragraph 84(6) of Schedule B1 to that Act, as it applies to CIOs.

(3) An application may be made by–

(a) the Commission;
(b) any person who was a charity trustee of the CIO immediately prior to its dissolution;
(c) any person having an interest in land in which the CIO had a superior or derivative interest;
(d) any person having an interest in land or other property–
    (i) that was subject to rights vested in the CIO; or
    (ii) that was benefitted by obligations owed by the CIO;
(e) any person who but for the CIO's dissolution would have had a contractual relationship with it;
(f) any person who has a potential legal claim against the CIO;
(g) any manager or trustee of a pension fund established for the benefit of employees of the CIO;
(h any person who was a member of the CIO immediately prior to its dissolution (or the personal representatives of such a person);
(i) any person who was a creditor of the CIO at the time of its dissolution;
(j) any former liquidator of the CIO; or
(k) any other person appearing to the court to have an interest in the matter.

(4) If the court orders that the CIO is restored to the register–

(a) the Commission must restore the CIO to the register; and
(b) the CIO is treated as restored to the register on delivery to the Commission of a copy of the court order.

35 TIME LIMIT FOR APPLYING TO COURT

(1) Subject to paragraph (2), an application to the court to restore a CIO to the register may not be made after the end of the period of 6 years from the date of dissolution.

(2) An application may be made at any time for the purpose of bringing proceedings against the CIO for damages for personal injury.

(3) The court must refuse an application under paragraph (2) if it appears to the court that the proceedings would fail by virtue of any enactment as to the time within which proceedings must be brought.

(4) In making that decision the court must have regard to its power under regulation 36 to direct that the period between the dissolution of the CIO and the making of the order is not to count for the purposes of any such enactment.

(5) For the purposes of this regulation–

(a) "personal injury" includes any disease and any impairment of a person's physical or mental condition; and
(b) references to damages for personal injury include any sum claimed by virtue of section 1(2)(c) of the Law Reform (Miscellaneous Provisions) Act 1934.

36 COURT ORDER WITH DIRECTIONS

(1) Where a court orders the restoration of a CIO to the register, it may give such directions and make such provision as seems just for placing the CIO and all other persons in the same position (as nearly as may be) as if the CIO had not been dissolved.

(2) Despite paragraph (1) the court may not give any directions or make any provision in relation to the matters covered by regulation 41.

37 CIO'S NAME ON RESTORATION

(1) Subject to paragraphs (2) and (3), a CIO is to be restored to the register with the name it had immediately before it was dissolved.

(2) Where–

(a) the CIO is to be restored to the register following an application to the court; and
(b) the order made by the court specifies a new name for the CIO on restoration,

the CIO must be restored to the register with that name.

(3) Where–

(a) the CIO is to be restored to the register otherwise than following an application to the court; and
(b) the Commission is satisfied that it would, were an application being made for the registration of the CIO with the name it had immediately prior to its dissolution, refuse to register the CIO on the grounds specified in section 208(2)(a) of the 2011 Act,

the CIO must be restored to the register with a new name specified by the Commission.

(4) Where–

(a) the CIO is restored to the register with a new name specified by the court, and
(b) the Commission is satisfied that it could, were an application being made for the registration of the CIO with the new name, refuse to register the CIO on the grounds specified in section 208(2)(a) of the 2011 Act,

the Commission may give a direction to the charity trustees of the CIO requiring the name of the CIO to be changed, within such period as is specified in the direction, to such other name as the charity trustees of the CIO may determine with the approval of the Commission.

(5) The Commission may not give a direction under paragraph (4) after 12 months from the date of the CIO's restoration to the register.

(6) Sections 43 and 44 of the 2011 Act apply to a direction made under paragraph (4) as they apply to a direction made under section 42(1) of that Act.

38 NOTIFICATION OF RESTORATION TO THE REGISTER

(1) Where a CIO is restored to the register the Commission must publish notice of the restoration in such manner as it thinks fit.

(2) A notice published by the Commission under paragraph (1) must state–

(a) the name of the CIO; and
(b) the date on which the restoration took effect.

(3) Where a CIO is to be restored to the register with a name other than the name it had immediately before it was dissolved, the notice published by the Commission must include–

(a) the name with which the CIO is restored to the register; and
(b) the name the CIO had immediately prior to its dissolution.

39 EFFECT OF RESTORATION

(1) A CIO which is restored to the register is treated for all purposes as having continued in existence as if it had not been dissolved.

(2) Paragraph (1) does not affect the validity of anything done by the charity trustees of the restored CIO before its restoration in reliance on consent given by the Commission in accordance with section 131(3) of the 2011 Act (preservation of accounting records) or section 134(3) of that Act (preservation of statement of accounts or account and statement).

40 PROPERTY TO VEST IN RESTORED CIO

On the date of restoration any property of the CIO which is vested in the official custodian vests in the restored CIO.

41 ACCOUNTS, REPORTS AND RETURNS OF RESTORED CIO

(1) In its application to a relevant financial year of a restored CIO, Part 8 of the 2011 Act (charity accounts, reports and returns) is to be read subject to the provisions of this regulation.

(2) The following provisions do not apply unless the Commission requests that the accounts, annual report or annual return (as the case may be) for that year are prepared–

(a) section 132(1) (requirement to prepare statement of accounts);
(b) section 138(2) (requirement to prepare group accounts);
(c) section 162(1) (requirement to prepare annual report);
(d) section 169(1) (requirement to prepare annual return).

(3) The charity trustees must transmit to the Commission, within 10 months from the date of any re-quest under paragraph (2), the accounts, annual report or annual return (as the case may be). The following provisions are modified accordingly–

(a) section 163(1) (requirement to transmit annual report to Commission); and
(b) section 169(3) (requirement to transmit annual return to Commission).

(4) Where the Commission requests that accounts are prepared, but not an annual report, a copy of the relevant auditor's or examiner's report must be transmitted to the Commission with the accounts as if section 164 (documents to be transmitted with annual report) applied.

(5) The Commission's power in the following provisions applies only where the accounts have not been audited within 10 months from the date of the Commission's request–

(a) section 146(1)(a) (power to require accounts to be audited);
(b) section 153(1)(a) (power to require group accounts to be audited).

(6) In the following provisions the requirement is to preserve for at least 6 years from the date of the Commission's request–

(a) section 134(1) (preservation of statement of accounts or account and statement);
(b) section 140(1) (preservation of group accounts).

(7) The charity trustees are not guilty of an offence under section 173 (offences of failing to supply certain documents) in relation to a failure to transmit an annual report or annual return unless the Commission has requested that the annual report or annual return (as the case may be) is prepared for that year.

(8) For the purposes of this regulation "relevant financial year" means a year other than–

(a) a financial year of the CIO in relation to which the period for transmission to the Commission, under section 163 (transmission of annual reports to Commission in certain cases), of the annual report for that year ended before the dissolution of the CIO;
(b) a financial year of the CIO which began after restoration of the CIO.

Schedule
Application of the Insolvency Act 1986 to CIOs

Regulation 3

APPLICATION TO CIOS OF THE 1986 ACT

1

(1) The provisions of the 1986 Act specified in sub-paragraph (2) apply in relation to bCIOs as they apply in relation to companies registered in England and Wales with–

(a) the general modifications set out in sub-paragraph (3);
(b) the substitution of the provision specified in sub-paragraph (4) for section 84 of that Act;
(c) the substitution of the provision specified in sub-paragraph (5) for section 122 of that Act;
(d) the substitution of the provision specified in sub-paragraph (6) for section 154 of that Act;
(e) the further modifications specified in the Table in sub-paragraph (7); and
(f) any other necessary modification.

(2) The specified provisions of the 1986 Act are–

(a) Parts 1 to 4 other than–
  (i) section 28;
  (ii) Chapters 2 and 3 of Part 3;
  (iii) sections 72B to 72F, 72GA, 76 to 78, 83, 93, 105, 111, 113, 120, 121, 124A to 124C, 138, 142, 157, 161, 162, 169, 185, 193, 198, 199 and 204;
  (iv) paragraphs 3, 4A to 5, 21, 23 and 44 of Schedule A1;
  (v) paragraphs 9, 111A to 116 of Schedule B1;
  (vi) paragraph 19 of Schedule 1;
  (vii) paragraph 3 of Schedule 4;
(b) Parts 6 and 7 other than section 242, 243 and 250;
(c) the Third Group of Parts (miscellaneous matters bearing on both company and individual in-solvency; general interpretation; final provisions) other than sections 389B, 402, 412, 415, 417, 418, 420, 421, 421A, 422, 426, 426A, 426B, 426C, 427, 428, 429, 434E, 437, 438, 439, 440, 441 and 442.

(3) The general modifications are–

(a) any reference to a company or a company registered under the Companies Act 2006 in England and Wales, is to be read as a reference to a CIO;
(b) any reference to a company being wound up by the court in England and Wales is to be read as a reference to a CIO being wound by the court;
(c) any reference to a company being wound up in England and Wales is to be read as a reference to a CIO being wound up;
(d) any reference to a winding up in England and Wales is to be read as a reference to the winding up of a CIO;
(e) any reference to the registrar of companies is to be read as a reference to the Charity Com-mission;
(f) in any provision which requires an original document to be sent to the Charity Commission, any reference to an original document is to be read as a reference to a copy of that document;
(g) any reference to the registered office of a company is to be read as a reference to the principal office of a CIO;
(h) any reference to a general meeting of a company is to be read as a general meeting of a CIO;
(i) any reference to a director of a company is to be read as a reference to a charity trustee of a CIO;
(j) any reference to an officer of a company is to be read as a reference to a charity trustee of a CIO;
(k) any reference to a shadow director is to be treated as omitted;

(l) in any enactment of the 1986 Act which makes provision (for any purpose) for "officer" to include a shadow director, any such provision is to be treated as omitted;
(m) any reference to a company's articles of association is to be read as a reference to a CIO's constitution;
(n) any reference to the interests of a member is to be read as a reference to the interests of the relevant CIO;
(o) any reference to the business of a company is to be read as a reference to the activities the CIO undertakes in furtherance of its charitable purposes;

in each case, unless the context otherwise requires.

(4) The provision to be substituted for section 84 of the 1986 Act is–

"Circumstances in which CIO may be wound up voluntarily

84

(1) A CIO may be wound up voluntarily if its members pass a resolution that it be wound up volun-tarily.

(2) A resolution under subsection (1) must be passed–

(a) at a general meeting of the CIO–
 (i) by a 75% majority of those voting (including those voting by proxy or by post, if voting that way is permitted); or
 (ii) where the CIO's constitution permits the members to make decisions otherwise than by voting, by a decision taken without a vote and without any expression of dissent in response to the question put to the meeting; or
(b) unanimously, otherwise than at a general meeting.

(3) In this Act "a resolution for voluntary winding up" means a resolution passed under subsection (1).

(4) Before the members of a CIO pass a resolution for voluntary winding up, they must give written notice of the resolution to the holder of any qualifying floating charge to which section 72A applies.

(5) Where notice is given under subsection (4), a resolution for voluntary winding-up may be passed only–

(a) after the end of the period of five business days beginning with the day on which the notice was given; or
(b) if the person to whom the notice was given has consented in writing to the passing of the resolution.

(6) If a resolution for voluntary winding up is to be proposed at a general meeting of a CIO, the person calling the meeting must give notice of not less than 14 days to–

(a) all members of the CIO entitled to vote at the meeting or, where the CIO's constitution permits the members to make decisions otherwise than by voting, all members entitled to take part in the decision to be made as to whether to pass the resolution at the meeting; and
(b) any charity trustee of the CIO who is not also a member of the CIO entitled to vote at the meeting or, where the CIO's constitution permits the members to

make decisions otherwise than by voting, who is not also a member entitled to take part in the decision to be made as to whether to pass the resolution at the meeting;

and the notice must contain particulars of the resolution that is to be proposed.

(7) For the purpose of calculating the period of notice to be given under subsection (6) the following are to be excluded–

(a) the day of the meeting; and
(b) the day on which notice is given.

(8) If a qualifying majority agrees, a resolution for voluntary winding up which is to be proposed at a general meeting may be passed without the notice provisions in subsection (6) being satisfied.

(9) Where a resolution for voluntary winding up is passed otherwise than at a general meeting it is treated as having been passed on the date on which the last member agreed to it, unless the CIO's constitution provides that it is to be treated as having been passed on a later date.

(10) A copy of every resolution for voluntary winding up or (in the case of a resolution that is not in writing) a written memorandum setting out its terms must be sent to the Charity Commission within 15 days of the date on which it is passed.

(11) If a CIO fails to comply with subsection (10) an offence is committed by the liquidator and by every charity trustee of the CIO who is in default.

(12) In this section–

"qualifying majority" means–

(a) in relation to a CIO whose members take decisions by voting, a majority in number of the members having a right to attend and vote at the meeting, who together represent not less than the requisite percentage of the total voting rights at that meeting of all the members;
(b) in relation to a CIO whose members take decisions otherwise than by voting, all of the members having the right to attend the meeting and to take part in the decisions to be made at that meeting;

"requisite percentage" means 90% or such higher percentage (not exceeding 95%) as may be specified in the CIO's constitution for the purposes of this section.".

(5) The provision to be substituted for section 122 of the 1986 Act is–

"Circumstances in which CIO may be wound up by the court

122

(1) A CIO may be wound up by the court if–
(a) the members of the CIO have passed a resolution that the CIO be wound up by the court ("resolution for court winding up");
(b) the CIO does not commence its business within a year of its registration in the register of charities or suspends its business for a whole year;
(c) the CIO is unable to pay its debts;
(d) at the time when a moratorium for the CIO under section 1A comes to an end, no voluntary arrangement approved under Part 1 has effect in relation to the CIO;
(e) it is just and equitable in the opinion of the court that the CIO should be wound up.

(2 The resolution for court winding up must be passed by the members of the CIO in accordance with section 84(2).

(3) Subsections (6) to (12) of section 84 apply in relation to a resolution for court winding up as they apply to a resolution for voluntary winding up.".

(6) The provision to be substituted for section 154 of the 1986 Act is–

"Application of surplus

154

The court shall make such directions as it considers necessary to secure the application of the surplus in accordance with the directions contained in the CIO's constitution pursuant to section 206(2)(c) of the Charities Act 2011.".

(7) The Table of further modifications is as follows–

Table of further modifications to provisions of the 1986 Act applied to CIOs

Provision of the 1986 Act	Modification(s)
FIRST GROUP OF PARTS (Company insolvency; companies winding up)	
Section 1 (Those who may propose an arrangement)	Omit subsections (4) to (6)
Section 4A (Approval of arrangement)	Omit subsection (5)
Section 5 (Effect of approval)	
Subsection (3)	In paragraph (a) omit "or sist"
Subsections (5) and (6)	Omit subsections (5) and (6)
Section 6 (Challenge of decisions)	
Subsection (1)	In paragraph (a) omit "member"
Subsection (2A)	Omit subsection (2A)
Subsection (4)	Omit "or in the case of an application under subsection (2A), as to the ground mentioned in that subsection"
Subsection (8)	Omit subsection (8)
Section 7A (Prosecution of delinquent officers of CIO)	
Subsection (2)	In the full out words omit paragraph (ii)
Subsection (3)	After "1985" substitute "to investigate the CIO's affairs as if the CIO were a company"
Subsection (7)	Omit paragraph (b)
Subsection (8)	Omit the reference to "the Lord Advocate"
Section 30 (Disqualification of body corporate from acting as receiver)	Any reference to a body conference is to be read as a reference to a body corporate other than a body corporate appointed as an interim manager under section 76(3)(g) of the Charities Act 2011
Section 38 (Receivership accounts to be delivered to Charity Commission)	In subsection (1) omit "for registration"

Section 47 (Statement of affairs to be submitted)	For subsection (3)(d) substitute: "those who are or have been within that year officers of, or in the employment of, a company or a CIO which is, or within that year as, a charity trustee of the CIO"
Section 72A (Floating charge holder not to appoint an administrative receiver)	
Subsection (2)	Omit subsection (2)
Subsection (3)	For "subsections (1) and (2) substitute "subsection (1)
Subsection (6)	For "sections 72B to 72G" substitute "section 72G"
Section 72G (Sixth exception: registered social landlords)	Omit "or under Part 3 of the Housing (Scotland) Act 2001 (asp 10)
Section 72H (Sections 72A to 72G: supplementary)	
Subsection (1)	For "sections 72B to 72G" substitute "section 72G"
Subsection (2)	In paragraph (d) for "sections 72B to 72G" substitute "section 72G"
Subsection (5)	Omit paragraph (b)
Section 73 (Scheme of this Part)	Omit "or Scotland"
Section 74 (Liability as contributories of present and past members)	
Subsection (1)	For subsection (1) substitute: "(1) When– (a) a CIO is wound up; and (b) its constitution states that its members are liable to contribute to its assets if it is wound up, every present and past member of the CIO is liable to contribute to its assets to any amount sufficient for the payment of its debts and liabilities, and the expenses of winding up, and for the adjustment of the rights of the contributories amongst themselves"
Subsection (2)	Omit paragraphs (d) and (f); in paragraph (e) for "the Companies Acts" substitute "the Charities Act 2011"
Subsection (3)	For subsection (3) substitute: "(3) No contribution is required from any member of a CIO exceeding the amount specified in the CIO's constitution under section 206(1)(d) of the Charities Act 2011 as the amount to be contributed by that member in the event of the CIO being wound up"
Section 79 (Meaning of contributory)	Omit subsection (3)
Section 81 (Contributories in case of death of a member)	

Subsection (1)	Omit the words from ", and the heirs and legatees" to "in Scotland"
Subsection (2)	Omit subsection (2)
Subsection (3)	Omit the words "in England and Wales"
Section 88 (Avoidance of share transfers, etc after winding-up resolution)	Omit the words from "Any transfer" to "liquidator, and"
Section 95 (Effect of a CIO's insolvency)	Omit subsections (2), (4A)(b) and (5) to (7)
Section 98 (Meeting of creditors)	
Subsection (1)	Omit subsection (1)
Subsections (3) to (5)	Omit subsections (3) to (5)
Subsection (6)	For "(1), (1A) or (2)" substitute "(1A) or (2)"
Section 99 (Charity trustees to lay statement of affairs before creditors)	Omit subsection (2A)(b)
Section 101 (Appointment of liquidation committee)	Omit subsection (4)
Section 107 (Distribution of CIO's property)	For "shall (unless the articles otherwise provide) be distributed among the members according to their rights and interests in the company" substitute "shall be applied in accordance with the directions contained in the CIO's constitution pursuant to section 206(2)(c) of the Charities Act 2011; and for this purpose the liquidator may require the charity trustees of the CIO to take any necessary action to secure that application"
Section 109 (Notice by liquidator of his appointment)	In subsection (1) omit "for registration"
Section 110 (Acceptance of shares, etc, as consideration for sale of CIO property)	
Subsection (1)	For paragraph (a) substitute: "to a company ('the transferee company'), whether or not the latter is a company registered under the Companies Act 2006, or"
Subsection (2)	In paragraphs (a) and (b) for "distribution among members of the transferor company" substitute "to be applied in accordance with the directions contained in the CIO's constitution pursuant to section 206(2)(c) of the Charities Act 2011"
Subsection (3)	In paragraph (a) for "company" substitute "members of the CIO"
Subsection (4)	Omit subsection (4)

New subsections (7) to (11)	After subsection (6) insert: "(7) For the purposes of this section, a resolution of the members of a CIO is to be treated as a special resolution if it is passed– (a) at a general meeting of the CIO– (i) by a 75% majority of those voting (including those voting by proxy or by post, if voting that way is permitted); or (ii) where the CIO's constitution permits the members to make decisions otherwise than by voting, by a decision taken without a vote and without any expression of dissent in response to the question put to the meeting; or (b) unanimously, otherwise than at a general meeting. (8) Subject to subsection (10), if a resolution under subsection (3)(a) is to be proposed at a general meeting of a CIO, the person calling the meeting must give notice of not less than 14 days to– (a) all members of the CIO entitled to vote at the meeting or take part in the decision to be made as to whether to pass the resolution at the meeting; and (b) any charity trustee of the CIO who is not also a member of the CIO entitled to vote at the meeting or, where the CIO's constitution permits the members to make decisions otherwise than by voting, who is also not a member entitled to take part in the decision to be made as to whether to pass the resolution at the meeting; and the notice must contain particulars of the resolution that is to be proposed. (9) For the purpose of calculating the period of notice to be given under subsection (8) the following are to be excluded– (a) the day of the meeting; and (b) the day on which notice is given. (10) If a qualifying majority agrees, a resolution under subsection (3)(a) which is to be proposed at a general meeting of a CIO may be passed without the notice provisions in subsection (8) being satisfied. (11) In this section "qualifying majority" has the meaning given by section 84"
Section 117 (High Court and county court jurisdiction)	
Subsection (2)	Omit the words from "Where the amount" to "(subject to this section)"
Subsection (3)	Omit subsection (3)
Subsection (7)	Omit subsection (7)
Section 123 (Definition of inability to pay debts)	Omit subsection (1)(c)
Section 124 (Application for winding up)	
Subsection (1)	Omit the words from "or by the designated officer" to "fines imposed on companies"
Subsections (2) and (3)	Omit subsections (2) and (3)
Subsection (3A)	For "section 122(1)(fa)" substitute "section 122(1)(d)"

Subsections (4) to (4A)	Omit subsections (4) to (4A)
Section 126 (Power to stay or restrain proceedings against company)	
Subsection (1)	In paragraph (a) omit "or Northern Ireland", and in the full out words omit "sist"
Subsection (2)	Omit subsection (2)
Section 127 (Avoidance of property dispositions, etc)	In subsection (1) omit the words from "and any transfer" to "the company's members"
Section 128 (Avoidance of attachments etc)	Omit subsection (2)
Section 130 (Consequences of a winding up order)	Omit subsection (3)
Section 131 (CIO's statement of affairs)	
Subsection (2A)	Omit paragraph (b)
Subsection (3)	For paragraph (d) substitute: "those who are or have been within that year officers of, or in the employment of, a company or a CIO which is, or within that year was, a charity trustee of the CIO"
Subsection (8)	Omit subsection (8)
Section 133 (Public examination of officers)	
Subsection (1)	In the opening words omit "or in Scotland, the liquidator"; in paragraph (b) omit "or, in Scotland, receiver of its property"
Subsection (2)	Omit "or, in Scotland, the liquidator"
Subsection (4)(d)	Omit "or, in Scotland, submitted a claim"
Section 135 (Appointment and powers of provisional liquidator)	Omit subsection (3)
Section 143 (General functions in winding up the court)	In subsection (1) for "to the persons entitled to it" substitute "applied in accordance with the directions contained in the CIO's constitution pursuant to section 206(2)(c) of the Charities Act 2011"
Section 144 (Custody of CIO's property)	Omit subsection (2)
Section 147 (Power to stay winding up)	Omit all references to the sisting of proceedings
Section 149 (Debts due from contributory to company)	
Subsection (2)	Omit subsection (2)
Subsection (3)	Omit "whether limited or unlimited"
Section 152 (Order on contributory to be conclusive evidence)	In subsection (2) omit from "except proceedings in Scotland" to the end
Section 165 (Voluntary winding up)	

Subsection (2)	In paragraph (a) for "company" substitute "members of the CIO"
New subsections (7) to (11)	After subsection (6) insert: "(7) For the purposes of this section, a resolution of the members of a CIO is to be treated as a special resolution if it is passed– (a) at a general meeting of the CIO– (i) by a 75% majority of those voting (including those voting by proxy or by post, if voting that way is permitted); and (ii) where the CIO's constitution permits the members to make decisions otherwise than by voting, by a decision taken without a vote and without any expression of dissent in response to the question put to the meeting; or (b) unanimously, otherwise than at a general meeting. (8) Subject to subsection (10), if a resolution under subsection (2)(a) is to be proposed at a general meeting of a CIO, the person calling the meeting must give notice of not less than 14 days– (a) all members of the CIO entitled to vote at the meeting or take part in the decision to be made as to whether to pass the resolution at the meeting; and (b) any charity trustee of the CIO who is not also a member of the CIO entitled to vote at the meeting or, where the CIO's constitution permits the members to make decisions otherwise than by voting, who is not also a member entitled to take part in the decision to be made as to whether to pass the resolution at the meeting; and the notice must contain particulars of the resolution that is to be proposed. (9) For the purpose of calculating the period of notice to be given under subsection (8) the following are to be excluded– (a) the day of the meeting; and (b) the day on which notice is given. (10) If a qualifying majority agrees, a resolution under subsection (2)(a) which is to be proposed at a general meeting of a CIO may be passed without the notice provisions of subsection (8) being satisfied. (11) In this section "qualifying majority" has the meaning given by section 84."
Section 172 (Removal etc (winding up by the court))	Omit subsection (7)
Section 173 (Release (voluntary winding up))	Omit subsection (3)
Section 174 (Release (winding up by the court))	Omit subsection (7)
Section 176A (Share of assets for unsecured creditors)	Omit subsection (4)(b)
Section 177 (power to appoint special manager)	
Subsection (2)	Omit "or members generally"
Subsection (5)(a)	Omit "or, in Scotland, caution"
Section 184 (Duties of officers charges with execution of writs and other processes (England and Wales))	Omit subsection (8)

Section 187 (Power to make over assets to employees)	
Subsection (1)	In subsection (1) for the words from "payment" to "business)" substitute "ex-gratia payment authorised, before the commencement of the winding up, by the Charity Commission under section 106 of the Charities Act 2011 or the Attorney General"
Subsection (2)	For subsection (2) substitute: "(2) The liquidator may, after the winding up has commenced, make any relevant payment if the CIO's liabilities have been fully satisfied and provision has been made for the expenses of the winding up. (2A) For the purposes of subsection (2) a payment is a relevant payment if it is an ex-gratia payment authorized, after the commencement of the winding-up, by the Charity Commission under section 106 of the Charities Act 2011 or the Attorney General."
Subsection (3)	For "the members on winding up" substitute "be applied in accordance with the directions contained in the CIO's constitution in compliance with section 206(2)(c) of the Charities Act 2011"
Section 189 (Interest on debts)	Omit subsection (5)
Section 190 (Documents exempt from stamp duty)	
Subsection (2)	Omit "If the company is registered in England and Wales"
Subsection (3)	Omit subsection (3)
Section 196 (Judicial notice of court documents)	Omit references to the Court of Session, sheriff court and High Court in Northern Ireland; in paragraph (b) omit "or the Companies Act"
Section 197 (Commission for receiving evidence)	
Subsection (1)	In the opening words omit "in England and Wales or in Scotland'; omit paragraphs (b) and (c)
Subsections (2) and (3)	Omit references to the sheriff principal
Subsection (5)	Omit subsection (5)
Section 201 (Dissolution (voluntary winding up))	
Subsection (2)	For subsection (2), substitute: "(2) The Charity Commission must remove the CIO from the register of charities on the expiration of 3 months from the date on which it received the account and return and the CIO is dissolved on the date on which it is removed from the register."
Subsection (4)	Omit "for registration"

New subsections (5) and (6)	After subsection (4) insert: "(5) Where the Charity Commission removes a CIO from the register of charities in accordance with this section, it must publish a notice, in such manner as it sees fit, stating– (a) that the CIO has been removed from the register of charities, and (b) the date on which the CIO was so removed. (6) In determining the manner in which to publish a notice under subsection (5) the Charity Commission must have regard in particular to– (a) the location of the CIO's principal office; (b) the area in which the CIO operated; and (c) the charitable purposes of the CIO."
Section 202 (Early Dissolution (England and Wales))	For subsection (5), substitute: "(5) The Charity Commission must remove the CIO from the register of charities on the expiration of 3 months from the date on which it received the official receiver's application under subsection (2) and the CIO is dissolved on the date on which it is removed from the register. However the Secretary of State to be interested, give directions under section 203 at any time before the end of that period. (6) Where the Charity Commission removes a CIO from the register of charities in accordance with this section, it must publish a notice, in such manner as it thinks fit, stating– (a) that the CIO has been removed from the register of charities; and (b) the date on which the CIO was so removed. (7) In determining the manner in which to publish a notice under subsection (6), the Charity Commission must have regard in particular to– (a) the location of the CIO's principal office; (b) the area in which the CIO operated; and (c) the charitable purposes of the CIO."
Section 203 (Consequence of notice under s 202)	In subsection (5) omit "for registration"
Section 205 (Dissolution otherwise than under ss 204-204)	
Subsection (2)	For subsection (2), substitute: "(2) The Charity Commission must remove the CIO from the register of charities on the expiration of 3 months from the date on which it received the notice and the CIO is dissolved on the date on which it is removed from the register"
Subsection (5)	Omit subsection (5)
Subsection (6)	Omit paragraph (c); and in the fill out words omit "for registration"

New subsections (8) and (9)	After subsection (7), insert: "(8) Where the Charity Commission removes a CIO from the register of charities in accordance with this section, it must publish a notice, in such manner as it thinks fit, stating– (a) that the CIO has been removed from the register of charities; and (b) the date on which the CIO was so removed. (9) In determining the manner in which to publish a notice under subsection (8), the Charity Commission must have regard in particular to– (a) the location of the CIO's principal office; (b) the area in which the CIO operated; and (c) the charitable purposes of the CIO."
Section 216 (Restriction on re-use of company names)	Omit subsection (8)
Section 217 (Personal liability for debts, following contravention of s 216)	Omit subsection (6)
Section 218 (Prosecution of delinquent officers and members of CIO)	
Subsection (1)	Omit paragraph (b)
Subsection (4)	Omit paragraph (b); and in the full out words omit "or (as the case may be) the Lord Advocate" in both places it occurs
Subsection (5)	After "1985" substitute "to investigate the CIO's affairs as if the CIO were a company"
Section 219 (Obligations arising under s 218)	
Subsection (2B)	Omit paragraph (b)
Subsection (3)	Omit the references to the "Lord Advocate" and "defender"
Subsection (4)	Omit the reference to the "Lord Advocate"
Section 233 (Supplies of gas, water, electricity etc)	In subsection (3)(c) omit the reference to Scottish Water
Section 235 (Duty to co-operate with office-holder)	For subsection (3)(d) substitute: "those who are, or have within that year been, officers of or in the employment (including employment under a contract for services) of a company or a CIO which is, or within that year was, a charity trustee of the CIO in question"
Section 236 (Inquiry into CIO's dealings, etc)	In subsection (3A) omit from "(in England and Wales)" to the end
Section 244 (Extortionate credit transactions)	In subsection (5) omit "or under section 242 (gratuitous alienations in Scotland)"
Section 245 (Avoidance of certain floating charges)	In subsection (1) omit "but applies to Scotland as well as to England and Wales"
Section 246A (Remote attendance at meetings)	Omit subsection (2)
Section 246B (Use of websites)	Omit subsection (2)

Section 248 ("Secured creditor" etc)	Omit paragraoh (b)(ii)
Section 251 (Expressions used generally)	
Definition of "administrative receiver"	Omit paragraph (b)
Definition of "chattel leasing agreement"	Omit "or, in Scotland, the hiring"
Definition of "floating charge"	Omit the words from "and includes" to "(Scottish floating charges)"
Definition of "the Gazette"	Omit paragraph (b)
Definition of "receiver"	Omit the definition
Section 387 ("The relevant date")	Omit subsections (4)(b), (5) and (6)
Section 388 (Meaning of "to act as an insolvency practitioner")	
Subsection (2)	Omit subsection (2)
Subsection (2A)	Omit subsection (2A)
Subsection (3)	Omit subsection (3)
Subsection (4)	Omit the definitions of "company", "interim trustee" and "permanent trustee"
Subsection (5)	Omit paragraph (b)
Section 389 (Acting without qualification an offence)	In subsection (2) omit the words from "or the Accountant" to "Act 1985"
Section 389A (Authorisation of nominees and supervisors)	
Subsection (1)	Omit "or Part 8"
Subsection (2)(b)	Omit "(in Scotland, caution)"; and "or caution"
Section 390 (Persons not qualified to act as insolvency practitioners)	
Subsection (3)	In paragraph (a) omit "or, in Scotland, caution"; in paragraph (b) omit "or caution"
New subsection (6)	After subsection (5) insert: "(6) This section does not apply to a body corporate appointed as an interim manager under section 76(3)(g) of the Charities Act 2011"
Section 399 (Appointment, etc of official receivers)	
Subsections (1) and (4)	Omit each reference to bankruptcy; individual voluntary arrangement; debt relief order or application for such an order
Section 411 (CIO insolvency rules)	
Subsection (1)	Omit paragraph (b)

Subsections (1A) and (1B)	Omit subsections (1A) and (1B)
Subsection (2)	Omit the reference to subsections (1A) and (1B) and to the Treasury
Subsections (2C) and (2D)	Omit subsections (2C) and (2D)
Subsection (3)	Omit "bank liquidator or administrator" and the references to the Banking Act 2009
Subsection (3A)	Omit subsection (3A)
Section 413 (Insolvency Rules Committee)	In subsection (2) omit the reference to section 412
Section 414 (Fees orders CIO insolvency proceedings)	
Subsection (2)	Omit paragraph (b)
Subsection (5)	Omit the reference to the Secretary of State
Subsection (8A) to (8C)	Omit subsections (8A) to (8C)
Subsection (9)	Omit the words from "and the application of" to the end
Section 415A (Fees orders (general))	Omit subsection (A1)
Section 416 (Monetary limits (companies winding up))	
Subsection (1)	Omit the entries relating to sections 117(2) and 120(3)
Subsection (3)	Omit "117(2), 120(3) or"
Section 423 (Transactions defrauding creditors)	For subsection (4) substitute: "(4) In this section "the court" means– (a) the High Court; or (b) any county court having jurisdiction to wind up the CIO."
Section 424 (Those who may apply for an order under s 423)	For paragraph (a) substitute: "(a) in a case where the debtor is being wound up or is an administration, by the official receiver, by the liquidator or administrator or (with the leave of the court) by a victim of the transaction;"
Section 431 (Summary proceedings)	
Subsection (3)	Omit subsection (3)
Subsection (4)	Omit the reference to the Lord Advocate
Section 432 (Offences by bodies corporate)	
Subsection (2)	The reference to any director, manager, secretary or other similar officer of a body corporate is to be read as including a reference to a charity trustee of a CIO

Subsection (4)	Omit the words "51, 53, 54, 62, 64, 66" and "and 23(1)(a)
Section 433 (Admissibility in evidence of statements of affairs, etc)	
Subsection (1)	Omit paragraphs (aa) and (ab)
Subsection (3)	In paragraph (a) omit the words "66(6), 67(8)," and from ", 353(1)" to "(2)(a) or (b)"; omit paragraph (e)
Section 434A (Introductory)	For "416 and 417" substitute "416"
Section 434D (Enforcement of a CIO's filing obligations	In subsection (4) omit "(in Scotland, expenses)"
Section 436 (Expressions used generally)	In subsection (2) in the opening words after "Companies Acts" insert: "with the substitution, in relation to CIOs, of references to charity trustees to: 'articles', 'the Joint Stock Companies Acts', 'overseas company', 'paid up', 'private company', 'public company' and 'registrar of companies'"
Section 436B (References to things in writing)	In subsection (2) ignore paragraphs (a), (b), (c), (e), (h) and (i)
SCHEDULE A1 (Moratorium where directors propose voluntary arrangements)	
Paragraph 1	Omit the definitions of "market contract", "market charge", "settlement finality regulations" and "system-charge"
Paragraph 2	For paragraph 2 substitute: "2 A CIO is eligible for a moratorium unless it is excluded from being eligible by virtue of paragraph 4"
Paragraph 7	
Sub-paragraph (1)	Omit "(in Scotland, lodge)"
Sub-paragraph (4)	Omit "(in Scotland, lodged)"
Paragraph 12	
Sub-paragraph (3)	Omit sub-paragraph (3)
Sub-paragraph (5)	For sub-paragraph (5) substitute: "(5) For the purposes of this paragraph 'excepted petition' means a petition presented by the Attorney General or the Charity Commission under section 113 of the Charities Act 2011."
Paragraph 17	In sub-paragraph (2) omit "(in Scotland, hired)"
Paragraph 22	In sub-paragraph (1)(c) omit the reference to paragraph 21
Paragraph 38	In sub-paragraph (1)(a) omit ", member"

Paragraph 40	In sub-paragraph (2) omit references to a "member" or "members"
Paragraph 45	
Sub-paragraph (4)	Omit the words "(except regulations under paragraph 5)
Sub-paragraph (5)	Omit sub-paragraph (5)
SCHEDULE B1 (Administration)	
Paragraph 14	Omit sub-paragraph (2)(d)
Paragraph 15	Omit sub-paragraph (3)
Paragraph 39	In sub-paragraph (1)(d) omit "or under any rule of the law in Scotland"
Paragraph 40	For sub-paragraph (2) substitute: "(2) Sub-paragraph (1)(b) does not apply to a petition presented by the Attorney General or the Charity Commission under section 113 of the Charities Act 2011"
Paragraph 42	For sub-paragraph (4) substitute: "(4) Sub-paragraph (3) does not apply to a petition presented by the Attorney General or the Charity Commission under section 113 of the Charities Act 2011"
Paragraph 43	Omit sub-paragraph (5)
Paragraph 47	
Sub-paragraph (3)	For sub-paragraph (3)(d) substitute: "a person who is or has been during that period an officer or employee of a company or a CIO which is or has been during that year a charity trustee of the CIO"
Sub-paragraph (5)	Omit sub-paragraph (5)
Paragraph 49	Omit sub-paragraph (3)(b)
Paragraph 73	Omit sub-paragraph (2)(c) and (d)
Paragraph 74	
The whole paragraph	Omit all references to a "member" or "members"
Sub-paragraph (6)	Omit sub-paragraphs (b) and (ba)
Paragraph 82	For sub-paragraph (1) substitute: "(1) This paragraph applies where a winding-up order is made for the winding up of a CIO in administration on a petition presented by the Attorney General or the Charity Commission under section 113 of the Charities Act 2011"
Paragraph 83	
Sub-paragraph (2)	Omit sub-paragraph (2)

Sub-paragraph (4)	For sub-paragraph (4) substitute: "(4) On receipt of a notice under sub-paragraphs (3), the Charity Commission must publish it in such manner as it thinks fit. (4A) In determining the manner in which to publish the notice under sub-paragraph (3) the Charity Commission must have regard in particular to– (a) the location of the principle office of the CIO; (b) the area in which the CIO operates; and (c) the charitable purposes of the CIO"
Sub-paragraph (6)	For "registration" substitute "publication" AND FOR "registered" substitute "published"
Paragraph 84	
Sub-paragraph (3)	For sub-paragraph (3) substitute: (3) On receipt of a notice under sub-paragraph (1), the Charity Commission must publish it in such manner as it thinks fit. (3A) In determining the manner in which to publish the notice under sub-paragraph (1) the Charity Commission must have regard in particular to– (a) the location of the principle office of the CIO; (b) the area in which the CIO operates; and (c) the charitable purposes of the CIO"
Sub-paragraph (4)	For "registration" substitute "publication"
Sub-paragraph (6)	For "registration" substitute "publication"
Paragraph 96	Omit sub-paragraph (4)
Paragraph 111	Omit sub-paragraph (1A) and (1B)
SCHEDULE 1 (Powers of administrator or administrative receiver)	
Paragraph 2	Omit the words from "or, in Scotland," to "private bargain"
SCHEDULE 4 (Powers of liquidator in a winding up)	
Paragraph 3	Omit the paragraph
Paragraph 3A	Omit ",242, 243"
SCHEDULE 6 (The categories of preferential debts)	
Paragraph 14	Omit sub-paragraphs (1)(b) and (c)
SCHEDULE 8 (Provisions capable of inclusion in CIO insolvency rules)	
Paragraph 14	Omit the words "or in the Bankruptcy (Scotland) Act 1985"
Paragraph 29	Omit ",66"

SCHEUDLE 10 (Punishment of offences this Act)	In the table, after the entry relating to section 67(8) insert: "84(11) Failing to comply with requirement to send resolution to Charity Commission Summary One-fifth of the statutory maximum One-fiftieth of the statutory maximum"

APPLICATION TO CIOS OF SUBORDINATE LEGISLATION MADE UNDER THE 1986 ACT

2

(1) The legislation made under the 1986 Act specified in sub-paragraph (3) applies to CIOs with any necessary modifications for the purpose of giving effect to the provisions of the 1986 Act which are ap-plied to CIOs by paragraph 1 above.

(2) Where there is a conflict between a provision of the subordinate legislation applied by sub-paragraph (1) and any provision of these Regulations, the latter prevails.

(3) The specified legislation is–

- (a) the Insolvency Rules 1986;
- (b) the Insolvency Practitioners (Recognised Professional Bodies) Order 1986;
- (c) the Insolvency Proceedings (Monetary Limits) Order 1986;
- (d) the Insolvency Practitioners Tribunal (Conduct of Investigations) Rules 1986;
- (e) the Insolvency Regulations 1994;
- (f) the Insolvency Act 1986 (Prescribed Part) Order 2003;
- (g) the Insolvency Proceedings (Fees) Order 2004;
- (h) the Insolvency Practitioners Regulations 2005; and
- (i) the Civil Proceedings Fees Order 2008.

APPENDIX 7

CHARITIES ACT 2011, SS 29–38 AND 310

(AS MODIFIED IN RELATION TO CHARITABLE INCORPORATED ORGANISATIONS)

PART 4
REGISTRATION AND NAMES OF CHARITIES

The register

29 The register

(1) There continues to be a register of charities, to be kept by the Commission in such manner as it thinks fit.

(2) The register must contain –

(a) the name of every [CIO], and
(b) in addition to any particulars and information required to be included by any other provision of this Act or of regulations made under it, such other particulars of, and such other information relating to, every such charity as the Commission thinks fit.

(3) In this Act, except in so far as the context otherwise requires, 'the register means' the register of charities kept under this section and 'registered' is to be read accordingly.

NOTES

Sub-s (2) modified in relation to CIOs by SI 2012/3012, reg 6(2).

Charities required to be registered

30 Charities required to be registered: general

NOTES

By virtue of SI 2012/3012, reg 6(3), this section does not apply to CIOs.

31 Restrictions on extending the range of excepted charities etc

NOTES

By virtue of SI 2012/3012, reg 6(3), this section does not apply to CIOs.

32 Power to alter sums specified in s 30(2)

NOTES

By virtue of SI 2012/3012, reg 6(3), this section does not apply to CIOs.

33 Power to repeal provisions relating to excepted charities

NOTES

By virtue of SI 2012/3012, reg 6(3), this section does not apply to CIOs.

Removal of charities from register

34 Removal of charities from register

NOTES

By virtue of SI 2012/3012, reg 6(3), this section does not apply to CIOs.

Registration: duties of trustees and claims and objections

35 Duties of trustees in connection with registration

(3) The charity trustees of a CIO must with 28 days –

(a) notify the Commission if there is any change in the particulars of the CIO entered in the register, and
(b) so far as appropriate, supply the Commission with particulars of any such change.

(4) Nothing in subsection (3) requires a person –

(a) to supply the Commission with copies of schemes for the administration of a charity made otherwise than by the court,
(b) to notify the Commission of any change made with respect to a registered charity by such a scheme, or
(c) if the person refers the Commission to a document or copy already in the Commission's possession, to supply a further copy of the document.

NOTES

Sub-ss (1), (2) do not apply to CIOs by virtue of SI 2012/3012, reg 6(4)(a).

Sub-s (3) substituted by SI 2012/3012, reg 6(4)(b).

36 Claims and objections to registration

(1) A person who is or may be affected by the registration of [a CIO] may, on the ground that it is not a charity –

(a) object to its being entered by the Commission in the register, or
(b) apply to the Commission for it to be removed from the register.

(2) Provision may be made by regulations made by the Minister as to the manner in which any such objection or application is to be made, prosecuted or dealt with.

(3) Subsection (4) applies if there is an appeal to the Tribunal against any decision of the Commission –

(a) to enter an institution in the register, or
(b) not to remove an institution from the register[, or
(c) to restore a CIO to the register.

(4) Until the Commission is satisfied whether the decision of the Commission is or is not to stand, the entry in the register –

(a) is to be maintained, but
(b) is in suspense and must be marked to indicate that it is in suspense.

(5) Any question affecting the registration or removal from the register of an institution –

(a) may be considered afresh by the Commission, even though it has been determined by a decision on appeal under Chapter 2 of Part 17 (appeals and applications to Tribunal), and
(b) is not concluded by that decision, if it appears to the Commission that –
  (i) there has been a change of circumstances, or
  (ii) the decision is inconsistent with a later judicial decision.

NOTES

Sub-ss (1), (3) modified by SI 2012/3012, reg 6(5)

Effect of registration and right to inspect register

37 Effect of registration

(1) An institution is, for all purposes other than rectification of the register, conclusively presumed to be or to have been a charity at any time when it is or was on the register.

(2) For the purposes of subsection (1) an institution is to be treated as not being on the register during any period when the entry relating to it is in suspense under section 36(4).

38 Right to inspect register

(1) The register (including the entries cancelled when institutions are removed from the register) must be open to public inspection at all reasonable times.

(2) If any information contained in the register is not in documentary form, subsection (1) is to be read as requiring the information to be available for public inspection in legible form at all reasonable times.

(3) If the Commission so determines, subsection (1) does not apply to any particular information contained in the register that is specified in the determination.

[(4) Copies of the constitution of any CIO as supplied to the Commission must, so long as the CIO remains on the register –

(a) be kept by the Commission, and
(b) be open to public inspection at all reasonable times.]

(5) If a copy of a document relating to a registered charity –

(a) is not required to be supplied to the Commission as the result of section 35(4), but
(b) is in the Commission's possession,

a copy of the document must be open to inspection under subsection (4) as if supplied to the Commission under section 35.

NOTES

Sub-s (4) substituted by SI 2012/3012, reg 6(6).

Vesting declarations and effect of merger on certain gifts

310 Pre-merger vesting declarations

(1) Subsection (2) applies to a declaration which –

(a) is made by deed for the purposes of this section by the charity trustees of the transferor,
(b) is made in connection with a relevant charity merger, and
(c) is to the effect that (subject to subsections (3) and (4)) all of the transferor's property [including any permanent endowment or other property held on special trust which is specified in the declaration ('specified trust property')] is to vest in the transferee on such date as is specified in the declaration ('the specified date').

(2) The declaration operates on the specified date to vest the legal title to all of the transferor's property [including specified trust property] in the transferee, without the need for any further document transferring it. [The transferee shall hold specified trust property on the same trusts, so far as is reasonably practicable, on which the property was held immediately before the merger.]
This is subject to subsections (3) and (4).

(3) Subsection (2) does not apply to –

(a) any land held by the transferor as security for money subject to the trusts of the transferor (other than land held on trust for securing debentures or debenture stock),
(b) any land held by the transferor under a lease or agreement which contains any covenant (however described) against assignment of the transferor's interest without the consent of some other person, unless that consent has been obtained before the specified date, or
(c) any shares, stock, annuity or other property which is only transferable in books kept by a company or other body or in a manner directed by or under any enactment.

(4) In its application to registered land within the meaning of the Land Registration Act 2002, subsection (2) is subject to section 27 of that Act (dispositions required to be registered).

[(5) Where specified trust property vests in the transferee by virtue of subsection (2), unless the Commission directs otherwise the specified trust property and the transferee are to be treated as a single charity for the purposes of Parts 4 and 8 of this Act.]

NOTES

Sub-ss (1), (2) modified by SI 2012/3012, reg 61(2)(a), (b).

Sub-s (5) inserted by SI 2012/3012, reg 61(2)(c).

APPENDIX 8

CHARITIES (MISLEADING NAMES) REGULATIONS 1992

SI 1992/1901

In exercise of the powers conferred upon me by section 4(2)(c) of the Charities Act 1992, I hereby make the following Regulations:

1

These Regulations may be cited as the Charities (Misleading Names) Regulations 1992 and shall come into force on 1st September 1992.

2

The words and expressions set out in the Schedule to these Regulations, together (where appropriate) with the plural and possessive forms of those words and expressions and any abbreviations of them, and hereby specified for the purposes of section 4(2)(c) of the Charities Act 1992.

Schedule
Specification of words and expressions for the purposes of section 4(2)(c) of the Charities Act 1992

REGULATION 2

Assurance

Authority

Bank

Benevolent

British

Building Society

[Charitable incorporated organisation]

Church

Co-operative

England

English

Europe

European

Friendly Society

Grant-Maintained

Great Britain

Great British

Her Majesty

His Majesty

Industrial & Provident Society

International

Ireland

Irish

King

National

Nationwide

Northern Ireland

Northern Irish

Official

Polytechnic

Prince

Princess

Queen

Registered

Royal

Royale

Royalty

[Sefydliad elusennol corfforedig]

School

Scotland

Scottish

Trade Union

United Kingdom

University

Wales

Welsh

Windsor

AMENDMENT

Entry "Charitable incorporated organisation" inserted by SI 2012/3012, reg 63, Sch 4, para 3(a).

Date in force: 2 January 2013: see SI 2012/3012, reg 1.

Entry "Sefydliad elusennol corfforedig" inserted by SI 2012/3012, reg 63, Sch 4, para 3(b).

Date in force: 2 January 2013: see SI 2012/3012, reg 1.

APPENDIX 9

CHARITIES (QUALIFIED SURVEYORS' REPORTS) REGULATIONS 1992

SI 1992/2980

In exercise of the powers conferred upon me by sections 32(4) and 77(3) of the Charities Act 1992, I hereby make the following Regulations

1 (1) These Regulations may be cited as the Charities (Qualified Surveyors' Reports) Regulations 1992 and shall come into force on 1st January 1993.

(2) In these Regulations–

"relevant land" means the land in respect of which a report is being obtained for the purposes of section 32(3) of the Charities Act 1992; and
"the surveyor" means the qualified surveyor from whom such a report is being obtained.

2 A report prepared for the purposes of section 32(3) of the Charities Act 1992 (requirements to be complied with in respect of the disposition of land held by or in trust for a charity otherwise than with an order of the court or of the Charity Commissioners or where section 32(5) of that Act applies) shall contain such information and deal with such matters as are prescribed by the Schedule to these Regulations (together with such other information and such other matters as the surveyor believes should be drawn to the attention of the charity trustees).

Schedule

Information to be contained in, and matters to be dealt with by, qualified surveyors' reports

1 (1) A description of the relevant land and its location, to include–

(a) the measurements of the relevant land;
(b) its current use;
(c) the number of buildings (if any) included in the relevant land;
(d) the measurements of any such buildings; and
(e) the number of rooms in any such buildings and the measurements of those rooms.

(2) Where any information required by sub-paragraph (1) above may be clearly given by means of a plan, it may be so given and any such plan need not be drawn to scale.

2 Whether the relevant land, or any part of it, is leased by or from the charity trustees and, if it is, details of–

(a) the length of the lease and the period of it which is outstanding;
(b) the rent payable under the lease;

(c) any service charge which is so payable;
(d) the provisions in the lease for any review of the rent payable under it or any service charge so payable;
(e) the liability under the lease for repairs and dilapidations; and
(f) any other provision in the lease which, in the opinion of the surveyor, affects the value of the relevant land.

3

Whether the relevant land is subject to the burden of, or enjoys the benefit of, any easement or restrictive covenant or is subject to any annual or other periodic sum charged on or issuing out of the land except rent reserved by a lease or tenancy.

4

Whether any buildings included in the relevant land are in good repair and, if not, the surveyor's advice–

(a) as to whether or not it would be in the best interests of the charity for repairs to be carried out prior to the proposed disposition;
(b) as to what those repairs, if any, should be; and
(c) as to the estimated cost of any repairs he advises.

5

Where, in the opinion of the surveyor, it would be in the best interests of the charity to alter any buildings included in the relevant land prior to disposition (because, for example, adaptations to the buildings for their current use are not such as to command the best market price on the proposed disposition), that opinion and an estimate of the outlay required for any alterations which he suggests.

6

Advice as to the manner of disposing of the relevant land so that the terms on which it is disposed of are the best that can reasonably be obtained for the charity, including–

(a) where appropriate, a recommendation that the land should be divided for the purposes of the disposition;
(b) unless the surveyor's advice is that it would not be in the best interests of the charity to advertise the proposed disposition, the period for which and the manner in which the proposed disposition should be advertised;
(c) where the surveyor's advice is that it would not be in the best interests of the charity to advertise the proposed disposition, his reasons for that advice (for example, that the proposed disposition is the renewal of a lease to someone who enjoys statutory protection or that he believes someone with a special interest in acquiring the relevant land will pay considerably more than the market price for it); and
(d) any view the surveyor may have on the desirability or otherwise of delaying the proposed disposition and, if he believes such delay is desirable, what the period of that delay should be.

7

(1) Where the surveyor feels able to give such advice and where such advice is relevant, advice as to the chargeability or otherwise of value added tax on the proposed disposition and the effect of such advice on the valuations given under paragraph 8 below.

(2) Where either the surveyor does not feel able to give such advice or such advice is not in his opinion relevant, a statement to that effect.

8

The surveyor's opinion as to–

(a) the current value of the relevant land having regard to its current state of repair and current circumstances (such as the presence of a tenant who enjoys statutory protection) or, where the pro-posed disposition is a lease, the rent which could be obtained under it having regard to such matters;

(b) what the value of the relevant land or what the rent under the proposed disposition would be–

  (i) where he has given advice under paragraph 4 above, if that advice is followed; or

  (ii) where he has expressed an opinion under paragraph 5 above, if that opinion is acted upon; or

  (iii) if both that advice is followed and that opinion is acted upon,

(c) where he has made a recommendation under paragraph 6(a) above, the increase in the value of the relevant land or rent in respect of it if the recommendation were followed;

(d) where his advice is that it would not be in the best interests of the charity to advertise the proposed disposition because he believes a higher price can be obtained by not doing so, the amount by which that price exceeds the price that could be obtained if the proposed disposition were advertised; and

(e) where he has advised a delay in the proposed disposition under paragraph 6(d) above, the amount by which he believes the price which could be obtained consequent on such a delay exceeds the price that could be obtained without it.

9

Where the surveyor is of the opinion that the proposed disposition is not in the best interests of the charity because it is not a disposition that makes the best use of the relevant land, that opinion and the reasons for it, together with his advice as to the type of disposition which would constitute the best use of the land (including such advice as may be relevant as to the prospects of buying out any sitting tenant or of succeeding in an application for change of use of the land under the laws relating to town and country planning etc).

APPENDIX 10

CHARITABLE INSTITUTIONS (FUND-RAISING) REGULATIONS 1994

SI 1994/30024

The Secretary of State, in exercise of the powers conferred upon him by sections 64 and 77(3) of the Charities Act 1992 and, having regard to the definition of 'the prescribed requirements' in section 59(6), section 59 of that Act, and after such consultation as is mentioned in section 77(4) of that Act, hereby makes the following Regulations

1 CITATION, COMMENCEMENT AND INTERPRETATION

(1) These Regulations may be cited as the Charitable Institutions (Fund-Raising) Regulations 1994 and shall come into force on 1st March 1995.

[(2) In these Regulations, 'authorised deposit taker' means–

(a) the Bank of England;
(b) a person who has permission under Part 4 of the Financial Services and Markets Act 2000 to accept deposits; or
(c) an EEA firm of the kind mentioned in paragraph 5(b) of Schedule 3 to that Act, which has permission under paragraph 15 of that Schedule (as a result of qualifying for authorisation under paragraph 12(1) of that Schedule) to accept deposits.]

[(2A) Paragraph (2) must be read with–

(a) section 22 of the Financial Services and Markets Act 2000;
(b) any relevant order under that section; and
(c) Schedule 3 to that Act.]

(3) In these Regulations, any reference, in relation to an agreement made for the purposes of section 59 of the Charities Act 1992, to a charitable institution, commercial participator or professional fund-raiser, shall, unless the contrary intention appears, be construed as a reference to any charitable institution, commercial participator or professional fund-raiser, respectively, which is or who is a party to the agreement.

NOTES

INITIAL COMMENCEMENT

Specified date

Specified date: 1 March 1995: see para (1) above.

AMENDMENT

Para (2): substituted by SI 2001/3649, art 480(1), (2).

Date in force: 1 December 2001: see SI 2001/3649, art 1.

Para (2A): inserted by SI 2001/3649, art 480(1), (3).

Date in force: 1 December 2001: see SI 2001/3649, art 1.

2 AGREEMENTS BETWEEN CHARITABLE INSTITUTIONS AND PROFESSIONAL FUND-RAISERS

(1) The requirements as to form and content of an agreement made for the purposes of section 59(1) of the Charities Act 1992 are those set out in the following provisions of this regulation.

(2) Such an agreement (hereafter in this regulation referred to as 'the agreement') shall be in writing and shall be signed by or on behalf of the charitable institution and the professional fund-raiser.

(3) The agreement shall specify–

(a) the name and address of each of the parties to the agreement;
(b) the date on which the agreement was signed by or on behalf of each of those parties;
(c) the period for which the agreement is to subsist;
(d) any terms relating to the termination of the agreement prior to the date on which that period expires; and
(e) any terms relating to the variation of the agreement during that period.

(4) The agreement shall also contain–

(a) a statement of its principal objectives and the methods to be used in pursuit of those objectives;
(b) if there is more than one charitable institution party to the agreement, provision as to the manner in which the proportion in which the institutions which are so party are respectively to benefit under the agreement is to be determined; and
(c) provision as to the amount by way of remuneration or expenses which the professional fund-raiser is to be entitled to receive in respect of things done by him in pursuance of the agreement and the manner in which that amount is to be determined.

NOTES

INITIAL COMMENCEMENT

Specified date

Specified date: 1 March 1995: see reg 1(1).

3 AGREEMENTS BETWEEN CHARITABLE INSTITUTIONS AND COMMERCIAL PARTICIPATORS

(1) The requirements as to form and content of an agreement made for the purposes of section 59(2) of the Charities Act 1992 are those set out in the following provisions of this regulation.

(2) Such an agreement (hereafter in this regulation referred to as 'the agreement') shall be in writing and shall be signed by or on behalf of the charitable institution and the commercial participator.

(3) The agreement shall specify–

(a) the name and address of each of the parties to the agreement;
(b) the date on which the agreement was signed by or on behalf of each of those parties;

(c) the period for which the agreement is to subsist;

(d) any terms relating to the termination of the agreement prior to the date on which that period expires; and

(e) any terms relating to the variation of the agreement during that period.

(4) The agreement shall also contain–

(a) a statement of its principal objectives and the methods to be used in pursuit of those objectives;

(b) provision as to the manner in which are to be determined–

(i) if there is more than one charitable institution party to the agreement, the proportion in which the institutions which are so party are respectively to benefit under the agreement; and

(ii) the proportion of the consideration given for goods or services sold or supplied by the commercial participator, or of any other proceeds of a promotional venture undertaken by him, which is to be given to or applied for the benefit of the charitable institution, or

(iii) the sums by way of donations by the commercial participator in connection with the sale or supply of any goods or services sold or supplied by him which are to be so given or applied,

as the case may require; and

(c) provision as to any amount by way of remuneration or expenses which the commercial participator is to be entitled to receive in respect of things done by him in pursuance of the agreement and the manner in which any such amount is to be determined.

(5) The statement of methods referred to in paragraph (4)(a) above shall include, in relation to each method specified, a description of the type of charitable contributions which are to be given to or applied for the benefit of the charitable institution and of the circumstances in which they are to be so given or applied.

NOTES

INITIAL COMMENCEMENT

Specified date

Specified date: 1 March 1995: see reg 1(1).

4 NOTICE PRIOR TO INJUNCTION TO PREVENT UNAUTHORISED FUND-RAISING

A notice served under subsection (3) of section 62 of the Charities Act 1992 shall, in addition to satisfying the requirements of that subsection, specify the circumstances which gave rise to the serving of the notice and the grounds on which an application under that section is to be made.

NOTES

INITIAL COMMENCEMENT

Specified date

Specified date: 1 March 1995: see reg 1(1).

5 AVAILABILITY OF BOOKS, DOCUMENTS OR OTHER RECORDS

(1) A professional fund-raiser or commercial participator who is a party to an agreement made for the purposes of section 59 of the Charities Act 1992 shall, on request and at all

reasonable times, make available to any charitable institution which is a party to that agreement any books, documents or other records (however kept) which relate to that institution and are kept for the purposes of the agreement.

(2) In the case of any record which is kept otherwise than in legible form, the reference in paragraph (1) above to making that record available shall be construed as a reference to making it available in legible form.

NOTES

INITIAL COMMENCEMENT

Specified date

Specified date: 1 March 1995: see reg 1(1).

6 TRANSMISSION OF MONEY AND OTHER PROPERTY TO CHARITABLE INSTITUTIONS

(1) Any money or other property acquired by a professional fund-raiser or commercial participator for the benefit of, or otherwise falling to be given to or applied by such a person for the benefit of, a charitable institution (including such money or other property as is referred to in section 64(3) of the Charities Act 1992) shall, notwithstanding any inconsistent term in an agreement made for the purposes of section 59 of that Act, be transmitted to that institution in accordance with the following provisions of this regulation.

(2) A professional fund-raiser or commercial participator holding any such money or property as is referred to in paragraph (1) above shall, unless he has a reasonable excuse–

(a) in the case of any money, and any negotiable instrument which is payable to or to the account of the charitable institution, as soon as is reasonably practicable after its receipt and in any event not later than the expiration of 28 days after that receipt or such other period as may be agreed with the institution–

(i) pay it to the person or persons having the general control and management of the administration of the institution; or

(ii) pay it into an account held by [an authorised deposit taker] in the name of or on behalf of the institution which is under the control of the person, or any of the persons, specified in sub-paragraph (i) above; and

(b) in the case of any other property, deal with it in accordance with any instructions given for that purpose, either generally or in a particular case, by the charitable institution:

Provided that–

(i) any property in the possession of the professional fund-raiser or commercial participator either pending the obtaining of such instructions as are referred to above or in accordance with such instructions shall be securely held by him;

(ii) the proceeds of the sale or other disposal of any property shall, from the time of their receipt by the professional fund-raiser or commercial participator, be subject to the requirements of sub-paragraph (a) above.

NOTES

INITIAL COMMENCEMENT

Specified date

Specified date: 1 March 1995: see reg 1(1).

AMENDMENT

Para (2): in sub-para (a)(ii) words 'an authorised deposit taker' in square brackets substituted by SI 2001/3649, art 480(1), (4).

7 FUND-RAISING FOR CHARITABLE ETC PURPOSES OTHERWISE THAN BY PROFESSIONAL FUND-RAISERS OR COMMERCIAL PARTICIPATORS

(1) This regulation applies to any person who carries on for gain a business other than a fund-raising business but, in the course of that business, engages in any promotional venture in the course of which it is represented that charitable contributions are to be applied for charitable, benevolent or philanthropic purposes of any description (rather than for the benefit of one or more particular charitable institutions).

(2) Where any person to whom this regulation applies makes a representation to the effect that charitable contributions are to be applied for such charitable, benevolent or philanthropic purposes as are mentioned in paragraph (1) above he shall, unless he has a reasonable excuse, ensure that the representation is accompanied by a statement clearly indicating–

(a) the fact that the charitable contributions referred to in the representation are to be applied for those purposes and not for the benefit of any particular charitable institution or institutions;
[(b) the notifiable amount of whichever of the following sums is applicable in the circumstances–
(i) the sum representing so much of the consideration given for goods or services sold or supplied by him as is to be applied for those purposes;
(ii) the sum representing so much of any other proceeds of a promotional venture undertaken by him as is to be so applied; or
(iii) the sum of the donations by him in connection with the sale or supply of any such goods or services which are to be so applied; and]
(c) the method by which it is to be determined how the charitable contributions referred to in the representation are to be distributed between different charitable institutions.

[(3) In this regulation, a reference to the 'notifiable amount' in relation to any sum is a reference–

(a) to the actual amount of the sum, if that is known at the time when the statement is made; and
(b) otherwise to the estimated amount of the sum, calculated as accurately as is reasonably possible in the circumstances.]

NOTES

INITIAL COMMENCEMENT

Specified date

Specified date: 1 March 1995: see reg 1(1).

AMENDMENT

Para (2): sub-para (b) substituted by SI 2009/1060, reg 3(1), (2).

Date in force: 1 October 2009 (in relation to a representation made on or after that date to which para (2) above applies): see SI 2009/1060, regs 1, 4.

Para (3): inserted by SI 2009/1060, reg 3(1), (3).

Date in force: 1 October 2009 (in relation to a representation made on or after that date to which para (2) above applies): see SI 2009/1060, regs 1, 4.

8 OFFENCES AND PENALTIES

(1) Failure to comply with any of the provisions of these Regulations specified in paragraph (2) below shall be an offence punishable on summary conviction by a fine not exceeding the second level on the standard scale.

(2) The provisions referred to in paragraph (1) above are–

(a) regulation 5(1);
(b) regulation 6(2); and
(c) regulation 7(2).

NOTES

INITIAL COMMENCEMENT

Specified date

Specified date: 1 March 1995: see reg 1(1).

APPENDIX 11

THE CHARITIES (TOTAL RETURN) REGULATIONS 2013

In exercise of the powers conferred on it by section 104B of the Charities Act 2011 the Charity Commission for England and Wales makes the following regulations:

PART 1 – GENERAL PROVISIONS

1. These regulations may be cited as the Charities (Total Return) Regulations 2013 and come into force on 1st January 2014.

2. In these regulations:

'available endowment fund' has the same meaning as in section 104A(5) of the 2011 Act;

'the 2011 Act' means the Charities Act 2011;

'expendable endowment" means a capital fund which the trustees may convert into income;

'Index' means the Retail Prices Index or Consumer Prices Index or such other prices index published by The Office for National Statistics or any successor government ministry, department or agency as the trustees adopt for the purposes of regulation 5 and 8(2) below, having regard to the nature of the relevant fund and their duties set out in regulation 6(1) and (2) below;

'investment return' means the return from investments which represent the assets given to the charity on a trust for investment and includes:

- any interest receivable; plus
- any net rent and other income or gain derived from the use or exploitation of assets; plus
- any dividends; plus
- all forms of capital gain resulting on, or from, the disposal, redemption, or revaluation of investment assets (including the issue or repayment of share or loan capital); less
- any capital losses resulting on or from the disposal, redemption, or revaluation of investment assets;

'negative unapplied total return' arises where the unapplied total return carried forward is less than nil;

'relevant fund' has the same meaning as in section 104B(6) of the 2011 Act;

'relevant percentage' is:

(a) for the purposes of regulation 5 the percentage equivalent to the rise in the Index as at the date on which the allocation is made from either (i) the date of the last occasion on which an amount from the unapplied total return was accumulated in the trust for investment or (ii) if there is no such occasion, the date of the valuation used for the purposes of the section 104A(2) resolution; and

(b) for the purposes of regulation 8(2) the percentage equivalent to the rise in the Index as at the date the trustees revoke their section 104A(2) resolution from the date of the relevant section 104A(2) resolution;

'relevant value' is the value of the relevant fund having deducted from that value the value of any unapplied total return included within it;

'section 104A(2) resolution' means a resolution made pursuant to s 104A(2) of the 2011 Act to adopt a total return approach to investment in relation to a fund or portion of a fund (including the returns from the investment of such fund or portion of it);

'total return' means the whole of the investment return received by a charity from a relevant fund, regardless of when it has arisen;

'total return approach to investment' means an approach to investment which gives trustees flexibility in the way they allocate the total return arising from the trust for investment between the trust for application and the trust for investment;

'trustees' means the charity trustees of a charity as defined in s 177 of the 2011 Act;

'trust for application' means the trust that attaches to charity property which the trustees have to apply for the purposes of the charity within a reasonable period of receipt;

'trust for investment' means the trust that is created when a gift to a charity is made on the condition that it should not be applied directly for the purposes of the charity, but instead should be invested to produce a return;

'unapplied total return' means that part of the total return which has not been allocated to either the trust for application or the trust for investment.

PART II – ADOPTION OF A TOTAL RETURN APPROACH TO INVESTMENT

3.

(1) These regulations apply where the trustees of a charity with an available endowment fund make a section 104A(2) resolution.

(2) The trustees shall identify and record, at the time when a section 104A(2) resolution is made,

(i) the value of the trust for investment as at a date on or before the date of the resolution,

(ii) the date of that valuation, and

(iii) any unapplied income from the trust for investment and any increase in the value of the trust for investment since the date of the valuation which together shall constitute the initial value of the charity's unapplied total return.

(3) The trustees may decide, at any time, and from time to time, subject to these regulations but otherwise at their discretion, what part of the unapplied total return should be held on the trust for application and, subject to regulation 5, what part of the unapplied total return should be accumulated as part of the trust for investment.

(4) The unapplied total return which is not allocated to the trust for application nor accumulated in the trust for investment shall be dealt with in the same way as the trust for investment until it is so allocated or accumulated.

4. The trustees may in exercising their powers in respect of a relevant fund, allocate part of the trust for investment to the trust for application subject to its recoupment on a pound for pound basis over a period to be reasonably determined by the trustees PROVIDED ALWAYS THAT the total amount so allocated shall at no time exceed 10%

of the relevant value as at the date of the first such allocation which remains subject to recoupment. When exercising this power trustees should have regard to the duty set out in regulation 6 (2) below.

5. The trustees may, as part of the exercise of their powers in respect of a relevant fund accumulate in the trust for investment an amount from the unapplied total return the value of which does not exceed the relevant percentage of the relevant value as at either (i) the date of the last occasion on which an amount from the unapplied total return was accumulated in the trust for investment or (ii) if there is no such occasion, the date of the valuation used for the purposes of the section 104A(2) resolution.

6. The trustees shall comply with the following directions as to matters connected with, or arising out of, the exercise of their own powers in relation to a relevant fund:

(1) When using those powers, and when discharging the duties set out in regulation 3 (2) and (4) and 6 (2) to (3) below, each of the trustees has a duty to exercise such care and skill as is reasonable in the circumstances, having regard in particular:

- (a) to any special knowledge, or experience that he or she has or holds himself out as having, and
- (b) if he or she acts as trustees in the course of a business or profession, to any special knowledge or experience that it is reasonable to expect of a person acting in the course of that kind of business or profession.

(2) The trustees shall only exercise their powers in relation to a relevant fund in such a way as not to prejudice the ability of the charity to further its purposes now and in the future.

(3)

- (a) Before using their powers in relation to a relevant fund, trustees must (unless the exception applies) obtain and consider proper advice about the way in which, having regard to the duty expressed in regulation 6 (2), the power ought to be used.
- (b) the exception is that the trustees need not obtain such advice if they reasonably conclude that in all the circumstances it is unnecessary or inappropriate to do so.
- (c) proper advice is the advice of a person who is reasonably believed by the trustees to be qualified to give it by his or her ability in and practical experience of investment and matters relevant to the proper use of the power conferred by regulations 3 to 5.

(4) The trustees shall in their annual report for each financial year:

- (a) state the policy adopted by the trustees for making the identification required by regulation 3 (2) above, and state the date from which the analysis required by that sub-clause was performed if different from the date when the charity was established.
- (b) give an explanation of the consideration and policies relevant to the trustees' determination in that financial year of:
  - (i) the allocation of the charity's unapplied total return between the trust for application and the trust for investment;
  - (ii) any allocation of part of the permanent endowment to the relevant trust for application under the power in regulation 4 above.
- (c) identify the person(s) (if any) who provided the advice referred to in (3) above.

(d) if the trustees of the charity concerned are not, or may not be, required to prepare an annual report, the information required by this sub-clause should be provided in the notes to the charity's accounts in the relevant financial year.

7.

(1) This regulation applies where the Charity Commission for England and Wales has, prior to the commencement of section 104A(2) of the 2011 Act, conferred on the trustees of a charity a power enabling them to decide which part of the unapplied total return from the assets of the charity given to it on trust for investment should be held on trust for application for the purposes of the charity by way of an order under section 26 of the Charities Act 1993 or section 105 of the 2011

(2) Where the trustees make a section 104A(2) resolution, they make take these regulations as discharging that order subject to the continued payment of any amounts agreed to be repaid by way of recoupment.

PART III – REVOCATION OF A SECTION 104A (2) RESOLUTION

8.

(1) This clause applies where the trustees who have made a section 104A(2) resolution, which to revoke that resolution.

(2) Where there is a negative unapplied total return, before revoking a section 104A(2) resolution, the trustees shall make provision for an amount equivalent to the negative unapplied total return, together with such amount (not exceeding the relevant percentage of the relevant value) that the trustees consider to be appropriate, to be paid to the relevant fund over such period as the trustees consider reasonable provided that such a period shall not exceed 10 years.

(3) In other circumstances, before revoking a section 104A(2) resolution, the trustees shall consider what part of the unapplied total return should be allocated to the trust for investment provided that the amount allocated shall not increase the value of the trust for investment over its value as at the date the total return approach was adopted by more than the relevant percentage.

(4) The remainder of the unapplied total return remaining after giving effect to any decision of the trustees under (3) shall be dealt with as expendable endowment.

REVIEW

9.

(1) Before the end of the review period, the Charity Commission for England and Wales must–

(a) carry out a review of these regulations,
(b) set out the conclusions of the review in a report, and
(c) publish the report.

(2) The report must in particular–

(a) set out the objectives intended to be achieved by the regulatory system established by these regulations,

(b) assess the extent to which those objectives are achieved, and

(c) assess whether those objectives remain appropriate and, if so, the extent to which they could be achieved with a system that imposes less regulation.

(3) Review period' means the period of 5 years beginning with the day on which these regulations come into force.

APPENDIX 12

Note that the Regulations refer to the provisions of the 1993 Act. Section 14(1) of the 1993 Act has been replaced by s 63(1) of the 2011 Act. Section 14(6) has been replaced by s 63(6) and (7). Section 14(8) has been replaced by s 66(4) and (6). Section 14(9) has been replaced by s 66(5). Section 14(10) has been replaced by s 66(2) and (3). Sections 14A(1)-(8) have been replaced by s 65(1)-(8). Section 14A(9) has been replaced by s 66(4) and (5).

THE CHARITIES (FAILED APPEALS) REGULATIONS 2008

In exercise of the powers conferred on it by sections 14(8) and (9) and 14A(9) of the Charities Act 1993 the Charity Commission for England and Wales make the following Regulations:

PART I – GENERAL PROVISIONS

1. These regulations may be cited as the Charities (Failed Appeals) Regulations 2008 and come into force on 18 March 2008.

2. In these regulations:

'the Act' means the Charities Act 1993;
'advertisement' means an advertisement published in pursuance of section 14(1)(a)(i) of the Act;
'appeal' means an invitation to the public or a section of the public whether in writing, by means of television or radio or otherwise;
'solicitation' means a solicitation as defined by section 14A(8)(a) of the Act that is within section 14A(2) of the Act;
'property' and 'donor' have the same meaning as in section 14(10) of the Act;
'trustees' means the trustees holding the property;
'relevant declaration' has the same meaning as in section 14A(3) of the Act;
'written record' may include information stored electronically;
'in writing' may include electronic forms of written communication.

PART II – APPLICATION CY-PRÈS OF GIFTS OF DONORS UNKNOWN OR DISCLAIMING: REGULATIONS UNDER S 14 OF THE CHARITIES ACT 1993

3. Advertisements shall be in the form specified in Schedule 1 to these Regulations or in a form equivalent to that form in any other language required or permitted by paragraph 4 of these Regulations.

4. Advertisements shall be published:

(a) in English in every case; and
(b) where the appeal was published in another language, in that language;

and may, in addition, be published in Welsh in any case where the appeal was not made in Welsh.

5. Any advertisement published in pursuance of section 14(1)(a)(i) of the Act shall be published in the manner specified in Schedule 2 to these Regulations.

6. Any inquiry made in pursuance of section 14(1)(a)(i) of the Act shall:

(a) be made in writing;
(b) be sent by post to the address of each donor recorded in the records of the trustees of the property; and
(c) contain at least the information specified in Schedule 3 to these Regulations.

7. The period described for the purposes of section 14(1)(a)(ii) of the Act shall be three months.

8. Any disclaimer executed for the purposes of section 14(1)(b) of the Act shall either:

(a) be executed in English in the form specified in Schedule 4 to these Regulations; or
(b) be executed in Welsh in the form equivalent in that language to the form specified in Schedule 4 to these Regulations.

PART III – APPLICATION CY-PRÈS OF GIFTS MADE IN RESPONSE TO CERTAIN SOLICITATIONS: REGULATIONS UNDER S 14A OF THE CHARITIES ACT 1993

9. The trustees must maintain a written record of every relevant declaration made by a donor giving property for specific charitable purposes in response to a solicitation.

10. The trustees must update the written record to include any change of address notified to the trustees by or on behalf of a donor who has completed a relevant declaration.

11. In the event of the failure of the specific charitable purposes for which property subject to a relevant declaration was given:

(1) the trustees must send written notification to the donor at the address in the charity's records:
  (a) stating the nature or value of the property (as applicable) and the specific charitable purpose for which it was given;
  (b) informing the donor that the specific charitable purpose has failed;
  (c) enquiring whether, in accordance with the declaration which he made, the donor wishes to request the return of the property (or a sum equal to its value);
  (d) advising the donor that if he wishes to exercise his right to request the return of the property, he must do so within the period specified in paragraph 13 of these regulations; amd
  (e) advising the donor that if he does not reclaim the property, the Charity Commission may make a Scheme to apply it for other similar charitable purposes.
(2) the trustees must return to each donor who so requests under section 14A(5) of the Act, the property (or a sum equal to its value) to the address in the charity's records or in such other manner or by such other means as the donor requests and the trustees agree.

12. The trustees must retain the written record of each relevant declaration for at least six years from the date:

(1) the property was applied for the specific charitable purposes for which it was given; or
(2) the property was returned to the donor in accordance with section 14A(5) of the Act; or
(3) the Commission or the court made a Scheme allowing the property to be applied cy-près.

13. The prescribed period for the purposes of section 14A(5)(c) and 14(6)(b) of the Act is three calendar months from the date on which the trustees sent written notification to the donor as prescribed by these Regulations.

14. A written record for the purposes of these Regulations must contain such information as the trustees consider sufficient to enable them to comply with section 14A(5) of the Act, and in particular:

(a) to identify the property to which a relevant declaration applies;
(b) to identify the specific charitable purpose for which the property was given;
(c) to identify and contact the donor.

Schedule 1

Form of advertisement prescribed for the purposes of section 14(1)(a)(i) of the Charities Act 1960

Advertisement

Name of charity (if applicable):

Registered charity number (if applicable):

Purpose for which money or other property was given:

NOTICE is given that money and other property given for this purpose cannot be used for that purpose because [state reasons]/

If you gave money or other property for that purpose you are entitled to claim it back. If you wish to do so you must tell [insert name] of [insert address] within three months of [specify date: see note below]. If you wish the money or other property to go to a similar charitable purpose and to disclaim your right to the return of the money or other property, you must ask the person named above for a form of disclaimer.

If you do not either make a claim within the three months or sign a disclaimer, the Charity Commission may make a Scheme applying the property to other charitable purposes. You will still be able to claim the return of your money or other property (less expenses), but **only if you do so within six months from the date of the Scheme made by the Commissioners.**

Date of this notice: **[specify date: see note below]**

*[Note: **[This Note does not form part of the prescribed advertisement]** If this advertisement is to be published in a newspaper or other periodical, the words 'the date of this publication' should be inserted in paragraphs 2 and 4 above.*

If this advertisement is to be published on a public notice board, the date inserted here should be the date on which the advertisement was fixed to the public notice board.]

Schedule 2

Manner of publishing advertisements in pursuance of section 14(1)(a)(ii) of the Act

1. Every advertisement must be published in a newspaper or other periodical which is:

(a) written in the same language as the advertisement; and
(b) sold or distributed throughout the area in which the appeal was made.

2. Where the purposes of the appeal were directed towards the benefit of an area wholly or mainly within a local authority district or a London Borough, or the City of London, a copy of every advertisement published under paragraph 1 must also be published by fixing copies of it to two public notice boards in the relevant areas.

Schedule 3

Information to be contained in inquiries to be made in pursuance of section 14(1)(a)(i) of the Act

1. The name and address of the charity to which the property was given by the donor;

2. A description of the specific charitable purposes for which the property was given by the donor;

3. The reasons why the purpose has failed;

4. A description of the property (including the amount of any money) given for that purpose by the donor;

5. A statement of the donor's right to have the property returned;

6. A statement that the donor may disclaim the right to have the property described in paragraph 4 above returned by executing a disclaimer in the prescribed form;

7. A statement that, where the donor disclaims his right in respect of such property, the property may be applied for other charitable purposes similar to those for which it was given by a Scheme established by the Commissioners or by the court; and

8. A statement that, where the donor has not replied in writing to the inquiry within three months from the date of service of the inquiry, he will be treated for the purposes of section 14(1)(a) as a donor who cannot be identified or found, but that he will be able to claim the property, less expenses, within six months from the date of any Scheme made by the Commissioners or the court.

Schedule 4

I HEREBY DISCLAIM my rights to the return of *the sum of £....../the property consisting of [insert description of property]** given by me for [insert name of charity to which, or descriptions of purposes for which, the money or property was given].

Signed:

Name in capitals:

Address:

Date:

#Signed:

Name in capitals:

Address:

Date:

* Delete as appropriate

This paragraph may be repeated if further signatures are required.

INDEX

References are to paragraph numbers.